CW01628008

# EVEREST

## THE MOUNTAINEERING HISTORY

# EVEREST

## THE MOUNTAINEERING HISTORY

WALT UNSWORTH

THIRD EDITION

THE MOUNTAINEERS

BÂTON WICKS

Published by The Mountaineers
1001 SW Klickitat Way, Suite 201, Seattle, WA 98134

Published simultaneously in Great Britain
by Bâton Wicks Publications, London.
All trade inquiries to: Cordee, 3a DeMontfort Street, Leicester, England, LE1 7HD

© 2000 by Walt Unsworth

All rights reserved

First edition 1981. Second edition 1989. Third Edition 2000.

No part of this book may be reproduced in any form, or by any electronic, mechanical, or other means, without permission in writing from the publisher.

Manufactured in Canada

Cover photograph: © Doug Scott

*Library of Congress Cataloging-in-Publication Data*
Unsworth, Walt, 1928–
Everest/Walt Unsworth.--3rd ed., rev.
p. cm.
Includes bibliographical references (p. ) and index.
ISBN 0-89886-670-7
1. Mountaineering--Everest, Mount (China and Nepal)--History.
I. Title.
GV199.44.E85 U57 1999
796.52'2'095496--dc21 99-051570
CIP

*British Library of Congress Cataloguing-in-Publication Data*
A catalogue record for this book is available at the British Library
ISBN 1-898573-40-9

Printed on recycled paper

# Contents

# List of Plates

COLOUR



BLACK AND WHITE

37. Chinese climbers on Everest, 1960. (*Xinhua News Agency*)
38. Camp IV on the South West Face, 1975. (*Ronnie Richards*)
39. The revolt of 1971. Dyhrenfurth (extreme right) argues with (left to right) Mazeaud, Evans, Vaucher, Axt, Yvette Vaucher and Mauri. (*John Cleare*)
40. Sherpas taking Bahuguna's body out of the Western Cwm after the Indian's tragic death in 1971. (*John Cleare*)
41. The gully through the Rock Band on the South West Face. (*Paul Braithwaite*)
42. Dougal Haston approaching the South Summit during the first ascent of the South West Face, 1975. (*Doug Scott*)
43. Doug Scott on the summit of Everest after the first ascent of the South West Face, 1975.
(*Doug Scott*)
44. A Russian climber on the so-called Fireplace Pitch of the Central Pillar – some of the most technically difficult climbing on Everest. (*Novosti*)
45. The summit of Everest seen from advanced base camp during the 1986 North East Ridge expedition. The Second Step is quite distinctive. (*Dr John English*)
46. The North Face of Everest, scene of much recent activity. The North East Ridge and its Pinnacles can be seen on the left, leading to the skyline and Second Step. The Great Couloir and West Ridge are distinctive. Changtse is in front. (*Dr John English*)
47. The North East Ridge of Everest, with the Pinnacles where Boardman and Tasker disappeared in 1982. (*Dr John English*)
48. Barry Taylor and Russell Brice on the first traverse of the Pinnacles, Everest North East Ridge, 1988. (*Dr John English*)
49. On the East Face of Everest, with the Kangshung Glacier below. (*Stephen Venables*)
50. The approach to the South Col by the East Face, called by the climbers 'The Cauliflower Ridge'. Compare the complexities of this ridge with the 1953 route on the other side of the col.
(*Stephen Venables*)
51. Paul Teare above the buttress, and starting Day 2 of the summit push on the 1988 Kangshung Face expedition. The huge buttress behind is the route of the 1983 American expedition.
(*Stephen Venables*)
52. Everest – more than ever a symbol of world mountaineering. (*Walt Unsworth*)

LIST OF FIGURES



LIST OF MAPS

# Preface and Acknowledgements

This is the story of Man's attempts to climb a very special mountain. As any mountaineer will tell you, Everest is not technically the hardest climb in the world, and certainly not the best. It is, however, the *highest* – and that's what makes it so special, what sets it apart from all other mountains and makes its story much more than a catalogue of daring feats by brave men. It has the power to arouse both the best and worst in human nature; a theme which previous writers have tended to ignore.

To have simply recounted yet again the climbing annals of the mountain from Somervell and Mallory to Bonington and Messner would have served no useful purpose except that of bringing the story more up to date. What I have tried to do is fill in some of the background, often explaining why success or failure came about. I have in fact tried to take the Everest story out of the realms of the *Boy's Own Paper*, to which it has sometimes seemed to belong, by showing the other side of the coin as well. This does no disservice to those who have risked their lives on Everest – quite the opposite in fact, for it shows how they overcame not only the natural hazards of the mountain, but obstacles like bumbling officialdom, international rivalry and plain double dealing as well. You may well wonder, after reading this book, not why it took so long to climb Everest, but how they ever managed it at all!

I have tried also to encapsulate the principal characters along the way, to make them real persons and not cardboard cut-out heroes. In doing so I have concerned myself only with those qualities pertinent to the climbing of Everest.

To attempt all this, even in a fairly large volume, has proved a formidable task and it would not have been possible without the unstinting co-operation given me by a great many Everesters and others. This has ranged from documentary evidence of all sorts to reminiscences and taped interviews. Even casual conversation has produced invaluable clues from some chance remark or other.

A great deal of the research was undertaken by Mrs Audrey Salkeld, who assisted me throughout the project. Mrs Salkeld is well known for her wide background knowledge of Himalayan literature and history, and her help has been of inestimable value. She shares with me our thanks to all those who assisted in any way.

Among the climbers, Everesters and others, whose help is especially appreciated are: George Band, the late T.S. Blakeney, Peter Boardman, Chris Bonington, Paul Braithwaite, H.R.C. Carr, Mike Cheney, Dr Charles Clarke, John Cleare, D.F.O. Dangar, Leo Dickinson, Kurt Diemberger, Dr Jim Duff, the late Nick Estcourt, Sir Charles Evans, Julian Gearing, Dr Raymond Greene, Alfred Gregory, Peter Habeler, Alan Hargreaves, the late Dougal Haston, Tony Howard, Lord Hunt, John Jackson, Eric Jones, Ned Kelly, E.G.H. Kempson, Klavs Becker Larsen, Bob Lawford, Peter Lloyd, Sir Jack Longland, George Lowe, Ian McNaught Davis, Jan Morris, John Morris, John Noel, Prof. Noel Odell, Jim Perrin, Dr L.G.C.E. Pugh, V.S. Risoe, Dolfi Rotovnik, Woody Sayre, Michel Schulman, Doug Scott, Tenzing Norgay, Dr Michael Ward, Dr Charles Warren, Mike Westmacott, Don Whillans and Ken Wilson.

I also appreciate the help given by Mrs B. Castle, formerly Photo Archivist at the R.G.S.; A. Cook of the India Office Library; G.S. Dugdale, Librarian at the R.G.S.; Peter Fozzard for guiding me through the Record Library at the B.B.C.; Eugene Gippenreiter for the official Soviet view of their Everest involvement; the late Duncan Grant for his memories of Mallory; Michael Holroyd for Mallory's connection with the Bloomsbury Group; Arthur Ingham for aeroplane statistics of the thirties; Dr K. Neville Irvine; Mrs C. Kelly, Archivist at the R.G.S.; Mrs J. Norton, Dr and Mrs R. Scott Russell for diaries, papers etc. on Finch; Mrs T.H. Somervell; Mrs E.J. Wilson.

For the illustrations I am indebted to Brian Evans, who drew the splendid maps and diagrams; Nada Tosic of the R.G.S., from whence the bulk of the photographs come; the National Geographic Society and Barry Bishop, for allowing me to use his fine pictures of the American 1963 expedition; the Xinhua News Agency for photographs of the Chinese expeditions; John Noel for permission to use photographs of the 1924 expedition and Chris Bonington who patiently went through his extensive picture files with me. My special thanks are due to Dr Charles Warren for allowing me to use his previously unpublished transparencies from pre-war days and to Frank Solari who had them carefully copied. I am also indebted to the individual photographers whose names appear in the list of illustrations.

There is a vast Everest literature as a glance at the comprehensive bibliography included at the end of this book will show. However, my thanks are particularly due to the authors and publishers of the following books: *Mount Everest: The Reconnaissance, 1921* by C.K. Howard-Bury (Edward Arnold); *Everest, The Hard Way* by C. Bonington (Hodder & Stoughton); *The Mount Everest Reconnaissance Expedition 1951* by E. Shipton (Hodder &

Stoughton); *The Story of Everest* by W.H. Murray (Dent); *Everest: The Unfinished Adventure* by H. Ruttledge (Hodder & Stoughton); *Abode of Snow* by K. Mason (Rupert Hart-Davis); *This My Voyage* by T.G. Longstaff (John Murray); *Through Tibet to Everest* by J.B. Noel (Edward Arnold); *George Mallory* by D. Robertson (Faber & Faber); *The Epic of Mount Everest* by F.E. Younghusband (Edward Arnold); *Snowdon Biography* by G.W. Young (Dent); *Hired to Kill* by J. Morris (Rupert Hart-Davis); *The Making of a Mountaineer* by G.I. Finch (Arrowsmith); *The Assault on Mount Everest, 1922* by C.G. Bruce (Edward Arnold); *After Everest* by T.H. Somervell (Hodder & Stoughton); *The Fight for Mount Everest 1924* by E.F. Norton (Edward Arnold); *Beyond the Frontiers* by A. Swinson (Hutchinson); *Everest 1933* by H. Ruttledge (Hodder & Stoughton); *The Wind of Morning* by H. Boustead (Chatto & Windus); *Camp Six* by F.S. Smythe (Hodder & Stoughton); *Moments of Being* by R. Greene (Heinemann); *Upon That Mountain* by E. Shipton (Hodder & Stoughton); *That Untravelled World* by E. Shipton (Hodder & Stoughton); *Mount Everest 1938* by H.W. Tilman (Cambridge University Press); *First over Everest* by P. Fellowes (John Lane, the Bodley Head); *The Pilot's Book of Everest* by Sq. Ldr Lord Clydesdale and Flt Lt D.F. McIntyre (Hodge); *I'll Climb Mount Everest Alone* by D. Roberts (Robert Hale); *Alone to Everest* by E. Denman (Collins); *Sherpa Tenzing* by J.R. Ullman (G. Harrap); *Four Against Everest* by W.W. Sayre (Arthur Barker); *High Adventure* by E. Hillary (Hodder & Stoughton); *Forerunners to Everest* by R. Dittert (Allen & Unwin); *Coronation Everest* by J. Morris (Faber & Faber); *The Ascent of Everest* by J. Hunt (Hodder & Stoughton); *Life is Meeting* by J. Hunt (Hodder & Stoughton); *In This Short Span* by M. Ward (Gollancz); *Faces of Everest* by H.P.S. Ahluwalia (Vikas); *Americans on Everest* by J.R. Ullman (Michael Joseph); *Everest – The West Ridge* by T.F. Hornbein (Allen & Unwin); *Everest South West Face* by C. Bonington (Hodder & Stoughton); *Doctor on Everest* by P. Steele (Hodder & Stoughton).

The detailed story of Everest told in this book ends with Messner and Habeler's oxygenless ascent in 1978, though some later ascents are mentioned in the postscript. But the story of Everest is like the painting of the Forth Bridge – a continuing task, and even while this book has been in production the story has advanced with the climbing of the South Buttress by the Poles and Messner's incredible solo ascent of the North Ridge. Perhaps the most important recent event is the opening by the Chinese of the Tibetan approaches to Western mountaineers.

Walt Unsworth
Harmony Hall
Milnthorpe
Cumbria
England

# Preface to the Second Edition

In the ten years since this book first appeared there has been no lessening of activity on Everest – on the contrary, there have been almost three times as many expeditions in the last decade as there were in the entire previous history of the mountain. This shows, if proof was needed, that the lure of Everest remains as strong as ever.

The details of all this activity can be found in the relevant appendices, which have been updated with the help of Audrey Salkeld and Xavier Eguskitza, both of whom keep a watching brief on Everest statistics. Undoubtedly the greatest single factor affecting the scene has been the opening of the Tibetan approaches by the Chinese. This has not only led to the reascent of the old North Col route by westerners, but also new routes on the North Face, a new approach to the West Ridge, the climbing of the East Face and the tackling of yet another 'last great problem', the North East Ridge *integrale*.

The number of countries participating in expeditions has increased, including many Eastern Bloc countries. The Russians themselves climbed a splendid new route on the South West Face. Expeditions are becoming increasingly hybrid, too, and a 'German' or 'British' expedition may well have members from other nations. The international ideal, so artificially promoted during the '70s, has come about naturally – only a cynic would claim it was a way of raising money or beating the permit system!

The demise of the large expedition, hinted at in the last edition, has not come about. Sponsors are still to be found who are interested in the world's highest mountain, especially as the media are now more closely involved than ever. Sometimes the mountain seems awash with money. There are times too when it has resembled a three-ringed circus, what with TV cameras, hang-gliders and commercial 'expeditions'.

Because of all this, Everest remains newsworthy and a good place for the press to hang some of their wildest stories. Pride of place must go to the U.S. *Weekly World News* with its headline 'Space Alien Baby Found on Mt Everest'. Dubbed the Starbaby, this little monster apparently has laser beam eyes capable of setting things on fire. I wonder what will happen if the Starbaby meets the Abominable Snowman? It all goes to show that Everest is following the fate of that other great mountain, the Matterhorn, in becoming the butt of man's folly. No doubt soon some publicity seeker will actually try driving a yak up the 'yak route'.

It was very gratifying that the first edition of this book received such a universal welcome. Inevitably there were some errors and I hope that those of a minor sort have been corrected in this edition. Names can cause problems, especially when translated from another tongue; not only can the spelling be problematical but sometimes, as in Korean, for example, the usage is different – the Koreans put the family name first. Some Sherpas seem to have two names – Lhakpa Dorje, who tragically died on the mountain in 1988, was also called Ang Lhakpa, for instance, whilst Chinese personal names sometimes seem impossible to pin down! There has been a profound change in the transliteration of Chinese into English since the first edition and most people will know, for instance, that Peking is now Beijing. The old spellings for the Everest region have been retained in this book – Rongbuk instead of Rongphu, for example – because it would otherwise become extremely confusing. Such changes must await a complete resetting of the book.

Doug Scott rang up to tell me I had reversed his role with that of Dougal Haston's during their bivouac after the first ascent of the South West Face. I obviously confused my Dougs and Dougals. I apologise to Doug and also to the Indian Mountaineering Foundation, who became, for some unknown reason, a Federation instead. The disposition of the French West Ridge team of 1974, struck by avalanche, needs correcting too: George Payot was not at Camp II as stated but at Base Camp; the man at Camp II being another Sherpa, Dordje, and he it was who was buried up to his neck but managed to escape. There were three climbers at Camp III and the rest as stated in the text. The dead were Nima Wangchu in Camp I and in Camp II, Devouassoux, Lakpa, Sanu Wongyal, Pemba Dorje and Nawang Lutuk – the only victim whose body was recovered. He was 17 years old.

Further evidence which has come to light about the various expeditions described in the first edition is dealt with in Appendix 1. Integration of this material in the main body of the text is not feasible in this edition for economic reasons. New chapters have been added which take the story up to 1988/89, though since there have been over a hundred expeditions, not all of them of great interest, I have concentrated on those which seem of most importance to the story of Everest and human endeavour, or sometimes human frailty.

My thanks are due to Audrey Salkeld and Xavier Eguskitza for their detailed statistics as mentioned earlier and to the latter for pointing out various errors and linguistic problems from the first edition. Others have contributed to the revised work in differing ways, from pictures and documents to long discussions and even chance but valuable remarks. In particular I would like to thank Bill Aitkin, Chris Bonington, John M. Boyle, Champak Chatterji, the late Mike Cheney, Michael Chessler, John Cleare, Nick Clinch, Steve Dodd, Dr John English, Ronnie Faux, Rita Gombu, Tom Holzel, Pat Lewis, Sir Jack Longland, Bill March, Sally Nesbitt, Novosti Press, Bachendri Pal, John Pollock, Tom Prentice, Scott Russell, Doug Scott, Edward Smyth, John Town, Stephen Venables, Dr Charles Warren, and Prof. Zhou Zeng.

Walt Unsworth, 1989

# Preface to the Third Edition

Interest in the world's highest mountain has never been greater—not just in the mountaineering community. The general public has been attracted to Everest by books such as Jon Krakauer's splendidly exciting *Into Thin Air* and by the mushrooming World Wide Web. The growth of commercial expeditions has been staggering. Ten years ago nobody would have thought there were so many people with $65,000 (£41,000) to spare who also were prepared to spend it risking their lives on Everest!

Money has often played a big part in Everest's story—read the chapters on the early expeditions and John Noel's desperate ploy with the dancing lamas to try to recoup his losses. Similarly there often has been dissention, none more so than the International South West Face fiasco of 1971. Both money and dissention have been prominent during the last ten years, perhaps one leading to the other more often that previously. On the other hand, it is ironic that the 'international' aspect of mountaineering so avidly sought during the 1970s with scant success should come about naturally twenty years later. Indeed, during the past few years, it has been hard to distinguish one expedition from another as they mixed and matched their ways up the mountain.

Another factor worth noting is the effect of the collapse of the Soviet empire. There are many more climbers from the old Soviet bloc now climbing Everest, and many are professional guides, of whom the best known was the late Anatoli Boukreev.

Since the previous edition the North East Ridge has been climbed in its entirety, and there have been interesting routes on the North Face and Secondary North Face, as well as repeats of things like the South Pillar and South West Face. The South Pillar becomes difficult to record because some expeditions do not complete it in its entirety once it becomes less of a challenge. There have even been tentative gestures towards climbing Fantasy Ridge and the Everest–Lhotse traverse. These remain goals for the future.

The list of expeditions has been updated since the previous edition, though there are so many now that only successful climbers are named along with the team leader. Notes and references also are provided, but many of the other lists have not been updated. Many are now quite meaningless because dozens make it to the summit every season and quite a number have climbed the mountain several times. Some mention is made in the general list of outstanding examples, such as Ang Rita's ten ascents. The statistics change daily!

Sadly, deaths continue to mount. The dramatic events of 1996 are well known, but climbers die on the mountain every year. These are mentioned in the appropriate places, but I have discontinued the 'body count' as such.

Once again I am indebted to various people and sources in the preparation of this update. Audrey Salkeld provided references and statistics; Liz Hawley provided excellent, invaluable reports from Kathmandu; Steve Bell explained the complexities of permits and charges; and the writings of many mountaineers in books, journals and the Internet have all contributed to the result.

Walt Unsworth, 1999

# Introduction: Goddess Mother of the World

The Himalaya is the greatest mountain system in the world. It stretches without interruption across the top of India in a gentle curve for 1,500 miles from east to west, between the Brahmaputra and Indus rivers. In width it averages a mere hundred miles, a barrier between the hot plains of India to the south and the bleak upland plateau of Tibet to the north.

Most of us find such an immense range of mountains hard to envisage, because the scale is beyond our experience, but if we imagine the most westerly of the great peaks, Nanga Parbat, to be in London, then the most easterly, Namche Barwa, would rise somewhere near Moscow. Or, put another way: if the Himalaya was laid out down the eastern side of the United States it would stretch from New York to Houston in Texas.

It is not one single wall of ice-draped mountains. The geological forces which formed the Himalaya (and it is a young range of mountains on the geological time scale) twisted and contorted it into a complex pattern which has been further modified by the erosion of many centuries. Great rivers have carved gorges through the ranges, and each year the monsoon lashes the southern slopes contributing inexorably to their inevitable destruction. Within the width of this complex structure it is possible to distinguish three zones. Nearest to the Indian plains are the low, forested Siwaliks – foothills really, and the haunt of bear and tiger. Behind these hills there rises a much higher group called the Lesser Himalaya – lesser only in comparison with the final, most northerly ridge, the Great Himalaya. Fifteen thousand feet would be an average height for a peak in the Lesser Himalaya – typically a limestone mountain rising from a bed of thick forest. In the Great Himalaya, however, twenty thousand feet is commonplace – there are over a thousand such peaks. And beyond the Great Himalaya lies upland Tibet. One may visualize the whole Himalayan range as three crumpled folds of the earth's crust pushed up against the ancient Indian continental block by the forces of Nature, long ago.

Cradled among the mountains towards the eastern end of the Himalaya, where the high peaks gather in greatest profusion, lies the independent kingdom of Nepal. Of the fourteen mountains in the world which exceed 8,000 m. no fewer than eight of them are in Nepal. Heights such as these are almost unimaginable – if you could put the Appalachians on top of the Rockies, the Nepal Himalaya would still tower over all. Or take Aconcagua in the Andes, the highest mountain in the Western hemisphere, 22,835 ft. Put the highest mountain in Britain, Ben Nevis, on top of it and Everest would still overlook both by 2,000 ft.

Mount Everest lies tucked away in the north-east corner of Nepal, on the border with Tibet, half hidden by its impressive neighbouring peaks. From a distance, as Sir Francis Younghusband once described it:

> Mount Everest for its size is a singularly shy and retiring mountain. It hides itself away behind other mountains. On the north side, in Tibet, it does indeed stand up proudly and alone, a true monarch among mountains. But it stands in a very sparsely inhabited part of Tibet, and very few people ever go to Tibet. From the Indian side only its tip appears amongst a mighty array of peaks which being nearer look higher.[1]

In 1905, during the Younghusband mission to Lhasa, two of his officers actually approached to within sixty miles of Everest and had a clear view of the mountain, even to the extent of picking out the North Ridge as a likely way to the top. Had Younghusband been able to reach the mountain from the south as well, through Nepal, he might have been surprised to discover how true his words were, because to obtain a proper view of Everest it is necessary to travel to the very foot of the mountain and climb some 18,000 ft up the adjacent rocky knoll of Kala Pattar. Even then only the top half is visible.

Everest is an enormous pyramid with three great ridges and three wide faces. When the first expedition reached the mountain in 1921 they were surprised to discover that it is essentially a rock peak, and not the snowy spire it seems from afar. This rocky characteristic is most noticeable from the north where, from the Rongbuk valley, the strata can be seen stretching across the North Face in distinguishable bands. The most prominent of these is at 27,500 ft and is a thick layer of yellowish limestone known as the Yellow Band.[2]

The northern side of the mountain was the first to be explored. From the summit a great ridge runs down to the north-east for three miles, terminating at a col known as the Rapiu La, which separates the East Rongbuk and Kangshung Glaciers. The average slope of this ridge is about one in two, but

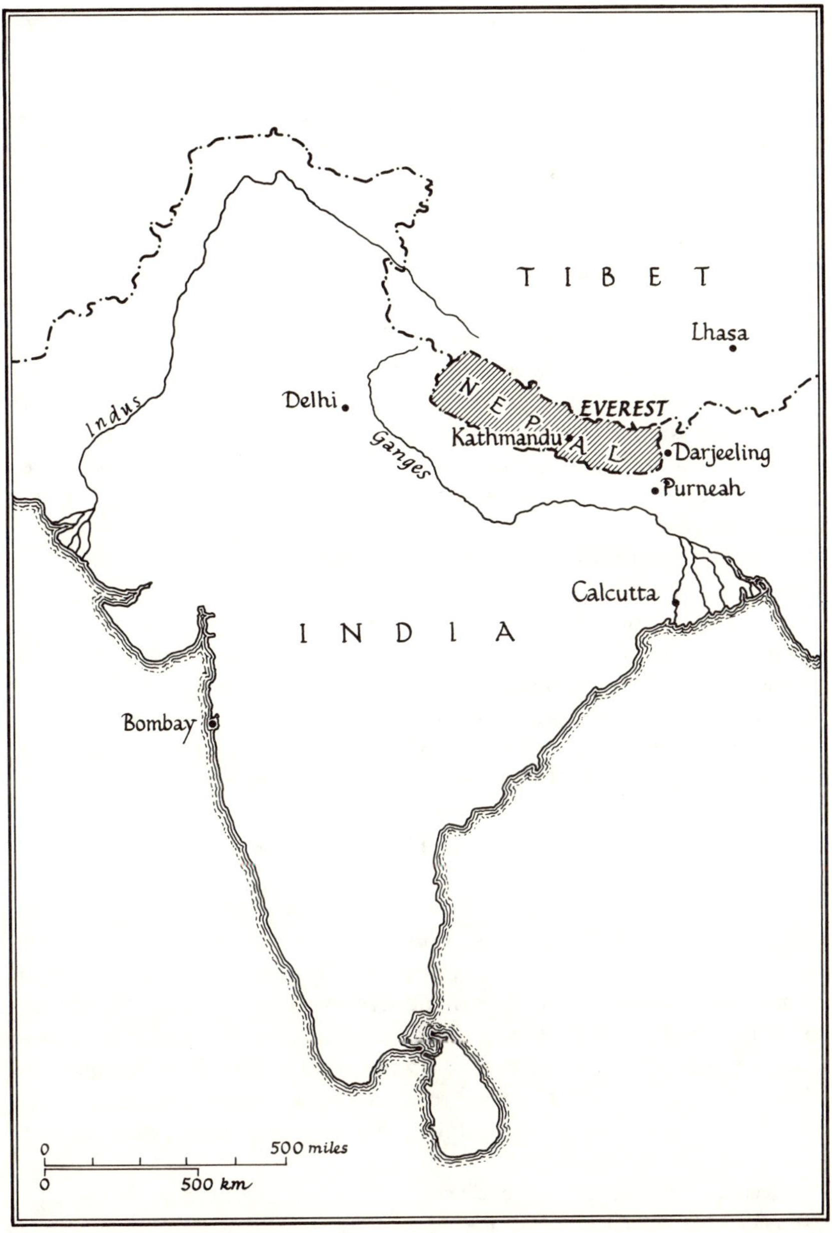


Map 1. The Indian Sub-continent

the top and bottom sections are steeper than the long undulating snow crest which forms the main part.

Rather less than a mile from the summit, this ridge has a distinct shoulder from which another ridge descends northwards to a high and icy col called Chang La – the North Col of the pre-war expeditions. Beyond the col rises Changtse, the 'north peak of Everest' (7,550 m.). This, the North Ridge, also averages one in two, rising up to two quite noticeable 'steps', where the harder limestone tops the Yellow Band. It is this ridge which formed the line of attack of the pre-war British attempts on the mountain, and the Chinese post-war ascents.

The West Ridge of Everest, like the North East Ridge, is about three miles long and of roughly the same average angle, though in this case the average is even more misleading because the central part of the ridge is almost level. The approaches to it are steep and icy and the upper part of the ridge consists of difficult rock. Technically it is probably the most difficult of Everest's ridges, and although the Americans went this way in 1963 they were forced off it in the upper part.

The third and final ridge of Everest is the South East Ridge, which falls from the summit to the South Col in a distance of a mile. Because the South Col is at a considerable altitude – 7,986 m., easily the highest of the cols limiting Everest's ridges – the slope is again about one in two. It is a fairly broad, mixed rock and snow ridge which leads up to a point called the South Summit. The crest then narrows and undulates to the final summit, with one awkward pitch – the Hillary Step, which is sometimes bare rock and sometimes snow-covered. This is the ridge by which the mountain was first climbed and it remains the normal line of ascent.

The frontier between Nepal and Tibet crosses the mountain by the West and South East Ridges.

On the northern side of the mountain the concave North Face stretches between the North Ridge and the West Ridge. As such faces go it is not very steep – 40°–45° at the Yellow Band was Wyn Harris's estimate – though the upper band of limestone is steeper and forms what amounts to a line of crags above the Yellow Band. Because the rock beds dip to the north at an angle of 30°, the effect at the Yellow Band is a series of easily angled overlapping slabs, like enormous roofing tiles. They are littered with detritus and in bad weather covered in snow, but for the climber, as Odell once put it, they are more awkward than difficult.

Because the North Ridge diverges from the North East Ridge some considerable distance below the summit, a small northern-facing facet is formed between the two, overlooking the upper cwm of the East Rongbuk Glacier. Triangular-shaped, with its apex at the North East Shoulder, 1,600 m. above the glacier, this facet dominates the old Camp III of the

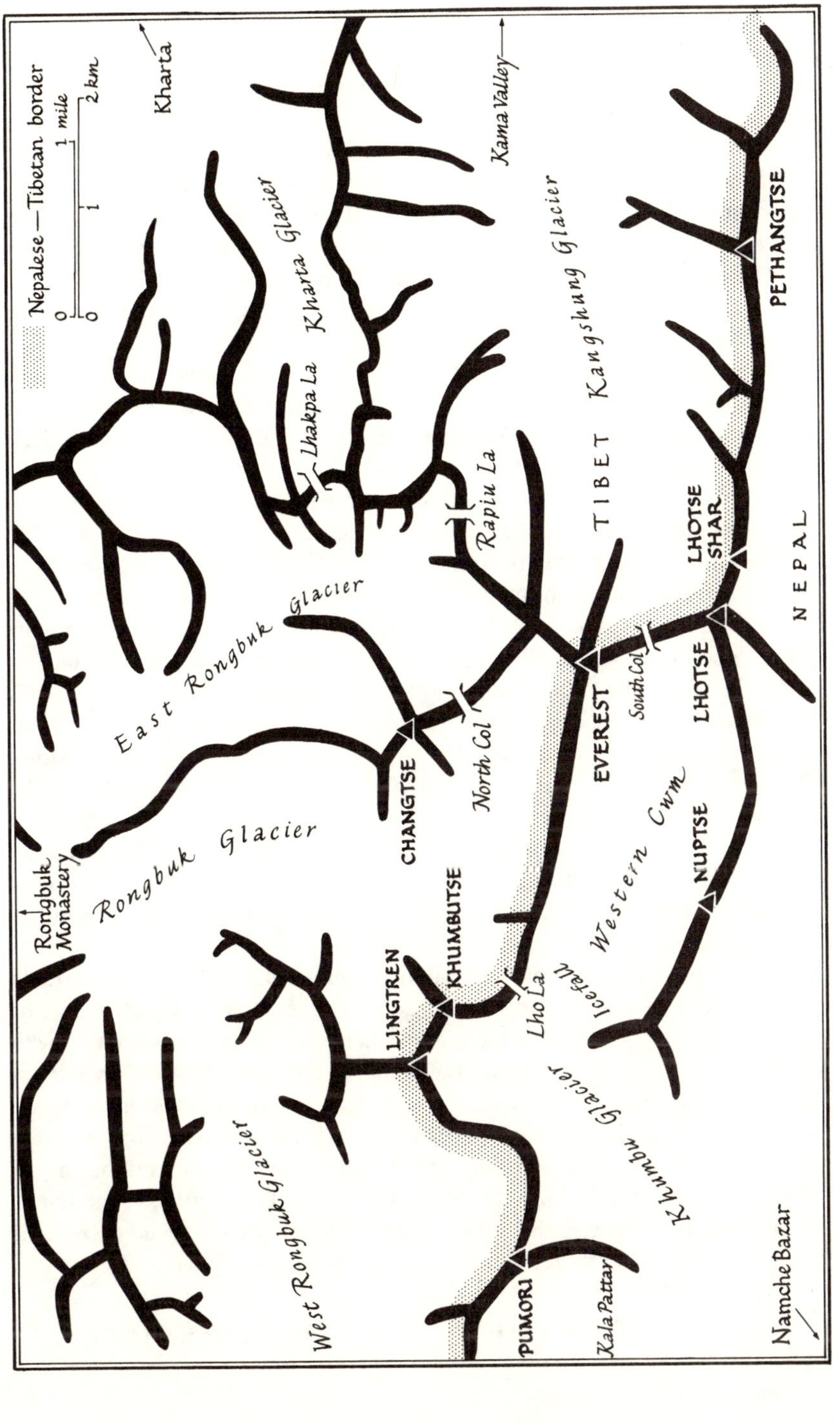


Map 2. Everest: glaciers and ridges

pre-war expeditions, but, understandably enough, was ignored by them. It would probably make a difficult rock and ice climb, though, because it does not reach to the main summit, one of minor importance. So far as is known, nobody has set foot on this face.

Nor has anyone attempted the enormous East Face of Everest, overlooking the Kangshung Glacier. When Mallory first saw it in 1921 he was awed by it: 'Everest ... is seen to fill up the head of the valley with a most formidable circle of cliffs overhung by hanging glaciers ... From this side the mountain seemed quite unclimbable ...'[3] Post-war climbers who have looked down the face from the South East Ridge, or across at it from other summits on the watershed, have been equally impressed.

Unlike the other faces, the East Face has its rock buttresses at the bottom. There are four main spurs above which the rest of the face is a complex of snow and ice slopes continuing upwards and merging with the South East Ridge and the North East Ridge. Above the lower buttresses the angle is not steep, but the various ice walls or serac barriers would undoubtedly make route-finding difficult and the climbing arduous.

The third great face of Everest is the South West Face, overlooking the Western Cwm, and again quite different from the others. For one thing it is very much steeper, the upper 2,000 m. being virtually a rock wall. Steep snow slopes rise from the bed of the Cwm for about 500 m. to the foot of the first cliffs, known as the Rock Band. Because the bedding planes dip to the north, the South West Face exhibits the scarp face of the rock – very much steeper, but more suitable for climbing, although the rock could be of better quality. The Rock Band is a similar schistose shale to that which appears below the Yellow Band of the North Face and has been described by one of the first men to climb it as 'very mixed and extremely rotten'.[4] The Rock Band is some thousand feet high, ending in a narrow ice field stretching across the centre of the face, above which rise steep cliffs formed from the scarp face of the summit limestone.

The Western Cwm is worth describing in some detail because it is central to most of what has happened on Everest since the Second World War. The Cwm is a high glacial hollow formed by a horseshoe of peaks and ridges, with its open end facing west. The northern wall of the Cwm is formed by Everest itself – the towering South West Face. At the head of the Cwm is the South Col, below which is a distinctive rock rib known as the Geneva Spur, running down towards the crevassed floor of the hollow. Continuing round the cirque, a ridge climbs steeply from the South Col to Lhotse (8,501 m.), the fourth highest mountain in the world. From Lhotse the ridge curls round to form the southern rim of the Western Cwm culminating in the long serrated summit of Nuptse (7,979 m.).

Within these high encircling walls the snowy bed of the Cwm is about two miles long and from a half to three quarters of a mile wide. It descends from the steep slopes of the South Col and looks fairly level, though in fact the gradient is almost one in four. It is crevassed, but not unduly so, and in many respects would make the ideal classic glacier approach to the mountain but for the Khumbu Icefall.

The Khumbu Icefall occurs where the glacier bed of the Western Cwm, moving inexorably downwards as glaciers do, tumbles steeply from the mouth of the cirque to the main valley. The fall is about two thousand feet in a distance of rather over a mile: an average slope of 1 in 2½, which is steeper than the huge press of ice can bear and maintain equilibrium. In consequence it fractures into thousands of pieces – an utterly chaotic jumble of ice blocks (seracs) and deep crevasses. Some of the seracs are immense, like crystalline town halls, and because the glacier is always on the move they eventually shift and collapse with a thunderous roar. Every climber knows that the serac he is passing beneath will one day collapse, and he prays fervently that it won't be at that very moment.

The Icefall is a formidable barrier between Base Camp and the mountain. To climb Everest it is essential to place camps in the Western Cwm, which means that laden Sherpas have to pass and repass through the dangerous Khumbu Icefall.

Even climbing the Icefall can be difficult, though it varies from season to season and some years is technically less difficult than in others. The first climber to see the Icefall was Mallory in 1921, when he was trying to find a way from the Rongbuk Glacier to the Western Cwm. He reached a col near Pumori on the watershed between Tibet and Nepal, but discovered he could not cross it because the Khumbu side was much too steep. He could, however, see the Icefall:

> . . . we have seen this Western glacier and are not sorry we have not to go up it. It is terribly steep and broken . . . It was not a very likely chance that the gap between Everest and the South Peak could be reached from the West. From what we have seen now I do not much fancy it would be possible, even could one get up the glacier.[5]

Yet it was by this very route that Everest was first climbed, though Mallory can be excused his pessimism, for looking at the Icefall from a distance it does seem fairly impossible.

It is never a comfortable place. The late Dougal Haston described his feelings about the Icefall in 1971:

> . . . it was always a mentally exhausting journey. In some places the only possible route was under overhanging shaky seracs. Frequent crossings of this type of passage are more wearing than big wall climbing. You cannot

> even take the normal safety precaution of going when there is no sun as the sun is on the Icefall for most of the day. One can only go in and hope. On some occasions complete sections of the route were destroyed by movement of ice. When one finally comes out of this icy mess into the Western Cwm it is like being in a newer, brighter land.[6]

A recent Everest climber told the author that too much emphasis should not be placed on the difficulties of the Khumbu Icefall, but there is no doubt that it is the greatest single obstacle in approaching the mountain. There is nothing comparable on the northern side. It may not be technically difficult for the modern ice climber – expeditions usually find a way through it in about a week – but it is always dangerous. At least eleven men have died there and for any Everest expedition the Khumbu Icefall must seem like a permanent ghost at a banquet.

By whatever route the climber decides to tackle Mount Everest he must first, as Mallory once observed, find the mountain. The approaches are in fact more numerous than is at first apparent: six have been tried at one time or another, two of them esoteric if enterprising (see Chapter 11) and all but one subject nowadays to the political restrictions of Chinese Tibet.

The eastern approaches to the mountain were explored by the 1921 expedition, but seldom, if ever, since. There are two alternative routes – the Kharta and Kama valleys, both leading up to the mountains from the deep ravine of the Arun river and the village of Kharta, where the expedition made their base in verdant surroundings which contrasted strongly with the bleak valley of Rongbuk to the north. The Kharta valley leads without difficulty to the Lhakpa La, a high but otherwise easy pass over into the head of the East Rongbuk Glacier below the North Col – this was the first approach route to Everest, and one wonders why it was never used again, if only to take advantage of the idyllic base and good supplies at Kharta.

The Kama valley also provides an easy approach, this time to the Kangshung Glacier and the stupendous East Face of Everest. The glacier here seems unlikely to be as simple as its neighbour, the Kharta, but the whole valley, rimmed with peaks such as Chomo Lonzo, Makalu, Pethangtse, Lhotse and Everest, provides one of the finest mountain panoramas in the world.

The main approach route from the north – that used by the pre-war expeditions – began at Darjeeling and entered Tibet from Sikkim. Then after a long western march over the bleak uplands it eventually turned south to the village of Chobuk, and entered the Rongbuk valley – a truly desolate place, plagued by incessant winds. Nevertheless, it had the advantage that the Rongbuk and East Rongbuk Glaciers which flow into the valley give uncomplicated approaches direct to the flanks of the mountain.

Nowadays, for the time being at least, these Tibetan approaches to Everest are of only academic interest to Western climbers, who are confined to the one standard approach from the south.

The southern route (see Map 5, p.256) involves a long trek from Kathmandu, the Nepalese capital, through leech-infested rhododendron jungles, and over a switchback of steep ridges which makes daily progress slow. The whole march is across the 'grain' of the country until the Dudh Kosi river is reached. Charles Clarke, doctor on Bonington's 1975 expedition, described the tremendous scale of the Dudh Kosi:

> At last we have reached the Dudh Kosi; how the scale of the country has changed from the little Beatrix Potter valleys and re-entrants to the vast sweeps of the ridges of the Dudh Kosi. No wonder there is the highest mountain in the world at the top of it. . . The majestic scale is impossible to capture on film and it is only by having to walk up the Dudh Kosi that one realizes how enormous it all is. Each little side valley is as large as most main Himalayan valleys and each ridge or re-entrant takes an age to cross.[7]

At Namche Bazar, the Sherpa 'capital', the vegetation begins to thin out as altitude is gained. It is an unusual village where the houses are built round a curve in the hillside like an enormous Hollywood Bowl. A day's march further stands Thyangboche monastery, a most sacred place for Buddhists, built on a grassy alp in an idyllic setting and dominated by impressive peaks such as Kantega and Ama Dablam. Eric Shipton, who led the first reconnaissance expedition up the valley in 1951, described it thus:

> During the past few days we had become familiar with the extraordinary beauty of the country, but this did not lessen the dramatic effect of the scene which confronted us when we awoke next morning. The sky was clear; the grass of the meadow, starred with gentians, had been touched with frost which sparkled in the early sunlight; the meadow was surrounded by quiet woods of fir, tree-juniper, birch and rhododendron silvered with moss. Though the deciduous trees were still green, there were already brilliant splashes of autumn colour in the undergrowth. To the south the forested slopes fell steeply to the Dudh Kosi, the boom of the river now silenced by the profound depth of the gorge. To the north-east, 12 miles away across the valley of the Imja Khola, stood the Nuptse-Lhotse ridge, with the peak of Everest appearing behind. But even this stupendous wall, nowhere less than 25,000 feet throughout its five-mile length, seemed dwarfed by the slender spires of fluted ice that towered all about us, near and utterly inaccessible.[8]

From Thyangboche (3,867 m.) the narrow track climbs steadily up the valley towards the Khumbu Glacier, still two marches away. In autumn the route is ablaze with flame-coloured berberis bushes, but as height is gained the hillsides become increasingly bare of vegetation and, were it not for the snowcapped peaks towering above, the scenery could be one of the bleaker parts of the Scottish Highlands or the Pennine moors. Eventually the track leads onto the moraines of the Khumbu Glacier, whose ice, six miles long, is covered by a chaotic jumble of rock debris. Near its head, and between the two beautiful mountains of Pumori and Nuptse, lies the area designated as Base Camp.

The walk to Base Camp from Kathmandu takes two weeks or more, but this is by no means time completely wasted. Quite apart from the incredible beauty of the scenery it is a very good training walk for would-be climbers, because acclimatization is sufficiently gradual.

Nowadays, the visitor can be saved much of the walk by taking a light plane from Kathmandu to Lukla airstrip, two easy days' walk below Namche Bazar, or even to an airstrip above Namche itself, where the Japanese have built the Everest View Hotel. Such a course is not always wise: the too sudden gain in height can lead to altitude sickness. Expeditions seldom, if ever, take this short cut. They prefer to walk in the whole way.

Apart from the other difficulties of reaching and climbing the mountain, any expedition to Everest must take into account the monsoon, which rolls up from the south-west about the middle of June to break against the mountain barrier. Everest is in the eastern part of the Himalaya: the rains last a little longer than elsewhere in the range, and don't die away entirely until about the end of September. During this period there is little chance of climbing the mountain. Apart from the weather itself the accumulation of fresh powder snow would make progress difficult and avalanches a constant menace.

Even the southern approach march through Nepal can be unpleasant in the monsoon: views are clouded over, the rivers are swollen and the leeches are voracious. On the other hand, the monsoon has little effect in Tibet and would not hamper an expedition approaching Everest from the north.

The monsoon dictates two periods during which Everest can be attempted – the pre-monsoon season and the post-monsoon season – and it is the former which has become the classic period for climbing the mountain. Then conditions are at their best, with snow cover at its firmest and days which get progressively warmer. For a month – roughly mid-May to mid-June – there is often a period of calm weather during which the assault can take place – the first ascent of the mountain, in 1953, occurred on 29 May, for example.

Nevertheless the weather can be fickle. Storms can occur even during this period, possibly during a crucial stage of the climb, with traumatic results for those caught in exposed situations. In some seasons, the weather can be almost wholly bad, so that an expedition has practically no chance of success – the expeditions of 1936 and 1938 suffered this fate.

# 1

# Peaks and Lamas

The first tentative steps towards Himalayan climbing were taken in 1879 and 1883 when the Hungarian mountaineer Von Dechy and the Englishman W.W. Graham paid their respective visits. Von Dechy was taken ill and little was accomplished, while Graham's accounts of his exploits were so full of discrepancies that they have been a source of argument from that day to this.

Martin Conway's expedition of 1892 was a very different affair altogether. Whereas Von Dechy and Graham had gone simply for the sport, Conway had more serious intentions, the chief of which was to make a name for himself as an explorer. He chose the savage Karakorum region beyond the western end of the Himalayan range, and by modelling his expedition along the lines of the one that the great Edward Whymper had led to the Andes some twelve years earlier, combined both exploration and climbing. Initially he had designs on K2, the second highest mountain in the world, but one sight of that immense spire of rock and ice was enough to convince him he did not have the resources to tackle it. Nevertheless he was successful in an industrious sort of way: the Royal Geographical Society later published his map of the area, and in reaching the summit of 'Pioneer Peak' (22,600 ft), a subsidiary of Baltoro Kangri, he established a new height record. He collected specimens of flora and fauna from the area and kept meticulously detailed notes of everything. It was in fact the very model of what Victorian intellectuals thought an expedition should be, and though with hindsight and vastly more experience to draw upon we can today dismiss its achievements as being somewhat pedestrian, Conway's Karakorum journey was a minor triumph in its time.

News about the expedition, which Conway fed to the public in letters to *The Times*, stimulated much interest and discussion about the Himalaya in general. Speculation inevitably veered round to Mount Everest. Could it be climbed? One man had been maintaining for some time that it could – Clinton Dent. As early as 1885 he had written:

> To my mind at least, as far as human endurance is concerned, it would be no more surprising to me to hear that a man had succeeded in walking up Mt Everest than to know that a man can succeed in standing an arctic climate while on a sledging expedition. Objections like the difficulty of arranging for a supply of food, of expense, of risk and so forth, are not taken into account – they are really beside the question: they have not proved insuperable obstacles in the case of arctic exploration: they will not prove insurmountable to the ambitious mountaineer we are contemplating. I do not for a moment say that it would be wise to ascend Mt Everest, but I believe most firmly that it is humanly possible to do so; and, further, I feel sure that even in our own time, perhaps, the truth of these views will receive material corroboration.[1]

When the Conway expedition raised the matter again in the public's mind Dent re-affirmed his views in the magazine *Nineteenth Century* with an article entitled 'Can Mount Everest be climbed?'.

The Conway expedition had a tangible link with the first direct steps towards Everest, for in his Karakorum party Conway included a young lieutenant from the 5th Gurkhas, the Hon. Charles Granville Bruce. Charlie Bruce, known as Bruiser to his friends, was to play a leading role in the early story of Everest exploration.

He was a remarkable character: a great bull of a man, strong, adventurous and inclined to horseplay. To his diminutive Gurkhas he was like a father, big, benevolent and bawdy – a man who would sit round the camp fire with them at night cracking dirty jokes, breaking into his hissing laugh, and who, even when he had risen to the rank of colonel, would take on half a dozen of them at once in impromptu wrestling matches on the barrack square.

The frontier campaigns which were then commonplace in India involved mountainous country and Bruce had soon realized the value of training his tough little Gurkha soldiers in mountain warfare, which in turn had led to his interest in mountaineering for its own sake. The Gurkhas, being a hill people, had taken quite naturally to the training and several of them shared Bruce's enthusiasm for climbing. They took part in several of the early Himalayan expeditions, and two of them died with Mummery on the ill-fated Nanga Parbat expedition of 1895.

Conway's Karakorum expedition of 1892 was Bruce's first real expedition involving systematic exploration and climbing, and despite being laid low with malaria for part of the time (a disease which recurred on later occasions) he threw all his considerable energy into the project – 'a steam engine plus goods train', as Conway described him. Already Bruce's thoughts were turning towards Everest.

The following year, 1893, found Bruce in Chitral, where he met a kindred spirit in Francis Edward Younghusband, who was serving there as Political Officer at the time. Younghusband, barely thirty years old, was a dynamic little man with a Kitchener moustache who had already made a name for himself through some remarkable journeys in Asia, including one across the Gobi Desert and over the formidable Mustagh Pass. In Chitral he and Bruce teamed up to climb a local peak, the shapely Ispero Zorn; it was on the polo ground in Chitral that Bruce suggested they should explore the approaches to Everest with a view to an ascent. This was the first direct proposal to climb Mount Everest ever made. Nothing came of their plans. Each went his own way as duty called along a troubled frontier and almost thirty years were to pass before they were united again in their common purpose under very different circumstances.

When Lord Curzon was appointed Viceroy of India in 1898 the Everest story took a step forward. Only thirty-nine, he was a brilliant politician of wide intellect, something of a traveller and, though not a mountaineer, the sort of man who could sense the adventure of exploring and climbing the highest mountain in the world. He had met and befriended Younghusband in Chitral and he must also have discussed the idea with Douglas Freshfield, who was a past President of the Alpine Club and an important figure in the Royal Geographical Society, for in July 1899 Curzon wrote to him saying he hoped to visit Nepal shortly and that he would seek permission there for an attempt on Everest. Nothing came of this, but later that year when Freshfield was in India the two men had further talks on the subject.

Everest, however, was small beer compared with other problems facing Curzon. One of these was the enormous power vacuum represented by the vast plateau of Tibet, where the Dalai Lama was thought to be plotting with the Tsar, leaving the way open for a possible occupation of the country by Russia. In British eyes this was a direct threat to India and so, in order to show the flag and keep out the Russians, in 1903 Curzon sent Colonel Younghusband into Tibet ostensibly to negotiate frontiers and trade. But the Tibetans refused to enter into negotiations and as a consequence Younghusband, his mission now strengthened by troops from India, marched on Lhasa. The advance was bitter and bloody – it took the British forces four months to reach the Tibetan capital, where a treaty was finally signed in September 1904. The Dalai Lama fled to Mongolia, and Colonel Younghusband was knighted by a grateful Empire.

Younghusband's mission was successful in keeping Russia out of Tibet. The British and Russians agreed to recognize the suzerainty of China over the bleak uplands – though at the same time the British were careful to supply the Tibetans with enough arms to keep the Chinese out, too. When in fact the Chinese did return in force, in 1910, the Dalai Lama fled to India and stayed there for about two years, until a revolution in their homeland caused the

Chinese troops to withdraw from Lhasa. From 1913 to 1950 Tibet was an autonomous state.[2]

Younghusband's mission and the subsequent events had considerable bearing on the early Everest expeditions. In the first place, despite the heavy fighting, Younghusband's troops did not ravage the countryside, nor did they seek to occupy the country permanently, and later the sanctuary given by the Indian Government to the Dalai Lama helped to predispose the authorities in Lhasa to look favourably upon the British. Despite the fact that the exclusion of foreigners was an almost fanatical tenet of Tibetan policy, Britain undoubtedly acquired special privileges denied other nations.

There was also an interesting sideshow during the mission itself. When Younghusband withdrew from Lhasa, the opportunity was taken to send a reconnaissance party under Captain C.G. Rawling and Captain C.H.D. Ryder to Gartok in Western Tibet, in the course of which journey they saw Everest from the north. Though they were sixty miles away from the great mountain (and had no time to go closer) Rawling observed the North Ridge and thought it might be feasible to climb it. He was fired with the ambition to try as soon as the opportunity arose.

It seems strange that after the success of Younghusband's mission Curzon, who was keen to see Everest climbed, should not consider an expedition through Tibet. Had he consulted Rawling, Younghusband or Bruce he would have found them unanimous in recommending such an approach, but for some reason Curzon seems only to have had in mind an approach through Nepal, a country, like Tibet, closed to foreigners. In 1905 he wrote to Freshfield outlining in some detail a major mountaineering project:

> I want to bring up again a question which I think I mentioned to you while in India. It has always seemed to me a reproach that with the second highest mountain in the world for the most part in British territory and with the highest in a neighbouring and friendly state, we, the mountaineers and pioneers par excellence of the universe, make no sustained and scientific attempt to climb to the top of either of them.
>
> My time in India will not in any case be very much longer and my successor may not care for such matters. I would be prepared either for the forthcoming summer or the summer following to lend every aid the Government can give to a thoroughly well-appointed mountaineering party, comprised of trained experts with Swiss Guides, that should come out with the set object of climbing one of these mountains.
>
> I imagine that Kinchinjunga will be chosen because it is mainly in British territory and at no great distance from a British base and British supplies.
>
> I should not mind asking the Maharaja of Nepal for permission for a party to climb Everest but the Nepalese are very suspicious and he might refuse.

Again I do not see how the coolies and supplies could be obtained in such a region. Would you care to interest yourself at all in such an expedition? It occurs to me that it might be done by the Alpine Club and the R.G.S. in combination and you are at liberty to pass on what I have written to the President of either society. I suppose that the months from August to October would be the time. It occurs to me that two years, or possibly three, might be required.

Camps would be instituted and gradually pushed forward until one day the advance camp would be placed on a spot from which a dash could be made for the summit. Coolies could be trained, attempts made on the mountain from different sides, everything leading up to the final denouement. I do not know what such expeditions cost. But it is possible that the Home Societies might pay half if the Government of India paid the other. I have not consulted my colleagues. But I think I could promise this assent to a moiety of £2,500 or £3,000 i.e. to half of a total expenditure of £5,000–£6,000.

Ought we not to be able to do this?[3]

Curzon's letter reveals his enthusiasm for the project, though, as he hints in the letter, his days as Viceroy were numbered, and he resigned in November.

Meanwhile Freshfield took the letter to the Alpine Club Committee, who appointed a sub-committee (of which both Conway and Freshfield were members) to deal with the matter. In their reply to the Viceroy on 6 June no mention was made of money:

The President and Committee of the Alpine Club have received with great satisfaction the information that his Excellency, the Viceroy of India, proposes to encourage a systematic attempt to reach the summit of Kinchinjunga or of Mt Everest.

They are convinced that in the course of such an attempt, scientific results of great value in several directions may be anticipated.

They will be prepared, when the proper time arrives, to give every support in their power to a scheme of such far-reaching importance.[4]

In fact they voted a miserly £100 – hardly the sort of money Curzon had in mind!

When the news of the Viceroy's proposal became generally known, A.L. Mumm, a wealthy publisher who was a member of the Alpine Club, suggested that an attempt on Mount Everest would be a fitting celebration of the Alpine Club's Golden Jubilee, due in 1907. He guaranteed to meet the expenses himself. The idea was eagerly approved. The party was to be Mumm, with his usual guide Moritz Inderbinnen, Dr Tom Longstaff with his guides, the two Brocherel brothers, Alexis and Henri, and Charlie Bruce with nine Gurkhas.[5]

But somewhere along the line Curzon's original intention for an expedition through Nepal was abandoned. Instead, moves were made to gain access through Tibet.

At first all went well. Sir George Goldie, President of the Royal Geographical Society, and his Council, gave active support to the plans, and much to the delight of everyone concerned the new Viceroy of India, Lord Minto – himself a member of the Alpine Club – promised to further the cause once he was firmly established in his post.

However, almost at the last minute, the plans were scotched abruptly. The villain of the piece was John Morley, Secretary of State for India:

> Morley was an elderly, austere, dry-as-dust little man, ambitious and determined to use the powers he had now acquired. His real interest lay in literature (especially the drier aspects of it) and sport made no claims on him. His Cabinet colleagues were said to nickname him 'Aunt Priscilla', and Campbell-Bannerman once spoke of him as a 'petulant spinster'. Morley had thoroughly disapproved of Curzon's Tibetan policy, resulting in the Younghusband mission of 1904, and though Curzon had now left India, Morley was determined to prevent any further excursions into that country if he could . . . on the plea that the expedition would be contrary to the spirit of the recently concluded Anglo-Russian Convention, Morley banned the venture . . .[6]

Morley's action was so high-handed that it caused considerable resentment and Sir George Goldie felt obliged to publish the relevant correspondence in *The Times*. In his covering letter he remarked caustically:

> I leave it to others to comment on the regrettable interposition by a Liberal Government of a Himalayan barrier to the advance of knowledge in this direction.

In a memorandum of 23 January 1907, Goldie had detailed the proposals for the expedition. Regarding Tibet he wrote:

> As the expedition would turn its back on Lhasa directly it left Indian territory, and as the regions through which it would pass are very sparsely populated, there can be no question of Tibetan timidity or anxiety being aroused or any friction or trouble occurring during the journey. It would not resemble Mr Sherring's mission in 1905, which penetrated into the heart of Western Tibet, and which, nevertheless, encountered no opposition whatever.

Morley chose to interpret this in a manner deliberately insulting to Goldie and the Society:

I have given full consideration to the proposal in your memorandum of 23rd January that a British party should be given facilities by the Government of India to attempt the ascent of Mount Everest from the Tibetan side, avoiding Nepaulese territory; and I am sorry to be obliged to refuse the present request for the same reasons which, as stated in the official letter from the Under Secretary of State to the Royal Geographical Society of March 28th last, made it necessary for me to my great regret, to decide that it was not possible, consistently with the interest of the policy of his Majesty's Government, for the Government of India to give encouragement or help to exploration in Tibet. There has been no change in the political situation since the letter of 28th March from this office to modify the considerations of high Imperial policy which led his Majesty's Government to decide that it was inexpedient to raise the question of facilities for travellers in Tibet with the authorities of Lhasa; and there can be no doubt that a British expedition proceeding by the route proposed through Tibetan territory, furtively as is suggested, and without previous notice to the Lhasa Government, would raise the question which his Majesty's Government wish to avoid in a more embarrassing form than if an application were made to the Tibetan Government for their consent.

I would add that this decision is based solely on considerations of public policy, and personally I am very sorry for the disappointment which it will cause to Major Bruce and Mr Longstaff.

Goldie was admirably restrained in his reply to this misrepresentation of the facts by Morley. He wrote:

I am grieved at the decision announced in your official letter of the 8th inst., less on account of the public-spirited men who were prepared to risk their lives or spend their money on scientific object than of the cause of the knowledge itself, which would have been promoted by the observations of various kinds made during the ascent of Mount Everest. I desire to disclaim very clearly and positively two assumptions on which your official letters appear largely to rest.

First, it never occurred to me that the expedition would be in any way 'furtive'. I assumed that the Government of India would notify the Lhasa Government that a purely scientific party desired to move from the British frontier along the sparsely populated inside edge of Tibetan territory to the summit of Everest, keeping its back turned on Lhasa for the whole of the journey. I do not believe in 'furtive' policy except in war, when deceiving the enemy is recognized as fair.

Secondly, I submit that such a journey has nothing substantial in common with an exploration, such as was refused in your letter of March

28, 1906, which would have penetrated a considerable distance into a populous part of Tibet and largely in the direction of Lhasa.[7]

*The Times*, in a chicken-hearted leader on the affair, said, '. . .it is known that Russian susceptibilities are easily awakened by reports of movements, however innocent, in the heart of Asia.'[8] Douglas Freshfield was less polite: 'Their [the Himalaya's] would-be conqueror has either to evade avalanches or get round Lord Morley, and I don't know which is the more awkward obstacle.'[9]

Mumm, Bruce and Longstaff shifted their attention to Garhwal, where there were no restrictions, and made the first ascent of Trisul (23,360 ft), which remained the highest summit to be attained for the next twenty-one years.[10]

It was a fine achievement – but very much a second best to what might have been. This came over strongly at the Alpine Club meeting at which Longstaff recounted his adventures. Lord Curzon was present and said:

> I always thought that Kangchenjunga, being within our territory, and Everest only a little way outside it, and the English being the first mountaineering race in the world, an Englishman ought to be the first on top of Kangchenjunga, and, if possible, of Everest also ... bitterly do I regret the opportunity gone. But another Pharaoh has arisen i.e. the present Secretary of State for India, who knows not Joseph, by which I mean myself, and who has no love for scientific expeditions on the Tibetan frontier.[11]

Freshfield said:

> At the last moment, however – as so often happens in stories – there appears a malignant fairy who was not invited to the Christening ... Our chief consolation lies in the reflection that the agreement made with Russia to prohibit all scientific exploration in Tibet only holds good for three years, and that it is more than probable that its originators will not be in a position to renew it ...[12]

And so the first serious attempt to mount an Everest expedition floundered on the harder rocks of bureaucracy.

Even though no expedition visited Everest in 1907 another small chink was made in the mountain's armour. In that year an Indian Survey servant, Natha Singh, was allowed by the Nepalese to penetrate the Dudh Kosi and map the peaks en route. It was the first visit by an outsider to the valley which many years later was to become the highway to Everest. Natha Singh's trek had to be a fairly rapid one, but he penetrated beyond Lobuche and outlined the end of the Khumbu Glacier.

In the years that followed, though the hopes of the Alpine Club had been crushed by Morley, individual mountaineers tried their luck with the authorities. In 1908 Bruce asked for an expedition through Nepal, but was again frustrated by 'political and religious prejudices'.[13] A year later the formidable Italian explorer and mountaineer the Duke of the Abruzzi tried for an attempt through Tibet, but negotiations broke down and he switched his attention to the Karakorum giant, K2, instead. Meanwhile, Curzon had not given up. In October 1911 he wrote to the Maharaja of Nepal expressing the hope that the latter would sanction an Everest expedition, but again nothing came of it. Dr A.M. Kellas, who had done some important climbs in Sikkim and Kumaun, also became interested in Everest and worked out a secret plan of attack from the north. 'Nothing ever came of this,' wrote Captain Noel later, 'for the authorized Expeditions took the place of furtive raids.'[14]

In 1913 he was followed by Colonel C.G. Rawling, the surveyor who had seen the mountain from the north during the Younghusband mission of 1904. Rawling outlined plans for an expedition to include Tom Longstaff and Jack Noel which gained the approval of the Royal Geographical Society and the Alpine Club. The idea was to have two expeditions – the first purely reconnaissance – but his scheme had to be postponed with the outbreak of the First World War.

All was frustration. Years later Tom Longstaff wrote bitterly:

> Today people may realize the hopeless frustration of battling against political difficulties of access; it was only such difficulties which so long debarred us from exploring and attempting to climb Mount Everest.[15]

During the 1914–18 war the middle classes, from which the nation's climbers were drawn, suffered out of all proportion to their numbers. In countless futile sorties 'over the top' they died in their thousands. Of the Everest pioneers Rawling and Bruce both became generals: Rawling was killed and Bruce severely wounded. Others who might have taken part in the first Everest attempts suffered similar fates: Geoffrey Winthrop Young, one of the most skilful Alpinists of the pre-war years, lost a leg; Herford, Oppenheimer, Jeffcoat and others – all young men of skill and promise – were swept away in the senseless holocaust. Who can tell what effect the presence of these men might have had on the early Everest expeditions? What if Young and Norton had been teamed together, two incredibly strong climbers, or Mallory and Herford? As it was, the first three Everest expeditions had to rely to a great extent on the Old Guard, men who had been active long before the war, and though their exploits were magnificent it was like attempting the mountain with one hand cut off.

The political situation with regard to Nepal was not affected by the war, but Russia in the aftermath of revolution posed no further threat so far as Tibet was concerned. China, too, had had a revolution and the Chinese garrison had withdrawn from Lhasa, harried by the Tibetans. 'They had conquered,' wrote Noel, with more enthusiasm than accuracy, 'had beheaded almost every Chinaman in Tibet, and their country was now their own . . .' No longer could the British Government forbid expeditions into Tibet on the grounds of 'considerations of high Imperial policy'. It was simply a matter of discussion with the Dalai Lama, and he had every reason to be friendly towards the British, not only because they had once provided him with sanctuary in India but also because he depended on them for ammunition.

Barely a month after the Armistice, in 1918, moves were made to reopen the Everest question. Sir Thomas Holdich, President of the Royal Geographical Society, acting with the knowledge of the Alpine Club, wrote to the Secretary of State for India, requesting permission for an expedition to Everest. His idea was that trials with oxygen equipment should be made on a peak called Kamet, in the Kumaun region, followed by an attack on Everest the following year. The Secretary of State put the proposals to the Viceroy.

The result was three months of silence from the Indian Government. Obviously something was required to prod them into action, and the quickest way to achieve this was to awaken public opinion. A splendid opportunity arose in March. On 10 March 1919, a young and virtually unknown Major J.B. Noel[16] rose to address the Royal Geographical Society with a paper entitled 'A Journey to Tashirak in Southern Tibet, and the Eastern Approaches to Mount Everest'. Everybody who mattered was present.

John Noel was a handsome young officer of the Machine Gun Corps, with a strong sense of romantic adventure, combined with something of the entrepreneur. The subject of his lecture was a journey he had made in 1913 from Sikkim into Tibet. The journey was made illicitly and in disguise:

> To defeat observation I intended to avoid the villages and settled parts generally, to carry our food, and to keep to those more desolate stretches where only an occasional shepherd was to be seen. My men were not startlingly different from the Tibetans, and if I darkened my skin and my hair I could pass, not as a native – my colour and shape of my eyes would prevent that – but as a Mohammedan from India.[17]

His purpose was simple: 'to seek out the passes that led to Everest and if possible to come to close quarters with the mountain.'[18]

The route he chose was north from Gangtok along the Tista river towards the well-known pass of the Sepo La, which led directly to Kampa Dzong, but before reaching the pass, which he knew would be guarded, he turned left into the little known district of Lhonak, to the north of the Kangchenjunga massif, and passed into Tibet by a difficult pass called the Choten Nyi-ma La. He had expected to meet a combination of river systems which would lead him to

Everest, but to his dismay he discovered the map to be hopelessly wrong and another high range of mountains lay between himself and his goal. With his slender resources there was no way he could cross these mountains, but he did have a minor reward:

> Presently, while watching the panorama, the shifting clouds revealed other high mountain masses in the distance; and directly over the crest of Taringban appeared a sharp spire peak. This, through its magnetic bearing by my compass, proved itself to be none other than Mount Everest. A thousand feet of the summit was visible.[19]

He got within forty miles of the mountain – the nearest any Westerner had ever been.

Noel's lecture did little to advance the knowledge of Everest except to show that a short cut from Sikkim was not a practical proposition. Nevertheless, an impressive quorum of speakers contributed to the discussion after the lecture. There were Kellas, Freshfield, Farrar (President of the Alpine Club) and Younghusband – all big guns – and such was the prestige of the R.G.S. in those days that the debate was widely reported. It even received a somewhat laboured satire from *Punch*, entitled 'Himalayans at Play' and ending:

> The chairman having expressed his regret that Sir Marcon Tinway was not present to describe his experiments with manlifting kites and trained albatrosses, the assembly dispersed after singing the Tibetan national anthem.[20]

The effect of Noel's lecture was to bring the whole question of Everest into public discussion again, which was what the R.G.S. wanted. A deputation from the Society promptly called on the Secretary of State to urge some action in the matter of an expedition. Within a month they had their reply from India – no. The Indian Government blandly asserted that relations with Tibet were strained at that moment, and they also found a new bogy-man to replace Russia – Japan. Adding insult to injury, they also refused permission for an expedition to Kamet, though Kamet was approached entirely through India itself. Whether the refusal was meant to put the Royal Geographical Society in its place, for daring to bring pressure to bear, or whether it was sheer bloody-mindedness on the part of the Indian Government (with or without the collusion of the home Government), is hard to say.

Nevertheless the Society treated this as a temporary rebuff and background preparation went ahead with the Alpine Club based on the two-expedition plan originally proposed by Rawling. J.P. Farrar, as President of the Alpine Club, was prepared for the Club to contribute £500 towards expenses, and he suggested that Marcel Kurz, a noted Swiss topographer, should accompany the expedition as surveyor. But Kurz's demand that he should be described as the sole author of any map 'trod very heavily on the toes of the Geographical people', and Kurz's services were refused by the R.G.S. In any case the Society wanted the expedition to be all British.

Farrar was a forceful personality, and a man who liked direct action. He was not in sympathy with the two-expedition plan. 'I am all for going for the highest peak at once,' he wrote.[21] In this he was unsuccessful, probably because the Royal Geographical Society were as interested in mapping the Everest region as they were in climbing the mountain, if not more so. With regard to the actual climbers he was strongly convinced that the leading man should be George Finch: 'If he and his brother Max . . . cannot do the job, then we have nobody who can.' He thought the Scottish climber Raeburn should look after Base Camp. As to Freshfield's suggestion that Dr A.M. Kellas should lead the expedition, Farrar was scathing:

> . . .Kellas has never climbed a mountain, but has only walked about on steep snow with a lot of coolies, and the only time they got on a very steep place they all tumbled down and ought to have been killed!![22]

This was a gross libel on poor Kellas, who had a number of high altitude ascents to his credit, but Farrar was already determined that the Alpine Club would not bow the knee to Freshfield and his geographers when it came to choosing men to climb Everest. In mountaineering matters, he said Freshfield was 'absolutely vieux jeu'.

There thus began a mild love-hate relationship between the two organizations which has endured to the present day.

On 26 April 1920, an expedition Committee meeting was held and a series of resolutions stated:

1 That the principal object of the expedition should be the ascent of Mount Everest, to which all preliminary reconnaissance should be directed.
2 That the mountain should be approached from the north through Tibet, and that no attempt should be made to get permission to pass through Nepal from the south, but that the Nepalese Government should be asked to assist with the supplies and transport.
3 That the Royal Geographical Society should be responsible for the preliminary negotiations with the British, the Indian, and the Tibetan Governments, and for the organization of the expedition up to the base camp from which the ascent of the mountain would be made, and that the Alpine Club should undertake the organization of the actual ascent.
4 That the Colonel Howard Bury be asked to visit India this year with the object:
   (a) of obtaining the support of the Government of India for the expedition,

(b) if it seems desirable, of going to Gyantse to interest the Tibetan authorities, and,

(c) of making an air reconnaissance of the approaches to the mountain with the assistance of the Royal Air Force in India.

5 That the Secretary of State for India be asked to support Col. Howard Bury's mission to the Government of India, and request the co-operation of the Royal Air Force.

6 That the work of the expedition be organized to cover two seasons, the first devoted to reconnaissance, the second to the ascent: that the co-operation of the Survey of India be asked, and that the party engaged in the reconnaissance include experienced Alpine climbers to examine the technical difficulties of the ascent.

7 That the Council of the R.G.S. be asked to earmark for the Everest expedition any money from the Society's funds which can be devoted to exploration and that a special fund be raised to cover the cost of the expedition, to which the Governments be invited to contribute.

8 That the personnel of the expedition be British subjects, and that no applications for the co-operation of non-British subjects be entertained.

9 That no public announcement for the present proposals be made until the consent of the Indian Government has been obtained.

10 That the Secretary of State for India be at once approached for continued support of the proposal, and that he be asked to receive a deputation.

11 That a joint working Committee of the Royal Geographical Society, and the Alpine Club be formed as soon as necessary for the organization and direction of the expedition.[23]

Despite Resolution No. 9, *The Times* outlined the plans for the forthcoming expedition, quoting from a speech Younghusband had made to the Royal Geographical Society the previous evening:

> Although there was no more use in climbing Everest than kicking a football about, or dancing, he believed the accomplishment would do a great deal of good. It would elevate the human spirit . . .[24]

Most of the newspapers took up the story, some of them objecting to Younghusband's candour in the uselessness of the project, though according to the *Observer* what he actually said was:

> Whilst, however, climbing Mt Everest will not put a pound into anyone's pocket, it will take a good many pounds out, the accomplishment of such a feat will elevate the human spirit . . .[25]

Not all the papers were enthusiastic. The reporter in the *Daily News* had feelings akin to present-day conservationists:

> It will be a proud moment for the man who first stands on the top of the earth, but he will have the painful thought that he had queered the pitch for posterity. For my part, I should like to think that some corner of the globe would be preserved for ever inviolate. Men will never lose the sense of wonder, but they will always try to do so, and such a sanctuary would have a world wide effect.[26]

The *Evening News* put it stronger if less elegantly:

> They will climb to the peak of Everest and be warm with happiness for a moment at 29,002 ft above the sea. Some instrument in their chilled fingers may prove that the odd two feet should be three feet, and then the explorers shall glow again for thinking of what they have wrought for science. But when they shall be safe back at the mountain foot, they will not be so happy; they will know that they have done a very foolish thing . . . Some of the last mystery of the world will pass when the last secret place in it, the naked peak of Everest shall be trodden by those trespassers.[27]

On the day following the committee meeting Younghusband wrote to the Secretary of State urging once again the desirability of an Everest expedition, and on 23 June a deputation consisting of Younghusband, Bruce, Howard-Bury and Farrar visited the India Office to discuss the matter. Two days later Howard-Bury left for India.

Lt Col. Charles Kenneth Howard-Bury was thirty-seven years of age, an old Etonian, descended from the illustrious Howard family, Earls of Suffolk. He had commanded the 60th Rifles with credit during the war and was a man of distinct but not severe military bearing. George Mallory couldn't stand him:

> He is not a tolerant person. He is well informed and opinionated and doesn't at all like anyone else to know things he doesn't know. . . He knows a great deal about flowers and is very keen about them, and is often pleasant and sometimes amusing at meals.[28]

He was also High Tory – which wouldn't go down well with the neosocialist Mallory.

Howard-Bury had an estate at Mullingar in Ireland where he trained race horses (many years later he called one of his horses 'Everest') and was comfortably well off; he undertook his Indian mission at his own expense. He was not a member of the Alpine Club and why he should suddenly appear on the Everest scene is uncertain, for his mountaineering qualifications were slight: some holidays in the Tyrol, where his family had once owned an estate, and some wanderings in the Tien Shan, Karakorum and Kashmir peaks when he was stationed in India in 1905–9. But he was not without a spirit of adventure – in 1905 he had made a secret journey into Tibet, which had earned him a severe reprimand from the Viceroy, Curzon. Nor was he without determination, as was shown by the four months he spent in India trying to persuade the Government there about the need for an expedition to Everest, and particularly the tough Political Officer in Tibet, Charles Bell.

His letters to Younghusband reveal a tenacious man determined to follow the Committee resolutions to the letter.[29] On 15 July 1920 he wrote:

> I arrived up here last Monday after rather a hot journey through the Red Sea and a very rough passage from Aden to Bombay. The railway journey across the plains was quite pleasant as it was cool and there was no dust. Since arriving here I have been busy interviewing the necessary departments.
>
> I first went to see Col. Coldstream who is acting as Surveyor General. I was only just in time to catch him as he left Simla yesterday morning. He told me that at present Moorshead [sic] is with Dr Kellas making the attempt to climb Kamet, but he promised to reserve him for the summers of 1921 and 1922. He seemed to think that he was a good Alpine climber too.
>
> He is meanwhile putting up a good case to Government in order to obtain their sanction for the payment of a surveyor and assistant surveyor if necessary together with their transport and rations. If this is granted, there would be a considerable saving of expense for next year.
>
> I went next to see the Foreign Secretary. Cater is still acting, as Dobbs had not yet come back from Mussoorie. They have already a file about the Mount Everest expedition, which I ran to ground in the Flying Corps Headquarters.
>
> Negotiations with Tibet are still held up as they are awaiting the reply of the Sec. of State. Should his answer over the arms question prove unfavourable and contrary to the wishes of the Government here, there might be friction with the Tibetans and they would think themselves badly treated and might refuse to allow the expedition. At the present time they are very friendly. Should the answer be favourable, no objection whatever would be raised and every assistance would be given. At the present time they can however give no definite answer for next year.
>
> I saw also Gould who was Asst. Foreign Secretary and who was up at Gyantse in 1913. He suggested my going up there and getting into touch with Bell and the Tibetans. Round Phari, he said there were some excellent porters and accustomed to carry loads at great heights. He told me also about the surveyors trained in England and also another that had been 3 years at Balliol whom I should probably meet up there, and who might be of great help.
>
> I am lunching with Cater tomorrow and shall see him again on Tuesday, so I hope to get something more definite out of him. They were very pleased at having someone personally to deal with, as they said it would make matters very much easier.

I next went to the Flying Corps Headquarters. Webb Bowen was away on tour, but I saw Mills who was acting for him. The proposal to make a reconnaissance he turned down at once on the grounds of expense. From the existing aerodromes at Allahabad and Calcutta they did not have a machine capable of doing the journey, and they refused at once to go to the expense of arranging a temporary base at Purneah. They suggested that the Handley Page Co. at Calcutta might be prepared to do it for the sake of the advertisement, but I am very doubtful if a Handley Page machine can go above 11,000 ft, which would be of little use. The Flying Corps would be prepared to lend cameras and advice, but nothing further. (The Viceroy seemed distinctly annoyed about their attitude when I told him this.)

I had a long talk with the Viceroy this morning over the whole expedition and I explained exactly what is proposed to be done. He was very sympathetic and promised to give us every support possible. He could however give us no definite promise with regard to next year, as it would depend on the attitude of the Tibetans towards us, which again depends on the result of the present negotiations. He however advised me to go up to Gyantse and see Bell and the Tibetan authorities and interest them in the project. With regard to the aerial reconnaissance he would do his best and write to the Prime Minister of Nepal. He thought the Air Force were raising unnecessary difficulties and promised to go into the question, as he could not understand their refusing to co-operate.

He also asked me to lay before him in writing exactly what we want the Government of India to do for us and what grant of money we should like. With regard to the latter, I do not quite know what to ask. I do not like to ask for too much, but if they were to give £1000, besides surveyors and transport, this would be of great assistance. However, I shall consult with one or two people first.

He followed this five days later:

I have just had another interview with Cater, who had just had a telegram from Bell. Bell says that he does not at all agree with Campbell's former view that he does not think the Tibetans would object to any reconnaissance of Mt Everest. Bell says that some poet-saint is buried near Everest, that the Tibetans are likely to be very suspicious and though we may fully explain what we want to do, they will not like it at all and that they will think that there is something else behind it. Also until the present negotiations are settled, he is very much against any reconnaissance or any expedition to Mt Everest at all. This telegram is being sent off today to the Secretary of State, and no doubt if you ask, you will be shown it. The basis of the whole trouble is the Sec. of State or Lord Curzon's refusal at present to allow half a dozen machine guns and a few thousands of rounds to be sent into Tibet and Cater suggested unofficially that it is now an excellent opportunity to get the matter settled favourably. If you could use your influence as Pres. of the Geographical Society and also with certain officials at the India Office to get the matter settled favourably, the chief obstacle to the expedition would be removed. (I am afraid that Bell is another obstacle and that as long as he is in his present position, he will put every difficulty he can in the way.)

Once the arms question is settled, the Tibetan government will be at once approached. They do not want them to hear of the proposed expedition indirectly and so the F.O. do not like to approach the Nepalese with regard to flying over their country until they have first approached the Tibetans.

Thus it will be seen that everything depends on the arms question.

A week later:

I sent you a telegram last week from Simla to try and explain that until the political questions with Tibet are settled, there will be no chance of the expedition to Everest being allowed. The delay is caused by either Montagu or Lord Curzon who do not seem inclined to agree with the Government of India over the arms question or of a resident in Lhasa. I therefore telegraphed hoping that you would understand and use your influence and that of the Geographical Society to get these matters settled favourably in accordance with the wishes of the Government of India. They are very anxious to get the matter settled out here, as it has been dragging on for a long time now.

The more I hear of Bell, the less I fear he will help us. They all say he is a most tiresome man to deal with because he is very slow and cautious and does not make any mistakes.

I went to Calcutta for two or three days and saw Col. Coldstream and got the latest maps and reports from the Survey office, but they do not add very much to our information.

I also saw Col. Edwards who is director of the Handley Page Indo-Burma Transport and tried to pick his brains over the question of an aerial reconnaissance. He said that they have got no machines at present capable of doing this and that it would be a very expensive job, probably needing two machines.

He said a Bristol with Rolls engines and fitted with a special tank for from 5–6 hours flight, would be the machine for the purpose. He suggested that if Mr Handley Page were approached by the Geographical Society, he might possibly present and have sent out a machine, as he would gain great advertisement by this. A temporary aerodrome would have to be made as near the Nepalese frontier as possible at the end of the Railway North of Purneah and supplies &c. sent up there. This would all cost a good deal of money.

But Howard-Bury had scarcely been in India a fortnight before the India Office in London was writing to the Secretary of the Royal Geographical Society refusing permission for an expedition. They put the onus on the Indian Government, citing 'political questions outstanding with regard to Tibet' – presumably the arms question mentioned by Howard-Bury in his letters – but it is more probable that they were influenced by Charles Bell. Howard-Bury's letters show that the Indian Government were not opposed to an Everest expedition, and, as events turned out, neither was Tibet. The Committee ignored the India Office's refusal, relying on Howard-Bury to carry it off. In August he wrote to Younghusband:

> I hope to leave on Saturday for Yatung, where Bell is at present. I am not very hopeful of getting him to look favourably on the expedition but I will do my best. Everyone seems to be quite agreed about him.
>
> The best plan for the expedition would seem to be to have two base camps, one at Kampa Dzong and the other at Tingri Dzong, and to have supplies brought up either from here or Kalimpong by mules to Kampa Dzong, then taken on by either a second relay of mules or yaks from Kampa Dzong to Tingri Dzong. At both these places a certain amount of supplies ought to be procurable, and they are both under the Tashi Lama who is very pro-British, so that a letter from him to either of the Commandants would ensure their help and co-operation.
>
> Government mules would be the best, but if not it would be cheaper to buy mules at Kalimpong and sell them again afterwards, than it would be to hire.
>
> I will write again when I have seen Bell and talked over matters with him.

At Yatung he met Bell, and began a long job of persuasion. The subsequent letter made the first mention of a native hill tribe called Sherpas:

> I have had several long talks with Bell, who is here at present.
>
> He told me frankly that he did not care for the idea of the expedition until the *whole* of the question of the relations between China, India and Tibet had been settled, which is different from the F.O. view, who want the arms and the sending of a man to Lhasa to be settled first, when they would be prepared to ask the Govt. for leave. The former question has gone on for 14 years and may go on as long again. At the same time he said that he could ask the Tibetan Government today and he was quite certain that they would allow the expedition, but that he did not think that it would be advisable at the present time and would put them in a suspicious frame of mind.
>
> Sherpa Bhootias would seem to be the best for high mountain work; they are less independent than the Tibetans.

He then set off on his own private reconnaissance of the Tista valley, following the route Noel had used in 1913, and wrote in October from Darjeeling:

> I arrived back here four or five days ago, and am at present staying with Lord Ronaldshay. I saw Raeburn yesterday, he came to lunch here. He did not get above 21,000 ft on Kingchinjunga. I think he found that anno domini was beginning to tell on him. He went up the Yalung valley on the Nepalese side. I had rather hoped that I might have met him on the North when I was in Lhonak.
>
> I had hoped to have had some glimpses of the Everest group from the Chorten Nyima La and from the extreme west of Lhonak, but clouds or other mountains always intervened, and I only saw it from a spur on the North of the Naku La. I looked down on Khamba Jong and the valley of the Arun that runs all the way down almost to the foot of Everest.
>
> I had to come back that way owing to the amount of new snow that had fallen on the Lungna La.

A fortnight later he wrote from Simla:

> I think our Everest expedition has advanced a step forward since I came up here again.
>
> Bell has been allowed to go to Lhasa to see and confer with the Dalai Lama and is likely to remain there for two or three months. I think it is rather a case of kill or cure, for he is not in good health and a journey into the heart of Tibet at this time of year promises to be a cold proceeding.
>
> The Foreign Office at home still remain obdurate over the question of the arms and I do not know how the Tibetans will take this. I have seen Cater and Dobbs, and have lunched with the latter. Dobbs is very ready to help and takes a keen interest in the expedition. I persuaded him to telegraph to Bell to ask the Dalai Lama in the course of his negotiations for leave for the Everest expedition next year and Dobbs added that it was a matter of great scientific importance. So now it all depends on how Bell puts it before the Dalai Lama and we shall have to wait for his answer, which will not be for a couple of months.

Howard-Bury's persistence eventually paid off. On 20 December 1920 a telegram arrived at the India Office from the Viceroy of India:

> Bell telegraphs that he had explained to Dalai Lama object of desired exploration [i.e. Mount Everest] and necessity of travelling through Tibetan territory, and obtained Tibetan Government's consent.

The message was sent on to the one man who had never given up hope through the years of frustration and disappointment – Sir Francis Younghusband. For him it was a personal triumph.

# 2

# 'We Are About to Walk off the Map'

News that the expedition to Mount Everest was definitely to take place was given at a meeting of the Royal Geographical Society on 10 January 1921. The press had a field day: WHERE WHITE MAN HAS NEVER TROD!; MILE HIGHER THAN MAN HAS EVER BEEN; AFTER MT EVEREST – WHAT? were typical euphoric headlines, though one paper carried the enigmatic banner, INSOMNIA DANGER.[1]

Leading mountaineers such as Conway, Bruce and Young gave their opinions in interviews and articles. George Abraham, one of two famous Keswick brothers who made their living from photographing and writing about mountains, said in the *Daily Mail* that '. . . the man who hopes to climb Mount Everest must be able with no training to run at fair speed up the last 300 ft of Mt Blanc.'[2]

Whoever such a mountaineering paragon might be he didn't say, but most papers were agreed that the leader of the expedition would be General Bruce. Not only did Bruce's experience make him the logical choice but he was also a popular figure.

As soon as permission for the expedition had arrived from India the Royal Geographical Society and the Alpine Club had set up a special committee to put it into effect. This met for the first time on 12 January 1921 and consisted of Sir Francis Younghusband, Colonel E.M. Jack and Edward Somers-Cocks from the Society, with Norman Collie, Captain Farrar and C.F. Meade from the Alpine Club. A little later two Honorary Secretaries were appointed: J.E.C. Eaton of the Alpine Club, and the professional secretary of the Royal Geographical Society, Arthur Hinks. Somers-Cocks, who was a banker, was made Honorary Treasurer.

The day-to-day administrative duties fell to Hinks, who turned out to be a formidable character, dominating the Everest Committee for two decades.

Arthur Robert Hinks, F.R.S., was a brilliant mathematician and world authority on the abstruse subject of map projections. Before moving to the Royal Geographical Society in 1913 he had been secretary of the Royal Astronomical Society for ten years and was on the staff of the University Observatory at Cambridge. At the University he lectured on surveying and cartography, but he never seems to have fitted into the academic world and it was Freshfield who got him the job at the Royal Geographical Society. 'Freshfield engineered his removal to the R.G.S. after a bequest for a lecture hall and extension necessitated a full-time Secretary there. The job was virtually created for Hinks – and Cambridge was not sorry to see him go.'[3]

He began as Assistant Secretary in 1913 and did not become Secretary until two years later – a post he held until 1945. He could be a difficult man to get along with: 'Always rubbing people up the wrong way,' Odell said. 'He considered his word should be taken as gospel – and sometimes it simply wasn't gospel.'[4] He was literally prepared to lay a wager on any of his opinions, and was not above expressing them in forthright, sometimes sarcastic letters, lacking in tact and discretion. Like many brilliant minds he seems to have had a faint contempt for his intellectual inferiors, and since this included most of his contemporaries it is easy to see why he was generally disliked. He was hard-working, particular, even pernickety. As a mathematician and surveyor his sharp eye fell with special severity on any errors or omissions made by the Everest surveyors in their reports – and in the countless arguments and disagreements Hinks was usually proved to be in the right.

Despite his undoubted intellect, however, Hinks had two grave faults. One was that he totally lacked practical experience of surveying in the field, with all its attendant problems and hazards – and was incapable of making allowances for this. The other was that for all his intellect he was completely unworldly, to the point of naïvety.

But it is his rash outspokenness which comes over so forcefully in the many letters he wrote during his time with the Everest Committee. He upset Mallory from the start, and his correspondence with Farrar, an equally forthright character, became icily hostile. Only Bruce seemed impervious to his remarks; but then the General didn't give a damn for anybody.

Hinks had a pathological distaste for publicity, which was a drawback considering much of the expedition funds came from that source, and it was fortunate that extroverts like Norman Collie and Sir Francis Younghusband could more than compensate for him in this respect. Younghusband could even take a rise out of Hinks: when Hinks wanted the long hall of the Royal Geographical Society to be known as the ambulatory, Younghusband said, 'If that is the ambulatory, then you shall be known as the perambulator.'[5]

The expedition planning got off to a bad start – a cashier employed by the Committee absconded with £717 of the funds. But a bigger blow was that General Bruce was not available to lead the team, having recently taken up a new appointment with the Glamorganshire Territorial Association. As a replacement, the Committee chose Howard-Bury, who had done such good service for the cause in India. Not only had he experience of travel in the Himalaya and Tibet, but he knew the people who mattered out there and would be able to smooth out any last-minute problems. He was a soldier, used to commanding troops. He was also a wealthy man, prepared to pay most of his own expenses.

Howard-Bury was not a mountaineer, of course, but this was not seen to be a great disadvantage because the Everest Committee were thinking in terms of a two-year effort – the first to reconnoitre the mountain, and the second to climb it, as Rawling had suggested years ago. Bruce was expected to be available for the second.

> But while it was decided to make the ascent of Mount Everest the main object of the expedition, Professor Norman Collie and Mr Douglas Freshfield from the first insisted that a whole season must be devoted to a thorough reconnaissance of the mountain with a view to finding out not only a feasible route to the summit but what was without any doubt the most feasible route. We knew nothing of the immediate approach to the mountain. But we knew that the only chance of reaching the summit was by finding some way up which would entail little rock-climbing and ice step-cutting. The mountain had therefore to be prospected from every side to find a comparatively easy route and to make sure that no other easier route than the one selected existed. This was considered ample work for the Expedition for one season, while the following season would be devoted to an all-out effort to reach the summit along the route selected in the first year.[6]

Howard-Bury was formally appointed leader on 24 January and two days later the Committee issued a resolution that:

> The main object this year is reconnaissance. This does not debar the mountain party from climbing as high as possible on a favourable route, but attempts on a particular route must not be prolonged to hinder the completion of the reconnaissance.[7]

In view of the emphasis on reconnaissance it is surprising that the initial enthusiasm for using aircraft for this task waned. Despite Howard-Bury's inquiries in India, the whole idea was suddenly dropped. There is no doubt that even the relatively primitive machines of the 1920s could have been invaluable in helping the reconnaissance. Perhaps the Committee didn't want to upset the Tibetans, or – more likely – aircraft would have cost too much.

In fact the question of costs was one of the problems facing the Committee. Nobody had any idea how much the expedition would cost, but they made 'quite a rough guess' that the two expeditions together would come to some £10,000. Freshfield thought this was far too much:

> I think the cost of the preliminary expedition ... is being much exaggerated. It cost me less than £200 going round Kangchenjunga (1899), a seven week journey with a party of 60 all told.[8]

As it turned out, the 1921 expedition cost between £3,000 and £4,000.

The money was raised by private subscription, particularly from Fellows of the Royal Geographical Society and members of the Alpine Club. The latter subscribed over £3,000, but rather surprisingly the Fellows, who were far more numerous, raised rather less. Notable figures contributed: King George V gave £100, and the Prince of Wales (who invited Howard-Bury to discuss the plans with him) gave £50. The Viceroy of India, Lord Reading, gave 750 rupees.

Even so it wasn't enough, and much to Hinks's disgust, contracts were drawn up with the press. The arrangements were made with the help of John Buchan, the popular writer and himself a keen climber. The right to publish expedition telegrams went to *The Times* and the *Philadelphia Ledger*; the expedition photographs went to the *Graphic*. These modest arrangements made the expedition financially secure.

Nowadays, when no major expedition anywhere would dream of setting out without its agent having first secured T.V. rights, magazine and book rights, film rights and any sponsorship that might be going, and when the departure requires at least one press cocktail reception, Hinks's attitude to publicity makes strange reading. When the team sailed he wrote in satisfaction: The expedition has got away without any interview and photograph in the press, which so often discredits the start.[9]

And when it was due to return he warned Mallory:

> You will of course remember that if the newspaper people get wind of your arrival you will be besieged by reporters. We were very proud of our success of getting the whole party off without interviews and photographs and cinematograph films and we are anxious to repeat this success. Please use a little cunning in making your return. It would be a great pity if we let the reporters in now when we have kept them out with so much success.[10]

Hinks was using the royal 'we'. Others on the Committee didn't share his views. When subscriptions were slow in coming, Norman Collie, who had an impish sense of humour and knew his man, wrote to Hinks about possible sponsorship:

I have a grand new idea that I am sure will commend itself to you, it is the following:

Go to Lord Leverhulme and say, give us £10,000 and we will take a large cake of Sunlight Soap and a flag also with Sunlight Soap emblazoned on it, and we will plant them on top of Everest, then he will be able to say:

1 Sunlight Soap beats the record – 29,002 tablets sold hourly.
2 Sunlight Soap towers aloft and dominates the kingdoms of the earth.
3 Avoid worry – use Sunlight Soap and for Ever-rest.

Hinks did not reply.[11]

Hinks determined to keep strictly to the letter of the contracts, which in his opinion the Committee had unwisely entered into, so that when *The Times* requested biographical details of the expedition members he refused to supply them, on the grounds that the contract was only for messages *from* the expedition. Younghusband stepped in and supplied them. There were also difficulties with the *Graphic*, and Hinks wrote to Howard-Bury:

We don't know the way about among all these sharks and pirates ... we are having a devil of a time over these sharks who want photographs.

No one regrets more sincerely than I do that any dealings with the Press was ever instituted at all. I was, as you remember, always against it but I am not in a position to do more than make the best I can of the instructions of the Committee ... at any rate, we have kept the newspapers in their proper place and not allowed them to pretend they are running the expedition. The illustrated people are still sore over the fact that every member of the party got away without being photographed or cinematographed.[12]

Because of the exclusive contract with *The Times*, Hinks decided that news about the expedition should not be released to other newspapers until twenty-four hours after *The Times* had seen the despatches. Naturally enough Fleet Street did not take this lying down. The *Daily Telegraph* deplored that any one paper should have exclusive rights: 'An enterprise too closely affecting India should not be made the subject of an exclusive newspaper scoop.'[13] The *Morning Post* took a more private but tougher line. They wrote to the Committee warning it that because of the news embargo in London they would get their reports direct from India where they had influence, and promised there would be trouble. There was. The Government of India promptly requested the Survey of India to supply reports for the Indian newspapers. As the Survey's paymasters they were entitled to do this and the Survey had an independently financed team attached to the expedition.

Hinks was furious and wrote to C.H.D. Ryder, Surveyor General:

This is the result of agitation which has been got up nominally by certain Indian papers, but really I suspect by the representatives in India of certain

> London papers protesting against the arrangement made by the Mt Everest Committee with *The Times* . . . the intervention of the Govt of India has put us in rather an awkward position . . .
>
> I am sorry to have to trouble you about this. All these questions of dealing with the newspapers and photographers are personally very distasteful to me, and I regret that the Expedition Committee thought it necessary to enter into them to some extent in order to provide the funds for the following year's work. As however they have done so, it is necessary for me to use every endeavour to see that the people with whom the Committee have made contracts get their full value, and are not let down by unexpected leakage, which might well take place innocently. The correspondent of the *Morning Post* in Calcutta is the man whom I particularly suspect of enterprise not perhaps very strictly honourable . . .[14]

He was chagrined when the *Morning Post* printed the story of Kellas's death several days before even the Committee knew of it. It was not to be the last time that enterprising newspapers would try to break *The Times* monopoly.

Despite the minor squabbles, raising enough resources in the short time available before the expedition sailed for India – barely five months – was a considerable achievement on the part of the Committee and one of the two major tasks facing them. The other was selecting the team.

In fact the Committee had only nominal control over the selection of team members. After all, the surveyors were being provided by the Survey of India and, since they were footing the bill, they made the selection there. So far as the climbing members were concerned the decision lay largely with Farrar – the rest of the Committee bowing to his expert opinion and, no doubt, his forceful personality. Farrar seems to have taken advice from Bruce, Collie and Winthrop Young – though Collie caused considerable embarrassment when, as President of the Alpine Club, he suggested himself as a member. He was sixty-two at the time and had done no serious climbing for ten years! He was persuaded to reconsider.

Requests to join the expedition came from all over the world. Some were of such merit that they had to be considered – Tom Longstaff, who had climbed in the Himalaya; Orde Lees, who had worked on oxygen equipment with Kellas; and J.M. Wordie, who was already a notable Polar explorer – but others came from people such as A. de Naranovitch, Russian Consul in Milan, and a Mr Charles Clarke who claimed to be 'the only Englishman ever to have been made an authentic Swiss Mountain Guide'. Perhaps the most interesting and persistent of the 'off-comers', however, was Sam Turner, a Manchester man who had climbed in many parts of the world and had described his adventures in a series of books which were not only sensational but highly critical of the climbing 'establishment' as personified by the Alpine Club. One feels that even had Sam been younger than his fifty-two years, it is unlikely the Committee would ever have admitted him – he definitely wasn't a pukka sahib!

Since reconnaissance was the principal objective the choice of surveyors was all important. Hinks wanted Major Kenneth Mason, who was already making a name for himself in Himalayan work, but the Surveyor General, C.H. Ryder, chose instead H.T. Morshead and E.O. Wheeler.

Ryder was an astute man, for both Morshead and Wheeler were not only sound surveyors (though criticized by Hinks) but fine mountaineers.

Henry Morshead was then thirty-nine years old. He had played a considerable part in proving that the Tibetan Tsangpo and the Indian Brahmaputra were one and the same river, and he had discovered the most easterly of the great Himalayan mountains, Namcha Barwa. In 1920 he was with Kellas on Kamet, and he was undoubtedly a tough character. 'I never met a harder man,' E.F. Norton wrote later, ' – his shirt open at the chest to the dreadful Tibetan wind – a heartbreaking man to live with.'[15] He was universally liked, and no one would then have believed that ten years later he was to be murdered in Burma.

Oliver Wheeler at thirty-one was Morshead's junior and had been with the Survey of India for only two years. He was chosen in preference to Mason because of his experience in photo-surveying, a new technique he had learned in his native Canada and which Ryder was anxious to try in the Everest region. Wheeler's father had been a surveyor too and the boy had accompanied him on many expeditions in the Rockies. He had climbed with famous Canadian pioneers like Outram, Fynn, Longstaff and Kain, and had made the first ascent – at the age of twelve – of a mountain named in his honour as Oliver's Peak. Later in life he was to become Sir Oliver Wheeler, Surveyor General of India.

These two were joined by Dr A.M. Heron from the Geological Survey of India, whose innocent geological activities so upset the Tibetans that he was banned from the 1922 expedition.

At a superficial glance, Farrar's composition of the climbing party seemed a sound balance of experience and youth – or what passed for youth in 1921. In charge of the climbers he placed Harold Raeburn, a Scot and one of the most distinguished mountaineers of his generation. In an age when guided climbing was still the accepted norm Raeburn not only climbed guideless but frequently solo as well – he had, for example, made the first solo traverse of the difficult Meije, in the Dauphiné Alps. Just prior to the First World War he had made nine new ascents in the Caucasus, and in the year before he went to Everest he had reached 21,000 ft on Kangchenjunga.

But he was fifty-six years old, and the great mountaineer was already a crabbed and crusty old man. H.W. Tobin, who was with him on Kangchenjunga, had found him so disagreeable that they travelled apart as much as possible. On the Everest expedition he had gastric trouble, which probably did nothing to help his temper. In a letter home Mallory wrote:

> I saw and still see Raeburn as a great difficulty . . . He is evidently touchy about his position as leader of the Alpine party and wants to be treated with proper respect. And he is dreadfully dictatorial about matters of fact, and often wrong . . . He has some very nice qualities; he has a good deal of fatherliness and kindliness. But his total lack of *calm* and sense of humour at the same time is most unfortunate.[16]

Later he wrote to Hinks, 'When he is not being a bore I feel moved to pity, but that is not often.'[17]

Howard-Bury couldn't stand him. After Raeburn's failure to pick up some expedition mail (he just rode past it) Howard-Bury fumed to Hinks, 'Can you imagine anyone being such a fool?'[18] But later, as it became increasingly obvious that Raeburn was ill, 'Raeburn has become very old and is a great responsibility . . . and like all Scotch, he is very obstinate.'[19]

In fact Raeburn never recovered from his experiences on Everest. On his return to Britain he suffered a complete breakdown and went into a slow decline until his death in 1926.

With hindsight it is easy to say that Farrar could hardly have made a worse choice for leader of the climbing party, yet Farrar was not to know this at the time. He had only the records to go on, and Raeburn's record was outstanding – indeed, it is doubtful whether in terms of climbing ability, taken in the context of his time, it was ever surpassed by pre-war Everest climbers.

The second climber chosen by Farrar for his experience was Dr A.M. Kellas, a lecturer in chemistry at Middlesex Hospital. 'Although he was keenly interested in chemistry he was even more interested in mountains,' Collie wrote, and indeed during the previous few years Kellas had been concentrating on the physiological effects of high altitudes, a subject on which he had made himself the leading authority.[20] Combining work with pleasure he had accumulated a good deal of Himalayan experience since his first visit in 1907, including ascents of Pauhunri (23,180 ft) and Chomiomo (22,430 ft). In 1920 he and Morshead would almost certainly have climbed Kamet (25,447 ft) had not the porters rebelled.

Morshead had been detailed to join Kellas by the Survey of India, but apart from this one occasion, and on his first visit in 1907 when he had brought Alpine guides out with him, Kellas climbed solely with local porters. He quickly found that these men were not only strong but soon learned the elementary climbing techniques then in use. They were cheerful, intelligent companions, and the best of them, Kellas discovered, came from a remote valley in Nepal. They were called Sherpas.

Kellas was an unorthodox man in several ways, apart from his climbing with 'coolies', as the term then was. He rarely bothered to write accounts of his climbs, except from a medical point of view. Brief notes in the *Alpine Journal* were the limit of his literary ambitions, though in terms of Himalayan experience he was the greatest of all.

Like Raeburn he was a Scot. Hinks called him 'a very obstinate little man',[21] but Mallory had great affection for him. To his wife, Mallory wrote:

> Kellas I love already. He is beyond description Scotch and uncouth in his speech – altogether uncouth. He arrived at the great dinner party ten minutes after we had sat down, and very dishevelled, having walked in from Grom, a little place four miles away. His appearance would form an admirable model to the stage for a farcical representation of an alchemist. He is very slight in build, short, thin, stooping and narrow chested; his head . . . made grotesque by veritable gig-lamps of spectacles and a long pointed moustache. He is an absolutely devoted and disinterested person.[22]

But, like Raeburn, Kellas was really too old for the job. He was fifty-three and had spent the previous year in an exhausting series of high-altitude climbs: almost a frenzy of activity. He arrived back in Darjeeling only a week or so before the Everest expedition set out.

These two elderly climbers were to occupy much of the time and energy of Dr A.F.R. Wollaston, the team doctor. Wollaston was an explorer in the old romantic style who liked remote places, especially if there were mountains which were particularly inaccessible. He had visited the Ruwenzori, in Africa, and made two trips into the interior of New Guinea, where he got within 400 ft of the top of Carstenz Pyramid, the highest summit, before having to withdraw. He had much in common with Howard-Bury and they became close friends on the expedition. Like Howard-Bury, Wollaston was a rich man who paid his own expenses, and both men were keen naturalists and more than competent photographers. Wollaston was forty-six years old.[23]

When Farrar had first thought about a party to climb Everest, as early as 1919, he had envisaged two Australian climbers, George and Max Finch, as his summit pair and the great Swiss mountain cartographer Marcel Kurz as surveyor, but Kurz was ruled out by the 'Britons only' rule adopted by the Committee, even if they had had choice in the matter. Max Finch also dropped out of the reckoning. George Finch was still available, though.

George Finch was thirty-three, a strong Alpinist and a research-scientist who, like Kellas, was interested in the physiological consequences of high altitudes. Of Australian origin, he had lived a great deal in Switzerland and spoke German better than he spoke English. His upbringing undoubtedly gave him a less rigid outlook on things than many of his contemporaries had, especially his older contemporaries, and the Committee on the whole viewed him with suspicion: he was too unconventional in attitude to be quite a pukka sahib. Nevertheless, he was Farrar's first choice, and Farrar carried great weight. Unfortunately, Finch had contracted malaria during the war, and a drastic cure he had taken for it, in France, had undermined his health. When Mallory was assessing their chances in a letter to Winthrop Young in February, he expressed doubts about Finch's health:

> Raeburn says he does not expect to get higher than 24,000 to 25,000; Dr Kellas presumably will get no further; so that final push is left to Finch and me and the outside chance that Wheeler or Morshead will take to climbing and make a success of it. Perhaps after all I shall be the weakest of the lot, but at present I feel more doubtful of Finch's health.[24]

The doubts proved justified, for a month later Finch failed his medical examination.

Despite being just over six feet in height Finch weighed only 11st 3lb. Both of the doctors who examined him (H. Graeme Anderson and F.E. Larkins) reported him to be in poor physical condition: slightly anaemic, sallow, flabby, losing weight and his mouth 'very deficient in teeth'. He was rejected by the Committee immediately.

Both Finch himself and Farrar were furious. A short time before his rejection Finch had blotted his copybook by having his picture published in an illustrated paper with a note about the forthcoming Everest attempt, much to Hinks's chagrin, and he now considered himself victimized because of this. Privately, accusations were bandied around, but Mallory thought the medical decision was justified. To Winthrop Young he wrote:

> Finch always seemed to me rather a gamble; he didn't look fit and I felt no confidence in his stamina – we're not going to have very good opportunities of getting fit. I can't for a moment think the medical examination was unfairly done. It was arranged by Wollaston and I can't imagine him a party to that sort of thing, however much the idea of an examination may have been the hope of the party opposed to Finch. Wollaston told me that there could be no question of taking Finch after the doctor's report.
>
> I feel sorry for Finch; the medical examination ought to have been arranged at a much earlier stage. But he forfeits sympathy by his behaviour. We shall be weaker on ice and in general mountaineering resources without him, but we shall probably be stronger in pure physique, much stronger in morale.[25]

In March, Finch undoubtedly was not fit. But the question is whether the condition was only temporary, and whether the Committee acted precipitately. That summer Finch did a particularly difficult climb on Mont Blanc and

Farrar remarked sarcastically, 'our invalid Finch took part in the biggest climb in the Alps this season!'[26] When Larkins examined him again, in November, he pronounced him fit for the next expedition. Nevertheless, the affair was not forgotten – by either side.

With Finch ruled out it was proposed to replace him with W.N. Ling, a Scottish climber and an old buddy of Raeburn's. Mallory was appalled at the idea, for Ling was forty-eight years old. He wrote to Hinks about it:

> Since receiving your letter telling me that Finch is not coming with the expedition to Mount Everest, I have been thinking very seriously of my own position. The substitution of Ling for Finch, though it may make little difference in the earlier stages of climbing, will in all probability very materially weaken the advance party. It seems to me that our best chance of success lies in finding easy conditions in the final stage, for which we have considerable grounds of hope as the photos all show comparatively easy angles on the north side. If this hope is realized the question will be one purely of endurance and not at all of mountaineering judgement as to snow conditions, etc., or of technical skill in dealing with snow and ice. All that is likely to come in lower down, but for the final push we want men who can last and we ought to give ourselves the best possible chance of being such a party when the critical time arrives. I don't doubt the value of either Ling or Morshead but from the point of view of this final effort they have too much against them – Ling his age (it seems to me age must make it more difficult for the body to adjust itself to the conditions) and Morshead the fact that he will be engaged on his surveying work and consequently will not be able to train systematically for this mountaineering effort: and in any case we know very little about him as a mountaineer.
>
> Looking at the matter in this way I consider we ought to have another man who should be chosen not so much for his expert skill but simply for his powers of endurance. I have all along regarded the party as barely strong enough for a venture of this kind, with the enormous demand it is certain to make on both nerves and physique. I told Raeburn what I thought about that and said I wanted to have Finch because we shouldn't be strong enough without him.
>
> You will understand that I must look after myself in this matter. I'm a married man and I can't go into it bald-headed.[27]

Hinks thought he could detect the hand of his enemy Farrar in this and he wrote back tactlessly:

> I don't think you need feel any anxiety about your own position, because you will be under the orders of very experienced mountaineers who will take care not to call upon you for jobs that can't be done. The fact that you have been in close touch with Farrar all along has no doubt made you imbibe his

view which is hardly that of anybody else, that the first object of the expedition is to get to the top of Mount Everest this year. Raeburn has been given full liberty to get as high as possible consistent with the complete reconnaissance of the mountain, and it is left at that. As for Morshead, after all he has been more than half as high again as you have been, and he did this at rather short notice. I suspect you will find him a hard man to keep up with when he has been in the field for several months on his survey work, which is I should imagine the best possible training.[28]

Naturally enough, Mallory took umbrage at this patronizing tone and would have written a strong letter to Hinks had not Wollaston stepped in and calmed him down.

Fortunately for all concerned Ling could not accept the invitation. Farrar suggested A.W. Wakefield, a Lakeland climber, but he couldn't go either, so the last-moment vacancy was filled by G.H. Bullock, a contemporary of Mallory at Winchester, where they had both been members of the school's Ice Club.[29] Bullock was thirty-four, a busy member of the Consular Service, but Lord Curzon, by now Foreign Secretary, contrived to get him extended leave of absence. It was a happy choice, for not only had Bullock climbed with Mallory many times before but he was a genial character who seemed to get on with everybody, even Raeburn. He had, said Howard-Bury, 'great qualifications – a placid temperament and an ability to sleep under any conditions'.[30] In an expedition where almost everybody actively disliked somebody else, Bullock was unique.

But the undoubted star of Howard-Bury's team was George Leigh Mallory, a thirty-five-year-old schoolmaster from Charterhouse, a man whose name was destined to be forever linked with that of Everest. With the single exception of Whymper and the Matterhorn, no man has ever been so closely identified with a mountain in the public mind, and in one sense the public were right: there was about Mallory and Everest the same sort of inexorable destiny that linked Whymper with the Matterhorn. In both cases it became a naked feud between man and mountain.

And yet, he almost didn't go. In 1921 he was dissatisfied with his job and undecided about what he should do, and he had a wife and three young children to provide for. When Farrar asked him to join the expedition he thought of refusing. He was persuaded otherwise by his former climbing companion and close friend, Geoffrey Winthrop Young, who pointed out that it would be a fine adventure and might be useful background if ever he took up the writing career he had often thought about. On 9 February Mallory lunched with Younghusband, Farrar and Raeburn, when he formally accepted the offer, 'without visible emotion', as Younghusband recalled.[31]

How was it that this reluctant young man became a *Boy's Own Paper* archetypal hero? The answer is that he couldn't help it: he was cast in heroic mould, both physically and mentally, and he became a child of destiny, a latter-day Siegfried, though he certainly didn't see himself as such. Mallory had greatness thrust upon him. The pity of it was that he had so little actual talent.

After an adventurous, somewhat harum-scarum upbringing as a parson's son in Cheshire he had gone to school at Winchester, where he had come under the influence of a young master, Graham Irving, the keen Alpinist who founded the Ice Club. From school he had gone to Magdalene College, Cambridge, where he took up rowing and eventually became Secretary of the college boat club. He read history, but not too well, and, undecided on a career, more or less drifted into teaching, a job for which he was temperamentally unsuited and not particularly good at.

At Cambridge he was drawn into some brilliant company – Rupert Brooke and Lytton Strachey were close friends. The homosexual Strachey was overwhelmed by his good looks. In a letter to Virginia Woolf he wrote:

> Mon dieu! – George Mallory! – When that's been written, what more need be said? My hand trembles, my heart palpitates, my whole being swoons away at the words – oh, heavens! heavens! I found of course that he'd been absurdly maligned – he's six foot high, with the body of an athlete by Praxiteles, and a face – oh incredible – the mystery of Botticelli, the refinement and delicacy of a Chinese print, the youth and piquancy of an unimaginable English boy. I rave, but when you see him, as you must, you will admit all – all!. . .Yes! Virginia alone will sympathize with me now – I'm a convert to the divinity of virginity and spend hours every day lost in a trance of adoration, innocence, and bliss. It was a complete revelation, as you may conceive. By God! The sheer beauty of it all is what transports me. . . For the rest, he's going to be a schoolmaster, and his intelligence is not remarkable. What's the need?[32]

With his good looks, his athleticism and perfect gentility, he could have been a knight at King Arthur's court, and in fact Winthrop Young nicknamed him Galahad.

Had he been born a little later he could hardly have escaped the clutches of television, but as it was his character was flawed by one serious weakness – he was a drifter, uncommitted and indecisive. He never seriously tried to shape events in his life; instead, it was the events themselves which did the shaping. He drifted into the Everest adventure as he drifted into everything else he did.

Mallory had a deep love of mountains and mountain experiences. It was the love of a Romantic and also, because of his natural athletic ability, a love of the action itself. Though he claimed to prefer snow climbing above all else, his greatest skill lay in rock climbing, where the open-face climbs then becoming popular were ideally suited to his easy grace of movement. 'He swung up rock with a long thigh, a lifted knee, and a ripple of irresistible movement,' wrote

Young, many years later. 'A perfect physique and a pursuing mind came together as it were in a singleness of power, as he rushed into motion.'[33]

And yet all the signs are that Mallory was a competent, rather than great, climber. His record is small, his climbs largely forgotten by present-day climbers. Even for his own day they were not particularly hard climbs – no climb of Mallory's matches Herford's Central Buttress Route on Scafell or even Botterill's Slab climb on that same cliff. In the Alps too he showed little innovation, and his best routes were done with Young, who was one of the finest Alpinists of the era. Comparing Mallory with other climbers he had known at that time, Young said that he was the greatest in unfulfilled achievement. As with so many other aspects of his life, Mallory failed to make the significant contributions to climbing which were expected of him, and far from being the greatest mountaineer of his day, he was not really in the leading cadre.

Mallory was never at ease throughout the 1921 expedition. He disliked Tibet – 'a hateful country inhabited by hateful people'[34] – and sometimes wondered about the whole project. He wrote to a friend:

> I sometimes think of this expedition as a fraud from beginning to end, invented by the wild enthusiasm of one man, Younghusband; puffed up by the would-be wisdom of certain pundits in the A.C.; and imposed upon the youthful ardour of your humble servant... The prospect of ascent in any direction is almost nil, and our present job is to rub our noses against the impossible in such a way as to persuade mankind that some noble heroism has failed once again.[35]

Nor could he get on with his leader: 'Relations with Bury have not been easy,' he wrote to Young, '... he is a queer customer as I'll tell you one day.'[36] And to his wife on another occasion:

> Frankly, I was quite glad Bury was away. I can't get over my dislike of him and have a sense of *gêne* when he is present which he too feels, even though we talk quite cheerfully. And now I've had trouble with him about stores – a most miserable petty business, so miserable I really can't bring myself to explain it. But his attitude amounted to an accusation of greed on my part in taking more than I ought up here for the use of the higher camps, and meanwhile B. and I are providing meat and tea for the coolies out of our own money, because we know they must be fed up and encouraged in this way if we are to get them up the mountain; and Bury will allow nothing outside their base rations...[37]

The feeling was mutual. Howard-Bury wrote to Hinks, 'Mallory and Bullock have been perfectly useless to me. They have never attempted to help in anything...'[38]

His contemporaries on the Everest expedition found Mallory to be a dreamer without an ounce of practical ability. Hinks referred to it in several letters: '. . .he seems to be a very innocent traveller who can hardly be trusted to get his own luggage aboard'[39]; and after an unfortunate incident when Mallory put the plates in his camera the wrong way, thus ruining any photographs, 'The failure of Bullock and Mallory to photograph anything is deplorable – they must be singularly unintelligent people not to be able to learn the elements of the thing in a day or two'[40]; 'he cannot take photographs and cannot make primus stoves work when other people can.'[41] Other people were less critical than Hinks but agreed that Mallory was forgetful: 'After the first few days,' John Morris wrote about a later expedition, 'we took it in turn to see that none of his kit was left behind.'[42] Bruce said of him: 'He is a great dear, but forgets his boots on all occasions!'[43] and Tom Longstaff described him as 'a very good stout-hearted baby, but quite unfit to be placed in charge of anything, including himself'.[44]

And this was the man who, more than anyone else before or since, was to match himself against the greatest mountain in the world. From the moment Mallory accepted Farrar's invitation the seeds of tragedy and immortality were sown.

So the team was completed – a somewhat scratch team, in which two vital substitutions had to be made before the match had even begun, and a team without reserves. The average age of the climbing party was forty-four and a half years.

Meanwhile the organization of equipment, by Farrar and Meade, was going on. To Winthrop Young, Mallory wrote: 'We're having trouble about equipment. Raeburn unfortunately was put in charge of the mountaineering section and is quite incompetent. Finch and I have had to put pressure through Farrar and I hope it will all come right, but such a vital matter as tents has not been properly thought out and no proper provision for cold and great heights came with Raeburn's scheme of things.'[45] Nothing special was designed, just the best generally available. As for the actual clothing and boots, that was left to the members themselves – each man was given £50 to buy what he thought he needed, a sum later raised to £100 'if necessary'. Howard-Bury and Wollaston provided their own gear, at no expense to the Committee.

The various members of the expedition assembled in Darjeeling at the beginning of May, where they collected porters and mules for the long journey through Tibet. Morshead and a party of surveyors left on the 13th following the Tista River into northern Sikkim and thence over the Serpo La to Kampa Dzong in Tibet, where they would meet the main party much later. The main party chose a longer but easier route, over the Jelep La to the Chumbi valley and thence by a wide arc to Kampa Dzong. With them they carried the vital passport from the Prime Minister of Tibet[46]:

To The Jongpens and Headmen of Pharijong, Ting-ke, Khamba and Kharta.

You are to bear in mind that a party of Sahibs are coming to see the Chha-mo-lung-ma mountain and they will evince great friendship towards the Tibetans. On the request of the Great Minister Bell a passport has been issued requiring you and all officials and subjects of the Tibetan Government to supply transport, e.g. riding ponies, pack animals and coolies as required by the Sahibs, the rates for which should be fixed to mutual satisfaction. Any other assistance that the Sahibs may require either by day or by night, on the march or during halts, should be faithfully given, and their requirements about transport or anything else should be promptly attended to. All the people of the country, wherever the Sahibs may happen to come, should render all necessary assistance in the best possible way, in order to maintain friendly relations between the British and Tibetan Governments.

Despatched during the Iron Bird Year Seal of the Prime Minister.

The start of the trek was not auspicious. The mules provided by the Army were fat, indolent beasts from the plains, quite unaccustomed to the rough journey through the hot, steamy, leech-infested jungles of Sikkim, and after only five days had to be sent back to Darjeeling as unfit for service. From then on the expedition had to rely on local transport, hardy hill mules and yaks, and though this was always forthcoming it frequently took time to organize.

Once across the Jelep La, the humid jungle of Sikkim gave way to the pleasant valley of Chumbi, dominated by the impressive peak of Chomolhari. Because the ridge they had just crossed acted as a barrier to the monsoon, the rainfall at Chumbi is only a quarter of what it is in Sikkim, and they found themselves in an almost European climate, with great silver fir trees forming darkly massed woods, and brilliant bushes of wild rhododendron, roses, spiraea and clematis. Purple irises and wild strawberries grew in profusion. In keeping with this lovely natural setting, the villages were prosperous, with well-cultivated fields and orchards. The scent of wild roses filled the air. They had arrived in Tibet.

All through Sikkim and over the Jelep La the expedition had suffered the torrential downpours of the *chhoti barsat*, those pre-monsoon rains which often came as a nasty surprise in the Himalaya, but in Chumbi the weather was fair and the land flowing with milk and honey. It was not to last: out of the valley the dusty trail climbed laboriously up to the Tibetan plateau, an arid desert some 16,000 ft above sea level. Mallory described it in a letter to his wife:

> The great change was coming up to the plains. . .in a few hours after walking in a small mountain valley among flowers and trees, where everything seemed near and friendly, to debouch into a great grey arid basin

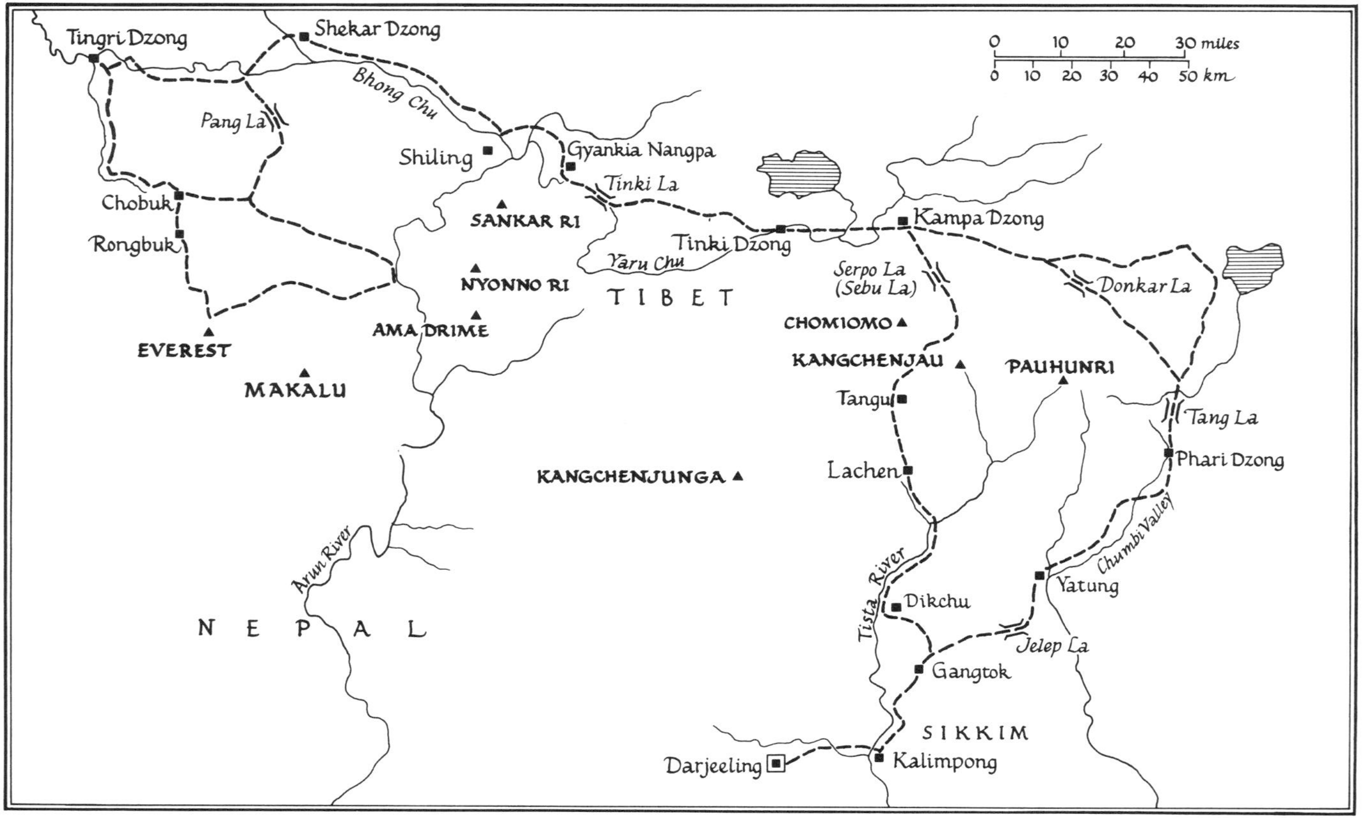


Map 3. The northern approach to Everest 1921–38

among rolling hills where the eye was carried an incredible distance and saw at the end of the prospect a steep snow mountain towering up alone – a country where everything was unfriendly and far. And then Phari, after ten miles' dusty walking in the glare of the plain itself... Phari seemed to prove that we had come to a new world altogether ruder than the mountain valley ... It is the most incredibly dirty warren that can be imagined ...

So far we had been on the high road, so to speak. In turning westwards to Kampa Dzong, we must leave the road to Lhasa... Nothing, I suppose, will ever be more dreary than the first stage from Phari: twenty-one miles, mostly across an absolutely flat desert of gravel.

...But in the evening light this country can be beautiful, snow mountains and all: the harshness becomes subdued; shadows soften the hillsides; there is a blending of lines and folds until the last light, so that one comes to bless the absolute bareness, feeling that here is a pure beauty of form, a kind of ultimate harmony.

Our great enemy, of course, is wind. On the best of days it is absolutely calm in the early morning, chilly at first and as the sun gets up quite hot. (The sun is always *scorching* and threatens to take one's skin off.) Any time between 10:00 and 12:00, the wind gets up – a dry, dusty unceasing wind, with all the unpleasantness of an east wind at home. Towards evening it becomes very cold, and we have frost at nights... The real problem for comfort now is to get a tent pitched so as to have some shelter when the day's destination is reached.[47]

Though Sherpas are undoubtedly the world's best porters, they are also probably the world's worst cooks, a fact the expedition had come to realize from the outset. The awful food did nothing to alleviate the enteritis and stomach pains which members now began to suffer. Wheeler and Raeburn were quite ill, and it did the latter no good either to fall off his horse twice, the animal kicking him on head and knee and rolling on him. But the worst affected was Kellas: the strenuous campaigns he had taken part in earlier in the year had sapped his body strength to such an extent that he could not withstand the ravages of dysentery. He grew progressively weaker, and had to be carried on a rude stretcher. He followed behind the rest of the party, wishing nobody to accompany him. Mallory wrote to a friend:

Can you imagine anything less like a mountaineering party? It was an arrangement which made me very unhappy and which appals me now in the light of what has happened – he died without one of us anywhere near him. And yet it was a difficult position. The old gentleman (such he seemed) was obliged to retire a number of times en route and could not bear to be seen in this distress, and so insisted that everyone should be in front of him.[48]

Kellas died on the approach march to Kampa Dzong, from heart failure brought on by the cumulative strain of the past months and accentuated by his illness. He was buried on a hillside south of the village, in a place which looked out across the arid Tibetan plain to the distant snows of the Himalaya where there rose the three peaks of Pauhunri, Kangchenjau and Chomiomo, which Kellas alone had climbed. Mallory described the scene to Geoffrey Winthrop Young:

> It was an extraordinarily affecting little ceremony burying Kellas on a stoney hillside – a place on the edge of a great plain and looking across it to the three great snow peaks of his conquest. I shan't easily forget the four boys, his own trained mountainmen, children of nature, seated in wonder on a great stone near the grave while Bury read out the passage from Corinthians.[49]

From the same place the expedition had its first glimpse of the summit snows of Everest.

*Dzong* is Tibetan for 'fort', and Kampa Dzong proved to be a spectacular fortress perched on a rocky cliff at the exit of a deep limestone gorge. Here the main body of the expedition was re-united with Morshead, who had arrived nine days earlier, despite his surveying work. Raeburn, however, was feeling no better and it was decided that he should be sent to Lachen in Sikkim to recuperate, and that Dr Wollaston should accompany him. Nobody regretted Raeburn's departure.

Without having even reached Everest, the expedition was seriously depleted and some of its purpose invalidated. All medical expertise was gone – by bizarre coincidence, of course, Wollaston, Kellas and Raeburn were all doctors. Kellas was dead and he was the only member of the team capable of making tests on the physiological effects of altitude as well as looking after the experimental oxygen sets carried in the baggage; and Raeburn, cantankerous though he was, was the leader of the climbing team.

None of this seemed to bother Howard-Bury much; and, of course, all was by no means lost. The survey team were still intact, and seemed to be enjoying themselves. It was the reconnaissance of the actual mountain which seemed in jeopardy. Everything now depended on Mallory and Bullock.

As the expedition moved off from Kampa Dzong, it was entering unknown country and a sense of excitement began to catch at Mallory: to Winthrop Young he wrote, 'We're just about to walk off the map. . .'[50]

On 13 June, en route for Shiling, Mallory and Bullock explored the Yaru Gorge and climbed a thousand feet up a cliff to a place that gave them a commanding view to the main Himalayan chain. To the south and west monsoon clouds hid the mountains but after a while they got a glimpse of Makalu:

> We were now able to make out almost exactly where Everest should be;

but the clouds were dark in that direction. We gazed at them intently through field glasses as though by some miracle we might pierce the veil. Presently the miracle happened. We caught the gleam of snow behind the grey mist. A whole group of mountains began to appear in gigantic fragments. Mountain shapes are often fantastic seen through a mist; these were like the wildest creation of a dream. A preposterous triangular lump rose out of the depths; its edge came leaping up at an angle of about 70° and ended nowhere. To the left a black serrated crest was hanging in the sky incredibly. Gradually, very gradually, we saw the great mountain sides and glaciers and aretes, now one fragment now another through the floating rifts, until far higher in the sky than imagination had dared to suggest the white summit of Everest appeared. And in this series of partial glimpses we had seen a whole; we were able to piece together the fragments, to interpret the dream. However much might remain to be understood, the centre had a clear meaning as one mountain shape, the shape of Everest.

It is hardly possible of course from a distance of 57 miles to formulate an accurate idea of a mountain's shape. But some of its most remarkable features may be distinguished for what they are. We were looking at Everest from about North-east and evidently a long arete was thrust out towards us. Some little distance below the summit the arete came down to a black shoulder, which we conjectured would be an insuperable obstacle. To the right of this we saw the sky line in profile and judged it not impossibly steep. The edge was probably a true arete because it appeared to be joined by a col to a sharp peak to the north. From the direction of this col a valley came down to the East and evidently drained into the Arun. This was one fact of supreme importance which was now established and we noticed that it agreed with what was shown on the map; the map in fact went up in our esteem and we were inclined hereafter to believe its veracity until we established the contrary. Another fact was even more remarkable. We knew something more about the great peak near Everest which we had seen from Kampa Dzong; we knew now that it was not a separate mountain; in a sense it was part of Everest, or rather Everest was not one mountain but two; this great black mountain to the South was connected with Everest by a continuous arete and divided from it only by a snow col which must itself be at least 27,000 feet high. The black cliffs of this mountain, which faced us, were continuous with the icy face of Everest itself.[51]

The country through which they moved westwards was the same barren landscape with which they had now become familiar. Sand dunes and mudflats alternated, and whenever the wind dropped they were pestered by myriads of irritating sand flies.

The monotony was relieved when they arrived at Shekar Dzong, the 'White Glass Fort', a remarkable series of buildings which staggered up a steep hillside like some medieval castle designed by Walt Disney or Ludwig of Bavaria. About a third of the way up the hill were the crowded buildings of a monastery which held four hundred monks, and this was connected by walls and turrets to the fort itself, whose whitewashed walls gleamed in the sun as high up the hill again. In turn a turreted wall climbed up from the fort to the sharp pointed summit of the hill, where there was a prominent tower. Howard-Bury described it, in what for him was a rare flight of fancy, as an enlarged St Michael's Mount.

A little excitement broke the monotony at Shekar Dzong when during the night the camp was attacked by a madman who tried to smash their stoves. Bullock drove him off with an ice axe.

From Shekar Dzong they moved on to Tingri Dzong, a village of considerable importance as a trading centre, built on a hillock in the middle of a vast flat plain. Everest lay some forty miles to the south and could be seen quite plainly, as could the immense Cho Oyu just to the west of it. Tingri was to be the expedition's first Base Camp, and they had reached it exactly one month after leaving Darjeeling.

What immense and exciting opportunities the 1921 expedition had for exploration! To the south of them, between Tingri and the Nepalese border (beyond which they could not venture, of course), lay a vast tract of the world's highest mountains virtually unknown to civilization. They were the first Westerners even to approach as near as Tingri, and the country to the south was their oyster, of which the pearl was Everest. The pearl was not for them to snatch, of course – that would be too much to expect – but their reward was almost as great, and some might say greater: to tread the untrodden glacier, to see for the first time what lay around the next spur or beyond the next blue mountain.

The western and eastern limits of the Everest group were fairly well known in general terms, though no European had ever been there. To the west, between the Everest group and the Gaurisankar group, was a high pass known as the Khumbu La, which was frequently used by traders passing from Namche Bazar in Nepal to Tingri Dzong in Tibet and vice versa. Immediately east of this a great tangle of peaks which included the known summits of Cho Oyu, Gyachung Kang, Everest, Chomo Lonzo and Makalu stretched away for some forty miles in a curve which turned gradually south. Beyond Makalu was the deep gorge of the great River Arun which cuts clean through the main Himalayan range, draining a vast area of Southern Tibet and pouring into Nepal to become the Kosi river. In places the Arun is quite impassable.

This much was known. What was not known was the detail of that forty-mile stretch of mountain between the Khumbu La and the Arun Gorge. In the heart of that icy tangle lay Everest. How would they reach the heart? As Mallory once said, first they would have to find the mountain.

The party divided up to undertake their various duties. Wollaston, who had rejoined them, remained at Tingri in charge of Base Camp, where a house had been obtained and a photographic darkroom set up. Natives brought him specimens of the flora and fauna which he preserved and collected in his role of naturalist, but he was also employed in looking after two native bearers who were ill with enteritis, one of whom died within a few days. Morshead, too, remained at Tingri, as he wanted to survey the locality, while Wheeler and Heron went off towards the Khumbu La to begin their own surveys. Mallory and Bullock made straight for Mount Everest. 'Looked at from here,' Howard-Bury recorded glumly, after noting their departure, 'it is certainly a very wonderful mountain, as it seems to stand up all by itself, but from this side it looks far too steep to be climbed.'[52]

Howard-Bury had intended to go with Wheeler and Heron, but toxic fumes produced in the darkroom made him ill for several days. When he recovered he set off on a tour of his scattered troops.

On 25 June Mallory and Bullock, with their porters, left the valley of the Dzahar Chu which they had followed from Tingri, and turning south entered the Rongbuk valley at Chobuk (see Map 4, p. 54). A short way beyond the village was a patch of fertile ground with grass and flowering shrubs, greener than anything they had seen since leaving Chumbi, but then as they pressed on the valley became mean and dreary. At length the path steepened and climbed up to two *chortens*, or Buddhist shrines. The view was enthralling:

> We paused here in sheer astonishment. Perhaps we had half expected to see Mount Everest at this moment. In the back of my mind were a host of questions about it clamouring for answer. But the sight of it now banished every thought. We forgot the stony wastes and regrets for other beauties. We asked no questions and made no comment, but simply looked.
>
> It is perhaps because Everest presented itself so dramatically on this occasion that I find the Northern aspect more particularly imagined in my mind, when I recall the mountain. But in any case this aspect has a special significance. The Rongbuk Valley is well constructed to show off the peak at its head; for about 20 miles it is extraordinarily straight and in that distance rises only 4,000 feet, the glacier, which is 10 miles long, no more steeply than the rest. In consequence of this arrangement one has only to be raised very slightly above the bed of the valley to see it almost as a flat way up to the very head of the glacier from which the cliffs of Everest spring. To the place where Everest stands one looks along rather than up. The glacier is prostrate; not a part of the mountain; not even a pediment; merely a floor footing the high walls. At the end of the valley and above the glacier Everest rises not so much a peak as a prodigious mountain-mass. There is no complication for the eye. The highest of the world's great mountains, it seems, has to make but a single gesture of magnificence to be lord of all, vast

in unchallenged and isolated supremacy. To the discerning eye other mountains are visible, giants between 23,000 and 26,000 feet high. Not one of their slenderer heads even reaches their chief's shoulder; beside Everest they escape notice – such is the pre-eminence of the greatest.

Considered as a structure Mount Everest is seen from the Rongbuk Valley to achieve height with amazing simplicity. The steep wall 10,000 feet high is contained between two colossal members – to the left the North-eastern arete, which leaves the summit at a gentle angle and in a distance of rather less than a mile descends only 1,000 feet before turning more sharply downwards from a clearly defined shoulder; and to the right the North-west arete (its true direction is about W.N.W.), which comes down steeply from the summit but makes up for the weaker nature of this support by immense length below. Such is the broad plan. In one respect it is modified. The wide angle between the two main aretes involves perhaps too long a face; a further support is added. The Northern face is brought out a little below the North-east shoulder and then turned back to meet the crest again, so that from the point of the shoulder a broad arete leads down to the North and is connected by a snow col at about 23,000 feet with a northern wing of mountains which forms the right bank of the Rongbuk Glacier and to some extent masks the view of the lower parts of Everest. Nothing could be stronger than this arrangement and it is nowhere fantastic. We do not see jagged crests and a multitude of pinnacles, and beautiful as such ornaments may be we do not miss it. The outline is comparatively smooth because the stratification is horizontal, a circumstance which seems again to give it strength, emphasizing the broad foundations. And yet Everest is a rugged giant. It has not the smooth undulations of a snow mountain with white snow cap and glaciated flanks. It is rather a great mass, coated often with a thin layer of white powder which is blown about its sides, and bearing perennial snow only on the gentler ledges and on several wide faces less steep than the rest. One such place is the long arm of the North-west arete which with its slightly articulated buttresses is like the nave of a vast cathedral roofed with snow.[53]

The next day they made a base camp a little distance beyond the Rongbuk monastery. The monastery was situated in a bleak spot at a height of 16,500 ft, in full view of Everest, which was sixteen miles away, though it seemed much nearer. It was a particularly holy place supporting some twenty lamas, chief of whom was the Head Lama, a reincarnation, like the Dalai Lama himself. In addition there were several hundred lay lamas who stayed for varying periods of time and a number of hermits who lived in caves and cells higher up the Rongbuk valley. It was a place noted for meditation, and at first the lamas did not take kindly to the intrusion of strangers, though in later years, when they were more used to expeditions, it became a custom for the Head Lama to bestow his blessings on the members. In 1921, however, the Head Lama was undergoing a year of seclusion.

From this camp Mallory and Bullock could look straight up the Rongbuk valley to Everest. Beyond the camp the head of the valley was filled by the Rongbuk Glacier, which seemed a flat white highway leading directly to the mountain. The two climbers had no reason to suspect that this glacier was any different from an ordinary Alpine glacier, but it is. In the Alps a glacier, provided it is not too crevassed, often provides a quick way into the heart of a mountain system, but in the eastern Himalayas the glaciers are a maze of melt channels and resemble an icy version of the shell-pocked battlefields of the First World War. To cross one is purgatory, to go up one almost impossible. The two climbers quickly learned that the way to get on in the Everest region was to follow the moraines at the edge of the glaciers.

With the mountain omnipresent they had plenty of time to study what they could see and reflect on the chances of climbing it. Mallory wrote in his diary:

> I wish some folk at home could see the precipice from this side – a grim spectacle most unlike the long gentle slopes suggested by photos. Amusing to think how one's vision of the last effort has changed; it looked like crawling half-blind up easy snow, an even slope all the way up from a camp on a flat snow shoulder; but it won't be that sort of grind; we'll want climbers and not half-dazed ones; a tougher job than I bargained for, sanguine as usual.
>
> E. is a rock mountain.[54]

On 29 June they established an advanced camp at 17,500 ft on a shelf above the western edge of the glacier, about two and a half miles from its snout. From this camp they inaugurated a series of probes to determine the features on the western side of the mountain.

They had already ascertained that the Rongbuk Glacier divided into two arms. One, the Rongbuk proper, led straight as an arrow to a snowy corrie over which towered the North Face of Everest, and another which turned off the main glacier to the west about two miles beyond their camp.

On 1 July Mallory set out with some porters to explore the head of the main valley, but bad weather denied him the success he had hoped for. However, he saw enough of the West Ridge and the North Col to dash his hopes of any easy access to the mountain in those directions. The North Col, the name he gave to the dip between the North Ridge and the North Peak (Changtse), might be attempted as a last resort, he thought, but the icy slopes up to it from the Rongbuk Glacier seemed steep and broken. Nevertheless, the way to the summit from the col, once the latter had been reached, did seem to be the only hope of climbing the mountain, and he hoped that the col might be more accessible from the other side.

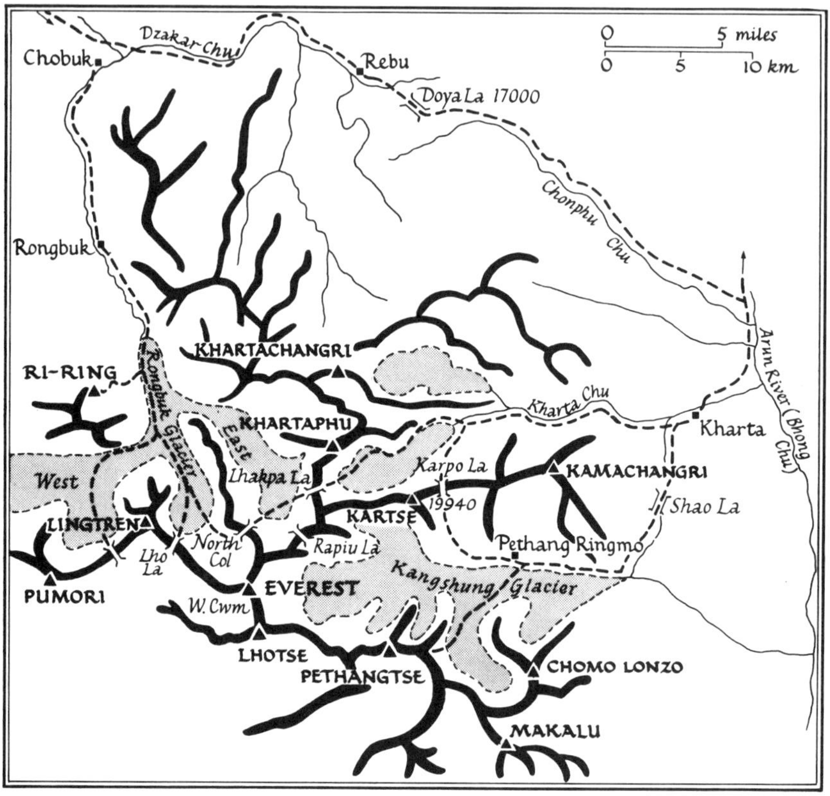


Map 4. The 1921 reconnaissance

Mallory was convinced that when it came to an actual assault on the mountain it would be necessary for the Sherpas to know the rudiments of ice craft, particularly the handling of axe and rope. He and Bullock had spent some time in teaching them and on 3 July they even embarked on a minor climb, from which they prudently withdrew at 21,000 ft. Mallory thought that the best of the Sherpas would eventually become safe mountaineers, though they were always 'coolies' to him. Despite his bouts of lassitude and mountain sickness, he was of course supremely fit, as Bullock bears testimony in his diary, and so he was more than a little surprised one day to find one of the Sherpas matching him step by step:

> . . .unconsciously I was led into something like a race by one of the coolies who was pressing along at my side. I noticed that though he was slightly built he seemed extremely strong and active, compact of muscle. . .I wondered how long he would keep it up.[55]

Mallory wasn't used to people who could keep up with him, but presumably the unknown Sherpa did, for he never mentioned the matter again!

Above their camp was a shapely peak which looked as though it would be a good vantage point for the whole area, and on 5 July they set out to climb it. After two and a half thousand feet they reached the crest of the ridge where they took forty minutes' rest and ate some food ('B. and the coolies rather tired at this point').[56] Roping up, they then made a long steady traverse to a snow col, followed by a long ridge leading towards their goal. The porters turned back after a while but the climbers pressed on: 'We moved very slowly, keeping up muscular energy and overcoming lassitude by breathing fast and deep. It was a colossal labour.'[57]

They reached the summit at 2.45 p.m. They had put up a fine performance by ascending 5,000 ft in one day at high altitude, and were justifiably proud of their achievement. Mallory thought it was probably the second highest peak ever climbed, but in fact his altimeter played him false and what he took for 23,000 ft was actually 22,500. Longstaff, Kellas and Calciati had all climbed peaks over 23,000 ft and men had been even higher attempting big peaks such as Kamet and Chogolisa. Nevertheless it was the first ascent made in the Everest region. The two climbers wanted to call it Mount Kellas to honour their late comrade, but in accordance with geographical practice it was later given the native name, Ri-ring.

They stayed on the summit for only fifteen minutes before the thought of bad weather drove them down again, but it was long enough to add considerably to their knowledge of the area. They got a clear idea of the complex ridges at the western edge of the group – Cho Oyu and Gyachung Kang – and they could judge the North Face of Everest from a new angle, which confirmed their opinion that once the North Col was reached the way to the top was distinctly feasible. Unfortunately they could also see a high ridge running eastwards from Changtse, the peak beyond the North Col, and they assumed that this ridge bordered a glacier which would flow east to the Arun river. To see the other side of the North Col they would therefore need to come in from the east of the massif. Changtse and its ridge seemed to bar any access from the north.

They were also able to place more accurately a great jagged ridge to the south which they had suspected might be another ridge of Everest. They now saw that it could not connect with Everest, but only with Lhotse, which meant there must be a high glacier enfolded between the ridge and Everest itself. They tentatively named the unknown glacier the West Cwm, and the jagged ridge itself was later called Nuptse.

But they could not see into the West Cwm; they were too far away and Everest itself baulked the view. Mallory suspected that the West Cwm and the West Rongbuk Glacier might be connected. It was possible that the glacier might start in the Cwm, flow westwards, then turn north between the peaks now called Lingtren and Pumori and join the West Rongbuk Glacier. It was something he had to find out.

To do this they established a second advanced camp on the West Rongbuk Glacier, about two miles from its junction with the main stream. It was a light camp at first and Mallory did not like it at all:

> A Mummery tent may be well enough in fair weather, though even then its low roof suggests a recumbent attitude; it makes a poor dining-room even for two men and is a cold shelter from snow. Moreover, the cold and draught discouraged our Primus stove – but I leave to the imagination of those who have learned by experience the nausea that comes from the paraffin fumes and one's dirty hands and all the mess that may be. It was chiefly a question of incompetence, no doubt, but there was no consolation in admitting that. . .Is it not a first principle of mountaineering to be as comfortable as possible as long as one can?[58]

To make things more comfortable, the heavier Whymper tents – and the cook – were moved up from the previous camp.

One fact which the 1921 expedition had discovered very quickly was that the monsoon period was not the best time to explore the Everest region. Surveyors and alpinists alike suffered from days of bad weather when nothing could be attempted, and even the good days were frequently spoiled by low cloud which made observation impossible. As far as Mallory and Bullock were concerned, at least half their time was wasted in this way.

But 12 July was fairly good as they set off to find the West Cwm. First they had to cross the West Rongbuk Glacier from their camp on the north bank to the south bank, their aim being to enter a branch of the glacier which ran south, round the shoulder of Lingtren. The going was easy at first, but then they ran into a maze of ice pinnacles which slowed them down and ultimately defeated them. By the time they reached the south bank the clouds were gathering: it was 10 a.m. and it had taken them four and a half hours to cover little more than a mile. There was nothing for it but to turn back.

The next day they tried again and by using their hard-won knowledge of the glacier succeeded in crossing it in less than an hour and a half. In the south branch the snow was good and they were able to make rapid progress, but as they ascended the weather closed in and they were enveloped in cloud and mist. They went forward into a dim white world, sensing great unseen peaks on either hand, conscious only of yawning crevasses as dim labyrinths all round. They had no idea of where they were, but eventually they realized they had reached a crest – presumably a col – and that there was a steep drop ahead of them. They turned back.

In the days which followed they realized that if ever they were to have time to reach this col again, to take advantage of even half a day's good weather, they would need another camp, placed in the south branch of the glacier. This they organized, and some time was also given to photography, but unfortunately these were the photographic plates which Mallory spoiled by using them the wrong way round. While Mallory wrestled with the camera, Bullock made an excursion up the long West Rongbuk Glacier towards its head where the Nup La makes a crossing into Nepal, but he failed to reach the col and low clouds prevented him from seeing anything.

On 19 July they set out from their new camp at 2.45 a.m. by glorious moonlight and tramped steadily up the south branch of the glacier. How different it was from their last attempt six days before! Now only light clouds drifted over Everest and the great white peaks were sharply defined against the dark sky. In two and a quarter hours they reached the col at the head of the glacier, between Lingtren and Pumori, and saw at once that their hopes were dashed. The West Cwm and the West Rongbuk Glacier were not connected with each other but separated by the steep frontier ridge. Mallory wrote:

> We reached the col at 5:00 a.m., a fantastically beautiful scene; and we looked across into the West Cwm at last, terribly cold and forbidding under the shadow of Everest. It was nearly an hour after sunrise before the sun hit the West Peak.
>
> But another disappointment: it is a big drop, about 1,500 feet down to the glacier, and a hopeless precipice. I was hoping to get away to the left and traverse into the cwm – that too, quite hopeless. However, we have seen this western glacier and are not sorry we have not to go up it. It is terribly steep and broken. In any case, work on this side could only be carried out from a base in Nepal, so we have done with the western side. It was not a very likely chance that the gap between Everest and the South Peak could be reached from the west. From what we have seen now, I do not much fancy it would be possible, even could one get up the glacier.[59]

Without any hope of reconnoitring the southern flanks of the mountain there was nothing they could do but withdraw from the Rongbuk area and move to Kharta over on the east, where Howard-Bury was setting up his second base camp. Before they could do this, however, a runner brought Mallory the bad news about the spoiled photographs and he felt obliged to retake as many as possible. He was bitter about the whole affair, as he wrote to his wife:

> I have had a bitter blow. All the photos taken up here with the quarter-plate – practically all I have taken – have gone wrong. Apparently I put the plates in the wrong way round. I knew nothing about plates and followed instructions given me by Heron. I have taken enormous trouble over these photos: many of them were taken at sunrise from places where neither I nor anyone else may go again – for instance, those on our ascent of

> Mount Kellas. However, I'm determined to replace them as far as possible. . .It will mean two days spent in the most tiresome fashion, when I thought all our work in those parts was done.[60]

While Mallory was retaking his pictures, Bullock and some of the porters made a journey to the head of the main Rongbuk Glacier where the broad col of the Lho La separates Tibet from Nepal. Rising mists prevented a distant view, but Bullock could see that the Lho La, like the col between Lingtren and Pumori which they had visited previously, provided no practical way into the West Cwm. The descent was far too sheer. He also had a good opportunity to look again at the North Col of Everest, and like Mallory thought an ascent from the Rongbuk Glacier would be a difficult piece of climbing.

And so the exploration of Everest from the north and west was complete. Mallory and Bullock had explored the Rongbuk Glacier system, had proved conclusively that there was no access to the south side of the mountain from Tibet, that Lhotse and Nuptse formed with Everest a distinctive cirque, that the North Col was accessible from the Rongbuk Glacier only with difficulty, and that the North Ridge and the North Face looked reasonable climbing routes.

Even Hinks, back in London, was satisfied with these results – Mrs Mallory passed on the letters from her husband – though he did have one quibble: 'He must not keep calling mountains by personal names like "Kellas" and "Clare" for they certainly will not be "allowed to stick". The idea is enough to make poor Kellas turn in his grave at Kampa Dzong. . .'[61]

Despite all this splendid work, however, Mallory and Bullock had made one serious error. Facing their first camp on the Rongbuk Glacier was a stream which came tumbling down through a gap in the mountainside to disappear in a cave in the glacier. Obviously another glacier must at one time have occupied the place of the stream, but it had now shrunk back out of sight behind the long north ridge of Changtse. The two climbers had intended to investigate the stream to see where its glacier would lead them, but they had never got round to it, and in any case it seemed likely to be a dead-end, for did not the east ridge of Changtse, seen from Ri-ring, cut off this approach before Everest was reached? Actually it didn't – but it was Oliver Wheeler, working on his own with a few Sherpas, and lugging around his photographic survey equipment, who discovered that the East Rongbuk Glacier was the highway they were all looking for.

In the meantime the expedition base had moved east to Kharta, a village in the valley of the same name, which was a feeder for the Arun river. Howard-Bury had discovered the place by accident when reconnoitring the river in search of an eastern base, and he could hardly have found a more idyllic spot. After the rigours of the Tibetan plateau with its persistent winds and barren landscape, Kharta was like the Garden of Eden – a real Tibetan Shangri La. The climate was mild and fresh, the valley was green, trees and flowers abounded. Here the expedition rested, in a house they had rented for about 1½p per day. In the garden, lined with poplars and willows, they were able to pitch their tents, while the house itself served for photographic and survey purposes and as a general store room.

The river which came tumbling down the Kharta valley was obviously of glacial origin and Howard-Bury surmised that it started life in the heart of the Chomolungma massif, possibly the East Face of Everest itself.

On 2 August, after four days of welcome relaxation amongst the comforts of Kharta, Mallory and Bullock set off to explore the eastern approaches to Everest. They had two principal objectives in mind: first, to look at the East Face, which nobody had seen, but which they thought was unlikely to be climbable; and second, to see whether the eastern slopes of the North Col were easier than those above the Rongbuk Glacier. They were hopeful that the Kharta valley would lead them directly to the North Col.

Their start was not auspicious. The porters were giving trouble over rations and at every village in this fertile valley they stopped to drink *chang*, the local beer. Mallory, who had gone on ahead, turned back to round up the recalcitrants, got himself lost, and what with this delay and that, they made only eight miles that day. Both Mallory and Bullock thought this was a poor show, as their diaries record, though actually eight miles is quite a reasonable trek in the high Himalaya.

On the next day the weather turned sour. Where they had camped a small lateral valley entered the Kharta from the south and their Tibetan guide turned into this, leading them up to a col, the Langma La, at 18,000 ft. Mallory was worried by this. He knew that Everest lay to the west, not the south, but the guide assured him this was the way to Chomolungma – indeed, he said, there were *two* Chomolungmas, and this was the way to both. Mallory guessed that one of the so-called Chomolungmas might be Makalu, so he instructed the guide to lead them to the furthest one. On the next day they turned into a large glacier-filled valley called the Kama, which flowed from the west, and camped above the true left bank on a grassy alp called Pethang Ringmo where yaks grazed and some Tibetans were encamped. The clouds were down and all they could see of their surroundings were occasional glimpses of a big white peak which they took to be either Makalu or Chomo Lonzo, immediately across the glacier from their camp.

Next morning the weather looked more hopeful and the two climbers went out on a preliminary reconnaissance up the Kama valley. As they searched for a suitable vantage point the clouds began to shred against the pinnacles and walls of the mountains and bit by bit an amazing scene was revealed. The head of the glacier, the Kangshung, opened out into a broad basin whose furthest limits were seven or eight miles from their camp site, but such is the scale of Himalayan mountains, that this distance seemed nothing and the peaks appeared to tower almost near enough to touch. All around them was a scene of incomparable grandeur: Everest at the valley head, Lhotse Shar, Pethangtse, Chomo Lonzo, Makalu – immense towers of rock and ice, four of them among the half dozen highest mountains in the world.[62] Mallory wrote to his wife:

> I'm altogether beaten for words. The whole range of peaks from Makalu to Everest far exceeds any mountain scenery that ever I saw before. . .[63]

They saw enough to convince themselves that this wonderful valley did not, alas, lead to the North Col. As Mallory had surmised, they were on the wrong side of a watershed and the valley they sought was parallel with theirs to the north. A plan was devised by which it was hoped to solve all the remaining mysteries; that is, access to the North Col, and fuller views of the East Face and North East Ridge.

On 6 August they made a camp higher up the Kangshung Glacier at 17,500 ft. The next day they set out to climb to a col on the northern rim of the valley, the Karpo La, almost 20,000 ft high and not an easy climb. Nevertheless, despite the steep rocks, the climbers and Sherpas arrived at the col by 9 a.m. Mallory wrote:

> We had already by this hour taken time to observe the great Eastern Face of Mount Everest, and more particularly the lower edge of the hanging glacier; it required but little further gazing to be convinced – to know that almost everywhere the rocks below must be exposed to ice falling from the glacier; that if, elsewhere, it might be possible to climb up, the performance would be too arduous, would take too much time and would lead to no convenient platform; that, in short, other men, less wise, might attempt this way if they would, but, emphatically, it was not for us.[64]

So the East Face was out. There remained the North East Ridge and the North Col. Below them on the other side of their ridge they could see the Kharta Glacier, but whether this ice stream went to the North Col of Everest it was not possible to see for, though it lay in the right direction, its head was obscured by a mountain spur. To solve the problem it was necessary to go higher.

Immediately west of their col rose the peak of Kartse (21,390 ft), which Mallory determined to climb. The angle did not look too steep, but the way up, by the East and South Faces, was guarded by two bands of rock. As it happened, the first band went to a direct assault, but the second was more difficult and they had some exposed climbing before they could turn it on the left and arrive below the summit cone. Everyone was exhausted and lay down on the snow to rest, but not before they had looked at the great North East Ridge of Everest, now face on to them and only some three miles distant.

It presented a fearsome spectacle. The crest was sharp and steep and the flanks seemed to offer no alternatives. Mallory dismissed it out of hand, though Bullock wrote in his diary: '. . .possible, but quite steep in places, and enormously long, and there are several gendarmes before the junction with the north buttress.'[65]

The approaches to the North Col, however, still proved elusive. Mallory, full of energy, proposed that they should complete the ascent of Kartse in the hope of solving this one remaining problem, but the response was less than enthusiastic. Almost everyone, including Bullock, was exhausted, and in the end only Mallory and a young Sherpa called Nyima made the top. They were too late: the clouds were boiling up, hiding the mountains, and they saw little that was of any use to them.

That evening, as they returned to camp, Mallory felt distinctly ill. For someone who, in his own words, 'Never imagined for myself the smallest deviation from my uniform standard of health and strength' it was something of a shock:

> I felt for the first time a symptom of weariness beyond muscular fatigue and beyond the vague lassitude of mountain sickness. By the time we reached the moraine I had a bad headache. In the tent at last I was tired and shivering and there spent a fevered night.[66]

He remained below par for almost another week, during which they retreated over the Langma La back to the Kharta valley, which they hoped would lead them towards the North Col of Everest.

On 13 August Mallory, still unwell, waved goodbye to Bullock as the latter set out to explore the Kharta Glacier. Mallory chafed at the inaction and wondered whether, after all, the final solution to the problem would be Bullock's alone.

A little way up from their camp the Kharta valley divided into northern and southern branches. The southern branch was the one they had seen from the Karpo La a few days earlier and they guessed that it did not reach the North Col – they had seen enough of the intervening mountain ridges to make that fairly certain. When Bullock set out therefore, he chose the northern arm of the glacier, up which he made good progress. Within no time at all, he realized it was not what he wanted and, though he stayed on another day to make doubly sure, he sent back a message on that first evening to Mallory.

Bullock had put two and two together, and made four. His reasoning went something like this: There must be a glacier descending from the North Col; that was self-evident. Such a glacier must flow eastwards since it was on the east side of the Everest–Changtse ridge, yet the *only* eastward-flowing glaciers were the north and south branches of the Kharta, and the Kangshung. Since it wasn't any of those the only explanation possible was that the glacier from the North Col *changed direction*. There was only one way it could do that – northwards, back to the Rongbuk Glacier!

When Mallory received the message he was dumbfounded. He remembered the little stream opposite their camp at Rongbuk. How could such a small stream drain what must be a fairly large glacier? He hardly believed it possible, and a little later, when a map arrived from Howard-Bury showing Oliver Wheeler's discovery of the East Rongbuk Glacier, he still didn't believe it.

He was in fact quite annoyed with the way things were going. It was beginning to look as though he had made an enormous blunder and it made him more determined than ever to discover a way to the North Col from their present position. In the account he wrote for the expedition book (*Mount Everest: The Reconnaissance, 1921*) he excuses himself for ignoring Wheeler's map: 'It was, unfortunately, a very rough map, professedly nothing more, and was notably wrong in some respects about which we had accurate knowledge.' It was the feeble excuse of a frustrated man.

Meanwhile, Morshead had arrived at the camp. So, while Bullock was up the northern branch of the Kharta Glacier, Mallory, much recovered in health, accompanied Morshead a short way up the other branch. A new idea occurred to him. At the head of the glacier was an easy col, above which could be seen the top of Changste, dead ahead. Suppose this easy col, later known as the Lhakpa La, could be crossed, would it not lead to the foot of Everest's North Col?

Bullock rejoined them but there were four days of frustrating delays before they could test the theory to the full, delays due to weather and movement of supplies, though they did manage to establish an advanced camp, which brought the Lhakpa La nearer. They set out on 18 August. The going, through soft snow, proved arduous and they were almost glad when some crevasses forced them to climb rocks for a time before regaining the glacier. A thin veil of mist danced around them as they trudged forwards, and with the sun coming up, the glacier, as so often happens, was converted into a sizzling cauldron. The final steep pull up to the col was sheer purgatory. 'One seemed literally at times to be walking in a white furnace,' Mallory wrote to his wife.[67] To Geoffrey Winthrop Young he confessed it was the biggest push he had ever made on a mountain.

Before they reached the col, Morshead dropped out, totally exhausted, but the one Sherpa who accompanied them – the incomparable Nyima again – matched them step by step to the top. Morshead managed to rejoin them twenty minutes later.

They reached the col at 1:15 p.m. and already the clouds were lowering.

The whole ridge from Changtse to Everest, including the North Col, was hidden from view, but at least they could look down into the head corrie of the East Rongbuk Glacier. From where they stood the descent to the glacier looked simple enough and they judged it to be 800 ft, though it turned out eventually to be half as much again. The East Rongbuk itself did not seem a difficult crossing either, but the slopes up to the North Col on the far side remained an enigma. They estimated that these slopes would be about 500 ft and steep – but that they would be climbable. 'I was prepared, so to speak, to bet my bottom dollar that a way could be found, and resolved that before we turned homeward this year we must get up from the East,' Mallory wrote later. Having no worthwhile evidence for this view, he was simply playing a hunch.[68]

The return to camp was a long wearisome affair, for poor Morshead was all-in and required frequent rests. They staggered into their tents at 2 a.m., ravenously ate a meal and thankfully crawled into their sleeping bags an hour later.

The first stage of the reconnaissance was over.

When George Mallory returned to Kharta on 20 August he was in a self-satisfied state of mind. His failure to discover the East Rongbuk Glacier had ruffled him, but now he had found a way into it from the east, up the Kharta valley, he felt he had redeemed himself. It was patently the way to approach the mountain – certainly for the present expedition, in any event, because the alternative was a long return round the mountain to Rongbuk monastery, which would waste valuable time. It might even be the best way for future expeditions, because Kharta was a good base with plenty of food and fuel supplies, and Rongbuk was singularly deficient in both.

He regarded himself as having the ultimate responsibility for success or failure and he wrote to Winthrop Young: 'The whole thing is on my shoulders – I can say this to you. Bullock follows well and is safe; but you know what it means on a long exhausting effort to lead all the time . . .'[69] This was not quite true, for on the strenuous ascent of Lhakpa La they had shared the lead. What was true is that Mallory was always the leader in the spiritual sense – he was the driving force which had dominated the reconnaissance, reinforced by his superb physical condition. Bullock always admitted as much.

There is no doubt that Everest, and the idea of climbing Everest, had by now seized Mallory in a powerful grip. For the first – and last – time in his life he had a true ambition.

Back in England Winthrop Young had realized this quite early on and he wrote a warning to his young friend:

> The result is nothing compared to the rightness of the attempt. Keep it 'right', then; and let no desire for result spoil the effort by overstretching

> the safe limits within which it must move ... Good fortune! and the 'resolution to return', even against ambition![70]

Mallory himself was almost frightened of the strange power which had gripped him. To Young he wrote: 'Geoffrey, at what point am I going to stop? ... I almost hope I shall be the first to give out!'[71]

On the last day of August 1921 Mallory and Bullock, impatient for the good weather they expected any day, were established once again in the Base Camp below the Kharta Glacier. The time had arrived for the first assault on Mount Everest, and Mallory was not happy about it.

He had every reason to feel qualms. The unknowns, the imponderables, the crass ignorance with which the expedition had struggled were beginning to take their toll. At this stage they were frankly pushing their luck, and Mallory sensed it.

A good maxim for a Himalayan expedition, and especially an Everest expedition, is to get in, get up and get out – and the quicker the better. Man must acclimatize, certainly, but once that is achieved the longer the assault is delayed the more arduous it will be for those taking part. There is a peak of acclimatization, after which the rundown is fairly rapid.

The Everest team of 1921 did not know this. They had been at fairly high altitudes for three months and by the end of August they were a spent force. Mallory wrote:

> I became more than ever observant of the party's physical condition ... Three of our strongest coolies were ill ... others seemed to be tired more easily than they should be ... Bullock, though he never complained, seemed no longer to be the fit man he was at the end of July. And for my part I began to experience a certain lack of exuberance when going up hill.[72]

Never before had Europeans spent such a continuous period of time at high altitude, and nothing was known or even suspected of the effects. Little did they realize they had become a classic case of the law of diminishing returns.

They were not to blame for this: how could they know? Perhaps more blame might be laid at the door of those who had sent the expedition out over the monsoon period, thus ensuring that many days were wasted through bad weather. It is true that nobody knew what the weather would be like in Tibet, a country protected from the monsoon by the Himalayan barrier, but Everest is part of that barrier and somebody should have had enough sense to realize that the monsoon would spill over the mountains, affecting them on all sides. The expedition thought – in the vaguest terms – that the monsoon would end at the beginning of September, but they didn't really know and in the event were disappointed. They could have waited a little longer – but had they done that they would have been even worse off from the point of view of over-acclimatization.

The organization of food and fuel was hopelessly inadequate: everything was arranged on the spur of the moment, locally, and usually by their sirdars, or foremen porters, who cheated sahibs and fellow porters alike. Later expeditions, who wisely paid their porters direct and not through the sirdars, discovered that the Tibetan porters were delighted to be paid at all – on the 1921 expedition they had worked because the local headmen (or Jongpen) had told them to work, and the pay which Howard-Bury thought was theirs was lining the sirdars' pockets. Even had the poor Tibetans suspected anything they hardly dare complain: they would not wish to annoy their Jongpen, and in any case they would not argue with a Nepali sirdar; the Tibetans were afraid of the people of Nepal, whom they associated with the ferocious Gurkhas.

The equipment, too, was amateurish: Bullock carried a suitcase around with him, and in his diary he tells how one day the porters were put on to nailing boots, because some new clinker nails had arrived from Base Camp; Mallory speaks on one occasion of choosing *only the porters with boots* (they were already fairly high), but perhaps the most telling incident comes from Bullock's diary: 'Having only brought one coat, which was wet, spent the evening in a sweater. Luckily I had two.' He was then at 20,000 ft![73]

How could they hope to succeed?

Mallory and Bullock sat it out in Advanced Base Camp for three weeks, waiting for the weather finally to clear. From time to time other members of the expedition joined them, and minor excursions were made in the locality. One of those to come up was Raeburn, who had recovered from his illness and returned from Sikkim. 'Raeburn,' writes Mallory in his official account, 'whom we rejoice to see again.'[74] But to Winthrop Young he wrote:

> Raeburn turned up again a week ago looking extraordinarily old and grizzled and being no less old than he looks. When he is not being a bore I feel moved to pity, but that is not often. He takes no part luckily.[75]

The weather finally cleared on 20 September, and at an early hour Mallory and Morshead set out with fifteen porters to establish a camp on the Lhakpa La, at 22,200 ft. At first the going was good, but once they had cleared the icefall they found themselves in deep powder snow. The porters were soon dropping from sheer exhaustion, but eventually eleven loads were hauled up to the col. The rest were abandoned for the time being, 800 ft lower down.

Having established the camp they all retired to Advanced Camp, but not before Mallory had a clear view of the North Col and the ice slopes leading up to it from the East Rongbuk Glacier. It looked even more severe than he had imagined – about a thousand feet high, steep and crevassed.

Mallory's plan was to reach the North Col direct from their camp on the

Lhakpa La, which meant a descent of 1,200 ft, a gradual uphill trudge across two and a half miles of unknown glacier, and a final steep snow climb of a thousand feet or more – and all above 21,000 ft. To do this his team would need to be fit and strong, so he chose Wheeler and Bullock to be his companions, with Wollaston, Morshead and Howard-Bury in reserve. Raeburn was left in charge of the camp.

As the party climbed up the Lhakpa La again on the 22nd they were astonished to see giant footprints in the snow, which the porters immediately recognized as those of *Metohkangmi* – the Abominable Snowman or *Yeti*. Similar tracks had been reported in Sikkim in 1889, and were to be reported and photographed many times in later years.

Despite this distraction it was a very tired party that assembled on the col, and none of them were keen to go on. 'I observed no great sparkle of energy or enthusiasm among my companions,' Mallory wrote later.[76] He was himself very tired and most of the Sherpas were suffering from varying degrees of mountain sickness.

That night they camped on the col in 34 degrees of frost and suffered miserably. By dawn Wollaston and Howard-Bury had had enough, so Morshead volunteered to take them back to the Advanced Camp. Similarly only nine Sherpas felt fit enough to continue, but ten were needed and so the number was made up by the unlucky loser of a straw poll among the rest.

The depleted climbing party – Mallory, Bullock and Wheeler, with their ten Sherpas – descended the Lhakpa La to the East Rongbuk Glacier, crossed the ice and began to toil up to the North Col. Though they found the climbing technically much easier than they had expected, the altitude and their tiredness made it hard going and they were glad enough to make it a short day by pitching their tents at 22,000 ft. The North Col lay above them, within striking distance next day.

They had a meal of soup, cocoa and dried fruit, then settled in for the night. The sky was clear, now the monsoon had gone, but for the first time they experienced that awful phenomenon of post-monsoon Everest, the violent wind. It rattled and shook the tents all night, and there was little sleep to be had. In the morning it was three tired climbers with three tired Sherpas who set out to reach the North Col.

They started by moving up to the right on a cone of avalanche debris, then turned and made a long leftward sweep up to the col. Two of the Sherpas, Ang Pasang and Lagay, made the trail, though the going was fairly easy until the final slopes, which proved rather steep and covered with deep soft snow. They reached the col at 11.30 a.m. – a climb of four and a half hours.

The col they found to be in the form of a double shelf, with the far side a little higher than theirs. This protected them from the strong westerly wind which was blowing, but they could see the spindrift being blown about in a violent fashion above them.

All were now desperately tired, but Mallory, no doubt momentarily elated by reaching the col, had thoughts about pushing on a bit further – up the North ridge or onto the Face: 'now finding my best form; I supposed I might be capable of another 2,000 feet, and there would be no time for more.'[77] But Wheeler's feet were so cold they had lost all feeling and though Mallory thought he was willing to go on, Bullock states categorically in his diary that Wheeler was against making any attempt. As for Bullock himself, he wrote: 'I was prepared to follow M. if he wished to try and make some height, but was glad when he decided not to.'[78]

The temptation for Mallory to push on was great, and not for the last time he forgot Winthrop Young's warning. Undecided what to do they tested the matter by going up to the higher shelf of the col, where they met the full blast of the icy wind. That was enough. There was no question of going on; they realized they could never have survived in that wind.

As they retreated wearily down the slopes of the col to their camp they noticed that an avalanche had wiped out part of the tracks they had made coming up. Mallory made no mention of this in his account of the climb, but avalanche risks on the approach to the North Col were to loom significantly in future expeditions. At the time they were too exhausted to understand that the mountain was giving them a warning.

The return over the Lhakpa La on the following day showed how tired everyone was. 'Were we fit to push the adventure further?' Mallory wrote '. . . The arguments, in fact, were all on one side; it would be bad heroics to take wrong risks; and fairly facing the situation one could only admit the necessity of retreat.'[79]

The main effort was finished, but it was not quite an end to the climbing. Mallory, Raeburn and Morshead took the stores back to Kharta, but Howard-Bury, Wollaston and Wheeler paid another visit to the Kama valley, crossing the Karpo La (the pass which Mallory and Bullock had visited from Kama some weeks earlier), and descended to the grassy camp site at Pethang Ringmo. Wheeler, who had done a splendid job throughout the expedition, was intent on making a photo-survey of the one valley he had so far missed, and Howard-Bury was keen to climb up to the long ridge joining Everest to Makalu, so that he could look into forbidden Nepal.

Taking two Sherpas, he climbed up to the ridge at the nearest point opposite the camp, separated by a small side glacier from the fantastic cliffs of Chomo Lonzo. It was probably the mountain marked as Pt 6530 m. on recent maps, though his description does not make this certain. He looked down on a large snowfield which curved away into a deep, unknown valley (the Barun Glacier) on the far side of which he could see another col leading west (probably col 6,190 m., north of Baruntse), through which one of the Sherpas could recognize peaks of the Khumbu valley – almost certainly Ama Dablam (see Map 5, p. 256). The Sherpas told Howard-Bury that long ago there was a route from the Khumbu to the Kama valley, and this must have been it, for there are no other possibilities.

He identified Chamlang and was impressed by the cliffs of Kangchuntse (which he regarded as part of Makalu). Away to the east he could see Kangchenjunga, and in the west the upper part of Everest's South West Face – 'these appeared very steep,' he wrote later, 'and even if it were possible and permissible to go into Nepal, it seemed improbable that a practicable route lies up that face of the mountain.'[80] It took fifty years to prove him wrong.

# 3

# Only Rotters Would Use Oxygen

Nothing illustrates better the thoroughness with which the 1921 expedition accomplished their reconnaissance than this last minor effort by the leader. They had seen the mountain from every side, had identified a practicable route from the north, and had even looked into country which no Westerner would see again until after the Second World War.

Yet back in London Hinks was not completely satisfied. At the end of the expedition he wrote to Howard-Bury: 'What has happened to the big rock peak photographed by both Kellas and Sella ... North of Makalu? Has it fallen down since last December? And if not why is it not in your photographs?'[1] He also passed on some of Mallory's letters to Norman Collie with the remark, 'There is no doubt about who thinks himself leader of the mountaineering party now.'[2]

Howard-Bury was having his own moan. With typical insensitivity on the part of the Committee, Bruce had been nominated as leader of the 1922 expedition before Howard-Bury's party had left India, and Howard-Bury was naturally hurt by this, thinking that it branded his own efforts a failure. He was also put out by Mallory and Bullock, who wanted to break their journey home – the former in Spain and the latter in Egypt – and return at the Committee's expense.

Mallory himself was momentarily fed up with Everest. He thought of the expedition as a defeat, because they hadn't either climbed the mountain or made a serious attempt at it. To his sister Avie he wrote:

> They've had thoughts of organizing an expedition for next year; but I've said it's no use going out except early in the Spring, to climb before the monsoon. They can't possibly organize another show so soon, particularly as I've also said that it's barely worth while trying again, and anyway not without eight first-rate climbers. They can't get eight, certainly not soon, perhaps not even the year after. Hinks (Hon. Sec.) already wants to know

> whether I'll go again. When they press for an answer, I shall tell them they can get the other seven first. How they'll pore over the A.C. list and write round for opinions about the various candidates! I wouldn't go again next year, as the saying is, for all the gold in Arabia.[3]

And to his friend David Pye:

> Never mind Everest and its unfriendly glories. I'm tired of travelling and travellers, far countries and uncouth people, trains and ships and shimmering mausoleums, foreign ports, dark-skinned faces, and a garish sun. What I want to see is faces I know, and my own sweet home; afterwards, the solemn façades in Pall Mall, and perhaps Bloomsbury in a fog; and then an English river, cattle grazing in western meadows . . .
>
> I've been writing solidly for ten days since leaving Bombay – a report for the A.C., vastly long and, I fear, not a little indiscreet . . . When I think of that wonderful Committee and all the solemn divergences of opinion that must have been passed between their nodding heads, the scrutiny of photographs and discussions of letters, with grave doubts coughed up in phlegmy throats as to whether the party are really 'on the right tracks', and all the anxious wisdom devoted to spoon feeding the Glaxo-loving public – lord, when I think of it, something bubbles up inside me. The effervescence is sternly repressed, of course, I settle down to ponder judgments; and then – a bubble outs and bursts.[4]

To Hinks he wrote:

> As to my going out again, may I leave that over till I see you? I have put clearly enough in my report the necessities as I see them for a future expedition and unless the required number of climbers is forthcoming, and the required number of coolies can be selected and equipped in time, I should not be inclined to go out next year. The chances are small enough whatever arrangements are made.[5]

To which Hinks, with some acerbity, replied: 'It is really very important that we should see you as soon as possible because though you may not be coming out next year other people are.'[6]

On 20 December the expedition gave an account of their adventures to a combined meeting of the Alpine Club and Royal Geographical Society. Mallory spoke for too long and away from the subject, thus preventing Wollaston from speaking at all, much to his disappointment. Raeburn was allowed only half an hour, which did nothing to improve his temper. 'Rarity of the air in Tibet does not seem to make his intelligence more permeable,' commented Hinks.[7]

Following on this, Mallory gave nearly thirty public lectures up and down the country. To Sir Francis Younghusband he wrote: 'The public interest is immense. A crowd was turned away from the Free Trade Hall, Manchester, which holds about 3,000.'[8]

Meanwhile, preparations went ahead for the assault of 1922. The Committee had no doubts about finance, there being adequate reserves from the first expedition,[9] and there were the newspaper contracts to fall back on as well, no doubt to Hinks's chagrin. In addition, a film was to be made of the adventure and it was confidently expected this would bring in extra money to pay off any debts which might accrue.

If the 1921 team agreed about anything it was that the timing of any attempt on Everest was crucial. They had been continually hampered by the monsoon and were of the opinion that Everest would be in condition only from about mid-May to mid-June: the calm period before the weather broke. After the monsoon the winds were too high and the temperatures too low. This crucial conclusion, though based on limited experience, was to dominate not only Everest climbing but expeditions in the eastern Himalaya generally for decades. One corollary was immediately apparent: to reach the mountain in time for the assault an expedition would have to cross the bitter uplands of Tibet in the aftermath of winter.

The team leader for 1922 was to be General Bruce, now freed from his military commitments and raring to go. 'If the council will have me, I'm your man. Don't think that I am possibly giving this job up,' he told Younghusband.[10]

His medical report (he was fifty-six) mentioned various scars due to accidents and bullet wounds (he had been seriously wounded at Gallipoli) and evidence of slight arteriosclerosis, though whether the doctors knew he also had occasional severe bouts of malaria is not revealed, and Bruce was not the man to enlighten them if it might jeopardize his chances. The report concludes: 'The above table of defects rather suggests that this man is unfit, but summing up the whole case and taking into account the history and general physique of this man, I consider he is fit to join the expedition.' It needed a much braver doctor than that to turn down Charlie Bruce![11]

Claude Wilson, a noted climber and doctor, was obviously a bit worried about him and wrote to him:

> I hope you will keep fit, but I take it there will be some second-in-command . . . of course, with all care, you might knock up like Raeburn did – though I don't think you'll die, like poor Kellas.[12]

Such gloomy views probably had no effect whatever on the General. He went through the expedition, as he went through life itself, with a joke and a belly laugh whenever possible. The serious-minded Hinks, who was obviously afraid of him, was driven to distraction.

Mallory had decided to go again, after all, despite the fact that the Committee chose six instead of the eight climbers he had urged as being necessary. Once again they were a mixture of age and 'youth', and once again, coincidentally, the medical profession was well represented.

Second-in-command to Bruce was Lt Col. E.L. Strutt, one-time High Commissioner in Danzig and a hero who had once rescued the Austrian royal family from a revolutionary mob. He was a man cast in an autocratic mould: inflexible in opinion, outspoken and totally unmoved by the changing times through which he lived. A strong, sound mountaineer of the traditional type, Strutt was later condemned for his uncompromising hostility to modern climbing tactics being introduced by continental climbers in the Alps. Mallory gives this picture of the man during the dreary walk across Tibet:

> A usual and by now welcome sound in each new place is Strutt's voice, cursing Tibet – this march for being more dreary and repulsive even than the one before, and this village being more filthy than any other. Not that Strutt is precisely a grouse; but he likes to ease his feelings with maledictions and, I hope, feels better for it . . .[13]

On Everest, Strutt nominally had charge of the Base Camp. Bruce does not seem to have liked him much, which is not surprising when one considers that two more opposite characters would be hard to imagine. 'It may possibly be that we are a little too young for him,' the General commented drily.[14] Still, he held Strutt's mountain judgement in high regard and later wished he had put him in command of the last attempt to reach the North Col.

George Finch was this time passed as being fit and it was expected that he and Mallory would team up together, possibly for the summit bid. Finch was given to telling tall stories, suffering from stomach upsets and 'living rough' on expeditions. 'Cleans his teeth on 1 February,' wrote Bruce, 'and has a bath the same day if the water is very hot, otherwise puts it off until next year. Six months' course as a lama novice in a monastery would enable one to occupy a Whymper tent with him.'[15] Technically, he was the best climber on the expedition, but his Australian unorthodoxy did not go down well with the climbing establishment and he suffered as a result.[16]

On the team also was Howard Somervell, a stocky Kendal man of thirty-two who was a surgeon in a London hospital. He was one of those men whom the Gods have gifted: a double first in Natural Science at Cambridge, a talented artist and musician, and physically strong. 'Stands by himself,' Bruce said later, '. . . extraordinary capacity for going day after day.' His only drawback, according to the General, was that he took size 22 in hats![17] Mallory got along with him famously and the two men frequently discussed literature in their tent at night, and even read Shakespeare to one another. In Somervell, Mallory could recognize a man who was both intellectually and physically his superior.

Another Kendal doctor on the climbing team was A.W. Wakefield, who had begun climbing with the Abraham brothers of Keswick and had established the famous Lakeland fell record, in which a runner tries to cover as many Lakeland summits as possible within twenty-four hours, and which is probably the most gruelling marathon in the world. Wakefield's record of fifty-nine miles and 23,500 ft of ascent in twenty-two hours seven minutes was set in 1905 – a record which stood until 1920, when Eustace Thomas bettered it, with Wakefield as his pacer. That same year Wakefield was with George Bower on the latter's first ascent of Esk Buttress, and so in both stamina and climbing ability he seemed the right man for Everest, despite the fact that he was forty-six years old. Yet he proved a failure: he was unable to cope with high altitudes, though he did reach the North Col. 'A complete passenger,' commented Bruce. 'Dear old thing for all that . . .'[18]

The sixth member of the climbing team was Major E.F. Norton, thirty-eight years old and a grandson of Sir Alfred Wills, the man whose ascent of the Wetterhorn in 1854 had begun the Golden Age of Alpine climbing. He was also distantly related to Mallory, but his experience of climbing appears to have been slight and the best that Younghusband could find to say of him in his Introduction to the 1922 expedition volume was that he was well known in India for his skill and interest in pig-sticking! Nevertheless, Norton was a determined man and turned out to be one of the best members of the team.

As doctor-in-charge (there being two others in the climbing team) was Tom Longstaff, forty-seven years old, and with more experience of Himalayan mountaineering than all the others put together. He had attempted Nanda Devi East, Nanda Kot and Gurla Mandhata, and had ascended Trisul (23,360 ft), which was to remain the highest summit attained by man until 1930. He had discovered the Siachen Glacier in the Karakorum, and his mountain journeys had taken him to the Caucasus, the Rockies, the Selkirks and the Arctic.

Though much the same age as Strutt and Wakefield, Longstaff had no wish to be regarded as a member of the climbing team, and, as he frankly admitted in his autobiography, he joined the expedition purely for selfish motives:

> I had no liking for all the hurly-burly of a big expedition, but the real inducement for me was that I should be able to revisit Tibet under the most favourable conditions, personally conducted and relieved of all the difficult negotiations with Tibetan officials and the worry of obtaining supplies and transport. I would buy a decent pony and enjoy at leisure every moment of the journey. Most of the men who have taken part in the several Everest expeditions will admit that they got much more pleasure from the approach through Tibet than they did from trying to climb the mountain.[19]

He enjoyed his journey, though he had nothing but ill to speak of the mountain:

To experience all this is worth the penalty of being condemned to try to climb the monster: for monster it is, this relic of primordial chaos, the home of devils, not of gods.

Everest is a forbidding mountain. It has no athlete's grace of form but the brutal mass of the all-in wrestler, murderous and threatening. Technically, I cannot agree that it is an easy peak . . . [20]

In charge of the filming and photography on the expedition was Captain Noel – that same Noel who had penetrated Tibet in disguise in 1913 and whose lecture to the Royal Geographical Society had been the launching pad for the present expeditions. Noel should have been on the 1921 reconnaissance but could not obtain leave from the Army in time and had requested the Committee to transfer him to the 1922 team. Hardworking and eccentric, he seems to have got on with everyone and his entrepreneurial flair delighted Bruce. Noel was a Roman Catholic and Bruce wrote: 'Stupor mundi. St Noel of the Cameras . . . Please approach the mountaineering Pope for his beatification during lifetime.'[21]

The size of the team, together with Noel's filming equipment, made transport a much larger problem than in the previous year, and Bruce used this as an excuse to get into the team some men in India he thought might prove useful. One of these was Colin Crawford, thirty-two years old, an Indian Civil Servant who had climbed in Kashmir and had been with Raeburn on Kangchenjunga. Crawford was to return to Everest many years later, but on this occasion he was not a success, as Bruce freely acknowledged to Hinks: 'Came as a transport officer at which he was entirely useless. Very cheerful. Does not stand great heights well. I freely acknowledge this is my blob.'[22]

The other two were Captains Geoffrey Bruce (the General's nephew) and John Morris, both officers in the Gurkhas. Five Gurkha soldiers accompanied the expedition, and of course General Bruce himself had been a Gurkha officer. Neither young Bruce nor Morris had any climbing experience, and though both spoke the native language, which enabled them to talk to the porters, there is little doubt that the General was playing the Old Boy network for all it was worth. As it turned out, both men proved admirable choices.

Because the expedition was purely a climbing party this time, the Survey of India were not sending a survey detachment as they had done in 1921. On his arrival in India, therefore, Bruce at once applied for the services of Morshead – not as a surveyor, but as a climber in his own right. 'A first rate goer, absolutely unselfish. Just the man for this sort of expedition, irrespective of his professional qualifications.'[23]

While he was negotiating this, Bruce received the unwelcome news that the Government of India had nominated the geologist Heron to accompany the expedition. Heron had upset the Tibetan Government in 1921 by digging holes in the ground, thereby releasing demons. Back in London Hinks had received the brunt of these complaints and to Heron he wrote tersely:

> I suppose you are the member of the party whose mining work has been objected to by the Tibetans, and has been the subject of an official letter to us. It disturbed the demons which live in the ground and the Jonpens [local officials] were very much afraid of them breaking out.[24]

The story, on the Tibetan side, grew with the telling. Heron was accused of digging up precious stones, and later the same charge was levelled against the party as a whole. In any case, poor Heron was cast in the role of the villain, and Bruce had no desire to be lumbered with a possible source of trouble, particularly since the man wasn't a climber. Bailey, who had replaced Bell as the Political Officer, didn't want Heron to set foot in Tibet either, and in the end sufficient pressure was brought to bear to prevent him joining the expedition. 'I have heard nothing officially,' Heron wrote to Hinks, sadly, 'and all I can gather is that local Tibetans object to the demons and pestilences let loose by my efforts.'[25]

But Morshead was allowed to go, as a climber, and Bruce's team was now complete. The bluff old General had really been quite adroit – with Morshead and Crawford, the climbing team now numbered eight, just as Mallory had said it should. [26]

Because of the late arrival back in England of the 1921 party and the early departure of the 1922, the Committee had barely three months during which to make the necessary preparations. Tents and other stores had been left in India by the first expedition, where repairs were being carried out, but there was still a great deal to be organized. Farrar and Meade were in charge of equipment, and the clothing they recommended varied little from the normal mountain gear, except that a long leather waistcoat was thought useful for keeping out the wind. They thoughtfully added that linings, *if any*, should be wool. This was scarcely adequate, and windproof smocks were later designed. Finch, a scientist, had made himself a jacket from balloon cloth, quilted with eiderdown – surely one of the first duvet jackets ever made, and nowadays a basic climbing garment for cold conditions.[27] Four kinds of footwear were provided – ski boots (with as few nails as possible to avoid conduction!), felt boots with lambskin uppers of knee height, high moccasins from Canada, and finneshoes from Norway. Crampons were made from dural.

Mindful of the awful food that had been the lot of the 1921 expedition, and the sickness it had caused, Bruce was determined that his team would be properly fed, and he paid great attention to this throughout the expedition. He also had a number of delicacies, such as tinned quail, included in the menu – a gourmet principle which was also followed on the 1924 expedition, and which was seized upon as bourgeois extravagance by later critics. Excesses there undoubtedly were – champagne, for example – but the idea of adding delicacies to an otherwise stodgy menu and thereby tempting men to eat when they may not feel like it, which is often enough at high altitude, is not a bad one. In fact a large expedition requires a different set of food values from a small lightweight party. The latter is usually in the field for a short time, whereas the former may be away for months, in which case a diet of yak beef, tsampa and potatoes becomes boringly monotonous and delicacies lift morale. Post-war expeditions, particularly to Everest, have rediscovered this simple fact.

On the first expedition the cooks had been incompetent, but Bruce overcame this problem by taking the most likely candidates out into the hills around Darjeeling for a trial run, and selecting the four best. In addition, Norton and Noel had their own servants, who were also good cooks. If ever there was a mountaineering army that marched on its stomach, that army was the 1922 Everest expedition. In a letter home Bruce wrote: 'They all eat very nicely and daintily, about 7–8 lbs a day. This simple ration seems to agree.'[28]

Important though the gear and food were, the three months between expeditions was dominated by the vexed question of oxygen. Almost nothing was known of high-altitude physiology, and the simple question being debated was whether Man could survive at 29,000 ft without some additional oxygen supply.

Oxygen was first used for Himalayan climbing as early as 1907, when A.L. Mumm took some small cartridges prepared by Siebe, Gorman and Co. to the Garhwal, on the Jubilee expedition of the Alpine Club which included Bruce and Longstaff. The matter was treated more or less as a joke, and the first serious work was that in which Kellas was engaged at the time of his death. No conclusive results had been obtained, and of course in the 1921 party there was nobody capable of carrying on Kellas's work.

The question of oxygen had also been raised independently by Professor G. Dreyer at Oxford, when Finch and P.J.H. Unna had gone to see him over a problem with Primus flames at high altitude for the 1921 expedition. Dreyer had done considerable work on oxygen lack at high altitudes for the R.A.F. and he expressed strong views about its desirability on Everest. 'I do not think you will get up without,' he told his visitors, 'but if you do succeed you may not get down again.'[29]

When this was reported to Farrar, he arranged to meet the professor and it was agreed that Finch should undergo a test in a decompression chamber. In this Finch did a simple exercise simulating a rapid climbing pace carrying a 35 lb. load. The difference in his performance with and without oxygen were so marked that the Committee decided to use oxygen on the 1922 expedition and set aside £400 for this.

Kellas had been experimenting with two types of oxygen supply. The first type was oxygen gas stored under pressure in steel cylinders and the second was a method of producing the gas from the chemical reaction on sodium peroxide in a device known as an Oxylithe bag. However, Kellas had not been able to go high enough to test his cylinders suitably, and in any case they were enormously heavy, outweighing any advantages given by the oxygen. The problem with the Oxylithe bags was that they could be used only when the climber was resting, and the idea that the oxygen would refresh him for his next burst of energy was obviously open to doubt.

In the event it was decided that the expedition should try both systems, but placing greater reliance on the cylinders. This proved a wise decision – when the Oxylithe bags were used at high altitude it was found that as well as oxygen they gave off particles of caustic soda, which were decidedly unpleasant!

The finished apparatus, designed by the Air Ministry along lines suggested by Professor Dreyer, consisted of a Bergen pack frame holding four steel bottles, tubes and regulator valves, and two different types of face mask. A full bottle of oxygen weighed 5¾ lb. and the total weight of the apparatus with four full bottles was about 32 lb. Ten sets were made, four of them spares.

The valves were regulated so as to supply enough oxygen to make any height equivalent to that of 15,000 ft – that is, a climber using it at 27,000 ft would, from the breathing point of view, feel he was at 15,000 ft – a perfectly normal height at which experienced climbers would be expected to function well. A great deal of care was taken to ensure that there was no interruption in the flow of gas when bottles were changed over, for it was Dreyer's view that a man at altitude being fed on oxygen might die if the flow was to cease. The climbers soon found that this was not true.

The two masks worked on different principles. In the Economizer mask there were two valves which helped in storing the expired breath, because much of the oxygen breathed in while working at altitude is breathed out again without being used by the body, which was obviously wasteful. This was to be the system generally used, but there was a snag in that the valves might freeze, so making the whole thing useless. To overcome this, a separate mask, the Standard – a flexible copper dome covered with chamois leather 'easily bent to fit the face of the wearer' – was supplied as a standby – there were no valves, control being exercised by biting or relaxing the end of the supply tube.

They had a good deal of trouble with the valves of the Economizer, even during the trials – poor old Wakefield was almost asphyxiated and would have been had not the mask been wrenched from his face! In fact, despite every precaution, the sets suffered considerable damage during transit and only three of the original ten functioned on the mountain.

Not all the team, or even all the Committee, were convinced of the need for oxygen. Everyone agreed (even Professor Dreyer) that it wasn't needed below 23,000 ft, and some argued that it shouldn't be used at all. Two distinct

*(Previous page)*
1. The pre-war route to Everest showing the camp at Shekar Dzong in 1924. The famous monastery was later destroyed in the cultural revolution. (John Noel)

*(Above)*
2. Members of the reconnaissance expedition of 1921 – the first Westerners to visit Everest. Back row: Bullock, Morshead, Wheeler, Mallory. Front row: Heron, Wollaston, Howard-Bury, Raeburn. (A.F.R. Wollaston)

*(Facing page, top)*
3. Wheeler's photo-survey party, 1921. (A.F.R. Wollaston)

*(Facing page, bottom)*
4. On the Lhakpa La in 1921. The discovery of this pass confirmed the existence of the East Rongbuk Glacier. (C.K. Howard-Bury)

5. Members of the 1922 expedition at breakfast. (*Left to right*) Wakefield, Morris,

Gen. Bruce, Geoffrey Bruce, a Gurkha, Norton. (Jonn Noel)

(*Facing page*)
6. On the way to Camp III – porters on the East Rongbuk Glacier. (Hugh Ruttledge)

(*Above left*)
7. A frostbitten porter, 1924. (Bentley Beetham)

(*Above rıght*)
8. Oxygen equipment and clothing on the 1922 expedition. (John Noel)

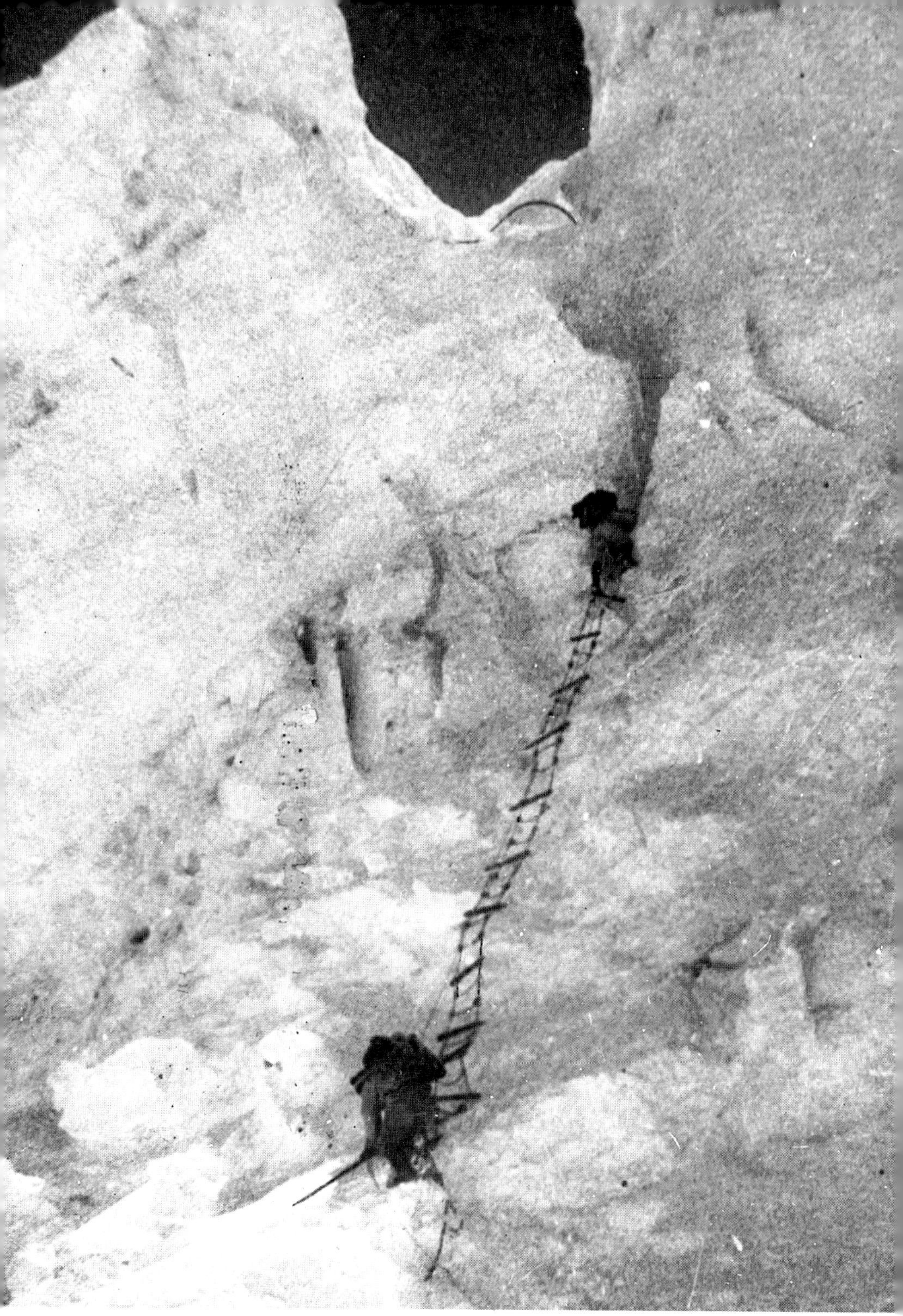

9. The ice chimney on the way to the North Col, 1922. (Howard Somervell)

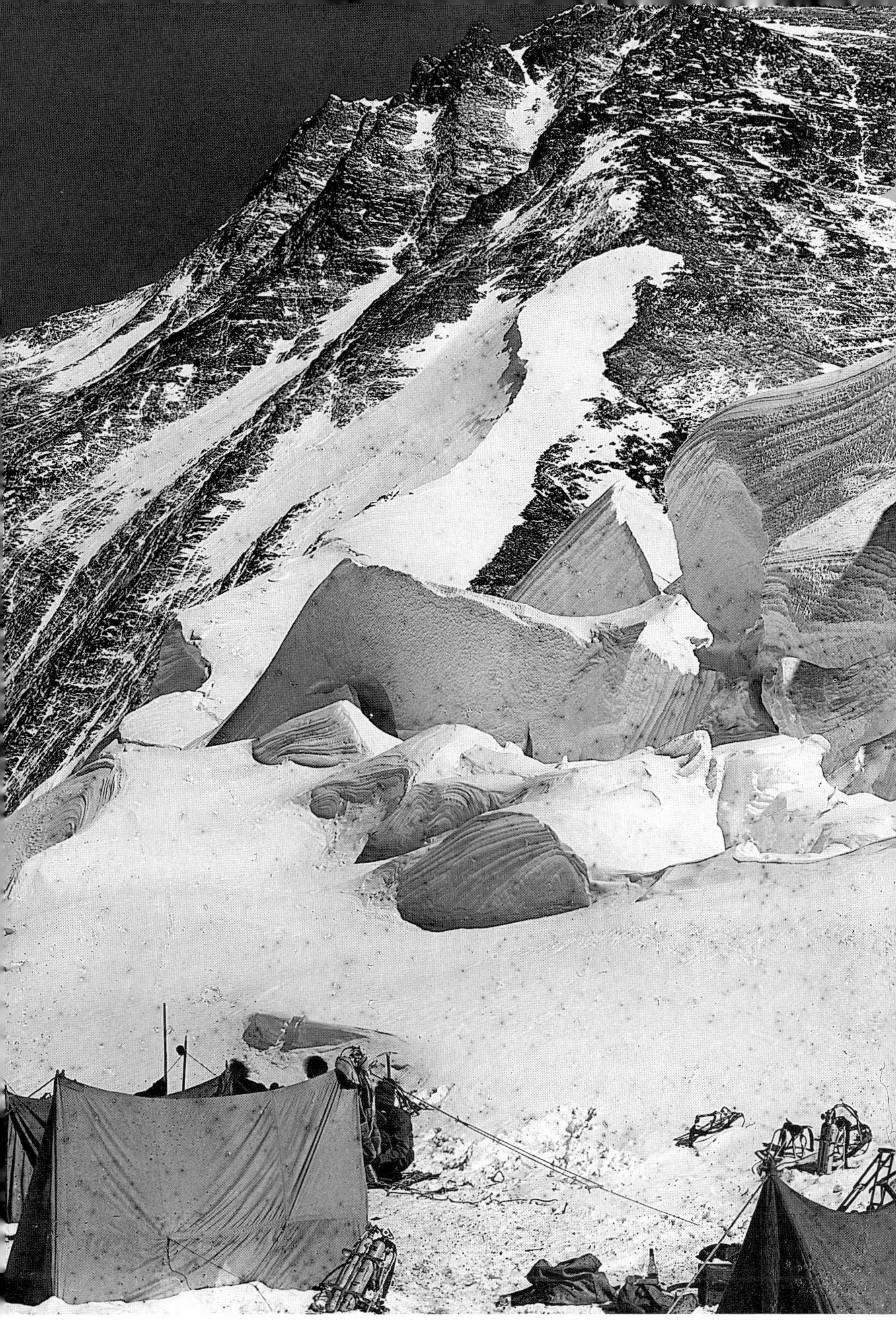

10. The North Col camp in 1922. The route follows the ridge up, then slopes away to the right. (John Noel)

11. The pre-war reconnaissances opened up a wide area of mountains for the first time: a view from near

Kama Chu of Chomolonzo and in the background, Makalu. (A.F.R. Wollaston)

*(Top)*
12. A party nearing the top of the North Col, 1922. (Howard Somervell)

*(Above)*
13. A frostbitten Geoffrey Bruce being helped back to Camp II, 1922. (George Finch)

*(Facing page)*
14. Mallory and Norton nearing the highest point reached during the 1922 expedition. A famous picture – and compare the clothing and equipment with that of post-war expeditions shown later. (Howard Somervell)

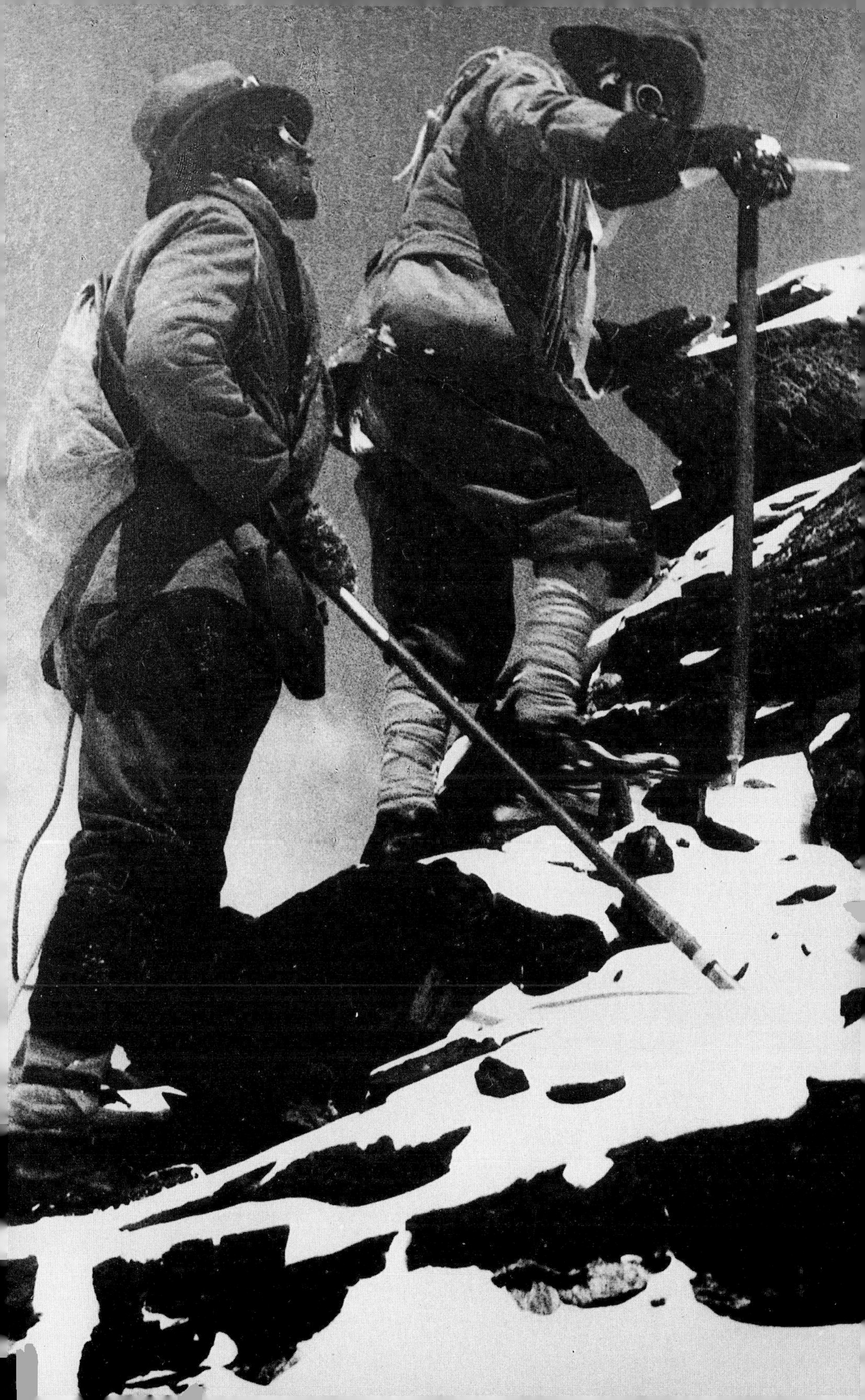

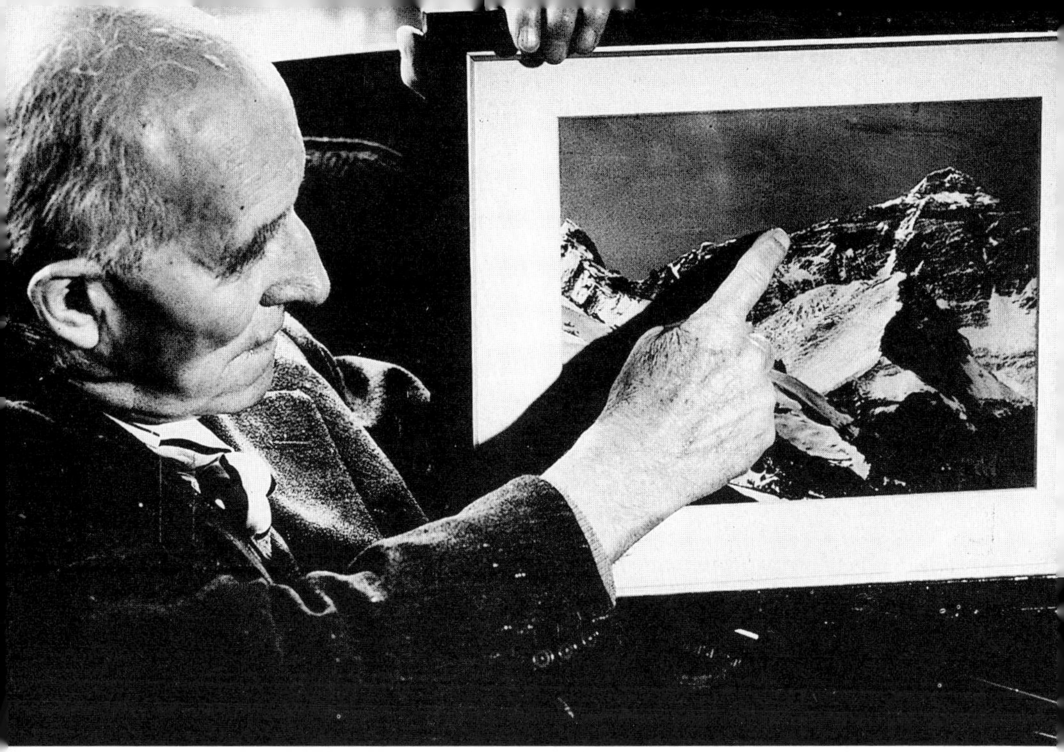

(*Facing page*)
15. The summit of Everest seen from the North Face in 1922. (Howard Somervell)

(*Above*)
16. Noel Odell points to the place on the North East Ridge where Irvine's ice axe was found. *(Leo Dickinson)*

(*Left*)
17. Sandy Irvine. (Unattributed)

18. The North Face of Mount Everest. (Dr John English)

scientific measures which render mountaineering less exacting to the human frame.[34]

The article by Hinks to which Farrar took exception also annoyed Finch, who claimed that it altered the whole aim of the expedition. He wrote savagely:

> Instead of the aim being to climb Mount Everest with every resource at our disposal, the opponents of oxygen . . . had so successfully worked upon the minds of the members of the expedition as to induce them to entertain a fresh objective, namely to see how far they could climb without oxygen. It were pleasant to think that the writer who could thus acclaim possible failure and, in advocating a new objective, destroy the singleness of purpose of the expedition, was not a mountaineer.[35]

Hinks never forgave him.

In this preparation there was one factor that the Committee did not seem to have grasped, which is that the logistics of a large expedition are pyramidal: the men and materials to be used in the actual assault depend upon an infrastructure of food and transport to get them there, and that as the assault team grows in men or materials, the base is broadened out of all proportion. And this in turn affects the costs.

The 1922 expedition had not only more men but also filming gear and the oxygen apparatus to transport. Small wonder then that they needed to employ forty Sherpas, innumerable local porters and three hundred animals. Small wonder too that the costs rose astronomically and Bruce was often short of money.

Hardly had the expedition set out than the General was writing to Hinks asking for money:

> Please note I am doing my best for this expedition. I have interviewed the Viceroy, I have preached to Boy Scouts and I have emptied the poes in a Dak bungalow. This is the meaning of the term General. They are cheap at home, but are more expensive out here. Hurry up with that thousand (£) please![36]

Three days later he doubled his request by cable to £2,000.

Farrar was appalled, and Hinks wrote back with malicious delight:

> Farrar is very much shocked at the receipt of your telegram wanting £2,000 more and has been urging us to cable you to say you shan't get any more. We have referred him to the paragraph in your instructions urging all possible economy on you. You know that Farrar is liable to go to extremes and that having loaded you up with enormously expensive Oxygen equipment, he is likely to be horrified at the second cost in transport . . .[37]

To Younghusband, Bruce confessed that the cost, instead of being double last year's, as estimated, was likely to be three and a half or four times as much.

Hinks wrote privately to Eaton, putting the Royal Geographical Society view:

> You must realize that a good deal of the trouble is due to the folly of Bruce who is making an awful hash of things . . . you really cannot expect the Geographical Society to bear the whole risk of the enterprise . . . if you Alpine Club people cannot somehow publicly or privately guarantee a thousand pounds of the overdraft, I fear that some of your eminent members will be left in India to work their passage home.[38]

In fact, despite the cash problem, the General was far from making a hash of things. His ability to speak directly to the Sherpas in Nepali (as could young Bruce and Morris), his initial care with the cooks and commissariat, his unfailing ability to make friends with the local people (he usually gave the chief officials of any village a bowler hat as a present, much to the delight of the recipient), all these things helped to make the journey across Tibet much less arduous than it would otherwise have been. The team members got on well with one another and they all thought the General was a splendid leader.

The first party had left Darjeeling on 26 March, the rest following later, and they all met again at Phari on 7 April (see Map 3, p. 46). Here they first came across the incessant Tibetan wind, and since it was earlier in the year than on the previous expedition, it was bitterly cold. The ground was frozen hard.

The expedition left Phari on 8 April, the bulk of the transport taking the easy but circuitous route to Kampa Dzong which had been followed by the 1921 expedition. The climbers, however, decided to take a short cut over the Donkar La, which involved two long, hard marches. At noon on the first day it began to snow and before long they were enveloped in a blinding blizzard. Had they not had with them local guides who knew the way, they would have fared badly. The day's march was sixteen miles and it was a desperately tired party which made the camp site that evening. On the second day, though it did not snow, the going was rougher and the cold was intense. It brought home to everybody the need for windproof garments – wool alone was simply not enough. Presumably Finch wore his home-made duvet, but others – the General for instance – had simpler clothing: 'I had a very efficient mackintosh which covered everything, but even then I suffered very considerably from the cold.'[39]

At Kampa Dzong the two elements of the expedition joined up again, and they were also joined by Finch and Crawford, who had been left behind because of the late arrival of oxygen bottles in Darjeeling. From there the party proceeded by way of Shekar Dzong to Rongbuk, though they took a more direct line than their predecessors by turning south at Shekar and crossing the Pang La, which led them to the Dzahar Chu, Chobuk and

Rongbuk. Each evening Finch insisted on an oxygen equipment drill (which probably went a long way to making it so unpopular) and Mallory complained of developing a 'Finch complex'.

It was a boring, tedious journey. Only once was there an opportunity for adventure, and that was when Mallory, Somervell, Finch and Wakefield attempted to climb the peak of Sangkar Ri (20,490 ft) from their camp at Gyankia Nangpa. But the mountain was too far away, Somervell had dysentery, and though he and Mallory got within 500 ft of the top, they retreated, tired and with headaches.

The expedition reached the Rongbuk valley on 30 April. The name means 'the valley of steep ravines', and it is indeed a most desolate place seldom free from the piercing wind coming off the mountain. To the Tibetans it was a holy place: at the entrance to the valley, opposite the village of Chobuk, was a large mani (or prayer) stone beyond which it was forbidden to kill any living creature, and five miles up the valley was the Rongbuk monastery, one of the most sacred places in Lama Buddhism.

The Rongbuk Lama, having completed the year of seclusion which had prevented him from meeting Mallory in 1921, received Bruce warmly. The General was impressed, as were all who met this remarkable person: 'He was a large, well-made man of about sixty,' wrote Bruce, 'full of dignity, with a most intelligent and wise face and an extraordinarily attractive smile.'[40] On a later visit another member of the team, equally impressed, put it more succinctly: 'Gee! that chap is either the holiest saint or the greatest actor on earth.'[41]

The Lama inquired of Bruce his reasons for wishing to climb Chomolungma (the local name for Everest) and Bruce, astutely grasping the situation, realized that any conventional Western explanation would be useless. Instead he drew upon the spiritual. They came as pilgrims, he explained, for Chomolungma was the highest mountain in the world, and any man who reached the summit must necessarily be nearer Heaven. The Lama could understand that. He invited Bruce to partake of Tibetan tea, but the General, who hated the stuff, declined on the grounds that he had sworn not to touch butter until his pilgrimage was over.[42] He also promised that no animals would be slaughtered in the valley, a rule which was rigorously enforced – even the animals destined to provide meat for the expedition were butchered beyond the Chobuk mani stone and brought to Base Camp as carcasses.

Bruce also took the opportunity to question the Lama about the yeti, the tracks of which had been seen in 1921, and he was calmly informed that five yetis lived in the upper reaches of the valley. From other monks in the monastery, the expedition learned that the yetis were much feared. They were said to be man-like and covered in long hair. Sometimes they raided villages, carrying off women, killing men and drinking the blood of yaks.[43]

Bruce had hoped to establish Base Camp on the true right bank of the Rongbuk Glacier, near the entrance to the East Rongbuk valley, but the

Tibetan yak drivers wouldn't have this and so the camp was made near the glacier snout. On 4 May, Strutt, Longstaff, Norton and Morshead set off up the East Rongbuk Glacier to reconnoitre a good line and establish the intermediate camps necessary before the North Col could be attempted.

In 1921, it will be remembered, Mallory and Bullock had found that in order to reconnoitre the West Rongbuk Glacier they had had to push out a series of small camps, which they had called their advanced camps. Later they had used the same system when approaching the North Col from the Kharta valley. Tom Longstaff called this method the 'polar method', because that seems to have been its origin, and it has been used by almost every Himalayan expedition since.

The reasons for doing this are simple. At high altitude it is not possible for laden porters to carry for long distances, or make great gains in height. Three to five miles of gradual glacier ascent, including at the most a gain in height of 1,500 ft or 2,000 ft of climbing if there is little horizontal distance involved, is enough hard work for one day, and therefore depots or camps must be established at suitable intervals from Base Camp until one camp is placed near enough to the summit for two climbers to get there and back. The higher camps tend to be smaller than the lower ones, naturally, and the final camp is likely to be a single small tent. This is the typical pyramidal structure of an expedition: the whole vast organization of men and materials narrows down to the point where there are just two climbers making a dash for the summit. Men and equipment flow up from Base Camp to the next camp and from there to the next, and so on. Climbers and porters move up and down between camps in a perpetual shuttle service.

On a large expedition there needs to be someone in charge of the lower camps to keep them functioning properly: in 1922 Charlie Bruce himself acted as Base Camp Manager (as it would now be called) assisted by Strutt, and his Gurkha N.C.O.s looked after the camps on the East Rongbuk Glacier. On this expedition, too, it became apparent that romantic names for the different camps would be too cumbersome and they were numbered instead – Camp I, Camp II and so on, indicating their position away from Base Camp. This system has been adopted ever since.

Though Wheeler had visited the lower reaches of the glacier in 1921 and Mallory's team had entered its head over the Lhakpa La, nobody had previously travelled the entire length of the East Rongbuk. This Strutt now accomplished. Camp I was established at 17,800 ft near the snout of the glacier and about three miles from Base Camp and Camp II at 19,800 ft, a further two and a half miles on. At this point the glacier became difficult because of *pénitentes* – large pinnacles of ice sprouting from the surface like shark's teeth – which forced the explorers onto the true left bank until such time as they discovered a deep trough through the remaining pinnacles to the smoother glacier beyond. The ice here was incredibly hard and polished like a skating rink, so that, despite its easy angle, crampons were essential. Camp III was established at 21,000 ft, three and a half miles beyond Camp II, in the great glacier bowl which is the head of the East Rongbuk.

Strutt returned from his reconnaissance on 9 May, but already the task of stocking the camps he had established was in hand. Young Bruce and Morris, as transport officers, had this tiresome job – made more onerous by the ever-changing number of porters available at any one time. Porters came and went as the mood took them: 'We never knew whether we should have three or four men working, or thirty,' the General recorded.[44] Despite this, the camps were sufficiently stocked by the 10th for Mallory and Somervell to leave Base Camp in order to establish a camp on the North Col, and to make an attempt on the mountain – without oxygen.

Despite Finch's persistent oxygen drills – or because of them – none of the climbing party believed in the apparatus. 'By the time we reached Base Camp,' Finch wrote, 'I found myself almost alone in my faith in oxygen.' Much of the apparatus did not function properly, anyway.[45]

Though Mallory may have been secretly pleased that the first attempt was to be without oxygen, there was actually no alternative, because the scarcity of porters made the carrying of the extra oxygen bottles impracticable at this stage.

Mallory and Somervell arrived at the site selected for Camp III by Strutt and set about establishing it properly. It was to be an important camp – the springboard for the climb up to the North Col – and therefore needed to be relatively comfortable. At Camp I Geoffrey Bruce had had the bright idea of building rough huts from the detritus of the glacier, and this was copied at Camp III – a cookhouse was erected, and some stone walls behind which the climbers could shelter as they ate their meals. A permanent cook, with the disconcerting name of Pou, was installed and shown how to use the Primus: 'We had never again to begrime our hands with paraffin and soot,' commented the fastidious Mallory.[46]

On the morning of 13 May, the two climbers, together with the porter Dasno, reconnoitred a way to the North Col. The climb was not particularly difficult, but they had to keep in mind all the time that it was to be used continuously by laden porters and therefore needed to be as simple and safe as possible. Many years later the same considerations were to apply on the opposite side of the mountain, when climbers had the problem of forcing a safe route through the Khumbu Icefall; the mauvais pas for pre-war expeditions was the climb to the North Col.

Ice or snow climbs are seldom the same from one year to the next, and Mallory could see that the route he had followed in 1921 was no longer feasible. Nevertheless, there was a ramp of sorts, though it was guarded by a steep slope of ice. Here fortune smiled on them – the ice was fissured by a crack, the edges of which gave them a virtual stairway to the ramp. On the ascent they protected the route with fixed ropes attached to the snow by wooden stakes – these were to act as handrails for the porters. The sophisticated use made of fixed ropes today with all the paraphernalia of jumar clamps and harnesses had not been dreamed of.

Though Mallory and Somervell made good progress, one thing bothered them. On a slope where there was so much ice in evidence, they might have expected any snow that was lying to be firm and crisp, but instead it was crusted – a thin, hard shell which cracked easily and revealed unstable powder snow beneath. Nevertheless, as is so often the case with climbers when the way ahead appears clear, they ignored this seemingly minor imperfection. It was to cost them dear.

Eventually all three reached the shelf on the col – where, as in 1921, there were two tiers. However, they had not arrived at the lowest point of the col and so, leaving Dasno to recuperate, Mallory and Somervell explored further and soon discovered that access to the lowest point was barred by a great crevasse. Mallory had met this the previous year, but then it had been easily circumvented; now it yawned wider and was a formidable obstacle. They thought of fetching a ladder from Base Camp, but weren't sure that even that might be sufficient ... 'it seemed rather a long way to have come from England to Mount Everest, to be stopped by an obstacle like this,' Mallory wrote later.[47] Eventually, by a considerable detour, they managed to work their way round it, and could see that an approach to the North Ridge, by which they meant to attack the mountain, was quite feasible. Leaving a tent at the ledge on the col, they retired to Camp III.

Meanwhile, at Base Camp, the porter situation was improving and even the oxygen was beginning to move to the intermediate camps. On 16 May, Finch set out from Base with the last of the cylinders.

Two days ahead of him were Strutt, Morshead, Norton and Crawford with a large press of porters. They arrived at Camp III on the 15th, fetching supplies for the North Col. Crawford, who was feeling the effects of altitude, went down again almost immediately with the now unburdened porters, leaving the other three climbers and eight Sherpas at Camp III. After a day of rest on the 16th, it was decided to make an immediate attack on the mountain – already the clouds were boiling up over Nepal and they were concerned at the small amount of time remaining before the onset of the monsoon.

On the 17th they began the first of two carries up to the North Col. Mallory and Somervell managed the first day well enough, but the others found the altitude gruelling, and Strutt, as he reached the col, exclaimed: 'I wish that bloody cinema was here. If I look anything like what I feel, I ought to be immortalized for the British public.'[48] But the next day, on the second carry, they all felt fitter. The North Col camp – Camp IV – was properly established: five small green tents to hold four climbers and nine Sherpas. Strutt, who had never intended to go beyond the col, returned to Camp III with a porter, whom he later despatched to Base with the heartening news that a camp had been established on the North Col. Mallory, Somervell, Norton and Morshead were ready for the first assault on Mount Everest.

The camp was set on the curious ledge which was such a feature of the col, protected from the prevailing west wind by the rampart of ice which formed the second tier. The tent doors were set facing inwards, towards the ramparts, and that night the climbers lay with their heads towards the open doors, each no doubt thinking what the morrow might bring, until exhaustion brought welcome sleep.

At 23,000 ft the North Col was the highest that Man had ever camped. High-altitude camping was something which the climbers had to develop as they went along: there were no precedents, and they could learn only from their mistakes. They had quickly discovered that certain foods, like ham or pea soup, appealed to their appetites, while others did not. They had unwisely opted to bring the slow-burning alcohol and meta fuel cookers, leaving the hated but more efficient Primuses at Camp III, and now they discovered how long it took to make water from snow at altitude, and how difficult it was to make tea when the water boiled at tepid temperatures. That first morning, too, they found their breakfast – tins of Heinz spaghetti in tomato sauce – frozen solid and realized they should have put the tins inside their sleeping bags to keep warm.

On the face of it such trivialities may appear to be of no account, but both physically and psychologically they added to the difficulties of the expedition. It must never be forgotten that these Everest pioneers had not simply to climb a mountain – they also had to overcome an immense barrier of ignorance. There were no precedents of any great worth; no deep fund of high-altitude knowledge upon which they could draw. Everything – even the opening of a can – was a new experience.

Their ignorance was so profound that for much of the time they were not even aware of it. When they set out on the first assault, at 7.30 a.m. on 20 May, the plan that Mallory had devised had failure built into it, though nobody was aware of the fact. Mallory's plan was simply to establish a light camp at 26,000 ft and from there make a summit dash on the next day. This meant the laden Sherpas climbing a height of 3,000 ft, then descending to the col again in one day, and the climbers on the following day doing a similar return journey to the summit from the new camp. Even with oxygen this would have been a tremendous performance at those altitudes. Without oxygen, there was not the slightest hope of success.[49]

Who knows what effect the frozen cans of spaghetti, which delayed their departure, had on the fates of the four climbers? Had they left earlier they might well have pitched Camp V higher, and had they done that it is doubtful whether any of them would have returned from that fateful first assault . . .

Mallory's plan had allowed for the nine Sherpas to share four 20 lb. loads between them, relieving one another in turn, but on the morning of the 20th five of the Sherpas were suffering from altitude sickness and could take no part in the assault. This left just the four climbers – Mallory, Somervell, Norton and Morshead – and four porters.

From the North Col they could see more clearly the nature of the task ahead. The North Ridge rose up, not too steeply, to a junction with the North East Ridge, which would then be followed to the summit. On the left of the North Ridge, the face fell away steeply to the East Rongbuk Glacier; on the right of the ridge, the North Face of the mountain fell away rather less steeply to the main Rongbuk Glacier. The North Face was a curious phenomenon on such a high mountain, for it was comprised of downward-sloping slabs, largely denuded of snow. Where the slabs came up to meet the snow of the ridge itself, there was a virtual parapet of stones – a 1,500 ft staircase, technically easy to climb. On a lower mountain it would hardly have been classed as a climb at all; the technique involved was merely that of placing one foot in front of the other.

Nevertheless, the men were roped together. A lack of oxygen dulls the brain and exhaustion makes for carelessness. Easy it may have been, but it was no place for a slip.

A breeze sprang up, insistently cold, forcing the climbers to put on more clothing – Morshead simply put his scarf on. A slight accident with the rope sent Norton's rucksack bounding down to the glacier, but he seemed unperturbed about it and the others promised to lend him spare clothing should he need it.

They advanced a little further and the wind grew perceptibly stronger, until they were forcing themselves against a gale. The sun had disappeared behind a cloud and the cold was intense. Morshead donned a sledging suit, and they could all feel the cold nipping their toes and fingers.

Mallory realized that if they were to survive they had to get out of the wind. Abandoning the easy staircase, he cut steps up the snow towards the crest of the ridge, every step a supreme effort of will in the thin atmosphere. At last he led his party to shelter on the lee side of the ridge – but the effort had practically exhausted him. His aneroid showed they were at 25,000 ft. They had climbed 2,000 ft and it had taken them three and a half hours. Morshead and a couple of the porters were lagging behind and came up later, but it was fairly evident that to go any further that day would have been suicidal for any of them.

They found themselves on a series of broken ledges, which, though out of the wind, offered too little room for a couple of tents. There did not seem to be much better chance higher up, so they resolved only to advance far enough to find the first possible spot that might accommodate them. At about 2 p.m. Somervell found a place for one tent, though it needed some work to make it habitable, and a little later Mallory and Norton found an even less congenial place, which would have to suffice for the second tent. The porters were sent down to Camp IV, a meal was prepared and eaten, and the climbers tumbled into their two-man sleeping bags for an uncomfortable night's rest. They were actually camping higher than Man had ever *been* before.

It snowed a little in the night and in the early morning a pall of mist overhung the ridge, shutting the tents off from the world. At 6.30 a.m., however, the mist lifted and the day ahead seemed fair. The climbers were not in good shape: fingers, toes and ears had been frostbitten during the gruelling previous day, and even before they started on this second morning another rucksack went tumbling over the edge. Fortunately it lodged about a hundred feet down the slope and Morshead recovered it. Mallory silently feared he could not go on:

> I hadn't the power to lift my weight repeatedly step after step. And yet from experience I knew that I should go on for a time at all events; something would set the machinery going . . .[50]

They roped up, Norton with Mallory, Morshead with Somervell, and began climbing at 8 a.m. Hardly had they gone more than a few steps when Morshead halted. 'I think I won't come with you any further,' he said. 'I know I should only keep you back.'[51] So Somervell attached himself to Norton's rope and Morshead returned to the tent.

They climbed for spells of twenty or thirty minutes, very slowly, drawing deep breaths, then halting for five minutes to recover. Their rate of progress was 400 ft an hour, diminishing as time went on, and they knew from the outset that they were only making a gesture. The summit was not to be theirs that day, and they were not interested in anything less – not even in reaching the North East Ridge. They plodded up, wrapped in a numbness compounded of physical hardship and psychological defeat.

Mallory later attributed their defeat to the weather, which had delayed their start by two hours, but of course he was wrong. Even had they started at 2.30 a.m. it is doubtful whether they would have got to the summit and returned safely. 'We were prepared to leave it to braver men to climb Mount Everest by night,' he wrote laconically.[52] Almost forty years later that is exactly what the Chinese did, on this very ridge.

They agreed to turn back at 2.30 p.m., and when at 2.15 p.m. they came upon a piece of easier terrain they used it to rest for fifteen minutes before their return. Their aneroid showed they had reached a height of 26,800 ft –

well above most of the surrounding peaks such as Changtse, Pumori or Gyachung Kang. Only Cho Oyu seemed to match them for height. No climbers had ever reached such a height before.

Yet, such was the scale of Everest, they hadn't even reached the junction with the North East Ridge; they estimated it was still 400 ft above them, another four or more hours of climbing.

They began the descent, Mallory in front, Norton second, and the imperturbable Somervell last as anchor man. Thinking to find a better way down, Mallory chose a new line and almost at once they were in trouble and had to struggle back to their old route. They reached their tents at 4 p.m. – a descent of 2,000 ft in one and a half hours.

Earlier in the day they had made up their minds that another night's camp on the uncomfortable ledges was to be avoided if possible, and since there were three hours of daylight left and the North Col was only 2,000 ft below, they decided to push on. They knew that at lesser altitudes a descent of 2,000 ft on terrain like the North Ridge takes about an hour, and they reckoned that they had plenty of time in reserve. Subconsciously, too, they thought that descending would make them stronger because the air was less rarefied. In fact it didn't, and they were much nearer to exhaustion than they imagined.

Morshead in particular was far from being fit for the descent. Despite his rest at Camp V he was still weak and suffering badly from frostbite. To protect him the better, they made a single rope of four: Mallory, Norton, Morshead and, as usual, Somervell in the rear to protect the party. Sometimes Norton changed places with Mallory to share the step cutting, but for the most part Mallory remained in the lead.

The fresh snow of the previous night had obliterated the tracks and steps they had made on the way up, and route-finding proved difficult. It seems likely that they took too low a line, but in any case the descent proved decidedly more awkward than they had expected.

Suddenly, as they were crossing the head of a long snowy couloir, Morshead slipped. Somervell, the anchor man, was in the act of moving from one snow step to another at that very moment and was caught completely unawares. He was jerked off. Norton, too, had scarcely time to realize what was happening and before he could take effective action he too was yanked out of his steps. In a matter of seconds the three men were sliding rapidly down the couloir towards the glacier, 3,000 ft below.

Mallory, who was cutting a step at the time, heard the sound behind him and instinctively realized what had happened. Almost by reflex action he thrust his axe deep into the snow and slipped a coil of rope around it. Of the three victims, Somervell at least was trying to use his axe as a brake, and probably the others were too, which was just as well, for it is doubtful whether

Mallory's belay would have held the weight of three bodies sliding at full speed down the slope. As it was, the strain was minimized and Mallory held his companions. He undoubtedly saved all their lives.

Though no one had been injured, they were all much shaken by the incident and their descent became slower than ever. Even so they were not greatly concerned – the North Col was now only a short distance away and there was still an hour of daylight left.

Unfortunately, Morshead's deterioration became more marked. He could move only a few paces at a time and the intervals of rest in between became longer. His critical faculties became irrational: he wanted to glissade down snow patches where the only safe method was to cut laborious steps. Every persuasion had to be employed to keep him moving, and wherever possible Norton physically supported him.

The daylight faded. Away to the west grey clouds piled up and lightning flickered. At least they were fortunate in one respect – there was no wind blowing to add to their misery.

Eventually they found their stone staircase of the ascent, and with this to guide them there was no chance of losing their way. It took them down to the col, where Somervell lighted his candle lantern in order that they could navigate in the dark amongst the dangerous crevasses which lurked there. They were now only some two hundred yards from their tents – but two hundred yards of tricky ice which called for special care from tired men.

It took longer than they had imagined. Casting this way and that to find the right route it seemed ages before they came across a place they clearly recognized – a fifteen-foot wall, which they had to jump down. For Morshead this was impossible, and his companions lowered him down on the rope. As for the others, each was glad to land safely in the soft snow, though in some ways too tired to care much.

Now there was only one final steep snow slope between them and the tents, and they were thankful that they had taken the precaution of fixing a rope down it when they first set up the camp on the North Col. All they had to do was let the rope guide them back to the tents . . . but at that moment their candle burned out, and in the darkness they couldn't find the rope, which was buried in the snow. There was nothing for it but to descend the slope as best they could, cautiously, haltingly, fearful of a slip. Then, suddenly, the rope was found – someone had unwittingly caught it and dragged it from the snow – and with its help they made a rapid descent to the camp. They crawled into the tents at 11.30 p.m. It had taken them seven and a half hours to descend the final 2,000 ft.

The four climbers were frostbitten, desperately tired, hungry and thirsty. Thirst above all was their demon and they couldn't even swallow a biscuit until their parched throats were slaked. But when they came to melt the snow for a brew they made a shattering discovery – there were no pans. By mistake, the Sherpas had taken all the cooking utensils back to Camp III! In desperation Norton concocted a form of ice cream from Ideal milk and strawberry jam mixed with snow. They guzzled it gratefully – with the result that it gave them agonies of stomach cramp during the night.

On the following morning, still tired, they began their descent of the North Col to Camp III. The fresh snow had obliterated their earlier tracks so that they were forced to fashion new steps – and fashion them carefully, for unguarded porters would have to climb the col to bring down the items of personal gear, such as sleeping bags, which the four climbers had left behind. Once near the camp, however, discipline gave way to a mad rush for refreshment and Mallory was pulled out of his steps, tumbling down the last few feet of the snow slope. Much to his chagrin who should be standing there to record his tumble on film but the arch-oxygen fiend himself, a grinning George Finch.

Finch and Geoffrey Bruce were on their way up to the North Col with a troop of porters, carrying oxygen sets.

Meanwhile the four returning climbers staggered on towards Camp III. Wakefield met them, shepherding them home, then Strutt and Morris. Noel filmed them. All they wanted was tea: lots and lots of tea. Somervell alone drank seventeen mugsful . . .

It had been an outstanding performance. They had climbed higher than anyone before them, and had returned from the brink of disaster.

As Mallory's team swallowed tea by the gallon, Finch and young Bruce were plodding slowly up to the North Col. As the General remarked at the time, the gas offensive had begun.[53]

# 4

# 'We Will Stamp to the Top with the Wind in Our Teeth'

At Base Camp, Finch had not been too happy with the oxygen apparatus. Parts had been damaged in transit, but the most serious fault was in the face masks, whose valves were so stiff they made breathing difficult. Fortunately Finch had foreseen this problem and had brought with him from Darjeeling some glass T-pieces and toy football bladders with which he made some simple but radical alterations. He fitted a bladder onto a T-piece and inserted this into the rubber mouth tube. When the wearer breathed in he received oxygen mixed with atmospheric air; when he breathed out, he bit the end of the tube so the oxygen filled the bladder instead. On breathing in again, the bladder deflated, supplying the man with oxygen. It proved very effective.

For four days Finch and Geoffrey Bruce, who had become close allies, worked at repairing the sets. The work had to be done in the open, with the ever-present Rongbuk wind producing zero temperatures and making the job a nightmare. Sometimes, when the sun did not shine, the temperature dropped so low that the tools were too cold to handle.

When the work was completed the two men went up to Camp III to give the sets some final trials. Climbing up to a 21,000-ft col they easily outpaced Strutt and Wakefield, who were without oxygen.

The ascent to the North Col on 22 May, when they met Mallory's party coming down, was the final trial of the redesigned sets. Three climbers wore them: Finch himself, Geoffrey Bruce and the Gurkha Tejbir. The results were remarkable – three hours to climb to the North Col from Camp III and only fifty minutes to return! And, as Finch proudly pointed out, with time to take thirty-six photographs on the way.

Two days later the same party, along with John Noel, once more climbed up to the col, this time for an assault on the mountain. They wore oxygen sets and consequently found the ascent easy, though no doubt the performance was looked on askance by the anti-oxygen faction, who maintained that if oxygen was needed at all (and Mallory, for one, thought it wasn't) it was only required above 25,000 or 26,000 ft. But Finch and young Bruce were quite content to be called rotters if it meant the difference between success and failure. In fact, quite unconsciously, Finch had hit upon a fundamental truth – that oxygen should be used from a relatively low altitude if it was to do any good. There was nothing to be gained from exhausting oneself on the lower slopes, then expecting oxygen to work miracles higher up.

It was hardly a party of pukka sahibs who now found themselves together on the mountain. First there was Finch himself: ex-colonial, an unorthodox but brilliant climber whose constitution had not proved too robust and who was distrusted by the establishment. Whereas Mallory and Somervell had read Shakespeare to one another in their tent, Finch tended to be a raconteur of tall stories. Then there was Geoffrey Bruce, a splendidly fit Gurkha officer, brought along to help with transport and now, with no previous mountaineering experience at all, cheerfully attempting the world's highest mountain. Accompanying his officer was Lance-naik Tejbir Bura of the 6th Gurkhas, accepting his position as an equal of the 'sahibs', as the Gurkhas had always done on such occasions, in the tradition of men such as Harkabir, Karbir and Raghobir who had climbed with Conway and Mummery. And finally, though going no further than the North Col, was 'St Noel of the Cameras' – John Noel. Was ever such a diverse party to make an assault on Everest again?

None of them had ever camped so high before. They spent a sleepless night on the col, and next day felt tired and listless: 'We all sat about in the snow in a sort of dazed condition, incapable of action,' wrote Noel. 'I felt overcome by a sort of mental coma. Finch felt the same, and so did Bruce.'[1]

Then Noel had the idea of taking a few whiffs of oxygen and felt wonderfully revived. So did Finch – and it gave him an idea which was later to save their lives.

At 8 a.m. twelve porters were sent off up the ridge carrying oxygen bottles and camping gear. An hour and a half later – very late for such an undertaking – Finch, Bruce and Tejbir, wearing oxygen sets, set off in pursuit. Each climber carried a 30-lb. rucksack – more than the porters were carrying – yet caught up with them at 24,500 ft. 'The English air', as the Sherpas called it, was proving its worth.

Shortly after one o'clock the wind freshened and it began to snow. Though they had only reached 25,500 ft – 500 ft short of their objective – Finch decided to make camp, in order that the porters, by this time an hour behind, would have a chance of returning to the col. The climbers levelled out a patch sufficient for a tent on the very crest of the ridge and prepared to spend an uncomfortable night.

In the darkness the wind rose in fury, threatening to hurl the little tent off the ridge. The canvas slapped and cracked like continuous gunfire and from time to time the whole camp and its occupants would be lifted clear of the ground, only to be dumped down again as the gusts rose and fell. Sleep was impossible. From time to time one of the men would crawl out into the teeth of the gale to check that the guy lines were secure. For the rest of the time they held on grimly to the tent doors, for the fastenings had broken and once the wind got into the tent itself nothing on earth would prevent it flying off the mountain and the climbers with it.

Even with the coming of daylight the storm did not abate. They managed to anchor the tent more securely, using a climbing rope, but, to add to their worries, a flying stone had cut a hole in the windward canvas.

As morning wore on the wind began to moderate slowly and by one o'clock had reduced to a stiff breeze. Desperately tired and already short of rations Finch and his men were at last given a chance to retreat to the North Col and safety. They didn't take it: instead, they decided to sit it out for another night in the hope that things might improve.

To while away the time and assuage the pangs of hunger they found comfort in cigarettes – Finch had a theory that smoking made breathing easier at high altitudes.[2]

At 6 p.m., as they were settling down to their second night, half a dozen porters arrived from the North Col bearing welcome flasks of tea and beef tea, sent up by the thoughtful John Noel. All six of the Sherpas were volunteers for the arduous journey, and of course they went down again immediately.

Despite this succour the three men suffered great hardship. For over thirty-six hours they had had totally inadequate sleep or food and, as they faced the second night in their lonely camp, the air temperature plummeted and they became rigid with cold. Finch could feel his limbs going numb and knew it meant the onset of frostbite. He could see that his two companions were haggard – Bruce in fact looked desperately ill – and he became worried. Had they overstepped the mark – gone beyond the limit of human endurance? Suddenly, he remembered how oxygen had revived him at the North Col, and he tried it again. The effect was remarkable and instantaneous. Warmth flooded back into his body and when Bruce and Tejbir also tried this strange cure it revived them too, immediately. Thus encouraged, they rigged up an oxygen set so that the gas could be breathed during the night, and as a result all three of them slept soundly.

They were away by 6.30 a.m., the two British climbers carrying 40-lb. loads and Tejbir 50 lb. The plan was that Tejbir would go no further than the junction with the North East Ridge, at which point he would hand over the spare oxygen cylinders which made up his load and then return to camp. But it was not to be; only a few hundred feet above the camp Tejbir collapsed, utterly exhausted. Though Bruce and Finch urged him to go on it was obviously useless, so they took the cylinders from him and sent him back to the tent.

With the collapse of Tejbir, any hope of success the party might have had collapsed too, but Finch was determined not to give in without a fight. He and Bruce unroped in order to move that much more quickly and set off up the ridge. For a time all went well, but then the wind – the eternal Everest wind – began to rise again, forcing them to quit the ridge and venture out onto the great North Face. At once things became difficult. They found themselves on the vast outward-sloping slabs of the Yellow Band, always slippery and sometimes covered in patches of soft unstable snow. For young Bruce, on his first climb, it must have been a trying experience, but he didn't seem put out and followed Finch with all the assurance of a veteran.

At 27,000 ft Finch decided to make for the ridge again, and they had climbed about 300 ft in that direction when Bruce suddenly cried, 'I'm getting no oxygen!' Turning round, Finch could see his companion was in great difficulty. He climbed down towards him and was just in time to grab Bruce by the shoulder as the young man began to keel over backwards off the mountain. Together they struggled to a ledge.

The problem turned out to be a broken glass tube in Bruce's set. Before Finch could begin to repair it (fortunately he was carrying a spare) he had to alter his own set so that both of them could breathe from it temporarily. That done, he calmly set about the repair of the faulty set. The height was 27,300 ft – the highest Man had ever climbed.

But, bitterly disappointed, Finch realized that their attempt on the summit was finished. He could not ask Bruce to continue after the traumatic shock he had just experienced, for though the young man was willing, it would have been a dangerous risk.

It had been a remarkable effort on the part of both men, but unique so far as Bruce was concerned – no other climber has set a world height record during his very first climb.[3] Finch wrote:

> Never for a moment did I think we would fail; progress was steady, the summit was there before us; a little longer and we should be on the top. And then – suddenly, unexpectedly, the vision was gone . . . It was too plain that, if we were to persist in climbing on, even if only for another five hundred feet, we should not both get back alive.[4]

One thing the accident had proved: the physiologists were wrong in assuming that if oxygen was suddenly taken away from a climber who had been using it, at altitude, the man would quickly die. Bruce especially, but Finch also to a lesser extent, had been without oxygen for quite lengthy periods during the incident and were none the worse for it once the supply was restored.

Defeat, as always, brought a realization of tiredness and so the two climbers wisely roped up for the descent. They quickly reached Camp V, where they found Tejbir snug in sleeping bags and much recovered. They left him to await some porters who were coming up from Camp IV and continued wearily to the North Col. Here they discovered that Crawford and Wakefield had come up, not to attempt the mountain, but just to take a look around, and so the tents were occupied. After a quick meal, there was nothing else for it but to continue down to Camp III. Noel, who had remained at the North Col throughout the attempt, went down with them, acting as anchor man behind the two tired climbers. Remarkably, they reached Camp III at 5.30 p.m. – only forty minutes after leaving the col. It had been an incredible day's high-altitude climbing: 1,750 ft of ascent and 6,000 ft of descent in eleven hours.

The times involved in the two attempts of 1922 make interesting comparisons. From Camp III to their highest point of 26,800 ft Mallory's party took 14¾ hours; Finch and Bruce took 12¼ hours and reached a point 500 ft higher – and, because of the traverse across the North Face, travelled a greater lateral distance. This gives an average climbing rate of 393 ft per hour for those without oxygen compared with 514 ft per hour for those with oxygen – and, because of the traverse, this last figure is lower than it might have been. In fact, up to 25,500 ft Finch and Bruce climbed at a rate of 666 ft per hour, which is about a third as fast again as Mallory. The advantages of oxygen were obvious to anyone not blinded by prejudice.[5]

When the two high-altitude parties returned to Base Camp at Rongbuk they were medically examined by Longstaff and everyone except Somervell was pronounced unfit for a further attempt. Nothing seemed to affect Somervell, neither cold nor altitude, but the others suffered varying degrees of frostbite and both Finch and Strutt had strained their hearts. Worst affected of all was Morshead, whose frostbite was so severe that he had to have a toe and several finger tips amputated when he returned to India.

Neither Mallory nor Finch received their medical reports gracefully. Both men insisted they were fit to take part in another attempt, though in Finch's case it proved a futile gesture, for once he started out he was unable to go beyond Camp I, he felt so ill. He returned to Base and with Strutt, Longstaff and Morshead made an early return home.

News that four members of the team had departed early annoyed Hinks, back in London. Writing to the General he said:

> Even if the oxygen business is played out early in June and the oxygen experts want to come home, I should myself have been glad to hear that you

propose to stay and do further geographical work in the country, with high climbing on the mountain without oxygen if the conditions were favourable. Even if the summit is reached in June, I myself should still hope that the party would not be in too much of a hurry to come home en masse.[6]

Poor Hinks. Sitting in his comfortable office in Kensington Gore, he had no conception of the conditions on Everest. The General replied:

> The flower of the men's condition must have gone, also the weather has distinctly got rougher and when it's rough on Everest, it really is rough, and one full exposure to it is enough to sap anyone's strength for a very long time ... I shall be very much relieved indeed when this last attempt is finished because to tell you frankly I am afraid of Everest under the present conditions with the monsoon only within days of us.[7]

But Hinks's imagination did not stretch to such limits. He replied: 'I should be a sad man if you all came back without clearing up the geography of the West Rongbuk ...'[8]

Strutt, Longstaff and Finch appeared before the Everest Committee on 17 July and gave their reports – Strutt making the interesting point that future parties should be younger, preferably about thirty. To Hinks in private they said a good deal more than they did to the Committee. Writing to Norman Collie, Hinks said:

> The returning people at present are disposed to say nasty things about Howard-Bury last year and Mallory this year ... I think they are all cross and jumpy ... and they want handling carefully.[9]

Of Strutt he said:

> He was fed up and glad to come away. Bruce was glad to get rid of him. Strutt does not yet realize how foolish it was for Finch and him to come home without a word of explanation.[10]

Obviously the two climbers did not report favourably upon their climbing leader, for Hinks says:

> All who have come back think Mallory's judgement in purely alpine matters was bad and inferior to Norton of whom everyone speaks very highly. They obviously had sharp disagreements about the appropriate way to ascend the North Col, Finch going a different way from Mallory.[11]

Collie, who had little regard for Mallory anyway, replied:

> I dare say Master Mallory has been lording it over other members of the party who were not there last year.[12]

Meanwhile, 'Master Mallory' had been leading a third attempt upon the mountain.

They had reached Camp III on 5 June: Somervell, Mallory, Crawford and Wakefield, with the necessary porters. The monsoon was starting, there was eighteen inches of fresh snow at Camp III and it was still snowing when they arrived. Nevertheless, the following day was fine and they decided to give the snow a day to consolidate, then start for the North Col on the 7th. On the morning of the 7th, at 8 a.m., they set off on their climb. Wakefield remained behind to look after Camp III. The assault party was Somervell, Mallory, a porter and Crawford, in that order, followed by thirteen Sherpas, divided into three ropes. The snow was waist-deep, movement slow and laborious, but by constantly changing leaders they ploughed a trench towards the col.

At 1.30 p.m. they halted briefly about 600 ft below the col, while Somervell took over the lead again. Hardly had they re-started when they were startled by an ominous sound 'like an explosion of untamped gunpowder' and before they realized what was happening they were sliding down the slope in the grip of an avalanche.[13]

It was all over in a few seconds. The snow stopped sliding and the leading rope managed to struggle free. Below them they could see the second rope, four porters, similarly unharmed, but of the last two ropes, one of four and the other of five men, there was no sign.

As the climbers rapidly descended the slope they had so arduously toiled up an hour earlier it became apparent that the nine missing porters had been swept over an ice cliff into the jaws of a waiting crevasse. With tons of snow pouring in on top of them there seemed little chance that any of the victims could have survived. Nevertheless, everyone clawed and scraped at the snow to make sure – and brought out two men still alive. One had been buried for forty minutes before they reached him. Seven Sherpas were dead.

It was the wish of the remaining Sherpas, many of whom had relatives amongst the dead, that the bodies should remain buried in the crevasse and those that had been dug out were re-interred. A memorial cairn was erected at the site of Camp III and the climbers withdrew from the mountain. It was a sad, abrupt end to the expedition.

Two of the climbers who took part in the events of that tragic day have recorded their feelings. Somervell said:

> I remember well the thought gnawing at my brain. 'Only Sherpas and Bhotias killed – why, oh why could not one of us Britishers have shared their fate?' I would gladly at that moment have been lying there dead in the snow, if only to give those fine chaps who had survived the feeling that we shared their loss, as we had indeed shared the risk.[14]

Mallory wrote to his wife:

> The consequences of my mistake are so terrible; it seems almost impossible to believe that it has happened for ever and that I can do nothing to make good. There is no obligation I have so much wanted to honour as that of taking care of those men.[15]

Mallory blamed himself for the accident because he felt it was his bad judgement of the snow conditions which was the root cause of it. Yet the actual line of ascent had been discussed and agreed between all the climbers taking part at the outset. No doubt Mallory felt that the responsibility was his as he was the most experienced high-altitude climber.

When news of the tragedy reached Britain, it was generally assumed to be Mallory's fault, though for differing reasons. Collie criticized him for taking a traversing line when to go straight up would have been safer under the conditions.[16] Strutt wrote to Mallory, commiserating with him, but adding 'after the great fall of fresh snow, seventeen persons on the North Col was fifteen too many, even after *two* days' perfect weather'.[17] Tom Longstaff wrote to a friend: 'To attempt such a passage in the Himalaya after new snow is idiotic. What the hell did they think they could do *on Everest* in such conditions, even if they did get up to the North Col?'[18]

In the same letter, Longstaff also pointed the finger of blame at the Committee for urging General Bruce to get results. And here may be the nub of the matter. Mallory had made a tactical error – but should he have been allowed to go into battle in the first place? With the monsoon coming on, the men weary and most people wanting nothing more than to go home, should General Bruce have allowed that third fatal attempt? The probability is that he had allowed himself to be persuaded by the climbers themselves, especially Finch and Mallory.

As for the death of the Sherpas, the General knew better than most Europeans the fatalistic outlook of the Asian mind. He knew that the porters would accept it as the will of the mountain gods. '. . . if it was written that they should die on Everest, they should die on Everest,' he wrote. 'If it was written they would not die on Everest, they would not, and that was all there was to be said in the matter.'[19]

The unfortunate end to the expedition did nothing to dampen the General's boisterous spirits. In reply to Younghusband's telegram of congratulation and condolence he replied:

> Thanks for the telegram, as to tell the truth from the terrific strafes we have been receiving, we thought that the expedition was not considered to be a very great success, in fact I was contemplating a flight to South America . . . It is raining terrifically here. I was chased for three miles by leeches this

morning, all the way from the top of the hill. They were furious, starved and uproarious but oh! have such pathetic faces.[20]

Any hopes that Hinks might have had for the expedition to continue, exploring the West Rongbuk Glacier and possibly making a post-monsoon attempt on Everest, were finally squashed by the North Col tragedy. Though the party did not return home directly – they went to the much pleasanter Kharta area and the Arun Gorge to relax and recuperate after the cold rigours of Rongbuk – as an expedition to the world's highest mountain it was over.

The 1922 expedition demonstrated the prime requirements for an ascent of Everest from the north: good judgement, good equipment and men with endurance. They had had only the latter. Of climbing skill, very little seemed to be needed – though Finch thought it would be required higher up, particularly in overcoming the two distinct rock steps of the North East Ridge.

In London, the Committee were anxious to maintain the momentum which the first two expeditions had started and another expedition was therefore considered for 1923. Francis Younghusband wanted to go out in the autumn of 1922 and set up Base Camp for them, so that the climbing party would be relieved of the burden of organizing the march-in and seeing to everyday chores. It was suggested that the climbers should leave England in January and train for six weeks in Switzerland en route, and Lhasa had already indicated its willingness to have another expedition. But in the end it was decided to put it off until 1924 because it would be impossible to get a satisfactory team of climbers together before then, and the equipment, particularly the oxygen equipment, needed to be modified in the light of experience. With a likely overdraft of £3,000 as well, a breathing space was necessary.

Meanwhile, the 1922 expedition had had a direct bearing on the lives of two of its members. On his way home from Tibet Howard Somervell had visited a friend at the Neyyoor mission hospital in Travancore and had been so impressed with the work being done there that he decided to join the staff, rather than accept a prestigious post he had been offered at University College Hospital. In his spare time he also wrote the incidental music to accompany Noel's expedition film.[21]

The other person to be directly affected was Mallory. On his return home, Mallory was out on a limb with no job and a wife and family to support. He tried to fill the gap by public lectures on Everest.

At the beginning of 1923 he went on a three months' lecture tour of the United States. Financially this proved a failure, though on occasions he had large audiences and the lectures were well received by the press. It was after one of these lectures that a reporter asked him why he wanted to climb Mount Everest and Mallory replied, 'Because it is there' – a phrase which has passed out of the realm of mountaineering history into common usage.

What did Mallory mean? Part of the phrase's popularity is undoubtedly its enigmatic quality, but it must have meant something to Mallory, at least. Was it, as some of his closest friends claimed, just the irritable reply of a tired lecturer to a question he had heard a thousand times before?[22] If so, it was an unconscious flash of genius. However, Mallory seems to have acquired the habit of using the word *there* to indicate anything which had a mystical quality. It occurs first in a letter which A.C. Benson wrote to him in 1911, urging him to read a certain book which achieved high quality 'by being there'.[23] And during the war Mallory had written home describing the sight of men digging trenches and how he would like to be able to draw them like figures from Millet, only 'more there'.[24] To him the word *there* seems to have gained an all-embracing meaning for mystical feelings which he could not put exactly into words – and this certainly applied to the climbing of Mount Everest. One feels that Mallory was searching for what the poet Franz Wefel put more elegantly: 'For those who believe, no explanation is necessary; for those who do not believe, no explanation is possible.'

On his return home in April 1923, Mallory's fortunes took an upwards turn. Hinks, who was now by way of being a Mallory fan, had recommended him for the vacant post of Assistant Secretary and lecturer of the Board of Extra Mural Studies at Cambridge, and he got it. Influential friends had written supporting his application, but both Winthrop Young and George Trevelyan reckoned his fame as an Everester (one might say by now, *the* Everester) had decided the issue in his favour. 'You see, he's known about now – he's ticketed,' said Trevelyan.[25]

There were some changes on the Committee after the 1922 expedition, the chief of which was Sir Francis Younghusband's stepping down from the Chair and handing it over to General Bruce. Farrar, too, resigned – no doubt to the satisfaction of Hinks, who had never got on with him.

The Committee also took the opportunity to tidy up some of the minor money matters which were bothering them, particularly the previously mentioned defalcation by a Mr C.E. Thompson of £704 17s 5d in cheques and £13 1s 6d in cash. Somers-Cocks, the Committee treasurer, seems to have felt some responsibility for this for he offered the Committee £350 if the matter was dropped, which it was. At the same time the Indian High Commissioner sent a bill for £360 16s 1d for the Army mules which had so lamentably broken down on the 1921 expedition. The Committee sent a protest to the Viceroy by way of reply. Some small honorariums were paid to Royal Geographical Society staff who had put in work on behalf of the expeditions and Hinks was made a grant of £250 for his hard work. Just as it seemed all these small irritations had been dealt with the Alliance Bank in Simla went broke, taking £700 of the Committee's money with it. The Committee also discovered to their dismay that through an oversight they had sold the German rights to the Everest film twice over, and were about to be sued!

In fact the film had hardly been the success that was hoped for. It had lost £700 in the provinces and though some continental rights had been sold there was little hope of showing it to America after Mallory's unsuccessful tour. The £500 profit it made eventually was held over to see what happened regarding the German rights.

Despite the film's lack of commercial success, John Noel came forward with an astonishing proposal for the next expedition. He proposed to buy the rights of all photographic work on the expedition for the huge sum of £8,000, payable to the Committee before the expedition sailed. The money was to be raised by forming a company – Explorer Films Ltd, with Sir Francis Younghusband as Chairman of the Board, and Noel confidently expected to make a considerable profit on the deal.

The Committee readily agreed to Noel's scheme. The plan was worth at least £10,000 to the expedition, because it relieved the Committee of making its own film or providing its own still photographs. It made the expedition solvent at a stroke, though *The Times* contract was continued, on the basis of £1,000 when the first report arrived plus a further £1,000 if the summit was reached.

To prevent rival newspapers from pirating copy before it reached Printing House Square, *The Times* developed an elaborate code which Bruce was to use in all cables to them. Unfortunately, the code itself was stolen from their Indian reporter, so the idea was scrapped in favour of one simple coded message – if the summit was reached Bruce was to cable 'Voiceful Lud benighted Charles'. Voiceful Lud was a code address for *The Times*, and the rest of the message illustrates a nice sense of humour on the part of the editor![26]

Meanwhile the Committee went ahead with choosing the personnel for the 1924 expedition. It was unanimously agreed that General Bruce should again be the leader, but in the background the medical board who examined him had strong reservations. Graeme Anderson thought he was fit to go only to 15,000 ft, which was quite inadequate for the job in hand, and Larkins, the other doctor making up the board, wrote to Claude Wilson: 'This time I honestly do not feel comfortable about passing him.'

Wilson, himself a doctor, was alarmed at the repercussions should the General fail his medical and wrote back immediately:

> I do not want General Bruce to see a modern Heart Specialist. His electro cardiogram would probably not be ideal, and they would, almost to a man,

turn him down on this, or on his blood pressure ... I don't want him frightened and I don't want him turned down, and though I know there is a risk, I am willing to take full responsibility for letting him go, assuming that he keeps feeling as fit as he is now.[27]

Larkins was still not happy about it. He sensed that Wilson was trying to get him to hush up the General's defects and he wanted no part of it:

> I therefore cannot possibly let the Committee take him on without expressing pretty strong warning. Actually I feel pretty sure that with your support they will take him simply because he is so indispensable but that is their own affair and if he gets apoplexy out there, they will have only themselves to kick.[28]

The Committee took note of Larkins' report, but the General was made the leader, with the proviso that he should be examined again at Phari.

An Alpine Club Selection Committee, which included Mallory, gave their minds to the job of choosing the climbing party, one of whom would be second-in-command to Bruce. With his experience of the two previous expeditions Mallory might have been expected to fill this position, but perhaps because the North Col disaster was still remembered and his well-known forgetfulness hardly suited him for any kind of overall command, he was ignored. Instead the offer was made to Norton.[29]

Mallory himself was at first not at all sure whether he should go on a third expedition. He had drawn up a list of possible candidates and put himself at the bottom with a large question mark behind his name. The indecision was partly domestic, partly personal – domestic in that he had a new job and a new home in Cambridge and seemed about to settle into a minor academic career; personal in that he hated Tibet and feared the influence which Everest seemed to have over him.

Secretly, he thought the issue would be decided for him; he thought the University would not allow him leave of absence so soon after joining it, but Hinks wrote to the authorities saying how anxious the Committee was that Mallory should go, and the University responded with six months' leave at half pay. Mallory was surprised and asked Hinks whether his presence was all that necessary. Hinks assured him that in the eyes of the Committee it was.

Hinks was right, of course. George Mallory *was* Everest in the public esteem, and it was unthinkable that he should not go. Once again destiny was ruling him and he was not able to fight back. He had a duty to his fellow mountaineers and to his country – and, of course, there was the insistent nagging at the back of his mind that this time he might just pull it off.

There was never any question what the decision would be, but he wrote to his father full of doubts. 'I only hope this is a right decision,' he said. 'It has been a fearful tug.'[30] Years later Kenneth Mason, the Himalayan historian, recalled: 'He didn't want to go on that last expedition, had a sort of premonition, you know.'[31] And if this seems like hindsight, there is a deal of truth in it. Just before the expedition set sail Mallory said to Geoffrey Keynes, 'This is going to be more like war than mountaineering. I don't expect to come back.'[32]

Somervell and Mallory were natural choices for the climbing party, and they were joined by Noel Odell, who was a geologist by profession, and Bentley Beetham, a Lakeland schoolmaster and close friend of Somervell, with whom he had just had a very successful Alpine season – thirty-five climbs in six weeks. Both men were good climbers, and Odell had been to Spitsbergen in the previous two summers with Tom Longstaff, who undoubtedly recommended him for the Everest team.

These men formed the hard core of the team around which the rest could be built, but there was one glaring omission – George Finch.

With the resignation of Farrar, Finch had lost his greatest ally on the Committee and his enemies saw the opportunity to settle old scores. His outspokenness in 1921, when he failed his medical, was not forgotten nor, despite all his hard work on the oxygen equipment, was it forgiven. Indeed, his advocacy of oxygen was, in some people's minds, further proof of his unreliability. In itself this might not have been sufficient excuse for removing him from the team, but the Committee did not have to wait long for another.

Before he went on the 1922 expedition, Finch had been warned by Hinks that all photographs, paintings and sketches – even unofficial ones – must remain under the control of the Committee, and must not be published or used in any way privately. Finch, who was a keen photographer, ignored this and when Mallory wanted some of his pictures for a lecture tour Finch refused to supply them. It would, he said, 'plagiarize them in the eyes of the public'.[33] The fact was that he wished to use them exclusively in his own lectures.

The Committee tried to keep a monopolistic control on lectures by team members. They offered the lecturer 30 per cent of the gate money as a fee but with no guaranteed minimum. Finch argued for a £25 guarantee, but the Committee would not agree.

But it was Finch's continental lecturing which caused the greatest friction. He had been raised in Switzerland and was a fluent German speaker, so it is not surprising that in the summer of 1923 he gave a series of lectures to continental audiences on his own initiative – only to receive a demand from the Committee for 50 per cent of the proceeds. He indignantly refused, and they therefore instructed him by solicitor's letter that he must not announce the lectures as being on the work of the Mount Everest expedition, or make Mount Everest the principal subject of his lectures. Finch ignored this blatant attempt at censorship and the Committee furiously sought ways of copyrighting the name of Mount Everest itself in order to prevent 'unauthorized persons lecturing on the subject'! They failed in this, but they kept a watch on Finch's lectures to see how many people attended and how successful they were.

The rift was complete. Though he continued his work on oxygen for them, Finch could never be wholly acceptable to the Committee again. The publication in May 1924 of his classic autobiography *The Making of a Mountaineer*, in which he devoted two outspoken chapters to the 1922 expedition, merely dotted the i's and crossed the t's of the affair. Of the book, Hinks wrote, 'Some people are enthusiastic and some are rather sniffy about it, especially the review in *The Times*.'[34]

Once again all sorts and conditions of people applied to join the expedition. Sam Turner was there again, writing voluminous letters to the Committee, and there was a strange application from someone signing himself General A.T.N.T. Ramuri, with an accommodation address in Merioneth: 'I have studied the summits of Everest and Chumulhari from very close quarters indeed, considerably closer than any man living.' Unfortunately, amongst other drawbacks, 'General Ramuri' wanted 'bare expenses plus £6,000', to take part.

Much to the Committee's astonishment, a woman, one Anne Bernard, applied, and the Committee wrote to her:

> It is impossible for the Mt Everest Committee to contemplate the application of a lady of whatever nationality to take part in a future expedition to Everest. The difficulties would be too great.[35]

Among the other unsuccessful applicants were past and future Everesters: Wollaston, Morshead (rejected because of his injuries), Wood-Johnson and Hugh Ruttledge.

Heron, the geologist who had roused Tibetan passions in 1921 by allowing demons to escape, also put in an application and the Committee decided he could go if the Government of India wished it. When Bailey, who was the Resident in Sikkim and in charge of Tibetan affairs, heard this he wrote a strong letter of disapproval, and in the end the India Office decided it would be better if Heron stayed at home.

Meantime two non-mountaineers were signed up for the jobs of transport and medicine. The first was E.O. Shebbeare of the India Forest Department. The second was R.W.G. Hingston, an R.A.F. medical officer. In the tradition of previous expeditions, Hingston was to act as naturalist as well.

It was tacitly understood from the outset that Geoffrey Bruce and four N.C.O.s from the 2nd/6th Gurkha Rifles would join the party, and his inclusion brought the climbing team up to six: Norton, Mallory, Somervell, Bruce (all with previous experience of the mountain), Odell and Beetham.

The Committee decided to increase this strength to eight and chose R.B. Graham and A.C. Irvine.

Richard Graham was another Lakelander, a schoolmaster like Beetham, and a strong Alpinist. He was also a very strict Quaker, and in accordance with his principles he had been a conscientious objector during the war. His selection roused immediate controversy: some members of the team indicated to the Committee that because of his war record they would prefer not to climb with Graham. Others defended him, and Somervell wrote from India to say that if Graham was dropped he would resign from the Alpine Club. The Committee stood by its decision, but Graham, bitterly disappointed and horrified that the matter had been aired in the press, withdrew his application on the grounds that harmony was essential in the party.[36]

His place was taken by John de Vere Hazard, who turned out to be a strange customer altogether, and one whose subsequent activities were to lead to trouble for the Committee.

The final place on the team was taken by Andrew Comyn Irvine, known as Sandy from his fair hair: a well-built young athlete of twenty-one who had rowed for Oxford in the Boat Race and had impressed Odell during the Merton College Arctic expedition to Spitsbergen. Irvine had been one of the sledging party on that occasion: a tough job which required strength and endurance. He had come through it so well that both Longstaff and Odell had no hesitation in recommending him to the Everest Committee.[37]

Some members of the Committee were against the inclusion of Sandy Irvine in the climbing team because of his youth and lack of mountaineering experience. But his performance in Spitsbergen had shown that his endurance was considerable, and he had more climbing experience than the Committee realized. He made the first ascent of the peak in Spitsbergen which bears his name and he had some experience of climbing in the Oberland and Wales. His first lead was the Chimney Pitch on the Great Gully of Craig-yr-Ysfa: not at all an easy climb, and perhaps indicative of his chief quality, which was great muscular strength. Irvine also had mechanical aptitude, and Odell, who was in charge of oxygen after the sacking of Finch, saw in his protégé a perfect assistant. He wrote later:

> Though lacking in mountaineering experience it was felt that the natural aptitude he had already shown, together with his undoubted gifts of mechanical and general practicable ability, not to speak of temperamental suitability, fitted him for inclusion in the party, before other older men of greater experience in mountain craft.[38]

Although this was to be the third expedition to the mountain and conditions in Tibet and on Everest were now well known, virtually no progress had been made in the question of personal kit for the climbers. Only Finch, with his innovative mind, had appreciated insulated jackets, but the idea did not gain general acceptance. Such invention as there was was directed at keeping the wind out rather than keeping body heat in. Apart from the 'Shackleton' outfit, the men were dressed in the same way Alpinists had been dressed for decades. £50 per man was allocated for kit, and Norton describes his own appearance on the mountain:

> Personally I wore a thick woollen vest and drawers, a thick flannel shirt and two sweaters under a lightish knickerbocker suit of windproof gaberdine the knickers of which were lined with light flannel, a pair of soft elastic Kashmir putties and a pair of boots of felt bound and soled with leather and lightly nailed with the usual Alpine nails. Over all I wore a very light pyjama suit of Messrs Burberry's 'Shackleton' windproof gaberdine. On my hands I wore a pair of long fingerless woollen mits inside a similar pair made of gaberdine; though when step-cutting necessitated a sensitive hold on the axe-haft, I sometimes substituted a pair of silk mits for the inner woollen pair. On my head I wore a fur-lined leather motor-cycling helmet, and my eyes and nose were protected by a pair of goggles of Crooke's glass, which were sewn into a leather mask that came well over the nose and covered any part of my face which was not naturally protected by my beard. A huge woollen muffler completed my costume.[39]

Various supplementary ideas were put before the Committee regarding the equipment. An original one came from a Mr A.F. Yarrow of Hindhead, who suggested the climbers should rub their bodies with oil as a means of retaining body heat, but nobody seems to have actually tried this on the mountain.[40]

The food supplies were on the same lavish scale as in the previous expedition, along with the gourmet tid-bits: sixty tins of quail in foie gras, for example, and four dozen bottles of champagne – Montebello 1915 was specified.[41]

The equipment which received the most thorough investigation before the 1924 expedition was also the most controversial – the oxygen sets. The climbers were still deeply divided over its use, either on the grounds of its efficiency or on sporting grounds, and though no argument could be advanced to shake the latter, the experiences of 1922, when Finch and Bruce had so obviously outpaced Mallory and Somervell, were sufficient proof that oxygen was a distinct aid to high-altitude climbing. All were agreed, however, that the 1922 apparatus was far from perfect and the Oxygen Sub-Committee, led by Unna and Finch, were determined to improve it.

The design changes were based on Finch's ideas and were carried out by Messrs Siebe, Gorman. Unfortunately they added considerably to the weight, and when Somervell tried out a prototype in the Alps in 1923 he was not impressed. He wrote to Unna:

> The climbing of even easy rocks is very much interfered with, especially in descending. Easy climbs become difficult, and difficult places become severe. The old 4-cylinder apparatus interfered with rock-climbing only slightly in comparison: the tremendous weight on the back pulls one out of balance and makes easy steep rocks almost as if vertical, and nearly all descending that cannot be managed as 'walking' has to be done face inwards as the projection of the cylinders behind is so awkward. With the extra weight of thermos flasks and *full* cylinders it would be exceedingly difficult to do some passages even on an easy mountain like Everest.
>
> If Everest were all snow, the apparatus would not markedly impede the climbing, but as it is very largely easy rock, and in a few places fairly steep rock, it would seem that the apparatus as at present constructed would add tremendous difficulty both to ascent and descent, difficulty which the most copious supply of oxygen cannot counterbalance.[42]

Somervell was an anti-oxygen man, and Unna admitted to ulterior motives in asking him to test the apparatus. To Spencer he wrote:

> ... Somervell has now sufficient interest in the apparatus, having been made to do some work on it, to be less keen to throw it on one side next time without a trial. That was my second object in sending it out to him.[43]

While arrangements were going forward for the 1924 expedition, preparations of another sort were engaging the attention of the nation. 1924 was to see the opening of the great two-year British Empire Exhibition at Wembley, and no doubt inspired by the topicality of the subject the India Section intended to show a large model of Mount Everest. They asked the Mount Everest Committee to contribute £200 towards the cost, but the Committee declined. However, the model was constructed by Sifton Praed – and caused Hinks, who acted as adviser to the project, several headaches. Siebe, Gorman and Armstrong Whitworth were granted permission to exhibit the oxygen apparatus and cylinders at the exhibition.

Recognition of a different sort came from the International Olympic Committee, who made the first ever Olympic awards for mountaineering to the 1922 team for 'the greatest feat of alpinism in the preceding four years' – a somewhat debatable conclusion, one would have thought. The ceremony took place at Chamonix skating rink during the Winter Olympics of January 1924, and since Bruce had already left for India, Colonel Strutt accepted the thirteen silver-gilt medals on behalf of the team. Additional medals were later given to two porters.[44]

The expedition left Darjeeling on 25 March to begin the long journey through the wastes of Tibet. Within a fortnight illness began to take its toll:

Beetham had serious dysentery, the after-effects of which were to make him virtually a passenger for the rest of the expedition, and Mallory had suspected appendicitis. Somervell made ready for an emergency operation but fortunately Mallory began to recover soon after reaching Kampa Dzong. Most serious of all was the condition of General Bruce, who was showing signs of malaria recurrence. He was sharing a tent with Odell and the latter recalls: 'He was wheezing and coughing and shaking like an earthquake. He was an enormous man. He had gone on a tiger hunt before the start of the expedition. Bagged his tiger, but also picked up his malaria.'[45] Hingston, the team doctor, became very anxious and on 13 April it was decided that the General should relinquish command to Norton, and return to Darjeeling. Hingston accompanied him.

Things had not gone well with the oxygen equipment either. By the time the cylinders arrived at Calcutta some were completely empty and some only half full owing to leaking valves. They were refilled, but by the time the expedition reached Shekar Dzong 30 per cent were empty again. The apparatus itself was full of faults and Odell wrote a report to the Committee: 'Every instrument leaked badly,' he said, ' ... six sets had serious defects directly due to faulty design and workmanship, or bad material.' He pointed out that most of the carrying frames were broken, and praised the salvage work of Irvine, 'without whose mechanical faculty and manipulative skill, an efficient oxygen apparatus would hardly have been at the disposal of the expedition. Under difficult circumstances Mr Irvine had constructed an improved model of about 5 lb. less in weight than the original.'[46]

If young Irvine, working with a minimum of tools in the bleak uplands of Tibet, could improve the model and reduce it by 5 lb. in weight, one is entitled to wonder what all those trained engineers at Siebe, Gorman's had been doing for the previous two years. When the matter was put to them, the manufacturers disclaimed any faults, and blandly wished the expedition well with the improved version.

Norton, now leader, set his mind to a plan of campaign. He appointed Mallory his second-in-command and gave him complete responsibility for the climbers, and he consulted everyone about their ideas on what should be done. Various schemes were put forward and discussed, but in the end it was Mallory's plan that Norton decided to adopt. On 19 April he reported to the Committee:

> The general idea has been to put in two attempts as early as possible, one with and one without oxygen, in order that, failing success, we may fill in the gaps in our previous knowledge in time to apply such experience for a final attempt or series of attempts.
>
> Briefly, two climbers (who, it is hoped, will take part in the final attempt if necessary) with requisite porters will first establish a camp and dump of stores at about 25,500 ft (No. 5), and partly stock it with oxygen. Next two

climbers destined to attempt the summit without oxygen, will escort a party of porters to the same camp, complete its stock of equipment, and oxygen, and send back spare porters to No. 4 retaining some eight at No. 5. Next day these same two climbers, with say eight porters including spare, climb to, say, 27,300 ft (No. 7), establish a camp and sleep – sending porters down to 5 or 4. This same day an oxygen party of two climbers with unloaded porters leave No. 4, climb to No. 5, and then carry to, say, 26,500 ft a camp and requisite oxygen equipment, sending porters back to No. 4. Next day two parties of two go for the top, one without oxygen from No. 7, one with oxygen from No. 6. These two parties will be mutually supporting, and constitute what many of us consider the ideal number for an assault. They will return to No. 6 or No. 5. Noel will probably be in one of these camps in support.

A reserve of 4 climbers remain in hand to repeat the plan if it fails through weather or unforeseen misfortune, or to modify it according to experience. If this reserve is reduced by sickness or other accident, it should always be possible to apply again whichever part of the original plan promised best – there is always a possibility of one or more of the original climbers recuperating sufficiently to take part in the final assault.[47]

Who the members of the three teams would be wasn't immediately decided. Norton thought that Mallory and Somervell should each lead a summit attempt, and though he was himself keen to be one of the non-oxygen summit pair he left the decision on that to Mallory. Indeed, it was now Mallory's job to choose the men for the job, and it didn't take him long. After dinner on 22 April Norton announced the teams:

1 to establish Camp V: Geoffrey Bruce and Odell.
2 to make a summit attempt from Camp VII without oxygen: Somervell and Norton.
3 to make a summit attempt from Camp VI with oxygen: Mallory and Irvine.

The choice of Irvine as his partner rather than the more experienced Odell or Bruce was explained by Mallory in a letter to his wife.

The difficult work of allotting tasks to me has now been done – Norton and I consulted and he made a general announcement after dinner two days ago. The question as to which of the first two parties would be led by Somervell and which by me was decided on two grounds: (1) On the assumption that the oxygen party would be less exhausted and be in the position of helping the other, it seemed best that I should use oxygen and be responsible for the descent. (2) It seemed more likely on his last year's performance that Somervell would recover after a gasless attempt to be useful again later. It was obvious that either Irvine or Odell should come with me in the first gas party. Odell is in charge of the gas, but Irvine has done the principal engineering work on the apparatus – what was provided was full of leaks and faults and he has practically invented a new instrument, using up only a few of the old parts and cutting out much that was useless and likely to cause trouble; so Irvine will come with me. He will be an extraordinarily stout companion, very capable with the gas and with the cooking apparatus.

Norton, if he is fit enough, will go with Somervell, or, if he seems clearly a better goer at the moment, Hazard. Beetham is counted out for the moment, though he's getting fitter. Odell and Geoffrey Bruce will have the important task of fixing Camp V at 25,500.

The whole difficulty of fitting people in so that they take part in the assault according to their desire or ambition is so great that I can't feel distressed about the part that falls to me. The gasless party has the better adventure, and as it has always been my pet plan to climb the mountain gasless with two camps above the Chang La it is naturally a bit disappointing that I shall be with the other party. Still, the conquest of the mountain is the great thing, and the whole plan is mine and my part will be a sufficiently interesting one and will give me, perhaps, the best chance of all of getting to the top. It is almost unthinkable with this plan that *I* shan't get to the top; I can't see myself coming down defeated. And I have very good hopes that the gasless party will get up; I want all four of us to get there, and I believe it can be done. We shall be starting by moonlight if the morning is calm and should have the mountain climbed if we're lucky before the wind is dangerous.

This evening four of us have been testing the oxygen apparatus and comparing the new arrangements with the old. Irvine has managed to save weight, 4 or 5 lb., besides making a much more certain as well as more convenient instrument. I was glad to find I could easily carry it up the hill even without using the gas, and better, of course, with it. On steep ground where one has to climb more or less the load is a great handicap, and at this elevation a man is better without it. The weight is about 30 lb., or rather less. There is nothing in front of one's body to hinder climbing, and the general impression I have is that it is a perfectly manageable load. My plan will be to carry as little as possible, go fast and rush the summit. Finch and Bruce tried carrying too many cylinders . . .

The telegram announcing our success, if we succeed, will precede this letter, I suppose: but it will mention no names. How you will hope that I was one of the conquerors! And I don't think you will be disappointed.[48]

The reason Mallory gives for choosing Irvine instead of the more experienced Odell, who knew just as much about the oxygen equipment, seems weak in retrospect. Norton was not altogether happy about it, but having given Mallory command, there was little he could do – in any case, Norton was not a technical climber and if Mallory felt that Irvine would be able to cope with the problems of Everest, then Norton would respect his judgement. Yet the mystery remains: why did Mallory choose Irvine? Was he really convinced that Irvine was a more competent mechanic than Odell, should trouble develop with the sets at high altitude? Mallory's knowledge of practical matters was so slight as to be non-existent, as witness the problems he had had with cameras and Primus stoves on previous expeditions, and his judgement could well have been influenced simply by the fact that he had *seen* Irvine repair the sets. On the other hand perhaps it was as W.H. Murray says: 'It may be that Mallory really wanted Irvine because he especially liked him.'[49] That he did like him was beyond doubt: he had shared a dining table with him on the voyage out and had wanted to share a cabin too, but Hazard had been allocated the berth already.

But did the springs of motivation go deeper? Had Mallory formed a romantic attachment for the handsome young undergraduate? If so, the chances are that it was entirely innocent and not reciprocated in any way. Though it has been said that Mallory was bisexual,[50] the artist Duncan Grant, who knew Mallory well, states emphatically that he was not and he suggests that the decision might well have been taken on aesthetic grounds. Given that Odell and Irvine were both good with the oxygen sets 'it would have been characteristic of Mallory (with his own superb proportions) to choose, of two equal objects, the more beautiful'.[51]

In the context of his overall plan, Mallory's choice of Irvine rather than Odell was not terribly important. If all went well, there would be four men on the summit push simultaneously: Mallory and Irvine with oxygen, Norton and Somervell without. All were proven to be very strong men, and it might be expected that the experience of the other three would see Irvine over any difficulties. It looked fine on paper. Unfortunately, Everest is not a paper mountain.

Mallory had no doubts about success. To Tom Longstaff he wrote: 'We are going to sail to the top this time and God with us – or stamp to the top with our teeth in the wind.'[52]

The expedition arrived at Base Camp on the morning of 28 April. The previous day they had visited Rongbuk monastery, where they had been disconcerted to find the Lama ill and unable to perform a ceremony of blessing, which Norton had hoped would boost the morale of the porters.

In consultation with the others Norton had decided on 17 May for the first attempt on the mountain. This was early, but in the back of his mind was the memory of the early monsoon of 1922, when the weather broke on 1 June – a week sooner than expected. This time he had no intention of being caught out:

if the first attempt failed, there would be time for a second and possibly third attempt. Once again this was a splendid plan in theory, but it made no allowance for the vagaries of Himalayan weather. As it turned out, their sense of urgency was to work against them; their energies dissipated in what became an almost frantic obsession, and a quite unnecessary one.

One thing they had learned from 1922 was that the men who were to make the summit push should be relieved of all hard work lower down the mountain. Geoffrey Bruce suggested that Camps I and II, on the East Rongbuk Glacier, did not require any sahibs at all to establish them. The work could be left to the Gurkha N.C.O.s, Tejbir, Hurke and Shamsher, the first two of whom had been on the 1922 expedition and knew the glacier well. Also, to spare the Sherpa porters and keep them fresh for higher altitude, 150 locals were recruited for these early camps. As in 1922, porters came and went mysteriously.

By 2 May the first two camps had been established. The local porters were dismissed and the expedition began its assault on the mountain. Just as a plan had been worked out for the summit assault, so too Norton had devised a meticulous plan for the first stage of the climb – the establishment of Camp III at the foot of the North Col and Camp IV on the col itself. He divided his fifty-two Sherpas into two initial assault groups of twenty each, with a reserve force of twelve.

On 3 May the first twenty porters set out from Base Camp on a cold, cloudy day. They were accompanied by Mallory and Irvine, who were to acclimatize at Camp III and test the oxygen equipment; Odell and Hazard, who were to make the route up the slopes of the North Col; and Noel, who was filming the whole procedure. The next day the second twenty porters set off, in the charge of a Gurkha N.C.O., Umar.

Two days later, Norton, Somervell and Beetham – the last named much recovered by now – left Base for the higher camps and on the following day Geoffrey Bruce brought up the rear echelon, including the reserve porters. Shebbeare was left in charge of Base Camp.

When Norton arrived at Camp II on 7 May he discovered that things had gone sadly wrong. The first party had reached Camp III, but the second party, following up, had met such appalling weather between Camps II and III that Mallory, who was now leading them, had decided to dump the loads a mile short of III and send the men back to II. Because this second group had failed to get through, the porters already at Camp III had suffered severe hardships, having only a handful of uncooked barley to eat and a blanket apiece to withstand a temperature of −22°F. As Norton arrived, most of the men struggled back to Camp II, which was now so crowded that supplies intended for the higher camps had to be opened and used. 'This was, in the circumstances, unavoidable,' wrote John Noel, 'but it broke the transport system. Thereafter the convoy parties started to choose their own sites for dumping and stores became scattered all along the line. From that day the whole transport system crumpled.'[53]

On the 8th Bruce and the reserves arrived, and so did Mallory, who came down from Camp III. Odell, Hazard and Irvine were still in the upper camp with two or three Sherpas. Mallory reported that Odell and Hazard were trying to make a route to the North Col – an attempt which failed because of the bad conditions.

Camp II was now to all intents and purposes Base Camp – most of the men were gathered there – and it needed a Camp Manager who could speak the native tongue. Shebbeare was sent for, and his place at Base Camp was taken by Hazard, who returned from Camp III.

Norton decided that a determined effort was needed to reach Camp III, to relieve the people already there if for nothing else, so on the morning of the 9th he set out with Mallory, Bruce and twenty-six Sherpas. It began to snow soon after they left Camp II and before they reached Camp III they were fighting a raging blizzard. Norton commanded eighteen of the men to dump their loads on the glacier and return to Camp II – it was obvious they would never have got through to Camp III in those conditions. With his two colleagues, and eight strong Sherpas from the reserve squad, he battled on to the upper camp. Geoffrey Bruce wrote:

> No one moved about the camp; it seemed utterly lifeless. The porters there were wretched, and this terrible blizzard, coming immediately on top of their hardships of a few days ago, completely damped their spirits and energy. Many of them became so apathetic that they would not even attempt to cook for themselves, even when stoves and oil were pushed inside the tents for them. Our eight stalwarts of the reserve again proved their value in helping with the cooking and comfort of the others. But the fierceness of the wind made movement outside a tent almost impossible, so after a hasty meal we turned in two to a tent, where the excellent sleeping-bags at any rate afforded warmth.
>
> The blizzard continued with unabating violence, and snow drifted into our tents covering everything to a depth of an inch or two. The discomfort of that night was acute. At every slightest movement of the body a miniature avalanche of snow would drop inside one's sleeping-bag and melt there into a cold wet patch. It was a very severe test on the tents, and although the largest of them only weighed 16 lb. not a single one gave way under the terrific strain. Morning came, and the snow stopped falling, but fallen snow was being driven along the surface of the glacier, producing the same effect as a blizzard. Up to ten o'clock it was useless to attempt to leave the shelter of a tent.[54]

Mallory and Irvine, both showing signs of strain, were sent down to Camp II next morning, but the others decided to stick it out for another night in case conditions improved. In this their hopes were dashed: the weather got worse. The wind rocked the tents with howling ferocity, the spindrift covered everything and that night there were 39 degrees of frost. It became increasingly obvious that even if they could survive the ordeal much longer, there was no hope of climbing the mountain until conditions improved. The next day Norton ordered a general withdrawal to Base Camp.

By 12 May everyone was back there. The scene was reminiscent of Napoleon's retreat from Moscow. The storm had battered and cowed them; the porters were utterly demoralized, and several were sick or injured.

Fortunately, Hingston had returned after seeing General Bruce into safe custody and now he and Somervell, as doctors, had their hands full. One man had a broken leg and another severe pneumonia, but the most serious cases were the Gurkha N.C.O., Shamsher, who had developed a clot on the brain, and the cobbler Manbahadur whose feet were frostbitten up to the ankles. Only major surgery could have saved either man, and this was not possible. They died and were buried near Base Camp.

On 15 May it was arranged that the expedition should receive a formal blessing by the Lama of Rongbuk, in order to put fresh heart into the porters. Each man was given two rupees with which to make an offering to the Lama and then the whole expedition trooped down to the monastery for the ceremony, at which the Lama made a short address and touched each of the men with his silver prayer wheel.

By now they had spent almost a week in Base Camp. Mallory, who was sharing a tent with Noel, seemed to the photographer highly strung; a man full of restless energy and ambition, who chafed at the enforced delay. It seemed as if he was impatient to meet his destiny. Prophetically he said: 'This retreat is only a temporary set back. Action is only suspended. The issue must shortly be decided. The next time we walk up the Rongbuk Glacier will be the last . . . We will gather up our resources and advance to the last assault.'[55]

# 5

# 'The Finest Cenotaph in the World'

Norton was a worried man. Obsessed by a fear that the monsoon might break early and ruin all their plans, he felt an urgent need to establish a camp on the North Col as quickly as possible so that advantage could be taken of any fine weather.

The porters had been heartened by their visit to Rongbuk monastery, and when the next day dawned fine that seemed a good omen too. Work began again on restocking the camps; the original plan was adhered to, but the date of the assault was put back to 29 May. Bentley Beetham, who was suffering from a severe attack of sciatica, was left in charge of Base Camp with Hingston while the others returned to the East Rongbuk Glacier. By the evening of the 19th all the camps were re-occupied: Norton, Somervell, Mallory and Odell had reached Camp III, Irvine and Hazard were at Camp II, Noel and Bruce at Camp I.

No time was lost in forcing a way to the North Col. Avoiding the 1922 route, of unpleasant memory, Mallory and Norton, followed by Odell and Sherpa Lhakpa Tsering, climbed a more direct line to the ledge on the col. The ascent involved the climbing of an ice chimney of 200 ft and this and other steep parts of the ascent they protected with fixed ropes attached to hollow wooden stakes driven into the snow. They reached the shelf at 2.30 p.m., found it smaller than it had been, and flopped down for a rest and a snack. Mallory and Odell then reconnoitred the route to the col proper – and were pleasantly surprised to find a relatively easy way through, in contrast to the maze of crevasses it had been in 1922. Well satisfied with a good day's work they returned to Camp III by 6.30 p.m.

A way had been found, but was it a safe way? That night Norton wrote in his diary: 'Don't like the look of the weather much. Pray heaven it's not the beginning of the monsoon, as no power on earth can make part of the North Col route safe under monsoon conditions.'[1]

Despite intermittent snow falls next day Somervell, Irvine and Hazard led a party of twelve porters up to the col to establish Camp IV. They had a hard time of it, for fresh snow lay everywhere, and the chimney was particularly difficult. Somervell and Irvine sack hauled the loads up this; a heartbreaking, exhausting job. Having reached the col, Hazard and the porters were left there, according to the plan, to set up the camp, while Somervell and Irvine returned to Camp III. Snow was falling steadily.

It snowed throughout the night and all next day until 3 p.m. At Camp III the climbers remained in their sleeping bags, reading mail which had just arrived. A cold, cheerless day was followed by an appalling night in which the temperature plummeted to −24°F.

But the next morning, 23 May, was bright and clear. At 9.30 a.m. Bruce and Odell set out for the col with seventeen Sherpas, their aim being to occupy Camp IV for the night, then push on and establish Camp V at 25,500 ft. However, by the time they reached the chimney pitch it was obvious that conditions were too difficult for them to continue. It had started to snow again, but through the swirling flakes they could see a party of men descending from the col. It was obvious that Hazard was evacuating Camp IV.

Bruce and Odell got back to Camp III shortly after 3 p.m. but it was not until two hours later that Hazard arrived. Only eight of his twelve porters were with him: four frightened men had refused to follow him down the dangerous slopes of the North Col. Now they were marooned, with little food and possibly suffering from frostbite.

Norton was in a terrible position. He was now convinced that the monsoon was breaking and therefore the longer the four abandoned porters remained on the North Col the more difficult it would be to rescue them, quite apart from their deteriorating condition. On the other hand the climbers at Camp III were also in bad shape: Mallory and Somervell had bad high-altitude throats, Irvine had diarrhoea, Odell had not slept for several nights and Hazard had already spent three days on the col. Snow conditions on the col were highly dangerous and to climb up there was to invite an avalanche. The chances of rescuing the four men were very slight.

But, of course, it had to be done, and conditions dictated that the three strongest men should attempt it: Norton, Mallory and Somervell.

They began at 7.30 next morning. Fortunately the day was fine and, more important still, the snow conditions were not nearly so bad as they had expected, though occasionally they sank waist deep. All went well until they were near the ledge on the col where the four porters awaited them. At this point a delicate traverse was necessary and it was obvious that the snow was in avalanche condition. Somervell, though racked by a cough, insisted on leading out across this while Mallory and Norton gave him a secure belay round their axes. Two hundred feet of rope ran out as Somervell edged across – but it was thirty feet short of where the porters were waiting.

There was nothing the men could do but make their way unassisted to where Somervell was waiting. One man came down, reached the rope, and with its aid quickly got down to the anchor point. The second man was also passing down the rope when the last two porters decided to come down together. At once the snow beneath their feet gave way and they began a rapid slide towards the ice cliffs two hundred feet below. Horrified, the climbers watched what seemed to be inevitable tragedy.

But a miracle happened. Instead of continuing to avalanche the snow balled up beneath the sliding figures and brought them to a halt within thirty feet. As soon as the man still on the rope had reached safety, Somervell untied himself, drove his axe deep into the snow as an anchor, and passing the rope round it lowered himself one-handed from the free end until he could grasp first one and then the other stranded man by the collar and drag him to safety.

The descent to Camp III was slow and painful, the tents not being reached until 7.30 p.m., and the next day Camp III was abandoned once again, in a general retreat.

The scattered and demoralized state of the expedition was now self-evident. Odell, Noel and Shebbeare were at Camp II with twenty porters. Mallory, Somervell, Bruce, Irvine and Norton were at Camp I with another twenty. Hazard, Hingston and Beetham were at Base Camp with about a dozen men who had proved useless at higher altitudes. All the climbers were either tired or ill or both – particularly the lead climbers who had wasted their energies on the North Col fiasco. The porters were in an even worse state: of the fifty-five Sherpas expected to reach Camp IV only fifteen were now fit for active duty. It wasn't that they were physically disabled, but the bad weather and hardships of the past few days had knocked the stuffing out of them, and such men were useless on Everest.

The weather mysteriously improved again and for the first time Norton began to suspect he had been wrong about the monsoon after all. Had he but known it, the severe weather experienced that year in the Himalaya had nothing to do with the monsoon at all, but was a freak series of storms beginning as depressions west of Afghanistan and travelling the whole length of the mountain ranges. If he had known this, Norton could have bided his time and sat them out in the comfort of Base Camp. As it was, his expedition had exhausted itself needlessly.

In a last desperate effort to salvage something from the wreck, a conference of members was held at Camp I and a new plan of action worked out. Because porterage was now at a premium, all unnecessary loads would have to be abandoned, and in the minds of almost everyone present that meant the oxygen equipment. Six climbers and all available Sherpas were to go to the North Col, and on successive fine days two teams, each of two men, were to set out from the col, make Camp V at 25,500 ft, then Camp VI at 27,200 ft and from there attempt the summit. Two climbers were to remain in support at the North Col. Once again, such a plan was doomed to failure because it meant a summit push of 2,000 ft without oxygen, by men already exhausted: nevertheless, the climbers of 1924 thought it feasible.

Geoffrey Bruce, who by chance had spent less time at altitude than most of the others, was the fittest member of the party and was an obvious choice for the first attempt. His partner was to be, inevitably, Mallory. Mallory's sore throat was much better, and Norton recognized that his nervous energy would see him through – besides, if anyone deserved another chance, that man was Mallory. He had borne the brunt of all the serious work on Everest from the very first expedition, and he practically had proprietary rights to the mountain. Everyone was aware of this and none questioned it.

The second party was also a tried and trusted team of strong men – Somervell and Norton. As on previous occasions, Norton himself took no part in his own selection – it was a decision of Mallory and Somervell. Somervell's sore throat was getting better, and his phenomenal record of endurance in 1922 and on the present expedition ensured him a place.

At the North Col the support team was to be Odell and Irvine, with John Noel in attendance primarily as photographer but also as a useful addition to the team in case of need. Hazard was to be in reserve at Camp III.

From Camp I Mallory wrote his final letter home:

> The only chance now is to get fit and go for a simpler, quicker plan ... But again I wonder if the monsoon will give us a chance. I don't want to get caught, but our three-day scheme from the Chang La will give the monsoon a good chance. We shall be going up again the day after tomorrow. Six days to the top from this camp![2]

The weather now seemed set fair and Somervell and Noel wanted to start the attack at once, but Norton insisted on another day's rest for everybody. The time was not wasted: the fifteen remaining porters, now nicknamed 'Tigers', moved up to Camp II, where Irvine joined Odell.[3] These two set their technical skill to making a rope ladder which would help the porters over the Chimney Pitch of the North Col climb.

By 30 May, all the climbing party were assembled at Camp III, and next day Mallory, Bruce and nine porters reached Camp IV on the col, establishing the rope ladder at the Chimney Pitch en route.

On 1 June, maintaining momentum, Mallory and Bruce, with eight porters, pushed on up the ridge. The day was fine but a bitter and at times violent north-west wind was blowing, rocking the men in their steps and sapping their energy as they struggled upwards. At 25,000 ft half the porters dumped their loads, exhausted. The two climbers and remaining four Sherpas dragged themselves up another 300 ft to the site chosen for Camp V. While Mallory organized the camp, Bruce and Sherpa Lobsang twice returned to the abandoned loads and carried them up to the camp.

Camp V consisted of two 10-lb. tents perched precariously on the east side of the ridge, out of the prevailing wind. About 200 ft below, the climbers could see the remains of the tents occupied by Mallory and Somervell in 1922. This time Mallory and Bruce occupied one tent, and three Sherpas the other.

Meanwhile, the second party, consisting of Norton, Somervell and six Sherpas, had arrived at the North Col. On the next day – 2 June – they too began to push up the ridge. Once away from the col they were exposed to the awful wind, and Norton later described what it was like to meet the icy blast:

> . . . that was a bad moment, its memory is still fresh. The wind, even at this early hour, took our breath away like a plunge into the icy waters of a mountain lake, and in a minute or two our well-protected hands lost all sensation as they grasped the frozen rocks to steady us.[4]

They had climbed about half way to Camp V when to their consternation they met Mallory's party coming down. Though it was difficult to hold a lengthy conversation in the biting wind, Norton learned enough about what had happened to give him serious food for thought. If Mallory and Bruce, with the pick of the 'Tigers', could not go higher on a perfect day, what chance was there for any of them?

Camp V had been left intact by Mallory, so two of Norton's porters were redundant and able to go back. The remaining four, with Norton and Somervell, arrived at the camp site at 1 p.m.

> The afternoon was spent as every afternoon must always be spent under these conditions. On arrival one crawls into the tent, so completely exhausted that for perhaps three-quarters of an hour one just lies in a sleeping-bag and rests. Then duty begins to call, one member of the party with groans and pantings and frequent rests crawls out of his bag, out of the tent and a few yards to a neighbouring patch of snow, where he fills two big aluminium pots with snow, what time his companion with more panting and groans sits up in bed, lights the meta burner and opens some tins and bags of food – say a stick of pemmican, some tea, sugar and condensed milk, a tin of sardines or bully beef and a box of biscuits.
>
> Presently both are again ensconced in their sleeping-bags side by side, with the meta cooker doing its indifferent best to produce half a pot of warm water from each piled pot of powdery snow. It doesn't sound a very formidable proceeding, and it might appear that I have rather overdrawn

> the panting and groans; but I have carried out this routine on three or four occasions, and I can honestly say that I know nothing – not even the exertion of steep climbing at these heights – which is so utterly exhausting or which calls for more determination than this hateful duty of high-altitude cooking. The process has to be repeated two or three times as, in addition to the preparation of the evening meal, a thermos flask or two must be filled with water for tomorrow's breakfast and the cooking pots must be washed up. Perhaps the most hateful part of the process is that some of the resultant mess must be eaten, and this itself is only achieved by will power: there is but little desire to eat – sometimes indeed a sense of nausea at the bare idea – though of drink one cannot have enough.[5]

The two tents of Camp V were pitched one above another on the slope, and when Norton descended to the lower tent where the four porters were squashed together, he found that stones from the upper tent platform had been dislodged and had struck two of the porters – one had a gashed head and the other a more seriously gashed knee. They looked certain non-starters for the morning.

As it turned out, only the porter with the head injury descended next day. The remaining three followed the climbers up the ridge, each man shouldering a 20-lb. load.

The day was fine, the wind less severe than previously, but two of the party found the going particularly hard: Somervell, who had developed a sore throat again, and Semchumbi, the porter with the injured knee. At 1.30 p.m. it became obvious that Semchumbi could carry no farther, and Norton was forced to make camp. The height was 26,800 ft.

While Norton and Somervell were pushing up the ridge, Odell and Hazard took a day trip from Camp IV to Camp V; Odell to collect geological specimens, Hazard 'just for air and exercise'.[6] In fact, Hazard had gone from Camp III to V in two consecutive days and had obviously acclimatized well. Odell, who had been slow to acclimatize at first, was now coming into form and finding little difficulty with the atmosphere.

The two men had little in common. Hazard was under something of a cloud over the abandonment of the porters on the North Col and in Odell's opinion he really didn't fit in with the expedition. Odell thought him 'a curious chap', self-centred and rather selfish.[7] Norton, too, had reservations: 'a man who likes to do things on his own,' he reported to Hinks.[8]

After a comfortable night in their high camp, Norton and Somervell began their assault on the summit at 6.40 a.m. next day. The weather was perfect: crisp, cold and virtually no wind.

Though they reached the Yellow Band about an hour after leaving camp their progress was painfully slow. Norton tried desperately to plod upwards twenty steps at a time; but not once did he make it; thirteen steps found him bent double, gasping for breath in the thin air. Every five or ten minutes they had to sit down and rest for a couple of minutes.

Somervell's throat grew steadily more painful. The thin, cold, dry air caught at the membranes and racked him with coughing fits which further drained his energy. Nor was his leader in a much better state. Scarcely had they climbed a thousand feet when Norton began to have double vision. He had removed his snow goggles, since the climb was on dark rock, and now his eyes felt sore and he had great difficulty in seeing where to put his feet.

They climbed the easy rocks of the Yellow Band and moved across the North Face some five or six hundred feet below the crest of the ridge. At noon they found themselves near the big gully which runs down the face near the foot of the final pyramid. Somervell's throat was so bad by this time that he urged Norton to press on without him. Norton described what happened next:

> I left him sitting under a rock just below the topmost edge of the sandstone band and went on. I followed the actual top edge of the band, which led at a very slightly uphill angle into and across the big couloir; but to reach the latter I had to turn the ends of two pronounced buttresses which ran down the face of the mountain, one of which was a prolongation of a feature on the skyline ridge which we called the second step, and which looked so formidable an obstacle where it crossed the ridge that we had chosen the lower route rather than try and surmount it at its highest point. From about the place where I met with these buttresses the going became a great deal worse; the slope was very steep below me, the foothold ledges narrowed to a few inches in width, and as I approached the shelter of the big couloir there was a lot of powdery snow which concealed the precarious footholds. The whole face of the mountain was composed of slabs like the tiles on a roof, and all sloped at much the same angle as tiles. I had twice to retrace my steps and follow a different band of strata; the couloir itself was filled with powdery snow into which I sank to the knee or even to the waist, and which was yet not of a consistency to support me in the event of a slip. Beyond the couloir the going got steadily worse; I found myself stepping from tile to tile, as it were, each tile sloping smoothly and steeply downwards; I began to feel that I was too much dependent on the mere friction of a boot nail on the slabs. It was not exactly difficult going, but it was a dangerous place for a single unroped climber, as one slip would have sent me in all probability to the bottom of the mountain. The strain of climbing so carefully was beginning to tell and I was getting exhausted. In addition my eye trouble was getting worse and was by now a severe handicap. I had perhaps 200 feet more of this nasty going to surmount before I emerged on to the north face of the final pyramid and, I believe, safety and an easy route to the summit. It was now 1 p.m., and a brief

calculation showed that I had no chance of climbing the remaining 800 or 900 feet if I was to return in safety.[9]

And so, half blind, full of the anguish of defeat, Norton turned back. He had reached an altitude of 28,126 ft – easily a record and one which was not to be broken for almost thirty years.

When he turned back Norton was near the end of his endurance. As is so often the case, retreat saw an evaporation of confidence and willpower, to be replaced by fear and tiredness – defeat is a psychological phenomenon as well as a physical one.

Rocks which had seemed easy when the summit was the goal now took on a fearsome appearance, and Norton records how as he approached the waiting Somervell he called for the help of the rope.

They started down together at 2 p.m. Somervell dropped his axe and it went spinning down the North Face – an ample warning to the tired climbers that the slopes were steeper than they seemed. Descending slowly they eventually reached Camp VI, collapsed the tent and weighted it with rocks, and continued down the ridge. At sunset they were level with Camp V, which lay below the ridge, to their right, but they went on past, intent on reaching the North Col.

Fig. 1. The northern route 1921–38

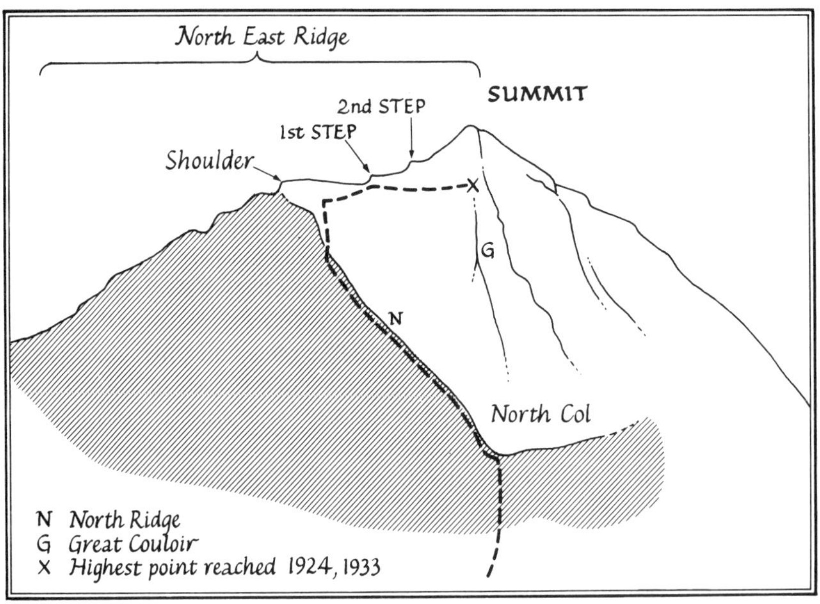

As the ridge eased they unroped, and when they reached the large snow patch which was such a feature of the route below Camp V, Norton glissaded it to save time. He expected Somervell to follow, but unknown to him Somervell was fighting for his life. The cough which had troubled him throughout the climb suddenly reached a climax:

> I had one of my fits of coughing and dislodged something in my throat which stuck so that I could breathe neither in nor out. I could not, of course, make a sign to Norton, or stop him, for the rope was off now; so I sat in the snow to die whilst he walked on, little knowing that his companion was awaiting the end only a few yards behind him. I made one or two attempts to breathe, but nothing happened. Finally, I pressed my chest with both hands, gave one last almighty push – and the obstruction came up. What a relief! Coughing up a little blood, I once more breathed really freely – more freely than I had done for some days. Though the pain was intense, yet I was a new man, and was soon going down at a better pace than ever to rejoin Norton. He had thought I was hanging back to make a sketch before the light went completely, and fortunately had not been worried.[10]

As they staggered down to the col, an electric torch their only guide in the now enveloping darkness, Norton began to shout for assistance. His voice seemed little more than a croak, but eventually there came a welcoming reply: the support party were coming up to help them, carrying oxygen. 'We don't want the damned oxygen,' Norton retorted, 'we want drink!'[11]

Soon Mallory and Odell loomed up in the darkness and helped the tired men back to Camp IV, where Irvine had soup and tea waiting for them.

That night Norton suffered excruciating pain in his eyes, and was totally blind for the crucial sixty hours which were to follow.

With the return of Norton and Somervell to Camp IV, the emergency planning worked out at the council of war a week earlier came to an end. Yet the weather was still good, and even while his leader was making the record climb, Mallory had decided to fall back on the initial plans concocted on the plains of Tibet. There would be a third attempt, by himself and Irvine.

It was to be an attempt using oxygen. It will be remembered that the oxygen apparatus had been abandoned in the contingency planning owing to a lack of porterage, but during the intervening week the situation had changed. Influenced by the good weather and the ease with which others were going up and down to the North Col, two more Sherpas had joined the fifteen original 'Tigers'. In addition, now that Camps V and VI were established and stocked, the Sherpas could be used simply to carry up the oxygen bottles. Mallory reckoned that he and Irvine could reach Camp VI without oxygen, then use the apparatus for the summit assault.

There was, however, one big difference between the original plan and this revival of Mallory's: in the original plan *four* men were to make the assault in two pairs, whereas now Mallory and Irvine were to go it alone. Once again it raised doubts about the wisdom of Mallory teaming up with someone so young and inexperienced as Irvine.

As Mallory outlined the plan to Norton at the North Col, the leader was full of doubts. Why not take Odell? he asked. Odell had been one of the slowest members of the expedition to acclimatize, but now that he had done so he was in excellent form – his stroll up to Camp V with Hazard had been evidence of that. Furthermore he was just as familiar with the oxygen apparatus as Irvine – indeed, the oxygen was his special responsibility – and, of course, he was a vastly more experienced climber.

All the logic pointed to Odell as the man who should go with Mallory. But Mallory was adamant: it must be Irvine. Norton, blind, in considerable pain, and still suffering from a sense of inferiority as far as technical climbing matters were concerned, offered no resistance.

> . . . it was obviously no time for me to interfere with the composition of the party, and when I found that Mallory had completed his plans I made no attempt to do so.[12]

To John Noel he said, 'There is no doubt Mallory knows he is leading a forlorn hope.'[13]

Odell must have been terribly disappointed that Mallory's choice had fallen on Irvine, and the irony was that Irvine had been Odell's protégé. A further irony was that though both men were oxygen experts, neither of them thought it should be used in the final ascent, and Irvine had expressed an opinion that he would rather reach the foot of the final pyramid without oxygen than reach the summit with it. He felt that if Everest was worth climbing at all, it was worth doing without artificial means. Nevertheless he welcomed 'almost with boyish enthusiasm' his unexpected chance to go for the top with Mallory.

Irvine was not in the best of health: he had the same throat trouble as Somervell and was breathing heavily and with great labour.

Taking everything into account common sense dictated that Odell was the man for the job. Why then did Mallory continue to insist on Irvine? One is forced to the conclusion that no recognizable logic played a part in Mallory's decision. Was it after all, as Duncan Grant has suggested, that Mallory chose Irvine partly on aesthetic grounds?

Incredible though this may seem, it was, in the final analysis, quite in keeping with Mallory's character. And this *was* the final analysis. Mallory was now thirty-eight years old. Fame and fortune alike had eluded him. Did he see this as his last chance for fame, and perhaps even immortality? Was he an ageing Galahad making a last desperate bid to find his Holy Grail and choosing as companion a young man who embodied all he himself had once been?

Sir Francis Younghusband wrote:

> He knew the dangers before him and was prepared to meet them. But he was a man of wisdom and imagination as well as daring. He could see all that success meant. Everest was the embodiment of the physical forces of the world. Against it he had to pit the spirit of man. He could see the joy in the faces of his comrades if he succeeded. He could imagine the thrill his success would cause among all fellow-mountaineers; the credit it would bring to England; the interest all over the world; the name it would bring him; the enduring satisfaction to himself that he had made his life worth while. All this must have been in his mind. He had known the sheer exhilaration of the struggle in his minor climbs among the Alps. And now on mighty Everest exhilaration would be turned into exaltation – not at the time, perhaps, but later on assuredly. Perhaps he never exactly formulated it, yet in his mind must have been present the idea of 'all or nothing'. Of the two alternatives, to turn back a third time, or to die, the latter was for Mallory probably the easier. The agony of the first would be more than he as a man, as a mountaineer, and as an artist, could endure.[14]

The 5th of June was spent resting at the North Col, Norton in a tent shaded from the light by sleeping bags. Somervell descended to Camp III and from there went on to Base Camp; Hazard came up to the col to act as reserve in place of Irvine.

The next day Mallory and Irvine, with eight porters, set off for Camp V. The blind Norton shook their hands and wished them good luck, but on the whole it was a silent departure with an air of inevitability about it. The climbers each carried an oxygen set and their personal gear for that day; the Sherpas the extra oxygen and spare bedding. They were soon out of view, and it was not until 5 o'clock that evening that four of the Sherpas returned with the message that Camp V had been occupied successfully. Mallory sent Odell a scribbled message: 'There is no wind here and things look hopeful.'[15]

Meanwhile Hingston, the team doctor who had no pretensions to being a mountaineer, manfully reached Camp IV to attend to the injured Norton. He could do little except confirm that it was snow blindness and was a temporary if painful affliction. That same day, with the help of Hazard he got the leader down to Camp III.

On the following day, 7 June, Mallory and Irvine climbed up from Camp V to Camp VI. Odell, in support with the Sherpa Nema, went up to Camp V, where eventually an unpleasant bombardment of stones dislodged from the ridge above announced the return of Mallory's four porters. The Sherpa Lakpa reported to Odell that the sahibs were fit and well and satisfactorily ensconced in Camp VI. He brought two scribbled messages from Mallory, one for Odell and the other for John Noel:

Dear Odell,

We're awfully sorry to have left things in such a mess – our Unna cooker rolled down the slope at the last moment. Be sure of getting back to IV tomorrow in time to evacuate before dark as I hope to. In the tent I must have left a compass – for the Lord's sake rescue it; we are without. To here on 90 atmospheres for the two days – so we'll probably go on two cylinders – but it's a bloody load for climbing. Perfect weather for the job.

Yours ever,
G. Mallory[16]

Dear Noel,

We'll probably start early tomorrow (8th) in order to have clear weather. It won't be too early to start looking for us either crossing the rock band or going up skyline at 8:00 p.m.

Yours ever,
G. Mallory[17]

Odell's porter, Nema, was suffering from altitude sickness, so the climber sent him down with the others, determining to spend the night alone at Camp V. The porters returned that same night to Camp III – a considerable performance on the part of Lakpa and his companions, for they had climbed from 25,000 to 27,000 ft carrying 20-lb. loads, then descended from 27,000 ft to 21,000, all in a single day and without oxygen.[18]

On the evening of the final assault, the camps settled down full of expectancy and not a little apprehension. At Camp III, below the North Col, there was Norton, Bruce, Noel and Hingston; Hazard occupied Camp IV on the col itself; Odell was at Camp V entirely alone, while the spearhead of the attack, Mallory and Irvine, were at Camp VI.

In order to understand what followed next day, it is necessary to have a clear idea of the upper part of the mountain. A little distance above Camp VI lay the Yellow Band of slabby, fairly easy-angled rock, littered with detritus and overlapping like gigantic roofing tiles. Taking a sloping line across this, upwards and to the right, brought one to the ridge at the foot of a distinctive tower called the First Step, where a stratum of darker rock, the Black Band, much steeper than the Yellow Band, ran across the North Face. Well to the right, both Black and Yellow Bands were cut by a deep gully. Above the First Step the ridge itself ran narrowly upwards to meet the more formidable Second Step, a cliff described as looking like the prow of a warship, and about 100 ft high. Beyond this lay the final summit cone, which seemed to offer no climbing difficulties.

The problem was how to overcome or circumvent the First and Second Steps. Should they be assaulted head on, as it were, along the crest of the ridge, or should the ridge be avoided by a long traverse to the right along the top of the Yellow Band in order to gain the gully at the far end in the hope that it might lead up to the summit cone? The rock itself tempts the climber to do the traverse, which is what Norton and Somervell had done, but Mallory was known to favour the ridge route – hence his note to John Noel telling him to watch the skyline.

Mallory and Irvine set out from Camp VI for the summit of Everest on the morning of 8 June. We have no knowledge of what conditions were like at Camp VI during the night, what delays or frustrations, if any, there were during the early hours of daylight or whether, as Mallory indicated in his note to Noel, they managed to set off early. Even less have we any knowledge of their physical health or mental state at that time. All that is known comes from one source – Odell. The rest is speculation.

After a good night's rest in his lonely eyrie at Camp V, Odell set off at 8 a.m. to make a leisurely solo ascent to Camp VI. He carried a rucksack with some provisions in it in case Mallory and Irvine were short of food, and he also took up the compass which Mallory had left behind. Earlier the morning had been clear and not too cold, but now, as he began his climb, banks of mist rolled in from the west to obscure the face of the mountain. But the mist had that luminous quality which indicates clear sky above, and Odell had no qualms about the two climbers, who should, he judged, now be nearing the summit pyramid.

Intent on geologizing, he took a circuitous route onto the North Face. He felt very fit, and when he was at a height of about 26,000 ft he came upon a small crag which he decided to climb rather than circumvent, more to test out his condition than for anything else. As he completed his climb he stepped into history. This is how he later described it:

> There was scarcely 100 feet of it, and as I reached the top there was a sudden clearing of the atmosphere above me and I saw the whole summit ridge and final peak of Everest unveiled. I noticed far away on a snow slope leading up to what seemed to me to be the last step but one from the base of the final pyramid, a tiny object moving and approaching the rock step. A second object followed, and then the first climbed to the top of the step. As I stood intently watching this dramatic appearance, the scene became enveloped in cloud once more, and I could not actually be certain that I saw the second figure join the first. It was of course none other than Mallory and Irvine, and I was surprised above all to see them so late as this, namely 12.50, at a point which, if the 'second rock step', they should have reached according to Mallory's schedule by 8 a.m. at latest, and if the 'first rock step' proportionately earlier. The 'second rock step' is seen prominently in photographs of the North Face from the Base Camp, where it appears a

short distance from the base of the final pyramid down the snowy first part of the crest of the North-east Arete. The lower 'first rock step' is about an equivalent distance again to the left. Owing to the small portion of the summit ridge uncovered I could not be precisely certain at which of these two 'steps' they were, as in profile and from below they are very similar, but at the time I took it for the upper 'second step'. However, I am a little doubtful now whether the latter would not be hidden by the projecting nearer ground from my position below on the face. I could see that they were moving expeditiously as if endeavouring to make up for lost time. True, they were moving one at a time over what was apparently but moderately difficult ground, but one cannot definitely conclude from this that they were roped together – a not unimportant consideration in any estimate of what may have eventually befallen them.[19]

Odell reached Camp VI about 2 p.m., just as the wind increased and snow began to fall. Sheltering in the tiny tent he found the inside to be as one might expect – a jumble of sleeping bags, spare clothes, some food, oxygen cylinders and bits of oxygen apparatus. More bits of apparatus and carrying frames lay outside the tent. There was no note or message of any kind.

It continued to snow and Odell wondered whether conditions higher up might have forced the climbers to retreat. If such was the case they might have difficulty in finding Camp VI in the storm because it was in a somewhat concealed position, so Odell left the tent and climbed a further 200 ft up the ridge, whistling and yodelling to attract their attention.[20] In the driving snow, visibility was down to a few yards and it was bitterly cold. Odell tried to distract himself with geology but within an hour he gave up the struggle, realizing that if Mallory and Irvine had gone a considerable distance along the ridge they would not be back for some time. He went back to the tent.

The storm, which had lasted about two hours, suddenly abated as he regained Camp VI. The mist rolled away and sunshine bathed the mountain. Odell scanned the ridge and summit cone, but could see no sign of the two climbers.

Though the seeds of anxiety were already germinating in his mind, Odell knew that he could not wait for the missing climbers. He must leave Camp VI and return to the North Col. Such had been Mallory's instructions in that final note, and in any case should the two climbers return late from their summit bid they might choose to spend the night at Camp VI, where there was only room for two people. Nor could he see any point in another lonely night at Camp V – he was still feeling splendidly fit – so he left Camp VI at 4.30 p.m. and by an astonishingly rapid descent arrived at the North Col camp at 6.45 p.m., where he joined the awaiting Hazard.

The evening was fine and a pale moonlight allowed Odell and Hazard to watch the upper slopes for signs of their companions. They saw nothing – not even a distress flare, which they were now half expecting.

Next morning it remained fine. The men at the North Col examined through field glasses the tiny tents of Camp V and VI high above but could see no signs of movement. By noon, Odell decided he must once again go up to Camp VI and so, collecting two Sherpas, he set out on the arduous ascent. As they climbed up from the col they discovered the bitter cross-winds of Everest had risen again and they had a hard struggle to reach Camp V. There they spent a sleepless night, the tents rocking in the gusts of wind and the temperatures so low that Odell was chilled through despite using two sleeping bags and wearing all his clothes.

On the following morning the wind was as strong and cold as ever and the two porters could not be induced to climb further. Odell sent them back to Camp IV and continued up the ridge alone.

At Camp V he had recovered the oxygen set he had brought up on his last visit and now he wore it on his climb to Camp VI. He found, however, that the gas gave him little assistance, and before he reached the camp he had stopped using it. In this respect, Odell's experience was different from that of everyone else who had used oxygen at altitude, and he concluded that he was sufficiently acclimatized to derive no benefit from it. For almost a fortnight he had lived more or less continuously at 23,000 ft or higher – and found oxygen superfluous.

Camp VI was just as he had left it two days previously. Mallory and Irvine had not returned. Out into the buffeting, freezing wind went Odell once more, in a desperately futile search for the missing climbers. For two hours he struggled upwards, looking for some clue that might offer a key to the tragedy – for tragedy it now undoubtedly was. Nobody could have survived two nights in the open on the upper slopes of Everest.

When he returned to the tent he dragged out the sleeping bags and laid them out on a patch of snow in the form of a letter T – his pre-arranged signal to Hazard, who was watching through binoculars, that the worst had happened.

Meanwhile, at Camp III, Norton and the others were becoming anxious at the lack of communication from Camp IV. Noel had trained the telephoto lens of his ciné camera on the summit pyramid, three miles distant, in accordance with Mallory's note, but 8 a.m. came and went without sight of the climbers and by 10 a.m. the mountain was obscured by mist. The day wore on and when no word had reached him about the fate of the party on the morning of 9 June, Norton sent a message by two Sherpas up to Camp IV:

Norton to Odell 9.6.24.
No. III Camp, 11.10 a.m.

Dear Odell,

The absence of signal from you spells disaster I fear. I have remained here to see the end of it, but am I fear useless myself to come and help – in fact the same applies to everyone here, as no one could get high enough to be of any help in time.

My instructions are as follows:

1 Watch the mountain – particularly the N. Arete up to camp VI – all day with Irvine's binoculars for possible distress signals, and keep a watch (coolies) posted in reliefs as a sentry at night for 2 or 3 hours after dark for flares (there are flares in both V and VI).

2 Search is useless except of VI Camp or beyond, and I won't have more parties committed so far in the present state of weather; so unless you have anyone fit enough to reach VI and back to IV tomorrow in the day don't attempt it. If you can see VI (I am not sure if you can) and there is no sign of life then search to VI is useless.

3 Remain in support – interpreting this in accordance with above 2 paras. – until 4 p.m. tomorrow or until snow begins to fall in a dangerous condition, and then come down at once with everyone in Camp IV. If by any chance a party starts for VI ( a forlorn hope I have very little use for) tomorrow and weather gets bad they must return to IV and on here *at once*, abandoning further efforts.

I send you this principally to give you a definite time limit, and for you to clearly understand that the guiding principle *must be not to risk a single other life English or Tibetan on the remote chance of retrieving the inevitable.*

You are the man on the spot and within these limits must use your own discretion.

Your position is a most trying one old boy and I fully sympathize with you.

Excuse writing as my thumb is frostbitten.

Please keep this letter as an official record.

P.S. These two porters bring a little porters grub and a one man sick carrier; they should return here tonight unless you have anyone sick etc. whom you want to send in their place.

P.P.S. If by any chance anyone goes up the mountain tomorrow please put out the 3 blanket signal (as used for summoning Hazard) and leave it out while party is away. Previously arranged signals to denote Mallory's return and success or failure stand.[21]

But even as the message was being laboriously carried up to the col, the watchers at Camp III could see Odell setting out on his second journey up the ridge. There was nothing they could do but watch, wait and pray. John Noel recorded the tension of the moment:

Two whole days and nights had now gone by, with hope fading at every hour. Norton, recovered sufficiently from snow-blindness, paced backwards and forwards in front of his tent, speaking little, visibly affected and, I think, already resigned to the worst. Hingston had all his medical aids ready and was prepared to go out at once in answer to a call from the support party up on the mountain. I had left my photographic station on the Cliff above the camp and now had my men posted at my telescope erected in the middle of Snowfield Camp. The men took it in turns to scan the mountain during every hour and moment of daylight. Norton, Bruce, Hingston and I sat about near the little Whymper tent we used for the mess. Now and then we called over to the watchers on the telescope, 'Kutch Dekta?' – 'Do you see anything?' The men turned and shook their heads each time: 'Kutch Nahin, Sahib' – 'Nothing at all, sir.'[22]

Once Odell had accepted the inevitability of Mallory's and Irvine's deaths there was little he could do but return to Camp IV and pass on the sad message. From the tiny tent he collected Mallory's compass and one of the special oxygen sets which Irvine had devised; pathetic mementoes of the vanished men. On his arrival back at the col he read Norton's message and at once prepared a signal made of six blankets in the form of a cross. It meant simply 'DEATH'.

At Camp III the watchers saw the signal and had their worst fears confirmed. Norton held a conference to decide what to do next, but the futility and further danger of organizing any sort of search party was soon apparent. He had Hingston lay out three rows of blankets as an answering signal to the col: 'Abandon hope and come down.' To London he sent the fateful news in a coded telegram:

OBTERRAS LONDON – MALLORY IRVINE NOVE REMAINDER ALCEDO – NORTON RONGBUK[23]

And on the next day, the 10th, when Odell and Hazard with their one remaining porter descended to Camp III they found only Hingston and Shebbeare remaining – the former in case medical help was required, the latter because he was in charge of evacuating all camps down to Base. Two days later, all but Shebbeare were gathered at Base Camp and the full tale was recounted.

There was no question of a further attempt on the mountain, or even of making extensive searches of the upper Rongbuk Glacier for the bodies of Mallory and Irvine. The latter was an almost impossible task and in any case it was not known whether the two climbers had fallen at all. The monsoon was rolling in, and nobody was fit enough to continue:

'Our attempts for the year are definitely finished,' wrote Norton in his report to the Committee. 'I enclose a medical report on the six surviving climbers. All were part worn before the attempt of the last 10 days: all are now entirely hors de combat for high climbing, and the same applies to the porters, though in their case more from consideration of 'moral' than of physical disability.'[24]

In fact Hingston had told him that all those who had been above Camp IV had dilated hearts, and though the damage was not permanent, further effort might cause lasting injury.

One of those least affected was, curiously enough, Odell, who had spent longer at high altitudes than anyone else. Between 31 May and 11 June he had been three times up and down from Camp III to Camp IV (23,000 ft) and from there once to Camp V (25,500 ft) and twice to Camp VI (26,800 ft). His two ascents to Camp VI were made over four consecutive days. Apart from one night at Camp III he had spent twelve consecutive days and nights at 23,000 ft or higher. Moreover, he did it without the use of oxygen apparatus.

Two years earlier such a feat would have been considered impossible, and it is not too much to claim that Odell's adaptation to altitude was the most valuable lesson of the 1924 expedition.

There were only three days remaining before the expedition broke up to go their various ways: the main body to the Rongshar valley to recuperate; John Noel to Shekar Dzong and the Chumbi valley, and Hazard to accompany the surveyor, Hari Singh Thapa, on a survey of the West Rongbuk Glacier. Before they moved out, however, Somervell and Beetham superintended the building of a memorial cairn on the most prominent moraine overlooking Base Camp. It was a substantial affair: a deep square plinth surmounted by a seven-foot-high pyramid built from moraine stones. Let into the pyramid were four tablets of the grey-green slate so often used for carving mani stones. The top one read IN MEMORY OF THREE EVEREST EXPEDITIONS and the others recorded the death of Kellas in 1921, the seven Sherpas who died in 1922, and Mallory, Irvine, Shamsher and Bahadur who had died in 1924 – a grim reminder that the three expeditions had cost twelve lives.[25]

Base Camp was evacuated on 15 June. By coincidence it was the day the monsoon broke.

News of the disappearance of Mallory and Irvine shocked and thrilled the world. Condolence letters and telegrams poured into the Committee and there was a message of sympathy from the King. At the Wembley Exhibition a wreath of bay leaves was laid on the Everest Model.

On behalf of the Committee, Norman Collie sent a telegram to Norton:

> Committee warmly congratulates whole party heroic achievements published today especially appreciate consummate leadership. All deeply moved by glorious death lost climbers near summit. Best wishes speedy restoration everyone health. Collie.[26]

Hinks followed this up with a letter:

> If anything could mitigate our sorrow in the loss of Mallory and Irvine it is the knowledge that they died somewhere higher than any man had ever been before, and it is possible for their relatives to think of them as lying perhaps even at the summit...
>
> I found your cablegram dated Phari June 19 awaiting me on arrival at work on June 20 and very soon had it decoded. The relatives were informed of the sad news that day and it was made public in *The Times* and associated newspapers on the Saturday morning. We have been overwhelmed with telegrams and messages of sympathy from the King, from many geographical societies and climbing clubs all over the world and from numbers of individuals in this country. The papers have vied with one another in paying their respect to the glorious memory of Mallory and Irvine ...
>
> What strikes us all in contrast to 1922 is the magnificent leadership and organization of the whole thing by which everyone supported everyone else and there was none of the rather go as you please style of Camps 3 and 4 in 1922. Whatever Hingston proved to you scientifically about the deterioration of the brain at high altitudes you have routed him triumphantly by showing as fine grip of circumstances as any man could have shown. Let me congratulate you especially upon your despatch of June 6 from Camp 3 – dictated when you were snow-blinded to a secretary with a strained heart. It was a superb performance.[27]

When Odell's story was published in *The Times* he gave his opinion on the likelihood of the climbers reaching the top. Later he expressed it thus:

> The question remains, 'Has Mount Everest been climbed?' It must be left unanswered, for there is no direct evidence. But bearing in mind all the circumstances ... and considering their position when last seen, I think myself, there is a strong probability that Mallory and Irvine succeeded.[28]

Hinks wrote to Mrs Bruce that this news 'put the tragedy upon an altogether higher level, and redeems it from what might have been unredeemable disaster into a very fine and glorious achievement'.[29]

As to whether the summit was reached opinions were divided. General Bruce, in Darjeeling, thought it likely: 'Anyhow it's dreadful – heartbreaking but wonderful,' he concluded in a letter to Hinks.[30]

Tom Longstaff, who had been on the 1922 expedition and was a great admirer of Mallory, had no qualms in the matter either. In a letter to a friend he wrote:

> It was my good luck to know both of them: such splendid fellows.
>
> Mallory wrote in the last letter I got from him, 'We are going to sail to the top this time and God with us – or stamp to the top with our teeth in the wind.' I would not quote an idle boast, but this wasn't – they got there

alright. Somehow they were 4 hours late, but at 12.50 they were less than 800 ft below and only a quarter of a mile away from the summit: Odell reports them moving quickly: therefore the oxygen was working well; nothing could have stopped these two with the goal well in their grasp at long last. It is obvious to any climber that they got up (see Sir Martin Conway and Winthrop Young's letters in *The Times*). You cannot expect of that pair to weigh the chances of return – *I* should be weighing them still – it sounds a fair day: probably they were above those clouds that hid them from Odell; how they must have appreciated that view of half the world; it was worthwhile to them; now they'll never grow old and I am very sure they would not change places with any of us. One can speculate endlessly as to what happened; I hope it was at the top and that they'll be found there, sitting in state, and be left in peace. Of course Everest will be ascended again but not very often. The Himalaya are too narrow from North to South there; Everest is too near the Plains; the undiluted regime of the Monsoon bumps too suddenly against the extremely different climate of the high lands of Tibet, 10,000 devils are continually contending up there . . .[31]

Others were less certain. Freshfield was one; he questioned whether the summit could have been climbed in the hours of daylight left, and concluded: 'I come back with sorrow to what I wrote in March that two is too small a party for so big a mountain. A larger party or a supporting party are essential for relative safety. Circumstances may however have made either impossible and I am not the one to blame climbers who cheerfully take the risk.'[32]

Norton himself also had doubts whether an ascent had been accomplished. 'It remains a case of "not proven",' he wrote, 'and that is all that can be said about it.'[33]

This so infuriated Winthrop Young, the arch-supporter of Mallory and the man who had got him on the Everest team in the first place, that he wrote:

> . . . after nearly 20 years knowledge of Mallory as a mountaineer, I can say . . . that difficult as it would have been for any mountaineer to turn back with the only difficulty past – to Mallory it would have been an impossibility. I could go into this at length but it is not necessary. The fact that Norton has to depend on this alone in opposing Odell's opinion rather confirms than shakes my own opinion that the accident occurred on the descent (as most do) and that if that is so, the peak was first climbed, because Mallory was Mallory.
>
> Of course there must always be an inclination in such an open question for those who hope to return to the attack to care to think the summit still unclimbed. It is an emotion which above all things these fine fellows should avoid giving to the public unless there is more evidence to contradict the probable interpretation of the facts as we all know them now equally.[34]

For *The Times* the question was of more than academic interest. Under the terms of their agreement with the Committee, they were obliged to hand over another £1,000 if the summit was reached. In view of the immense publicity they were quite anxious to pay, providing they got a definite ruling on the matter, but the Committee could not bring themselves to do this, as Hinks explained to the newspaper:

> The Committee cannot properly give you statements which are made in the reports from Col. Norton. We all hope that they reached the top and like to think of them resting there rather than at the head of the main Rongbuk Glacier after a fall, but there does not seem to be any possibility of a definite conclusion and I think you will agree the Committee can hardly be in a position to make any positive statement.[35]

*The Times*, rather regretfully one feels, declined to pay.

In the eyes of God all human beings are equal; in the eyes of men, some are more equal than others. Many men have lost their lives on Everest, often in strange or dramatic circumstances, but none have aroused the interest or the emotions of the public so much as Mallory and Irvine did. The reasons for this are not difficult to identify: the story embodies all the virtues of the British public school spirit of the day, still secretly and wistfully admired by the nation which has now lost it; a true-life tale that could have been lifted straight from the pages of the *Boy's Own Paper* without altering a sentence. Moreover it has the added attraction of being a mystery story, for nobody knows what really happened on that fateful day in June.

Such evidence as there is, is scanty and inconclusive. All that anyone *knows* is that Mallory and Irvine spent the night of 7 June at Camp VI, had gone when Odell arrived next day, and never returned.

Presumably the two men attempted to reach the summit on 8 June. That was certainly their intention and, of course, Odell's evidence substantiates it. But Odell's sighting was inconclusive and the pity is that so much of the conjecture must depend upon it. Indeed, until 1933, when there was another attempt on the mountain, Odell's sighting was the *only* evidence, but in that year Wyn Harris discovered an ice axe which could only have belonged to Mallory or Irvine. It was lying on some smooth, brown, 'boiler plate' slabs about sixty feet from the crest of the ridge and 250 yards before the First Step. It was undamaged and the maker's name – Jos. Willisch, Bergführer, Taesch-Zermatt – could clearly be seen engraved upon it. However, as Willisch ice axes were standard issue to the 1924 expedition, there was no means of identifying its owner.[36]

How did the axe come to be lying on the slab? One interpretation is that it was dropped from the ridge early in the climb, and came to rest where it was later found. In which case the two climbers must have decided to press on with only one axe between them – not an unlikely decision on a route predominantly rocky, where the axe would be of only occasional use, and especially with the ultimate climbing prize at stake. It could be, of course, that if this is what did happen, the loss of the axe contributed to some later accident in which the climbers were killed.[37]

Of course, a more sinister interpretation is that the axe itself marked the scene of the accident. If such is the case, it can only have happened during the *descent*, because when Odell saw the two men they were higher up the ridge than the place where the axe was found.

On the face of it a very simple but convincing explanation of the mystery can be built on the assumption that the axe marked the scene of an accident. Mallory and Irvine, it can be assumed, made an unaccountably late start, which is why they were not very far along the ridge when Odell saw them at 12.50 p.m. At 2 p.m., possibly while they were trying to climb the difficult Second Step, they were hit by the snowstorm and decided to retreat. They battled down the ridge in the teeth of the gale and all went well until they reached the fatal slab where one of them slipped. The other laid down his ice axe in order to grab the rope with both hands to save his companion – but the impetus was too great, he was plucked from his stance, and both men fell to their deaths.

The storm ended at 4 p.m. and the sky cleared. Could the two men have descended that far in two hours? Possibly they could, but if so, then Odell, when he resumed his watch, must only just have missed seeing the accident.

Against this theory one must set the nature of the place itself. At the point where the ice axe was found the slab was easily angled, and though the rocks steepened below, it was the sort of place climbers would normally tackle unroped.[38] If Mallory and Irvine were unroped, of course, an accident to one of them would not have affected the other, and there would have been a survivor, unless one stretches coincidence to assume *two* accidents. But the slab was so easy that even a slip was unlikely to prove serious, as a body just would not slide far; and if they were roped together it would be easy for one man to hold the other on the rope.

Nevertheless, *if* an accident took place on the slabs then Mallory and Irvine must have roped together. If it was night, they probably would have roped, but that presumes a very long descent from the ridge, and Odell, who was watching after the storm, would surely have seen two black dots picked out against the ridge made white with freshly fallen snow. If they descended, they must have done so during the storm, and one can imagine the weariness they felt, for nothing is so tiring as defeat.

Tired as they were, perhaps they kept the rope on. Perhaps the normally easy rock was made slippery by the freshly fallen snow on which one of them skidded, falling on to his back and, with his two oxygen cylinders acting like skis, shooting off the face pulling his companion with him.

If that is what happened, it was a classic example of the climbing adage that accidents usually occur in the easy places, when the climber has relaxed and is less alert than he might be. It is certainly the simplest explanation of the mystery and yet – would one man pull the other off in such a way and in such a place? Were they even carrying oxygen cylinders?

If Mallory and Irvine were not wearing oxygen sets, then the risk of a slip on the slabs was negligible – and there is no evidence that oxygen was being used. Though the two men had taken oxygen cylinders and sets up to Camp VI, and oxygen was ostensibly the reason why Irvine was Mallory's partner, Odell found many parts of the oxygen sets lying scattered round the tent when he got there. Could it be that the sets were malfunctioning and that Irvine had been unable to fix them? Odell at first thought that the spare parts were just a symptom of Irvine's incessant mechanical tinkering, but he has since expressed doubts whether oxygen was used on that unfortunate day. If Irvine had been struggling with the sets in the morning, that might also account for their late start.[39]

So much depends on Odell's sighting of the two climbers. Longstaff suggested that what he actually saw were two choughs and Smythe suggested it might have been two rocks; and it is true that in the mountains it is easy to mistake distant rocks for human figures. But Odell was quite adamant: 'I am prepared to maintain that I saw two *human* figures moving deliberately and expeditiously,' he wrote in 1934.[40] He was about 700 yards away at the time, and we can only assume that what he saw was Mallory and Irvine.

But they were not at the Second Step, as he imagined. From such evidence as we have we know that the Second Step is a formidable obstacle: a smooth wall of black rock, sheer and possibly overhanging, about 100 ft high. Members of the 1933 expedition who passed close below the step as they traversed across the North Face thought it looked an impossible obstacle. The only climbers actually to tackle it have been the Chinese. In their account of the first ascent in 1960 they describe it as a 'sheer and slippery' rock wall, 30 m. high, which tallies closely with the 1933 description. 'After searching around the bottom of the rock wall, we decided to ascend along a razor-edge ridge hardly a metre wide [*sic!*] and then turn to the right to climb up the step.'[41] At the top there was a three-metre slab which caused a great deal of trouble, and altogether the climbing of the step took *five hours*. Even allowing for the many inconsistencies of the Chinese report, it is obvious that the Second Step could not be climbed in *five minutes*, as Odell suggested.

An interesting theory has been put forward that the other side of the Second Step, overlooking the east face of the mountain, could be a straightforward snow slope without technical difficulties, but even so to climb 100 ft in five minutes needs a climbing rate of 1,200 ft per hour, which at that altitude, even with oxygen, is patently impossible. In any case, if there was an easy way round the Second Step the Chinese climbers would surely have discovered it.

If the hump that Odell watched the two men climb was not the Second Step, nor was it the First Step, for observers are agreed that this obstacle could be turned by a traverse on the North Face. It might, however, have been one of the lesser humps in between the First and Second Steps. If it was, why were the climbers so late in arriving at this point on the ridge?

Several possibilities present themselves. First of all there is the possibility that malfunctioning oxygen sets prevented an early start, allied to which is the slower rate of climb if the two men decided to dispense with oxygen altogether. The only evidence for this is the oxygen apparatus parts strewn about Camp VI; against it is Odell's observation that the two men seemed to be 'moving expeditiously', which must mean he saw a certain alacrity, and that is very unlikely for two men without oxygen at that altitude. They would be moving slowly, ponderously even.

Another alternative is that they set out early as intended, with oxygen, and struck the First Step too low down. The configuration of the mountain at this point is such that it tends to tempt the climber away to the right, below the ridge. Mallory might have followed this tempting line only to realize after a while that there was no chance of getting back onto the ridge as the rocks were too steep, and that he was bound to end up in Norton's gully.[42] Realizing that the only way onto the ridge was at the First Step, he deliberately turned back to tackle the problem anew.

But would Mallory do that? He might have, had he realized his mistake early enough; in which case he would not be much behind schedule, yet there are *five hours* to be accounted for. Surely he would not give up so much time *and oxygen* for the sake of a theory that might prove wrong anyway? Rather would he have pressed on and tried to force Norton's route up the Great Gully, even though he thought it inferior to the ridge route.

According to the note he sent Odell, Mallory was to go for the top with two cylinders of oxygen instead of the usual four, and so he would have little to spare for such diversions, even had he not been pressed for time. To be short of one thing might be unfortunate, as Lady Bracknell would have observed; to be short of two would be downright carelessness.

The loss of an ice axe would not account for the lateness of the climbers. On the rock ridge it would not slow them down at all – quite the reverse in fact – and they are unlikely to have spent five hours searching for it.

Unless one accepts a malfunction of the oxygen apparatus (and Odell's sighting seems to rule this out) there doesn't seem any explanation of the crucial time factor – *unless the hump which Odell saw them climbing was above the Second Step*. If the relatively inexperienced Chinese climbers were able to surmount the Second Step, Mallory would certainly have been capable of it. The time taken by the Chinese was five hours, which is exactly the gap so inexplicable in Mallory and Irvine's attempt.

If we assume that the two climbers were just above the Second Step at 12.50 p.m., they had before them the summit cone of about 800 ft still to climb – two to three hours of effort even allowing for a fast climbing rate, and not necessarily as easy as it appears in distant photographs. They would have been laboriously climbing this when the storm struck at 2 p.m.

From Odell's account we know that when the storm cleared after two hours there was no sign of anyone on either the ridge or summit cone, and against the white backcloth of freshly fallen snow, two moving black dots would have been clearly visible. So the second reasonable hypothesis would read like this:

Mallory and Irvine set out from Camp VI early on the morning of 8 June, wearing oxygen apparatus. They made good time, but as they approached the ridge one of them dropped his ice axe, which went sliding off down the slabs below. Undeterred by this mishap they reached the First Step, turned it on the north and continued along the ridge until they came to the Second Step. This proved to be a formidable obstacle, taking a long time to overcome, but once above it their goal seemed in sight. Though conscious that they were now short of time and oxygen they pressed on in a calculated risk – the calculations perhaps distorted by excitement, ambition and the seeming nearness of the great prize. But their luck ran out: hit by the storm, possibly gasping their last mouthfuls of oxygen, they either fell or died of exposure before they reached the summit.[43]

Another theory has been put forward by the American writer Tom Holzel. He argues that when the two climbers reached the top of the Second Step they realized that they did not have enough oxygen left to reach the summit, and so it was decided to split up. Irvine contrived to transfer most of his oxygen to Mallory, and to descend immediately to Camp VI. Mallory, alone and with sufficient oxygen, could have made a rapid ascent of the final slopes and reached the summit by 3 p.m. Both men were caught by the storm: Irvine as he descended the ridge, Mallory as he reached the summit. Tired, and stumbling down slabs made slippery by the fresh snow, Irvine fell to his death, leaving his axe behind. Mallory, now out of oxygen and desperately fatigued, was unable to complete the descent and likewise perished.

Holzel's theory is attractive in so far as it gets Mallory to the summit, but it hardly squares with Mallory's character and upbringing. Even allowing for Mallory's fanatical determination to reach the summit, he would never have sent young Irvine down the ridge alone. Once above the Second Step they were committed together, and would have seen it through together, or perished in the attempt. Moreover the transference of oxygen from Irvine to

Mallory would have been rather difficult, if not impossible, to effect under the conditions.[44]

So we are left with alternative explanations which fit the known facts. Either the men were late setting out because of oxygen difficulties, turned back at the Second Step when the storm came on, and fell to their deaths at the spot indicated by the ice axe, or they set out as planned and died in the storm as they approached the summit.

Some day perhaps a climbing party will come across the remains of Mallory and Irvine where they have lain now for more than half a century. Such things are not unknown in the mysterious world of the mountains. But until that happens, nobody can say for certain what happened on 8 June 1924.

There have been several psychical explanations of Mallory's and Irvine's deaths, which is perhaps a measure of the public emotion their disappearance caused.

The first recorded instance seems to have been that of the Austrian climber Frido Kordon, who in 1926 attended a seance with his son acting as medium. According to Kordon, the spirits told him Mallory and Irvine reached the summit at 5 p.m., where Irvine collapsed and died shortly afterwards. Mallory buried him there and marked the grave with a cairn of stones. Mallory then began his descent but fell 150 metres and was killed.[45]

A year later Odell was approached by a man in Canada who also claimed to have attended a seance in which the medium told them Mallory and Irvine reached the summit, and there seems little doubt that there were several such stories going round at the time.

Some time later a retired artist called Williamson living in Shetland wrote to Odell, whom he knew, to say that a psychic friend of his had died and had passed on a message to say he had been in touch with Irvine. Irvine had told him that he and Mallory had reached the summit very late. On the way down, unroped, Mallory had slipped to his death. Irvine, alone and frozen by the intense cold, had carried on for a short distance, then overcome by fatigue had rested on a slab below the ridge. He laid his axe down, and as he huddled himself against the cold, Mallory had suddenly re-appeared. 'Come on, old chap, it's time for us to be going on,' he said.

Odell claims that when he told this story to Somervell, whose strong Christian beliefs did not exclude a scientific attitude to the paranormal, the latter thought there might be something in it.[46]

There was a memorial service in memory of George Herbert Leigh Mallory and Andrew Comyn Irvine at St Paul's Cathedral on 17 October 1924. Besides relations and close friends there were representatives of the royal family, members of previous Everest expeditions, of the Alpine Club and the Royal

Geographical Society. The service was conducted by the Bishop of Chester – both Mallory and Irvine being Cheshire men.

Public interest remained intense. Arrangements had been made earlier for a public lecture in October. Hinks had planned to hire the Albert Hall if the expedition was successful, and the smaller Central Hall at Westminster if it was not. There was no question now but that the Albert Hall was needed.

The press ran articles full of speculation and jingoism. Inevitably the question arose whether it was worth the sacrifice, and the *Morning Post* replied:

> In the days of peace England will always hold some who are not content with humdrum routine and soft living. The spirit which animated the attacks on Everest is the same as that which has prompted arctic and other expeditions, and in earlier times led to the formation of the Empire itself. Who shall say that any of its manifestations are not worth while? Who shall say that its inspiration has not a far-reaching influence on the race? It is certain that it would grow rusty with disuse, and expeditions like the attempt to scale Everest serve to whet the sword of ambition and courage.[47]

Ruth Mallory wrote to Geoffrey Winthrop Young:

> Whether he got to the top of the mountain or did not, whether he lived or died, makes no difference to my admiration for him. I think I have got the pain separate. There is so much of it, and it will go on so long that I must do that . . .
>
> Oh Geoffrey, if only it hadn't happened! It so easily might not have.[48]

# 6

# The Affair of the Dancing Lamas

Major Frederick Marshman Bailey was one of those incredibly adventurous characters spawned by the Great Game in Asia. Tough and resourceful, he had diplomatic adroitness, a flair for languages and a good deal of luck. He was the real-life embodiment of the fictional hero in Kipling's *Kim*.

There were few areas in Central Asia that Bailey didn't know well. He had fought at Gallipoli, served as a Political Officer in Iraq and Persia, and been a spy in Russian Turkestan during the early days of the Revolution.[1] But his first love was Tibet, a country he knew probably better than any other Westerner.

His first introduction to Tibet had been as a young subaltern during Younghusband's mission to Lhasa, when he took the opportunity to explore the western part of the country. The Younghusband Treaty established a British Trade Agency at Gyantse and in 1905 Bailey became the Agent, a position he occupied for three and a half years, improving his knowledge of the language and eventually gaining the friendship of the Dalai Lama. In 1911 he returned to south-east Tibet in a journey of exploration which won him the Gill Memorial Award of the Royal Geographical Society, and then two years later, with Morshead, he proved that the Tsangpo and Brahmaputra rivers were one and the same by means of a particularly daring and dangerous Tibetan journey which earned him the disapproval of the Indian Government and the Gold Medal of the R.G.S. It was on this expedition that he discovered and brought back the celebrated Tibetan Blue Poppy, *M. baileyi*.

The war years then intervened, but in 1921 Bailey was appointed Political Officer in Sikkim in succession to Sir Charles Bell, a position he occupied for the next seven years. He was directly responsible for relations with Tibet, and was deeply concerned in the affairs of the early Everest expeditions.

It might be reasonably assumed that a man as steeped in adventure as Bailey was, and a double award winner of the R.G.S. to boot, would be a keen supporter of the attempts on Everest, but such was not the case. For reasons known only to himself, Bailey showed by his actions that he was not in favour of the expeditions and, though he fulfilled his duty in conducting the necessary negotiations with Lhasa, he never failed to support any objection the Tibetans cared to make. Perhaps he saw in the expedition the first threat to that exclusiveness which made Tibet the Forbidden Land and which for Tibet's sake he wished to preserve; or it could be that he genuinely believed that the huge caravans of climbers and porters might disturb the economic balance of the regions through which they travelled (as indeed they did to some extent) and possibly affect the political *status quo*. Whatever his motives it is clear that his ultimate aim was to get the expeditions stopped.

He came onto the scene at a particularly unfortunate moment. No sooner had he taken up his post at Gangtok than he had to deal with the Tibetan complaints about Heron's geologizing and Morshead's unofficial wanderings in the wake of the 1921 expedition. Of the two, Morshead was the more serious offender because he had deliberately flouted the restrictions laid down by Lhasa, whereas poor Heron was merely doing the job he was supposed to do. Curiously, however, Morshead was quickly forgiven, whereas Heron remained condemned. Could this have been due to the fact that Morshead had been Bailey's partner on his epic Tsangpo adventure of 1913? About Heron, however, Bailey was adamant in pressing the Tibetan complaint, and the affair went up to Viceroy level, causing a considerable stir.

In the affairs of government, a mountaineering expedition, even to the highest mountain in the world, takes a very low priority. Government departments might, out of sympathy or interest, do something towards helping the expedition along provided it didn't create a fuss or make too much extra work. If the expedition does cause trouble, however, then the departments are more reluctant to help next time round. Bailey's tactics seemed based on this attitude.

As the man in closest contact with the Tibetan authorities he wielded considerable influence in the Indian Government when it came to Tibetan affairs, and despite the fact that Heron was exonerated by his superiors and proved to be nothing but a harmless geologist going about his work, Bailey was able to over-ride the powerful Survey of India and prevent Heron from accompanying either the 1922 or the 1924 expedition.[2]

The trouble caused by Heron's and Morshead's petty irregularities imposed conditions on the 1922 party which would have been irksome to any other leader but General Bruce. Bruce, as always, went his own way, and though the expedition had to watch its step in dealing with the locals, it is doubtful whether even Bailey would have dared tangle with the General had anything gone wrong. As it was the 1922 expedition passed off without any political squabbles, but once Charlie Bruce was out of the way, after the 1924 expedition, Bailey once more had a free hand.

He began by complaining about the expedition's journey to recuperate in the Rongshar valley. After leaving Base Camp, Norton, and those of the team who didn't make their own arrangements for the journey back to India, travelled westward over the Lamna La to Kyetrak and then by the Phuse La to the Rongshar Valley, below the massive peak of Gaurisankar. The Rongshar is a deep gorge like the Arun, and the team followed it down into Nepal until a broken bridge prevented further exploration. There could hardly have been a more welcome change from the cold, windy valley of Rongbuk than the warm, vegetated gorge of Rongshar.

There is no doubt that the expedition were naughty in stepping over the border into Nepal: 'We knew that we were trespassing on a grand scale,' wrote Bentley Beetham later – but Nepal was not the concern of Bailey. He sent to the India Office a letter he had received from the Ministers of Tibet dated the 25th day of the 7th month of the Wood Mouse Year (23 September 1924):

> The reason of sending this letter by the Ministers of Tibet. We have received a report from the tax collecter at Rong-shar to the following effect:
>
> 'Recently 7 sahibs of the Mt Ev. Exped. with 17 coolies arrived at Rong-shar. They visited the Tibet and Nepal frontier, carried out survey operations and took photographs. On the way they collected different kinds of flowers which they carried away with them. They also went all over the place, took photographs and conducted survey operations. After staying 11 days they returned to Tingri. When their passport was examined it was noticed that Rong-shar was not mentioned as one of the places for them to visit.'
>
> In the Passport, which was given to the Sahibs as a result of communication between the Tibetan and British Govts, it was stipulated that apart from visiting Mt Everest they should not go about in further districts as they liked.
>
> Their act of going about in this way in other districts and of conducting survey operations and taking photographs on the Tibet/Nepal Boundary, is a direct breach of the orders of both the British and Tibetan Governments.
>
> Please therefore submit a report to the Great British Government and give orders to those Sahibs. They may have visited other districts about which we have not yet received any reports; if so, we will send you a further report about it.[3]

Norton told the Committee what they already knew, that though the passport did not specifically mention Rongshar it had been understood all along that the party would go there to recuperate. Both the 1921 and 1922 expeditions had visited the valley without bother, and what was more, the officials of the Shekar and Tingri districts, and those in Rongshar itself, had given them every assistance. In their reply to the India Office the Committee explained this and pointed out that it was Major Bailey who had provided the translations of the original Tibetan documents, thereby hinting that if there was a discrepancy between the Tibetan and English versions it was Bailey's fault.

The Rongshar complaint was soon abandoned by the Tibetans and Bailey, for it was a footling thing which could not be really justified. It could be argued that Rongshar was part of the Everest region and, as we have seen, the other expeditions went there.

In any case Bailey had found more certain bait. The Tibetans complained about the post-expedition activities of J. de V. Hazard and John Noel.

Hazard was the man who had left Base Camp, just before the others went to Rongshar, in order to help the surveyor Hari Singh Thapa to survey the West Rongbuk Glacier. 'Hazard likes a job of work on his own,' commented Norton dryly.[4]

In fact Hazard never seemed to fit in with other members of the team, and the way in which he had left four porters stranded on the North Col had done nothing to increase his popularity. The fact that three key men – Norton, Somervell and Mallory – had to risk their lives and waste their energies on rescuing the porters could have had serious consequences for the expedition. Norton was coldly furious with him.

As we have seen, Odell, who shared the North Col camp with Hazard towards the end of the expedition, found him 'a curious chap' and very self-centred. On one occasion he left Odell alone at the col, and meeting an astonished Norton and Bruce on his descent informed them that he had felt like going back to Base Camp for a hot bath! Significantly, too, Hazard made no attempt to accompany Odell on the latter's historic climbs to Camp VI. A strange chap indeed – but possibly one who had been totally overwhelmed by Everest, once he got there, finding the whole concept was too much for him.

This might explain why, at the end of a long and arduous expedition, he eagerly volunteered to accompany Hari Singh Thapa on his survey work. Perhaps he felt that here at last was a positive contribution which he could make to the work of the expedition – he knew that Hinks, back in London, had set great store on the surveying of the West Rongbuk.

Unfortunately his latter-day enthusiasm went too far. After the West Rongbuk Glacier had been surveyed he persuaded the Djongpen of Shekar to supply him with transport for a 'survey' to Lhatse on the Tsangpo River, far to the north of Everest. The Djongpen pointed out that Lhatse was not an area mentioned on the passport, but Hazard made the journey anyway.

There was no way the Committee could excuse Hazard's journey – it was a flagrant breach of the passport, and Bailey knew it. This was a trump card, but he had no need to play it, for already he held the ace: Captain John Noel and the affair of the dancing lamas.

John Noel was an extraordinary man of boundless energy and ideas, utterly dedicated to the conquest of Mount Everest. It was his illegal journey to Tashirak in 1913 which had helped to spark off the first expedition, and though Army duty prevented him from joining the 1921 team he was an enthusiastic member of the 1922 and 1924 expeditions.

He fizzed with ideas, all of them highly original and most of them impracticable, such as laying an oxygen pipe line up to the higher camps to save carrying cylinders. There is no doubt, as Odell has said, that Noel was a bit of a showman. Most of his companions regarded him as a kindly, helpful, industrious eccentric and on the whole they rather liked him, putting up with his incessant photography with a tolerant amusement. General Bruce had nothing but praise for him.

In 1922 Noel had been put in charge of making the expedition film, and despite the rather modest success it had enjoyed he became convinced that if a longer, more professional, film was made of the 1924 expedition it would be a huge commercial success – if the mountain was climbed. He was under no illusions about the risk involved, as is shown in a letter to General Bruce:

> Travel films have in the ordinary way little scope except as lecture films and it is almost impossible to get them into the cinemas which is the chief source of revenue for films, but next year by taking an elaborate and carefully produced film with more capital available for production and exploitation that the Expedition would ordinarily care to spend I expect to be able to make a film that can compete in the cinematograph trade with the usual productions and so obtain a large enough scope to repay the cost of producing the film. Success will depend virtually on whether the mountain is conquered. I will accordingly take two separate films, one of the story of the Expedition which will be shown to the public only in the event of the mountain being conquered and a second film dealing with the life of the people in Tibet, Sikkim and Bhutan. The latter will allow my organization to mark time until the mountain is finally conquered in a later Expedition when the film taken next year can then be brought out and be exploited. All this, however, would be my risk.[5]

Though Noel himself was not a mountaineer in the technical sense, he had seen enough of Mallory, Somervell, Finch and young Bruce in 1922 to convince himself that the chances of success next time round were very high. He was determined to record this great victory for posterity – and at the same time make his fortune. His showmanship, energy and entrepreneurial flair were at once channelled in this one direction – and he backed his judgement with whatever means he could lay his hands on.

If the expedition had been successful, Noel's dreams might well have been realized, but not being a man for half measures he let his dreams rule his pocket from the outset. He needed to acquire the film rights from the Everest Committee, but whereas a more cautious businessman would have negotiated clauses embodying success or failure and cut his cloth accordingly (as indeed *The Times* had done over despatches) Noel made an outright gamble which would have astonished the most hardened poker player. As we have seen, he offered £8,000 for all photographic rights to the expedition, or £6,000 for the film rights, payable in advance. The Committee (not themselves noted financial wizards) could hardly refuse such a generous offer, and they accepted the £8,000 with alacrity.

Noel formed a company called Explorers Films Ltd to raise the money, with Sir Francis Younghusband as Chairman.[6]

A couple of contracts were readily available for the company on the 'news' side of the expedition in the shape of a picture service to *The Times* and films to Pathe Gazette, and of course there would be fees payable by members of the team who gave illustrated lectures on their return home, but the real money lay in the success or failure of the full-length feature film which was at the heart of Noel's ambitions.

'The film will be in story form,' Noel wrote to Bruce, 'the general thread of the story being "Man's struggle against Nature". It will show adventures to the party in Tibet and it will work out the theme of Man's success in carrying his fight for dominance over Nature one stage further by conquering the highest mountain in the world.'

To all the members of the expedition he sent a letter outlining his plans and assuring them that his photography would not interfere with the climbing: 'I want to make special reference to this point that to some people the cinemat. camera is disconcerting and perhaps annoying ... On this new expedition I want to assure everybody that the presence of my cinematographic camera will never on any occasion cause worry or annoyance to anybody.'[7]

He set his mind to organizing the filming with great thoroughness, taking advantage of every innovation he could discover. He hoped to use the 'new Friese-Green colour process', and for the high-altitude filming he had a new camera developed by Arthur Newman which weighed only four pounds and worked by clockwork motor as against the usual handcrank. The film was self-threading. Its one disadvantage was that it held only 16 ft of film, or about a minute of running time. A 20-inch telephoto lens was built to fit this camera, 'resembling a baby Lewis gun'.[8] For still photography he planned to use stereoscopic pictures (then much in vogue) as well as the usual type. He had hoped that John Morris would help with the landscape work, but as it turned out Morris was unable to join the expedition.

Nothing was to be left to chance. Feeling that it was too risky to trust the undeveloped, fragile film on the long boat journey back to England, Noel arranged for it to be developed in Darjeeling. To do this meant building a special photographic laboratory with a constant water supply and steady electric voltage. The construction of this building, made of local stone, wood and corrugated iron, was put in the hands of Arthur Pereira, Honorary Secretary of the Royal Photographic Society, and himself a noted producer of travel films. Pereira, with an assistant, King, and a number of Indian helpers, agreed to take on the job of developing the film as it arrived by runner from Tibet, as well as developing and printing the stills and, when time allowed, making lecture slides from the best of the photographs. It was long, hot work – fifteen hours a day on average, or as Pereira put it 'all day, seven days a week, for four months'.[9]

Noel provided his own Sherpas and equipment for Camp III and the North Col, which was the highest point he expected to visit, but it is important to note that he came under the overall command of the expedition leader. He was with the expedition but not of it – a somewhat ambivalent position which was to have repercussions for the Committee in London.

Hinks was never really happy with the situation: it didn't accord with his tidy mind, and Noel's courting of publicity was anathema to Hinks. Among Noel's fringe activities was the sending of an artist, Francis Helps, to the Chumbi valley to paint portraits of Tibetan types (who turned out to be exceptionally unhelpful to the artist) and the organizing of a Citroen tractor to carry the photographic equipment in the early stages of the trek across Tibet.

Fortunately perhaps for Noel, the tractor didn't arrive at Darjeeling until the expedition had departed. It turned up eventually in the charge of a Lt Col. Haddick, and a Lt Fitzgerald – the latter a representative of the Tank Corps who had come out from England specially to drive the vehicle through Tibet.[10] Arthur Pereira, feeling that something had better be done with the tractor, suggested that it should follow the expedition at least as far as the Tibetan border, and so a special tractor mini-expedition was organized with Pereira, Haddick and Fitzgerald accompanied by a Citroen company representative, Mr Cundell, and a Mr Millwright of Darjeeling. Ahead of them went a convoy of mules dumping cans of Shell petrol at suitable staging points.

At first the track was fairly broad and the vehicle made good progress, but young Fitzgerald suffered from altitude sickness and was forced to return to Darjeeling. The driving devolved on Cundell, who soon found difficulty coping with the narrowing track, the missing bridges and hair-raising precipices along which the tractor crawled. Sometimes a kilometre a day was reckoned good going. What the locals thought about it all beggars the imagination.

Eventually the vehicle was put in a rude shelter, still a day's march from the Tibetan border, where for all that is known it remains to this day.

Meanwhile, Pereira's absence from the laboratory had interrupted the photographs to *The Times*, and Hink's wrote testily about the whole affair to Norton:

> Noel's photos have begun to appear again in *The Times* the last few days, but nothing so far above Camp II. I suspect that the interruption was due to his man at Darjeeling taking part in a somewhat curious enterprise trying to get a caterpillar car over the Jelap, of which high-falutin accounts have been sent home to *The Times* by a certain Lt Col. Haddick. *The Times* submitted them to me, and I told them that it had nothing whatever to do with the expedition but was concerned entirely with Noel's photography and lecturing concern. I went further and said . . . it would be rather a pity if *The Times* published a high-flown story about what looked like a rather silly enterprise . . . I think *The Times* will take this view and won't tarnish the thing with side-shows. I send this for your private information and hope that I have taken the right line.[11]

Distasteful though Noel's fringe activities were to the fastidious Hinks, they did no harm to the expedition. Harmless, too, seemed an idea he had mentioned to Bruce in his letter of 26 January – an idea for pulling in the public to see his feature film. 'We intend if possible,' he wrote, 'to bring back a small party of Sherpa porters or Tibetans to England who will appear with the presentation of the film in London.'[12]

When the expedition failed to climb the mountain, all chances of success for Noel's film virtually vanished. Had he been with Odell at Camp VI and by some stroke of luck filmed those black dots moving along the ridge, it might have been a different matter, but as it was he was left with an adventure film which included hardly any adventure. He had no alternative but to adopt his secondary plan, which was to turn the film into a travel documentary about Tibet, called 'The Roof of the World'. For this he needed all the supporting material he could get, and even thought of going to Lhasa with a group of British Buddhists who had arrived in Tibet; but Hinks dissuaded him. His original idea of bringing Sherpas to England was no longer fully in accord with the new subject of the film. Instead he decided to bring home several lamas from the monastery at Gyantse, their function being to dance on the stage to the accompaniment of their own cacophonous cymbals and horns.

Meanwhile, the Everest Committee, blissfully unaware of the storm which was about to break, were preparing for the next attempt on the mountain in 1926. Rumours had reached the Committee that other countries were interested in mounting expeditions and the Royal Geographical Society wrote post haste to the Under Secretary of State for India expressing the hope that the Indian Government would do nothing to assist such interlopers 'until the enterprise to which the Mount Everest Committee have devoted so many years has been abandoned by them, which is very far from being the present situation'.

On 5 November 1924, the Committee formally applied for permission to send an expedition in 1926, and on the same day Hinks wrote to Bailey mentioning the fact and hoping that no assistance would be rendered to Swiss or German expeditions in the offing, adding 'we have heard that a member of the expedition of 1922 has a private scheme for getting out next year and stealing a march on the Committee. You will perhaps be able to make a fairly accurate shot as to his identity.'[13]

A fortnight later Hinks received a cabled reply from Bailey which made no reference to the next expedition at all. Instead it dealt with Noel's film:

> Some offence has been caused by a portion of the Everest film showing a man eating lice. The Tibetans say that this is not typical and will give the world the wrong and unfortunate impression. Can you ask Noel to cut this out? I am cabling this as otherwise I am afraid the film will be exhibited before we hear.[14]

Hinks might have been surprised at this seeming non-sequitur to his own letter but he wasn't unduly worried. In any case he had a couple of objections to the film himself: he wanted Noel to cut out references to Shebbeare always knowing where the whisky was kept, and to Mrs Mallory saying she regretted the whole enterprise. He does not seem to have asked how the Tibetans could possibly know what was in Noel's film, since they could not have seen it. Bailey probably knew it from a showing at Darjeeling and not for the last time was putting words into Lhasa's mouth.

Noel, ever ready to please, cut the scene. 'I have cut out one scene (to please Bailey) but left another which people have seen recently and do not think there is any harm in it. An old beggar man is seen "fleaing" a child's head, and he performs the usual Tibetan custom of killing what he finds with his teeth. This scene does not show him eating anything.'[15]

A week later came a letter from Bailey referring to the lamas. This first missive was quite mild, merely objecting to stage imitations of religious ceremonies and requesting that the non-religious nature of any dances should be stressed. In particular, Bailey did not want the catch phrase 'devil dance' being used. On New Year's Day, 1925, however, he followed this up with a more detailed complaint:

> I am afraid that there is every chance of the Tibetan Govt. refusing permission for the next Everest expedition – for this reason I am sorry Noel

has not unreservedly agreed to cut out all objectionable things on his film.

The Tibetans are very upset about several things this year – Hazard's journey to Lhatse, the undesirable things on the film and also more than anything what they consider the enticing away of monks from Gyantse to England with their religious paraphernalia to parade their religion for pecuniary gain.

You know that there were complaints about some religious dances at Wembley.

There is no doubt that no one in Tibet welcomes these expeditions and permission is only obtained out of friendliness to us, and that will cease to weigh sufficiently with the Tibetan authorities if the actions of the expedition hurt their religious and other feelings. I am writing to you because it seems to me that the prospects of a further, and we hope successful, attempt on the mountain are being jeopardized by the owners of the film.[16]

Bailey went on to say that although no official complaint had been received from the Tibetan Government, people in high places were enraged, and the affair could affect Anglo-Tibetan relations, which was quite contrary to what Explorer Films had assured the Tibetans when the film was first mooted. In due course Hinks passed on to Bailey a placatory reply from the film company with assurances that the lamas were not taking part in any performances which were religious or unseemly.

Meanwhile the lamas were appearing in cinemas in London and the provinces. Their 'performance' with thigh-bone trumpets and drums was unusual to British audiences, but more curious than exciting and hardly the sort of thing likely to cause a breach of diplomatic relations. As 'holy men' the lamas had an audience with the Archbishop of Canterbury, who presented them with a finely illustrated copy of the Bible, which they later pulled to pieces so that each could have his own share. The holiness of Gyantse was quite different from that of Lambeth Palace!

As it became transparently obvious that the lamas were merely a harmless diversion, Bailey shifted the grounds of his objections from their performance to the manner in which they left Tibet. He forwarded a letter from the Ministers of Tibet which, after repeating the charges about members of the expedition visiting unauthorized areas, went on:

Over and above this, they have enticed and taken away to England four or five monks whose photos as dancers have appeared recently in the newspapers. We regard this action on the part of the Sahibs as very unbecoming. For the future, we cannot give them permission to go to Tibet, should they ever ask for it, and we request that you will kindly stop them. We would also request that you will kindly arrange, by reporting the matter to the

> Great British Govt., for the immediate return to Tibet and handing over of the monks, who have been taken away deceitfully. Kindly let us have an early reply to this.[17]

From the wording of this letter it is obvious that the request for an expedition in 1926 had not been put to the Tibetan authorities by Bailey, but that he had allowed the affair of the dancing lamas to pre-empt the issue, which was precisely what he hoped for. Without further discussion he took this letter as a formal refusal for a 1926 expedition and informed the Indian Government of that fact. This was cabled to the India Office in London, who informed the Everest Committee that permission would not be granted.

It was only at this juncture that the Everest Committee, faced with a *fait accompli*, realized that the Political Officer in Sikkim was not on their side at all.

Noel was incensed at Bailey's letter and wrote to Hinks:

> I have to report to the Committee that the Lamas were brought to England by my personal invitation through Mr D. Macdonald of Chumbi, Tibet, who is a personal friend of the Chief Lama, who has come with them.
>
> These lamas travelled as private people and were not on any political mission. They came as my friends and guests to England at their own consent and wish. There was no reason to correspond through official channels concerning their journey beyond obtaining them the requisite and necessary passports for their journey, and these passports were issued by the Sec. of the Bengal Govt. at Darjeeling, after authority from Lhasa to issue such passports was first obtained. The Sec. of the Bengal Govt. wired to Lhasa before he consented to issue the passports and he obtained information from Lhasa that there was no objection to the issue of such passports. They were accordingly issued and the Lamas proceeded to England in my care.
>
> I think it was Mr Laidenlaw of the Lhasa Govt. who was referred to but the Sec. of Bengal Govt. did not tell us. He merely told us that information had been received by him from Lhasa that it was in order for the Lamas to go to England and accordingly he gave us the passports.
>
> The Lamas on their part travelled with the full knowledge of their own fellow lamas and their own officials. They receive letters now normally every week from Tibet and in none of these letters is there any expression from their own people of displeasure about their visit to England. The lamas are in my care in England and are very well looked after and well treated, treated as one would one's own friends. Their travel to England will help to promote cordial friendship between ourselves and the Tibetans. I must ask leave to take vigorous exception to the expression of Major Bailey, P.O. of Sikkim, by which he says the lamas were taken away deceitfully. This is

untrue and is a discreditable assertion to me, because I arranged the passports through the Govt. of India and with the knowledge of Lhasa in a perfectly correct manner, in fact in the same manner as any foreign travellers obtain their passports to travel abroad.

These lamas will travel back to India and Tibet in September, which is the earliest date the season and climatic conditions will permit them to traverse the India Ocean and India to reach Tibet.[18]

This letter by Noel was both injudicious and open to investigation, which Bailey proceeded to make with relish. The Everest Committee, as English gentlemen, took it at face value and proceeded to attack Bailey through the India Office.

On 1 July Hinks wrote to the India Office a letter placing the whole affair on Bailey's shoulders, and enclosed statements from Noel and Norton:

In further reference to your letter of June 12 P.1641, and to General Bruce's letter of June 17 in reply:

I have now the pleasure to send you the answers which Co. Norton and Capt. Noel have returned to the request of the Mt Everest Committee that they should furnish statements of the circumstances in which members of the Expedition visited the Rongshar Valley and the Lamas were brought to England.

2 In regard to the complaint that some members of the Expedition visited the Rongshar though this was not included in their passport, I would call your attention to the clear explanation of Co. Norton that his visit to the Rongshar was arranged by the Dzongpen of Shekar, who gave letters of introduction to the officials at Tropde, arranged the transport and sent his Chongay with them. It is difficult to see how Co. Norton could have acted more correctly and we feel that Major Bailey could have no difficulty in making a perfectly clear and sufficient explanation to the Tibetan Government on this point. The only difficulty might be that the explanation might involve the Dzongpen of Shekar in trouble, and for this reason it would not be desirable that the text of Colonel Norton's letter should be communicated verbatim to the Tibetan Government. You will I am sure take all care that nothing is done to get the Dzongpen of Shekar into trouble, for he has been at all times a most sympathetic and valued friend of the expedition.

3 In the letter dated 23rd September, 1924, just recently communicated to us, the Ministers of Tibet say that the passport which was given to the party stipulated that apart from visiting Mt Everest they should not go about in other districts as they liked. We do not recognize any such stipulation in the translations furnished by Major Bailey of two documents which appear to constitute the passport and covering letter.

The parwana informs the Dzongpens of four districts that the Expedition will enter their jurisdictions at the end of March, 1924. It directs them, inter alia, to make without delay camp arrangements at whatever place they happen to camp. This phrase in the absence of any more restrictive clause would seem to be ample justification for the action of the Dzongpen of Shekar, and the Mt Everest Committee trust that when Major Bailey replied to this letter he drew attention to this point. It was not until receipt of your letter of June 12, many months later, that the Committee learned for the first time that any question had been raised about the Rongshar visit and though they at once asked for a report from Colonel Norton they realized that much valuable time had been lost.

4 In regard to the complaint that monks have been taken away deceitfully, I would draw your attention to the explicit statement of Capt. Noel that the passports for the lamas were issued by the Secretary to the Bengal Government at Darjeeling after authority had been obtained from Lhasa to issue such passports. I should suppose it probable that the telegram to Lhasa went through the office of Major Bailey at Gangtok, and in any case it must have been possible for Major Bailey to ascertain the facts.

5 The Committee have not been informed what answer if any Major Bailey has made to the two letters of which copies have been furnished to us, but the Mt Everest Committee will greatly regret it if the Political Officer in Sikkim did not take immediate steps to make a suitable and conclusive reply on the question of the lamas, which seems to be perfectly plain, and if further he did not assure the Tibetan Government that if there had been any trespass on the part of the Expedition beyond the limits of travel for which they had permission, such trespass was certainly unintentional and the journey must have been made with the assent of the local authorities. No one knows better than Major Bailey how careful the two last expeditions have always been to do nothing to hurt the susceptibilities of the Tibetan Government.

6 It will cause the Mt Everest Committee great concern if the allegations of the Tibetan Government charging the Expedition with breach of faith and with deceitful and unbecoming action have not been already repudiated in firm language by the Political Officer in Sikkim. In any case the Mt Everest Committee hope that you will now be in a position to ask the Government of India to instruct Major Bailey to explain the misapprehension by which the party inadvertently exceeded the intention of the Tibetan Government, in visiting the Rongshar, and that he will be further instructed to make it quite clear to the Tibetan Government that the Mt Everest Committee were in no way responsible for the visit of the lamas to England, but that this visit was arranged after all necessary permission had been obtained.

7 I enclose copies of the following documents ... (see above).
I am, dear Sir, your Obedient Servant ...[19]

Powerful though the Everest Committee might be, and as the Royal Geographical Society undoubtedly was, they were not so powerful as to be able to instruct the India Office in the conduct of its affairs. Hinks's letter caused a furore in the corridors of power and the affair escalated out of all proportion. Norton's statement was accepted, Noel's was not.

Disconcerting facts were slowly coming to light. Bailey obtained signed statements from David Macdonald and Sirdar Bahadur Laden La disclaiming any knowledge of the alleged passport provided for the lamas.[20] Furthermore, the Chief Secretary of the Bengal Government denied there had ever been an application for them. In the face of this evidence the Everest Committee asked Noel to produce the passports for examination, and learned to their horror that the documents did not exist.

The sad fact was that John Noel had been duped, albeit innocently, by young John Macdonald. The latter had been entrusted with the job of getting the lamas to England and finding himself delayed by Indian red-tape had risked cutting a few corners. When he had applied for passports in Darjeeling he had been told that the documents could be issued only after approval from the Indian Government, so he took the lamas to Calcutta to await developments. While there he managed to secure from the Commissioner of Police permits for the party to sail for England, and they had reached Colombo before the Bengal Government realized what it had done. They asked for the lamas to be detained pending instructions from Delhi, but the authorities in Ceylon felt they were powerless to intervene, and so the lamas sailed on to England.

When it became clear that Noel's statement could not stand up, the India Office turned in full cold-blooded fury on the Everest Committee, laying the blame squarely on them.

> The Govt. of India find Capt. Noel's statement about the monks taken to England to be in direct variance with the facts as known to them. They are investigating the matter further, but in any case find it difficult to accept without qualification the statement of your Committee that it has no responsibility in the matter of the monks.
>
> The film in connection with the display of which the monks were brought to England, and from which the Committee derived financial benefit, was made by Capt. Noel as a member of the expedition and it was during the course of the expedition that the arrangements for the monks' travel were made. With the formation of a Company (of which however Capt. Noel and Sir Francis Younghusband are directors) direct control in respect of matters connected with the Mt Everest film may have passed from the hands of the

Mt Everest Committee, but the responsibility it appears to the Govt. of India must remain with the Committee.[21]

There was no way the Committee could wriggle out of it: the facts were plain. Noel *was* under the command of Norton, and hence the ultimate responsibility rested with the Everest Committee. The letter ended:

> Finally I am directed by Lord Birkenhead (Secretary of State for India) to say that he must take the strongest exception to the tone of your remarks in regard to Lt Colonel F.M. Bailey . . . the criticisms and insinuations in your letters regarding Lt Colonel Bailey appear to his lordship to be misplaced and uncalled for.[22]

There was nothing now for the Committee to do but eat humble pie and Hinks wrote to the Under Secretary an abject apology:

> The Committee regret very deeply the humiliating position in which they were placed by the discovery that Captain Noel's statements were incorrect. They ask that you will accept for yourself, and also will convey to the Government of India, that as soon as the correctness of the facts was challenged, they did everything in their power to discover the truth, and immediately communicated to Mr Wakely the result of their enquiries. They trust that both the Secretary of State and the Government of India will recognize that they did all that was possible in a most difficult and humiliating position.[23]

To apologize so fully to Bailey himself, however, stuck in Hinks's craw. He knew the man had outmanoeuvred him and had effectively blocked the way for future expeditions, so he merely wrote a superficial apology, which did not go unnoticed in the India Office:

> The Committee will be glad also if you will ask the Government of India to convey to the Political Officer in Sikkim the Committee's regret that so much trouble has been given to him by these unfortunate occurrences and to convey to him their thanks for his good offices in representing the Committee's explanations and regrets to the Tibetan Government.[24]

But Bailey had won, and won handsomely. To the eyes of officialdom he was a maligned victim and the Everest Committee were little more than rogues – and inept rogues at that.

Bailey remained as Political Officer in Sikkim until 1928, during which time there was not the slightest chance of another expedition to Everest.

Ironically before the year was out Explorer Films had gone bankrupt, leaving the lamas stranded in Colombo. The Committee cabled £150 to help them return to India.

At the height of the trouble over the dancing lamas, John Noel called at the R.G.S. to see Hinks, and finding that he was out, dictated a confidential note in which the following forthright paragraph, stripped of diplomatic niceties, occurs:

> As regards the trouble with Bailey, I want to tell you quite candidly what is the cause of the whole trouble, and has been since the beginning of the expeditions. It is not the hostility of the Tibetans but merely the obstruction of Major Bailey. He himself told my wife in India that he did not like the Mt Everest expeditions because of the trouble and work they gave him. That sounds an extraordinary thing to say, but it is perfectly true and you know yourself how he obstructed General Bruce in all matters in which it was his object to help him. The opinions that Major Bailey quotes as coming from the Tibetans are entirely from himself, and if people in England understood the real position of a Political Officer in India, they would know that he has such a peculiar position that the Government refers all matters to him and he practically dictates any answer he wishes, putting the authority on to the native people because they accept his advice and he advises them to do what he wishes.[25]

On the evidence one cannot help but agree with Noel that Bailey fixed the whole affair from start to finish. On the other hand one is entitled to question his motives, which surely must go deeper than a wish to avoid extra work. How did it come about that a man who was himself a noted explorer, with a high degree of adventure in his make-up, set himself to destroy the greatest adventure and exploration of the day?

Was it simply that the high-spirited young man who had traced the Tsangpo with Morshead and defied the Bolsheviks in Russia had in the space of a few short years turned into a crabbed, finicky bureaucrat? Perhaps it was reaction to his own lost ambition – when Bailey died in 1967 amongst his notes was one he had written many years earlier regarding Everest: 'It must be climbed one day and I hope I will be one of the men to do it.'[26]

# 7

# 'Another Bloody Day'

On 19 March 1931, at the Royal Geographical Society, the Mount Everest Committee was reconstituted under the Chairmanship of the President, Sir William Goodenough. Younghusband and Longstaff represented the R.G.S., Withers and Collie the Alpine Club, so the change didn't make much difference.

The time seemed propitious for a fresh initiative. Bailey had gone from Sikkim, there was a bank balance of over £4,500 to form the nucleus of funds and fresh young climbers with good Alpine and even Himalayan experience were not wanting. Within four days of being appointed Chairman, Goodenough was writing tentatively to the Secretary of State for India asking 'how the feeling lay' for another Everest expedition.

The response was not encouraging. The Secretary of State, Wedgwood-Benn, regretted that 'under present conditions' there was no possibility of pursuing the matter further, and in a private letter to Hinks Colonel Weir, the new Political Officer in Sikkim, explained how the affair of the dancing lamas still rankled in Tibet.

> Pictures of the dances and dancers appeared in our weekly picture papers and were seen by Dalai Lama, who looked on the whole affair as a direct affront to the religion of which he is the head.
>
> He has directed that if any of the Tibetans should return to Tibet they should be arrested and sent to him for punishment. Naturally they prefer to remain in exile in Darjeeling and Kalimpong where they eke out an existence.[1]

Weir also pointed out that in Sikkim, where the Maharaja was of Tibetan descent, the lice-eating incident in Noel's film had not been favourably received. In fact the Maharaja had refused Noel permission to revisit Sikkim, though he had readily granted permission to the continental expeditions of Dyhrenfurth and Bauer.

It looked as though the Tibetans had long memories and were neither willing to forget nor to forgive. In desperation the Committee mooted the idea of going through Nepal instead of Tibet, but General Bruce warned them that Dyhrenfurth's recent expedition to Kangchenjunga had upset the Nepalese and made them more intransigent than ever.

Nevertheless, seven years had passed since the last expedition and critics were beginning to complain that the Committee was not pressing the case strongly enough. This was true enough – but these were the same men who had had their knuckles rapped by the India Office in 1924 and they had no intention of getting them rapped again.

Had they only known it, they had at their disposal a very powerful argument: that of chauvinism. Younghusband had unwittingly touched on it at the first meeting of the new Committee when he made a reference to the ghosts of Mallory and Irvine which he hoped might soften the hearts of the India Office and Sikkim: 'Attention should be called to the fact that this country should have a priority in view among other things that her countrymen lay at or near the top.'[2]

Younghusband's statement did not go unnoticed in the India Office. The fact was that Britain's monopoly of Mount Everest was being threatened. Suggestions were coming from the United States that the next British expedition should contain an American, Terris Moore, or alternatively that there should be an American expedition led by Page Stelle and including a British climber – preferably Odell, who was well known in American climbing circles. Rumour also had it that the Swiss climber Dyhrenfurth intended to press for a chance too.

More disturbing than these, however, was the growing strength of German high-altitude expeditions, both in the Andes and Himalaya. Paul Bauer was about to make his second attempt on the mighty Kangchenjunga, third highest mountain in the world, and if he succeeded it would put the Germans in a very strong position indeed to claim the right to attempt Everest. It would have been politically impossible for the Indian Government to have denied them: the rest of the world would have seen a refusal as cynical imperialism and it would certainly have stoked the already smouldering German nationalism. It would have been perfidious Albion once again up to her tricks, even if she was disguised with a sari.

One should not perhaps make too much of this: it was not a great national issue which caused the lamps to burn all night in the India Office. But it must have crossed the minds of the civil servants whose job it was to smell out the nuances of policy. At any event the Indian Government began to put pressure on Tibet, despite the timidity of the Everest Committee, and a year after Wedgwood-Benn's initial refusal permission was granted for an expedition in 1933. The Dalai Lama put the position delicately, granting 'reluctant permission in deference to the wishes of the British Government in order that the friendly relations may not be ruptured'. Hardly the warmest of welcomes. A codicil stipulated that all members of the expedition must be British.[3]

For the Everest Committee it was a dream suddenly come true, relieving them of the growing criticism. For the Government it was a model exercise in keeping foreigners in their place without really trying.

Norton was the obvious man for the job, but his military duties prevented him from accepting, and for similar reasons Geoffrey Bruce was also ruled out. Finch had virtually given up climbing in 1931 after an Alpine accident in which one of his companions was killed, and the other leading figures from previous expeditions were either too old or too immersed in their careers – this was an inevitable penalty following on the high average age of the climbers chosen in the 1920s together with the passing of almost a decade.

Had they been bold, the Committee could have chosen one of the new climbers who had gained Alpine and Himalayan experience since 1924. There was, in fact, an obvious candidate for the job – Francis Sydney Smythe.

Frank Smythe had sprung into prominence as a mountaineer in the seasons of 1927 and 1928 when with Graham Brown he had made two new climbs on the Brenva Face of Mont Blanc: the first breaches in a vast wall of ice and rock, and perhaps the greatest British contribution to Alpinism between the two world wars. Following on this success Smythe was invited to join G.O. Dyhrenfurth's International Expedition to Kangchenjunga in 1930, when he reached the summit of Jongsong Peak (24,344 ft). A year later he led his own expedition on the ascent of Kamet (25,447 ft) – the first peak over 25,000 ft to be climbed.

Smythe, then thirty-two, was obviously a voice to be listened to and a man to be reckoned with, but he was a man the Committee had been watching for some time and despite his brilliant record there was something about him which they didn't altogether like or approve.

Curiously enough he had been considered for the 1922 expedition, at the astonishingly young age of twenty-two, but Somervell's report to the Committee had downed him:

> A bad mountaineer, always slipping and knocking stones down and an intolerable companion. Nobody in our party could stick him for more than a few days, owing to his irritating self-sufficiency. However, he is a very good goer for his age (?23 or 24) and carries on well without getting tired himself though his incessant conversation makes others tired.[4]

Raymond Greene, who was a close friend, reckoned Smythe was the only man he knew whose temper improved with altitude; off the mountain he certainly had a reputation for irritability, tactlessness and being easily offended. His was in fact a classic case of the massive inferiority complex being over-compensated for – he was a frail-looking man, and had suffered as a child from over-protective parents. No good at formal games, not a good scholar, he felt himself physically and intellectually inferior to his contemporaries – and he spent the rest of his life proving the opposite. It was the springboard for his climbs and for his writing; Smythe was a successful writer and photographer of the mountain world. In terms of popularity he was possibly the most successful mountain writer Britain has ever known.

None of this went down well with the Committee. The fact that Smythe lived off his writing made him next best thing to a professional mountaineer, which in their view was not something to be encouraged. More than that, however, he had been one of the Committee's most constant critics in the years before 1933, and had even gone to the extent of applying to the authorities for his own private expedition to Everest. Moreover, he had sent the Committee a list of suggestions for 'the proper organization of a future Mount Everest expedition' – a rather tactless document to present to people like Bruce, Longstaff and Norton.

There is nothing in the records to show that Smythe's name was ever seriously canvassed as leader of the 1933 expedition or that he himself ever thought he should be leader, but privately at least it must have been discussed, and dismissed. The Committee wanted Smythe all right, but not as leader. For that they wanted a good safe man, and preferably an old India hand. They chose Hugh Ruttledge.

Hugh Ruttledge was forty-eight years old, an ex-Commissioner from the Indian Civil Service, and in no sense a mountaineer. It is true that during his time at Almora, in the foothills of the Himalaya, he had made a number of adventurous forays into the mountains and had even penetrated into Tibet, but they were journeys of exploration, done with his wife, not attempts on peaks or passes. He was known to Somervell, who had accompanied him on one of his trips, to Longstaff and of course to General Bruce, who knew everybody. It was Bruce who nominated Ruttledge for the job.

Probably nobody was more surprised than Ruttledge himself. 'He felt that he had had greatness thrust upon him,' as Jack Longland later wrote.[5] He had the advantage of Himalayan travel, a knowledge of the native people and a command of their tongues, but his age, his limp (occasioned by a pig-sticking accident) and his self-effacing modesty were not the qualities looked for in great leaders. He came to the task at a difficult moment, following the long pause in activity after Mallory's death, when a thrusting group of post-war climbers were hammering at the doors of the Alpine establishment but when effective power still remained in the hands of the Victorian mountaineers.

Ruttledge, at first unaware of the conflicting passions, was the man in the middle. 'It was unfair on Ruttledge, and perhaps on us, to ask him to lead that particular expedition,' wrote Longland.[6]

Whatever the young climbers may have thought about Ruttledge's appointment they kept any criticism to themselves; most were too anxious to be chosen for the team to upset the apple-cart. From the Committee's point of view he was just the man they wanted: malleable.

His first task was to prepare a list of proposed members of the expedition – something which was obviously beyond him since he knew little of the climbing world. The choice was in fact made by the Committee, and they decided on a party of twelve or thirteen, *all* of whom (*'except possibly the leader'*: Minute Book) should be capable of going high on the mountain. Two were to double as medical officers.

Three previous Everesters were included: Noel Odell and E.O. Shebbeare of the 1924 expedition and Colin Crawford of the 1922 expedition. Odell's capacity for acclimatization was proven beyond doubt and 'Ferdie' Crawford was an experienced rock climber, and although forty-three years old, was well built and had recently completed some difficult climbs in the Rockies with Odell. Crawford's contribution to the 1922 expedition had been less than was expected. 'Crawford's great powers were neglected sadly almost up to the end of the expedition – a crime for which I was chiefly responsible,' wrote Strutt – possibly the stern, unbending Strutt did not appreciate the clowning to which Crawford was addicted.[7] Crawford's medical report was poor but he just scraped through. At forty-nine, Shebbeare was the oldest man in the team, but he was chosen for his great ability as transport officer. He had served in the same capacity in 1924 and had done such a good job that Paul Bauer chose him for the German expeditions to Kangchenjunga in 1929 and 1931. Like Ruttledge and Crawford, Shebbeare was an Indian Civil Service man.

But the core of the expedition was Frank Smythe and his Kamet team: Eric Shipton, E. St J. Birnie and Dr Raymond Greene, who was to act as chief medical officer.[8]

Apart from Smythe himself, Shipton, who was then twenty-five, was the most exciting prospect: he had crammed into a twelve-month period of frenzied activity the Ruwenzori, Kilimanjaro, the first traverse of Mount Kenya and the ascent of Kamet. He was at the time a planter in Kenya, but he was destined to become one of the greatest mountain explorers of the century. The 1933 expedition was in a sense Shipton's launch pad and Everest itself was eventually to prove both the touchstone of his genius and his greatest disappointment.[9]

Two other climbers with Himalayan experience were invited: George Wood-Johnson, who had been on Kangchenjunga with Dyhrenfurth's international expedition in 1930, and Hugh Boustead, who had climbed in Sikkim and was a soldier-adventurer then in charge of the Sudan Camel Corps.

None of the rest of the team had Himalayan experience, but they were all fine alpinists: Percy Wyn Harris, who had traversed Mount Kenya with Shipton; Jack Longland, ace rock climber and known as an advocate of Mallory's ridge route on Everest; T.A. Brocklebank, the inevitable rowing blue; and Dr W. McLean, who was to act as Raymond Greene's assistant.

All passed their medical, but in November Odell was forced to withdraw for business reasons and his place was taken by Lawrence Wager, an old climbing partner of Longland's who had been to Greenland with the explorer Gino Watkins.[10]

It was indeed a strong expedition that Ruttledge commanded, one of the most powerful and talented teams ever to attempt Mount Everest.[11]

Socially there was little to distinguish the members of the 1933 expedition from those of its predecessors. The climbers came from the same class that had traditionally provided the membership of the Alpine Club for three quarters of a century: the well-to-do middle classes, with a background of Oxbridge and a decent sprinkling of Army officers and Government officials. Ruttledge recalled that applications to join the expeditions were received from 'pugilists, a barber, and a steeplejack' – thereby implicitly inviting his readers to scoff at such notions as preposterous.

It is doubtful whether the Committee even knew there existed a body of climbers whose horizons were the bleak moors around Sheffield rather than the Georgian porticos of South Audley Street, and probably ignorance rather than snobbery kept small the corpus from which selection was made. In any case no working-class climber could afford to take the time off to go to the Himalaya. So the gulfs were practical as much as social.

Nevertheless, by 1933 associated changes were taking place within the ambit of the expedition organization. A much more professional approach was made to the venture. In the first place the burden of work was lifted from the shoulders of Hinks and placed on those of a paid Secretary who had been recruited for the job: J.M. Scott, who had been with Wager in Greenland. For the first time, too, there was a good deal of support in kind from firms supplying goods to the expedition either free or at reduced prices: steps along the road to sponsorship.

The Committee had at their disposal some £5,000, but another £7,000 or so were needed to see the expedition financially secure. After their experiences in 1924 it is hardly surprising that the idea of an expedition film was vetoed.[12] However, there were still the newspaper and book rights, and these were put in the hands of a sub-committee consisting of Leo Amery, Sir Francis Younghusband and Sir J. Withers, who enlisted the aid of Christy and Moore, literary agents. By tradition, of course, Everest books were published by Arnold and newspaper rights went to *The Times*, but the agents changed that – Hodder and Stoughton paid £3,000 for the book, and, more surprising, the *Daily Telegraph* secured the newspaper rights by paying £3,500 plus a percentage of receipts. What Arnold thought of this nobody knows, the *The Times* was furious. It immediately transferred its interests to the proposed Houston flight over Everest, which occasioned some acrimonious correspondence between Geoffrey Dawson, the editor, and Hinks.[13]

Although Smythe's party had made the ascent of Kamet in 1931 it was the Germans who had been tackling the really big peaks in the years prior to 1933, especially Kangchenjunga and Nanga Parbat, and though they had not reached the summit of either they had accumulated considerable high-altitude experience, particularly with regard to equipment. The Committee suggested that Ruttledge should visit Paul Bauer in Germany and pick his brains, but Ruttledge declined, preferring to rely on Smythe's experience and native British inventiveness.

There had been some advances made in mountaineering gear during the decade since the last Everest expedition, but hardly anything significant. Rope still meant the Alpine Club rope of Messrs Beales, as it had done for fifty years or more, and the expedition took 2,000 ft of it, plus a similar amount of less expensive rope for general use (the fixed ropes of the North Col used up a thousand feet of this).

It is fair to say that technical gear, in the climbing sense, was of little account in the expedition planning, though Crawford made a special visit to Austria to buy a stock of ice axes and crampons, mainly for use by the porters – the climbers had their own preferences. What concerned them much more was the cold conditions they expected to encounter, and particularly the notorious Everest winds. Windproof clothing of Grenfell and similar cloths were designed, and the Sherpas were provided with windproof canvas overalls. Shetland pullovers provided the warmth beneath the shell clothing: Finch's earlier excursions into duvet seem to have been forgotten or ignored.

Each climber had three types of boots: a general trekking boot, for the march across Tibet and glacier work up to Camp III; a sheepskin-lined boot not unlike a flying boot, made by Morlands and meant for camp comfort; and high-altitude boots designed by Robert Lawrie which were specifically intended to prevent frostbite. To achieve this Lawrie lined the boots with felt and put a layer of asbestos between the outer and inner soles. The outer soles were of leather, lightly nailed round the edge with iron nails called 'clinkers' – the cleated rubber sole specially designed for climbing had not yet made its appearance.

The principal tentage of the expedition was a modified Meade pattern – a sturdy two-man ridge tent which, for general mountaineering, had replaced the heavier Whymper tent of earlier years.[14] An innovation, however, was a special framed tent of igloo shape, made by the firm of Camp and Sports. Double-skinned with Jacqua material:

> It had eight curved struts, jointed in the middle to make easy porterage, a sewn-in ground-sheet, which was supplemented later by a separate ground-sheet made by the Hurricane Smock Company, lace-up doors, two mica windows, and a ventilating cowl which could be turned in any direction according to the wind. In addition to guy-ropes there was an outer flap which could be weighted down with snow or stones. The tent accommodated six men in reasonable comfort at night. Many more could squeeze in for the day.[15]

Raymond Greene, with typical irreverence, described it as looking like a plum pudding without the sprig of holly. Nevertheless, the three the expedition took with them served them well, especially at Camp III. The idea of such a structure does not seem to have survived this period and was not to return until, in modified form, it reappeared as the Whillans Box, long after the Second World War.

Among the more unusual items of equipment were three sixty-foot rope ladders presented to the expedition by the Yorkshire Ramblers' Club (a noted caving and climbing club), one of which proved invaluable on the ice wall of the North Col.

It was inevitable that the oxygen question should be raised again, though it did not seem to arouse the same passions as formerly. Most members were vaguely against it on purely aesthetic grounds, but nobody seems to have expressed strong opinions one way or the other. The apparatus was redesigned by Greene, who made it simpler and achieved an all-up weight of only 12¾ lb. In the event, it was never used by the climbers, though it was used medically.[16]

Nevertheless, the Committee recognized that living in the high, thin air of Everest did have its problems, not least of which was the tendency for climbers to develop a severe sore throat. Somervell, it will be recalled, almost died of this in 1924. The answer in 1933 was the Matthews Respirator, developed by Bryan Matthews at Cambridge. Matthews pointed out that 15–25 per cent of body heat production was lost through the respiratory system, and that in rarefied air there was not sufficient oxygen to replace the heat loss. To combat this, the cylinder of his respirator consisted of fine copper mesh which absorbed the heat from the air breathed out and passed it to the cold air coming in. At the same time the interstices of the mesh held moisture condensed from the outgoing breath, and this too was taken up by the incoming air. The result was that the wearer breathed warm moist air instead of cold dry air: his body heat improved and the cause of the sore throat disappeared. Nevertheless, the device proved unpopular, mainly on psychological grounds (the same resistance to any sort of protective mask is well known in industry).

As far as food was concerned the choice was much the same as before, ranging from basic pemmican (eaten mostly by the porters – the climbers couldn't stomach it) to delicacies from Fortnum and Mason's. Raymond Greene described it thus:

> The principles which govern the choice of a well-balanced diet are becoming generally known. But where the safety of an expedition over a long period is involved, it is as well for the menus to be overhauled by an expert. The last expedition was well served by Dr Zilva, of the Lister Institute. It was not Dr Zilva's fault that a diet which looked well on paper tasted less well in the mouth. In fact, one of the most popular food-stuffs was the concentrated lemon juice suggested by him as an antiscorbutic. But the diet must not only contain a well-balanced mixture of fats, proteins and carbohydrates, arranged to give the necessary number of calories and containing the necessary minerals and accessory food substances. It must be palatable. Former parties, fighting their way unacclimatized and in poor health up the slopes of Mount Everest, found that from the North Col upwards their appetites deteriorated. The 1933 party, well acclimatized and in robust health, retained its appetite, but became fastidious. Unlike our forbears, we were not prepared to live on condensed milk, jam and acid drops. We wanted meat, cut off the joint, and two veg. Urgent messages were daily sent to the harassed party at Camp III, and by them passed on by wireless to the Base, demanding mutton and ham and eggs. At Camp IV men dreamed, with childlike blissful smiles on their brown and hairy faces, of steak and onions and roly-poly pudding, while the more fiery spirits emptied into the crevasse tin after tin of a peculiarly loathsome tinned-meat ration, unpalatable at any height and inedible when great altitude had made gourmets of us all. At Camp VI Shipton, almost dumb with laryngitis, was heard to whisper hoarsely, 'Oh, for a few dozen eggs.'[17]

Greene was equally scathing about the medical supplies proposed by Ruttledge and wrote to his leader:

> McLean and I, with howls of laughter, have been through the list of medical stores . . . It reads like a sale list of a practitioner who has at the age of ninety-seven at last decided to retire.[18]

All these subjects – gear, oxygen, food – had been gone over in great detail by previous expeditions and in general the expedition of 1933 simply copied their forbears, adding such little improvements as experience or the whims of the moment dictated. There was only one significant acknowledgement of the march of science: the expedition took with them a radio and telephone 'network'. This was the gift of Mr D.S. Richards, a radio enthusiast, and was operated by him and four members of the Royal Corps of Signals, two of whom, E.C. Thompson and W.R. Smyth-Windham, accompanied the expedition into Tibet. Smyth-Windham, in fact, though no mountaineer, eventually reached the North Col.[19]

It was the first time that radio communication had been tried in a Himalayan expedition, and part of Richards' motive was to see whether it was possible to use radio in such a wild area, and whether trans-Himalayan communication was possible. The principal transmitters and receivers were made by Standard Telephone & Cables, and supplemented at Camp III by a McMichael four-valve superhet, a gift of the McMichael Company. This was long before 'walkie-talkies' and today's transistor models were thought of, and the apparatus was very heavy – the transmitter at Base Camp, for example, required six twelve-volt acid batteries, plus a charging unit.

The network consisted of transmitters and receivers at Darjeeling, Base Camp and Camp III, with a telephone line extension up to the North Col. Despite the long, rough journey across Tibet, the apparatus worked well and Ruttledge found it possible to send messages to the Committee in London and receive a reply within twenty-four hours. Equally important, the expedition could be kept informed of the progress of the monsoon.

The radio was also used as a morale booster. B.B.C. overseas programmes were heard at Base Camp (stern discipline dictated that they were too late in the evening for Camp III) and a sort of 'Forces Favourites' was established by relaying gramophone music from Base to Camp III and even, on one occasion, over the phone to the North Col![20]

The expedition assembled in Sikkim towards the end of February and then began the long journey through the Chumbi valley and across the windblown plateau of Tibet, following the now traditional route of Everest expeditions. As a journey it was not particularly unpleasant, and the members came through it with fewer illnesses than previously.

They did, however, suffer the loss of some gear through theft – several pairs of high-altitude boots for Sherpas, a Meade tent, and sundry other items, including part of the liquor store. The local Dzongpen was informed and suspicion fell upon four transport drivers who were convicted and given a hundred lashes each, with rawhide whips.

> The punishment was administered by two men, one on either side of the victim whose trousers were stripped; after every ten or fifteen lashes there was a pause and the accused's hair and ears were pulled while he was told to produce the missing articles.[21]

But they were never recovered, the men receiving their punishment with stoical indifference. Smythe reckoned the stolen goods were worth about £100, which was equivalent to a fortune in Tibet, and doubtless the thieves thought the prize was worth a few lashes. By Tibetan standards the sentence was light.

Petty theft had always been a feature of Everest expeditions – notably from mail sent from Base Camp by runners – but not on this scale. What it highlights is the great temptations huge expeditions put in the way of these impoverished peoples – an ugly symbol of the economic effects they had on the country through which they passed. After all, there were a hundred or so men and three times as many beasts forming a mile-long column travelling through a sparsely inhabited and far from fruitful land where economic stability had settled centuries earlier at an appropriately low level. Transport animals, chickens, eggs, maize – all these goods were required by the expedition, who were immensely rich by local standards, and willing to pay good prices. The local officials, the Dzongpens, forced the population to provide the goods, despite the fact that it would upset the local economy. The Dzongpens were acting under the Dalai Lama's instructions, as laid out in the passport which every expedition carried, but even had they not been commanded to do so, the local Tibetans, born traders, would certainly have sold the stuff anyway, and let the later consequences go hang. The temptation was too great, and still is in similar remote mountain areas.

The thieving transport men were merely an excessive symptom of a general disease. The corrupting influence which expeditions had on the Tibetans did not go unnoticed by thoughtful mountaineers in Europe, and it was one of the factors which led, albeit temporarily, to a change in strategy after 1933.

Base Camp was established near Rongbuk on 17 April, which was twelve days earlier than in 1924. The plan was to build up the camps fairly slowly, partly for more thorough acclimatization and partly so that the climbers would not be exhausted, or even fatigued, by the preliminaries to the detriment of the final assault. This was fine in its way, and worked well in fact, but there can be dangers in the lethargy produced by underwork. Shipton, already inwardly rebelling against the whole paraphernalia of large expeditions, commented that one of the greatest dangers was contracting bed sores.

Camp III, at 21,000 ft and lying on the old site below a shoulder of Changtse, was established on 2 May. At once it was obvious to the climbers that there had been considerable changes to the North Col slopes since the earlier expeditions. The right-hand or northern slope, where there had existed the ice chimney climbed by the 1924 party, had become a smooth, steep ice slope, threatened from above by ice walls which peeled off into avalanches, sweeping the slopes below. On the left, the way up was barred by huge ice bulges which were far too difficult to climb at that altitude, and could never be made into a route for laden porters.

The only way was right up the middle – the dangerous route taken in 1922 when seven porters were avalanched to their deaths. But it too was changed. A large crevasse ran across the middle of the slope and above it was a forty-foot ice wall. The North Col ledge, which had provided such a comfortable camp site for the earlier expeditions, was above the ice wall, but now 200 ft below the col itself. Apart from the constant danger of being swept away by avalanches the main problems were the great crevasse and the ice wall. Could the former be crossed or the latter climbed?

For a fortnight, efforts to climb to the col were frustrated by bad weather. Eleven climbers had assembled at Camp III as the days had gone by, but all they could do was make futile forays during the short periods of fine weather, cut a few steps up the col slopes and then retreat in the face of a fresh storm. Within hours the work they had done was undone by the elements and so each attempt meant starting all over again.

Even in the brief periods of fine weather they could see the wind whipping the snow from the col itself. Much to their surprise and chagrin, though the wind came from the west, as usual on Everest, the fact that they were on the east or leeward side of the col made no difference. Instead of being sheltered, as they had a right to expect, they found that the wind came over the col then veered downwards, hammering the glacier bowl at the head of the East Rongbuk Glacier. 'The mountain,' wrote Smythe, 'reeked and smoked like a volcano; the embodiment of elemental fury.'[22]

That was the good weather. But conditions were often so bad that the climbers scarcely ventured out of their tents, or even out of their sleeping bags. On 6 May Smythe's diary began: 'Another bloody day.'[23]

However, during a lull in the bad weather, Ruttledge took the opportunity of establishing an intermediate camp – IIIa – at the foot of the North Col, just out of avalanche danger. When the opportunity came for a proper attack on the col, Camp IIIa would save a tiring preliminary trudge for the climbers by being that much nearer the objective.[24]

Illnesses of various kinds had struck the party almost as soon as Base Camp had been reached. Crawford had bronchitis, Wyn Harris flu, Wager diarrhoea and Thompson a suspect heart. Though all of them gradually recovered, the party was constantly plagued by the 'high-altitude throat' which had characterized the earlier Everest attempts.

As the days wore on the climbers became increasingly depressed. There had never been such a continuous period of bad weather on any Everest expedition, and all the time they had gained on the march in was being blown away in the gusting winds of the East Rongbuk. Desperately they talked of snatching a victory in a brief period of fine weather: of a dash, without porters and each man carrying his own gear, for the top. It was a futile plan, but at least it helped to while away the hours.

One of the problems of climbing snow slopes in a period of unsettled weather is that time must be allowed for any fresh snow to consolidate after it has fallen. To do otherwise is to invite destruction by avalanche. This means that if there is a fine day following on a day of heavy snowfall, it may be frustratingly dangerous to climb. Such a day was 10 May, but when the fine weather continued on the next morning Smythe led a party onto the slopes of the col to see what condition the snow was in. They found it bad: loose fresh snow lying on ice – the ideal conditions for a wind slab avalanche. After climbing a short distance with growing concern, they made a judicious retreat.

On the 12th, conditions were better and the weather still held its promise, so they set out again – Smythe, Shipton, Boustead and Wager with a couple of porters. They climbed steadily up the steepening slopes to where the big crevasse cut across the face. There they rested, and were joined by Longland who had followed their steps.

Fortunately, the crevasse was bridged at one point by a mass of hardened snow, presumably the remnants of some old avalanche. Above this bridge nature had carved out a bowl in the ice, the upper lip of which was a forty-foot ice wall, perpendicular in part or even overhanging. It looked a tough climb, but it was the only possible way ahead. On either side of the bowl, the ice reared in hundred-foot walls, overlooking the crevasse.

Smythe and Shipton advanced into the bowl. At one point they were surprised to see the end of an old rope projecting from an ice wall – a remnant of 1922 or 1924, and now embedded fifty feet below the surface where it had once lain.

Smythe attacked the forty-foot wall and found that it was tough, rubbery ice of the worst sort. Instead of splintering, as normal ice does when struck by an ice axe, it just gripped the pick of the axe, which had then to be wrenched out, ready for the next blow. It was slow and fatiguing work.

When at last Smythe had fashioned his first step he found he couldn't stand in it without a balancing hand from Shipton, the wall was so steep. Longland and Wager arrived at this point and the former produced a piton from his rucksack. Though the piton was designed for rock, not ice, it was better than nothing and Smythe hammered it into place above his head. By means of a karabiner he attached the rope to the piton, and so, providing the piton stayed in the ice, he was supported by a pull from above.

He described what happened next:

> With my left foot well planted in one step, I cut another step to the right above the overhanging bulge large enough for both feet. The difficulty now was to get first the right and then the left foot across to this step. But first of all a rest was essential as I was panting so rapidly that I felt quite dazed; also, in addition to foot-holds I had cut hand-holds and my hands were losing sensation. At the foot of the wall I soon recovered breath, energy and circulation. Then, feeling better, I set off again, but found that the only way of reaching the new step was to stand on the piton with my right foot. This was by no means easy in the broad, clumsy, high-altitude boot, and at my

> first attempt my foot slipped and, being now without support from above, I was within an ace of toppling off backwards. Fortunately my left hand-hold and foot-hold prevented this, though the shortness of breath due to such an unexpected exertion nearly caused me to come off anyway. A second attempt was successful, and once both feet were on the capacious hold the worst was accomplished.[25]

Above this the ice slope relented to 70°, but was plastered with snow which had to be brushed away by a gloved fist before steps could be cut. As Smythe remarked later, it was savage going.

Eventually he reached a safe belay place and brought up Shipton on the rope. Panting at every step they continued up the slope to the great ledge, which was the only possible place for Camp IV. They found it to be a hump-backed ice shelf, which was the lower lip of a crevasse, ninety feet long and sixteen wide. It was backed by a thirty-foot ice wall. On this shelf there would eventually be two frame tents, a Meade and a porters' bell tent.[26]

It was almost certainly the same ledge that the 1922 and 1924 expeditions had used – only now, owing to the constant movement of the ice, it was at least 200 ft below the col proper.

A storm was brewing. The others had not followed Smythe and Shipton beyond the crevasse, but had begun fixing ropes in the lower part of the route. The two climbers began a swift retreat as the snowflakes began to swirl and the cold became intense. They abseiled down the ice wall to the bowl, then, helped by the fixed ropes, made a thankful descent to Camp IIIa. The way to Camp IV was open.

Nevertheless the situation was not very rosy. Sherpas who should have come over from Khumbu to help the expedition were held up by heavy snows on the high passes, while the persistent illnesses which had plagued the team since Base Camp continued. Ruttledge and Shebbeare, the two oldest men, had both come up to Camp II but were obviously feeling the altitude and had, like most, the Everest laryngitis. Greene, who had been lucky to escape serious accident in a glacier tumble a few days earlier, ordered them down. Various others in the team were either poorly acclimatized or suffered from laryngitis. More serious than any of these, however, Wood-Johnson was suffering severe stomach pains which proved to be due to a gastric ulcer. He had been one of those expected to take part in the final assault, but that was now out of the question.

On the 13th Longland and Wager fixed up a caving ladder so that porters could climb the ice wall. That evening the bad weather returned, but next day, though conditions were not perfect, Shipton, Smythe, Boustead and Birnie led twelve laden porters to the site of Camp IV at 22,800 ft then returned to IIIa. Good news greeted them on their return – forty-six Sherpas had joined the expedition from the Khumbu. The bad news was that the monsoon had reached Ceylon – there was only ten days, or at best a fortnight, before it reached Everest. It was early.

Though the monsoon is the limiting factor in planning an Everest expedition, in that one goes before or after it because it guarantees bad weather, it is not the only bad weather that strikes the mountain. Both the 1924 and 1933 expeditions suffered long periods of storm during the pre-monsoon period, for, like other great mountains, Everest can make its own weather.

On the night of 14 May storms battered Camp IIIa, threatening to destroy the frame tent and its inhabitants. When the wind finally abated at 10 o'clock next morning Smythe, Shipton, Boustead, Birnie and Wyn Harris set off for Camp IV with a dozen laden porters. After an unpleasant climb – the wind was still fairly rough – they set up camp on the ice ledge and the porters descended to Camp IIIa. Camp IV was finally established.

Supplies were ferried up to Camp IV next day and eleven porters remained there. There were now sixteen men on the ice ledge and the build-up for the assault was beginning at last.

Because of its situation, tucked away on its ledge with its protecting ice wall, Camp IV was a much more sheltered place than the lower Camp IIIa. The storms that began that night – the 16th – and continued to the 20th had far less effect on the upper camp than they had on the lower one, where Greene and his companions were for a time literally fighting for their lives. Years later, in his typical tongue-in-cheek style, Greene wrote:

> We lay in the comfortable arctic tent like pips in a gigantic cantaloupe. In the evening the hurricane returned. Once or twice in the night I woke to find the tent swaying ominously. At two o'clock there was a resounding crash and the side of the tent fell in. Longland, who had very virtuously insisted on sleeping in his own leaky Meade tent to leave more room for the rest of us, slept on undisturbed. The remaining four of us sat up and looked at one another with a wild surmise. We knew that if we could not erect the tent again it was the end of us. In such cold and in such a gale survival would have been impossible. With no word spoken, Wager and I climbed out into the night. It was fairly light but bitterly cold. The moon and stars were partially obscured by light clouds scudding violently across a dark blue sky. The mountains stood around vaguely self-illuminated. The wind was so strong that we could hardly stand. Knee-high for me, shoulder-high for the shorter Wager, a thick layer of driven snow raced horizontally, so that only his head was visible, apparently decapitated. All the guys of the tent had given way, but after an hour they were replaced and the tent was secure though lop-sided. After this unpleasing interruption I slept uninterruptedly till seven o'clock.[27]

At the upper camp, on the other hand, life could be tedious. On the day after Greene had had his night-time struggle with the tent, Smythe wrote:

> Life was very boring. I amused myself with a minute examination of my face in a small pocket mirror. It had been wrecked by sun and wind. Where my beard did not protect it, the skin could be pulled off in large flakes, and my ears were beyond all hope of immediate repair. My nose was moderately sound except for the edges of the nostrils, which were raw and sore, whilst the constant need to wear woollen sweaters had saved my neck. In the matter of lips, I was more fortunate than most, and by dint of constant greasing I had saved them from cracking too disastrously, but some of my companions had oozing crevasses and bergschrunds which were painful to contemplate. Worst of all it had become a habit with me during the night to remove scabs when half asleep, so that old cracks were being constantly reopened and were not getting a chance to heal.[28]

On the 18th, though the weather was still too bad for a relief party to climb the North Col slopes, it later became calm enough for the men at Camp IV to ascend the remaining few hundred feet to the crest of the col itself. Despite the weather, bit by bit the expedition was making progress.

On the following day Smythe and Shipton reconnoitred the ridge and contact with the lower camps was re-established by the arrival of Wager and Longland with porters carrying additional stores and the tents for Camps V and VI. The weather seemed on the mend, and on the 20th Camp IV became a hive of activity: at 8.45 Wyn Harris. Birnie, and Boustead, with eleven porters, started up the ridge to establish Camp V, while no fewer than five climbers came up from IIIa: Greene, Wager, Longland, Crawford and Brocklebank, shepherding porters in an impressive build-up of men and materials.

But the bad weather they had experienced during the previous fortnight had taken a greater toll than anyone realized. Frustration and petty illnesses had built upon the natural antipathy one has for one's fellow men at high altitudes and it needed only a spark to set light to the powder keg. That spark came on the very day that things seemed to be going so well, 20 May, and it was struck by Bill Birnie.

In any large expedition there is not only an official hierarchy, duly appointed, such as Leader and Deputy Leader, but a more subtle unofficial one based on the experience and personalities of the team. Doug Scott has referred to it in shop-floor terms as the 'us and them' syndrome; Raymond Greene, speaking specifically of the 1933 team, called it 'a definite pecking order'.[29]

In this pecking order, Birnie stood quite high. Shebbeare had been made Deputy Leader by Ruttledge, but Shebbeare was fifty years old and after his illness at Camp III he never went higher than Camp II again during the whole expedition. 'Birnie tacitly assumed responsibility,' wrote Greene, 'and nobody argued.'[30] Boustead, a soldier like Birnie, certainly thought the latter was in command. The others had probably given the matter little thought and were glad enough to leave the organization of Sherpas and loads to Birnie.

On 20 May, then, Wyn Harris, Birnie and Boustead, with eleven porters, struggled up the ridge in an effort to establish Camp V. The day was perfect but for the usual cold wind, and those who were watching progress from Camp IV expected no problems. Camp V was earmarked for 25,500 ft, but a thousand feet short of this target the party stopped, dumped their loads and started to descend. The observers were astounded and concerned: they felt something must have gone seriously wrong.

The porters, in great fettle, came bounding back down the ridge, followed by Wyn Harris and later by Birnie and a tired-looking Boustead. What had happened, apparently, was that Birnie had decided the porters had had enough, in the cold wind, and had ordered the retreat. Boustead had acquiesced in this, but Wyn Harris was furious and there had been a violent disagreement. Wyn Harris was for pushing on and establishing the camp as planned, but Birnie overruled him.

Back in the tent that night there was an almighty row, with accusations flying thick and fast and ranging far beyond the initial cause. All the pent-up frustrations of high-altitude living in bad weather burst forth. Perhaps the most frustrated of all was Shipton:

> Nerves were already frayed, and we were all liable to lose our tempers at the slightest provocation and to take our silly grievances sorely to heart. This seems to be a common manifestation of the effects of life at high altitudes. In our case it was undoubtedly aggravated by the rough handling we had received from the weather, and by having been forced to spend so much of our time during the past month cooped up in a tent with too little to do and too much to anticipate. Being unable to speak above a whisper, I found it difficult to quarrel successfully with anyone, and it would have been too exhausting an attempt to pull my opponent's beard. Had I been psycho-analysed at the time, I would no doubt have been found to be suffering from some fierce repressions.[31]

On the next day Ruttledge himself went up to Camp IV and held what was virtually a court martial. Normally the most mild-mannered of men, he was very angry and reprimanded both Birnie and Boustead. The latter apologized, but Birnie stormed out of the meeting in a temper. Two days had been lost, and in Greene's opinion it cost the expedition the chance of success. Meanwhile Smythe and Shipton climbed 1,500 ft up the ridge 'for exercise'.

Next day, 22 May, another attempt was made to establish Camp V. It was the same party as before, with the addition of Greene. Ruttledge put Wyn

1. The path to Everest is now followed by hundreds of trekkers every year. The great peak of Ama Dablam dominates the scene. (Walt Unsworth)

(*Facing page*)
2. Deep in the Khumbu, peak rises on peak in a wonderland of mountains. This is the Kangtega group. (Walt Unsworth)

(*Above*)
3. The head of the Khumbu Valley is a wasteland dominated by a ring of icy mountains. Left to right the peaks are Pumori, Lingtren and Khumbutse. (Walt Unsworth)

(*Above*)
4. Hillary (right) and Tenzing prepare for their successful ascent, 1953. (George Band)

(*Facing page*)
5. Tenzing on the summit of Everest, May 29th, 1953. The first successful ascent of the world's highest mountain. (Ed Hillary)

(*Facing page, top*)
6. The American expedition of 1963 in the Khumbu Icefall, one of the most dangerous places on the mountain. (Barry C. Bishop © National Geographic Society)

(*Facing page, bottom*)
7. A party on the West Shoulder, reconnoitring the way to the West Ridge in 1963. Later expeditions tackled the ridge from the Lho La. (Barry C. Bishop © National Geographic Society)

(*Above*)
8. Lute Jerstad approaching the summit of Everest along the South East Ridge in 1963. (Barry C. Bishop © National Geographic Society)

9. Phantog (left) leading her party on the ascent of Everest during the Chinese expedition of 1975. (Xinhua News Agency)

Harris specifically in charge. Accompanying them, more for exercise than anything else, were Longland and Wager. Ruttledge himself went as far as the col: throughout the expedition nobody could accuse Ruttledge of leading from behind. He knew his limitations, both physical and technical, but he stretched them to the limit to urge his party on.

The day was calm and clear. The porters romped up the easy ridge and Wager was climbing at the rate of 600 ft per hour. Greene, however, who had only spent one night at Camp IV and was not yet acclimatized, found the going hard. On the way up they came upon Finch's camp of 1922, and though the tent was in shreds, the poles looked bright and new, and some tins of food still lay about, labels as intact as the day they were bought eleven years before. So dry is the atmosphere at that altitude that nothing was affected, nothing rotted. Greene was glad to find some oxygen still in a container Finch had abandoned and took a whiff of it to revive himself, if only for a moment. He also picked up a can of film, thinking it might be of historic interest, but it later proved to have been unexposed.

Camp V was set up at 25,700 ft. The plan had been for Wyn Harris, Greene, Boustead and Birnie to remain there with eight porters for one night, then continue up on the following day and establish Camp VI. Longland had gone back to Camp IV with a sick porter, and now Greene was forced to retire, his place being taken by Wager.

Greene was given charge of the porters who were returning directly to the North Col, but in fact they needed no help on the easy ridge and had soon left the ailing climber behind. Years later Greene wrote a dramatic account of his descent which gives a vivid picture of what utter exhaustion can do to a man at altitude – in his case, a big strong fellow:

> The going was easy to a trained mountaineer, scrambling over rocks about as easy as the Crib Goch ridge on Snowdon, interspersed with patches of snow. But I was a sick man. In every patch of snow I fell over and rested a while. At last in a very comfortable spot, sheltered from the howling wind, I decided that I had had enough. I was warm and comfortable and the view was superb. If I stayed where I was I would fall comfortably asleep. I had no wife or children for whom I could feel responsible: my parents had five other children and, though I knew they would mourn, they would lose only a small proportion of their offspring. I decided to stay.
>
> I am reminded of what sometimes happens in a hot bath on a winter morning at home. One lies there comfortably and there is no hurry to get out. Then suddenly one is out of the bath with no conscious effort to leave it. I do not remember any such effort, but suddenly I was struggling downwards again, falling again in every patch of snow, but rising at once when breath returned. Then below me were the tents of Camp IV bright green against the snow.[32]

On 23 May Smythe and Shipton moved up to Camp V in the teeth of a strong wind. They were hardly surprised to find that nobody had tried to establish the next camp, in view of the conditions, but it did mean someone would have to go down to Camp IV because V wasn't big enough. In the event Wager and Wyn Harris went down.

Camp V comprised two platforms, one some four feet above the other. Each platform accommodated two Meade tents, pitched end on.[33] Besides the porters, the camp now held Birnie, Boustead, Smythe and Shipton.

During the night a storm blew up and raged all through the following day. Smythe and Shipton discussed whether, once the wind dropped, they should abandon the plans for Camp VI and attempt a summit dash from their present position, but any such decision was made unnecessary by the wind rising again on the 25th, forcing a total retreat of the entire party to Camp IV, where they found the tents threatened by avalanche and spent the next day moving them.[34]

There were now eleven climbers at Camp IV, in varying degrees of fitness, which was far too many for practical purposes and only served to make the supply position more difficult, especially as nobody seemed to be suffering any loss of appetite through altitude.[35] To ease matters, Ruttledge, Greene, Crawford and Brocklebank descended to Camp III with the exhausted porters who had established Camp V.

The assault began again on 28 May with Birnie, Longland, Wager and Wyn Harris moving up to Camp V. On the next day, leaving Birnie in charge of the camp to await the arrival of Smythe and Shipton, the other three, with the eight Sherpas, set off to establish Camp VI, which they managed to do half way up the Yellow Band at 27,400 ft – 600 ft higher than in 1924, and about 400 yards nearer the summit, which was 1,600 ft above.

A ledge, nowhere more than three feet wide, sloping outwards and clogged with snow, formed the site for the camp. A modest platform was built on which to raise the tent, but the floor sloped and about a quarter of the tent hung freely over the void of the North Face. Wager and Wyn Harris settled in for the night; Longland took the porters down.

The route which had been followed between Camps V and VI was not an easy one to follow: an indiscriminate line zig-zagging up the featureless acres of slabs that form the North Face. Longland realized that in descent the porters could easily lose their way, especially as they were tired and therefore likely to be careless, and that there was a potential accident waiting to happen. Astutely, he decided not to follow the line of ascent, but to make instead for the North Ridge itself, which should provide an infallible guide.

Hardly had they reached the ridge than a great storm swept up with startling suddenness:

A moment before all had been quiet and peaceful. In a few seconds Nature seemed to go mad. The far horizons vanished as the voice of the wind rose to a scream and the snow tore past in blinding sheets. The effect upon tired men may be imagined. Their world disappeared, their goggles iced up till they had to be discarded, whereupon their eyelashes froze together, making it very difficult to see at all. They were literally fighting for their lives.

Well for them that they had a great leader and a great mountaineer at their head. Longland never faltered though, to use his own words, 'visibility suddenly narrowed to a snowswept circle of some twenty yards, and – I was taking a party of porters down a ridge which I had never been on before, but which I knew to be ill-defined and easy to lose, particularly in such conditions.' He kept his men in close order, and they staggered downwards, leaning sideways against the wind to keep their balance and peering through the storm for a glimpse of the North Peak and the ridge, but seeing nothing beyond the rocks just ahead. Every few minutes they halted to count their numbers, lest someone should be lost or left behind. The men were responding magnificently to example, and not one fell out.

Suddenly, below a little cliff, they came upon a spot of green, Norton's Camp VI of 1924, where Mallory and Irvine spent their last night of life and where Odell came in his great effort to find them. The tent was no longer usable after nine years of exposure, yet it looked surprisingly new. The men, much cheered by this discovery, rummaged about and found a folding candle-lantern and a lever-torch. The latter worked at the first touch. Then they hurried on downwards, for to remain still in these conditions meant death. The storm continued relentlessly.

About 200 ft lower down a terrible thought occurred to Longland. He remembered that, in one of the 1924 photographs of Mount Everest as seen from the Base Camp, the position of that year's Camp VI was marked by an arrow pointing, not to the main north ridge, but to a subsidiary ridge farther to the east. Could it be that he was leading his party straight for the appalling ice-slopes above the East Rongbuk glacier, instead of down the main ridge to Camps V and IV, and safety? It was a dreadful moment, and the worst of it was that he could see no landmark through the flying snow. But he kept his head and watched for the appearance of a great snow couloir, which he knew must be on the left if he were on the wrong ridge. The anxious descent continued slowly, down little snow-covered cliffs and icy screes, reassured to some extent by the invisibility of the couloir. But it was a painful passage. Some of the more exhausted porters were beginning to sit down, unable to face any longer the torture of the wind. They had to be urged to their feet and encouraged to keep on down that doubtful, perhaps fatal ridge, the problem of which the leader had to keep to himself. At last, over a little edge, and not a hundred feet below, appeared a green tent. It was Camp V. Longland had brought his party safe through a test which even Mount Everest could hardly make more severe. He had not enjoyed one care-free moment for two hours.[36]

Two of the exhausted porters remained at Camp V; the rest, after a brief interval, continued down to Camp IV, followed by Longland.[37]

So far the plan was working admirably. On the 30th, Wager and Wyn Harris began their assault from Camp VI, Smythe and Shipton moved up to VI from V, and in support at IV were Longland, Crawford and McLean.

After a poor night of little sleep and a scanty breakfast, Wager and Wyn Harris left the tent at 5.40 a.m. to begin their climb. They traversed diagonally upwards towards the North East Ridge and about an hour later, just as the sun had appeared with its welcoming rays, Wyn Harris, who was leading, came across an ice axe lying on a slab. It could only have belonged to Mallory or Irvine: a poignant reminder of the 1924 tragedy.[38]

Leaving the axe where it lay, to be recovered later, the two men continued their climb, reaching the foot of the First Step, which close acquaintance showed to be two large towers on the ridge. Their thoughts were to turn the First Step and gain the crest beyond it, in other words to follow the route Mallory had always advocated, but they now saw that the ridge itself would be difficult and time-consuming.

At this point the two climbers were at the junction between the Yellow Band, whose slabs they had ascended, and the much steeper grey rock which forms the crest of the ridge and of which the First Step is the terminal tower. So far they had not felt the necessity to rope up, and as they surveyed what lay ahead they could see that the going along the ledge where the Yellow Band met the grey rock was equally easy, and therefore swift.

They traversed along the ledge to a point directly below the formidable Second Step. From a distance they thought they had seen an oblique gully cutting into the Second Step in a north-easterly direction, but this vanished from view as they grew nearer. The step was a formidable cliff which they considered unclimbable – and in any case, consideration of it was academic, because the steep grey limestone separating them from the foot of the cliff was equally unclimbable.

The Second Step was the terminal prow of another band of grey rock lying on top of that which formed the First Step, like two unequal layers in a cake. Wyn Harris and Wager thought that they could see a minor gully cutting up through both bands which would lead to the ridge above the Second Step and so give access to the summit pyramid. Once again they were deceived: the gully proved to be nothing more than a shallow scoop, which disappeared before it reached the crest of the rocks.

Though they were not to know it at the time, by avoiding initial contact with the ridge at the First Step, Wyn Harris and Wager had cut out any possibility of following Mallory's ridge route and were committed to the North Face traverse first attempted by Norton and Somervell. In view, too, of the renewed controversy about the fate of Mallory and Irvine which the discovery of the ice axe provoked, it is important to remember that though Wyn Harris and Wager traversed directly below the Second Step, they did not actually come close enough to it to make a realistic judgement of its difficulty. It is a well-known axiom in climbing that to judge correctly the difficulty of a cliff, one must rub noses with it.

The two men, now roped, found themselves forced to traverse a descending line over increasingly difficult ground, onto the North Face and towards Norton's gully, which lay round a corner some 500 ft away.

Having reached the gully they discovered it to be full of loose powder snow. It was 50 ft wide, and the crossing of it proved sensational, for had it avalanched, or had one of them slipped, they would have fallen 10,000 ft to the Rongbuk Glacier below.

Beyond the gully the rocks were steeper than before, more snowed up because they were more sheltered from the wind, and devoid of any place to belay. Finally they reached a point about 150 ft beyond the gully and 50 ft higher than the top of the Yellow Band, where they halted to review the situation. It was 12.30 p.m. and the summit lay 1,000 ft above – say another four hours of climbing, which would scarcely have left time for a descent to Camp V. Had conditions been good they would undoubtedly have taken the risk and pressed on, but the loose snow covering the rocks and filling the gullies tipped the balance in favour of caution.

Wyn Harris and Wager turned back. They had equalled the height recorded established by Norton in 1924.

Unwilling to retrace the desperate traverse of the morning, the two men took a lower and easier line across the gully and the slabs beyond. This led them back to the foot of the First Step, but by now they were too exhausted to climb up the grey rock and see what the ridge was really like between the two steps. Instead, Wyn Harris retrieved the ice axe from its slab (leaving his own in its place) while Wager crawled to the ridge below the First Step and peered down the tremendous East Face of Everest.

They reached Camp VI at 4 p.m., reported to Smythe and Shipton, then continued on down to Camp V and the waiting Birnie. On the following day they descended to the North Col, and almost met with disaster when Wyn Harris, glissading down some hard snow, suddenly found himself sliding towards a precipice overlooking the East Rongbuk Glacier. Fortunately he managed to use his ice axe as a brake to stop himself and climb back to safety – but it was a near thing and again symptomatic of the tiredness which induces carelessness in 'easy' places.

Meanwhile Smythe and Shipton spent the day stormbound in Camp VI and were unable to begin their attempt until the following morning, 1 June. The intense cold deterred them from starting too early, and it was 7.30 a.m. before they left the tent. Neither was in good shape: they had eaten badly and slept worse, and they had been too high for too long. Right from the outset Shipton felt ill and when they reached a level platform near the foot of the First Step he collapsed, utterly beaten. Encouraging Smythe to go on alone, Shipton returned to Camp VI.

Smythe had no hesitation in choosing Norton's route: the ridge above him looked too formidable and the Second Step seemed impregnable, like 'the sharp bow of a battle cruiser'. He traversed across the slabs and the great gully and, like those who had gone before him, found the rocks beyond the gully too dangerous by half:

> When these slabs are snow-free they are probably not much more difficult than the slabs to the east of the great couloir. There are numerous ledges, and though the general angle is appreciably steeper, there is no necessity for anything but balance climbing, and I confidently believe no insuperable obstacle will prevent the climber from reaching the subsidiary couloir. But now snow had accumulated deeply on the shelving ledges and it was the worst kind of snow, soft like flour, loose like granulated sugar and incapable of holding the feet in position. As I probed it with my axe, I knew at once that the game was up. So far the climbing had been more dangerous than difficult; now it was both difficult and dangerous, a fatal combination on Everest. The only thing I could do was to go as far as possible always keeping one eye on the weather and the other on the strength I should need to retreat safely.[39]

He pushed on gamely, but the psychological pressure brought about by the uncertain dangers and his loneliness eventually grew too strong:

> I was a prisoner, struggling vainly to escape from a vast hollow enclosed by dungeon-like walls. Wherever I looked hostile rocks frowned down on my impotent strugglings, and the wall above seemed almost to overhang me with its dark strata set one upon the other, an embodiment of static, but pitiless, force.[40]

Smythe struggled on a few more feet, reaching roughly the same point as his predecessors before he accepted the inevitable defeat. Norton in 1924, and now Wyn Harris, Wager and Smythe in 1933, had all reached a height of 28,200 ft: a record no Western climbers ever exceeded on the north side of Everest.

The question must be asked: if the climbers had used oxygen would they have succeeded in climbing the mountain in 1933? The condition of the rocks on the far side of the great gully was undoubtedly bad, but were they made insuperable only by the debilitating effects of high altitude? Both Smythe and Shipton have described at length the mental lethargy which altitude invokes, in addition to sheer physical tiredness – a kind of 'couldn't care less' attitude which is both dangerous and at the same time not conducive to the sort of effort needed to climb Everest. Each man who got near the goal in those early years and who turned back felt relief rather than disappointment. Smythe himself later hinted that a man would need more than willpower to get to the top; he would need an inbred determination to succeed springing from his subconscious so that it would drive him on even when willpower faltered. 'Perhaps it is not too much to say that Everest will be climbed in England,' he concluded.[41]

As regards oxygen, Wyn Harris suggested it should be used for the crossing of the couloir and the rocks beyond, along with fixed ropes. Smythe, a romantic purist if ever there was one, was forced to agree that oxygen might have been useful:

> Prior to 1933 there were those to whom the thought of it was abhorrent. I confess to a similar prejudice. There seemed something almost unfair in climbing what was then thought to be an easy mountain by such artificial means. I doubt whether there is a member of the present expedition who now thinks thus, for Everest has been proved to rely for its defence not only on bad weather and altitude, but on its difficulties too; it allows of no latitude; it defends with every means in its power, and its weapons are terrible ones; it is as exacting on the mind as it is on the body. Those who tread its last 1,000 ft tread the physical limits of the world.[42]

George Finch, ever the savage watchdog of the doings of the Everest Committee, was infuriated by the continued non-use of oxygen and by the common belief that oxygen was of no benefit to a naturally acclimatized man: 'a conclusion so aggressively at variance with established fact that even to the unscientific mind it is surely incomprehensible'. Tampering with oxygen, in the way suggested by Wyn Harris, was no good at all in Finch's view:

> This wretched state of indecision about oxygen must be ended, and in good time, too, if the next expedition is to succeed. Either oxygen should be taken and used full blast in the attack above 25,000 or even above 23,000 feet, or it should be utterly tabooed on moral or material grounds, or indeed for any other reason that the wit of man can conceive. And if the prospective Everest committee cannot bring itself to decide one way or the other then sack the lot![43]

Whether in fact oxygen would have given Wyn Harris, Wager or Smythe the necessary strength, physical and mental, to tackle the snowed-up rocks beyond the great gully, there is no means of knowing. The only certainty is that George Finch remained a voice crying in the wilderness.

There can be little doubt that during his return from his solo attempt, Smythe was near to exhaustion. For one thing he descended only as far as Camp VI, and for another he suffered from the delusory experience, common to climbers under stress, of imagining he was accompanied by a partner.

His second experience, however, was less common:

> I was still some 200 feet above Camp VI and a considerable distance horizontally from it when, chancing to glance in the direction of the north ridge, I saw two curious-looking objects floating in the sky. They strongly resembled kite-balloons in shape, but one possessed what appeared to be squat underdeveloped wings, and the other a protuberance suggestive of a beak. They hovered motionless but seemed slowly to pulsate, a pulsation incidentally much slower than my own heart-beats, which is of interest supposing that it was an optical illusion. The two objects were very dark in colour and were silhouetted sharply against the sky, or possibly a background of cloud. So interested was I that I stopped to observe them. My brain appeared to be working normally, and I deliberately put myself through a series of tests. First of all I glanced away. The objects did not follow my vision, but they were still there when I looked back again. Then I looked away again, and this time identified by name a number of peaks, valleys and glaciers by way of a mental test. But when I looked back again, the objects still confronted me. At this I gave them up as a bad job, but just as I was starting to move again a mist suddenly drifted across. Gradually they disappeared behind it, and when a minute or two later it had drifted clear, exposing the whole of the north ridge once more, they had vanished as mysteriously as they came.[44]

Unidentified flying objects in the Himalaya? Knowledge of U.F.O.s was much less common in 1933 than it is today, but Smythe's description of what he saw has a familiar ring to modern readers. Or was it simply the mental state of a tired man under great stress that produced what Raymond Greene called 'Frank's pulsating teapots'?

When Smythe returned exhausted to Camp VI about 12.30 p.m., Shipton, much recovered, volunteered to go down to Camp V. Neither felt able to endure the cramped conditions of the camp for another night: with only one there it might be better. So Shipton set off down at 1.30 p.m. while Smythe sank into an oblivion of fatigue.

Scarcely had Shipton traversed across the slabs to the ridge (everyone now followed Longland's descent route) than, like Longland, he was met by a blizzard that suddenly blew up out of nowhere. The fierceness of the storm was incredible: all he could do was cower behind a boulder till the wind abated, then descend in short rushes between the violent gusts. But in the swirling mist and snow he soon lost all sense of direction, so he found a relatively sheltered nook and waited hopefully for a sign to guide him. Luckily, the mists parted for a moment and revealed the dark spire of Changtse – the North Peak – which enabled Shipton to recover a sense of direction and complete his journey to Camp V, where Birnie, now weak and frostbitten from his long and faithful vigil, was waiting for him.

The next day, after a good night's rest (the only one recorded at Camp VI) Smythe began his descent as soon as the sun came up. He encountered verglas on the slabs, which was unique in Everest experience, and he put it down to extra moisture in the monsoon air, which had now reached the mountain from the Indian plains.[45]

Just as he was reaching easier ground below the Yellow Band, another sudden storm such as had hit Longland and Shipton came roaring in from the north-west and flattened Smythe against the rocks. The force almost tore him from the mountain and the cold was paralysing. Stumbling and sliding, he managed to find a sheltered ledge, and remained there for half an hour, while the wind roared overhead. When at last it slackened a little, he continued his descent and much to his chagrin was just in time to see the distant figures of Birnie and Shipton abandon Camp V. There was nothing for it but to stagger down after them towards the North Col, and hours later it was a thankful Smythe who, almost at the end of his tether, was greeted by Jack Longland who had come up the ridge to meet him, bearing a flask of hot tea laced with brandy.

On 3 June the retreat from Camp IV was, as Smythe described it, 'a descent of broken men'. Though they left some gear at the col in case another attempt was feasible, in their hearts they knew it was a futile gesture. Birnie was in a bad way through frostbite and altitude debilitation, McLean had developed pneumonia, Shipton had lost the power of coherent speech – and other members, lower down the long trail of camps to Base, were in little better shape.

All returned to Base Camp under Greene's orders where a medical check-up took place and where, from those pronounced fit, a further attempt was planned. Men and materials actually went up to Camp III, but to no avail.

Ruttledge found himself in something of a dilemma. The monsoon had arrived and climbing the mountain was no longer possible. On the other hand quite a number of the climbers were still reasonably fit, and one or two – Crawford and Brocklebank, for example – were only just reaching the peak of condition. It seemed a pity to waste such good potential for the want of a few weeks' waiting, especially as the Political Officer in Sikkim had told Ruttledge that the chance of another expedition was slight.[46] Ruttledge therefore proposed to the Committee that he and six or seven of the climbers should recuperate in the Kama valley, then return for another attempt on the mountain in the autumn.[47]

The Committee replied by cable next day:

> Money not available for autumn. Withdraw expedition Darjeeling at your convenience. You have done everything possible. Congratulate all on safe execution hazardous enterprise. We are applying for permission next year. Chairman.[48]

# 8

# 'We Are Beginning to Look Ridiculous'

Ruttledge reported to the Everest Committee on 2 October. It was inevitably the report of a commander whose troops had fought bravely, only to lose the battle. On the positive side, three climbers had gone as high as Man had ever climbed before and there was a fuller appreciation of what was involved in proper acclimatization, even if the thorny nettle of oxygen usage remained ungrasped. There was also a proven nucleus of young climbers capable of reaching the summit given the right conditions.[1] On the other hand, the equipment still left something to be desired and nobody was yet able accurately to predict when the monsoon should strike Everest. Was the monsoon of 1922 late, or were the monsoons of 1924 and 1933 early? Nobody could say for sure.

If the Committee was disappointed it put on a brave face to the world, applied to the authorities for another attempt on the mountain, and asked Ruttledge to lead it. It was a very gentlemanly, even cosy, winding-up of yet another unsuccessful Everest attempt.

But beneath the surface, well hidden from public gaze, an almighty storm was brewing.

The seeds of the storm lay in the successive failures that had now accrued on Everest. Mallory had been right when he said that climbing Everest was more like war than mountaineering – it had indeed become a war of attrition. Amongst the younger climbers, who felt perhaps that the mountain was not all that difficult measured as a technical exercise, there was a feeling of despair and frustration. It seemed obvious to them that the whole business of climbing Everest was being grossly mismanaged.

They looked at the Committee and did not like what they saw there. In the first place they could see no good reason for the presence of the Royal

Geographical Society representatives, since Everest was now purely a technical climbing problem, and in the second place, they thought their own representatives were past it. 'It is difficult to overemphasize the frustration felt by young climbers in the mid-nineteen thirties,' wrote Jack Longland many years later, 'believing, as they did, that the conduct both of the [Alpine] Club and of Everest affairs was largely in the hands of people who had not been near a serious climb for years.'[2] Carrying this to a logical conclusion, there was also a strong feeling that the leader of the next Everest expedition should be a man capable of leading from the front.

And the eye of the storm alighted on Hugh Ruttledge, the mild-mannered, limping non-climber, whose leadership embodied everything the young guard detested.

It was entirely a gut reaction brought on by Ruttledge's indecisiveness. In 1933 there was no evidence that Ruttledge had put a foot wrong, or that if he had acted in any other way the expedition would have been more successful. One can, perhaps, point hesitantly at the Birnie incident, when time was lost in establishing Camp V, and which Greene maintains cost them the summit, but that was hardly Ruttledge's fault, and he rectified the matter immediately with the only real flash of anger ever connected with his name.

Nevertheless, Ruttledge was the scapegoat: he was the chap who was too nice by half to lead such a talented, self-opinionated team as that on Everest in 1933.

'He felt that he had had greatness thrust upon him . . .' wrote Longland:

> I think the trouble was that his qualities of modesty, kindliness and gentleness were not those which easily overcame the difficulty of directing men who in that particular field had experience of a kind that he lacked. He was chosen to lead a group of young men who knew far more about mountaineering than he did. And therefore it was when technical decisions had to be taken which appeared to him to have several equally possible answers that his real dilemma appeared. He worked himself to the verge of collapse preparing for an expedition that was very hastily mounted, and then, during its conduct, found himself listening too continuously and too deprecatingly about the ways in which the problem might be solved. There were too many voices, and, if the voice of personal ambition was rarely raised, and, when raised, as often thoroughly discounted, Hugh Ruttledge found it difficult, in that inevitable Babel, to make up his own mind, and, when he did, he sometimes made it up by a snap decision on evidence that was not the best.[3]

No voices were raised against Ruttledge during the course of the expedition in 1933; it was only during the aftermath, during the cosy acceptance of failure, that the storm broke. Like all such rows it was superficially petty, spiteful and with more than a hint of skullduggery – but the causes went deep.

The last meeting of the 'Old' Mount Everest Committee took place on 15 March 1934, and they considered a letter from Ruttledge expressing his desire to resign the leadership of any future expedition. No reasons are given in the Committee Minute Book, which records only the Committee's regret and the fact that they were prepared to accept the resignation only because of the improbability of obtaining permission for an expedition in 1935. But the Minutes do not relate all that passed at the meeting and consequently are not a true record: in fact Longstaff told the meeting of the criticisms which had been levelled at Ruttledge and of which Ruttledge was by now aware.

Two days previously Ruttledge wrote to Crawford:

> My dear Ferdie,
>
> Tom Brocklebank has written to say, in the nicest possible way, that he can no longer support me in the leadership. He thinks I'm no longer heart and soul in the show. He's wrong about that but I didn't see that anything much could be done until the position was clearer.
>
> Still I understand from T.G.L. that he did not agree with my views and it may be that other members of the party feel the same about it. If so my resignation, which I sent in to the Committee yesterday, will save them and me embarrassment.
>
> The field is now clear. I shall always do anything I can to attain the success we all desire – Yours ever, Hugh.[4]

The letter leaves no doubt that Ruttledge knew what was afoot, and the reference to the field being clear indicates that he knew Crawford had designs on the leadership. It was, on the face of it, a gentlemanly withdrawal to avoid distasteful controversy.

A new Committee was constituted in May. Representing the R.G.S. were Major General Percy Cox, who became Chairman; Kenneth Mason, who had recently retired as Superintendent of the Survey of India to become Professor of Geography at Oxford; and L.R. Wager, who had been on the 1933 expedition. For the Alpine Club there was the redoubtable Colonel Strutt, together with Hugh Ruttledge and Colin (Ferdie) Crawford. Sir Geoffrey Corbett represented the Himalayan Club. Spencer and Hinks continued as joint honorary secretaries, though a few months later Spencer became Treasurer and E.S. Herbert took over as A.C. Secretary. Hinks, of course, remained the real power.

The criticisms of Ruttledge became so clamorous that the new Committee were forced to make official recognition of them. Confidential statements were taken from Smythe, Crawford, Shipton and Wager. Meanwhile, despite his resignation, Ruttledge appeared to act as an expedition leader, even advising on the disposal of surplus equipment to the Himalayan Club.

No doubt the affair would have blown over had it not been for the Tibetans unexpectedly granting permission for another expedition in 1935 or 1936. The Committee decided to send out a light reconnaissance party in the post-monsoon period of 1935 and follow up with a full-scale expedition in the next year. Ruttledge was asked to be leader – and he promptly accepted.

In the back rooms of South Audley Street, all hell broke loose. The offer had been made to Ruttledge out of courtesy for his past services and nobody had expected him to withdraw his resignation. When he did, those who were involved with Everest, whether as administrators or climbers, polarized into two hostile factions, the pro-Ruttledge and anti-Ruttledge groups – and it is fair to say that the anti-Ruttledge group were pro-Crawford. In effect, therefore, it became a struggle between Ruttledge and Crawford, with great reluctance on Ruttledge's part, one feels, and increasing animosity on Crawford's.

Among the members of the 1933 team, Longland, Wager and Brocklebank supported Crawford, while Smythe, Wyn Harris and Shipton supported Ruttledge. Smythe's influential support in particular must have encouraged Ruttledge, but nevertheless he had no stomach for a fight and resigned again – 'I have of course requested the Committee to consider me no further,' he wrote to Crawford, explaining his reluctance.[5]

This placed the Committee in a serious dilemma. They now had to find a replacement for Ruttledge, but were equally determined that it would not be Crawford, whom they regarded as the cause of all the mischief, at best an upstart, at worst a traitor.

One of the criticisms levelled against Ruttledge (presumably stemming from the Birnie affair) was that he failed to maintain adequate discipline and this prompted the Committee to seek a military alternative – thus effectively silencing the criticism and thwarting Crawford at the same time. Ruttledge himself suggested Norton, but Norton was unable to accept. Geoffrey Bruce was also unable to accept, and so was Maj. Gen. R.C. Wilson, a friend of Ruttledge's who was with him in Kumaun in 1926 and who had made a spirited attack on the Tibetan mountain called Kailas in the same year. The Committee, in some desperation, turned in on itself, but both Kenneth Mason and Strutt refused the job.

The decisive Committee meeting took place on 28 March 1935. In desperation the Chairman telephoned Longstaff to ask whether he would lead the expedition, but Longstaff replied that he did not really want to go, and would accept only if all the members of the previous expedition wanted him. Such unorthodox democracy affronted Cox and his colleagues. Corbett said huffily that the leader must select the team, and not the team the leader, while Mason said Longstaff's suggestion smacked of a Soviet. Longstaff's name was promptly dropped.

In a gesture of compromise John Morris's name was hopefully floated by Crawford. Morris had been an excellent transport officer in 1922 but the Committee felt he did not carry enough weight to command an expedition. They were seeking high executive material, and at the time Morris was just an ordinary Major. In any case, one feels they would have regarded any suggestion by Crawford with suspicion.[6]

During all these discussions Ruttledge and Crawford, who were both members of the Committee, were asked to withdraw on several occasions and were absent when Morris's name was abandoned. The Committee were now faced with the only real choice they had ever had – Ruttledge or Crawford. While the two men were absent the others took the opportunity briefly to discuss them, though everyone's position was well known. Strutt said he could not support Ruttledge because Ruttledge did not have the confidence of some of the 1933 party, and he read out a letter from Wager, who was unable to attend the meeting, to the same effect. Both Strutt and Wager thought Crawford would make a good leader. Sir Geoffrey Corbett expressed his opinion that the 1933 expedition failed because of the three days lost at the North Col when Crawford was in charge, and Mason said that he too felt strongly about the North Col incident.

Cox brought up the subject of a Soviet again – and though he was overstating the case, what he really meant, and what the others felt though they didn't say so, was that they did not want the power of the Committee successfully challenged by a bunch of upstart young climbers. And it was the young climbers who mainly supported Crawford. It was the 'us and them' situation all over again. They were the managers and they had no intention of being dictated to by the shop floor.

At the same time Cox and his colleagues could not afford to ignore Crawford altogether, as they would dearly loved to have done. There were powerful Alpine Club factions who supported him – including, of course, Strutt. As a final despairing measure it was agreed to bring the two men into the room again and ask each whether he was prepared to lead the expedition if chosen – there was always the faint chance that one of them might back down at the last moment.

When Ruttledge and Crawford came into the room, Cox asked Ruttledge whether, *prima facie*, he would lead if chosen. Ruttledge prevaricated and asked the Committee to consider Crawford first, but this they refused to do. Eventually, Ruttledge said, 'Yes, on certain conditions.'

The question was then put to Crawford and, astonishingly, he replied, 'I cannot say I would like to lead, but I am prepared to accept if the Committee cannot get anyone better.' This was not only an open insult to Ruttledge, but it was taking modesty beyond the bounds of credibility.

When both men had retired once more, the choice was put to the vote.

Wager's letter was counted as a vote for Crawford, but Sir Geoffrey Corbett was not allowed to vote because the position of the Himalayan Club on the Committee had not yet been officially ratified. Cox was nothing if not scrupulous – he could afford to be, since the result was a foregone conclusion. Strutt and Wager voted for Crawford; Cox and Mason voted for Ruttledge. Hinks and Spencer did not have votes, so the result was a tie. Sir Percy Cox therefore exercised his Chairman's casting vote for Ruttledge.

When the two protagonists were brought back into the room and told the result, the Chairman asked Ruttledge what were the conditions of acceptance he had mentioned. 'I consider it is not in the interests of the new expedition that it should include all the members of the former,' he replied, blandly.[7]

Crawford took the decision badly. 'He became quite paranoid towards the end of the affair,' said Raymond Greene. 'I went along partly with what Crawford said, but I wouldn't have carried it to such extremes.'[8]

To Ruttledge, Crawford sent a bitter letter on 2 May:

> There is no blinking the fact that all this Everest publicity has fanned a flame in you, hitherto dormant, of personal ambition and this has brought you to the pass of forcing yourself upon the expedition against the sincere advice of the mountaineers, and by means of the support (even to the extent of a casting vote at the critical moment) of the non-mountaineers, who perforce are completely ignorant of the needs of the Everest expedition.[9]

Yet the most that Ruttledge was guilty of was vacillation: it was only Crawford's suspicions that saw duplicity. On the other hand, there is no doubt that Sir Percy Cox and Kenneth Mason had it in for Crawford all along. They considered his actions traitorous, or at least not the conduct becoming an officer and gentleman. Mason summed up the Establishment position:

> There has been, in my opinion, a change of attitude among certain members of the last expedition. When they came home after the last expedition they were whole-heartedly in support of Ruttledge as leader. Some of them were unsuited to go again. They made the mistake of assuming that they had a prior right to future selection. During the period June to December 1934 'post mortem' discussions among themselves led some of them to magnify minor errors of judgement on the part of the leader, and to forget their own greater failures. This led to the ambition on the part of Crawford to lead, an ambition that could not be fulfilled since the Committee had already selected the leader. The subsequent behaviour of Crawford, both on and off the Committee, has shown clearly that the decision of the Committee regarding the leadership was perfectly correct.[10]

The affair did not end there, for having succeeded in appointing Ruttledge as leader, Cox was determined to get rid of Crawford altogether and by a high-handed action based on dubious evidence 'sacked' him from the Everest Committee. Strutt resigned in sympathy and the Alpine Club was thrown into disarray. Nevertheless, the Club's committee refused to back Crawford's protest and in consequence C.F. Meade, Graham Brown, Jack Longland and Crawford himself resigned from it.[11]

It was a sordid affair and unfortunately not the last of its kind in the annals of Everest. Though superficially petty, it illustrates the growing divergence between the geographers and the Alpinists over Everest, and the growing influence of the 'new guard' amongst the Alpinists themselves – young men of great ability and resource, no longer content to sit in awe at the feet of their elders. The days of handing down the Tablets were over.

In the immediate aftermath, when they came to select the 1936 team, the Committee excluded only Crawford – there was no way in which he could participate in view of what had happened. Of the other 'rebels' invited, Wager was unable to go because of prior commitments and Jack Longland, principled to the end, declined on the grounds that he was not prepared to give unconditional support to the leader.[12]

The announcement of the 1935/6 expedition was sent to the press on 4 April 1935. By a curious coincidence on that same day the death occurred, at the age of eighty-two, of Lancelot Fielding Everest, eldest son and last lineal descendant of Sir George Everest after whom the mountain was named (see Appendix 3).

While the wrangles over the leadership were smouldering in the back streets of Mayfair, Eric Shipton had returned to the Himalaya intent on solving the long-standing problem of entry to the Sanctuary of Nanda Devi in Garhwal. He was joined in this venture by his erstwhile partner from East Africa, Bill Tilman, with whom he had made the first traverse of Mount Kenya in 1930. This was Tilman's first visit to the Himalaya, but the names of Shipton and Tilman – 'the terrible twins' – were so closely linked with mountain expeditions for the next quarter of a century that it is worth while pausing to examine the men and what they stood for.

They were not twin-like in appearance. Shipton was half a head taller than his partner: a man of medium height, with broad shoulders, crinkly fair hair, ears which rather stuck out and deep-set, intense blue eyes. Tilman was small, dapper even, with a puckish face adorned by a trim officer's moustache (he had served as an Artillery subaltern in the war) and hair plastered down in the fashionable mode of the time. He was nine years older than Shipton.

But in mountain matters the two men were remarkably similar: stars like Castor and Pollux, revolving round and supporting one another. Two strands in particular are worth picking out: both men were keener on the exploration of the mountains than on any particular ascent, and both men were opposed to the concept of the large expedition. In these strands lay the seeds of their achievements and, ultimately, so far as Everest was concerned, their eclipse.

Their trip to the Garhwal (both men would probably have objected to the word 'expedition' – anything properly called an expedition is too big, Tilman is reported to have once said) epitomizes all that Shipton and Tilman stood for. They were the only Europeans and, for most of the five months they were away, they were accompanied by only three Sherpas – first-class men, including Angtharkay, who was destined to become one of the best-known Sherpas of all time. They romped all over the area and, of course, succeeded in their prime objective which was to force a passage through the Rishiganga gorge into the Sanctuary of Nanda Devi – a place where no man had been before, though many had tried.

'The whole of this brilliant and successful reconnaissance had been well planned,' Kenneth Mason wrote later. 'The party travelled light and shared the loads with their porters; comforts were cut to a minimum. The expedition re-set the fashion in Himalayan mountaineering of the small compact party.'[13]

Mason was right when he hinted that Tilman and Shipton had not started a new idea but resurrected an old one. After all, some of the earliest expeditions were small: W.W. Graham, Mummery, Eckenstein and others. But since those days the focus of attention had shifted to the massive assaults on Everest by the British and the equally massive assaults on Kangchenjunga and Nanga Parbat by the Germans. Shipton and Tilman dragged the focus back to a more realistic level by showing what the small party could accomplish with the minimum of resources.

Both Shipton and Tilman had by now given up their farming interests in Kenya and were intent on a life of adventure. In those heady days there was still so much unknown about the mountain areas of the world, and particularly the Himalaya, that the possibilities appeared endless. Everest seemed not to belong to this romantic existence – the stark realities of the windswept North Col had nothing in common with the excitement of discovering new lands.

But Shipton had been on Everest in 1933, and the added recognition which his Nanda Devi venture had gained him did not go unnoticed by the Everest Committee.

> It soon became apparent that Mount Everest was the most immediate barrier to the enchanting plans that had begun to crowd upon my imagination. Having once taken a share in the attempts to climb the mountain, it was hard to stand aside. Although the problem now appeared one of restricted scope, it was no less fascinating. Any one year might yield the right conditions for an unhampered climb up that last, 1,000 foot pyramid of rock upon which so much eager speculation had been lavished. It was like a gambler's throw, in which a year of wide opportunity in untrodden fields was staked against the chance of a week of fine weather and

snow-free rock. In those days it was not realized how slender was that chance. In 1933 we thought we had been unlucky with the weather; but never again was it to treat us so well.[14]

The Committee still had a balance of £1,400 at its disposal, and so Shipton offered to lead a reconnaissance expedition comprising six climbers at an overall cost of £200 each. This would go out during the monsoon period, summer 1935, the very beginning of the time limit granted by the latest Tibetan passport. Ostensibly its purposes were:

1 to collect data about monsoon snow conditions at high altitudes, and to investigate the possibility of a monsoon or post-monsoon attempt;
2 to re-examine the western ridge of Everest and the unknown 'Western Cwm', but without entering Nepal;
3 to report on ice formations on the North Col and advise on any special equipment to deal with them;
4 to try out new men for the 1936 expedition, especially with regard to their powers of acclimatization;
5 to investigate food and equipment problems;
6 to make a photogrammetric survey, improving and extending the survey of 1921,[15]

but Shipton had his own reasons as well –

> But I had a private motive: my dislike of massive mountaineering expeditions had become something of an obsession, and I was anxious for the opportunity to demonstrate that, for one-tenth of the former cost and with a fraction of the bother and disruption of the local countryside, a party could be placed on the North Col, adequately equipped to make a strong attempt on the summit. The Committee accepted my proposal, and I began to recruit my party, which naturally included Bill. I expected him to be delighted by this chance to go to Everest, but in fact he was far from pleased with this change of plan. Though he did not say so, I suspected that the root of the objection was that, while he had been forced to accept the stark necessity of my company, the prospect of having five companions was scarcely tolerable.[16]

Shipton was particularly revolted by what he considered the high living of the big Everest expeditions. He consulted Dr Zilva of the Lister Institute, who worked out for him a diet giving 4,000 calories per day of particularly monotonous, one might say unpalatable, food: pemmican, cheese, powder milk, sugar, dried vegetables, flour, biscuits, lentils, nuts and ghee, supplemented by local foodstuff, such as mutton and eggs. Vitamins A to D were supplied by cod liver oil, adexolin, yeast and ascorbutic acid tablets. Iron deficiency was to be rectified by ferrous sulphate!

This contrasted strongly with what had gone before, as Shipton later explained:

> While on the march we lived largely off the country. Mutton was easy to procure, though at first the sheep were rather thin. We cooked the meat in pressure cookers and the result was a great success. Where transport presents a problem and fuel is scarce these gadgets are well worth their weight; they overcome in twenty minutes the resistance of even the toughest meat. We could generally get potatoes and onions, though until later in summer other vegetables were not obtainable. However, we had brought out dried vegetables from England, and these provided us with quite a good substitute. Eggs were always plentiful in the villages, and though many of them were rather stale we consumed enormous quantities. Our record was 140 in a single day between four of us, and many times our combined party of seven put away more than a hundred. Tilman could bake an excellent loaf with the local flour and the dried yeast which we had brought as a supply of Vitamin B. Excellent butter made from Yak's milk was always available. So food presented no problem while we were in inhabited parts of Tibet; appetites were healthy and no one was inclined to be fussy about lack of variety.
>
> Food for life at high altitudes was a more serious question. I had developed an exaggerated antipathy towards tinned food, largely as a result of two expeditions on which it had been used almost exclusively. There is no doubt that food embalmed in tins, however cunningly, lacks some essential quality, and when one is fed on nothing else one very soon becomes heartily sick of even the most elaborate delicacies. I believe that to be one of the reasons why we had found it so hard to eat enough at high altitudes in 1933. That year I had been given the job of running the commissariat. At first everyone was loud in praise of the fare, and I was always having to emerge from the mess-tent to open another tin of this or that to satisfy rapacious appetites. Long before we had reached the base camp this enthusiasm had died down; before the expedition had run half its course the complaints against the food were bitter and endless, and to these I had lent strong support. Actually the quality of the tinned food could hardly have been improved; we had every conceivable variety – half a dozen kinds of breakfast food, bacon, ham, beef, mutton, chicken, lobster, crab, salmon, herrings, cod-roes, asparagus, caviare, foie gras, smoked salmon, sausages, many kinds of cheese, a dozen varieties of biscuit, jam, marmalade, honey, treacle, tinned and preserved fruit galore, plain, nut-milk and fancy chocolates, sweets, toffee, tinned peas, beans, spaghetti – I cannot think of anything we did not have. And it was supplied in such quantities that, rather than transport what was left all the way back from the base camp, we threw away scores of cases of provisions. And yet, one and all, we agreed

that the food was wholly unsatisfying. It seemed to me that the conclusion was obvious – and it was amply confirmed by my subsequent experience. But it was by no means universally accepted, and the majority were inclined to blame the firms that had supplied the food.

In 1935 I went rather too far the other way: it was bad policy to force people who were quite unused to rough food to make such a complete break with their normal diet. Taken in moderation tinned food undoubtedly has its uses, particularly when – as on Mount Everest – transport presents no particular problem. But it should be used to supplement fresh, salted or dried food, rather than as the main diet. A perfectly simple compromise is possible.[17]

There was also another reason why Shipton was keen to lead the reconnaissance apart from the trying out of his ideas – it was a chance in a lifetime to explore the forbidden country around Everest without being inexorably tied to the mighty peak itself. This would indeed be combining the best of both worlds – and it is precisely what the expedition did.

Besides himself and Tilman, the other members of the reconnaissance party were Edwin Kempson, a teacher at Marlborough College who had climbed for twelve years in the Alps, summer and winter, and was a friend of Wyn Harris; Dr Charles Warren, a paediatrician who had been with Marco Pallis in 1933; Edmund Wigram, a medical student who was strong as an ox and a good Alpinist; L.V. Bryant, a tough young New Zealander with a fund of anecdotes; and Michael Spender, a double-first from Oxford who regarded mountaineering simply as an extension of surveying, a pursuit to which he was dedicated. He had the reputation of being arrogant and provocative – 'highly individual' was Kempson's description – but he got on well with Shipton.

Angtharkay was in the Sherpa team, naturally, and so was a young friend of his called Tenzing Bhotia, later better known as Tenzing Norgay and destined to be the first man to reach the summit of Everest. Tenzing was only nineteen in 1935, and this was his first expedition. He almost didn't make it; two extra Sherpas were hired at the last minute, and he was one of them. Fate seemed to be sowing seeds in the 1935 expedition which were to bear fruit eighteen years later, for it was Bryant's cheerful willingness which predisposed Shipton to think highly of New Zealand climbers and resulted in Hillary joining the 1953 expedition. Thus, both Hillary and Tenzing can look back at 1935 with some satisfaction.

Indeed, tenuous though it is, this connection with final victory is perhaps the most significant contribution which the 1935 expedition made towards the problem of climbing Everest.

The expedition left Darjeeling towards the end of May 1935 and taking a different route from that of their predecessors, crossed the Kongra La and struck westwards, close to the Tibetan border, until they came to the village of

Sar, where they paused for a fortnight to explore the unknown ranges of Nyonno Ri and Ama Drime, peaks of 21,000–22,000 ft which form an eastern barrier to the gorge of the Arun. 'There was,' explained Shipton in the next *Alpine Journal*, 'no need to go straight for Everest' and Ruttledge later excused this extra-curricular romp in terms of acclimatization for higher things. The fact is that the Nyonno Ri mountains have nothing whatever to do with Everest or its approaches, and one suspects that Shipton, the born explorer, could not resist the temptation of a blank on the map.

And yet from the Nyonno Ri they could see that the Everest group was enjoying fine weather and was in perfect condition. In fact the monsoon didn't break until 26 June, the day the party left Sar to continue their journey towards Rongbuk, and at least one mountain historian, Dyhrenfurth, has felt that had Shipton not 'wasted time' he might have reached Everest and climbed it. Kempson, who was on the expedition, tends to agree with him – but points out that hindsight is different from reality.

The reality was that nobody expected the mountain to be in condition during the month of June, and in any case the main purpose of the expedition was reconnaissance and training.

And yet – what a glorious opportunity it was for Shipton to demonstrate what a small expedition could do! He must have weighed the pros and cons, whether to spend the time in his favourite pursuit of exploring unknown areas or whether to push for Everest, possibly climb it, and prove his point for all time. Did his nerve fail him? A special clause had been written into his contract forbidding him to make an assault – but here was a case for the Nelson touch, surely. When he saw Everest from the Nyonno Ri, did he regret his decision to turn aside? By the time he reached the mountain his chance had gone.

Looked at in a broad historical perspective, Shipton's action had a crucial bearing on the whole future of Himalayan exploration. Had he gone for Everest and climbed it, not only would this have removed the major stumbling block to Himalayan development, but it would have altered the whole concept of Himalayan mountaineering, and the massive expeditions to peaks such as Nanga Parbat, Kangchenjunga, K2 and Everest itself – which became usual and which still are the norm – might never have taken place. There might have been a more sporting ethic about the conquest of the world's highest mountains: less rape and more seduction.

On the other hand, had Shipton made a dash for Everest, found the mountain in condition and launched a rapid assault, the result could have been disaster. He was short of materials, short of men and short of time – particularly short of time, for he would probably have had some ten days only in which to climb the peak before the monsoon broke. The oncoming bad weather might have caught his small party stretched out on the mountain between the North Col and Camp VI, with little in reserve and retreat might have been difficult. As events turned out, the assault party would have been a weak one, for neither Bryant nor Tilman, two of his strongest climbers, acclimatized well in 1935.

Yet when all this has been said, and the chance of real disaster acknowledged, the fact remains that Shipton missed his one great opportunity of proving the viability of a small expedition on Everest. By ignoring orders he could just possibly have pulled off the mountaineering coup of all time.

Many years later his adherence to the idea of a small expedition was to rob him of ultimate victory over Everest, and the man who might have been knighted by his new Queen and feted by august societies around the world was instead working as a humble labourer. Even in 1935 he had been concerned about the prospects for his later years. 'Eric always worried about what he would do for money when he got old,' says Charles Warren.[18] Not that such trappings would have bothered Shipton: it was the theme he was worried about. Shortly before his death in 1977 he said in an interview that his efforts had merely earned him a reputation as an amiable eccentric. 'Maybe I should have lobbed a bomb into the Alpine Club,' he said.[19]

The party arrived at Rongbuk monastery on 4 July and two days later began the familiar walk up the East Rongbuk Glacier.

Their health was not too good at this stage. Bryant was obviously badly affected by altitude and it was decided to leave him at Camp I: '... his face was very blue and he was again sick in the night,' says Kempson's diary. 'Edmund [Wigram] coughs very badly and so gets out of breath. Bill [Tilman] is going slow and so am I. Eric [Shipton] is the fittest, though we all enjoy sitting down idle when we can.'[20]

Nevertheless they reached Camp III in three days from Rongbuk, which was good going. After a night at Camp III they decided to move it to a new site 500 ft higher near the spot where the 1933 expedition had left a food dump. Warren remembered the food they found there with affection. After Shipton's spartan diet the goodies left by the 1933 expedition seemed like a Christmas hamper!

On the way they found the pathetic remains of Maurice Wilson (see pp. 244–5).

Above the new Camp III rose the steep ice slopes of the North Col. As in previous years the slopes had altered owing to ice movement, and the route of 1933 was no longer practicable. The ice wall, down which the caving ladder had hung, was now broken into a dangerous mass of seracs. Fortunately, over on the right-hand side of the face there was a climbable tongue of ice which led up to the point where the old Camp IV had nested. The ledge which had held this camp had finally vanished and the slopes above were too steep for climbing, so there was nothing for it but to traverse horizontally across the face at the level of the old Camp IV, then climb straight to the col at the place where Camp IVa had been in 1933.

They began work on the climb up to the col on the next day, though none of them, except possibly Shipton, were feeling up to it. Whether it was over-indulgence in the cache of goodies they had recovered from the 1933 stockpile – toffee, chocolate and Carlsbad plums, which would seem like manna after Shipton's strict diet of pemmican, cheese and nuts, or whether it was the sobering effects of finding Maurice Wilson's body, it is hard to say, but both sahibs and Sherpas were affected. Tilman and Wigram were too ill even to attempt the climb, as were five of the porters, so Shipton, Kempson and Warren took turns of twenty minutes each, kicking steps up a nasty slope where four inches of snow lay over hard ice, the laden porters coming up behind. Soon, however, it began to snow hard, adding to their misery, and the Sherpas refused to go on. Shipton ordered a return to Camp III, where he gave the Sherpas a good talking to, threatening that unless they co-operated in future they would be sacked and the sahibs would carry the loads themselves. On earlier expeditions this would probably have caused the Sherpas to fall about laughing, but they could see that Shipton meant it. 'They were immensely contrite after Eric's talk,' says Kempson's diary.

Two days later, on 12 July, only six days after leaving Rongbuk, Shipton, Kempson, Warren and nine Sherpas occupied the North Col with supplies for fifteen days. The intention was to take a light camp up the ridge to 26,000 ft and from there reconnoitre the upper part of the mountain, and, if luck was with them, climb it.

There was little chance of the plan succeeding. The upper part of Everest, including the slabs, was snow-covered and totally impracticable, and in any case, the weather was too bad: the monsoon snow sweeping in over the mountain more or less continuously.

So on the 16th it was decided to withdraw to Camp III. Hardly had they begun than they received a severe shock. In his diary Kempson wrote:

> After an excellent night, we started down from the col on what was certainly the most dangerous mountaineering trip I have been. About 40 ft below the top the whole surface to a depth of about 3½ ft had come away. We got down this 'step' and then had to traverse below its impending surface to a prominent and safe crevasse away to the left. It was not merely new snow that avalanched, but a very large depth of quite old snow, and there had been absolutely no superficial indication of the danger on our ascent. After this we had to pass across and down a slope that was dominated by an unbroken and dangerous-looking 4 or 5 hundred feet of nasty-looking snow. It was a nervous stretch, as one sank about 18″ into damp snow. Later the slope eased off, and the final steep descent we covered by a sitting and standing glissade. I had been last on the lower rope

> and Charles was first on the second rope. I had entreated him to return and he most strongly agreed but moral persuasion I suppose led him to come down all the same – and we reached the bottom safely. We had a colossal argument about the safety of the up and down route. Eric stoutly maintained that the former was the more dangerous.

Shipton's argument was that if the place had already avalanched it was unlikely to do so again for some time – a nicety of judgement when twelve men's lives are at stake. Almost equally disturbing were the facts that nobody had heard the avalanche, though it must have been immense, and that on the way up there had been no indication of such a danger.

Shipton had left some stores on the col in readiness for another hopeful attempt when the weather improved, but now he decided the North Col slopes were too dangerous, and all attempts on the mountain were abandoned.

While this abortive struggle with Everest was taking place Spender, working from stations on the main Rongbuk Glacier, had made an excellent photogrammetric survey of the North Face, and the two 'invalids', Wigram and Tilman, had climbed the Lhakpa La, the pass between the East Rongbuk and Kharta Glaciers first crossed by the 1921 party, and from there had ascended the unnamed peaks which flank the pass on each side.

There then commenced what can only be described as an orgy of mountain exploration and climbing.[21] Khartaphu (23,640 ft), to the east of the East Rongbuk Glacier, was climbed by Shipton, Kempson and Warren, which not only proved a satisfying climb but provided them with a fresh view of Everest and especially the formidable North East Ridge. On their way down they met Tilman, Wigram and Bryant, who were intent on their own ascent of this easily accessible peak and it was decided that the whole party should regroup immediately at Camp II.

Once there, the expedition divided into two halves. Kempson, Warren and Spender set off to explore the mountains to the east which overlooked the wide, flat Far East Rongbuk Glacier. While Spender busied himself with surveying, Kempson and Warren climbed two unnamed peaks of 22,000 ft plus, then ascended Kharta Changri (23,070 ft), which they found surprisingly easy to climb. Food shortages and an outbreak of dysentery which affected Spender and some porters forced them back to Base Camp at Rongbuk on 31 July.

Meanwhile, Shipton's party had climbed Kellas Rock Peak (23,190 ft), a 22,580-ft unnamed mountain above Camp II and a couple of 21,000-ft peaks at the confluence of the East and Far East Rongbuk Glaciers.

Kempson had now to return home, but after two days' rest at Base Camp the remainder of the expedition divided into three parties: Shipton and Bryant (at last recovering from his illness), who decided to tackle the West Rongbuk Glacier and the fascinating Lingtren peaks; Tilman and Wigram, whose job was to go up the main Rongbuk Glacier to the Lho La, examining Everest from the west and seeing whether there was access into Nepal; and Spender and Warren, who were to continue the survey. It was, of course, a reappraisal in depth of the work done by Mallory and Bullock in 1921. After an interval of fourteen years it was perhaps time that someone took another look at it.

Shipton and Bryant climbed three peaks in the Lingtren group, including the principal summit of 21,730 ft, which lies on the watershed with the Sola Khumbu and gives superb views into the Western Cwm, and the peak of Lingtren Nup (20,610 ft). Regarding the Western Cwm Shipton wrote: 'As far as we could see the route up it did not look impossible, and I should very much like to have the opportunity of one day exploring it.'[22]

But the Lingtren Group nearly proved disastrous. As they were descending one of the peaks, a cornice broke away:

> While we were making our way along a narrow ice-ridge I heard a roar like a heavy gun going off, felt a jerk of the rope round my waist which nearly cut me in two, and found myself standing alone on the ridge. Bryant had broken away a bit of the cornice, had gone down with it, and was now almost hanging on the other end of the rope some way below the crest of the ridge; but he had retained possession of his axe and was thus able to cut his way back to me. Later in the descent we got involved in a small snow avalanche which, fortunately, we were expecting.[23]

Meanwhile Tilman and Wigram soon discovered that the Lho La held no prospect of a descent into Nepal, and that the West Ridge of Everest, which had been favourably commented on in 1933, held no chance of success. They climbed a small peak near the Lho La, the better to examine the West Ridge, then made a difficult crossing of the pass just north of Changtse, to end up on the East Rongbuk Glacier near Camp II – it was the first time a direct passage had been made across the northern ridges of the Everest group, linking the Rongbuk and East Rongbuk Glaciers. They ended their tour by climbing two more unnamed 22,000-ft peaks.

The parties re-assembled at Rongbuk on 14 August. They had made some interesting climbs and had seen Everest from some new angles, but in practical terms of approaching the mountain they had found nothing to alter the conclusions expressed by Mallory fourteen years earlier.

Two days' rest was again considered sufficient before the party, with the exception of Spender, trekked back up the East Rongbuk Glacier on their most ambitious project of all – the ascent of the 24,730-ft Changtse, the formidable-looking North Peak of Everest. Ostensibly, their objectives were to take telephotos of Everest and to test out the monsoon snow at high altitude, but one suspects the real reason was to snatch a plum ascent while the opportunity offered. As it turned out, the snow was so bad that the attempt was abandoned at a little over 23,000 ft. From the slopes of the mountain they were able to look down on the North Col and see that the tents Shipton had left there in July were already buried under fresh snow.

On their return to Rongbuk Shipton laid plans for a return to Darjeeling that can only be compared with the 'fighting withdrawal' techniques so familiar to battalions of the British Raj in earlier days. He determined to sweep eastwards, beyond the earlier limits already reached by the Kempson party, exploring, climbing, surveying as he went, hoping to end up in the Arun valley, whence, if Tibetan permission was gained, he could move east once more into the Nyonno Ri range, where it had all started weeks before.

That the eastward sweep wasn't quite as successful as Shipton had hoped was no fault of his. A few peaks were climbed, including one of 22,470 ft, but porter trouble curtailed their activities and they arrived in the Arun valley earlier than they had intended. Here they met with further disappointment because the Tibetans forbade them to continue their exploration of the Nyonno Ri range.

Frustrated, but with energy undiminished, the party moved eastwards as quickly as they could, 'reckless of the suffering entailed by the Tibetan wooden saddles', to return to Sikkim over the Chorten Nyima La – that same obscure pass which Captain J.B. Noel had used on his journey to Tashirak in 1913. Once over the border they paused to do some climbing in the little known Dodang Nyima range of North Sikkim, before eventually calling it a day and returning to Darjeeling.

It had been an energetic, whirlwind, campaign. Twenty-six peaks over 20,000 ft had been climbed – as many, said Longstaff, as since the days of Adam, and on this score alone it must be reckoned one of the most successful Himalayan expeditions ever undertaken – and certainly one of the cheapest. There was, in addition, the large amount of surveying done by Spender.[24]

But in terms of Everest, which is what the expedition was supposed to be about, how successful was it? The answer seems to be hardly at all. The useful information gained was minimal and not always trustworthy, as later events were to prove.

Despite their successes on various peaks the weather on the whole had not been good, and snow conditions above 23,000 ft were always abominable. From this it was concluded that the monsoon period was unsuitable for high-altitude climbing and this reinforced the already tacitly accepted maxim that so far as Everest was concerned, the brief interlude between the end of the winter storms and the onset of the monsoon was the only period suitable for attempting the mountain. It was a belief that continued for many years – and it was quite wrong.[25]

Another wrong conclusion drawn from the experiences of 1935 was that two men – Bryant and Tilman – were unsuited to high-altitude work. Certainly the evidence pointed that way, and again 23,000 ft seemed the magic mark. Above that height Tilman and Bryant were useless, and even below it Bryant took a long time to acclimatize. At various times during the expedition both men were very ill, and so it is hardly surprising that they were rejected for the 1936 expedition.

And yet in that same year, 1936, while Ruttledge was leading another abortive attempt on Everest, Tilman and Odell (also an Everest reject) climbed Nanda Devi – at 25,645 ft the highest mountain in the world to be climbed by that date.

Fourteen years and five expeditions had gone by since the first attempt on Everest, and still none of the important questions had a satisfactory answer. What was the best way to approach the mountain, from north or south? Not known, because nobody had approached from the south. What was the best time of the year? Not known for certain. Could it be climbed without oxygen? Not known. What caused altitude sickness in one man and not another, or conversely at one time but not another? Not known.

And there were a host of smaller but still important unknowns: how to combat frostbite effectively, how to judge Himalayan snow conditions (demonstrated by the North Col avalanche of 1935, especially), what was the best food, and so on.

As criticism began to mount over the successive failures of the pre-war Everest expeditions it must be remembered that the pioneers were fighting more than a mountain. They were fighting ignorance too: each expedition added so little to the sum of knowledge.

By a cruel stroke of irony all the bitterness aroused by the struggle for leadership after the 1933 expedition was in the end for nothing. If Ruttledge had looked to glory, the glory was emphatically denied him; if Crawford nursed his grievances, he must have gained a grim satisfaction at the turn of events. The 1936 expedition was a complete failure.

It was nobody's fault. The team that the Committee chose was rich in talent and experience and admirably suited to the task. Tilman was absent, of course, but there was Smythe, Shipton, Wyn Harris, Kempson, Warren and Wigram, all of whom had been on Everest and two of whom had been as high as man had yet climbed. In addition there were two newcomers to the team, P.R. Oliver and J.M.L. Gavin, both of whom had favourably impressed Smythe in the Alps.

Oliver already had Himalayan experience. An Army officer serving on the North West Frontier, he had spent several leave periods in the hills and in 1933 had attempted Dunagiri (23,184 ft) in the Garhwal, but failing in this had later made the second ascent of Trisul (23,360 ft) accompanied by a porter.[26] His summit dash of 4,000 ft through fresh snow illustrated his strength, stamina and speed and made him an ideal choice for Everest. Oliver's pencil sketches of his companions illustrate the expedition book *Everest: The Unfinished Adventure* – he would much rather have been an artist than a soldier, but family ties prevented it. He died in a Japanese ambush in Burma in 1945.

Among the non-climbing members of the expedition were John Morris, who had been in the 1922 party and was again in charge of transport, and W.R. Smyth-Windham, the radio operator who in 1933 had taken a telephone up to the North Col.

Perhaps the most remarkable newcomer, however, was Dr G. Noel Humphreys, then fifty-three years old. Surveyor, botanist, airman and mountaineer, Humphreys had come from humble beginnings to make a name as an explorer of the Ruwenzori, the fabled Mountains of the Moon, where he had made seven journeys. After his first two trips he felt that a knowledge of medicine would help him in his career as an explorer, so he ensconced himself in a London attic for four years, living on an average of twenty-four shillings and sixpence a week while he qualified. He became a doctor in 1931 at the age of forty-eight.

Every man in the team, including the leader and the doctor, despite their ages, could have gone up to the North Col had the need arisen, and given reasonable luck they stood a better chance of climbing Everest than any of their predecessors. Yet the whole affair was finished before it had begun – the monsoon came a month early.

Rongbuk was reached on 25 April and the mountain was seen to be in fine condition. The build-up of the lower camps was begun and then, on the 30th, came the first sudden snowfall. This was followed by a heavy fall of snow on 10 May, which was disturbing because if repeated it could invalidate the avalanche-prone approach to the North Col and cause delays. At the same time it was not particularly important overall – there were often pre-monsoon storms of short duration, the *chhoti barsat*.

A reconnaissance to the North Col had been made on the 9th by Smythe, Shipton and Warren, following more or less the same route as the previous year; that is, up the right-hand side of the slopes, fairly easily for some 500 ft followed by a long traverse to the left and finally a sharp pull up 50° slopes to the crest of the col. The snowfall of the 10th, which was repeated on the 11th, prevented further activity in this direction (and erased the steps that had been cut), so that Ruttledge could do little but work out the order of the final assault. He decided that Smythe and Shipton would have first crack, then Wyn Harris and Kempson, followed by Warren and Oliver (using oxygen), and finally Wigram and Gavin. The plan was to push up the ridge as before but this time have a further high camp, Camp VII, at about 27,000 ft, from which to make the final assault.

No more snow fell on the 12th, so on the following day they began making a route to the col. Smythe and Gavin led, followed by Wigram and Oliver and with them went the Sherpas Rinzing, Da Tsering and Da Tendrup. Smythe chose the line, but he had been asked by Ruttledge to save his strength for the upper mountain and not to do too much step cutting. No doubt to everyone's surprise he handed the lead over to the Sherpa Rinzing, who cut steps up the initial ice slope 'in the tireless manner of the first-class Alpine guide', said Oliver. It was the first lead climb done by a Sherpa on Everest: in fifteen years the Sherpas had evolved from 'coolies' to professional climbers, albeit embryo ones. They were to evolve much further still.

Smythe and Gavin led the traverse and the final steep 300-ft climb to the col. The climb took five and a half hours but when it was completed there was a safe route to the col, with a good deal of fixed rope in place ready for the laden porters. It was extremely encouraging: the blazing of the trail to Camp IV had taken in all only five days, three of which had been invalidated by the weather. In 1933 the same job had taken a fortnight.

On the next day Wyn Harris and Kempson took forty-six porters up to the col to establish Camp IV and they were followed on the 15th by Smythe and Shipton with fifty porters, thirty-six of whom remained at the col with the two climbers ready to begin the long assault up the ridge.

For the first time ever, the climbers took with them lightweight radio sets. These were not the 'walkie-talkies' which were later so familiar, because transistors had not yet been invented, but lightweight valve sets meant for use in the high camps. It was hoped to have one in each of Camp VII, Camp V and Camp IV, and since the lower camps were already linked by radio to Base, and Base to India, there would be an effective chain of communication throughout the operation. In particular, weather information could be relayed to the men building up the assault.

The party went up at a rapid pace, showing that both climbers and porters were fit and in good spirits. One Sherpa, Ondi, did the climb in only 2 hours, despite his load. [27]

But the mountain was simply not in condition. Deep snow lay everywhere – there was even two feet of soft snow on the exposed crest of the ridge – and though it might have been possible laboriously to establish the next camp, the boiler-plate slabs and Norton's traverse on the upper slopes were out of the question. When it snowed again on the 18th Smythe decided on a withdrawal – and it was not without some anxious moments that everyone got down the snowy slopes of the col to Camp III.

It was realized by Ruttledge that to keep inactive men at altitudes above 23,000 ft for any length of time leads to physical and mental deterioration, and already some of the younger porters at the col were showing signs of strain. In addition, the slopes of the col were getting worse, and another heavy snowfall might result in the party being cut off. In everybody's mind was the tragedy of

Nanga Parbat two years earlier, when four Germans and six porters died in a terrible retreat – the worst Himalayan disaster of all time. Ruttledge had thirty-eight men on the col, with a line of retreat which was an obvious avalanche trap, as was shown in 1922 and 1935. The risk was too great: if anything went wrong the ensuing disaster in terms of men killed could make the Nanga Parbat affair look tiny by comparison.

The weather was wrong. Not only did it snow heavily at times, but between storms it was much too warm – sometimes too warm even for the climbers to remain in their tents. On steep slopes like the North Col, there could hardly be a more dangerous combination than fresh snow and warm weather. It was a recipe for disaster.

In view of this Ruttledge ordered a general retreat to Camp I so that everyone could benefit from the lower altitude, but on arrival he heard some disquieting news. A message had come from India telling him that the monsoon was forming off the coast of Ceylon. This was extremely early, but Ruttledge counted on it taking a fortnight to reach the Everest region, and with luck it might even spend most of its force in Nepal before it struck the mountain. Nevertheless, there was obviously little time to spare.

For once, the north-west wind which usually blew with cold insistence down the Rongbuk Glacier and across the North Face of Everest was absent, just when it was most needed to blow away the freshly fallen snow.

By the 23rd, the new advance was ready to begin; Smythe, Shipton, Gavin and Ruttledge moved up to Camp II. They did so with heavy hearts, born in the knowledge of the mid-day weather report. The monsoon had reached Darjeeling. Instead of the expected fortnight, it had taken just four days to travel up the entire sub-continent. Such a thing had never happened before in living memory.

The climbers assembled at Camp III, but to no good purpose. It snowed every afternoon and evening, and they had nothing better to do than speculate on other ways of climbing the mountain, avoiding the hateful avalanche-prone slopes of the col. Shipton, Oliver and Gavin even made a cursory examination of the great North East Ridge, but it was really just a gesture born of frustration. On the 28th they all returned to Camp I, forcing their way back through a blizzard.

The mountain now began to play with them. On the 29th the climbers awoke to find a strong north-west wind blowing the snow off Everest in swathes. Excited that chance was turning their way at last, they set off once again next day to re-occupy Camp III for the third time, but even as they marched up the now hated East Rongbuk Glacier, the weather changed again and snow fell heavily.

Still, an attack was mounted on the col on 4 June: refashioning the steps in the snow, digging out the buried fixed ropes. The traverse, the most dangerous part of the ascent, obviously was in no fit condition when they got to it and in sheer desperation Smythe began to climb up the steep ice directly above the approach line. Such a route could never have been made safe for laden porters and in the end the project was abandoned. They had a nervy time retreating to the safety of Camp III.

Smythe, disconsolate and frustrated beyond words, knew the expedition was finished and that they would never reach the North Col again that year, but in the tents that night the arguments raged around poor old Ruttledge's head. He wrote:

> There could be no doubt that on this day fifty men had been in great danger on those treacherous slopes; and I spent the evening trying to sum up the situation correctly. Some believed that excessive risks had been taken; others that they had remained just within the safety factor, and that it was worthwhile persevering now that the wind had again gone round to the north-west and was blowing great guns. The evening weather report was on the whole favourable, indicating that we might expect a temporary continuance of this wind. Certainly the North Face was clearing rapidly.
>
> On the morning of June 6th a full gale was raging, and the tents shook and trembled as the gusts tore at them. Inside, the debate whirled and eddied between the poles of advance and retreat, while for the time being I remained apart in my own tent, striving to maintain some balance of judgement.[28]

Then Wyn Harris came to Ruttledge and suggested that he and Shipton should examine the slope once more – one last desperate try. Against his better judgement, Ruttledge agreed. Shipton later described the incident:

> It was a ridiculous thing to do, but we were feeling rather desperate. A strong wind had been blowing from the west for many days, sweeping great masses of newly fallen snow over the Col and depositing it on the eastern slopes; there had been heavy night frosts; ideal conditions for the formation of 'wind-slab'. We climbed quickly over a lovely hard surface in which one sharp kick produced a perfect foothold. About half-way up to the Col we started traversing to the left. Wyn anchored himself firmly on the lower lip of a crevasse, while I led across the slope. I had almost reached the end of the rope and Wyn was starting to follow when there was a rending sound – rrrumph – a short way above me, and the whole surface of the slope I was standing on started to move slowly down like a descending escalator towards the brink of an ice-cliff a couple of hundred feet below. Wyn managed to dive back into his crevasse and to drive his ice-axe in to the head and twist the rope round it. I collapsed on to my back and started to perform the frog-like motions prescribed by the text-books, though this was obviously

> not going to help me much if I were carried over the ice-cliff. My principal feeling was one of irritation at having been caught in such an obvious trap. Before it had travelled far the slope began to break up into great blocks. Presently the rope became taut between my waist and Wyn's axe, my swimming was arrested, the blocks began to pile up on top of me and it seemed clear that either I or the rope must break in two. However, before either of these events occurred the avalanche miraculously stopped. It is probable that Wyn's quick action had saved the situation.[29]

The two men descended safely, rather shaken. If evidence was needed that the expedition was over, then this was it.

The frustration of the climbers spilled over into wild gestures as they waited for the Tibetan transport to take them away from Base Camp. Shipton led a party on an attack on Changtse, the peak which had defeated him the previous year, but again found that the snow was unreliable and was forced to retreat. Smythe had a mad plan to assault Everest in a lightweight dash, using the western approach to the North Col from the Rongbuk Glacier, but he was calmed down by Ruttledge, who got him to reconnoitre the col instead. Mallory had pronounced it impossible in 1921 and Tilman had not regarded it favourably in 1935, but nobody had actually tried it. As it turned out it was a feasible route, possibly useful as an escape line for anyone trapped on the col. Under normal conditions however, Smythe thought the usual way from the East Rongbuk Glacier was preferable.

On 17 June, the expedition left Base Camp for home. One of their last corporate acts was to compose a long letter for the reform of the Alpine Club.

There is no doubt at all that the 1936 Everest expedition was desperately unlucky with the weather. On previous occasions the monsoon had reached Everest on these dates:

| | |
|---|---|
| 1921 | 7 July |
| 1922 | first week of June |
| 1924 | 16 June |
| 1933 | 30 May |
| 1935 | 26 June |

In 1936 it arrived on 25 May. As Smyth-Windham pointed out, the only parties favoured with a late monsoon on Everest were the reconnaissance parties.

Poor Ruttledge! It seemed just his luck that his two expeditions should suffer the two earliest monsoons. In his writings he bears it all with equanimity and a keen sense of humour, but he reveals also a man rather out of his depth. He wasn't a bad leader, and moralists can point to the fact that nobody was killed on his two expeditions, but Everest required rather more than this sort of negative leadership. One feels that it wasn't so much a case of Ruttledge not knowing what to do but rather a reluctance to see that others did it. In short, he was not a born leader of men.

He commanded two of the finest teams of climbers ever to approach the Himalaya: intelligent, strong-minded men who knew far more about mountain climbing than Ruttledge could ever hope to know, and he felt his inferiority. A fair-minded man, he doubted his right to command such experts.

Smythe knew this and lorded it over Ruttledge, who regarded him with awe and admiration, putting up with his tantrums over air beds and his occasional burst of irrational irresponsibility. 'Smythe was an odd chap,' Edwin Kempson recalls. 'Tried to throw his weight about. Very categoric about things and when proved wrong, still managed to adopt an "I told you so" attitude.' 'He didn't give an outward show of aggressiveness,' said Warren, 'but he was dogmatic.'[30]

To say that Ruttledge was just a figurehead and that Smythe was the real leader is to oversimplify, but it was true to a certain extent. Fortunately (or perhaps not?) there were strong counter-checks to Smythe's dominance – Shipton, Wyn Harris, Greene and Kempson spring to mind – but somehow it is the ghost of Smythe which hovers over the 1933 and 1936 expeditions.

The failure of the 1936 expedition, for whatever reason, went down badly with the British public. The traumatic events of the Crawford–Ruttledge controversy, and the rumblings of discontent among the younger climbers, were known only to a privileged few, of course. Outwardly, and particularly in the 'responsible' newspapers, everything was shown as quiet determination and true grit. But you can't fool all the people all the time. The British know when their leaders are trying to con them, and there was a widespread feeling that all was not well in the climbing world.

Somebody, of course, was bound to give the game away – and who better than George Ingle Finch? He had nothing to lose, and some old scores to settle. The *Morning Post* of 17 October 1936 reported:

> Feeling is growing among members of the Alpine Club that the control of future Mount Everest expeditions should be in the hands of climbers only – not, as heretofore, of a mixed committee of the Alpine Club and the Royal Geographical Society.
>
> The leader of the next expedition, it is also being urged, should himself be a climber – preferably the climber whose chances of getting to the summit are most fancied.
>
> While the expedition was still in progress, public criticism was naturally stilled. Now the whole question of the control and organization of Everest expeditions is likely to be brought before the Club at an early date.

Captain G.I. Finch, a former Everest climber, yesterday explained to a representative of the 'Morning Post' what are regarded by many climbers as the main grounds of criticism.

'We ought not to treat the climbing of Mount Everest as a domestic issue,' Captain Finch stated. 'It is an issue of National and Imperial importance. The present position is that we are beginning to make ourselves look very ridiculous.

'The Germans and Americans have both wanted to make an attempt on Mount Everest, and unless we put up a better show, it will be difficult to argue that we are justified in keeping Mount Everest to ourselves.'

SUGGESTED AGE LIMIT

For the future, Captain Finch urged that the first necessity was to choose the best possible man to get to the top and then leave him, with the advice of a climbers' committee if wanted, to pick his own men and make his own arrangements. There should be an age-limit of 25–35.

'You cannot apply the military method of Staff control under conditions when the leader cannot be expected willingly to risk the lives of others,' he said. 'The instruction "must not take any risks" is tantamount to saying that you must not get there.

'On the other hand, a climbing leader is in a position to ask others to take the same risks that he is himself taking. Forceful personality and strong character, not "compatability of temperament", are the qualities needed on Everest. The pertinacious spirit of a Jean Batten is what is going to get men to the top.

'It is a fact that men have been barred because they have been thought to be fired with personal ambition. In a venture of this kind, personal ambition is a valuable quality. As regards men, we have first-class material for a hundred expeditions.

'I want to make it clear,' Captain Finch added, 'that no personal attack is intended. The question, essentially, is one of principle. Everest is now a climbing job, and that job should be in the hands of climbers.'[31]

# 9

# Small Is Beautiful

The 1936 expedition had been a £10,000 failure. When permission was granted for another attempt in 1938 the public were becoming cynical over the repeated failures and beginning to regard the whole Everest project as a waste of money. Not everyone's reasons were as chauvinistic as Finch's: many thinking people had been shocked by the Depression and felt that there was something morally wrong in sending out expensive expeditions to Tibet when people at home were starving – an expression, perhaps, of that recurrent Puritanism which is at once a strength and a weakness of the British character. The cost of an expedition to Everest was hardly likely to affect the underlying economic ills of the time. Nevertheless the feeling persisted right up until the outbreak of war. It was perhaps summed up best by Raymond Greene:

> I think a lot too much has been said in the past about the spiritual and mystical significance of climbing Everest and about its possible effects on British prestige. However true that may be, the fact remains that we go to Everest not for those reasons at all, but either simply because it is fun or in order to satisfy some purely personal and selfish psychological urge.
>
> I do not think we are any longer justified in spending large sums of public money in satisfying these private urges.[1]

For whatever motives, the Mount Everest Committee realized that a public appeal for funds would be a waste of effort and possibly embarrassing into the bargain. The newspapers, fingers on the public pulse, were not keen to take up options on the expedition, though eventually *The Times*, a rejected suitor since 1924, came to the rescue.

A shortage of cash in a mountaineering venture is often no bad thing. It forces the participants to examine the options more closely and stick to the basics. Indeed, it often leads to a purer, more sporting, form of mountain climbing. In 1938 this was precisely the effect which it had on the Everest Committee: they were forced to consider only the essentials and, willy nilly, become converts to the philosophy of Shipton and Tilman.

Tilman (the more rigorous purist, according to Shipton) had a philosophy which can be summed up in the phrase 'Small is beautiful'. He expressed it typically thus:

> It is not easy to see either the origin of or the reason for these unwieldly caravans organized on the lines of a small military expedition rather than a mountaineering party. Were it not that the pioneering days of Himalayan climbing were past one might find a parallel in the earliest days of mountaineering in the Alps, when numbers were considered a source of strength and not the weakness they usually are. For de Saussure's ascent of Mont Blanc in 1787 the party numbered twenty. The elaborately organized expedition of the Duke of the Abruzzi to the Karakorum in 1909 was the original Himalayan expedition in the grand style, but before and since that time many private parties had climbed and explored with a minimum of fuss and expense – notably those of Mummery, Conway, Longstaff, Kellas, Meade, to mention a few. Of course the means must be proportioned to the end; there is a difference between rushing a moderate-sized peak and besieging one of the Himalayan giants, but any additional means we think we need for the more formidable task ought to be taken reluctantly and after the severest scrutiny. Anything beyond what is needed for efficiency and safety is worse than useless. In 1905 Dr Longstaff and the two Brocherel brothers, with no tent and one piece of chocolate, very nearly climbed Gurla Mandhata, a peak in Tibet north of Garhwal, 25,355 ft high, a practical application of that important mountaineering principle, the economy of force – an imperfect example, perhaps, because one might argue that with a tent and two pieces of chocolate they might have succeeded. But away with such pedantic, ungracious quibbles. Did not Mummery, who more than anyone embodied the spirit of mountaineering, write '. . . the essence of the sport lies, not in ascending a peak, but in struggling with and overcoming difficulties'?[2]

There were more recent examples which Tilman might have quoted to substantiate his theories. In 1931, Frank Smythe had climbed Kamet (25,447 ft) with a small expedition and Tilman had climbed Nanda Devi (25,645 ft) in 1936. Perhaps the most remarkable of all, carrying the idea almost to its ultimate conclusion, was Spencer Chapman's ascent of Chomolhari (23,997 ft) in 1937 when the 'expedition' consisted of two sahibs and three Sherpas with a total budget of £39 5s 0d!

All these were in direct contrast with the enormous Everest expeditions and others. The Abruzzi expedition which Tilman mentions consisted of twelve Europeans, 258 porters and ninety-five baggage animals; the German expedition to Nanga Parbat in 1934 involved fourteen climbers and 600 porters . . . it was as if there was an unwritten rule which said that big peaks required big expeditions. It was this that Tilman set out to disprove.

In February 1937, the Mount Everest Committee invited four key men to discuss plans for 1938 – Shipton, Tilman, Smythe and Warren. From these four men a leader might be expected to emerge, but more than that, each had a good knowledge of the abilities of other climbers who would make up the team. A month later, in March, Tilman was chosen as leader.

And so the course was set for a truly radical departure from Everest tradition: the Old Guard had been pushed aside and affairs were in the hands of the climbers at last. No doubt the Committee had grave misgivings, but in their straitened circumstances there was little else they could do.

The financial situation was bad. At the beginning of 1937 they were in the red to the tune of £1,538 – though this was put right by the receipt of £2,000 from the publishers, Hodder and Stoughton, for the manuscript of the 1936 story. Nevertheless, by August, when the name of the expedition leader was due to be publicly announced, there was only £335 in the kitty.

At this critical point Tom Longstaff stepped into the picture. Longstaff had been on Everest himself in 1922 as the doctor-in-charge, though he disliked what he called 'the hurly-burly of a big expedition'. In earlier years he had amassed a formidable record as a mountaineer and explorer, and always with a small party, travelling light. Like many others he had become disgusted with the way the Everest expeditions were organized and in the row which followed the 1933 expedition he had sided with the 'rebels'. In Tilman he saw a chance of reform – perhaps he even saw a reflection of his former self.

He now came forward with an offer virtually to underwrite the costs of the new expedition. He promised that by November he would place £3,000 at the disposal of the Committee, providing certain conditions were met, the chief of which was that either Shipton or Tilman (he didn't mind which) was confirmed as leader. The Committee accepted.

Longstaff's other conditions simply emphasized Tilman's own views: that there should be no advance publicity for the expedition, and that anyone selected for the team should be willing to pay whatever they could afford for the privilege of going.[3]

Tilman set about forming a small, competent team of experienced men. The nucleus was already to hand, of course – Smythe and Shipton – both of whom had a burning ambition to be the first man up Everest; Smythe particularly.

Jack Longland, who had done so well on the 1933 expedition, was invited to take part, but his employers, the National Council for Social Services, refused him leave of absence. 'I could not afford to lose my job,' he wrote recently.

'Perhaps regular jobs were taken rather more seriously than they seem to be in the expedition world of today.'[4] His place was taken by Peter Oliver, who had been on the 1936 expedition.

Charles Warren was also included, though at first Tilman did not wish to take a doctor because it impinged on the purity of his concept of self-sufficiency. However, Warren was a good climber who had been to Everest in 1935 and 1936 and was certainly no base-camp doctor; furthermore, it was pointed out to Tilman that even if the climbers didn't need a doctor, the Sherpas might – a prophecy which turned out to be true enough in the end. 'I never quite knew,' said Warren, 'whether to be flattered at being asked to go on the Everest expedition because I spent my spare time mountaineering, or whether to be insulted because Tilman asked me to go as a doctor.'[5]

To complete the seven-man team there was a newcomer to Everest, Peter Lloyd, and a veteran, Professor Noel Odell – the last person to see Mallory and Irvine on their fateful climb in 1924. Odell was now forty-seven years old, but extremely fit and had been to the summit of Nanda Devi (25,645 ft) with Tilman in 1936. Lloyd was a stocky, strongly built man, who had also been on the Nanda Devi expedition.

Small though it was, it was an immensely strong and talented team. Every man on it had Himalayan experience; every man had proved himself capable of functioning well at heights above 20,000 ft. They were also 'socially harmonious', as Shipton put it (there were none of Smythe's 'horrid northern climbers'), and their experiences had interlocked, their paths had crossed, on many previous climbs.

Even so, to the man whose dictum was 'any number more than one constitutes a large party' and who maintained that any expedition which couldn't be organized on the back of an old envelope was over-organized, a party of seven did not seem small: 'not so small as it could have been,' he said. Nevertheless, Tilman accepted the numbers philosophically: 'it represents a high margin of safety against casualties'.

After the 1936 expedition Eric Shipton had drawn up a budget for a small Everest expedition, and Tilman used this for his calculations, even managing to pare it down from £2,500 to £2,360. This suited the Committee's finances admirably.

There was nothing innovatory about their basic equipment, and basic equipment was all they got. Out went such superfluities as radio, and Tilman was all for throwing out the oxygen sets too. This latter act would have resulted in a considerable saving in transport cost, if nothing else, but it would also have caused a considerable rumpus among the climbing establishment. The pro-oxygen and anti-oxygen factions were strongly entrenched, and one never missed an opportunity to snipe at the other. For Tilman, or anyone else for that matter, to leave out oxygen sets would have been construed by the pro-oxygen faction as a deliberately hostile act. The political pressures were too strong for Tilman as they had been for some of his predecessors: oxygen sets had to be taken to Everest, if only as totems.

Tilman was never convinced of oxygen's usefulness. He told the story of how he had walked up Grains Gill in the Lake District in forty-five minutes wearing an oxygen mask, and how, a day later, he did the same climb without oxygen in five minutes less! Of course, Tilman was well aware that at such low altitudes this test proved nothing at all about the value of oxygen to the high-altitude climber: it is the fact that he told the story at all that shows he had scant regard for oxygen.

Nevertheless, he took it to Everest. Perhaps at the back of his mind there remained painful memories of his own poor showing at altitude during the reconnaissance of 1935. At any event he admitted that if the party found itself within striking distance of the summit in good weather, and were defeated by a lack of oxygen, they would look 'uncommonly foolish'. It was, he later wrote, 'a rather cowardly reason'.

Cowardly or not, only four sets were taken – indicative perhaps of the symbolic rather than practical aspects of the apparatus. Of these, two were of the old 'open' type developed by Finch (who had by this time returned to the fold), that is to say, oxygen was breathed via a mouth tube and mixed with air breathed through the nose; and the other two were of a new 'closed' type in which pure oxygen was delivered to a face mask. Charles Warren, who was in charge of oxygen, favoured the latter after he had held some successful trials in the Alps, but as events turned out they worked less adequately on Everest. Peter Lloyd, who as a qualified chemist was appointed Warren's oxygen assistant, came to the conclusion that climbing speed increased using oxygen above 26,000 ft, and even below that height it was justified by the way it reduced tiredness.

Even if Tilman had to bend his own rigid rules in order to accommodate oxygen apparatus and a doctor, he had no intention of doing so over food. Put simply, Tilman believed that most people, even on expeditions, ate too much and usually the wrong sort of food. Both he and Shipton seemed able to exist on next to nothing, and their reputation in this was such that Tilman felt obliged to try to dispel some of the myth:

> The technique of travelling light which Shipton and I employed on our own expeditions does not mean that we deliberately starve ourselves or our porters. It does not and should not imply inadequate or indifferent food. As we once lived perforce for a few days on tree mushrooms and bamboo shoots there is a general impression that this is our normal diet, eked out with liberal doses of fresh air, on which, thanks to a yogi-like training, we thrive and expect everyone else to do likewise. Nothing could be farther from the truth. Like Dr Johnson, we mind our bellies very strenuously: 'for I look

upon it', he said, 'that he who will not mind his belly will scarcely mind anything else.' The more restricted a ration is the more need is there for careful thought in its selection. For normal men a ration of 2 lb. a day is ample (I have kept Sherpas happy for two or three weeks on 1½ lb.), and the whole art lies in getting the most value for weight.[6]

For anyone who knew Tilman, the core of that statement lies in the last two sentences: 'getting most value for weight' means in fact abandoning any concepts of taste or palatability and basing one's calculations solely on the requisite calories, vitamins and minerals. Tilman saw food simply as human fuel and nothing else.

Gone indeed were the days of quails in aspic, washed down by champagne, which had characterized the expeditions of General Bruce. Tilman in fact refused an offer of free champagne from a well-wisher, though he unbent sufficiently to accept a case of tinned tongue – 'our diet included much that was not really necessary,' he wrote laconically.[7]

Plain basic food was the order of the day: eggs, vegetables, bacon, ham, cheese, butter and pemmican, eked out by sweet stuffs and goodies, amongst which Tilman counted porridge and soup! 'In 1938 we had food in abundance,' he wrote later.

Well, nobody actually starved, but probably only Shipton thought the food was really adequate. Complaints were constant, and even to this day Warren remembers vividly how bad it was and how they all fell like delighted pirates on the food cases left at Rongbuk by the 1936 expedition. In his account of this Tilman treated his companions to a touch of sarcasm: 'this windfall, consisting of nourishing foods like jam, pickles and liver extract (of which there were several cases), alone saved the party from starvation.'[8]

Noel Odell came back from the expedition in a highly critical temper:

> But it is mainly in respect of the provisioning that I would criticize this year's expedition. Frankly we did what we did on the mountain not because of our meagre rationing but in spite of it. And we could have done more at times than we did, and returned, some of us, in better condition if our rationing had been ampler and more suitable. I am no believer in the necessity for truffled quails or champagne (though practically all of us regretted the refusal of a generous gift of a case of the latter), but for a sustained sojourn at really high altitudes a carefully selected and varied diet is essential; and some alcohol has its uses after a particularly exhausting day. As most people know, one's palate and appetite become very fickle at high altitudes, and it is no good thinking that badly cooked porridge, or an inferior brand of pemmican, or a single rasher of bacon for breakfast, is going to keep together the body and soul of even the most devoted Everest climber.[9]

This cut no ice with Tilman, who was used to being criticized on this score by Odell, '[who] has not yet finished criticizing the food we ate on Nanda Devi in 1936 and who, in spite of his semi-starved condition, succeeded in getting to the top'.[10]

The pemmican was meant as high-altitude rations, but even Tilman admitted it was a failure:

> If you do succeed in getting outside a richly concentrated food like pemmican a great effort of will is required to keep it down – absolute quiescence in a prone position and a little sugar are useful aids. Without wishing to boast I think the feat of eating a large mugful of pemmican soup at 27,200 ft performed by Lloyd and myself, is unparalleled in the annals of Himalayan climbing and an example of what can be done by dogged greed. For greed consists in eating when you have no desire to eat which is exactly the case anywhere above Camp IV.[11]

In a sense, food dominated the 1938 expedition and one senses that, had the expedition failed for any other reason than bad weather, the food – or lack of it – would have been blamed. As it was, the influenza and other ailments which beset the party were attributed by critics to the inadequate diet: a charge which rankled with Tilman, and which he stoutly denied.

The party, with the exception of Smythe, who was following later, arrived at Gangtok in Sikkim on 3 March. Their route from there lay up the Tista valley through Gangu and over the Sebu La (17,000 ft) into Tibet – the 'short-cut' route to Kampa Dzong and perfectly feasible for a small expedition. They intended to reach Rongbuk early in order not to miss the clear period before the monsoon, should the monsoon itself be early. The lessons of 1935 and 1936 had not gone unheeded. However, the early start raised its own problems: heavy snowfall hindered their progress up the Tista, and of course the Tibetan plateau was bitterly cold. It may well have been the rigours of the approach march which contributed most to the flu which affected several members later, including Tilman.

Rongbuk was reached on 6 April, ten days earlier than any previous expedition. Everest was a black obelisk, blown clear of snow by the strong winter winds, and to Tilman's surprise so too was the north peak, Changtse, which is 5,000 ft lower. Tilman was impressed and later wrote the last pre-war description by any European of Everest as seen from Rongbuk.

> I am not one of those who decry the mountain as unimpressive, shapeless, or even ugly – what some mountaineers rudely call a cow peak. Seen from Rongbuk it looms up magnificently, filling the head of the valley. The final pyramid, with or without its streaming banner, is a glorious thing; the face looks what it is – steep; and the two great ridges seen now in profile would

make any mountaineer's heart leap. Were it 20,000 ft lower it would still command respect and incite admiration.[12]

The principal Sherpas had travelled with the climbers from Sikkim, the rest joined the expedition direct from their homes in the Khumbu valley bringing with them, as arranged, a large quantity of rice and other foodstuffs. There was a fine nucleus of experienced men, including Pasang, Kusang, Rinzing, Tenzing and others who knew Tilman well and admired him. Their leader, or sirdar, was the indomitable Angtharkay.[13]

The porters arrived on the 7th and two days later the first carry began to the site of Base Camp. In rather less than three weeks Camp III was established below the North Col slopes and tentative probings had begun on them to establish a way up.

On the face of it the expedition was going well, but there were in fact two serious drawbacks. In the first place the weather was extremely cold, even at Camp III, and watching the spindrift plume off the North Col Tilman knew it would be colder still up there. There was no point in establishing higher camps under such conditions; the mountain could not be climbed and it would only sap the men's strength. Added to which was the second serious drawback: as the establishment of camps up the glacier had gone on, each of the climbers had developed some debilitating ailment. Tilman had contracted influenza, Oliver, Lloyd and Warren had bad colds, Smythe had a sore throat and Odell a cough. Only Shipton seemed immune from the general malaise.

There was nothing for it but to wait until mountain conditions improved and the health of the party recovered. But wait where? Certainly not at Camp III; nor did Tilman much like the idea of retiring to the dreary wastes of Rongbuk. Instead he determined to cross the Lhakpa La into the lush Kharta valley, on the east side of the mountain – reversing, in fact, the route by which Mallory and his companions had first approached the mountain in 1922.

The Kharta valley was an ideal retreat for a sick party. At about 11,000 ft above sea level it was 5,500 ft lower than Rongbuk, warmer and altogether more pleasant. There was fuel and food in plenty, Alpine meadows, forests of juniper and birch, and rhododendron thickets already in bud.

They stayed in this paradise for about a week, recuperating, and then Smythe and Shipton were left behind to recross the Lhakpa La back to Camp III while the others took a more circuitous route round to the north to cross the Doya La (17,000 ft) and end up at Rongbuk.

This took them five days. Gradually, however, Everest came into view once again – and it was white from top to bottom. When they reached Rongbuk, the faithful Karma Paul, who had been looking after things in their absence, told them that it had snowed on 5 May and every day for a week thereafter. The monsoon had broken.

At first they refused to believe it. In 1936 Ruttledge had bemoaned his fate at being caught by the earliest monsoon ever experienced by an Everest expedition, and that broke on 25 May. Was it possible that it could break almost three weeks earlier still?

By 18 May they had returned to Camp III, and next day began an assault on the North Col slopes. They chose a central line and found the snow surprisingly good and the going so easy that Oliver led all the way without the need of a relief until about 300 ft from the top. At this point the slopes steepened considerably and were barred by ice cliffs which necessitated a leftwards traverse of some 300 ft. The snow on the traverse was soft and at one point it broke away, precipitating Oliver and a Sherpa a few feet down the slope. Fortunately they were laying a fixed rope, both ends of which were securely held at the time, so they were easily held. The rope was duly fixed on the traverse, and the party retired to Camp III, satisfied with the day's work.[14]

They arrived at camp to find Shipton and Smythe, who had that day crossed the Lhakpa La from the Kharta Valley. This seeming isolation of Shipton and Smythe, treating them almost as a separate unit apart from the rest of the expedition, was deliberately planned by Tilman. Even in such a select party as the 1938 expedition, where all men were equal, some were still more equal than others. It was recognized from the outset that if the summit was to be won the most likely pair to do it would be Shipton and Smythe. Consequently, Tilman determined to conserve their strength for the final push: not for them, if it could possibly be helped, the chore of breaking trail up to the North Col.[15]

That night snow fell for several hours, and the climbers could hear avalanches crashing down from the near-by peaks and ridges. All the old fears about the North Col slopes came crowding into their minds. They recalled the close shave that Shipton and Wyn Harris had in 1936 and above all they recalled the disastrous avalanche of 1922 in which seven porters died.

Nevertheless by 24 May they reckoned conditions were once more satisfactory. The slopes had been provided with fixed ropes, and the few hundred feet of new climbing between the end of the traverse and the North Col were quickly overcome by the lead team of Shipton and Smythe, who were pressed into service. All the climbers (with the exception of Lloyd, who had flu) and twenty-six porters reached the col and dumped their loads on the site of the 1936 camp, marked by the apex of a pyramid tent poking through the snow. Everyone then returned to Camp III.

On the following day Tilman and Smythe, with fifteen porters, returned to the col. As they surveyed the mountain they had come to climb and the superb scenery lying all around, they felt little hope or joy. The peak was covered in soft deep snow, the air was warm, stifling even, and ominous clouds piled up on the near-by ranges. They descended to Camp III.

They now realized in their innermost hearts that they were committed to attempting the mountain during the monsoon period, a course which their predecessors had declared impossible. But the weather itself wasn't bad on the whole, and Tilman felt he couldn't simply just give up without at least one main effort.

He now decided to divide the team into two parties. The lead pair, Smythe and Shipton, returned to Rongbuk with fourteen porters, their objective being to climb the North Col from the west, that is from the main Rongbuk Glacier, by the route which had been partly reconnoitred in 1936. Meanwhile the rest of the team was to ascend to Camp IV by the usual route.

On the 28th Odell, Oliver, Warren and Tilman occupied Camp IV. In the afternoon it began to snow and didn't stop until 8 p.m. With a foot of snow to contend with, there was little the climbers could do and so the next day was spent in the large dome tent they had erected, and defeat was in the air.

The following day they pushed on up the North Ridge, the trail through the deep snow being made by the young enthusiastic Tenzing. By one o'clock they had reached 24,500 ft, but Tilman realized that with the snow conditions then prevailing on the peak there was no point in establishing Camp V.

Snow again fell that evening and so on the next day, a retreat to Camp III was made once more.

Meanwhile Smythe, Shipton and the recuperated Lloyd had set up their first camp on the main Rongbuk Glacier, en route for the western approach to the col. When they heard that the others had retreated from the col, they were not sure what to do, so waited until they were joined by Tilman.

It was decided to withdraw completely from the East Rongbuk Glacier and concentrate all their energies on the new line of approach, which was, they hoped, more free from avalanche danger.

The first camp, already established by Smythe, was called Lake Camp, an idyllic setting with grass, a stream and a small lake tucked in between a high moraine and the eastern wall of the valley, catching the full benefit of the sun for most of the day. Its altitude was 18,000 ft.

The second camp (North Face Camp) lay some two and a half miles further up the true right bank of the Rongbuk Glacier, at 19,000 ft, just before the point at which a subsidiary glacier, the approach to the North Col, flows in. Tilman, Shipton, Smythe and Lloyd occupied this camp with seventeen porters; the rest of the party were to follow in due course.

The next morning they rounded the corner of Changtse and began their ascent of the little glacier leading towards the North Col. The ascent was not as steep as on the familiar route from the East Rongbuk Glacier, but the slopes were more open and looked frighteningly avalanche-prone. Bearing this in mind the party crept up close by the walls of Changtse, which towered over them on their left. About a mile up the glacier an icefall pressed them even more to the left, but shortly after 1 o'clock they found a wide snow shelf above the icefall where they set up their third camp, called somewhat factually West Side Camp. Tilman estimated its altitude to be similar to that of Camp III on the East Rongbuk Glacier, about 21,500 ft.

They left camp at seven next morning to tackle the final slopes to the col. Before they had gone far they came upon the debris of an enormous avalanche, which could only have fallen within the last few days and which was indicative of the inherent dangers of the route. The avalanche had also stripped the slope of snow, leaving only hard ice, which required arduous step cutting and sensitive balance, especially on the part of the laden porters.

They tip-toed up the ice for 500 ft until they could reach an area of snow cover. 800 ft above them lay the col, which was their goal; but the slopes had steepened and the snow had softened in the increasing warmth of the morning. Behind them lay stark evidence of what these snow slopes could do once the sun had softened them, and it was a thankful party which reached the North Col at 11 a.m. 'The sun, feeble though it was, had been on the slope for an hour and from its effect on the snow I felt it was high time for us to be off it,' commented Tilman.[16]

So once again the expedition was established on the North Col, having made the first ascent from the west.

On 6 June, the day following their reoccupation of Camp IV on the col, they began the ascent of the North Ridge. Surprisingly, the snow had consolidated for quite some distance, so that they were able to make good progress until, about 800 ft below the position selected for Camp V, things deteriorated. Two of the porters struggled on for a further hundred feet and then sank down exhausted. The rest crawled on until at 4 o'clock they reached the site for Camp V.

Smythe and Shipton stayed at Camp V; Tilman and Lloyd returned to Camp IV with six of the porters and picked up the two exhausted men on the way down. By far the best of the porters had been the indefatigable Tenzing, and now he and Pasang put up a remarkable effort by descending from Camp V to pick up the abandoned loads, 700 ft below, and climbing back up with them – this on top of a day which had reduced most of the party to near exhaustion.[17]

A strong easterly wind prevented any advance next day, but on 8 June the party from Camp V moved up the ridge to establish Camp VI at 27,200 ft, on a gentle scree slope below the Yellow Band. It had been a hard day's work, and the Sherpas really had extended themselves; Pasang seemed ill.

It was all to no avail. Next day Smythe and Shipton found that the snow was deep and powdery and it took them an hour to progress a single rope length. Norton's traverse line, piled deep with snow, looked horrendous, and even if it could have been crossed the gully beyond was out of the question. More as a gesture than from any feeling of hope, the two climbers tried to make a diagonal ascent towards the crest of the ridge, aiming for a point below the First Step, though the ridge also looked fearsome. However, as the rocks steepened the possibility of the waist-deep snow avalanching and sweeping them off the mountain became acute; their only course was to retreat.

They reached Camp V just in time to meet Tilman and Lloyd coming up. Their news must have been depressing to Tilman, even though he hardly expected better. Despite the conditions he and Lloyd decided to continue their plans to go to Camp VI and, even if an ascent of the mountain was impossible, at least to try to reach the crest of the summit ridge. It was, however, a vain quest.

That evening Tilman and Lloyd returned to Camp IV on the North Col to find Odell and Oliver in residence with a few porters. The others had gone down to the East Rongbuk Glacier with a sick porter, and now it looked as if there was another sick porter, for Pasang lay in his tent paralysed on his right side. The other porters were all in favour of abandoning their comrade as a sacrifice to the mountain gods, who, as they pointed out with Eastern logic, were obviously punishing the expedition. If Pasang escaped his patently pre-determined fate, the gods would take someone else instead.

Naturally enough, this line of reasoning was not accepted by the sahibs, and next day there began the laborious job of carrying Pasang down the slopes to the East Rongbuk Glacier. Like the others, Tilman decided to risk the avalanche slopes to the east rather than the icy slopes on the west side of the col. Their human burden proved to be an awkward carry, but the porters treated him as they would any other load, and it was a wet, cold and very ill Pasang who was eventually put to bed in Camp III. That he survived and eventually recovered reasonably well is indicative of the toughness of his race.

The expedition was over. Like its predecessors it had failed to climb Everest, the only difference being that it had failed cheaply.

Was the experiment a success? Certainly it demonstrated, as Tilman has claimed, that a small expedition was as capable of putting two men into position for a summit bid as a large one. Before the team had set out from England someone had said, 'If you fail, whatever you do don't blame the weather,' meaning that after all the recent failures, the weather was beginning to look like a convenient excuse. Yet, however it looked to the people back home, most of whom could not even begin to appreciate the realities of the problem, it was the weather which called an end to the game. Experiences in 1938 made it quite clear that once the monsoon has broken, the north side of Everest is not climbable. The rocks become covered in snow, and above Camp V at least the snow never consolidates, but remains like a sea of waist-deep flour through which the climber must struggle, all the time gasping for air and hoping the slope won't avalanche.

Tilman, like Ruttledge in 1936, was unfortunate to have to contend with an early monsoon – or was it the norm, and others in previous years who had been lucky enough to meet a late monsoon? That question was never satisfactorily answered, even after seven expeditions.

Supposing conditions had been good on the North Face, could Tilman's experiment have succeeded? There seems no reason to doubt it: Smythe and Shipton had never felt fitter, on their own admission, and though there was 1,800 ft to climb from Camp VI to the top, they stood at least as good a chance as their predecessors. Tilman had certainly proved his point.

All the same it wasn't as clear a point as it first seems. Tilman himself blurred the issue with his austerity diet. There is no evidence to show that this benefited the team in any way, and it may in fact have been psychologically detrimental. In the event, it didn't matter to the result, but it might have done had the weather been different. Reading Tilman's thesis, one sometimes feels he concentrated too much on individual trees and almost forgot the value of the forest.

Another factor which helped Tilman enormously, and which both he and Shipton recognized when they wrote their accounts of the expedition, was the enormous strides made by the Sherpa porters in confidence and ability. They were not yet climbers, in the European sense, but the men who were with Tilman in 1938 – Angtharkay, Tenzing, Pasang and the rest – were very different from the 'coolies' who had travelled with Howard-Bury. Once the value of the Sherpas had been proved on the first three Everest expeditions, they were in demand by expeditions throughout the Himalaya: German, French, American, Dutch, Italian, Japanese and many British expeditions had used the natives of Sola Khumbu, and the Sherpas had learnt from all of them. The best of them, though lacking in technique, had become infected with the spirit of the game: 'Previously,' wrote Shipton, 'it has always been rather a question of driving these men to extreme altitudes; now the position was almost reversed.'[18]

Tilman, as he freely admitted, compromised his basic principles by taking oxygen apparatus on the expedition, and ironically it was his expedition which more than any other since the time of Finch gave oxygen its most thorough testing. Though the closed oxygen system never worked properly, Lloyd used the open system continuously above Camp IV and found that it reduced fatigue considerably, and above 26,000 ft made a decided increase in his climbing rate. To Tilman, however, this was little more than a scientific curiosity and had nothing to do with climbing Everest:

> My own opinion is that the mountain could and should be climbed without, and I think there is a cogent reason for not climbing it at all rather than climb it with the help of oxygen ... I feel sure that if it were climbed with the help of oxygen there would be for mountaineers an instinctive urge to climb it again without. The plausible argument that it is better to climb

> the mountain with oxygen rather than not at all is therefore unsound ... Mountaineering is analogous to sailing, and there is not much merit to be acquired by sailing with the help of an auxiliary engine. If man wishes gratuitously to fight nature, not for existence or the means of existence but for fun, or at the worst self-aggrandizement, it should be done with natural weapons.[19]

Tilman was applying to the Himalaya the rigid ethics of classical mountaineering – the idea that if you can't get up a rock or a mountain by 'fair' means, you should wait until someone comes along who can. Unfortunately, it was a somewhat bent ethic even in the days of Whymper, and even more so since – the 'self-aggrandizement' Tilman speaks of is a strong force for wrongdoing. By 1938 not enough big Himalayan peaks had been climbed to establish an ethical norm, and by the time there were, the norm included oxygen.

The prizes were too great for too much ethics: when the big peaks were there for the taking, a little thing like oxygen wasn't going to stop the would-be conquerors. Bearing in mind the nature of some men, it says quite a lot for mountaineering tradition that the post-war expeditions were as restrained as they were.

Now that the Golden Age of Himalayan first ascents is over, with all the really big peaks climbed at least once and often several times, the pressure is off and mountaineers have once again turned to a more leisurely examination of ethics. Tilman's basic assumptions were right, of course: conquest alone is not enough. When he spoke at the British Mountaineering Council's National Conference in 1976 Tilman received a rapturous welcome from the audience. They were applauding a prophet come into his own, for though Tilman was not the inventor of the small expedition he had been its most consistent champion for forty years.

The small expedition, the so-called 'Alpine-style ascent', is rapidly becoming commonplace even for the most ambitious Himalayan objectives, and Everest itself has not been immune. Today's climbers have out-Tilmanned Tilman in many ways – but of course, they have advantages that he never had, stemming from the age in which we live. But the change was a long time in coming, and even now is not complete.

The 1938 expedition returned home to the rumblings of Munich and a country too concerned about events in Europe to worry much over the success or failure of an Everest expedition.

Only one minor mishap upset the tranquillity of the expedition's homecoming. Peter Oliver had left Rongbuk before the others because his Army leave was up. On the way home he stayed in Kalimpong with Norman and Bunty Odling, who had been particularly hospitable to Everesters since 1933. Naturally, he discussed the expedition with his hosts, unaware that Norman

Odling was a Reuter correspondent. Odling filed a despatch based on Oliver's story – and scooped *The Times*, who had an exclusive contract with the Committee. *The Times* was furious, Tilman was acutely embarrassed, and it cost the Committee £850 in reparation.

Tilman's expedition was the last pre-war attempt on Everest. The North Ridge remained inviolate. Summing up, Eric Shipton wrote:

> No, it is not remarkable that Everest did not yield to the first few attempts; indeed, it would have been very surprising and not a little sad if it had, for that is not the way of great mountains . . .
>
> It is possible, even probable, that in time men will look back with wonder at our feeble efforts, unable to account for our repeated failure, while they themselves are grappling with far more formidable problems. If we are still alive we shall no doubt mumble fiercely in our grey beards in a desperate effort to justify our weakness. But if we are wise we shall reflect with deep gratitude that we seized our mountaineering heritage, and will take pleasure in watching younger men enjoy theirs.[20]

The Mount Everest Committee met for the last time on 14 June 1939, three months before the invasion of Poland. By a curious coincidence Hinks resigned as Secretary, after serving the Committee from its inception; wiser in the ways of mountaineers, no doubt, though the years had done nothing to mellow his forthright temperament.

If the clouds of war were gathering over the country, no wisp of them penetrated into the Committee room. Impressed perhaps by Chamberlain's scrap of paper, the Committee decided to ask permission for Everest expeditions in 1940, 1941 and 1942.

There could hardly have been an end more in keeping.

# 10

# The Pegasus Factor

Had Mount Everest been climbed at the first attempt it would have been hailed as a notable achievement and quickly forgotten. The peak itself, because it is the highest in the world, would have become no more than a curious statistic for use in quiz games.

It was, ironically, the repeated failures which gave the mountain real stature in the public's eyes. Hinks notwithstanding, the publicity was enormous, and if, towards the end of the decade before the war, the public became a little bored with the whole business, the mountain was by then firmly implanted in its mind as a symbol of the unattainable and moved out of the purely mountaineering domain to become a challenge to Man in general.

When it comes to a question of self-esteem, Man is a pretty sneaky sort of creature. If he sees a game in which the rules consistently damage his vanity, he changes the rules. If he couldn't 'conquer' Everest by climbing it, he would 'conquer' it some other way. The only other way was by flying over it.

Today, with our high-flying jets and pressurized cabins, such an objective seems ludicrously petty and the word 'conquest', laughable. Even commercial airliners regularly cruise at 31,000 ft, which is 2,000 ft higher than Everest, and military jets go much higher. But in the years between the wars the situation was very different: the idea of flying over Everest in the unsophisticated machines of the day was a real challenge.

It was an era when aviation was itself a challenge – the period of the great air races and public heroes like Mollinson and Lindbergh. The challenge of Everest may have been known to the public, but the challenge of aviation was known to a much greater degree. Why should the two not be combined? After all, the urge to fly faster or longer was well catered for. Why not fly higher as well? And since altitude records tend to be dull things compared with a race from London to Sydney, why not give it recognizable substance by flying over Mount Everest?

The possible use of aircraft to assist the mountaineers had not been overlooked by the Mount Everest Committee. John Noel had himself raised the subject during his lecture to the Royal Geographical Society in 1919 – the lecture which had sparked off the whole Everest saga. He had suggested that an aerial survey of Everest should be possible, with the planes taking off and landing in India. For closer survey work he thought a 'man-lifting kite' with a ceiling of about 500 ft might be useful – an interesting idea in view of the development of hang-gliding half a century later. At the same lecture Younghusband agreed with Noel about the desirability of aerial survey, though Percy Farrar wanted to go further and transport the whole expedition to Everest by airship.

Both Younghusband and Farrar were closely involved in the preparations for the first expedition led by Howard-Bury in 1921, and it seems likely that when Howard-Bury went to India in 1920 to canvass support he was instructed to investigate the possible use of aircraft. In that year the world altitude record had been raised by the Americans to 33,114 ft, and it must have seemed to the Committee that using aircraft in the Himalayas was a distinct possibility.

But the Air Force in India weren't interested, and Howard-Bury got a cold reception.[1] When the Viceroy heard of this he was distinctly annoyed, with the result that when Howard-Bury returned to the Air Force authorities a little later, he found them much more co-operative. He was able to report home enthusiastically:

> I have seen a good deal of Webb Bowen too and his views with regard to an aerial reconnaissance have altered considerably and he is now ready to help us in every way possible next autumn. He thinks a D.H. 9a would do the job and he would be prepared I think to lend us a machine, pilot, photographic apparatus and petrol, but we should have to take all the expense of preparing a landing ground or temporary aerodrome.[2]

Whether the Committee eventually considered that the cost of making a landing strip at Purneah was not justified is hard to say, but the idea of using aircraft for either reconnaissance or supplies was soon abandoned. It was probably a wise decision: the Handley Page bomber in use at the time had a ceiling of 10,600 ft – dangerously low for Himalayan flying. On the other hand, if the D.H. 9a mentioned by Webb Bowen had been capable of high-altitude reconnaissance, it might have solved in minutes the problem of the East Rongbuk Glacier that kept Mallory and Bullock guessing for weeks.

In 1924 Alan Cobham, one of the most famous aviators of the day, discussed with Hinks the possibility of using aircraft for reconnaissance and store-carrying but they agreed it wasn't feasible, and General Bruce, who was having similar talks with the Air Ministry, came to the same conclusions. Cobham's scheme had the backing of the *News of the World* – in itself enough to put Hinks off. Eventually, Cobham did fly over some of the lower Himalayan peaks, as did the American aviator Halliburton; but neither could tackle Everest itself.

By this time the altitude record was held by the French at 36,000 ft and production aircraft were evolving which would just about take the Himalaya in their stride. Inevitably, the idea of actually landing somebody on the mountain was mooted and the American flyer Roscoe Turner offered his services to the Committee to do just that. He had, he said, five years' experience in all kinds of aviation including wing-walking, plane-changing and balloon-piloting. Despite these uniquely advantageous qualifications, the Committee turned him down.

Nevertheless, not everyone regarded the idea of landing on Everest as preposterous. John Noel was convinced it would be done, and in 1927 he explained how:

> The altitude of 30,000 feet is now no difficulty to modern high-flying machines. They can now also be constructed to be able to hover almost stationary against even mild winds. (I do not necessarily refer to helicopters.) From already proved performances in high flying and hovering, it would be possible to provide a machine that could hover within 100 feet over the summit of Everest and so allow a passenger from the plane under certain right conditions, and protected by thickly padded clothing which he would discard on landing, to descend by a rope from the machine to the ground. The shape of the summit of Everest, as far as observed by telescope hitherto, seems to offer sufficient space, evenness and snow-covering to make such a landing possible, although there would be no chance of a plane itself landing, nor of even taking off again nor of picking up its passenger. That passenger (there could be two) would with the aid of liquid oxygen breathing and previous high-altitude acclimatisation, descend the mountain as far as the East Rongbuk Glacier snowfield at the foot of the Ice Cliff, where another suitably constructed aeroplane could easily land and pick him up to fly back to India.
>
> The descent of the mountain would be undertaken in two days, using sleeping-bags and food dropped in a suitable place on the mountain during previous flights. A number of these Depots would be dropped for the choice of the climbers.[3]

It is doubtful whether anyone took Noel's suggestion any more seriously than they did those of Roscoe Turner. What seemed much more likely was that before long somebody would attempt to fly over the mountain.

French and German aviators were known to have been planning to fly over

Everest for some years, but British interest in such a project did not crystallize until 1932, when a monocled Army officer, Major L.V.S. Blacker, came forward with definite proposals for an attempt.

Blacker's timing was perfect; all the portents for success suddenly came together. First of all, there was a re-awakening of public interest in Mount Everest with the prospect of the 1933 expedition after an interval of nine years – valuable background enthusiasm which made Blacker's goals understandable to everyone. Then, as a demonstration that his plans were not unrealistic, Blacker could point to the exploits of Squadron Leader S.B. Harris, who in March 1931 had led a flight of Wapitis from Risalpur to Gilgit in the Karakorum, circuiting the mighty Nanga Parbat (26,658 ft) and crossing other high peaks such as Rakaposhi, Domani and Haramosh. Last, and most important of all, Britain had just raised the aircraft altitude record to 44,000 ft, thanks to the new Bristol Pegasus engine.[4]

Engines already existed which were capable of carrying a single-seater aircraft the necessary height and distance, but Blacker had realized at the outset that this would not be good enough. Later he wrote:

> An attempt could, of course, have been made some years earlier in a single-seater aeroplane with good hopes of success.
>
> However, without an observer and fully adequate photographic equipment, the flight would have been easier but mere foolish sensationalism, inasmuch as no scientific results could be expected.[5]

In fact, the venture had to be given a cloak of scientific responsibility or it could not have taken place at all. It was only by convincing the influential Royal Geographical Society that the flight could produce valuable aerial survey material that there was any hope of approaching the India Office and through them the Nepalese Government. So despite Blacker's words an attempt could *not* have been made earlier – a single-seater flight intended merely to break a record would not have been allowed. Before 1932 there was no engine capable of carrying two men to the required height. The whole success of the affair rested on the Bristol Pegasus engine.

The Pegasus S3 – the 'S' stood for supercharged – was an air-cooled radial-type engine with nine cylinders of twenty-eight litres capacity capable of developing a maximum of 580 brake horse power at 13,500 ft. The supercharging was essential for high-altitude work: an unsupercharged engine draws in its combustible mixture of petrol and air at normal atmospheric pressure, or rather less, which means that it is most effective at sea level, where the atmospheric pressure is highest. It is correspondingly less so at altitude, where the atmospheric pressure is lower. At the height of Mount Everest an unsupercharged engine loses some 73 per cent of its power.

By forcing the mixture of petrol and air into the cylinders under pressure –

supercharging – this power loss is substantially reduced. In the Pegasus the supercharging was done by means of a rotary pump driven from the crankshaft, and it enabled the engine to maintain 50 per cent of its power even at the height of Everest – almost twice as powerful as an unsupercharged engine of the same type.

There was no doubt that the Pegasus, fitted in a suitable airframe, would be capable of carrying a pilot and observer/photographer over the summit of Everest. Technical details and costings needed to be worked out of course, but Blacker realized that in the Pegasus engine lay certain success; it had the power to overcome not only the physical problems but the political ones too.

Blacker set up his headquarters at the College of Aeronautical Engineering, Chelsea, in March 1932 and in the same month submitted his plans to the R.G.S., who almost immediately approved of them and sent a letter of support to the India Office. In the following month facilities were made available by the R.A.F. and negotiations were begun with the Bristol Aeroplane Company. The Committee, which until then consisted of Blacker and an old wartime comrade, Colonel P.T. Etherton, suddenly began to acquire prestigious names; Lord Peel and John Buchan (the famous author, later Lord Tweedsmuir) joined it, followed in the next few months by Lord Clydesdale, M.P. (who was later nominated as one of the pilots), the Master of Sempill, Lord Lytton, Lord Burnham, the Maharaja of Nawanagar and sundry high-ranking Air Force officers. As a Committee it was very high-powered indeed. Unfortunately it was also broke.

In the spring of 1932, when the project had begun, the financial side had seemed satisfactory. A number of individuals and firms had promised support in money and materials, but that summer there was a financial crisis and a lot of the promises were withdrawn. The plans were already far advanced and the organizers were faced with a desperate situation.

At the last moment, like some fairy godmother, the rich and beautiful society hostess Lady Houston stepped in with £10,000, and further assurances of £5,000 if necessary. At once the cloud was lifted; the Committee were able to afford the best of everything they required.

Lady Houston was well known as a patron of aviation (the Schneider Trophy, for example) but it seems that in this case her action sprang from a family friendship with Lord Clydesdale. At the same time she thought that if the flight was successful it would impress the natives of India with the innate superiority of their British overlords. She saw it as further strengthening the foundations of a great empire. Unfortunately, she made these political views widely known through the press and this aroused the anger of the Indian Congress Party, though they could do little to prevent the flight.

With the advent of Lady Houston's money, the Committee grew again in size and was forced to move to more commodious accommodation in

Grosvenor House. Because of the complexities of organization the Chief of Air Staff, Sir John Salmond, suggested that an experienced executive officer should take overall charge of the organization and he suggested Air Commodore P.F.M. Fellowes. Blacker, the man who began it all, was gently put on one side and Fellowes took over. It was a significant step on the road to success.

Air Commodore Fellowes was a wartime flying hero – D.S.O. and bar – a born leader of men and, most important, a genius at organization. Any student of Everest cannot help but compare the way in which Fellowes, with a mere six months at his disposal, organized the whole complex and highly technical operation, with the bumbling, haphazard efforts of the Mount Everest Committee, who had taken years to reach even a modicum of efficiency. It is true, of course, that the problems were different; but so was the approach to the problems. Fellowes and his team tackled theirs in a scientific manner, thought every contingency through in advance, and went forward in great confidence.

The technical work to be done before the flights could take place was quite staggering. Though the Pegasus engine was already decided upon, a suitable aircraft had to be found to carry it. In the end the choice fell on a Westland P.V3, a prototype plane developed as a day bomber. However, as there was only one of these in existence the second plane was to be a Westland Wallace. In honour of their sponsor the Committee renamed the P.V3 the Houston-Westland. It was a biplane capable of carrying two persons, and with a high undercarriage which would give adequate clearance for the extra large propeller thought necessary for high-altitude flying.[6]

The aircraft had to be rigorously modified and equipped with much innovatory equipment. For example, ingenious use was made of fourteen-volt electric heating! Kapok suits were lined with heating wires, as were the flyers' goggles. The cameras were warmed by electrically heated jackets, and even the oxygen supply was pre-heated so that no moisture would clog the regulatory valves. How Finch must have envied them their technical capacity!

Then, too, there were specially adapted flying instruments and oils to be considered and tested, and, most important, the cameras.

No fewer than four types of photographs were to be attempted by the aviators. First and foremost were the aerial survey pictures taken on a Williamson Automatic Eagle III survey camera, pointing downwards and recording overlapping vertical shots of the country over which the plane would fly. For the results to be of any value this type of photography is not as simple as it may seem, especially in mountainous country, and various corrections need to be considered in advance. It is also important for the aircraft to fly a level course whenever the camera is being used, itself a tricky operation.

Photography was the responsibility of the observer, or second man. In addition to the survey photography he also had to handle a large plate camera for stills photography and a ciné camera too. These (and their spares) were kept in the observer's cockpit and it is little wonder that there was no room for a parachute or even a safety harness. Using the heavy ciné camera was a tricky job: the observer needed to hook his feet under some projection in the cockpit, otherwise the drag as he leaned out might have tipped him from the plane altogether.[7]

By February 1933 all was ready for the move to India. The two Westlands were shipped to Karachi in the S.S. *Dalgoma*, while Fellowes and the two pilots, Clydesdale and McIntyre, flew out in three light Moth planes.

Meanwhile, how did the Mount Everest Committee, involved as it was with its own 1933 expedition, view this esoteric interloper on their sacred preserves?

They certainly weren't pleased. They first learned that the flight was taking place in September 1932 – presumably when Lady Houston's finance put the show on the road – although Hinks at least must have known earlier because he had been consulted on the survey aspects of the photography. The Mount Everest Committee at once approached the India Office to find out whether they approved of all this flying nonsense, and finding that they did, they then wrote to Blacker saying they disapproved of any action which might upset the Tibetans. As far as can be judged, Blacker ignored them – after all, he wasn't proposing to fly over Tibet, and in any case he didn't care what the Everest Committee thought.

When, early in October, the Committee discovered that the flight had actually gained permission from Nepal and India, they were most upset and, in the way of Everest Committees, became thoroughly pompous. They were, they said, 'most anxious' and hoped the flight might be postponed: 'We cannot forbid it, but will do our best to discourage it.' A somewhat empty threat, to say the least.[8]

As if to rub salt into the wound *The Times* enthusiastically took up the cause of the Everest flight, enabling Dawson, the editor, to get his own back on the mountaineers who had rejected him in favour of the *Daily Telegraph*. Hinks was furious.

The base selected for the expedition was Purneah, about 300 miles north of Calcutta in the province of Bihar. The members of the expedition were housed in a bungalow belonging to the Maharaja of Darbhanga. It stood in its own grounds, which included a golf course and tennis courts, while near at hand was the Raja of Banaili's private race course: 'The surroundings, in fact, had the surface aspects of a well equipped country club.'[9] The landing field itself was ten miles away at Lalbalu (the 'other ranks' were soon sent out there to rough it), but the journey was no problem:

> The Raja of Banaili, a cheery personality, who had shot over a hundred tigers, offered us his fleet of motor-cars, remarking that, if possible, he would like to retain one or two for his own use. He had seventeen. He seemed astonished, as if at an unusual display of moderation, when only three cars and a lorry were required.[10]

To read of such luxuries, as they appeared in *The Times* reports, must have galled the mountaineers who had endured the hardships of the Tibetan plateau, especially when reference was made to 'the horrors of exploration' – 'there was no milk for breakfast on one occasion,' wrote Strutt sarcastically in the *Alpine Journal*, 'and on another dinner could not be served until 10.30 p.m.'[11]

If the aviators did not share the extreme discomfort of the climbers, they did share the same weather. Just as it was impossible to climb the mountain if the weather was bad, so too was it impossible to fly over it. Clear weather and fairly modest winds at 30,000 ft were what the pilots needed to ensure success – clouds would make photography useless, and a strong wind, blowing in the wrong direction, would cause the aircraft to use up too much fuel with possibly disastrous consequences. Though an emergency landing strip had been constructed forty-six miles nearer the Nepalese border than Purneah, it was little more than a sop to conscience: the real fear was a forced landing in the tangled mountain masses of Nepal, with little chance of survival.

Day by day the weather reports came from Calcutta, and the expedition's own high-altitude wind balloons were sent up, but it was not until 3 April that conditions were judged to be favourable and the two Westlands roared off from Lalbalu airfield at 8.25 a.m. In the lead plane, the Houston-Westland, the pilot was Clydesdale and the observer-photographer was Blacker; in the second plane, McIntyre was pilot and the observer's place was occupied by S.R. Bonnett, a professional cameraman working for Gaumont British Films.

A ground haze, or dust haze, obscured the forward view until at about 19,000 ft the planes rose above it into a brilliant sky and the whole range of the Nepalese Himalaya lay before them, stretching away on either hand to Kangchenjunga and Dhaulagiri or beyond, gleaming white and quite magical. Clydesdale wrote:

> The aeroplanes seemed to be enclosed within a semi-circle of the most gigantic mountains in the world. This time they really looked enormous, because we were seeing them from much closer range than we had ever seen them before. Just to the right of the aeroplane's nose as it rose clear of the murk, the summit of Mount Everest appeared with its plume, like the smoke of a volcano, stretching out to the east but in proportion rather shorter than we had seen it on previous occasions, indicating that the wind velocity was less than when we had usually observed it. Everest was probably nearly 50 miles distant when first sighted.[12]

On the technical side, however, things were not going so well. Because of the haze they failed to find the river junction which was to be the control point of their survey. In fact, for the same reason, they could not ascertain the drift of the aircraft, which was much greater than the pilots allowed for, and as a consequence, instead of approaching Everest from the south-west, up the Dudh Kosi and over Namche Bazar, they came at it almost due south, just to the west of Chamlang.

The planes kept as low as possible in an attempt to pick up identifiable landmarks, but suddenly the pilots found that they were approaching the Everest massif with nothing like enough altitude. Clydesdale began a steep climb to bring the plane up to 31,000 ft, which meant he would clear the summit by the safe margin of approximately 2,000 ft, when suddenly a downdraught on the leeward side of the massif plunged the Houston-Westland down by 2,000 ft. Despite putting the controls into maximum rate of climb, he knew he was losing height to the force of the downdraught. Out of the corner of his eye he could see that McIntyre had been forced even lower and was altering course to avoid Lhotse.

Clydesdale himself could do nothing but approach Lhotse head on – and he barely skimmed the summit. Immediately, the downdraught ceased, the plane climbed sharply and he passed over the summit of Everest with 500 ft to spare. The time was 10.05 a.m.[13]

His approach also carried the Houston-Westland through the well-known 'plume' of Everest, that seeming tail of cloud which streams away from the mountain's summit. Clydesdale soon discovered it was no mere cloud but 'A prodigious jet of rushing winds flinging a veritable barrage of ice fragments for several miles to leeward of the peak'. It cracked the celastroid windows of the rear cockpit.[14]

Meanwhile, McIntyre had his own problems. The Wallace, weighted down by the heavier ciné equipment, could not match the Houston-Westland in rate of climb, and the pilot found himself in a desperate situation as the huge peaks rapidly closed in:

> We were in a most serious position [he wrote]. The great bulk of Everest was towering above us to the left, Makalu down-wind to the right and the connecting range dead ahead, with a hurricane wind doing its best to carry us over and dash us on the knife-edge sides of Makalu. I had the feeling that we were hemmed in on all sides, and that we dare not turn away to gain height afresh. There was plenty of air-space behind us, yet it was impossible to turn back. A turn to the left meant going back into the down-current and the peaks below; a turn down-wind to the right would have taken us almost instantly into Makalu at 200 miles an hour.[15]

Fortunately a sudden uprush of air allowed him to scrape over a ridge to comparative safety. However, McIntyre's task was to fly over Everest, not avoid it, so he turned his machine once more towards the mountain and again scraped crab-wise over one of the ridges. He repeated the manoeuvre three times before he judged he had gained sufficient height to attempt the summit.

As the machine flew over the top of Everest, McIntyre had time only for the briefest glance, because it had become obvious that something had happened to Bonnett, the observer. In fact, Bonnett had fractured an oxygen feed pipe and had almost passed out before he found the break and repaired it by bandaging it with a handkerchief. Realizing that the summit must be close, Bonnett had then tried to struggle up against the slipstream with the heavy ciné camera to get the shot of a lifetime, but, already weakened, the effort proved too much for him and he collapsed unconscious on the floor of the cockpit.

In trying to discover what had happened to his observer, McIntyre wrenched the nose piece of his own oxygen apparatus away. He couldn't get it to stay back in place and so was forced to fly the plane with one hand and hold his precious oxygen mask to his face with the other. It was an uncomfortable flight home.

Both aircraft touched down at Lalbalu at 11.25 a.m. They had been away exactly three hours – three hours of great adventure, though as Clydesdale sombrely recorded later: 'It was not our business to have adventures, for adventures are eschewed by all well-organized expeditions.'[16] McIntyre was more blunt: 'At the time it was very much like a nightmare,' he said.[17]

Unfortunately the survey photographs were not a success owing to the ground haze, and so, despite protests from Lady Houston, who seems to have had a particularly soft spot for Clydesdale, the flight was repeated on 19 April, though this time the planes did not pass over the actual summit.

There is no doubt that in its organization and execution the Everest flight was a brilliant *tour de force*. From start to finish the whole plan had taken a mere thirteen months, in which the aircraft and engines had to be built, special equipment designed and tested, political and financial problems overcome. The attention to detail was meticulous and scientific: it was in fact an object lesson in how to organize an expedition.

The mountaineering establishment were not too pleased with the success of the Houston flights. Though the Everest Committee sent off the obligatory telegram of congratulation to Fellowes and his team, the review of the expedition book, *First over Everest*, in the *Alpine Journal* was one of grudging admiration, with a thinly veiled suggestion that the expedition had altered its motives from science to mere publicity. Pure jealousy drips between the lines. But this was nothing compared with the mauling the expedition film got from the formidable Strutt, then editor of the *Alpine Journal* and a man not noted for temperate speech: 'The films give mostly the appearance of having been taken through a keyhole covered with sheep netting', he wrote, and: 'Whatever may have been the short-comings of the "Houston-Everest" flight in performance, it has not suffered from want of publicity.'[18]

The truth of the matter was that the Mount Everest Committee, and through them the Alpine Club, had come to regard Mount Everest as a private domain reserved exclusively for them.

In these days, when intercontinental aeroplanes commonly cruise at 30,000 ft while their passengers recline in comfortable chairs watching the latest movie, it is difficult to imagine the adventure of that first Everest flight, for, unlike mountain climbing, flying has become so common as to be debased in our present estimation of adventure. Yet adventure it was, and though not comparable with, say, Alcock and Brown's crossing of the Atlantic, it was a tiny step forward in aviation history.

Nine years after the Houston flight, Everest was flown over again, but under very different circumstances. Cruising alone in a P43A pursuit plane, the commander of the famous 'Flying Tigers', Colonel Robert L. Scott, decided on the spur of the moment to fly over Everest. He had no preparations and had no authorization, but he set a course which took him over Kangchenjunga, Makalu, Lhotse and Everest, crossing the summit *two miles* above it – a measure, if nothing else, of the immense strides made in aircraft design since the Houston flight.

On 16 June 1945, Sq. Ldr C.G. Andrews, a New Zealander, and C. Fenwick, who was British, flew over Everest in a de Havilland Mosquito. They claimed to have skimmed the summit by about thirty feet.

In 1947 an enthusiastic R.A.F. pilot, Kenneth Neame, flying a Spitfire XIX, made an unauthorized photographic flight over the mountain, and in 1953 a Liberator of the Indian Air Force also flew over Everest.

Some day, no doubt, an enterprising individual with a strong sense of adventure and notable lack of self-preservation will hang-glide from the summit of Everest onto the Khumbu Glacier or Rongbuk Glacier, but until that day arrives there is nothing to be gained by flying over the world's highest mountain. Today, at Kathmandu airport, you can hire a light plane to take you on a flight to Everest on any fine day you choose, and though you won't cross the summit, for a few pounds or dollars you can match the photographic exploits of the pioneers.

# 11

# The Outsiders

Although the Houston flight of 1933 was a minor triumph of aviation history, nobody saw it as the 'conquest' of Mount Everest. Following Mallory's dictum, few climbers would use the word in any event, but even the general public, unaware of the niceties of mountaineering ethics, realized that until someone actually stood on the top the job wasn't finished.

It seems now, in retrospect, that 1933 was the watershed of public expectation. The Ruttledge team of that year was particularly strong and well equipped. There had been almost a decade in which to reflect on mistakes of the past and build a team of experts who would not only climb the highest mountain in the world, but avenge the deaths of Mallory and Irvine at the same time. And when Ruttledge's team failed people gave a mental shrug and declared the thing impossible. After 1933, expeditions were not expected to succeed.

But there are men for whom the unattainable has a special attraction. Usually they are not experts: their ambitions and fantasies are strong enough to brush aside the doubts which more cautious men might have. Determination and faith are their strongest weapons. At best such men are regarded as eccentric; at worst, mad.

Partly because the repeated failures of the official expeditions made the mountain a natural target, Everest has attracted its share of men like these. Their mountaineering experience varied from none at all to very slight – certainly none of them had the kind of experience which would make an ascent of Everest a reasonable goal. Three things they all had in common: faith in themselves, great determination and endurance. Their attempts were all illicit – not one of them had permission to visit Everest, a fact which they regarded as little more than an inconvenient nuisance. None were successful.

The first of the outsiders to try his luck against Everest did so for ulterior motives. Maurice Wilson had no personal ambitions when it came to mountain climbing, for he had never climbed a mountain in his life. What he did have was a fanatical belief that a combination of faith and fasting could cure the human condition. He believed that if a man fasted almost to the point of death then all his physical and mental ills would drain out of him; and if he also had faith in the powers of God, then God would renew him in body and spirit, and he would emerge a stronger, better person.

It seemed to Wilson a simple panacea for the world's ills, but he was astute enough to realize that if he tried to spread his gospel by the usual means, through lectures and articles, few would bother to listen: he would be just another prophet crying in the wilderness. What he needed was publicity of the sort that would make people sit up and take notice. So why not climb Mount Everest – alone?

He had no fears about the outcome: Divine faith, he believed, could accomplish any task. It was this burning faith that set in train one of the most bizarre and moving chapters of the Everest story.

Maurice Wilson was one of the 'lost generation' whose ranks were decimated by the First World War. Those who survived the horror of the trenches often wondered why, or how, and for all of them life was never quite the same afterwards. Many of them, restless, haunted by the shadows of their terrible experiences, found it difficult to re-adjust to civilian life. This was certainly the case with Wilson.

He was born in Bradford, Yorkshire, in 1898, the third son of a self-made woollens manufacturer. In the normal course of events he would have followed his father and brothers into the mill, but the war changed that. On his eighteenth birthday he enlisted in the infantry and was commissioned a year later, joined his battalion in time for the third battle of Ypres and won the Military Cross. Shortly afterwards he was seriously wounded in his chest and left arm by machine-gun fire, and invalided home.

Wilson was a tall man – over six feet – and strong as an ox, which doubtless helped him to recover from his injuries, though his left arm never properly healed and gave him bouts of pain during the rest of his life.

He was demobilized in the summer of 1919 and quickly found that life in Bradford held no fulfilment. After a short stay in London he emigrated, first to America and from there to New Zealand, tackling a variety of jobs but never finding the satisfaction he had come desperately to need. To any onlooker he must have appeared successful, for he had ingrained in him a practical Yorkshire business acumen which stood him in good stead, and he managed to accumulate the bank balance which was later to finance his great dream. But monetary success meant little to him, and he returned to England as dissatisfied as ever.

Frustration such as Wilson felt carried with it bouts of melancholia and there seems little doubt that on his return from abroad he was nearing a nervous breakdown. He became physically ill, too, losing weight and racked by coughing spasms, but, spurning the usual medical treatments, he underwent, secretly, a mysterious period of fasting and prayer. In two months he was a healthy and happy man again – and he had found his purpose in life.

Whenever he was questioned about his remarkable recovery, Wilson said that he had been to see a man in Mayfair who had once cured himself of an illness the medical profession had declared incurable, and that this man had instructed him in the method. It consisted of fasting for thirty-five days, subsisting only on sips of water, and then, when the body was purged, of asking God to make him whole again. This man, said Wilson, was wealthy enough to devote all his time to spreading the word, and had so far cured over a hundred people like himself.

Yet Wilson never named this benefactor, nor did the man seem known to the world in general. Whatever publicity about his drastic remedy there might have been seems to have gone completely unnoticed. It was Wilson who took it upon himself to spread the gospel.

Did the mystery man ever exist, or was the cure invented by Wilson himself? On the boat home from New Zealand, Wilson had befriended a party of Indian yoga experts and had shown great interest in their beliefs. Had some of what he learned stuck in his mind, and was his cure nothing but a mish-mash of yoga and Christianity? It seems at least as feasible an explanation as the mysterious man in Mayfair.

Nevertheless, Wilson was not a charlatan. He *did* undergo the fasting and the prayer, and he *was* made well. He believed implicitly in what he was doing.

The conviction that he had found his true vocation came to him as he recuperated in the Black Forest in 1932, after his illness and remarkable recovery. His problem was how to make people listen to his message. His biographer, Dennis Roberts, writes:

> It was while his mind was thinking along these lines that he saw, in the Freiburg café, a cutting about the 1924 Expedition to Everest. He read of the Sherpas and yaks that had carried the elaborate train of equipment to the base of the mountain; he read of the dangers and apparently insurmountable difficulties that had faced the mountaineers. And he asked himself did he truly believe that fasting and Divine faith could accomplish anything? No sooner had he asked himself, than he knew his belief was indeed pure and absolute. And he realized what he must do.[1]

But the newspaper cutting must have been simply a crystallizing point for what was already in his head. Everest was very much in the news at that time, with the Houston flight and the 1933 expedition both actively in preparation. It is inconceivable that Wilson didn't know of these things – in fact the Houston flight probably determined his course of action.

When he returned to London, his first thoughts were to persuade the Houston team to take him with them so that he could parachute onto the mountain, but he quickly abandoned that as impracticable. Nevertheless, the idea of using a plane to reach his goal struck him as common sense and he conceived a plan to fly to Everest, crash land on the East Rongbuk Glacier and make his way to the summit on foot. That he should even consider such a scheme shows that he had a total misconception of the Everest environment, and there were two other practical objections – he knew nothing about mountain climbing and he couldn't fly a plane. He set out to learn both.

One has the feeling that if Wilson could have bought a plane and left forthwith for India, that is precisely what he would have done, without bothering about technical niceties like learning to fly properly. But even in the 1930s a pilot's licence was required by law, and to get one a proper course of instruction was necessary. So Wilson bought a Gipsy Moth, three years old and bearing the letters G-ABJC, which he promptly named *Ever Wrest*, and joined the London Aero Club. Here he learned to fly, rather badly. But he did eventually get his pilot's licence.

Learning to fly was one thing, learning to climb quite another. In those days there were no organized courses of instruction, and one learnt from friends who were already climbers or by imitating a good Alpine guide, but Wilson doesn't seem to have taken advice from anyone. He went up to the Lake District and Snowdonia for five weeks, did a bit of scrambling and came back to London scarcely any wiser than before. Walking up Helvellyn or Snowdon is hardly adequate training for an ascent of Everest. Had he gone to Switzerland and put himself in the hands of a competent guide, he might have appreciated something of the nature of his undertaking. If nothing else, he would have found out what an ice axe and crampons were.

Nevertheless, Wilson had two great assets: his determination, and his physical fitness. This latter he constantly improved by long walks – he walked from London to his parents' home at Bradford several times.

By the middle of April 1933 all his preparations were ready. He had purchased such kit as he considered necessary and had had the Gypsy Moth suitably adapted with a long-range fuel tank and strengthened undercarriage. First, however, he decided to fly to Bradford to say farewell to his parents and family. It was an unlucky decision, for somewhere over the Yorkshire moors the engine cut out and *Ever Wrest* crashed into a farmer's field, hitting a hedge and tipping over. Wilson himself was unhurt, but the damage to the plane was considerable. It took three weeks to repair.

By this time the exploits of Maurice Wilson were beginning to appear in the daily papers. Apart from his crash he had also made a sensational (and illegal) parachute jump over London, and of course he made no secret about his plans to climb Everest. As the day for his departure drew near the Air Ministry sent him a stern note informing him that he would not be allowed to fly over Nepal. He replied to the effect that since the Houston flight had flown over Nepal only a month previously he didn't see why he couldn't do the same. The Air Ministry pointed out that the Houston flight was a special case, and he wasn't.

On Sunday, 21 May, on a perfect morning for flying, Maurice Wilson took off from Stag Lane Airfield, Edgware, en route for India and Everest. It was not an auspicious start: in his excitement he took off down-wind instead of up-wind and barely cleared the landing strip. A few minutes previously he had torn up a last-minute telegram from the Air Ministry, completely forbidding the flight.

A week later and Wilson landed at Cairo; a week later still and he was in India, having completed a remarkable solo flight despite the best efforts of the British Government to frustrate him. At Cairo he had been refused permission to fly over Persia (Iran) and at Bahrein he had been refused fuel, yet he managed to reach Gwadar in India and from there flew on to Lalbalu, near Purneah – the same place as the Houston flight had used earlier.

But Lalbalu was the end of his dream so far as the faithful *Ever Wrest* was concerned. The authorities would not grant him permission to fly over Nepal, and they impounded his plane to make sure he didn't get up to any more tricks.

Wilson's flight received considerable press coverage, for it was no mean feat he had accomplished. For an inexperienced pilot to fly a second-hand Gypsy Moth to India, and by a circuitous route, was quite an achievement in itself. To do it in the face of bureaucracy showed real determination. Indeed, when Wilson landed in India he had already achieved the purpose of his mission. The irony is that he completely failed to recognize that fact. Nothing but the conquest of Everest would satisfy him.

The weeks went by, the monsoon came, and Wilson realized that his chances of attempting the mountain for that year had gone, even if the authorities relented. Furthermore, he was running out of funds, so he sold *Ever Wrest* to a planter named Cassells for £500, and in July made his way to Darjeeling.

Once there he made formal application to the authorities for permission to enter Sikkim and Tibet on foot, and was firmly refused. The truth was that he was becoming something of an irksome thorn in the side of the Raj, for by this time he was too well known to be quietly gaoled or deported on a trumped-up charge: the press, who followed his progress avidly, would have had a field day at the Government's expense. There were many people who admired Wilson's determination and guts, even though they thought him a crank. It was just these qualities in Wilson that the authorities didn't like: they were suspicious, and rightly so.

With official permission refused him, Wilson began to make plans for an illegal journey into Tibet. In Darjeeling he met and talked with Karma Paul, the man who had done so much to help all the British expeditions to Everest. At first Karma Paul was enthusiastic to help the Englishman and promised to accompany him to Base Camp, but as they grew better acquainted with one another a mutual distrust and dislike built up which finally dissolved the partnership.

In January, when he had finally broken with Karma Paul, Wilson began to look round for other help. He wanted someone who knew the way through Tibet to Base Camp, and who would take him there without asking too many questions. By chance he found not one, but three – Tewang, Rinzing and Tsering, who had all been porters on the Ruttledge expedition.

Maurice Wilson left Darjeeling on the early morning of 31 March 1934. To avoid suspicion he had paid for his hotel room six months in advance and he gave out the story that some friends of his had invited him away on a tiger shoot. It was some time before the authorities tumbled his ruse, by which time he was already well out of their reach, travelling through Sikkim by night marches disguised as a Tibetan monk.

With the three Sherpas to guide him and care for him, he passed rapidly up the valley of the Tista, avoiding the towns and villages, and over the Kongra La into Tibet. Once across the border he felt a freer man, away from the watchful eye of the all-powerful British Raj; free enough to discard his disguise and travel by day instead of night. In his diary he wrote: 'Now in forbidden Tibet and feel like sending Government a wire: "Told you so!" '[2]

As he traversed the bleak Tibetan uplands in the days which followed, often frozen by the piercing winds or stung by the wind-chipped particles of sand scoured from the barren crust, he compared it with the mountains of the moon. Despite the hardship, he often managed twenty miles in a day and on 12 April he was rewarded with a splendid view of Everest. It aroused all his old ardour: 'Am already planning for future after the event,' he wrote. 'I *must* win.'[3]

Two days later – 14 April – he reached Rongbuk monastery. He had taken twenty-five days to cover the 300 miles from Darjeeling – ten days less than it had taken the 1933 expedition.

At Rongbuk monastery he made a very favourable impression on the Head Lama, who allowed him access to the equipment left behind by Ruttledge. But he was so anxious to be off on his great adventure that he stayed for only two days at the monastery and on the 16th he set off – alone – for Everest.

Wilson knew the route he had to take – up the East Rongbuk Glacier to the North Col slopes – for he had read all the books on the subject assiduously.

Unfortunately for him, those books had been written by mountaineers who were not only accustomed to finding their way over the sort of terrain that would make most people blanch, but who, in the still lingering manner of Victorian England, were inclined to describe any difficulties with proper restraint.[4]

On the first day, Wilson, carrying a 45-lb. rucksack, made good progress, but then as he moved up the East Rongbuk Glacier he was appalled and frustrated by the difficulties. Totally inexperienced in glacier travel, he had no idea which way to go, but found himself wandering in a maze of ice pinnacles. He had only a rough idea of how to use his ice axe, wasting energy cutting useless steps that led to nowhere. Time and again he retraced his path, caught in the grip of the ice maze, struggling against hunger, altitude and the enervating effects of glacier lassitude.

It took him three hard days to reach the site of the old Camp II, where he had the good fortune to find a pair of crampons, which would have helped him enormously in his struggle with the glacier. Such was his ignorance, however, that he simply tossed them aside.[5]

The weather, which had been fairly good for his attempt so far, suddenly became worse. On his fourth day out – 19 April – he advanced only three quarters of a mile and gained only 250 ft in height. It took him six hours.

Next day he worked his way slowly up the glacier to within a couple of miles of the site of Camp III below the North Col. Here, camped in the ice trough which is such a feature of this part of the East Rongbuk, he was pinned down by a blizzard for almost four days. In his cramped little diary he pencilled: 'Discretion is the better part of valour. No use going on. Eyes terrible and throat dry and v. sore . . . It's the weather that has beaten me – what damned bad luck!'[6]

Was Wilson deliberately writing for posterity, or was his power of self-deception such that he really believed it was only the weather that had beaten him? He was short of food, even though he existed on the sparsest of rations – a few figs, a little gruel – he was suffering agony from the old wound in his arm, and he was practically exhausted by the altitude, the weather and the hard going he had encountered. And he had not even reached Camp III. He must have realized then that his quest was hopeless.

A lesser spirit might have died at that point, or at least soon after. Wilson was faced with a gruelling retreat down the East Rongbuk and main Rongbuk glaciers. Somehow he fought through, stumbling, half blind, racked with pain, to the monastery and the welcoming arms of the Sherpas. He had been away nine days.

It was an incredible performance. He was lucky to be alive and yet on the very evening he returned, exhausted though he was, he managed to scribble in his diary, 'I still know that I can do it.' Then he slept for thirty-eight hours.

Eighteen days passed before he was ready for his second attempt. He took longer to recuperate from his first ordeal than he imagined he would and then two of the Sherpas, Tsering and Tewang, were ill. He had decided on his second attempt to use the porters to carry up to Camp III enough food and gear to allow him to make a semi-permanent base there from which he could make a lone attempt on the summit during a period of fine weather. In the event Tsering was never well enough to leave Rongbuk and only Tewang and Rinzing set out with Wilson on 12 May.

The Sherpas knew the intricacies of the East Rongbuk Glacier and they reached the site of the old Camp III in three days. Cached near-by they found a food dump left over from the Ruttledge expedition, which they had no hesitation in plundering. All Wilson's dietary plans were cast aside in the face of such bounty. He tucked in willingly to Fortnum and Mason's best foods and finished off with a 1-lb. box of 'King George' chocolates. At the same time he was disgusted at the way in which valuable radio equipment had been abandoned by his predecessors – 'enough to stock a shop', he remarked in his diary.

For the next few days the three men were confined to camp by a fierce blizzard. In his diary Wilson recorded the humdrum happenings of food and sleep, and confessed that his original plan of going straight from Camp III to Camp V was not a good one:

> Not taking short cut to Camp V as at first intended as should have to cut my own road up the ice and that's no good when there is already a handrope and steps (if still there) to Camp IV.[7]

That entry alone reveals Wilson's total ignorance of mountains, and of the task he had undertaken.

He was also affected by the altitude. His head ached and on the 21st he wrote pathetically: 'Terrible when you can't put your head down for aching nerves.'[8]

On the 21st, despite some bad weather, Wilson and Rinzing had been part of the way up the slopes of the col. In his diary, Wilson thought it was half way, but this seems unlikely. He was bitterly disappointed to discover that all trace of the 1933 expedition had been erased by the elements – no rope, no steps.

Next day the weather was better and Wilson set out once again to climb the col. This time he was alone. He was away for four days, working his way slowly up the face, camping on ice shelves in incredibly exposed positions, until he came to the final barrier – the forty-foot ice wall split by the chimney that had taxed the powers of Frank Smythe in 1933. Wilson camped below the chimney – 'I am parked at an angle of 35°,' he wrote. Next day he tried to climb the chimney but it utterly defeated him, though he struggled for hour after hour. In his diary, already an almost illegible scrawl and often incoherent, his frustration and despair provoked a flash of clarity: 'Had a horrible job yesterday', he wrote, 'and whoever selected that route ought to be pole axed.'[9]

On 25 May Wilson staggered back to Camp III. The diary tells the story succinctly:

> Only one thing to do – no food, no water – get back. Did two sheer drop-rolls down the face of the ice but fortunately without effect like sore a bit but not too much. They [presumably the Sherpas] said that I could get to C.IV and top but of course they were thinking of [indecipherable word] days when all steps were cut.[10]

He spent the next two days in bed. On the 28th he wrote in his diary: 'Tewang wanted to go back, but persuaded them to go with me to Camp V. This will be a last effort, and I feel successful . . .'[11]

In fact the Sherpas had not agreed to any such plan, which they could see was plain madness. Instead they tried to persuade Wilson to return to Rongbuk, but he wouldn't hear of it. On the 29th he set out alone, but, too weak to make a real effort, he camped for the night at the foot of the col, not far from Camp III.

On 30 May he stayed in bed and then, on 31 May, came the final entry in his diary: 'Off again, gorgeous day.'[12]

The body of Maurice Wilson was discovered by Eric Shipton's expedition the following year. Charles Warren described it vividly in his diary of the time:

> 9th July. It was decided to move camp one hour's walk further up the glacier. We set off at about 9.30 a.m. There was some monsoon cloud blowing up from the South, but at first I walked in my shirt sleeves.
>
> I was a little way ahead of the others and Eric had just sat down on a stone to rest. I saw a boot, one of Maurice's, lying in the snow and a little ahead was a green mass which I took to be a tent left behind by the last expedition. I shouted to Eric as I advanced – 'Hello. Here is a perfectly good pair of boots and a tent; it must be a dump'. Then approaching the green heap I got a bit of a shock to see that it was the body of a man lying huddled in the snow. At once the thought flashed through my mind – Wilson! I shouted back to Eric – 'I say, it's this fellow Wilson!' Quite soon the rest of the party came up to us. Then we had to decide what to do.
>
> The body was lying on its left side with the knees drawn up, in an attitude of flexion. The first boot I had found some 10 yards down the slope from it; the second was lying near the man's feet. He was wearing a mauve pull-over and grey flannel trousers with woollen vest and pants underneath. There was a stove near his left hand to which a guy-line to a tent was

attached. The torn remains of a tent was pulled out of the snow some few feet down the slope from him. We wondered whether to tell the porters but by this time they had come up to us and had seen what we had discovered. For the most part, they took the matter very casually. Before disturbing the body we searched in the snow for his note-book and other belongings. Eventually a light weight rucksack was found along with a small Union Jack on which were signatures of his girl friends, and most important of all his diary – an extraordinary documentary revelation of monomania and determination of purpose. It ended several days before his death with a statement that he was off to the North Col for the second time.

From his position, I think he must have died in his sleep of exhaustion and exposure, in his tent, the tent having been blown away at a later date. There are three curious facts about the tragedy. (1) No sleeping bag was to be found. (2) He was within 200 yards of the 1933 Everest expedition's food dump, which he knew about because he had already made use of it. (3) He was within hailing distance of Camp 3 where Tewang was supposed to have been waiting for him.

After some discussion it was decided to bury him in a crevasse. The moraine was changing too rapidly for a surface burial there. So we wrapped him in his tent and, after cutting away the lip of a suitable one, slid the body into the depths, where it disappeared from sight. We all raised our hats at the time and I think that everyone was rather upset at the business. I thought I had grown immune to the sight of the dead; but somehow or other, in the circumstances, and because of the fact that he was, after all, doing much the same as ourselves, his tragedy seemed to have been brought a little too near home for us.

We built a cairn at the spot where his body had been found and that evening we read his diary to try to find out some of the circumstances of his death.[13]

It is reasonable to assume that Maurice Wilson died of sheer exhaustion. Only his indomitable faith had driven him on, but faith and courage were not enough to climb Everest: skill was needed too, and this is what Wilson so conspicuously lacked. When at last he realized this, as he must have done during those last few days, his spirit crumbled and inevitably he died.

The three Sherpas returned to Kalimpong late in July and gave the world its first news of Wilson's death. Wilson had asked them to wait ten days at Camp III and then, if he hadn't returned, go back by themselves. Their stories were confusing: they claimed to have waited a month, which is unlikely, and there is no explanation why they didn't go to the foot of the col, only a few hundred yards away, before they left for home. Had they done so they would have discovered the body of their leader. This confusion led to them being unjustly censured: the scapegoats of the Wilson tragedy, on whom the authorities vented their spleen. The fact was surely that the three men were mortally afraid – after all, the loss of a sahib was a serious matter, and like children they lied to try and avoid all blame. No blame was theirs: although Tewang and Tsering were ill for most of the time after reaching Rongbuk, they and especially Rinzing had done their utmost to look after Wilson, even trying to protect him from his own wilful folly. No man was better served by his Sherpas than was Wilson.

Strangely enough, that was not quite the end of the Wilson story. In 1960 a Chinese expedition discovered the body of a man 'dressed in a faded green suit of English cloth' which they reburied. It was probably the body of Wilson; it is not unusual for bodies to emerge from glaciers, sometimes after many years, and there are several recorded examples in the Alps. Two years later the unauthorized Sayre expedition found an 'old style tent' at the foot of the North Col and wondered if it was Wilson's, as indeed it could have been if the Chinese had removed it from the body before burial.

There are some similarities between Maurice Wilson and the next man to make a clandestine attempt on Everest, Earl Denman. Like Wilson, Denman was single-minded and determined in his project, though in his case he had no ulterior motive: he had no new theory to expound to the world. If Denman had anything to prove it was only to himself:

> I grew up with an ambition and determination without which I would have been a good deal happier. I thought a lot and developed the far-away look of a dreamer, for it was always the distant heights which fascinated me and drew me to them in spirit. I was not sure what could be accomplished by means of tenacity and little else, but the target was set high and each rebuff only saw me all the more determined to see at least one major dream through to its fulfilment.[14]

Here seems to be encapsulated the spirit of the man. He was introspective, not a good mixer, and seemed to be conducting a continuous struggle against a powerful inferiority complex that stemmed from childhood. Born in Canada, Denman was brought to England at an early age. His father was permanently ill and his mother had a difficult struggle to bring up the family – a depressing background which no doubt turned the lad to dreaming and gave him a strange guilt complex about poverty. Nobody likes being poor, but few feel guilty about it. Denman did. One senses that Denman's attempts to turn his boyhood dreams into reality were external manifestations of a deeper inner struggle.

Everest did not at first enter his plans, if indeed he had any. Though he later claimed a long interest in mountains it must have been the interest of a romantic, for there is no background of scrambling on British hills or Alpine heights that one can ascertain – no evidence that he had any physical contact with mountains until he found himself in Africa during the war and paid a visit to the Ruwenzori mountains. Even here he did no real climbing, but for some reason he thought of Mount Everest.

Why the thought came to him is not clear from his account. He began by considering the Virunga mountains, which lie south of the Ruwenzori on the Zaire–Rwanda border and rise to some 15,000 ft. He conceived the ambition to climb all eight of these little-known volcanic summits and, if he succeeded, to attempt Everest! Since all but one peak of the Virunga mountains are little more than stiff walks, and even the odd one out – Mikeno – hardly difficult to an experienced climber, Denman's reasoning is a little obscure.

Nevertheless, it was the plan he followed. All he possessed was determination and a bank balance of £650, which had to suffice for both his African Safari and his Everest attempt. He told no one of his plans and his training was more unorthodox than any climber's before or since:

> Mine was a hard way to learn because it was a lonely one. But always at the back of my mind was the fear that I should be talked out of it if I told my plans to anyone else. There are always so many people ready to offer discouragement, and so few to see that failure, though painful, is better than frustrated longing.
>
> My methods, I know, were in nearly all respects crude, but I saw no strangeness in them because they came naturally to me. During my early days on mountains the opportunity of climbing with more experienced men never came my way, and so I made my own trips with none but native Africans as guides and porters, and these I came to look upon also as friends and companions. Because I was unable at first to provide myself with clinkered boots, I dispensed with footwear altogether and climbed barefoot. Eventually I became so accustomed and hardened to walking and climbing in this simple manner that I found an added joy in it, and before long I could proceed happily beyond the snow line on any African mountain and over practically all kinds of ground without harm. To travel light became so much of a habit with me that any really non-essential article of equipment I looked upon as an encumbrance.[15]

Between April and June 1946, he completed the first part of his plan, the ascent of all the Virunga peaks – the first man to do so, but more because of their relative inaccessibility (not to say obscurity) than because of any inherent difficulties. On his return trip to Rhodesia he stopped off to climb Kilimanjaro (19,340 ft), the highest mountain in Africa, but technically no more difficult than the Virunga. Thus prepared, Denman was ready for Everest.

He made his way to India and on 13 March reached Darjeeling, where he put up in frugal lodgings. The next day he met Karma Paul, the general factotum who had been on so many Everest expeditions, and through him the two Sherpas, Tenzing Norgay and Ang Dawa.

Tenzing later recalled the interview in his autobiography:

> Right from the beginning it was like nothing I had experienced before. Denman was alone. He had very little money and poor equipment. He did not even have permission to enter Tibet. But he was as determined as any man I have ever met . . .[16]

Karma Paul washed his hands of the whole affair – he wanted nothing to do with illegal entry into Tibet – but the two Sherpas decided to accept Denman's offer. It was a crazy idea, as Tenzing later admitted, but the lure of Everest was too strong:

> What there was to think about I do not know, because nothing made sense about it. First, we would probably not even get into Tibet. Second, if we did get in we would probably be caught, and, as his guides, we, as well as Denman, would be in serious trouble. Third, I did not for a moment believe that, even if we reached the mountain, a party such as this would be able to climb it. Fourth, the attempt would be highly dangerous. Fifth, Denman had the money neither to pay us well nor to guarantee a decent sum to our dependents in case something happened to us. And so on and so on. Any man in his right mind would have said no. But I couldn't say no. For in my heart I needed to go, and the pull of Everest was stronger for me than any force on earth. Ang Dawa and I talked for a few minutes, and then we made our decision. 'Well,' I told Denman, 'we will try.'[17]

On 22 March they left Darjeeling and travelled via Lachen to Tibet. Once over the Kongra La they took a westerly course which was well away from the usual trade route in order to avoid detection as much as possible. It was a hand-to-mouth, day-to-day sort of existence, and not at all like the well-planned expeditions which the Sherpas usually associated with an attempt on Everest. 'Almost every day something went wrong,' Tenzing later wrote. But the Sherpas well knew what they were about and did their best to see Denman through. In fact, they gained quite a liking for the bearded Canadian; he was strong, resolute and daring.

When plans had first been mooted in Darjeeling, the fate of Maurice Wilson had crossed the minds of both Karma Paul and Tenzing (Denman had never heard of him), but the Canadian was far from being a second Maurice Wilson. He was an engineer with a strong sense of practicalities, and at no time did he contemplate trying to climb Everest alone: the two Sherpas were to accompany him to the top.[18]

Because they travelled light, they travelled quickly, which was just as well, for the Tibetan plateau in early spring is not a place to loiter. They were stopped only once, by a party of six horsemen who told them they must not proceed beyond the next village. Fortunately no attempt was made to arrest them, so by taking a more circuitous route and making a long march next day they avoided further trouble. They reached Rongbuk monastery on 8 April.

At Rongbuk Denman discovered that the old head Lama who had befriended all the pre-war Everest expeditions was dead and his place taken by his reincarnation, a seven-year-old boy. The monastery was to be Denman's base – he had no resources for a proper base camp – and from it he and the two Sherpas set out on 10 April to follow the traditional route up the East Rongbuk Glacier to the North Col.

It took them only four days, for they carried their tents with them and had no chain of permanent camps to establish. The going was rough, but it was the bitter cold of the Rongbuk nights which most affected Denman. The first night he spent alone in the smaller of his two tents, feeling the cold eat into his marrow. On the next night he moved into the larger tent with the Sherpas, but still the cold numbed him all night, preventing sleep. Even for the next two nights, when he shared Tenzing's sleeping bag, it was too cold for proper sleep.

In fact Denman was experiencing real high-altitude climbing conditions for the first time, for though he had thought of the Virungas in that sense they are no higher than an average Alpine or Rocky Mountain peak. He does not seem to have been prone to altitude sickness and he was physically very fit, but the gnawing cold and the typical high-altitude disinclination to eat hit him like a pole-axe. Any romantic ideas he may have had dropped away like magic and he realized for the first time the scale of his undertaking and the total inadequacy of his equipment and resources.

They had a bitter struggle to set up the tent at the foot of the North Col in the face of a gale-force wind which threatened to tear the tent out of their grip. Even when it was up and they were huddled inside they lay awake all night listening to the wind and fearing for the safety of their fragile shelter. Had the tent been torn to shreds by the wind, their chance of survival would have been minimal.

On the following morning, the wind having abated, the three men set out on an abortive attempt to reach the North Col, which seemed unusually free of snow that year. Before they had gone far, however, the wind came howling back, threatening to hurl them off the slopes and cutting like an icy knife through their inadequate clothing. 'Even Denman knew we were beaten,' wrote Tenzing.[19]

And so they retreated, back to the Rongbuk monastery, back across the plateau, back to Darjeeling, where they arrived on 28 April. Incredibly, the whole trip had taken just five weeks.

Denman was nothing if not persistent. He was back in Darjeeling the following year, this time much better equipped (through sponsorship) but still without the vital permission to enter Tibet. Unfortunately for him too much had leaked out about his previous attempt, and neither Tenzing nor any other Sherpa was willing to risk another clandestine journey. He returned home to Rhodesia dismayed, wrote a book about his adventures, and was planning to attempt the mountain through Nepal in 1953 when the news came through of the British success. He turned his back on the mountains for ever.

In 1951 another adventurer turned up in Darjeeling, ready to make an attempt on Everest. Klavs Becker-Larsen was a young English-speaking Dane, big, blonde and handsome. He had no climbing experience before or after his Everest adventure but, like Wilson and Denman, he had plenty of guts.

By 1951 the Chinese had occupied Tibet, but Nepal was slowly opening her frontiers. Larsen had no official permission to visit either country, but he calculated that his chances of survival, should he be caught, were better in Nepal and so he determined to attempt Everest from the south. This was only a few months after the Houston–Tilman journey to the Khumbu, the first party ever to approach Everest from the south, and before the official British reconnaissance due in the post-monsoon period of 1951. Larsen was therefore not only attempting the highest mountain in the world, but approaching by a route which was at the time virtually unknown.

Not that Larsen had any intention of making a new route on the mountain itself. His aim was simply to get to Rongbuk as secretly as possible and climb the established North Col route.

In Darjeeling, with the help of Karma Paul, he managed to secure the services of four Sherpas by promising them high wages and together they set off on 14 March. At Sandakp'u they engaged three more Sherpas in order to lighten the loads and speed up the marches.

Without an adequate map, Larsen left the route-finding to the Sherpas, who knew the journey well because it was the traditional way to their homeland in the Sola Khumbu. They passed through country which was reputed to hold brigands and they had to be constantly on their guard. To avoid arousing suspicion they by-passed all the important villages, but if ever he was questioned too closely by curious natives Larsen told them he was conducting a water survey. The worst moment came at Tamur, where Larsen met a police officer who spoke perfect English; but the young Dane succeeded in passing himself off as a journalist and even managed to extract an official pass from the policeman.

The party crossed the Arun valley near Dingla and after traversing the mountainous country between that river and the Dudh Kosi, ended up at

Namche Bazar, the chief Sherpa village, on 4 April. Three days were spent here, allowing the Sherpas to visit their families (possibly for the first time in years). Larsen climbed an adjacent hill to get his first, somewhat distant, view of Everest.

At Namche, Larsen learned that there was a glacial pass called the Lho La which led from the Khumbu valley to the Rongbuk valley. The Sherpas were quite certain it was a feasible route because they knew of a lama who had once crossed it when returning to Rongbuk monastery. It was undoubtedly the shortest way into Tibet.

Trusting his informants, Larsen, his party now enlarged to twelve Sherpas to carry the food he had bought in the village, trekked up the Khumbu valley and onto the long, debris-covered waste of the Khumbu Glacier. Only Tilman and Houston had previously been so far.

Ahead of him, the Dane could see the spectacular frontier ridge dividing Nepal from Tibet, a tremendous cirque of high peaks, fluted with ice. He could also see the Lho La, the pass he was supposed to cross, and his heart must have sunk. On the Nepalese side, the Lho La is a cataclysmic tumble of steep ice and rock.[20]

An experienced mountaineer would have dismissed the pass out of hand as too difficult to cross, particularly with loaded porters, but Larsen determined to give it a try. For one thing, it seemed only an hour away and there would be nothing lost by having a closer look. Five hours later, still not having reached the pass, they camped for the night.

Next day, with three of his best Sherpas, Larsen began his attempt on the Lho La. They started to climb on the left, or western edge, and then sloped over to the right. The porters, badly shod and without ice axes, must have found it a nightmare. Falling stones and lumps of ice went whistling past at frequent intervals and it became obvious that sooner or later someone was going to get killed. At half-height Larsen decided to retreat, and by the grace of God they all made it safely back to the glacier. 'My first experience with ice and ice-axe,' he wrote later.[21]

Perhaps the irony of the situation was that while he was making his hair-raising attempt on the pass Larsen must have looked out over the great Khumbu Icefall, which was on his immediate right and which was later to prove the real key to Everest. But he could not have foreseen that. The Icefall looks even more difficult than the Lho La, and in any case seems to go in the wrong direction for an ascent on Everest. As far as Larsen was aware (or anyone else at the time) the only feasible way up Everest was via the North Col, which was on the opposite side of the mountain.

Beaten by the Lho La, Larsen returned to Namche and rested for a day in the adjacent village of Khumjung, where he managed to purchase a rope left behind by the recent Tilman–Houston team.

Still determined to reach Tibet, the young Dane then set off up the Nangpo Tsangpo valley for the Khumbu La (Nangpa La), an easy glacial pass lying to the west of the great peak of Cho Oyu, and the traditional trading route between Namche Bazar and Tibet (see Map 5, p. 256). At Marulung they met a group of traders who had been forced back by a heavy snowstorm on the pass, but ignoring this Larsen pushed on up the valley and camped for the night at Lunag, which proved to be nothing more than a miserable stone hut.

Next day, as they moved over the Nangpa Glacier towards the pass Larsen realized that the merchants had been wise men – the glacier was covered in deep soft snow which made progress slow and fatiguing. For the Sherpas, who had spent a miserably cold night, these conditions were too much. They went on strike, and Larsen was forced to retreat down the valley to the village of Thame, where he spent five days recuperating while waiting for conditions on the pass to improve.

On 30 April, despite a snow squall, Larsen and his porters crossed the Khumbu La into Tibet. That evening they bivouacked in a hut on the right bank of the Kyetrak Glacier and next day reached the important trading post of Kyetrak, where, fortunately for Larsen, the Communist officials were absent. From Kyetrak he turned east, crossing the Lamna La to Chobuk at the end of the Rongbuk valley. He arrived at Rongbuk monastery on 3 May. Though he did not realize it at the time, this journey of Larsen's was unique. Though the Khumbu La had been reached by members of the 1921 expedition from the Tibetan side, political considerations had prevented them from crossing into Nepal. Sherpa traders and porters used the route regularly of course (and still do, despite the regime in Tibet), but Larsen is the first Westerner known to have crossed the pass. He is also the only Westerner to have visited both the south and north sides of Everest in the same season. Not bad going for an inexperienced explorer![22]

At Rongbuk monastery Larsen seems to have got on well with the Head Lama (the boy that Denman had met), though he couldn't persuade him to part with equipment left behind by the pre-war expeditions. The Lama explained that he was only a trustee of the equipment: it had actually been given to his predecessor, the old Head Lama, and was therefore not his to dispose of. So much for the practical aspects of reincarnation! However, Larsen finally managed to acquire a tent and five bags of yak dung for fuel.

Ignoring ominous soothsayings from the monastery that he would not reach the summit, Larsen set off for the East Rongbuk Glacier and reached the site of the old Camp III in three days. Here he paid off five Sherpas and spent a day acclimatizing and recuperating. His plan of attack was simple: with two of the best Sherpas he intended to climb the col and then push on up the ridge to Camp VI. From there he was to make a solo summit dash. One can't help but admire his *sang froid*.

On 9 May he set off up the slopes with two Sherpas. The going was good, but as they reached a point about three quarters of the way up a strong wind arose and the Sherpas wanted to descend. Larsen argued that they should go a little higher and pitch the tent, but at that moment a large piece of rock broke off from Changtse and went bouncing down the slopes on which they were standing, too close for comfort. This was too much for the Sherpas' nerves; ignoring Larsen's pleas, they began to descend.

There was nothing the Dane could do but follow them, furiously shouting dire threats of punishment. So angry was he that he missed his footing and found himself shooting down the slopes, but he used his ice axe to break his fall and continued down without more ado.[23]

Despite this little contretemps, Larsen was optimistic about making another attempt next day, but no inducements he could offer would persuade the Sherpas to go. Larsen's uninhibited methods of attack on steep ice slopes were not at all to their liking – they wanted fixed ropes such as Ruttledge had used in 1936.

Without the support of his Sherpas Larsen was forced to return to the Rongbuk monastery, where he learned the unwelcome news that a Chinese officer and two soldiers were out looking for him. The Lama had put them off the scent for the time being but obviously it would only be a matter of time before the Dane was caught and imprisoned.

And so, five days later, by a series of long marches, Larsen was back in Namche. There he sold his surplus gear and trekked back to Darjeeling, which he reached on 28 May.

Throughout his journey, with the exception of the blizzard on the Khumbu La, Larsen enjoyed good weather – the sort of weather so conspicuously absent in 1936 and 1938. His achievements were much more than those of Wilson or Denman, who, for whatever motives, achieved nothing more than personal adventures. The pity is that Larsen kept no detailed diary of his unique adventure. It was only when returning home on the long and boring sea voyage that he saw fit to expand the simple notes he had jotted down at the time.

One unusual theme recurs in Larsen's story – his inability to come to terms with his Sherpas. Sherpas are usually the most helpful and happy-go-lucky of peoples, but for some reason there seems to have built up a mutual distrust between the Dane and his porters. Perhaps he pushed them too hard – not an easy thing to do where Sherpas are concerned, because they are incredibly tough, but Larsen was extremely strong and not averse to long, hard marches. Perhaps the Sherpas mistook his energetic enthusiasm for fanaticism and saw him as another Maurice Wilson. Whatever the reason, Larsen was certainly disenchanted with them. He wrote shortly after his return:

> I have still to meet one of those Sherpas that were so highly praised by other expeditions. Mine were a shabby lot. I believe the explanation to be

> that the colossal expeditions of the thirties offered them luxurious conditions. When confronted by real hardships and dangers they have their tails down like the majority of primitive people with whom the conception of honour has not yet arisen.[24]

Wilson, Denman and Larsen had one obvious thing in common – they each intended to make a solo attempt on the mountain, albeit with Sherpa assistance in the early stages. But they had something deeper in common too: a depth of willpower that went far beyond what we normally regard as self-confidence. Wilson couldn't recognize its source – he needed the mystical faith of a quasi-religion, and when that failed him he died. The others were made of sterner stuff, recognizing that the springs came from within themselves. Of his own attempt, Larsen writes:

> I wanted to prove myself to myself and others by doing something which would take everything I had to give. I also wanted adventure.
>
> I was brought up to believe that I could do anything I believed I could do – that *my own* reason was the best judge as to what I could cope with and what not. With this sort of code it is not quite as difficult for one's dreams to materialize.[25]

In 1953 an attempt on Everest was planned by members of the Creagh Dhu Club, a group of tough, largely working-class climbers from Clydeside in Scotland. The club's reputation for hard climbing – and fighting – was considerable, and they included in their ranks the redoubtable Hamish MacInnes, one of the finest climbers in Britain at that time, and well known for his unorthodox approach to problems.

The Everest attempt was MacInnes's idea. Since the club had no money, his plan was to use the food and supplies left by the Swiss on the mountain in 1952; as a good Scot he couldn't see the sense in wasting it. Using these supplies he and his companions intended to make a light-weight attack on the South East Ridge.

The fact that the official British expedition was also under way at the same time meant nothing to the Scottish lads. Chris Lyon, unofficial club historian, said:

> We intended to land at Colonel Hunt's own attack on Everest, knock on the tent door, touch the skip o' the bunnet and say 'Hillo Mr Hunt, son – are ye startin' any good climbs the day?'[26]

No doubt tongue-in-cheek stuff – but it indicates pretty accurately what the post-war breed of hard young climbers thought about the Establishment, who had a monopoly on Everest.

MacInnes and John Cunningham (another fine climber from the same club) were both in New Zealand at the time and so it was decided to launch the expedition from there. The other team members, who were still in Scotland, could see no sense in wasting money, so they applied for government-assisted £10 immigrant passages to the Antipodes. Unfortunately, by the time these came through, Cunningham and MacInnes were already trekking through Nepal.

So the Creagh Dhu Himalayan expedition became a two-man attempt on Everest. Without visas (a constant theme among small expeditions and almost, it seems, *de rigueur*) they needed to travel circumspectly. Both men carried enormous loads – said to be 140 lb. – though what that weight consisted of is hard to imagine, since their equipment was so minimal that a Sherpa who helped them as far as Namche Bazar made them a parting gift of a knife, fork and mug – he felt so sorry at seeing them eating with pitons and tent pegs!

It was, of course, all in vain. John Hunt's party climbed the mountain first, but the two Scots, having come so far, were reluctant to return home empty handed and so switched their plans to make a spirited assault on Pumori, which failed at about 22,000 ft.

Cunningham never returned to Everest, but MacInnes was to play a part in later events.

In the spring of 1962 a small American expedition trekked up the Dudh Kosi, en route for Namche Bazar and an unclimbed mountain called Gyachung Kang which stood on the borders of Tibet (see Map 5, p. 256). They were well equipped and their gear and prepacked food was transported by Sherpas under the proper control of a sirdar. Accompanying them was an Army liaison officer supplied by the Nepalese Government. Altogether it was the very model of a small, light-weight Himalayan expedition.

At 7,922 m. (25,991 ft) Gyachung Kang is one of the Himalayan giants, and an impartial observer might have said that the Americans were, if anything, over-ambitious in their plans, especially since they had little mountaineering experience. In fact, they were more ambitious than anyone suspected, for their real and secret aim was to climb Mount Everest.

The leader was a bespectacled forty-three-year-old assistant Professor of Philosophy from Tufts University, near Boston, Mass., called Woodrow Wilson Sayre. His origins were blue-chip Boston society – his father had been an Ambassador at the United Nations and his mother was the daughter of President Woodrow Wilson. His education was likewise top drawer – St Alban's School, Williams College (Phi Beta Kappa, of course) and Harvard, where he gained his Master's and Doctorate. He was academic, mild-mannered, fussy even to the point of wondering whether the local Sherpa beer, chang, would upset his constitution. But beneath this prissy exterior was an iron will and a frame as tough as old boots.

Accompanying Sayre on the expedition was Norman C. Hansen, aged

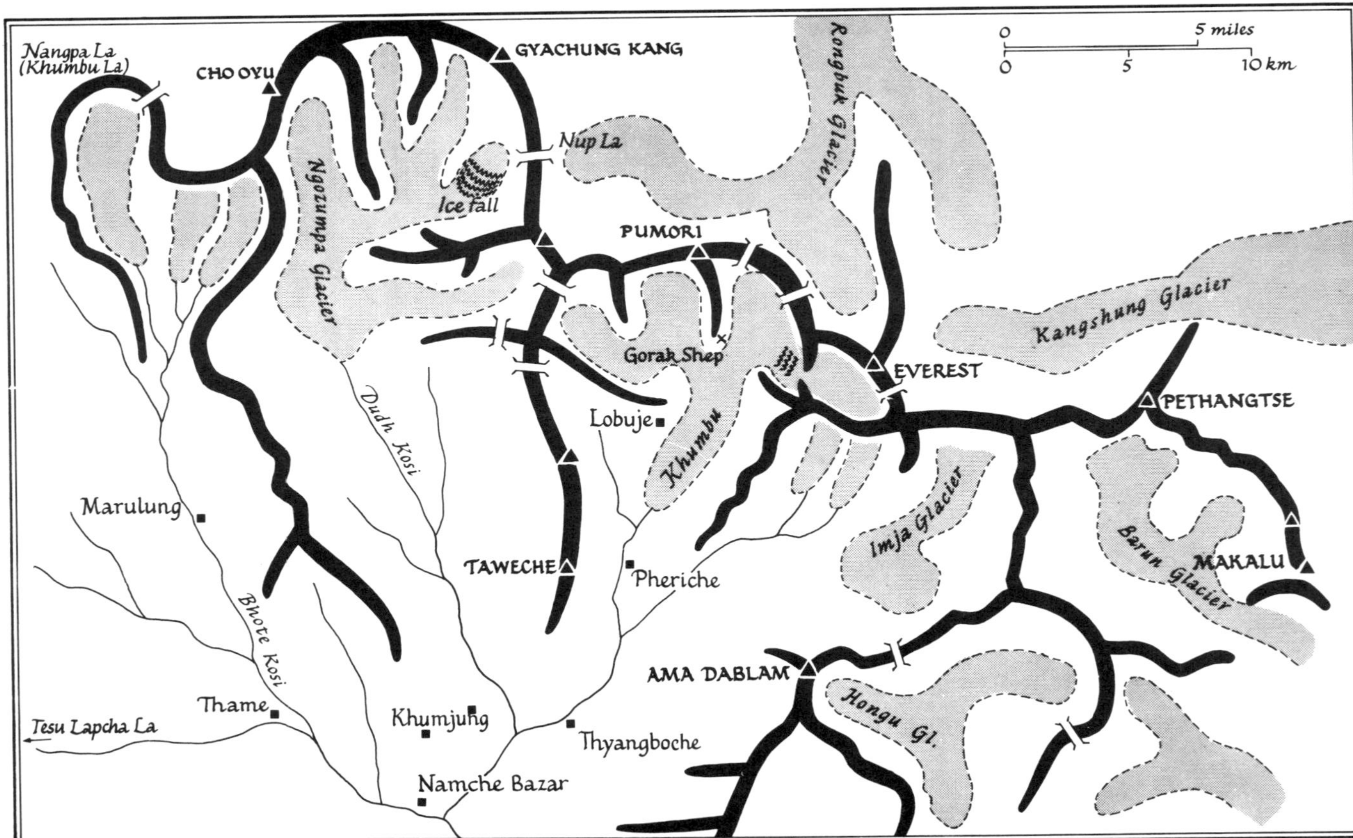


Map 5. The approach from the south

thirty-six, a Boston lawyer and long-standing friend; Roger Alan Hart, aged twenty-one, a final-year geology student from Tufts University, and Hans-Peter Duttle, a twenty-four-year-old Swiss school teacher whom they had first met by chance in Zermatt while on their way to India.

Sayre had caught the Everest bug while still at college in pre-war days. He had read all the books and was full of admiration for the men who had got within 900 ft of the summit without oxygen:

> But part of my dream was to do better. So I studied the literature. I thought I saw where mistakes had been made that could be corrected. I thought I saw new approaches that would make it possible to surmount the obstacles. I made my general plan and was impatient to test it. But I knew it would be a few years yet before I would have the time and the finances to do so. So I sat back and waited.[27]

A few years later he met Hansen and infused him with the idea of climbing Everest too. Even when the British succeeded in climbing the mountain in 1953 Sayre's dream was not shattered, for his beloved North Ridge was still inviolate, and in any case the British had mounted a large expedition which had used oxygen – both anathema to the philosophy professor. Sayre was a believer in the Shipton–Tilman theory that small is beautiful, and he would undoubtedly have supported Tilman in his belief that to use oxygen was cheating.

The one great advantage which inexperience confers on the would-be mountaineer is that he is not bogged down by tradition or precedence. To him, all things appear simple, and he chooses straightforward solutions to the problems he faces. Often, of course, it defeats the success he is seeking, and sometimes it has tragic results, but the man himself doesn't know this when he sets out on his adventure. Maurice Wilson, Earl Denman, Klavs Becker-Larsen – none of them knew much about mountain climbing or they would not have set out on their hopeless quests, yet, untrammelled by techniques, determination carried them a long way.

Sayre's case was a little different. He had far more resources than his predecessors and much more time in which to plan his assault. His was a long-term dream. Nevertheless, he had this in common – that when he first conceived his plan of attack he was uninhibited by previous experience. He applied a logician's mind to all he had read about Everest and came up with a logician's answer. And before attempting Everest he tested his theory on other high mountains – Mt Whitney (14,495 ft) in California and Mt McKinley (20,320 ft) in Alaska – and was successful. There seemed no logical reason why it shouldn't work on Everest. It was certainly original.

From his reading Sayre reckoned that though there were technical climbing problems on the North Ridge, or North Face, they were probably not so great that they could not be overcome by a little preliminary practice. Several of the men who had gone highest on Everest in the pre-war expeditions – Norton, for example – were not technical mountaineers. There were, however, two major problems – the effects of high altitude, and the sheer logistics of reaching and climbing the mountain. There was the weather too, of course, but that was a matter of chance. The altitude and logistics were something that a man could solve, given strength and the right spirit of commitment.

Sayre evolved a simple plan which he believed would take care of both problems. It did away with the traditional system of fixed camps involving porters ferrying loads up stage by stage and the climbers advancing in almost military fashion from redoubt to redoubt. Instead, Sayre substituted a system of rigorous self-sufficiency in which there would be only one camp, wherever the climbers happened to be at the time. Little by little the camp would be advanced: if the going was tough, the advance might only be a couple of hundred yards; if the going was easy, it might advance a mile or more.

Everything went forward stage by stage, humped upon the backs of the climbers. Naturally, this could not be done in one journey – the loads would be too heavy for that – but it could be done in relays. The establishing of a camp would involve two or possibly three journeys up and down from the previous site.

At high altitudes the thought of going up and down over a gruelling course twice or three times in one day is enough to make most climbers blanch, but it doesn't seem to have deterred Sayre or his companions. The valuable physiological effect is that one gains altitude slowly and becomes acclimatized steadily.

The plan worked when Sayre and Hansen tried it on Mt Whitney in 1950, and though Mt Whitney is an easy peak technically, they did it in arduous conditions of deep snow involving a sixty-mile trek. It worked again four years later when the two men made a twenty-three-day ascent of McKinley – and McKinley, the highest mountain in North America, rises 17,000 ft above the plains at its feet. Everest rises only 13,000 ft above Rongbuk.

Sayre and Hansen had done some rock climbing with the Appalachian Mountain Club, and their successful ascent of McKinley convinced Sayre that they were now ready for Everest.[28] Yet he waited eight years before making his attempt. Then, in 1961, he suddenly seemed to have realized that time was not an inexhaustible commodity. 'You know, Norm,' he said to Hansen, 'we're getting old. It's this year or never.'[29] A few months later they were trekking up the Khumbu valley.

The inexplicable part of the Sayre story is that a man of relative affluence, if not exactly wealthy, should build up a dream over decades and then try to realize it after only the scantiest of preparations. Everything could have been meticulously prepared during the previous years, but it wasn't. Even the two younger members of the team were last-minute choices. Hart was a member of Tufts University Mountain Climbing Club, a cross-country runner who had been twice to Antarctica, and was worth taking a chance on; but Duttle, picked up so casually in Zermatt, was a totally unknown quantity.

Sayre's plans for the expedition were bold and daring. Realizing that there was no hope of receiving official permission from the Chinese for entry into Tibet, he resolved, as Larsen had done eleven years earlier, to enter that country illegally from Nepal.

Times had changed since Larsen had crossed the Khumbu La. The authorities in Nepal had a much better idea of what visitors were up to, and there was no chance of the Americans using the ancient trade route to Rongbuk. Even had the Nepalese allowed it, the Chinese border guards would have turned them back.

But about half way along the frontier ridge between Everest and the Khumbu La there is another pass, the Nup La (5,985 m.), which lies at the head of the long West Rongbuk Glacier on the Tibetan side and overlooks the tremendous icefall of the Ngozumpa Glacier on the Nepalese side (see Map 5, p. 256). It was this dangerous icefall which prevented the Nup La from being used as a proper pass between the Khumbu region and Rongbuk. Otherwise it would be a fairly direct route between the two, since there are no problems on the Tibetan side. The icefall – two huge steps (almost 3,000 ft high) – had been climbed by Edmund Hillary and George Lowe in 1952, and they had been impressed by its difficulties. The New Zealanders had then made a quick trip down the West Rongbuk Glacier, across the main Rongbuk Glacier, and up the East Rongbuk Glacier to near the site of the old Everest Camp II. Fearing that the onset of the monsoon might cut off their retreat, Hillary and Lowe had then returned to Nepal over the Nup La. It was this route that Sayre intended to follow.

Naturally enough, Sayre could not make the Nup La his official objective – that would have been suspicious to say the least – but only a short distance from the pass, and in the same general direction, lay Gyachung Kang. To climb Gyachung Kang it would be necessary to climb Nup La icefall. This gave Sayre the opening he was looking for.

His plan was to establish a Base Camp below the icefall, leave the liaison officer and Sherpas there, then set off up the icefall, ostensibly to climb Gyachung Kang. Once out of sight of Base Camp, however, the plan was to cross the Nup La and make for Everest.

Sayre's approach to the mountain involved a trek of twenty-five miles and he intended to backpack every yard of it, there and back. It was all at high altitude, of course, and was reputedly patrolled by Chinese border guards. He allowed himself a month to do it in.

Base Camp was established on 24 April and no time was lost finding a way through the tottering seracs of the huge icefall, which is, if anything, bigger than the one guarding the Western Cwm. Stonefall was frequent – the deadly hum of an unaimed missile as it hurtled down through hundreds of feet of space was a constant background noise.

Sayre's original intention had been to dismiss his Sherpas once Base Camp was reached, but he quickly found out how useful they were in the icefall. Though only three in number, they saved the party valuable time and with their help Camp II was established above the icefall in fourteen days.[30] His original estimate for the task, however, was ten days, and he had already lost time during the march-in, so that the expedition was already behind schedule.

Confidently, Sayre sent the Sherpas down to Namche, telling them to return to Base Camp in a month's time. The four men then set about their long haul to Everest.

Camp II, at just over 19,000 ft, was below the Nup La. Everest lay twenty-five miles to the east, beyond the three great Rongbuk Glaciers.[31] Sayre's intention was to leave from the Nup La with 120 lb. of gear and food per man, divided into three loads of 40 lb., which would need three trips per man per day. At each camp a cache of food was left for the return journey and in addition they were eating about 2 lb. of food per man per day, so that as the trip continued the loads would become lighter and eventually the relentless shuttle might be reduced to two times per day. Working on these figures, and the distance involved, Sayre estimated that it would take ten days to reach Everest, eight days to try to climb it, and five days to return (loads would be much lighter on their return). This gave a total of twenty-three days, leaving seven spare for emergencies from the month he had allocated.

A little arithmetic shows that this was a pretty tough schedule. Leaving out the climbing of the mountain, which depended on all sorts of imponderables, the approach march of twenty-five miles in ten days meant an advance of an average two and a half miles per day, and since every advance required three trips, each man would be walking twelve and a half miles per day (seven and a half miles of descent and five miles of ascent) all at altitudes of 17,000–21,000 ft. Not impossible, but extremely hard. The average trekking day in Nepal, usually at much lower altitude, is five to eight miles.

It was inevitably a gruelling journey. Hansen was suffering from altitude sickness and Duttle had less stamina than the others, but fortunately young Hart proved a hardy specimen, as did Sayre himself. Nevertheless, they could not possibly keep to their schedule. It took them nineteen days to the site of the old Camp III at the foot of the North Col. That they made it at all is a tribute to their guts and determination. They were delighted to find that food had been left behind by the Chinese expedition of 1960, and they feasted on crab meat and corned beef.[32]

They arrived at the site of Camp III on 28 May. Two days earlier Sayre had noticed a change in the weather: the snow which fell was wetter and in bigger flakes than the fine dry powder snow they had become accustomed to, and dark brooding cloud masses had replaced the fluffy white clouds of the Himalayan spring. He feared that the monsoon was about to break. Not only would this prevent them from attempting Everest, it might also cut off their long retreat and leave them prisoners of the Communists. This could be personally unpleasant, to say the least, but it would also provoke an international incident involving the United States, China and Nepal and jeopardize the large American expedition which was scheduled to attempt Everest in the following year.

These thoughts crossed Sayre's mind but did not deflect him from his purpose. By superhuman efforts he and his party had reached the foot of the North Col, and until they were physically beaten by the storm, Communists or sheer exhaustion, nothing was going to stop him attempting Mount Everest.

Sayre's plan of attack was, like all his plans, simple. All four men were to climb to the North Col in a day, carrying loads of 20 lb. each. Dumping the loads, they were to return to Camp III,[33] where they would split into two pairs. Then, as soon as the weather was good enough, the first pair would go up to the col and set off up the North Ridge, carrying their tent and provisions. The second pair would follow in support, one day later. To reach the summit would require a minimum of six days, but Sayre mentally allowed for eight or nine.

On the 29th the attack on the col began but almost immediately went wrong. Duttle felt so weak that he dumped his load at the foot of the slopes, and Hansen was stopped by a big crevasse which cut across the upper part – the same crevasse as Smythe had encountered in 1933 and whose upper edge rose a sheer thirty or forty feet above the lower. Sayre managed to overcome it by some desperate climbing in soft, unstable snow, then bring up Hart. Between them they hauled up Hansen's pack and cached it above the crevasse. By mid-afternoon Sayre and Hart reached a ledge some 300 ft below the crest of the col, where they dumped their loads and returned to Camp III. It had been another hard day's work.

Next morning they all felt understandably lethargic and were so late in starting that they were forced to spend the night camped in the crevasse on the face. Fixed ropes had been left here by Sayre, so that there was no problem in overcoming the crevasse next day. They found Hansen's abandoned load, which Sayre and Hart, as the two strongest, divided between themselves. By lunch-time they had reached their previous high point – the ledge 300 ft below the col – where they had cached two more loads. As it was impossible to carry these up as well, they were left for later collection. A little while later they emerged over a rim of snow and stood on the North Col – the first Western climbers to do so for almost a quarter of a century. Sayre felt a justifiable flush of pride:

> At that moment I felt a glow of satisfaction. Our plans had worked out unbelievably well. We had gotten along without oxygen. We had gotten along without Sherpas. We had gotten along without a string of fixed camps to support us. Moreover, we had negotiated the 'impossible' distance from Base Camp to our present perch. In the process we had trained ourselves to handle respectable technical difficulties of many kinds. And we had conditioned ourselves to hard, lean effectiveness. Certainly the loads that Roger and I had just carried up to 23,000 feet without undue fatigue bore witness to this. Most of all, in a few more minutes we would all be here on the col together, safe and sound, healthy, eager, and ready to go on. On hand, we would have five full days of food and fuel for the final push. This was more than I had really dared to expect. But now that it was all accomplished, the miracle of the summit was a genuine possibility.[34]

It was an incredible achievement, but it had been won at a price. The original plan had slipped into oblivion. Now there were four men on the North Col together, two of whom were strong and two who were not. It would have been better had they followed Duttle's suggestion that he should remain at Camp III – possibly with Hansen. As it was, two men had to do most of the work for four – the other two were really just an encumbrance: it is doubtful whether they could ever have played an active support role higher up the mountain.

Though the day was well advanced Sayre and Hart descended 300 ft to the ledge where the rest of the loads lay cached. They started back up, roped together, in a gathering gloaming which soon turned to inky night. Neither man felt worried by the darkness: they knew the route, which wasn't too difficult, and both were brimming with strength and self-confidence after their great success.

It was, as any climber would readily recognize, the classic situation for an accident. The hard work done – success achieved – mental relaxation – easy ground – unrecognized fatigue . . . the rope ran slack between them, untended on such easy terrain.

Suddenly, Hart was gone.

> A sudden slip, a body tobogganing down the slope with fearful acceleration – I would be next. I grabbed for my ice axe, which was standing upright in the snow. I tried to sink it in deeply so that it would hold the strain when it came. But right here the snow was thick over hard ice. The axe only penetrated a couple of inches – not nearly enough to hold a man after 100 ft of unchecked fall. For with all that slack between us, Roger had to fall the

> full length of the rope before I could even begin to stop him. Desperately I tried another spot. No luck. Now there was no more time. I hunched down against the axe to hold against the coming impact as well as I could, but I knew it was hopeless, then the rope seized me, jerked me over backward, and instantly I, too, was tobogganing down the slope.[35]

They slid down about 150 ft of snow slope. Then, sickeningly, came a sheer drop over which both men plunged – to land in soft snow, thirty or forty feet below, where they came to a halt almost side by side. It had been a lucky escape, though their situation was still perilous.

There was no way they could move on the darkened mountain. They could not climb the ice wall they had just dropped over, and below them lay unknown dangers not to be tried in the dark. They had no sleeping bags, no stove, no food. All they had in their loads was a tent, and though there was no place to pitch it they wrapped themselves up in it as best they could.

Together, they spent a bitterly cold night. Sayre's left arm hurt and Hart was occasionally sick and even at times delirious.

But they survived, and moreover without frostbite or exposure, despite the altitude of 22,700 ft. Next day, they made their way groggily back to the North Col. They weren't beaten yet. 'I wasn't going to give up on Everest because of one knockdown,' wrote Sayre.[36]

Brave words – but at the time Sayre did not realize how much the strength of his little band was depleted. The backbreaking approach march, the high altitude, the various minor injuries and the continuous nervous strain – all these factors were sapping the strength of the party.

On the next day Sayre and Hansen started out up the North Ridge, Duttle accompanying them part of the way to help with the carry. Hart was still feeling the effects of his fall and remained at the col. To Sayre's chagrin they climbed only 600 ft where he had hoped to climb 2,000 ft. On the following day they did another miserable 600 ft and that night, as they camped, they realized they were beaten. At their current rate of progress, even if they could maintain it, it would require another eight or nine days to reach the summit. They didn't have enough food for that – nor enough stamina.

The next day, therefore, Sayre went up the ridge alone to see whether he could reach the Yellow Band and to take a colour ciné film of the mountain – something no Westerner had ever done on the northern side. But the Yellow Band proved too far away; at his best estimate he made 25,500 ft, which was still 1,500 ft below his target.

It was a tired American who turned to descend, and he was a little light-headed as well. Like many mountaineers who have seen their hopes of the summit dashed he wanted to get off the mountain as quickly as possible. While the hope is still there, energy can always be dredged up from somewhere and no difficulty is too great to attempt, but once that hope has gone, energy evaporates, leaving only a numb ache, a desire to get down and an incredibly careless attitude to things in general. But the mountain, of course, never relaxes.

Looking for an easy way down, Sayre decided to glissade on a patch of hard snow. Scarcely had he started, however, than he was sliding out of control, down the ridge towards his tent. As he shot past he grabbed at the tent but it was torn from his grasp, though it slowed him down a bit and he finally slid to a halt by some rocks. He was torn and bruised, and lucky to be alive. He had gone 600 ft.

Hart came up later that day but they sent him back to the col. There was no way they could go further. Next day Sayre and Hansen struck the tent and retreated. It was a nightmare descent to the col:

> The next morning I had deteriorated badly. I had no strength, I was weak, I was dead on my feet. I literally fell asleep every minute that something was not going on. Norm had to bark at me to keep me conscious. He wrote that I was very slow in understanding and very slow in executing what I did understand. It was obvious that I could not carry a pack and Norm could not carry both. So he tied the two packs together on a light line and let them down the slope. They stuck again and again. Each time they did, it was my job to go down the rope and push them on down the slope. Of course, now when we wanted things to slide down, they never would. All this was very slow and tedious. I didn't notice it so much, because at every stop for a new belay I dropped off to sleep. But it was a big strain on Norm. He was getting groggy, too.
>
> Suddenly he slipped and toboganned down 25 feet, ending up in the rocks. He broke his watch. At that moment I suddenly felt that things were falling apart. We were falling all over the mountain. We were accident prone. We were too close to the edge. 'Wake up!' I said to myself. 'This is going to be the fight of your life just to get off the mountain, This is for keeps!'[37]

The next day – 6 June – they began an epic descent of the North Col. Sayre fell twice – the second time when he was unroped and went tumbling 400 ft down the slopes to end with a twisted knee. Duttle fell into a crevasse and was hauled out by Sayre; Hansen and Hart both had their slips and near-disasters. That night they were forced to bivouac on the ice slopes, only completing their descent next day. It was more of a rout than a retreat. But the Gods were smiling and they all got down safely.

Even so they were still in a desperate situation. By the very nature of their plan, they were now faced with a gruelling trek back to the Nup La, across twenty-five miles of exhausting glaciers, followed by a descent of the

Ngozumpa icefall. Compared with these, the added danger of meeting a Chinese border patrol seemed of little account – as did the fact that the monsoon was overdue.

It took them ten days to return to Base Camp. Despite hunger and tiredness, they navigated perfectly and picked up their food caches (though they had food for only five days left). If the Gods continued to smile, which they did, it wasn't all just luck.

The biggest blow to their morale was that on reaching their old Base Camp they found it deserted. They were long overdue, of course, and the Sherpas, having decided the party must have perished, had packed everything up and taken it back to Namche Bazar. Hungrily, the climbers made a forced march down the valley to the village of Tanna . . .

From Base Camp back to Base Camp, Sayre's incredible attempt on Everest had occupied forty-seven days. It was a brilliant folly and an epic of Himalayan endurance.

More than that one would hesitate to claim. The party had a large slice of good luck – a late monsoon, for instance, and avoiding the Chinese guards; they were strong but not very skilful mountaineers, as witness their various accidents; but perhaps above all, the plan itself was inherently self-defeating. The slow, backpacking approach involving double or treble marches, while at first acclimatizing the mountaineer to altitude, soon begins to over-acclimatize or debilitate him. In short, he is too high for too long. On McKinley it would work well, but not on Everest.

There was one other aspect of Sayre's attempt which cannot be overlooked. His incursion into Tibet, leading a four-man team and deliberately deceiving the Nepalese authorities, had much more serious political overtones than the lone adventures of Wilson, Denman or Larsen. It was more serious even than the incursion of Hillary and Lowe in 1952, who had followed much the same route, because a decade had elapsed and the Chinese grip on the country was much firmer. When Sayre told Dyhrenfurth (the leader of the 1963 American expedition, then about to set out) what he had done, the latter was appalled. He felt that if the news leaked out it might jeopardize the American attempt, and the State Department concurred. Pressure was put on *Life* magazine to withhold the story they had bought from Sayre, and eventually its publication was put off until the 1963 expedition was on its way to Base Camp.[38]

As it happened, the Chinese ignored the whole affair.

# 12

# A Fresh Start

The failure of the British to climb Mount Everest in the years between the wars was part of that tide which ebbs and flows in every sphere of man's activity. Each time it flows, it flows a little stronger until problems which it has lapped around for years are eventually overcome by the flood. The British failure on Everest was matched by the German failure on Kangchenjunga and Nangpa Parbat, the French on Gasherbrum and the American on K2. In fact, none of the world's fourteen highest peaks – those over 8,000 metres in height – was climbed before the war, and yet within fifteen years of the war ending they had all been climbed. By then the tide had turned and was running strong.[1]

To try to understand why this should be is at best a speculative business. There is nothing to suggest, for example, that the post-war generation of climbers was any fitter or more determined than their pre-war counterparts. *Technically* they were probably better climbers, though at first only marginally so – a small plus factor. A larger plus factor was the improvement in equipment, in food and in physiological knowledge as a result of wartime research; these did not make the actual climbing any easier, but they did make it more comfortable and safer. It was the accretion of such things, together with less tangible factors such as a freer socio-economic climate and a definite post-war ebullience, that contributed to the swelling tide. As a result, the climber was relieved of many of his background handicaps and could concentrate more energy on the job in hand, which was to reach the summit.

As far as the British were concerned, they gained from the rising tide like everyone else, but the war had seriously weakened them politically. The end of empire was in sight and with it all the advantages which empire brings. Nobody noticed at the time, but Everest was no longer an exclusively British preserve.

Time was running out for Britain, though it is unlikely that Eric Shipton knew or cared much about that when he wrote to the Alpine Club only a few weeks after the end of hostilities, suggesting that plans should be made to resume the struggle for Everest, possibly in two years' time – 1947. The A.C. Committee enthusiastically agreed and appointed Shipton as leader, but the Viceroy of India, Lord Wavell, made it quite clear that there was no possible chance of permission being granted to visit Tibet in 1947.

1947 was, of course, the year of Partition, when the Raj came to a precipitate end and the sub-continent was divided into two nations, India and Pakistan. The transformation was bloody, with an aftermath of civil disorder. Much of the Himalaya was declared a prohibited area, and nobody had time to bother about Everest.

At the same time, in Tibet, the Dalai Lama was having his horoscope cast. This was a serious matter, because upon the outcome rested Tibetan attitudes for the next few years, including foreign policy. As it turned out, the horoscope predicted that the Dalai Lama would be threatened by foreigners, and all foreigners were banned until 1950. As the horoscope progressed it became increasingly gloomy, with the result that the ban on foreigners was prolonged indefinitely. So the road to Everest was effectively barred and the chances of an expedition were nil. The Alpine Club, joining once again in co-partnership with the Royal Geographical Society, decided to bide its time. There was little else it could do. Private initiatives, like that of a certain Group Captain A.F. Bandit, who was planning an air-lift to Base Camp, were still-born in the face of overwhelming political obstacles.

The Dalai Lama's horoscope turned out to be truly prophetic. In October 1950 the Chinese Communist armies invaded Tibet and sealed it off to Westerners more effectively than the old regime ever had. As we have seen in the last chapter, a few daring spirits risked crossing the border, but there were no official mountaineering expeditions from the West into Tibet for many years. The northern route to Everest was closed.

But even as Tibet was becoming more than ever the 'forbidden land', so Nepal was at last beginning to open up. The two events were not entirely unconnected – watching the advance of China up to her northern borders (which in any case are largely disputed), the Nepalese began to see the dangers of isolation and prudently sought friends in the West. There was a palace revolution in which the hereditary rulers, the Rana family, were overthrown and the King, who until then had been a mere puppet, assumed control. In the years since then, as a buffer state between two powerful nations, Nepal has managed to come to terms with both India and China – not without incidental benefits.

The opening of Nepal to foreigners was a turning point in Himalayan climbing, and one of the most significant events in the whole history of mountaineering. Not only did it give climbers their first opportunity to tackle many of the world's highest peaks, it also gave them the key to Everest itself.

At first communications were very primitive. Metalled roads existed only around Kathmandu, the capital city of the country and almost as fabled as Lhasa itself. There were a few motor cars in Kathmandu, but these had been transported piecemeal on the backs of porters from the railhead at Jogbani on the Indian frontier. Indeed to those early visitors Kathmandu valley, broad, fertile and with a delightful climate, must have seemed like Shangri La: a heaven cut off from the rest of the world by the thick, malarial Terai jungle to the south and the Himalayan peaks to the north.

The approach to Everest from Nepal is certainly very different from the bleak marches across Tibet suffered by the pre-war climbers. Instead of the dreary Tibetan wastes, with their incessant and biting wind, Nepal offers densely wooded, deep-cut valleys, alive with the brilliant colours of rhododendron and berberis bushes. Even the villages seem cleaner than their Tibetan counterparts, while the natives are universally friendly.

Another advantage is that the trek through Nepal provides much better training for the climbers. In the first place it has to be done on foot – no ponies can manage this route – and because it crosses the grain of the country there is a good deal of ascent and descent, but always creeping gradually higher, which helps acclimatization as well as strengthens leg muscles.

The first party to be allowed access to the Sola Khumbu region, where the Sherpas live and where Everest lies, was that led by an American, Dr Charles Houston, who had been with Tilman on Nanda Devi in 1936. He invited Tilman to join him, and though the expedition (if such it could be called – it was quite informal) was not a mountaineering one and spent most of its time in the Sherpa capital of Namche Bazar, Tilman could not resist the opportunity of pushing on up the valley towards the foot of Everest.[2]

They reached the Khumbu Glacier but did not have time to study the great Icefall which cascades out of the Western Cwm. Nevertheless, Tilman came to the conclusion that an ascent of Everest by this route was impracticable, so confirming the opinion of Mallory, who had looked down on the Khumbu from Tibet thirty years earlier.

Tilman's reconnaissance was only a superficial one, and it was obvious that fuller exploration was needed before a proper judgement could be made.

The Himalayan Committee of the Alpine Club and R.G.S. – successor to the old Everest Committee – had been established on an informal basis in 1947 when Everest was first being considered again after the war. They had in the bank some £1,500 inherited from their predecessors and from the royalties of the 1938 Everest book which, because of the war, was ten years in gestation. With the money they financed Tilman on an expedition to Langtang in Nepal and there was talk of sending Shipton with a party to climb Tirich Mir, though this came to nothing.

In May 1951 Michael Ward, a London surgeon and climber, suggested that a proper expedition should be made to the Sola Khumbu for the purpose of ascertaining whether there was a practicable route through the Icefall to the Western Cwm, and from there to the South Col. Ward had gathered together such photographs as were available and was very enthusiastic about his idea, but he didn't know the right contacts and in any case was tied by Army duties at the time. However, Campbell Secord came to the rescue by putting Ward's plan before the Himalayan Committee, and he was supported by W.H. Murray, a noted Scottish mountaineer. At first the Committee were at best lukewarm to the idea, but eventually they agreed.

The team was to be Ward, Secord and Murray together with Bourdillon, Nock and the noted Swiss climber Alfred Tissieres, who happened to be doing research work in Cambridge at the time and was a friend of Secord's. In the event, Tissieres, Nock and Secord dropped out. Murray was the proposed leader, but suddenly, in July, Eric Shipton turned up, having been forced out of his job as a British Consul in China by the advance of the Communist army. Murray immediately offered him the leadership. The cost – £2,000 to £2,500 – was largely met by granting exclusive coverage to *The Times*. 'It was all very democratic and casual,' says Ward.[3] It was also very hurried. There was barely a month in which to get everything ready for shipment to India. The Secords' garage was turned into a sort of HQ-cum-warehouse and in the end, so frantic was the rush to have everything ready for the boat, disaster was only averted by the ladies of the local W.V.S. being brought in to do the packing.

In the meantime the formal constitution of the Himalayan Committee was decided upon: the Chairman was to be the President of the Alpine Club, and the other members were to be the President of the R.G.S., the Secretary of the A.C., the Director and Secretary of the R.G.S., a treasurer, two members of each of the A.C. and R.G.S., plus a representative of the Himalayan Club. Thus it hardly differed from the old Everest Committee, and it faced much the same problems as its predecessors had done in 1921.

There was, however, one new problem – Everest was no longer exclusively British. The first hint of this was when the Swiss Foundation for Alpine Research asked for the Swiss climber René Dittert to be allowed to accompany the Shipton reconnaissance team. This was turned down on the grounds that the expedition was purely a domestic affair. The Swiss must have been puzzled about the distinction between Tissieres and Dittert, since both were Swiss, but they let it pass. When, however, two New Zealanders, E.P. Hillary and H.E. Riddiford, and an Indian geologist, Dr Dutt, were added to the party at the last minute, they were understandably put out.

It was Shipton's personal decision to include the two New Zealanders, and at first it didn't go down well with the other members. 'I had already turned down several applications,' he later wrote. '. . . I was about to send a negative reply when, in a moment of nostalgic recollection, I recalled the cheerful countenance of Dan Bryant.'[4] Shipton had been very impressed by Bryant during the 1935 reconnaissance, and he seems to have been favourably disposed towards New Zealand in general – at one period shortly after the war he had considered emigrating there, and during the reconnaissance it was Hillary who was to be his most constant climbing partner. 'My momentary caprice was to have far reaching results,' he later wrote, laconically.[5]

Apart from the last-minute additions, it was a fairly tightly knit, coherent group, whose objectives were suitably loosely defined and which did not require the detailed planning of a large expedition. It was admirably suited to Shipton's talents and temperament.

Though the problems of the 1951 reconnaissance were nothing like as severe as those of their predecessors thirty years earlier – the 1921 reconnaissance – there was still an element of Mallory's 'first find the mountain' about it. Of course they knew that Everest lay at the head of the Khumbu valley and was guarded by a big icefall, but actually reaching the Khumbu from India was a problem in itself. Four routes were known to be feasible: from Darjeeling, along the trail used by the Sherpas when visiting their homeland (the route followed by Larsen); from the railhead at Jainagar in Bihar Province (near Darbhanga, where the Houston flights were based); from Kathmandu, rather far to the west; and from the railhead at Jogbani, further east than Jainagar.

As the trek was to take place during the monsoon period the first two routes were dismissed as too difficult and unpleasant, and Kathmandu, though easier, was further and therefore more expensive, so the party set out from Jogbani. It was the route used by Houston and Tilman the year before and they had done it in a fortnight.

The difference was that Houston's party had travelled in the dry, calm post-monsoon. The 1951 party found things very different during the rainy season: rivers swollen by rain, bridges swept away, porters hard to come by ('no one ever travelled far during the monsoon if he could help it,' local officials told Shipton). Above all, perhaps, the misery of tramping muddy paths in continuous rain through leech-infested forests.

> On the march to Dingla it had rained mostly at night and the days had been fine. This happy arrangement could not be expected to last, and by now it was raining for most of each day. We set off again on the morning of the 12th and climbed to the crest of the high, narrow watershed ridge. For three days we made our way slowly along it in a northerly direction, unable to see anything of our surroundings because of alternating spells of heavy rain and equally drenching Scotch mist. After a while we lost all sense of direction and distance; it was a curious sensation, blindly following this narrow crest, the ground on either hand falling steeply into the silent,

10. Near the top of the Rock Band gully, the key to the difficult South West Face. (Doug Scott)

11. Members of the British expedition in 1975 climb the difficult ramp leading out of the Rock Band Gully to Camp VI. (Doug Scott)

12. Dougal Haston traversing above the Rock Band during the first ascent of the South West Face, 1975. The climb has only been repeated once, in 1988, with tragic results. (Doug Scott)

(*Above*)
13. The North Face of Everest. Triollet and Loretan are below the Great Couloir, ready for their remarkably fast ascent in 1986. (Dr. John English)

(*Facing page*)
14. Climbers on the North East Ridge (Dr. John English)

(*Above*)
15. On the Kangshung Face. Ed Webster on fixed ropes in Big Al Gully on the way to Camp I, 1988. (Stephen Venables)

(*Facing page*)
16. The deep crevasse separating the buttress from the upper slopes on the 1988 Kangshung Face route. The only way across was by Tyrolean traverse, demonstrated here by Ed Webster. (Stephen Venables)

(*Above*)
17. Some of the world's leading Himalayan mountaineers (left to right) Wanda Rutkiewicz, Eric Escoffier, Wojciech Kurtyka, Ehrard Loretan, Pierre Beghin, Doug Scott and Reinhold Messner. These are representative of the climbers responsible for the new wave of extreme climbing on Everest and other Himalayan peaks. (Sylvie Chappaz © Vertical)

(*Left*)
18. Bachendri Pal, escaping from the avalanche which shattered Camp III, became the first Indian woman to reach the summit in 1984. (Walt Unsworth)

forested depths below, while rocky peaks loomed, one after another, ahead. The undergrowth was infested with leeches; on a single twig a score of the creatures could be seen, stiff and erect, like a cluster of little black sticks, ready to attach themselves to our legs and arms and clothing as we brushed past.

The way consisted of a continuous series of long, steep climbs and descents. It was very hard work for the porters, for the track was slimy with mud and they slipped constantly, losing their balance under the shifting weight of their sodden loads. We spent the nights in little cowherds' shelters, mostly deserted, which were interspersed along the ridge. They kept out most of the rain, and fires lit inside discouraged the leeches from entering. Without them our lot would have been a great deal worse.[6]

The two New Zealanders, Edmund Hillary and Earle Riddiford, who were making their own way from India, caught up with the main party at Dingla. Both were tall, big-boned men, with not an ounce of spare flesh between them. Riddiford wore spectacles, giving him a fairly schoolmasterish appearance, but both he and Hillary were typically forthright Antipodean males. Strong and tough, their journey through Nepal by a slightly different route from Shipton's, and a more hazardous one as it happened, had left them looking ragged and unkempt.

This bothered Hillary, who stood somewhat in awe of Shipton's reputation as the most famous living Himalayan mountaineer. Moreover, he had that outmoded idea of conventional Englishmen so common to colonials and Americans: 'But these Englishmen – for all I knew they might shave every day; they might be sticklers for the right thing. We'd have to smarten up a bit and watch our language.'[7]

He needn't have worried, as he quickly discovered when they at last joined forces:

> Feeling not a little like a couple of errant schoolboys going to visit the headmaster, we followed the Sherpa into a dark doorway and up some stairs into the upper room of a large building. As we came into the room, four figures rose to meet us. My first feeling was one of relief. I have rarely seen a more disreputable bunch, and my visions of changing for dinner faded away for ever.[8]

On 19 September they finally crossed a pass which led them into the valley of the Dudh Kosi, and as if they had suddenly come into Shangri La, the monsoon rains were left behind. The brilliant blue post-monsoon skies arched over the most dazzling array of snow-white peaks to be seen anywhere in the world. On the 22nd they entered Namche Bazar. The journey from Jogbani had taken almost a month.

Looking back, it is easy to say that the expedition could have started a month later, achieved the same results, and spared itself such misery on the walk-in, but so little was known of conditions on the south side of Everest that this was a risk they could not take. Their aim was to use the whole of the post-monsoon period for work on the mountain itself and though they were vaguely aware that the monsoon finished towards the end of September they did not know how long the fine weather would last before the onset of the winter gales. Indeed, this was something which all the later post-monsoon expeditions had to face – judging exactly what would be the right 'slot' for an assault between the monsoons and the winter winds. It was most brilliantly done by Bonington in 1975.

At Namche Bazar the expedition was entering the final stages of the southern approach to Everest (see Map 5, p. 256), a route which was to become increasingly familiar to mountaineers and trekkers over the succeeding years but which at that time had been travelled by only a handful of Westerners: Tilman, Houston and Klavs Becker-Larsen. Shipton later admitted that one of the chief inducements to lead the expedition was the opportunity it afforded him to visit the homeland of the Sherpas – nor was he disappointed at what he saw. How he must have welcomed the contrast between the beautiful setting of the Dudh Kosi and the hateful Tibetan plateau and grim Rongbuk valley of pre-war days!

The party left Namche on 25 September with enough provisions for seventeen days. In that time they hoped to find a way through the Icefall, inspect the Western Cwm and see if there was a practicable route to the South Col. If things went well, Shipton intended to send down for further supplies and reconnoitre as far as possible towards the col itself.

They moved gradually up the valley, camping at places which were later to become so familiar but were then being encountered for the first time: the monastery at Thyangboche, with its awe-inspiring view of the great peaks; the yak pastures at Pheriche and Lobuje; then up the long debris-encrusted Khumbu Glacier to a final camp near the little lake of Gorak Shep, on the west bank.

On 30 September, Riddiford, Ward and Bourdillon with two Sherpas set out to make a preliminary investigation of the Icefall while Shipton and Hillary climbed some way up the peak of Pumori to gain a view into the Western Cwm. Almost at a single glance they got the good news and the bad news:

> We found to our surprise that from the point reached we could see right up to the head of the Western Cwm, the whole of the west face of Lhotse, and the South Col. We estimated that the floor of the cwm at its head was nearly 23,000 ft high, about 2,000 ft higher than had been expected. There

appeared to be a perfectly straightforward route from there up the face of Lhotse to some 25,000 ft whence, it seemed, a traverse could be made to the South Col. All this, of course, must be confirmed by close inspection from the cwm itself, and the need for good snow conditions, particularly on that traverse, is obvious. At present snow conditions on the mountain are quite impossible.

Our study of the icefall was less encouraging than our view of the cwm. From the top of the lower half there was an easy route running through to the left; but this was obviously swept by ice avalanches from the west ridge of Everest, while to the right nothing could be seen but a wild tangle of seracs and ice cliffs. However, we made a further reconnaissance the following day from a ridge near the Lho La, which revealed the upper icefall in a more hopeful light.[9]

Riddiford and Pasang had climbed four fifths of the lower Icefall at their first attempt and were optimistic about the rest of the route, and even though Ward and Bourdillon, choosing a different line, had been unable to make much progress, there was little doubt that the Icefall would go. But it was obviously a dangerous place: the whole 2,000 ft was slowly on a downward slide, utterly unstable. Ice pinnacles the size of a cathedral could topple over without warning, obliterating anyone unfortunate enough to be in their path. Even at the edges it was no safer, for it was squeezed between the steep slopes of Everest's West Ridge on the one hand and those of Nuptse on the other, either of which were likely to precipitate enormous avalanches.

In climbing, as in many other aspects of life, the risks are weighed against the goal. When that goal is Everest, the risk-threshold is high. There isn't a climber in the world who, given the chance of an Everest ascent, would turn back because of the Icefall risk, though in other circumstances he would steer clear of such a place. Unfortunately, however, as Shipton well knew, it wasn't so simple. There was a moral problem as well. Granted that the climber was willing to risk his own life in the pursuit of his goal, was he justified in risking the lives of his laden porters, who, after all, were simply doing a job of work? Moreover, the risk to the porters was far greater because they would need to go up and down the Icefall many times, ferrying loads up into the Western Cwm.

Already by 1951 some of the Sherpas had become experienced mountaineers – Angtharkay, who was Shipton's sirdar, or chief porter, was one – and they were increasingly treated as such by the expeditions. They could judge the risk as well as anybody, and could be counted on to face it, not just for pay but because they were imbued with the same sense of achievement as their leaders. But what of the others? Shipton was the first leader to have to face this dilemma and, ultimately, he baulked it.

Hillary, however, did not share Shipton's qualms. The New Zealander weighed the danger against the prize:

> Shipton was far from happy about subjecting Sherpas to such a route – it hardly worked in with the deep-seated British tradition of responsibility and fair play. But, in my heart, I knew the only way to attempt this mountain was to modify the old standards of safety and justifiable risk and to meet the dangers as they came; to drive through regardless. Care and caution would never make a route through the icefall. If we didn't attack it that May, someone else would. The competitive standards of alpine mountaineering were coming to the Himalayas, and we might as well compete or pull out.[10]

'Only the first time counts' somebody once said, speaking of mountain climbing, and it is true that the first in the field has far greater problems (and greater rewards) than those who follow. When a thing has been done once, the fear of the unknown has been broken and a huge psychological barrier removed. When Shipton looked at the Khumbu Icefall, nobody had climbed it, much less taken porters up it. The Swiss were the first to do that in any numbers, and thereafter it became accepted. The questions were always there, but they became increasingly less acute under the levelling influence of repetition and, in later years, the growing capabilities of the whole Sherpa corps.

'It would be wrong to make too big a thing of the Icefall,' the late Nick Estcourt once said, meaning that no single part of an Everest ascent should be exaggerated at the expense of the whole, and this is true.[11] Nevertheless, the Icefall is the most inescapably dangerous place on the mountain, and more people have been killed there than anywhere else.

Heartened by the quick success of Riddiford, Shipton established a small camp nearer the Icefall in the hope of breaking through the barrier with a quick, concerted effort. On 4 October, he, Hillary, Riddiford and Bourdillon, with three Sherpas, began the climb. They found that before the sun got on the ice – about 10 a.m. – the cold was so intense that frostbite was a real danger. Once the sun struck the ice, however, the temperature shot up until the place was like a furnace; 'glacier lassitude' and thirst became the problems. But they kept at it:

> We got through the first half of the icefall quickly and easily, with Riddiford's reconnaissance as a guide. But the upper half was a far tougher proposition. Threading our way through a maze of seracs, ice walls and crevasses which split the surface in every direction, we could never see more than about 200 ft ahead. The snow was often hip deep, so that even with so many to share the labour progress from point to point was very slow, and a false line costs a great deal of time.

> However, by the middle of the afternoon we seemed to be approaching the top of the icefall. We had decided to turn back not later than 4 o'clock in order to reach camp before dark. Even that was running it a bit fine, since it did not allow for accidents, such as the breaking of a snow bridge. We reached the last of the seracs at an altitude, according to our Watkin aneroid, of 20,600 ft. We looked across a deep trough to a level crest of ice marking the point where the glacier of the cwm takes its first plunge into the icefall like the smooth wave above a water-fall. Crossing the trough was difficult, as it was riven with crevasses, but by 3.50 we had reached the steep slope below the crest. This had to be climbed diagonally to avoid an ice cliff directly above. The snow was obviously unstable, but the slope was not high enough to constitute a serious danger. The leading rope was half-way across, and not more than 30 ft from the crest, when, as we had half expected, the slope avalanched. Pasang and I, at either end of the break, managed to scramble off the moving sheet of snow, and Riddiford was left suspended between the two of us while the sheet broke into great blocks and slid silently into the trough.[12]

It was only a minor incident and nobody was hurt, but it was enough to tell them to turn back. It had been a long hard day, and enough was enough, despite the temptation to climb the last few feet into the Cwm. They reached camp shortly before dark.

Shipton decided that even if they could get through to the Western Cwm – and there seemed no reason to doubt it now – there would be too much soft snow in the Cwm and on the slopes of the South Col to make further progress. With a bit of luck, however, the snow might be reduced by evaporation, given a few more days, and so his plan was to leave Everest alone for a couple of weeks and spend the time profitably by exploring the surrounding tangle of peaks and glaciers.

One wonders to what extent, having seen the way clear to the South Col from his eyrie on Pumori and having proved that the Icefall could be climbed, Shipton lost interest in the mechanics of the approach. The grand design, the broad sweep – these were Shipton's strong points: the minutiae of a mountain ascent held no interest for him. For him the most important thing was always to see what lay over the next ridge – an unbounded curiosity about the 'untravelled world', as he himself later called it. It was his greatest asset as an explorer – and his greatest weakness as a mountaineer, particularly as an Everest leader.

It must have been with a feeling of relief that he turned his back on the Icefall and set about exploring the surrounding mountains. He was, ostensibly at least, looking for other ways to approach Everest. In particular he wanted to break out to the east to see whether there was an easy route from the Khumbu to the great Kangshung Glacier which flowed from the East Face of Everest, and also whether there was any truth in the report he had heard from a Sherpa, that to the west of Everest lay a high pass connecting the Chola Khola (a branch of the main Khumbu valley) with Tibet.

Consequently, the expedition divided into two teams: Shipton and Hillary striking eastwards; Murray, Ward, Riddiford and Bourdillon westwards.

Suffice to say that neither party discovered a way round the mountain. The high white ridge whose apex is Everest stretched unbroken to east and west. To the east, Shipton and Hillary found their way barred by the steep flanks of the Cho Polu ridge which prevented them from reaching the Barun Glacier, whence, by Pethangtse, they might have been able to link up with the explored area of the Kangshung Glacier covered by the 1921 expedition. Instead they were forced south to the Hunku Glacier, and by the time they had discovered a feasible way over to the Barun Glacier their supplies were low and they were forced to turn west again, crossing a high pass just south of Ama Dablam and ending up at the village of Dingpoche. From there another high pass over the Pokalde ridge took them back to the Khumbu Glacier and Base Camp.

Meanwhile, striking westwards over the romantically named Changri La, Murray's team had discovered that they were not in the Chola Khola, as they expected, but an arm of the immense Ngozumpa Glacier, which drained Cho Oyu and Gyachung Kang. This was the celebrated Gyubanare Glacier, at whose head rose the spectacular Gyubanare icefall leading to the Nup La. Murray knew that the Nup La had been reached from the Tibetan side in 1924 but never crossed, so he decided to attempt the icefall.

> The whole of the first day was spent in reaching that icefall and camp was pitched at its base. Never had we seen a fall in such a state of ruin. The debris of fallen ice-cliffs and pinnacles marred its surface. We found a safe line and on our second day enjoyed one of the best ice-climbs of our lives, climbing in ice-claws and making good progress for 300 ft. Then the pinnacles and cliffs were encountered. Between them were huge crevasses, some lightly bridged with ice, some open and fathomless. Curtains of icicles hung from the overhanging walls and flashed in the sunshine. Great caves and chasms loomed blue and green. Beneath our feet we could often hear the tinkle of fragments falling into a hidden crevasse. A last ice-cliff of 40 ft could not be turned, so it was climbed by a vertical crack and at last we emerged on more level ground. Far beyond, still another icefall could be seen. It was obvious that we were beaten. Three days would be needed to reach the Nup La. For this there was no longer sufficient food. We turned back.[13]

The Icefall was climbed in the following year by Hillary and Lowe, and later by the Sayre expedition (see Chapter 11).

Shipton and Hillary reached Base Camp in the Khumbu a week before the others. They again pushed a forward base nearer the Icefall and with the two experienced Sherpas, Angtharkay and Utsering, began once more to climb the unstable, dangerous ice.

Their first day's work – a thousand feet or so – went smoothly enough. There had been few changes since they were last there and things looked hopeful. On the next day, however,

> . . . we found that immediately above the point we had reached the day before enormous changes had taken place. It was as if an earthquake had occurred. Over a wide area, stretching almost completely across the glacier, the cliffs and towers we had encountered before lay in a ruin of shattered ice-blocks. It reminded me very much of a bombed-out area in London during the war. With some misgivings we ventured to cross the devastated area, with 100 ft of rope between each man. Hillary was ahead, chopping his way through the ice-blocks, when one of the blocks fell into a void below. There was a prolonged roar and the whole surface we were standing on began to shudder violently. I thought it was about to collapse, and the Sherpas, somewhat irrationally no doubt, flung themselves to the ground. Evidently a considerable part of the shattered area was overhanging a void though it was impossible to tell how much of it. In spite of this alarming experience it was not so much the shattered area that worried us as the area beyond, where the cliffs and seracs were riven by innumerable new cracks which seemed to threaten a catastrophe.[14]

On 26 October, when Murray's party rejoined them, what amounted to a council of war was convened. It was decided then that the whole party would climb up the Pumori ridge, from where they could get a good view of the Icefall, the Cwm and the South Col, and decide their course of action according to what was revealed.

To Shipton, the view was depressing. Although some snow had gone from the mountain, the Cwm and South Col looked in much the same state as they had three weeks earlier. The Icefall looked a tottering mess.

Nevertheless, it was decided to make an all-out assault with the whole climbing team and three Sherpas, Angtharkay, Pasang and Nima. On 28 October they at last forced their way through the Icefall and stood on the lip of the Western Cwm. They had turned the key that unlocked the door to Everest.

Once they had reached the Cwm, however, they discovered that their troubles were by no means over. Two enormous crevasses barred the way. Shipton decided to retreat to Base Camp.

This decision did not go down well with everybody. There were those who wanted to press on and, when retreat was inevitable, to make further efforts to find a safer route through the crumbling ice. Shipton acquiesced in this, half-heartedly. He had been to the Cwm and that was sufficient for him, although he felt that by not finding a safer route he had virtually failed in the job he was appointed to do. In his despatch to *The Times* he wrote:

> Our virtual defeat by the icefall, formidable though we knew it to be, has come as a surprise and a disappointment, particularly as we are now convinced that, in reasonable conditions, a practicable route exists from the Western Cwm to the summit of Mount Everest. However, icefalls throughout the world are subject to great seasonal variations, and autumn is usually the season when they are at their most difficult. This dragon guarding the Western Cwm is now in a restless mood; it is not unreasonable to expect that in the spring he may be found sleeping.[15]

The party returned to Namche. Their failure to press on up the Western Cwm had left time in hand for a final fling. They decided to investigate the Bhote Kosi, the other arm of the river which divided at Namche Bazar. At Thame village, Hillary, Riddiford and Dutt (who had spent his time making geological surveys while the others had been climbing) crossed the Tesu Lapcha pass to the west and found themselves in the remarkable gorge of Rowaling, which they followed to Lamsbazar. From there they made their way to Kathmandu. Murray and Bourdillon went to the head of the Bhote Kosi to look at the famous Nangpa La, that traditional trading pass into Tibet used by Larsen in his lone attempt on Everest (see Chapter 11). Shipton and Ward accompanied them part of the way, then struck westwards over a high col, which they named the Menlung La, and entered upon a sort of sanctuary reminiscent of Nanda Devi. They were making towards Gaurisanker but, to their surprise, a higher and far finer peak rose like a pale granite spire out of the sanctuary: they named this peak Menlungtse. They were shortly joined by Murray and Bourdillon, when the whole party made their way down to the deep Rongshar gorge, from where they reached Lamsbazar and ultimately Kathmandu.[16]

Before they had set out from London three months previously, Shipton had put the chances of finding a route through to the Western Cwm as 30 to 1 against. Their exploration had at least reduced the odds considerably.[17]

When the party returned to England early in December Shipton was amazed to discover how much interest his expedition had aroused among the general public. *The Times* had not only published his reports as they came from Nepal, but had collected them together and republished them as a special supplement. A public lecture which Shipton gave in Liverpool had to be repeated three times – and on the last occasion the hall was as packed as it had been on the first.

So much publicity rather took Shipton aback. His previous Everest adventures, in the days before the war, had been during a period when repeated failures had dulled the public's appetite and interest in Everest was at its nadir. Now it was very different.

Shipton was one of the most modest men ever to tread the high places of this Earth. He saw the intense public interest as a search for relief from the austerities of the post-war years – a simple diversion he called it – but he discounted his own personal appeal. Adventure was fashionable: a French mountaineering team had climbed Annapurna, the first 8,000 m. peak ever to be ascended, and Thor Heyerdahl had made his sensational crossing of the Pacific in Kon Tiki. Books about these great adventures were best-sellers – as was the unpretentious Penguin paperback *Climbing in Britain*, a simple handbook on how to climb our own hills.

Adventure, and a sense of the great outdoors, had a new, eager audience. They read avidly about what had been done and who had been doing it in the years just before the war, and the names of Smythe, Tilman and Shipton ranked high on any list. All three men were good writers and their armchair devotees were legion. Shipton was to this new public almost a folk hero, and though a reconnaissance of Everest in itself would anyway have stirred the mood of the time, the fact that it was led by Shipton raised it to greater heights.

And of course, in the public's eyes if not in his own, his reconnaissance had been successful. He had found the way to the roof of the world.[18]

Not that Shipton was seen as another George Mallory. So far as Everest was concerned nothing would replace that Adonis figure in the public esteem. But, like Mallory, he inspired confidence. Informed public opinion was quite certain that the man to get a team to the top of Everest was Eric Shipton.

The Himalayan Committee agreed. Shipton was asked to lead the full assault on the mountain earmarked for 1952.

It came as a nasty surprise to discover that there would be no expedition in 1952. The sway of the great Raj had ended, and it was to the Swiss, not the British, that the Nepalese authorities granted access the following year.

The Himalayan Committee tried to retrieve the situation by requesting a joint expedition. The Swiss could see the advantages of this – after all, the British climbers were the only ones who knew the terrain and had tackled the now notorious Khumbu Icefall – but any joint expedition would have to be on their terms. They held the ace card – permission.

Basil Goodfellow represented the Himalayan Committee at a meeting with the Swiss Foundation for Alpine Research in Zurich on 29 December. He loftily conceded that the Committee were prepared to discuss partnership, provided Shipton was leader and it was understood that it would be a Swiss group in a British expedition.

Such demands had no chance of success. The Swiss politely told Goodfellow that their plans for a pre-monsoon attempt were now complete, equipment and finance were available, and the climbers already chosen. They also pointed out that when they had asked for Dittert to be included in the British reconnaissance team, they had been refused, although two New Zealanders were later admitted. Dittert was present at the meeting, and the old grudge was now being paid off in full.

The Swiss also pointed out that they had been trying to get permission to attempt Everest since 1926, but had always been frustrated by British imperial chauvinism. However, they told Goodfellow, they deplored the sort of nationalism demonstrated by French and German climbers, and on this account were willing to include a group of British climbers in the Swiss expedition.

The card the Swiss were playing for was Shipton, and Goodfellow was astute enough to recognize this. After some bargaining it was agreed that Shipton and Wyss-Dunant would be co-leaders of an expedition consisting of six climbers from each country.

At this point Shipton was called on the telephone and he agreed in principle – providing the British team could include the two New Zealanders, Hillary and Lowe.

The Swiss seemed to see this as a raising of the stakes. In return they demanded that Wyss-Dunant should be the overall leader and that Shipton and Dittert should be joint climbing leaders. To this Goodfellow could not agree, and though the discussion went on to cover the technicalities of co-operation, any hope of a joint expedition was dead.

In the end it was decided that the Swiss would make a pre-monsoon attempt and the British would make a post-monsoon attempt. But the Nepalese Government thought otherwise: the Swiss would go to Everest, they said, and the British would have to be content with Cho Oyu.

The British, though privately gnashing their teeth, took the blow with their customary sporting good grace. Edmund Hillary later wrote what he felt about the Swiss attempt at the time – feelings which found an echo in most British hearts:

> I think for the first time I was really admitting to myself quite honestly that I didn't want the Swiss to climb Everest. Let them get very high – good luck to them in that but not to the summit! I wanted it left for a British party to have a crack at next year.[19]

It was a very human weakness compounded of patriotism (some may say nationalism, which is less generous) and the competitive urge. There was also a degree of fear – fear that the Swiss might climb the mountain at their first attempt, which in the eyes of the world would make the British, with their long record of failures, look rather foolish. To most people the *reasons* wouldn't matter.

None of this was allowed to come to the surface. As climbers, the British and the Swiss had long had a special relationship, for between them they had practically invented the sport – the British as the daring amateurs, the Swiss as professional guides. Shipton went over to Zurich to show his rivals the photographs he had taken and to brief them to the best of his ability.

He knew in his heart that their chances of success were very good. Though he had not penetrated into the Western Cwm he had seen enough to tell him that this must be the way to climb Everest. Already he had accepted that his reservations about leading Sherpas through the Icefall would have to be set aside, because the advantages of the route made the prize clear for those determined to grasp it. W.H. Murray, who was with Shipton in 1951, enumerated these advantages:

> Despite our disappointment in not reaching the slopes of the South Col, our reconnaissance had been successful in that we had found answers to all the questions we had set out to answer, and that these answers were for the most part favourable beyond expectation. The western route may yet prove to be a better one than the old north route over which it offers these six advantages, some of which are still to be proven true:
>
> First, the main difficulties occur low down, whereas on the north route they start at 28,000 feet, where the climber commands less energy.
>
> Second, on the last three thousand feet of the South-east ridge the strata dip northward, in favour of the climber, and so should give better support for the snow, more tent platforms, and permit the last camp to be placed much nearer the summit.
>
> Third, the route is protected from violent wind until close to the South Col (about 25,800 ft).
>
> Fourth, the South-east ridge is broad and should give a wider choice of route than the northern line.
>
> Fifth, on the north side the snow above 25,000 ft refuses to consolidate, and by remaining powdery makes climbing impossible until it is cleared by the north-west wind; whereas the fact that snow lies always on the South-east ridge, despite wind, would imply that there it does consolidate and may give satisfactory climbing.
>
> Sixth, the slopes above the South Col are in sunshine from dawn, thus allowing climbers to make an earlier and easier start than from camps on the northerly side (where the old Camp VI was in shadow until 9 a.m.).[20]

The bugbear was the Icefall. It was just plain dangerous. 'Compete or pull out,' Hillary had said. The time had come to raise the stakes. Shipton knew this and accepted it – but it troubled him.

René Dittert had conceived the idea of an expedition to Everest in a

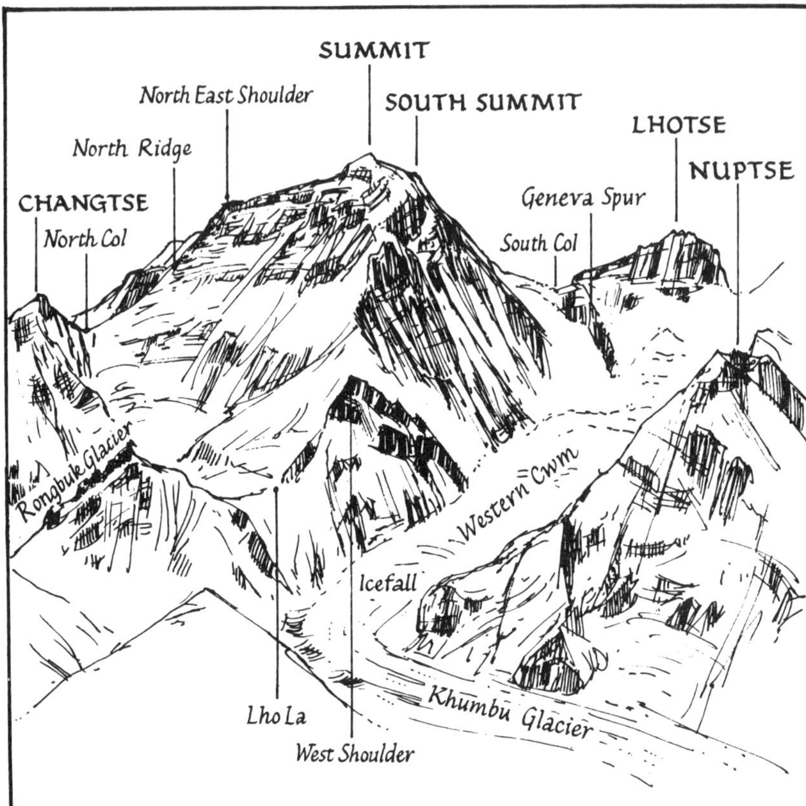


Fig. 2. The approach through the Western Cwm

conversation with Ed Wyss-Dunant in 1949. It was to be a combined climbing and scientific expedition, and the members were to be drawn from a select band of mountaineering fanatics from Geneva known as the Androsace – a club which is never allowed to exceed forty.

At first the plans were modest, in keeping with the finances of the group, but all that changed when they came under the auspices of the Swiss Foundation for Alpine Research.

The Swiss Foundation for Alpine Research was formed in 1940 for the express purpose of furthering exploration and scientific research in mountain areas beyond Europe, including the Arctic and Antarctic. In a more limited way it is similar to the British Royal Geographical Society or the American National Geographical Society, except that it is more closely linked with government – it works directly under the Department of Internal Affairs. At the time of their Everest venture the Foundation had already sent five previous expeditions to Himalayan regions, as well as to Tibesti and Baffin Island. It had considerable financial resources, and was able to provide for the best possible equipment. The Androsace had found themselves a particularly benevolent fairy godmother!

'A handful of friends' René Dittert called the team. They were also the cream of Swiss climbers. Besides Dittert there was Asper, Aubert, Chevalley, Flory, Hofstetter, Lambert, Roch and Wyss-Dunant. On the scientific side there was a geologist, Lombard; a botanist, Zimmermann; and an ethnologist, Mme Lobsiger. Of the climbers, the best known outside Switzerland were undoubtedly Raymond Lambert and André Roch, both outstanding mountaineers.

With the opening of an airport at Kathmandu the erstwhile trail from the railhead at Jogbani became redundant; henceforth most expeditions to Everest would start from the Nepalese capital, following a route which turned out to be so beautiful that it has become one of the most famous and popular treks in the world, and for many people a goal in itself. On that first occasion it took the Swiss twenty-three days, including a two-day rest at Namche Bazar.

It was at Kathmandu, therefore, that the Swiss expedition assembled and where they met their Sherpas for the first time, including the sirdar, Tenzing Norgay.

Tenzing was thirty-eight years old. He was small and dapper-looking, with a pencil moustache and sleeked-back hair. His countenance was open, frank and intelligent, and he had perhaps a rather more serious air than was common among the fun-loving Sherpas from which he came. He had been born in the village of Thame, a day's march from Namche up the Dudh Kosi. He had been to Everest three times with the pre-war British expeditions and once since the war with Earl Denman, and he had also accumulated experience in many parts of the Himalaya and Karakorum. He had done well for himself and taken the name 'Norgay', which means 'the fortunate one'.[21]

In 1947, shortly after the Denman adventure, Tenzing had joined a Swiss expedition to the Garhwal which included André Roch and René Dittert. He was not the sirdar, but his ability quickly manifested itself, and when the sirdar was injured Tenzing took his place. He made a brilliant success of it, climbing four new peaks (the first actual summits he had ever reached!). It added a new dimension to Tenzing's life and for this he was forever grateful: he had a deep admiration for the Swiss.

The feeling was mutual. When the 1952 Everest expedition was launched, Roch and Dittert insisted that Tenzing should be sirdar.

There was at first a bit of trouble over the recruitment of porters. The Shipton expedition had left behind it some resentment over payment, baksheesh and a missing camera, and there was a general reluctance to take part in another expedition, presumably on the principle of once bitten, twice shy. But eventually loads were sorted out, and despite a last-minute 'strike' to try to raise the pay by two rupees the caravan set out on the long trail to Everest.

The expedition established its Base Camp by the small moraine lake of Gorak Shep (16,570 ft), on 20 April, and their Camp I was established on the Khumbu Glacier at 17,226 ft below the Icefall. The plan was the customary one of pushing camps forward in a series of staging posts until the final camp, probably not more than a single tent, could be pitched high enough up the mountain to allow two men to make a summit 'dash'. In the pre-war days, the long approach up the East Rongbuk Glacier had necessitated three such camps before the slopes of the North Col, where the real climbing began, were reached. On the Khumbu approach, with its Icefall, the climbing begins almost at once, so that the material for all the camps has to be ferried up a fairly steep and sometimes difficult route. The Swiss plan was to place Camp II half way up the Icefall, where there is a natural break in the seracs, Camp III above the Icefall, and Camp IV on the South Col. To reach Camp IV meant traversing the whole of the Western Cwm and climbing the steep slopes of the col in a single journey – much too hard a task, as the Swiss were quickly to discover. They found, too, that there was no need to have Base Camp at Gorak Shep – it would be much better removed to the site of Camp I.

The attack on the Icefall was begun on 26 April by Dittert, Chevalley, Lambert and Aubert. That day they took six hours to climb 1,150 ft through the maze of crevasses and seracs. Like Shipton previously they discovered that one of the problems of the Icefall was that once inside it the climber could not see more than a few feet ahead and consequently had no proper idea which was the best direction to take. Quite apart from the obvious danger, there was the less obvious frustration caused by taking false lines which in the end led nowhere. And with frustration comes tiredness.

The next day they pushed their route out a bit further, then retired to Camp I. The struggle was taken up by Roch, Flory, Asper, Hofstetter and Wyss-Dunant, who established Camp II half way up the Icefall.

On the 30th this same party, except for Wyss-Dunant, made an all-out attempt to reach the Cwm. They were forced to the left, below the steep slopes of Everest's West Ridge, and into a couloir threatened by seracs and avalanches. It was a natural highway – but it was so dangerous that Roch christened it 'Suicide Passage'. It took them to the edge of the Cwm.

Like Shipton in the previous year, Roch now found his way barred by a huge crevasse. Asper tried to swing across by rope manoeuvres but couldn't get a purchase on the other side, so they returned to Camp II. Next day they were back, and by lowering Asper sixty feet down the crevasse to a snow bridge, they were able to get a rope across. This in turn was converted into a rope bridge, made of four ropes securely anchored into the ice on either side of the chasm and crossed by sitting astride two ropes and pulling on the others. By this method the Sherpas and their loads were transported across the crevasse. Roch had entered the Western Cwm. It was a tremendous break-through, gained, as Hillary had foreseen, by raising the stakes, by accepting new levels of danger. That night an avalanche swept the whole of Roch's Suicide Couloir, but by that time the climbers were safely back in camp.

Camp III, at the entrance to the Cwm, was occupied on 6 May and its provisioning – with material for the higher camps – was continued. By good luck, there was not a single incident in the Suicide Passage, though sixty loads went up it, but there were some near misses. Stones, ice debris and even the occasional avalanche swept down it, but nobody was hit.

When Roch had first entered the Cwm and prospected a little way into it he had been overawed by the scale of things and pessimistic about their chance of success, but once Camp III was established and other climbers in their turn had an opportunity to explore the Cwm and assess the difficulties ahead, the mood changed to one of quiet optimism.

From their tents they could see the snowy bowl of the Cwm, undulating but rising slightly, stretching away to the slopes of Lhotse, Mallory's old 'South Peak of Everest'. It was hemmed in on the left by the South West Face of Everest, an impressive wall of dark rock laced with ice bands, and on their right by the steep icy ramparts of the Lhotse–Nuptse Ridge. To the left of Lhotse, at the head of the Cwm, the skyline dipped to the South Col. Steep slopes of snow and ice joined the floor of the Cwm to the col, and these were divided by a conspicuous rib of black rock which the Swiss called the Éperon des Genevois – the Geneva Spur.

Though the Cwm was not very wide, it was longer than the Swiss had imagined and it was obvious that there was no way Camp IV – the next camp – could be placed on the South Col. For one thing it was too far, and for another the Western Cwm and the Lhotse slopes had their own problems.

Reconnaissance showed the climbers that the Cwm was cut across by wide crevasses. The only way to avoid these was by making a detour to the right, beneath the menacing slopes of the Lhotse–Nuptse ridge, where there was considerable danger from avalanches. The slopes to the col itself, too, seemed dangerously avalanche-prone, and the Swiss realized that anyone caught by a heavy snowfall on the South Col, or even at the head of the Cwm, might well have no retreat.

Dittert remembered the tragedy of 1922 when the slopes of the North Col avalanched and killed seven Sherpas. And the North Col presented the only objective danger on the old route, whereas on this new route from the south there were three – the Icefall, the Lhotse–Nuptse slopes and the slopes to the South Col. Moreover, all the Sherpas had to risk the first (and of course all the climbers) and most of them had to risk the second as well. It was only when they reached the ascent of the South Col that the situation was back to parity with the old northern route. It was up to the Swiss to test these risks and see whether they were justified.

In the ensuing days Camps IV and V were established in the Cwm, the latter at 22,630 ft below the slopes of the South Col. It was the latter-day equivalent of the old Camp III, which rested below the North Col on the East Rongbuk Glacier, and now, as then, the problem was how to tackle the slopes above. Dittert wrote:

> Seen from the camp the Col had a gentle and deceiving appearance, all its slopes being foreshortened. But the figures proved the contrary. The Col rose more than 3,500 ft above us, though one might easily reckon it at half that figure. The average slope varied between 40 and 45 degrees, almost that of the Brenva route on the south face of Mont Blanc.[22]

Four alternatives faced the Swiss. The most direct slopes to the col were divided at half height by the rocks of the Geneva Spur which split them into two couloirs, rather like the upper arms of a letter Y. The left-hand branch led directly to the col itself, and was thus the shortest way up. The right-hand branch led to a rocky crest somewhat above the col. Further right still was the steep Lhotse Glacier descending the face of the mountain, and it seemed possible to climb the glacier, then traverse left to the top of the South Col. The glacier route had the advantage of being more open than the two couloirs and possibly less of a trap, though there was avalanche danger on all three. The spur itself was the fourth alternative.

On 15 May, Lambert and Tenzing, who had become firm friends though they couldn't speak a word of each other's language, accompanied by Roch and Dittert, climbed up towards the Geneva Spur. They were above 24,000 ft and only able to breathe oxygen during their halts because the sets did not function when the climbers were moving. Though such gasps of oxygen gave immense relief, the effects were very transitory, as Finch had discovered years earlier. Mostly it was a question of mind over matter, as Dittert explained:

> Cutting steps exhausted me and stupified me. I was empty-headed. I thought only of the moment when I would surrender my place to those who came behind. At last, Lambert's rope relieved us. Seeking the safest line, Lambert climbed straight up towards the beginning of the spur. The slope was steep, between 40 degrees and 50 degrees. Ascending last now, I had more frequent rests. I leaned my forehead on the axe and waited for my heart to calm down. I listened to the labours of the leader, to the resounding blows and to Roch's breathing. I watched the rope running up between my legs. It rose slowly, by jerks of eight or twelve inches and I dreaded the moment when it would tighten again and I would have to start moving once

more. When my turn came, I raised my head and looked upwards. Lambert was cutting at the hard ice, fifteen feet below the base of the spur.[23]

At one o'clock they reached a small platform on the spur at a height of some 24,600 ft. Here they rested for a while, then traversed across the spur to see what the left-hand couloir was like. To their dismay they found it to be hard ice and, though climbable, not suitable for laden porters. Enough work done for one day the four men descended to Camp V.

Exploration continued for another two days with little positive result until on the 19th Chevalley, Asper and the Sherpa Da Namgyal succeeded in climbing the Geneva Spur to a point higher than the South Col. They descended by the right-hand couloir. Their conclusions were that the climb up the spur was feasible for porters, provided there were fixed ropes on the steep lower slopes. The couloir they dismissed – it was too long and there was no place to rest or camp in the whole of its 3,000 ft sweep. On the spur there was at least the chance of a rest on the small platform they had discovered, and as the spur stood out from the mountainside it was unlikely to be bombarded by debris falling from above.

On the next day Flory and Dawa Thondup, Lambert and Tenzing, Roch and Pasang prepared the route to the Geneva Spur. Where the climbing was steepest they fixed ropes – about 150 m. in all – and they did what they could to enlarge the little platform which was to be the springboard of the attack. They noted that, should an emergency arise, the platform would not be big enough to hold a tent. Even the loads of equipment which were to be dumped there would have to be secured by ropes and pitons, or they were likely to tumble off down the mountain.

Then, for two days, they were pinned to Camp V by a sudden storm, whose ferocity caused Dittert great concern. Had the monsoon broken early? And supposing a storm like this were to catch them when they were at the South Col, or even higher. In his diary he painted a vivid picture of what it was like to be caught in an Everest blizzard:

> The gale made us tremble – both us and our tents – and gave us the time for reflection. For thirty-six hours a furious wind immobilized us in our fragile shelters. It was the sole master of space. Lying motionless and uneasy, we listened. The night passed and the wan daylight filtered through the cotton walls. And with the wind came the cold. Forced to go out to see a tent-pole that was giving way, I was rendered breathless by the fearful sight that met me. The fresh dusty snow was flying in uninterrupted whirlwinds and the dark stormclouds, coming from the south-west, were racing madly across the sky. I could hear them roaring as they broke more than 3,000 ft above me against the rugged bastions of Everest, then invisible in the fog. Like a fear-stricken beast I went back to hide. In a few hours the white and

impalpable dust would penetrate everywhere and it was impossible to defend oneself against it. With our caps pulled down to our eyes and with our sleeping-bags fastened around our necks for two nights and a day and for a further morning we cowered down and did not move. In the intervals between squalls the harsh coughs of inflamed throats and bronchi could be heard in the various tents and these were the only signs of life, except that the indefatigable Sherpas, profiting by a brief calm during the first day, brought us something to drink.

Did we think? Scarcely, for altitude seals the brain. One's imagination is even less active, fortunately. Rather, one is invaded by waves of vague feeling; a desire to leave everything to descend once and for all, to see grass and water and leaves once more; anxiety at the idea that if the snow was beginning to fall, the avalanches would not miss us; terror at the sudden thought that we might have been at the South Col or even higher. And then at moments, seen clearly through this maze of anxieties, the hope that the nightmare was about to end, that the sunlight would return, that all our chances were not extinguished. The will to go on was still alive, deep down, fragile, threatened, but living like flames that one has to shield with both hands lest they die.[24]

By 24 May everything was ready for the first assault. The party was Lambert, Flory, Aubert, Tenzing and six other Sherpas. Their tactics were simple and clear – first, to establish Camp VI on the South Col, then to place Camp VII no lower than 27,500 ft on the South East Ridge, and finally to push up the ridge as far as possible and perhaps to the summit itself.

Scarcely had they set out, however, than bad weather intervened and Lambert ordered a retreat. He was justifiably afraid – afraid of the great unknown into which they were venturing. 'The flanks of Everest are one of the places of the Earth where one is not ashamed of occasional fear,' he admitted. Dittert, however, was annoyed – especially when the weather cleared up around midday. At 8.15 a.m. next day the final ascent began.

After about an hour, one of the Sherpas could go no further. His condition had been a cause of concern almost from the outset because he seemed to be suffering from a sudden recurrence of malaria. Fortunately it was not too difficult for him to descend alone. His load was shared out among the others.

At 11.30 a.m. they reached the equipment dump on the tiny platform of the Geneva Spur. Here they rested for an hour and then, adding to their loads from the dump, continued their laborious ascent. Hour followed hour and the crest of the ridge above seemed no nearer.

At 4 p.m. they had been on the climb for eight hours and the day was fast slipping by. The cold grew intense and two more porters stopped; fearing frostbite, they wanted to go down. Tenzing, now occupying a dual role of climber and sirdar, argued with them to go on, but Lambert felt sympathy for them. They had done what they could, he argued, let them descend.

Nevertheless the loss of the two porters posed a serious problem. Their loads could not be added to what the others were already carrying and though Lambert and Flory each took a tent, most of the gear had to be anchored to the ice slope for collection later. Moreover, it was tricky work swapping loads around on such precarious footing and it is small wonder that a sleeping bag slipped from Aubert's grasp and went sailing off into the wind, lost forever.

Night fell and still they had not reached the elusive col. The cold was now almost unbearable, sapping what little energy remained. By 7 p.m. it became obvious that they would have to make a forced bivouac – but where could they bivouac on that terrible slope? Then fortune smiled on them. The angle of the slope eased off and they were able to dig out two platforms in the snow on which to pitch their tents. The tiny tents were each designed to hold one climber – or, at a squeeze, two. That night one tent held three Swiss and the other, four Sherpas.

There was no room for sleeping bags. The men just lay huddled together trying to obtain mutual warmth. As the wind howled over the ridge, it seemed likely to blow both tents away into the Western Cwm, and Lambert, for his part, felt obliged to drive his ice axe into the snow and tie himself to it, just in case! Incredibly under the circumstances, Tenzing managed to brew some hot soup for everybody. Nobody slept.

> The night was endless [wrote Lambert], like the slope to which we were moored, like all dimensions in this terrible land. We endured, we waited in patience, we breathed deeply in order to control our hearts, and we suffered the cold which at first froze our shins, and then penetrated slowly to take up its abode in our flesh.[26]

They survived the bitter night and were relieved when the next morning dawned bright and clear. Two of the Sherpas went down to rescue the gear that had been abandoned on the previous day, and another stayed at the bivouac site to await their return. The three Swiss and Tenzing continued the ascent towards the col. At 10 a.m. they came out on the ridge and were able, at long last, to look down on the South Col, which lay 300 ft below them.

The wind on the col was like a raging fury and it took them two hours to get the tent up, the climbers crawling about on all fours, struggling with the wildly flapping canvas. When the Sherpas came up, they were all in – all except the incredible Tenzing, who had been down to the bivouac to help the others and who, alone, went down twice more to bring up essential supplies.

Next morning, after the three Sherpas had set off back to Camp V, Lambert and Tenzing, followed by Flory and Aubert, turned their attention to the South East Ridge. They carried only one tent and enough food for a day.

The first obstacle was a large rock buttress which they climbed by means of a gully. Once on the ridge above the buttress they decided to camp (Camp VII). The height was about 27,500 ft.

With only one tent available it meant that two climbers would have to withdraw to the col and act as a support party. Selflessly Flory and Aubert volunteered to do this. They knew that next day Lambert and Tenzing would make a bid for the summit.

Lambert and Tenzing spent a miserable night in the little tent. They had no sleeping bags, no Primus stove, very little food. By using a candle flame they managed to melt a little ice in an empty tin to help relieve their raging thirst. Of sleep there was no question. It was hardly the ideal preparation for an assault on the world's highest peak.

When dawn at last came, the two men crawled out to face a world in which the weather signs were ominous. Nevertheless they decided to continue. All they carried with them were three oxygen cylinders – enough for six hours. The valves of their oxygen sets were too stiff for the climbers' lungs to manage while actually climbing, which made the sets fairly useless, but on the other hand nobody knew for certain whether man could actually survive at 29,000 ft without additional oxygen.

They advanced up a route of mixed snow and rock. Their progress was funereal; they were bent double with the labour, sometimes reduced to climbing on all fours. Mists drifted over them, and the occasional snow shower, adding to the already unreal nature of the world created by their numbed brains. Through a gap in the weather they saw that they were higher than Lhotse's summit.

At 11 a.m. they came out onto the ridge crest, keeping away from the cornices which they instinctively knew would overhang the east: one false step and they might plunge thousands of feet to the Kangshung Glacier. Fortunately, the climbing was not technically difficult and the angle of the slope quite moderate.

Nevertheless, the lack of air was telling more at every yard. They were forced to use the oxygen every three steps, and progress was slower than ever. Through another rent in the mist Lambert suddenly saw the top of their ridge – the South Summit – about 650 ft above them. It seemed almost near enough to touch. Yet Lambert knew they weren't going to make it, because the previous 650 ft had taken them five hours. They turned to descend.

Lambert and Tenzing had reached a height of 28,210 ft. It was higher than anyone had ever climbed before.

On 29 May a second assault was launched on the mountain. It comprised Dittert, Roch, Asper, Hofstetter, Chevalley and five Sherpas. Only two of the Sherpas, Sarki and Mingma Dorje, were willing to stay at the South Col, and Sarki arrived there in a state of collapse. Roch, too, was in a bad way: an injury to his ribs, suffered just before the expedition set out, was taking its toll. At the col itself conditions were unbearable, with intense cold and high, nerve-racking winds.

For three nights Dittert's party remained on the col, hoping against hope that conditions would become calm enough to let them make an assault. But really it was never on. Their strength was rapidly ebbing: they had been too high too long, and when the weather finally did improve on 1 June, they realized that they must seize the opportunity, not to go higher, but to go down. One look at the hollow shells that were now his companions convinced Dittert that they had pushed themselves to the edge of disaster. He realized that he and his companions must get down to Camp V while they still had some small margin of strength. It was a nightmare descent, and they were forced to bivouac on the ledge of the Geneva Spur – an open bivouac, but the Gods were kind and the night was surprisingly mild. Next day they tumbled, utterly exhausted, into Camp V and the waiting arms of Lambert.

Within twenty-four hours they were sufficiently recovered to begin the withdrawal from the Western Cwm. With heavy loads and heavy hearts they plunged down the slopes, wanting nothing more than to flee the mountain. Down past Camps IV and III, down past Camp II and down through the Icefall to Advanced Base, Camp I. Only when they were free from Everest did they stop their headlong flight.

The Swiss expedition to Everest was over.

But in the autumn they were back. They had to be: 1952 was their year for Everest, and they had come so close to victory in the spring that they felt impelled to give it one more try. Next year was to be the turn of the British, and after that, the French ... it seemed impossible that the mountain could hold out so long.

Dittert was unable to be present in the autumn, and the leadership passed to Gabriel Chevalley, a doctor. Only he and the indefatigable Raymond Lambert returned to the mountain for the second time in a year. The other members were Arthur Spöhel, Gustave Gross, Ernest Reiss, Jean Busio and Norman Dyhrenfurth, son of Oscar Dyhrenfurth who had led so many pre-war Himalayan expeditions. Dyhrenfurth was technically an American citizen, but was invited nevertheless, not only for his climbing ability – and his parentage – but also because he was an experienced film-maker.

In the matter of equipment, the Swiss had learned some valuable lessons from their experiences in the spring and had put them into effect with remarkable speed. The closed-circuit oxygen system they had been using, which was lightweight but useless, was abandoned, and they took instead some 300,000 litres of oxygen in bottles which held 400 and 600 litres and was used on the open principle. They also abandoned the radio links they had carried in the spring. The reindeer-hide boots, which had proved so warm, they retained. The main problem was that nobody knew quite just how cold it might be on Everest in autumn, but the Swiss provided themselves with enough gear for any eventuality. The weight of gear rose 50 per cent over the spring total – 7½ metric tons as against 5 – and the number of porters increased correspondingly. The number of Sherpas who had been allocated the dangerous job of keeping the Icefall route open were augmented by eight more. Tenzing, again the sirdar, was also officially declared to be a member of the climbing team.

The Swiss were taking no chances as far as preparation and equipment were concerned, yet gambling everything on the unknown post-monsoon season, for though Shipton had made a post-monsoon reconnaissance, nobody had tried actually to climb Everest in the autumn. It doesn't sound much, yet it was a tremendous leap in the dark, adding a whole new dimension to the problem.

Almost from the outset the expedition was dogged by bad luck and ill-health. Chevalley himself was ill for much of the time and his leadership seemed to suffer as a consequence. The approach march was made under abominable weather conditions and two porters died from exposure. Morale among Sherpas and climbers alike was never high, and it sank lower as time went on. Only Lambert and Tenzing seemed to have any appetite for the job in hand.

But the Icefall was overcome and camps pushed forward up the Western Cwm. Camp V at the head of the Cwm was some 600 ft lower than in spring which meant that there was a vertical height of over 3,500 ft between the camp and the South Col – an impossible climb for laden porters at that altitude.

Nevertheless, Chevalley chose to attack the same route as Dittert had used in spring, even though he must have realized that it was the choice of this route, with its lack of places for an intermediate camp, that had been Dittert's major tactical error. Later, Chevalley wrote this about his decision:

> I was never very enthusiastic about the immediate adoption of this tactic – the direct route to the Éperon by way of the main slope. It must be said that we envisaged this and adopted it tactically at Zurich and that it was precisely for this route that such a great length of rope had been brought. Nevertheless, the primordial criterion determining the route to follow ought to be the possibility of an intermediate camp, and from the first a route by the Lhotse glacier appeared to me very promising in this respect, as compared with the present one. I regret that my delay did not allow me to proceed, on the spot, to a searching and objective examination of the situation; I also regret having omitted or deferred opening a definite discussion of this subject on my first arrival at Camp IV. Later on, taking into consideration the establishment of Camp V below that in the spring, and in view of the argument for an ascent route effectively secured by stepcutting and a continuous fixed rope, with no real certainty of favourable conditions on the Lhotse glacier, it was difficult for me to bring the operation to a halt, to

> reverse tactics and seek a new and unknown route. The fact is that, while in the spring the first day's reconnaissance got as far as the 'depot' and that the necessary section of fixed rope was placed in a single day thereafter, two days progress has this time scarcely reached to two-thirds of the distance to the upper rock island which is still well below the 'depot'. There are several reasons for this: we start out from a camp some 500 to 600 feet lower than previously; the base of the slope is sheer ice, and because of the conditions of the snow, safety requires the cutting of steps and the fixing of a continuous rope from the bottom to the top of the slope.[27]

He excused himself by claiming that he never really intended to use the route for the main attack, but merely as a reconnaissance. For what? Why waste valuable energy and time on something which was known to be impracticable? It was now the end of October, and one suspects that after a month on the mountain the responsibility, sickness and total lack of morale in the team had made Chevalley less than decisive.

Then on the 31st a serious accident occurred. Four ropes set out from Camp V to climb up towards the Geneva Spur when some splinters of ice came whistling down the slopes. The climbers ducked: such things are not uncommon and usually do no damage if the pieces are small, but by unlucky chance the Sherpa Mingma Dorje was hit in the face and neck. Chevalley, who was on the rope below, went at once to the rescue, and he, together with the four other Sherpas comprising the two ropes affected, managed to get the injured man to the foot of the slopes.

There were still two ropes up ahead, climbing. The top one consisted of two Sherpas led by Spöhel, and the second of the three Sherpas. Whether the latter were unnerved by the accident to Mingma Dorje, or whether there was a double stroke of fate, they slipped out of their steps and went slithering and tumbling 600 ft to the foot of the slopes. Incredibly, they did not come to much harm. One had a broken collar bone, but the other two had only minor cuts and contusion. They were, however, badly unnerved by their experience and were of little further use to the expedition. But Mingma Dorje, the original victim, was in a bad way. A splinter of ice had pierced one of his lungs and despite all that Chevalley could do he died of his injuries shortly after.

Mingma Dorje was buried at the foot of the mountain, between Camps IV and V. Twenty-five years of age, he had been one of the more promising of the Sherpas, and one of the two men who had stayed with Dittert at the South Col in spring. He was the first victim to die on Everest since Maurice Wilson, almost twenty years earlier.

Chevalley now tried something he should have done earlier. He sent reconnaissance parties up the Lhotse Glacier to see whether there was an easier way of reaching the South Col – the route André Roch had advocated in spring. The going proved not too difficult and there were places for intermediate camps. In due course Camps VI and VII were set up on the glacier and on 19 November Lambert, Reiss, Tenzing and seven Sherpas reached the South Col.

There they spent a bitter night. The temperature in the tents was thirty below zero and the wind howled across the col at sixty miles per hour.

Next morning they set off for the ridge. The wind had scarcely abated and the cold was still intense. Fumbling forward it took them an hour just to cross the width of the col. They climbed a little higher, but already they knew they were beaten.

Winter had arrived, and its bitter winds had blown away the last Swiss hopes of being the first to climb Everest.

Though they had failed to climb the mountain, by their courage and determination the Swiss had demonstrated that the Khumbu route was feasible and relatively safe. Nobody had been injured in the dreaded Icefall and the death of Mingma Dorje was sheer bad luck. The Swiss had, however, made several mistakes, and in spring at least these had cost them the summit.

For one thing their timing was wrong. Lambert and Tenzing arrived at the South Col about a week too early during the spring assault – ironically when the pre-monsoon calm arrived the Swiss were back in Namche Bazar – and they were two or three weeks too late in reaching the col during the autumn period. Once the post-monsoon calm gives way to the winter winds, climbing on Everest becomes intolerable.

Then, too, the closed-circuit oxygen sets were a big disappointment. The advantage of this system is that it recycles the oxygen, thereby doing away with the need to carry large numbers of gas cylinders, and the Swiss apparatus weighed only 5¼ lb. Though it worked perfectly at lower altitudes, the climbers discovered that above 23,000 ft the resistance of the valves was too great. A positive effort was needed to breathe through the thing – and you can't make a positive effort when your whole being is concentrated on the agony of stumbling forward a few more feet.

No doubt in the spring Camp VII should have been placed higher up the ridge, but that is a fairly academic question in view of the lack of logistical support by the time it was established. The real fault – and this was misjudgement on Dittert's part – was in trying to establish a camp on the South Col direct from Camp V, without any intermediate camp. It was a vertical height of more than 4,000 ft – from 22,639 ft to 26,854 ft – which is far too much at those altitudes for a single day, especially for porters.

The Swiss were the real pioneers of post-war Everest, and like so many of their kind they suffered a pioneers' fate: failure.

Meanwhile, in South Audley Street, London, the British were stirring themselves into an agonizing re-appraisal of the whole situation.

# 13

# 'Rather More Than a Mountain'

The disappointment suffered by the British at being denied an attempt on Everest in 1952 was tempered somewhat by the realization that they weren't really ready for it. Some equipment had been tried out during the reconnaissance and on the whole found to be satisfactory, but nothing had been done on the vital question of oxygen equipment or physiology.

There was also the question of suitable personnel. For a full-scale assault on Everest more climbers would be required than were needed for the reconnaissance. Where were they to come from? Few young British climbers had any experience of the Himalaya, and even Alpine experience was still not common, as Britain dragged herself out of a gloomy period of post-war austerity in which foreign travel was greatly limited by currency restrictions. Such impetus as existed seemed to be coming from Oxbridge, where Tom Bourdillon and his friends were seeking to raise the standard of British Alpinism to that of the best Continental climbers. Yet there did not seem to be any British climbers to compare with continental aces such as Hermann Buhl, Gaston Rebuffat and Lionel Terray. No British mountaineers had attempted, much less climbed, the great North Walls of the Matterhorn or Eiger – and if they had the Himalayan Committee would have been mildly shocked, like an elderly aunt seeing her niece's panties for the first time. Such desperate climbs were still regarded with deep suspicion by the British climbing Establishment.[1]

In truth, it was a period of transition. The great groundswell of post-war British climbing was beginning to surge up from the dark gritstone edges of the north, lapping over the steep cliffs of Wales, its devotees contemptuous of the standards of their predecessors. But it was only a groundswell – it had not yet smashed in full fury against the Alpine north walls. If the Himalayan

Committee were conscious of this new wave, they chose to ignore it. Their selection for Everest was to be firmly rooted in the traditional recruiting grounds of the old, long-established clubs, particularly the Alpine Club, the universities and the services. 1953 was to see not only the climax of the long Everest saga but the final flowering of the Old Guard.

The Cho Oyu expedition in 1952, undertaken at the time the Swiss were making their spring assault, was meant as a practice run for Everest. The peak seemed eminently suitable: it is 26,857 ft high and is a close neighbour of Everest, lying at the head of the next valley to the west.

Unfortunately, the best approach to the summit (and the route by which it was eventually climbed) lay just over the border in Tibet and Shipton, the leader, did not feel inclined to risk the chance of a brush with the Chinese Communists. Consequently, only a light attack was mounted – with a base camp just on the Nepalese side of the border – and it was almost bound to fail, as it did.

Here again Shipton was perhaps being over-cautious, as he later admitted. Edmund Hillary certainly thought so: as he pointed out, even if the Chinese were in that part of Tibet (which was by no means certain) they would hardly bother to come up to 18,000 ft on a barren glacier, and so the risk of detection was slight. But the leader of a party sees things differently from those with less responsibility, and it could be that Shipton had in the back of his mind the possible political implications that a brush with the Communists might create – if Nepal were to be embarrassed, for example, she might retaliate by cancelling permission to climb Everest in 1953. And nothing could be allowed to jeopardize that.

So the Cho Oyu expedition broke up into parties going their separate ways. The two New Zealanders, Hillary and George Lowe, took the opportunity to make the first crossing of the Nup La by the incredible Gyubanare icefall, and then to make a rapid trip down the West Rongbuk Glacier to the main Rongbuk Glacier, and up the East Rongbuk Glacier to the north side of Everest. It was partly a romantic desire to see the classic route of the old pre-war expeditions, partly a vague plan to climb Changtse which came to nothing. Once across the Nup La, of course, they were entirely in Tibet, but they were more worried about getting back before the weather broke than they were about Communist soldiers. The whole sortie was brilliantly executed by these two very strong New Zealanders. It was this sortie, too, which inspired Woody Sayre to make his own expedition in 1962 (see Chapter 11).

Later still, the two New Zealanders joined Shipton and Charles Evans in a sweep to the east of the Everest massif, to the great Barun Glacier, which drains a wide area below the peak of Makalu. They were able to find a way north to the frontier ridge, overlooking the Kangshung Glacier, with its dramatic views of the stupendous East Face of Everest. This was probably the col which Howard-Bury had reached from the opposite direction during the reconnaissance of 1921, and it was a minor landmark in Everest exploration, for it completed the last link in the circumnavigation of the mountain. There was now no possible approach to Everest that had not been travelled at least once by the explorer-mountaineers. The completion of the chain had taken thirty-one years.

This was Shipton at his best – the brilliant penetration of a blank on the map – and the thing he was happiest in doing. But it wasn't what he had been asked to do – or rather, what was expected of him. He was expected to climb Cho Oyu, or at least have a good try. His failure to press home the attack, combined with a similar failure on the Khumbu Icefall in 1951, began to sow seeds of doubt amongst the members of the Himalaya Committee. As it turned out, the Cho Oyu expedition was a test not so much of men and equipment as of Eric Shipton.

If not the mountain, what then did the Cho Oyu expedition achieve? As an exercise in team building it was not without merit, for though not all the members of the Cho Oyu team eventually went to Everest, and not all the members of the Everest team had been on the Cho Oyu expedition, there was a solid nucleus who had been on both, and significantly, perhaps, these were the men who went highest on Everest.

Attached to the party for the purposes of physiological research with particular reference to acclimatization was Dr L.G.C. Pugh of the Medical Research Council, whose expenses of £600 were met by the Royal Society. Pugh laboured under considerable difficulties: he was dealing with a bunch of individuals whose sole aim was to climb a mountain and who, on the whole, cared nothing for test tubes or statistics. 'Many opportunities for systematic research on physiology and equipment were wasted because the party had not been fully briefed before departure,' he complained later. 'When Cho Oyu had been abandoned, the party had no inclination to undertake systematic work.'[2]

Nevertheless, Pugh achieved valuable results, summed up by Michael Ward thus:

> . . . this was *the* most important Expedition from the scientific point of view. On it Griff Pugh solved the vital problems necessary for the ascent. These involved investigations on $O_2$ uptake, clothing, fuel etc. He wrote a report to the MRC [Medical Research Council] which had a very restricted circulation. All this scientific work was really separate from the mountaineers – and a good thing too![3]

On his return to London Pugh, with two other expedition members, Campbell Secord and Alfred Gregory, outlined their views to the Himalayan Committee:

1 Fitness essential – important to select 1953 team now and give them every chance to climb together and get to know each other well in advance of departure.
2 Oxygen should be given highest priority – should be tested post-monsoon (1952) in Himalaya in readiness.
3 Cho Oyu equipment too haphazard. All Everest clothing must be fitted to selected individuals well before departure.
And must check back on previous experience. In the past many mistakes made by previous parties had been repeated.
4 Hygiene important. Sherpa huts and unclean cooking must be avoided. (This caused trouble on Cho Oyu; Swiss apparently had no such trouble.)
5 Illness could affect acclimatization. A man who appeared to acclimatize badly should not be rejected out of hand – he could yet go high.
6 Journey through Nepal insufficient for the blood changes of acclimatization. 36 days were needed. Everest team should go a month ahead and acclimatize in the foothills at 15,000 ft and as much above as conditions permitted.
7 Pugh favours closed-circuit oxygen and says it's urgent to start work on this. Shipton has said oxygen will be essential above the South Col. Pugh: 'it was clear that having regard to the lower level of fitness and mountaineering experience of any British party, that only the very best oxygen equipment could enable us to put up a better performance than the Swiss.'[4]

The Committee agreed that the team members and reserves should have an opportunity of training together in the Alps in the following January, and some preliminary Himalayan training in March, before the actual assault on Everest. This would take care of points 1, 5 and 6 put forward by Pugh. They also agreed to look into the question of oxygen.

Then, for the first time, the question of leadership arose. Until that moment everybody had assumed that Shipton would lead the British assault on Everest in 1953, including Shipton himself. But it was not that clear-cut. In December 1951, after his return from the reconnaissance, the Committee had invited him to lead an assault on the mountain in 1952 but because of the Swiss attempts that assault never took place and the 'training' expedition to Cho Oyu had replaced it, which, as we have seen, Shipton duly led. Everyone seems to have assumed the offer would extend into 1953: Shipton was leader by tacit consent. In any case, his standing and experience as a Himalayan mountaineer was immeasurably greater than that of anyone else available.

The Committee decided to discuss who should lead the 1953 expedition *should Shipton not be fit*. Seven names were considered, but a preference was expressed for military officers because they were readily released from duty and were likely to have organizing ability. Three names were noted in particular: John Hunt, Jimmy Roberts and Charles Wylie. But the Committee decided to make no decision until Shipton returned from Nepal.

'Should Shipton not be fit' – Shipton, the man who could live off next to nothing in the mountains and still carry out a rigorous campaign, and had hardly had a day's illness in his life! One can only assume that this preliminary discussion by the Committee was some roundabout skating on thin ice. Confidence in Shipton's ability to make a successful attempt on Everest was waning, but the Committee were not yet ready to take the plunge. They knew that to sack Shipton would land them in deep, icy water.

There were two main reasons for this. Though Shipton was something of an introvert, a shy man in unfamiliar company, because of his books and lectures he was immensely popular with the general public, and it is never a good idea to alienate the public, especially if they are going to be asked for funds. Secondly, and more immediately important, Shipton's sheer ability in the mountains, together with his lack of cant or humbug, generated admiration and loyalty among his team members. To alienate *them* might have a disastrous effect on the expedition's morale.

Yet the pressure on the Committee for success in 1953 was enormous. The Swiss had almost pulled it off, and it was obvious that Everest would be climbed, and soon. Already the mountain was allocated to the French in 1954 and the Swiss again in 1955. It would be a long time before the British could try again, and by then it would almost certainly be too late. Only the first time counts.[5]

There was, too, a rather special reason for wanting success. Britain had a new Queen who was due to be crowned in Westminster Abbey in June 1953. The ascent of Everest would make a splendid Coronation gift: the finest possible herald to the New Elizabethan Age everyone was talking about. To fail would be an appalling letdown.

Never before had it been so essential to have the right leader.

On 28 July, a week after Shipton returned to England, the Himalayan Committee met to hear his report on Cho Oyu and to make plans for Everest. The question of leadership was paramount in everyone's mind. Shipton thought that the Committee – like everyone else – had assumed he would lead the expedition, but he also sensed that this time there was no room for failure and that his own capacity for ruthlessness was in question. There had been straws in the wind, whispers – others had heard them, and Shipton must have heard them too, albeit at second hand. In an extraordinary baring of the breast, he decided to make his position quite clear to the Committee.

> It was clear that the Committee assumed that I would lead the expedition. I had, however, given a good deal of thought to the matter, and felt it right

to voice certain possible objections. Having been to Everest five times, I undoubtedly had a great deal more experience of the mountain and of climbing at extreme altitudes than anyone else; also, in the past year I had been closely connected, practically and emotionally, with the new aspect of the venture. On the other hand, long involvement with an unsolved problem can easily produce rigidity of outlook, a slow response to new ideas, and it is often the case that a man with fewer inhibitions is better equipped to tackle it than one with greater experience. I had more reason than most to take a realistic view of the big element of luck involved, and this was not conducive to bounding optimism. Was it not time, perhaps, to hand over to a younger man with a fresh outlook? Moreover, Everest had become the focus of greatly inflated publicity and of keen international competition, and there were many who regarded success in the coming attempt to be of high national importance. My well-known dislike of large expeditions and my abhorrence of a competitive element in mountaineering might well seem out of place in the present situation.

I asked the Committee to consider these points very carefully before deciding the question of leadership and then left them while they did so.[6]

This only confirmed the Committee's worst fears. It was hardly the fighting speech of a determined leader.

While Shipton was out of the room the Committee discussed what they had heard, and possible alternative leaders. The names of John Hunt and Jimmy Roberts were prominent in these talks, but in the end the Committee decided on a classic British compromise – that Shipton's experience was too valuable to waste and he should be made overall leader of the expedition in the same way as Wyss-Dunant was overall leader of the recent Swiss attempt, but that there should be a separate Assault Leader or Deputy Leader for the actual attempt on the summit.

When Shipton rejoined the meeting he was told of the decision, in which he concurred, stating that he preferred the term Deputy Leader to Assault Leader, and proposing Dr Charles Evans for the job. This sudden proposal must have taken the Committee aback – they had their own ideas as to who should be Deputy Leader – but they agreed. They also agreed to defer for the time being the actual definition of the two roles – who should do what.[7]

Undoubtedly at this point in the meeting Shipton considered the question of Leader and Deputy Leader settled. They went on to discuss team members: Hillary, Lowe, Ayres (another New Zealander) and Gregory were the men Shipton wanted most, but he thought Bourdillon's ice craft was suspect and agreed to take him only because he was an oxygen expert. Riddiford, who had been on the 1951 reconnaissance, was ruled out because he had sciatica. No other names were discussed, but it was felt that the age range should be twenty-five to thirty-five.

They also agreed to set up a small subcommittee of Pugh, Bourdillon and Wing Commander Roxburgh (of the Institute of Aviation Medicine), to pursue the oxygen question. Pugh wanted closed-circuit sets, but it seemed unlikely that these could be perfected in time and so it was decided that every effort was to be made to improve the open-circuit sets in time. On this occasion no prima-donna purists would be tolerated: everyone had to learn to use oxygen, whether they liked it or not. This, perhaps more than anything else, illustrates how different the attitude of 1953 was from that of 1933.

It was also agreed that Alfred Gregory would be in charge of an autumn training programme, but Shipton turned down the idea of a scientific team from the British Museum being attached to the expedition.

The Committee felt that there was so much to see to, so many details, that a full-time organizer was required as soon as possible. Ideally this should be the Deputy Leader, but if Evans wasn't readily free the job could be farmed out to someone else. Colonel John Hunt was available.

Henry Cecil John Hunt was born in Simla on 22 June 1910. His father, also Cecil, was an Army officer and something of a mountaineer – he had actually climbed with Edward Whymper, the conqueror of the Matterhorn. Young John followed his father (who was killed in action in 1914) in both profession and pursuit. He was good at both. He came top of his year at the Sandhurst Military Academy, gaining the Anson Memorial Sword and King's Medal. He began climbing in the Alps at the age of fifteen (his first ascent was the traverse of Piz Palu) and while serving in India in 1935 he made the first ascent of the South Buttress of Kohlahoi and took part in a spirited lightweight attack on Saltoro Kangri (25,400 ft) in the Karakorum, getting to within a thousand feet of the top. On the strength of this he was invited to take part in the 1936 Everest expedition, but failed on health grounds.[8]

Then came the war, followed by post-war service in Europe when he climbed mostly with French mountaineers and became a member of the G.H.M., an elite French club. By 1952 his experience extended over ten alpine seasons and five Himalayan expeditions, but, though he had been elected to the Alpine Club in 1935, he was not part of the British climbing establishment and was virtually unknown in this country.[9]

However, he did have a friend at court. Basil Goodfellow was Secretary to the Himalayan Committee, Secretary of the Alpine Club, and himself a keen Himalayan man. He had met Hunt in the Swiss Valais the previous summer and they had done a number of the classic routes together – 'this was an important factor in B.R.G.'s advocacy, I think,' says Hunt.[10] He considered Hunt to be a 'terrific Thruster' and was determined to have him as leader, for the final assault if nothing else.

This in turn suited Claude Elliott, Chairman of the Himalayan Committee and President of the Alpine Club. Elliott didn't know Hunt, but he didn't like

Shipton and he seized on Goodfellow's 'discovery' like a drowning man clutching a life raft. On 29 July, the day following the Committee meeting, he wrote to Hunt asking him whether he would be available as Assault Leader and possibly London organizer. He explained that an Assault Leader was necessary because Shipton's age made it unlikely he would go high on the mountain. Shipton, in fact, was only three years older than Hunt.

A week later Elliott wrote to fellow Committee member Kirwan:

> I wish we had been able to get this information earlier before Shipton fixed up with Evans, but I hope that Shipton will invite Hunt and that H. will accept. I am more and more convinced that a thruster like him is needed, but as T.G.L. says, much would have to depend on Evans' tact.[11]

Kirwan, too, was in favour of Hunt, and he wrote back:

> I am sure that we should have him whether we get Wylie or not, but I am equally sure that the proper title and position for him would be as Deputy Leader instead of Evans. This would be justified on grounds of his age and general experience, and I am perfectly sure that Evans would fall in with this.
>
> Shipton's position as leader above Hunt is equally well justified by long experience of Everest itself (which Hunt has not) and by his more extensive Himalayan experience generally. Beyond that, there seems to be no need for further definition of roles. Anyone who can go high, presumably will; and no doubt, the more the merrier.
>
> If the above were approved Hunt would have a definite role with the proper prestige attached and his relation with Shipton clearly defined by the title. He would act for the leader on a number of occasions during the preparatory period when doubtless we shall not see Eric at all! We have of course to sell this to Shipton but he is more and more coming round towards Hunt. If he agrees, then the somewhat difficult and nebulous title of Organizer will drop out for good.[12]

A few days later he wrote to Elliott again:

> I discussed with Goodfellow and Shipton the position as regards Hunt and Goodfellow has written him a letter explaining the situation and asking him if he could come over for a talk with Shipton and myself. Shipton seems quite opposed to H. being made Deputy Leader. He still seems to be a little afraid of what he has heard about Hunt's temperament and feels this would matter less if he had the position of Organizer and just an ordinary member of the expedition, than if he was Deputy Leader and in control of his party. It is very difficult to argue about this without knowing Hunt, and it seems to me that Goodfellow must be the judge, but I think it's a pity that the scheme

> outlined in my letter has not been found acceptable. Goodfellow and I both agree that if Hunt goes on the expedition in any role except Deputy Leader, then his functions must be fairly defined and he should be made aware of all the snags beforehand.[13]

Their correspondence shows that both Elliott and Kirwan were by now much in favour of Hunt as Deputy Leader or Assault Leader. The extraordinary thing is that neither man had ever met Hunt or knew anything more about him than what Goodfellow had told them.

Meanwhile Goodfellow had actually sent Hunt a telegram inviting him to come over from Germany and discuss things with Shipton. Hunt 'nearly jumped over the moon'.[14]

But the meeting didn't go well. To some extent they were talking at cross-purposes, for Shipton thought he was interviewing Hunt for the job of Organizing Secretary, whereas Hunt thought he was to be Deputy Leader, and said so. This was something Shipton could not accept – he had already nominated Charles Evans for that job. So Hunt withdrew and Charles Wylie, another Army officer, was made Organizing Secretary. He and Shipton established an expedition H.Q. at the Royal Geographical Society and began work.

Naturally enough, Elliott and Goodfellow found this outcome less than satisfactory. They were determined that Hunt should be appointed in a senior capacity, even if it meant the removal of Shipton altogether.

The crunch came at the Committee meeting of 11 September. 'I was surprised to find that the first item on the agenda was the "Deputy Leadership",' wrote Shipton later, 'and still more so when I was asked to go out of the room while this was discussed.'[15]

No wonder he was puzzled. He thought the question of Deputy Leader had been agreed (it had), and in any case the Leader of an expedition should surely be present at any discussion about his Deputy.

Meanwhile, in the Committee, Elliott (who was Chairman) reported that strong representations had been made that the leadership of the expedition should be strengthened. He did not say who had made these representations, but it provoked a lengthy discussion, the outcome of which was that John Hunt was appointed Co-leader, with special responsibility for organization in London and the final assault on the peak.

The meeting temporarily adjourned while Elliott, Wordie (of the R.G.S.) and Goodfellow broke the news to Shipton.

Shipton was flabbergasted. In his memoirs he wrote:

> Then, for the first time, it dawned on me that there must have been a great deal of backdoor diplomacy since the last meeting, of which I had been totally unaware. It seemed particularly strange to me that I should have

been expected to accept the proposal, especially remembering the views expressed the previous winter on the subject of joint leadership by most of the Committee and myself.[16]

He meant, of course, the breakdown of negotiations with the Swiss on the question of leadership, during the discussions for a joint Anglo-Swiss expedition in 1952 (pp. 279–80), but this was merely a red herring: rather pathetic point-scoring by a man still bewildered by the unfortunate events of nearly two decades ago.

'The influences which caused the Committee's *volte face* are still obscure,' he wrote. This must surely be self-deception, for the chief influence was Eric Shipton.[17]

A more astute political mind than Shipton's would have seen the signs long before that traumatic Committee meeting, and would have adapted accordingly or withdrawn earlier. But there is no evidence to suggest that Shipton sensed any of this – and a lot to suggest that he regarded the Everest expedition as just another mountaineering adventure. It was this easy-going attitude which was his final downfall: he wouldn't, perhaps couldn't, adapt to the urgency of the situation.

Ingrid Cranfield, in a profile of John Hunt, summed it up admirably: 'to Hunt an "assault" on the mountain merely meant a concerted, military-style operation: whereas to Shipton "assault" sounded more like a criminal offence.'[18]

When the Committee reconvened, after about an hour, Shipton told them that he could not accept Co-leadership with Hunt, nor could he agree to Hunt being Deputy Leader. He was, however, prepared to resign if the Committee felt this was in the best interest of the expedition.

He again withdrew while the Committee considered this, and he was away for more than an hour. When he returned it was to the inevitable decision. His resignation had been accepted and John Hunt had been appointed Leader in his place. The Committee urged him to remain as an ordinary member of the expedition, but Shipton, not unnaturally, declined.

The reaction on the part of the climbing world to the sacking of Shipton alternated between incredulity and anger. Hillary disapproved – to him it smacked of changing horses in mid-stream, and anyway, he said, 'Everest without Shipton won't be the same.' Young Tom Bourdillon, who had been to Cho Oyu and was the expert on oxygen equipment for the forthcoming expedition, felt so strongly about it that he withdrew his name, and agreed to reconsider only after considerable persuasion by Shipton himself. Charles Evans also protested, as did Jack Longland (of the 1933 expedition).

So strong and adverse was the publicity that at the next meeting of the Committee, a fortnight later, Elliott thought it necessary to reaffirm their decision and opened the whole question once again. Two members, Wager (who had been on the 1933 expedition) and Kirwan, had not been present when Shipton was sacked, and they strongly disapproved. Kirwan, though in favour of Hunt leading the assault, thought the price too high.

But how could they go back on their decision without making themselves look foolish, creating further confusion and possibly seeing the whole expedition dissolve in acrimony and dissent? They couldn't, and when it came to the vote Hunt was reaffirmed as leader by six votes to two.

Ironically perhaps, Charles Evans was confirmed as Deputy Leader.

Though Shipton resolutely refused to be a member of Hunt's team he did agree to help the expedition during the planning stages: to refuse would have appeared too dog-in-the-manger. Nevertheless, he was a badly shaken man; his self-esteem was bruised beyond repair and, rather sadly, he never really accepted the validity of the arguments for his dismissal.

In the five years that followed, Eric Shipton went through a series of personal crises: he was divorced, lost his job as Warden of Eskdale Outward Bound School and ended up as a labourer for the Forestry Commission. It was almost by chance that his interest in mountain exploration was rekindled when his exploits in Patagonia re-established his reputation as one of the greatest mountain explorers of all time.[19]

What of the new leader? Hunt, a kindly man, given to seeing the other fellow's point of view, was dismayed by the manner in which he had been appointed leader, and it left permanent mental scars: 'This is a slightly (for me!) embarrassing matter to write about, even 25+ years after the event!' he wrote in a recent letter.[20]

Dismayed though he was, he never for a moment let his eye stray from the target, which was the ascent of Everest. In a letter introducing himself to Hillary (who was in New Zealand) and commenting upon the Shipton affair, he wrote: 'However, you will, I am sure, agree with me that there is only one way of looking at it – we must go ahead with the planning with a firm determination to get to the top.'[21]

He brought to the task a military precision which would have been anathema to Shipton, and a positive genius for organization. He was, wrote James Morris, who accompanied the expedition as the *Times* correspondent, 'authority and responsibility incarnate'.[22] And yet, if he ran the expedition like a large-scale military operation, he did so from the conviction that it would achieve the desired result – not from any liking for such methods. Like Shipton, he preferred the small intimate expedition, but unlike Shipton he grasped at once the realities of the present situation. Victory was of paramount importance – a discussion on ethics could come later.

Every account of the 1953 expedition stresses the efficiency of its organization. This was undoubtedly the fruit of Hunt's military training, and yet it would be false to assume that Hunt himself was the archetypal pre-war British officer. Despite his military upper-middle-class background, his political views were towards the left, and he had even written a tract called 'I am a Revolutionary' – hardly par for the course at Camberley!

In a sense, the leadership of the Everest expedition was thrust upon him and under circumstances which made the task doubly difficult. Not only had he to climb the mountain, he had to overcome the massive prejudice against him for supplanting Shipton. Had he failed, both he and the Committee would have been easy prey for the waiting critics.

The new leader took up his duties officially on 9 October and by 5 November had produced a series of papers which, taken together, amounted to a detailed draft plan for a successful assault on Everest. They were characterized by meticulous attention to detail and though Hunt stressed to the Committee that the final form of the plan could be worked out pragmatically only on the mountain itself, in fact only minor changes were made.

The plan was structured to allow three attempts on the summit on successive days. Hunt calculated that two attempts might not be enough, while more than three would be impracticable in terms of resources and the debilitating effects of having men so high for so long. To achieve this he reckoned on a team of ten climbers, supported by an adequate number of Sherpas.

With the leadership issue settled the work of selecting the team could proceed. It was plain that the nucleus would come from the Cho Oyu party, but there were other places to be filled and the unprecedented step was taken of circularizing member clubs of the British Mountaineering Council. As a result a large number of names were considered and among those not selected there were inevitably many mountaineers who later did fine work on other Himalayan peaks – Ian McNaught Davis, for example, and Tony Streather. Bentley Beetham, who had been a member of the 1924 expedition and was now sixty-six years old, applied to go but was rejected, as was the ace rock climber Arthur Dolphin. Others, later to make names for themselves in different fields, were Chris Brasher, the Olympic gold medallist, and Sebastian Snow, the long-distance walker. It was, on the face of it, an interesting exercise in skimming the cream of the British mountaineering fraternity.[23]

A selection committee of Hunt, Goodfellow and Shipton was formed, but it was Hunt who laid down the ground rules. He looked for candidates with:

Expedition temperament,
Suitable age and physique,
Adequate experience of the right type,
Exceptional fire and determination.

Overall, Hunt wanted a homogeneous team capable of working together harmoniously, and for this reason he restricted membership to men from Britain and the Commonwealth. He foresaw that international rivalry could develop with a mixed team, a fact amply demonstrated on Everest two decades later. In any case there were political reasons for making this a successful British expedition – though in the early stages of planning, before Hunt appeared, the Committee had for reasons best known to themselves agreed to include two Americans. Hunt insisted that if these materialized they would be 'supernumeraries' to the team proper: as events turned out no Americans were available that year because they were mounting their own expedition to the Karakorum giant, K2. Even the Indian liaison officer, N. Jayal (a distinguished mountaineer and later head of the Himalayan Institute), was turned down.

Furthermore, so determined was Hunt that his team would succeed that he tried to strip it of anyone who did not contribute directly to the climbing. In this he was not entirely successful: *The Times* (who had bought exclusive newspaper rights) insisted on sending a reporter, James Morris, though Hunt thought he could have managed to send the despatches himself.[24] Similarly, there had to be a professional film cameraman, Tom Stobart, because the Committee had entered into a contract with Countryman Films Ltd in order to boost finances. As it turned out, they did nothing to hinder the expedition and proved to be vital lynch pins in the final story. The achievement of 1953 belonged to Hunt and his climbers, but it was Morris and Stobart who packaged it and presented it so effectively to the world at large.

Hunt was not keen, either, to indulge in large-scale scientific activities – there was never any question of botanists, geologists and anthropologists, such as had accompanied the Swiss expedition, being included this time. There was, however, an agreement with the Medical Research Council that physiological experiments should be carried out, and Hunt agreed to take Griff Pugh, who had been on the Cho Oyu trip, though he refused to take a second physiologist.

Charles Evans was a doctor, but he wasn't eager to act as medical officer as Hunt initially suggested. For one thing he was really a specialist brain surgeon and besides, as Deputy Leader and a climber, he would have his hands full. Michael Ward (who had initiated the original reconnaissance in 1951) was therefore appointed M.O., with instructions to assist Pugh wherever necessary in the physiology work. The fact that Ward was also a good climber made him a useful reserve to the climbing team.

The team was founded on a nucleus of Shipton's Cho Oyu party. Charles Evans was a Liverpool surgeon, aged thirty-three, a stocky man with fair hair. Besides Cho Oyu, he had been to the Himalaya on two other occasions – with Tilman to the Annapurna massif in 1951 and to Kulu. Alfred Gregory, known as 'Greg', was a travel agent from Blackpool, aged thirty-nine, and the oldest man in the party except for Hunt himself. He was small, wiry and sharp-featured, with a small moustache, and had proved himself an excellent high-altitude climber on the Cho Oyu trip. Greg was also a first-rate photographer, something he turned to professionally later in life. Tom Bourdillon, in Hunt's words, was 'built like a second-row rugby forward'. He was twenty-eight and had been with Shipton in both 1951 and 1952. He was a physicist and, with his father, who was also a scientist, was trying to develop an effective closed-circuit oxygen apparatus.

Also from the Cho Oyu team were the two New Zealanders, Hillary and Lowe. George Lowe was of medium height, well built, and a primary school teacher. At twenty-eight he was five years younger than his friend and compatriot, Edmund Hillary, but had been climbing for longer and indeed had introduced Hillary to some of the harder New Zealand climbs. Incredibly, the tall and lanky Hillary had only begun climbing when he was about twenty-six, but he had rapidly shown that he was skilful and of immense stamina. For a living, he was a professional beekeeper.

Then there were the newcomers, those who had not been on Cho Oyu. Mike Westmacott was twenty-seven, a statistician who had once been President of the Oxford University Mountaineering Club; and, as if to balance the Oxbridge listings, George Band was ex-President of the Cambridge University club. He was big, studious-looking and bespectacled. At twenty-three he was the youngest member of the team – younger than the 'ideal' minimum age of twenty-five laid down by Pugh – but, like Westmacott and Bourdillon, he was one of a dynamic coterie of university climbers who were beginning to push up British standards in the Alps.[25]

Charles Wylie, aged thirty-two, was a Gurkha officer who had been captured by the Japanese and spent most of the war in a P.O.W. camp. This in itself was a testament to his toughness. He had done some Himalayan climbing in the Garhwal, and of course he was the man who eventually got the job of expedition organizer during the Shipton leadership controversy.

Finally there was Wilfrid Noyce, public schoolmaster and distinguished author. Then aged thirty-four, Noyce had been an instructor in mountain warfare during the war, both in Kashmir and in Wales (where he had assisted Hunt). He had also climbed in Garhwal and in Sikkim, where he had reached the summit of Pauhunri (23,400 ft). Before the war, which had severely interrupted his climbing career, Noyce was something of a 'Golden Boy' in British climbing, particularly in association with Menlove Edwards. In the Alps, too, Noyce had a reputation for extreme stamina. His writings were scholarly, even erudite, and he more than anyone else came nearest to being a post-war equivalent of Mallory.[26]

In Nepal, the climbing team was to be increased by one when Hunt invited Tenzing to become a fully fledged member of the team. After the Swiss expedition, when, with Lambert, Tenzing had climbed higher than any other human being, it was obvious that this Sherpa was more than a load carrier, and more even than a sirdar, the foreman status to which the most experienced Sherpas had previously been elevated. His original motives in becoming a porter may have been rooted in money – what other reason would there be for humping heavy loads up dangerous mountains? – but he had long since advanced beyond that stage. The money was still important, as it must always be to the professional, whether Sherpa or Alpine guide, but he had also caught the spirit of mountaineering. He was determined to get to the top.

It was this determination to succeed which marked out Tenzing from the best of his fellow Sherpas at that time. Other Sherpas before him had entered into the sahibs' spirit of adventure, others had equal strength and technical accomplishment, and indeed half a century earlier some of Bruce's indomitable Gurkhas had been excellent climbers in their own right, but none of these had the single-minded determination of Tenzing.

Meanwhile, Hunt's strategical planning had to allow for two unpleasant possibilities. The first of these was that the Swiss, in their post-monsoon attempt (which was taking place while the British preparations were being made), might succeed in climbing the mountain after all. What then should the British do? Hunt proposed switching the attempt to Kangchenjunga, the third highest mountain in the world and reasonably accessible, and Basil Goodfellow was detailed to ask permission of the Indian authorities, who had political jurisdiction over the mountain. Alternatively, of course, they could still go to Everest and try to make a second ascent. Inquiries were made at *The Times* regarding which would have the better publicity value.

But either alternative would have been a mere consolation prize. Had the Swiss succeeded, it would have cast such a gloom on the British camp that any expedition would have been a spiritless affair. As far as public interest was concerned it would have been a non-event.

The second unpleasant possibility was that the spring assault might fail. Should they then abandon the project, or go for a second attempt in the autumn as the Swiss had done? The Committee hesitated over this – because of the expense – and it wasn't until January 1953 that they finally decided that a second attempt should be made if the first one failed. It was felt that not all the original team might be up to the strain of staying in Nepal throughout the monsoon and returning for a second strenuous tour of duty on the mountain, so a short list of reserves was drawn up, four of whom would be sent out as reinforcements.[27]

And so the broad strategy for 1953 was determined. There was to be a major offensive in the spring, with up to three assaults on the summit, and if this should fail there was to be a second offensive in the autumn, using fresh reserves. In the event of a last-minute success by the Swiss, contingency plans were available for a fresh target. It was all very military, all very logical and compared with the fumblings and bumblings of earlier British expeditions a complete revolution.

Hunt alone was responsible. He was the leader and he led from the front, knowing exactly what he wanted and how to get it. The man matched the hour. This was the last battle, and the British were determined to win it.

There was an enormous amount of preparation to be done. Hunt and Wylie worked full-time at it, but team members, reserves and even friends not directly involved were from time to time pressed into service. Hunt somehow lighted a flame of belief that kindled enthusiasm even for the chores which preceded the adventure.

This time nothing was to be left to chance in the way of equipment. Every item was to be the best possible, and vital gear such as windproof clothing and boots was specially designed and tested.

Each climber was provided with shell clothing consisting of anorak and overtrousers of a close-woven material made of cotton warp and nylon weft, which weighed only 4¾ oz. per square yard but which was totally impervious to winds up to 100 m.p.h. It was proofed with Mystolen to make the garments showerproof.

The expedition tents were of the same cloth. The basic pattern was that of the Meade tent, which had given good service, virtually unaltered, since the earliest expeditions. For communal use these were supplemented by larger pyramid tents – generally used as cookhouses – and by two extra large twelve-man dome tents which served as mess tents. The system of tentage in fact (apart from the material) bore a strong resemblance to that of the 1933 expedition.

Despite Griff Pugh's strictures about the necessity of having the correct oxygen equipment, little progress had been made. Peter Lloyd, who had been a member of the 1938 expedition (when he had conducted comparative tests on the open- and closed-circuit systems), was put in charge of this vital department, assisted by Tom Bourdillon and Alf Bridge. The first two had scientific expertise and Bridge was an engineer, working for the Gas Board.[28] In its way the appointment of these three men was symptomatic of the new determination which had arrived with Hunt. Amateur bungling was out: the men handling the oxygen were not only climbers but scientists too, well able to relate the needs of one discipline to the other. But even scientists must sometimes agree to disagree . . .

Lloyd's initial report set a cost of £4,000 on the oxygen equipment – which the Committee found acceptable – but he later revised this downwards as the main contractors (Normalair) and the Ministry of Supply decided to make no charge. Forty open-circuit sets were requested by Pugh, but Lloyd thought this was too generous. Hunt, displaying his usual pragmatism, decided to take whatever was going and decide what to use once the climbing started. By way of a bonus, it was learned that the Swiss had left a good deal of oxygen on the mountain and so it was decided to take adaptors which would fit the Swiss cylinders to the British masks.

The task facing Lloyd, however, was not simply that of acquiring sufficient sets and paying for them. His most immediate concern was to decide on what type of set to acquire – and in this he clashed with his co-worker, Bourdillon.

Bourdillon had been working with his father (also a scientist) to develop the closed-circuit oxygen system which had been tried out on previous expeditions with varying degrees of success. In this system a chemical exchange took place between the carbon dioxide breathed out by the climber and a cylinder of soda-lime, with the effect that oxygen was returned to the system for use over and over again. A supply of fresh oxygen replaced what was actually absorbed by the climber's body, but obviously the wastage rate was much reduced and consequently less oxygen needed to be carried. From time to time the soda-lime cartridge became exhausted, but this was easily replaced by a quick-loading cartridge system. A second benefit of the closed circuit was that it provided a richer oxygen supply which gave the climber greater vigour: a post-expedition comparison of times on the upper part of the mountain showed that men carrying roughly the same loads climbed almost twice as fast wearing the closed-circuit set as they did when wearing the open-circuit set.[29]

But the Bourdillon system was very new and scarcely beyond the prototype stage. His experience of similar apparatus in 1938 made Lloyd distrust it:

> My own experience in 1938, when I had done comparative trials on the open and closed circuit systems, had led me to distrust the closed circuit design with its inherent complexity and with the inevitable resistance to breathing caused by the duct and valve gear ... The 1953 apparatus was improved in comparison with that of 1938 by fitting bigger and better valves but I think my 1938 conclusion was right, that it is inherently too claustrophobic and complex, and that is why it has never caught on.[30]

Lloyd also had misgivings about apparatus which was really pure laboratory development, as the Bourdillon set undoubtedly was. Writing on oxygen equipment in general he said: 'Oxygen equipment for Everest and other big mountains cannot be developed in decompression chambers because these do not reproduce the essential conditions of acclimatized men with very high lung ventilation rates etc.'[31]

It follows from this that in Lloyd's view any oxygen apparatus must have a mountain provenance, and, bearing in mind his experiences of 1938, that to him meant the open-circuit set:

> ... the right tactic was to concentrate on improving the storage efficiency of

> the open circuit system (i.e. the ratio of oxygen weight to total weight) and on providing generous quantities of a well engineered equipment of this type.
>
> . . . the design of the equipment for the 1953 expedition had to depend very greatly on experience gained on the mountain in the twenties and thirties.[32]

Nevertheless, the Bourdillon apparatus had its supporters on the Committee and in the end the inevitable compromise was reached: twelve open and eight closed sets were taken. These were for active use on the mountain, but many more R.A.F.-type open sets were taken for training, sleeping, spares and so on – nobody remembers how many, and the records are totally confusing.[33]

It was, inevitably, the open-circuit sets which came in for most use on the mountain. They had been developed by the Institute of Aviation Medicine and Normalair from R.A.F. sets, but so changed that they were virtually original. A face mask was developed by the Institute which replaced for the first time Finch's mouth tube, and the steel cylinders used by the R.A.F. were replaced by smaller, and considerably lighter, dural cylinders. Unfortunately these alloy bottles proved both expensive and slow to manufacture, so the expedition ended up with a mixture of sixty alloy cylinders and a hundred steel ones.

The dural cylinders held 800 litres of gas as against the steel cylinders' 1,400 litres, but the latter weighed 10 lb. more. A climber wearing a fully charged oxygen set, with three dural cylinders, was carrying a staggering 41 lb. weight. Even with two cylinders it weighed 29½ lb. – or slightly more than Irvine's improved apparatus of 1924! During use the sets could be adapted to provide up to six litres of gas a minute, or three times more than Odell thought necessary in 1924.

A novel feature of the oxygen supply on the 1953 expedition was the deliberate policy of using oxygen as an aid to sleeping. This was Lloyd's idea, based on his own vivid recollections of the misery of trying to sleep at high altitude. Oxygen helps to keep the body warm and reduces headaches, and is almost invariably used for this purpose by high-altitude expeditions today – those that use oxygen at all, that is. In 1953, however, it seems to have been a new idea. It was a fairly simple matter to make a T-piece connector which would allow two masks simultaneously to draw oxygen from one cylinder. The rate was two litres per minute.

In fact, throughout the expedition the oxygen apparatus behaved remarkably well. There was, however, one sudden wave of panic right at the start when, at Base Camp, fifteen out of forty-eight 'training bottles' (steel cylinders) were found to be flat. The other cylinders were still on their way across country from Kathmandu. Were they flat too? There was no chance of getting replacements in time if they were. 'It was all too evident,' Hunt wrote, 'that here was a crisis which would inevitably affect, and might well prejudice, our plans.'[34] As it turned out, all was well: the cylinders were full.

Later on Hunt wrote of oxygen: 'only this, in my opinion, was vital to success. But for oxygen . . . we should certainly not have got to the top.'[35]

# 14

# 'The Last Innocent Adventure'

On 8 March the expedition assembled at Kathmandu. The Sherpas had already arrived from Darjeeling: twenty men hand-picked by the Himalayan Club for their abilities at high altitude and led, of course, by the redoubtable Tenzing, now more or less recovered from his gruelling experiences of the previous year, which for a time had affected his health. These twenty men were expected to reach the South Col and six of them were to be selected as possible members of assault parties when the time came. Other Sherpas would be engaged en route as the party travelled through the Khumbu valley.

As was customary on large expeditions each member was allocated his own personal Sherpa, the idea being that each climber would get to know and understand at least one Sherpa and vice versa. A rapport naturally grew between each pair: Hunt and Da Namgyal, Noyce and Annullu and so on. Michael Ward recalls that he was allocated 'a roly-poly Sherpa', Gombu, a youth of seventeen who 'distinguished himself by being the only Sherpa ever to ask his Sahib to walk a little more slowly as he was finding the pace too fast!' A few weeks later this most unpromising sounding youth became the youngest person ever to reach the South Col, and in later years twice climbed Everest.

The Sherpas are among the most uncomplicated and happiest people on Earth and it is impossible to know them and not like them; yet reading the various biographies and accounts written over the years by members of the 1953 expedition, one sometimes feels that the camaraderie between climber and Sherpa is overdone. Occasionally a Sherpa might be 'a rascal' or a 'bit of a rogue', much given to drinking chang, but never in these accounts is he allowed to have any real feelings, especially of anger or frustration. Tenzing is always described with his 'shy, quiet smile' – there is no hint of the humiliation he felt in Kathmandu when dealing with the British, or the fact that the deputy sirdar Ang Dawa and another Sherpa, Pasang Phutar, left the expedition at Thyangboche.

The fact is that the Swiss expeditions of the previous year had not only opened up the way to Everest, but had also opened up a new relationship with the Sherpas, making them companions in the great adventure.[1] The British who followed them understood nothing of this: individual Sherpas were fine chaps with whom one could strike up a lasting friendship, but the Sherpa corps as a whole were socially inferior. Perhaps it was a remnant of the Raj – three hundred years of tradition cannot be shaken off overnight, and to John Hunt, who had soldiered in India for many years, the arrangements made for the Sherpas in Kathmandu would not have seemed amiss. Socially conscious though Hunt was (and is) he had a military mind conditioned to a strict class division between 'officers' and 'other ranks'. And the Sherpas were definitely 'other ranks'.

The trouble began when the Sherpas discovered that they were billeted in a garage at the British Embassy, whereas the climbers were in the Embassy itself. The garage was a converted stable and had no toilet facilities. The Sherpas objected and Tenzing (who had been offered a room in the Embassy) considered marching off to a hotel as a form of protest, but finally decided to stay in the garage with his companions and try to allay their suspicions. Next morning they urinated over the road in front of the garage.

The Embassy staff were furious, and when some of the newspaper men got hold of the story Hunt was furious too. The Sherpas got a dressing-down – which did nothing to improve relationships.

From this unfortunate beginning arose a series of petty squabbles over equipment and so on which lasted until the expedition reached its first Base Camp at Thyangboche, and ended with the defection of Ang Dawa and Pasang Phutar. Indeed, it was only when the climbing began that something like harmony between climbers and Sherpas began to emerge.

Two years later, in his autobiography, Tenzing summed it up:

> My own personal relations with the British were quite satisfactory. True, there was not the informal, easy comradeship there had been with the Swiss. I did not share a tent with one of them, as I had with Lambert, and there was not much joking and horseplay between us.[2]

It would perhaps be foolish to make too much of these early incidents, and yet they could have had serious repercussions on the expedition had things not turned out so well in the end. It was Hunt's only serious mistake.

One of the principal differences between the post-war and pre-war expeditions was that the latter could use transport animals for the approach to the mountain, or the 'walk-in' as it is now commonly called. The arid plateau of Tibet lent itself admirably to travel by horse, mule or yak, whereas the steep-sided valleys of Nepal, traversed only by narrow and sometimes precipitous paths, can be tackled only on foot. Apart from the meagre supplementary rations obtainable from villages along the way every gram of food and every kilo of equipment has to be carried in by human labour. And for a major expedition to Everest, that means a lot of porters.

So many porters, in fact, are needed that it is not feasible for the whole party to move together along the track, because when the head of the column reached its destination each day, the tail would still be an hour or more away and any co-ordination would be impossible. So the expedition was split into two halves, separated by a day's march.

To give some idea of the numbers involved: the first part of the expedition left Kathmandu on 10 March with 150 porters; the rest a day later with 200 porters. And they were carrying just the bare essentials – the main body of stores left a month later, again in two halves.

The walk in, to Thyangboche, took sixteen days, but by 27 March both halves of the expedition had reunited on the level grassy alp dominated by the famous monastery. All around rose a riot of superb peaks, little known and totally unclimbed: Thamserku, Kantega, Ama Dablam . . . and in the far distance, just visible, the tip of Everest itself. '[It] made me gasp in wonder at the beauty of it when I first stepped out onto the meadow beneath the monastery,' said Hunt. [3]

For the next three weeks this idyllic camp site was the expedition base while the climbers explored the surrounding valleys and passes, sharpening their fitness and gradually acclimatizing to the thin cold air of higher altitudes. This training period was broken into two halves, with a three-day rest at Thyangboche in between, and the second half was cleverly designed to run smoothly into the assault proper, by having Hillary's group move forward to the head of the Khumbu Glacier, establish a Base Camp and attempt the Icefall.

On 9 April Hillary set off for the Khumbu Glacier. In his party were Mike Westmacott, George Band and George Lowe, together with Griff Pugh, the scientist, and Tom Stobart, the film cameraman. They were accompanied by five high-altitude Sherpas and thirty-nine porters, many of whom were women. That night, as they camped at Phalong Karpo, it began to snow, and next day they progressed up a valley which had been transformed to a dazzling white blanket. Most of the porters, who had no snow goggles, suffered abominably from the glare: some became snowblind, and many partially so. When they camped for the night at Lobuje, Hillary was seriously worried that he had ruined the expedition right from the start!

However, the toughness of the Sherpas and the resourcefulness of Tom Stobart, who managed to rig up thirty pairs of 'goggles' from tinted plastic and sticking tape, avoided a potential setback and next day the party was able to proceed up the moraine to the camp site at Gorak Shep, where they set up a temporary Base Camp.

Gorak Shep is a tiny green lake set in a hollow of the moraines below the stony summit of Kala Pattar, a small peak buttressing Pumori, which rises impressively to the north of it. Below the moraines lies the trough of the Khumbu Glacier, and across the glacier the gleaming savage ridges of Nuptse dominate the scene. Indeed the West Ridge of Nuptse juts out to such an extent that, combined with the curve of the glacier, it effectively hides the Icefall from view. Everest, however, towers in the background, its great triangular South West Face unmistakable, and a plume of spindrift more often than not trailing from the summit.

Gorak Shep would be the perfect Base Camp – and the Swiss had thought of it as such initially – but for the fact that it is separated from the Icefall by rough, uncomfortable going which under the circumstances is too far.

Hillary, like the Swiss before him, moved nearer to the target, and in fact came across the Swiss camp site, which proved ideal. As a happy bonus George Lowe discovered a huge pile of juniper wood: fuel which the Swiss had abandoned.

While camp was being established Hillary made his way over to the foot of the Icefall to see what conditions were like. He remembered the struggle he had had two years earlier with this monstrous cataract of ice, and now, to his consternation, it seemed to be in a worse condition than ever.

That, of course, is the problem with the Icefall. There is no knowing in advance whether it will be better or worse from one season to the next. All that is certain is that it will usually be pretty bad, and always dangerous. It was this that made Shipton back off and ultimately it cost him the leadership. He was right, in that men have since been killed by the treacherous, shifting ice, both Sahibs and Sherpas; but he had been proved wrong in thinking that men should not be subjected to the greater dangers involved. Hillary had seen and accepted the risk, back in 1951. The Icefall has never since stopped a single Everest expedition.

They began next day: Hillary, Westmacott and Band (Lowe was ill and remained in camp). They found the way ahead complicated, often dangerous, and with several technically difficult pitches, to which they gave grisly names such as Mike's Horror and Hell Fire Alley, perpetuating a long tradition of mountain climbing.[4]

That first day they didn't quite reach the snowy ledge where the Swiss had put their Camp II, but the following day Hillary returned to the attack with Westmacott and the Sherpa Ang Namgyal, and, since the lower part of the route was now familiar, made swifter progress. Just before reaching the ledge they came across an astonishing feature which Hillary later described:

> There appeared to have been an enormous subsidence in the middle of the icefall, and below us a wide, shallow gully swept smoothly through the icy ruins up to the broad ledge which was our first objective. The floor of the

gully was flat enough, but it was split into a jigsaw puzzle of horizontal and vertical crevasses like a pattern of sunbaked mud. And it looked terribly unstable – as though it could sink again at any moment. It was obviously our old 'Atom Bomb' area. But it would take us where we wanted to go, and that was the main thing.[5]

That was indeed the main thing: in one sentence Hillary had summed up his whole approach to the Icefall and to the difficulties higher up the mountain – an approach shared wholeheartedly by his leader. Prudence was cast to the winds – but the notches on the narrow belt between what is acceptable and what is not are drawn ever tighter by succeeding generations in mountain climbing. Each generation has its sticking points and awaits another generation to make further advances.

That day they reached the shelf where the Swiss had placed Camp II.

The route they had taken lay somewhat to the left of centre on the Icefall. On the third day they decided to try a fresh approach – up the middle – to see whether it offered a safer route, but in this they were disappointed. As they returned to camp that night a hint of competition arose – a note came from Hunt announcing that he, Ward and Noyce had arrived at Gorak Shep earlier than expected. This disconcerted Hillary, who had determined in his own mind that it would be his party, and none other, that forced the route through the Icefall. Hunt would undoubtedly arrive next day, and Hillary was determined to greet him with the news that the way to the Western Cwm was clear.

The next day he set out to establish Camp II on the shelf half way up the Icefall. Westmacott was ill, so he took Lowe and Band with three Sherpas to help to carry the gear. Pugh and Stobart decided to go along too, the latter to do some filming among the ice. They all made it to the shelf without undue problems and pitched camp. Stobart and Pugh went down again with the Sherpas, leaving the three climbers to camp out on the ice.

As they crawled out of their tents next morning the obstacles of the upper Icefall looked insuperable. The seracs and ice blocks of the lower fall had been of reasonable size, thirty feet or so at most, but those above were towering, formidable giants: 'Square cut, with cliffs a hundred feet high, they surged over the crest of the Cwm, and like great icebergs ground their way slowly and relentlessly to the bottom.'[6]

Difficulties there certainly were. At the 'Ghastly Crevasse' they were forced to teeter across an immense chasm on an insubstantial sliver of ice, and the final ice wall called for some difficult climbing up a steep buttress, which in turn led to an ice chimney climbed by bridging. But once out of the chimney they found themselves on the edge of the Western Cwm. A few yards further and they discovered the ideal spot to place Camp III – a pleasant snowy hollow, safe from the avalanches that poured off the surrounding ridges.

(*Previous page*)
19. Camp IV on the North Col in 1933. (Frank Smythe)

(*Facing page, top*)
20. Hugh Ruttledge at the Rongbuk monastery blessing ceremony, 1933. (Eric Shipton)

(*Facing page, bottom*)
21. Jack Longland crossing a river during the approach to Everest, 1933. (Frank Smythe)

(*Above left*)
22. Woodrow Wilson Sayre. (Woody Sayre)

(*Above right*)
23. Klavs Becker-Larsen in Nepal, 1951. (K. Becker-Larsen)

(*Facing page*)
24. Thyangboche monastery on the approach to Everest. (Walt Unsworth)

(*Above*)
25. Namche Bazar, the Sherpa 'capital'. (Walt Unsworth)

(*Facing page, top*)
26. Pheriche and the upper Khumbu valley. (Walt Unsworth)

(*Facing page, bottom*)
27. The Everest group from Kala Pattar. Changtse rises in the left background above the West Col, which in turn is over the Icefall. The scale shows the enormous slopes to the West Shoulder, with Everest behind. In the foreground are the superb ridges of Nuptse. (Walt Unsworth)

(*Above*)
28. Base Camp on the Khumbu Glacier. (John Cleare)

29. In the Khumbu Icefall. (Leo Dickinson)

(*Facing page, top*)
30. The ascent to the South Col; crossing the Lhotse face. (Barry C. Bishop © National Geographic Society)

(*Facing page, bottom*)
31. Evans and Bourdillon exhausted after their summit attempt in 1953. (Alfred Gregory)

(*Above*)
32. The South Col and Everest seen from the Lhotse face. (Alfred Gregory)

33. In the Western Cwm. Camp II of the international 1971 expedition. (John Cleare)

MADE by
PIONIER

*(Above)*
34. Climbing the South East Ridge. (Barry C. Bishop © National Geographic Society)

*(Facing page)*
35. Hunt, Hillary and Tenzing. (Alfred Gregory)

36. Return from the roof of the world – Hillary and Tenzing after their successful first ascent of Everest in 1953. (Alfred Gregory)

Hillary's cup was full. He had done what he had determined to do – broken through the Icefall without interference from anybody else. Joyfully, the three climbers made their way down to Camp II – there to find Hunt and Ang Namgyal. Hunt had come straight up from Gorak Shep. Hillary's thoughts must have echoed the Old Duke's: it had been a damned close-run thing.

On 22 April Camp III was established above the Icefall at 20,200 ft and, coincidentally, Base Camp was brought forward from Gorak Shep to the Khumbu Glacier camp. On this day, too, the last of the stores arrived from Kathmandu. The expedition was now complete and well under way.

A period of steady build-up was now embarked upon as Hunt began the lift of supplies into the Cwm and across it to the foot of the Lhotse face. Camp IV was established at 21,200 ft, Camp V at 22,000 ft and Camp VI at 23,000 ft on the furthest edge of the Cwm, below Lhotse. Much of the trail-breaking was through soft snow, which is always hard work at any altitude, but even so the siting of the camps so close together was conservative to say the least. Nevertheless, it was all according to Hunt's carefully calculated plan. Progress, if steady, was inexorable – why wear yourself out in the early stages of the expedition if you have enough men and materials to make things easier?

An interesting feature of this build-up period in the Western Cwm is that it brought together Edmund Hillary and Tenzing for the first time. It was on a hard day; the snow was soft and the hot sun had turned the great white bowl of the Cwm into a veritable inferno. Nevertheless, Hillary was feeling particularly strong. He went at a cracking pace and was delighted to find that Tenzing had no difficulty in keeping up with him.

> This was the first time I had climbed with Tenzing (April 26th) or indeed, ever seen him climbing, and I was very interested to watch him in action . . . Although not perhaps technically outstanding in ice-craft, he was very strong and determined and an excellent acclimatizer. Best of all, as far as I was concerned, he was prepared to go fast and hard.[7]

In other words he had found someone who could match him in strength and determination – and that determination included getting to the top of Everest, for there is little doubt that both Hillary and Tenzing had set their ambitions high right from the outset. One wonders what might have happened had there been no Tenzing: would it have been Hillary and Lowe for the summit? One suspects this might have been the case; but Lowe's chances were diminished once Hillary found Tenzing to be such a match.

Tenzing, for his part, greatly admired Hillary. He thought he was a fine climber, with great strength and endurance – and a cheerful disposition, something all Sherpas admire. He later wrote:

> I suppose we made a funny pair, he and I, with Hillary about six feet three inches tall and myself some seven inches shorter. But we were not

worrying about that. What was important was that, as we climbed together and became used to each other, we were becoming a strong and confident team.[8]

They certainly tested one another on that first meeting. On the way down the Icefall they had called at Camp II, where a solitary George Lowe was keeping vigil, and Hillary had bet Lowe that he and Tenzing would make Base Camp in time to put out the 5 p.m. call on the radio. 'That'll be the day,' remarked Lowe, who knew it meant descending the rest of the Icefall in less than an hour.

There are few New Zealanders who do not rise to a challenge like that, especially from a fellow countryman, so off went Hillary like a rocket, with Tenzing, who had no say in the matter, flying behind. Where the going was easy they actually jogged down the ice, leaping crevasses as they came to them, scorning the ice bridges. And it was a crevasse which led to Hillary's undoing. He leapt for the far bank of the chasm, which was seriously undercut, landed heavily, and caused the ice to break off.

In an instant he was plunging into the void, surrounded by a heavy mass of ice which threatened to crush him. Almost by reflex he jammed himself across the chasm, thrusting his crampons into one ice wall and pressing his shoulders against the other. The ice fell away into the distant depths but he was held firm on the rope by Tenzing, who had reacted to the accident with admirable skill and speed. Hillary must have been convinced more than ever that in Tenzing he had found the ideal partner for a summit assault.

At Camp II George Lowe switched on his receiver promptly at 5 p.m. 'Hello George,' came Hillary's voice from Base Camp.

On 2 May, during the build-up of camps in the Western Cwm, Hunt decided that he, Bourdillon and Evans would make a reconnaissance of the Lhotse Face, the next stage of the assault. During recent days the weather had not been kind and there was much fresh snow about, but Hunt wanted to test the closed-circuit oxygen apparatus and this seemed the right opportunity, since Bourdillon was not only the inventor of it but its chief advocate.

Meanwhile Hillary, back in Base Camp, chafed at the bit, anxious to know how the reconnaissance would go and impatient at missing what he considered to be a vital slice of the action. Suddenly he had an idea – why not go up to Camp IV and find out? He needed an excuse, of course, but since Hunt was testing the closed-circuit sets, why shouldn't he, Hillary, test the open-circuit system? The plan was that by using oxygen to assist their ascent, he and Tenzing should climb from Base Camp to Camp IV and return in the same day. It was a flimsy pretext – the open-circuit system was known to work anyway – but Hunt agreed. There is no doubt that the lanky, easy-going New Zealander had a way of convincing Hunt of almost anything.

On 2 May then, as Hunt and his party were investigating the Lhotse Face, Hillary and Tenzing set off up the Icefall at their usual rapid pace. Assisted by their oxygen they reached Camp II in an hour and a half and Camp III fifty minutes later – they had climbed the Icefall in about two hours! But beyond Camp III they ran into deep soft snow which slowed them down, so that they took another two hours to reach Camp IV, where they awaited the return of Hunt's party.

It was late afternoon when Hunt, Bourdillon and Evans finally staggered back, tired and not a little disturbed. The reconnaissance had achieved little except to confirm their faith in the closed-circuit oxygen sets.

Hillary and Tenzing, now without oxygen, started on their journey back to Base Camp at 4.20 p.m., with little daylight to spare and in a gathering storm.

Fifteen minutes after leaving Camp IV they were struck by a snowstorm of tremendous ferocity. The wind battered them like a sledgehammer, the tracks were obliterated and the driving snow made visibility virtually nil. A series of marker flags had been set out to indicate the proper route, but these were so widely spaced that in the storm one was not visible from the next, and it was only Hillary's familiarity with the details of the route that enabled them to stagger from flag to flag.

When Hillary eventually reached a wide crevasse bridged by a metal ladder he felt easier: it meant that Camp III was only a few yards away. Then he remembered, with a sinking heart, that shortly after they had left it that morning Camp III had been struck and the tents removed. It was thought to be superfluous.

So there was nothing for it but to plunge down the Icefall. Here Hillary was on more familiar ground despite the storm and the fresh snow which distorted obstacles and hid numerous potholes and small crevasses. In the gathering gloom of impending night the two men eventually staggered into Camp II.

It was empty and cheerless, and though there were sleeping bags and food it held no attraction for the two climbers. They decided, incredibly, to turn their backs on sure safety and risk a descent of the remaining part of the Icefall, at night, for the comforts of Base Camp. Only men supremely sure of their own strength and ability could make a decision like that.

By the time they finally reached the foot of the Icefall it was pitch dark, and it was two tired men who stumbled over the stones of the Khumbu Glacier towards the welcome lights of Base Camp. It had been an incredible day. 'Well,' thought Hillary, 'we've made it, and I expect we've proved something. But at the moment I've no idea what it is.'[9]

On 7 May Hunt called a conference in the mess tent at Base Camp to announce his plans for the final assault. Only George Lowe and George Band, who were at Camp III, were missing: the rest crowded into the tent, tense and expectant. At the back sat James Morris of *The Times*, ready to make notes for his next despatch.[10]

For everyone present it was, as Hunt later wrote, the biggest event of the expedition apart from the summit bid itself. At it each man was to learn his fate – whether he had been chosen as one of the elite, to make a summit bid, or whether he was to play some subsidiary, even though important, role.

Hunt carefully elucidated his plans to the expectant climbers – the need to build up Camp IV into an Advanced Base, the difficult work to be done establishing a route up the Lhotse Face, and the establishing of a camp on the South Col. The build-up was a matter of logistics, but the difficult nature of the Lhotse Face demanded skilled ice craft and in Hunt's opinion this required George Lowe, assisted by Westmacott and Band. For the onerous task of conducting Sherpas up to the South Col and establishing a camp there, he chose the imperturbable Noyce and Charles Wylie.

After a detailed and lengthy exposition, in which his audience began to grow restless, Hunt now revealed what they were all waiting for, the summit plans in detail. There would be two summit assaults, twenty-four hours apart, weather permitting. Oxygen would be used from Camp V (22,000 ft) onwards. The first summit bid would be made from the South Col by Bourdillon and Evans, using closed-circuit apparatus. Their prime objective was to be the South Summit, but if they had enough oxygen and things were going well, they were to press on to the final peak. While they were doing this they were to be followed up the ridge by a support party consisting of Hunt, Gregory and four or five hand-picked Sherpas who were to establish a light camp at about 28,000 ft (Camp IX), then return to the col.[11] On the following day, whether Bourdillon and Evans had been successful or not, Hillary and Tenzing, using the open-circuit apparatus, were to ascend the ridge to Camp IX, stay the night there, and make the ascent next morning, returning to the South Col.

Everyone seemed content with the plan and their role in it, except for Mike Ward, who was more than a little incensed. He was particularly angry that Hunt should be leading the team which was to establish Camp IX: 'I did not think he would be fit enough and my conclusion was based on his age and performance to date.'[12] This was a little hard on Hunt who, in fact, had already been as far as the Lhotse Face, and though observers spoke frequently of him looking tired and drawn at most stages of the expedition, he seemed to have remarkable powers of recovery. Ward later wrote:

> He looked dreadful but this was normal. I wondered how much longer he could go on flogging himself during the day, yet seeming to recover after a night's rest. Almost every time that I had seen him, over the last two weeks, he had looked the same and I had grave doubts about his ability to function efficiently high on the mountain even with oxygen.[13]

In the event Hunt did very well on the final push, as Ward acknowledges, and one wonders whether his initial reservation was based entirely on his medical opinion or whether it wasn't coloured by chagrin. For he himself, as doctor, had been condemned to be a reserve. When he was chosen for the expedition Hunt had made it quite clear to him that he was going as a doctor first and a climber second – and now Hunt decided that the proper place for a doctor during the crucial assault period was Base Camp. For a climber of Ward's ability and Himalayan experience it was a galling prospect. As things turned out he eventually went to Camp VII on the Lhotse Face.

But Ward also had grave reservations about the plan itself. Why, for example, could Bourdillon and Evans not start from a camp set up on the ridge instead of from the South Col? The efficiency of the closed-circuit set, while theoretically better than the open-circuit, was not all that much superior. Indeed, in one sense it was technically unproven at high altitude, whereas the open-circuit had had a long history of continuous development stretching back over many Everest attempts. It seemed to Ward that the plan for Bourdillon and Evans had failure built into it.

There is no doubt that Ward had a point. Surely the correct sequence would have been to establish Camp IX on the ridge and send both teams off from it in turn. When Hunt came to explain his decision in *The Ascent of Everest* he seems to have had a most unconvincing ambivalence towards the closed-circuit apparatus. At one instant he explains how the theoretical advantages of the set made it possible to attempt the summit direct from the South Col, and at the next he is warning of the dangers inherent in using the set at all.

The facts seem plain enough: consciously or unconsciously, Hunt never believed that Bourdillon and Evans would reach the summit. Their summit bid was the strategy of a careful commander simply testing out the enemy's defences before throwing in his crack troops. And the crack troops were Hillary and Tenzing: one suspects that Hunt had decided that long before the conference of 7 May.

But before a summit bid could be made at all they had first to overcome the Lhotse Face. Lhotse is the second of the great triumvirate of peaks – Everest, Lhotse and Nuptse – whose walls enclose the Western Cwm in a gigantic horseshoe. Thus, looking up the Cwm, the jagged crest of Lhotse forms the centrepoint, with the depression of the South Col on its left, between it and Everest's South East Ridge. From the mountain, steep slopes of snow and ice sweep down for some 4,000 ft to the bed of the Cwm, breaking up at about half height into the crevasses and seracs of the Lhotse Glacier. Steep slopes also descend from the South Col to the Cwm, but here they are divided by the long buttress of rock which the Swiss had named the Geneva Spur (Éperon Genevois). The spur looks an obvious way of reaching the South Col, but the Swiss had found it far from easy and had eventually opted for a less direct route through the Lhotse Glacier.

Benefiting from their predecessors' experience, this is what the British intended to do as well. It meant forcing a way through the Lhotse Glacier, probably with one camp, then making a long leftwards rising traverse across the upper slopes to reach the South Col. The snowfalls which the expedition had experienced every afternoon would have filled the steep Lhotse Face with soft snow – arduous to cross at altitude, and possibly dangerous too if the snow was in avalanche condition. To force a route up this face was the task allotted to George Lowe.

Lowe was handicapped right from the start: his two companions who were to help him in his arduous task were *hors de combat*. George Band had developed a cold and had to go down while Mike Westmacott, try as he might, could not seem to acclimatize sufficiently for work at really high altitudes. Lowe, however, determined to carry out his task with the aid of Sherpas and so on 10 May he went up to Camp V with four experienced men: Da Tensing, Gyalgen, Ang Namgyal and Ang Nyima. At first he still hoped that Westmacott would join him in spearheading the attack and that the four Sherpas would keep them supplied with stores, but that was not to be: Westmacott carried loads for a few days between Camps V and VI but was unable to go further; by the 13th he was utterly exhausted, and Hunt (who had come up to observe progress) sent him down to recuperate.

Meanwhile Lowe, out in front, forcing the route up through from Camp VI towards the top of the Lhotse Glacier, had found an ideal companion for the job – Ang Nyima, a chain-smoking Sherpa who had shown little interest in the expedition up to this point, but who now demonstrated an endurance to match that of Lowe himself.

Camp VI, at about 23,000 ft, was the site of an old Swiss camp, about a third of the way up the Glacier, and was used by the British as a temporary camp until enough progress could be made to establish Camp VII a thousand feet higher. Progress was slow and arduous owing to the fresh falls of snow every day and the need to make the route safe for laden porters, just like the slopes of the North Col in the old days.

On the 15th Ang Nyima went down for a rest and Wilf Noyce took his place as Lowe's companion. Next day, as they plugged up the slopes, Lowe kept falling asleep from the effect of some sleeping pills he had taken the previous night, and there was nothing Noyce could do but lead his companion back to Camp VI. The watchers in the Cwm below groaned and grew apprehensive. Not knowing the situation, they wondered why Lowe and Noyce had turned back. But next day they made up for it: they established Camp VII (again on the site of an old Swiss camp) at 24,000 ft and pushed on a further 600 ft.

Mike Ward, who had leapt at the opportunity caused by the illnesses of Band and Westmacott to come up in support, now replaced Noyce, but much to the chagrin of the observers below (Camp IV, Advanced Base, now had a considerable population), they saw three climbers set out from Camp VII (Lowe, Ward, Da Tensing) then after a while falter and turn back. The wind, it seemed, was fiercely cold and there was no prospect of progress. Was the attack coming to a halt?

To an impatient Hillary, waiting like a greyhound on a leash in Camp IV, it certainly seemed so. In his diary he noted: 'Apparently windy and cold, but it seemed to us at Camp IV that there was a certain lack of drive.'[14]

By now George Lowe had been nine days on the Lhotse Face and in Hillary's opinion this was too long. He thought that his fellow New Zealander had run out of steam, and he pressed Hunt to allow him and some of the others to go up to Camp VII and finish the job off. Griff Pugh, the physiologist, was also worried that Lowe had remained for so long at high altitude, but Hunt, although worried by the lack of progress, refused to be stampeded. He intended to keep his shock troops in reserve until they were needed.

On the 19th, George Band, now recovered, led a party of laden Sherpas up to Camp VII and returned with the news that Lowe and Ward still considered it too cold and windy for further progress. This was depressing news. Time was running out: the monsoon, which had seemed a pale phantom of a threat not so long ago, now became a harsh spectre. The most they could reasonably expect was a fortnight's grace, and there was still a long way to go. Hunt realized that he would have to do something to break the impasse, not only to save time but also to restore morale.

He decided on a bold move. According to his plan, once Lowe had prepared a safe route to the South Col, the next phase was to send up Wilf Noyce with a party of Sherpas, to establish the camp on the col. Hunt now decided that Noyce and the Sherpas should go up to Camp VII, and whether the route was prepared or not force their way through to the col. Wylie, with a second group of Sherpas, was to follow twenty-four hours later, and would therefore, literally, be pushing Noyce hard from behind. If Noyce failed to make it, Camp VII was going to be very crowded!

Noyce went up to Camp VII on the 20th; Lowe and Ward came down. George Lowe had spent eleven days at 23,000 ft or more: eleven days of hard toil mingled with frustration. It was, wrote Hunt later, 'an epic achievement of tenacity and skill', but at the time, with failure imminent, Hunt was less well disposed to the New Zealander – he was 'excessively rude' to poor Lowe, according to Mike Ward.

Next day, 21 May, was the turning point of the expedition. It was the day which made success possible – and the day on which Hunt came nearest to losing his nerve.

On the morning of the 21st, up at Camp VII, Noyce's Sherpas were in poor shape. Only Anullu and Ang Norbu were fit to go higher and it was obvious that there would be no carry to the South Col that day. This was disappointing, but the day did not have to be wasted. Noyce had discussed an alternative plan with Hunt for just such an emergency – he and Anullu, using oxygen, should carry on the work begun by Lowe in breaking a trail to the col. But to reach such a decision took time and it was 10 a.m. before the two men set out. The weather was fine.

Down below in the Cwm, Hunt, chafing with impatience, wondered what was happening. The radio wasn't functioning and there was no sign of activity at Camp VII. It was with relief that he saw Noyce and Anullu start out on their climb. Yet it was a relief tinged with misgiving when he realized that Noyce was following the contingency plan.

It must have seemed to Hunt at that moment as though the expedition was going to founder without even reaching the South Col. Twelve days had been spent on the Lhotse Face and still it wasn't conquered. His resolution weakened, and when Hillary again pressed him to allow Tenzing and himself to go up in support, Hunt reluctantly agreed. He felt that Tenzing's presence might have a stimulating influence on the Sherpas at Camp VII, but he stressed to Hillary that he should only go beyond Camp VII if the extreme urgency of the situation demanded it. His intention was to boost morale, nothing more. His reluctance to play his ace early was obvious to the last.

Meanwhile Noyce and Anullu were making splendid progress. They climbed above the Lhotse Glacier and swung out onto the great leftwards traverse towards the col. The snow was firm and, so it seemed to the watchers below, the higher the two men climbed, the faster they travelled. At last they struck the Lhotse ridge some 200 ft above the South Col. The spell was broken.

It was 5 p.m. when they arrived back to a somewhat crowded Camp VII. There were fourteen Sherpas, Wylie, Hillary and Tenzing – all immensely cheered by the success that Noyce and Anullu had achieved.

There was never any doubt that once Hillary and Tenzing had got to Camp VII they would continue to the South Col. It was unreasonable to expect Noyce to return to the col after such a splendid pioneering effort, which meant that Charles Wylie would have to lead fourteen Sherpas up there on his own. Both Hillary and Tenzing considered this too was unreasonable, and so, despite Hunt's orders, they felt compelled to go on. It was just the situation they had dreamed of, and they made full use of their opportunity. Next day, as Noyce and Anullu went down to Advanced Base, Hillary and Tenzing led Wylie and his Sherpas up to the South Col. It was a superb effort – thirteen good loads delivered to the col in one carry.

And that evening Hillary and Tenzing were back in Advanced Base. It had been another incredible performance from this pair: from Camp IV to Camp VII in one day, from Camp VII to the South Col and back to Camp IV in another – from 21,000 ft to 26,000 ft and back in less than thirty hours. Hunt just hoped they hadn't burned themselves out.

As Hillary and Tenzing descended the Lhotse Face, the first assault party was already setting out from Advanced Base. This was Bourdillon and Evans, supported by Hunt and two Sherpas, Da Namgyal and Ang Tenzing. They made their way up to Camp VII and from there, next day, to the South Col, which Hunt later described so vividly:

> We looked down upon as dreary and desolate a place as I ever expect to see: a broad plateau, perhaps as much as 400 yards along each edge, its northern and southern limits set by the steepening slopes rising towards Everest and Lhotse, falling away abruptly westwards into the Cwm and eastwards down the Kangshung Face. The surface of this waste is partly covered by stones, partly with sheets of bare, bluish ice. The edges are snow fringed, but the snow has been hardened almost to the consistency of ice by the wind. And it is the wind which adds to the sense of dread which possesses this place. It was blowing fiercely as we went down the slope which must be descended from the top of the Spur to reach the level surface of the Col. We were making towards the right where there were some patches of colour among the stones; a splash of orange caught the eye. These patches marked the remnants of the Swiss camp. It was a queer sensation to go down like this at the end of our long, hard climb, as though entering a trap; and this feeling was heightened by the scene which we were approaching. For there before us were the skeletons of the Swiss tents, three or four of them; they stood, just the bare metal poles supported still by their frail guy ropes, all but a few shreds of the canvas ripped from them by the wind.[15]

They had a fierce struggle with the wind to put up the tents, and it was five very tired men who that evening collapsed into their sleeping bags.

Indeed, their exertions had been such that there was little hope of them mounting an assault on the final ridge next day. Not only did they need a rest, but they needed time to prepare their gear for the climb. Moreover, Ang Tenzing was completely done in, and it was hoped the day's rest might lead to his recovering in time for the assault. What was most galling, though, was the fact that the weather was fine, with very little wind – a perfect day for attempting Everest! Their only consolation was that the second assault party, instead of being twenty-four hours behind as originally planned, was forty-eight hours behind in order to let Hillary and Tenzing recover from their efforts on the Lhotse Face.

The climb up to the South Col had not been without problems: both Hunt, who was using open-circuit, and Evans, who had closed-circuit apparatus, had had oxygen problems, and on the day of the first assault, 26 May, the start was delayed because of a fault in Evans's set. For an hour or so there was some doubt whether it would take place at all, and throughout the climb both Hunt and Evans continued to be bugged by oxygen difficulties. It is doubtful, though, whether these seriously affected the outcome of the day's events.

Much to Hunt's chagrin Ang Tenzing still did not feel able to move ('a shirker' Hunt wrote in his diary), so he and Da Namgyal shared out the extra load between them, in addition to their own, and set off for the South East Ridge at 7 a.m. Evans and Bourdillon, unloaded, were later in starting because of the oxygen apparatus problem, but soon caught up with the others and overtook them. Cloud was boiling up to the east, so that only the tops of great peaks like Makalu and Kangchenjunga pierced through them.

Seen from the South Col, the South East Ridge of Everest looks very little like the popular idea of a ridge. Because of foreshortening it looks more like a separate peak: a conical face rising from the col, not too steeply, and terminating in a snowy apex which is in fact the South Summit of Everest. A rock band separates the col from the ridge proper and this is penetrated by a shallow gully about 1,300 ft high, on the right-hand side of the 'face' presented to the observer. About half way up there is a distinctive snowy shoulder, and it was here that Hunt and Da Namgyal hoped to dump their loads in readiness for the second assault. And yet, as is so often the case in the mountains, all is not what it seems: the ridge is indeed a proper ridge – it is simply that it presents something of a flank to the observer.

Hunt and Da Namgyal struggled up the ridge to the tattered remnants of the Swiss tent where Lambert and Tenzing had spent a night during their pioneering attempt the year before. Both men were feeling the effects of altitude – Hunt later discovered that the breathing tube in his oxygen set was choked with ice – and it was all they could manage to climb another hundred feet or so before dumping their loads and making a weary retreat to the South Col.

Meanwhile Evans and Bourdillon had been making splendid progress. The early morning troubles with the closed-circuit oxygen sets seemed to have been overcome, and though Evans was condemned by the adjustments to only half the normal supply of four litres per minute, they managed the first 1,300 ft in an hour and a half. Had they continued at that rate they would have reached the South Summit by 10.30 a.m.

Unfortunately, as they climbed higher they found the going more difficult. Soft fresh snow covered many of the ledges and great care was necessary to avoid a slip. The cloud was now wreathing all about them and it began to snow.

By 11 a.m. they had reached the snow shoulder where Hunt had hoped to place his camp. The ground was easier here, being more level, so they took the opportunity to change the soda-lime canisters in their oxygen sets for fresh ones. Unfortunately, this seemed to knock Evans's apparatus off key again and he had great trouble in breathing.

When they reached the foot of the final pyramid that forms the South Summit they first of all tried the snow slopes on the Kangshung side, but finding these crusted and in potential avalanche condition, Bourdillon led the way to a rocky crest over on his left, which though splintered and rotten did offer good holds. The crest comprised steep walls separated by sloping ledges which gave them a zig-zag course towards the final hundred-foot cone of snow. Plodding laboriously up these soft slopes, Evans gasping for breath, they eventually came out onto a corniced little dome. It was the South Summit of Everest. The time was 1 p.m.[16]

At 28,750 ft it was the highest summit that had ever been attained, and if Hunt's expedition did nothing else, at least Bourdillon and Evans had given it one small feather to stick in its cap – small compared with the major prize, that is. Anywhere else, any other situation, and it would have been a significant achievement for a major expedition. But on Everest, the South Summit was only a stepping stone to the ultimate prize – and from it, for the first time, the climbers would see the final ridge in close-up.

It was a fearsome sight: narrow, apparently steep, with precipitous drops on either side and huge cornices billowing like frozen waves out over the Kangshung face. A westerly wind was howling, blowing spindrift across the ridge, limiting visibility and giving it all the attributes of a snow-filled aerial maelstrom.

The question, of course, was whether to go on or turn back. The two climbers had achieved their primary objective and the ridge ahead looked difficult. Evans estimated that it would take them three hours to reach the summit and another two hours to return to the South Peak, to which must be added a further two and a half hours of descent to the South Col – a total of seven and a half hours. They had enough oxygen for only a third of that time – enough to get them to the summit, but not back again. Were they willing to risk a one-way ticket?

The crux of the matter was Evans's faulty oxygen set. Both men were prepared to risk an oxygenless descent, but supposing Evans's set broke down before they even reached the summit? Bourdillon, beset by the double frustration of having his life's ambition not quite within his grasp and being let down by the very apparatus he had helped to design, was all for making a solo attempt. He even went down into the dip beyond the South Summit, but to no real purpose.

Writing from memory a quarter of a century later, Evans described their feelings on the South Summit:

> From memory, Bourdillon and I did discuss on the South Summit the question of whether he should go on alone and we came to the conclusion that the right thing to do was for both of us to descend. It would be quite wrong to say that he was 'beside himself with frustration' and my

recollection of the half-hour spent on the South Summit is of weighing up the pros and cons of any course of action very dispassionately. You must remember that the faculties and energies of people suffering from anoxia are very much reduced and at great heights both ambitions and frustrations are diminished: pressures and arguments are not strong. I think all I can say is that we did discuss the possibility of Bourdillon going on alone and that we decided that taking into consideration time, the remaining supply of oxygen, our estimates of time for covering the distance to the top and back, our own condition and the weather which was not good, we agreed that the sensible thing was to come down.

Beyond the South Summit there was then a small drop before the ridge continued and Bourdillon went down this on a rope and back again so that we could report on this little bit of the route to Hillary. I am not now sure whether we both went down onto the next bit of the ridge, but I rather think it was Bourdillon alone, not however unroped.[17]

Retreat was the only course open to them.

It was a nightmare descent. Evans's oxygen set continued to malfunction and ultimately, by some skilful tinkering, Bourdillon managed to convert it to the open-circuit system. Both men were desperately tired and slipped continuously. When the final gully leading to the South Col was reached they more or less fell down it, too tired to be concerned any more. Evans wrote later:

We knew that we were too tired to be safe, but somehow we had to get down it. Moving one at a time, and belaying with the axe-shaft driven well in, we had made several rope-lengths when I came off. I was last, and just beginning to move down to Bourdillon. I found myself shooting past him, was slightly annoyed with myself for the slip, and thought that I must keep my crampons off the snow. After what seemed a very long time, the rope pulled slightly at my waist, but there was no check to my speed, and I thought to myself, 'Hello, so Tom is coming too.' Fortunately we were below the steepest part of the gully and before long the slope ceased, and we came to rest in softer snow. My axe came sliding by, and I was able to catch it before giving myself over to the business of getting back my breath. After I had made my apologies to Bourdillon (we were always punctilious on these occasions), we went on down.[18]

The climbers at the South Col went out to greet them and help them back to camp. Hillary later described them:

The two men were an awe-inspiring sight! Clad in all their bulky clothes, with their great loads of oxygen on their backs and masks on their faces, they looked like figures from another world. They moved silently down towards us – a few stiff, jerky paces – then stop! Then a few more paces!

> They must be very near to complete exhaustion. With a lump in my throat, I climbed up to where they now stood waiting, silent and with bowed shoulders. From head to foot they were encased in ice. There was ice on their clothing, on their oxygen sets, and on their rope. It was hanging from their hair and beards and eyebrows: they must have had a terrible time in the wind and snow![19]

Because there had been a delay of twenty-four hours in making the first assault, the second assault team had caught up with them at the col and consequently the three tents there were overcrowded that night. There was Hunt, Bourdillon and Evans, tired from their attempt on the ridge; Hillary and Tenzing, the second assault team; Gregory and Lowe, the second support team; and three Sherpas: Ang Nyima, Ang Temba and Pemba. The rest of the Sherpas who had brought loads up that day had gone straight back down again, taking with them Ang Tenzing and Da Namgyal, the two men who, with Hunt, had formed the first support team.

The wind rose during the night and continued to buffet the tents with ferocious gusts throughout the next day. To the climbers crowded in the tents on the col, Everest presented a terrifying spectacle as the clouds wreathed and shredded around the South East Ridge and streaks of spindrift were flung high into the air. There could be no attempt that day.

Nevertheless it was essential that the camp should be relieved of some of the overcrowding and, as the weather wasn't bad enough to prevent a descent to Camp VII, Evans and Bourdillon set off down, accompanied by the Sherpa Ang Temba, who had been feeling ill. However, scarcely had they left the tents when Bourdillon collapsed in the snow. He was given an oxygen set, which revived him for a time, but he collapsed again. It became obvious that the party would need help if they were to reach Camp VII in safety.

Now according to Hunt's original plan, the second assault was to be launched by Hillary and Tenzing, with Gregory and two Sherpas in support, but as it turned out Lowe and Hunt were there as well. Lowe had brought up the Sherpas the previous day and had persuaded Hunt to let him stay on to help Gregory, while Hunt had conceived the notion that as leader he ought to stay at the col until the second attack succeeded or failed. In short, both men found convenient excuses to be where the action was: excuses which they justified to themselves, if to nobody else. There was no reason to suppose that Gregory and the Sherpas couldn't have managed without Lowe and, leader or not, there was nothing Hunt could have done at the South Col except sit and wait.

So the emergency caused by Bourdillon's weakness presented John Hunt with a dilemma. Who was to go down with Bourdillon, himself or Lowe? Both were, in a sense, superfluous to the needs of the assault party.

And just for a moment – for one fleeting instant during the whole long expedition – Hunt cracked under the strain. The temptation was too great, even for a man of Hunt's ingrained sense of justice, and he ordered Lowe to go down with Bourdillon. Rank, as the Americans say, hath privileges. Naturally enough, Lowe argued long and volubly – and Hillary supported him.[20] It wasn't until George was actually getting ready to go that Hunt suddenly changed his mind. 'I have never admired him more than for this difficult decision,' Hillary wrote later – and one tends to agree with him.

What caused the sudden *volte face*? Was it that Hunt realized that by sending Lowe down he was possibly weakening the attack should an emergency arise? Or was it that his highly developed sense of fair play at last overcame self-interest? The fact was that, leader or not, he was also part of the support for the first assault team – and it was a member of the first assault team who was in trouble. True, the assault itself was over, but did his duty not extend to seeing them safely off the mountain? That is the word which must have nagged at Hunt's conscience remorselessly – duty. To an officer brought up in the code of the pre-war British Army (and more especially, as in Hunt's case, in India) it was not a word to brush aside lightly.[21]

So Hunt went down with Evans, Bourdillon and Ang Temba. It must have been a nightmare descent for all four; there wasn't one really fit man among them. 'The blind leading the blind,' Hillary grimly recalled. They got down safely, but not without incident. Just before they reached Camp VII, Ang Temba fell into a crevasse, and the other three didn't have enough strength left to pull him out. Fortunately Mike Ward and Wilf Noyce came out from the camp and effected a rescue.

It is interesting to compare the effects of the two days, 26 and 27 May, on Evans and Bourdillon. Because of the malfunctioning of his apparatus Evans had not derived the full benefit from the oxygen he carried and in consequence had been desperately fatigued during the climb to the South Summit. Nevertheless, on his return to the South Col he recovered fairly quickly and was probably the fittest man of the four who descended to Camp VII. Bourdillon, on the other hand, supplied with pure oxygen, had been fit during the assault, but deteriorated immediately he removed his mask, on his return to the South Col. In Ward's opinion removing the pure oxygen of the closed-circuit system was equivalent to a sudden de-acclimatization, hence Bourdillon's collapse. No doubt psychological factors came into it too – nothing is so wearying as failure, real or imagined – but even so it was a further point against the closed-oxygen system. Bourdillon's experience seems to indicate that once this system is used by a climber going high, he is committed to its continual use until he returns to a safe lower level – certainly much lower than the South Col. The logistical implication of this could well be staggering. Since 1953 all development has been towards the ever improving open-circuit system, and as far as mountaineering is concerned the closed system became an anachronism.

On the morning of 28 May the second assault began. The support team moved off first, at 8.45 a.m., Lowe in the lead carrying 45 lb. of stores, Gregory and Ang Nyima behind with about 40 lb. apiece. The second Sherpa, Pemba, was ill and could take no part in the effort. Hillary and Tenzing followed at 10 a.m., and though they were supposed to be lightly loaded, to conserve their energies for the summit push next day, they were in fact carrying rather more than their supporters. Of course, they were spared the tedium of cutting steps on the ice – they simply followed those cut by Lowe's party.

The two groups came together at the tattered remnants of the old Swiss camp and from there on climbed together. A little further and they came across the load dumped by Hunt and Da Namgyal. They added this material to their own loads, sparing Ang Nyima, who wasn't going too well. They were now carrying over 50 lb. apiece – and Hillary in fact was carrying 63 lb. Even for a tough New Zealander like Hillary, it was a phenomenal load to carry at high altitude.

Hunt's dumping site had been considered too low for an effective assault on the summit (being only 150 ft higher than the old Swiss camp), but now they were faced with the problem of finding an alternative, higher up the ridge. Frequently their hopes were raised by the sight of some ledge, only to discover on reaching it that it was an illusion – there was no ledge at all, or it sloped wickedly, or it was too small and was totally inadequate even for a small two-man tent.

They were all extremely tired and near to despair when Tenzing thought he remembered a place he had passed when he was with Lambert the previous year. They traversed over to the left to find it, but the promised land turned out to be just another unsuitable site. They were about at the end of their tether and didn't know quite what to do next when George Lowe spotted a tiny platform some fifty feet above.

Anxiously they crawled up to it. It wasn't ideal because though it was big enough it sloped, but it would have to do. The height was estimated at 27,900 ft. The time was 2.30 p.m.

After thankfully dumping their loads the three members of the support team wasted no time in starting off down again. From now on Hillary and Tenzing were on their own. The success or failure of the expedition rested in their hands.

The first task – and an urgent one – was to try to make the ledge more suitable for erecting a tent on. They scraped away with their axes in an attempt to construct a level platform, but after two and a half hours' work the best they could achieve was a sort of two-tier effect, with one level about six inches higher than the other. They straddled the tent across this and lashed the guys at one end to oxygen cylinders and at the other to a somewhat dubious knob of rock. It didn't seem too secure, but it was the best they could manage under the circumstances.

Their great exertions of the day had made the two men hungry despite the altitude and it wasn't long before Tenzing had boiled some chicken noodle soup. They followed this with sardines and dates, and as a special delicacy a tin of apricots which Hillary had brought up specially for such an occasion. In addition they consumed mug after mug of hot sweet lemon drink, which was full of carbohydrate energy and a safeguard against dehydration.

Once they had eaten their fill they settled in for the night, Tenzing laying out his airbed on the lower platform, quite unconcerned about the thousands of feet of space which lay beyond the tent wall on that side, while Hillary settled onto the narrower upper platform. They had little oxygen to spare for sleeping and Hillary decided to use it in two shifts: from 9 p.m. to 11 p.m. and from 1 a.m. to 3 a.m., during which time they dozed. The two hours from 11 p.m. to 1 a.m. they spent in drinking hot lemon, the inevitable brewing ritual that is a feature of mountain bivouacs. As a mountain camp it had one unique feature – it was the highest that Man had ever camped at that time.

They were wakened at 3 a.m. by a sudden coldness which told them their sleeping oxygen had run out. From their sleeping bags they tackled once again the business of eating and drinking – and Hillary had the added chore of thawing out his boots, which he had removed the night before for the sake of comfort.[22]

By 6.30 a.m. they were ready to begin the climb. As they stood on the tiny ledge by the tent they looked very different figures from their predecessors of thirty years earlier. Basically, their underneath clothing, based on wool for warmth, was the same, with the addition of a string vest, but on top of this they wore a duvet suit: thick padded jacket and trousers filled with fine Eider down, over which was a shell suit of windproof cloth. On their hands they wore three pairs of gloves: silk inside, then wool, and an outer casing of windproof cloth. A man dressed like this is impressively bulky. Add the huge insulated boots, the goggles and the oxygen mask, and he looks like a creature from outer space. They had come a long way from the days of clinker nails, puttees and Norfolk jackets.

They climbed up the ridge, cursing the crusted snow which broke beneath their boots and let them sink with an energy-sapping jolt up to their knees at every step, until they came to the snow shoulder where Evans and Bourdillon had changed oxygen cylinders. Hillary was concerned over their own oxygen supply, so he fell on the abandoned cylinders eagerly and was delighted to discover that each was one third full – another hour's supply and a useful standby for their return down the ridge.

At last they came to the great sweep of snow which led to the South Summit. This was where Bourdillon had traversed left to reach the rock ridge and where he and Evans had zig-zagged up from ledge to ledge of unstable rock. Hillary, possibly put off by his predecessors' account of the ridge and being in any case a snow and ice climber by training, opted to go straight up the steep white slope that towered ahead.[23]

Immediately, he knew he was in trouble. The snow slope was steep and dangerously unstable. It was so powdery that there was no hope of a firm belay with his ice axe. If either man slipped, there was little chance of arresting the fall and a fair risk of starting an avalanche. There was a more than even chance that it would avalanche in any case and sweep them off the mountain. It was a nervy, risky business – 'My solar plexus was tight with fear,' Hillary later confessed.

But he was willing to risk much for Everest: that had been Hillary's philosophy all along.

'Ed, my boy, this is Everest – you've got to push it a bit harder,' he said to himself. When Tenzing came up to him Hillary asked his opinion.

'Very bad, very dangerous!' said Tenzing.

'Do you think we should go on?'

'Just as you wish.'[24]

They went on. 'It was one of the most dangerous places I have ever been on a mountain,' Tenzing later recalled.

But at last, after what seemed a lifetime, they reached the firmer snow of the final cone and climbed to the South Summit. The time was 9 a.m.

Though they were blessed with better weather than Evans and Bourdillon, who had seen the final ridge through swirling snow, it still looked a formidable climb. The huge cornices overhanging the right-hand side of the ridge precluded any chance of keeping to the crest, for a cornice could easily break away and precipitate them down the Kangshung face. The only chance of tackling it lay on the left side, which was fearfully steep. If the snow was in bad condition it might even be impossible.

But, to Hillary's delight, the snow was crisp and firm. They traversed it without much difficulty to the foot of a rocky tower which barred further progress. It was not an unexpected obstacle: it showed up prominently on aerial photographs and could be seen quite distinctly through binoculars from as far away as Thyangboche in the Khumbu valley. It was in fact an upwards step in the ridge, about forty feet high, and now known as the Hillary Step.[25]

There was no way of climbing this barrier directly and it seemed a chancy business to try to circumvent it on the left, for having got round the base of the step there was no telling whether it would be possible to climb back to the ridge. However, over on the right-hand side Hillary saw a possible though risky way up. A huge snow cornice lapped up against the rock step, and as is often the case some melting had taken place and a gap had formed between rock and ice. It was wide enough for a man to slip into. Was it possible, Hillary wondered, to climb it as one would a rock chimney? Or would the thrusting of cramponed feet be sufficient to send the cornice sliding off to eternity, and with it the climber?

Tenzing took a secure belay and Hillary eased himself into the slit. Tentatively he leaned back against the ice, facing towards the rock where he might hope to find handholds. The cornice made no movement. Then came the real test. He stamped his crampons hard into the ice behind him and levered upwards. The ice remained firm. With gathering confidence he squirmed and clawed his way up the fissure, pulled himself over the top onto a flat ledge, and lay there gasping for breath after his great effort.

When he had recovered he took a firm stance and called for his partner to come up, and eventually Tenzing arrived gasping by his side.[26]

Beyond the rock step the angle of the ridge eased off. It presented a series of rising undulations, still with the fearsome cornices on the right. But the going was easier and now the two men could move together; there was no need for belays. Hump after hump was crossed until suddenly Hillary was aware that there were no more undulations ahead, only a sharply dropping ridge, and beyond it, thousands of feet below, the ochre brown carpet of the Tibetan plateau.

On his right, a small ridge rose for some forty feet to a snowy dome. Hillary turned to it, and slowly, methodically, began to cut steps to the top. Tenzing followed close behind. At 11.30 a.m., 29 May 1953, Edmund Hillary and Sherpa Tenzing stepped onto the summit of Mount Everest and became the first men ever to reach the highest point of the terrestrial globe.

This is how Hillary described their moment of triumph:

> My first sensation was one of relief – relief that the long grind was over; that the summit had been reached before our oxygen supplies had dropped to a critical level; and relief that in the end the mountain had been kind to us in having a pleasantly rounded cone for its summit instead of a fearsome and unapproachable cornice. But mixed with relief was a vague sense of astonishment that I should have been the lucky one to attain the ambition of so many brave and determined climbers. It seemed difficult at first to grasp that we'd got there. I was too tired and too conscious of the long way down to safety really to feel any great elation. But as the fact of our success thrust itself more clearly into my mind, I felt a quiet glow of satisfaction spread through my body – a satisfaction less vociferous but more powerful than I had ever felt on a mountain top before. I turned and looked at Tenzing. Even beneath his oxygen mask and the icicles hanging from his hair, I could see his infectious grin of sheer delight. I held out my hand, and in silence we shook in good Anglo-Saxon fashion. But this was not enough for Tenzing,

and impulsively he threw his arm around my shoulders and we thumped each other on the back in mutual congratulations.[27]

Hillary busied himself taking photographs and then peered down the great North Ridge where the early Everest attempts had been made. He thought of Mallory and Irvine and looked around the summit to see whether there was any trace of them having been there, but there wasn't. Meanwhile Tenzing had dug a hole in the snow and placed in it some small items of food as a gift to the Gods of Chomolungma. Into the same hole Hillary placed a little crucifix which John Hunt had given him for just such a purpose.[28]

They carved seats for themselves in the snow, ate some Kendal mint cake, and then, fifteen minutes after their arrival, set off on the long tiring journey back to the South Col.

In an hour they were back at the South Summit. Then came the nasty part – the descent of the dangerous snow face beyond the South Summit – but they managed it and before long they reached the oxygen cylinders left by Evans and Bourdillon. They still had some of their own oxygen left, however, which was sufficient to take them back to their camp of the previous night, so they carried the two spare cylinders back to the tent.

They paused at their overnight camp long enough for Tenzing to make a brew of lemon drink while Hillary changed the oxygen cylinders. They had climbed throughout the day on a flow rate of three litres per minute (three quarters the normal rate) but now he reduced it to two litres per minute. He had calculated that at that rate it should just see them safely back to the South Col.

Packing up their personal belongings they set out again on the last stage of the descent, leaving the little tent to its fate on Everest's icy flank.[29]

And all went well. Though buffeted by squalls of wind that unaccountably roared down the final couloir, as if Everest was trying to show some final disapproval, they emerged safely at the bottom and began slowly to make their way towards the camp on the col.

George Lowe came out to meet them, carrying hot soup and spare oxygen. Hillary waved his axe and George knew they'd been successful.

'In rough New Zealand slang,' wrote Hillary later, 'I shouted out the good news.'

What he actually said was: 'Well, George, we knocked the bastard off.'

On the day after the second assault the atmosphere at Camp IV was charged with hopes and fears. Nobody knew whether Hillary and Tenzing had succeeded or not: there was no radio communication with the South Col, and a visual signal which Hunt had arranged was obscured by drifting mists.

Practically the whole team was gathered at Camp IV to await the news. One of the last to come up from Base Camp was James Morris, *The Times* correspondent, who, though no mountaineer, was determined to be at the heart of the drama for its closing scenes. Anxious eyes scoured the Lhotse Face and eventually five tiny dots could be seen descending: Hillary, Tenzing, Lowe, Noyce (who had replaced Gregory) and the Sherpa Pasang Phutar. That in itself was a great relief to the watchers: nobody had been killed.

The hours dragged on and the descending figures were lost in the ice maze of the Lhotse Glacier. The tension in the camp mounted until suddenly a shout went up: 'There they are!'

James Morris described the ensuing moments vividly:

> I rushed to the door of the tent, and there emerging from a little gully, not more than five hundred yards away, were four worn figures in windproof clothing. As a man we leapt out of the camp and up the slope, our boots sinking and skidding in the soft snow, Hunt wearing big dark snow-goggles, Gregory with the bobble on the top of his cap jiggling as he ran, Bourdillon with braces outside his shirt, Evans with the rim of his hat turned up in front like an American stevedore's. Wildly we ran and slithered up the snow, and the Sherpas, emerging excitedly from their tents, ran after us.
>
> I could not see the returning climbers very clearly, for the exertion of running had steamed up my goggles, so that I looked ahead through a thick mist. But I watched them approaching dimly, with never a sign of success or failure, like drugged men. Down they tramped, mechanically, and up we raced, trembling with expectation. Soon I could not see a thing for the steam, so I pushed the goggles up from my eyes; and just as I recovered from the sudden dazzle of the snow I caught sight of George Lowe, leading the party down the hill. He was raising his arm and waving as he walked! It was thumbs up! Everest was climbed! Hillary brandished his ice-axe in weary triumph; Tenzing slipped suddenly sideways, recovered and shot us a brilliant white smile; and they were among us, back from the summit, with men pumping their hands and embracing them, laughing, smiling, crying, taking photographs, laughing again, crying again, till the noise and the delight of it all rang down the Cwm and set the Sherpas, following us up the hill, laughing in anticipation.[30]

Stobart was on hand to film it all for posterity: the slow, forlorn looking approach of the four men, George Lowe's sudden exulting cry, the hugging and backslapping ... it was a dramatic emotional moment – and one which Stobart, with an eye to what makes a good movie, had contrived. He had gone ahead to meet the returning heroes and had persuaded them not to reveal their success until the last moment. The results were electric and brought lumps to the throats of cinema audiences round the world.

The party moved into the big dome tent at Camp IV and while Hillary and Tenzing ate 'a leathery omelette apiece' listened to the tall New Zealander's account of their adventure. In the background James Morris scribbled furiously. Already he had grasped the possibility of the Everest story coinciding with the Coronation of Queen Elizabeth II and the impact such a coincidence would have in Britain. It was gilding the lily perhaps – but what's wrong with golden lilies? As soon as Hillary had finished his tale, Morris set off for Base Camp, guided by Mike Westmacott.

Meanwhile, Hunt made a brief emotional speech about the success and the way in which everyone had contributed to it. Then he returned to his tent, too ill to take part in further celebrations that night. The release of tension had been too much for him, coming as it did on top of months of strain and weeks of arduous physical activity.

For the others, as they sipped their celebratory rum and endlessly recounted incidents of the expedition, did they realize that theirs was what Morris had called 'the last innocent adventure'? Certainly they all knew that the ascent of Everest was more than just another climb, but they had gone into the adventure with much the same spirit as Mallory. They were skilled amateurs on a paid holiday, and though some might argue that the whole show was run with a military efficiency alien to the mountaineering ethos, that adventitious aids like benzedrine tablets and a 2 in. mortar were taken along, not to mention oxygen, the impression remains that the ghost of Mallory wasn't far away.[31]

They also thought about their reception back home; about how pleased everyone would be, even if it was only by the fact that now Everest was out of the way, attention could be turned to some real mountain climbing. There might even be a dinner or two held in their honour and of course there would be the inevitable lectures to give.

This was the extent of their projections into the immediate future. None of them had any real idea of the impact which the climb was to have not only on the world in general and Britain in particular, but especially on themselves. Perhaps only Wilf Noyce, the philosopher-poet, had uneasy feelings about the aftermath of climbing Everest: he could sense vaguely that the Everest they knew, a great shoulder of rock and ice symbolizing not only majesty but also pain and discomfort, would give way to another Everest, the Everest of public acclaim, adulation, sycophancy and misunderstanding.

Even as they sipped their rum, the harbinger of all their fates was staggering down the Icefall with news for the outside world.

For a non-mountaineer, James Morris had put up quite a remarkable performance over the past two days, going from Base Camp to Camp IV and back again. His return trip was an agony of tiredness but he was spurred on by two driving thoughts – first, that he had an outstanding news scoop on his hands, and secondly, that with luck he could get the story to London in time for the Coronation.

As far as the latter was concerned haste was imperative because the ceremony was in three days' time and Base Camp was a long way from civilization. As for the scoop – well, scoops have a habit of rapidly slipping away. There were Sherpas coming down from the mountain who would pass the news on to their colleagues and it would run like quicksilver down the Khumbu valley – Chomolungma conquered! And in the valley, as Morris well knew, were two rival journalists, Ralph Izzard of the *Daily Mail* and Peter Jackson of Reuters, only too eager to snap up any news and beat *The Times* exclusive coverage. Secrecy and speed: both were essential to Morris.

Arrangements had been made with the British Embassy in Kathmandu to send any messages direct to Whitehall for immediate delivery to *The Times* – use of diplomatic facilities much criticized by other newspapers – but Kathmandu was at least a week away and Morris knew that in order to get his message to London in time for the Coronation he would need to use the Indian radio post at Namche Bazar. He sent a runner there as quickly as possible with the coded message:

*Snow conditions bad stop advanced base abandoned yesterday stop awaiting improvement*

which decoded read:

*Summit of Everest reached on 29 May by Hillary and Tenzing*

Obligingly the Namche operator relayed the message to Kathmandu and very soon it was on its way to London. The need for the code was more than justified: the message 'leaked' en route, and several newspapers were unwise enough to take it at face value and report the expedition's failure. An exclusive dispatch appeared in *The Times* on the morning of 2 June, Coronation Day. Just as Stobart had pulled off a cinematic *tour de force* when he filmed the meeting of Hunt and Hillary at Camp IV, so too James Morris had pulled off a sensational coup.

And so the British, as usual, had not only won the last battle but had timed victory in a masterly fashion. Even had it not been announced on Coronation Day it would have made world headlines, but in Britain at least the linking of the two events was regarded almost as an omen, ordained by the Almighty as a special blessing for the dawn of a New Elizabethan Age. It is doubtful whether any single adventure had ever before received such universal acclaim: Scott's epic last journey, perhaps, or Stanley's finding of Livingstone – it was of that order. The fact that neither of the two men who reached the top was actually British seemed of little importance to the public: in those days Britain still had a far-flung empire and New Zealanders were certainly regarded as chips off the Old Mother Block. Even Nepal, through the long association of the British Army with the Gurkhas, was regarded as the next best thing to a British colony.

The climbers themselves were genuinely amazed at their reception by the public: it far outstripped anything they had imagined and Noyce's 'other Everest' proved to be almost as much an ordeal as the real thing. There were lectures and banquets galore: they were fêted and honoured around the world, and even a year later Noyce wrote 'the honeymoon is not yet quite ended'.

Hillary and Hunt received knighthoods; Tenzing received the George Medal. These were the immediate trappings of success, but it would be an interesting study for a sociologist to determine what effect the ascent of Everest had on the later lives and careers of the participants. Suffice to say here that the three principal figures in the drama – Hunt, Hillary and Tenzing – were projected onto a world stage where even now, more than twenty-five years on, they are still instantly recognized.

For Tenzing the change was particularly profound: an overnight leap from being an obscure peasant to a national hero – indeed, a two-nation hero, since he was born in Nepal but lived most of his life in India. His reception in Kathmandu on his return from Everest was almost frighteningly ecstatic, with crowds chanting 'Tenzing Zindabad! Tenzing Zindabad!' and banners proclaiming 'Hail Tenzing, star of the World'. Nepal, it was said, had produced two Gods – the Lord Buddha and Tenzing.

Heady stuff for anybody, let alone an unsophisticated Sherpa, and made more confusing by nationalist politicians who latched onto the Everest bandwagon for their own ends. Who got to the top first? They wanted to know, and without waiting for an answer produced banners showing Tenzing hauling a weary Hillary up the final slopes.

Tenzing's natural qualities came to his rescue, particularly his ability to learn quickly and well. He emerged from the morass of cant and humbug tempered but unscathed and settled down to become the distinguished Director of Field Training at the Himalayan Mountaineering Institute at Darjeeling. In 1957, Lord Hailsham, speaking at the Centenary Dinner of the Alpine Club in London, where Tenzing was present, said of him:

> Tenzing is one of the group of very famous men who are referred to quite simply without prefix or suffix . . . Tenzing has won fame all over the world, not only for what he has done but for the qualities of spirit and character which have made him known and loved and respected wherever he has been. What an ambassador he has been for a people who for many centuries lived secluded in their mountains and valleys and are now for the first time to be fully known and admired by the majority of mankind.[32]

All the members of the successful Everest team have retained their interest in mountaineering through the years which have followed. Tragically, two of them died in the mountains. Bourdillon was killed in the Alps in 1956 and Noyce in the Pamirs in 1962.

What of the sport itself? Mountaineering as a leisure activity certainly expanded manyfold in the years following 1953.

There are indications that this would have happened anyway, but anyone who has lived through this period and been closely connected with the sport recognizes that the ascent of Everest did give a certain undefinable yet very real impetus to the sport in Britain.

Profits from John Hunt's official account of the adventure, *The Ascent of Everest*, from the film and from the lectures were set aside to fund the Mount Everest Foundation to 'encourage, or support, expeditions for the exploration of, and research into the geology, ethnology and similar sciences of the mountain regions of the world' and grants have been made each year since 1954 to expeditions. When Everest was climbed some people wondered whether that was an end to Himalayan mountaineering, but Wilfrid Noyce had the perfect answer by countering with another question: Did the ascent of Mont Blanc mean the end of Alpine climbing?

In his diary for 30 May 1953 – the day he met Hillary and Tenzing on their return from the summit – John Hunt wrote 'Thus ends the Epic of Everest.' It was the biggest misjudgement he ever made.

# Interlude

When it comes to climbing them, all great mountains seem to pass through the same stages of development. First of all there is the attempt to gain the summit, usually by the easiest or most convenient route, and by almost any means short of mechanical transport. Once that is out of the way, the climbers turn their attention to more difficult ascents and to climbing the mountain in a 'purer' way – that is to say, by cutting down on adventitious aids, such as oxygen. Non-climbers frequently cannot understand this. To them the summit is the obvious goal – and in one way it is, which is why it is always the first challenge to be overcome. But it isn't the real goal: the real goal is the outcome of the struggle between Man and mountain, with the latter always presenting fresh challenges and the former wondering whether he dare accept them. It is an endless, fascinating, titanic struggle. The conquest of Everest in 1953 was not the end, nor even the beginning of the end. More accurately, it was the end of the beginning.

Since Hunt's great achievement the mountain has followed the classical lines of development, as we shall presently discover, but it is always worth bearing in mind that Everest has one particular attribute shared by no other mountain – it is the highest peak in the world. This makes it very special, even to hard-boiled mountaineers who generally dismiss mere height as something of little importance. For this reason the original route taken by Hunt's party is still in demand – the top still counts a lot in this case. It has been climbed many times since 1953 – more frequently in fact than any other of the world's 8,000-m. peaks. Hunt's climb has become the 'ordinary route' and the Sherpas refer to it disparagingly as the 'Yak route', but this doesn't mean it is any easier than it was in 1953 – people still fail on it. Nevertheless, to detail all the expeditions which have attempted the South East Ridge in the last quarter of a century or so would be too repetitive for our purpose, since very few of them contributed anything new to man's fight against Everest. For that, we must turn elsewhere, and where better to start than that old adversary, the North Ridge, which held out against the British for so long?

# 15

# News from the North

When the Chinese army marched into Tibet in 1950 the northern approaches to Everest were effectively sealed to Western climbers. A few daring adventurers broke the seal to try their luck, as we have seen, and Woody Sayre even got to the North Col, but there was no official expedition from the West for over forty years.

But this does not mean that there have been no expeditions at all – both the Russians and the Chinese themselves have had their parts to play in the continuing saga of Everest's northern slopes. The problem is that from countries like Russia and China, where every facet of life is moulded to suit ideological purposes, it is impossible to get a clear picture of events. Success is due to ideology and the story is told from that point of view – failure is never mentioned.

We know very little about the organization, aims and ethics of Chinese mountaineering. From time to time word is sent out from Peking telling of the ascent of some mighty peak deep in China or Tibet, usually accompanied by photographs and vague details which give nothing away and are sometimes so riddled with inconsistencies as to be totally baffling. This does not mean that the gist of the story is untrue – it may have been badly translated, probably by a non-climber who didn't understand the finer points even in his own language, let alone English, or it may have been doctored by some bureaucratic cog in the Ministry of Information to give it a better slant. The Chinese have without doubt made some very high ascents – but for what purpose? We know nothing of their ideals: we do not even know whether there are sporting climbs done, just for the enjoyment of the thing. This is important, because if we knew more about the corpus of Chinese climbing we could assess their great ascents, or failures, in a more sympathetic light.

About the Russian climbers, on the other hand, we know a great deal.

Western climbers visit Russia every year to climb in the Caucasus or the Pamirs, and Russian climbers pay reciprocal visits on a state-sponsored basis. We know how climbing is organized in Russia; that it has a strong sporting element, even to the point of fostering competitive climbing, and though it has a structure which Western climbers wouldn't tolerate, there is no doubt that the Russian climber has much the same motivation as his European or American counterpart.

But there is a good deal of difference between cultural exchange visits to foreign countries and a national expedition to climb Mount Everest. The latter has political implications involving the prestige of the country (and the Party) and it would be bad propaganda for a Soviet team to fail. In fact, there has never been a Soviet expedition to any of the world's highest peaks: no Russian climber has passed the magic 8,000-m. mark. By not taking part in the Himalayan ascents of the post-war era Soviet climbers have missed out on a whole phase of mountaineering history, though they certainly had climbers capable enough. Political timidity denied them an opportunity.[1]

Or did it? Did the Russians in fact try some great endeavour, and get badly mauled in the process? If that was the case they would certainly hush it up and not try again for a very long time. Some observers believe that this is exactly what happened.

In 1952 reports of a Russian expedition to the north side of Everest appeared in certain European climbing journals and in *The Times*. It was a post-monsoon attempt, following the Swiss failure of the spring, and was seen by some commentators as an effort to forestall what seemed like the inevitable success of the second Swiss expedition or the British expedition scheduled for the following year.

The reports mentioned an expedition of thirty-five climbers and five scientists, led by Dr Pawel Datschnolian, a well-known Soviet mountaineer. They left Moscow on 16 October and after various unforeseen delays reached the mountain via Lhasa, eventually attaining a height of 26,800 ft, where they established Camp VIII. Then disaster struck swiftly and silently: the six men at Camp VIII simply disappeared and despite an intensive search were never seen again. The missing men included the leader, Datschnolian, and experienced climbers such as Lanitsov, Alexandrovich and Kazhinsky. It was, in fact, a complete disaster.

Such is the story – but is it true? The motive was certainly strong enough: had the Soviets been successful in snatching Everest it would have been an outstanding propaganda coup, comparable with Sputnik 1. The political will to attempt the coup was not lacking either, particularly as this was during the Stalinist era and at the height of the cold war. Nor was the time scale an impossible one – although the expedition must have been a hastily arranged, badly prepared affair, the game was worth the candle.

Yet the evidence is circumstantial. Datschnolian, it is said, has never been seen since. But why should he have been? Meetings between Soviet climbers and those of other countries were virtually unknown at that time, so he was hardly missed on the international scene. On the other hand, the reports are so detailed that, if they are not true, they must have been concocted by somebody with a good knowledge of Russian climbers.

The Soviet mountaineering authorities vigorously deny that the 1952 expedition ever took place. According to K. Kuzmin, President of the U.S.S.R. Mountaineering Federation:

> Neither the Mountaineering Federation of the U.S.S.R. nor any other sports bodies of our country have ever sent expeditions of Soviet mountaineers with the aim of climbing Jomolungma [Everest] in 1952. Some reports published by certain foreign publications on this matter do not correspond to the truth. At that time Soviet climbers did not have an opportunity to organize an expedition either to Everest or any other 'eight thousander'. However, later on, having gained good experience of climbing the highest summits located in the territory of our country, Soviet alpinists accepted the proposal made by Chinese mountaineers to conduct a joint expedition to Jomolungma. In this connection three of our climbers – E. Beletski, L. Filimonov and A. Kovyrkov – took part in reconnaissance of the route of ascent to this summit from the north in 1959. They came back home safe and sound. The joint Soviet–Chinese expedition to Jomolungma was being planned for the next year; however, for reasons not depending upon us this expedition did not take place.[2]

This is not evidence, of course – merely a statement. And just as there is only circumstantial evidence that the expedition did take place, so too there is only circumstantial evidence that it did not.

The time factor seems wrong. Even allowing for the great propaganda victory to be gained, and a consequent willingness to take risks, 16 October is very late to be setting out for Everest. It is reported that the expedition arrived back at base only on 27 December, when the weather would be appalling. Yet it is just possible, of course – much would depend upon the weather that year, though winds of more than 100 m.p.h. can be expected even in November.

Another, perhaps more telling, pointer has nothing to do with mountaineering or Everest, but everything to do with Russia and China. As Kuzmin hints in his letter, the Sino-Soviet expedition planned for 1960 did not take place because of the widening rift between the two nations. This has become increasingly bitter over the years, with no opportunity for embarrassing the other being missed by either side. In these circumstances it seems incredible that the Chinese have never mentioned any Soviet mountaineering disaster on Everest. When their own efforts were crowned with success, it would have been a golden opportunity to make political capital at their arch-enemy's expense. Yet they have not done so, nor have any of their expeditions reported finding evidence of a Russian attempt.

So we simply don't know. Trying to peer back into the murky fog of Stalinist Russia is a particularly unrewarding exercise. The chances are that the 1952 expedition did not take place; that the whole story was, as Kuzmin has called it, 'a *canard*'. On the other hand, if it *did* take place then it was a singularly inept venture in which one suspects mountaineering judgement was over-ruled by political demands.

Times have changed and the wheel turned full circle. In 1982 a Soviet expedition will attempt Everest from the south, via Nepal. They will do so in the full light of world publicity and, win or lose, there can be no secrets this time.

It is certain that the Russians helped the Chinese when that nation decided to take up mountain climbing in 1955, and the preliminary reconnaissance of Everest that took place in 1959 was a culmination of that co-operation. But for growing political differences there would have been a Sino-Soviet attempt on Everest in 1960. As it was, the Russians withdrew, and the Chinese decided to go alone.

They had built up, in a very short time, a fairly impressive record of high ascents. In 1957 they had made the second ascent of Minya Konka (7,590 m.), the highest peak in China proper,[3] in 1958 they climbed Shule (6,305 m.), in 1959 they climbed the North East Peak of Nyenchin Tangla (6,177 m.), and, more importantly, Muztagh Ata (7,456 m.) – a peak which had once defeated Shipton. Two other important ascents were to follow hard on the heels of their Everest adventure – Amne Machin (7,160 m.) in 1960 and Kongur Tiube Tagh (7,595 m.) the following year, the latter by an all-woman expedition. All those up to and including 1959 were shared, if not led, by Soviet climbers, but nevertheless it is clear that the Chinese had learned quickly.

They began their plans for an ascent of Everest in 1958 with a thorough reconnaissance of the northern approaches. Leaving nothing to chance, the reconnaissance group consisted not only of climbers but also of various assorted scientists: geologists, topographers, hydrologists, zoologists, botanists, surveyors and altitude physiologists, all of whom 'provided an important guarantee for the selection of a safe route'. Most important of all, perhaps, was the establishment of a weather station near the mountain with a network extending right back to Peking, which made forecasting much more reliable.

In 1959 the reconnaissance took place in which the Soviet climbers Beletski, Filimonov and Kovyrkov participated, although the Chinese account makes no mention of the Russians and it is difficult to establish how deep was the Soviet involvement in the preparations of 1958 and 1959. Certainly it was meant to be a Sino-Soviet expedition in 1960, and it seems likely that much of the original planning and the climbing gear was Russian. However, the political break which caused the Chinese to make the attempt alone did not find them helpless or unprepared.

They had carried out detailed historical research into the British pre-war expeditions and into the post-war ascents from Nepal. They also carried out research into technical problems 'including even the smallest detail such as the use of matches at altitude'. From all this they drew up a four-phase plan, the first three phases being concerned with gradual acclimatization and the fourth with the assault on the summit. Just in case this didn't work out they also had alternative plans for three-phase and five-phase assaults.

In the meantime the climbers expected to participate in the expedition followed a specially prepared physical training programme intended to bring them to peak fitness at the right time. When the teams assembled together:

> special training was taken up with a view to tackling the Second Step, which had been described as an insurmountable barrier, besides making various preparations. According to experiences gained from all sides, we improved some of our equipment and successfully carried out training in climbing long stretches of precipices with an incline of 80 degrees.[4]

It was, by any standards, a massive expedition. There were 214 men and women involved, a third of them Tibetan. Seventeen were Masters of Sport and eighteen First Grade Sportsmen. The average age was twenty-four – young for an Everest venture. The leader was Shih Chan-chun.

The main party reached Base Camp on 19 March. This had been established at 5,120 m. near the snout of the Rongbuk Glacier by an advance party who had arrived a fortnight earlier and had struggled against bad weather to prepare the way for the main expedition. The advance party had pushed up the East Rongbuk Glacier establishing Camp 1 at 5,400 m., Camp 2 at 5,900 m. and Camp 3 at 6,400 m. – virtually the same camp altitudes as those of the pre-war British expeditions. On 25 March all the members gathered at Base Camp to watch the Chinese flag being hoisted to the strains of their National Anthem.

Two days later the climbing party had reached Camp 3, though the purpose of this remains obscure since on the next day they returned to Base Camp. At the same time a 'scout group' set out from Camp 3 to reconnoitre the way to the North Col.

The weather was bad: high winds and a swirling mist made progress inordinately slow. At 6,600 m. they could go no further and a temporary camp was erected in exactly the same place as the old British Camp IIIa of 1933. Next day, in improving weather, they tackled the initial slopes of the col and rested for the night at the foot of an ice chimney similar to that which had figured so prominently in the 1924 attempt.

Led by Masters of Sport Hsu Ching, Liu Ta-yi and Peng Shu-li, it took the party all the next day to climb the ice chimney and reach a point fifty metres below the col. They retreated the following day, having judged their task to be completed.

From the Chinese accounts, which always lack essential details, it is not possible to determine whether the reconnaissance party were ultra-cautious or merely inept. It is unlikely that the difficulty of the North Col slopes had changed significantly since the pre-war days (and the relatively inexperienced Woody Sayre had little trouble there two years later – see Chapter 11), yet they had taken three days to climb from 6,400 m. to approximately 6,950 m. – an advance of roughly 600 ft per day. Even on Everest, and without oxygen, skilful climbers have equalled this rate *per hour*!

After the reconnaissance there was a rest period of a week, and then between 6 April and 14 April a reconnaissance in force was carried out, led again by Hsu Ching. The route up to the col was eased by fixed rope, ladders and crevasse bridges, ready for the main assault, and the ridge above was explored for about a thousand feet.

Once again the party withdrew to Base Camp, this time for eleven days. On the 25th the main assault party left base and four days later were established on the North Col, from where, on 29 April, they set out for their final assault.

At first the weather was fine, but when they had climbed some 1,300 ft up the ridge they were struck by a storm. Deep soft snow hindered their progress and the cold became numbing – 37°C below zero. They camped at 7,200 m. and were pinned down there all next day by fierce winds.[5]

For the next three days they continued their somewhat erratic progress up the ridge. On the first day they managed only 200 m. of ascent, but on the second and third day they achieved 500 m. and 400 m. respectively before pitching camp. From their account there is little to distinguish one day from another – there is no mention of the Yellow Band, for example, or the First Step. Nor is there any discussion over selection of route: Norton's Traverse is never mentioned and it seems that they were committed, either through choice or ignorance, to Mallory's line along the ridge crest.

On 3 May, leaving their three companions to establish a camp at 8,500 m., Shih Chan-chun and Wang Feng-tung pushed on a little further to the foot of the Second Step. This is a feature of the ridge which had to some extent dominated the plans of the pre-war British expeditions, making them prefer Norton's lower traverse line in an effort to avoid it, though nobody had actually ever got to grips with it, with the possible exception of Mallory on his ill-fated last attempt.

The two Chinese climbers found themselves facing a sheer rock wall about thirty metres high, which they eventually tackled by way of a narrow arete: 'We pressed on with great determination and care, boldly using the necessary mountaineering techniques,' wrote Shih Chan-chun, in what must surely be one of the most enigmatic climbing descriptions of all time.[6]

The top of the step was only 100 m. higher than their last camp, yet it took them the rest of the day and half the night to climb it. Even then they didn't quite reach the top: a smooth ten-foot wall barred the final part and the two climbers were forced into a miserable bivouac in a snow-filled crevice.

They had hoped to continue next day, reconnoitring a way to the summit, but though the weather was fine they must have been exhausted by their ordeal, for they decided to retreat. As on the previous occasions, everyone withdrew from the mountain to Base Camp.

Back at base there were signs of the advancing season which in turn meant the advent of the monsoon. Their excellent weather reports indicated that the period between 19 May and 25 May would be the last fine weather before the storms came, and so on 14 May they began the stocking of camps, right up to 8,500 m., with gear and supplies for the final assault.

On the morning of 24 May the summit party, consisting of Wang Fu-chou, Chu Yin-hua, Konbu (or Gonpa) and Liu Lien-man, left the top camp at 8,500 m. to make the final assault. They were using oxygen sets, as indeed had their predecessors at this height.[7]

Before long they came to the Second Step and climbed it until, like the reconnaissance team, they were stopped by the final three-metre wall. The wall was steep and rotten. Liu Lien-man tried four times to climb it, but each time fell off exhausted. After each fall it took him ten or fifteen minutes to recover, but after his fourth attempt he could try no more.

Chu Yin-hua took over the lead. He removed his boots and stockings and tried to climb the wall barefooted, but failed. Flurries of snow began to fill the air, and in desperation the climbers resorted to combined tactics:

> He crouched down slowly on a piece of rock, big enough for one person only, and offered Chu Yin-hua a leg up on his shoulders. At this altitude, even the slightest movement would consume a great deal of strength and energy. He trembled all over, short of breath, but he clenched his teeth and steadily stood up, with much heroic effort. Liu helped Chu Yin-hua to the top of the slab. Finally with the help of a rope paid out by Chu from above, the three others climbed up the cliff one after another. Only when they had all reached the top of the Second Step did they find that it had taken them three hours to climb this three-metre slab.[8]

Non-climbers may wonder that an obstacle rather less than ten feet high should cause such a problem, but it should be remembered that this obstacle was at a height above sea level of 8,600 m. and the climbers were encumbered with rucksacks, oxygen sets and bulky eiderdown suits. There is a world of difference between ten feet of rock by the roadside at Llanberis and ten feet of rock high on Everest.

Nevertheless, the time taken – three hours – does indicate a lack of experience and possibly technique. The Chinese ascent of the Second Step can be reckoned as a triumph of sheer determination. Unfortunately, no Western climber has ever had the opportunity of assessing the technical difficulties involved.

Having reached the top of the step the climbers found themselves confronting further difficulties. In the first place their oxygen supplies were running low and in the second place their team leader, Liu Lien-man, was too exhausted to continue:

> The three Communist Party members, Wang Fu-chou, Chu Yin-hua and Liu Lien-man, and Konbu, then held a brief Party group meeting. It was decided that the assault group should advance to the summit as quickly as possible and Liu Lien-man should remain where he was.[9]

Brief though this conference may have been, time seems to have flown by on this extraordinary climb. Darkness had begun to fall as the three remaining climbers crawled their way upwards, sometimes on all fours. Knee-deep snow hampered and exhausted them, and though the wind had dropped, a one-metre rock step defeated their tired efforts and delayed them for thirty minutes. Chu Yin-hua described the final few metres thus:

> It was getting darker and darker and we were getting weaker and weaker for every inch we made forward. Then we were confronted with another sheer icy cliff. We were forced to trudge along the northern slope, circle around the cliff westward toward the ridge in the north-west. We were just about to ascend when we discovered our oxygen reserves were all out! At that moment, we remembered the decision made at the Party meeting and Liu Lien-man's words of encouragement, which filled us with confidence to plant our national flag on the summit. We had already reached 8,830 metres above sea level and nothing would make us turn back! But our legs refused to carry us any further, so we had to go on all fours. Gonpa took the lead, and we two followed closely behind. Onwards, and onwards! We forgot time and cold. Suddenly we noticed Gonpa had disappeared. With a great surprise we looked upward. We spotted a shadow on top of the towering peak just a few metres away. It was Gonpa himself! We were overjoyed with excitement. Immediately, we forgot our fatigue, and great strength seemed to come back to us. When we went up to the top, we found there was another peak, still a few metres higher than the one we had just sur-

mounted. That was the highest point of Jolmo Lungma. Then we made our final assault with still greater exertion. Breathing became so difficult that each inch forward meant tremendous efforts. The last few metres of ascent took us no less than forty odd minutes.

At this time, we saw the star-studded sky above us on the top peak of Jolmo Lungma. To the south of the crest was gleaming white snow, and to the north was nothing but dull grey rocks. We stood on an oval-shaped space, the boundary line between the snow and the rocks.[10]

They had climbed through the night and reached the summit in the pre-dawn light. It had taken them nineteen hours, during which time they had had nothing to eat or drink.

Konbu took from his rucksack a Chinese flag and a small plaster bust of Mao Tse-tung which he placed on a large rock to the north-west of the summit and covered them with stones. Wang Fu-chou took out his diary and they signed their names: 'Wang Fu-chou [etc.] conquered Mt Jolmo Lungma 04.20 25 May 1960'. The page was torn out, placed in a glove, and buried amongst some stones. They collected nine rock specimens as a present for Chairman Mao and then, fifteen minutes after their arrival, began their descent.

The sky lightened as they descended and by the time they had reached 8,700 m. it was light enough to use the ciné camera they carried, and Chu Yin-hua turned round and took a few photographs. Soon afterwards they came upon Liu Lien-man (who must have had a terrible ordeal, huddled on the ridge throughout the night) and found that he had saved his oxygen for them – a gesture which moved them to tears.[11]

Five days later the whole expedition had withdrawn from the mountain and was back at Base Camp. Everest had been climbed from the north. Or had it?

Western experts had some misgivings. The Chinese account was as short on facts as it was long on rhetoric, a combination of generalities and propaganda which was bound to arouse suspicion. There were in fact several accounts of the climb given by the Chinese authorities to the Western newspapers and journals, all more or less identical, though purporting to be written by different members of the expedition. British climbers regarded the whole affair as a very rum show indeed, and polite doubts were expressed in the pages of the *Alpine Journal*, though nobody actually called the Chinese liars.

Like the Chinese themselves, their account of the expedition is inscrutable. It defies reasonable analysis because so much is left out, and some of what is included borders on the improbable. But not the impossible. We know now with more certainty that it *is* possible for men to climb Everest without oxygen as the Chinese claim to have done, that it *is* possible to survive an overnight bivouac high on the mountain as Liu Lien-man is said to have done, and given a clear night there is no reason why an ascent should not continue through the hours of darkness – it is seldom really dark in the mountains and pre-dawn starts are common enough in the Alps, often on terrain technically more difficult than Everest.

What made Western observers more suspicious of the Chinese claim than anything else, however, was the absence of summit photographs. If you reach the top in the dark, you can't take summit photographs, naturally – but also you can't take summit photographs if you don't reach the summit at all. Suspicious and sceptical minds put two and two together. Such pictures as the Chinese did produce were pored over intently, especially one taken by Chu Yin-hua at 8,700 m., a frame from the ciné film blown up and used as a magazine picture. A good deal of ingenious mathematical reasoning went into ascertaining where precisely the shot was taken from, using a map in reference to known peaks shown on the picture and comparing it with pre-war pictures taken by the British. Basil Goodfellow showed that it probably *was* taken at 8,700 m. as the Chinese claimed, though R.L.G. Irving showed that it was taken some 200 m. lower – at about the First Step on the ridge. It was Wager, however, who clinched the argument by using three photographs enlarged to the same scale: his own which he took in 1933 at the First Step, the Chinese picture, and one taken by Edmund Hillary from the summit in 1953. By identifying prominent features which were juxtaposed on the pictures Wager showed that the Chinese picture was taken from a point a little above the Second Step – or at 8,700 m. as the Chinese claimed.

If the Chinese had climbed the Second Step, as the picture indicated, there was no reason to suppose they hadn't reached the top – though some die-hards maintained that the picture could have been taken from an aircraft flying close to the ridge! Because the picture has no foreground this is conceivably true, though it would have required a very skilful and daring pilot to do it.

There seems little doubt now that the Chinese did climb Everest in 1960, though their account of the climb still contains some tantalizing mysteries. Why, for example, were they so slow? It took two hours to reach the Second Step from the assault camp, a mere seventy metres below it – an incredibly slow rate of about 115 ft per hour. It took a further five hours to climb the Step – thirty metres high – thus still further reducing the rate of ascent to about 55 ft per hour. On the descent, too, they seem to have been slow. One account mentions returning to the assault camp at 4 p.m., that is the descent took eleven and a half hours from the summit, which means they had been on the move for over thirty continuous hours. Furthermore, according to the account, *they continued their descent*. An absolutely marathon performance, especially when one realized that the party had come straight up the mountain from Base Camp in a single push. To Western climbers reading these accounts at the time, it all seemed a little bit too much.

Most tantalizing of all are the two significant gaps in the Chinese story. For example, once the assault camp had been established at 8,500 m. on 3 May why was there a sudden withdrawal from the mountain, followed by a hiatus not broken until supplies began to move up the mountain on 14 May? Then, too, what of the descent? Shih Chan-chun's account mentions nothing between the time the summit party were re-united with their patiently waiting comrade on the ridge, and arriving back in Base Camp five days later, yet we know from the Indian mountaineers who were on the South East Ridge at the same time as the Chinese were on the North, that the weather was bad on the 25th and the monsoon broke on the 26th. The Chinese say nothing of this, yet their descent from the roof of the world must have been an epic of endurance.[12]

The decade spanning the 1960s was a period of upheaval in China owing to the so-called Cultural Revolution, a reaffirmation of revolutionary fervour which had nothing to do with culture but which made the country more enigmatic than ever. The world relied on information supplied by the New China News Agency or the bevy of professional 'China Watchers' stationed in Hong Kong, who picked up what tit-bits they could. It is hardly surprising that little reliable news came out of such a situation: the truth was stranded somewhere between the Scylla of propaganda and the Charybdis of speculation.

During this decade the Chinese seem to have made two more attempts on Mount Everest.

In 1967 the German magazine *Alpinismus* reported that a Chinese expedition had been virtually wiped out while attempting Everest in 1966. Of twenty-six team members only two survived. The latter had returned to Base Camp half frozen owing to inadequate protective clothing and reported that the rest had gone on, stimulated by the thoughts of Chairman Mao. They were never seen again – 'the thoughts of Chairman Mao are no substitute for mountaineering skill and experience' commented the *Alpine Journal*.

The Chinese ignored these reports but issued a statement saying that a scientific expedition, to study solar radiation, was established on the North Col for one week during March 1966.

Then in May 1969 there was the curious expedition of the three surveyors Chen Chien-ming, Wang Ming-yuda, and Yen Tung-liang, who were determined to climb the world's highest peak: 'No matter how high the mountains,' they are quoted as saying, 'they are not as high as the fighting will of the revolutionary party of Surveyors and Cartographers, or the soaring thoughts of Chairman Mao.'[13]

Thus inspired they set out for Everest. Their first attempt was blighted when Wang Ming-yuda was taken ill and Yen Tung-liang suffered a heart attack. Both men retired to Base Camp for a further study of Mao's thoughts, which helped them to recuperate, but their companion, Chen Chien-ming, continued alone to the top where he 'hoisted the red banner of Chairman

Mao's thoughts on the world's highest peak'. Later, his two colleagues also climbed the mountain, apparently separately.

This story, which came from the New China News Agency, is completely unsupported by any corroborative details. If it is true (and one must gravely doubt it), it represents a remarkable leap forward in Himalayan mountaineering: three solo ascents of Everest, apparently without oxygen or any back-up facilities!

It was stories such as this, coming out of China in the 1960s, which did so much to discredit Chinese mountaineering in the eyes of the rest of the world's climbers. The boy who cried 'Wolf' too often was in the end not believed at all, and this was the fate of the Chinese, for in 1975 they did make a remarkable ascent of Everest – and nobody believed them. It was only when a British expedition climbed the mountain later in the same year and discovered the survey pole left behind by the Chinese that people sat up and took notice.

The expedition was a particularly large one, though the exact number of participants is unknown. It was charged with the double duty of making scientific observations and reaching the summit of Everest – whose name, for some reason, the Chinese had now changed to Qomolangma Feng.

It assembled at the Rongbuk monastery, Base Camp, in March and by the 20th of that month reconnaissance teams had reached the head of the East Rongbuk Glacier and the slopes leading to the North Col. They found the latter much changed since 1960:

> A steep glassy ice slope now blocked the way. Huge ice blocks from recent avalanches piled up at 6,800 m. and an ice wall criss-crossed with cracks stood at 6,900 m. right up to the top of the North Col. It meant the North Col had become more difficult to climb than fifteen years ago.[14]

Their first route on the slope was too steep to be a viable way for porters so they abandoned it and started to cut a zig-zag trail up some less steep slopes a little to the left. After an hour's work they had reached 6,800 m. and were taking a rest when one of their number, Pasang Tsering, fell into a crevasse and had to be hauled to safety, fortunately unhurt. Markers were left at the crevasse, and a metal ladder, as they continued their ascent.

By the time they reached the steep headwall of the col, the day was drawing to a close, and choosing a convenient ice ledge, they camped for the night. The temperature was −30°C.

At dawn next day they began their attack on the ice wall which they found to be about 150 ft high. Cutting their way up this they then found themselves faced by a wide crevasse at the top. Fortunately it was crossed by a snow bridge – a natural arch of snow and ice spanning the chasm. They used this to cross the gap, but then, fearing that it might not be strong enough for future use, they strengthened it with a couple of metal ladders lashed together with nylon rope and stiffened by struts made from ice axes. By noon they had reached the North Col, and their reconnaissance task was completed.

Between mid-March and mid-April the main body of climbers embarked on three acclimatization climbs. No details are given of where these climbs were, but the Chinese were obviously following tactics similar to those which brought them success in 1960 – gradual but rigorous acclimatization followed by a swift summit bid.

By late April a series of camps had been established on the mountain up to a final assault camp at 8,600 m. This was 100 m. higher than the equivalent camp of 1960, and was situated between the First and Second Steps. Later on, this top camp was moved higher still, to 8,680 m.[15]

These camps must have been large, and the stocking of them must have involved an army of porters (or 'Tibetan people in support of the Expedition' as the Chinese report euphemistically calls them), because what the Chinese had in mind was virtually a wholesale assault on the summit. When the first summit party left Base Camp on 24 April, to be followed two days later by a second group, there were at least forty climbers involved (thirty-three men, seven women), and as these were the ones who eventually passed the magic 8,000-m. mark it is reasonable to suppose there were others who dropped out along the way. It must have looked more like an attack on the Somme than an ascent of Everest!

Each group was in touch with Base Camp by radio, and was directed from there by the 'party committee of the expedition', who told them whether to advance or retreat.

The first group reached the North Col camp on the 27th and next day began ascending the ridge towards the camp at 7,600 m. A few hundred feet short of the camp, however, they were struck by a sudden and furious gale which made them bend double to keep their balance and threatened to hurl them off the mountain. Their colleagues, who had reached the lower camp at 6,500 m., were also struck by the same gale, which prevented them ascending to the col.

The committee back at Base Camp advised them to retreat to the camp at 6,000 m. to await the better weather which the forecasts predicted would shortly appear. However, this was easier said than done, and in the end the two teams were spread between the three camps at 6,000 m., 6,500 m. and 7,000m., where they remained trapped by storms for three days.

On 2 May the weather cleared and the committee ordered a general advance. By 4 May, thirty-three men and seven women had reached the camp at 8,200 m., and next day seventeen men and three women reached the summit assault camp at 8,600 m. Following their usual tactics of going straight through to the top the summit bid was scheduled for the next day, 6 May, but when dawn came the weather was very bad and the attempt was postponed for twenty-four hours. However, there was no let up in the weather and when

11.00 a.m. came and went, with no prospect of a summit bid, the committee ordered a general retreat back to Base Camp.

It was decided that before another summit attempt could be made some reorganization of the two top camps was needed. Consequently, the camp at 8,200 m. was lifted to 8,300 m., and that at 8,600 m. to 8,680 m. As a boost to morale at this time a special plane, ordered by the Central Committee in Peking, flew in with fresh fruit and vegetables. 'Fruits in hand, the mountaineers turned their hearts to Peking and cheered: "Long live the great leader Chairman Mao!" and "Long live the Chinese Communist Party!".'[17]

It was, one imagines, the latter-day equivalent of old General Bruce raising his glass of champagne and toasting the King.

On 17 and 18 May two more assault parties set out for the mountain. There were eighteen climbers, led by a twenty-nine-year-old Tibetan soldier called Sodnam Norbu, whose deputy was a thirty-seven-year-old Tibetan housewife and mother of three, Phantog. Together with their support groups, these reached the two camps at 8,300 m. and 8,680 m. on 25 May, by which time two women and seven men were too exhausted to continue. The committee decided that the remaining nine climbers should attempt the summit in two teams, each in turn.

The first rope, led by Sodnam Norbu, was to consist of three more Tibetans: Darphuntso, a thirty-year-old car body sprayer; Kunga Pasang, a twenty-nine-year-old soldier; and Tsering Tobgyal, a twenty-nine-year-old electrician. While they were making their ascent, the second rope would move up to the top camp from 8,300 m. and make their own attempt on the following day. The leader of this rope was Phantog, and the others were Lotse, a thirty-seven-year-old soldier and veteran climber who had been on the 1960 Everest expedition and the 1964 Shisha Pangma (Gosainthan) expedition; Hou Sheng-fu, a thirty-six-year-old climbing instructor who had also been on the 1960 and 1964 expeditions; Samdrub, a twenty-three-year-old soldier; and finally Ngapo Khyen, another soldier and at twenty-one the youngest member of the assault team. With the single exception of Hou Sheng-fu, all were Tibetans.

But once again the weather thwarted their plans. A gale-force wind on 26 May made a summit bid impossible. The committee at Base Camp, anxious now about the rapidly approaching monsoon, issued drastic orders. The first team was to prepare the Second Step for a rapid assault and the second team was to follow the original plan of going up to the top camp – that day, irrespective of weather. It was 3.30 p.m. before either team could venture out, but they followed their instructions and joined forces at the top camp at 9 p.m. that evening.

For Phantog's party in particular it must have been a gruelling day, battling up the ridge against the wind. Apart from the two young soldiers, however, it was a very experienced team, for besides the two Everest veterans Lotse and Hou Sheng-fu, Phantog herself had climbed Muztagh Ata (24,758 ft) and Kongur Tiube Tagh (24,924 ft).

At eight on the morning of the 27th, the nine climbers set out for the summit of Everest. By 9.20 a.m. they had climbed the Second Step and then stopped for ten minutes to inhale oxygen.[18]

Buffeted by strong winds and stung by flying spindrift the climbers struggled up the ridge. At 12.30 they were still some 200 ft from the summit when they found their way barred by an ice wall. They detoured round this 'to the north', climbed a rocky outcrop, then traversed 'westward'. This diversion took thirty minutes, and it was another hour and a half before they finally reached the top, where they planted the Chinese flag and the red-painted metal survey pole.[19]

They found the roof of the world to be a snowy platform about three feet wide and forty feet long. They remained there for seventy minutes, taking photographs and making scientific observations, before descending.

> At this time the base camp was resounding with cheers of 'Long live the great Leader Chairman Mao!' and 'Long live the great Communist Party of China!', and the beating of drums and gongs and the cracking of fireworks. Happy and excited, people hailed the great victory of Chairman Mao's proletarian revolutionary line, the fruitful achievements of the great Proletarian Cultural Revolution and the Movement to Criticize Lin Piao and Confucius and the tremendous success of conquering the summit of Qomolangma Feng.[20]

The 1975 Chinese expedition to the summit of Everest was a magnificent achievement – but was it mountaineering? Even stripped of the crude hyperbole and silly propaganda, there is that about the Chinese account of expeditions which rankles with the Western climber. He suspects their ethics and finds their tactics almost unbelievable.

It is true that there is no hint of the sporting ethic in Chinese climbing, judging by their own accounts, but as far as Everest is concerned this hardly matters. Nobody climbs Everest for fun, and conquest – or achievement, call it what you will – comes in many disguises. As for tactics, the Chinese undoubtedly have a system uniquely their own. Taught and then abandoned by the Russians, they had had to evolve their own methods, undoubtedly influenced by their interpretation of books written by members of the pre-war British expeditions to Everest – some of the parallels are quite striking. The result is their own brand of high-altitude climbing, solidly based on acclimatization. It is a tidal system: a series of waves, each one lapping the shore a little higher than the last: advance, withdraw, advance a bit further, withdraw again, and so on. Given enough climbers it contains within it the seeds of inevitable success or, if things go badly wrong, disaster on a terrible scale. It resulted in the great Chinese successes of 1960 and 1975; it might also have caused the tragedy of 1966, though we don't know this for sure.

It is not really surprising, given such methods, that the Chinese ascent of 1975 involved the largest group ever to tread the summit of Everest at one time, nor is it surprising that one of them was a woman. Alas for poor Phantog, she wasn't the first woman to reach the roof of the world – a Japanese housewife had beaten her to it by just a few days.

# 16

# West Side Story

The success of the British on Everest in 1953 established the pre-eminence of the large expedition, well equipped, supplied with oxygen and expensively funded, for the next quarter century. In this way all the remaining major Himalayan peaks were conquered in rapid succession, for where success (and particularly national success) is imperative, the end justifies the means. It was, and to a large extent still is, the accepted norm for tackling the highest mountain in the world.

At the same time there have been plenty of smaller expeditions tackling smaller, though perhaps technically more difficult, Himalayan climbs. Over the last decade in particular, the success of these teams has led to a questioning of Himalayan tactics: whether the massive build-up employing armies of porters, the inexorable pushing forward of camp upon camp, the hundreds of feet of fixed rope and the use of oxygen are necessary even for the highest peaks. Present-day climbers have demonstrated that the simple 'Alpine approach', whereby two men climb virtually as they would in the Alps, can be used even on the great 8,000-m. peaks.[1]

But none of this has so far influenced Everest. Simply because it is the highest mountain in the world, the summit of Everest remains something special. Against the Himalayan trend, expeditions to Everest seem to have got bigger rather than smaller, and much more expensive. This is particularly the case when there is some new objective in mind – the South West Face, for example – but it applies to the ordinary route up the South East Ridge as well. In these inflationary times, climbing Everest doesn't leave much change out of £100,000.

This will certainly alter. Even Everest cannot withstand the current mountaineering trends for ever, and in any case sheer economics will dictate the size of expeditions in the long run. But the expeditions from 1956 to 1978 were direct descendants of John Hunt's team. They were all big and expensive.

When the British climbed Everest in 1953, the French abandoned their plans for the following year: coming second, especially to the British, did not appeal to the Gallic temperament and in fact it was many years before a French mountaineer stood on the world's highest summit.

The next attempt on the mountain did not take place until 1956 and it was fitting justice that the successful team should be Swiss. It was a pre-monsoon expedition of ten men led by Albert Eggler, a noted Swiss climber.

They reached the South Col by the middle of May. At this point Eggler took a bold gamble – he decided that before attempting the South East Ridge of Everest, his leading team should face about and attempt the north ridge of Lhotse (27,890 ft), which formed the other side of the col. On 18 May Fritz Luchsinger and Ernst Reiss set out in gale-force winds to try Lhotse. They found the going was tough – extremely steep with hard ice and numerous cliffs and towers of rock – but they reached the summit at 3 p.m. It was a first ascent – and a fine consolation prize for the country that had so nearly been the first up Everest.

The Swiss then placed a high camp (27,550 ft) on the South East Ridge of Everest and on 23 May Ernst Schmied and Juerg Marmet reached the summit – the second ascent, and the first by Europeans. On the following day Adolf Reist and Hans Rudolph von Gunten also reached the summit, making the Swiss success a triumph.

Nowhere, apart from in Britain itself, did the ascent of Everest in 1953 have a greater impact than in India, whose middle and upper classes are, in some ways, more British than the British themselves. The fact that Tenzing took part in the first ascent was particularly fortuitous from their point of view, for although the Sherpa had been born in the Sola Khumbu region of Nepal he had lived most of his life in Darjeeling and was an Indian national. Inspired by this, the Indians founded the Himalayan Mountaineering Institute at Darjeeling (with Tenzing as Chief Instructor) and, in 1958, the Indian Mountaineering Federation.

The Federation was born out of a successful ascent of Cho Oyu (26,750 ft) which the Indians made in 1958. It is a Government-sponsored body, with the armed forces – whose traditions go back to the days of the Raj – providing many of its members, who might be expected to have the same affection for mountain exploration as many of their predecessors had. Himalayan adventure, especially the ascent of high peaks, is the Federation's sole purpose for existence. Within a few years of its foundation, Indians had climbed important peaks such as Annapurna III, Nanda Devi, Nilkanta and Panch Chuli, and had built up a formidable reservoir of talent and experience in high-altitude mountaineering.[2]

Within two years they were attempting Everest. The leader was Brigadier Gyam Singh, Principal of the Mountaineering Institute, and his deputy was K.F. Bunshah, who had led the successful assault on Cho Oyu. There were twenty-three team members in all, twelve of whom were climbers, the rest acting in the support roles of transport, signals and so on. They were accompanied by 800 porters – a formidable number.[3]

There had been very little time in which to organize the expedition. Ordnance factories were given the job of producing shirts and climbing breeches, while 500 lb. of wool from the Punjab was hastily distributed by Tenzing to the Nepalese community in Darjeeling with instructions for the women to start knitting stockings and pullovers!

Despite such an inauspicious beginning, the expedition made remarkably good time on the mountain. They reached the South Col barely a month after leaving Base Camp, but then bad weather struck. Nawang Gombu, Captain Narinder Kumar, and Sonam Gyatso reached Camp VII on the South East Ridge on 24 May and set out for the summit next day. However, at the foot of the South Summit, at about 28,300 ft, they gave up the struggle and returned wearily to camp. The weather remained bad, and a second assault team got no further than the South Col. Obviously, the monsoon had broken, and it was time to go home.

Two years later the Indians returned to the attack. It was another large-scale effort, this time led by Major John Dias. Like their predecessors they suffered from abominable weather, and it wasn't until 1 May that Camp VI was established on the South Col. Then, at this most crucial period before the monsoon, the weather closed in again and the first assault party was not able to occupy the col camp until 26 May.

All next day 70 m.p.h. winds battered the camp and made advance impossible, but on the 28th three men, helped by a support team, moved up the ridge and established Camp VII at 27,650 ft.

For Sonam Gyatso, the tough little Sherpa, this was the second time he had been within striking distance of the summit, for he was also one of the 1960 assault team. This time his companions were different: Hari Dang, and the bearded Mohan Kohli, an instructor-lieutenant in the Indian Navy and deputy leader of the expedition. They were desperately short of oxygen but the weather was bad on the 29th, so there was no chance of a summit attempt. To save oxygen they decided to use none at all during the day and only a little at night while they were confined to camp.

It was a miserable experience, but the next day dawned brighter and they set off for the summit full of hope. But they fared no better than their predecessors – the wind rose, and they were hampered by soft snow on the ridge. At 3.30 p.m. they turned back, having failed to reach the South Summit.

They had almost passed the point of no return. Lack of sleep and lack of oxygen had combined to bring about sheer physical exhaustion. Their descent had the qualities of a nightmare. Kohli described it:

> We were utterly exhausted. As we approached the steep slope at around 28,000 ft Sonam slipped taking with him Hari who was caught unaware. Like a driver who instinctively jams on his brakes at the slightest hint of an impending collision, I drove my ice axe into the ice which stopped our fall to the Western Cwm 7,000 ft below.
>
> At 8 p.m. it was pitch dark and we were nowhere near our tent. One can write a book on what happened during the next two hours. We knew that if we stopped here, we would be frozen to death. But in pitch dark it was not easy to move. At one time we almost said our last prayers. However, we did not really give up. We took the lead turn by turn, including Hari who was tied to the middle of the rope. At 10 p.m., crawling on all fours, we hit our tent.
>
> We could only manage to remove our crampons and slipped into our sleeping bags, without any food or liquid. In fact we were unconscious with exhaustion.[4]

It would be a mistake to think the Swiss and Indian attempts added nothing new to the fight for Everest simply because they were repeating the British route of 1953. Every expedition adds a little more to Man's knowledge of the mountain – and himself. This was particularly true of these early repeats. The Swiss, for example, found that they could lighten the design of the oxygen sets considerably – a big bonus for the climber. The Indians, because of the bad weather, pushed at the boundaries of our physiological knowledge, particularly in their second expedition. The summit team of Kohli, Sonam Gyatso and Hari Dang spent three consecutive nights at a height of 27,650 ft, much of the time without oxygen, and the preceding two nights on the South Col at 25,850 ft. The climber Gurdial Singh, together with a Sherpa, spent six consecutive nights at the South Col, mostly without oxygen, while one of the team doctors, Captain M.A. Soares, spent no fewer than forty-five consecutive days at Camp III (21,200 ft). Then, too, there was the astonishing exploit of the veteran Sherpa sirdar, Angtharkay, who at fifty-three carried a full load to Camp VII (27,650 ft). None of them suffered any permanent harm, yet only a few years earlier such exploits would have been thought highly dangerous.

Nevertheless, these climbs were repeats, or attempted repeats, of something which had already been accomplished. It was left to the Americans to come up with a quite different approach.

In the world of mountain climbing Norman Dyhrenfurth was the famous son of an equally famous father. The family were of Swiss origin, and Norman was educated in his home town of Zurich. Dyhrenfurth senior had led international expeditions to Kangchenjunga and the Baltoro in the 1930s and had written a number of authoritative books on the Alps and Himalaya, so it is not surprising that his son should have begun Alpine climbing at an early age and taken part in two expeditions to Alaska when he was only nineteen – on one of which he was co-leader. He became a professional explorer and film-maker.

His first introduction to the Himalaya was in 1952, when he took part in the abortive post-monsoon attempt by the Swiss. Three years later he was back for an unsuccessful attempt on Lhotse, then he took part in the 1958 search for the Yeti, and finally was on the brilliantly executed Swiss ascent of Dhaulagiri (26,811 ft), sixth highest mountain in the world and at that time the highest to be attained without oxygen. All the same, it was Everest that counted most, and he had resolved to go back to that mountain to try again.

He began planning from the moment of the Swiss defeat. He resigned his job as Head of the Motion Picture Division of the Department of Theater Arts, University of California at Los Angeles, to go freelance and thus provide himself with the opportunity to do more exploration and to devote more time to raising money for his Everest dream. It was frustrating, unrewarding work: no sooner had he begun than John Hunt's team climbed the mountain, and the Indian Air Force flew over it to record a series of dazzling pictures. Everest had been 'done': there was nothing to be gained by climbing it again, so far as the tycoons of American industry were concerned – and since they were the people who would have to finance the project, the outlook for Dyhrenfurth seemed bleak.

Eight years of dreaming slipped by before Dyhrenfurth realized that, unless he took some positive step, the idea of an American Everest expedition would remain a dream forever. Gambling that everything would come right in the end, in 1960 he boldly applied to Kathmandu for permission to climb Everest the following year. This was refused, and the Indians had the mountain for 1962, but he was given a chance for the following year, 1963. This meant that Dyhrenfurth had almost three years in which to plan the expedition – and he needed all the time he could get.[5]

Although the people who controlled the purse strings of America's vast wealth were apathetic to mountain adventure, Dyhrenfurth realized that if only he could arouse their interest the money for his expedition would be forthcoming. He also understood the American mentality and the value of the hard sell. He knew that to try economies – to mount a small, inexpensive expedition – would be courting not only failure on the mountain, but financial failure as well. To catch the eye of the nation (and tug its purse strings) his proposals had to be big, bold and beautiful.

He announced that the forthcoming Everest expedition would cost a staggering 186,000 dollars. It would be a big team to do a big job. The American climbing establishment was shocked, and Charles Houston, who had led American attempts on K2 and was an old ally of Bill Tilman, charged Dyhrenfurth with a violation of the true spirit of mountaineering. Nick Clinch, another former expedition leader, told Dyhrenfurth dryly: 'You don't even have to climb the mountain: you'll deserve a medal for just raising the dough.'[6]

But Dyhrenfurth knew what he was about: and there is nothing like controversy for catching the public interest. The man in the street loves to take a peek at the in-fighting between members of an esoteric, exclusive group like mountain climbers. Equally controversial, among the climbers themselves, was Dyhrenfurth's insistence that this was to be an all-American show. Many felt that nationalism had no place in mountaineering.[7]

Even so the money was slow coming in. 'The raising of money for an Everest expedition proved only slightly less difficult than, say, soliciting funds for a statue of Karl Marx on the White House lawn,' wrote Ullman, the expedition biographer.[8]

Undoubtedly, the underlying cause of this was that the American public had no inherent national sympathy for mountain climbing, unlike the Alpine countries of Europe, or the British, who had invented the sport. In those countries there was something akin to understanding, and though the man in the street might on the whole consider it a reckless risk to life, he acknowledged that it was something which had to be done. There was no such acceptance in America. Dyhrenfurth had two Everests to climb.

He might never have made it had not the National Geographic Society stepped in. Like its British counterpart, the Royal Geographical Society, the National Geographic is a prestigious society devoted to the advancement of geographical knowledge. It publishes a well-known and highly profitable magazine, and it has considerable resources available for geographical research. In the past it had helped to finance Peary and Byrd in polar exploration, but it had never backed a mountaineering venture. Now it decided to help Dyhrenfurth – but not without strings. The strings were precisely those which the Royal Geographical Society had attached to the first British Everest expedition, namely, that there must be a *scientific* content to the expedition. Climbing the mountain would not be enough.

Dyhrenfurth was astute enough to realize that such a condition would be attached and he was prepared for it. He knew the dangers of splitting his team into small groups, each pursuing its own speciality and oblivious of the common need, so he worked out a plan in which all the scientific work would be concerned with the climbing of the mountain and all, or nearly all, the scientists would be mountaineers. It was a shrewd move: never in recorded history has there been a scientist-mountaineer who would put his science first and the mountain second. But it convinced the National Geographic Society, who gave Dyhrenfurth 114,000 dollars.

This was, of course, the cornerstone of financial viability for the Americans, though it was a mixed blessing. Because they were now committed to scientific research as well, the original budget of 186,000 dollars was quite insufficient, and eventually the cost of the expedition rose to the staggering sum of 400,000 dollars. As with all expeditions some of this came in the form of free equipment, food and services – about 70,000 dollars' worth.

Besides raising money, Dyhrenfurth had also to raise a team. It had to fulfil the dual role imposed upon it by the National Geographic: to be experienced and strong enough to climb the mountain, and at the same time be sufficiently well qualified to undertake the scientific programme. Under such conditions it is hardly surprising that Dyhrenfurth's team was the most academically brilliant ever to set foot on Everest: of the twenty members finally selected there were five with Doctorates and eight with Master's degrees. Only two were non-graduates.

As his second-in-command, Dyhrenfurth chose Dr William E. Siri, a physiologist from the University of California, whose job it was to co-ordinate the scientific programme. He was forty-four years old, small, wiry and bespectacled – 'looking every inch the research scientist'. He had considerable mountaineering experience and had been on five overseas expeditions (three as leader), including an attempt on Everest's neighbour, Makalu.

Of the rest, the oldest by far was James Ramsey Ullman, fifty-five, the doyen of American mountain writers, best known for his novels *The White Tower* and *Third Man on the Mountain*, both of which had been filmed by Hollywood. He was the official biographer of the expedition whose job it was to write both an account for *Life* magazine and the definitive expedition volume. Though a climber, he was not expected to go beyond Base Camp, and in the event was prevented by illness from going much beyond Kathmandu.[9]

The remaining members of the huge team were: Allen C. Auten (36), Barry C. Bishop (31), John E. Breitenbach (27), James Barry Corbet (26), David L. Dingman (26), Daniel E. Doody (29), Richard M. Emerson (38), Thomas F. Hornbein (32), Luther G. Jerstad (26), James Lester (35), Maynard M. Miller (41), Richard Pownall (35), Barry W. Prather (23), Gilbert Roberts (28), William F. Unsoeld (36) and James W. Whittaker (34). In addition, there was one British member: Lt Col. Jimmy Roberts (45), who was the transport officer, lived in Nepal and had considerable expedition experience, including the successful Hunt expedition to Everest in 1953.

Dyhrenfurth's anxiety over fund-raising had not only led him into accepting the scientific chores imposed by the National Geographic Society but also into widening his original objective. Everest by itself lacked public appeal, so he turned to the idea of doing 'The Grand Slam' – Everest, Lhotse and Nuptse, three of the highest mountains in the world.

Everest and Lhotse had both been climbed by the Swiss expedition in 1956, and it must have seemed a good idea to Dyhrenfurth to add Nuptse to the bag, making a clean sweep of the three great peaks which encircle the Western Cwm. It was the sort of package deal he felt he could sell to the American public. In the end, his problem was that he couldn't sell it to his climbers.[10] They were much more interested in another idea of Dyhrenfurth's: an attempt on the unclimbed West Ridge of Everest, first discussed among themselves during a training session on Mount Rainier. It wasn't until they reached Chaubas, on the walk-in, that a final decision was made. Dyhrenfurth recorded in his diary:

> Now that we have no more 'camp followers', we talked very frankly about the thing that had been on the minds of all the climbers: the West Ridge, which, if we can pull it off, would be one of the biggest things in Himalayan mountaineering. It was interesting to see how highly motivated the whole group was. There was comparatively little interest in Lhotse and Nuptse although I had explained to them that initially, when we were trying to raise funds, the idea of an American 'Grand Slam' of three peaks had its appeal. But to most of the men that meant very little. In fact, Tom Hornbein, who is such an idealist and so enthusiastic about the idea, declared himself in favour of throwing everything into the West Ridge attempt, even if it meant jeopardizing success altogether. At this point I had to speak up strongly. I told them that I was in favour of making a serious stab at the West Ridge, or at least a thorough reconnaissance. If it proved feasible, we would push up a line of camps, but at the same time we would build up the South Col route. We might possibly make the main attempt over the West Ridge, but as a back-up we would have a four-man assault with support team from the South Col, so that we can be sure – or as sure as one can be – of success on a mountain such as Everest. If the West Ridge proves impossible, we will at least have taken some good pictures of the Tibetan side of Everest from an entirely new point of view. But if the ridge is possible, we could attempt a traverse by having some men go up from the West and come down toward the South Col, and two – or perhaps four – do the same in reverse. That of course would be almost too much to hope for. In any case it was agreed that we should certainly make a stab at Lhotse as well, oxygen and other logistics permitting . . .[11]

It was a momentous decision. It turned what might have been just another Everest expedition into the greatest mountaineering feat of the decade. And it was primarily all down to one man: the slightly balding, ex-Navy doctor, Thomas F. Hornbein.

Tom Hornbein was thirty-two. He had first qualified as a geologist before turning to medicine, where he quickly became an expert in anaesthetics (and consequently was in charge of oxygen during the expedition). After a lectureship at Washington University he joined the U.S. Navy as a lieutenant, and was still a serving officer when Dyhrenfurth managed to secure his premature release in time for the Everest adventure. He had started climbing at the age of fourteen in his native Colorado and had climbed in many parts of the United States. In 1960 he had taken part in the successful American ascent of Masherbrum, a notable peak in the Karakorum, though he wasn't a member of the summit party. Slight, not very tall, and with an elfish face, he was not much like the popular conception of a mountain climber.

On the other hand, Hornbein's boon companion did look like a climber. Though not over tall (he was 5ft 10 ins.), thirty-six year-old Willi Unsoeld was solidly built. He held degrees in physics, theology and philosophy and was also a qualified professional mountain guide in the Tetons of Wyoming. He was a man utterly devoted to the hills and he had already participated in three previous Himalayan expeditions, including the one with Hornbein to Masherbrum, where he had made the first ascent.[12]

Dyhrenfurth's original idea regarding the West Ridge had been to use it as a means of descent after climbing the mountain by the usual South East Ridge, thus making what climbers call a traverse – up one side and down another – but his companions thought this was too risky. Who wants to risk their lives on an unknown and probably difficult descent after climbing Everest? If anything went wrong – if the descent proved too difficult – there could be no going back.

Hornbein turned the idea around, making it more feasible – up the West Ridge and down the South East Ridge. And he was for throwing everything they had into this attempt – he could see little value in merely repeating Hunt's original climb. On this Dyhrenfurth had to disagree. He had to think of the wider implications of such a decision. In the first place, though the world of mountaineering might acknowledge that failure on the West Ridge was more worthy than success on the normal route, the world in general certainly would not. To them, failure was failure, no matter how it came about. The American public, not to mention the sponsors, who had poured thousands of dollars into the project, would ask some very awkward questions if the team returned empty-handed. Once again the Everest syndrome dominated the tactics: on any other mountain it wouldn't have mattered – but Everest is Everest and national pride is involved.

There was another consideration too. Not all the team were interested in the West Ridge. Some saw it as a threat to their scientific programmes; others, reflecting the view of the general public, thought that nothing should be allowed to jeopardize the attempt to get to the top by the only known and tried route.

Apart from Dyhrenfurth himself the leader of the anti-ridge faction was James W. Whittaker, a mountain guide from Mount Rainier and manager of a sports equipment shop in Seattle. Big Jim, as he was universally known, was thirty-four years old, 6ft 5ins. tall and over 14 stones in weight. His features were the handsome, clean-cut lines of the archetypal all-American hero. He was immensely strong, and kept in trim during the walk-in by doing fifty or sixty push-ups at the end of each day's trek. And with all this went a singular determination. During the pre-expedition check-ups, when psychologists had asked each member of the team whether they would get to the top of Everest, they had all demurred, hesitating to commit themselves. Only Big Jim had replied instantly, 'Yes I will!'

Dyhrenfurth was no autocrat – which was perhaps as well considering the team of highly intellectual rugged individualists he had at his command. He tended to let things evolve, and by the time the expedition reached Thyangboche two teams – the 'West Ridgers' and the 'South Collers' – had polarized. The former comprised Hornbein, Unsoeld, Bishop, Breitenbach, Corbet, Dingman and Emerson, the latter, Dyhrenfurth, Siri, Whittaker, Jerstad, Pownall and Gil Roberts. The remaining members decided to support both teams as necessary. There was, inevitably, a certain amount of friction between the two groups, usually with Unsoeld, the philosopher, trying to calm things down. In effect, Dyhrenfurth was now leading *three* expeditions: the West Ridgers, the South Collers, and the scientists – and it was his fervent hope that they would not pull apart and disintegrate into total failure.

The two climbing groups naturally tended to be based on old friendships: Hornbein and Unsoeld on the one hand, Whittaker and Jerstad on the other. Hornbein called them the rock climbers (West Ridge) and the ice climbers (South Col) and looking at the home backgrounds of the men involved this seems fair enough. He also thought there were more fundamental philosophical differences – that the South Collers had all at some time taken part in competitive sports, whereas the Ridgers had not. In this he was hinting at a more fundamental difference: which is more important, the prize or the winning of it?

These then were the individuals who tramped the long trail to Base Camp. They were the spearhead of a vast army, whose corps consisted of thirty-two Sherpas (later thirty-seven) and 909 porters, the latter carrying 29 tons of food and equipment, broken down into 65-lb. loads.

The expedition left Kathmandu on 20 February and established Base Camp at 17,800 ft on the Khumbu Glacier on 21 March. It had been an exceptionally early start, allowing them time for a leisurely approach march, especially above Namche Bazar, where acclimatization was important. They had paid for this by encountering a blizzard at Thyangboche and a snow blanket in the upper Khumbu valley, but there were no serious hitches and they found a good camp site on the glacier.

On the very next day, the reconnaissance of the Icefall began. For this important task Dyhrenfurth chose a strong team – Willi Unsoeld, Jim

Whittaker and Lute Jerstad, accompanied by three experienced Sherpas, Gombu, Nima Tenzing and Passang Temba.

One of the problems about threading a way up an icefall, and particularly an icefall as big and complicated as the Khumbu, is that the climbers can seldom see more than a few feet in any direction. It is like being in an ice-maze, with tunnels and cracks running in every direction, any one of which might lead to an easy route, or to nowhere. The climbers have to probe ahead, relying on a mixture of luck and experience. They have also to keep in mind the dangers of the relentlessly grinding ice, and all too often routes that seem easy have to be rejected because they are threatened by tottering ice pinnacles, or are obvious avalanche chutes. The experience of others is no guide, for even if an icefall – such as the Khumbu – has been climbed many times, each season the ice has moved and the whole scene is different. On some occasions the route-finding may be easier than on others, but it is invariably time-consuming.

Dyhrenfurth, however, had an ingenious aid to help overcome the Icefall. He knew that a man standing well back from the scene of action, able to view the whole tumbling mass, could trace out possible lines of ascent. If he was able to communicate this knowledge to the men actually engaged on breaking the trail, their job would be much simpler.

Consequently, Dyhrenfurth, Siri and a Sherpa climbed some way up the lower slopes of the Lho La where they could command a view of the Icefall and see the climbers at work. By two-way radio he directed Unsoeld's team on the best line, and consequently the Icefall party found a route that took them two thirds of the way to the top on their first attempt. Here, on a ledge, they made a cache of equipment before returning to Base Camp, it being Dyhrenfurth's policy not to site an intermediate camp in the Icefall itself.

On the following day a team was sent out to improve the route so far pioneered. It consisted of Jake Breitenbach, Dick Pownall and Gil Roberts, with the Sherpas Ang Pema and Ila Tsering. By about 2 p.m. they had reached the thirty-foot ice wall which was the final obstacle below the gear cache. Pownall was in the lead, with Ang Pema behind him and Breitenbach, third man on the rope, waiting in a gully below the cliff. Roberts and Tsering were on a separate rope, about forty feet away.

Roberts was watching Pownall climb when suddenly he heard a deep rumbling noise which turned into a terrifying roar as a whole top section of the ice cliff – 'about the size of two railroad cars one on top of the other' – peeled away. Caught by the blast he was blown backwards and slid thirty or forty feet, but managed to pick himself up, unhurt. His companion, too, was uninjured. Hastily they scrambled up to see what had become of the other rope.

A pile of ice debris marked the scene of the fall. The three men had disappeared.

Searching desperately, Roberts was relieved to discover Dick Pownall alive but almost buried. His chest was pinned by an enormous ice block and it took ten minutes' hard work with the ice axes before he could be dragged free. Miraculously, he wasn't seriously injured. Of the other two there was at first no sign, but a low moan suddenly indicated someone buried deeper in the ice. Attacking the debris, Roberts and Ila Tsering eventually came across Ang Pema, lying upside down, his rucksack grotesquely jammed up behind his neck. When they dragged him free he was found to have a nasty head wound and a dislocated shoulder.

But of Jake Breitenbach there was no sign. He had been standing at the bottom of the wall in a narrow gully, and now that gully was choked with hundreds of tons of ice fragments. He must have been killed instantly.

The mood in the American Base Camp that night was one of shock and grief. In the following two days the shock was replaced by despair. The inter-group rivalries between the Ridgers and the Collers were forgotten and there was a serious discussion about abandoning any idea of the West Ridge. Many would have abandoned the whole expedition had they not felt so indebted by all the hundreds of thousands of dollars which had put them there. Now they just wanted to make a rapid ascent of the ordinary route to honour that debt, then quickly depart.

The Sherpas, of course, couldn't understand what all the fuss was about. As Buddhists, they believed in reincarnation, so that death was only a transitional phase – a philosophy which made the Americans angry and caused a temporary hiatus in the relationships between the sahibs and porters.

But of course the Sherpas were in a sense right. Tragic though it was, the death of Breitenbach could be seen as merely an unfortunate accident; and not entirely unexpected in such dangerous circumstances. Indeed, there is much to be said for the view that the only justification for Breitenbach's death was that the expedition *should* go on.

There was one unpleasant statistic. This was the eighth expedition to attempt the notorious Khumbu Icefall: literally hundreds of climbers and porters had been up and down through those dangerous towers of ice since 1951, and not one had been killed or even seriously injured. Breitenbach was the first to die there.

Once the expedition got going again, death in the Icefall was never far from their thoughts. Gil Roberts probably summed up the general feeling when he said, 'I'll go through the Icefall twice – once up and once down.' And there were some near misses. Hornbein later recalled one such incident shortly after Camp I had been established at the entrance to the Western Cwm on 30 March. The final obstacle had been an ice wall:

> On April 2, Pownall, Dick and I were preparing to descend from Camp I

> to sculpt the upper part of this wall into a form more reassuring to laden porters. For some reason Pownall asked for a delay. Twenty minutes later, as we stood outside our tents roping up, the mountain started coming apart. The rolling boom drew our eyes to the chaotic dissolution of the ice canyon just below. Two hundred yards away, towers began to topple, walls sagged into rubble. In a chain reaction, the gigantic breaker curled towards us. I stood transfixed, unconsciously bracing myself against the moment our camp should become part of it. Thick clouds rose from the cauldron, ice particles shimmering like tiny diamonds before the hidden sun, then settling as dust upon our camp. When the air had cleared, the camp had not moved.[13]

Had they not been delayed, all three would have been crushed and buried beneath the crashing ice blocks.

2 April was also the day on which Camp II was established in a hollow of the Western Cwm, at 21,350 ft. It was virtually the same site as Hunt's Camp IV, and like that camp it became the Advanced Base. Most of the expedition's material and men were to move up to this camp in the ensuing weeks, and it was from here that the twin assaults on the mountain – via the West Ridge and the South Col – were to be mounted.

It was not achieved without a certain amount of friction. The science and the climbing began to conflict, despite Dyhrenfurth's well-laid plans, and there was also Sherpa trouble, which, though not serious, disturbed the even tenor of the expedition.

It was mostly the Americans' own fault. Brought up in a mountaineering tradition where every man carries his own heavy pack into the wilderness, and in a nation where Jack is as good as his master, they could never quite stomach the seeming servility of the East. Much to the disgust of the Sherpas, expedition members carried their own heavy loads – often as much as 75 lb. – even though the Icefall, and though they excused this on the grounds of having to 'keep fit', one is bound to ask, fit for what? Was it a misplaced American sense of guilt – a straining to demonstrate equality?

There is no doubt that the Sherpas regarded the Americans as a soft touch. They wrung from them extra pay in lieu of double sleeping bags, even though the single bag they were given was of a quality superior to that of most double bags, and, more serious, they had a habit of turning up at Advanced Base with less than full loads, thus necessitating extra carries. Had firmness been applied from the start things might have been better, but the Americans by their very upbringing lacked the qualities of a *pukka sahib*.

There was even trouble between the Sherpas themselves, four of whom were expatriates living in Darjeeling, while the rest were local men from the Khumbu. The latter were undoubtedly jealous of the more sophisticated

Darjeeling men, particularly as two of them, Gombu and Ang Dawa, were blatantly treated more favourably by the Americans.

The problem was that a Khumbu Sherpa named Pasang Phutar had been foisted on the expedition as sirdar, or chief Sherpa. They had accepted him because most of their Sherpas were Khumbu men and it seemed the diplomatic thing to do, even though he did not acclimatize well and in the event never got beyond Camp I. He was, in fact, a sort of figurehead without any real authority – the real sirdar in all but name was the tough, thrusting Gombu.[14]

The Khumbu men were not fools and knew very well what was going on, and resented it, just as they resented the favouritism shown to Ang Dawa, who was Dyhrenfurth's personal Sherpa.

Mostly these feelings were undercurrents which did not materially affect the progress of the expedition: background unpleasantness which stretched the already taut nerves of the expedition members.

If the Americans were weak on personal relations, they made up for it in technology. At Base Camp they had a main radio transceiver and no less than eleven walkie-talkies directing the flow of material through the Icefall to Advanced Base.

From Advanced Base the two factions of the expedition separated. The South Collers, following the established pattern, planned to push straight ahead up the Cwm, climb the Lhotse Face, traverse left to reach the South Col and from there go up the South East Ridge. The West Ridgers, on the other hand, planned to turn left from the camp, try to reach the West Shoulder and from there push up the West Ridge. The difficulty was that from the moment one expedition became two there was fierce competition for priority in men and materials.

According to Dyhrenfurth's compromise plan, the reconnaissance of the West Ridge was to take priority once Advanced Base was established. Only in this way could he quieten the vociferous demands of Hornbein and the quieter insistence of Unsoeld. Whittaker and the other South Collers went along with it – a reconnaissance could do no harm to the basic impetus of the expedition and it would take some of the steam out of Hornbein to let him exhaust himself on the steep unknown slopes leading to the West Shoulder. Once this little *divertissement* was out of the way, they thought, the expedition could get on with its real job of climbing the mountain – via the South Col.

Hornbein saw it differently. He intended to reconnoitre the West Ridge all the way to the summit.

Despite their first claim on food and equipment, all was not well with the West Ridgers. Their team had been seriously depleted: Breitenbach was dead, Emerson and Corbet had failed to acclimatize. This left Hornbein, Unsoeld, Bishop and Dingman – and even Dingman was not completely fit. Thin resources for tackling an unknown route on the highest mountain in the world – and for fighting off the persistent demands of the powerful South Col faction.

But Hornbein and Unsoeld were two exceptional men. They were determined, intelligent and tough. Both were exceptionally hard goers, and when together on the mountain they not only tended to 'burn off' everyone else within sight, but tried it on each other as well.

Unsoeld in particular went like a steam engine. On the walk-in he had confided to Hornbein that he was worried about his forthcoming performance, that his age might tell against him – he was thirty-six, four years older than Hornbein. But Hornbein knew Willi Unsoeld only too well – he had climbed with him on Masherbrum – and put this down to his friend trying a bit of one-upmanship. He was right. Later he wrote:

> I seemed to be going as strongly as any but the incredible Unsoeld, who appeared to have gone manically awry, threatening to demoralize the Expedition by his extreme hyper-activity, hyper-optimism, and seeming indestructibility.
>
> ... What was Willi trying to prove? Soloing half the Icefall unroped and beneath an 80 pound load, for example? Was this his way of leading us all back into the fray again after Jake's death? If so, it must be lonely out there in the front, shouting 'Charge!' to a contingent out of earshot.
>
> ... Most of us didn't need such a boost. Some were more cowed than invigorated by Willi's energy, asking themselves, 'How can we hope to keep up with that?' Finally, Dick and I hauled him aside:
>
> 'Slow down, Willi, you're demoralizing half the Expedition.'[15]

He wasn't demoralizing Hornbein, as Unsoeld well knew. After one particular session when they were roped together with Unsoeld out in front going like a rocket, Hornbein cried in exasperation, 'Damn it, Willi, what are you trying to do?'

Unsoeld smiled and said, 'Just testing you.'

'For what?'

'Bigger things.'[16]

As Dyhrenfurth and the South Collers were to discover, opposition means nothing to men like these. It only steels their resolve. Numbers don't count.

The West Ridge reconnaissance began on 3 April, when Unsoeld and Barry Bishop investigated the steep slopes leading to the West Shoulder. It was the first time anyone had been on that part of the mountain, so they didn't know quite what to expect. However, they found it reasonable going and managed to ascend 1,000 ft before retreating to Advanced Base.

Two days later it was Hornbein's turn, again with Bishop. They reached the previous high point then traversed left across some slopes of steep ice until

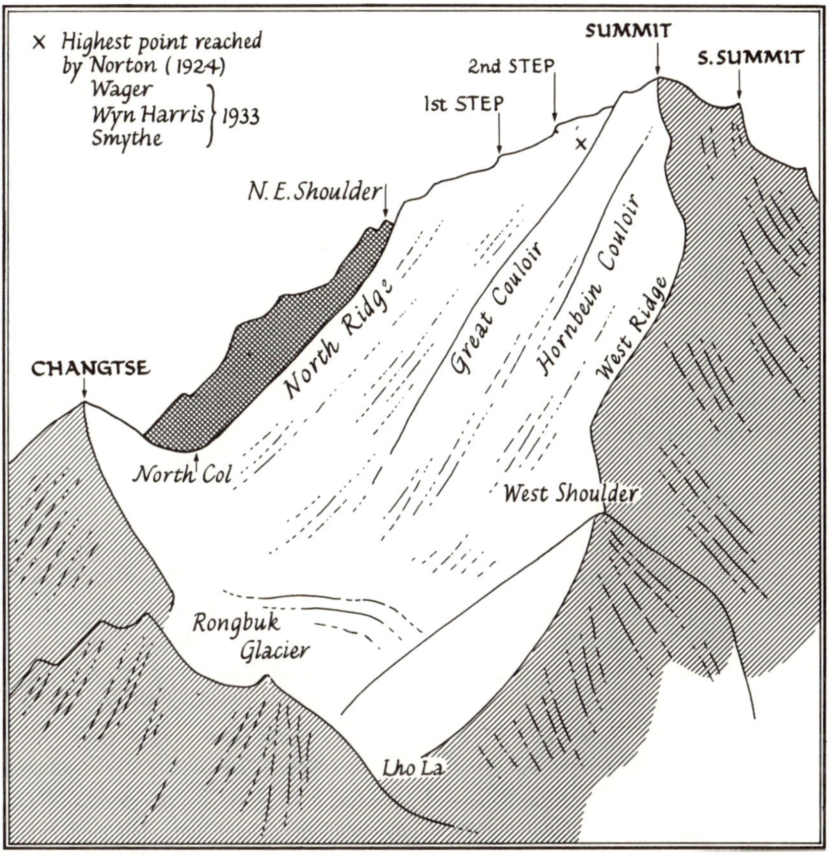


Fig. 3 The West Ridge

they reached a place where it was easier to climb upwards. The climbing was mostly on snow slopes of 35° to 45°, with some outcropping rock near the top where the slope eased off to form the rounded bulk of the West Shoulder. At 3.30 p.m. the two men reached a height of 23,500 ft. Above them bulged the Shoulder, and no more discernible problems. They had opened the way to the West Ridge.

Hornbein and Bishop returned to Advanced Base elated. With a little preparation the way to the Shoulder could be made safe for porters and a camp established there. Such a camp would be roughly equivalent to the South Col camp of the ordinary route and serve the same purpose, that is, as a springboard for the final assault on the ridge.

On the 7th Hornbein and Bishop, with seven Sherpas, established a staging camp above the initial slopes, just before the traverse. The Sherpas went down again, but the two climbers stayed the night and were joined next day by Unsoeld and Dingman, accompanied by the same seven Sherpas. They had planned to push the route out to the Shoulder, but the weather was too bad – there were high winds – so once again the Sherpas went down, to return for a third time on the following day when the weather was better.

The staging camp was struck and the eleven men, each bearing a heavy load, advanced across the traverse and up the slopes to the Shoulder. Here, at 23,800 ft, just below the crest, they made Camp 3W (W for West Ridge, to distinguish it from the Camp 3 of the South Collers). The Sherpas again returned to Advanced Base, leaving the climbers to continue the reconnaissance of the ridge.[17]

On the next day the four men reached the crest of the Shoulder, but what should have been a spectacular view, down to the Rongbuk Glacier on the one hand and the Western Cwm on the other, was obscured by curtains of mist which drifted around, offering them only the briefest of glimpses. The following day they had better luck. Hornbein wrote:

> On the 11th we got away an hour earlier. At the Shoulder the mountain waited, fully assembled. The cloud cauldron of the great South Face boiled, accentuating the black, twisting harshness of the West Ridge. We stared. Yesterday's fragments had not exaggerated. Our eyes climbed a mile of sloping sedimentary shingles, black rock, yellow rock, grey rock, to the summit. The North Col was a thousand feet below us across this vast glacier amphitheatre. As we stood where man had never stood before, we could look back into history. All the British attempts of the twenties and thirties had approached from the Rongbuk Glacier, over that Col, on to that North Face. The Great Couloir, Norton, Smythe, Shipton, Wager, Harris, Odell, our boyhood heroes. And there against the sky along the North Ridge, Mallory's steps.[18]

Above the Shoulder the West Ridge formed a snowy crest for a short distance and then reared up in a twisting edge of dark rock, formed by the meeting of the North and South West Faces of the mountain, the latter being much the steeper of the two. If the climbers were forced off the crest of the ridge, there would be no escape for them that way: obstacles would have to be turned on the left, on the North Face.

Technically, of course, the left-hand side of the ridge was in Communist Tibet, but that hardly concerned the climbers: they were unlikely to be disturbed by the Chinese border guards at 25,000 ft! What did concern them was the North Face, with its notorious outward-sloping slabs which they could now see in all their chaotic malevolence, like stacks of tottering roof tiles, showing like black teeth through an overburden of snow. Any diversions from the ridge would mean venturing onto those.

And a diversion seemed necessary almost immediately. The initial part of the rock ridge looked much too formidable for direct assault, although a detailed scrutiny would be required to be sure of this. Bishop and Dingman were dispatched to look more closely at the start of the ridge, while Hornbein and Unsoeld set about finding an alternative route.

A vertical streak of snow, discernible from a distance, had been noted by Hornbein as a possible way up and had been christened 'Hornbein's Couloir'. This looked as though it would help them to by-pass the ridge where necessary, though to reach it would mean traversing out across the tile-like slabs of the face.

In the event, neither party got far. The mist boiled up again, preventing the climbers from seeing their objectives, so they returned to Camp 3W.

That evening they mulled over their chances disconsolately. The formidable crest of the ridge, and the disconcerting alternative over the North Face slabs, seemed too difficult for laden porters, and porters would be necessary to put assault camps higher up if the summit was to be achieved. With a large expedition concentrating all their efforts on the ridge such an ascent might be possible, but the chances of a small splinter group like themselves achieving success were remote. Dingman was for giving up the attempt forthwith, the other three wanted just one more try. They left it to the weather to decide.

Dingman was still suffering acclimatization problems, so, when the morning of the 12th turned out to be fine, he remained at Camp 3W while Hornbein, Bishop and Unsoeld prospected up the ridge again. By 1 p.m. they had reached their highest point of the previous day. Light snow began to fall and the mists started to build up again, but the three men determined to press on until they reached the place where the rock ridge proper began. They felt that they owed themselves at least that much.

It was 4 p.m. when they reached the rock. A snow-filled diagonal depression, which they had noticed the previous day as a possible way to reach Hornbein's Couloir, ran up into the thickening mist above them. It didn't seem too difficult – but that would be for another day to decide. For the present they had reached the limit of their reconnaissance and their resources. They had climbed to 25,100 ft and there, at the foot of the final ridge, they had discovered a perfect site for Camp 4W – should there ever be a full-scale assault. Hornbein and Unsoeld were determined that there would be.

The four men returned to Advanced Base on 13 April. Their reconnaissance had been a brilliant success. They had opened up access to the West Ridge and felt justified in asking for the men and material necessary to complete the route. Dyhrenfurth refused: while the West Ridgers had been absent, a decision had been taken by Dyhrenfurth and the rest of the expedition to make an all-out bid for the summit via the South Col.

The South Collers always had in their hands the one trump card which counted when the chips were down: that theirs was a proven route and a 90 per cent certainty. And Dyhrenfurth had to have success – with such a prestigious expedition under his command failure would have been unthinkable. On the other hand, in purely mountaineering terms it meant very little – even old Tashi, who had been with the party on the West Ridge, called it 'the milk run'. All this had been argued out before, but Hornbein's continued fiery advocacy of the West Ridge had won some sort of equality for the two routes. In particular, it had been agreed that the South Col attempt would be made by teams of two instead of four, as Big Jim Whittaker preferred. Only by cutting down like this would there be enough men and materials for both routes simultaneously.

It was this vital decision which had been revoked during the absence of the West Ridgers. Once Hornbein and Unsoeld were out of the way, it had been an easy matter for the South Collers to persuade Dyhrenfurth that four-men teams were essential for success – especially as he was in sympathy with them anyway.

When Hornbein and Unsoeld learned of this they were furious, Hornbein especially. 'Only an American expedition would attempt to vote itself to the top of Everest,' he later wrote in bitter memory of that day. 'Our approach to decision making was at times exorbitantly democratic.'[19]

The more philosophical Unsoeld wrote in his diary, 'Surely mountaineering is more than a matter of summits, even when the summit is that of Everest.'[20]

Both men felt as though they had been betrayed and, as leader, they considered Dyhrenfurth the culprit. 'My chances of winning any popularity contest were rather slim,' he later wrote.[21]

The first four-man team to attempt the summit would be Lute Jerstad, Dick Pownall, Big Jim Whittaker and Gombu. That much had already been decided, but the second four-man team was still in doubt. Dyhrenfurth offered the place to the West Ridgers, but Hornbein and Unsoeld felt honour-bound to refuse, though not without considerable heart searching – 'we came awfully close to tossing in our chips and joining the stampede,' said Unsoeld.[22] Ultimately, it had to be the West Ridge or nothing. It looked like being nothing.

The other two members of the West Ridge reconnaissance, Dave Dingman and Barry Bishop, were less dogmatic. Dingman had grown increasingly despondent about his chances of climbing the West Ridge and, as he confided to Unsoeld, he was afraid that Hornbein's increasing fanaticism would lead to serious trouble. He had little doubt that once Hornbein got to grips with the ridge he would push up it to – and maybe beyond – the limits of safety, and he wanted no part of it. He transferred to the South Collers.

With Bishop the situation was different. He was not a free agent. As an employee of the National Geographic Society he had been assigned to the

Everest expedition to do a specific job – bring back a collection of photographs worthy of the influential *National Geographic Magazine*. It was largely in pursuit of this that he had joined the West Ridgers in the first place – no man had ever been in a position to photograph Everest from the West Ridge before. He had accomplished that during the reconnaissance, and now on his return to the Cwm he had received a reminder from his employers that pictures from the summit were equally desirable. He had become a keen West Ridger, but by the nature of things he stood a better chance of successfully completing his assignment if he joined the South Col team.

Not for the first time, the West Ridge attempt seemed dead. Dyhrenfurth, however, did leave Hornbein and Unsoeld one small lifeline with which to keep alive their hopes. They were allowed to use any material or any porters not required for the major effort – and of course any climbers who wanted to join them could do so. In this they were fortunate: both Barry Corbet and Dick Emerson had recovered from their altitude sickness and returned to Advanced Base intent on helping the West Ridge effort. A further boost came in the shape of Al Auten, the base radio operator who, tired of twiddling knobs down on the Khumbu Glacier, had handed over his responsibilities to Barry Prather and come up into the Cwm anxious to do some climbing. So now there were five: Hornbein, Unsoeld, Corbet, Emerson and Auten.[23]

The first problem facing them was how to lift sufficient supplies up the 2,000 ft between the Cwm and the West Shoulder without adequate porterage. They attempted to solve this by using some experimental winching gear the expedition had brought along, but it was only a partial success, involving the climbers in enormous effort and endless frustration, as the winch repeatedly malfunctioned. 'Never has so little been accomplished by so many,' quipped Corbet. Hornbein reckoned that in the end the winch may have saved a day or two – and the operation lasted from 16 April to 13 May. But at least it kept the West Ridgers occupied, preventing them from dwelling too morbidly on the inexorable advance of the South Col team.

During the time of the West Ridge reconnaissance the South Collers had not been idle. They had managed to establish Camp III at 22,900 ft and Camp IV at 24,900 ft on the Lhotse Face. On the 16th Lute Jerstad and Dick Pownall with the Sherpas Chotari and Nima Tenzing, disobeying orders from Dyhrenfurth to go no further than the 'Yellow Band', reached the South Col. It was the earliest that any expedition had ever reached that vital objective. That same night they returned to Advanced Base: an impressive performance involving 1,600 ft of new ascent and 5,000 ft of descent.

It was, of course, only a reconnaissance. But the way had been made, and for the next nine days the build-up of supplies went ahead. On the 27th the first assault team left Advanced Base.

The composition of the team had changed from that originally planned. Big

Jim Whittaker and Gombu were still there, but now they were accompanied by Dyhrenfurth and Ang Dawa (Dyhrenfurth's personal Sherpa). For the forty-five-year-old leader to promote himself into the assault team seems incredibly self-indulgent, but he excused it on the grounds that a good film of the ascent was desirable and he was the only competent cameraman fit to make the climb. Dan Doody, who had been expected to do the high-altitude filming, was suffering acutely from altitude and spent most of the time in his sleeping bag, wholly incapacitated.

This relegated Jerstad and Pownall to the second assault party, along with Bishop of the *National Geographic* and Bishop's personal Sherpa, Girmi Dorje.

There is no doubt that Dyhrenfurth's plan included the strongest climbers on the expedition (except for the West Ridgers, of course) and in the right order. The question is, did he himself expect to make the summit, or was it just another leader making a gesture towards ambition? Dyhrenfurth's situation, as he set out from Advanced Base, was curiously analogous to that of Hunt in 1953.

Inserting himself like that into the lead team had created another problem. It had displaced two more potential summiteers, Dave Dingman and Barry Prather. Hastily, Dyhrenfurth revived his plan for an assault on Lhotse to accommodate these two, who would thus make up the third assault team going to the South Col. When Hornbein heard of the Lhotse attempt, he was more furious than ever: the West Ridge, it seemed, was no longer even second choice.

It was the nadir of team relationships and the expedition came near to bursting apart at the seams. The West Ridgers already felt badly let down by the decision to go all out for the South Col route; to revive the old Lhotse plan, which had never been seriously considered since the approach march, was hardly tactful. Had the teams not left when they did, had the West Ridgers not had their winches to play with, the merest chance remark could have ignited an explosive situation. Dyhrenfurth skated very adroitly over some thin ice, and came through unscathed. Years later, when there was no Willi Unsoeld to calm things down, he was to try it again, with less happy results.

Though the start was delayed two days by bad weather, the first American assault on Everest went smoothly for a while. Whittaker, Gombu, Dyhrenfurth and Ang Dawa moved to Camp III on 27 April and on to Camp IV next day. On the 29th they established Camp V on the South Col and on the 30th Camp VI on the ridge at 27,450 ft.

Camp VI was lower than Dyhrenfurth would have liked – it was short of the height achieved by the British top camp in 1953 by 450 ft – but he was in no position to argue the matter. Weighed down by camera equipment, he and Ang Dawa, who had a faulty oxygen set, fell well behind Whittaker, Gombu and the support Sherpas as they trudged up the ridge. It was these latter who decided where the top camp would be – Whittaker knew no better – and by the time Dyhrenfurth arrived the Sherpas had gone down again and it was too late to do anything about it. So the four men camped, knowing they were short of their target.

Another disturbing factor was the insistence by the support Sherpas on having oxygen to descend the ridge, when Dyhrenfurth's plan had been to keep the partially filled bottles the men had used coming up to augment supplies at Camp VI. A shortage of oxygen loomed.

On the next day – 1 May – Whittaker and Gombu got off to an early start, but Dyhrenfurth and Ang Dawa were later in setting out and did not go far before turning back. A combination of age, altitude and a gear load of 50lb. had beaten the American leader. They returned to Camp VI to await events.

At 11.30 a.m. Whittaker and Gombu reached the South Summit. Continuing along the ridge they found the Hillary Step to be well snowed up and of no technical difficulty. At 1 p.m. without further incident they reached the summit, where Whittaker planted a large American flag.

Short of oxygen, Whittaker and Gombu were forced to make an arduous, slow descent to Camp VI. It took them five hours, and although the original plan had been to go straight down to the South Col, because of the lateness of the hour and the lack of oxygen there was no chance of doing that. Fortunately, the second assault team, who should have come up to occupy Camp VI that night, decided to remain at the South Col because of the weather.[24]

Next day as Whittaker and Gombu, ahead of Dyhrenfurth and Ang Dawa, descended the ridge towards the South Col they met the second assault team on their way up. They had had oxygen problems too: there was not nearly enough at the col for a four-man assault, and in the emergency which this caused it was decided that Lute Jerstad and Barry Bishop would make the ascent while Pownall and Girmi Dorje would support them to Camp VI and then return to the col. When they met the descending party, however, all plans for a second attempt were abandoned. Without the extra oxygen they expected to find at Camp VI, even a two-man attempt was unlikely to succeed. Furthermore, Whittaker and Gombu were near exhaustion and would need looking after even when they reached the col – not to mention Dyhrenfurth and Ang Dawa, who were coming down more slowly. So they all returned to the South Col.

It was one and a half hours later when Dyhrenfurth and Ang Dawa came down the final slopes of the ridge to the col. Both men were blue in the face from lack of oxygen, and Dyhrenfurth was delirious. He collapsed into the arms of Lute Jerstad, who was the first to reach them, but revived under oxygen sufficiently to stagger down to the tents. Here, with more oxygen, hot drinks and a rest, the two men rapidly recovered.

Meanwhile, the Lhotse team of Dingman, Prather and three Sherpas had experienced their own drama. At Camp IV Prather had felt unwell and therefore remained behind, while Dingman and two of the Sherpas went ahead with some supplies to Camp V. But the weather was so bad they were forced to turn back – and, in doing so, saved Prather's life, for they found him very ill indeed, suffering from pulmonary oedema, the worst form of altitude sickness, and one which is rapidly fatal. By another stroke of good fortune, Dingman was a doctor and was able to treat Prather immediately with injections and oxygen.

The Lhotse attempt was over even before it had begun, but after sending Prather back Dingman continued up the Lhotse Face because he thought the supplies he was carrying might help the assault teams on the South Col. In the event, of course, he met them coming down, and learned of the ascent and the abandonment of any further attempts for the time being.

The Americans had achieved their success early. They had time in hand for another assault – the monsoon wasn't due for a month – and they had the material and manpower to do it. First, however, there was a need for rest and recuperation, which meant a general withdrawal to Base Camp on the Khumbu Glacier. The Americans called it 'R & R': a better name might have been 'the 3 Rs' – rest, recuperation and recrimination.

The recrimination centred on the oxygen supplies. Everyone agreed that these had been sadly mismanaged during the assault. A lack of oxygen had caused the second team to abandon their attempt and had been responsible for the traumatic oxygenless descent of Whittaker, Dyhrenfurth and the two Sherpas from Camp VI. Dyhrenfurth laid the blame squarely on Tom Hornbein, the man responsible for the expedition oxygen supplies: 'If I had known Tom was going to be so fanatical about the West Ridge,' he told an expedition meeting, 'I would have increased our budget, ordered three hundred oxygen bottles and hired fifty Sherpas. If only Tom had been honest with me about his ambitions back in the States.'[25] By implication Dyhrenfurth was accusing Hornbein of hogging too much oxygen for the West Ridge, thus depriving the South Collers of their fair share.

It was a potentially explosive situation again. Willi Unsoeld put a restraining hand on Hornbein's shoulder, expecting the worst, but for once the ex-Navy man kept cool. He explained that the oxygen had been fairly apportioned and that the quantities had been carefully calculated on the basis of the team's climbing and sleeping requirements and on the experience of the British and Swiss expeditions. However, he pointed out, during the two nights the first assault team had spent at Camp VI, on the ridge, they had consumed almost all of the eighteen bottles carried there, when six of those bottles were meant for the second assault team. He implied that if there was a shortage of oxygen then the first assault team had nobody to blame but themselves. They should not have let the Sherpas go down with oxygen, nor (in a direct reference to Dyhrenfurth) should oxygen have been used for just sitting around in the tent at Camp VI. Oxygen was for climbing and sleeping – nothing else. When the calculations had been made, sitting around in tents was 'quite reasonably' excluded.

Dyhrenfurth was incensed at Hornbein's use of the words 'quite reasonably'. There was enough truth in it to prick his conscience, yet an element of injustice too. He knew that the ex-naval man was pointing the finger of blame at him, accusing him of going too high, of letting ambition over-ride ability. Hornbein later wrote:

> Norm, at 45, had climbed higher than any man his age. To film the summit climb he and Ang Dawa, burdened with cameras, had gone above 28,000 ft before their oxygen ran low. As he talked, I began to realize that he had travelled to the edge of his physical limits – oxygen almost had led him beyond. He was exhausted, possibly disappointed, perhaps suffering the lingering effects of oxygen lack, and his restraint was gone. His feelings poured forth. There was nothing to say in reply, in my own defence; there was no need.[26]

The oxygen argument simmered and occasionally bubbled for the rest of the time the party were together at Base Camp. The strain of a long high-altitude expedition was beginning to show, and it wasn't helped by yet another of those 'democratic' decisions which the leader seemed to favour. The team had come to the extraordinary conclusion that only the bare facts of success should be given to the world's press, and that the names of the successful pair should be withheld until the expedition was finished. Then, should there be further ascents, all the names could be announced simultaneously. The purpose of this was to promote team harmony, and to prevent the press from turning Whittaker into an American hero. They rightly judged that the pressmen and editors would not be interested in the hard slog involved in getting a man on top of the world – all they would be interested in was the man himself. Perhaps because they were academics, who knew only too well how the popular press could trivialize the most serious subjects, their thinking was coloured – who knows? It couldn't work of course, as a few moments of rational thought would have told them. The clamour of the press was too great – and in any case the native bush telegraph passed all the details down the valley in a matter of days.

Dyhrenfurth had achieved the primary aim of the expedition, which was to put an American on the summit of Everest. It was a success – but a qualified one. After all, the British had done that much ten years earlier. Moreover, the Swiss had put *four* men on top, and it would be gratifying to at least equal that number.

It is interesting to speculate what might have happened had the initial assault gone according to plan. Supposing all four men had reached the summit, or indeed all eight men? And what if Dingman had climbed Lhotse into the bargain? Would they now be regrouping at Base, and would Hornbein have been given his chance for the West Ridge? Almost certainly not. It would have been pushing one's luck too far. By a strange irony of fate it was the very mediocrity of the Americans' first attempt that led them to make one of the greatest mountaineering feats ever performed.

There was a certain sagging in expedition morale and energy at Base Camp. This is hardly surprising. They had been long in the field, and the euphoria of Whittaker's ascent gradually evaporated to leave a flatness. For various reasons eight men from the expedition were never to return to the Western Cwm: for them the expedition was over. For the others, the sheer willpower necessary to start again was considerable. This was particularly so for Bishop, Jerstad, Dingman and Girmi Dorje, who were destined to retrace their steps to the South Còl.

The essence of the new plan was simple. There would be simultaneous attempts on the West Ridge and the South East Ridge and the parties would hope to meet on the summit. If that happened ('A chance in a thousand,' said Dyhrenfurth), all the men would descend the South East Ridge to the South Col, in which case the West Ridgers would have traversed the mountain; that is, gone up one side and down another, the classical ideal of the mountaineer. On the other hand, if the two parties should not meet, which seemed likely, each would descend by their own route of ascent. It was thought to be too dangerous for the West Ridgers to try to descend the South East Ridge without support – they would be bound to be desperately tired and, of course, they would be on what was to them unfamiliar ground.

The teams for this double assault virtually picked themselves. Two ropes were to try the West Ridge: Unsoeld and Hornbein, Corbet and Emerson, with Al Auten in support at the high camps. The South East Ridge party was more flexible: Bishop and Jerstad were to make the attempt (their second of the expedition), but Dingman, Jimmy Roberts and Girmi Dorje, their support team, would also try to go as high as possible. Commanding Advanced Base would be Maynard Miller, who had some scientific work to do in the Cwm anyway. Target date for the ascent was to be 18 May.

While most of the expedition was resting at Base Camp, Barry Corbet and Dick Emerson had been steadily plugging away trying to get materials from Advanced Base to Camp 3W on the West Ridge. Because of slow acclimatization these two men had already spent a lot of time at Base Camp, and the last thing they needed was rest and recuperation. So, while their companions took a break, they worked hard trying to get the recalcitrant winches to work properly and slowly building up supplies for the forthcoming attack on the ridge.

It had not been without its moments of drama. On 3 May a powder snow avalanche had carried away one of the intermediate gear dumps, and with it a tent containing two Sherpas. Fortunately, the Sherpas suffered no more than a rough slide for a few hundred feet and emerged grinning, but valuable gear was lost and there was now no tentage between Advanced Base and Camp 3W.

Nevertheless, when the West Ridge team forgathered at Advanced Base on 6 May, Corbet and Emerson were able to assure them that the winches were working and things were under way. From 8 to 13 May this lift of materials to 3W continued, though two days were lost through bad weather and the date for the summit assault had to be correspondingly put back to the 21st.

On 14 May Unsoeld once again reached the foot of the West Ridge proper at 25,100 ft – the same point he had reached over a month before during the reconnaissance with Hornbein and Bishop. It was a delectable place for a camp, nicely level, and with astonishing views down into the Western Cwm on the one hand and the Rongbuk Glacier on the other. The Sherpas with him dumped their loads, and everyone returned to 3W. Next day Unsoeld and Hornbein returned with more loads, and the camp – 4W – was established. The two men stayed the night at the camp and on the following day prospected the route ahead. They found the Diagonal Ditch was easy and that it led to snow fields which in turn led to Hornbein's Couloir. What lay above the couloir they could not tell, for in its upper reaches it twisted out of sight. Nevertheless, it seemed a reasonable way up.

Meanwhile, as the two leaders were prospecting the route, Barry Corbet and Dick Emerson were moving up from Advanced Base to join Al Auten at Camp 3W. Emerson was again feeling unwell and he was forced to retreat from the face, leaving Corbet to continue alone to the camp.

The next day, 16 May, was a crucial one for the West Ridgers. They lived through a storm that threatened to wipe them out and bring disaster to the whole expedition. It was a high-altitude storm – those down in Base Camp felt nothing, though they could hear the roaring round the mountain peak. Those up above were fighting for their lives.

At Advanced Base, in the Western Cwm, Dick Emerson was feeling sick and dispirited. He knew that unless he rejoined his companions on the ridge pretty soon his chances on the mountain would be nil. On 16 May, therefore, he started back up alone – just in time to avoid an order from Dyhrenfurth instructing him to descend to Base Camp. He was far from well and it became evident as the day wore on that he would not make Camp 3W by nightfall. This was something he had taken into account before setting out, and he was prepared for an enforced bivouac on the face.

As darkness closed in he came to a dump of equipment left on the face. Selecting two oxygen bottles, he dragged them into a nearby crevasse and prepared to bed down for the night. He had no sleeping bag, but he did have an airbed and adequate clothing, and he reckoned that the walls of the crevasse would protect him against the chilling effects of the wind. In this he was wrong: the strong wind, which began to blow about 10 p.m., came howling across the mountain parallel to the face, so that the crevasse acted like a funnel. Snow was blown in, covering Emerson in a white blanket. Incredibly, he not only survived, but spent a relatively comfortable night.[27]

Next day the weather was fine but the wind extremely strong. Emerson struggled up against it, often clinging to the icy face with his axe to save being blown away. Once, caught off balance by a shifting gust, he went sailing not downwards but *across* the slope, so powerful was the wind.

Nevertheless, he somehow managed to struggle on, and at 10 a.m. reached the welcoming shelter of Camp 3W.

The storm that had battered Emerson had also struck the ridge, where Camp 4W had grown to three tents. One was the original small one still occupied by Hornbein and Unsoeld; the other two were somewhat larger frame tents and were joined together at their entrances. In one lay Corbet and Auten; in the other the four Sherpas who had helped in the carry.

About midnight, Corbet and Auten awoke to the shrieking of the gale and to the terrifying realization that the tents were moving and sliding off the mountain. There was nothing they could do to stop them, and they realized that the next few seconds would determine their fate. If they were sliding down the south side of the ridge, they would plunge over the tremendous precipice that overlooked the Western Cwm, and that would be the end for them all. On the other hand, if they were sliding down the northern side of the ridge, towards Tibet, the gentler slopes on that side offered a tiny chance of survival.

The slide accelerated, then, as the tents went completely out of control, they started to roll over and over – a wild, dark, tumbling nightmare of men, oxygen bottles, stores and equipment. They were rolling into Tibet.

Suddenly, they came to a jolting halt. A trough-like ledge fielded them as neatly as a first team catcher. They had travelled fifty yards, dropped a hundred feet. Miraculously, no one was injured.

The first that Hornbein and Unsoeld knew of all this was when a taut, gasping Corbet appeared in their tent. Immediately the two leaders dressed and went to the aid of their companions. In the darkness, with the wind still howling all round, the whole team struggled to anchor the two wrecked tents to the mountain to prevent them sliding any further. Then, exhausted, they retired to their sleeping bags, Auten crawling into the small tent shared by Hornbein and Unsoeld, Corbet and the Sherpas remaining behind to anchor what was left of the wreckage.

Daylight brought no end to the wind. Hornbein's tent, still on the ridge, caught the full blast and was threatened with destruction. The three men trapped inside clung desperately, but futilely, to the poles. Nothing could withstand that raging hurricane, and when, inevitably, the guy ropes snapped and the tent began to move, a hurried exit was called for. Fortunately they managed to arrest the tent sufficiently for boxes of food and oxygen bottles to be piled on top of it, collapsing it and anchoring it.

There then began a general retreat to Camp 3W in the teeth of the gale, which was now reaching its maximum power. Men were lifted off their feet, and frequently the whole party had to flatten themselves in the snow, clinging to their ice axes as their only means of survival.

It was mid-afternoon before they crawled into 3W, dazed and exhausted, there to meet Emerson, himself a survivor. Yet, incredibly, no one had been hurt during all these terrifying events. The West Ridgers were battered, but intact.

All the same, they had lost valuable tentage and stores, which threw their whole project once more into doubt. Hornbein said later that if they had not been so exhausted the whole team would have retired to Advanced Base and given up. As it was, a night at Camp 3W brought rest and a fresh plan. It was Hornbein's plan, of course: he had his teeth into the West Ridge like a terrier with a bone and was not yet ready to let go.

Basically the plan was a paring down of the original one based on the knowledge that there was not only less material available after the storm, but less time too. Instead of two more camps above 4W there would now be one; instead of two summit attempts, there would be one.

There was not much argument about who the summit pair should be. Auten was in a support role anyway and had never meant to go high; Emerson was not fully recovered. That left Hornbein, Unsoeld and Corbet – and it was Corbet who volunteered to back down. He recognized the special relationship which existed between Hornbein and Unsoeld, and knew that in the last analysis, if things got really tough, that relationship might make all the difference between success and failure, even between life and death. 'What's more,' he said, grinning at his elders, 'you're both just about over the hump – I'll be coming back again someday.'[28]

Over the radio link Dyhrenfurth approved the new plan, sanctioned the extra delay it would involve and put in train such additional material as possible to help the depleted team supplies. Al Auten, who had wanted to go down, agreed to remain in support, and carrying the fresh supplies came two more Sherpas. It was barely enough – five climbers and five Sherpas – and three of the Sherpas were inexperienced men on their first expedition.

On the morning of the 20th, a perfect day, they set out to re-establish the stricken Camp 4W. The site had to be the same as before because there was nowhere else suitable, and as they crawled into their sleeping bags that night they must all have felt a quiver of apprehension, remembering what had happened a few nights earlier. But this time all went well, and on the next morning three ropes set off up the mountain – Corbet and Auten, lightly laden and reconnoitring the way ahead, then the five Sherpas and finally Unsoeld, Emerson and Hornbein.

The reconnaissance rope had a two and a half hours' start. Their route was predetermined, for part of Hornbein's plan was that they should make use of what knowledge they had gained already about the West Ridge, which meant going for the Hornbein Couloir and ignoring any other, possibly more direct, lines. At least they had seen the couloir and knew it could be climbed: there was no time to waste in exploring other possibilities. So when Corbet and Auten set out that morning across the Diagonal Ditch which led to the couloir they had no route-finding problems. Their task was two-fold: to cut good steps for the laden porters to follow, and to find a bivouac site for the single tent of Camp 5W, as high as possible.

At two o'clock Corbet and Auten reached the foot of the Yellow Band at a height of 27,250 ft, where they found a tiny platform just about capable of holding a two-man tent. Though it was not so high as they would have wished (it still left 1,800 ft to the summit) they dared go no further. The Sherpas were two hours behind, and by the time they had caught up and dumped their loads there would be barely sufficient daylight left for them to retreat to 4W.

That night Hornbein and Unsoeld perched in their precarious eyrie. The tent was secured on the upper side by a shaky peg tapped half an inch into the rotten rock of the Yellow Band, and on the lower side by two ice axes driven into mushy snow. Surveying their insecure lodging Unsoeld had planted a prayer flag brought up by the Sherpas. 'I think we'd better rely on that,' he said, laconically.

Before trying to snatch some sleep Hornbein wrote a short letter to his wife, ending it: 'Tomorrow shall spell the conclusion to our effort, one way or another.'[29]

They awoke at four next morning, spent two hours preparing for the climb, then set out. Their first problem was the Yellow Band, the crumbling series of limestone cliffs through which Hornbein's Couloir carved a tenuous passage. The couloir became steeper and narrower – it was sometimes barely ten feet wide and in one place so narrow they had literally to squeeze through. It was hard going, requiring the cutting of many steps. In four hours they had climbed a mere 400 ft.

Near the top of the Yellow Band they came across their major obstacle: a sixty-foot wall of crumbly rock broken into two tiers by a snow-covered step. Hornbein took over the lead but failed to climb the obstacle, not because it was too difficult but because the sheer effort exhausted him – he discovered later that his oxygen set was malfunctioning by not supplying the correct flow rate. Unsoeld tried in turn, and by a supreme effort managed to haul himself over the top. Hornbein followed, and a rope-length later they both halted to call base on the radio. Their altitude read 27,900 ft.

Time was getting on and they still had a long way to go. One thing, however, was certain. They were now committed to the traverse. With or without assistance they would have to descend the South East Ridge to the South Col camps. They felt that to try to return by the rotten rock of the West Ridge would be suicidal.[30]

Above the Yellow Band they veered to the right to reach the ridge proper for the first time since they had left Camp 4W. For a while they delighted in clean rock, removing their crampons and overboots, climbing almost as freely as they would have done at home. Then came the snow-ice again, so they replaced their crampons and crunched steadily up the summit slopes of Everest.

Suddenly they were conscious of a tattered American flag fluttering in the breeze some forty feet ahead. It was the one placed there by Big Jim Whittaker three weeks earlier:

> It was 6.15. The sun's rays sheered horizontally across the summit. We hugged each other as tears welled up, ran down across our oxygen masks, and turned to ice.[31]

They stayed for twenty minutes on the summit, then began their descent of the South East Ridge, encouraged by the fresh footprints they discerned in the snow – evidence that Lute Jerstad and Barry Bishop had been to the summit that day as planned. Before they began the long trip down Unsoeld radioed to Advanced Base the fact of their success and quoted Robert Frost:

> . . . And I have promises to keep,
> And miles to go before we sleep,
> And miles to go before we sleep.[32]

As they crossed the South Summit the daylight faded quickly. The footsteps they were following became less distinguishable in the deepening darkness, and though they used their torches they found these almost as exhausted as they were. They could do little else but pick their way cautiously, fumbling through tiredness, down the dark, confusing ridge.

Would the support party of Dave Dingman and Girmi, who should be at Camp VI, come up to look for them? There was always a hope. They shouted into the dark void, but the wind flung their voices away.

Then, like something out of a dream, they thought they heard an answering call. Calling again, this time they were certain of a response. Guided by the shouts, they stumbled on down until eventually they came upon two dark crouching figures in the snow. Much to their surprise, it was not Dingman and the Sherpa but Lute Jerstad and Barry Bishop, the men who had preceded them to the summit that day.

Jerstad and Bishop had had an unhappy twenty-four hours. After reaching Camp VI from the South Col, Bishop had been taken unaccountably ill and had spent a restless night of sickness, pain and mental anguish. He had managed to sleep a little but not much and, out of concern, his partner hadn't slept much either. When morning came both men were tired, but the day was fine and Bishop was feeling better, so they decided to press on with the climb. However, as Jerstad was changing the butane cylinders on one of their breakfast cookers, there was a sudden sheet of flame which filled the tent. Both men had their eyebrows and beards singed and Bishop's plastic oxygen mask, lying near the cooker, burst alight and filled the tent with dense, acrid smoke. Bishop recalled the incident:

> Panic gripped us. Lute struggled toward the zippered entrance, and I tried to smother the flames with my sleeping bag; but my legs were still inside it and I could get no leverage. Meanwhile the fire was feeding on the air in the tent, soon exhausting it, and our lungs were aching. I was groping desperately for a knife to cut through the tent wall, when Lute managed to tear open the zipper and literally dived outside. His momentum was so great that he almost pitched down the steep slope toward the South Col. I was on his heels. We snatched the flaming stove from the tent, doused it in the snow, and soon the fire had died in the thin air. When at last we crawled back into the tent we said nothing to each other, but we shared the same thought. The omens were bad, all bad.[33]

Not until 8 a.m. did they manage to begin their climb, already tired and more than a little shaken. Only a supreme effort of willpower dragged them upwards, like automatons. They were not fully aware of their actions – Jerstad actually took the wrong route when leaving the South Summit and had to retrace his steps – and they were painfully slow. They reached the summit at 3.30 p.m., the climb having taken seven and a half hours.

On the summit they could see signs of the earlier ascent by Whittaker and Gombu, but no trace of Hornbein and Unsoeld, whom they assumed to have given up the West Ridge attempt or at least put it off for a day, because the afternoon was already well advanced. After forty-five minutes spent in photography, during which Jerstad took the first ciné film ever from the roof of the world, they began their slow, laborious descent.

Night fell. They were in a worse way now even than the West Ridgers, for they had no torches at all. After three and a half hours they had descended only 600 ft, and it was then that they heard the shouts on the ridge above them and realized that Hornbein and Unsoeld had made the top after all. They decided to wait for them, to join forces.

The West Ridgers were desperately tired when they eventually reached their companions, but they realized at once that Jerstad and Bishop – especially Bishop – were in a much worse state and near the end of their tether. Nevertheless, Hornbein urged them to move: to spend a night on the ridge in the open seemed to him to be courting disaster. Obediently they staggered to their feet, and the party groped its way down the dark ridge once again.

There was still a thousand feet of descent before they could reach the tiny Camp VI, where, God willing, they would find safety and respite. But their progress became slower. They were out of oxygen. Bishop collapsed but eventually recovered enough to continue the nightmarish descent.

After three hours they had descended no more than four hundred feet and even Hornbein had to concede that there was no way they were going to reach camp that night. Already it was midnight, and they had been climbing for sixteen or seventeen hours. They were totally exhausted. There was nothing they could do but risk a bivouac on the open ridge.

They slipped their packs off and waited for dawn, Hornbein and Unsoeld huddled together for mutual warmth, the other two a little above them, separate in their cold misery.

Hornbein's feet were cold, so Unsoeld offered to rub them to prevent the frostbite they feared. When at last his companion managed to remove his boots and socks, Unsoeld snuggled the cold feet against his stomach to bring them back to life. It was a noble gesture, but the recipient soon ached from the awkward positioning he was in and the experiment was abandoned. When he offered to do the same for Unsoeld, the latter declined: his feet were all right, he said, because he had a high resistance to cold. Hornbein, the doctor, was too weary to argue, even to think straight. It was a decision that was later to cost Unsoeld nine of his ten toes.[34]

And so they sat out the five long remaining hours of darkness. Hornbein later described the experience:

> The night was overpoweringly empty. Stars shed cold unshimmering light. The heat lightning dancing along the plains spoke of a world of warmth and flatness. The black silhouette of Lhotse lurked half-sensed, half-seen, still below. Only the ridge on which we were rose higher, disappearing into the night, a last lonely outpost of the world.
>
> Mostly there was nothing. We hung suspended in a timeless void. The wind died, and there was silence. Even without wind it was cold. I could reach back and touch Lute or Barrel lying head to toe above me. They seemed miles away.
>
> Unsignalled, unembellished, the hours passed. Intense cold penetrated, carrying with it the realization that each of us was completely alone. Nothing Willi could do for me or I for him. No team now, just each of us, imprisoned with his own discomfort, his own thoughts, his own will to survive.
>
> Yet, for me, survival was hardly a conscious thought. Nothing to plan,

> nothing to push for, nothing to do but shiver and wait for the sun to rise. I floated in a dreamlike eternity, devoid of plans, fears, regrets. The heat lightning, Lhotse, my companions, discomfort, all were there – yet not there. Death had no meaning, nor, for that matter, did life. Survival was no concern, no issue. Only a dulled impatience for the sun to rise tied my formless thoughts to the future.[35]

When dawn came and they were able to continue their desperate journey they were barely aware that they had survived the highest bivouac in mountaineering history at that time.

In a little while Dave Dingman and the Sherpa Girmi appeared, climbing the ridge to search for the bodies of Jerstad and Bishop, whom they presumed had died in the attempt on the summit. Much to Dingman's amazement and joy, there were not two dead bodies, but four living climbers to collect.

The West Ridge had been climbed and Everest traversed – the first ever traverse of a major Himalayan peak. It was a complete triumph for the Americans. And a personal triumph for the determined, argumentative, insistent little doctor from San Diego, Thomas F. Hornbein.

# 17

## 'Not a Private Affair'

The Indians had not given up hope. Despite their reverses of 1960 and 1962 (when they came so near to reaching the summit) the Indian Mountaineering Federation displayed a tenacity of purpose not unlike that of the old pre-war Everest Committee. In 1965 they mounted their third expedition to Everest: a carefully selected team (mostly Darjeeling Sherpas from the armed forces) led by a naval officer, Lt Cdr M.S. Kohli, who had been Deputy Leader in 1962, when he reached a height of 28,600 ft on the South East Ridge.[1]

This time the Indians were brilliantly successful. On 19 May after a frustrating period of bad weather, a camp was established on the South East Ridge at 27,930 ft – the highest assault camp so far achieved on the mountain. From it, at 9.30 a.m. next day, Captain A.S. Cheema and Nawang Gombu reached the summit. Gombu thus became the first man to climb Everest twice, for he had accompanied Whittaker to the top during the American expedition two years earlier.

On 22 May Sonam Gyatso and Sonam Wangyal reached the summit, then two days later C.P. Vohra and Ang Kami. Finally, on 29 May Captain H.P.S. Ahluwalia, H.C.S. Rawat and Phu Dorje also reached the summit – the first three-man ascent from the south, or the first ever, if one discounts the Chinese claims of 1960. In all, the Indians put nine men on the summit, far and away the most comprehensively successful attempt the mountain had seen at that time. It was a record matched only by the Chinese in 1975 and the Austrians in 1978, and not exceeded until the post-monsoon German expedition of 1978 put twelve people on top.

The Indian success marked an important stage in the rapidly growing story of Mount Everest because it supported so completely the point that Hornbein and Unsoeld had pressed on Dyhrenfurth during the American expedition two years before: that in mountaineering terms the ascent of the South East Ridge was no longer an event of great significance. Given the right men, the right equipment and a reasonable degree of luck with the weather, there was now no reason why any number of ascents should not be made. The Indian success, by its very magnitude, had completed the mountaineering subjection of the South East Ridge.

Not that the ridge was henceforth ignored – far from it. Everest is still the highest mountain in the world, and nations large and small – particularly (though not exclusively) those with a mountaineering tradition – have keenly felt the need to make the ascent for reasons of prestige. So the South East Ridge has seen ascents by the Japanese, Italians, South Koreans, Austrians, Germans and French, not to mention repeats by the British and Americans. Three have failed: the Argentinians in 1971, the Spanish in 1974 and the New Zealanders in 1977 – although the last named were trying something new: to climb the mountain without support, as if it were an Alpine peak.

The Indian success was notable too for being the last attempt allowed by the Nepalese for three years. The Nepal Himalaya were closed to climbers until the summer of 1969 while the authorities considered the position. In particular they were conscious of being a small country caught between two antagonistic giants, India and China, and they wanted no provocative actions by foreigners that might upset either. So for the time being they reverted to their old isolationism, and when the gates were reopened, there were more stringent regulations regarding expeditions – and higher fees![2]

Meanwhile the thoughts of the world's leading mountaineers were far from the Himalaya. They were concentrated instead on the blank soaring granite walls of the Yosemite valley in California where for nearly a decade, multi-day routes of an astonishing severity had been created by local men such as Warren Harding and Royal Robbins. Harding, for example, had spent a total of forty-five days, spread over eighteen months, in making the first ascent of the Nose on El Capitan, a sheer 3,000 ft cliff overlooking the Merced river. He had used hundreds of pitons, over a hundred bolts (drilled into the rock) and some 3,000 ft of fixed rope. In 1960 the route was repeated by a four-man team who took seven days. Before long the Nose had become the classic hard climb of the valley and even harder routes were undertaken. The fashion spread. In 1965, for example, a British party climbed the incredible 4,500 ft Troll Wall in Norway by a multi-day push.

Following a little behind these new super-severe rock climbs came a revolution in ice climbing techniques. The cutting of steps was out; instead, reliance was placed on the tenuous bite of the forward-pointing spikes of the modern crampon – the so-called 'lobster claws', which the climber could kick into the ice for half an inch or so, depending on the ice's hardness. On steep ice handholds (always difficult and delicate to cut with an ice axe) gave way to special short axes, one in each hand, that the climber could hook into the ice for purchase. In this way ice climbing became much more akin to rock climbing than it had been. Steeper ice could be climbed, and moreover climbed much quicker.

In other words, what the leading climbers were doing was pushing modern techniques to the limit in the furtherance of their sport.

Naturally there was interaction between the new and the old techniques through adaptation, improvisation and experimentation. It was a time of searching and the opening-up of new forms of mountaineering expression. Some of the older climbers shook their heads and there was a muttering about ethical values – but who bothers about ethics in the fizz and bubble of a new and heady champagne?

Since the new techniques were adapted to faces rather than ridges, face climbing predominated: the face was to be climbed as directly as possible. One event more than any other symbolized the new era: the first ascent of the Eiger Direct in 1966.

This big mountain face, the most feared in the Alps, has been the cause of numerous fatalities both before and after it was first climbed in 1938 by an Austro-German team. The original route snakes its way up the icy cliff, seeking what weaknesses there are: for the modern climber there was an obvious, if daunting, challenge in straightening it out.

In the winter of 1966 the challenge was accepted simultaneously by two teams, an Anglo-American team led by the dynamic American John Harlin and a German team led by Jörg Lehne. Both groups found it a bitter struggle, but by using fixed ropes and jumars the climbers were able to advance and retreat according to conditions. Indeed, some climbers who theoretically were not engaged on the climb, such as Chris Bonington, who was photographing the venture for a newspaper, were able to help from time to time, then return to base at Kleine Scheidegg. Ironically, it was through the parting of a fixed rope that Harlin was killed, after which the rival teams combined and forced their way to the top.

With the ascent of the Eiger Direct the die was cast. If such methods could work in the Alps, why not on the big Himalayan faces as well? It was put to the test by a British expedition under Bonington. In 1970 they tackled the huge South Face of Annapurna (8,078 m.) in Nepal and were brilliantly successful. Don Whillans and Dougal Haston reached the summit. Haston had been one of the participants in the Eiger affair, and Whillans, like Bonington, had helped in it too. All three were to make their mark on the ultimate goal, Everest.

But it was the Japanese who first seized the opportunity. In 1963 the Japanese Alpine Club had been granted permission to attempt Everest during the pre-monsoon period of 1966. Unfortunately they, like everyone else, were prevented from fulfilling their ambition because of the Nepalese ban on expeditions, and it wasn't until 1969 that they could renew their hopes. However, they did gain a bonus – they were granted permission for three consecutive expeditions: spring and autumn 1969, and spring 1970.

During the post-war years, Japanese climbers had been very active in the Himalaya. They were skilful and tough, and had accounted for two top-class mountains, Himal Chuli and Manaslu, the latter being seventh highest in the world. In the number and frequency of their expeditions they outdid everyone else – even it is suggested, everyone else put together. Expense seemed no object: presented with three consecutive Everest expeditions most nations would have blanched at the cost. The Japanese took it in their inscrutable stride.[3]

They were well aware of the modern trends in climbing (about this time they put up their own direct route on the Eiger) and realized that on Everest the next logical step would be to attempt the great South West Face whose crags loomed over the Western Cwm. Their three expeditions gave them a unique monopoly of the problem, enabling them fully to reconnoitre the face in 1969 in readiness for a full-scale assault the following year. Not since the British monopoly of Everest in the days before the war had anyone had such a continuous bite at the apple.

The great triangular shaped South West Face (Fig. 4, p. 444) sweeps up from the Western Cwm for almost 8,000 ft to the summit. The lower two thirds of this distance consists of steep snow slopes running up into a series of rocky towers and buttresses, the exploration of which could take a lifetime and the climbing of which might prove impossible. Fortunately, in the middle of the face, there is a wide break where the snow sweeps up to a higher point. This is known as the Central Gully, but it is wider than most gullies, so the name is a little misleading. It stretches up until, at a little more than 26,000 ft, it meets a steeper wall of rock known as the Rock Band, where it divides right and left, running below the band, but still ascending. On the right it is almost like a ramp, quite long and extending upwards another thousand feet or so, towards the South East Ridge. To the left it is shorter and steeper, arching up to meet a narrow gully cutting through the rock. Above the Rock Band there lies another snowfield, stretching across the face, and above that a steep triangle of summit rock.

The Japanese sent only a small reconnaissance party to the mountain in the pre-monsoon period of 1969. It made its way into the Cwm, but did little more than make a preliminary survey of the problem. In the autumn they returned in greater force, establishing Base Camp by 16 September and Advanced Base (Camp 2 – in the Western Cwm) only twelve days later. The weather was exceptionally fine, with none of the high winds that can be such a demoralizing feature of post-monsoon climbing on Everest, and there was good, firm snow on the lower slopes of the face. Nevertheless, the Japanese concentrated on building up supplies in the Cwm before attacking the mountain, and it was a further two weeks before Camp 3 was set up, at 23,000 ft. Camp 4 was established at the mouth of the Central Gully (24,600 ft) and Camp 5 at 25,600 ft. It was with these last two camps that the Japanese came across a problem nobody had foreseen – the snow in the higher reaches was not deep enough to allow proper tent platforms to be excavated. Henceforth portable platforms, adjusted to the angle of the slope, would be a necessary part of any expedition to the South West Face.

Spearheading the Japanese reconnaissance were Masatsugu Konishi and Naomi Uemura, the latter already building up a reputation as one of the world's most formidable mountaineers, despite his slight build and amiable, almost cherubic countenance. On 31 October they reached a point just below the Rock Band by working out to the left. The following day two of their companions, Hiroshi Nakajima and Shigeru Satoh, managed to climb even a little higher.

What the four Japanese climbers observed convinced them that it would be possible for a full-scale expedition to penetrate the Rock Band, the major difficulty, and climb the Face. For the moment they had gone far enough.

The Japanese reconnaissances of 1969 were in the time-honoured mould of Everest exploration. Like the 1922 expedition, which showed that a way could be made via the North Col, and Shipton's expedition of 1951, which showed that entry to the Western Cwm was feasible, so they too had shown that there was a way to climb the South West Face. But was that enough? No doubt they thought it was, for they had another season in hand in which to prove it.

Yet once again the fact of Everest being Everest overshadowed the thinking and logistics of the final expedition, just as it had done for the Americans in 1963. Then, Dyhrenfurth's prime target was to get an American to the top so as to please his sponsors and satisfy the folks back home. Anything else was subsidiary, and it was only Tom Hornbein's determined individualism which had converted an expensive exercise in public relations into an outstanding mountaineering achievement. And now here were the Japanese confronted with the same problem – the summit for national prestige, or a new and worthwhile route up the difficult South West Face? Hoping to repeat Dyhrenfurth's good luck, they opted for both.

It was a massive expedition – no fewer than thirty-nine climbers and seventy-seven Sherpas (including a woman climber, Miss Setuko Wanatabe) led by the seventy-year-old veteran Saburo Matsukata, who never went higher than Base Camp. The plan was that the combined resources of the expedition would be used to force the Icefall and establish Advanced Base (Camp 2), from where the two teams for the South West Face and South Col route would act independently.

The larger the expedition which has to traverse the Icefall, the greater the potential danger, because at any given moment there are likely to be more targets for the unpredictable ice to strike. The Japanese therefore stood a greater risk of accident, but to make things even more dangerous there was a *second* Japanese team on the mountain: a thirty-four-man ski expedition, completely independent of the climbers and separately financed. Altogether there must have been some 150 people passing through the Icefall, not counting the Icefall Sherpas who were going up and down in a constant daily stream, stocking the camps in the Cwm.

An accident was almost inevitable. On 5 April 1970, the day after Camp 1 was established at the lip of the Cwm, an Icefall avalanche hit a party of Sherpas from the ski expedition, killing six of them. A few days later another Sherpa was killed. Not since pre-war days had a wholesale disaster struck the little Sherpa community: they were appalled and distressed.

Nevertheless, despite these catastrophes, and the slowness of certain team members to acclimatize properly, Advanced Base was established in the Cwm by 17 April. Or rather, *two* Advanced Base Camps, for it was decided that the Face team and Col team would live and work separately from now on. The camps were fairly near each other, with the Face team's camp situated a little closer to the South West Face itself.

Above base, responsibility for the expedition rested in the hands of Hiromi Ohtsuka, who, as he confessed in his diary, found himself facing all the problems of a large split-offensive expedition that had beset Dyhrenfurth, both in terms of logistics and in the philosophical realm of whether to place emphasis on virtually certain but unremarkable success via the well-tried South Col route or on the *possibility* of acquiring great prestige by a first ascent of the untried South West Face. Like Dyhrenfurth, he felt obliged to go for the former: logistically the South Col team were given an advantage, and the fact that Naomi Uemura was allocated to that route emphasizes the point. Unlike the Americans, the Japanese climbers do not seem to have had any option which route they would climb. The choice was made by the leader. The South West Face team consisted of nine men led by Masatsugu Konishi, who had led the autumn reconnaissance. Naturally enough, even among the Japanese, more accustomed than their Western contemporaries to accepting autocratic discipline, not everyone was pleased with their allocated climb. However, there was no Oriental Tom Hornbein to stir things up.

On 21 April another and totally unsuspected hammer blow fell on the expedition. During the evening meal at Camp 1, the youngest member of the expedition, twenty-eight-year-old Kujoshi Narita, suffered a sudden heart attack, and before his shocked companions could do anything to help, died. Earlier in the expedition, Narita had not been well but had spent a week recuperating at Lobuje, the staging post below the Khumbu Glacier, and had returned from there seemingly fit and strong – indeed, he was known as one of the strongest men on the expedition, which made the impact of his death all the more shocking. The expedition was halted while Narita's body was taken down the Icefall and from there down the Khumbu valley for cremation.

Narita's death, combined with the continual illnesses which seemed to dog the expedition, delayed matters to such an extent that Ohtsuka decided to abandon the South West Face altogether and put all his resources into climbing the ordinary route. This was too much, even for the disciplined Japanese, and four days later he changed his mind again – the Face climb would continue, but the South Col route would get priority (which it already had). Shades of Dyhrenfurth!

Suffice to say that progress via the South Col was now rapid, and on 11 May Naomi Uemura and Teruo Matsuura reached the summit of Everest. Next day Katsutoshi Hirabayashi and the Sherpa Chotare repeated the ascent, and took the opportunity, when near the South Summit, of descending a little way onto the South West Face to inspect the problems. Hirabayashi thought the route looked very difficult.

This was hardly surprising, for the winter of 1969 had been a particularly dry one. Hardly any snow had fallen and consequently the South West Face was stripped of much of its overmantle. The team now tackling it found that where during the reconnaissance there had been accommodating snow and ice slopes, there was now a good deal of bare rock. It made life difficult and dangerous, and progress very slow.

Ohtsuka's plan had been to establish Camp 4 just below the Rock Band by 12 May. This proved impracticable, and it was established much lower and sooner (6 May) on the slopes below the Central Gully, using special dural platforms for the tents. From there on 8 May Konishi and Akira Yoshikawa climbed up to 25,600 ft, following the left-hand branch of the fully previously reconnoitred. Two days later Katsuhiko Kano and Hiroshi Sagono, with two Sherpas, went higher still, but discovered that after a height of about 26,000 ft the Face was so stripped of snow and ice that they had to remove their crampons and treat it as a rock climb. The rock was broken but unpleasant. Fortunately the weather was good and they were able to reach a height of 26,400 ft, where they could examine the narrow gully that cut through the Rock Band. Stripped of ice it looked formidable, but they thought it could be climbed.

However, they did not get a chance to put it to the test. While descending to Advanced Base for a rest, Kano was hit in the back by a falling stone and slightly injured. That same day Hiroshi Nakajima was also struck by a stone. Alarmed at these mishaps, Ohtsuka immediately withdrew all climbers from the South West Face, declaring that the stonefall hazard was too great and that, in any case, there wasn't time enough to complete the route before the monsoon.

Stonefall is a natural hazard on many face climbs, varying from mountain to mountain, season to season, and even hour to hour. Some faces are notorious for it – the Eigerwand, for example – but the South West Face of Everest has never been one of these. It could be that in 1970 the Japanese were particularly unfortunate in following such a dry winter, and that the blanket of snow and ice which holds most of the loose rock in place was largely absent. No other expedition has reported trouble with stonefall on this vast face.

Ohtsuka decided that the unfortunate Face team would now concentrate their efforts on making two more assaults on the South Col route. In this, however, they were frustrated by the weather, and by 21 May the expedition had withdrawn from the mountain.

Meanwhile, the Japanese ski expedition had accomplished its own peculiar achievement. Yuichiro Miura, a professional skier, skied down from the South Col to the foot of the Lhotse Face on 6 May. When his speed reached 100 m.p.h. he opened a parachute brake. Unfortunately, a shift in the wind caught him off balance and he hit some rocks which threw him over. He slid some 600 ft to the foot of the slope, stopping just short of a huge crevasse. He was unconscious but otherwise uninjured. The whole episode was dramatically recorded on film and eventually shown throughout the world on television.

Altogether, the Japanese had an unhappy time on Everest in 1970. In terms of cost, both in money and lives, the game hadn't been worth the candle. True, they had achieved their primary aim – to climb Everest – but in mountaineering terms they had achieved little that was worthwhile. Not for them the Dyhrenfurth luck! They had one small consolation prize – Miss Setuko Watanabe had reached the South Col. She was the first woman to do so, and she set a height record for her sex.

Summing up after the expedition the Deputy Leader Hiromi Ohtsuka said:

> A 39 member expedition is too large to work as a cohesive unit. One leader should not have more than 12 to work with otherwise there will be a lack of common bond among the members. Furthermore, the pleasures of mountaineering will be stifled . . . the necessity of such a big expedition should be considered with restraint in the future.

Ohtsuka's words were to prove prophetically wise, but unfortunately he was shouting against the prevailing wind. The fact is that in the 1970s mountaineering became a growth industry, and Everest itself was bound to be involved.

The world of 1970 was a very different world from that of half a century earlier when Mallory and his companions had first set out to find Mount Everest. Basically, mountaineering itself had not changed all that much, except in so far as technical advances had made life easier and safer in some respects: there is nothing to suggest that the climbers of 1970 were braver, stronger or (as far as high-altitude climbing went) more skilful than those of

1920. Nor had their dedication changed: high-altitude mountaineering involved exhaustion, suffering and nervous tension, with death riding on the climber's shoulder at every step. As technology makes things easier, the climber steps up the challenge as a counterbalance. The rewards are largely personal and private: fame is ephemeral and limited except in very few cases – a modestly successful pop star is better known to the general public than the most successful of climbers. The reasons for climbing are much the same as they were fifty years ago.

Nevertheless the external influences on the modern climber are very different from those on his predecessors. 'The last innocent adventure' James Morris called the successful Everest expedition of 1953, and though he was perhaps a decade or so early in his judgement, there was little that was innocent about the late 1960s and the 1970s.

The prime cause of all this was the increasing wealth and leisure in the more advanced countries of the world. People had the time and money to do the sort of things their grandfathers would have considered suitable only for the squirearchy. Some of them turned to climbing mountains. In schools, too, 'education for leisure' became a fashionable mode, some of it again directed towards mountain activities.

Easier travel helped: cheaper flying and long motorways took the average adventurer to places which were once almost inaccessible – even to the very foot of Everest itself. And over all this activity watched the pervasive eye of the television camera, recording, informing, ceaselessly turning out entertainment. Even if you couldn't afford to go to the mountains, you could at least live your adventures vicariously through the medium of the small screen.

It is still going on, of course, and we call it progress. Whether it will be for good or ill remains to be seen, but at least mountaineers have gained some public understanding from it all. Many more people now have a sympathy with the aims of the climbers; they realize he is not just a fool trying to break his neck in some expensive ritual.

The effect all these forces had on the leading mountaineers was to make them much more professional. Because in the early days of the sport professional guides were considered an absolute necessity, there has never been a rigid division between professional and amateur mountaineers. Even in the heyday of Victorian and Edwardian snobbery the sport always managed to blur distinctions – after all, what was the great Edward Whymper, conqueror of the Matterhorn, if he wasn't a professional mountaineer? Or, in the later years, men like Smythe, Shipton and Tilman, all of whom distinguished themselves on Everest? But in the post-war years the few became many: some were satisfying the demand for training or equipment, others working in the media or providing material upon which the media could feed.

The trend was international. Every country produced its stars – Gaston

Rebuffat in France, Carlo Mauri in Italy, Royal Robbins in the U.S.A. and many others. In Britain two Lancastrians had long dominated the scene: the wry, enigmatic Joe Brown and the pugnacious, sharp-witted Don Whillans. They were joined by others, but particularly by a young man of ascetic appearance, a Sandhurst voice and definite opinions called Christian Bonington.

It was against this background of accelerating world interest that the International Expedition to Everest's South West Face was conceived. The midwife to this ill-starred child of the seventies was Norman Dyhrenfurth.

It all began innocuously enough as a simple expedition to Antarctica. Back in 1965 two teams had put up new routes on the immensely difficult Troll Wall in Romsdal, Norway. One was a British team from Manchester and the other a Norwegian team consisting of Leif Patterson, Jon Teigland and Odd Eliassen. They all became firm friends and it was not surprising, therefore, that a year or so later John Amatt of the British party should contact Patterson suggesting they combine on an expedition.

As luck would have it Patterson was planning a trip to the Antarctic with the other two Norwegians, so he invited Amatt to join them. However, this gave the expedition an international flavour and Patterson had the idea of extending this theme by inviting climbers of other nationalities to join in as well. Dave Isles of the U.S.A., Dudzinski and Peterek (Argentinians of Polish descent) completed the team. All the members were personally known to Patterson.

Unfortunately the Antarctica project fell through, so they turned their attention to the Himalaya instead. Being of the new school of dedicated face climbers it was natural, if ambitious, that they should decide on the Rupal Flank of Nanga Parbat, regarded as the greatest single face in the Himalaya. Once again their plans were thwarted: a German expedition had already secured permission for Nanga Parbat.[4] Their choice then turned to the South West Face of Everest.

And so, by a curious combination of circumstances, the friendly trip to Antarctica had become transformed into an attempt on the hardest route of the highest mountain in the world. Patterson and Amatt had not merely changed objectives, they had changed leagues and had elected themselves to the First Division. It was a daring promotion and they startled nobody more than themselves, for none of the team had any Himalayan experience whatsoever.

Recognizing that they were getting out of their depth they turned for help to Colonel Jimmy Roberts, the man whose organizational ability had played so large a part in the first ascent in 1953 and the American success ten years later. Roberts, a former Gurkha officer, had retired from the Army and was running a trekking organization in Kathmandu. His knowledge of the Himalaya and its peoples was extensive, perhaps greater than that of any other Westerner, and he had taken part in about a dozen major expeditions, often as leader, so he was ideal for the job.

Roberts became the new leader of the venture, but it is doubtful whether even he, with all his experience, realized the magnitude of the undertaking and the scale of resources that would be necessary to climb the formidable South West Face. At this time (1968) nobody had done more than look at the face from the Western Cwm. The Japanese had not begun their explorations, nor had Bonington's team climbed the South Face of Annapurna to demonstrate that big Himalayan faces were feasible. Roberts, Patterson and Amatt were pushing out into unknown waters, with none of the resources which ultimately proved necessary.

They did, however, recognize that some Himalayan experience might be useful before tackling Everest and to this end made plans to attempt Dhaulagiri II, an unclimbed Nepalese peak of 25,429 ft, in 1969.[5] As a warm-up exercise this too was a little ambitious!

Meanwhile, the team had grown. Three Americans had joined – Gary Colliver, Barry Hagen and John Evans – as well as the Rhodesian climber Rusty Baillie. All were experienced climbers, but their addition simply exacerbated the organizational problems which were already becoming tiresome, owing to the fact that the team was scattered throughout the world. Communications were slow, especially with Roberts in Nepal and Patterson, who was now in Uganda, and the bulk of the work fell on Amatt. He bore it for some months until, in 1969, dismayed at the lack of progress, he decided to quit the venture.

Amatt's resignation was a serious blow and but for a curious twist of fate the expedition might have withered away and died stillborn for lack of progress. At this crucial time, however, Roberts received a letter from Norman Dyhrenfurth inviting him to take part in an expedition – to the South West Face of Everest! It transpired that Dyhrenfurth, unaware that others were interested, had been working on his own plans.

Roberts suggested a merger for an expedition in 1971. On the face of it this was a sensible move because it would revive the old Roberts–Dyhrenfurth partnership which had proved so successful for the Americans in 1963. The two men were complementary: Roberts for his logistical planning and knowledge of the Sherpas, Dyhrenfurth for his international connections and ability to raise the necessary money. However, it had one serious drawback. The comfortable little team originally envisaged by Patterson, in which everyone knew one another (despite their various nationalities), was on amalgamation to become a group of strangers, each jealous of his own reputation. There were serious misgivings in the Patterson team about the way in which their initial ideals were being radically altered, but the amalgamation was inevitable. Roberts and Dyhrenfurth became joint leaders, though Dyhrenfurth took the lion's share of the responsibility, including that of financing the venture.

Dyhrenfurth, in fact, assumed a staggering financial burden. As was the case with the earlier American expedition the costs escalated like a rocket; but this time, because there was no national prestige involved, there was no single national institution prepared to underwrite the expedition. It was the international nature of the enterprise which appealed to Dyhrenfurth. He wanted to demonstrate that men from different nationalities and backgrounds could work together harmoniously and to the common cause, even under conditions of extreme hardship. It was a feeling which ran deep in the Dyhrenfurth family background: his father Günter Dyhrenfurth, had organized international expedition in the thirties and he himself had run an international expedition to Lhotse in 1955. What could be a better vehicle for international co-operation than Everest, the greatest prize of all?

Yet because it was international it had this built-in financial weakness. Each country, either through its media or some charitable body, was willing to contribute *something* towards the costs, but never enough, and Dyhrenfurth found himself in a situation in which he was inviting participants from different countries simply for the extra cash they could bring in, although every addition to the team pushed up the costs even further. By the time it was all over, Dyhrenfurth was facing a bill in excess of a quarter of a million dollars.[6]

Each climber contributed 500 dollars to the expedition, but large sponsors were few and far between for the reasons mentioned – only Trans World Airlines, who gave 12,000 dollars, and the Mainichi Newspapers of Japan, who gave 25,000 dollars, were significant contributors. The countries of the so-called 'Latins' – about whom much was to be heard – made very small contributions, and France, none at all. More surprisingly perhaps, Germany and Austria, countries with a strong Himalayan tradition, also contributed very little. The direct disadvantages of being international were summed up in N.A.S.A.'s refusal to help the expedition because it was 'neither a corporation nor based in the U.S.A.'. Dyhrenfurth had hoped for 30,000 dollars because of the work he was doing on oxygen equipment.

It was not until the B.B.C. bought the TV and newspaper rights for 48,000 dollars that the finances looked healthier, though even that sum was less than Dyhrenfurth had hoped for. The B.B.C.'s total contribution jumped to 110,000 dollars, but the extra money paid for the seven-man film crew they attached to the already swollen expedition. In addition the B.B.C. sold the newspaper rights to the *Sunday Times*, who sent a reporter, Murray Sayle.

Like Topsy, the expedition just growed. By the time it was in the field there were thirty-three members from thirteen different countries, including the media men – some of whom were good climbers in their own right. It was not, however, a *team*. Patterson's original ideals had disappeared under the crushing burden of financial expediency, and so, for that matter, had Patterson himself, along with Baillie, Hagen and the two Argentinians. Of the innocent founder members, so to speak, only two remained: the Norwegians Teigland and Eliassen. Dave Isles was still there, and so were two of the other Americans who had joined Patterson before the link-up with Dyhrenfurth: Colliver and Evans. All the rest were newcomers, and they formed as disparate a bunch as one is ever likely to find on an expedition.

On paper it was a firmament of stars. Apart from those already mentioned the climbing team consisted of Wolfgang Axt and Leo Schlömmer of Austria; Duane Blume of the U.S.A.; Tony Hiebeler of West Germany; Carlo Mauri of Italy; Pierre Mazeaud of France: Harsh Bahuguna of India; Naomi Uemura and Reizo Ito of Japan; Dougal Haston and Don Whillans of Britain; and the husband and wife team of Michel and Yvette Vaucher of Switzerland. The two doctors (who were also climbers) were Peter Steele of Britain and David Peterson of the U.S.A.

Few of them had climbed together and those who had tended to cleave together in a natural defence against the ambitions of the rest, anxious to protect their own reputations. Jealousy was rampant, being a much more cogent feeling than any superimposed international camaraderie. Islands of isolation grew up, not helped by the language barrier, for when the prevailing language is English it is easy for ancient Gallic fears to be revived and a plot suspected.

Ironically, the one thing which the members had in common – their skill as mountaineers – was one of the major causes. Put plainly: there were too many chiefs and not enough Indians.

Early in the planning, Chris Bonington was enrolled as climbing leader, but the experience he had gained from his Annapurna expedition, which took place while the Everest venture was being planned, gave him food for thought and he later wrote:

> What worried me was whether I was going to be able to control a group of climbers of this calibre, all of whom would presumably want their turn out in front, and all of whom would have come with dreams – or the determination – of being in the summit party. My own authority would be tenuous, and I could even end up in an uncomfortable position as go-between for the expedition leadership and climbing members.[7]

Shrewdly, Bonington had spotted the major flaw in advance, and he withdrew from the expedition. When he later rejoined it for a short time his initial doubts were reinforced, so he withdrew again. Not even a tempting offer from the B.B.C. for him to go as a reporter could change his mind a second time.

It wasn't so much team selection as team collection: Dyhrenfurth was like a philatelist garnering the cream of the world's rare stamps – only to discover that they didn't make matched sets and some of the specimens were no longer in mint condition. But he could not afford to be too selective: some of those he would have liked to include simply couldn't get any backing and he was forced to take those who could. Only two nominees failed to bring in extra cash beyond the obligatory personal contribution of 500 dollars: the likeable Indian Army officer, Harsh Bahuguna, who had almost reached the summit of Everest in 1965, and the French politician Pierre Mazeaud, who took Dyhrenfurth's tentative inquiry as a definite offer and promptly accepted, ignoring the request for sponsorship. Whether it was because he did not wish to offend a member of the French Chamber of Deputies (and one, moreover, tipped to succeed to the plum job of Minister of Sport), or whether it was because Vaucher, Axt and Hiebeler all recommended Mazeaud, Dyhrenfurth let the matter stand.

The hard core of the team were professionals to a greater or lesser degree. Uemura and Mauri earned their livelihoods directly from their worldwide adventures (Mauri had just returned from Thor Heyerdahl's *Ra* voyage); Hiebeler owned a prestigious climbing magazine, *Alpinismus*; Haston was director of a mountaineering school, and so on. Each, therefore, had a special motive for doing well, above and beyond the call of the mountain.

Had the team been able to meet in the Alps, as originally planned, some of the weaknesses and personality clashes might have been foreseen and action taken to eliminate them, but the financially stringent situation that Dyhrenfurth found himself in prevented that. Indeed, finance – or the lack of it – dominated the preparations to a damaging extent. Quite apart from the difficulties already mentioned, Dyhrenfurth found himself once again tackling Everest when public interest in it was at its lowest. Not only the general public but the climbing fraternity too were disenchanted with the whole idea.

There were two possible explanations for this. One lay in the nature of the climb itself. The South West Face of Everest is not a particularly attractive-looking climb. It is a great triangular face whose main feature, the Rock Band, runs across it horizontally. There is no natural line up: no challenging ridge or buttress that beckons to be conquered – just an awkward obstacle to be climbed or avoided as the case may be. Dyhrenfurth had countered this by announcing in the expedition newspaper that the climb was to be the *direttissima* – that is to say, straight up. Only the American members believed this way possible.[8]

More cogent at the time, however, was the growing mood of revulsion that the climbing world was beginning to feel towards the whole concept of the huge super-marathon expedition. The Japanese Everest expedition of 1970 symbolized all that was going wrong. There was hostility towards the wheeler-dealer tactics necessary to raise the huge sums involved, the show-biz attitude of the media, the prima-donna attitude of the climbers. *If this is expedition climbing,* the mood ran, *then we want no part of it.* Indifference turned to positive antagonism, and it is fair to say that a large section of the climbing public were looking forward to the failure of Dyhrenfurth's expedition with malicious glee.

Knives were out from the start, and one can't help but feel sorry for Dyhrenfurth, who was so wrapped up in the mechanics of the venture that he failed to see how the public mood had changed.

Why this should be so is difficult to see at this distance in time. After all, Bonington's Annapurna expedition had the full media treatment and yet was a popular success with climbers and public alike. But then, it wasn't international.

Bonington's part in the Everest story was to come to full fruition some years later, but suffice to say at this stage that his withdrawal from the International Expedition dealt a serious blow to its tactical strength. His undoubted ability to command from the front when necessary would have made him the ideal climbing leader for the South West Face. His absence left a gap which was never adequately filled, though Bonington did suggest a replacement.

The man he suggested was one of the post-war legends of British climbing, a stocky, sharp-witted, aggressive Lancastrian named Don Whillans. As we have seen, in 1970 Whillans, with Dougal Haston, reached the summit of Annapurna I by the South Face – a remarkable *tour de force* and one of the landmarks of mountaineering history. He was also an Alpinist of great repute, and it was because of an Alpine climb – the Central Pillar of Frêney, a difficult route on Mont Blanc – that he was disliked by Pierre Mazeaud. In 1961, Mazeaud and two others had survived a terrible ordeal on the Frêney Pillar while trying to make the first ascent. Four of their companions had died. Later that same year Bonington, Whillans, Clough and Dlugosz snatched the first ascent, much to the disgust of Mazeaud. He thought the British were mere opportunists, trading on his own party's misfortunes. 'Mazeaud can never forgive the British,' wrote Whillans, 'and me especially, for making the first ascent of the Central Pillar of Frêney.'

Whether Dyhrenfurth was aware of Mazeaud's hatred of Whillans or not, he did know that the little Lancastrian had an outspoken nature whose very bluntness frequently upset people. Whillans seemed to move around in a perpetual aura of prickly controversy which fame and maturity (he was then thirty-seven) had done nothing to modify. On the one hand he was too good a climber to leave out, particularly since he would be teamed with Haston, his partner on the successful Annapurna climb, but on the other hand his forthright nature, in Dyhrenfurth's opinion, made him unfit to be in command. To solve this dilemma Dyhrenfurth once again sought refuge in compromise: Whillans joined the expedition, but the post of climbing leader was abolished. Instead, there was to be a 'co-ordinator' between the active men on the mountain and the Base Camp gurus. John Evans, an American, was appointed to this task.

Bonington had taken part in the route-planning during his brief membership and had given it as his opinion that a team of twelve would be sufficient for the South West Face. More than that would lead to complications – which is exactly what Hiromi Ohtsuka, leader of the Japanese climbers, had discovered.

Dyhrenfurth therefore cast around for an alternative which would keep the rest of the climbers happy. He had a choice of two: first, and most obvious, the ordinary route up the South East Ridge by way of the South Col; second, the West Ridge climbed by his own party in 1963.

The first alternative was ruled out almost immediately. The predominantly Anglo-Saxon membership of the expedition in its early stages regarded the ordinary route with disdain. It had been climbed many times, and for the vast International Expedition, composed as it was of a galaxy of star performers, to climb it again was like using a steam hammer to crack a nut. Dyhrenfurth consulted his old buddies, Barry Corbet and Barry Bishop of the 1963 team, and they concurred.

Looking back, it seems as though this was a blinkered decision taken by men who thought only in terms of massive resources. In fact the resources of the expedition, particularly in terms of Sherpas, were scarcely adequate for the South West Face. The Sherpa force was fifty-five men compared with the seventy-five the Japanese had employed. This gave Dyhrenfurth a ratio of little more than one and a half Sherpas per team member. For the first ascent, in 1953, John Hunt had needed double that ratio. Climbers were the only surplus, and as Ken Wilson, editor of *Mountain* magazine, later pointed out, a lightweight attempt via the South Col would have been a worthwhile objective. It might have been done without Sherpa support, or even without oxygen. In any case, a line of small camps leading to the South East Ridge could have been a valuable retreat route should anyone climb the South West Face and for some reason be unable to descend the same way. Nobody had ever descended the West Ridge.

Another point, and one that was to prove crucially important later on, was that the decision not to climb the ordinary route was made quite early in the planning by men whose nations had already climbed it. As more continental climbers were brought in, the relative importance of climbing Everest *by any route* grew. The late-comers were not, however, consulted. Perhaps they took it for granted that the summit was the prime objective if it came to a crunch – certainly Mazeaud did, as Whillans explained:

> The attitude of Mazeaud on receiving the invitation seems to have been

that he had been invited to *climb Everest*, not that he had been invited to join a team attempting the difficult unclimbed South West Face.

Dyhrenfurth opted for the West Ridge. Hornbein must have smiled at the irony of it when he heard, but this time it was to be the West Ridge Direct, not the alternative by the Hornbein Couloir, which the Americans had climbed in 1963. It was a formidable objective, guaranteed to stretch resources to the limit, but at the time it wasn't seen in that light. Only the advantages were seen – that it was more worthy of effort than the ordinary route, and that, should the South West Face attempt fail, the West Ridge was a nice consolation prize. It was also another hedge against the possible success of the Japanese in 1970.

Not everyone was happy with the dual role the expedition had now assumed. Rusty Baillie, at that time still a member, wrote:

> Regarding the West Ridge and the West Ridge Direct: the former has been done and the latter is splitting hairs. To my way of thinking, the time will come in Himalayan history when variants will be climbed. But it is not now. Thus I would want to attempt the Face. Also I think that the Face will need the utmost, not only from every member, but also from the expedition as an entity. All expeditions are a strain on inter-relationships, an International one even more so . . . an international one with a divided aim may well spend its energy solving problems of personality rather than of mountaineering. I therefore respectfully submit that we all put our efforts into one route. I can appreciate that our sponsors and commercial interests may expect a route by any way, but hopefully we will not have to be ruled by them in mountaineering decisions.[9]

Baillie was a prophet crying in the wilderness. He later resigned.

The team was well equipped. For their high-altitude camps they had the rigid-framed Whillans Box, a tent that Don had designed after experiencing the trauma of a Patagonian gale. Its box shape gave the occupants greater freedom of movement than an ordinary tent – no small advantage in a high camp. The oxygen equipment, too, was excellent and a credit to its designer, physiologist Dr Duane Blume.[10]

As always, there were some faults. By a quirk of design the Austrian crampons didn't fit the German boots properly and gave trouble throughout the expedition. Then, too, Blume found that the oxygen masks didn't fit the Sherpas. This was because they were standard U.S. Air Force issue, which came in two types discreetly marked *Caucasian* and *Oriental* – and the Oriental pattern was based on Vietnamese facial characteristics, which are quite different from those of Sherpas. Fortunately some masks of the 1963 pattern were available.

The radios were not always reliable either, particularly in the weather conditions the expedition was to encounter, and probably contributed to some of the misunderstanding that arose.

The only major drawback was the food, which arrived in Kathmandu in bulk instead of in the more easily organized man-day rations, and the subsequent labour involved in sorting it out was never satisfactorily accomplished. Tasty tidbits destined for the high camps would mysteriously vanish on their way up. Normally, this might have been something of a joke, but on this occasion the tidbits were eagerly sought after because the rest of the food was unpalatable. Dyhrenfurth had delegated the organization of the food to Wolfgang Axt, the thirty-five-year-old school teacher from Austria, not realizing that Axt was a vegetarian and health food fanatic. His choice of diet met with less than universal approval from his fellow team members.

In all there were some thirty-five tons of food and equipment, about half of which was flown to the STOL (Short Take Off and Landing) airstrip which had been built at Lukla in the Khumbu valley, about seven days' march below Everest Base Camp. The rest of the supplies were carried in by the expedition's 450 porters.

Base Camp was established on 23 March 1971 in the now traditional place below the Khumbu Icefall. During the march from Kathmandu relations between the various members of the expedition had been cordial. Both Whillans and Haston, however, were concerned at the holiday atmosphere of the trek; they had the uncomfortable feeling that some of the participants were not fully aware of the hardships that lay ahead, and they wondered how the camaraderie would stand up when it came to the crunch.

During this walk-in, the members were asked to choose the route they wished to take. In doing this, Dyhrenfurth was establishing democracy in the same way he had during the 1963 American expedition. It was the exact opposite to the dictatorial method used by the Japanese (Uemura must have been surprised) but there is nothing to indicate it was more successful.

After some changes of mind the teams settled down as follows:

For the South West Face: Evans (co-ordinator), Colliver, Peterson (all Americans); Ito and Uemura of Japan; Whillans and Haston from Britain; the German Hiebeler; and the Austrian Schlömmer.

For the West Ridge: Axt (co-ordinator); the Norwegians Teigland and Eliassen; the Vauchers, husband and wife; Bahuguna of India; Mauri of Italy; Isles of the U.S.A.; Mazeaud of France; and Steele, the British doctor.

Of the two leaders, Roberts intended to look after Base Camp, and Dyhrenfurth, Advanced Base in the Western Cwm. The Sherpas were to be divided equally between the two teams, once progress had been made beyond Advanced Base.

Hardly had Base Camp been established when there was a roar from the

Khumbu Icefall and the startled climbers saw huge blocks of ice tumbling down, smashing everything in their path. It was an awesome warning to everyone that the holiday was over and there was grim work ahead.

The Icefall was in bad condition, very unstable and totally unpredictable as always. A great curving depression, which seemed to offer a quick way through it, proved illusory, and it was a fortnight before a relatively secure route was pioneered and Camp 1 set up on the lip of the Cwm. On 5 April Camp 2 – Advanced Base – was established in the Cwm at 21,600 ft, and from there each team began to make its own way towards its objective. International relationships immediately began to wear thin.

On the Face route things began smoothly. There was a much better covering of snow than the Japanese had enjoyed the year before and the four lead climbers, Whillans, Haston, Uemura and Ito, had little difficulty in fixing ropes up the fairly easy snow slopes and establishing Camp 3(F) on the same spot their predecessors had used.

Meanwhile the West Ridge team were encountering problems. The snow slopes leading to the West Shoulder were proving to be difficult – more so than in 1963 when the Americans climbed them. The two Norwegians, Eliassen and Teigland, together with the Indian climber Bahuguna, had at first tried to go straight up, but found this impossible. Later, in a savage article in *La Suisse,* Vaucher was to claim these three lacked experience and had poor ice-climbing technique. Be that as it may, nobody else was willing to try a direct route up the slope.

Vaucher and Axt now went to work to re-establish the original American route of 1963. They found that even this was difficult. Their way was blocked by an icefall which caused a circuitous detour, first downhill, then by a horizontal traverse, and finally up the slope again to rejoin the original line.

Axt then teamed up with Bahuguna. They managed to establish Camp 3(W) at 22,600 ft, then on 17 April, after a night at this camp, they climbed up to the crest of the ridge, prospecting the way ahead and seeking a suitable place for Camp 4(W). In this they were successful: Camp 4(W) would be on the ridge itself, and so far as they could see the ascent of the rocky West Ridge would not be an insuperable task. Much heartened by this progress the two men descended.

It was at this point that chance threw the dice against them. The two men had worked hard and were due for a rest. They could have gone straight down to Advanced Base (and indeed Dyhrenfurth had wanted Bahuguna to go down to Base Camp itself for a recuperation period some days earlier but he had declined). Now, however, as they returned from the ridge they spotted a better site for Camp 3(W), which they had always thought was too low anyway. They decided to stay the night at 3(W), move it to its new site next day, then return to Advanced Base.

Meanwhile, their companions had not been idle. Their aim was to shorten the somewhat complicated route to Camp 3(W). Mauri and Mazeaud climbed up the slopes and dumped loads of ropes, stakes and pitons in readiness for this task, then Vaucher and Eliassen went to work, paying out the rope and fixing it in place with stakes and ice screws. It was a horizontal traverse about 400 ft long, curling round a bulge of the mountain. The snow slope was some 40° – by no means excessive – and wherever the rope was pinned to the slope Vaucher and Eliassen cut a platform or large step, where a man could stand and rest in comparative safety. This was useful because if a climber was following the rope and was attached to it by a safety line he would have to stop and unhook himself whenever he came to a stake or piton, then hook on again beyond it. Laden porters in particular would appreciate this: under normal circumstances many of the climbers might not bother with a safety attachment because the traverse was not all that difficult. The new traverse was a valuable piece of work: it cut out the downhill bit of the route and shortened the time to Camp 3(W) by about an hour.

Up above, Axt and Bahuguna were told of these developments by radio and they in turn informed the others of their plans for a new Camp 3(W).

Next day, 18 April, Axt reported on the radio that the weather looked threatening: dark clouds were piling up to the north-west. Nevertheless, he and Bahuguna continued with their plan to move Camp 3(W).

At Advanced Base on this morning a different kind of storm was brewing. The two Vauchers, Carlo Mauri and Pierre Mazeaud went to Dyhrenfurth with a strong complaint that their equipment for the West Ridge was not getting through, whereas the equipment for the Face team seemed to get through without difficulty. They had mentioned it before, but now they put it in stronger terms. They suspected bias: that preferential treatment was being given to the Face team because it was primarily an Anglo-American affair and therefore the only part of the expedition to interest the B.B.C., which had put so much money into the venture.

Dyhrenfurth explained that there was a hold-up at Camp 1. He suggested that to help matters out they should all go down the Cwm to Camp 1, pick up loads and bring them up. After all, during the American expedition he had led, characters like Unsoeld had cheerfully trudged uphill with loads of 60 lb. or more. But the Latins (as they had become known) refused to countenance this.

It was beneath their dignity, they said, to do work which was intended for Sherpas. Disgusted at their attitude, Dyhrenfurth decided to set an example by shouldering a pack frame himself and setting off for Camp 1.

Here was the chiefs and Indians syndrome showing its naked rawness! Throughout the expedition there had been (and continued to be) a reluctance on the part of many members to carry loads. In some instances the Latins had not even carried their own personal gear, but they were not alone in dodging heavy packs. Even where ostensibly heavy loads had been carried, on some occasions suspicious colleagues had surreptitiously 'weighed' them and found them to be remarkably light. One-upmanship was rampant. Was it that load-carrying was really beneath their dignity, or was it that nobody wanted to burn himself out, thereby reducing his chance of the summit? The Sherpas, who were the silent butt-end of all this manoeuvring, were not impressed.

At Camp 1 Dyhrenfurth met Peterson, Haston, Schlömmer and Hiebeler and tried to sort out the logistic bottleneck. He then packed two oxygen cylinders ('One each for Face and Ridge, in fairness to both teams') and plodded back up the Cwm towards Advanced Base.

As he climbed the weather rapidly deteriorated and soon the Cwm was filled with a raging blizzard. Only the willow wands stuck in the snow at regular intervals showed Dyhrenfurth the way forward. A snow avalanche from the slopes of Nuptse struck him, but by bracing himself he was able to keep his stance, and fortunately it was only powder snow, not the wet, cloying, obliterating kind. He struggled on, and then out of the white darkness appeared the familiar figure of Ang Lakpa, his personal Sherpa, come to see that the sahib was all right.

Together they trudged back through the storm, losing their way momentarily, until they picked up the line of markers again. Suddenly, high above them they heard a fearful scream, then another and another. They shouted back but the wind whipped their voices away. They knew that the screams had come from Harsh Bahaguna.

While Dyhrenfurth and Ang Lakpa struggled up the Cwm a distraught and exhausted Wolfgang Axt staggered into Advanced Base Camp. He had descended from Camp 3(W) in the storm. 'Bahuguna is still up there!' he gasped.

At once a rescue party scrambled into their gear and set off to rescue the Indian climber. Rivalries and national jealousies were put aside as Eliassen, Vaucher, Whillans, Mazeaud, Mauri, Steele and Ang Phurba faced the storm, in automatic response to the age-old climbers' code that help must be given at all costs. It was 5.15 p.m. Night in the Cwm wasn't far off.

They all climbed as rapidly as possible. It was a lung-tearing effort made worse by the storm. Perhaps because they knew the route better than the others, Eliassen and Vaucher were the first to reach the hapless victim.

Bahuguna's condition was bad. His chest harness was attached to the long fixed rope of the traverse and he just hung there, helpless with cold and exhaustion. A rime of ice covered his face. One glove was gone, and the harness had pulled up his clothes, exposing his bare midriff to the elements.

Eliassen, more to comfort him than anything else, asked him if he was O.K. and incredibly the Indian seemed to murmur that he was. The two men tried to move him across the traverse but were prevented by the force of the storm. They then decided to lower him on a rope and attempt to swing him across the slope to the shelter of a crevasse, where possibly the others could reach him. Hardly had they begun to lower him than he turned upside down, and Whillans, who had now arrived at the scene, climbed down and turned him right way up. Whillans then tried to move him sideways, at considerable risk to himself, but found it impossible. There was only one other option - to lower Bahuguna straight down the slope to another crevasse where it was hoped Steele, Mazeaud and Ang Phurba could take charge of him.

Thirty-five feet above the sheltering crevasse the rope ran out. Whillans, teetering around on the steep slopes in the face of the storm and darkness, without ice axe or protective rope, took one last look at the Indian. He was unconscious, his face blue, his eyes staring. In half an hour he would be dead.

'Sorry, Harsh old son, you've had it,' muttered Whillans.

The rescuers were themselves now in an unenviable position. Exhausted, battered by the storm, they had to fight their way back to camp.

It was a dejected group that met Dyhrenfurth in Advanced Base that night. Axt knew nothing of the final tragedy, for Steele had sent him to bed with sleeping pills before the rescue team set out, but the rest were there in a sombre, angry mood. Harsh Bahuguna had been popular with everyone. Mazeaud accused Axt of murder through negligence, but Dyhrenfurth calmed him down, promising a full inquiry next day.

Next morning, as the team assembled in the mess tent, Axt was the last to enter.

'*Wie geht es Harsh?*' ('How is Harsh?') he demanded.

'*Weisst du es nocht nicht? Er ist tot!*' ('Don't you know? He is dead!') Dyhrenfurth replied.

Axt burst into tears.

The inquiry was set for 10 a.m. and Dyhrenfurth directed Bill Kurban of the B.B.C. to tape-record the proceedings, in case there should be further inquiries or disputes. Asked what had happened, Axt said:

> We were not roped during the descent, there was no need, there were no difficulties at all. Since I knew Michel [Vaucher] and Odd [Eliassen] had placed fixed ropes on all the steeper sections, I left my climbing rope and my harness and karabiner at the new camp. At first Harsh went ahead. Around 2 p.m. the weather turned bad. Soon we were caught in a raging storm. When we reached the long rope-traverse I took over the lead and got across it hand over hand. It was very long and tiring as hell. At the far end I waited for Harsh to follow. Voice communication was impossible, the storm was much too strong. I waited for a long time, perhaps as much as an hour. My hands and feet lost all feeling. Then I saw Harsh tied into a fixed rope with a

37. Chinese climbers on Everest, 1960. (Xinhua News Agency)

38. Camp IV on the South West Face, 1975. (Ronnie Richards)

(*Facing page, top*)
39. The revolt of 1971. Dyhrenfurth (extreme right) argues with (left to right) Mazeaud, Evans, Vaucher, Axt, Yvette Vaucher and Mauri. (John Cleare)

(*Facing page, bottom*)
40. Sherpas taking Bahuguna's body out of the Western Cwm after the Indian's tragic death in 1971. (John Cleare)

(*Above*)
41. The gully through the Rock Band on the South West Face. (Paul Braithwaite)

(*Facing page*)
42. Dougal Haston approaching the South Summit during the first ascent of the South West Face, 1975. (Doug Scott)

(*Above*)
43. Doug Scott on the summit of Everest after the first ascent of the South West Face, 1975. (Doug Scott)

(*Above*)
44. A Russian climber on the so-called Fireplace Pitch of the Central Pillar – some of the most technically difficult climbing on Everest. (Novosti)

(*Facing page*)
45. The summit of Everest seen from advanced base camp during the 1986 North East ridge expedition. The Second Step is quite distinctive. (Dr John English)

(*Facing page, top*)
46. The North Face of Everest, scene of much recent activity. The North East Ridge and its Pinnacles can be seen on the left, leading to the skyline and Second Step. The Great Couloir and West Ridge are distinctive. Changtse is in front. (Dr John English)

(*Facing page, bottom*)
47. The North East Ridge of Everest, with the Pinnacles where Boardman and Tasker disappeared in 1982. (Dr John English)

(*Above*)
48. Harry Taylor and Russell Brice on the first traverse of the Pinnacles, Everest North East Ridge, 1988. (Dr John English)

(*Above*)
50. The approach to the South Col by the East Face, called by the climbers 'The Cauliflower Ridge'. Compare the complexities of this ridge with the 1953 route on the other side of the col. (Stephen Venables)

(*Facing page*)
51. Paul Teare above the buttress, and starting Day 2 of the summit push on the 1988 Kangshung Face expedition. The huge buttress behind is the route of the 1983 American expedition. (Stephen Venables)

52. Everest – more than ever a symbol of world mountaineering. (Walt Unsworth)

harness and karabiner, groping his way round the last corner of the steep ice-slope that separated us. He waved with one hand. Everything seemed O.K., no indication of any serious difficulty. I was really worried about frostbite so I went down. Just before I got to the camp I heard his screams and alerted everybody. I couldn't have gone up as I was completely done in.[11]

When he was asked why he did not stay with Bahuguna he replied:

> I had no idea how bad things were with him, and besides what could I have done without a rope or karabiner? Harsh had taken his gear but I would have had to go back hand over hand over that long traverse. I simply didn't have enough strength in me for that and my hands and feet felt like blocks of ice.[12]

It was not the end of the affair for Axt. On his return to India some weeks later he was questioned closely by Brigadier Gyan Singh and Major H.P.S. Ahluwalia, who were the committee appointed by the Indian Mountaineering Federation to look into the causes of the tragedy. After considering various statements and a transcript of the B.B.C. tape, they issued the following statement:

> According to Axt, he did not go back to look for Bahuguna because he had no harness or carabiner without which he would have been of little help. Presumably for the same reason he crossed the rope traverse quickly without waiting for Bahuguna to follow close behind. But even before he started, Axt knew about the existence and nature of the traverse and as an 'ice-specialist' he should also have known that the harness and the carabiner would be needed on this obstacle. However, he chose to leave this essential safety equipment, weighing no more than a few hundred grams, behind for 'reasons of weight'. The Committee, therefore, consider that Bahuguna may not have lost his life if Axt had brought his essential safety equipment and travelled close to his rope-mate.
>
> The Committee find it difficult to agree that he did not realize that Bahuguna was in difficulty until he heard his shouts for help at 4.15 p.m.
>
> The Committee rule out wilful foul play on anyone's part.
>
> The Committee are not certain if Bahuguna was, in fact, wearing silk or nylon gloves under his thick outer gloves. But, apart from that his clothing was appropriate for tackling the traverse, and in his rucksack he was carrying adequate insulated clothing. Unfortunately, after Bahuguna was incapacitated on the fixed rope, the clothing he was wearing was not sufficient to protect him from the elements and keep him warm.[13]

This seems less than fair on poor Axt. It was precisely because he was an 'ice-specialist' that he felt he did not need the safety harness – as events in his case proved. He did not expect to have to return along the rope to help Bahuguna. It was Harsh Bahuguna's enthusiasm and willingness that finally overstretched him and led to his death.

The great storm lasted for ten days, marooning the climbers in their camps. Through rifts in the clouds the men at Advanced Base could see from time to time the body of Harsh Bahuguna dangling down the slopes of Everest like a puppet on a string. The sight contributed to the general mood of depression occasioned by the accident, the never-ending storm and the food shortages the storm created.

Tony Hiebeler, editor of *Alpinismus*, had had enough. He had never acclimatized properly and had gone down to Base Camp on the first morning of the storm. When he heard of Bahuguna's death it was the last discouraging blow. He wrote a note for Dyhrenfurth: 'I am a physical and mental wreck, I can't take a single step towards the mountain – forgive me.' He packed his rucksack and left for home on 25 April.

Hiebeler left for the best of motives – he genuinely felt he was no use to the expedition, and that he could do more to help the venture from his office in Munich. But of course, the media, realizing that things were going badly for the expedition and knowing that international tensions and squabbles make better news stories than the climbing of a mountain, boosted his 'defection' out of all proportion. Had they but known it, they were shortly to have a field day.

Bahuguna's tragic death had particularly affected the spirit of the West Ridge team. Steele and Eliassen had lost all interest in it: all they wanted was to help the Face team to achieve their objective and then get off the mountain as quickly as possible. Mazeaud and Mauri, too, wanted no more to do with the West Ridge, but for a different reason. They felt it was too difficult and requested a switch to the South Col route, much to Dyhrenfurth's disgust:

> I tried to convince them that Everest has already been climbed by five expeditions by way of the South Col. All told, 23 climbers of six nations have reached the summit that way. I considered this colossal investment in time, manpower and money unjustifiable for a route which at this stage of Himalayan mountaineering is of no further interest . . . All my pleas were in vain. Against my better judgement I proposed a vote to be taken.[14]

The vote was among the West Ridgers only. Axt, Isles and Surdel (a B.B.C. cameraman assigned to the Ridge) voted to stick with the original plan; Steele and Eliassen voted to join the Face team in an all-out effort; Teigland voted to go with the majority. And the majority proved to be the four Latins: Mazeaud, Mauri and the two Vauchers, all of whom voted for the South Col route.

It was as Dyhrenfurth had feared and he wrote:

> It is more and more obvious that Carlo Mauri and Pierre Mazeaud are in no way interested in an all-out team effort. All they want is personal glory by reaching the summit the easiest way possible and to become national heroes in France and Italy. Also the Vauchers' sole interest lies in the summit . . . Despite serious misgivings and deep disappointment, I declared myself ready and willing to lend support to their new project. . . .[15]

Man proposes, but the mountain disposes . . . The decision was taken on the fifth day of the storm at a time when nobody realized that it was going to last five more days, making it one of the worst storms in the history of the mountain. By the end of it morale and health were badly eroded. Most members went down to base to recuperate or to attend the funeral of Harsh Bahuguna, who was cremated at Gorak Shep and whose ashes were sent home to Dehra Dun.

Supplies once again began to move up into the Cwm from Base Camp, but Jimmy Roberts, who was in charge of the logistics, was not happy with the situation. There simply were not enough porters to supply two teams simultaneously, added to which the passage through the Icefall was changing daily owing to unusually frequent ice movements, which made the journey slower and more hazardous. He had put it to Dyhrenfurth that the South Col attempt should be scrapped and all resources concentrated on the Face, but Dyhrenfurth was reluctant to break his word to Mazeaud and the rest of the Latins.

Eventually, Roberts could stand it no longer. Unable to hold a full discussion of the situation with his co-leader at Advanced Base because of intermittent radio contact, he broadcast to all the expedition his thoughts on what needed to be done. Basically it was to scrap the South Col route and concentrate on the Face.

It seems that faulty radio transmission prevented Dyhrenfurth from hearing Roberts' message, but he had by this time come to the same conclusion. The South Col route would have to be abandoned – but, of course, not without a vote. He therefore went on the air, ignorant of Roberts' appeal, to ask members yet again to vote for which route they wanted.

The result was a foregone conclusion. Dyhrenfurth had caught the Latins divided: the two Vauchers were actually on their way down to Base Camp and therefore unable to vote, which left only Mazeaud and Mauri in favour of the South Col route. To make sure the decision was overwhelmingly democratic, Dyhrenfurth even included the leading Sherpas in the voting, much to the justified amazement of Mazeaud. The Sherpas voted for the Face route too – after all, their part in it was a simple straightforward snow slope which was both easier and safer than the long arduous flog up to the South Col!

Mazeaud was furious. The coincidence of the two broadcasts convinced him that he was the victim of background plotting. As his accusations grew wilder he inevitably included the arch-villain, Whillans, 'that English working-man' (true) who 'stood to gain millions from Karrimor for the climb' (untrue).[16] Coming from a French Gaullist Deputy it is difficult to judge whether Mazeaud meant 'English' or 'working-man' to be the bigger insult. Perhaps fortunately for both (and certainly for Mazeaud), Whillans was at one of the advanced camps at the time.

Mazeaud and Mauri packed and descended to Base Camp. As he left Dyhrenfurth he gave one final histrionic outburst:

> They expect me, Pierre Mazeaud, Member of the French Assembly, aged forty-two, to work as a sherpa for Anglo-Saxons and Japanese. Never! This is not me, but France they have insulted!

It was just what the popular press had been hoping for. Bang went international co-operation. Bang went *entente cordiale*. And bang went any chance Mazeaud had of becoming Minister of Sport.

At Base Camp Mazeaud and Mauri joined the two Vauchers, who were incensed at not being in on the vote. All were convinced that the affair was a typically devious Anglo-Saxon plot, engineered by the B.B.C. to ensure that the two Britons, Whillans and Haston, got to the summit in preference to anyone else. The Americans and Japanese were in collusion with the British (though why this should be so remained unexplained). Meanwhile Whillans, up in the Cwm, had ordered the only camp established by the South Col party to be struck: a gesture of finality which enraged Mazeaud even more. Wild accusations flew in every direction and when the hapless Dyhrenfurth, a sick man, returned to Base Camp, Yvette Vaucher pelted him with snowballs, yelling *'Voici le salaud!'* ('Here's the bastard!')

The Latins were for leaving straight away, but even at this late juncture Dyhrenfurth procrastinated. He persuaded them to stay until Jimmy Roberts returned from Harsh Bahaguna's funeral next day. He was hoping for some mediation that would patch up the quarrel – by this time he himself was so ill that effective decision-taking was quite beyond him.

When Roberts returned and apprised himself of the situation his action was immediate. Tough as old boots and a hard whisky drinker, he had been brought up in a different world from Dyhrenfurth's. His school was that of the British Army, where to command meant just that. He called together the four dissidents and said: 'No South Col. Face only – and if you don't like it you can go. There will be no discussion.'

Roberts' attitude did nothing to ease the situation. Now more determined than ever to quit, the Latins threatened to crucify the leaders at press conferences in Europe, and there were wild innuendoes about reprisals. A Sherpa guard was mounted on the vulnerable and valuable oxygen supply.

Next day, as they made preparations for leaving, the Latins' anger still bubbled and, in the mess tent that night at dinner, it boiled over into one final, furious row. Peter Steele, the British doctor at Base Camp, has described what happened:

At dinner one could predict a confrontation, and it came; yet I feel sure it might have been avoided. Instead of amicably forgetting our differences for the last night and all sitting together, the leaders and the predominantly Anglo-American members sat down at one end of the mess tent while opposite and separated by a short distance were the Vauchers, Mazeaud and Mauri with Jurec Surdel, Odd Eliassen and myself.

John Evans arrived late, having come down from the Hill and gave a first-hand account of events on the mountain. 'Camp VI has been established and occupied this morning by Don and Dougal. The oxygen sets are working well and only minor troubles have been found with the rubber valves freezing up. Hopes are rising for the summit and morale is on the up.'

Yvette got up from the table to go to bed and upbraided John Evans in an emotional tirade, sarcastically thanking him for letting them down over the vote. John took it with characteristic calm and charity but the fuse was ignited and the charge exploded soon after. As Michel Vaucher, Carlo Mauri and Pierre Mazeaud left the tent the latter threw some provocative taunts at Norman and the encounter began in earnest. The Latins were down one end of a long table, the leaders at the other end and various members ranged on both sides.

All the old arguments were produced, the old ground ploughed over and the tent took on the air of a courtroom. Pierre Mazeaud, magistrat, député, membre de L'Assemblée Nationale, was in his element holding the floor with a powerful command of language and rhetoric. He cut a fine figure leaning on the large teapot, his index finger pointed and wagging. Carlo and Michel sat by and said little. I translated for them when they misunderstood the English.

Norman sat back at the end of the table and listened with attention and dignity as Mazeaud's loquacious accusations poured out: the Anglo-Saxon plot to oust the Latins, collusion with the B.B.C. to put a Briton on the top for the success of their film, Whillans standing to make a million from his boxes if he reached the summit, allegations of drunkenness and pot smoking at Camp II, distorted radio messages over the vote. He rounded off with a personal thrust, *'Norman, tu es intelligent mais tu es faible, pas comme ton père.'*

One man, a B.B.C. cameraman, had been sitting quietly; his head was buried into his chest as he dozed off the effects of the whisky that had been circulating freely. In the middle of Mazeaud's most poignant plea for reconsideration of the decision on the South Col he stood up, lurched towards and fell across the table, dislodging his spectacles.

'Look, another drunken Englishman,' shouted Mazeaud. 'You are all drunkards and idiots.'

Jimmy Roberts, who had remained notably silent in the face of the onslaught, leaned forwards and slowly, deliberately and with power of feeling said: 'Fuck off, Mazeaud.'

Mazeaud's mouth drooped in horror. The bubble burst and a peal of hysterical laughter rent the air, doing nothing to placate the now furious Frenchman. Jimmy called for Sirdar Lakpa and, speaking in Nepali, told him to muster a squad of Sherpas outside the tent in case of trouble. But they were already there. Eager faces stood back in the shadows hanging on every moment of the action.[17]

The next day the Latins left. If their conduct during the last few days had been deplorable, it was also understandable. Human vanity had led them to expect more than the expedition could give. They had seen it, wrongly, as a way to achieve personal ambitions – Mazeaud would have been the first Frenchman to climb Everest, Mauri the first Italian and Yvette Vaucher the first woman. As the Swiss had already climbed the mountain, no similar accolade was in store for Vaucher himself, though there was the possibility of man and wife climbing the mountain together, which would no doubt have been personally satisfying and publicly profitable. The pity was that Vaucher was one of the ablest climbers on the expedition and his rightful place was on the Face, with Whillans and the others.

Strangely enough, despite the fireworks and histrionics, the charges and counter-charges, there were some deep-lasting friendships formed, even between the Latins and the rest. Mauri, in particular, was unhappy at the way things had gone and he seems to have been dragged along by events against his will.

Needless to say, there was no deep-laid plot, by the B.B.C. or anyone else, to exclude the Latins or deny them their moments of glory. But had they been misled in the first place? Mazeaud certainly thought so and always maintained that the invitation was to climb Everest, not the South West Face. How he could have believed this, in view of the world-wide publicity that heralded the expedition and extolled the Face climb, is difficult to understand, but it is possible. The responsibility must rest with Dyhrenfurth, who acted from the start like a straw bending to accommodate every prevailing gust of wind.

The defection of the Latins was no serious loss to an expedition with so much manpower in reserve. Unfortunately, it was at this point that sickness swept like a scythe through the ranks and seriously reduced any chance of success.

Almost from the beginning the expedition had been dogged by minor illnesses, and there was some complaint from the hardier members that the doctors were molly-coddling their patients, sending them down to recuperate when it wasn't really necessary. But as time went on even the critics had to admit that the victims really were ill.

The earliest casualty was Dyhrenfurth himself. Four days before he left home, a routine check by his doctor had revealed a thyroid complaint, but not wishing to jeopardize the expedition he had kept the news to himself. Dyhrenfurth also seemed particularly prone to the fairly common high-altitude sore throat (he suffered badly both in 1963 and in 1971) and these two ailments, combined with the debilitating tensions of the previous few weeks, finally brought him down with glandular fever. Steele sent him home, and as the same illness swept through the team, Teigland, Howell, Colliver, Blume, Eliassen and Evans left too, though Eliassen and Evans recovered and rejoined the expedition. Bronchitis, pneumonia, colds and the inevitable headaches and sore throats all began to take a toll. Only four men remained unaffected throughout – Whillans, Haston, Ito and Uemura, and they were the four who were out in front tackling the Face.

With all these upheavals Roberts was now the expedition leader and Whillans the climbing leader. Whillans, Haston and the two Japanese had worked steadily on the Face, pushing the route up the great Central Couloir towards the Rock Band. Camps were established on the same sites as the former Japanese camps, using the alloy levelling platforms that the Japanese had left behind. Camp V was occupied on 5 May at 26,000 ft.

The problem from there was how to tackle the Rock Band, that immense fractured wall that ran across the mountain, barring access to the upper Face. The two Britons pushed out to the left to investigate the gullies that the Japanese had thought so promising, but they rejected them as being too steep. The centre of the wall was impregnable (so much for the hoped-for Direct route!), so they explored out to the right along a broad but difficult ramp. At the far end of this, they established Camp VI (27,200 ft).

For days at a time the weather was bad, preventing any progress. At times such as this the two Japanese retreated down the fixed ropes to Advanced Base where they waited out the storm. Whillans and Haston, however, remained in the high camp and because of this came in for criticism on the grounds that they were using up oxygen supplies to no good purpose, even though they were using it only for sleeping. During the bad weather days, said Whillans, 'we conserved it and just sat there feeling bloody miserable.'

Apart from the two Japanese and the Sherpas, there was virtually no support for the two Britons. Whillans had asked Axt to help, but Axt was still visibly affected by the death of Bahuguna. He told Whillans that he could not go onto the Face because he had promised his wife that he would not – it was too dangerous. Schlömmer, the other Austrian, did volunteer to help, providing he could lead, but his request was refused. Shortly afterwards the two Austrians returned to Kathmandu, where the media representatives were waiting like vultures to snap up the latest 'international' controversy. They were delighted when Schlömmer accused the British of hogging the lead. It seemed to confirm everything the Latins had said earlier: that the whole thing was a typically devious British plot.

Certainly the rejection of Schlömmer's help seems curious until one learns the background. The truth is that the Austrian had gained a reputation among the Face team for dodging work. On one occasion, when he was due to go up to one of the high camps, he asked Whillans to send down a Sherpa to carry his personal gear, which the outraged Lancastrian indignantly refused to do. It was felt, therefore, that a climber who had avoided the hard and boring job of establishing the camps up the Central Gully had no right suddenly to slip into the lead when things got more interesting.

Nevertheless Schlömmer's accusation was hard to shake off. The fact is that Whillans and Haston were in the lead, and stayed there for three weeks. Yet who else was capable of taking over? Ito and Uemura had their chances, but didn't seem to have the tactical flair of the British: 'I think they just lacked the Whillans cunning,' said Haston. They seemed quite happy in the role they were playing, and both sides had great respect for the other's contribution.

Both parties too were deeply appreciative of the effort put in by the Sherpas, who tried their best to keep the camps supplied, often without any sahib support. Both they and Uemura managed to reach Camp VI carrying heavy loads and without using oxygen.

Above Camp VI, near the end of the big ramp, an 800-ft buttress, black and formidable, reared up. It was split by a gulley which, though climbable, was a serious task at that altitude. The climbers were encumbered with oxygen gear, and the cold was intense, often more than 35° below freezing.

Whillans climbed up part of the way, then, rounding a corner, was astonished to see that it was a fairly simple matter to traverse to the right over some broken slabs and join the well-known ordinary route on the South East Ridge! The temptation must have been immense, but after all the trauma of the expedition how could he opt out in this fashion? He knew he would be accused of hypocrisy, of having planned it all from the start.

Turning his back on easy fame he faced the gully again. When Haston came up they looked at the obstacle and knew that they simply did not have the resources to tackle it.

'How about buggering off?' said Whillans. And the great international dream was over.

# 18

## 'All the Winds of Asia'

The media had a field day at the expense of the International Expedition. Helped by the frustrations and indiscretions of the continental members, they presented to the world a picture of shattered idealism, more than somewhat tinged by a touch of 'we told you so'.

Not everyone saw it in that light, and certainly not many of those who took part did. John Cleare of the B.B.C. team, and himself a good climber, wrote:

> Had the summit been reached it would have been hailed as one of the greatest achievements in mountaineering history, and the critics would conveniently have forgotten their cynical remarks. The International ideal did not fall far short of complete realization, despite the disruption caused for a short time by the South Col group, and some later bickering about the lead on the face, for these were differences of personality rather than nationality. For most of us the facts are simple. We were able to work and climb in complete accord with thirty-one mountaineers and film men from thirteen nations, sometimes even with no common language, for over a hundred days. I have a host of new friends and offers of floors to sleep on and partners to climb with all over the world. Perhaps there is more to success than reaching a summit?[1]

Murray Sayle, the *Sunday Times* reporter who accompanied the team and who as a non-climber was able to assess the situation dispassionately, was near the mark when he said that the expedition was plagued by bad luck from the start. Certainly very little went right for them, and the great storm in which Harsh Bahuguna died shattered them physically and morally. The wave of sickness was accelerated by this. Cleare wrote:

> In retrospect there were two major causes of failure – each serious enough in itself to have stopped a less powerful expedition – bad weather and

sickness, the latter aided by the results of the former. Although the assault team was stopped well short of the summit their record is impressive. They went 450 metres higher than the two previous Japanese attempts on the face. Whillans and Haston spent twenty-one days continuously above 7,450 m., with the Japanese close behind, and so broke all previous altitude endurance records. Seventeen Sherpas carried fifty-five loads to 7,925 m., and two actually carried to Camp 6 without oxygen – a very gallant effort without which nothing would have been possible.[2]

Despite the brave words, and the brave deeds, the feeling remains that there was a fundamental weakness, not so much in the idea of an international expedition, but in the way it was finally structured. And for this the responsibility must rest with Norman Dyhrenfurth. The *ad hoc* collection of climbers brought together by the feverish chase for financial support virtually ensured that the team members would be incompatible. Nothing was made clear enough to the participants: Dyhrenfurth, in seeking to please all men, had succeeded in pleasing none.

The international dream seemed irrevocably shattered, and the chances of anyone repeating the experiment were dismissed. Yet within twelve months it *was* repeated.

Dr Karl Maria Herrligkoffer was a fifty-seven-year-old Munich doctor with flowing white hair, a bushy moustache and a passion for organizing climbing expeditions, though he himself was not a noted climber. He had begun back in 1953 when, despite considerable opposition, he had organized a 'memorial' expedition in tribute to all those who had died in pre-war days on Nanga Parbat, the 8,000-m. peak in the Punjab. Nanga Parbat had always been considered a 'German' mountain and on two particularly disastrous expeditions in 1934 and 1937 a total of eleven Germans and fifteen porters had lost their lives. One of the victims was Willi Merkl, half brother of Karl Herrligkoffer and leader of the 1934 expedition.

The 1953 expedition was crowned with success when Hermann Buhl of Innsbruck, possibly the finest climber of his day, made an incredible solo dash for the summit. Unfortunately, in making his attempt Buhl had disobeyed Herrligkoffer's orders, and what should have been unalloyed joy turned into acrimony and a law suit.

Since then Herrligkoffer had organized a succession of expeditions, including six more to Nanga Parbat, a mountain that is burned deep in the German dream and which has attracted many of their best climbers. One such (though actually he was Tyrolean) was Reinhold Messner, who, with his brother Günther, made a desperate traverse of the mountain during Herrligkoffer's 1970 expedition. Günther was killed during the descent, and once again there were legal battles and considerable acrimony after the expedition.

There is no doubt that in the international climbing scene Herrligkoffer had gained a reputation as a controversial figure. Yet he was the man who, having obtained permission to attempt Everest in the pre-monsoon period of 1972, decided on yet another international expedition to the South West Face.

The reasons were purely financial. Unlike Dyhrenfurth, Herrligkoffer had no ardent international dreams – all his previous expeditions had been Austro-German – but the costs of mounting a large expedition to Everest were very different from those involved in sending a team to Nanga Parbat. The organization called grandiloquently the Deutsches Institut für Auslandforschung (German Institute for Exploration), which the food doctor had set up to handle his expeditions simply did not have that sort of money. It was necessary, if distasteful, to bring in outside help.

Herrligkoffer was now in much the same situation as Dyhrenfurth had been, though he acted more shrewdly and did not cast his net quite as wide. As the organization proceeded various Japanese, Spanish, Austrian and German climbers dropped out, dissatisfied with the arrangements. Sometimes it was Herrligkoffer himself who dismissed a climber, as in the case of Mischa Saleki, an Iranian. Doug Scott, who later joined the English team, explained: 'He had become a casualty of the frenetic fund raising period prior to the expedition and when he wrote an article for *Alpinismus* Herrligkoffer had crossed him off the list.'[3] At the time Herrligkoffer was involved in a court case against *Alpinismus*.

One of the early casualties was Chris Bonington. Initially, Herrligkoffer had invited Whillans and Haston to join the team and it was Haston who suggested that Bonington would be a useful member, not only for his climbing ability but also because his successful venture to Annapurna had given him strong contacts with the media and publishing worlds. Bonington went to Munich with his agent George Greenfield, and discussions took place which illustrate more vividly than anything else how the scene had changed since the innocent pre-war days of Hinks and George Finch:

> There was little feeling of shared anticipation of a great adventure. I realized we were negotiating like a group of business men over the copyrights and how to raise money.
>
> That afternoon we discussed and came to an agreement on the split of media rights. We left with no feeling of friendship, and I, with very little enthusiasm for the expedition. Nevertheless, in the next six weeks, George Greenfield and I set about raising the necessary support for the German–British Everest expedition. Both the B.B.C. and I.T.N. were interested, as were several publishers and newspapers. There is no doubt that we could have raised a large part of the money that Herrligkoffer needed.
>
> Now it became increasingly difficult to deal with him and it became quite

obvious that he was trying to raise funds himself which cut across the copyrights we were arranging on his behalf, in order to be independent of the British contribution. In some ways I don't blame him, but he should have told us in the first place, instead of accepting our offer of help, allowing us to raise support for him, and then revoking our verbal agreement at the last moment.[4]

Bonington also felt concerned about Herrligkoffer's conception of the enterprise: 'both Dougal and I were badly shaken to learn how little he appeared to know about the problems presented by Everest.'[5] Apart from the financial aspects, it was obvious the German was still thinking in terms of Nanga Parbat, and though Whillans went to Munich to brief him on the peculiar difficulties and requirements of the world's highest mountain, Herrligkoffer never seemed to grasp what was needed. When the expedition was on the mountain this was to cause delays and frustrations which robbed it of any chance of success.

In view of this both Bonington and Haston withdrew from the team. In the end there were three British participants: Whillans, Doug Scott and Hamish MacInnes, all of whom found the financial arrangements to be based on shifting sand, as Scott later explained:

> Over a dozen firms supplied us with clothing, tents, oxygen and other equipment. All this was worth thousands of pounds, and more was supplied at greatly reduced prices. The Mount Everest Foundation considered giving us a grant, but as Herrligkoffer was calling for contributions of £600 per member we had to turn to the mass media for financial support. Eventually, the *Observer* and the B.B.C. came in with substantial grants which not only financed us but made the whole expedition possible. A few weeks before we left I delivered all the equipment gathered in the U.K. to the Deutsches Institut für Auslandforschung which is the rather grandiose title of Herrligkoffer's expedition organizing enterprise. In fact, the Institut turned out to be his doctor's surgery.
>
> Once he had received the vital oxygen supplies, Herrligkoffer said that he expected Don to pay the £800 bill for them. This came as something of a shock and although this particular issue was later resolved in Nepal, incidents like this occurred all along and made us uncertain whether or not we would ever reach Everest.
>
> In Munich I signed one of Herrligkoffer's contracts, but as it was all in German, of which I know only about a dozen words, I signed it subject to the understanding that we would get a translation, only part of which ever materialized. Herrligkoffer drew my attention to a bundle of other signed contracts, pointing out that everyone was paying the equivalent of £600 and that this was written into the contract. He agreed that ours could be taken

out of the British grants, and said that we should keep a detailed account of our expenses as they would be paid in due course.

A few days before departure, Herrligkoffer's British agent received notification from Herrligkoffer that our personal contribution must be paid for out of our own pockets, and that it now stood at £1,000! We let Hamish handle that one, which he did very effectively: he told the leader that we were withdrawing, which of course meant the loss of the TV and newspaper grants. Herrligkoffer responded by offering Hamish a private deal, which he refused. The day before departure we found that we were invited back on, and that the £1,000 would be taken from the grants! However, we are still waiting for repayment of over £1,000 expenses, including two visits to Munich and flights to Kathmandu.[6]

Meanwhile, as the composition of the expedition changed, so did its title, which finally became the European Mount Everest Expedition. It was predominantly Austrian and – more than that – Austrian Army, but there were the three British, one Swiss (Hans Berger) and one Italian (Leo Breitenberger).

The expedition reached Kathmandu on 12 March and it was obvious from the outset that Herrligkoffer either did not understand or did not believe in acclimatization. He marched straight through to Base Camp, with the result that the man designated to look after it, Professor Huttl, never reached the camp at all but had to return home through altitude sickness. His replacement, a thirty-two-year-old German consular official called Horst Vitt, arrived at Base Camp only to collapse and die from pulmonary oedema. The task was eventually taken on by Alice von Holb, a thirty-three-year-old pharmacist, who also, through force of circumstances, inherited medical responsibility for the expedition for most of the time. Fortunately for her, there were no serious accidents or illnesses.

The expedition did not move out to Base Camp as a single group. An advance party went ahead to set up the camp and begin work on the Icefall. When the rest of the team arrived, on the 26th, the work was going well and prospects looked bright.

But beneath the surface things were very far from being all right: the British were ill, the Austrians suspicious and the Sherpas disgruntled. As if these were not enough, Mischa Saleki, the Iranian student whom Herrligkoffer had 'crossed off', turned up on his own accord, intent on creating a fuss.

The disaffection of the Sherpas was potentially the most serious trouble. During his visit to Munich, Whillans had warned Herrligkoffer that the Sherpas were not like other hill tribes – certainly not like the Hunza porters, who do the carrying for Nanga Parbat expeditions. The Sherpas were much more sophisticated: they had built up a mountaineering tradition that had been in existence for half a century, and when it came to expedition work they had an expertise which far outmatched that of any other porters. On Everest, of course, they were unique and knew better than their employers what was expected of them. The Austrians were not aware of this and, in addition, communication was difficult because many of the Sherpas could understand English but not German, and few of the Austrians could speak English. As a result they tended to hector and bully the Sherpas, who resented it.

Matters came to a head when the Sherpas discovered that their allocation of high-altitude gear did not meet the requirements of the Himalayan Society. There were insufficient foam mattresses, only enough duvet clothing for the fifteen Sherpas who would work on the Face itself and none for those who would work in the Icefall and the Cwm. There were no double sleeping bags for any of them.

Whillans had explained to Herrligkoffer what the requirements would be, but the German had chosen to ignore the advice. No doubt he knew that the leading Sherpas were already well equipped from the spoils of previous expeditions and counted on this to save expense, but the Sherpas don't look at it that way. A tradition has grown up whereby *every* expedition provides for its Sherpas fully. The Sherpas regard this expensive gear as the perks of the job: most of it is carefully stored away to be sold later in the bazaars of Kathmandu.

When the gear was not forthcoming the Sherpas went on strike and Herrligkoffer was forced into a hasty return to Germany to get it – even chartering a helicopter from Base Camp to Kathmandu to speed things up. It was an expensive and time-consuming mistake, made doubly galling by the realization that most of the gear would never be used!

Meanwhile, as the Austrians hacked their way up the Icefall, Don Whillans lay in his sleeping bag at Base Camp suffering from a recurrence of an old illness to the inner ear, which caused him vertigo, and Doug Scott was ill from dysentery. While his companions were thus *hors de combat*, Hamish MacInnes decided to service the photographic equipment with which he hoped to capture the adventure on film for the B.B.C.

It was Scott's first trip to the Nepal Himalaya. Thirty years of age, he was big and broad, his face almost hidden by long hair and voluminous whiskers. A Nottingham physical education teacher, he had forged his own path to the top of the sport through his local club and personal friends, outside the fashionable mainstream of British climbing. His expeditions, too, had been to offbeat areas – the Hindu Kush, Baffin Island and the almost unknown Tibesti mountains deep in the Sahara. He had done some outstanding long hard rock climbs, and his almost aggressive individualism was allied to phenomenal strength.

It was also MacInnes's first official visit to Everest, though at the time of John Hunt's successful first ascent in 1953 he and fellow Scotsman John

Cunningham had made an abortive two-man trip to the Khumbu (see p. 254). Tall, thin and craggy, with a fringe of beard, he was forty-two years old and, like Whillans, one of the living legends of post-war British climbing. From his Highland base in Glencoe he had ranged over many of the world's mountains, from the Caucasus to the Southern Alps of New Zealand.

No doubt the illness of the British contingent was aggravated by their too rapid ascent to Base Camp, chivvied along by Herrligkoffer. However, the rest of the team didn't see it that way: openly they accused Whillans and his companions of laziness; secretly, they feared a plot.

The trouble was that the leading climbers – Felix Kuen, Adolf Huber, Werner Haim and Leo Breitenberger – had been briefed before the expedition by their compatriot from the International Expedition of the previous year, Leo Schlömmer, who, with his friend Wolfgang Axt, had quit the mountain after a disagreement with Whillans. There was no love lost between Schlömmer and Whillans, and the Austrian warned his countrymen to beware of the little Lancastrian's machinations. In consequence Kuen and the others – known as the Big Four, because they were ones who did all the lead climbing – suspected that the British illnesses were something of a charade, and that Whillans was simply conserving their energies for later on. If the Big Four tired themselves out on the initial stages of the climb the way would be open for the British to go ahead, relatively fresh, for the final summit assaults.

That was the way Kuen and his friends saw it – and they were determined to baulk Whillans if they could. Already they had succeeded in having him demoted from Joint Climbing Leader (with Kuen), although he was the only man present with any experience of Everest, and had been higher on the Face than anybody else.

To try to allay these fears, the three British climbers helped with the Icefall work. Whillans was soon forced to retire, but Scott, climbing with Horst Schneider and ten Sherpas, managed to complete the route through the maze of seracs to the site of Camp I on the edge of the Western Cwm.

Mischa Saleki turned up unexpectedly at Base Camp intent on his pound of flesh. He was in a justifiably bitter frame of mind, for he had done a lot of work in Iran raising funds for the expedition and had obtained some equipment as well. His own participation had been partly sponsored by the Iranian Government. When Herrligkoffer had summarily crossed him off the list he felt humiliated.

Saleki was in fact a perfect example of the sort of problem that the two international expeditions created. In their desperate search for money they cast their nets too wide and accepted people who, on a more rational system, would never have been chosen. As a climber, Saleki was not in the same league as the others on the team, and though he did manage to reach Camp II he suffered a good deal of derision.

The British contingent feared that Saleki's wrathful arrival might wreck the expedition, but they managed to take him aside and calm him down. They persuaded him that he should try to make the expedition a success despite the injustice he had suffered, and eventually he agreed to do this. He regarded the three Britons as sympathetic allies, in return for which he often told them – being a fluent speaker of German – what the Austrians were planning. Most importantly, he warned that the Big Four intended to keep the British off the summit.

But Saleki did not stay to see the end of the affair. Unable to stand the taunts and jibes of the others, he left Base Camp as suddenly and dramatically as he had arrived – some say by stowing away in a helicopter.[7]

Meanwhile it was obvious that a battle of willpower was about to take place between the British and the Big Four. Not all the other members were complacent about the way things were going – Adi Weissensteiner, for example, tried to establish better relations with the Sherpas, and Peter Perner remarked to Scott that unless relationships between Kuen and Whillans improved there could be no successful outcome.

All the accusations and counter-accusations that had marred the International Expedition broke out again like measles, though perhaps in a less virulent form: the Big Four were accused of hogging the lead, not only by the British but also by their compatriots; Kuen was accused of 'saving himself' by carrying only light loads; the British were accused of using too much oxygen – it was a nauseatingly familiar pattern which, when reported in the press, did nothing to enhance the image of mountaineering.

Schlömmer had done his work well. He had instilled into Kuen a mortal fear of Whillans, a fear enhanced by inexperience of high altitudes.[8] Kuen felt that once Whillans was in the lead, with his knowledge of big mountains and his previous Everest experience, there would be no chance for anyone else.

It was not a wholly irrational fear. Whillans was as tenacious as a terrier, and if he saw a chance for the top no doubt he would take it. But you cannot run a successful expedition with one hand tied behind your back. Scott was bitter about Kuen's tactics:

> It became more and more apparent that the job was too big for him, and that he was anyway approaching it in the wrong fashion.
>
> But it was also apparent that Kuen was to be pitied more than anything else, for it was obvious that Herrligkoffer had thrust him into his present position largely because he could be relied upon. This had been proven in the German courts on several occasions. If only Kuen could have picked Don's brains and benefited from his experience . . . but how could he when his manner was awkward and cold, and when from the start he was suspicious of Don?[9]

Camps I, II and III were established fairly rapidly despite a savage storm which drove the climbers out of Camp II and caught Whillans – now recovered from his illness – in the Icefall as he moved up to Camp I. But for a chance shifting of the mist he might never have seen the tent and perhaps would have been forced into a dangerous bivouac.

After Camp III progress was slower, and it took six days to make the route to Camp IV. Kuen and his companions were beginning to tire, and sickness or injury took its toll. Breitenberger, for example, did not seem to be adapting to altitude very well and was clearly a sick man. His companions bullied him into continuing for a while, but eventually he had to retreat to base, where it later transpired he had pleurisy. Huber too retreated with an infected throat, and Haim was injured on the knee by a falling stone. Of the Big Four only Kuen remained active, but such was his suspicion of Whillans that he was not prepared to let him take over the lead. In the end he agreed that Schneider and the three British climbers could establish Camp IV, but only on the promise that they would go no further.

At this point Herrligkoffer returned from Germany with the extra equipment for the Sherpas. Michel Anderl, Herrligkoffer's fifty-seven-year-old deputy, sent a message to all the camps asking the team to assemble at base to greet the leader.

It was 1 May, the weather was excellent, and time was running out. To retire to Base Camp under such circumstances was putting social niceties before mountaineering practicalities. The vital task was to keep up some sort of momentum, to keep pushing forward the camps on the Face, if there was to be any chance of success. Whillans realized this and requested permission to stay up in the Cwm, pushing the route out to Camp V, but this was denied – he was ordered to come down like the rest. Whillans refused, and eventually the three British, along with Adi Sager, Adi Weissensteiner and a handful of Sherpas ignored the festivities at Base Camp.

If, on the face of it, Anderl's action in calling everyone back to Base Camp seemed madness, there was some method in it. The Big Four were exhausted and ill, and needed a rest: Herrligkoffer's return was a splendid excuse for a rest period. The fact that there were others who didn't need a rest – and the British were not alone in this – appeared not to count. It was beginning to look as though nobody but Kuen was going to be allowed at the front.

Having refused to descend to Base the British climbers worked at establishing Camp V, using rope left behind by the International Expedition the year before. They cut platforms for two tents and dumped some loads of gear, but a shortage of porters (most of whom were at Base celebrating Herrligkoffer's return) prevented them from doing much more.

The British trio spent ten days at Camp IV and this aroused the wrath of Herrligkoffer and Kuen, who accused them of using fifteen bottles of oxygen, as well as vital provisions. They had, said Kuen, grievously upset the plans for

Camp V and, intentionally or unintentionally, sabotaged it. In fact, the British climbers had used only four bottles of oxygen from the expedition's stock – the rest were bottles that had been abandoned by the International Expedition.

On the 10th Kuen and Huber returned to the Cwm with a detailed plan of attack. Scott describes what it was:

> Huber and Kuen arrived at Camp 4, armed with a plan they had worked out at Base Camp. In effect it placed us in Camp 3, and Sherpas in Camp 4 with Peter Perner or Adi Weissensteiner if the latter's cough would allow it. Horst Schneider and Adi Sager were to go to Camp 5 and Kuen and Huber to 6. When all was ready two of us were to be allowed to join them at the front in an attack on the summit. But just how we could get enough oxygen and other equipment up there, to support four climbers, was not explained, and we grew suspicious. We had a feeling that we were being edged out again. So we worked out a compromise plan, which put us in support of the summit pair, with one other Austrian accompanying us in Camp 5. After Kuen and Huber had made their bid, we four of the support party would have a go.
>
> After some debate, this proposal was accepted and Kuen and Huber moved up to 5. Unfortunately, Schneider and Sager were not satisfied with the new arrangements and they went to persuade Kuen to revert to his original plan. The crunch came when Schneider and Sager returned from their mission. Schneider said, 'You British are in trouble. Kuen says you must go down to Camp 3 or he will come down, call off the Sherpas and end the expedition.' Next day we went down to Camp 2 and later to Base Camp. We had come to the end and reached the point where personality differences could no longer be ignored. Both Schneider and Sager refused to carry for Don.[10]

So the British were out of it, having done a Mazeaud type withdrawal from the expedition, though with more justification than their French predecessor. All efforts at compromise had been rejected by Kuen, burdened as he was by a morbid fear of Whillans or a deep sense of inferiority.

On 18 May a final assault was made on the Face by Kuen, Huber, Berger, Sager, Perner and Schneider. They were helped considerably by the fixed ropes left by the International Expedition, and by the 21st Kuen, Huber, Sager and Schneider reached the site of Camp VI, where the four of them planned to spend the night in a single two-man tent. While their companions erected this, Kuen and Huber prospected the way ahead, re-discovering the easier by-pass route that Whillans had found and rejected the previous year.

That night the weather broke and the temperature plummeted. By next morning there was no improvement in conditions. Cramped into a tiny tent, the Austrians had neither the facilities nor the reserves of stamina to sit out prolonged bad weather. There was nothing for it but to retreat: Herrligkoffer's expedition was over.

The three years 1970–72 inclusive had given the British a distinct advantage when it came to climbing big mountain faces at high altitude. They had participated in the two international Everest attempts and had successfully climbed the South Face of Annapurna. A strong cadre of experienced climbers had emerged, all of whom knew each other well. Technically, on rock or ice, they were as skilful as any in the world, and much more accomplished than most.

They included, of course, the men who joined the international Everest teams – the small, stocky, aggressive Whillans with his round face, old-fashioned haircut and flat Lancashire accent; the emaciated-looking, withdrawn and monosyllabic Scot, Haston, said to be the toughest interview assignment any reporter could get; the big, whiskered, rugby-playing giant, Scott; and the rangy, craggy Highlander, MacInnes, who had an inordinate fondness for driving E-type Jaguars. In addition, from the Annapurna team came Nick Estcourt, Cambridge graduate and computer expert; Mike Thompson, a quiet-mannered anthropologist who had escaped from his Army commission by the simple expedient of standing for Parliament; Martin Boysen, a teacher; and a stocky little bespectacled film cameraman from Lancashire, Mick Burke. By and large they were the very epitome of Smythe's 'horrid northern climbers'.

Strangely enough they were not necessarily the best climbers in Britain – there were others who were as technically proficient – but they did have the sort of cohesiveness that comes from co-operative experience. Out of that sort of experience arises mutual respect and understanding – the sort of understanding one finds among the forwards of a top soccer team, where knowledge of what the other fellow is going to do next plays a decisive role.

The unquestioned leader of this talented group was Chris Bonington. Like Thompson, Bonington had been for a short while an Army officer, then a trainee manager with Unilever, before finally launching into a full-time career of mountain adventure. He had first come to the attention of the climbing world when at the age of nineteen he had made the first ascent of Raven Gully in Glencoe, an extremely difficult Scottish ice climb. He followed this with a series of technically difficult rock climbs and attempts on some of the hard Alpine routes that had not had previous British success, such as the Cima Grande Direct in the Dolomites and the Bonatti Pillar of the Dru. He was with Whillans on the first ascent of the Frêney Pillar – the climb that had so annoyed Mazeaud – but he came to the attention of a wider public when, with Ian Clough, he made the first British ascent of the notorious Eigerwand in 1962.

Meanwhile, he had also participated in overseas expeditions, making the first ascents of Annapurna II (26,041 ft) in 1960, Nuptse (25,700 ft) in 1961, and the Central Tower of Paine in Patagonia (with Whillans) in 1963. By this time he had become a photo-journalist, which allowed him to take part in a number of exciting projects, not least of which was the first ascent of the Eiger Direct in 1966. Although not officially a member of the climbing team, his vivid photographic coverage of the dramatic events that took place brought him wide publicity.

But Bonington found journalism too restricting: the role of observer, even an active one, he found irksome. He felt the need to participate to the full and to choose his own adventures. He decided to organize his own expedition and, almost by accident, chose as his goal the South Face of Annapurna, a tremendous face of avalanche-swept rock and snow in Nepal.[11]

The expedition gathered together many of his companions from previous adventures and was brilliantly successful. When Whillans and Haston reached the summit, Bonington's expedition had overcome the most technically difficult climb ever attempted on one of the world's highest peaks.

Bonington himself did not reach the summit, but that hardly mattered, for at last he had found his true *métier* – as an expedition organizer of the first rank. He surprised even himself, for he had never thought that his talents lay in that direction; yet through hard work, shrewd calculation and, it must be said, the services of a good agent, he had launched and executed a brilliant climbing coup. The climb was filmed by Independent Television and followed up by the leader's exciting lectures and fine book.

Bonington's meteoric rise to international fame was not accomplished without criticism. There were those among the climbing fraternity who viewed with suspicion his embracing of the media, and one shudders to imagine what old Hinks would have said had he still been active. He was labelled as a wheeler-dealer and, in a savagely brilliant satire in the magazine *Mountain*, parodied as Cassius Bonafide, the conqueror of Annaplus.[12]

How much of this was envy and how much arose from a natural suspicion of the financial world that seems endemic among climbers is hard to say. Bonington, who behind his confident exterior is a sensitive, even touchy person, was probably hurt, although he didn't show it. He could afford to ignore such criticism: his climbing background was outstanding and his current ability obvious.

In the next few years he was to strengthen his grip on the expedition scene and become a recognized figure in a way no mountaineer had done in Britain since Edward Whymper a century earlier. It was a different sort of recognition from that accorded to Hunt and Hillary – theirs had been a single, monumental, unrepeatable achievement for which they were duly recognized and honoured; Bonington's was a high plateau of achievement: a string of adventures which kept him before the public eye.

Bonington's success was due to a rare combination of the right qualities. As an organizer he was on a par with Hunt, meticulous over detail, and shrewd to a degree Hunt never was. He could exhibit all the charm and compassion of Dyhrenfurth and, like the American, advocate democratic decisions among his team, yet he was made of far sterner stuff and knew how to command as well. If he had faults, they showed in frequent changes of mind and sudden outbursts of temper; yet there was never any question of shilly-shallying on his expeditions.

Bonington chose his teams carefully, striking a balance between those who were aggressively ambitious and those who were strong but less motivated. The same names appear time after time on his expeditions, and he was accused – with some justification – of having a 'Bonington clique', but he was simply applying the golden rule of most team sports: that a settled team brings the best results. He gained the respect of team members because they knew he was as capable as themselves and could lead from the front if necessary.

These qualities make for a great expedition leader, but Bonington was doubly fortunate in that the Gods had bestowed on him the gifts of communication. He was a good photographer, a first-rate speaker who expressed himself well both in the lecture hall and television studio, and a fine writer. And because he could communicate he could raise interest – and money – in his projects. Perhaps above all else this was the difference between Bonington and other expedition leaders: his public persona matched and supported his climbing abilities.

Bonington had been briefly involved in the preparations for Dyhrenfurth's International Expedition of 1971, and it was the failure of that venture which first gave him the idea of making a serious attempt himself. The problem was that once Nepal had opened up for climbing again in 1970, Everest had been rapidly 'booked' for years ahead.

This booking policy is a necessary evil which the Nepalese Government operates for all its high peaks. On the one hand it ensures that the authorities know exactly which expedition is where at any given time (and collects the appropriate fee) and on the other it guarantees the climbers freedom from interference by other expeditions. With most peaks this would scarcely ever be a problem, but it certainly would be with Everest. The frustrations and dangers of several expeditions all trying simultaneously to ascend the Icefall into the Cwm and race for the summit are patently obvious. So control of access is necessary, and two 'slots' per year are allocated, one pre-monsoon and one post-monsoon. These are rapidly snatched up by hopeful aspirants.

Herrligkoffer had the next slot, in spring 1972, and, as we have seen, Bonington flirted with the idea of joining the German doctor in a 'European' attempt on the mountain, but found their views so much at variance that he withdrew.

The next two slots were held by an Italian millionaire called Guido Monzino. Monzino hoped to use the post-monsoon period of 1972 in a reconnaissance of the ordinary route (though one wonders why) preparatory to making a full-scale attempt in the spring of 1973, but early in 1972 rumours began to circulate that Monzino might be abandoning his project altogether. Hopeful candidates began to lobby in Kathmandu – especially for the plum pre-monsoon slot of 1973 – but to no avail. Monzino decided to retain his option on the 1973 slot. Bonington was offered the autumn slot of 1972.

But having got it, what should he do with it? The South West Face was the obvious goal, of course, but the decision wasn't that simple. In the first place Herrligkoffer's team seemed to be settling down to their job and might well climb it, leaving any embryo expedition uncomfortably stranded. Then, too, autumn was the lucrative trekking season in Nepal and the best Sherpas would not be available. Finally, there was the weather. Nobody had climbed Everest in the post-monsoon period, and most of those who had tried were appalled by the high winds and increasingly low temperatures that heralded the approach of winter.

Taking all these factors into account Bonington decided that an expedition to the South West Face was too big an undertaking to organize in the time available and that the only sensible plan would be to attempt Everest by the ordinary route, but using a modest, lightweight approach, which would be closer to the tradition of mountaineering than the massive expeditions of the past.[13]

But Herrligkoffer's failure changed the whole situation. The esoteric charms of mountain puritanism faded before the harsh challenge of the unclimbed face. It was too strong a challenge to resist.

Neverthless, Bonington found himself involved in a mental struggle. The prize was once more on offer, but there were barely eight weeks in which to organize a full-scale expedition and raise the £60,000 he calculated it would cost. He had to make the commitment, then try to fund it. Nothing daunted, Bonington submerged himself in a frenzy of fund-raising – book rights, media rights, postcards and posters – until the project was financially secure, just one week before departure. It was an impressive performance – although it didn't favourably impress everyone. McNaught Davis, himself no mean climber, took a cynical view of the whole effort:

> However, whilst its objectives (and the effort made) were to be applauded, the means that had to be used to raise enough cash to achieve them seem questionable . . .
>
> Still there are ways of raising cash that we haven't even started using yet. From the success of the professional footballer's venture into pop records I can see the 'Everest Squad' backed by the Alpine Club Wind Ensemble and accompanied by the Namche Sherpas' Choir singing their way to a golden disc . . .[14]

To which the answer is probably that George Greenfield, Bonington's agent, hadn't thought of it.

The views expressed by McNaught Davis found a ready echo among the mountaineering fraternity, with its built-in conservatism and inbred suspicion of anything financial. But Bonington's success had been due at least in part to his ability to see exactly what was required and to go for it, irrespective of his or anybody else's romantic idealism. He knew that the South West Face would need a large expedition, superbly equipped, and that to pretend otherwise was to avoid the issue. And large expeditions cost a lot of money – there simply has to be commercial backing.

Bonington had already selected his team for the originally planned lightweight assault: Haston, Estcourt, Burke, Thompson, and Peter Steele, the doctor who had been on the International Expedition. These still formed the nucleus of the Face team, but it was strengthened by bringing in Scott and MacInnes as extra lead climbers, Jimmy Roberts as Deputy Leader, and two support climbers, Graham Tiso, an Edinburgh equipment dealer, and Kelvin Kent, an Army officer. Unfortunately Thompson and Steele had to drop out at the last minute. They were replaced by Dave Bathgate, a Scottish climber, and Dr Barney Rosedale.

There was one outstanding omission, Don Whillans. It was, perhaps, inevitable that between two such forceful personalities as Bonington and Whillans an uneasy relationship would develop. Both were strong-minded, opinionated leaders of men. On Everest, Bonington decided, there was room for only one leader – himself. In this he was supported by some of the team members who had been on Annapurna and had taken exception to Whillans: Haston and Burke in particular.

It was all a calculated gamble, in which the stakes were high and the speed of play frighteningly swift, and it confirmed, if nothing else, Bonington's coolness and nerve, and powers of organization. To assemble and finance a major expedition to attempt the hardest route on the highest mountain in the world in rather less than eight weeks requires a considerable degree of self-confidence!

In a curious way the shortage of time may even have helped Bonington, by preventing the changes of mind to which he is often prone. Before the expedition left Britain he was quite clear that he would attempt the Whillans route above Camp VI rather than try for the original line investigated by the Japanese (and since ignored), as many people thought he should. He argued that he had neither the time nor the resources for exploration – it had to be an assault by the best-known route. The imponderables were in any case bad enough: the Icefall was reputed to be much worse in autumn than in spring, he himself had no previous experience of Everest, and – most important of all – no one knew whether Everest was climbable in the post-monsoon period.

The expedition established Base Camp on 14 September and began the job of finding a way through the Icefall. The weather was good and they reached the Cwm on the 20th, but then the winds rose, the weather broke, and they were unable to make a further advance for ten days. Camp 2 – Advanced Base – was established on the 30th and two days later Estcourt and Bathgate reached the site of Camp 3.

Now Scott and Burke took over, pushing up the Face towards the site of Camp 4, the work interrupted by snowstorms for days at a time and the length of daylight shortening as winter crept closer. It was bitterly cold, and the higher they climbed the more violent became the gusts of wind. Already most of the team hated the mountain and wanted nothing better than to climb it quickly and get away: a recurring theme in the Everest story, as cold, altitude, sickness and storms build up relentlessly and climbers awake to face, in Smythe's words, 'another bloody day'.

On 12 October Haston and MacInnes assumed the lead, building up Camp 4, then pushing on to make Camp 5.

It is in the repetitive recounting of the now established system of camps on the South West Face of Everest that one is reminded most forcibly of the parallels with the pre-war attempts on the north side of the mountain. In both cases expedition after expedition went through the same ritual – a Base Camp was established, the North Col (or Icefall) was climbed, a series of camps was pushed forward until invariably it seemed, for whatever reason, the expedition ran out of steam.

Everyone who took part had a valid, and often unforgettable, mountaineering experience, yet, looked at as a whole, the expeditions resemble nothing so much as wars of attrition.

The comparison should not be pressed too closely. Half a century brings a lot of changes even in mountain climbing, and the camps which Bonington's team was laboriously pushing up the South West Face were quite unlike those that Mallory knew. The terrain was dissimilar, for one thing – a vast snow slope as against the ridge and the boiler-plate slabs of pre-war days – and the techniques were different too. Whillans Boxes replaced the old Meade tents, and there were hundreds of feet of fixed ropes, anchored to the snow by metal plates gruesomely known as 'dead men' so that porters and climbers could go up and down in a shuttle service with safety.[15] And the frequency of the Face expeditions was such that each camp site was littered with the bric-à-brac of previous expeditions – tent frames and platforms (often damaged), oxygen cylinders, spare rope: all the mountain excreta of our modern consumer technology. Allowed time, of course, the mountain would erase the lot.

The expedition was going well, despite the occasional storms. Then, on 16 October, winter arrived, and with it the winds. They came roaring down the great central gully, battering tents and climbers alike. Spindrift – powdered snow – was hurled about in swirling swathes which covered everything and hardened like concrete.

It was a curious, intermittent wind, which came in violent bursts of energy. Often the day would appear fine, with clear blue skies and the absolute silence that is such a feature of high mountains, when suddenly, with a noise like an express train, the wind would come roaring down the Face. At times it was an almost continuous succession of blows, at other times there were hopeful periods of stillness when it seemed the wind had finally subsided, then back it would come as violent as ever.

For most of this period Bonington was trapped up at Camp 4, hoping to establish Camp 5. In his diary he wrote:

> The wind is the appalling enemy. It is mind-destroying, physically destroying, soul-destroying, and even existing in the tents, which I think are now pretty weathertight, it is still very, very hard. This will certainly be the most exacting test I have ever had to face, and I only hope it is one that the others will be able to face . . .
>
> Oh, the absolute lethargy of 24,600 ft. You want to pee and you lie there for a quarter of an hour making up your mind to look for your pee bottle. I've no appetite at all and it's an effort to cook anything for yourself. I suspect it is high time I did go down for a short rest – I think if you try to stay up high the whole time, to conduct operations, you end up being ineffective in that you are just getting weaker and weaker, more and more lethargic.[16]

Camp 4 was particularly vulnerable to falling debris – ice and stones – loosened by the wind from the heights above. To guard against this some wire netting had been brought up to protect the roofs of the tents, but somehow it had never been put in place. The camp escaped, however, until the night of 25 October when Estcourt and Bathgate had taken over Bonington's lonely vigil. Half drugged with sleeping pills, the two men tried to shut out the noise of the incessant wind. In his diary Bathgate described what happened:

> An almighty crash: immediate wakening – everything covered in snow; the bottom end of the Whillans Box torn, the framework broken and sheared through; it must have been a good-sized rock that had hit us. This was taken in, in seconds. I remember Nick saying, 'Well, there she goes.' Both of us trying feverishly to think of what to do, though still half drugged with Mogadon and, anyway, at an altitude of 24,600 ft, constructive thought is difficult.
>
> Eventually Nick sat at the broken end of the box, holding it up with his head. I put boots on over duvet socks and crawled out to inspect the other box for possible habitation. It was pitch dark outside, and the beam of my torch hardly cut through the rushing particles of snow. Both boxes had rips or broken zips and were rapidly filling with snow. The temperature was −25°C, and God knows what the strength of the wind was. The only thing I

could grab to help with repairs was a shovel, and spare piece of frame-work. The shovel helped to prop up the damaged corner. Everything was in chaos, but we managed to find some matches, a stove and brew materials – and then, ironically, there was a shortage of snow to melt in the cooking pot.

We brewed for two and a half hours, and this raised the temperature in the box to an almost bearable level. Outside the wind was still whistling past, bringing with it a torrent of spindrift and rocks. At 8 a.m. we made radio contact with Camp 2, and Chris agreed that we should abandon Camp 4. He asked whether we could transfer to one of the other boxes, but we told him that they also were damaged and were now part filled with snow. In addition, all our gear was covered in spindrift and we could never have got it effectively dried out.

By 11 a.m. we were ready to go. Down the ropes with numb hands and feet, a river of snow rushing past, ankle deep. During the big gusts it was total white-out conditions, and if you could manage to open your eyes, you could see black objects rush past. At one point Nick tried to warn me of stone fall. Dozens of rocks, anything from the size of golf balls to that of footballs, whizzed past our ears. We were very lucky not to be hit.

Eventually we got round the rock buttress, to the relative safety of Camp 3, and Graham was waiting for us with gallons of hot drinks. He seemed quite happy at 3 where it was sheltered from the full force of the storm. We left him and clipped on the fixed ropes once again; visibility averaging fifty feet, arrived down at the Bergschrund safely, and traversed the slope before walking blind for a while. Began to wonder about our chances of finding Camp 2, and chances of survival if we didn't. Then suddenly, during a clear spell, we saw people coming towards us, Barney, Chris and two Sherpas. Our gratitude was indescribable. The Sherpas took over our bags. Everything was laid on at Camp 2.[17]

By the end of October the weather had dealt severely with the expedition: Camp 5 had not been established properly, Camp 4 was damaged, Camp 1 was practically buried in snow, and communication between the Cwm and Base Camp had been broken. Furthermore because of contingencies caused by the weather, the lead climbing teams were out of phase and there were heated arguments about who would have the lead when they reached the Rock Band.

This of course was the crux of the climb, one of the two plum leads on the Face, the other being the final summit dash. Up to the foot of the Rock Band it was all hard work and no glory, without even personal climbing satisfaction. It was the Rock Band and the summit dash that counted most in the climbers' minds.

The fact that there was an argument at all shows that the expedition was still full of hope. Despite the winds and the onset of winter they still expected to climb the mountain and during the next fortnight re-occupied the camps on the Face. Bonington, with the Sherpa Ang Phu, made carries up to the site of Camp 6 at 27,300 ft, and on 14 November MacInnes, Haston, Scott and Burke carried from Camp 5 to Camp 6 in the hope of establishing the camp. MacInnes and Haston had planned to spend the night there, then attempt the Rock Band next day, but the wind was too strong and the cold too intense even to contemplate setting up a tent. MacInnes turned back with a faulty oxygen set. Haston described how the others struggled on:

> The wind – always the wind, was viciously asserting its authority. This was no silent journey up a crisp snowfield in the pure high air. I had visions of storms on old trans-Atlantic cutters. The constant banging in your ears would suddenly be intensified with a huge crack, as an extra gust smashed over the West Ridge and pulled at the figures on the ropes. This cracking was at least a warning. The axe was banged in and you crouched and held on. Once I was toppling on a long, loose section of fixed rope and went twanging down onto my Jumars. Doug told me later that at one point he was caught unprepared, picked up and thrown for a few feet, before clattering onto the ever elastic fixed ropes. I continued quickly, with a mind going almost as quickly as the wind. I had experienced many bad storms, many high winds, but this was a new dimension of wind speed, and it was basically fine weather! The sky, when you could see it through the spindrift, was blue.[18]

And when they reached the foot of the Rock Band, where Camp 6 was supposed to be sited, they could see that it was all in vain. Even if they had managed to establish the Camp, they would never have been able to climb the Rock Band. The chimney line that Whillans and Haston had discovered in 1971 turned out to be a false goal. The weather had stripped it of the snow and ice which had made it such a tempting proposition and it lay revealed as steep, difficult rock climbing – too difficult for an altitude of 28,000 ft and much too difficult for an Everest winter.

The attempt was over.

Ironically, as the expedition withdrew from the mountain there occurred one of those tragedies which fate seems to deal so cruelly and unfairly from the pack. A young climber called Tony Tighe, who was an acquaintance of some of the team, had made his way to Base Camp and helped out there by doing various chores, including looking after the radio. As the team withdrew Tighe took the opportunity to climb the Icefall in order to see the Western Cwm, a seemingly safe trip along a well-marked route, which at that moment was busy with Sherpas. Tragically, he was never seen again, and it is certain that he was killed by a collapse of ice that occurred near the point at which he was last seen alive.

If Bonington's expedition had failed in its objective, it had at least added immeasurably to the depth of Everest experience amongst British climbers. A number of 'new boys' had been 'blooded', not least Bonington himself.

A year later a huge team sponsored by the Japanese Rock Climbing Club arrived at Everest. The leader was Michio Yuasa, and there were no fewer than forty-eight climbers and thirty-three Sherpas, divided into various groups. It seemed to embody all the old faults – it was too big and had too many objectives. And, of course, it was post-monsoon.

Incredibly, the South West Face team ignored the experience gained by Bonington and headed once again for the Whillans–Haston chimney at the right-hand end of the Rock Band. A severe storm damaged their Camps 4 and 5, but eventually they did reach the Rock Band before more bad weather forced them to abandon the attempt.

Their companions, however, were having better luck on the ordinary route. On 26 October, Yasuo Kato, a student, and Hisahi Ishiguro, a clerk, set out from the South Col and reached the summit of Everest at 4.30 p.m. Their elation at success, however, was tempered by the thoughts of descent: their oxygen had run out and they were suffering from frostbite. As they stumbled down the ridge, slowly and painfully, darkness overtook them and forced them into an involuntary bivouac. They had no sleeping bags, food or drink, and all they could do was crouch under the shelter of a rock and pummel each other to keep warm. Next morning, suffering from exposure, half blinded and maimed, they managed to stagger back to camp.

It was one of the most important climbs in the history of the mountain. It was the first time Everest had been climbed in the post-monsoon period, thus removing forever the doubt whether such a feat was possible; it was the first time the summit had been reached direct from the South Col without an intermediate camp on the ridge; it had demonstrated that it was possible to function on the summit and descend the ridge without oxygen; and it had shown that a high bivouac, even in the colder autumn period, was not necessarily fatal. All these reassuring factors were to prove of immense psychological value to later expeditions.

The battering which the British team had experienced on the South West Face in the autumn of 1972, in the merciless roar of the winter winds, had completely shaken their faith in the post-monsoon period. Nobody had really expected winds of such ferocity, and when Bonington returned home he told his friends 'Never again!'

But never is a long time. 'You've got to remember that we were justifying the actions we had taken in turning back, to some degree – and the easy way out when you come down is to say it is almost impossible at this time of year,' Bonington said later.[19] When the Japanese showed that Everest could be climbed in the autumn the psychological barrier was weakened. Nevertheless Bonington remained convinced that any success on the Face would have to come during the warmer, calmer, pre-monsoon period.

The problem was that the pre-monsoon seasons were booked up for years ahead by expeditions which were expected to have the ordinary route as their objective. Only by joining one of these ventures could Bonington have any chance at a spring attempt; and that would mean an international expedition with split objectives and divided loyalties. Recent experience had shown that this was not a good way of doing things!

However, there was one faint hope. In the spring of 1976 the British Army was booked for an attempt on the ordinary route, and Bonington felt there might be a better chance of co-operation there, especially since, during his time as an Army officer, he had been a founder member of the Army Mountaineering Association, under whose auspices the expedition was to take place. But the Army's plans were already well advanced and, furthermore, the incursion into their ranks of a team of civilian 'star' climbers would inevitably detract from the expedition's military identity. There would be considerable publicity, but it would be concentrated on Bonington's team, and the Army might find itself relegated in the eyes of the media to being little more than a vehicle from which Bonington could operate. Major General Brockbank, Chairman of the A.M.A., turned the idea down.

Early in December 1973 Bonington learned that the Canadians had withdrawn their application for the post-monsoon period of 1975 and there was a chance that he might get it if he applied. It put him in a quandary. Convinced there was no chance of climbing the South West Face during this period, he had to decide whether it was worth going at all. But the pull of Everest is strong, no matter what the chances of success might be, and so, after several days of wrestling with his conscience, Bonington decided to go. He revived his original idea of a lightweight attempt on the South East Ridge.

Permission came through in April 1974 while Bonington, Scott and Haston were in Delhi, on their way to climb Changabang, a peak in the Garhwal Himalaya. Faced with this fresh reality, misgivings welled up again, fed by Scott and Haston. Scott pointed out that the South West Face was the real challenge of Everest, any other being secondary. A lightweight attempt on the mountain was a fine idea, in accordance with current trends – but suppose they got into the Western Cwm and discovered ideal conditions for an attempt on the Face? They would not have the resources to tackle it and would feel frustrated, cheated even.

These arguments weighed strongly with Bonington. There is little doubt that from that day the objective would be the South West Face, yet he prevaricated, insisting that first they must find a single sponsor to cover the costs. Even though he had over a year in hand this time, the thought of having to chase sponsors *and* organize a major expedition was too much. And of course, it was this that had helped to ruin the original Dyhrenfurth venture.

By the time he returned to England – after successfully climbing Changabang – Bonington had mapped out his general strategy for a post-monsoon

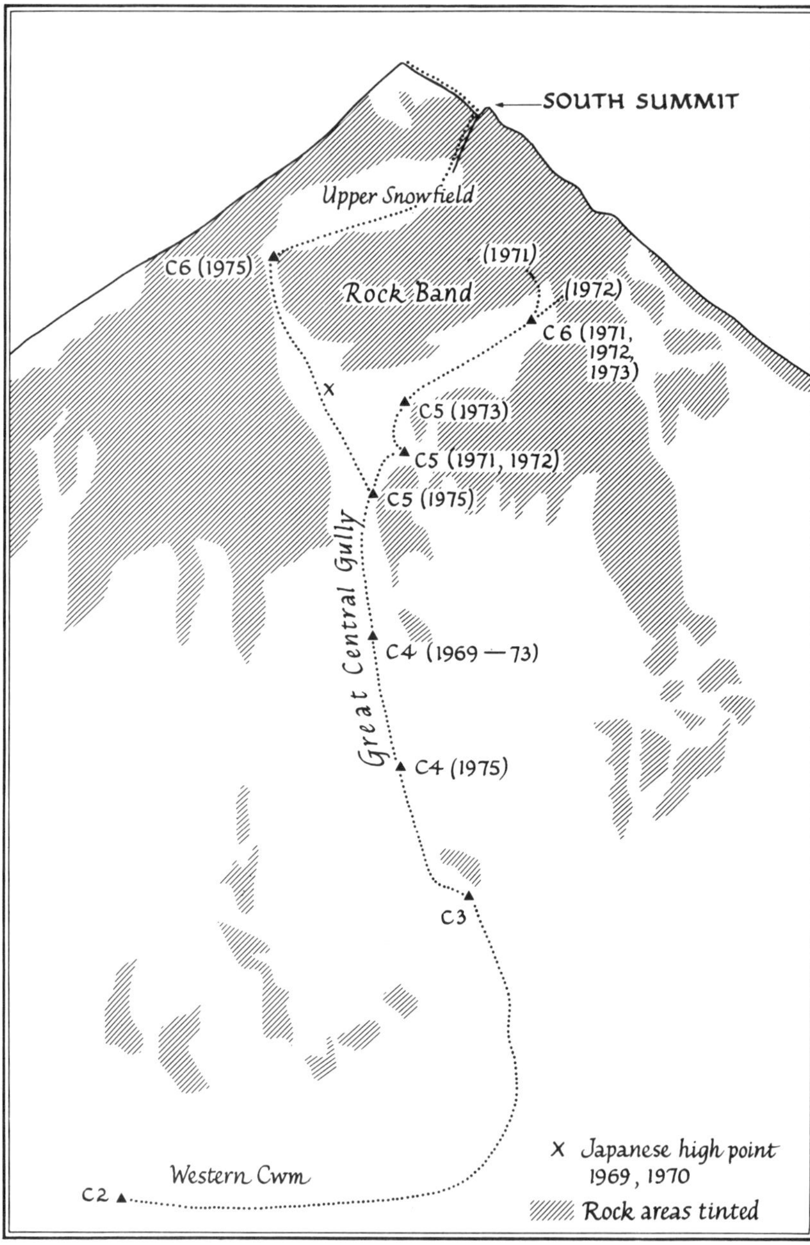


Fig. 4 The South West Face

attempt on the Face. Two factors were of overwhelming importance. First, for any hope of success they had to avoid the onset of the winter winds, which meant going early, approaching the mountain at the tail end of the monsoon. The Japanese had done this, arriving at Base Camp on 25 August, and had succeeded in climbing the South East Ridge. Second, there had to be a fresh approach to the problem of the Rock Band, because the Whillans Chimney seemed extremely difficult and didn't really lead to the best part of the Face for continuing the climb – it tended to push one over rightwards, towards the South East Ridge. In addition, it would have meant establishing a Camp 7, and that would make the logistics very difficult indeed. Over the years, these problems had become increasingly obvious.

On top of this there was the need for a rapid ascent, and if they were to beat both the Rock Band and the autumnal gales a smooth build-up would be required, with adequate reserves of men and material.

Bonington reckoned that all this would cost £100,000. The question was who would be willing to put up that sort of money for a mountaineering expedition? And a risky expedition at that – for five previous attempts on the Face had failed.

The answer was – Barclays Bank International. Both Bonington and his agent, George Greenfield, had a mutual friend in Alan Tritton, a director of the bank, and they succeeded in interesting him in the expedition; he in turn persuaded his Chairman and board members to agree to providing the finance. In fact, Barclays went one better – they agreed to underwrite the expedition no matter what the cost, thus completely relieving Bonington of any worries about inflation or financial shortfall. It was an expedition organizer's dream come true.

Not everybody saw it in the same light. Angry customers wrote to the bank demanding an explanation, and there was even a question in the House from a Labour M.P. They wanted to know what the justification was for spending this huge sum of money on such an ephemeral and socially useless thing as a mountaineering expedition.

Had they known that £100,000 was a serious underestimation and that the final cost was to be £130,000, no doubt they would have been even more irate, although their anger was based on a complete misconception of the money's origin. It came from the bank's advertising account, and the only people who stood to lose anything were the advertising agents who might otherwise have got the business. The people taking the risk were the board – and the risk they took was whether they were going to get value for money in terms of publicity. It eventually proved to be a golden gamble: because the bank owned various media rights (including Bonington's best-selling book) they not only received tremendous publicity, but actually recouped their outlay as well.[20]

Two other points are worth considering. First, in view of the objective it wasn't all that large a sum in the context of sport sponsorship. It costs a lot more, say, to enter a yacht for a round-the-world race, or sponsor a major golf or tennis championship, but mountain climbing is a cinderella sport when it comes to money. Ironically, so far as the British are concerned, it is the one sport in which they have had consistent success since the war and in which they are second to none.

The critics really hadn't thought it through. How can you measure in terms of cash the national euphoria engendered by, say, the successful Everest ascent of 1953, made when the country was still recovering from the war and in even worse financial straits than it was in 1975? After it was all over, Bonington said:

> ... if we said these are stringent times – which was one of the criticisms which was made – therefore, it is a waste of money to go off on mountaineering expeditions and therefore, in parallel really, it is a waste of money to do absolutely anything which isn't tied up with the direct productivity of the country, then what an appalling, boring, dreary country we should have, and if we had such a boring, dreary country we should be deeper in the mire than we already are.[21]

The climbing world itself was not mute. Some critics merely echoed the sentiment that £100,000 was too much to spend on a single expedition and that the money would have been better disbursed among a number of lightweight expeditions with less prestigious objectives – failing to understand that in such circumstances the money would not have been forthcoming at all. Others, no doubt bored by the repeated failures and the media coverage which the Face had received, dismissed the route as an ugly one of no consequence, a subjective assessment which only history can confirm; while some criticized Bonington because he seemed to favour a tightly knit little group which excluded some equally good climbers – though in fact only eight out of the final eighteen members were close acquaintances. All the conservatism which is so rampant in climbing rebelled against the giant publicity machine that the South West Face invariably provoked, and it was this more than anything else which was the cause of the criticism. Bonington had more than the Face to climb: old Cassius Bonafide would be hacked to death by vitriol-dipped quills if he didn't get this one right!

Bonington laid his plans carefully, unhampered by financial constraints and with sufficient time in hand to do a much more thorough job than had been possible in 1972. Men, food and materials were fitted into a logistical pyramid the apex of which was to be two men sitting in a lonely tent – placed in the right spot at the right time – ready for the final summit dash. It was an exercise in a vast yet precise upwards funnelling of resources – and it was perhaps a sign of the times that it was done with the aid of a computer. It was probably the most meticulous preparation of any Everest expedition since Hunt's.

In order to achieve the speedy ascent he thought essential, Bonington reckoned on expanding his team to eighteen front-line members – that is, those who were to be actually engaged in the climb, either as lead climbers or in support roles.

The core of these came from the 1972 expedition and the Annapurna expedition: forty-four-year-old Hamish MacInnes (who became Deputy Leader), the inaugurator of the madcap Creagh Dhu expedition to Everest twenty-two years earlier, who had twice been on the South West Face, Dougal Haston, Doug Scott, Mick Burke, Nick Estcourt, Martin Boyson and Mike Thompson. Only the last two had not been on the Face before.

Newcomers to the team were Paul Braithwaite, a twenty-eight-year-old interior decorator from Oldham who looked like a character from *Dr Zhivago*, had an impressive Alpine record, and was invariably known as Tut; Allen Fyffe, also twenty-eight, was a Scot, a bald, broad shouldered man who had also done some outstanding Alpine routes, and was a climbing instructor; Ronnie Richards, twenty-nine, a bespectacled chemist from the Lake District who had climbed the West Ridge of Pic Lenin in the Pamirs the previous year; and Dave Clarke, thirty-seven, who was the owner of an equipment shop in Leeds – sandy haired, solid and no-nonsense. Barclays Bank (who have their own climbing club) nominated Mike Rhodes, twenty-seven-year-old clerk from Bradford. Youngest of them all was Peter Boardman, twenty-four years old and the National Officer of the British Mountaineering Council: broad-shouldered and genial, he had already acquired a considerable reputation for accomplishing big climbs.

The two doctors were Charles Clarke and Jim Duff, both experienced mountaineers, and to complete the team there was Adrian Gordon, a fluent Nepali speaker who lived in Kathmandu, who was to look after Advanced Base Camp, and Mike Cheney, Base Camp Manager, a small, sharp-featured man who was deeply involved in the trekking business and was acquiring the mantle of Jimmy Roberts as a Nepali expert.

Behind them there was a considerable support team: the Sherpa corps of thirty-three high-altitude Sherpas led by their sirdar, the twenty-seven-year-old Pertemba, who came from Khumjung, and twenty-six Icefall porters under Phurkipa, whose job it was to keep the route into the Cwm open and see that the supplies got through. There were more Sherpas to do the cooking and general chores.

In addition there was a four-man B.B.C. TV team, a *Sunday Times* reporter, a liaison officer (each with *their* Sherpas) and, working from England at the outset of the expedition, Bob Stoodley and his drivers, whose job was to transport all the equipment to Kathmandu in two sixteen-ton vans.

And right at the base of the organizational pyramid was a small army of secretaries, media men and general helpers to ensure that everything was co-ordinated both on and off the mountain.

This was the extent of the manpower that Bonington had to influence and control. 'Perhaps I am a frustrated Field-Marshal,' he wryly commented.

Naturally enough, the gear and food were the best available and in ample quantities. The tents in particular were given thorough attention in view of the previous disastrous experience, when much of the tentage had been wrecked by gales. MacInnes was given the job of redesigning them, and produced a strengthened box for the lower Face camps and a more compact 'assault box' for Camp 6, which Bonington confidently expected to be placed above the Rock Band. Bullet-proof mesh to deflect stonefall was provided for the roofs of the lower boxes.[22]

With sufficient men and materials under his command it only remained for Bonington's judgement on timing and the route to be followed to be borne out in practice. If he got those wrong, then no amount of skill and determination, no vast quantities of superlative gear, would be of any avail. A degree of luck was needed as well, for mountaineering is essentially a gamble, and the winner is the one who correctly calculates the odds.

And the odds were not reckoned great, even amongst the team members. Fifty-fifty was the optimistic view – the pessimists were quoting ten to one against.

Influenced by the experience of the Japanese, Bonington planned to be at Base Camp ready to begin the climb by the end of the third week in August. Normally this would have meant transporting tons of material over the long trek from Kathmandu during the height of the monsoon, which was a far from pleasant prospect, but Bonington hit upon the idea of sending the gear out *before* the monsoon and storing it in one of the Sherpas' houses at Khunde, a village near Namche Bazar, and only four or five marches from Base Camp. Two somewhat overloaded trucks left Barclays city headquarters (sped on their way by a farewell cocktail party) on 9 April and arrived in Kathmandu on 3 May. From there the gear was air-lifted to Lukla airstrip, a tilled grass field perched on an Alpine shoulder over the gorge of the Dudh Kosi, and portered from there to Khunde. It was safely established in its monsoon storage by 10 June.

Meanwhile, the route to be followed on the Face had been discussed and analysed by the climbers. It eschewed the rightwards traverse that led to the Whillans Chimney and concentrated instead on a deep gully to the left of the great central couloir. This was the area which had first attracted the Japanese when they pioneered the Face, but it had since been unaccountably neglected. Bonington and Scott had observed the gully during their previous outing and felt that it held promise.

If the gully led them through the Rock Band, as they hoped, they would find themselves at the left-hand extremity of the curious snowy shelf which is such a prominent feature of the upper Face. Here they planned to establish

Camp 6. To reach the summit from there would mean traversing right across the shelf, then climbing a gully to the summit ridge and following the ridge, over the Hillary Step, to the top. It would be a long, long day, with a more than likely chance of an enforced bivouac on the return. But the Japanese had shown such a bivouac to be feasible, and the risk had to be accepted.

Base Camp was established on 22 August. Already the weather signs were favourable, for during the walk-in – despite the season – they had been blessed with fine mornings, and rain only in the afternoons. Estcourt and Haston, who had gone ahead of the main parties, were already at work on the Icefall, which proved to be in a rather better condition than on the previous occasion.

In five days they were through the Icefall and two days later Camp 1 was established. The monsoon was not really at an end and there was still much soft snow around, with frightening avalanches roaring off Lhotse and Nuptse. It was conditions such as these that had destroyed a French expedition to the West Ridge the previous autumn, and Bonington was concerned about making a premature entry into the Western Cwm with the risk of being hit by an avalanche. Nevertheless by 2 September Camp 2 (Advanced Base) was established in the Cwm at 21,700 ft.

There had been some discussion as to how to tackle the lower slopes of the Face – the great central couloir. Haston and Scott had discovered what they believed to be a new and more direct line sloping up to the couloir from the left, with rocky outcrops beneath which camps could be sheltered, but in the end Bonington decided it would be preferable to follow the established route, which kept just to the right of the couloir and out of the main avalanche danger.

There was, however, a change in the disposition of the camps. Camp 3 occupied its traditional site at 23,000 ft, but Camp 4, which had been a very exposed camp sited in the heart of the big couloir, was pulled back almost a thousand feet to 23,700 ft and a more sheltered position, and Camp 5, previously sited at 26,000 ft, was lowered to 25,500 ft. Tactically the new sites were an improvement – the long, exhausting carry from Camps 3 to 4 was much reduced, and Camp 5 was in a better position for attacking the left-hand side of the Rock Band.

Things were going remarkably well. The weather was good, supplies were flowing and tensions amongst the lead climbers, though always near the surface, were not breaking through. Bonington himself spent much of this period at Advanced Base: the frustrated Field-Marshal now in full battle command, disposing of his troops. Later he analysed his command philosophy:

> I try to be as democratic as I possibly can and in this was very aware of what the other members of the team felt. Whenever I possibly could I would consult and discuss how we were going to do it.

> I think in a strong expedition and a large expedition it must come back to one person, the leader, in the final analysis to make a decision. If you don't do that I don't think you are doing the job as the leader, but at the same time you can do this in an easy-going, relaxed kind of way. I think we succeeded in being democratic in the sense that as far as possible people were consulted right the way through the expedition and could also make their voices heard and known, but someone has got to make a decision in the end and I made it.[23]

Back at Base Camp, Dr Charles Clarke viewed his leader – and others – with a shrewd eye.

> Chris is in a state of hypermania at Camp 2 in the Western Cwm, drawing charts of stores, oxygen, men, being uncontrollably effusive down the radio and Mick has christened him the 'Mad Mahdi'. He is desperate that the master plan unfolds smoothly and above all that the route from Base to Camp 2 is safe, for it is here that the Sherpas go alone and much can go wrong.
>
> He really is a great leader in spite of all the criticism levelled at him. Nobody else has the personality to command us and deep down we respect him. I have a very good relationship with him particularly as I, thank God, am not in the raffle – i.e. the great decision of who goes to the top. This sadly alienates him from most of the lead climbers. Even a little is enough and it's just beginning to show itself. No splits, no factions, no nastiness, but it's all there in their hearts.[24]

By the time MacInnes, Boysen and Boardman occupied Camp 4 on 11 September, the expedition was well ahead of the schedule Bonington had set. Six days later the leader, with Richards, established Camp 5 at 25,500 ft and they were joined there next day by Scott and Burke. Progress was almost unbelievably smooth and swift. Bonington, Scott and Richards ran out fixed rope from Camp 5 to the Rock Band, while Estcourt and Braithwaite moved up in support. The very next day the assault on the Rock Band started.

Moving across the ropes fixed by their companions on the previous day, Estcourt and Braithwaite approached the dark gully which they hoped might prove the key to the ascent. When they reached the end of the ropes Tut Braithwaite won the 'toss' to decide who should lead in the unknown territory ahead and soon found himself clambering over awkward sloping rocks to the gully entrance. Estcourt followed, and behind them in support came Bonington and Burke.

The gully was a dark and narrow slit cleaving through the Rock Band. It had a good snow bed which gave a firm grip for their crampons, and Braithwaite and Estcourt alternated leads, taking in their stride a snow-covered boulder that blocked the chasm at one point. The rock was not too good for pitons and there were no natural anchors, but the standard of climbing was not technically difficult – 'about Scottish Grade III' was how Estcourt described it. 'Scottish Grade III at 27,000 ft isn't something to be taken lightly,' commented Bonington.[25]

Estcourt wasn't taking it lightly at all. His oxygen ran out and he climbed on without it, feeling 'like a hundred and five year old war veteran'. And, as they neared the head of the gully, Braithwaite's oxygen also ran out:

> I don't think I shall ever forget the feeling of suffocation as I ripped the mask away from my face. I was on the brink of falling, beginning to panic, felt a warm trickle run down my leg. God, what's happening? Scrabbled up the rock arete until at last I reached some firm snow. I collapsed exhausted.[26]

Had he fallen off he would have bounced two hundred feet down the gully and almost certainly been killed.

Braithwaite had halted just below a ramp, which sloped off to the right and seemed to lead to the upper icefield above the Rock Band. Estcourt joined him, then pushed on to tackle the ramp. It was easy at first but then it became a precarious struggle: the ramp was narrow, sloped outwards and was largely composed of rubble cemented together by ice. It was overhung by a steep wall which thrust out at the encumbered climbers.

Estcourt clawed his way forward, desperately striving to keep his balance, while his companion watched anxiously. He managed to knock a shaky piton into a crack, pulled on it cautiously and, digging desperately into the snow, snatched at another hold. He knew he just had to keep going: no stopping, no turning back, for to try either would be fatal. After a further twenty feet he reached a good crack, banged home a secure piton, and heaved a sigh of relief. 'Given the conditions it was the hardest pitch I've ever led,' he said.[27]

And as they had hoped, the ramp led to the upper icefield. Nick Estcourt and Tut Braithwaite had solved the problem of the Rock Band.

Bonington now had to give serious thought to the summit attempt. Initially he had envisaged only one attempt, and though he would not commit himself on who the summit pair would be, it was widely expected to be Haston and Scott. Such had been the progress of the expedition, however, that there was time in hand for a second and even third summit attempt. The problem was that, whereas the first attempt by Haston and Scott was more or less tacitly accepted by the team, there were lots of anxious contenders for the subsequent placings. Whatever Bonington's choice, somebody was going to be disappointed.

He had promised to give the Sherpas a place in any subsequent summit attempts after the first, but by juggling the logistics a bit he could make these ascents with four-man rather than two-man teams. His final decision was that the second attempt would be made by Burke, Boysen, Boardman and the Sherpa sirdar, Pertemba and the third attempt by Estcourt, Braithwaite, Ang Phurba and himself.

He placed himself ahead of other contenders, justifying it on the grounds of experience and fitness, but in reality it was that old Everest syndrome at work again – 'the glittering prize' – which had tempted earlier leaders like Hunt and Dyhrenfurth. Bonington perhaps had more justification, but was that enough? Charles Clarke, the team doctor, thought not. By the time any third attempt took place, Bonington would have been at Camp 5 for almost two weeks – far too long for anybody to stay at 25,500 ft. Other problems were pressing too, lower down the mountain, so reluctantly Bonington gave up his place to Ronnie Richards.

The announcement of the summit parties was met with varying degrees of disappointment by those who might have expected a chance and didn't get one, none more so than Hamish MacInnes, who had had such a long and close association with attempts on the Face and was Bonington's second-in-command. But MacInnes had had a close shave with a powder snow avalanche which had swept over him, filling his lungs with icy particles, and he was really too ill for a summit attempt. Nevertheless, it is hard to watch a lifetime ambition slipping by, so he left the expedition quietly, to return home.

On 22 September Haston and Scott established Camp 6 on a small snow ridge just beyond the exit from the gully. Next day they ran out 1,500 ft of fixed rope across the upper snowfield towards a snowy gully that led up to the distant ridge. It proved nervy work, with inadequate anchors, and in the early section of the traverse there was an awkward rock step which required five pitons to overcome. There was no accommodating ice into which crampon claws could bite: only soft snow overlying shaly, downward-sloping rock. Long before the exit gully was reached the rope ran out, so they anchored its end and returned to Camp 6.

The climbers were pleased with their hard day's work – particularly as it had not seemed to exhaust them unduly, which gave them added confidence in their own strength and ability. Next morning at 2.30 a.m. they prepared for their summit bid. Haston wore his bulky duvet suit but Scott, preferring greater freedom of movement, wore only his windproofs. Realizing they might have to make a forced bivouac, they also packed a tent-sack and a stove. Each had two oxygen cylinders, various pitons, personal gear and between them three 50-m. ropes. There was no room in their sacks for sleeping bags.

At 3.30 a.m., while it was still dark, they set out on their great adventure. By the time dawn tipped the surrounding ridges they had reached the end of the fixed rope and were embarked on virgin territory, leading into the gully below the South Summit. Suddenly Haston stopped, fighting for breath. A quick investigation showed that there was plenty of oxygen left in his cylinder and therefore it must be the set which was malfunctioning. Only by partially dismantling the apparatus did they discover that a lump of ice had formed in the junction of the mouthpiece tube. They prised it out with a knife, reassembled the set and continued on their way. Had it been a more serious fault their attempt would have been finished, as the repairs took over an hour to complete.

Scott tackled a steep rock step in the gully and brought up his companion. Ahead there seemed two possible alternative routes – directly up a gully to the Hillary Step, or more or less straight up towards the South Summit. They decided to go straight up, and immediately ran into waist-deep powder snow of the most tiring, frustrating kind. With Haston in the lead they floundered upwards, thrashing the snow and gaining a couple of feet every few minutes. Although the angle was 60° and the snow in classic avalanche condition there was no hope of belays. Scott was hard behind his leader, sometimes pushing him in the small of the back to prevent him sliding down and losing what little he had gained.

They stepped onto the South Summit at 3 p.m. The climb had taken them eleven and a half hours.

Now they were on ground made familiar by books and photographs. The ridge between the South Summit and the top of Everest undulated away towards the Hillary Step and the goal of their ambition, for although they had climbed the Face, the ascent could not be counted as complete unless they reached the summit of the mountain. However, it was already late in the day, and the snow on the ridge promised to be little better than the awful powder snow in the gully. Should they bivouac and tackle the ridge early next morning, when the night temperatures might have hardened the snow? It was a tempting idea, and while they considered it Scott put on a brew and Haston dug a bivouac snow-hole.

But it is hard to have a prize within one's grasp and not reach out for it immediately. Supposing the weather changed before morning? There might be disadvantages as well as advantages in waiting. Tentatively, Haston moved off along the ridge and found conditions not perfect, but acceptable, and that was stimulus enough.

The Hillary Step was banked up with steep, soft snow and as Haston clambered up it Scott had a growing feeling of elation: '. . . it gradually dawned on me that we were going to reach the summit of Big E'.[28]

At 6 p.m., side by side, Scott and Haston stepped onto the summit of Everest. The South West Face had been climbed.

On the top they found a tripod, five feet high, with a bunch of red ribbons fluttering from it – proof positive that the Chinese had indeed made the ascent they claimed in the spring. Scott stood in front of it and handed his camera to Haston. 'Here you are, youth,' he said. 'Take a snap for my mother.'[29]

The two men were in a precarious situation. They were on the roof of the world, with night fast approaching. Analysing the situation they reckoned they could get back to the South Summit in the gloaming, and, if the moon came out, possibly all the way back to Camp 6. The going would be firmer than it was on the ascent – already the snow was hardening as night approached.

They set off back along the ridge, abseiled down the Hillary Step and reached the South Summit. The expected moonlight did not materialize and a tentative exploration of the descent gully convinced them that it would be too risky to try returning to Camp 6. There was nothing for it but to bivouac on the South Summit at a height of 28,750 ft – the highest bivouac ever undertaken.

They enlarged the snow cave that they had begun earlier in the day until by about 9 p.m. it was large enough for them to crawl into and lie down out of the wind. Their oxygen was exhausted and before long the fuel in their little stove was used up too. The cold gnawed into their bones.

Scott, lacking his duvet suit, hacked away at the cave for much of the night in an effort to keep warm, but without the life-giving oxygen nothing eased the appalling coldness.

'There was no escaping the cold,' Haston wrote. 'Every position was tried. Holding together, feet in each other's armpits, rubbing, moving around the hole constantly, exercising arms. Just no way to catch a vestige of warmth.'[30]

They began to hallucinate under the stress. Scott wrote, 'Our minds started to wander with the stress and the lack of sleep and oxygen. Dougal quite clearly spoke out to Dave Clarke. He had quite a long and involved conversation with him. I found myself talking to my feet.'[31]

'I don't think anything we did or said that night was rational or planned,' Haston wrote. 'Suffering from lack of oxygen, cold, tiredness but with a terrible will to get through the night all our survival instincts came right up front. These and our wills saw the night to a successful end.'[32]

And with the first light they began their descent, moving cautiously at first, aware of the dangers brought on by tiredness and oxygen deficiency. Yet the warmth of movement was itself a pleasure. When at 9 a.m. they stumbled into Camp 6 they were not only safe, but sound. They had not slept or eaten for thirty hours, they had survived the highest bivouac ever made – and without oxygen – and they were not even frostbitten.

That same day, 25 September, the second assault team of Boysen, Boardman, Burke and Pertemba occupied Camp 6. Burke was climbing slowly and giving cause for concern; he had already spent eight nights at Camp 5 and Bonington was worried that this might have caused deterioration. But Burke explained over the radio that he had been delayed by various things

– and in any case he was determined to fulfil his role as cameraman by filming the route to the summit.

At 4.30 on the following morning the four men set off individually for the summit, protected by the fixed rope. Boysen went first, then Boardman and Pertemba, with Burke fetching up the rear.

Misfortune struck quickly. Before he had gone far, Boysen's oxygen set stopped working, and to compound his misery he lost a crampon. There was nothing he could do but go back, passing the others in turn; he finally crawled back into the tent and 'howled with anguish, frustration and self-pity'. Through the open door of the tent he could see the others making progress.

Boardman and Pertemba were climbing rapidly. The snow was in much better condition than it had been two days earlier, and when they reached the end of the fixed ropes they continued to climb solo, not feeling the need to be roped together. At 11 a.m. they reached the South Summit, where they were delayed for an hour by the malfunctioning of Pertemba's oxygen set, which, like Haston's, had an ice blockage. Once this was corrected, however, they continued along the ridge, to reach the summit of Everest at 1 p.m.

They mumbled into a miniature tape recorder and Pertemba fixed a Nepalese flag to the Chinese survey pole, but they were denied the superb views that Haston and Scott had witnessed two days previously. In fact, all through the day the clouds had been boiling up, obscuring the surrounding mountains. At first, Everest and Lhotse had remained above the cloud, like islands in a troubled sea, but gradually the vapour had swirled higher until even the summits of these mighty peaks were covered in mist.

Earlier in the day Boardman had been aware of a tiny figure a long way behind them, and had presumed that it was Burke watching their progress before rejoining his partner, Boysen, in the tent. As they descended from the summit, however, they were surprised to come across Burke sitting in the snow.

> We were amazed to see him through the mist. Mick was sitting on the snow only a few hundred yards down an easy angled snow slope from the summit. He congratulated us and said he wanted to film us on a bump on the ridge and pretend it was the summit, but I told him about the Chinese maypole. Then he asked us to go back to the summit with him. I agreed reluctantly and he, sensing my reluctance, changed his mind and said he'd go up and film it and then come straight down after us. He borrowed Pertemba's camera to take some stills on the top and we walked back fifty feet and then walked past him whilst he filmed us. I took a couple of pictures of him. He had the Blue Peter flag and an auto-load camera with him. He asked us to wait for him by the big rock on the South Summit where Pertemba and I had dumped our first oxygen cylinders and some rope

and film on the way up. I told him that Pertemba was wanting to move roped with me – so he should catch us up fairly quickly. I said 'See you soon' and we moved back down the ridge to the South Summit. Shortly after we had left him the weather began to deteriorate.[33]

At the South Summit the two men waited for Burke to return but as time went by and there was no sign of their companion the anxiety over his fate – and theirs – began to grow apace:

> All the winds of Asia seemed to be trying to blow us from the ridge. A decision was needed. It was four in the afternoon and the skies were already darkening around the South Summit of Everest. I threw my iced and useless snow goggles away into the whiteness and tried, clumsily mitted, to clear the ice from my eyelashes. I bowed my head into the spindrift and tried to peer along the ridge. Mick should have met us at least three quarters of an hour before, unless something had happened to him. We had been waiting for nearly one and a half hours. There was no sign of Doug and Dougal's bivouac site. The sky and cornices and whirling snow merged together, visibility was reduced to ten feet and all tracks were obliterated. Pertemba and I huddled next to the rock of the South Summit where Mick had asked us to wait for him. Pertemba said he could not feel his toes or fingers and mine too were nailed with cold. I thought of Mick wearing his glasses and blinded by spindrift, negotiating the fixed rope on the Hillary step, the fragile one foot windslab on the Nepal side and the cornices on the Tibetan side of the ridge. I thought of our own predicament, with the eight hundred feet of the South Summit Gully – guarded by a sixty foot rockstep halfway – to descend, and then half of the two thousand foot great traverse above the Rock Band to cross before reaching the end of the fixed ropes that extended across from Camp 6. It had taken Doug and Dougal three hours in the dawn sunshine after their bivouac to reach Camp 6 – but we now had only an hour of light left. At 28,700 ft the boundary between a controlled and an uncontrolled situation is narrow and we had crossed that boundary within minutes – a strong wind and sun shining through clouds had turned into a violent blizzard of driving snow, the early afternoon had drifted into approaching night and our success was turning into tragedy.[34]

After ten minutes Boardman decided that it was too risky to wait any ›nger. With the storm increasing in fury and the darkness closing in, to delay their departure any further meant almost certain death: a bivouac under such conditions was out of the question. So they cast about for the way down, fumbling and half blinded. For one instant the storm lifted and revealed the South Summit. There was no sign of Burke. The time was 4.30 p.m.

Boardman and Pertemba then began a descent which was to prove every whit as dramatic as that of Hornbein's party in 1963. The young climber plunged down the exit gully as fast as he could, belayed to a 'dead man', then yanked Pertemba down after him. The Sherpa was unaccustomed to climbing without the assistance of fixed ropes, and though he had performed nobly on the way up, the storm and the disappearance of Burke had temporarily unnerved him, making him cautious. But Boardman realized there was no time for niceties: speed was essential if they were both to survive. What worried him most was a nagging fear that he had chosen the wrong gully and they were off route ... the sight of an abandoned oxygen cylinder, which marked the rock step in the gully, came as a great relief.

They abseiled down the step. Pertemba was going more strongly now and they fought their way through the dusk and storm across the open face for a thousand feet towards the fixed ropes.

> During our traverse we were covered by two powder snow avalanches from the summit slopes. Fortunately our oxygen cylinders were still functioning and we could breathe. It was a miracle that we found the end of the fixed ropes in the dark, marked by two oxygen cylinders sticking out of the snow. On the fixed rope Pertemba slowed down again and I pulled him mercilessly until he shouted that one of his crampons had fallen off. The rope between us snagged and in flicking it free I tumbled over a fifteen foot rock step to be held on the fixed rope. At one point a section of the fixed rope had been swept away. At half past seven we stumbled into the 'summit boxes' at Camp 6. Martin was there and I burst into tears.[35]

For thirty hours the three men were trapped at Camp 6 by the raging storm. Pertemba was snowblind, Boardman was worried about possible frostbite in his feet and the luckless Boysen, who looked after them both, got frostbitten hands. On the second night, when the storm abated, they could hear avalanches roaring down the Face. Next day they began their sad descent.

So the South West Face was climbed at last. Not once, but three times, for everyone agrees that Burke must have made the summit and that the accident occurred on the descent, when, blinded by the storm, it would have been so easy for him to lose his way and stumble to his death over the South or East Faces of the mountain.

Burke had made the first solo ascent of Everest – that is, not roped to a partner. Had this contributed to his death? If Boysen had not been incapacitated, would the two of them together have reached the summit and survived – or would two have died instead of one? There are too many factors for and against to make any rational judgement.

Bonington had told them all over the radio to stick together and if anything went wrong to turn back. But when a lifetime's ambition is within grasp, some men tend to ignore such orders. Everyone on the expedition, Bonington included, has agreed that if they had been in Burke's position that fateful morning they too would have gone for the top.

Perhaps nothing can confirm this better than Burke's own words. When he first arrived at Camp 6 and heard that Bonington was going to ask him to withdraw, he said, 'Chris can get stuffed.'

# 19

# 'None But Ourselves'

The struggle for the South West Face dominated the first half of the 1970s. It was, after all, the last great unsolved problem on Everest that was available to Western mountaineers. It was not, however, the only problem: new men come along who look at old problems and discard the solutions of their predecessors, aiming for something purer or more aesthetically pleasing.

One such challenge was the long West Ridge. Ever since Hornbein and Unsoeld climbed it in 1963, mountaineers have been looking for a way to straighten it out, for despite the Americans' great achievement they were the first to admit that by taking Hornbein's Couloir on the North Face they deviated from the true ridge line. Moreover, since they started the climb from the Western Cwm a purist could argue that they left out the lower part of the ridge altogether.

But nobody seemed willing to embark on a West Ridge attempt while the Face remained unclimbed. Although parties continued to attempt the usual route by the South East Ridge because there was a reasonable chance of success, the West Ridge was too much of an uncertainty for the average expedition. It needed a well-organized team of experienced climbers – and most of those preferred to spend their time and money on the Face. Had the Face not been such a lure, the West Ridge would undoubtedly have been repeated in the early 1970s.

During the International Expedition of 1971 Dyhrenfurth had tried to combine an attempt on the West Ridge with one on the Face but the attempt had been blighted by storm and Harsh Bahuguna's death.

The first attempt at a complete 'integrale' – that is, the ridge from bottom to top, without deviations – was made in the post-monsoon period of 1974 by a French expedition under the leadership of Gérard Devouassoux, Deputy

Mayor of Chamonix, a famous Alpine resort. Devouassoux, like the other nine members of the team, was a professional guide. It was the first French expedition to Everest, and extremely ambitious – not only did they intend to climb the unknown West Ridge but they hoped that all the team members would reach the summit.

With hindsight one might say that it was over-ambitious on three counts: first, the expedition was probably too small for its objective; secondly, none of the members had any experience of Everest; and thirdly, very little was known at that time about post-monsoon conditions on the mountain.

This last point was crucial. In 1972 Bonington's team had been met by the fierce winds which mark the onset of Everest's winter, but a year later the Japanese had established Base Camp by late August, and had succeeded in making the first post-monsoon ascent of the mountain. The solution to the problem lay in choosing exactly the right time – were the Japanese lucky with the weather? If the warm monsoon winds have not abated the snow is extremely soft and liable to avalanche. In other words there is a short period in the post-monsoon Everest weather during which an attempt is possible.

The West Ridge of Everest (see Fig. 2, p. 282) begins properly at the Lho La, a relatively low icy saddle in the ridges dividing Nepal from Tibet, which on the Nepalese side presents a fearsome spectacle of steeply tumbling ice. From the Lho La the ridge rises fairly steeply to a prominent cone-shaped eminence called the West Shoulder (where the original American route joins it), then less steeply to the final great soaring pyramid that forms the distinctive upper part of Everest. Broadly speaking, the lower part of the route is mainly (though not entirely) snow and ice, the upper part rock.

When the French arrived at Base Camp in mid-August they found, to their gratified surprise, that snow conditions were firm and sound. The Nepalese authorities, for political reasons, had asked them not to go to the actual Lho La itself, so the climbers began a complicated and technically difficult route up the rock walls above the foot of the Khumbu Icefall which brought them onto the slopes of the West Peak. Camp I was in a sheltered situation among rocks at 19,140 ft, Camp II was above the Lho La at 21,120 ft and Camp III, established on 9 September, was close to the crest of the West Shoulder at 22,770 ft. They had overcome their first major problem, which was how to gain access to the Shoulder and upper ridge.

Unfortunately they were to pay a severe penalty for their rapid success, for in their planning they had made an appalling error. They were totally unaware of the wavelength and times of the All India Radio weather reports, and consequently missed the broadcast warning of an unexpected return of the warm monsoon weather. Had they received the warning they would, presumably, have evacuated the mountain, for they were in a dangerous avalanche zone, but the rising temperatures caught them unawares and there was little the twenty-one climbers and Sherpas spread between the three camps could do except sit tight and hope the thermometer would drop again.

On the evening of 9 September, Camp II was occupied by Devouassoux, Georges Payot (who was Deputy Leader), Pierre Tairraz and five Sherpas. The other climbers were at Camp III, which had just been established, and one climber with ten Sherpas at Camp I. At 7.30 p.m. there was a crack followed by a roar as a massive avalanche slid off the mountain between Camps I and II, smashing the former with its shock waves and setting off a secondary avalanche which overwhelmed Camp II.

Payot was buried up to his neck in snow but fortunately managed to extricate himself, as did Tairraz. Between them they freed a trapped Sherpa, but though they dug desperately into the piled up snow there was no sign of their leader or the remaining Sherpas. Night was upon them too, and they were forced into a terrible bivouac before retreating next day.

At Camp I the blast of the avalanche had hurled another Sherpa 600 ft down the mountainside. In all, Devouassoux and five Sherpas had died in one of the worst tragedies in the mountain's history.

Understandably, the French withdrew. There was no further attempt on the West Ridge until the spring of 1979, when a thirty-one-member Yugoslavian expedition led by Tone Skarja finally succeeded in climbing it from the Lho La to the summit. From the top camp (Camp VI) two attempts failed before Jernej Zaplotnik and Andrej Stremfelj made the summit in an eight-hour push. Two days later a second party of two climbers and the Sherpa Ang Phu repeated the ascent, but tragically Ang Phu fell and was killed between Camps V and IV during the descent.[1]

During the same period as these ambitious assaults on the South West Face and the West Ridge, the original way up by the South Col had not been neglected. Between 1971 and 1979 no fewer than ten expeditions attempted Everest by the South East Ridge: three failed, the rest succeeded. Some were simply personal or national efforts to reach the summit with the minimum of fuss, 'because it was there'; others added considerably to the sum of Man's knowledge about the mountain – and himself.

During the post-monsoon period of 1971 a government-sponsored Argentinian expedition led by Lt Col. H.C. Tolosa was defeated by the weather. They had left Kathmandu on 17 August and established Base Camp on 15 September, reaching the South Col on 28 October after delays due to weather. As Bonington's experience was to confirm the following year, this was much too late for success in the face of the fierce winter winds.

In the spring of 1973 the Italian millionaire newspaper magnate, Guido Monzino, led a well-equipped sixty-four-strong expedition to the mountain. They were supported by seventy Sherpas. As the numbers suggest, it was an expedition in the grand style of bygone days, reminiscent of Vittorio Sella or the Duke of the Abruzzi. At Base Camp the leader had a carpeted five-roomed tent equipped with leather upholstered furniture. Supplies were ferried up to the Western Cwm by Italian Air Force helicopters, one of which crashed into the Icefall, though fortunately without loss of life.[2]

Despite delays due to bad weather, the Italians Rinaldo Carrel and Mirko Minusso and the two Sherpas, Lhakpa Tensing and Sambu Tamang, reached the summit on 5 May. Two days later Fabrizio Innamorati, Virginio Epis, Claudio Beneditti and Sonam Gyalzen repeated the ascent.[3]

The Italians had thus put eight men onto the summit – not quite equalling the Indian record of nine, achieved in 1965. Sir Edmund Hillary, who visited the Italian Base Camp, was disgusted by the profligacy of it all. 'It's now reached the heights of the ridiculous,' he said.

In the spring of 1974 it was the turn of a modest sixteen-man Spanish expedition led by Juan Ignacio Lorente and sponsored by the electrical firm Tximist. Two attempts were made on the summit, but both were foiled by weather: the second only 350 ft from the summit, on 13 May. When the weather eventually cleared, on the 22nd, there was nobody left at the high camps fit enough to make another bid, and so the attempt was abandoned.

According to A.F. Mummery, the celebrated pioneer Victorian Alpinist, any great mountain gradually regresses in the climber's estimation from being 'an inaccessible peak' to 'an easy day for a lady', as the climbing of it becomes increasingly familiar. Mummery was perhaps being a little tongue-in-cheek, but there is a good deal of underlying truth in his words. There is no reason to believe that Everest will not follow this general pattern.

In addition to being the year of the conquest of the South West Face, 1975 was also the Year of the Woman as far as Everest was concerned. Two women climbed Everest that year. One was Mrs Phantog, a member of the Chinese team (see pp. 355–9), although she was preceded by Mrs Junko Tabei, a thirty-five-year-old bespectacled ex-schoolteacher from Tokyo.

Mrs Tabei was a member of the first 'all-women's' expedition to Everest. The team had fourteen women climbers, twenty-three Sherpas and some five-hundred porters. It was sponsored by the Tokyo Women's Mountaineering Club and paid for by newspaper and television interests. It was thoroughly prepared for four years before setting out and it included many of Japan's best women climbers. Mrs Tabei, for example, had previously reached the summit of Annapurna III (24,787 ft) in 1970.

The expedition went forward without incident until the night of 4 May when an avalanche, roaring down from Nuptse, devastated Camp II in the Western Cwm. By the greatest good fortune nobody was killed, but Junko Tabei and Yuriko Watanabe had a narrow escape when they were injured by tumbling ice blocks. A good deal of equipment was lost and for a brief period it seemed that the expedition might have to be called off. In the event the team decided to use their resources in making just one attempt on the summit instead of the two they had originally planned.

Mrs Tabei made a remarkable recovery from her avalanche injuries. By 13 May, together with the sirdar Ang Tshering, she had established Camp VI on the ridge, and after being delayed by bad weather made her summit bid with the Sherpa three days later.

They left the tent at 5 a.m. and reached the South Summit at 8.30. From there to the top took another four hours, and for Mrs Tabei, small and lightly built, the deep soft snow they encountered and the Hillary Step (seemingly in difficult condition on this occasion) proved almost beyond endurance. Ang Tshering led the whole way and she followed as best she could:

> The route was too steep and too long for a woman. Ang Tshering was climbing faster and often urged me to move on by pulling my hand. I was tired and we progressed slowly towards the summit, sometimes on our elbows. It was a very hard climb.[4]

Nevertheless, exhausted and, as she admits, terrified of the descent, Junko Tabei became the first woman to climb Mount Everest.

It is fair to say that 1975 turned out to be a seminal year in the history of Mount Everest: the most important year since 1953, when Hunt's success first showed the way. Not only was the great Face climbed, but the South East and North ridges too, and by women. Everest may never be 'an easy day', but the underlying truth of Mummery's dictum has been amply borne out. From 1975 to 1979 (when this book was being completed) the mountain has been climbed several times each year.

In 1976 a joint British-Nepalese Army expedition under the command of Lt Col. Tony Streather were successful in putting two men on top. Sgt J.H. (Brummy) Stokes and Corporal M.P. (Bronco) Lane reached the summit at 3.15 p.m. on 16 May. The weather was bad and they were forced into a harrowing bivouac on the way down, both men badly frostbitten. Earlier, the expedition had suffered the loss of Terry Thompson, a Marines captain, who had fallen into a crevasse at Camp II and been killed.

In the autumn of that year the Americans organized a Bicentennial expedition to Everest, led by a thirty-eight-year-old State Department lawyer, Phil Trimble. It was a fairly modest affair of eleven climbers and thirty Sherpas, accompanied by a six-man TV crew sent by C.B.S. Sports, who were helping to finance the venture.[5] Two members were Barbara and Gerard Roach of Colorado, who hoped to become the first husband and wife team to climb the mountain, but in this they were disappointed. Instead, Bob Cormack and Chris Chandler arrived on the summit at 4.15 p.m. on 8 October and managed to avoid a bivouac by reaching Camp VI, on the ridge, after dark. Owing to what Gerard Roach called 'bureaucratic foulups', no further attempts were made, and the expedition withdrew.

Though the Americans had reached the summit they seemed to feel that their success was qualified, that perhaps they had used a sledgehammer to crack a nut, even though, in terms of manpower, their expedition was barely one third the size of the army expedition which had just preceded them. Gerry Roach wrote:

> Yet about half the expedition members left the mountain with feelings of frustration or failure. It was much too big. It was not man against the mountain so much as expedition against the mountain, and the expedition seemed to be propelled more by dollars than by individual initiative. The true initiative, it seemed to me, lay in coming up with the dollars. All these things ran counter to the spirit of mountaineering.
>
> The expedition succeeded in large measure by impersonalizing mountaineering. It replaced single efforts and more limited crusades with the staggering power of regimented attack. We obtained large quantities of the finest food and equipment and then hired 40 Sherpas to transport it up the mountain. In some endeavours, such as the exploration of space, the power of regimented attack is necessary to achieve the objective. But we had gone to Everest for sport, for adventure. Those goals, I think, did not require such an expensive and potent offense . . .
>
> Everest can be climbed by a much smaller team using few if any Sherpas. Someday I would like to return to Everest with such a team and tackle the mountain head on, like the rock back home. Maybe it won't work, but to find out is the reason for going.[6]

It was the age-old cry of the traditional climber to get back to basics, to eschew the expedition trend that divorced a man from his mountain, to return to the faith of their forefathers, Shipton and Tilman. But nobody has yet proved it can be done on Everest.

In fact, at the time of writing, there has only been one attempt at a lightweight Everest Expedition. This was in the spring of 1977 when a team of seven New Zealanders and a Canadian, led by Keith Woodford, struggled through the Khumbu Icefall and up the Western Cwm without the aid of porters. All eight reached a height of 24,800 ft on the Lhotse Face – their highest camp – and from there Mike Browne and Mike Mahoney reached the South Col. High winds prevented any further advance, but in any case the constant work had debilitated the team and it is doubtful if they could have carried on.

Summing up his experience, Woodford still thought the mountain could be climbed by a lightweight team, but conditions would have to be perfect.

> ... it is only just possible and it will take a very strong party. If we'd had reasonable conditions we could have done it. But with difficult snow and ice conditions and high winds, the mountain was just too big for us. We had a strong party and pulled together well for 65 days above 18,000 ft. But at the end of those 65 days we were just too tired to make a push to get to the summit.[7]

There can hardly have been a greater contrast than that between the pioneering New Zealand effort and the South Korean expedition which followed them in the autumn of 1977. The Koreans had a team of nineteen climbers led by Kim Young-Do, a member of the South Korean National Assembly, and financed jointly by the Governmennt and business interests. It turned out to be a very curious affair indeed.

Despite five years of preparation, the detailed organization was not too sound. They underestimated the porterage required for the trek to Base Camp by 20 per cent, then, having arrived at the mountain, discovered that their French and American oxygen equipment did not fit their Japanese cylinders! Fortunately they were able to purchase some American bottles which the Bicentennial expedition had left at Namche Bazar, but it meant they were seriously short of oxygen from the start.

They were, however, very well staffed with high-altitude Sherpas, no fewer than twenty-eight of whom carried right up to the South Col. According to the Sherpas only two of the climbers reached the col (the Koreans claim four reached it) which gives a carrying ratio of 14:1 or 7:1 depending on which account you care to believe. In any event, this massive logistical support, allied to the best weather seen on Everest for years, led to a very rapid build-up:

| | | |
|---|---|---|
| Base Camp established | 9 August | |
| Camp 1 | 16 August | 6,100 m. |
| Camp 2 | 19 August | 6,450 m. |
| Camp 3 | 26 August | 7,400 m. |
| Camp 4 | 7 September | 7,980 m. (South Col) |
| Camp 5 | 8 September | 8,500 m. (on South East Ridge) |

And the first summit bid was made the very next day by Park Sang-Yul and the Sherpa Ang Phurba, who had been supported up to Camp V by no fewer than eight porters. Faulty oxygen gear and an unexpected heavy snowfall prevented the summit from being reached. Had they succeeded they would have beaten by two days the thirty-three-day record established by the British South West Face expedition in 1975 for the fastest ascent of the mountain.

However, on 15 September the summit was reached by Ko Sang-Don and the Sherpa Pemba Norbu, at 12.50 p.m. Nine high-altitude porters had supported them to the top camp.

Despite a bumbling beginning and good luck with the weather, the Koreans had some justification in being proud of their achievement. After all, they were not a nation with a long history of mountaineering success behind them, and they had joined an elite club at their first attempt: only Britain, America, China, India, Japan, Switzerland and Italy, besides Nepal itself, had put climbers on the roof of the world at that time, and even nations with a strong mountaineering background, such as France, Germany, Austria and Russia, were still excluded.[8]

Looked at from a purely climbing viewpoint, the achievement was minimal – but, as readers of this book will know, Everest is more than just a mountain.

Mike Cheney, who lives in Kathmandu and is deeply involved with most of the expeditions that visit Nepal, wrote:

> Of all Everest expeditions to date this was the most blatantly 'political' and 'all about national prestige' – nothing to do with Western concepts of mountaineering. The Koreans did not climb Mount Everest 'because it was there'. The expedition was a calculated exercise in 'prestige politics' . . . But why should Asians in Asia conform to Western standards? The trend in Asian mountaineering is to use the Himalaya for the purpose of gaining national prestige. Who are the Westerners to complain?[9]

Cheney's analysis is a bit sweeping, perhaps, and the Japanese cannot be included in it. The truth is less simple, one feels. Individual climbers the world over climb for their own satisfaction, but Everest, being Everest, inevitably brings a nationalistic overburden which is exploited by politicians and propagandists. The weaker or less well developed the country, the louder they will bang the drum.

After 1975, it seemed that there was little left to do on Everest. The South West Face, widely publicized as 'the hardest on the highest', had at last been climbed, the three great ridges had succumbed, there had been multiple ascents, women's ascents, pre- and post-monsoon ascents, the peak had been traversed, there had been a solo ascent and even an ascent by a 'teenager'! True, there was the odd bit of tidying-up to be done: everyone agreed that the West Ridge needed straightening out, and an Alpine-style lightweight ascent would be nice, but as far as new routes were concerned, until the Chinese opened Tibet to foreigners there wasn't a great deal of scope. The top British and American climbers turned their attention elsewhere, to other more obvious challenges like the ridges of K2 in the Karakorum, second highest mountain in the world.

There was, however, one great physiological challenge which so far nobody had accepted. Could Everest be climbed without oxygen? In 1978 two men determined to try.

Reinhold Messner and Peter Habeler were two Tyroleans who had built up formidable reputations as mountaineers. Both were slight of build, handsome and charming – the very personification of every schoolgirl's ideal ski instructor. But behind the good looks there was a capacity for incredible endurance allied to climbing talents that were well beyond the ordinary.

Messner burst on the world scene when he was in his early twenties with some outstanding solo ascents of hard rock climbs and his outspoken advocacy of free climbing – that is, without the metal protection pegs driven into the rock, which were then in common use in the Alps. In some quarters he was hailed as a young Messiah, and his philosophy, backed up by his great ability, had undoubtedly had a profound effect on Alpine climbing.

In 1970 Messner went to Nanga Parbat, where he made the first traverse by climbing the Rupal Flank and descending the Diamir Face, a climb in which his brother, who was with him, was killed. Other high-altitude ascents followed with a variety of companions, until in 1974 he began his remarkable partnership with the Mayrhofen guide, Peter Habeler.

Their success as a team was meteoric. In that first season together they astounded the Alpine world by making extremely rapid ascents of two of the most formidable north faces: those of the Matterhorn in eight hours and the notorious Eigerwand in ten hours. The previous best time on the Eigerwand had been more than double that, so it was immediately apparent that here was a team who were not merely good climbers but had a special *rapport* which allowed them to move together instinctively. Habeler put it down to a sort of telepathy: that each one knew exactly what the other was thinking as they climbed together.

And yet, curiously for so close a bond, it was only a working relationship. They were not intimate friends, seldom met except on their expeditions, and never confided in one another about their lives outside the world of climbing. For one thing they were so temperamentally different: Messner was a 'superstar', writer of popular climbing books, television personality, outgoing and forceful, while Habeler was a quiet man who cared little for glamour or publicity.

In 1975 they travelled to the Karakorum and made an astonishing two-man ascent of Gasherbrum (Hidden Peak) at 8,068 m. the eleventh highest mountain in the world. They did not use oxygen equipment.

It was of course a logical extension of Messner's Alpine philosophy, with which Habeler fully agreed. Put simply it was that nothing artificial should come between a climber and his mountain, that to use ulterior aids was to deny the full richness of the mountain experience, and just as metal pitons were anathema on rock climbs so too oxygen was anathema on high-altitude climbs. 'I know I can climb Everest with *Technik*,' he said. 'With enough *Technik*, so can anyone . . . so many porters, so much oxygen, so many porters to carry the oxygen . . . like so, I know I can climb Everest. I just as well stay at home.'[10]

Taken to its logical conclusion, of course, such a philosophy would mean that the only valid ascent would be by one man, alone, climbing to the summit naked, but that would be *reductio ad absurdum*: common sense must prevail.[11]

Possibly the two men had Everest in mind right from the start of their partnership. It would provide Messner with what his philosophy demanded: a lightweight oxygenless ascent of one of the great steep faces of the world, similar to the South Face of Aconcagua in the Andes and the South Face of Dhaulagiri in the Himalaya. In late 1975 Habeler was certainly thinking of a lightweight ascent, possibly via the South West Face.[12]

There was, however, one snag to their preparations. They did not have permission to attempt the mountain, and they realized that there was virtually no chance of obtaining one of the coveted spring or autumn 'slots' for many years to come. For men in the peak of condition such a wait could be disastrous. Their only chance lay in joining one of the expeditions already scheduled.

Fortunately the Austrian Alpine Club had booked for spring 1978 and the two men were able to attach themselves to this as a sort of independent unit. They could not, of course, claim to be a lightweight expedition, since they were enjoying the logistical support of the main group, with all its Sherpas and camps. They determined therefore to attempt the ascent without oxygen.

The Austrian expedition comprised a thirteen-man team led by Wolfgang Nairz, a thirty-three-year-old journalist from Innsbruck. The members, who varied in age from twenty-six to fifty-four, all had experience of high-altitude mountain climbing in the Himalaya or Andes. Two of them were British: Leo Dickinson and Eric Jones, cameramen attached to the team by Harlech TV, who were making a television film of the attempt and who were both good climbers in their own right. The cost of the expedition was £65,294, more than a quarter of which was raised by the members themselves, the rest coming from various media contracts, promotional gimmicks and private donations.[13]

The expedition aims were explicitly stated. They were: to make the first Austrian ascent of Everest; to attempt the summit without oxygen; to attempt the first ascent of the South Spur; to attempt the world hang-gliding record by gliding down from the South Col. Subsidiary aims were to test equipment and record the adventure on film and tape.

On the face of it, the Austrians had apparently fallen into the common trap of having a multiplicity of objectives, but in fact only the first two really counted – to make the first Austrian ascent and the first ascent without oxygen. Hang gliders were taken but were never used on the mountain, and the South Buttress, which is a triangular wedge of the mountain between the South Col and South West Face, was not attempted either.[14] So there remained the two basic objectives: the one to be tackled by the main team under Nairz and the other by Messner and Habeler. Magnanimously, Nairz agreed that the oxygenless attempt should come first.

The expedition set up Base Camp in late March and began the task of making the route through the Icefall and establishing camps in the Western Cwm, with Messner and Habeler playing their part in these preparations. On 2 April they set up Camp II (Advanced Base Camp), rode out a fearful storm that night and retreated to Base Camp next day. Others took over, but on the 10th Messner and Habeler returned to Camp II and reconnoitred the site for Camp III. They were staging their camps at greater intervals than usual, so that Camps I, II and III covered more or less the distance usually taken by Camps I–IV; their Camp IV was to be on the South Col, which is usually Camp V. They were going well: Messner actually prospected up to 7,800 m., while Habeler raced down the ten kilometres from Camp II to Base in one hour twenty minutes – a journey down the Cwm and through the Icefall that normally takes four or five hours.

Things were progressing satisfactorily when unhappily, on the 18th, a Sherpa working in the Icefall disappeared into a crevasse, his body beyond recovery. A storm began that day too, and blew throughout the next day as well. On 21 April, however, the weather was better, so Messner and Habeler, accompanied by three Sherpas, began their assault.

They reached Camp III, perched on the Lhotse Face, on the 23rd. That night Habeler was taken violently ill with stomach cramp and sickness, all the symptoms of food poisoning, and he realized with dismay that some sardines he had eaten earlier in the day must have been bad. The resulting debilitation made any chance of an ascent hopeless, and so the next day he made a lone and weary retreat to Camp II, weak and disconsolate, a prey to the elemental savagery of the Lhotse Face and the endless Cwm. Fog came down and for a while he wandered about, lost in a white wilderness and facing certain death – until he finally came across marker flags, which guided him into camp.

Meanwhile Messner had determined to push on, to establish Camp IV on the South Col and, if fortune favoured him, to make a solo ascent from the col to the summit. It was a wild dream that now assailed him: to climb the mountain not only without oxygen but also without a companion – the ultimate test of his own severe philosophy.

To help him to establish a camp on the col he had with him two Sherpas, Mingma and Ang Dorje. As they struggled up the remainder of the Lhotse Face and over the Geneva Spur the wind rose rapidly, and by the time they reached the col they were fighting a raging storm. They managed to erect a tent and crawl inside, appalled at the violence of the elements. The tent fabric flapped and rattled and Messner wondered whether they would all be blown clean off the mountain or whether the tent would simply be torn to shreds, leaving them exposed to the elements. Either way, survival seemed unlikely. Outside the wind reached 125 m.p.h. and the temperature dropped to 40° below zero.

There was no chance of sleep, desperately tired though they were. Messner and Ang Dorje tried to cook: Mingma simply crawled into his bag and lay as if dead.

Towards dawn the tent fabric, no longer able to withstand the blast, ripped open. Snow came pouring in. Messner and Ang Dorje struggled out and began erecting a second tent, fighting the billowing canvas and the freezing, stinging spindrift. It was essential for their survival that they should succeed, and an hour later they were able to crawl inside the tent, along with the apathetic Mingma. As he sank into the tent Messner burst into tears.

They remained there all next day as the storm raged around them. The two Sherpas, and particularly Mingma, were convinced that nothing could save them and gave themselves up to their fate with a calmness that angered Messner. He was determined that he would survive, and the Sherpas with him.

What exactly happened in that stormbound tent during those terrible hours we shall probably never know. Undoubtedly Messner shouted and railed at the Sherpas, hoping to keep alive the spark of survival. In the end he probably saved their lives, but this was not appreciated by Mingma, who later accused him of 'subjecting Nepalese nationals to inhuman treatment', which included urinating into the Sherpa's cooking pot.[15]

Ang Dorje did not corroborate his partner's statement, and it must be remembered that they were three men whose nerves were as taut as violin strings, clinging desperately to the edge of survival. They had eaten little and slept not at all for two days and two nights of terror. They were virtually reduced to automatons, and their later memories of those terrible hours are scarcely to be relied on.[16]

Had the storm continued they must surely have perished, but the dawn following the second night held promise of good weather and at 7 a.m. they set off back to Advanced Base in the Western Cwm, which they reached that afternoon. Next day Messner returned to Base Camp – and was almost killed when a ladder gave way in the Icefall.[17]

Once Habeler and Messner returned from their abortive attempt, Nairz felt free to go ahead with his own plans. On 3 May, Nairz himself, with Robert Schauer, Horst Bergmann and the sirdar Ang Phu, reached the summit of Everest from a camp (Camp V) pitched on the South East Ridge. A week later Oswald Ölz and Reinhard Karl made the summit – Karl being a German national, and therefore the first German to climb Everest. Three days later Franz Oppurg, climbing solo, also made the summit – the first ever solo of the South East Ridge, and the first solo ascent since Mick Burke's fateful climb of 1975.

So, by any standards, this well organized, highly skilled, Austrian team was outstandingly successful. But between the ascent by Nairz on 3 May and that by Ölz a week later, there took place the event which was to make mountaineering history.

After his retreat from Camp III, Peter Habeler had been uncertain whether or not to make a second attempt without oxygen. A highly intelligent, sensitive man, he had read a great deal about Everest and the problems of high altitude and was worried by some of the medical prognostications. In particular he was worried that by prolonging his stay in the thin cold air his brain cells might suffer irreparable damage, which some doctors thought was a distinct possibility. Given good weather, he felt he would have no problems on the physical side. He was extremely fit and strong, and would doubtless survive the ordeal – but did he want to survive as a cabbage, his brain irretrievably damaged?

He considered the possibilities. If he and Messner could make a rapid ascent, straight up and straight down again, without any delays, they might just get away with it. But supposing another storm blew up and they were trapped on the col without oxygen? Might they not deteriorate beyond repair? He decided the risk was too great, and that the only thing to do was make an ordinary ascent using oxygen apparatus. He informed Messner of his decision, but of course Messner wanted no part of it. He then asked to join the rest of the Austrians in their plans – and was surprised, hurt and angered by their response: a firm no, couched in strong terms.

One can easily imagine Habeler reacting in this way. An uncomplicated man, he probably thought the undoubted extra qualities he would bring to the team would be welcomed. Like many others, he had not realized that Everest was a special mountain and aroused jealousies and fears even among the best of companions. The immediate reaction of the team was not 'Here is Peter Habeler, he will strengthen the team' but 'Here is Peter Habeler – whom will he displace? Will it be me?' Franz Oppurg, who at twenty-six was the youngest member of the team, and Josl Knoll, at fifty-four, the oldest, were particularly bitter. They accused Habeler of boasting about climbing Everest without oxygen, then backing out when put to the test.

Habeler was furious. All his recent reservations about the effects of an oxygenless ascent went out of the window. In an angry mood of 'damn them all' he committed himself irrevocably to Messner's project.

Early in the morning of 7 May, Habeler, Messner and the cameraman Eric Jones left Camp III for the South Col, accompanied by three Sherpas. None of them wore oxygen sets, though two cylinders and a face mask were taken up for use in dire emergency. This did something to reassure Habeler, who was still assailed by medical doubts, now that his anger had subsided:

> It was a big psychological help for me, anyway, because I was relying on it in case something would have gone wrong. I would have used it. I would have had no doubts in using it.[18]

It was a long hard slog up to the col, but at least they had no problems with the weather, which was good. The two Austrians managed it in three and a half hours: Jones, laden with his movie camera, took about an hour longer. The three Sherpas were sent down and the climbers settled in for a cold, oxygenless night.

From his own sparsely equipped tent, thirty feet away from the Austrians, Jones could hear them cooking, talking and preparing for the day ahead. He felt fit and strong, able to make the summit without oxygen, despite some frostbite, but he knew he would never keep up with the other two. Their speed was phenomenal. Disappointed, he realized that he did not figure in the Austrians' plans:

> You can't blame them. It's every man for himself up there, and I made no effort to prepare for the morning. When they left, I just stayed in my sleeping bag until about 11 o'clock.[19]

At 5.30 next morning, 8 May, Messner and Habeler left the camp for their summit bid. Each carried a small rucksack with personal gear, and Messner had a 50-m. rope. He left first, heading for the gully which leads up to the ridge from the col, while Habeler had a few words with Jones. The weather was misty, a keen wind blew, and Habeler did not think they would get far. He told Jones they were going to reconnoitre the ridge.

Habeler soon caught up with his companion, who had stopped to take photographs. Together they tackled the long introductory gully, not bothering to rope up, but plodding up the 40° snow slope, changing the lead from one to the other every twenty minutes or so. Eventually the snow became too deep and Habeler led the way over to some rocks which, though glazed with ice, offered easier progress. Further up the rock ran out into crusted snow, which would hold for a second then break, plunging the climber's foot deep into the snow with a jerk. Even in the Alps such snow conditions are tiring: on Everest they are exhausting, and the two men were glad to get back onto rock, even though it was of a rotten, crumbly sort.

Eventually they came to Camp V, at which Nairz had left some food and a stove. Messner crawled into the tent and brewed some tea. Habeler describes his feelings as they continued the ascent:

> I left Reinhold in the tent and went on alone. At first I was able to follow the tracks left by the successful Nairz party, but then the snow became soft and tiring so I moved further to the right, towards the Kangshung face where the snow was much firmer and I could more or less front point. It was quite steep but I found it a relief after the weary snow of the ridge.
>
> Reinhold caught up and passed me, and he was the first to reach the sort of Col before the South Summit. At this point the climbing became more

difficult. There were bands of rock, 2 metres or 2½ metres high, through which we had to thread our way. I had taken the lead again but we still didn't use the rope because there was no means of belaying, and although there was no exposure – visibility was down to a hundred metres – I was very conscious of the consequences of a slip, and I was scared.

I tried to escape by climbing some snow over on my right, but it was soft and bottomless, and after two or three steps I was exhausted. So it was back to the rocks, with Reinhold always close behind. At last he stopped to do some filming and I was able to draw ahead again.

Just before the South Summit I felt so tired that I dug a hole in the snow and dumped my rucksack in it. I knew it was safe there and that, come what may, I should be able to reach it again.

Without the rucksack it felt much easier and suddenly, it seemed, I was through the clouds and into clear blue sky. There was a strong breeze from the south-west and I wondered whether it could prevent us from going on. Until this stage I don't think I'd really considered the actual summit – not because I didn't feel strong enough, but because I was waiting for something to happen which would give us an excuse to retreat. I was hoping something would turn up ... but as I sat on the South Summit, the final ridge looked much too optimistic. I turned away from it and took a picture of Reinhold coming up the South Summit.

The summit ridge was heavily corniced on the right, so we put on the rope – just slipped it round the waist and tied a knot, then moved together, Alpine style, towards the Hillary Step.

Between the South Summit and the main summit, Reinhold did a lot of filming – he used three cassettes – and he particularly wanted to film the Hillary Step. The Step was completely snow covered and we could see the steps made by Nairz leading up it. Reinhold went ahead then stood on top, pointed the camera, and signalled for me to come on. I was not too happy about it, and I shouted something about the need for a belay, but perhaps he didn't hear me. Anyway, he just kept filming, so I thought 'so what?' and went up, with the slack trailing round me.

But the Nairz steps were not what they seemed. They had become soft and kept breaking, and I found myself planting my axe in firmly and hanging on like grim death.

The Hillary Step knocked the stuffing out of us both. We just lay on our bellies in the snow, gasping and immobile until at last we felt a bit of power coming back into our limbs.

Thankfully from there to the summit it was easy going. We had to keep more or less to the crest of the ridge because there was wind slab on the left which looked as though it might avalanche. On the right there were cornices which we somehow ignored – I am sure that our film will show us walking

> on cornices when it appears. We just wandered along the ridge, a few steps at a time, with Reinhold in front. Sometimes the rope between us would be slack and catch up on a snow cornice and I would pull it to free it – this would make Reinhold very angry, but it had to be done or the rope would have been permanently snagged. And in all this, strangely enough, I was not really aware that we were approaching the summit of Everest. I was not eager for the summit, but just felt as though we were two climbers who might have been almost anywhere, just strolling along the ridge.[20]

They left the South Summit at noon and reached the top at 1 p.m. Only then did they fully realize the magnitude of their achievement: that they had accomplished a feat long thought impossible. They fell into each other's arms and wept.

Once the first flush of success wore off, Habeler's unease began to assail him again:

> After about five minutes I wanted to go down again. I was gripped by this morbid fear that if I stopped too long I would seize up and never move again. Reinhold, however, wanted to stay a while longer, so after half an hour I set off alone, leaving him to play with his tape recorder. 'Don't forget to leave the rope at the Hillary Step!' he shouted, as I made my way down the ridge.
>
> But when I came to the Hillary Step there was nowhere to fix the rope. I suppose I could have belayed it round my ice axe, but I needed my axe. There was nothing for it but to climb down, solo. I remembered Reinhold's instructions, but I thought 'To hell with it, if I can climb solo, so can he.' So I faced into the snow and went down carefully, step by step. I suddenly felt very tired.
>
> A little further on I felt so tired I had to lie down and rest for a while, then up again and along towards the South Summit. But the final little pull up to that summit, a gentle 25 degree slope only four or five metres high, beat me and I had to rest again. I could see Reinhold tackling the Hillary Step. Finally, I turned into the slope and crawled on all fours to the South Summit. I was exhausted – when I looked at the Nuptse ridge I could see *two* ridges.
>
> Looking back I could see Reinhold had reached the foot of the Hillary Step, so I took another picture of him and decided not to wait, but to push on. I still had this incessant urge to get down quickly. . .[21]

Habeler later confessed that he was scarcely conscious of his physical actions during his descent – it was as if he was an observer, watching somebody else climb. Little did he realize that he had embarked on one of the most remarkable descents in the history of mountaineering.

He plunged down the ridge at a rapid pace. The mist had lifted, revealing the deep abyss on each side: on his left, thousands of feet down to the Kangshung Glacier, on his right, an equally impressive void where the South West Face dropped to the Western Cwm. He felt exposed and vulnerable. He was not sure whether he could manage the icy rocks that he had climbed on the way up, but he had no thought of waiting for his partner so that they could rope up – an incessant force drove him downwards.

To avoid the rocks he veered left onto the snowy East Face. Almost at once he slipped, sat down with a bump – and found himself sliding down the slope at a rapidly increasing speed. Desperately he used his ice axe as a brake, and brought the slide to a halt:

> It was a tricky situation and the most dangerous moment of the whole ascent. Though I hadn't slid far, the whole face was deep in snow and could easily avalanche off at any moment. There was nothing I could do except try to traverse across, to strike the ridge again. Once or twice I slipped again, the snow piling up into huge cushions at my feet, but luckily it didn't avalanche. It was very tiring and I was overjoyed when at last I saw the two tents of Camp V below me. I hoped Reinhold had ignored my arrows in the snow! I couldn't see him anywhere.[22]

Feeling that nothing could stop him now, he continued his mad rush down. When he came to the final gully – the one leading down to the col – he literally jumped into it. Inevitably, the snow gave way and in an instant he was tumbling and sliding down the gully in a flurry of snow. Non-stop it carried him almost down to the col. When he picked himself up he found he had lost his ice axe and snow goggles, and had a twisted ankle.

Eric Jones, from his vantage point on the col, had seen Habeler's incredible slide and was sure he'd been killed. He went over towards the gully and was relieved and surprised to find the weary climber stumbling towards him. Habeler was weeping and mumbling to himself incoherently. Jones at once took charge and led him to the tents. The time was 2.30 p.m. It had taken Habeler exactly one hour to descend from the summit of Everest.

About half an hour later Messner came into camp, practically snowblind. Throughout the day he had been constantly removing his goggles in order to film with the 8-mm. camera he carried, and now he was paying for it. That night he was in great pain, unable to sleep, unable even to lie down. Habeler gave him three pain-killing tablets, but he moaned and sobbed throughout the night, huddled up. Even so, he refused to take oxygen to ease the pain. The only concession Habeler could get from him was that if things got worse in the next twenty-four hours he would reconsider the oxygen question!

That night a storm blew up, rocking the tents and adding to Habeler's worries. How would they get down next day? Messner was snowblind, Jones was frostbitten and he himself had a wrenched ankle. Habeler prayed to God for deliverance.

One thing was certain: they had to descend next day, storm or no storm. They could hardly have survived another night.

And so at 6 o'clock next morning the three men staggered out into the teeth of the gale and found their way, miserably and haltingly, down the fixed ropes of the Lhotse Face to Camp III. Here they rested and were shortly joined by Dr Oswald Ölz and Reinhard Karl, who were going up the mountain to make their own assault on the summit. The doctor treated Messner's eyes, and then, three hours later, the two men continued their descent to the relative comforts of Advanced Base Camp. The great adventure was over.

Reinhold Messner and Peter Habeler had fulfilled the dreams of Mallory, completed the work of Norton, and made what Tilman would undoubtedly have regarded as the first real ascent of the mountain. The half-century of dispute between the pro-oxygen faction and the anti-oxygen faction, which had seemed so irrevocably settled by Hunt's expedition in 1953, had suddenly and dramatically swung the other way. Messner and Habeler had shown that the mountain *could* be climbed without oxygen – and in mountaineering ethics *could* means *should*. Doubtless oxygen sets will still be used on Everest, particularly on the harder routes, but not for long, one suspects. Man has crossed another barrier.

When the Sherpas heard what had happened, some of them were frankly incredulous. They could not believe that a Westerner could go higher without oxygen than any Sherpa had ever been, and into the bargain climb Everest so quickly. Dark suspicions were aroused in their minds: why did the sahibs take the two oxygen cylinders to the South Col if they didn't intend to use them? Why did the sahibs send the Sherpas down from the col unless it was to ensure there were no witnesses? And how could the sahibs climb and descend the South East Ridge without oxygen in a shorter time than most people could do it *with* oxygen? It was this last that the Sherpas found hard to believe, and it even persuaded notable sirdars like Pertemba and the legendary Tenzing to sign a petition to the Ministry of Tourism demanding an inquiry.

Depositions were made by various Sherpas to the Minister which reveal a childish dislike of Reinhold Messner. Obviously, Messner had upset some of the Sherpas, for he alone is singled out for criticism, and the depositions have all the hallmarks of small boys trying to get their own back for some injustice, real or imaginary. Needless to say, the evidence supporting Messner's and Habeler's ascent is overwhelming; and perhaps the most ironic proof of all is that one of Messner's chief critics, the Sherpa Mingma, was himself to take part in the second oxygenless ascent only a few months later![23]

# 20

# New Horizons

When China finally emerged from the nightmare of the cultural revolution she threw off the shackles of isolationism and embraced ever-widening contacts with the west. Amongst those to benefit from this liberalisation were mountaineers who, for the first time in several decades, were allowed access to Chinese mountains. As Tibet was included in this remit the whole north side of Everest became once more available to foreign climbers. Apart from the Chinese themselves, few people had been there since before the war.

Time has brought change. Except for the challenging presence of the great mountain itself there are few similarities between the old expeditions and their successors. The long trek from Sikkim across the barren country Mallory called 'hateful' is no longer necessary, nor is there any hassling with *dzongpens* for mules, for both have been abolished. Now the bulk of an expedition comes on the new road from Kathmandu, handing over to Chinese trucks at the border. A visit to Lhasa, once forbidden, is now obligatory for at least some of the members in order to sort out details with the Chinese authorities.

Even if the climbers were to follow the old road into Tibet they would find much changed. The cultural revolution has destroyed most of the monasteries including the famous ones at Shekar Dzong and Rongbuk. Galen Rowell, the American climber-photographer, saw Rongbuk in 1983:

> This is a depressing place . . . as desolate a place as man could imagine. Next to our camp here is the Rongbuk Monastery without a single ceiling; just broken walls stretching a hundred yards up a hillside devoid of life, where hundreds of pilgrims and lamas once worshipped . . .
>
> The rape of Rongbuk was the culmination of a tour of destruction that had begun for us as soon as we left the restored showcase of Lhasa. Shekar, the "Shining Crystal Monastery" seen by Mallory on the 1921 expedition was in far worse condition. Not even a wall was intact.[1]

The old monastery at Rongbuk seems to have become a rubbish dump for expeditions.

Another difference from the early expeditions is the restriction which the Chinese place on Sherpa porters. A few HA porters might be allowed as members of the climbing team, plus cooks and so forth, but there can be no mass influx of porters such as used to take place in the old days (the actual number seems to vary at the whim of the authorities). Beyond base camp, transportation is usually by yak to advanced base up the East Rongbuk Glacier: a distance of 14 miles.

Perhaps as important as anything else is the change which has come over climbers since the days of General Bruce and Mallory. These newcomers to the Everest game look at mountains with fresh eyes, unimpeded by the dead hand of tradition and armed with superior techniques and technology. Though conscious of those who have gone before on these inhospitable slopes, the new climbers look at the North Face of Everest and see a multitude of interesting problems, where their predecessors only saw one. They *know* the mountain can be climbed by the North Ridge, because that's what the Chinese did back in 1960, so they examine this whole new northern world to see whether there are other ways, undiscovered and exciting.

The earliest attempts by the Chinese to introduce outsiders to the north side of Everest seemed dogged by ill fortune. In 1958 there was a Soviet-Chinese training meet which was intended to be followed by a joint expedition, but worsening political differences between the two nations brought an end to that and led to the Chinese making their own successful attempt in 1960. Then in 1978 there was another training expedition, this time with the Iranians, but that too was not followed up as Iran plunged into turmoil.

On 20 September 1979 the Chinese Mountaineering Association (CMA) announced that eight peaks were open to foreigners, including Mount Everest. Despite the high tariffs imposed by the Chinese there was a rush of applications, from which the Chinese selected a Japanese sponsored Sino-Japanese Expedition which consisted of a preliminary expedition to reconnoitre the mountain in the autumn of 1979 and a full scale expedition the following spring. This was precisely the sort of expedition the Chinese were looking for – large and expensive. Small expeditions were of little use to the Chinese who saw in mountaineering a way to earn foreign currency. The Japanese expedition was rumoured to be costing a million pounds.[2]

And so in the autumn of 1979 a 9-man Japanese team visited the north side of Everest, ready for a spring offensive. They explored the East Rongbuk Glacier, the route of the pre-war British expeditions, and the main Rongbuk Glacier, which formed a great bowl with the North Face and West Ridge and led to the Lho La. It was the first proper examination of the area by outsiders for over 40 years and though it was considered likely that the following year's expedition would tackle the Chinese route up the North Ridge, looking at the face itself in the light of modern technology, the Japanese could see many more possibilities than were available to the pre-war climbers.

Seen from the Rongbuk Glacier the North Face seems to have been sliced off at an angle and dusted with icing sugar. The angle is not all that great – perhaps 60 degrees in the lower part and steepening where the rocks protrude, though high up, under the NE Ridge, the Yellow Slabs are only 30 degrees.[3] In truth, it is a rather sombre picture, for there are none of the dramatic buttresses which feature so much on the South and East Faces, only two prominent gullies – the Great Couloir, down the middle of the face and the Hornbein Couloir, over on the right towards the West Ridge. This is the couloir which the Americans climbed in 1963 on the first ascent of the West Ridge, but from the Rongbuk Glacier it can be seen that the couloir has a long extension sweeping down the face to the glacier. In fact it became apparent that the Hornbein Couloir was logically a North Face route rather than a West Ridge Route. The Japanese climber K. Takami explored the foot of the route, his thoughts on the forthcoming expedition.[4]

Under the overall command of Hyoriko Watanabe, 39 Japanese climbers and 21 Chinese 'assistant climbers', with 13 press and TV staff set up camp on the Rongbuk Glacier on 5 May, 1980.[5] They were faced with precisely the same quandary that the Americans had in 1963, i.e. that of splitting the party into two groups, one to tackle the ridge route and the other to tackle the North Face.[6] However, the Japanese seem to have formed two distinct expeditions who henceforth had little cooperation with one another.[7]

The ridge party found conditions trying because of incessant high winds. Susuma Nakamura and Yasuo Kato did all the leading and on 3 May they left Camp VII at 8,250 m. on a bid for the summit. Nakamura was forced to give up but Kato pressed on alone to the top, thus making his second ascent of Everest – the first non-Sherpa to do so. He also became the first foreigner to climb Everest from the north and the first to climb it by two different routes. His first ascent had been by the South East Ridge in 1973 – in itself the first post-monsoon ascent of the mountain.

Everest seemed like Kato's mountain, but two years later, on the South Col route, after making the second winter ascent, Kato failed to return to base and was never seen again.

Meanwhile Miyashita's preparations for the North Face, begun at the same time, were going smoothly. They took the route reconnoitred by Takami the previous year – up the snow and ice slopes directly below the Hornbein Couloir, where there is a convenient gap in the lower band of rocks which guards the face. Fixed ropes were established up to 8,350 m., with the Chinese climbers helping to ferry loads up to Camp IV at 7,800 m.

In late April Takami contracted frostbite and another climber, Akira Ube, was killed by an avalanche on 2 May near the base of the Hornbein Couloir. Of the original climbing party of six in the end only two were able to attempt the summit, Tsuneo Shigehiro and Takashi Ozaki. On 10 May they climbed through the couloir and onto the West Ridge then, about four hours below the summit, their oxygen ran out. Undaunted, the two men struggled on to complete the first ascent of the North Face. They began their descent in the late afternoon and were forced to bivouac after about an hour, but this does not seem to have done them any harm and they were able to withdraw in safety to Base.

Whilst the Japanese were busy opening up the north side of the mountain another climber was in Beijing to see what openings he could extract from the Chinese authorities. Reinhold Messner who, with Peter Habeler, had made the first ascent of Everest without oxygen in 1978, had wanted permission to attempt the virgin peak of Kongur but finding that a British team had got there ahead of him, switched his attention to Everest. He wanted to climb the mountain alone.

Messner had already climbed five of the world's highest mountains, the 8,000 m. peaks, and was destined to become the first man to climb all fourteen. Since his ascent of Everest with Habeler he had climbed the fearsome K2, second highest mountain in the world, and perhaps more significantly had made a solo ascent of the Diamir Face of Nanga Parbat.

Nanga Parbat was in many ways the corner stone of Messner's Himalayan career. It had come to mean much to him since he had first climbed it in 1970 with his brother Gunther and Gunther had been killed by an avalanche in the descent. Also Nanga Parbat was known as a 'German' mountain because in the 1930s it had been a particular target of Austro-German expeditions and many great climbers had lost their lives there including Welzenbach, one of the founders of modern climbing. The mountain was etched deep into the Austro-German pschye, and it was inevitable that one of that race would make the first ascent, Hermann Buhl, in 1953. Messner was from the Tyrol, and though technically Italian, it is easy to see how Nanga Parbat would affect him.

There was another dimension too. Messner seems to imbue his climbing with a lyrical mysticism that some observers find quite baffling. It is as if his technical brilliance needs justification, just as the old climbers used scientific enquiry as an excuse to climb at all. Critics have savaged him as they have Bonington for commercialism and he has done nothing to mollify them; some of his disputes have been very public. Perhaps it is a gesture of defiance that he has bought himself a castle in the Tyrol; Siegfried come home at last.

There is something of all this in Messner's relationship with Nanga Parbat. After Gunther's death in 1970 Messner returned to the mountain in 1971, 73 and 77 and on the last two occasions tried unsuccessfully to solo the mountain.

In 1978, after his divorce of the previous year, he tried again:

> Only in 1978, after I'd learned that life can be borne alone and that man is an individual, after I had given up thinking in terms of pairs, only then did I have the courage to take this greatest leap forward in my climbing career. Alone, I climbed a new route on the Diamir Face, with no 'technical aids' apart from my crampons, axe, tent and sleeping bag, and I returned from summit to Base Camp by a different new route.[8]

It was an astonishing achievement. Two years later he was proposing to the Chinese that he do the same on Everest. He realised what a coup such a climb would be – and he knew that the fine Japanese climber Naomi Uemura was also after the same prize. The autumn slot for Everest was already taken by a French team and in any case Messner realised that the Chinese would not be happy to let a solo climber have a prime slot because there would be very little money in it. He therefore proposed that he should do the climb *during the monsoon* – a time not favoured by many, even though it was no longer dismissed out of hand as it had once been. The Chinese agreed – and promptly charged him $50,000 for the privilege.[9]

A number of climbers had already reached the summit of Everest climbing solo, including most recently Kato, who had climbed the North Ridge, but Messner's intention was to climb alone all the way, from the foot of the North Col to the summit and back. No established camps, no prepared caches, no support team on the mountain. Everything he needed he intended to carry on his back.

The Chinese insisted that Messner take with him to the foot of the mountain an interpreter, a liaison officer and a medical officer but he wriggled out of the last by insisting that the first aid certificate held by his girl friend Nena Holguin was good enough. Nena was to keep a vigil at the foot of the North Col.[10]

The little party approached the mountain at the end of June and set up Base Camp on the site used by one of the early British expeditions which Messner found by comparing the landscape with old photographs. For some days they explored up to the foot of the North Col and even tried to reach the Lho La, but the snow was soft and deep, making any sort of progress very hard work. Though he made one arduous and dangerous attempt on the North Col, it was obvious that conditions were not right for an attempt on the mountain. Disheartened, he didn't let his disappointment or the thought of losing $50,000 interfere with his mountain judgement for a moment. He withdrew, and spent two weeks investigating the environs of another mountain called Shisha Pangma.

When he returned after two weeks, conditions had improved dramatically. There was a weather window in the monsoon, the temperature had dropped and hardened up the powder snow into acceptable firmness. On 16 August he and Nena arrived at Advance Base below the North Col and the very next day, wearing trainers instead of boots, he jogged up the slopes of the Col to the crevasse which guards its lip. Here he left a rucksack containing the things he would need for his trip, then swiftly returned to his tent. He was intent in getting away to a good start next day!

> The rucksack weighed about 20 kilos and contained a small bivouac tent, a sleeping bag and a plastic mattress. His ice axe and crampons were made of titanium for lightness. There was also a stove, spare mitts and goggles. His food supplies were thin strips of beef, dried fruit, chocolate, sardines, tomato soup and Tibetan salt tea. His ice axe again had a screw fitting into which he could fix his camera to photograph himself while climbing.[11]

At 5 a.m. next morning, under a still dark sky, Messner set off on his great adventure. He climbed the slopes to his rucksack in just 90 minutes, shouldered his burden but didn't bother putting on his crampons over his plastic boots. Through the blue darkness he could see the rim of the crevasse. Then suddenly . . .

> I've fallen down, down, down. It felt like eternity in slow motion, rebounding back and forth off the walls of ice, although it was in reality only eight metres deep.
>
> And so I'm standing on a narrow platform. Is it thick or thin? I look up. I look down. It's all the same. It's black – everywhere. My headlamp's died. I see a twinkle from a lone star through a small hole somewhere up above.[12]

Messner had fallen into a crevasse. He found himself standing on a snow bridge which might collapse at any minute and for a bitter moment he thought that if ever he managed to escape he would run away from this hateful mountain; pack up and go back home. But even though he was entombed in the dark ice, he never lost control of his superb mountaincraft. Edging up a narrow ramp he was able to reach the surface, and this time successfully span the crevasse. He reached the North Col and headed up the ridge. The sun rose, tinting everything in a warm golden glow.

The sun softened the snow and made the going laborious, but he climbed almost 1,500 m. that day, until he came to a small platform where he pitched his tent and made himself a meal of cold dried beef and salt tea. Here he had a sense of not being alone; as though there was a companion whose presence was felt but not seen. It is an irritating phenomenon, fairly common to climbers under stress and recorded previously by Frank Smythe amongst others. Messner knew it well and called it the partner within himself. Still, he managed to sleep well that night.

Next morning he lightened his load and set off at 9 a.m. when the first sunlight touched the ridges of Everest. The going was again soft and he wasted two hours trying to find a satisfactory way of tackling the ridge. But he could see that whole North East Ridge was deep in snow and would be impossible. There remained one alternative, never done before, but looking feasible – and dangerous. To traverse across the North Face to the Great Couloir and climb that to the summit.

He set off conscious that he was on a potential avalanche slope. 'With a slow and cautious pace I move out across its wide dimension. It is definitely not steep yet still it leaves me with an air of uncertainty. Anything falling off from above will without doubt sweep me from my feet.'[13]

All day he picked his way delicately across the immense slope. The scale of Everest is such that this single traverse was 2 km. and when he camped on a snow mushroom that evening he was depressed by his seeming lack of progress. He had gained only 400 m. in height.

The little promontory stuck out from the face and he felt safe there from the avalanche menace. But it was at 8,200 m. and the altitude was beginning to tell. Eating and drinking were an effort and his invisible companion made the site feel cramped.

Next morning the clouds were gathering round the mountain and soon the snow began to fall. If he was to make the summit at all then he would have to do it quickly. Wearing his crampons he abandoned everything but his camera and ice axe. He climbed the snowy Great Couloir but at the Yellow Band he broke out of the couloir to the right, onto the rocks of the North Pillar, which were stripped of snow. Visibility was down to 50 m. and he had only the vaguest notion of direction.

He began to despair. He was taking only a few paces then resting on his axe, gasping for air. Suddenly he saw the metal tripod which the Chinese had placed on the summit five years earlier, and he crawled to it on hands and knees. The time was 3 p.m.[14]

> I was in continual agony; I have never in my whole life been so tired as on the summit of Everest that day. I just sat and sat there, oblivious to everything . . . I knew I was physically at the end of my tether.[15]

He left the summit at 4 p.m. and following his own footprints retreated down the couloir in three and a half hours. On reaching his tiny tent he climbed into his sleeping bag, too tired to eat or drink, wracked with exhaustion and unable to sleep. He just lay there through the night and as soon as it was light next day he forced his aching body to begin the hazardous traverse of the face. Everything but his camera and climbing gear was abandoned. Fortunately, the weather was beautiful.

It is doubtful whether he was really aware of his surroundings during the retreat; it was a mechanical thing; a trained athlete doing what he was supremely good at. He stumbled and slid down the North Col and it wasn't until he reached the East Rongbuk Glacier and the welcoming arms of Nena that the machine was switched off and the reaction came. His face was burnt, his lips cracked and his eyes full of tears. Quiet sobs broke from him and he seemed semi-delirious. He had pushed himself to the limit and had achieved a remarkable climb; perhaps the greatest single achievement ever made on a mountain at that time.

Each of Reinhold Messner's two ascents of Everest was a unique concept, daringly and brilliantly carried out by a master craftsman. In 1978 he and Habeler made the first ascent without oxygen, and two years later he made the first solo ascent. These and more recently his climbing of all the 8,000 m. peaks has made him a super-star in the climbing world; grudgingly admired by his peers yet the prey to jealous criticism. An old climbing companion of his, Oswald Ölz, who was on the 1978 expedition sums it up thus:

> Discriminating critics who reject Messner object to his sensationalism, shown by the remorseless display of photos of dead mountaineers, or by including artificially steepened climbing photos in some of his publications. Indeed, today's most successful mountaineer has no need for such tricks; the reality of the 8000ers and their ascent is drama enough. However, in his case self-display dominates over other values. Also there is little that is flattering in his views on rivals and former friends. Messner's abusive tirades directed against his former climbing partner Peter Habeler are embarrassing only for himself. They stem from the vulnerability of the hero, apparently so cool and superior, who is quite capable of feeling emotion which, however, tends to show itself only at moments of disappointment. One should therefore remember that men with the imagination and ability to open up new horizons are, more often than not, difficult and uncomfortable personalities.[16]

An American critic was less kind: 'Messner', he said, 'sees Everest as an eight thousand metre extension of himself.'

After Messner's daring climb there were no further successful attempts on the North Face or the North Col route for four years, though seven expeditions tried. Among the most dramatic failures was that of the American expedition in the spring of 1982 led by Lou Whittaker, whose twin brother Jim had been the first American to climb Everest back in 1963. Among the team members were Frank Wells and Richard Bass, two wealthy Americans who were trying to climb the highest peak in each continent, and the woman climber Marty Hoey.

They attempted the North Face by the Great Couloir, starting from a Base Camp on the Rongbuk Glacier. No oxygen sets were being used and Camp V was established at 7,620 m. on 8 May but then the weather worsened and slowed things down. On 15 May four members tried to establish Camp VI at just over 8,000 m. Larry Nielson and Dave Mahre were searching for a suitable site while Jim Wickwire and Marty Hoey were sitting on a rock outcrop in the middle of the couloir, belayed to an ice screw. As Wickwire started to climb again Hoey moved aside to let him pass when suddenly and inexplicably, her safety harness jerked open, she stumbled, and fell 1,800 m. down the face.

The expedition was not abandoned though the team were badly dispirited. A summit attempt was made on 18 May by Nielson, Simonson and Dunn in which Nielson managed to get above the Yellow Band at 8,400 m. before retreating, suffering from frostbite. Wickwire made a further attempt four days later but he too failed and the expedition was finally called off.

In the autumn of 1984 the Americans returned to the fray. The leader was again Lou Whittaker (now 55) and a nucleus of the former team to whom were added several new members including the experienced John Roskelley and Whittaker's son, Peter. Permission to climb their original route to the Great Couloir, direct from the Rongbuk Glacier, had already been granted to an Australian expedition, but the Chinese, perhaps sympathetic to the Americans' declared aim of dedicating the climb to the memory of Marty Hoey, agreed to let them approach the couloir from the North Col – in other words, repeat Messner's climb. The Australians had no objection to this, though it seemed possible the two groups might meet somewhere in the upper couloir.

Logistically the new arrangement was much better for the Americans. One of the problems of approaching Everest via the main Rongbuk Glacier is that it is not possible to get yaks very far up the glacier, so that there is a four-mile hike to the foot of the North Face. The yaks dump their loads at around 5,500 m., whereas on the East Rongbuk Glacier the yaks can carry almost to the foot of the North Col, nearly a thousand metres higher. This time, however, they intended to use oxygen for the ascent, though as compensation to omit the fixed rope on the upper slopes – previously they had fixed ropes to 8,000 m.

The post-monsoon snow conditions were not good at first and though the North Col was reached on 4 September, the slopes were deemed to be too avalanche prone for load carrying and it wasn't until 15 September that Camp IV was established on the col. Three days later Roskelley and Wickwire pushed on up the ridge and almost reached the place where Camp V was to be established but they were driven back by high winds and a sudden storm. Two days later the same pair, now backed up by Ershler, Dunn, Smolich and Peter Whittaker, established the camp at about 7,600 m. Here they discovered two tents left by a recent unsuccessful expedition, covered in snow but otherwise in good condition.[17] Next day another carry was made to the camp and then everyone retreated to Base Camp for a week.

This retreat was part of their tactical plan, based on Messner's, of making rapid raids on the upper mountain, then retreating to Base Camp for R & R. In this way they hoped to acclimatize and also avoid the deterioration brought about by long periods at high altitude.

Despite continuous boisterous cold winds whipping across the ridge from the west an attack was mounted on 1 October. The climbers divided into three teams: Lou Whittaker, Wilson and Mahre were to break the trail across the North Face and try to establish Camp VI in the Great Couloir, preferably as high as possible. Wickwire, Roskelley and Peter Whittaker were to follow as first summit team and Ershler, Dunn and Smolich as the second. But it didn't work out like that; Wilson was climbing with a cracked rib brought on by severe coughing (shades of the pre-war British expeditions!) and Lou Whittaker injured his right eye, so instead of breaking trail the three men were forced to retreat, leaving the first summit team in lonely occupation of Camp V.

Third October turned out to be a relatively calm day. The three men at Camp V suddenly saw something which gripped their attention: three tiny figures were making their way slowly but steadily up the Great Couloir. It was the Australians making their final push for the summit.

The winds rose again and drove the Americans down to Camp III. Now it was the turn of the second team. On the 8th, Ershler, Dunn and Smolich set out from Camp V and crossing the North Face attempted to set up a camp in the Couloir. Their plan was to use the tent abandoned by the Australians but they couldn't find it and consequently spent a cold bivouac in the open. They all suffered bitterly from the cold, especially Dunn and Smolich, so they withdraw to Camp III.

When another attempt to establish a camp in the couloir failed it was obvious some radical rethinking was necessary. The main difficulty was the incessant winds. Wickwire and Roskelley came up with the notion that if the traverse across the face was done *lower down* then the winds might not be so ferocious. To their great satisfaction this turned out to be the case and a new Camp V was established at the foot of the upper couloir.

A new summit team had been arranged: Wickwire, Ershler and Roskelley occupied Camp V on 17 October and next day climbed the couloir to 8,100 m. where they levelled out a small platform below a rock outcrop. The plan was for Wickwire and Ershler to make an attempt using the two bottles of oxygen cached previously near the site of their new camp and for Roskelley to climb without, as he preferred. Unfortunately only one oxygen bottle was found and this was bestowed on Wickwire since he had damaged a lung on K2 in 1978.

At 6 a.m. on the 19th they made their bid, but neither Roskelley nor Wickwire were going well and at the Yellow Band it was decided to return to Camp VI. At this stage Wickwire decided to retire and so the final attempt on

20 October was made by Phil Ershler and John Roskelley. They left at 6.15 a.m. and by 11 a.m. were above the Yellow Band, having been helped to a certain extent by an abseil rope left dangling by the Australians a few days earlier. Ershler had the remains of the oxygen, Roskelley climbed without.

At 2.10 p.m. Roskelley halted. His hands and feet were numb from cold and he shivered incessantly as he felt the onset of hypothermia. Reluctantly he decided to descend, but he persuaded Ershler that he should continue to the top, to give the expedition the success it deserved. As Roskelley struggled down, Ershler, the Mount Rainier guide with some 300 ascents of that peak to his credit, seemed to gain new impetus; he shot up the remaining 300 m. at an incredibly fast pace and reached the summit at 3.45 p.m. Shortly after 6 p.m. he was back in Camp VI and the next morning they all retired safely to the East Rongbuk Glacier and so home.

The Australians meanwhile, who were the first team from that country ever to attempt Everest, had established an Advanced Base Camp below the North Face in the late monsoon period and had pushed a route up the dangerous snow slopes below the Great Couloir, establishing three camps, the highest at 7,500 m. Despite fixed ropes for most of this distance, the slopes were steep and likely to avalanche and it wasn't until the end of September that, like the Americans, they decided the snow had consolidated enough to be safe.

It was a small expedition with great ambitions. There were just five Australian climbers and two HA Sherpas plus a film crew from Channel 9 TV, who were the major sponsors, and a reporter from *The Age* newspaper. All the climbers were experienced in Himalayan climbing; intelligent, tough, introspective and mostly graduates. They were mountain men, big mountain men, which is unusual because Australia doesn't have any big mountains, but in their own fashion they had inadvertently followed the pattern which had been set for years by their contemporaries in the Old Country – they had learned to rock climb on the small crags of home then gone out into the wide world to extend their knowledge.

The plan was simply to climb the North Face direct by the Great Couloir, and to do it in style without oxygen and without fuss.

On 28 September Lincoln Hall, Tim McCartney-Snape, Andy Henderson and Greg Mortimer climbed to Camp II (6,900 m.) and three days later moved up to Camp III (7,500 m.) From there, on a brilliant day of little wind, they moved up the Great Couloir.

> The climbing conditions were perfect. The surface of the snow had frozen hard so that our boots did not sink in and our crampons bit firmly into the slope. The only problem was that a fall would certainly be fatal as it was impossible to stop a slip on the ice. A hundred metres below Camp III the Great Couloir plunged over a huge ice cliff, the most prominent feature of

> the North Face, then continued in an unbroken sweep to the bottom of the mountain. For the sake of speed we climbed unroped, though each of us was very much aware how serious a fall would be . . .
>
> The walls of rock flanking the Couloir began to close in, bringing with them a feeling of hostility. It was no place for humans. There was no air, no water, no hope. I shook my head and fought away the pressure of those negative thoughts. It's just another mountain, I told myself. Just another climb.[18]

They established Camp IV at 8,150 m. on the edge of the couloir. Above them the broken rocks of the Yellow Band blocked the couloir exit, like a crumbling wall, guarding the summit. The expedition was not carrying supplementary oxygen and the four men had a bad night. In the morning (3 October) Lincoln Hall turned back, suffering from the cold, while the other three pushed on up the couloir.

It was difficult mixed climbing and the party were not best equipped for the task: they had no supplementary oxygen, McCartney-Snape was climbing in cross-country ski boots because his double climbing boots had been lost when an avalanche had destroyed one of the lower camps, and Henderson had a broken crampon. But they climbed the difficult Yellow Band and wandering across the summit slopes of the mountain finished up the West Ridge. Henderson, lagging behind the other two and badly frost bitten, gave up less than 50 m. from the summit; perhaps the cruellest failure ever recorded on Everest. That night it was 3 a.m. before the Australians got back to their top camp, triumphant but weary.

The Americans, perched on the North Ridge at Camp V, watched the Australians withdraw from the mountain next day:

> A sight that none of us will forget was the Australians' tortuously slow descent of the Great Couloir the entire next day, obviously at their physical limits.[19]

Australia is not a nation with any great tradition of mountaineering and yet the Everest Expedition of 1984 was a model of what an expedition should be. Not only that, their actual achievement was astonishing; one of the greatest climbs ever done on the mountain.

These four expeditions had seen the establishment of the four chief routes on Everest's North Face: the Japanese Route or Hornbein Coulour Direct, the Australian Route or Great Couloir Direct, Messner's Route and the Ershler variation. It seemed unlikely that it could offer anything more – yet the story was by no means over.

In the following year a Spanish Expedition succeeded in making an oxygenless ascent of the classic North Ridge route but the French pair of

Pierre and Annie Beghin failed trying to climb the face and Hesegawa was also unsuccessful trying to solo the face. In fact it wasn't until 1986 that there was any further success on the north side of Everest, though numerous expeditions came and went.

The post-monsoon period of 1986 must have turned the Rongbuk area into something akin to the old mining camps of Alaska. There seemed to be teams everywhere. As the monsoon died away a Chilean expedition retreated after one of their number died in an accident at the North Col – he stepped through a cornice and his fall set off a tremendous avalanche across the whole width of the Col. A British expedition was encamped for an attempt on the North East Ridge, an American expedition was determined to launch a hang glider from the West Ridge (they succeeded) and yet another American expedition was trying to put the first American woman on the summit and look for clues to the Mallory mystery, revived after Wang Hong Bao's reputed finds, as reported to Hasegawa in 1979. (See Appendix One.)

But of all the expeditions the most interesting was the Franco-Swiss expedition. Annie and Pierre Beghin were back together with Jean Afanassieff, Erhard Loretan, Nicole Niquille and Jean Troillet. They were a talented bunch of climbers but not a team in the accepted sense because everyone was to do their own thing – a team of all chiefs and no Indians. The two girls were to try and make the first women's oxygenless ascent of Everest, Loretan and Troillet were to attempt a repeat of the Japanese route up the Hornbein Couloir Direct, Pierre Beghin was to attempt a solo ascent of the same route and Jean Afanassieff was to film the various goings-on.

Nicole Niquille was 30 years old, born at Fribourg, and the first Swiss woman to become a professional guide. Though noted for her tenacity on this occasion she and her companion failed to acclimatise and got no further than the foot of the North Face. Beghin too had to give up yet again. Though he set out with Loretan and Troillet, by the time the Hornbein Couloir was reached he was totally spent – it must have been agonising watching the two others draw steadily away. And draw away they did.

Erhard Loretan was a 27-year-old climber from Gruyères in Switzerland. He had astonished the climbing world in the previous year by climbing the formidably difficult K2 in record time, and later that same year Dhaulagiri, another of the world's giants, also in record time. Everest was to be Loretan's ninth 8,000-m. peak.[20] Only three people had climbed more – Messner, the Polish climber Kukuczka and Loretan's compatriot Marcel Reudi (unfortunately Reudi was to die on Makalu a few weeks later).[21]

Troillet had been Loretan's companion on the rapid ascent of Dhaulagiri and now the two men, confident in each other, had decided to go for Everest in the purest possible way; no oxygen, no intermediate camps, no ropes even – a truly Alpine-style ascent.

On 28 August they skied across the Rongbuk glacier to the foot of the face accompanied by Beghin. At 11 p.m. that evening they started the ascent, climbing through the night, their head-torches casting a pale glow on the steep ice, their crampon points biting into the night-hardened snow. When daylight came they rested for a long time then set off again. Whilst Beghin returned, exhausted, Loretan and Troillet pressed on remorselessly, reaching the summit by the West Ridge exit at 2 p.m. on 30 August. They spent an hour admiring the view and then, turning to descend, they calmy slid down the mountain on their backsides! In 3½ hours they were back at the foot of the face – the quickest descent of the mountain ever achieved safely. The whole climb took 43½ hours.

Loretan and Troillet demonstrated supreme confidence and superb competence. They had luck with the weather, but everyone needs that and their astonishing achievement is one of the greatest mountain climbs of all time. Just think of it – the highest mountain in the world climbed in less than two days! It's enough to make one doubt the difficulty of the climb – could it possibly be difficult, given the circumstances? As if in answer to the unspoken question, Roger Marshall, an Anglo-Canadian on his third visit to the mountain, was killed the following year trying to repeat the climb.

* * *

Both the pre-war and post-war expeditions to the north side of Everest had always identified the North Ridge, rising from the North Col, as a natural way onto the great North East Ridge and so to the summit. So well developed was this route that nobody had considered tackling the whole North East Ridge from the Rapiu La. The first explorers had dismissed it out of hand as being too long and difficult. So long as the natural line by way of the North Col remained unclimbed, nobody was going to add to the difficulties.

But the Chinese ascent of the mountain in 1960 and again in 1975 eased the pressure in that respect and though western mountaineers seemed at first more concerned with repeating the Chinese climb, other parts of the mountain came under consideration, including the North East Ridge.

From the Rapiu La at 6,510 m. to the summit at 8,848 m. the distance is about 5 km. The great snow ridge sweeps up from the col to Pt 7,090 m. and then to a distinctive summit at Pt. 7,912 m., about a third of the way along. Beyond this there rises three black pinnacles, like decayed teeth, obviously the major obstacle before the junction with the North Ridge, known as the North East Shoulder, at 8,393 m. No climber had ever been on this part of the ridge, though beyond the Shoulder it became the well-known route of pre-war heartbreak, with the infamous First and Second Steps.

Perhaps because the top third was so well known, the ridge lacked a certain appeal and it aroused little enthusiasm amongst British climbers when Chris Bonington announced that it would be his objective for 1983.[22]

He chose a small but highly motivated team. Besides himself there was Pete Boardman, who had reached the summit on Bonington's successful South West Face expedition in 1975, Joe Tasker, a great friend of Boardman's with whom he had done the remarkable ascent of Changabang West Face in 1976 and Dick Renshaw with whom Tasker had done a daring two-man ascent of Dunagiri in 1975. In support at Base Camp was Dr. Charles Clarke and Adrian Gordon, both of whom had been in the 1975 expedition. Only the year before Bonington, Boardman, Tasker and Clarke had been members of the successful team which made the first ascent of Kongur in Western Xinjiang.

Even compared with other small teams – the Australians, for example – it was a remarkably integrated group, each member linked to the others by complex, long-standing bonds of experience. But it was very small, and the ridge was very big.

Not only big, but high – and no oxygen was to be carried on the expedition. The Pinnacles were over 8,000 m. and would be time-consuming to cross. As the hours rolled by the spectre of physical deterioration would loom ever greater, so a slow Alpine-style ascent of the entire ridge was unlikely to be successful. Bonington's plan was to push a series of light camps up the ridge to a point before the Pinnacles, then make a lightweight summit dash:

> It had seemed a sound strategy back in Britain but, faced with the colossal scale of the ridge, the effects of altitude and the debilitating wind and cold, we were all beginning to have our doubts. At night, even on the glacier, it was down to −20°C, and during the day the temperature never crept above freezing. Only the day before, Pete had commented that we could have done with another three or four climbers to share the burden of making the route and ferrying loads.[23]

The expedition was pre-monsoon and the usual cold winds were blowing over Everest, but in 17 days they managed to establish three snow-cave camps at 6,850 m., 7,256 m. and 7,850 m. up the ridge. The last had taken 14 hours to construct because the snow was ice and the ice was rock and it had been backbreaking work. But the morning of May 4 found the four climbers in the top camp ready to attack the Pinnacles. They climbed the first Pinnacle that day and retreated to their top camp for the night. Bonington felt desperately tired and next day he and Boardman ferried supplies up the ridge towards the Pinnacles whilst Tasker and Renshaw pushed out the route. But not far: the ridge was corniced and the snow soft, seemingly bottomless. At 8,000 m. it was exhausting work and they managed only a couple of rope-lengths before dropping back, Renshaw experiencing a strange sudden numbness down one side of his body, which wore off through the night but left everyone feeling disquiet. They decided to return to Base. 'We were making so little progress for so much effort, it seemed much better to get back down for a rest, and then go for the summit Alpine style, without any more of this exhausting to and fro.'[24]

At Base Camp Charlie Clarke confirmed that Renshaw had had a mild stroke and should not try to go back up the hill. Tasker too, was suffering. In his diary, Charlie Clarke wrote:

> And Joe, poor Joe. What on earth is going on? Dull, central abdominal pain, tarry black stool which can only mean blood. The easiest conclusion is an ulcer, but he has a very bloody throat with a hard black crust right across the pharynx. I suppose this could have seeped down and caused the problem. We'll have to wait to see the outcome but clearly he cannot go anywhere with a bleeding bowel. I've told him he mustn't go unless he's really better.
>
> And so we bathe our wounds and hope for a reasonable enough recovery to get three up high and I suppose two on the summit. One would do. Trying to look at it all objectively, I do not think we have a hope in hell. The days required to kill the Pinnacles, added to the summit ridge, cannot be less than six and this is simply too long without oxygen. I think:
>
> Pete could do it.
>
> Joe probably could, but is ropey.
>
> Chris has said he doesn't think he can and I'm sure he's right.
>
> Dick can't because of illness.
>
> Adrian has had severe chest pains.
>
> Me? Well, as usual, I'm apprehensive about being drawn into something much too big for me and really a bit apprehensive about the North Col, particularly as the weather is getting warmer. Still, I'll be pleased to have to go up there and back.
>
> This leaves two alternatives, either go for it, as Pete would like – or abandon it and go for the Col route as a threesome. The first seems the purer – for two to climb as far as they can on the Ridge – and I expect that is what will happen on the day.[25]

The expedition seemed to be falling apart through illness and acclimatisation problems but a new game plan was put together in which Dick Renshaw would return home, accompanied for the first stage by Charlie Clarke; Tasker and Boardman would make a spirited Alpine-style attack on the Pinnacles and Bonington and Gordon would climb to the North Col, there to await the return of the attack party. There was also the chance that the climb might be broken at the North Col, for rest and recuperation, in which case Bonington thought he might join them for the summit assault since he had never personally reached the summit of Everest despite his long and distinguished career.

The summit pair were admirably matched in a complementary way. Of similar height and stocky build, they were very different in character. Boardman, who was known affectionately as Peter Pan, because he seemed eternally young, much younger than his 32 years, had an amiable grin and a very laid-back attitude. Joe, on the other hand, was brought up by the Jesuits to be a priest and though he opted out before ordination, he still had about him the Jesuit's secretive air. He could be brusque, and had a tendency to be defensive against strangers. Between them however they had a line of banter that seemed inexhaustible. Both were superb mountaineers and moreover, excellent writers whose books won high praise.[26] The plan was for the two climbers to go straight up to the Second Snow Cave in order to save at least some time at high altitude, and from there to the Third Cave on the following day, from where they could spring their attack. The cave was already stocked from their previous efforts.

They set out from Advance Base on May 15 and reported by radio that they had reached the Cave in good time and were climbing well. Next evening they reported they had reached the top snow cave and would be attempting the Pinnacles on the morrow.

Meanwhile, Bonington and Adrian Gordon were having an unhappy time on the slopes of the North Col, which proved much steeper than Bonington thought and more complex too. For Gordon, who had limited climbing experience, it was an unnerving experience despite his partial recovery from his illness:

> Despite my renewed vigour and enthusiasm I'm not without fear (he wrote in his diary) for the North Col has claimed a fair number of casualties in the last sixty years. The first time I set eyes on it, I thought, 'I'm bloody glad I'm not going up there'. But here I am.[27]

On the 17th Boardman and Tasker could be seen tackling the ridge between the First and Second Pinnacle. They were going slowly and at 9 o'clock, twenty minutes before dark, the leader had reached the foot of the Second Pinnacle and his companion was moving to join him. They had been on the go for 14 hours and were obviously in for an uncomfortable bivouac. Throughout the day there had been no word from them on the radio, though Bonington called them regularly every half hour. That night, the anxious watchers at Advanced Base saw no lights twinkle on the dark, high ridge and next morning there was no sign of the climbers. Boardman and Tasker were never seen again.

What happened to Boardman and Tasker will probably remain a mystery. We now know that the ridge from the First Pinnacle onwards is knife-edged, with cornices on either side and awkward snow mushrooms to negotiate. Climbing into the night it seems likely that the two men could find nowhere to bivouac and eventually met with an accident through sheer exhaustion. But why were their lights not seen? In 1984 the American climber, Donald Goodman, attempting to climb the mountain by the normal North Col route reached a height of 8,290 m. from where he clearly saw objects on the North East Ridge which could only be relics of the Boardman-Tasker climb. Unfortunately Goodman was too far away to identify anything properly. The following year, during another attempt at the North East Ridge, the British climber Rick Allen found Tasker's movie camera at about 8,200 m. The uncanny parallels with Mallory and Irvine hardly need emphasising.

There were no more expeditions to the North East Ridge until 1985, when a large expedition led by Mal Duff was beaten back by high winds as they reached the Pinnacles.

1986 saw another large expedition, led by 'Brummie' Stokes, who had climbed Everest in 1976 (see Chapter 19), arrive on the scene but this time post-monsoon. They found the 30-degree slopes to the Rapiu La in avalanche condition and turned instead to the 450-m-high buttress which rises from the glacier to Pt 7,090 on the ridge.

Exploration of the buttress was done by Mo Anthoine, Joe Brown, Paddy Freaney and Bill Barker:

> At this point they were well ahead of the main supply line and through a 'logistical mix-up' only Barker had managed to acquire ice-axe and crampons. Food had also run short at that early stage, so the first exploration of what became known as 'Bill's Buttress' was led entirely by Barker with his fellow-climbers supporting him, equipped with umbrellas and a couple of dessert spoons. They were sustained by a large carton of fruit drops.[28]

This actually cut out much of the lower ridge and put the team a week ahead of schedule, but all to no purpose. The dreadful post-monsoon weather came hammering in with high winds and fresh snow. Winter seemed to be approaching with unwarranted swiftness.

> Time after time the climbers were forced off the ridge, frustrated because they had now come to close quarters with it and knew that it was not difficult technically. Only the appalling weather was holding them back from the most significant unclimbed route on the world's highest mountain.[23]

Harry Taylor and Trevor Pilling reached the foot of the Pinnacles on 15 October. They too thought the way ahead seemed without technical difficulty, but the weather turned bad again with the arrival of high winds and swirling snow. Far from continuing, the two men had a struggle to retreat in safety, sometimes crawling on all fours against the howling gale.

Doug Scott's post-monsoon expedition in the following year got no further than part way up the First Pinnacle, where he was defeated again by the high winds and intense cold. 'The storm that put paid to our attempts and those of all the other expeditions last autumn was said to be the biggest to have hit this part of the Himalaya in living memory', Scott recalled later.[30]

Scott also called for a return to basics: for small expeditions to meet the challenge without oxygen and all the paraphernalia of the siege-type approach, but during the monsoon period of 1988, Brummie Stokes returned to the fray with a large team which included many of those who had been with him in 1986. Climbers dubbed it 'The Golden Oldies Expedition' because it not only included the legendary Joe Brown, now 57, but quite a few climbers who were on the wrong side of forty. There were 16–20 members (doctors and media personnel changed) and ten Sherpas, including two cooks, to carry loads up the mountain. Unfortunately, Stokes suffered three strokes – probably cerebral oedema – and had to return home, at which point the leadership was taken over by Paul Moores.[31]

There was some difficulty in getting all the team and gear to Base Camp but once this had been accomplished and the Advance Base set up by Paul Moores and Pete Long, work began on the now familiar task of establishing the three ridge camps. They used Bill's Buttress again and despite unsettled weather established a rota system of working in fours; so that any group spent a week on the mountain with the Sherpas, then went down for five days R & R at Base Camp. At any given period there would be two groups on the hill, one returning to Base and another resting at Base. But a storm put an end to this activity and it wasn't until the end of the month that work could start again.

First of all they had to re-establish the line of communication up the ridge, most of which had been obliterated by the storm Camp 2, for example, a box tent designed by Mo Anthoine, was buried under five feet of snow. It was Mo Anthoine who described the scale of Everest and the Pinnacles to Al Alvarez:

> You see these huge expanses of rock and ice and you think, that one small flank is bigger than any of the mountains I've ever been on . . .On the North-East Ridge route, everyone talks about the pinnacles: once you're up them, you've cracked it, they say. Not true. You're still seventeen hundred vertical feet and three-quarters of a mile in distance from the summit, and that's a long, long way when you're above twenty-eight thousand. I mean, there are only a couple of other places in the world that high. So it's by no means over when you've done the pinnacles. You've still got a full day to go.[32]

By the first week of August Harry Taylor and New Zealander Russell Brice were established in Camp 3. They climbed the First Pinnacle, laying fixed rope, then retreated for the night to Camp 3. Brice, who had led the last part and had glimpsed the other Pinnacles ahead, commented, 'They're a piece of weasel piss'.[33]

It is curious how the previous Stokes' expedition and now this one, thought the Pinnacles would be easy. Next day, when Brice and Taylor came to tackle them in earnest, Brice found how wrong he had been. Intent on travelling light for maximum speed, the two men had no sleeping bags or tent, just one small oxygen bottle, a length of polyprop rope[34], an axe each and a deadman. Even this, with camera and radio added came to 30 g.

> By 9 a.m. we were at our high point: Russell led off and I filmed him. It was a testament to the route that the video never saw the light of day again until the following day on the North Ridge. The Ridge was truly knife-edged with cornices blown to either side and difficult mushrooms to negotiate. Progress was decidedly slow but momentum was maintained by methodically knocking off the top 18 inches of loose snow and virtually climbing heel to toe. It was a sobering experience with gullies sweeping down to our right and the steep flutings of the Kangshung Face immediately to our left. After four hours of tightrope walking, a 55° ramp led off right to the second Pinnacle. Conditions underfoot were now appalling with almost bottomless snow on the ramp which left us both gasping like old men.[35]

The ramp led them behind the Second Pinnacle, which they discovered was not actually on the ridge itself, but set forward some 30 m. But the climbing remained delicately difficult and it was two hours more before they were able to sit down without having to straddle the ridge. After a brew they continued towards the Third Pinnacle, until darkness forced them to halt and scrape out a place to bivouac. It started to snow. The regulator on Taylor's oxygen set was broken so they tried to share one between them to help them sleep.

They had intended to start at midnight and go for the summit of Everest in one long push, but that night it snowed heavily so that it would have been impossible to see anything. The snowflakes swirling in the light from their head torches would have been mesmerising and disorientating. Even at 5 o'clock it was a virtual white-out on the ridge and after crossing the last Pinnacle they sat down for a brew. They could hardly see a thing but over the radio Joe Brown down at Base told them the weather was clearing and to sit tight until they could see the way down the North Ridge.

True to Brown's prediction at 11.30 a.m. the weather cleared. They could see the top, which seemed so close – but then, so it had to all those pre-war expeditions which had seen it from much the same place. There was no option but to go down; the weather was bad, the snow was bad, time had run out.

Told of their success, Bonington said it was 'A bold necky push and a fine piece of mountaineering. But they haven't climbed the North-East Ridge because you've got to get to the summit to do that.' Nevertheless, he cancelled the expedition he had planned for the next year.[36]

★ ★ ★

In broad terms Everest can be regarded as a three-sided pyramid. The southern side stretches from the South Col to the Lho La, the northern from the Lho La to the Rapiu La, and the eastern from the Rapiu La to the South Col. Two of these sides are in Tibet and so when the Chinese lifted the ban on access, not only the northern side became available, but the eastern side as well. Nobody had been there for fifty-nine years.

Most climbers were not too concerned, even those who knew there *was* an East Face. Mallory's report after his initial reconnaissance in 1921 was utterly damning. After describing the huge threatening walls of ice, which looked as if they might crash into the valley at any moment, and the immense buttresses of shattered steep rock which guarded the bottom, he concluded:

> . . . Other men, less wise, might attempt this way if they would, but, emphatically, it was not for us.[37]

Such photographs as there were (and there were not many good ones) tended to prove Mallory's judgement sound. And in any case, there were other fish to fry. It wasn't until the autumn of 1980 that the American mountaineer Andrew Harvard accompanied by the veteran Chinese climber Cheng Rong Chan and interpreter Tsao Hong Juen, set out from Lhasa to take a close look at the face.

It was a voyage of discovery. Three days in a jeep brought them to Kharta, the favourite place for R & R of the pre-war expeditions, who described it in almost lyrical terms after the rigours of Rongbuk, then a four day trek took them to the old camp site on the edge of the Kangshung Glacier.[38] The valley of the Kangshung is called the Kama Valley and around it is some of the most spectacular mountain scenery to be seen anywhere, including three of the world's five highest mountains; Everest, Lhotse and Makalu. Harvard had read of all this but:

> Nothing prepared me for that first unforgettable view. As I rounded a slope overlooking Tibet's great Kangshung Glacier, I suddenly faced an immense mass of ice and rock thrusting toward the vault of the sky. For many moments I stood motionless at the majesty of the scene – the virtually unknown East Face of Everest.[39]

The great white wall was 8 km. long, stretching from the Rapiu La in the east round in a cirque to Lhotse in the south. Most of the distance is taken up by Everest itself – the long North East Ridge, rising to the summit, then the much shorter South East Ridge, dropping to the South Col. Below these ridges great swags of ice and snow drape like a Georgian curtain for almost

2,500 m., cut off at the base by horrendous ice-plastered cliffs, themselves a thousand metres high.

Over to the east a subsidiary ridge of sharply majestic elegance swings out from the main mountain towards the glacier from Pt 7912 m. On almost any other mountain it would be a major ridge, but here it is a detail in a vast panorama. This is the forgotten East Ridge nicknamed by some as the Fantasy Ridge.

Left of the East Ridge is a series of ribs or buttresses the biggest of which lies almost directly beneath the summit of Everest with an incipient ridge line above it, relatively free from avalanche.

For two days Harvard studied the wall, watching in horror as the avalanches poured down. But he also saw the big buttress and its protective ridge above.

> By dusk on the second day I had completed my study. By then I knew: There was a route. It would be difficult and dangerous, but not impossible, not suicidal.[40]

In the following autumn an American team under the leadership of Richard Blum, with Lou Reichardt as climbing leader, attempted the face. The membership was as diverse as it was talented; along with well-known US climbers John Roskelley and George Lowe, there was the Austrian expert Kurt Diemberger and Sir Edmund Hillary.[41] They had an option on either the North Face or the East Face and chose the latter on the strength of Harvard's recce. By the end of August they were established at Base Camp (*c.*5,200 m.) from where Buttress Camp – Advanced Base – was established at the foot of the Main Buttress, at about 5,350 m. They decided that a direct frontal assault on the buttress was their best option and work began immediately. By September 4,700 m. of rope were laid and on the next day Kim Momb and George Lowe began climbing the first section of mushroomed ridges which intersperse the rock. They found snow conditions very bad, breaking through the crust and going thigh deep at every step. It took two hours to lead a single rope length and Momb was forced to lead one pitch crawling on all fours. 'We're screwed', he said when asked his opinion.

That night it snowed and so on the 6th, everyone returned to Base, where, contrariwise, the clouds lifted properly for the first time and gave them a clear view of the East Face. John Roskelley was for abandoning the project in favour of the North Face and as bad weather continued to keep the climbers off the face, dissension and argument became rife. On 10 September a meeting was called, which all team members were asked to attend, in order to clear the air and get everyone united behind a common goal.

> Sir Edmund Hillary made a very stirring speech, saying that it would be insignificant for the American team to reach the summit by the north, but

> that an attempt of any kind on the east face would be a triumph of the human spirit and a significant step forward in international mountaineering. His talk roused enthusiasm dampened by the late monsoon snow. The team voted on what to do. All but Roskelley and Eric Perlman voted to stay with the east face.[42]

Unfortunately, shortly after this Hillary developed cerebral oedema and had to be evacuated. Gary Bocarde and Lowe established Camp I, Snow Camp, at 5,800 m. from where the route soon reached a long gully-like feature down which hefty lumps of rock and ice would from time to time come bounding. The climbers felt as exposed as the pins in a game of bowls and for this reason the gully became known as the Bowling Alley. Its floor was ice at an angle of 50–65 degrees. To minimise the risk to the team George Lowe soloed it, trailing rope behind him, and the buttress became known as Lowe's Buttress. Above the gully Camp II was established, appropriately nicknamed Pinsetter Camp (6,100 m.).

Pinsetter Camp established them at the base of the big rock headwall which is such a feature of the buttress. The attack on this was done by Lowe, Reid and Perlman. The rock was extremely rotten and friable as first Lowe, then Perlman forced their way up difficult pitches in an increasingly violent snowstorm. When Reid took over the storm was so bad he suffered a fall of ten feet after climbing only thirty feet on the snow-covered rock and though he climbed back up, the decision was made to abandon it for the day and they retreated to Buttress Camp.

The pitch became known as Reid's Nemesis because when he returned to complete it, this time with Jones, he took three more falls before overcoming the difficulties. Above the Nemesis, Lowe took over again, climbing with Sue Giller on what proved to be the crux of the buttress. Giller declared that never before had she been so frightened on a climb as she followed Lowe up the crumbling headwall, with rocks breaking off and bouncing all round her, as her leader struggled with extremely difficult free and artificial climbing.[43]

Storms forced the team down for a deserved rest but 22 September was bright and clear. A huge avalanche rumbled off the mountain to the right of the buttress, engulfing a three-mile-wide cirque, its wind blast shaking Base Camp and swirling spindrift up to eight miles away. If anything was needed to emphasize the scale of this mountain face, the avalanche provided it. Even the buttress they were climbing was virtually a mountain wall within a mountain wall, such was the scale.

Roskelley who had taken no part in the climbing, decided to leave. He returned home to Spokane to deliver a stinging criticism in the local press about American expeditions in general and the Blum expedition in particular:

> We end up picking teams because some guy's wife wants to go or some other guy's buddy wants to go. Then we toss in a few climbers. Frankly, I feel that risks my life.[44]

He criticised the Blum expedition as being poorly organised and composed of a mish-mash of climbers and trekkers, despite being the best financed ever to leave the United States.

> My complaint was that the people we were with – high altitude affects everyone differently – were too slow. We had 8,000 feet of very dangerous avalanche slope above us, terrible weather and I did not think the risk was justified.[45]

Momb and Lowe reached the ice above the rocks, but Momb was suffering from a stomach disorder and decided to leave the expedition with Roskelley. Bruce McCubbrey went too. With Jim Morrissey away with Ed Hillary and Andy Harvard nursing a neck injury, this left only eight climbers to push out the route. Nevertheless, Helmet Camp was established at about 6,500 m. before storms brought everyone back to Base.

Here an animated discussion took place. Bocarde and Perlman who had been beyond Helmet Camp maintained that conditions were too dangerous and declined to continue the climb. Lowe and Reid thought things were not that bad and advocated an assault, whilst the rest of team were less committed either way. It was all very reminiscent of the Dyhrenfurth expeditions of 1963 and 1971, though the problems were less marked and a major part of the route had been achieved already. Seven climbers returned to the fray.

Sue Giller and Lowe were the first to pass the high point again, but one look at the avalanche scars above Helmet Camp convinced Giller that it was too dangerous to continue. Bravely though, she volunteered to act as back-up as far as Helmet Camp in support of a summit attempt. But the expedition was worn out and breaking down; Jones retired to Base with a respiratory infection. On 5 October, Reichardt, the climbing leader, reached the high point:

> In two hours he led past the big crevasses which Bocarde predicted would take two weeks to cross. Nonetheless, he made the decision to call off the expedition. He based the decision on several factors. The first is that despite the directness of the route, we had a long way to go. We were still below 23,000 feet. We had only five climbers willing to go up higher, and Morrissey was not yet well acclimatized. Beyond this, only Lou had been high without oxygen before (on the summit of K2 in 1978). He felt that it was likely that Dan Reid, George Lowe, or I would have problems. Without oxygen or support, it would be difficult to deal with illness or injury above the buttress. The snow was still not well settled and slab-avalanche danger

existed. Finally, it was late in the season and the winter jet-stream wind storms were likely to arrive soon. In short, he did not feel the risk of injury was justified by the small chance of reaching the summit.[46]

In 1983 the Americans returned to the East Face. The climbing team was practically the same as before except that this time the leader was Morrissey. Speaking of the great buttress, the Lowe Buttress, which is a feature of the climb Morrisey said, 'In more than a quarter century of mountaineering, I have found no challenge to equal it for modern climbing techniques.'[47]

It took 28 days to climb the buttress aided by the ropes and pitons left in place at the first attempt. To help in hauling the gear up the dangerous route the Americans rigged two winches, separated by an airy ridge. The first, designed by team member John Boyle and powered by a 5-hp engine lifted loads of 80 lb a thousand feet up the buttress, whilst the second hoist, operated by a counterweight of snow packed in a canvas bag, lifted the loads another 700 ft. Half a ton of gear was lifted in this way and the hoists saved a prodigious amount of man power.[48]

Pinsetter Camp was established on 25 September and then the route pushed out via the confusingly named Camps 1, 2 and 3 above Helmet Camp in the avalanche-prone upper snows, at 7,160 m., 7,590 m. and 7,865 m. respectively. On 8 October – five and a half weeks after the start of the climb – Carlos Buhler, Kim Momb and Louis Reichardt came out onto the South Summit of Everest and followed the South East Ridge to the top, passing a Japanese party who had just climbed it, on the way. Despite the fact that the climbers used oxygen apparatus for the final thousand-metre dash to the summit it was an exhausting and frightening final day, for as Reichardt struggled up to the ridge, a hapless Sherpa, Pasang Temba, came cartwheeling past him, slipping, sliding, rolling and accelerating out of control to his death thousands of metres below.[49]

Next day, 9 October, three more Americans – George Lowe, Dan Reid, and Jay Cassell – also reached the top. For Lowe it must have been particularly satisfying, for if the East Face of Everest belonged to any one person then he was that person. Right from the start it was Lowe's aggressive climbing and positive attitude which ensured success. But the teams as a whole, both in 1981 and '83, deserve great praise, because the route they chose on a vast and virgin face was the God-given natural line. They fought it despite its inherent dangers and technical difficulties, and they succeeded.

Ironically in view of all that had happened, the Underhill Award for outstanding accomplishments by an American climber in 1983 went to – John Roskelley![50]

In the spring of 1988 a much smaller American expedition came to the East Face of Everest. The climbing team consisted of the leader Bob Anderson, who had once been within 250 m. of the summit of Everest, Ed Webster, Paul

Teare and Stephen Venables. Venables was a 34-year-old British climber, with a good expeditionary record, who had been recommended to Anderson by Lord Hunt.[51] In support was an American photographer and woman doctor, plus two Nepalese cooks.

There were no porters and so no supplementary oxygen, because such a small team could never have ferried it up the mountain. Instead it was to be a genuine lightweight attempt. Such an attempt held great dangers – no back-up in case of emergency, and the need to make a rapid ascent before high altitude deterioration set in. They would have to 'flash it', to use Doug Scott's graphic description of what was necessary. Venables was aware of the dangers:

> To make a serious attempt on what we were trying to do, sooner or later you were going to have to put your head on the block . . . When I went on the Everest trip I was more conscious than ever before that I might not come back.[52]

The party had no intention of trying to repeat the 1983 route. Instead they chose a line over to the left, below the South Col. Though this too was guarded by a big buttress, it was not quite as big as the original one and they estimated that technical climbing would end at about 6,500 m., leaving 2,350 m. of easier angled snow climbing to the summit; 1,500 m. to the South Col, then 850 m. by the South East Ridge – the ordinary route – to the top.

The fixing of the buttress with rope went extraordinarily well. Starting on 3 April, and fixing rope as they went they climbed steadily up the steep buttress until on 8 April they were able to establish Camp 1 at its top. All that remained, it seemed, was a steady plod to the summit of Everest: 'But one thing Everest seems to do better than any mountain,' wrote Anderson later, 'is to get harder just when you expect it to get easier.'[53]

Instead of an easy move on to the snow they discovered to their horror that a wide crevasse, like a crystalline canyon, separated their buttress from the parent mountainside. The only way across was to rig up a Tyrolean Traverse – a sort of high wire act across the abyss. Webster and Anderson did this, and it took them three days of dangerous work. No sooner had they finished than the weather broke and the climbers retreated to Advanced Base.

During a lull in the series of storms the four climbers were able to ascend the fixed ropes and establish Camp 2 at 7,500 m., but it wasn't until 8 May that the weather finally cleared and they were able to set out on their summit attempt. The plan, working on the 'flash it' principle, was to reach the South Col by midday on the tenth and from there go for the top, then back and down.

They made Camp 1 easily enough that day but next morning it was snowing, obliterating their previous tracks, and making the going very laborious. It took fourteen hours to reach Camp 2, where they put the tents up then crawled in wearily, Webster and Venables in one tent, Teare and Anderson in the other. Their intended early start next day dissolved in tiredness and when they got away they found that the great snowy bowl they were climbing acted like a reflector for the sun's rays. They stripped off their high altitude clothing and added it to their sacks, which now weighed upwards of 40 lb each. In the afternoon it snowed again and as they breasted the final slopes to the South Col they were hit by a fierce wind that made putting up the tents a struggle. It was another twelve-hour day. The South Col, said Venables, was a very nasty place.

> Their original schedule called for them to head for the summit that night. But the wind made it almost impossible to stand upright and they were, in any case, far too tired. As they huddled in their tents that night all four suffered frightening bouts of breathlessness, aggravated for Venables by attacks of claustrophobia which made him want to leap out of his sleeping bag and rip open the tent door.[54]

Next morning the wind was still blowing hard, ruling out any attempt at the summit. Paul Teare was not well; he felt dizzy, 'his head rattling with traces of cerebral oedema',[55] and so as quickly as possible he set off back to Base Camp, since the only cure for oedema is to lose height. The other three decided to risk another day at altitude; though the wind slapped the tent fabric incessantly and the temperature dropped to minus forty.

But that evening, like a signal from the Gods, the wind died away. The three climbers decided to start for the summit, climbing through the night. And because mobility was essential and speed their ally, they travelled without rucksack or emergency bivouac gear. Venables broke the trail, then came Webster and finally Anderson. They were not roped; each man made his own laborious progress.

Through the darkness they trudged. At first Venables found he could take twenty paces before needing a rest but as the night wore on this became progressively less and by the morning he was resting after every step. Finally he ground to a halt and sank down to rest. The height was 8,600 m. and the time 11 a.m. He fell asleep for an hour and when he awoke realised he was on the slopes of the South Summit. Webster was just reaching him and they exchanged some words. Webster said his brain was hurting and he didn't want to break the trail and Venables called him a bloody nuisance, but it was nothing more than irritability brought on by tiredness and altitude. Soon after this Webster gave up and a little later so did Anderson. Both spent the night in a tent left on the ridge by a Japanese party.

Meanwhile Venables struggled on. He reached the South Summit at 1.30 p.m. – well behind schedule – and then the Hillary Step which he was glad to find in good condition. It was also equipped with a fixed rope left behind by a Japanese party and for which Venables had had the foresight to take up a prusik loop.[56]

He reached the summit at 3.40 p.m. where he left some dried flowers as a momento, given him by Tensing Norbu, son of Sherpa Tenzing. The summit was littered with Japanese oxygen bottles. After ten minutes he started his descent:

> And then of course, my plans started to fall to pieces. I had not made enough allowance for the blinding wind and snow. I suddenly found myself dangerously exhausted and terrified by oxygen deficit as I abseiled too fast down the Hillary Step. But I managed to control the panicky hyperventilation and carry on down, eventually groping my way through the stormy twilight, back up to the South Summit and over to the correct descent route.[57]

He had reached the top of the South Summit on all fours, verging on a state of collapse but he managed to force himself on. He became convinced that he was no longer alone; a common phenomenon amongst climbers who are near exhaustion or in a high state of tension. In Venables' case an old man seemed to guide and accompany him, but others appeared from time to time, including the old Everest pioneer, Eric Shipton.

In this delirious state Venables staggered on. On one occasion he slipped and found himself sliding towards the Kangshung Face:

> I stopped in a panic and was suddenly desperate to have a pee. The old man said, 'Well, pee in your pants then, it'll keep you warm'. And so I did.[58]

As daylight faded Venables was still only half way back to the South Col. He knew he would have to bivouac for the night on the open ridge. He had no tent, no stove, no rucksack, no shovel with which to dig a life-saving snow hole, only his ice axe with which to scrape an inadequate shelter. But he was encouraged by the knowledge that others had done likewise and survived – and he was fortunate in that the night was calm and the temperature, minus 20 to 25 degrees, bearable.

At dawn he resumed his descent. In a short while he caught up with Webster and Anderson and the three men roped up in symbolic unity, descending the couloir to the South Col and the tents, which they reached mid-afternoon.

At the Col they discovered that each had been frostbitten. Anderson and Venables had frostbitten toes, Webster frostbitten fingers.

The most immediate danger stemmed from the fact they had now been at 26,000 ft or above for 72 hours. But one of the consequences of altitude is to induce an illusion of well-being and that night, says Venables, they succumbed to 'a false sense of security', accentuated by the euphoria of having reached the summit. Another consequence is an overwhelming lethargy that makes the slightest task appear a monumental ordeal. 'It took an enormous mental effort just to lean on one elbow to light the stove,' Venables says. 'The rot had really set in.'[59]

Just how dangerous the situation had become is graphically told by Anderson:

> Complete incompetence reigned and a belief we could slide down the buttress in a day was filed in our brains under 'major excuses not to move'. By this time the stove had well and truly packed up, only hissing intermittently. Ed stumbled over to leap off the South Col first. I staggered behind, and Stephen wandered over after me. Ed was a good 500 feet down when I reached the cornice. The slope below looked glissadable – anything to get down quickly with less effort. So I leapt off, glissaded 50 feet (admiring my control), hit rocks, flipped over them and stumbled in the slope below, which then avalanched. As I cartwheeled down the slope, taking breaths every time my head popped up, it really hit me that we were right out of control. Getting down was going to be a bit harder than expected.[60]

The retreat was inexorably turning into a rout. It was 3 p.m. before they left the Col and dark before they reached Camp 2, although they had originally intended to descend all the way to advance base. They were late in starting next day, too, but it didn't matter because the mist had come down and they couldn't see where to go. They crawled back to Camp 2.

All three were now in a bad way. As pale dawn rose on the ninth day of their epic climb, Webster put it clearly: 'We get up, get moving – or die.'[61]

Despite the mist they struggled down, spurred on by the will to live, ploughing through deep soft snow. Anderson fell behind, but late in the morning the other two found the fixed ropes at the top of the buttress. Down they went, thankful in the knowledge that providing their strength did not run out the ropes would see them safely off the accursed mountain. Down through the gathering twilight, down through the inky blackness of night until at 4 a.m. they staggered into camp and the welcoming arms of their companions who had feared the worst.

Meanwhile, Anderson endured another night in the snow, unable to find the fixed rope. He arrived back at the camp next afternoon. 'We should have stayed together,' said Venables later. 'He was very good natured about it. He didn't seem to mind.'

The expedition had achieved a true lightweight, oxygenless ascent of the highest mountain in the world by a new and difficult route. It is not perhaps a natural line – the 1983 expedition had chosen the supreme line on the East Face – but the ascent was a climbers' climb and the descent one of the great epics of endurance.

# 21

## 'The Highest Grade V in the World'

The opening of the Tibetan approaches to Everest in the last decade has done nothing to lessen the popular appeal of the Nepalese side. It simply meant that more people could be on the mountain at any given time, and of course, it opened tantalising prospects of traverses between the Nepalese and Tibetan ridges. In fact, the opening of the Tibetan side probably came at the right moment to relieve the pressure building up for access to the mountain and which could not be satisfied from Nepal. Goodness knows what the waiting list would be like if Tibet was not available. One could imagine putting in for an Everest 'slot', then being too old to go on it, or registering your offspring at birth for a possible future attempt! Even allowing for the Tibetan dimension, such is the pressure that the old seasons of pre-monsoon and post-monsoon are no longer as exclusive as they were. Climbs are now done in the monsoon and winter seasons too.

The original route by the South Col and the South East Ridge which brought success to Hunt's 1953 party, is still the most popular way up the mountain and the most certain of success – though teams still fail on it. In fact, when the Koreans climbed the South Col route in the winter of 1987/88 this was the first successful ascent of any route on the Nepalese side since October 1985. There had been ten failures in a row.[1]

We will return to the slings and arrows of the South East Ridge later but first let us turn our attention to the West Ridge; that four-mile-long barrier which separates the North and South West Faces, first climbed by the Americans in 1963. As time went by it became increasingly obvious that the famous Hornbein Couloir by which Hornbein and Unsoeld avoided the middle part of the ridge was so disjointed as to make the route one of questionable value; a line which served its purpose at the time but one of little aesthetic appeal. In 1963 it was a tremendous achievement, of course, though perhaps the real worth of Hornbein and Unsoeld's climb was the fact that they were the first to traverse the mountain (see Chapter 16).

It was obvious that the route had to be straightened out; the ridge climbed direct. It was also obvious that such a climb would be very difficult or the Americans would not have avoided it as they did.

The first ascent of the ridge 'direct' by Tone Skarja's Yugoslav team was mentioned briefly in Chapter 19, written as the first edition of this book was about to go to press but events since have confirmed just how difficult this ridge is; at the time of writing only three teams have been successful out of the 21 who have attempted it. The Yugoslav's climb was a remarkable achievement; one of the finest in the annals of Everest.

In the spring of 1978 a reconnaissance party of Yugoslavian mountaineers led by Tone Skarja, investigated the approach to the Lho La from the Khumbu Glacier, below the Ice Fall. This was the way the French had tried in 1974 when the leader, Devouassoux and five Sherpas were killed in an avalanche (see Chapter 19), but Skarja chose a line up the rock wall well to the left of any avalanche fall-line. The route was difficult, with several pitches of Grade IV and Grade V – a feature of the climbing which was to recur regularly all the way to the top and which led Skarja to christen the West Ridge, 'the highest Grade V in the world'.[2]

Knowing that the final 200 m. to the col would be specially difficult for laden porters, the Yugoslavs decided to use a winch in the same manner as the Americans in 1963. This would be used to establish Camp I on the Col or more accurately, a little to the left of the col, on the upslope to Khumbutse.

In February of the following year 25 climbers, again led by Skarja, left Yugoslavia with 18 tons of equipment and arrived at Base Camp on 31 March. Early arrivals had in fact begun fixing rope up to the col on the 29th and work continued at such a pace that by 6 April, fixed ropes had been laid between the foot of the Col at 5,350 m. and the top at 6,050 m., the 200 m. hand lift had been erected, 6 tons of gear hauled up and Camp I established in tents and snow caves with places for 40 people!

The camp was christened Alpina. From it the route led slightly downhill to the Col itself and then steeply up the slope from the Col to the West Shoulder. This involved two more camps – Camp II, 'Induplati' at 6,770 m. and Camp III, 'Rasica' just below the West Shoulder at 7,170 m. This climb to the West Shoulder from the Col was in itself quite a feat, for there is a tricky rock band to cross with some Grade IV/V climbing involved. Between Camps II and III the going was easier on 35-degree snow slopes and then the ridge levels out for a mile and a half. This is where the original American route joined the ridge in 1963 and at the end of the level section the Yugoslav team set up Camp IV, 'Krka', at 7,520 m. This was established on April 27.

From here the big divergence from the American route had to take place in order to achieve the 'direct'. The Americans had climbed diagonally to the left to reach the sombre gash of the Hornbein Couloir; the Yugoslavs were committed to going straight up the steep ridge, which now towered above them in grim-looking turrets of snow-streaked rock.

Between 3 and 7 May the climbers were pinned down by 90 mph winds which shrieked across the ridge, but the moment relative calm returned they went into the attack to establish Camp V, 'Energoinvest' at 8,120 m. It was from here that the attack on the summit was to be launched.[3]

On 10 May, the day after the camp was established, Viktor Groselj and Marjan Manfreda made the first summit bid. Route finding was difficult and the two men had problems with their oxygen set valves and frostbite. They got no higher than 8,300 m. but in this they managed to climb and equip with rope the first hard pitch (Grade V) before retreating; a pitch now known as the Manfreda Chimney. Two days later Dusan Podbevsek and Roman Robas made the second attempt, but they too lost their way and had to retreat.

Next day a very strong team comprising the Stremfelj brothers, Andrej and Marko, with Nejc Zaplotnik set off in strong winds and temperatures of minus 35 degrees Centigrade. After a while Marko had to retreat because of a faulty valve on his oxygen set, but the other two, climbing quickly at Grade II and III, reached the second crux – a pitch of V and two of IV – to reach the summit of Everest at 1.51 p.m. For their return they descended the Hornbein Couloir and reached Camp IV late in the evening.

The next party was delayed by heavy snowfall until the 15th. It comprised Stane Belak, Stipe Bozic and the Sherpa Ang Phu, who was making his second ascent of the mountain and at that time the only man to have climbed Everest by two different routes. Bozic filmed the ascent and this helped to make them slower than the first team. They didn't reach the top until 2.30 p.m. As a consequence they were forced to bivouac in the Hornbein Couloir at a height of more than 8,200 m.

Meanwhile, another party of climbers, Borut Bergant, Ivan Kotnik and Vanja Matijevec had spent the night in Camp V in readiness for yet another summit bid, but this they selflessly abandoned to help their comrades, of whom nothing had been heard for some time. They crossed over to the Hornbein Couloir just in time to meet the others emerging after their bivouac. They seemed in fine shape despite their ordeal but as they crossed a 35 degree snow slope, Ang Phu suddenly slipped and making no attempt to stop himself, slid 1,800 m. down the face to his death. His body was recovered next day.

In the light of this tragedy – and the fact that oxygen supplies were exhausted – the Yugoslavs withdrew from the mountain, abandoning Base Camp on 21 May.

This expedition was a model of organisation, application and ability. Though it was the first Yugoslav expedition to Everest, the climbers had considerable Himalayan experience and several of them such as Zaplotnik,

Groselj and the Stremfelj brothers, had climbed other 8,000 m. peaks. It was a large expedition, but extraordinarily smooth in operation – look at the dates given above for the establishment of camps and quick-fire repeats of summit attempts and you can see how this skilled team wasted no time at altitude. They understood full well altitude deterioration and applied the well tried formula of *get in, get up and get out* in the shortest possible time.

Nobody else climbed the West Ridge for the next five years, though there were some notable attempts (see Appendix 4, Summary of Expeditions). In particular there were two attempts to traverse the mountain; the first by a French team in 1983 and again by the Japanese in the winter of 83/84. The French, led by Yannick Seigneur and Patrick Barthe, intended to climb the West Ridge by the Hornbein Couloir and descend by the North East Ridge, starting from the Rongbuk Glacier and without any intermediate camps or supplementary oxygen. Though a height of 8,205 m. was reached in the Hornbein Couloir the attempt was abandoned.

The Japanese adopted a different plan. Two expeditions were mounted, one led by Kazuyuki Takahashi from Nepal by the South Col route and another by his wife, Michiko Imai Takahashi from Tibet taking the 1980 route to the Hornbein Couloir (see Chapter 20) and the final rocks of the West Ridge to the summit, where it was hoped the two teams would meet. It can only have been a fleeting hope; the chance of such close coordination in mid-winter is very much in the hands of the gods and on this occasion the gods decided against it. The South Col expedition met with success but Mrs Takahashi's team got no higher than 8,100 m. in the Couloir owing to bad weather, frostbite and mishaps. Ironically, Takashi Ozaki, who was in the successful South Col team (the third winter ascent of the mountain) had made the first ascent of the Hornbein direct route in 1980; the route on which his comrades were failing.

The French winter attempt of 1982/3, led by Michel Metzger, witnessed one of the most bizarre events in the history of Everest. Known as the Couzy Everest Expedition[9] its original purpose was to repeat the South West Face, but when they reached the Western Cwm they found it was being pounded by avalanches rolling off Nuptse and the West Shoulder so they changed the objective to the West Ridge.[10]

They all celebrated Christmas at Base Camp then set about establishing camps along the ridge. On 30 December three French climbers plus a Belgian and a Swiss were progressing from Camp 1 to Camp 2 at about 7,000 m. when the Belgian, Jean Bourgeois, a 45-year-old engineer from Dinant, began feeling the symptoms of altitude sickness and decided to return to Camp 1. Strong winds were howling across the ridge and it wasn't long before the rest of the party decided to retreat as well. They arrived back at Camp 1 in the late afternoon only to discover no sign of Bourgeois. Radio contact established that he had not turned up at Base Camp either. It looked as though the Belgian might have fallen down the steep face of the Lho La, but despite continuous searches for the next few days no trace was discovered. The expedition was abandoned and Base Camp evacuated on 7 January.

Then, to everyone's amazement, Bourgeois turned up fit and well in Kathmandu on 14 January with a remarkable tale.

He had begun his descent a little way above the Lho La. His head was splitting and he knew the only cure was rapid descent. 'After walking a few hundred feet' he said, 'I lost my balance and slipped down towards the Tibetan slope. It was my sheer luck. Had I landed on the southern slope, I would have been killed instantly.'[11] How long he slid or how far he couldn't guess, but he ended up on the Rongbuk Glacier and decided that his best course of action was to walk down the glacier to the monastery.

He failed to reach the monastery that day and spent the night shivering in a shelter he made in the rocks of the glacial debris. Next afternoon he reached the monastery but was disappointed to find it ruined and deserted, so he pushed on, bivouacking that night again, and on the following evening reaching the outskirts of a small village. But the guard-dogs were barking and as Tibetan guard-dogs have a fierce reputation, Bourgeois thought it wisest to await till morning to enter the village, so he spent his third night out.

As he entered the village next morning the women and children fled in terror, convinced he was a yeti. Eventually he managed to persuade the village headman that he was a mountaineer, and he was given food and tea. Continuing his journey he eventually reached Xigaze (Shigatse) on 4 January where the authorities detained him for several days whilst they made enquiries in Beijing, Lhasa and Kathmandu as to who this stranger might be who had walked in out of the blue.

On 11 January he was put in a jeep, taken to the Nepalese border, given 500 Nepalese rupees and sent on his way. He arrived in Kathmandu on the afternoon of the 14th after one of the strangest episodes ever recorded in the Himalaya.[12]

In the spring of 1984 the Bulgarians came to Everest intent on celebrating the 40th Anniversary of the country's revolution by a successful ascent of the world's highest mountain. As the South Col route had already been claimed by the Indians that year, the Bulgarians chose the West Ridge.[4]

The team had been carefully whittled down to 18 climbers plus some auxiliaries from an original one hundred who had been sent for training in the Caucasus and Pamirs. Their leader was Avron Avramov.

Base camp was established early in March and work begun on the climb to the Lho La on 10 March. The Bulgarians had received considerable advice from the successful Yugoslavs about the problems of the climb and they adopted the Yugoslavian idea of a winch to lift gear over the final steep part of the pass. Unfortunately the motor on the winch lasted only one day after which the winching had to be done manually.

At the Lho La they first became acquainted with the fierce winds which were to blow almost continuously throughout the expedition, usually at 60 mph or more. Movement was often restricted for days at a time and tents were constantly being blown away. At Camp IV two tents were uprooted within minutes of being pitched, whilst at Camp II three tents were blown away completely and the climbers had to frantically dig snow caves in which to survive.

Camp V was established at 8,120 m. on 19 April and next day, at 6 a.m., Christo Prodanov set off for the summit with Sherpa Chouang Ringde. Prodanov was an experienced climber who had soloed Lhotse. He was 41 years old, and he had elected to go for the top without oxygen. They moved very slowly.[5] At the Manfreda Chimney Prodanov dislodged an old oxygen cylinder which was lying there and this caught his companion full in the chest. Shortly after this the Sherpa gave up, 'affected by altitude'.[6]

> Prodanov battled on through the wind during the afternoon, and although he was making progress towards the summit, he must have realized that his chances of returning by way of the W ridge, in darkness and alone, were being reduced as time went on. He had no food or water, and was only carrying medicine. At 6 p.m. he reached the summit and took some film with the 8 mm. video camera. He left it on the summit, where it was found later by other team members. Prodanov began his descent in approaching darkness and increasingly violent winds. The other team members were obviously anxious for his well-being, and were in constant touch with him by radio. A four-man team set off up the ridge to meet him, one man suffered frost-bite in his fingers. The rescue team were unable to reach Prodanov in these severe conditions. The last radio contact with Prodanov was at 7.45 a.m. on 21 April. Prodanov said he was having difficulty pressing the button on the radio, and that he had lost feeling in his legs and feet.[7]

Prodanov was never seen again. The team withdrew from the mountain and the Bulgarian Government instructed the expedition to use oxygen for future attempts.[8]

Several days passed before the team returned to the attack. When they did they tried to establish a Camp VI at around 8,600 m., above the major difficulties, but they couldn't find enough level space with suitable anchorage for a tent and since the wind still howled across the ridge, the thought of the tent being blown away, together with its inhabitants, made Camp V seem a much more suitable starting point.

Starting at 4 a.m. on 8 May, Ivan Vultchev and Metodi Savov began a fresh assault on the West Ridge. At first they had been undecided whether to put off the attempt for a day or two because fresh snow had fallen, waist deep, but they decided to go ahead. In the dark they frequently lost their way, and wading through the snow was exhausting work. They had difficulty in identifying the real Manfreda Chimney from the two other look-alikes and above it they found the grey rock band more difficult than they imagined. The wind increased in velocity; the temperature dropped to minus 35 degrees.

Feeling more dead than alive, Vultchev and Savov staggered to the summit of Everest at 5.15 p.m. – an average ascent of 55 m. per hour under the most appalling conditions. As they crawled the last few feet they came across Prodanov's rucksack – a sad reminder of their lost comrade.

Their own situation was fairly desperate. Their oxygen had run out. They had no bivouac gear and their only food was a little chocolate, yet it was obvious that they would have to spend the night out in a bivouac. Exhausted by over thirteen hours of struggle they collapsed into a small crevasse just 20 m. below the summit. There they shivered the night away.

The two Bulgarians had already decided that even if they survived the night, they were unlikely to get back down the West Ridge in safety in the prevailing conditions. Nor did they know how the deep snow had affected the Hornbein Couloir, which the Yugoslavs had used as their route of descent. In the circumstances they thought their best chance of survival lay in the South East Ridge – the original route on the mountain, and one which the Indians were at the moment climbing. With luck, they would meet up with some of the Indian camps. Using their radios they informed their comrades of their decision, though unfortunately it was not possible to warn the Indians as the latter didn't have a network on the mountain.

As Vultchev and Savov were making their desperate ascent, two more climbers, Kiril Doskov and Nikolay Petkov, were moving up to take their place in Camp V. Next morning, at 3.30, these two set out to climb the ridge. Conditions were now much better; the snow had consolidated and they were able to follow their predecessors' footprints, but the climb had the urgency of a rescue mission; Savov was reported to be in a bad way after his night on the roof of the world.

Doskov and Petkov wasted no time. By 9.30 a.m. they were at the summit (120 m. per hour) and caught up with Vultchev and Savov as the latter were nearing the South Col. Poor Savov was having difficulty walking and the two newcomers helped him down, and gave him oxygen, while Vultchev hurried down to the South Col and the Indian camp, where, in the true spirit of the Raj, he was offered tea.[13]

The four Bulgarians had traversed the mountain. It was only the second time it had been achieved and indeed, they claimed that theirs was the first 'complete traverse', since they had climbed all the West Ridge from the Lho La, whereas the Americans had started from the West Shoulder. Technically, they could be right – but it seems a little ungenerous, especially as the Americans were pioneers in every sense; *first* on the ridge and *first* on the traverse. And that counts for a lot.

In 1986 the West Ridge was climbed again, this time by a pre-monsoon Canadian team starting from Rongbuk. Included in the team was a 29-year-old woman mountain guide from Alberta, called Sharon Wood, who two years previous had succeeded in climbing the difficult South Face of Aconcagua in the Andes. Dwayne Congdon and Sharon Wood reached the summit in May – Wood becoming the sixth woman to climb Everest and the first to climb the West Ridge. She was also the first woman to climb a new route – or at least a major variant – for the expedition had reached the ridge by the North Spur of the West Shoulder. This had been climbed previously by the Americans and the French in 1983, but the Canadians were the first to complete the climb to the summit of the mountain.

In the same year Steve McKinney, leading a large American expedition which failed to climb the ridge from the north, succeeded in hang gliding from the ridge to the glacier; a further step towards the 'Matterhorn Syndrome' mentioned in the Preface.

From the foregoing it can be seen that the West Ridge is attainable these days from either the Rongbuk Glacier or the Khumbu Glacier, but no such choice exists for routes on the southern side of the mountain. All these must perforce start in the Western Cwm, which means traversing the notorious Khumbu Icefall and just because the mountain is climbed so frequently these days it doesn't mean that the icefall gets any easier or safer. It still kills people. The Canadian expedition of 1982 was particularly hard hit – they lost three Sherpas and a cameraman, Blair Griffiths, in the icefall.

This was the way of the first ascent in 1953, via the South Col and South East Ridge, and the many subsequent ascents which earned it the nickname of 'the Yak Route'.[14] It was also the springboard for the many attempts on the South West Face in the early 70s and culminated in Bonington's successful expedition of 1975. The Americans in 1963 had also done the West Ridge from here, but in 1979 the Yugoslavian ascent of the entire ridge from the Lho La reduced the American route to one of historical importance only. As of that date there were only two viable routes from the Cwm – the South West Face and the South East Ridge. In the ten years since then two more important routes have been added: the South Pillar or Polish Route, and the Central Pillar, the Russian Route. But this is not the whole story, of course: Man's struggle with the mountain knows many refinements and, as I pointed out at the beginning of this book, Everest can bring out the best and worst in human nature.

In the autumn of 1978 a Franco-German expedition broke all previous records by putting fifteen people on top of Everest, including two Himalayan veterans, Pierre Mazeaud and Kurt Diemberger. At 49, Mazeaud was the oldest man to climb Everest at that date. Three men repeated the Messner-Habeler feat of going to the summit without oxygen: Wilhelm Klimek, and the Sherpas Mingma and Ang Dorje, and this comprehensive expedition also put the first European woman on the summit, a Polish housewife called Wanda Rutkiewitz.

Wanda Rutkiewitz was the third woman to climb Everest after the initial success of Junko Tabei and Phantog in 1975. In the following year another woman reached the top – Hannelore Schmatz of West Germany, who with her companion, the American climber Ray Genet, died of exposure on the way down. Six years later Chris Bonington came across her body, frozen in a sitting position, just above the South Col – presumably carried there by avalanche.[15] Her death was a sad end to what was otherwise a fine expedition – all seven members reached the summit and several Sherpas too. It was the smallest, fastest team to meet success and the leader, Hannelore's husband, Gerhard Schmatz, became the oldest summiteer – he was 50.

It may be appropriate at this juncture to consider the part women have played in the Everest story. At the time of writing, eight women – and possibly nine – have stood on the roof of the world. Apart from Phantog (North Ridge) and Sharon Wood (West Ridge) the others have climbed by the South Col route. Two women have died on the mountain – Hannelore Schmatz, just mentioned, and the American Marty Hoey who fell to her death whilst attempting the Great Couloir in 1982 (see Chapter 20).

After Hannelore Schmatz the next woman to climb Everest was the slightly built Bachendri Pal, who reached the summit during the Indian expedition of 1984. There were no fewer than seven women involved and the real purpose of the expedition was to put one of them on top. Indian women mountaineers have a fine record in the Himalaya and it was considered about time that one of them stood on the summit of Everest. Those selected were Dr Meena Agrawal (41), Chandraprabha Aitwal (42), Bachendri Pal (28), Rekha Sharma (24), Rita Gombu (27), Harshwanti Bisht (30), and Sharavati Prabhu (24) – all experienced climbers with excellent records, though ironically enough, Miss Pal had the least impressive record of all.

Several of these women might have succeeded in reaching the top had it not been for the misfortune which seemed to dog the expedition from the start. Indeed, even before the expedition reached Base Camp, a Sherpa called Ang Ringzin, who was part of a team sent on ahead, was killed by an ice avalanche near the Lho La and a kitchen boy, Jang Bir, was found dead by the path near Lobuje, presumably from altitude sickness.[16]

Ang Ringzin's death angered his colleagues, though it is not clear why, for normally Sherpas accept death with a fatalism derived from their Buddhist faith. Major Khullar, the expedition leader, wrote:

> I saw a party of Sherpas moving down carrying the deceased. I was certain I wouldn't be meeting a happy group considering what they had just gone through but I wasn't really expecting what followed. Was their mood foul? It was terrible . . . On coming to know that I was the leader they let loose their emotional selves bursting out with genuine and not so genuine grievances . . . For half an hour there was a kind of empty violence in the air . . .[17]

Apart from Ang Dorje, the Assistant Sirdar, and his men from Thame, there seemed to be constant friction between the team and the porters. In such conditions rumour abounds, even to the extent of causing a strike because word spread amongst the porters that the expedition was broke and couldn't pay them. Needless to say, this was quite untrue, but it is symptomatic of the friction on both sides.

Because of Sherpa problems, not enough loads had been lifted to the South Col when the time came for the first assault. On 8 May, the deputy leader Prem Chand established a minimal camp on the ridge above the col, accompanied by Chandra Aitwal, Phu Dorje and a couple of Sherpas, but he decided against pressing for the top because of possible benightment. He did not want to risk a forced bivouac for Miss Aitwal – no doubt he had the grim example of Hannelore Schmatz in mind in similar circumstances.

Returning to the South Col, Chand had to make an unenviable decision. The assault camp on the ridge was just one tent. There was not room for two teams up there and someone would have to go down. To give up his own chance of the summit must have been difficult but to chose which of the two women would go for the top and which would go down must have taken considerable courage.

In the end he decided that Rita Gombu would go for the summit and that Chandra Aitwal would go down. Miss Aitwal was one of the best of Indian climbers, with ascents of Nanda Devi and Kamet to her credit but she was 42 years old and Rita Gombu had youth on her side.

Despite these problems, on 9 May three climbers moved off from the top camp on the ridge above the South Col – Phu Dorje, a 34-year-old mountaineering instructor from Sikkim; Ang Dorje, another 34-year-old Sherpa, who had climbed Everest with Wanda Rutkiewitcz in 1978, and Rita Gombu, the 27-year-old daughter of Nawang Gombu, the first man to climb Everest twice (1963 and 1965).[18] They set out at 7 a.m. but after an hour Ang Dorje, who was not carrying oxygen, decided to turn back, fearing frostbite. Phu Dorje was some fifty yards ahead and he waited for Rita Gombu to catch up. The wind was whistling across the South East Ridge at 50 mph and thin cloud scudded over the mountain. Rita was in two minds and Phu Dorje urged her to go on, promising to help her to the top, but she found the elements too much and gave up. She had reached 8,665 m. – just 183 m. below the summit.

Phu Dorje decided to continue on his own, though his oxygen supply had given out. He plodded on through knee deep snow and shortly met the Bulgarian climber Ivan Vultchev on his way down after his dramatic ascent of the West Ridge. It took him two hours to reach the South Summit where he discovered the second Bulgarian, Metodi Savov, lying prostrate in the snow, apparently dead. There was nothing the Sherpa could do so he pressed on and just before the Hillary Step he met the second pair of Bulgarians, Doskov and Petkov, making rapid progress in pursuit of their companions. He reached the summit at 12.30 p.m., where he stayed for 15–20 minutes, presenting a scarf to the Goddess Chomolungma in thanksgiving. He then hurried down the ridge, overtaking the Bulgarians and guiding them to the top camp tent where he plied them with tea.[19]

On 15 May another two groups were moving up the mountain. In the second group, at Camp 3 in the Western Cwm, was Miss Pal, a sports' officer from the TATA group, with an MA in Sanskrit, and a slight, unlikely looking candidate for the top of Everest. That night, half an hour after midnight, there was a sudden ominous bang which reverberated round the cwm, followed by a roar and crash. A huge serac had broken away from the Lhotse face to come smashing down on the unsuspecting Camp 3. The camp was utterly destroyed in seconds but, by a miracle, the only injuries were one man with a broken leg, another with some cracked ribs and a few bruises all round. Miss Pal stepped from the chaos unharmed.

The expedition drew back to Camp 2 where the Sherpas were rebellious. Khullar wrote:

> There was nothing left of Camp 3 save a torn tent. Supplies at South Col were limited. Most of our capable Sherpas had been injured, the others were too exhausted. The majority were convinced that the expedition was jinxed thanks no doubt to the dubious prediction of a lama. He did not have to be a genius; accidents on Everest are a common occurrence. Even Sherpa Sirdar Ang Dorjee wanted us to wind up and leave. We were not the best of friends when he left with the casualty for I warned him that the team this time would climb without the Sherpas if necessary and in my Sherpa English I told him 'if you coward then NOT come – members climb alone'. And I think this and more than that his rapport with the press brought him back to us on 20 May in company of three of his gallant Thame colleagues – the last of what were left.[20]

Whatever organisation the expedition might have had now began to disintegrate in an undignified scramble for the summit, though the plan to get a woman on top was not forgotten. Unfortunately Chandra Aitwal was mistakenly reported sick and left behind, once again robbing her of a summit chance. On 21 and 22 May various climbers made their way up from Camp 2 to the South Col where they found a distinct shortage of oxygen. This did not concern Ang Dorje, who always climbed without oxygen anyway, and at 6.20 a.m. on 23 May he and Miss Pal set off for the summit. Sonam Palzor, not wishing to be left out of things picked up three cylinders left behind by the Bulgarians and set off in pursuit at 7 a.m., followed half an hour later by Lhatoo Dorje. Not quite knowing what to do about these pre-emptive strikes four men were left standing on the South Col: Magan Bissa, Minoo Mehta, Kiran Inder Kumar and Jai Bahuguna '(they) were left out, but had shown restraint and to a cynic, lack of initiative.'[21]

The day was one of perfect weather and the four climbers made rapid progress. Lhatoo Dorje, another of Tenzing's relations, and Field Director of the Himalayan Mountaineering Institute, soon overtook Palzor and caught up with Miss Pal and Ang Dorje just below the South Summit. The going was hard at this point and Lhatoo made his companions rope-up whilst he moved alongside them. They were helped at the Hillary Step by the ropes left behind by previous parties, and at 1.07 p.m. reached the summit. Fifteen minutes later, Palzor joined them and then, after 45 minutes on the summit, they retreated down the ridge where Magan Bissa, one of the disappointed quartet from the South Col, climbed up to meet them with fruit juice and oxygen.

Sharon Wood, the Canadian mountain guide, was the next woman to climb Everest, by the West Ridge in 1986 as described earlier, but no American woman climbed the mountain until the post-monsoon period of 1988, when Stacey Allison, a 30-year-old building contractor from Portland, Oregon, following the ordinary South East Ridge route, reached the summit with Sherpa Pasang Gyalzen on 29 September. She was followed on 2 October by Peggy Joan Luce, a 29-year-old Seattle bicycle messenger. Both were members of the North West American Everest Expedition led by a Seattle attorney called Jim Frush. Climbers from the North West have a long association with Everest and it is entirely appropriate that the first American women to reach the top should, like the first men in 1963, come from the North West.[22]

It was interesting that the American women should climb Everest in 1988 because feeling was growing amongst American women climbers that something should be done about it – just as a similar feeling had grown in Indian climbing circles a few years earlier. Sue 'Killer' Giller, who had tried three routes on the mountain without success, expressed their frustration when she said, 'I'm so sick of this first woman thing. All I want is for *some* woman to get up there and get it over with so we can get on with quality expeditions'.[23] Hardly had she spoken than her wish was granted, but that special Everest magic which can bring out the best and worst in climbers was at work again: it seemed that nationalism was being revived through the distaff side.

The two Americans made the seventh and eighth ascents by women. The ninth ascent, if it took place at all, followed shortly after, though even Lydia Bradey, the 27-year-old mountain guide from Christchurch, New Zealand, is not sure whether she reached the top or not. It is a confused tale and one so recent (at the time of writing) that all the facts may not yet have come out – and perhaps they never will.

Lydia Bradey was part of a New Zealand expedition which attempted the South Pillar without success. She transferred her attention to the adjacent South East Ridge, for which she did not have official permission, and claimed to have reached the top on 14 October, solo and without oxygen. This would certainly have been a double first for a woman, but there was no proof that she did the climb and some evidence that she did not. She carried no watch, so could not give her times, and her camera was frozen, so she took no pictures. In view of her claims these omissions were unfortunate, but not unduly suspicious – such things do happen. However, she met some Spanish climbers just below the South Summit and later at the South Col, and from their timings it would seem impossible for the New Zealander to have reached the summit and back in the time.

For being on a route without permission Miss Bradey could be banned from entering Nepal. The Government demanded a written statement from her and in it she claims she might have confused the South Summit with the top – but did she? The Spaniards said she was crawling on all fours at the South Summit when they saw her; she says she was on her feet and going strongly through deep snow. Even to reach the South Summit without oxygen means that Lydia Bradey is a very tough lady indeed; whether she became the ninth woman to climb Everest earns for the moment at least, a verdict of unproven.

At the end of the '70s one of the major objectives remaining on Everest, apart from new routes, was a winter ascent of the mountain. The Poles, who have a distinguished record of winter climbing, and Himalayan climbing, decided to attempt this and got permission to try the South East Ridge in the winter of 1979/80 and, as a bonus, a spring expedition to try a new route to the left of the ridge. Both were led by Andrzej Zawada, one of Poland's most distinguished mountaineers. With Tadeusz Piotrowski he had climbed Noshaq (7,492 m.) in February 1973 – the first 7,000 m. peak to be climbed in winter and during the following winter season he had almost, but not quite, reached the summit of Lhotse. It was Zawada who had persuaded the Poles to go for a winter ascent, arguing that a summer ascent of Everest was no longer important. He had also to convince the Nepalese Government, who up to that time had never granted permission for a winter attempt. On the application he wrote:

> The beginning of winter expeditions to the Himalaya will open up new horizons for mountaineering. The highest peaks which have already been

> conquered in the pre-monsoon and post-monsoon seasons will be virgin peaks to winter expeditions as has happened before in the Alps, the Caucasus and the Hindu Kush. Winter expeditions to the Himalaya are a natural historical consequence of mountaineering progress.[24]

And, curiously enough, the expedition which did take place was almost like a winter reprise of John Hunt's ascent back in 1953. There were differences, of course – the route was well known for one thing – but there was the same sense of frustration and disappointment turning to sudden joy.

Conditions were extremely severe. Crisp snow had been replaced in many places by hard ice, there were savage winds which often made movement impossible and the temperatures were appallingly low – at the South Col it was minus 40 degrees, *inside the tent!* Under such conditions injuries and sickness proliferated.[25]

The permit was due to expire on February 15 and though it was extended a couple of days, Zawada felt that the expedition was slipping away. He decided to lead from the front, to see whether he could inject some dynamism into the proceedings. The weather improved so with Szafirski, Heinrich and Pasang Norbu he helped to establish a camp on the South Col, from where Heinrich and Pasang Norbu were expected to go for the top. Szafirski and Zawada descended without oxygen, not leaving the col until 4 p.m. It was almost Zawada's undoing:

> I felt the lack of oxygen very much. Szafirski was in front of me – he was in a hurry to get down. After sunset, darkness came very quickly as usual. I was on a narrow ledge just before Yellow Rocks without fixed rope, and I could not find the piton with the next fixed rope. Szafirski had already descended through the rock band, and he told me afterwards that he had no strength left to climb up again to guide me to the proper spot. I switched on my torch, but I still could not find the place. I had to save the batteries which were running out in the very severe frost. I decided to traverse out onto the icy wall, hoping to reach the fixed ropes. With great difficulty I managed to chip out two tiny footholds in the ice. I stood on them tentatively with only the front spikes of my crampons. Below me there was a sheer drop of 1000 m. of the huge icy slab which ended in the open crevasse. If I only had one piton and one small-loop! But finally commonsense prevailed and I made my way back to the rocks, taking great care. The only thing left to do was to wait for the dawn. I cut out a small platform in the ice and built a small wall of ice blocks on the windward side. I took out all the clothes I had in my rucksack and put them on. Trembling with cold, I began the long wait. I was at 7,600 m. and it seemed as if the unusually bright stars were just above my head. Suddenly, down below, I saw lights moving in the vicinity of Camp 3. I shone my torch in their

direction to let them know where I was. It was Cichy and Wielicki. At great personal risk they were climbing up to come to my rescue. At about 2 a.m. that night they reached me. They gave me some hot soup and rubbed me until I felt warm again. In the morning, I was in Camp 3 again.[26]

But the effort had not been in vain. On the very last day of the permit, February 17, Leszek Cichy and Kryzysztof Wielicki set out from the South Col at 6.30 a.m. for the summit, each taking one bottle of oxygen. They were carrying a radio but no word came to the anxious watchers below as the morning dragged on. Fearing the worst, Zawada sent two men to Camp 3 as a safety precaution in case rescue was needed. Then, at 2.25 p.m., Cichy's voice came over the radio. 'Guess where we are!' he said.

After the success of the first winter ascent the Poles withdrew from the mountain, leaving Kazimierz Olech in charge of Base Camp whilst the rest returned to Poland or recuperated in Nepal. Zawada was back at Base Camp by March 25, with a team which was two-thirds new and one-third winter veterans. The Polish team was a strong one: ten members had 8,000 m. experience and between them they had accumulated seven ascents of 8,000 m. peaks. Their aim was to climb the South Pillar; a distinct long ridge of rock running directly down from the South Summit and tailing out into the steep snow slopes below the South Col. It is the right-hand bounding feature of the South-West Face, looked at squarely on. A number of people had expressed interest in its possibilities for some time, and it had been the original objective of Messner and Habeler.

The weather was consistently bad throughout, with snowfall nearly every day in May bringing increased avalanche danger. Despite this the sites of Camps I and II were the same as for the winter expedition, but then the new line climbed the steep slopes below the pillar and to the right of it, with Camp III at 6,900 m. and Camp IV at 8,050 m. This was straightforward ice climbing but just above Camp IV a rock band, 200 m. high, barred the way and caused a bit of difficulty. Each climber in turn nibbled away at the problem and although it was only Grade III/IV – nothing to an experienced climber at sea level – at 8,000 m. it can be quite formidable. It took 16 days to overcome, but on 14 May Ryszard Gajewski, Janusz Kulis and Kazimierz J. Rusiecki established Camp V above the rock wall at 8,300 m.

On 18 May Andrzej Czok and Jerzy Kukuczka spent an uncomfortable night at the camp, buffeted by strong winds. Undeterred by this, at five next morning they started for the summit and for 7½ hours fought deep snow, howling winds and sub-zero temperatures to reach the South Summit. Here their oxygen ran out, but they decided to continue without it and at 4 p.m. reached the summit of Everest. Their return to the tent was a struggle against cold, weariness and darkness but they reached it safely, 17 hours after they had left it.

The Polish route on the South Pillar is the shortest way from the Western Cwm to the summit. 'It can be expected that this route in the future will become the most common route on Mount Everest', declared one enthusiast, but alas, it has never really happened.[27]

In 1982 the Russians came to Everest. It was confidently assumed by Western observers that the Soviets would opt for the ordinary route up the South East Ridge, because this was their first big Himalayan expedition and they would not want to fail. *Glasnost* and *perestroika* had not yet arrived on the Soviet scene, and whilst the political capital to be made out of success was minimal, there were plenty of people around ready to make propaganda capital out of Soviet failure. It was quite a surprise, therefore, when the Russians chose an untried and difficult-looking line up the South West Face.

The line chosen was the Central Pillar. This begins as a low rib on the left of the great Central Gully, which at about half-height on the face rises dramatically to a sharp ridge, joining Everest's West Ridge at 8,296 m.

The Russian system of mountain climbing is fundamentally different from that of other countries. It has none of the anarchic freedom which is such a feature of the Western climbing scene but is rigidly controlled so that climbers may only attempt grades of climbs on a progressive scale. They try and get as many members of a team to the top as possible and they have observers to keep an eye on progress.[28] As a system it should be very safe, if stifling in initiative, but on occasions it has gone terribly wrong.

For a venture like Everest, of course, only top grade climbers could be selected. The leader was a Professor of Theoretical Physics, Yevgenni Tamm, who sought the advice of the recently successful Poles:

> They gave us so much valuable advice as to our gear and drew our attention to the need to take the average age of the team into account. As a rule mountaineers around age 20 do not stand up to the stress of prolonged ascents. We took this into account and arrived at the average age of 35 for our team.[29]

In fact the three lead climbers were considerably older. Eduard Myslovsky was 44, Ervand Illinsky was 40, and Valentin Ivanov, 42. These three were selected two years in advance of the rest. Each was to lead a team of four men. In addition, there was to be a back-up team led by Viacheslav Onishenko and, for some unexplained reason, an odd climber, Valery Khomutov, who didn't belong to any of the teams but brought the total of climbers to 17. All sorts of tests were employed to find the right people, including four trips to the Pamirs; the highest of Russian mountains. At the end of the day the climbing teams looked like this:

*Myslovsky's team* included the redoubtable Vladimir Balyberdin (32), an engineer from Leningrad, noted for his single-mindedness, along with

Vladimir Shopin and Nikolai Cherny. *Illinsky's team* were all from Alma Ata, where Illinsky was a trainer at the Mountain Centre: Yuri Golodov and Kazbek Valiev and Valery Khishchanty – the latter two having made a name for themselves with a difficult route on the South Face of Pik Kommunizm in the Pamirs. *Ivanov's team* had Sergei Ephimov (37) from the Urals, the ace rock climber Sergei Bershov (34) who had actually climbed in the USA, and Mikhail Turkevich, who at 28 was the youngest member. In *Onishenko's reserve team* were Aleksei Moskaltsev, Sergei Chepchev and Vladimir Puchkov. Khomutov was also attached to this team and later seemed to become its leader, just as Valiev seems to have replaced Illinsky.

The climbers arrived at Base Camp on 16 March and started work on the Icefall. By 24 March camps had been established at the top of the Icefall and at the foot of the Face (Camp 1). However, all was not well with the expedition. The Icefall had been much more difficult than anticipated,[30] Myslovsky had been warned by the doctors to keep below 6,000 m., and the general strangeness of Nepal to the Soviet climbers all contributed to a depressed atmosphere. Then just before the end of March a violent storm smashed the upper camps and a general retreat was ordered.

By 4 April they were back at work on the Face. Ivanov's team climbed 16 rope-lengths up the slopes to the start of the difficult rock ridge but could not find a site for Camp 2. Taking over, Myslovsky's team managed to establish the Camp at 7,350 m. before retiring in turn to allow the Alma Ata climbers a go.

Above the camp the rock reared up in blank and overhanging walls. Only on the right did there seem to be a chance and the Alma Ata men forced their way through for 17 pitches of some of the most difficult climbing ever seen on Everest. Then Myslovsky, who seems to have recovered (or was ignoring the doctors) reappeared to set up Camp 3 at 7,850 m. Myslovsky was the exception: most of the others were suffering from sore throats and coughs. Cherny and Shopin went down with altitude sickness and Onishenko, reserve team leader, was so bad he had to be rushed off the mountain, in a state of semi-paralysis.

Myslovsky and Balyberdin managed to push out the route to the 8,000 m. mark before following their comrades down the mountain. They were the first Russian climbers ever to reach 8,000 m.

Myslovsky's team was sent for R & R to the woods around Thyangboche and it seems likely at this stage that the expedition leader, Tamm and his deputy Ovchinikov, had decided that Myslovsky and Balyberdin were the best men for the first summit push. Myslovsky argued for them to stay as a team, but Shopin and Cherny were sent back up the mountain to help with stocking the camps. There was some problem over this because many of the Sherpas couldn't manage the difficult technical climbing above Camp 3. Ivanov's team had established Camp 4 in a sensational situation at 8,250 m., on the crest of the rib with sheer drops for thousands of feet on both sides. Less than 50 m. above lay the West Ridge. On 29 April Shopin and the Sirdar, Pemba Norbu, managed to deliver vital loads of oxygen to this camp.

Tamm's policy was that each of the teams should have three spells at high altitude, retiring to the lower camps between times. With the establishment of Camp 4 all the teams had completed their quotas, but there still remained Camp 5 to be established on the West Ridge, at about 8,500 m., from where the summit bid would be launched. Accordingly, whoever established Camp 5 would also have first go at the summit, provided they were fit enough to continue.

There wasn't much doubt that it would be Myslovsky and Balyberdin and on 27 April they went up to Camp 1 where they met Shopin, shattered from his efforts at establishing Camp 4. Of the Sherpas at Camp 1, Navang agreed to go back up with the two climbers and if possible attempt the summit.

But next day, as they struggled upwards, Navang was in trouble. He had difficulty in seeing and though Myslovsky changed goggles with him, it became obvious that he was suffering from snow blindness. Myslovsky took the porter's load, which brought his own load to 25 kg – twice the normal weight. By this time Balyberdin was a long way ahead, but they could keep in contact by shouting and they agreed to abandon some of their load en route. As darkness fell and it started to snow, Myslovsky was forced to abandon his rucksack altogether, and he was lucky to make Camp 4, where an anxious Balyberdin was waiting.

Next morning whilst Balyberdin continued to make the route towards Camp 5, Myslovsky went down for the abandoned loads. As he jumared up the ropes again his clamps suddenly jammed and he found himself upside down, unable to move. His oxygen was finished and he began losing consciousness. With a last despairing effort he tried to free himself of the heavy rucksack and this he managed to do – only to drop it. The precious load bounced down the face, gone forever, and with it Myslovsky's spare gloves. All he had to protect his hands from the bitter cold was a pair of thin woollen gloves – and one of those was torn.

Despite this they continued to advance the route next day, Balyberdin making Myslovsky an improvised rucksack from the tent bag at Camp 4. They established Camp 5 at 8,500 m. The summit was a mere 350 m. above them and on 4 May, at 6.10 a.m. they set off for the top.

If they had expected an easy passage they were soon disillusioned. Though they quickly reached the crest of the ridge, the route to the summit proved difficult. It took two hours to cross a band of red rock, then came snow-coated slabs, overlapping and tilted like the tiles of a house, where they were forced to use pitons for protection. Hour after hour slipped by as difficulty followed difficulty, but finally, after eight and a half hours the top came in sight. As they reached the snow cone which formed the summit, one of Myslovsky's oxygen bottles ran out and he stuck it on the highest point. Strangely, they felt no elation to their success. Balyberdin said:

> When we reached the top we did not feel the delight we anticipated down below. It was just like finishing a job. We did not even kiss or embrace each other.[31]

They took cine film of each other, then removed the film and left the camera for whoever would follow. They buried souvenirs in the snow and the Sherpa offerings to the Gods, and finally, after just over an hour on the roof of the world, they were ready to descend.

The descent seemed as arduous as the ascent had been. By 6 p.m. it was dark, they had run out of oxygen, and due to the intense cold their torches wouldn't function and they were reduced to groping their way down. They had descended less than 100 m. when Balyberdin decided to call for support on the radio.

Listening in Camp 5 were Bershov and Turkevich, who suspecting something was amiss, had prepared extra oxygen cylinders and a flask of hot tea for such an emergency. When Balyberdin called for help they set off at once, climbing by moonlight, fresh and strong. They reached their stricken comrades in 3 hours.

Fortified by the oxygen and hot tea, Balyberdin and Myslovsky continued their descent. Bershov and Turkevich, with the summit only 100 m. above them requested permission to continue to the top. At first Tamm was inclined to say no, but eventually a terse affirmative came over the radio and the two men set off. In fact they made such good time that they reached the summit at 1.20 a.m., paused for a short while, then returned down the ridge in time to catch up with the first pair a few hundred feet above Camp 5, which they reached as dawn was breaking at 5 a.m.

Already in position were Ephimov and Ivanov who at once set off for the top whilst the others continued down. Myslovsky was in a bad way, exhausted and with badly frostbitten hands. When he eventually reached Base Camp he was evacuated to Moscow where parts of his fingers were amputated.

Meanwhile Ephimov and Ivanov reached the summit at 1.20 p.m. on 5 May. Two days later Valiev and Krishchaty abandoned their attempt due to high winds, but that night, when the wind dropped, they made the ascent in the dark, reaching the top at 1.50 a.m. They returned to Camp 5 at 8 a.m., utterly exhausted, where Ilinsky and Chepchev gallantly gave up their own summit attempt in order to help their comrades down.

Not wishing to push his luck too far, Tamm now ordered a general retreat from the mountain, but members of the reserve team who were high on the ridge had other ideas and next day, 9 May, Khomutov, Puchkov and Golodov reached the summit at 11 a.m.

This was a remarkable Himalayan debut for the Russians: all but two of the climbers who were still fit had reached the summit – 11 in all.

> On the other hand, the picture of a well oiled machine carrying successive parties of climbers to the summit is a misleading one. Some of the final pushes stretched the participants to their limits, if not beyond, and showed the strange contrast so often displayed in past Russian epics – an organisational emphasis on safety and caution combined with a set of climbers who will willingly drive themselves into the ground in pursuit of their goal. One can sympathise with the leadership during the final week, the expedition already a success and the weather deteriorating, with a series of climbers high on the face and extremely determined to get to the summit. Mountaineering accidents are often viewed in the USSR as a form of failure on the part of an individual or group. The fact that Tamm and Ovchinkov let the later ascents go ahead says something for their courage and understanding. It would have been easy to get them all down and head for the applause in Moscow.[32]

Not the least remarkable aspect of the Russian expedition was the strict timetabling of events, with one pair following another like clockwork, despite some bad weather on the upper ridges. The Russians might have cause to see in it a vindication of their strict timetabling on climbs at home, where a three-day route is a three-day route; no more, no less. There is too a similarity between the great Central Rib and some of the multi-day ridge climbs of the Caucasus, which must have stood them in good stead.[33]

In 1984 a Czech team repeated the South Pillar climb first done by the Poles four years earlier, but they lost a man on the descent when Jozef Psotka fell into a crevasse and was killed. He was 50 years old and the oldest man to reach the summit.

The 'oldest man' record was destined to be well and truly broken next spring when a large and very successful Norwegian expedition came to the mountain. Many of the larger expeditions these days tend to be international in character and the Norwegian one included two Americans, Dick Bass and Dave Breashears and the British climber, Chris Bonington.[34]

Bonington had been brought in by the expedition leader, the millionaire Arne Naess, at an early stage to help plan the expedition. He had been to the mountain three times previously (see Chapters 18 and 20) but had never reached the top. He was 50 years old and he saw this as his last chance – 'Will you be using oxygen, Chris?' I asked him. 'Every drop I can get!' he replied. He reached the summit on 21 April and became, by ten days, the oldest man to have climbed Everest.

Bass, a wealthy businessman, and Breashears, who acted as his mountain mentor, had also been to Everest before, in 1983 and '84. Breashears had reached the summit in 1983, but Dick Bass had been frustrated, even though he was on a personal quest of an unusual kind – an ambition to climb the highest point on every continent. He had managed them all except Everest – and time was slipping by, even more so than for Bonington, for Bass was five years older.

Naess was understandably not keen to have a 55-year-old man on the expedition, especially one who, apart from the Seven Summits record, was not particularly interested in mountain climbing. Not only was the age wrong, the motivation was wrong as well. But the thought of having Breashears in the team – a man who had climbed Everest and who was a good cameraman to boot – was tempting. Bonington, who had climbed with Bass on Vinson Massif in the Antarctic, put in a good word and in the end Naess agreed, but for a price; Bass had to pay $75,000 and provide his own food, equipment and Sherpas.

Eight men reached the summit on 29 April, including Naess and then, on the next day, Dick Bass, Dave Breashears and Ang Phurba also reached the summit. Bonington's record had lasted just nine days and Dick Bass, at 55, became the oldest man to climb Everest and the first man to climb the highest points of all seven continents.[35] In fact the Norwegian expedition had several minor records to its credit besides those of Bass: it was the first Scandinavian ascent, the earliest ascent by a pre-monsoon party, and the largest number of summiteers of any expedition – 17. The Sherpa Sungdare made his fourth ascent, a record number, whilst Ang Rita had climbed it three times without oxygen.[36]

In the post-monsoon period of that year (1985), an Indian expedition was caught by storm and Major Kiran Inder Kumar fell to his death from near the South Summit. About half an hour earlier he had radioed that his oxygen mask was punctured and leaking and that he had lost his snow goggles. There were high winds and the visibility was poor. The leader had asked Kumar to retreat but he had refused. Later his partner of the climb reported that Kumar had slipped and fallen. A kitchen boy at the base camp saw a red object falling down the mountainside and later Kumar's body was recovered. Four others died of exposure, when they were stranded for three days at the South Col without food or fuel. When the rescue team got there two were already dead, a third died shortly after they reached him and a fourth was abandoned to die on the mountainside when strong winds and darkness made it impossible for them to bring him down. Among those who died was Major Jai Bahuguna, whose brother had died on Everest in 1971 (see Chapter 17). Though the expedition continued it was unsuccessful.

This was the Indian's first post-monsoon attempt and there were later allegations that it had been badly planned and mismanaged. Despite their fine mountaineering record, something certainly seemed amiss in their command structure: there had been more than a hint of this on the previous expedition in 1984, when relations with the Sherpas were bad, and there had been a final undignified scramble for the top. The Indians have never been back to Everest.

Another echo of the fateful 1971 expedition came with the Japanese Naomi Uemura Film Expedition, which followed the Indians on the ridge. Uemura, who had climbed Everest in 1970 and was also on the International expedition of the following year, was a very popular figure in Japan and his disappearance on Mount McKinley in 1984 was regarded almost as a national disaster. A film of his life was made and this expedition was a part of it, during which seven men reached the summit. Unfortunately, the film itself aroused bitter controversy in Japanese climbing circles.

A very curious hiatus now occurred on the south side of Everest. The Uemura expedition of 1985 was the last successful ascent for two years from Nepal. It wasn't for the lack of trying – expeditions came and went with the usual frequency each season, but the whole south side of the peak seemed to be jinxed until the winter of 1987, when Heo Young-Ho of Korea reached the summit on December 22, accompanied by the Sherpa Ang Rita. It was Ang Rita's fourth ascent, each done without oxygen.

If there was a dearth of successful expeditions during the past few years, then 1988 more than compensated for it. The media were starting to take a more active interest in the mountain than before. Whereas previously climbers had carried little film cameras or video cameras up the mountain, the television gurus began to see their own Everest – the challenge of a live broadcast done from the summit. This was something the sponsors could understand and so there was no shortage of money, much to the chagrin of climbers with worthier but less glamorous objectives.

First in the field was the massive and heavily publicized Asian Friendship Expedition involving climbers from Japan, China and Nepal. The aim was to make a simultaneous crossing of the mountain from the North Col to the South Col and vice versa, and at the same time relay live pictures from the summit. It would be the first time any of this had been accomplished and it was heavily sponsored by the commercial Japanese TV network, Nippon Television. Target day was 5 May, which is Japan's Children's Day and a national holiday.

There were two teams, each comprising climbers from the three countries. The first team, of 136 people, was based at Rongbuk under the leadership of the veteran Japanese climber Tsuneo Shigehiro. Included in this team was a 36-man TV crew. The other team, of 118 people, was led by Sherpa Kunga and based below the Khumbu Icefall.

Sadly, before the expedition was properly underway, the Japanese doctor with the Khumbu party, Hidetaka Mizushoki, aged 49, suffered a heart attack and died. From then on, however, helped by splendid weather, things seemed to go like clockwork. On 4 May, right on schedule, six climbers occupied Camp 5 (8,500 m.) on the South East Ridge and set off next morning for the summit. That same morning, 5 May, three climbers left Camp 6 (8,650 m.) on the North East Ridge at 5 a.m.

The northern group arrived at the summit first, at 9.30 a.m. They were Noboru Yamada, the 38-year-old Japanese climber making his third ascent of Everest, Cerin Doji from Tibet, aged 30, and Sherpa Lhakpa Nuru (Ang Lhakpa), 27. About an hour later three of the southern group appeared: two Tibetans, Ringen Punco and Da Cering, with the Sherpa Ang Phurba, who was making his second ascent, having climbed the mountain with Dick Bass in 1985. Their three companions had apparently given up. The summiteers shook hands, planted their national flags and an emblem to commemorate Children's Day and calmly waited the appearance of the TV crew.

After about 20 minutes of waiting, Ang Phurba, who had run out of oxygen two hours before reaching the summit, decided to descend and set off alone down the North East Ridge to complete his traverse. At noon Lhakpa Nuru also decided to descend and he set off down the opposite ridge to complete the traverse in the other direction.

It was another hour before the TV crew appeared: three experienced Japanese climbers, Susuma Nakamura, 42-year-old, Shoji Nakamura, 46, and Teruo Saegusa, 31. It was Saegusa's second ascent of Everest – he had climbed the South East Ridge in 1985. The TV transmitter was fitted to Susuma Nakamura's helmet and pictures went out live to an estimated audience of 280 million people in Japan, China, Nepal, South Korea, USA and Australia.

Before long three more climbers arrived via the North East Ridge: Sherpa Lhakpa Sonam, 25, Munehiko Yamamoto, 29, of Japan and the Chinese climber Li Zhixin, 26. The last named had frostbitten toes and the team intended to return the way they had come instead of traversing the mountain. By this time there were ten people assembled on the summit of Everest – the largest single gathering ever held there. Including the two had had gone down, twelve climbers had visited the summit that day.

The descent began at 2 p.m., Yamada and Cerin Doje continuing their traverse down the South East Ridge and the rest descending the North East Ridge. All returned safely to their Base Camps.

Whatever one may think of the motives for such an expedition, it was nevertheless an outstanding feat of organisation and technology. The electronic problems of broadcasting from the roof of the world are not our concern here, but the skill, discipline and yes, perhaps luck, to get ten people simultaneously on Everest's summit has to be saluted.

Not surprisingly the organisers, having achieved such a coup, were anxious not to push their luck. A second attempt due on 8 May was called off, but there was a strong party at the South Col who had no intention of coming down without making a summit attempt. All but one of the five men concerned had already climbed Everest previously: Ang Rita and Sungdare no less than four times apiece, Narayan Shastra and Ang Karma Guru by the North Col route in 1985. Only the Nepalese soldier Padma Bahadur was odd man out, and yet it was he and Sungdare who made the top at 10.45 a.m., the others giving up.

Padma Bahadur became the first member of the Nepalese Army to reach the summit of Everest. As for Sungdare, the ascent put him one ahead of his great rival in their private race, the score now standing at Sungdare 5, Ang Rita 4. Altogether the expedition had put 14 people on the summit.

Undeterred by this pre-monsoon accomplishment, the French arrived on Everest in the post-monsoon period, to celebrate the tenth anniversary of the first French ascent. On 26 September five Frenchman and three Sherpas reached the top in a perfectly ordinary ascent of the South East Ridge, notable only because the average age of the French was 51 years, and Jean Marc Boivin descended from the summit by parapente, reaching Camp II in 11 minutes.

> The French expedition secured enormous media backing from Alcatel, TDF, France Telecome and UAP to mark the anniversary of the French ascent of 1978. Though Marc Batard and Jean Marc Boivin claimed that they wished to make fast and sporting ascents, the media appear to have dominated, with a budget of 32 m francs, 300-400 Sherpas, 6000 litres of fuel, 150 tents, 26 generators, post-production facilities at Kunde and plans to televise for a whole 24 hour period with 400 minutes of live coverage. All this was planned to follow up the Olympics, with little consideration for environmental effects or the weather. Nor does the fact that such coverage has happened once already, with the huge spring three-nation traverse and live coverage from the summit, seem to penetrate the vision of European sponsors.[38]

Amongst the French contingent was a 37-year-old guide from the Megève called Marc Batard, who had conceived the notion that he could climb Everest from base to summit in a day, alone and without oxygen. It was a daunting ambition, but Batard was supremely fit and mentally attuned. In the pre-monsoon period he 'trained' for Everest by making the first solo ascent of the West Pillar of Makalu (8,463 m.) – it was also the first complete traverse since he descended the normal North West Ridge. Then, just before his Everest attempt, he and the Sherpa Sungdare made a rapid ascent of Cho Oyu (8,201 m.) in 18 hours from base to summit.

His first attempt at the world's highest peak was on 11 September. He left Base Camp at 8.15 a.m. and had reached the South Col by nightfall, when strong winds drove him back. Three days later he set off again, this time in the afternoon and climbing through the night reached a height of 8,750 m. before returning to base 'very much exhausted'. His final attempt began on the evening of 25 September. Climbing rapidly through the hours of darkness he reached the summit 22½ hours later, just an hour behind the main French team mentioned above. He had comfortably beaten the previous record by Loretan and Troillet of 39 hours set in 1986 (see Chapter 20).[39]

Batard's was a remarkable *tour de force*. The Nepalese authorities rather unkindly remarked that the route had been pre-prepared by Sherpas on the main expedition and though this is true there is nothing to suggest that it made much difference. Batard had climbed Cho Oyu through deep snow when nothing was prepared and he would have done the same on Everest. On the way down he passed the main team and continued all the way to Base Camp. His original intention had been to do the climb with Sungdare, but for some reason that didn't happen.

Other ascents of the mountain were also made in 1988, but just as it seemed that Man was all triumphant, Everest struck back. Michel Parmentier, a French climber who had survived the terrible tragedy of K2 in 1986 was killed in the Hornbein Couloir, but the cruellest blow fell on a group of Czech mountaineers who had reached the top after one of the most remarkable climbs ever seen on the mountain.

Since the Bonington expedition of 1975, nobody had succeeded in climbing the South West Face of Everest, though three parties had tried: the South Koreans in the winters of 1985/6 and 86/7 and the Czechs in the pre-monsoon season of 1987. In the post-monsoon period of 1988 another Czech team arrived, determined to climb the face in alpine fashion – that is to say, without pre-placed intermediate camps. The four men concerned were Josef Just, Dusan Becik, Peter Bozik and Jaroslav Jasko. They set out from Camp 2 in the Western Cwm at 3 a.m. on 14 October armed with a tent inner lining, two sleeping bags, two 40 m. climbing ropes, four ice axes, two ice hammers, three small cameras, one video camera, a cooking stove and gas, and food for three days. Besides having no established camps, they had no fixed ropes, no oxygen supplies and no Sherpas. It was a daunting proposition and one wonders whether the Czechs really knew what they were letting themselves in for.[40]

By the end of the first day they had climbed the Central Couloir and reached the Rock Band, an ascent of 1,650 m., but next day they found the chimney which cuts through the Rock Band to be much more difficult than they had imagined and it took them most of the day to climb it – about 300 m. only, and they bivouacked again above the chimney.

Their third day on the face was spent making the long exposed sloping traverse towards the gully leading to the South East Ridge, but Becik was feeling ill and exhausted and they were forced to bivouac a third time below the South Summit. Next day they reached the South Summit and Just followed the ridge to the top of the mountain whilst the others decided to descend. Just reached the summit at 1.40 p.m. At 4 p.m. he radioed Base Camp to say he had rejoined Becik and Jasko and that the latter was feeling lethargic and didn't want to descend. There was no mention of the fourth member, Bozik.[41]

At 5.30 p.m. Just came on the radio again to say they were still at about 8,300 m., but descending slowly. They were all suffering from altitude sickness and were having trouble with their eyesight.

They were never heard from again. At about 6 p.m. an American party on the South Col could see the entire route to the South Summit but there was nobody on it. Either the Czechs had fallen through a cornice or possibly, in their weakened state, been blown off the ridge by the strong winds which had risen.

'Whatever the cause it was a terrible end to one of the greatest feats of modern alpine-style mountaineering,' said *Mountain* magazine. But others asked whether credit could be given to such a suicidal attempt. Even if one of the party reaches the summit, can the climb be called successful, if everyone on it dies?[42]

* * *

What is there left to do on Everest? Apart from the filling in of detail such as the first winter ascent of this or that route, or the first woman's ascent, is there any new objective on the mountain? Two of the routes mentioned as possibilities in the first edition of this book – the South Pillar and the East Face – have been climbed, but nobody has yet attempted the South West Face Direct or the Grand Traverse of Nuptse, Lhotse and Everest. The Russian Route on the South West Face and the North East Ridge Integrale were important new lines, not at first recognizable as viable objectives but proving themselves very worthy indeed. The North East Ridge has not been done *in toto*, as yet, though there is a party about to attempt it even as I write – one of 14 expeditions to Everest this year (1989).

Options are narrowing. The huge East Face will always provide new challenges, though mostly without much form to them. A splendid exception is the pinnacled East Ridge which rises from the Kangshung Glacier to Pt 7,912 on the North East Ridge; this might make a very hard route to the top because it would also involve the Pinnacles of the main ridge.

The North East Facet, between the East and North East Ridges might make a short, sharp climb and there may be something between the North East Ridge and the North Ridge, though this might be clutching at straws.

One thing is for sure – the pace will continue unabated, as Everest maintains its fascination for the world's mountaineers.

# 22

## 'Everest is Another Ballgame'

Once it became apparent that mountaineers were prepared to pay huge sums of money to attempt Everest, the authorities in China and Nepal abandoned any pretence of proper control. Cash became the chief criterion for obtaining a permit, and the demands of the authorities increased exponentially throughout the '90s. In 1991 the fee for an expedition on the Nepalese side was $2,300 (£1,475); by the end of the decade, it had risen to a minimum of $70,000 (£45,000), plus an extra $10,000 (£6,400) for every climber after the first seven.[1] Despite the costliness, the climbers came in ever increasing numbers. Both base camps, north and south, became tented villages with hundreds of climbers, Sherpas and camp attendants. At times it resembled a three-ringed circus. Most of these expeditions were of no significance, except to the participants. For them, of course, it was probably the greatest experience of their lives, especially if they were one of the lucky ones to reach the summit.

Attitudes on the mountain inevitably changed, too. A different ethos emerged and, as we shall see, had a profound effect on events. Expeditions were no longer self-contained, try though they might. Some groups became literally intermingled so that climbers from one team reached the summit accompanied by those of a different team. For example, on 12 May 1992 a Dutch team led by Ronald Naar reached the top mixed with a large international team led by New Zealander Rob Hall. In fact, 32 climbers reached the summit that day.[2] Cooperation existed in the Icefall, too. Leaders would meet at the start of the season to agree who would fix the ropes and ladders — the 'Icefall doctors' — with everyone contributing to the cost, although this was sometimes a source of controversy, especially with East European expeditions who often had no money to spare for such luxury.

With such a melting pot there were inevitably examples of selfishness, and even callousness, but there were also incidents that called to mind the highest principles of mountain tradition. Such an incident took place in October 1992 when the Spanish climber Juan Carlos Gómez, having reached the Hillary Step and within a stone's throw of the top, gave up his chance of reaching the world's highest summit to help a companion who was descending in great distress. Gómez could have told the man to wait where he was and collected him on the way back but instead chose to immediately see him safely down. This is not an isolated example.

In a decade of excess there were, of course, many more successes — and many more deaths. Various minor 'firsts' were achieved[3] (see the list of ascents in Appendix 5). Marc Batard's record ascent of 1988 stood for ten years until Kaji Sherpa did the climb from Khumbu Base Camp to the summit in 20 hours, 20 minutes — and he was reputedly delayed by poor weather![4] More people, especially Sherpas, climbed the mountain several times, including the incomparable Ang Rita, who has climbed Everest no fewer than ten times (and probably more by the time you read this).

Because the high cost of climbing Everest has not deterred many ordinary climbers, professionally led groups, usually called 'commercial expeditions,' have proliferated to satisfy demand. Costs vary, but a typical price to join one of these groups is $64,000 (£41,000). There are plenty of takers.

Nothing has excited as much controversy in recent years as these commercial expeditions. Because of their history (detailed later), they do leave an indefinable sour taste for older mountaineers. Many accusations have been levelled against them, most of which are both true and untrue, for the fact is that not all commercial expeditions are alike. Some comprise highly experienced climbers with other 8,000 m. peaks to their credit who are going along to beat the permit system. On the other hand, to pretend that all commercial expeditions are so expert is nonsense. The late Anatoli Boukreev gives the game away when he describes an Indonesian team who had no climbing experience. He was asked to lead this expedition by the Indonesian government as a commercial undertaking. Boukreev's suggestion that they should do a year's training on lesser peaks first was turned down — the Indonesian authorities were only interested in Everest. So he formed the expedition. After a couple preliminary climbs on smaller local peaks in the Khumbu, Boukreev led his team to Everest, helped by two other Russian guides and some Sherpas. They reached the South Col and made for the summit:

> The ridge was quite different from last year; there was much snow and it was steeper. Iwan was moving slowly; he fell at one point, tenuously stopping on the old fixed rope. I began to show him how to use

> his ice axe properly on the ridge. Here I realized I was dealing with a man who had never seen snow until four months ago.[5]

This must have been the highest climbing lesson in history! One of the Indonesians made the summit and two others came within a few metres. It was a prodigious effort on their part, but Boukreev admits he wasn't proud of the expedition and that they were lucky. 'I know this success will only encourage other inexperienced individuals into the mountain,' he wrote.[6]

In the spring of 1996, Matt Dickinson, a TV cameraman, reached the summit via the north ridge led by Alan Hinkes, one of Britain's best climbers. It says much for the determination and strength of both men, for of the two standard routes up Everest, this is the more difficult — and Dickinson had done no serious climbing in his life before. He had not even been up Ben Nevis, Britain's highest hill at 1,344 m. high and, by the tourist route, just an afternoon's stroll.[7]

So Boukreev was right. Inexperienced people are tempted to go for the top — and they often succeed. The irony in this is that experienced climbers often fail. Some of the worst accidents on the mountain have happened to experienced climbers.

So where does this leave the commercial operators? How can they demand a certain level of experience from clients when those clients well know that highly inexperienced climbers reached the summit the year before? It's a hard one to call and it must ultimately come down to human judgement — i.e., the judgement of one human by another. But the stakes are very, very high. If you play the Everest game, you are gambling your money *and* your life with the forces of nature.

The majority of the commercial expeditions, indeed expeditions as a whole, opt for the well-established normal routes of the South East Ridge from Nepal or the North Col and North Ridge from Tibet. The two routes are very different: whilst from the assault camp the northern route may be slightly shorter than the southern, it is much higher — 8,300 m. compared with 7,900 m. — so that the climber has to spend two nights and a day above 8,000 m., whereas the summit is reached in a day from the South Col so the climber is only subject to a really high altitude for a few hours. Also, the weather is worse on the north; fierce cold winds often pin the climber down whilst the south side is protected by the bulk of the mountain. Added to this are four recognizable problems on the north: (1) the Yellow Band of poor rock, (2) the First Step, (3) the Second Step (though a ladder now helps) and (4) the difficult summit rocks. On the south there is only the Hillary Step, which is steep but short. Perhaps the final and most crucial advantage the South East Ridge has is that it is relatively easy to follow as a route; the descent is well defined, which you cannot say about the North Ridge, as climbers from Jack Longland in the 1930s to the Taiwanese climber Shih Fang-Fang in 1994 discovered. Having made the summit, Shih could not find his way back down and died.

With the imposition of restrictions on the number of climbers by the Nepalese, more teams are going to the north because they have no choice. Nevertheless it is more difficult and statistics (1995) showed success was roughly five times greater on the south.

It is a common perception that business and nature don't mix and one of the criticisms of commercial expeditions is that they are just that — commercial. They are money-making enterprises, done by the organisers for no other purpose (after all, the guides and Sherpas have probably climbed the mountain before). Yet I fail to see, except for the scale of the thing, what the difference is between paying to be guided up the Matterhorn and paying to be guided up Everest. Success or failure is common to both. So is the possibility of death.

It may be that there is an awful lot of self-righteous breast-beating going on in the mountaineering community for the wrong reasons, mostly wrapped in some false notion of tradition. The plain fact is that from the very outset of the sport, people have been paying others to guide them up mountains. Everest is no different. What is morally wrong is when guides accept clients whom they *know* to be unsuitable — who won't make it no matter what — and in many commercial expeditions, only one or two climbers make the top out of a dozen or so. Were the others taken along for the ride? Were the others taken *for* a ride? Boukreev's comments earlier indicate that commercial pressures can affect the judgement of whether a climber is suitable.

Ten years ago, at the conclusion of the last edition of this book, I wrote:

> One thing is for sure — the pace will continue unabated, as Everest maintains its fascination for the world's mountaineers.

If this has been proved only too true, it is not without disappointment, for of the dozens of expeditions in the intervening 10 years, very few have shown any real initiative. There have been few attempts to break new ground or even to repeat some of the harder routes. The mountain has entered a gimmicky phase (most famous mountains do) where the object seems to be to race up and down in the fastest time or descend on a snowboard. As Stephen Venables so admirably put it, 'Everest is prime Guinness Book [of World Records] territory.'[8]

Even so, deaths continue to mount, though on the south side of the mountain there has been a dramatic change in pattern. Until 1969, 50 percent of fatalities occurred in the Icefall; in the next ten years this rose to 56.25 percent, then it suddenly dropped. In the last decade, the Icefall has accounted for only 4.3 percent of fatalities. In absolute numbers, too, there has been a dramatic decline. The reason for this is not known. Perhaps there has been a change in the rate of glacier movement, or perhaps the modern tradition of fixing the route in advance by the so called 'Icefall doctors' has helped.[9] Accidents occur higher up the mountain for other reasons, too. But as Adrian Burgess commented:

> It would appear the capability of teams range from the very experienced to the wildly incompetent. The main cause of accidents is because climbers are taking so long on the final day that they do not arrive at the summit until after four p.m. Then, tired from their efforts, they must descend in failing light and with failing strength. Teams should decide on a reasonably early turn-around time, such as two p.m. and then adhere to it.[10]

All these problems were during the 1990s, but in 1989 there was a terrible accident of a more classical kind. A very strong Polish team, led by Eugeniusz Chrobak, made a spring attempt on the West Ridge via the Hornbein Couloir. Besides the Poles, the team had four Americans, three Mexicans, a Canadian and a British climber — symptomatic of the way Himalayan climbing was developing. Though starting in Nepal, they decided to approach the ridge from the Tibet side and established Camp I at 6,000 m. on the West Rongbuk Glacier. Because crossing the Lho La, between the Khumbu and Rongbuk, is difficult and dangerous, they crossed by Khumbutse (6,408 m.), a minor peak that forms the other side of the Lho La to Everest's West Ridge. They then climbed back to the ridge where they established four more camps.

On 22 May, Miroslaw Dasal and Miroslaw Gardzielewski reached the top of the Hornbein Couloir in an unsuccessful bid for the summit, then retired to Camp IV at the base of the couloir to help support the next team. This team comprised Chrobak as the leader and Andrej Marciniak who left camp at 1 a.m. on 24 May and reached the summit in the late afternoon. They reached camp again, but the next day the weather grew foul, and the four climbers retreated down to the Lho La where they were met by a third pair, Andrej Heinrich and Wraclaw Otreba. In worsening weather and heavy snowfall, all six climbers retreated to Camp I.

It was obvious that with all the fresh snow there was danger of avalanches, but the Poles decided it would be safe enough to ascend to the Lho La and then climb up to Khumbutse, the rocky face of which was provided with fixed ropes. On 26 May they set out, fighting deep snow that made progress slow and arduous. They changed leads frequently as each leader became exhausted, leaning into the snow, gasping for air. Suddenly, at approximately 1 p.m., a roaring avalanche struck them, sweeping them off their feet. They dangled helplessly on the rope for a few seconds — and then the rope broke.

The six climbers plunged 200–300 m. to the Lho La.

Dasal, Gardzielewski and Otreba were killed instantly; Heinrich died shortly after; and Chrobak, though alive, never regained proper consciousness and died during the night. Only Marciniak remained. The avalanche had removed his goggles and he became snow blind. Floundering on, he fell into a crevasse, injuring himself, but managed to crawl out and reach Camp I, where he found a radio in working order and managed to contact Base Camp in Nepal.

Because of the heavy snowfall, it was obvious to those in Nepal that a rescue from Base Camp was not possible — it would have to be done from Tibet. This posed a diplomatic problem because the Chinese were still smarting from the bad publicity from the Tiananmen Square incident and had closed the borders. It was only through the good offices of the Russian embassy in Kathmandu that an international team of climbers[11] crossed the border on 29 May and reached the stranded Pole, now starving as well as injured, on 1 June. 'When I first heard the shouts,' Marciniak said later, 'I thought it was music. I was sure I was dreaming or hallucinating when I heard the voices, but soon I saw figures approaching through the mist and realised they were people.' It was a moving moment for both the rescued and the rescuers.

In the autumn a special Funeral Expedition was mounted by the Poles to find the bodies of their dead companions, but in this they were unsuccessful. The party had to content themselves with a funeral mass and symbolic burial service. Two memorial tablets were fixed to the moraines of the Rongbuk Glacier and at Everest Base Camp. In the long and distinguished history of Polish Himalayan mountaineering, this was by far their worst accident.

By early May 1989 the south side of the mountain was alive with climbers. There was said to be a beaten track up to the South Col and fifty tents at Camp II. An experienced Sherpa, Phu Dorje, who had climbed Everest before, was killed in a fall whilst returning from the summit after accompanying the first Mexican ascent. At the end of 1989 another Sherpa died, reputedly from altitude sickness, but this is so rare in Sherpas, who live most of their lives at altitude, that one suspects it was something else, such as a heart attack.

The following season, the spring of 1990, saw the first all-Nepalese ascent. It was an army expedition led by Lt Col Chitra Bahadur Gurung but with several Sherpas, including the indomitable Ang Rita, then 41 years old.[12] Ang was one of the summit party and, as usual, he did not use oxygen. The snow was deep and there was a strong wind blowing that hampered its progress. Four members turned back, but three Sherpas and a soldier, Top Bahadur Khatri, struggled to the top in 15 hours, 15 minutes. It was 5.15

p.m. when they arrived, and they had long since run out of oxygen (only Ang Rita was climbing without it). It was an exhausted group that faced the gruelling descent in gathering darkness.

The team members bivouacked at the foot of the Hillary Step, and, during the long hours of a shivering night, two became seriously frostbitten. Nevertheless, the next day they managed to complete their descent, helped by their comrades and, after medical treatment in England, eventually recovered. It was a close-run expedition, and the general opinion amongst others on the mountain at the time was that if it hadn't been for Ang Rita there would have been another tragedy. 'That man is superhuman,' one climber said.[13]

Meanwhile, on the north side of the mountain, a very different expedition was assembling under the leadership of 61-year-old Jim Whittaker, who had made the first American ascent of Everest back in 1963. In an era when summit meetings of world leaders were all the fashion, Whittaker conceived the idea of having a summit meeting that would outclass all others — on the roof of the world! His plan was to put mixed teams of American, Russian and Chinese climbers together to climb Everest.

Aware no doubt of the acrimonious international teams of the past (see Chapters 17 and 18), Whittaker had a much more rigid outlook. There would be not a vaguely liberal get-together such as had happened previously, full of both hope and ill-will, but a structured expedition backed by the Soviet and Chinese communist authorities, whereby it was each country for itself. No one nation was to have priority over another and, indeed, Whittaker did not want there to be an overall leader — but in this, much to his surprise, he failed. Both communist teams voted the American as leader!

It must be remembered that this was in the days before *glasnost*, when the three nations were barely on speaking terms. 'Mr Whittaker, we have not had Soviets in our country for thirty years,' said the Chinese. 'Exactly,' he replied. 'What an opportunity!'[14]

Whittaker is not called Big Jim for nothing. A tall, impressive figure at six feet, five inches and fourteen stones, he certainly impressed the Chinese and Soviets. The Everest International Peace Climb was inaugurated, with Whittaker as overall leader, Vladimir Shatayev leader of the Soviets and Losand Dawa the Chinese. The Soviet climbers came from various parts — Kazakstan, Ukraine and Russia itself, whilst the Chinese were, in fact, all Tibetan.

The teams became acquainted during practice climbs on Rainier and Elbrus (the Soviets insisting on the latter so as not to 'lose face'), and on 24 February, met in Beijing in readiness for the trek across Tibet to Base Camp. With them went 20 tons of supplies — half gear, half food. Base Camp was

17,500 ft. Poor weather and some team illnesses delayed things, but eventually six camps were stocked up the ridge, and Camp VII was to be mobile, carried by the assault party, which consisted of two ropes with a climber from each country on each rope. Oxygen was used, carried in special lightweight titanium bottles provided by the Soviets. Whittaker was leaving nothing to chance in ensuring that the Peace ropes got to the top. And so they did. On 7 May, six international climbers reached the summit of Everest together. In the next three days, the weather remaining fine, 14 more ascents were made, but now all restraints were off and some did it without oxygen. On their return to Lhasa, 5,000 schoolchildren lined the roads in greeting.

Whittaker's organisation was brilliant, perhaps matching that of Hunt in 1953. The cost was well in excess of a million dollars, but he had shown that real international cooperation was possible — of course, he could not have foreseen the break-up of the Soviet Union or the opening up of China, but nevertheless it remains an outstanding achievement. The leader summed it up himself: 'We succeeded far beyond out wildest dreams: no deaths; 20 to the summit, first Soviet woman to the summit, second Chinese-Tibetan woman to the summit; five ascents without bottled oxygen; two tons of garbage removed from the mountain.'[15] And of course the cooperation of former enemies — the reason for it all.

Whilst Whittaker's team was busy in the north, all sorts of things were happening in Nepal. Another American team, led by Glenn Porzak, put climbers on Everest and Lhotse, though perhaps an opportunity was missed to do a difficult traverse. Certainly there were some fine climbers who might have done it — Wally Berg, Peter Athans and Scott Fischer, for example.

The last of Porzak's team to make the top of Everest was Andrew Lapkass on 11 May, who found himself sharing the ascent with the Australian climber Tim Macartney-Snape, who had soloed the mountain starting at *sea level* in the Bay of Bengal! Macartney-Snape's journey had included a 3 km. swim across the Ganges at one point, and he helped Beda Fuster's Swiss team to fix ropes to the Lho La, because, like them, he intended to climb the difficult West Ridge. However, this was not to be. Heavy snowfall made the West Ridge impracticable and so he diverted to the ordinary route. Macartney-Snape had been the first Australian to climb Everest 6 years earlier when he climbed the Great Couloir in one of the finest ascents ever made at that time. Amid the ever growing guided hordes plodding up the South East Ridge, the heart warms to individualists like Macartney-Snape who, like the Pilgrim in *Hassan,* always goes a little further.

Another international expedition, led by the New Zealander Rob Hall, climbed the South East Ridge on 10 May 1990. First to the top was Peter Hillary, son of Sir Edmund Hillary, the first man to climb Everest in 1953.

By means of satellite communication, Peter spoke to his father from the summit. Meanwhile, a lone figure came up to the top from the north and, handing a postcard to Gary Ball, said 'I Soviet,' and asked him to take his photograph. Without another word, he then stomped off down the ridge; he was obviously one of Whittaker's peace corps. A little later, Rudy Van Snick from Hall's team came up with the Sherpa Apa and became the first Belgian to reach the summit. The next day, two Swedes, Mikael Reuterswärd and Oskar Khilborg, from the expedition reached the top. Reuterswärd, who was somewhat ahead of his companion, was the first of his nation to climb Everest, and by satellite he spoke directly to the King of Sweden.[16]

In the post-monsoon period the south side of Everest was really crowded. No fewer than nine expeditions were vying for the Icefall, but fortunately they managed to work together to establish the route, though apparently not without vociferous disputes over route priorities.[17] Hooman Aprin's American commercial expedition had designs on the South Pillar, which was encouraging, but was frustrated by the weather and switched to the normal route. Seven members reached the summit including the leader and the husband and wife team of Aleksei Krasnokutsky and Cathy Gibson (the second husband and wife team to reach the top), beaten only by the Slovenes Andrej and Marija Stremfelj, who arrived at the top earlier that afternoon of 7 October. Marija Stremfelj was also the first Slovenian woman to reach the top, though it was her husband's second visit.

Andrej Stremfelj's original objective had been the West Ridge of which he had made the first direct ascent in 1979 (see Chapter 19). This time he hoped to complete the original American route by the Hornbein Couloir, but like Aprin, he was foiled by the weather and switched to the South East Ridge.

It was a time for many minor records: Jean-Noël Roche and his son, Bernard, became the first father and son team to reach the top (4 October), and Bernard, known as Zébulon Roche, became at 17 the youngest person to reach the summit. Father and son descended from the South Col by paraglider!

On the following day Marc Batard made his second ascent of the mountain, his intention being the double ascent of Everest and Lhotse on succeeding days, but heavy snow foiled this. With Batard were several compatriots including Christine Janin, the first French woman to make the top. Three other French women reached the South Col, as did Sherpani Pasang Lhamu, the first Sherpa woman to reach 8,000 m. She later accused the leader of preventing her from attempting the summit. Yves Le Bissonais had the distinction of being the first one-legged climber to reach the col. He was more fortunate than the luckless Korean, Ham Sung-Hun who, having witnessed his companions reach the top on 6 October, decided to have a go himself next day, without oxygen and without his leader's permission. He was never seen again.

Heavy snowfall seems to have been the cause of many failures and several deaths during the post-monsoon period. A Spanish expedition was abandoned when a climber and two porters were killed by an avalanche below the North Col. Two spirited attempts at the South West Face were made by Basque and Korean teams. The Basques were climbing without supplementary oxygen, and several climbers suffered altitude problems. This, and the weather, stopped them from climbing the Rock Band for approximately 3 weeks. At last, due to determined work by Paco Txabarri and Iosu Bereziartua, the band was forced, and on 9 October four climbers went to 8,300 m. where they hoped to establish Camp V. However, the wind was so strong that they had to abandon the attempt and the expedition retired.

In the four-day period of good weather, 4–7 October, 31 people reached the summit via the South East Ridge — more than in the entire previous history of the mountain.[18]

In the spring of 1992, Marc Batard attempted again to climb Everest and Lhotse on the same day. Rumours abounded about his row with Pasang Lhamu, who had left his previous expedition in a flaming temper after he refused to let her try for the summit. He claimed she wasn't strong enough, a claim substantiated by climbers from another expedition. Her husband, the head of a trekking agency in Kathmandu, lodged a complaint with the tourism ministry that a foreigner had prevented a Nepalese woman from climbing a Nepalese mountain. This time, Batard's first attempt failed because of high winds, and on his return to Base Camp, he was surprised to find he did not have a climbing permit! He immediately retired from the mountain claiming victimization, swearing never to climb in Nepal again.[19]

Later in the year, Pasang Lhamu led her own expedition to the mountain, determined to be the first Nepalese woman to climb Everest, but she only reached the South Summit. Foreign climbers on her expedition were said to be less than enchanted by the experience. For example, one French climber complained that he had to sleep with another expedition on one occasion because there were not enough tents. There was more trouble when her Sherpas demanded $300 (£190) per person from other expeditions using the Icefall route they had prepared. A Russian expedition made their own route through the Icefall, though a rather dangerous one that they later abandoned, sneaking past the guardian Sherpas on the normal route, with their faces heavily disguised in protective gear so that they could not be identified!

The Russians were in fact a strong team that included Anatoli Boukreev and Volodya (Valerie) Balyberdin: the latter famous for the Russian ascent of the South West Face in 1982 (see Chapter 21). Balyberdin is noted for a formidable will, and though 51 years old, managed to climb Everest for his second time. The expedition, six Russians and three Americans, had curious origins. The original plan had been to assemble a team for a daring Lhotse-Everest traverse, part of the Everest Horseshoe, but when this idea fell through, Boukreev and Balyberdin determined to make a speed ascent to beat Marc Batard's record of 22 hrs 29 mins by climbing to the summit from Base Camp and back in a day. After their summit climb, both men had a crack at this. On 12 October, Boukreev set off at 5 p.m., and after climbing through the night, reached 8,300 m. by 8 a.m. before cruel winds forced a halt. He was back in Base Camp 24 hours after leaving it. Five days later, Balyberdin took 17 hours to reach the same height before he, too, had to retreat. Thinking he would go faster without crampons, he had left these behind, and because he didn't expect to be out for long, wore only a thin padded jacket and carried a thin sleeping bag. With these he bivouacked and descended the next day safe and well – without frostbite!

The Russians were undoubtedly a tough bunch. Giutashvili, another on the team, also survived several hours in a snowhole until rescued by his companions. He had made the summit despite being 54 years old and only having one lung!

There were several more enterprising expeditions in 1991. Two attempts were made on the South West Face, first by the Koreans in spring and then by the Japanese in winter. The Koreans were defeated by too little snow, which made it difficult to use crampon claws above the Rock Band. The Japanese spent 12 weeks on the task, using relays chosen from 41 climbers, but strong winter winds prevented them from even reaching the Rock Band. A Swedish team climbed the North Face by the Japanese Route and Hornbein Couloir, whilst an Italian team led by Oreste Forno climbed the face by the Great Couloir, using a partially new route that included an 80-m. wall of Gr V. Battista Bonali, and the Czech Leopold Sulovsky made the ascent on 17 May after the first attempt by De Stefani and De Marchi failed when De Stefani went down with cerebral oedema and his companion suffered bad frostbite, necessitating a difficult rescue involving the whole team.

Also on the north side, Harry Taylor and Russell Brice tried to complete the North East Ridge but were forced to abandon it and descend the North Ridge though they had made a brilliant first crossing of the notoriously difficult Pinnacles. Other members of the team had climbed the North Ridge itself — the normal route on this side of the mountain — and two Sherpas, Babu Tshering and Chuldin made the summit. They all descended and joined the Swedish expedition, which was hosting 'one of the best parties ever given at 17,000 ft.'[20] It is interesting that the Swedes also had a complete field hospital at their base camp that they shared with other expeditions and undoubtedly helped to keep down the casualty rate.

The most interesting of these enterprising expeditions, however, was the attempts made by the Meiji University Alpine Club on the formidable Fantasy Ridge, perhaps one of the best unclimbed lines on Everest. The ridge sweeps down from the northern edge of the East Face as a long, sickle ridge, prominently pinnacled and curving up at its end to a majestic little peak, Pt 6426 m. (Why not name it Fantasy Peak?) From here to the top of the ridge is 1,458 m. (4,782 ft) and approximately 3 km. of length, after which the climbers must tackle another 3 km. of the North East Ridge, including its formidable Pinnacles! Quite a route — well beyond the capacity of the eight-person team.

They set up Base Camp on the Kangshung Glacier on 14 April after a 12-day trek from Kharta with 370 Tibetan porters — shades of the 1920s! It took 16 days to establish Camp I at 6,100 m., but beyond that, they encountered more of the unstable ice that had delayed their ascent and they were bombarded by stonefall. It was also, they said ruefully, 'very long.' Not surprisingly, they decided to retire. 'A few more months might have got them up the route, but the risk of either the climbers or the ridge falling down was too serious to contemplate.'[21] It remains the only attempt made on the ridge.

Because of the traffic on the mountain's normal routes, it is becoming difficult to count anything as a genuine solo ascent now. The three attempts in 1991 all failed. On the North Face, true solo ascents are still possible. Here the Austrian climber Rüdiger Lang tried a new variant. He set out on 1 May and bivouacked the first two nights at 7,300 m. and 7,700 m., but then the weather closed in and he was not seen again until 8 May when he was discovered in an emergency bivouac, apparently frozen to death. The New Zealander Robert Anderson, also attempting the North Face at the same time, managed by repeated efforts to reach 8,300 m., but eventually intense cold and frostbite forced him down.

The strangest attempt, however, was made by British climber Jonathan Pratt, who arrived at the south side of Everest without porters or companions. He had the meagrest of resources and even tried borrowing a few rupees from a Sherpa to buy food. He cheerfully set off up the Icefall using the fixed ropes and, having reached the Western Cwm, slept in other climbers' tents and ate their food. In the company of others, he made a couple of attempts at the summit but failed. This did not stop him from returning the following spring and reaching the top with the Chilean team.

In the pre-monsoon season of 1992, Everest's Khumbu Base Camp had all the appearance of the tented hordes of Ghengis Khan and some of its attributes, too. An Italian visitor said it looked like a fairground.[13] Expeditions fought for space, sometimes literally, as the Spaniards and Dutch resorted to bombarding each other with stones, whilst a British Service Expedition tried to act as mediators. The American and New Zealand expedition leaders complained about the Russians for stealing their route, whilst the Russians complained that the Americans were money-grubbing mercenaries, and moreover, that judging by his language, their leader was no gentleman! Others said the Russians helped themselves to food and tents. For acting outside their permit, the Russians earned a 5-year ban.

Despite the cleansing powers of the winter snows, such a repeated concentration of humanity in a relatively small area must have increasingly serious health implications. The authorities will have to give consideration to this. Currently it seems to be quietly ignored.

On the mountain itself, things were not much better. Summing it up for the *American Alpine Journal,* Elizabeth Hawley wrote:

> American and New Zealand expedition leaders complained about Russians pushing ahead of them on a climbing route for which the Russians had no permit, doing so in violation of their repeated promises to wait briefly for those who did have permission to move up first, and in contravention of the Nepalese authorities' instructions to stick to their own more difficult route, the result of this conflict was that eight Russian summiters and their leader have been banned from entering Nepal again for five years. The Russians complained that the American and New Zealand leaders were making large profits conducting incompetent clients whom they charged US $35,000 each, that this was merely business, and that the American leader was no gentleman in the language he used. The British made a formal complaint about a Czechoslovak who "was wandering all over the mountain: he asked if he could climb up our ropes to the west shoulder. When I said, 'No,' he came up anyway." A New Zealander, whose commercial expedition caused much of the long delay for others having to wait their turn to ascend the Hillary Step, complained of "the most frightening time of my life" when he was descending the step. Indians were ascending roped to each other but belayed to nothing else. One of them, who kept slipping, was grabbing him for a handhold "and I could see myself falling down the southwest face tied to four Indians."[22]

Out of all this melee came 55 ascents in the four days 12–15 May, beating the previous 31 ascents (also in four days) of 1990.[23] On 12 May alone, 32 people saw the top between 10.30 a.m. and 1 p.m. — six Americans, four Russians, three Indians (including a woman), three New Zealanders, two Dutch, the first Belgian woman, the first Israeli and the first Hong Kong-

Chinese together with eleven Sherpas. Three Indians died on the mountain, and a Tamang cook died of a heart attack at Base Camp.

Ascents continued in the post-monsoon period, with 32 climbers reaching the top, all via the South Col, but there were no successful ascents from the north. Included in the 'firsts' were the first Luxembourger, Eugène-Berger, and the first Peruvian, Augusto Ortega. Two expeditions, an American one led by Todd Burleson in the spring and a Franco-Italian one led by Agostino Da Polenza in the autumn, placed laser apparatus on the summit so the height of Everest could be remeasured. Three stations in Nepal and a similar number in Tibet did the measuring, but the results – 8,848.65 m. – are just a metre or so higher than the old figure and, one would have thought, well within the limits of error. Hardly worth the bother, really, though it possibly was a useful confirmation to remove any future speculation.

The 1990s saw the return of extreme skiing to the mountain. In the spring the German Reinhard Patschneider skied down the South East Ridge from approximately 8,400 m., or rather more than half way to the South Summit. Meanwhile Hans Kammerlander and Norbert Joos skied down the north side of the mountain from approximately 7,800 m. All these were beaten, however, when on 27 September the French ace Pierre Tardivel skied all the way down from the South Summit at 8,748m.

Most of this activity, both before and after the monsoon, was on the standard route via the South Col and South East Ridge. With such numbers, it is little wonder that it became called disparagingly the 'Yak Route,' but it should be remembered that the proportion of successes to attempts was probably only marginally better than it was in earlier days and that the route was much better known, especially by the Sherpas. The South East Ridge was, and is, a serious proposition, as events were soon to demonstrate.

There were many enterprising ascents and attempts during the year. A British Joint Services Expedition attempted the West Ridge, reaching it by a new line straight up from the Western Cwm. Fighting their way up through gale force winds, they doggedly established camps along the ridge until 11 May when they put up Camp V at the foot of the Hornbein Couloir and on the 17th erected Camp VI at the top of the couloir. But three days later the fierce wind destroyed Camp V, and with communications cut between the top camp and those lower down, it was decided to withdraw. Several team members were involved in the rescue of the French climber mentioned earlier and spent 14 strenuous, dangerous hours getting him down the Icefall. The leader of the British team was bitter about incompetent, badly equipped parties trying to climb Everest. 'They were literally climbing on our backs,' he said.[24]

A team, mostly from the Spanish army led by Francisco Soria, quietly and efficiently climbed the South Pillar in May, putting five people on the summit. They were well equipped and competent and, eschewing the ordinary route, chose a challenge within their abilities.

The Ukrainian climber Mikhail Turkevitch, who had climbed the South West Face 10 years earlier, returned to try again with a party of his countrymen to whom were joined three Russians and two Frenchmen, including the well-known expert, Christophe Profit. It was a post-monsoon attempt, mostly done without oxygen, and the plan was to make a direct route to the summit via the headwall that towers above the rock band. They soon concluded that this was beyond their resources and opted instead to repeat the British route of 1975.

After two weeks the team succeeded in placing three men at 8,500 m., above the rock band, but two of them became frostbitten and had to descend. Whilst his companions went down, the third man, Ukrainian Igor Svergun, decided to make a solo attempt on the summit. He crossed the face, and as daylight faded, he must have been in the gully leading to the South East Ridge, or even on the ridge itself, but Svergun was confused and had no idea where he was. As night descended, his torch batteries gave out. Struggling up in the dark, he came face to face with a steep wall festooned with fixed ropes. He couldn't tackle it in the dark so he waited for 4 hours expecting the moon to break through — forgetting that it was the time of new moon, making it practically useless as a guiding light. As Svergun stood there, wondering where he was and what to do next, a bitter wind blew up forcing him to retreat in the dark across the fearsome face. It was a formidable task.

By now Svergun had difficulty breathing (he may have been developing oedema), but by sheer chance, he came across a partially filled oxygen bottle, abandoned in some past attempt, and though he had no oxygen mask, he just opened the tap and gulped the raw gas. He eventually reached his top camp at 8,300 m. By securing the precious gas cylinder to his body with a rope, he continued down the difficult gully that cuts through the rock band, gulping air as he felt the need. After 24 hours, he reached the foot of the face (6,400 m.), but incredibly, instead of stopping, he continued down across the Cwm and through the Icefall, the bottle sliding, clanking before him and every so often providing him with vital oxygen. Amazingly he reached Base Camp little the worse after his terrible ordeal. Svergun's descent ranks high amongst the annals of Everest endurance.

In 1992, an expedition comprising four Japanese, four Kazakhs and Sherpas made yet another attempt on the obstinate North East Ridge, in attempting which expeditions seemed to run out of steam. It will be remembered that on the first attempt 10 years earlier, British climbers Peter Boardman and Joe Tasker had disappeared (see Chapter 20). They had never been found, although American climber Donald Goodman, standing on the north east shoulder of Everest in 1984, had seen coloured objects on the pinnacled section of the ridge where the two Britons had last been seen climbing. Though several attempts were made on the ridge in the next few years, none crossed the Pinnacles until Harry Taylor and Russell Brice in 1988. Struggling through a whiteout, they saw nothing of the missing climbers.

The Kazakhs and Sherpas made the route because they were more experienced than the Japanese, except for co-leader Motomo Ohmiya, who had climbed Kanchenjunga, the world's third highest peak, and several other Himalayan giants. A series of camps were established along the ridge, and 4,000 m. of rope was fixed. Camp IV was at 7,090 m., and it was just above this (at approximately 7,200 m.) that they came across signs of the 1982 British expedition by Boardman and Tasker: two sleeping bags, two rucksacks, a notebook and other small items. It seemed like the debris from a snow cave that had been destroyed by wind. A month later on 15 May as they crossed the Second Pinnacle, the Kazakhs came across the body of Boardman.[25] Then the weather closed in, and the climbers realised they could not make the summit (they were not using oxygen), so two retreated the way they had come and the other two went down via the North Col.

Meanwhile, also on 15 May, three Japanese and three Sherpas set out from Advance Base but were held up at Camp IV by bad weather for several days, after which one of the Japanese descended suffering from altitude sickness. He was accompanied by a Sherpa. The four remaining climbers struggled upwards with the two remaining Sherpas leading the way. The Japanese, Ohmiya and Manabu Hoshi, made heavy weather of the ascent, perhaps because they were not properly acclimatised. Whilst the Sherpas reached Camp VI and dumped their loads before descending the North Ridge, the Japanese were well behind.

In the meantime the Kazakhs decided to have another crack at the ridge. Setting off on 22 May, they raced up the fixed ropes conscious that time was running out for their permit. They reached Camp IV the next evening after a strenuous day's ascent, where the radio gave them the disturbing news that Ohmiya and Manabu had failed to reach Camp VI. The weary Kazakhs did not hesitate. Although it was now dark, they set off for Camp V by the light of their headtorches. They reached the camp at 5.30 a.m., brewed some tea and rested for 2 hours before setting off once again. It was a prodigious effort, but they were rewarded when at 2 p.m. they found Ohmiya on the ridge a little way below Camp VI. He was alone and in a pitiable state. He seemed confused and did not want to climb the fixed ropes despite the help, but eventually the Kazakhs got him into the tent, got the primus stove going and plied him with warm water to alleviate his dehydration. His face was badly frostbitten, and his fingers turned black. He drifted in and out of consciousness, but his rescuers could not get him to take oxygen — he insisted it was needed for the next day's ascent! Of Manabu there was nothing to be seen — only a tell-tale jumar left on the fixed rope and an abandoned ice axe.

Nobody slept that night. The next morning, Ohmiya did not want to descend, swearing at his companions as they gently forced him down the ridge towards the North Col. 'We led him downwards along the route toward the North Col, tearing ourselves away from the alluringly simple way along the ridge to the not-too-distant summit. We figured we were only about five hours from the top, but we were not fated to finish the route.'[26] Before they reached the col, however, the oxygen ran out. It was desperate work to reach the col, where an Austrian team offered them tents for the night and an American team brought them food. At last the exhausted, starving Kazakhs and their charge could eat and sleep.

Had the Kazakhs lost? Think rather that humanity had won.

As the decade advanced so did the siege of Everest. In the spring of 1993, 294 climbers attempted Everest from the southern side, of which 81 — more than one of four — reached the summit and nine more did so from the north. On 10 May, 40 men and women saw the top — a record for a single day. The season saw a dramatic rise in the number of women making the ascent, 14, compared with the previous sum total of 16. One of them, Santosh Yadav of India, became the first woman to make a second ascent.

Of all the successful climbers in spring of 1993, no fewer than 22 had climbed Everest before. This can only be accounted for by professional guiding, whether by Sherpas or Western guides: amateurs usually repeat high mountain ascents only when they are tackling a different route. Depressingly, this was not the case on Everest in 1993. All the successful teams climbed either the South East Ridge (the South Pillar variant) or the North Ridge, both considered the normal routes. Nobody attempted a new route. Not until the end of the year, in the bitter winter season, was anything significant achieved, when a strong seven-man Japanese team made a rapid ascent of the South West Face.

There were, of course, the usual plethora of 'firsts' — first Finn, Lithuanian, Taiwanese and Irish. The last was Dawson Stelfox, who has dual Irish and British nationality and so achieved the unusual distinction of making the first Irish ascent of Everest and the first British ascent of the North Ridge route! Rebecca Stephens became the first British woman to make the summit, and three Korean women did likewise for their country. The Indian Radha Devi Thakur became the youngest woman to make the ascent — 19 — whilst American Dolly Lefever became the oldest at 47. The Spaniard

Ramón Blanco, climbing on a British commercial expedition, became at age 60 the oldest person to climb Everest, though he barely survived the adventure when his oxygen ran out on the way down.[27]

After three previous attempts, Pasang Lhamu became the first Nepalese woman to make the summit – and tragically died on the descent. It was the first ascent of 1993; Lhamu knew that a powerful women's team from India that included Nepalese climbers might well be successful and deprive her of her cherished ambition. Lhamu was not an experienced climber and was notoriously slow at altitude. Led by five Sherpas, including Sonam Tshering who had climbed Everest four times previously, she set out after midnight on 22 April from the South Col and reached the top 14½ hours later – well behind schedule. On the descent from the summit to the south summit, it took 4½ hours when it should have taken less than an hour.

Tshering began spitting blood on the descent. Three of the other Sherpas decided to race ahead, but Pemba Nuru stayed with the exhausted pair at the south summit where they were all forced into an unprepared bivouac. They had no bivouac gear (not even sleeping bags) and no radio, and they had run out of oxygen. In the morning when Nuru tried to get them moving again, Tshering was too sick to stand and Lhamu kept falling over.

Nuru raced down to the South Col to get help, but the other Sherpas there were too tired to go back up. More Sherpas arrived the next day, but their rescue attempt was frustrated by high winds, and it was not for another 2 weeks that anyone was able to reach the fatal bivouac. Nuru was with the rescue crew, and he discovered Lhamu frozen to death in the position he had left her – resting against the mountain slope. Of Tshering there was no sign, just a rucksack marked his last resting place. He had probably fallen down the vast Kangshung face.

Lhamu became a posthumous heroine in Nepal. A mountaineering institute and a street were named after her, and condolences came from the king (who gave her a medal) and the prime minister (who gave $10,000 from the government to educate her children). A memorial was planned, and, the ultimate accolade, a commemorative postage stamp was to be issued.[28]

A fortnight before Lhamu's fatal dash for the summit, two climbers were seen *descending* the South East Ridge. Because nobody had gone up that way as yet, so early in the season, they could only have come from the north. And indeed they had. Heo Young-Ho was an experienced Himalayan mountaineer who had climbed Everest in 1987 by the South East Ridge. This time he was climbing the North Ridge accompanied by Ngati Sherpa, as part of a four-man Korean team.

They lost their tent in a gale, but undaunted by this, decided to climb the North Ridge and bivouac in a snow hole at 8,300 m. just below the North

East Ridge junction. The next day in a half gale, they reached the summit by mid-afternoon. In view of the weather, Heo decided that it would be safer to descend the South East Ridge, which they did, bivouacking at 8,500 m. in a shallow snow hole scooped out of the ridge. The following day, 14 April, they were dismayed to find nobody at the South Col so continued down until they came to the highest established camp, a Korean women's team at 7,200 m. Here they received food and drink — the first they had had for 37 hours. Later, at lower camps, they were able to radio their companions in Tibet who had given them up for lost. It was only the second time the mountain had been traversed north-south and the first time it had been done without support on the descent. Heo had displayed sound judgement and utter competence.[29]

In the seasons of 1994 there was little of note achieved on Everest, except perhaps the giant clean-up of the South Col by an American expedition that removed 200 discarded oxygen cylinders from the mountain. Half a dozen of the team made the summit, including Brent Bishop, the son of Barry Bishop who was on the first American ascent of 1963. There was a spring attempt on the Kangshung Face by the 1988 route, led by David Breashears, but the snow was too unstable, and the attempt was abandoned.

Breashears had climbed Everest twice before, and, in addition to the Sherpas, a number of names were beginning to appear regularly, usually associated with commercial expeditions. This year, Rob Hall and Peter Athans made their fourth ascent, Ed Viesturs made his third and Mark Whetu and Bob Sloezen their second.

The 1995 season began auspiciously, especially on the north side where the weather was unusually fine. During April and May, 74 climbers reached the top including the firsts from Brazil, Denmark, Wales, Romania, Latvia, Turkey and Argentina. On the north, Luc Jourdon made the first French ascent of that side, whilst Reinhard Patschneider, a 38-year-old Italian guide, climbing without supplementary oxygen, reached the summit in 21 hrs by the North Ridge — this beat Batard's 22½ hrs done in 1988, but Batard's ascent was 3,500 m. against Patschneider's 2,400 m. Another to reach the top from the north was George Mallory, grandson of the man who, in a sense, started it all and then disappeared on Everest in 1924.

The English climber Alison Hargreaves, 33, became the first woman to make a 'solo' ascent of Everest's North Ridge without supplementary oxygen.[30] Though not alone (there were 182 climbers on the ridge at the time), she was utterly self sufficient, refusing help or food from others. Hargreaves was a daring, ambitious climber anxious for fame and fortune who had been desperately upset when Rebecca Stephens beat her to the summit of Everest as the first British woman. Hargreaves had recently done the great north faces of the Alps in rapid succession and intended to do the three highest Himalayan peaks one after the other, too. Unfortunately, 3 months after her Everest success, she died with six others in a storm on K2, snatched from the ridge by gale force winds as she descended from the summit.

A Korean team made a post-monsoon ascent of the South West Face in 1995, but perhaps the outstanding event of the year was the completion of the North East Ridge *integrale* at long last. This was done by Japanese Nihon University, celebrating its mountaineering club's 70th anniversary. It was a large expedition (it had a scientific element as well) almost in the old style, with 13 climbers, 6 scientists, 31 Sherpas, 2 Chinese liaison officers and an interpreter. After establishing Base Camp on the Rongbuk Glacier on 25 March a series of camps was established along the ridge in the following weeks. 4,000 m. of fixed rope was used. The weather was fine, and on 9 May, Kioshi Furuno and Shigeki Imoto with 10 Sherpas, all on oxygen, left Camp V, traversed the Pinnacles and established Camp VI at 8,350 m. on a platform cut in the snow. The following day, starting at 8 a.m., they traversed upwards until below the foot of the First Step (8,560 m.) where they established Camp VII. Six Sherpas went down after erecting the tents, leaving the others to investigate the First and Second steps. They found the Chinese ladder, which had become a feature of the route, dislodged and lying on the ground, so they put it back in place ready for the morrow.[31]

They now had a bit of a problem: Camp VII could only hold four climbers, the original size planned for the summit team, so two Sherpas, probably Pasang Kami and Nima Dorje, late additions, were sent back to Camp VI from which they had to start their summit bid, tackling the First Step in the dark!

Without further problems, all six climbers reached the summit at 7.17 a.m., where they stayed for an hour before descending to Advanced Base, arriving at 6.16 p.m., just before sunset. It was an outstanding success based on the efforts that had gone before and on the unusually good weather.

The unexpected good weather, especially on the north side of the mountain, had seen 150 people reach the summit in 1995. Had the weather on the north turned nasty, according to one expert, 'There would have been dead people everywhere.' By the spring of 1996 there had been no fewer than 4,000 climbers who had attempted the mountain – 660 successfully. Of the 4,000, 142 had died — a figure that was to rise substantially as the pre-monsoon season opened again. Nemesis was waiting.

The two days of May 1996 when a storm struck the mountain, leaving people strung along the ridges like dolls on a clothes line, have gone down in mountain history as a tragedy comparable with anything occurring before. Eight people died (five on the south side and three on the north side). Ten years previous, 13 people had died in various incidents on K2, and in the 1970s, eight women died on a climb in the Pamirs. All deaths occurred on ordinary routes. It seemed as though the mountains were determined to 'apply the brakes' from time to time.

Although these tragedies were covered by the media at the time, massive publicity came in 1996 via the World Wide Web. Here is what Charlotte Fox, one of the survivors, had to say later about the three Web sites resident at Base:

> They spurred a world-wide interest in mountaineering as there had never been before, allowing Everyman to be a part of an expedition to the highest point on earth...the sites were a hit. And, for better or worse, they largely precipitated the avalanche of press that occurred later. Everyone had an angle. As you may have noticed.[32]

The Web spawned numerous articles and at least two books. In terms of worldwide publicity, there had been nothing like it in mountaineering since Edward Whymper's companions fell off the Matterhorn.[33]

Eleven expeditions assembled on the south side of Everest in the 1996 pre-monsoon season. The authorities had promised only four, but the thought of all the money waiting on the sidelines proved too much. The 'Icefall doctors,' under the command of two British climbers, Henry Todd and Mal Duff, fixed a route through the notorious seracs and announced that the Icefall was in the best condition they could ever recall. Even so, they needed 70 ladders. The expedition leaders decided a rota for ascents, and the large commercial groups led by American Scott Fischer and New Zealander Rob Hall chose 10 May. Also on that date, a small Taiwanese expedition of Chen Yu Nan and Gau Mong-Ho with their Sherpas were to attempt the ridge.

The Taiwanese suffered a setback on the evening before their final assault when Chen stepped out of the tent at Camp III to relieve himself and, not wearing proper boots, slipped on the ice and fell 80 ft down the Lhotse Face into a crevasse. Though he was rescued quickly and seemed to have no ill effects, he was unable to continue next day and in fact died as he was being taken down to Base. In Camp IV, Gau — known as Makalu Gau from his brush with that mountain – was devastated and thought his chances of reaching the summit were gone, but at midnight, under a still and starlit sky, his Sherpas persuaded him to try for the top. After all, there would be plenty of company. As he started his climb, he was encouraged to see the bobbing headlights of Fischer and Hall's teams climbing upwards to the ridge.

Hall's team had left the South Col first, half an hour before the others because they were expected to be slower. Besides the 35-year-old Hall, a black-bearded, reserved New Zealand man said to resemble Abe Lincoln, there were two other guides: Andy Harris, a fellow New Zealander, and Australian Mike Groom. In the team were Jon Krakauer (a journalist and an experienced climber), Doug Hansen, Dr Seaborn, Beck Weathers, Yasuko Namba, Dr Stuart Hutchinson, Frank Fishbeck, Dr John Taske and Lou Kasischke. Krakauer had been assigned by the magazine *Outside* to write a story about what it was like to be on a commercial Everest climb, and originally he was going to climb with Fischer's team, but in the end, the magazine got a better deal from Hall. In fact, though the cost on both expeditions was $65,000 (£41,700), few if any paid the full tariff. The exception was the tall socialite, Sandy Hill Pittman, who not only paid Fischer in full but also paid for her father to accompany them on the trek in and, for several extra Sherpas, to see to their personal needs. She was rich, she was 40, she was tough — she had already done six of the Seven Continental Summits and only wanted Everest to complete the set. She was also a journalist and operated a Web site for the American TV network NBC whilst on the trip. Hall's team could not be called a strong one when compared with Fischer's. 'It was clear to me,' wrote Krakauer, 'that none of us in Hall's group had a prayer of climbing Everest without considerable assistance from Hall, his guides and his Sherpas.'[34]

Besides Pittman, Fischer had a strong team, many with altitude experience — Charlotte Fox, 38, had climbed two 8,000 m. peaks, for example. Her friend, Tim Madsen, had no altitude experience but was strong so she persuaded him to come along. Dale Kruse, 45, a dentist friend of Fischer's, was known to have an altitude problem, but he was the first to sign up so Fischer could hardly refuse him. In the team, too, was one of the most famous names in American mountaineering, Pete Schoening, now 68 but the man who in 1953 saved five lives on K2 when he miraculously held the entire party in a fall. His nephew, Klev, was in the Everest group, too. If all went well there were several 'firsts' the team could gain: oldest person (Schoening) and first Scandinavian woman (Lena Nielson–Gammelgaard).

The leader, Scott Fischer, was the pin-up boy of the mountaineering world: 6 ft, 4 in tall with blond, flowing locks and a charismatic personality. He had climbed Everest and K2. With him was another experienced guide, Neal Beidleman, and the Russian guide Anatoli Boukreev, known as Toli. Boukreev, 38, another tall blond but with pronounced Slav features, had climbed no fewer than seven 8,000 m. peaks, some more than once and all without supplementary oxygen. He'd been up Everest twice before. Though he was immensely strong, some clients thought he had a somewhat cavalier attitude to guiding. He saw his job in terms of getting clients to the top; he was not there to socialise and certainly not to mollycoddle. Some clients resented this — they probably expected more consideration for their $65,000!

One of them referred to the guides as the 'hired help,' which probably wasn't well received! Boukreev was far and away the highest paid guide on Everest.

Even before the South Col, the mountain had taken its toll from the expeditions. Schoening and Kruse were no longer summit contenders, and several thought Fischer was looking decidedly off form, perhaps because he had been going up and down the Icefall like a yo-yo, seeing to things.

There had been a storm on 9 May, but that had blown away, and by 10 p.m. the sky was clear with the mountain illuminated by a bright moon. The omens seemed good, but already there was a serious flaw that was to cost them dearly. The fixed ropes between Camp IV and the summit were not all in place. Fixing the ropes ahead of the teams had been the responsibility of the two sirdars, Lopsang Jangbu Sherpa, from Fischer's group, and Ang Dorje, from Hall's, but this had not been done. Lopsang claimed later that he had been told by other climbers that the ropes were already in place and there was no need for him to bother. Now the ropes had to be fixed, causing delays. Beidleman and Dorje fixed the first length, then later Boukreev and Krakauer took over.

At the South Summit there was another delay whilst they waited for fresh oxygen supplies — this too should have been done – but it cost another hour. At the South Summit, Beck Weathers had had enough and decided to stay put, hoping for a guide to take him down in due course. Others were finding the going tough too: Namba, the Japanese woman, was very slow, advancing zombie-like up the narrow ridge, and Pittman, too, was exhausted. There was a turn-round time — the time by which the summit must be reached or you give up and turn round — but nobody seemed to remember clearly whether it was 1 p.m. or 2 p.m. In any case, with the summit of the world so close, who was going to turn round? All of the Fischer team that had set out made it to the summit, but of Hall's team, apart from the guides and Sherpas, only Krakauer, Hansen and Namba were successful.

Fischer himself was hurting badly. Slowly he moved up the ridge accompanied by Lobsang. They were well behind the rest of the team. As he passed Beidleman, he gasped, 'I am so tired.' The others were coming down at this point, and when they got to the Balcony below the South Summit, Charlotte Fox noticed it was already 6 p.m., an hour before dark. They plunged off the Balcony through new soft snow intent on reaching Camp IV, which they could see below, but as they neared the end of the last fixed rope, they came to a halt as Namba and Weathers were sitting exhausted in the snow. Beidleman and Groom tried to assist the stricken pair, but as they all started to move again, a violent thunderstorm broke and dark descended with all the swiftness of an Asian night.

In the darkness and storm the descent became slower still. They sensed they had reached the South Col, but at one point the little group also sensed they were about to step into a vast emptiness, and Beidleman screamed at them to back off and huddle down where they were. They could so easily step over the Kangshung Face! If they stayed immobile there was a good chance they could survive the storm.

It was a long, bitter night. The temperature was minus 40 degrees F, and the wind howled over the South Col at 70 m.p.h. They tried to keep their spirits up with shouting and slapping one another, but they were out of oxygen and their stamina was sorely depleted by lack of food and drink. Even the energy drug, destramethasone, with which they had been supplied, began to wear off and metabolism dropped to zero. Charlotte Fox wrote later: 'Finally, we just lay together in a heap and waited, I hoped, for that warm fuzzy feeling that comes with hypothermia, and death.'[35]

Eventually, the storm abated. The sky cleared, and the ghostly shapes of the mountains appeared. Encouraged by this, some members moved off to where they thought the tents were, but others were hardly able to stand, let alone walk. Five of them found themselves together: Pittman, Fox, Madsen, Namba and Weathers. Suddenly, out of the darkness appeared the tall, gaunt form of Boukreev. He gave an oxygen canister to Pittman and then took hold of Fox. Arm in arm, they stumbled through the biting wind as the Russian led her to the tents of Camp IV. He then returned to lead Pittman and Madsen back. It was a magnificent show of courage and strength on the Russian's part.[36] He had ensured that all his charges reached safety, but the leader, Fischer, lay exhausted on the mountainside with Gau, the Taiwanese climber. The next day, Gau was helped to safety, but Fischer was unable to move, a victim of cerebral oedema. Namba died during the night, but incredibly, Weathers, who had been left for dead, turned up at Camp IV the next day, having survived the night in the open.[37]

With the exception of Gau and his Sherpas, Nima Gombu and Mingma Tshering, the last people on the summit of Everest that day were the guides. It was almost 4 p.m. before Fischer started down, having spent some 15 or 20 minutes on top, complaining to Lopsang that he felt ill. He had climbed using oxygen, but now, for some unknown reason, he took off his mask, though he had plenty gas left. Shortly after Fischer, Gau and his Sherpas started down, and then Lopsang. Hall was left alone, waiting for Doug Hansen to struggle to the top, the very last of the climbers to make the summit that day.

It was now a couple of hours past the last reasonable turn-round time, so why was Hall still waiting? Krakauer[38] suggests that it might have been because 12 months previous Hall had turned Hansen round at the South Summit at 2.30 p.m. and did not want to repeat the bitter disappointment a second time. The decision was to cost both men their lives.

No sooner had Hall and Hansen begun their descent than Hansen more or less collapsed. Lopsang watched them cross the dangerous ridge to the Hillary Step, then continued his own descent. At the Step, Hall could not do anything for Hansen, who had run out of oxygen. He called for help on his radio.

There was oxygen at the South Summit. If Hall had known this he could have climbed down and taken some back to his stricken companion. Instead, the South Summit was occupied by Andy Harris, one of Hall's guides, who was in a befuddled state. He thought the canisters were empty and said so on the radio. When the descending Lopsang reached him, however, he realised his mistake and wanted the Sherpa to help him carry the canisters up to the others, but Lopsang had his own party to look after and they were now some way ahead. He declined, even though Harris offered him $500 (£320) for the carry. As Lopsang continued his downward progress, Harris shouldered the canisters and slowly made his fumbling way up towards the stricken pair.

Nobody knows what happened on that perilous storm swept ridge during the night except that Harris, by superhuman courage, probably met the other two and together they tried to reach the South Summit, with Hall and Harris helping Hansen. Only Hall made it. At 4.43 p.m., he came on the radio to say he had reached the South Summit. He was confused and slurred in speech. He had oxygen but couldn't get the valves to work. Of Hansen and Harris, there was no sign. They were never seen again.[39]

By 9 a.m. Hall had got the valves to work and was breathing gas. On the radio, his friends tried to make him descend, but he remained immobile. Half an hour later Dorje, Hall's sirdar, and Lhakpa Chhiri set out in a desperate rescue attempt, but though they reached to within 700 ft of the South Summit, the strong, cold winds eventually brought them to a halt and they were forced to turn back.

Throughout the day, Hall talked on the radio to various friends down below. At 6.20 p.m. he was put in contact with his wife in New Zealand. She had reached the summit of Everest with her husband 3 years before, so she knew what it was like on the ridge — a place from which no rescue was possible, Hall had told her. Now she had to face the reality. 'I love you,' he croaked, over the distant airwaves. 'Sleep well, my sweetheart. Please don't worry too much.'

It was Hall's final message. Twelve days later, two climbers found his body in a scoop on the South Summit, half buried in snow.[40]

Five climbers had died. The American media trumpeted it as the worst accident ever on the mountain, but this was because all the victims, bar one, were Westerners. In fact, seven Sherpas died in the very first expedition of 1922, six more in 1970 and six, together with a Frenchman, in 1974. All deaths were caused by avalanches. What was the cause of this most recent disaster? Not the storm, though that didn't help. It seems the prime cause was the slowness of Hall's party, made worse by the failure of the Sherpas to fix the ropes and to bring up the spare oxygen in time. As so often in the mountains, it was *time* that mattered most, and too much of it was lost or frittered away.

At the same time that Hansen and Hall reached the summit, a group of Indian climbers on the north side of the mountain radioed to base that they too were on top of Everest. Despite the storm raging round the peak, the top was actually clear, but the Indians did not report seeing anyone else. In fact they were still mist enshrouded, and the tragic truth is that they had mistaken a subsidiary hump for the summit. This was confirmed a few days later when some offerings to the gods were discovered some 500 ft below the summit.

The Indian team was a large one with 39 members, and by 10 May they had six climbers high on the ridge ready for the final ascent. The men all were from the Border Police in Ladakh, a Buddhist region of India bordering Tibet and sometimes called Little Tibet. They were late in getting away, and by mid-afternoon, still 1,000 feet below the top, they were hit by the storm. Three men turned back, but the remaining three, Tsewang Smanla, Tsewang Paljor and Dorje Morup, decided to press on. At 4 p.m., having reached their 'summit,' they turned and headed down the ridge. Darkness descended, and climbers stationed lower down observed the Indians' headlamps bobbing around somewhere near the Second Step. They failed to make radio contact. Nor did they make it back to their camp at 27,230 ft where a Japanese team was ensconced and ready for their own attempt.

The next morning just before 2.00, the Japanese Hiroshi Hanada and Eisuka Shigekawa, accompanied by the Sherpas Pasang Tshering, Pasang Kami and Ang Gyalzen set out up the ridge in strong winds. They reached the First Step at 6 a.m. where they discovered Paljor, badly frostbitten, lying in the snow, moaning and barely alive. Leaving him, they carried on with their ascent. Just more than an hour later, they reached the more formidable Second Step, where they were disconcerted to discover the famous Chinese ladder in a state of decay. It took 1½ hours to overcome the Step, beyond which they came across the other two Indians, Tsewang Smanla and Dorje Morup, also in a bad way. The Japanese did not stop to offer assistance but continued their ascent, into the teeth of the gale. They made the summit just before noon.

On their way down they came across the two Indians above the Step. Morup seemed dead, and his companion, barely alive, was tangled in a fixed rope. Kami freed him, then the party left him and continued on their way. Below the Steps there was no sign of the remaining Indian climber, who had presumably fallen.

Asked why they had not given assistance to the stricken men Shigekawa said, 'We were too tired to help. Above eight thousand meters is not a place where people can afford morality.'[41]

A week later, others from the Indian team made a successful ascent and discovered the bodies of their companions.

But if 1996 was a year of disaster on Everest – and others died during that fateful year [42] – it also had its triumphs. Hans Kammerlander, 39, famous for his extreme ski exploits in the Alps, made the fastest ever ascent of the North Ridge route. Climbing through the night of 23 May, he went from Base Camp to summit in 16 hrs 45 mins without supplementary oxygen, thus cutting more than 4 hours off Patschneider's record set the previous year. He then skied down the same route (except for 250 m. of rock including the First and Second Steps, presumably) in 6 hrs 45 mins, an amazing round trip of only 23½ hours!

Three days earlier on 20 May, a strong Russian team from Krasnoyarsk successfully reached the summit via the Secondary North Face, using a steep couloir of rock and snow, at one point totally vertical. They emerged onto the North Ridge at 8,250 m. from where they went to the top and made their descent by the usual route. They didn't use oxygen until reaching the ridge. This was the first ascent — indeed the first attempt — of a face that tends to be overlooked in the vastness of things and one where we can expect to see much more done in future. Unlike Fantasy Ridge on the opposite side of the mountain, which is such a blatant challenge, the Secondary North Face (between the ordinary route and the North East Ridge) with a finish to the summit will remain an intimate challenge for the discerning cognoscenti.

Along with the accidents and ascents, Everest attracted its usual quota of 'records' in 1996. David Breashears led a team to the summit with a 42-lb. IMAX-type camera on which they managed to get more than 2 minutes of sweeping vista to incorporate into a film. The film was a huge success and is still playing in most places that have access to the large IMAX screens.

Helping the IMAX team was Jamling Tenzing Norgay, the son of the Sherpa Tenzing who made the first ascent in 1953, who reached the summit with the camera team on 23 May. Also with the IMAX team was an Austrian who climbed Everest in 1978, Robert Schauer, who made a return ascent at the age of 42. The first Spanish woman to make the top, Araceliu Segarra, was also with the IMAX team. Accompanying Ang Rita on his record tenth ascent was the young Swede Goran Kropp, who cycled all the way to Everest, climbed the mountain and cycled back again. The first people from Africa to climb the peak were South Africans Cathy O'Dowd and Ian Woodall, who made the summit on 25 May. Less fortunate were Belgians Dirk Dansercoer and Daniel Hernadez, who after trying an illegal ascent in the post-monsoon period were apprehended in the Icefall and banished for 10 years!

After all the excitement of the previous year, there was no significant expedition on Everest in 1997 — just the usual plethora of commercial expeditions, some good, some not so good, and a couple that were downright fraudulent! Plans were promulgated for two ambitious traverses from Lhotse to Everest (or vice versa), one by Boukreev and another by Patschneider, but neither came to anything because Boukreev was frustrated by the weather and the fact that he seemed to have picked up an infection that sapped his normally colossal strength. Also Patschneider became ill and forced to return home. As a guide, Boukreev had been the first up Everest that year, on 26 April, with the Indonesian Army Expedition .[43]

A Russian team climbed the North Face by a variant that took in a new rib, though higher up they abandoned it to follow the usual line to the summit, which was reached by Alexandre Zelinski and Sergei Sokolov on 24 May. However, the New Zealand guide, Russell Brice, who was on the mountain at that time, disputes the Russian claim. According to Brice the two Russians climbed the ordinary North Ridge, using Brice's tents on the North Col and 'borrowing' four of his precious oxygen bottles without permission. The Russians denied this, but Brice later found the missing bottles (marked with his name) scattered up the ridge. In the post-monsoon period, nobody reached the summit of Everest — the first time this has happened in many years!

There is little doubt that disputes about claims and counterclaims have been growing in recent years. In the 1998 post-monsoon season a new record was established on the South Col route by Kaji Sherpa, 35, who claimed to have climbed the ridge in 20 hrs 24 mins, thus cutting a couple hours off Marc Batard's 10-year-old record. He was supported by other Sherpas who broke the trail and fixed rope, and he used oxygen bottles from time to time, though apparently not continuously. High winds and the time taken to fix ropes wasted 2 hours, according to the climber, who thinks it can be done in 18 hours. However, Japanese climbers on the mountain dispute Kaji's claim, and unfortunately the summit photographs are inconclusive. In turn the Nepalese disputed a claim by Carlos Pitarch of a Spanish expedition that he had reached the top via the ordinary route, two days earlier, and in this they were backed up by the Japanese. It is beginning to leave a nasty taste.

The mountain now seemed more crowded than ever. Surenra Chavan of the first non-military Indian expedition reached the summit on 18 May with Sherpas Dawa Tashi, Dawa Nuru, Thomting and Tenzing. It was the first ascent of the season, but the next day, realising the weather was fair, there was a mad dash for the summit on all sides. Nineteen climbers reached the top from the north, but on the south side, no fewer than 57 climbers formed an endless line up the South East Ridge — it must have seemed like those old pictures of the Klondike gold rush! 'It was more reminiscent of a supermarket check-out than a supposedly wild mountainside,' said one of the participants.[44]

At the Hillary Step the ridge was not roped, and the whole line was turned back by American guide Eric Simonson. Maybe time was running out and he had the spectre of what happened in 1996 at the back of his mind. Had Simonson not turned people back, it would have established a new record for the number of climbers reaching the summit in a day. Among those disappointed were Singaporeans and a Bolivian Indian, the first of their kind, as well as the first disabled climber, Tom Whittaker, who had lost a foot in a road accident. Whittaker had been on the mountain twice before, in 1989 and 1995, and turning back must have been bitter, but worse still, as he continued down from the South Col, he developed pulmonary oedema and had to take time out to recuperate. Fortunately, all these adventurers were successful a few days later. (See the list for the numerous ascents of this season in Appendix 5.) Amongst the successful climbers, was 28-year-old Sundeep Dillon, a British climber on Dave Walsh's commercial expedition who, by climbing Everest, became the youngest person to complete the Seven Summits.[45]

Perhaps the most poignant tragedy was that of 22 May when Sergei Arsentiev, a 39-year-old Russian, and his wife, Francis, a 40-year-old American, reached the summit without oxygen. It was Sergei Arsentiev's second ascent, but unfortunately Francis Arsentiev collapsed on the descent, possibly from oedema. Her distraught husband left her to summon help, but after meeting an Uzbek team and warning them of what had happened, he was never seen again. Higher up, the Uzbeks came across Francis Arsentiev – unconscious but still alive. They were joined by South Africans Cathy O'Dowd and Ian Woodall, who tried to revive her with oxygen but to no avail – she later died.

Two men climbed the mountain twice in the spring 1998 season: Tashi Tshering, a 28-year-old Sherpa, who also recorded his sixth ascent overall, and Jeff Rhoads, a 44-year-old American, who became the first non-Sherpa to climb the mountain twice in a season. In the meantime, Ang Rita's record was threatened by Apa Sherpa, who made his ninth ascent, and the American Wallace Berg, who made his fourth ascent. With the increase in commercial expeditions, multiple ascents like these will inevitably become more common. Wally Berg's ascent was in connection with a remeasuring of Everest's height. He spent 2 hours drilling two holes in the world's highest bedrock (known as Barry Bishop Ledge). A CPS receiver was mounted and data was collected. The data was retrieved by the Singapore climbers a week later. The results seem to indicate that the height of Everest will have to be reduced, but only slightly, and not enough to demote it to second place below K2.

Amongst the expeditions heading for Everest at the start of the 1999 season was one to the north side called The Mallory and Irvine Research Expedition, led by Eric Simonson, a 43-year-old guide from Washington state. The purpose of the expedition is clear from its title: to try to discover the remains of the two British climbers who disappeared so mysteriously in 1924 (see Chapter 5) and to establish whether Mallory and Irvine had reached the summit. The body of a dead Englishman from a pre-war expedition had been seen by the Chinese climber Wang Hongbao in 1975 (see Appendix 1), but Wang had been killed before he could be questioned further. An expedition to find the body in 1986 was frustrated by the weather, but nevertheless belief in Wang's testimony remained high — and the body could only be that of Mallory or Irvine.

The expedition set out in March and established itself on the mountain. On 1 May, five climbers left Camp V (25,700 ft) at 5 a.m. to go up to Camp VI, which, despite a strong wind and intense cold, they reached at about 10 a.m. The party consisted of Dave Hahn, Andy Politz, Tap Richards, Jake Norton and Conrad Anker. All were experienced mountaineers, the first four as professional guides, but Norton and Anker seemed stronger than the others, despite climbing without oxygen.

From Camp VI the team spread out into a gridlike pattern to search the slopes of the North Face. They were working according to a preconceived plan by the team's historian, Jochen Hemmleb, who concentrated on the fact that Wang had discovered a body within twenty minutes of the Chinese Camp VI. It was Hemmleb's clarity of vision that was the key to success. According to Hahn the slopes were 'Maybe the size of twelve crazily tilted football fields.'[46] It was uncomfortable, dangerous work, made more so by the lack of snow. Crampon points skated and scraped on the steeply angled tilelike rocks and one false move could mean disaster. They began by traversing directly west in order to reach an indistinct ridge that they thought was a crucial indicator of the Chinese 1975 camp, bearing in mind that

Wang had said he found a body within a few minutes of this camp. As they struck out beyond the ridge, they parted company. Hahn, Politz and Richards took a higher line than the other two, and Anker, travelling fast, was soon way beyond the others so that Politz shouted over the radio for him to come back because he was beyond the search area. He didn't and he wasn't.

As they searched the slopes the party began to come across the bodies of climbers killed in more recent times. Anker found two such bodies as he made a deep recce, almost to the edge of the shelf where it dropped away in steep cliffs to the Rongbuk Glacier. He started to zigzag back up the slope, but after about fifteen minutes, he stopped to remove his crampons so that he might get a better purchase on the rocks. As he continued, he spotted the remains of an old tent that he decided to investigate, but then he saw something else — '. . . all of a sudden I saw a patch of white, further away to the right, like marble.'[47] He went over and found Mallory's body.

The team had expected to find Irvine, not Mallory, and at first they thought it was Irvine. Influenced by the marks on the ice axe discovered in 1933, they were sure the axe had been Irvine's.[48] As it turned out, it was Mallory's body that was found below the site of the axe, but the axe was irrelevant to the discovery.

Mallory was lying on scree, face down with his arms outstretched and his hands clawing at the slope. Much of his clothing was missing, revealing a body like white marble. He wore only one clinker-shod boot, on his right foot, above which the leg was broken. As if to ease the pain of his last hours on earth, he had crossed his other leg over it and composed himself to die.

Whether there were internal injuries there was no means of knowing. The body was frozen to the earth and it could not be turned over — the discovers never saw the man's face,[49] though name tags on the clothing made his identity unmistakable. The team took a small sample of skin from his forearm for later DNA testing, just to put the matter beyond doubt.[50] They took from the body a few personal items: some letters, sun goggles, pocket knife, a handkerchief (marked 'GLM') and an altimeter. When they had finished their investigation, they performed a short burial service and covered the body with rocks. The team determined not to reveal the body's exact location.

A few interesting facts are worth noting. First, Mallory still had the remnants of a climbing rope around his waist and therefore he must have been roped to Irvine when the accident occurred — they had not parted company. Second, Mallory could not have had a big fall, or the body would have been in worse condition, but he obviously had some sort of fall, broke a leg and slid down the scree that he desperately tried to claw. His ice axe and oxygen set were missing. Did Irvine fall and pull his leader off, with the rope parting during the fall, or vice versa? And if so, where was Irvine? It was obvious from Wang's description of the body he found in 1975 that it was not the one found by the expedition. Somewhere on that vast tilted screeslope there is another body from 1924, unless, as Conrad Anker suggests might have happened, it has since been moved by an avalanche.[51]

As daylight faded on that fateful day in 1924, it seems that Mallory and Irvine fell from the Yellow Band, probably quite low down on it and not far from the safety of Camp VI. Neither were killed outright, but Mallory was mortally injured. Irvine, judging by Wang's evidence, was probably less seriously injured and had tried to make his way to Camp VI in the dark but succumbed to exhaustion.

But had they reached the summit?

Fresh bits of evidence came to light, seized on eagerly by aficionados anxious to prove Mallory's success. From a note found on Mallory, it seems they had more oxygen available than was previously thought (though he told Odell he would only carry two — 'a bloody load'). A 1924 oxygen bottle, numbered 9, was found on the ridge about 850 ft above Camp VI and 620 ft from the base of the First Step and was obviously dropped on the way up (had it been abandoned on the way down, it would certainly have been the last usable cylinder, in which case, the whole carrying frame would have been abandoned by desperately tired men to save weight). Mallory's note said the bottle contained 110 atmospheres of oxygen, so if the rate of flow was the full 2.2 litres per minute, it gives the two men a respectable climbing rate of 230 ft per hour.

We are thrown back on three crucial questions, none of which can be adequately answered: what time did the two climbers set out from Camp VI, where did Odell see them and could they have climbed up *and down* the difficult Second Step?

If they had started early, then their rate of climb, presuming they had maintained something similar, might have got them to the 'third step', which is possibly where Odell saw them. Unfortunately Odell's evidence became confused as he kept changing it. He at first thought he saw them at the Second Step and that they were late — over four hours behind schedule. That precludes the summit, at least until 7 p.m. when it would be dark, and any descent in the dark would be virtually impossible because they had left their torches at Camp VI.

Some days after the discovery of the body, Conrad Anker and Dave Hahn set out from Camp VI for the summit of Everest. Anker was particularly interested in whether the Second Step could be free climbed and whether Mallory could have done it. He found the main problem to be a corner crack, at which he removed his oxygen apparatus to tackle whilst trying to avoid the ladder placed nearby by the Chinese. He managed it, but 'At one point I was just gassed, so I stepped out onto the ladder with my right foot. I caught my breath and thought, *damn.* Then I manteled up and was on top. So I did the moves, but I rested on the ladder. I want to be upfront about that.

'The Second Step is about 90-ft long and the crux felt like 5.10 with my boots and at altitude. Even with a shoulder stand I think it improbable that Mallory and Irvine would have done it.'[52]

Anker's words bear special weight. Here is a man who not only made the first known free ascent of the Second Step (pardoning his minor transgression) but also did it *with the specific purpose of seeing whether Mallory could have done it.*

The ascent by Anker and Hahn is illuminating in other ways. They left Camp VI at 2 a.m. and reached the summit at 2.50 p.m. but did not return to Camp VI until 9.20 p.m. — and they had down clothing, fixed ropes, torches and all the paraphernalia of modern high altitude climbing. What price had Mallory and Irvine paid in their simple tweed jackets and clinkered boots?

Asked what he thought about Mallory and Irvine's final day, Anker said, 'I think they left camp late. They left their flashlights at camp, so it was dawn when they started climbing. You look at the clothing they have, and it would have been too cold for them to start at 2 in the morning.

'They then climbed through the Yellow Band, which in itself is tricky. If they had a good climbing day they got to the First Step or above it; but only maybe to the Second Step. Then they had to turn round and downclimb through the Yellow Band. I think that at the last tier they slipped and that's where the accident happened.'[53]

Nothing else matter but the timing and the technical difficulties, and that means, sadly, they didn't do it. Perhaps if the famous camera is discovered undamaged or if more oxygen bottles are discovered high up near the summit, there will have to be a reappraisal.

# *Appendix 1*
# Further Background Information to the Earlier Expeditions

Interesting information continues to turn up about the earlier expeditions. Unfortunately it is not possible to weave it into the text in the proper places because that would mean re-setting the entire book, including the index, notes etc – and one glance should tell you why the publisher wants to avoid that!

1921–24

Norman Collie's facetious remark in Chapter 2 about taking Sunlight Soap to the top of Everest in exchange for sponsorship, does not seem entirely original. I recently came across Miss Annie Peck's failure to raise sponsorship for her attempt on the South American mountain called Illampu in 1898 in which she says 'What a chance was lost for saying Soapine did it!' Collie might well have read Miss Peck's account of her adventures and the phrase stuck in his mind.[1]

There has been further elucidation of the Finch affair. Scott Russell's new edition of Finch's book *The Making of a Mountaineer* contains a fine biographical memoir of the climber, which draws on material not previously available and sheds new light on the controversy between Finch and the Everest Committee, described in Chapter 4. Scott Russell is Finch's son-in-law and he shows that the controversy was not the reason for Finch's rejection in 1924 – that had already been decided upon, for reasons which will now probably never be discovered. Unknown to me when I researched the book, the Everest Archives had been 'weeded'; an easy thing to do since they were not particularly well classified. Among the missing papers was a letter which Finch sent to the Committee to try and heal the breech between them. The letter never reached the Committee and so Finch remained persona non grata. Furthermore, it seems that Finch's rejection by the 1921 Committee on the grounds of health, was done despite evidence from a leading medical authority disputing the reports of the Committee's own doctors, Anderson and Larkins. The new evidence simply emphasises the antipathy to Finch by some powerful players in the Everest game. Personally, I suspect Hinks was behind the trouble, as usual, though Scott Russell is too polite to say so.[2]

1933

In a bookseller's catalogue there comes quotes from an autographed letter by Raymond Greene to which my attention has been drawn. It was obviously written a long time after the events but Greene draws on his diary of the time. It concerns the infamous Birnie incident when two days were lost over the establishment of Camp V, and it emphasises the quite deep divisions between the 'soldiers' and 'others' mentioned by Longland. There is no indication as to who the letter was written to or its date:

> I am alas, the only survivor of the 'incident'. Out of loyalty and affection for our companions, it has been somewhat glossed over by all who have written about it . . . There remains my diary, written at the time . . .
>
> 'Camp IV. May 20th. To us in a state of rage entered Wyn (Harris). He with Hugo (Boustead) and Bill (Birnie) had gone up to establish Camp V. The bloody army officers (as Wyn called them) at a certain point had overcome his objections and had turned back,
>
> 1. because the porters were tired, whereas Wyn said they weren't.
> 2. because there was a bad wind, whereas Wyn said there wasn't.
> 3. because they had reached Camp V, whereas Wyn said they hadn't.
>
> As to the merits of 1 and 2 we could not judge. As to 3 Wyn was obviously right. About 2 hours later, Bill and Hugo arrived, Bill nursing Hugo, apparently done, into Camp. An appalling row between Wyn and Bill broke out. W. kept his temper, Bill did not. It raged till Wyn, Waggers (Wager) and I departed to the quiet of our own tent, where Waggers cooked us an excellent dinner . . .
>
> 'May 21. I spent the morning acting as peace-maker and have I hope settled the B-W row . . . At about mid-day Hugh (Ruttledge) arrived. In the afternoon an unpleasant pow-wow took place at which Bill and Hugo were told by Hugh that their effort of the day before was the most disgraceful day in the annals of Everest . . . It may be that we lost not two days but twenty years.'[3]

What a remarkably prescient statement was that last sentence by Greene. Whether the 1933 expedition would have succeeded had Camp V been established we shall never know, but as fate would have it, it was exactly twenty years before Everest was climbed.

1936

The aftermath of the 1933 Ruttledge-Crawford controversy described in Chapter 8 is reflected in a letter from Smythe to Greene which Charles Warren has passed on to me. It is worth quoting in full; it shows Smythe's dislike of Crawford, Longland, Finch and Graham Brown (with whom he had climbed Route Major on Mont Blanc). J.M.L. Gavin was Smythe's protege and it was Smythe who had got him on the Everest expedition. He was up for election to the Alpine Club at the time of the expedition and some people thought his qualifications were weak, hence Smythe's concern.

My Dear Raymond,

Why the devil aren't you here? You would enjoy this show. It's Kamet over again and even pleasanter as not even the occasional querulousness of a 'Drawing Room Soldier' breaks the peace of as happy and united little show as has ever gone anywhere in the world.[4]

The fates are propitious. In spite of Bruce's gloomy prognostications we got over the Sebu La with the greatest of ease – a maximum of 3 ins of snow and that low down – an easier pass than the Natu, and, as according to local information it's nearly always open, why it wasn't used before – avoiding the foul Phari-Khampa marches, I don't know. R.G.S. tradition I suppose. Someone gets an idea into their noddle and there it sticks for years.

So here we are and not a sore throat in the party. We had our troubles on the Sikkim side. Hugh (Ruttledge), a nasty chill developing into a spot of bronchitis. Morris, malaria and (there was) a crop of chills among which I must number mine – now I feel fitter than in '33. The weather is quite different. From Khampa to Tinki we had very high winds but they were astonishingly warm. Here we have been positively basking in the sun which is hotter than the Riviera and there is often no wind at all until late in the day. This . . . (?) for instance we sunbathed after midday 1000 ft above the camp and were almost glad of a breeze to temper the heat. Like you, I have a hunch that this is only the beginning of good fortune. Everest has never yet been attempted by a really fit, well fed party.

The scheme barring accidents is for Eric (Shipton) and me (to have) first whack, then Wyn (Harris) and Kempson, then a full dress oxygen attempt. But the first and second parties will have 2 oxygen sets available at (Camp) 7 which is to be under the 1st Step, (Camp) 6 being at the foot of the yellow band. Smidge's (Smijth-Windham) wireless sets are most efficient and the scheme is to get one to (Camp) 5 with the first party and one to (Camp) 7 with the second party.

I think you would hardly recognize Hugh (Ruttledge) this time. He is an altogether different man. He's far happier than in '33. No man ever profited better by experience. The whole assault scheme was agreed on and by him,

Eric (Shipton), Wyn (Harris), Kempson and me – who formed a committee before we crossed into Tibet, so there was none of those interminable and profitless arguments in which Jack (Longland) was so conspicuous which used to drive me to the peace of my tent in '33. And the whole atmosphere is subtly different. No cliques, no suspicions, no backchat. Everyone out to do their damndest, an altogether different show. And in John Morris we have a pearl of great price, the exact opposite in efficiency of dear old Shebby (Shebbeare). The whole banderbast is taped from beginning to end. I am mess sec. We have an excellent cook – a scrounger of course and sometimes slow but a far better cook than Tencheddare. And no words of mine can do justice to the food – there isn't an item that isn't the best procurable. Our 3800 eggs for instance are indistinguishable from fresh eggs and the Danish bacon and ham, all the Chivers products etc etc real winners. And pressure cookers reduce Tibetan sheep to the tenderness of quails in aspic.[5]

We heard with considerable amusement the idiotic goings on at the A.C. Had Gavin been blackballed the whole expedition would have resigned en bloc. As it is I've come to the conclusion that a club that includes such as Finch and Graham Brown is not worth belonging to – as have several others. So I shall probably save my next year's sub, and do a damn good dinner on it, which is worth a year's membership of a club that has behaved so rottenly to Hugh (Ruttledge) and the show.

Well, all this sounds Utopian. We've our bloody times to go through but I do feel whatever the result there will be no backchat and recriminations for there are no shits on this show who seek to explain their own failures in the mistakes of their leader. Now that I come to think of somes (?) rotten action after Hugh (Ruttledge) had been sweating away at the book and at getting new permission and at Ferdie's (Crawford) and Longstaff's intrigue against him ably backed by Jack (Longland) at the A.C. all I can say is thank God they are not here.[6]

The porters are a splendid crowd. They have even volunteered – no suggestion from us – to carry heavier loads on the mountain. We've 3 mess tents and it is a success as (it) makes for more comfortable meals.

I'm working away at a cine film in both natural colour – the Kodachrome process – and B&W. I pray for Hugh's sake we get up for the immense work he has put into the show and the way he is running it has made him worthy of leading a successful show.

I hope all is going strong with you and that the practice is flourishing. I've heard rumours that you may join the ranks of family men. If true all the very best to you both. Kids when you haven't got them seem a nuisance – but when you have it's a different story.

Love from Hugh, Eric, Wynn and Smidge.

Yrs. Frank[7]

It is easy to see in this letter the petulance for which Smythe was noted. At the thought that Gavin might be blackballed from the Alpine Club he is like a little schoolboy issuing dire threats. His support for Hugh Ruttledge was because Ruttledge virtually handed over command to Smythe, who was thus in the happy position of being boss but not carrying the can. He doesn't seem to have much time for 'dear old Shebby' as transport officer, yet Shebbeare had twice been chosen to accompany the Germans on Kangchenjunga by their leader Paul Bauer.

It was all in vain, of course. The 1936 expedition was a total failure despite Smythe's high hopes.

There's an amusing tailpiece to this letter. According to the envelope the letter was delayed because the postmaster at Gangtok had failed to affix sufficient stamps. The postmaster was sent to jail for this offence.

### 1953

Sally Nesbitt, John Hunt's daughter, told me the fascinating story of how the news was received at the family home in Wales of the 1953 success. Sally was in the bath on the evening in question when her mother came rushing upstairs shouting 'They've done it!' The Foreign Office had rung through with the good news. Full of excitement, the family rang round all their local farmer friends and by midnight a celebratory party was in full swing. A passing stranger would have been amazed for apart from the climbers themselves and a handful of people in London, nobody else in the world outside that remote Welsh valley knew Everest had been climbed!

In the aftermath of the climb, the family were totally unprepared for the shattering deluge of publicity from the world's media. This was Noyce's 'other Everest', mentioned in Chapter 14, the Everest of publicity, which faced all the climbers and almost overwhelmed the Hunt family.[8]

### Chinese Expeditions, 1960–75

During the last ten years more detail has come out about the Chinese expeditions to Everest in 1960 and 1975, although substantially the story is the same as I have related in Chapter 15.

There seems to be some variation in the spelling of names from time to time so that for a Western observer it is not always obvious whether or not it is the same person being mentioned. In Prof. Zhou Zeng's history of Chinese mountaineering there is no mention of the expeditions of 1966–69. Instead he says:

> With the outbreak of the disastrous 'cultural revolution' in 1966, mountaineering activities were brought to a standstill. They were not resumed until 1974 . . .[9]

On the other hand a book of photographs was published in 1974 reputedly covering just this period![10] Admissions and denials seem to go hand in hand in China, even today when access is very much easier than it was. The 1978 training expedition with the Iranians did take place, however, and Zhou Zeng says it wasn't followed up because of the changed political situation in Iran.

Most interest has been created by the various things the Chinese are reported as finding on the northern side of the mountain. In 1960 they found what was almost certainly Maurice Wilson's body lying on the glacier above the old Camp III. You will remember that the body had been discovered by Charles Warren in 1935 and reburied, but glaciers have a habit of giving up their dead and the reappearance of Wilson is not all that extraordinary. The body was still there in 1965 but it had gone by 1975; how or why nobody seems to know.[11]

In 1965, near Wilson's body the Chinese found a down sleeping bag and ten unused Kodachrome films. This could only have come from the Woody Sayre illegal attempt of 1962.[12]

In 1960 the Chinese also found a pre-war oxygen apparatus at 7790 m., near Camp V. They took it back to Beijing where the oxygen was tested and found to be still usable. This could be a set which Odell left behind in 1924.[13]

Also in 1960 Shi Zhan Chun saw a wooden pole sticking out of the snow about 200 m. down the North Face from the 2nd Step. It was about an inch in diameter and three feet long. Nearby was a foot of hemp rope lying on some rock. Their position was on the approximate line taken by the summit attempt parties in 1924 and 1933, which could conceivably account for the rope, but the pole is a mystery. A similar piece of pole was found on the main Rongbuk Glacier at 5,800 m. and could have fallen from the ridge.[4]

By far the most intriguing of these Chinese mysteries occurred during the Sino-Japanese Reconnaissance of 1979. A Chinese climber called Wang Hongbao told Ryoten Hasegawa, the leader of the climbing party, that during the 1975 Chinese expedition he had seen *two* English dead from pre-war days. One was near Camp III on the East Rongbuk Glacier and was obviously Maurice Wilson, but who was the second? Wang said the body was on the ridge at about 8100 m. and when he touched the man's clothes they had crumbled to dust and blown away in the wind. He had covered the body with snow.

Communication between the two climbers was difficult as neither spoke the other's language, but Hasegawa managed to ask was it a Russian, possibly thinking of the often rumoured Russian expedition of 1952 when six climbers were reputed to have been killed. But Wang denied that Russians had ever got that high on the North Ridge. 'English, English,' he repeated.

When Hasegawa realised the implications of what Wang was saying he was awestruck: the body could only be that of Mallory or Irvine.

But Everest keeps its secrets. The very next day after he had told his remarkable story to Hasegawa, and before he could be questioned further, Wang and two comrades were killed by an avalanche.[15]

The immediate effect of this disclosure was to alert climbers to the chance of rediscovering the body on the ridge, and perhaps even the camera whose films would still be decipherable given careful developing. The 1986 American North Col expedition had the search for the body as part of its aims and included Tom Holzël, who has long believed that Mallory climbed the peak (see Chapter 5). The expedition was frustrated by the weather and so far no further discoveries have been made. The 1986 expedition was criticised in some quarters on the grounds that even if it was Mallory or Irvine, the body should be left in peace.

Wang's story also gave rise to a conspiracy theory. It was argued in some quarters that the Chinese would deliberately hide the body and say nothing about it officially just in case it proved that Mallory and Irvine had reached the summit by the North Ridge in 1924, and thus rob the Chinese of their first ascent in 1960.

The Chinese reaction was to deny the story. Leaders of the 1960 expedition wrote that Wang was never on the ridge alone and would have had no opportunity to discover anything by himself. They imply that language difficulties between the two men made misunderstanding likely and their article concludes:

> Even if there is to be some conclusive evidence which proves that Mallory and Irvine did reach the summit in 1924, that would not in the least narrow the significance of the success of British climbers in ascending the summit from the southern slope in 1953 and that of Chinese climbers from the northern slope in 1960. Chinese climbers would be highly elated and draw immense encouragement from these achievements.[16]

It would be inappropriate to close this appendix without mentioning those Everesters who have passed away since the first edition of the book. Many of them were my friends and I will always recall the indomitable Whillans sitting in our kitchen with a mug of tea and a butty, having called in for a chat on his way north; or the bright-eyed, slightly fey, Peter Boardman telling me how, during the ascent of the South West face of Everest, he had waited for the vanished Mick Burke while the storm gathered and night approached. Peter didn't smoke, but as he told his story in a Kathmandu bar, only a few days after the event, he smoked incessantly, nerves a-jangle. 'Don't tell my mum, Walt,' he grinned, indicating the cigarette, 'or there'll be hell to pay.' Now Whillans and Boardman are both gone; Don from a heart attack and Peter making another attempt on the world's highest mountain.

Other people not to be forgotten are Uemura, Unsoeld, Raymond Greene,

John Noel, Mike Cheney – some moderns, some old timers. Noel Odell, the last person to see Mallory and Irvine, passed away as did Tenzing, the first man ever to set foot on the roof of the world. And at the age of 90, his contributions to the Everest story almost forgotten, that old rogue and general factotum of the pre-war expeditions, Karma Paul, passed away peacefully in Darjeeling.[17]

'The mountains give and the mountains take,' Don Whillans once said, and as this book goes to press there is the sad news of the deaths of Sungdare and Jerzy Kukuczka, two outstanding Everest climbers. Sungdare drowned in the Dudh Kosi. He was 34 and had climbed Everest no fewer than five times. Kukuczka, who was 41, died on the South Face of Lhotse. He had climbed all the world's 14 eight-thousanders and was responsible for the Polish Route (South Pillar) on Everest in 1980. Their stories are related in Chapters 20 and 21.

## *Appendix 2*

# The Height of Everest

Because both Nepal and Tibet excluded foreigners until comparatively recent times the inaccessibility of Mount Everest led to continuous controversy over the mountain's height and name.

Until the middle of the last century Kangchenjunga (28,307 ft), a peak to the east of Everest, on the Sikkim border, was regarded as the highest mountain in the world, having supplanted Dhaulagiri (26,811 ft) in that respect some years previously. In 1849, however, the Great Trigonometrical Survey of India began a series of triangulations which included the mountains of Nepal. The task of the surveyors was particularly difficult because they were not allowed into Nepal itself and had to content themselves with observations made from the plains and foothills of India. Faced with a distant jumble of high peaks, the nearest ones hiding all but the very tips of those on the far-away Tibetan border, the surveyors did what they could in trying to make sense out of the tangle. Few of the mountains had names known to the surveyors, so they were all given Roman numerals – Kangchenjunga, for instance, was Peak VIII. Everest was Peak XV.

Not until 1852 were the recordings taken in the field completely analysed and computed. One day, the legend goes, the Bengali chief computer, Radhanath Sikhdar, rushed into the office of Sir Andrew Waugh, the Surveyor General in Dehra Dun, and exclaimed, 'Sir! I have discovered the highest mountain in the world!' The story was first told by Younghusband, but later writers connected with the India Survey, such as Burrard, Gulatee and Mason, have pointed out that the discovery of Everest's height was the corporate work of field surveyors and computers and not that of any one man – certainly not Radhanath Sikhdar, anyway, since he left Dehra Dun in 1849 and played no part in computing Everest's height. The chief computer at the time was an Anglo-Indian named Hennesy.[1]

Six observation stations had been used for the sightings of Peak XV with the average distance over which the readings were taken being 111 miles. The computed *average* height, with corrections, was 29,002 ft. This remained the officially accepted height for Everest until 1955.[2]

It was not correct. How could it be with the observations taken at such great distances? Even with the finest of instruments, every error in measuring the vertical angle greatly magnifies the error of the final result when the longitudinal distance is great – and there are enough problems to be grappled with in computing the height of a mountain without adding to them in this way. The surveyors realized this, of course, and knew that their final figure was little more than informed guesswork.

The problems in determining the height of a mountain such as Everest were outlined by B.L. Gulatee, Director of the Geodetic and Training Circle, Survey of India, writing in the *Himalayan Journal* of 1952. Speaking of measuring vertical angles he says:

> The most accurate method is, of course, spirit levelling, which apart from the disadvantages of being very slow is quite inapplicable to high peaks. So long as the surveyor's work is confined to short rays to hills of moderate height all is plain sailing, but with lofty peaks observed from great distances numerous complications set in and the problem comes within the domain of higher geodesy, involving a knowledge of advanced theory of refraction, plumb-line deflexion, gravity, geoids, datums of reference, and so on. Indeed many of the technical considerations cannot be elucidated in simple language and even geographers find them difficult.[3]

Nevertheless, some hint of the practical difficulties can be grasped fairly easily – enough to recognize the complexities of the problem and why the height of Everest is by no means certain.

One of the prime difficulties is in choosing a datum level from which to calculate the height. Obviously this level must be the same over a wide area (India, for example) or the relative heights in that area would lose all meaning. The geoid is the level used most frequently – that is, mean sea level *at the point in question*. Obviously, since the sea does not actually penetrate into the Himalayas it has to be imagined as doing so through some hypothetical canal. If this canal ran through the base of Everest, the height of the mountain would be the difference between the water surface and the summit.

The problem is that the water surface in such a canal would not be at the same level as it is on the coast, where the actual measurement takes place. The huge mass of Everest above the water would pull it up by gravitational force, perhaps by as much as 150 ft, but since there are insufficient data available to make a correct assessment of the mountain's mass the exact effect of the pull is not known. So, right from the start, there is a source of error in any calculation of the mountain's height.

Another major source of error is the refraction of light rays passing between the summit and an observer's theodolite. The light does not travel in a straight line but is refracted according to the changing density of the air through which it passes. There is a time of minimum refraction which leads surveyors to observe vertical angles only between noon and 3 p.m., as readings taken over a distance of 100 miles can vary by 200 seconds of arc between morning and afternoon. Also, the shorter the distance involved, the less the refraction, but as the early Everest surveyors were working from an average distance of 111 miles, the error due to refraction was considerable – in fact they applied a correction factor of 1,375 ft.

Two other sources of error are easily understood. In high mountain country the liquid levels, by which instruments are set, are pulled upwards by the gravitational forces of large mountain masses, and as a result the observed angles are too small. Only approximate corrections can be applied to take account of this.

Finally, on a mountain such as Everest, the amount of accumulated snow on the summit must fluctuate from season to season, and year to year. As nothing can possibly be known of this, it must remain a permanent source of error.

These examples should be sufficient to show why the height of Everest has been altered over the years to the present figure of 29,028 ft. Even this can only be regarded as the best figure obtainable to date, with no claim to certainty.

It follows from these considerations that if the height of the mountain is not known exactly, then neither are the heights of intermediate points on its ridges and faces. Over the years since it was first measured, Everest has officially 'gained' 26 ft (at one stage it actually 'gained' more than this, but was reduced again) and so the heights reached by various expeditions should be raised in proportion. But this is a somewhat pointless exercise, compounding inaccuracies, and so throughout this book all the heights given have been those calculated or estimated *at the time of the event.*

Only one thing is certain regarding the height of Everest: it is the highest mountain in the world.

Assertions to the contrary have not been wanting over the years. One of the earliest is in a letter from the mountaineer W.W. Graham to the editor of the *Alpine Journal* and dated 3 November 1883. Graham was the first climber to visit the Himalaya simply to enjoy the climbing or, as he put it, 'more for sport and adventure than for the advancement of scientific knowledge'. He visited Sikkim and in his letter wrote:

> By the way, I believe that Mount Everest will have to take a back seat. From the western peak we climbed, west of Kang La, we had a glorious view; and two peaks north-west of Everest are, we were all agreed,

considerably higher.[4]

Probably Graham mistook Makalu for Everest and the two peaks to the north-west were in fact the real Everest and Lhotse. Graham was a very good climber (he made the first ascent of the Aiguille du Géant in 1882) but, presumably because he was out simply for enjoyment, was more than a little confused about his exact whereabouts in the Himalaya. His claims regarding his achievements in Sikkim, where he claimed to have climbed Kabru (24,002 ft), and in Garhwal, where he claimed the first ascent of Changabang (22,520 ft), are now generally discounted, though they caused heated discussions in mountaineering and geographic circles at the time.

More recently, in 1944, American Air Force pilots based in China reported that when flying at more than 30,000 ft they observed a peak which was a thousand feet higher than them. Its location was north-west of Chengtu in West Szechuan province, but the Chinese have never confirmed the existence of such a mountain. It is more than likely that the pilots' altimeters were wrong and the mountain they saw was Amne Machin (23,491 ft), whose ascent was accomplished by the Chinese in 1960.

★ ★ ★

Since the publication of the first edition a closer study of the evidence leads me to suspect that the computation of Everest's height might have been done by Radanath Sikhdar after all. It depends on whether you believe S.G. Burrard or R.H. Phillimore, both historians of the Survey of India. According to Burrard:

> About 1852 the chief computer of the office *at Calcutta* (author's italics) informed Sir Andrew Waugh that a peak designated XV had been found to be higher than any hitherto measured in the world.[5]

The chief computer at Calcutta was undoubtedly Radanath Sikhdar (1813–1870). He had joined the Survey in 1831 as a computer and had worked with Sir George Everest personally for five years. Everest called him 'his right arm'. Along with the rest of the Surveyor General's field office, Sikhdar moved from Dehra Dun to Calcutta in 1849.[6]

If the figures were sent to Calcutta for computation, then Sihkdar almost certainly was in charge. But were they?

According to Phillimore,[7] the computations took place in Dehra Dun. Andrew Waugh, who took over from George Everest as Surveyor General, had elected to stay in Dehra Dun and sent his deputy, Henry Thuillier, to Calcutta to take charge there. So there were two centres where the work could be done: Calcutta, the erstwhile capital of British India, with Thuillier and Sikhdar, and Dehra Dun, traditional home of the Survey, with Waugh, John Babonau Nichterlein and John B.N. Hennesy.[8]

Hennesy was an Anglo-Indian, son of an army storekeeper, who had served in the Survey for a few years before making his way to England where he studied mathematics at Jesus College, Cambridge. He returned to India and was put in charge of the Survey HQ at Dehra Dun. Hennesy it was who invented the system of numbering the peaks with Roman numerals, starting in the east, which gave the future Everest number XV.[9]

Phillimore says the computations were done in Dehra Dun by Waugh, Nichterlein and Hennesy. The work was not completed until March 1856, when Waugh wrote to Thuillier in Calcutta:

> *We have for some years known that the mountain is higher than any hitherto measured in India, and most probably the highest in the world.* In justice to my able assistant J. Hennesy, it is proper that I acknowledge that I am greatly indebted to him for his cordial cooperation *in revising these computations.*[10]

The italics are mine. It seems to me that what Waugh is acknowledging in this letter is the fact that there already existed some previous calculations for Everest, perhaps preliminary and rough ones, and that Hennesy had revised these to produce a final published version. It could be that Radanath Sikhdar had made these preliminary calculations, and hence the confusion. Both Sikhdar *and* Hennesy had worked on the figures.

# *Appendix 3*
# Everest's Name

For thirteen years after it was found to be the highest mountain in the world, Peak XV had no officially accepted name, but in 1865, at the suggestion of Sir Andrew Waugh, Surveyor General of India, it was named after his immediate predecessor, Sir George Everest, the man most responsible for the Great Trigonometrical Survey. It has been said of Sir George that no man before or since has done as much for the geography of Asia, and it would seem a fitting tribute that his name should be attached to the highest of the great peaks his methods had helped to survey.

But Everest himself was not all that keen on the idea. In 1857, at a meeting of the Royal Geographical Society where it was being discussed, he said that while he found it gratifying:

> Yet he must confess there were objections to his name being given to this mountain which did not strike everybody. One was that his name was not pronounceable by the native of India. The name could not be written in Persian or Hindi, and the natives could not pronounce it.[1]

He was in a delicate position. While he did not wish to offend his devoted followers in the Survey, he knew that to give his name to an Asian mountain could create an unwelcome precedent. The official policy was that mountains should be given the name by which they are known locally, and this policy was strongly supported by the leading geographical societies of the world.

Waugh, however, had been determined to honour his old chief. As early as 1856 he had informed Sir Roderick Murchison, President of the Royal Geographical Society, about his suggestion, justifying it on the grounds that so long as his officers were debarred from entering Nepal it was not likely that he would be able to discover a local name for the mountain. Murchison agreed to support him in what was really a charade, for both men knew that local names for Peak XV were not wanting.

Fortunately for Waugh's plans the reports were conflicting. In 1855, after the height of Peak XV and the fact that it was the highest mountain in the world had been revealed, Brian Hodgson, who had for some years been a Political Officer in Nepal and was a noted linguist, announced that it was known locally as Devadhunga. At the same time the three Schlagintweit brothers, well-known German explorers, reported that the peak was called Gaurisankar in Nepal and Chingopamari in Tibet. Waugh discounted these names as unsubstantiated.

Others were less sure. Some pointed out that Hodgson knew the country well, which Waugh's surveyors did not, and that the name Devadhunga, meaning 'The Abode of Deity', gave the mountain the religious significance one would expect in a Buddhist country like Nepal.[2]

On the other hand, the name of Gaurisankar was already well known and did seem to be based on fact. Much to the dismay of Waugh, it was provisionally adopted by the Royal Geographical Society in 1862 and universally used on continental maps. In Britain, Douglas Freshfield, a leading figure in both the Royal Geographical Society and the Alpine Club, vigorously supported the name of Gaurisankar whenever the matter appeared in print and, even after the Society changed its mind and adopted the name of Mount Everest in 1865, continued to use Gaurisankar. He would never write the name Everest except in inverted commas, to show his disapproval. In 1882 he wrote:

> I trust that all geographers, or at any rate all mountaineers, will revert to the ancient and natural name for the mountain. With every respect for the worth of the 'Indian Survey' it is impossible to acquiesce in the attempt permanently to attach to the highest mountain of the world a personal and inappropriate name in place of its own.[3]

The controversy rumbled on for nearly half a century and it was not until 1903, when Lord Curzon, as Viceroy of India, sent Captain Henry Wood, R.E., into Nepal to sort the matter out that it was conclusively demonstrated trigonometrically that Everest and Gaurisankar were two different peaks thirty-six miles apart.

So Waugh had been vindicated. Devadhunga was unknown and Gaurisankar was a different peak altogether. Sir Sidney Burrard, writing in 1907, said,

> After fifty years of controversy no true native name has been produced for Mount Everest: each of those suggested has in time been shown to be inapplicable, and the evidence that no such name exists is overwhelming.[4]

But Burrard was wrong, indulging in wishful thinking out of loyalty to the

Survey. There was plenty of proof that the native name for Everest was Chomolungma.

As early as 1733, D'Anville of Paris had published a map of Tibet which correctly marked the position of the mountain and labelled it 'Tschoumou-Lancma'. The map was based on the work of a group of French Capuchin friars who lived in Lhasa from 1707 to 1733 and who had returned through Western Tibet, constructing a rough map of their journey. If the name Chomolungma (whatever its spelling in Western script) was so easily obtainable by a group of travelling monks, it seems incredible that it was not known to the Indian Survey more than a hundred years later.

In fact it seems to have been deliberately ignored by Waugh in his rigid determination to honour Sir George Everest. Later travellers heard the name commonly used. Charles Bruce and Dr Kellas heard it from their native porters in the early years of this century, and the first expedition to the mountain in 1921 received a passport addressed from the Dalai Lama to various officials which stated, 'You are to bear in mind that a party of Sahibs are coming to see the Chha-mo-lung-ma mountain . . . '

In Tibet itself members of that expedition heard the mountain invariably referred to as Chomolungma and Douglas Freshfield, though by then in his late seventies, eagerly took up the old theme:

> The expedition to the Himalaya of 1921 has accomplished one remarkable feat which has as yet hardly obtained a recognition it deserves. It has succeeded where the endeavours of the Survey of India during the past sixty-six years had singularly failed.[5]

The evidence rather suggests that the Survey of India knew all about Chomolungma but chose to ignore it on the grounds that it was imprecise to the point of uncertainty. Their case was helped by variations in spelling, such as are bound to occur when an eastern word is transcribed into English – for example *Chomolungma* means 'Goddess Mother of the World' and is wholly appropriate for the name of a mountain, whereas *Chamalung* (an alternative version of the name given on the Tibetan passports of 1921–4) could mean 'Bird Land', which patently refers to a district rather than a peak.

Evidence that the name referred to the mountain and not the district comes from a booklet which the Head Lama of Rongbuk presented to some members of the 1936 expedition. The booklet was intended for pilgrims and in describing the founding of the monastery it says:

> At that time in a place where the auspicious long-lived five sisters . . . walked the earth, in view, namely of the high, self-created, ice mountain named Jo-mo-glan-ma, he . . . blessed the place to be a chief scene of spiritual attainment. Especially Mkhan-pa-lun . . .[6]

Mkhan-pa-lun means the Abbot's Ravine, that is, the site of Rongbuk monastery, and the mountain which dominates Rongbuk is Mount Everest. There can be no doubt that the Jo-mo-glan-ma referred to in the booklet is identical with the peak we call Everest.

The Survey of India eventually modified their attitude by suggesting that Chomolungma referred to the Everest massif as a whole rather than the peak itself. It is actually the *peak* which dominated Rongbuk, but nevertheless experiences from other remote areas of the world have shown that local people usually give a name to a massif rather than individual peaks because the massif has relevance to their lives in that it brings rain or avalanches or prevents them from reaching the next valley. Individual summits have no meaning for them. Even the Head Lama of Rongbuk, in his diary, says: 'In the southern part . . . there is a mountain called by the *general* name Jo-mo-glan-ma.'[7]

Only climbers need to differentiate between the various summits of a massif and they usually give the name of the massif to the highest peak. Had Everest been discovered and named by climbers it would certainly have been called Chomolungma.

Recent large-scale maps have opted for the compromise: on them the massif is called Chomolungma, and the peak itself Mount Everest.

One wonders how the story would have developed had Sir George Everest been called Sir Cuthbert Shufflebottom instead. Perhaps even Waugh would have been less keen on Mt Shufflebottom, for indisputably Everest as a name has a fine ring to it. It *sounds* right for the highest mountain in the world. As long ago as 1920 Sir Francis Younghusband had put into words what most people thought on the subject:

> It would be a great misfortune if the beautiful and suitable name of Mt Everest was ever changed, even though it is actually the name of the late and honoured Surveyor General and not a native name . . . Even if this proposed expedition (1921) finds its real name written clearly upon the mountain, I hope it will take no notice, as I am sure you will agree that no name is so beautiful and suitable as Mt Everest.[8]

And most of the world agrees. Only the Chinese call it Chomolungma, or a variant of it, and even though history is on their side, there is much in what Kenneth Mason says: 'Surely after a hundred years, the world should be content with Everest.'[9] Content or not, the world is probably stuck with it.

No more English names were bestowed on peaks in the Everest region. When the 1921 reconnaissance expedition explored the area, Mallory tried to name various peaks with English names but he was overruled and Tibetan ones were invented for them. Usually they were simple and descriptive, but nobody can deny that to Western ears they sound more fitted than their English equivalents – Changtse sounds better than North Peak, which is what it means, and similarly Lhotse is preferable to South Peak, Nuptse preferable to West Peak.

Curiously enough, the Government of Nepal has in recent years invented yet another name for Everest – Sagarmatha – and a large area of the Khumbu is designated the Sagarmatha National Park. Nobody will take any notice: certainly not the local inhabitants. In October 1975 I was walking through the Sagarmatha National Park with a Sherpa guide and a porter. The porter was a simple, illiterate peasant, the guide one of the modern breed well educated at the school in Khumjung. When Everest came into view I turned to the guide and said, 'Ask Lapka what he calls that mountain,' which he did.

'Chomolungma,' said Lapka, without hesitation.

*Appendix 4*

# Summary of Expeditions to Mount Everest 1921–98

1921

FIRST EVEREST RECONNAISSANCE EXPEDITION (British)

Leader: Lt Col. C.K. Howard-Bury
Climbing Leader: H. Raeburn. When sickness forced his retirement from the expedition, this post was assumed by G.H. Leigh Mallory
Dr A.M. Kellas, G.H. Bullock, Dr A.F.R. Wollaston, Major H.T. Morshead and Major E.O. Wheeler (both from the Survey of India and accompanied by three native surveyors), Dr A.M. Heron (Geological Survey of India)
Interpreters: Gyalzen Kazi and Ghhetan Wangdi

The expedition explored the northern approaches and the Rongbuk and West Rongbuk Glaciers. Mallory and Bullock found the approach over the East Rongbuk Glacier to the North Col.
(Dr Kellas died near Kampa Dzong on the approach march, and a coolie died at Tingri Dzong. Kellas was the oxygen expert for the expedition and as a result of his death oxygen was not therefore used at all.)

1922

SECOND EVEREST EXPEDITION (British)

Leader: Brigadier General C.G. Bruce
Deputy Leader: Lt Col. E.L. Strutt
G.H. Leigh Mallory, Major E.F. Norton, Major H.T. Morshead, G. Ingle Finch, Dr T.H. Somervell, Dr A.W. Wakefield, Capt. J.B.L. Noel,

C.G. Crawford, C.J. Morris, Capt. J.G. Bruce, Dr T.G. Longstaff
Interpreter: Karma Paul
Sirdar: Gyaljen (Gyalzen Kazi of the previous year)

Following the East Rongbuk Glacier and the North East Ridge, a height of 8,320 m. was reached by G.I. Finch and J.G. Bruce using oxygen. Seven Sherpa porters were killed by avalanche below the North Col on 7 June: Lhakpa, Nurbu, Pasang, Pema, Sange, Dorje and Remba.

1924

THIRD EVEREST EXPEDITION (British)

Leader: Brigadier General C.G. Bruce, but when Bruce contracted malaria on the march-in, the leadership was taken over by Lt Col. E.F. Norton
G.H. Leigh Mallory, Capt. J.G. Bruce, E.O. Shebbeare, N.E. Odell, Major R.W.G. Hingston (Doctor), Dr T.H. Somervell, Capt. J.B.L. Noel (Photographer), A.C. Irvine, B. Beetham, J. de V. Hazard
Interpreter: Karma Paul
Sirdar: Gyaljen

Norton reached a height of 8,580 m. (without oxygen); Mallory and Irvine were lost somewhere above 8,450 m. and when last seen were 'going strong for the top', but it is regarded unlikely that they reached it.
There were two other losses by death on this expedition: Lance-Naik Shamsherpun, a Gurkha, died of a brain haemorrhage, and Man Bahadur, Assistant Bootmaker, died of pneumonia following severe frostbite.

1933

FOURTH BRITISH EXPEDITION

Leader: H. Ruttledge
F.S. Smythe, C.G. Crawford, E.E. Shipton, Dr R. Greene, Capt. E. St J. Birnie, P. Wyn Harris, L.R. Wager, J.L. Longland, Major H. Boustead, T.A. Brocklebank, Dr W. McLean, G. Wood-Johnson, E.O. Shebbeare
Wireless Operators: W.R. Smyth-Windham, E.C. Thompson
Interpreter: Karma Paul
Sirdars: Lewa, Nursang and Sanam Topgye

Camp VI was established at 8,350 m. Three climbers – P. Wyn Harris climbing with L. Wager, and later F.S. Smythe climbing alone – reached approximately 8,580 m., the same height as Norton in 1924.
(On this expedition an ice axe was found which must have belonged to either Mallory or Irvine.)

This same year the Houston Mount Everest Expedition twice flew over the summit of Everest in light aeroplanes and took aerial photographs.

1934

SOLO ATTEMPT

Maurice Wilson, eccentric, ex-Captain of the British Army, attempted the North Col route alone. He had crossed Tibet in disguise with three Sherpas, Tewang, Rinzing and Tsering, who waited for him in vain at Camp III. Wilson's body was found in 1935 at a height of 6,400 m. close to the 1933 food dump (and was rediscovered in 1960 by the Chinese expedition).

1935

BRITISH RECONNAISSANCE EXPEDITION

Leader: E.E. Shipton
L.V. (Dan) Bryant, E.G.H. Kempson, H.W. (Bill) Tilman, Dr C.B.M. Warren, E.H.L. Wigram and M.A. Spender (Surveyor)
Interpreter: Karma Paul, assisted by Dawa

This small expedition busied itself in the Everest area, exploring, surveying and mapping, only reaching the Rongbuk valley on 4 July. The North Col was reached on 12 July but it was too late in the season for a serious attempt on the mountain. M. Spender made a photo-theodolite survey of the Everest region from the north. (Among the porters was a young Sherpa, Tenzing, who carried to the North Col. This was the first of his seven expeditions to Everest, culminating in the first ascent in 1953.)

1936

SIXTH BRITISH EXPEDITION

Leader: H. Ruttledge
F.S. Smythe, E.E. Shipton, P. Wyn Harris, E.G.H. Kempson, E.H.L. Wigram, Dr C.B.M. Warren, P. Oliver, J. Gavin, C.J. Morris, Dr G.N. Humphreys
Wireless Officer: W.R. Smyth-Windham
Interpreter: Karma Paul
Lead Sherpas: Ang Tarkay, Ang Tsering

This expedition was repulsed by an early onset of the monsoon, but the western slopes of the North Col were examined and pronounced to be 'not impossible'.

1938

## BRITISH EXPEDITION

Leader: H.W. Tilman
E.E. Shipton, F.S. Smythe, N.E. Odell, C.B.M. Warren, P. Lloyd and P.R. Oliver
Interpreter (and 'general factotum'): Karma Paul
Sirdar: Angtharkay (sometimes written Ang Tarkay)

This small expedition again met with very heavy snow conditions and an early monsoon. They reached 8,320 m. only, but they did it much more cheaply than earlier expeditions.

During the Second World War and in 1947 various serving airmen made unauthorized flights over Everest.

1947

## SOLO ATTEMPT

Earl Denman, a Canadian, disguised as a Tibetan and with two Sherpas – Tenzing and Ang Dawa – made an illicit journey across Tibet to Everest and climbed to just below the North Col (*c.* 7,150 m.).

1950

## ANGLO-AMERICAN NEPAL RECONNAISSANCE

O. Houston, Dr C. Houston, H.W. Tilman, A. Bakewell and Mrs E.S. Cowles
Sherpas: Gyalgen, Da Namgyal, Pa Norbu and Saki; also a young Sherpa Danu (said to be a brother of Angtharkay); and 'Dicky', a Sherpani (believed to be wife of Saki)

While this was not a mountaineering expedition, it was the first party to be allowed access to the Sola Khumbu region and it reconnoitred the route to the Khumbu Glacier, which they followed to the foot of the Icefall. Climbing to a vantage point on the west of the glacier, they had hoped to see into the Western Cwm and to the South Col, but it was shielded by a shoulder of Nuptse.

1951

## ANOTHER CLANDESTINE ATTEMPT

K.B. Larsen (Denmark) left Darjeeling with four Sherpas. Crossing into

Nepal he engaged three more Sherpas, and at Namche Bazar enlarged his Sherpa team to twelve. Failing to cross into Tibet by the Lho La, he managed to traverse the Nangpa La and travelled on to Rongbuk. Just below the North Col his Sherpas refused to go any further and he was forced to abandon his attempt on Everest.

1951

RECONNAISSANCE EXPEDITION (British)

Leader: E.E. Shipton
M.P. Ward, T. Bourdillon, W.H. Murray and New Zealanders E. Hillary and H. Riddiford
Sirdar: Angtharkay
(Dr Dutt of the Geological Survey of India was also attached to the expedition)

This was a post-monsoon exploratory expedition on behalf of the Alpine Club and the Royal Geographical Society. It explored the Nepal approaches to Everest and climbed the Khumbu Icefall, almost into the Western Cwm.

1952

THE SWISS EXPEDITIONS

Two expeditions sponsored by the Swiss Foundation for Alpine Research made serious attempts to climb Everest from the south:

THE SPRING ASSAULT:

Leader: Dr E. Wyss-Dunant
G. Chevalley, R. Lambert, R. Dittert, L. Flory, R. Aubert, A. Roch, J.-J. Asper, E. Hofstetter
Sirdar: Tenzing
(Also included were two naturalists: Dr A. Lombard and A. Zimmermann)

The expedition climbed the Geneva Spur to the South Col. Lambert and Tenzing reached a high point of 8,595 m. on the South East Ridge.

POST-MONSOON ATTEMPT:

Leader: G. Chevalley
R. Lambert, E. Reiss, J. Buzio, A. Spöhel, G. Gross, N.G. Dyhrenfurth
Sirdar: Tenzing

A Sherpa, Mingma Dorje, was killed by falling ice while fixed ropes were being set up on the Lhotse Face. Despite this the route up the face was opened up and the South Col reached; this has since become the classic route. Bad weather prevented the climbers from progressing beyond the South Col.

1952

Frequent reports have told of a Soviet attempt on Everest from the Tibetan side during October. The attempt was unsuccessful and it was said that six climbers, including the leader, Pawel Datschnolian, were killed.

1952

In preparation for their 1953 expedition, British and New Zealand climbers went to Cho Oyu.
Leader: E.E. Shipton
L.G.C. Pugh, C. Secord, A. Gregory, T. Bourdillon, R. Colledge and New Zealanders: G. Lowe, H. Riddiford, E. Hillary, C. Evans

1953

BRITISH EXPEDITION: FIRST ASCENT

Leader: Colonel H.C.J. Hunt
Deputy Leader: Dr R.C. Evans
G. Band, T. Bourdillon, A. Gregory, E.P. Hillary, W.G. Lowe, C.W.F. Noyce, Dr M.P. Ward, M. Westmacott, C.G. Wylie
Physiologist: L.G.C. Pugh
Cameraman: T. Stobart
Correspondent for *The Times*: J. Morris
Sirdar: Tenzing (known variously as Tenzing, Khansana, Tenzing Bhotia or Tenzing Norgay)

This was a strong, well-led, well-equipped and determined expedition and was rewarded with success. The South Summit was reached on 26 May by R.C. Evans and T. Bourdillon (using closed-circuit oxygen apparatus), and the main summit on 29 May by E.P. Hillary and Sherpa Tenzing (using open-circuit apparatus).

1954

An Indian Air Force Liberator plane with full crew flew over Everest taking many valuable (and now famous) photographs of the mountain from the air.

1956

EVEREST/LHOTSE EXPEDITION (Swiss)

Leader: A. Eggler
Deputy Leader: W. Diehl
H. Grimm, Dr E. Leuchtold, F. Luchsinger, J. Marmet, F. Müller, E. Reiss, A. Reist, E. Schmied, H. Von Gunten
Sirdar: Pasang Dawa Lama (Dawa Tenzing took over when Pasang fell ill)

A single Swiss expedition climbed both Everest and Lhotse. The summit of Everest was reached on 23 May by E. Schmied and J. Marmet, and again on 24 May by A. Reist and H. Von Gunten. (Lhotse was climbed on 18 May by F. Luchsinger and E. Reiss.)

1958

In preparation for a planned joint expedition later, Chinese and Russian mountaineers (Leaders: Chuj Din and J. Beletzki) visited Everest on reconnaissance. They reached a height of 6,400 m. below the North Col. (The planned joint expedition did not later take place.)

1960

Simultaneous attempts were made on Everest by Indian mountaineers from the South and Chinese from the North.

FIRST INDIAN EXPEDITION

Leader: Brigadier G. Singh
Da Namgyal, Ang Temba, Nawang Gombu (Sherpa instructors from Himalayan Institute, Darjeeling), Capt. N. Kumar, Sonam Gyatso, K. Bunshah, Flt Lt A.K. Chowdhury, R.V. Singh, B.D. Misra, C.P. Vohra, Capt. A.B. Jungawala, M.S. Kohli
Doctors: Flt Lt N.S. Bhagwanani, Capt. S.K. Das
Cameraman: C.V. Gopal
Transport Officer: Flt Lt A.J.S. Grewal
Signal Officer: Lt S.C. Nanda
Meteorologist: K.U. Shankar Rao
Secretary: Sohan Singh
Liaison Officer: Dhanbir Rai

A height of 8,625 m. was reached by Gombu, Kumar and Sonam Gyatso.

## CHINESE EXPEDITION

Leader: Shih Chan-chun

With an expedition of 214 men and women (one third of whom were Tibetan) the Chinese claimed to have reached the summit on 25 May. The three 'summiters' were Wang Fu-chou, Kombu and Chu Yin-hua; there were no summit photographs (it was night time when they reached the top) and some Western experts doubted the truth of the Chinese claim. (Shih Chan-chun was again leader of the 1975 expedition which was proven to be successful; there is now much more readiness generally to believe that the Chinese did succeed in 1960 also.)

1962

## FOUR-MAN BID

Three Americans and one Swiss – W.W. Sayre, N.C. Hansen, R.A. Hart and H.P. Duttle – crossed the Nup La (5,915 m.) from Nepal into Tibet and made an unsanctioned attempt on Everest from the north. They reached the top of the North Col (7,600 m.).

1962

## SECOND INDIAN EXPEDITION

Leader: Major John Dias
Lt M.S. Kohli, Sonam Gyatso, C.P. Vohra, Flt Lt A.K. Chowdhury, Capt. A.B. Jungawala, Gurdial Singh, Hari Dang, Capt. Mulk Raj, K.P. Sharma, D.P. Sharma, Suman Dubey, Dr A.N.D. Nanavati, Capt. M.A. Soares
Sirdar: Ang Tharkay

The highest point (8,720 m.) was reached on 30 May, by the South Col route. One Sherpa, Nawang Tsering, was killed during the course of the expedition after being hit by a stone from the Lhotse Face.

1963

## AMERICAN EXPEDITION

Leader: N.G. Dyhrenfurth
A.A. Auten, B.C. Bishop, J.E. Breitenbach, J.B. Corbet, D.L. Dingman, D.E. Doody, R.M. Emerson, T.F. Hornbein, L.G. Jerstad, J.T. Lester, M.M. Miller, R. Pownall, B.W. Prather, G. Roberts, J.O.M. Roberts, W.E. Siri, J.R. Ullman, W.F. Unsoeld, J.W. Whittaker
Sherpa Sirdar: Pasang Phutar

(Angcherring also acted as a Sherpa organizer, Nawang Gombu and Ang Dawa IV were 'semi-sahibs')
Liaison Officer: Prabakher Shumshere Jung Bahadur Rana

This expedition put six men on the summit and achieved the *first traverse* of the mountain. On 1 May J. Whittaker and Nawang Gombu reached the summit via the South Col route: L. Jerstad and B. Bishop repeated the South Col route to the summit on 22 May; and the same day T. Hornbein and W. Unsoeld reached the summit after the first ascent of the West Ridge. They met Jerstad and Bishop just below the South Summit, all spent a free bivouac at about 8,600 m. and together descended the South Col route. (J.E. Breitenbach was killed in the Icefall during the approach to the climb.)

1965

THIRD INDIAN EXPEDITION

Leader: Commander M.S. Kohli
Lt Col. N. Kumar (Deputy Leader), Nawang Gombu, Sonam Gyatso, Gurdial Singh, C.P. Vohra, Major Mulk Raj, Sonam Wangyal, Capt. A.S. Cheema, Capt. H.V. Bahuguna, Capt. J.C. Joshi, Dr Lala Teland, H.C.S. Rawat, Ang Kami, Major B.P. Singh, Major H.P.S. Ahluwalia, Capt. A.K. Chakravarti, G.S. Bhangu, Hav. Balakrishnan
Liaison Officer: Lt B.N. Rana
Sherpa Sirdar: Ang Tsering
Assistant Sherpa Sirdar: Phu Dorje

This expedition was rewarded with success. On 20 May the summit was reached by A.S. Cheema and Nawang Gombu (Gombu's second ascent); on 22 May Sonam Gyatso and Sonam Wangyal stood on the summit; on 24 May it was the turn of C.P. Vohra and Ang Kami, and on 29 May H.P.S. Ahluwalia, H.C.S. Rawat and Phu Dorje. All ascents were by the South Col route.

1966–9

During this period the mountains of Nepal were closed to climbers.
There were many reports of Chinese activity on the north side of Everest. A Chinese scientific expedition was reported to have set up an observation post on the North Col; other reports suggest that as many as twenty-six climbers were lost on the North Col in 1966. In 1969 another story came from the New China News Agency to the effect that three surveyors had scaled Everest.
All these accounts are unsubstantiated, but a book of photographs was published entitled *A Photographic Record of the Mount Jolmo Lungma Scientific Expedition 1966–1968*.

1969

In the spring of 1969 Nepalese restrictions on climbing expeditions were lifted. A Japanese team set off to reconnoitre the South-West Face of Everest. The party included Naomi Uemura.

The Japanese returned in the autumn with a larger reconnaissance party:
Leader: H. Mihashita
N. Uemura, M. Konishi etc. (twelve members in all)

At the end of October a height of 8,000 m. was reached (the Rock Band) by several members of the team.

Another Japanese team were on Everest preparing for the South Col ski expedition the following year. Phu Dorje, Sirdar to the ski expedition, was killed in the Icefall on 18 October.

1970

## JAPANESE (SOUTH WEST FACE) EXPEDITION

Leader: Saburo Matsukata (aged seventy)
S. Hirano, M. Doi, M. Konishi, Miss Setuko Watanabe, T. Kano, T. Kanzaki, H. Nishigori, N. Uemura, K. Narita, K. Kano, Y. Kamiyama, A. Yoshikawa, C. Ando, H. Sagono, R. Itoh, M. Nakashima, K. Hirotani, S. Ohmori, M. Kono, M. Osada, J. Inoue, K. Kimura, H. Aizawa, S. Satoh, M. Harada, K. Taira, T. Naito, T. Noguchi, S. Tateno, H. Nakagawa, S. Matsukata, H. Ohtsuka, S. Sumiyoshi, Y. Matsuda, Y. Fuhita, K. Hirabayashi, T. Matsuura, H. Tamura, H. Nakajima

The expedition failed to improve on the 1969 performance and after a number of setbacks turned all their attention to the South Col route. On 11 May the summit was reached by T. Matsuura and N. Uemura; and on the following day by K. Hirabayashi and Sherpa Chotare. Miss Watanabe set up a women's altitude record by climbing to the South Col (8,000 m.). Kvak Tsering (Sherpa) was killed in the Icefall on 9 April; Kujoshi Narita, one of the Japanese members, died of a heart attack at Camp 1 on 21 April.

## JAPANESE SKI EXPEDITION

An expedition of thirty-four members, including two skiers and a team of cameramen, were on Everest to film a ski descent from the South Col.
Y. Miura descended the Lhotse Face on ski from the South Col by the couloir which separates the Geneva Spur from the South Face of Everest. He reached

a reported speed of 150 km. per hour and slowed down by means of parachutes. A successful film was made of his descent into the Western Cwm. Six Sherpas were killed by an avalanche in the Icefall on 5 April.

1971

## INTERNATIONAL EXPEDITION

Leader: N.G. Dyhrenfurth
Joint Leader: Lt Col. J.O.M. Roberts
J. Evans, D. Whillans, D. Haston, N. Uemura, R. Ito, L. Schlömmer, D. Peterson, G. Colliver, T. Hiebeler, W. Axt, M. Vaucher, Mrs Y. Vaucher, P. Mazeaud, C. Mauri, O. Eliassen, J. Teigland, D. Isles, H. Bahuguna, F.D. Blume, Dr P. Steele.
The expedition was accompanied by an eight-man B.B.C. television team under A. Thomas: J. Cleare, I.F. Howell, N. Kelly, I. Stuart, J. Surdel, W. Kurban, A. Chesterman
*Sunday Times* reporter M. Sayle and a geologist, H. Gurung
Liaison Officer: Capt. Vishnu Prasad Sharma
Sherpa Sirdars: Sona Girme and Lhakpa Khumjung

The original intention was to launch simultaneous attacks on the South West Face and the West Ridge and the team divided itself between the two objectives. The Indian member of the expedition, Harsh Bahuguna, died in particularly tragic circumstances on 18 April, and subsequently sickness, depression and ill-feeling beset the team. The West Ridge bid was abandoned in favour of the South Col route, but later that too was forsaken and all attention focused on the South West Face. Haston and Whillans (supported by the Japanese pair and high-altitude Sherpas) pushed to a height of 8,350 m. before lack of resources forced a retreat.

1971

## ARGENTINE POST-MONSOON EXPEDITION

Leader: Lt Col. H.C. Tolosa
C. Comesaña, Capt. N. Azuaga, J. Carlos, J.B. Barrientos, E. Burgos, J.S. Fernandes, J.L. Fonrouge, J.M. Iglesias, J.M. Llavar, O. Pellegrini, J. Peterek, G. Robles, A. Rosasco, A.M. Serrano, J. Skvarca, G. Vieiro, U. Vitale, J.E. Viton

The expedition reached the South Col but was forced to withdraw at the end of October because of high winds and an unfavourable weather forecast. A high point of 8,100 m. was reached on October 30 by J. Peterek and U. Vitale.

1972

EUROPEAN EXPEDITION

Leader: Dr K.M. Herrligkoffer
Deputy Leader: M. Anderl
Climbing Leader: F. Kuen
D. Whillans, D. Scott, H. MacInnes, A. Huber, W. Haim, L. Breitenberger, P. Bednar, P. Perner, H. Schneider, A. Weissensteiner, A. Sager, H. Berger, S. Maag
Scientists: Alice Von Holb, Dr J. Zeits, Dr M. Fach, U. Mehler
Cameraman: J. Gorter
Liaison Officer: Mr Pandi

Like the International Expedition of 1971, this one was riven by personality and organizational problems; despite relatively good conditions the team were unable to improve on the 1971 position. On 20 May Kuen and Huber reached a position of *c*. 8,300 m.
(Mischa Saleki, an Iranian climber, joined the expedition for a time. Horst Vitt died at Gorak Shep hurrying to take over as Base Camp Manager from Professor E. Huttl, who had been flown home with altitude problems before reaching Base Camp.)

1972

BRITISH SOUTH WEST FACE EXPEDITION

Leader: C.J.S. Bonington
Deputy Leader: J.O.M. Roberts
M. Burke, N. Estcourt, D. Haston, K. Kent, H. MacInnes, D. Scott, G. Tiso, D. Bathgate, Dr B. Rosedale
Base Camp: Beth Burke, T. Tighe
Liaison Officer: Dr R.B. Subba
Sherpa Sirdar: Pembatharke
Asst. Sirdar: Sona Hishy

A post-monsoon expedition. Appalling weather prevented climbing above 8,300 m.; the climbers were stopped at the Rock Band, which halted the spring expedition.
(Tony Tighe died in the Icefall during the withdrawal from the mountain. There were very good performances from several of the high-altitude Sherpas. Ang Phu went eight times to Camp V; Ang Phurba, Pertemba and Jangbo went four or five times to Camp V and twice to Camp VI.)

1973

## ITALIAN EXPEDITION

Leader (of sixty-four-man team): G. Monzino
Deputy Leaders: P. Nave and G. Pistino
Climbing Leader: R. Stella
Doctor: P. Corretelli
Sherpa Sirdar: Lhakpa Tenzing

This massive expedition, which used helicopters for transporting luggage through the Icefall and employed 100 Sherpas, succeeded in putting eight men on the summit via the South-Col route:

5 May M. Minusso, R. Carrel, Sherpa Lhakpa Tensing and Sambu Tamang (Nepal)
7 May F. Innamorati, V. Epis, C. Beneditti, and Sherpa Sonam Gyalzen

1973

## JAPANESE POST-MONSOON EXPEDITION

Leader: M. Yuasa

This was another large (forty-eight-man) expedition and divided its attention between the South West Face and the South Col route.
The South West Face Party (led by J. Endo) were again halted at approximately 8,300 m. on 26 October. Sherpa Jangbu was killed by avalanche on 12 October.
The South Col party met with better success. The summit was reached on 26 October by H. Ishiguro and Y. Kato, thus making the *first post-monsoon success*. Though forced to bivouac on the way down, they escaped severe permanent injury.

1974

## SPANISH EXPEDITION

Leader: J.I. Lorente
L. Abalde, A. Alonso, J. Cortázar, L.I. Domingo, J.C. Fernández de la Torre, R. Gallardo, R. Kirch, A. Landa, F. Larruquert, A. Lerma, F. Lusarreta, A. Rosen, L. M. Sáez de Olazagoitia, F. Uriarte, J. Villar

This expedition was prevented from climbing the South Col route by high winds. Camps were established on the col and the summit ridge and twice teams were poised for the final assault. The highest point reached was 8,500 m. on 13 May by Rosen and Uriarte, the second summit pair. The first pair, Gallardo and Abalde, were both slightly frostbitten.

1974

## FRENCH WEST RIDGE EXPEDITION

Leader: G. Devouassoux
Deputy Leader: G. Payot
C. Ancey, D. Audibert, F. Audibert, J.-P. Balmat, D. Ducroz, Dr E. Lasserre, C. Mollier, P. Tairraz

The aims of this post-monsoon expedition were to put all members on the summit and to climb the entire West Ridge from a point below the Lho La, the 'Integrale' (Americans in 1963 had joined the West Ridge at the West Shoulder). Political considerations forced them to avoid the Lho La itself, but they succeeded in reaching the ridge and established Camp 3 at 6,900 m. on the crest of the West Shoulder. On 9 September an avalanche completely destroyed Camps 1 and 2, killing (Camp 2) G. Devouassoux and four Sherpas; (Camp 1) Sherpa Nigma Wanchu. The expedition was abandoned.

1975

## JAPANESE LADIES' EXPEDITION

Leader: Mrs Eiko Hisano
Mrs Junko Tabei, M. Mamita, F. Nasu, Mrs Y. Watanabe, S. Kitamura, Mrs M. Naganuma, Mrs S. Fuhiwara, T. Hirashima, Y. Mihara, R. Schioura, F. Arayma, S. Naka, Y. Taneya, and Dr M. Sakaguchi
Sherpa Sirdar: Ang Tshering

On 16 May Junko Tabei became the *first woman* to stand on the summit of Everest; she was accompanied by Sherpa Sirdar Ang Tschering; they had climbed the South Col route.
(A serious avalanche had previously devastated Camp II, injuring Mrs Tabei and two Sherpas.)

1975

## CHINESE EXPEDITION

During the spring of 1975 another expedition was busy on the northern slopes of the mountain.
Leader: Shih Chan-chu
Deputy Leader: Phantog, a Tibetan lady climber

The expedition was organized by a 'Party Committee' which included Wang Fu-chou, one of the 1960 'summit' party. This was a very large expedition (410 persons) run on military lines; in fact it seems troops were used as a transport column up to the North Col and 'scouts' employed to prepare the route. The first summit attempt (thirty-three men, seven women) were beaten back by continuous storms, but from an assault camp at 8,680 m. nine climbers set off for the summit, which they reached at 14.30 hours. The nine – Phantog, Sodnam Norbu, Lotse, Samdrup, Dharphuntso, Kunga Pasang, Tsering Tobygal, Ngapo Khyen (all Tibetan) and Hon Sheng-fu (Chinese) – remained on the summit seventy minutes and performed various scientific tasks. Phantog thus became the second woman to climb Everest. Oxygen was used sparingly; the climbers inhaled briefly from their cylinders during rest periods only. Wu Tsung-yueh died after a fall from 8,500 m.

1975

BRITISH SOUTH-WEST FACE EXPEDITION

Leader: C.J.S. Bonington
Deputy Leader: H. MacInnes
P. Boardman, M. Boysen, P. Braithwaite, M. Burke, M. Cheney, C. Clarke (doctor), D. Clarke, J. Duff (doctor), N. Estcourt, A. Fyffe, A. Gordon, D. Haston, M. Rhodes, R. Richards, D. Scott, M. Thompson
Liaison Officer: Lt Mohan Pratap Gurung
Gurkha Signallers: L/C Jai Kumar Rai, Cpl Prembahadur Thapa
B.B.C. TV team: A. Chesterman, N. Kelly, C. Ralling, I. Stuart
*Sunday Times* Reporter: K. Richardson
Sherpa Sirdar: Pertemba
Asst. Sirdar: Ang Phu

This post-monsoon expedition met with success after discovery of a ramp which solved the problem of the Rock Band. D. Scott and D. Haston reached the summit on 24 September (with a bivouac afterwards on the South Summit); P. Boardman and Sherpa Pertemba repeated the climb on 26 September; Mick Burke disappeared the same day after making what was probably the first solo ascent of the mountain. (This expedition employed a Sherpa team of eighty-two – including Tamangs and Gurkha soldiers. There were thirty-three high-altitude Sherpas and twenty-six Icefall Sherpas; the B.B.C. team also had eight high-altitude Sherpas under their Sirdar Jagatman (Tamang); the Base Camp Sirdar was Lhakpa Thondup and the Head Cook Purna.)

1976

JOINT ARMY M.A./ROYAL NEPALESE ARMY EXPEDITION

Leader: Lt Col. H.R.A. Streather, O.B.E.
Major G.D.B. Keelan, Capt. T.D. Thompson, Capt. Sir Crispin Agnew of Lochnaw Bt, Cpl Basantakumar Rai, Capt. M.G. le G. Bridges, Major

M.W.H. Day, R.L. Faux (*The Times*), Major J.W. Fleming, Sgt M.R. Francis, Capt. N.F. Gifford, Capt. P.W. Gunson, Lt Col. R.N. Hardie, Major I.J. Hellberg, Dr P.J. Horniblow, Capt. C. Johnson, L. Cpl S. Johnson, Capt. M.H. Kefford, Capt. M.T. King, Cpl M.P. Lane, Capt. B.H. Martindale, Major A.J. Muston, Cpl Nandaraj Gurung, Cpl Narbu Sherpa, Capt. P. Neame, Capt. P.B. Page, Lt Col. J.D.C. Peacock (Base Camp Manager), Lt J.P. Scott, Sgt J.H. Stokes, Capt. P.R. West, F/O G.P. Armstrong, Major Bhagirath Narsingh Rana, Subadar Krishna Bahadur Karlo, Cpl Bishnu Bahadur
Liaison Officer: Lt Gopal Raj Pokhrel
Sherpa Sirdar: Sonam Girmi
Gurkha Signallers: Jaikumar Rai (Base Camp), Cpl Prembahadur Thapa (Namche Bazar)
(There were ten high-altitude Sherpas, fifteen Icefall porters, the Base Camp cook was Gurkha Rifleman Ramkrishna Gurung and Advance Base cook Dawa Tenzing and there was a strong support party.)

M. Lane and J. Stokes reached the summit on 16 May by the South Col route; they were forced to bivouac just below the South Summit on the way down and suffered serious frostbite injury. Earlier in the expedition T. Thompson had been killed when he fell into a crevasse near Camp II.

1976

AMERICAN BICENTENNIAL EXPEDITION (Post-Monsoon)

Leader: P. Trimble
H. Bruyntjes (Netherlands), Arlene D. Blum, C. Chandler, R. Cormac, D. Crouch, D. Emmett, F. Morgan, R. Ridgeway, Barbara and G.A. Roach
Film Crew: M. Hoover, P. Pelafian, J. Wright, P. White
Reporter: J. Kazickas
Interpreter/Advance Base Manager: J. Reinhard
Liaison Officer: Dilu Prasad Benju
Base Camp Manager: Sherpa Pasang Kame

Thirty-four Sherpas excluding cooks, mail runners etc. The summit was reached on 8 October by C. Chandler and R. Cormack following the South Col route (a third member of the summit team, Ang Phurba, turned back when his oxygen system failed). A second summit bid was frustrated by high winds and cold.

1977

## NEW ZEALAND EXPEDITION

Leader: K. Woodford
Deputy Leader: R. Cunningham
M. Andrews, R. Price, Fr M. Mahoney, M. Browne, N. Banks and A. Twomey (Canada)

Base Camp was established on 10 March and no porters were used above this point. After initial good progress, bad weather and limited manpower slowed them down; Camp V (still below the South Col) was the highest camp placed, at 7,570 m. Brown and Mahoney reached the South Col on 14 May, but this was as high as the expedition could go and they began the retreat the following day.

1977

## SOUTH KOREAN EXPEDITION (Post-Monsoon)

Leader: Kim Young-Do
Sixteen members in the team
Sherpa Sirdar: Ang Phurba
Base Camp Sirdar: Lakpa Tenzing

This expedition enjoyed the best weather conditions ever known by an Everest expedition, and made good progress. A first summit bid by Park Sang-Yul and Ang Phurba failed 100 m. below the summit; the second on 15 September was successful and the mountain was climbed (by the South Col route) by Ko Sang-Don and Pemba Norbu. The Sherpas reported that only two of the climbing team got to the South Col (the Koreans later claimed this was four); to get these two (or four) men to the South Col and above, all twenty-two high-altitude porters carried to the South Col, as did six Icefall porters, a very high Sherpa/Korean ratio.

1978

## AUSTRIAN EXPEDITION

Leader: W. Nairz
Dr O. Ölz, H. Bergmann, J. Knoll, H. Hagner, Dr R. Margreiter, F. Oppurg, R. Schauer, H. Schell
Attached to this expedition was a two-man team attempting *Everest without artificial oxygen:* R. Messner (Italy) and P. Habeler
HTV Film Crew: L. Dickinson, E. Jones

Reporters: R. Faux (*The Times*), W. Lopacka, R. Karl (a climber but reporting for *Bunte Illustrierte* as well)
Sherpa Sirdar: Ang Phu
Asst. Sirdar: Dati
Liaison Officer: Sen

Early in the expedition the Messner–Habeler team realized they would not be able to climb the 'South Pillar' as they had hoped and opted to follow the South Col route for their oxygenless attempt. Both teams co-operated in route-finding and establishment of camps and the summit was reached:
3 May by R. Schauer, Ang Phu, W. Nairz, H. Bergmann
8 May by R. Messner and P. Habeler – the *first ascent totally without oxygen apparatus*
11 May by O. Ölz and R. Karl
14 May by F. Oppurg (probably the second solo ascent)
(Sherpa Dawa Nuru was killed in the Icefall.)

1978

## PERSIAN/CHINESE 'TRAINING' EXPEDITION

It is reported that in April 1978 fifteen Iranian mountaineers joined twenty Chinese mountaineers for an expedition to the north side of Everest. They had a support team of forty people as well as local porters (100), sixty soldiers and thirty yaks. Camp 4 was established on the North Col and nine Chinese and two Iranians are said to have reached 7,500 m. on 21 May, before the expedition was halted by the early approach of the monsoon.

1978

## GERMAN POST-MONSOON EXPEDITION AND FRENCH POST-MONSOON EXPEDITION

These two expeditions shared a permit and Liaison Officer but retained a certain amount of independence on the mountain.

GERMAN TEAM:

Leader: Dr K.M. Herrligkoffer
Deputy Leader: Sigi Hupfauer
Asst. Deputy Leader: Wanda Rutkiewicz (Poland)
H. Daum, J.F. Daum, H. Engl, G. Härter, H. Hillmaier, H. Kirchberger, W. Klimek, B. Kullmann, J. Mack, G. Ritter, Marianne and S. Walter, R. Allenbach (Switzerland)
Support team: M. Rink, F. Seiler, H. Wehrs

Asst. Doctor: H. Laube
Cameraman: H. Schumann
Base Camp Organizer: Doris Kustermann

The following summit climbs were made by the German team:
14 October: H. Hillmaier, J. Mack, and H. Engl, *who climbed without using artificial oxygen.*
16 October: S. Hupfauer, W. Klimek, R. Allenbach, W. Rutkiewicz, Sherpa Ang Kami, and Sherpas Ang Dorje and Mingma who climbed without oxygen.
17 October: G. Ritter, B. Kullmann.
(Mrs Rutkiewicz became the first Pole and, at the same time, the first European woman to climb Everest.)

FRENCH TEAM:

Leader: P. Mazeaud
J. Afanassieff, W. Ceccinel, C. Deck, R. Despiaux, K. Diemberger, N. Jaeger, J.-F. Mazeaud
Sherpa Sirdar: Pemba Norbu
15 October: J. Afanassieff, N. Jaeger, P. Mazeaud and K. Diemberger reached the summit
(At forty-nine, Pierre Mazeaud became the oldest man to have so far climbed Everest.)
The German and French ascents were all by the South Col route.

1979

## YUGOSLAV WEST RIDGE EXPEDITION

Leader: T. Skarja
Z. Andrejcic, S. Belak, B. Bergant, S. Bozik, M. Gafic, V. Groselj, T. Jamnik, S. Klemenc, F. Knez, I. Kotnik, M. Manfreda, S. Marence, V. Matijevec, V. Mesaric, D. Podbevsek, B. Pollak, R. Robas, M. Sisic, A. Stremfelj, M. Stremfelj, I. Tekavcic, E. Vavken, N. Zaplotnik, J. Zupan.

This expedition was the first to climb the entire ridge from the Lho La. After two summit bids had failed, J. Zaplotnik and A. Stremfelj reached the summit after more than eight hours from their highest camp (6). Two days later the summit was reached again by two more Yugoslavs, Stane Belak and Styse Bozik, with Sherpa Ang Phu. Tragically Ang Phu was killed in a fall from the ridge when returning to Camp 4; he was the first man to have climbed Everest twice by two separate routes.

# *Part Two*

1979

## SINO-JAPANESE RECONNAISSANCE FROM THE NORTH

Leader: Dr. Junsei Saito and Yoshinori Hasegawa as climbing leader

In preparation for a joint Japanese-Chinese expedition to the northern side of Everest the following spring, a 9-man team visited the Central and East Rongbuk glaciers and reached a height of 6550 m.

(While 6 climbers were approaching the North Col on 12 October, a wind-slab avalanche swept three Chinese – Wang Hong Bao, Nima Thaxi and Luo Lan – into a crevasse where they died.)

1979

## SWABIAN (West German) EXPEDITION (Post Monsoon)

Leader: Gerhard Schmatz
Nick Banks (NZ), Ray Genet (USA), Hans von Kaenel (Switzerland), Dr. Tilman Fischbach, Gunger Kaempfe, Dr. Hermann Warth, Frau Hannelore Schmatz (wife of Leader)
Sirdar: Pertemba Sherpa

Following the South Col route, the summit was reached on 1 October by G. Schmatz, Dr. Warth, Sherpa Lhakpa Gyalzo, H. von Kaenel and Pertemba Sherpa; and on 2 October by T. Fischbach and Ang Phurba; N. Banks, G. Kaempfe and R. Genet; and H. Schmatz, Sherpa Sundare and Ang Jangbo.

This was the smallest successful expedition to date, the fastest (32 days) and the first to put all members on the summit. At age 50, G. Schmatz was the oldest man to climb Everest; also this was the first time an Everest expedition team had included a married couple. Frau Schmatz was the fourth woman to reach the top; however, descending from the summit after a high bivouac, both she and R. Genet died.

1980

## POLISH WINTER EXPEDITION

Leader: Andrzej Zawada
Leszek Cichy, Krysztof Cielecki, Ryszard Dmoch, Walenty Fiut, Ryszard Gajewski, Andrzej Heinrich, Jan Holnicki-Szulc, Dr. Robert Janik, Bogdan Jankowski, Janusz Maczka, Kazimierz Olech, Maciej Pawlikowski, Ryszard Szafirski, Krysztof Wielicki, Krzysztof Zurek

The first winter ascent of Everest was made (via the South Col route) on 17 February by L. Cichy and K. Wielicki.

1980

## POLISH SOUTH BUTTRESS EXPEDITION

Leader: Andrzej Zawada
Eugeniusz Chrobak, Kryzsztof Cielicki, Andrzej Czok, Ryszard Gajewski, Andrzej Heinrich, Jerzy Kukuczka, Janusz Kulis, Kazimierz Olech, Kazimierz Rusiecki, Wojciech Wroz (and one other).
Sirdar: Pemba Norbu

Taking a new line through a series of ice slopes on the righthand side of the South Buttress and overcoming a difficult rock band, the summit was reached on 18 May by Czok and Kukuckzka. (Their oxygen had run out by the time they reached the South Summit and they completed the climb without.)

This new route (the seventh to date) is the shortest way to the top of the mountain from the south side.

1980

## BASQUE (Spanish) EXPEDITION

Leader: Juan Ignacio Lorente
Juan Arrue, Xabier Erro, Ricardo Gallardo, Xavier Garayoa, Emilio Hernando, Kiki de Pablos, Angel Rosen, Luis Maria Saenz de Olazagoitia, Jose Urbieta, Felipe Uriarte, Martin Zabeleta
Sirdar: Pemba Sering

On 14 May summit was reached via the South Col route by M. Zabaleta and Pasang Temba.

1980

## SINO-JAPANESE NORTHEAST RIDGE AND NORTH FACE EXPEDITION

Leader: Hyoriko Watanabe
The expedition's 39 members and 21 Chinese 'assistant climbers' accompanied by 13 press and television people, established Base Camp at the tongue of the Rongbuk Glacier on 5 May. They then divided into two teams:

### THE NORTHEAST RIDGE TEAM

Leader: Yoshio Hamono

From Camp VII at 8250 m. on 3 May, Yasuo Kato and Susuma Nakamura set off for the summit supported at the Second Step by Shoji Nakamura and Toichiro Mitani. Susuma Nakamura was forced by exhaustion to give up and Kato continued alone to the summit (his second Everest ascent). Both men bivouacked (separately) without oxygen near the Second Step and descended safely the next day.

### NORTH FACE TEAM (12 Persons)

Leader: Hideki Miyashita

On 10 May Tsuneo Shigehiro and Takashi Ozaki climbed via the Hornbein Couloir and the rocks of the West Ridge to the summit. They ran out of oxygen when about four hours below the summit on the way up and were forced to bivouac about an hour below the top on the way down. They suffered no injuries.

(Akiro Ube was killed by avalanche near the bottom of the Hornbein Couloir on 2 May.)

1980

## FRENCH RECONNAISSANCE EXPEDITION

Jean-Claude Marmier and the French Army visited the Kama and Rongbuk valleys during May with a scouting party. The object was to determine which route their military expedition should take the following spring. They decided on the classic North Col/Northeast Ridge route.

1980

## SOLO ASCENT BY THE GREAT COULOIR

Reinhold Messner

On August 20 Reinhold Messner became the first person to make the entire ascent of Mount Everest solo. He used no artificial oxygen and the climb took him three days during the monsoon period. Like Norton in 1924, he followed a line below the Northeast Ridge, crossing to the Great Couloir. He then joined the ridge near the Second Step, which he turned to the left.

1980

## NEPALESE-ITALIAN EXPEDITION (Post Monsoon)

Leader: Francesco Santon
32 Italians, 15 Nepalese, 1 Austrian (Kurt Diemberger), 2 Czechoslovaks and 2 Thais with 25 high-altitude porters.

This huge expedition failed to reach the summit, but did attain the South Summit. Two men died: Sherpa Nawang Kersang in the Khumbu Icefall, and Mario Piama higher on the mountain.

1980

## EAST (KANGSHUNG) FACE RECONNAISSANCE

Andrew Harvard (USA) and liaison officer Cheng Rong Chan with an interpreter Tsao Hong Juen travelled to the Kama Valley from where Harvard climbed alone up the north side of the Kangshung Glacier to photograph Everest's east face. The return to the Karta was made by way of the Langma La.

1980–81

## JAPANESE WINTER ATTEMPT

Leader: Naomi Uemura

Six Japanese climbers accompanied by five scientists and reporters failed to make the second winter ascent. They were following the South Col route and the col was the highest point reached.

Noburu Takanaka was killed when he fell from a fixed rope.

1980–81

## BRITISH WINTER WEST RIDGE EXPEDITION

Leader: Alan Rouse
Adrian and Alan Burgess, Brian Hall, Paul Nunn, John Porter, Joe Tasker, Dr. Peter Thexton

This expedition attempted the West Ridge via the Lho La without sherpa support and without the intention to use oxygen. They were accompanied by a 4-man television crew. In 10 weeks of sub-zero temperatures, the highest camp placed was Camp III at the top of the West Shoulder (7,150 m.).

1981

## JAPANESE WEST RIDGE EXPEDITION

Leader: Shinichi Nakajima
Atsuhiro Aso, Kazuo Nishimura, Ryoten Hasegawa, Shunichi Machi, Junichi Tanaka, Makoto Nebuka, Junichi Sakamoto, Kouichi Matsuda, Norio Ohinishi, Touichiro Mitani, Morio Nakanishi, Kazuyoshi Sakuma, Shin Taguchi, Tsuyoshi Takano, Sakaki Matsumura, Yasuaki Arai, Yasuaki Hayashida

The expedition attempted to repeat the Yugoslav route. On 20 May a height of 8,750 m. was reached by Tanaka and Taguchi, but they were unable to climb the last 100 metres because of fatigue and lack of oxygen.

1981

## FRENCH MILITARY EXPEDITION

Leader: General Pierre Astorg
Climbing Leader: Jean-Claude Marmier
Liaison Officer: Ju Yin Yan

28 Frenchmen (15 climbers, the rest support/media) and 33 Chinese (13 being high altitude porters) established base camp at the foot of the Central Rongbuk Glacier on 3 March. The highest point reached (on two separate occasions during the second half of May) was the First Step (8,550 m.).

1981

## TWO-MAN ATTEMPT

Russell Brice and W. C. Freaney

These two New Zealand-based climbers failed to scale Everest from the

Western Cwm. They established four high camps and reached 7,620 m. on 5 October before being driven back by high winds.

1981

## AMERICAN MEDICAL RESEARCH EXPEDITION

Leader: Dr John West
Climbing Leader: John Evans
Base camp manager: Rodney Korich
F. Duane Blume, Christopher Kopczynski, David Jones, Jeff Lowe, Glenn Porzak, Michael Weis with scientists: Steven Boyer, David Graber, Peter Hackett, Christopher Pizzo, Frank Sarnquist, Robert Schoene and non-climbing scientists: Sukhamay Lahiuri, Karl Maret, James Milledge, Richard Peters, Michele Samaja, Robert Winslow

Mount Everest was climbed by a variant of the South Col route on:
21 October by Kopczynski and Sherpa Sundare (his second ascent); and on
24 October by Pizzo, Hackett and Sherpa Yong Tenzing.

1981

## AMERICAN KANGSHUNG FACE EXPEDITION

Leader: Richard Blum
Climbing Leader: Louis Reichardt
Liaison Officer: Wang Fu Chow
David Breashears, Gary Bocarde, Kurt Diemberger, Susan Giller, Andrew Harvard, Sir Edmund Hillary, Christopher Jones, George Lowe, Scott McBeth, Bruce McCubbrey, Kim Momb, James Morrissey, Eric Perlman, Daniel Reid, John Roskelley, Geoffrey Tabin, Mikael Reynolds

The first-ever attempt on the Kangshung (East) Face of Everest took place during August-October. A height of about 7,000 m. was reached.

1981–2

## 'CIRCUMNAMBULATION' OF EVEREST

Ned Gillette, Jan Reynolds, James Bridwell, Stephen McKinney, Craig Colonica, Richard Barker

Starting with the first winter ascent of Pumori, this team circumnavigated Everest, covering the Nepalese section between December 1981 and January 1982, and the Tibetan section in April and May 1982. Wherever possible they skied.

1982

## AMERICAN NORTH FACE EXPEDITION

Leader: Louis Whittaker
James Wickwire, Philip Erschler, Marty Hoey, Eric Simonson, George Dunn, Edward Hixson, Dan Boyd, Dave Mahre, Larry Nielson, Joe Horiskey, Gary Isaacs, Tracy Roberts, Nawang Gombu, Richard Bass, Frank Wells, Steve Marts

In the period March-May an attempt was made on the North Face by way of the Great Couloir (or Norton Couloir) which achieved a height of 8,380 m. Marty Hoey fell to her death on 15 May from near the high point when her harness inexplicably came undone.

1982

## BRITISH NORTHEAST RIDGE EXPEDITION

Leader: Christian Bonington
Peter Boardman, Dr. Charles Clarke, Adrian Gordon, Richard Renshaw, Joseph Tasker
Liaison Officer: Chen Rongchan
Interpreter: Mr. Yui

This British lightweight expedition to the unclimbed Northeast Ridge came to a tragic conclusion with the loss of P. Boardman and J. Tasker somewhere above 8,000 m. They failed to return from a summit attempt on 15 May. Their high point was estimated at the time to be *c.* 8,230 m. although later sightings of relics which could only have derived from their attempt means the pair in fact climbed somewhat higher along the ridge.

1982

## RUSSIAN SOUTHWEST FACE EXPEDITION (New Route)

Leader: Evgeny Tamm
25 members (17 climbers, a camera crew, doctor and radio man) and 10 high-altitude Sherpas
Sirdar: Pemba Norbu

This expedition successfully climbed a new route to the left of the Bonington Couloir. The summit was reached on:

4 May by Eduard Myslovsky and Vladimir Balyberdin
Mikhail Turkevitch with Sergei Bershov

5 May by Valentin Ivanov and Sergei Ephimov
8 May by Kazbek Valiev and V. Khrisshchaty
9 May by Yuri Golodov, Vladimir Puchkov and Valery Khomutov

1982

## CANADIAN EVEREST EXPEDITION

Leader: W. March
Lloyd Gallagher, John Amatt, Tim Auger, Robert Baillie, Alan Burgess, James Blench, Dwayne Congdon, Jim Elzinga, Roger Marshall, Dave McNab, Pat Morrow, Dave Read, Gordon Smith, Laurie Skreslet, and Don Serl, supported by: Dr. Steve Bezruchka, Dr. David Jones, Kurt Fuhrlich, Blair Griffiths, Bruce Patterson and Peter Spear
Sirdar: Gyaljen

This large team, which had originally planned to climb the South Pillar, met with disaster early in the post-monsoon season. First three Sherpas (Ang Tsultim, Dawa Dorje and Pasang Soina), then cameraman Blair Griffiths, were all killed in the Icefall. 6 climbers quit the expedition and the remaining members focused attention on the South Col route. On
5 October Skreslet, Sundare and Lapka Dorje reached the summit
(It was Sundare's third ascent of Everest)
7 October Morrow, Pema Dorje and Lakpa Tsering reached the summit.

1982

## SPANISH WEST RIDGE EXPEDITION (Post Monsoon)

Leader: Lluis Belvis
Josep Manuel Anglada, Emili Civis, Manuel Mateu, Jordi Pons, Jaume Altadill, Oscar Cadiach, Narcis Serrat, Alfons Valls, Jordi Sugranyes, Xavier Perez Gil, Lluis Hortala, Josep Vidal Ponce, Antoni Llasera, Josep Casanovas, Francesc Sabat and Joan Ribas

From the Lho La this expedition was following an easier line than the Yugoslav route and to the right of it. Sherpa Lhakpa Tsering died from a stomach perforation, and towards the end of the expedition Nima Dorje slipped and fell to his death from near the highest point reached (8,500 m.).

1982

## DUTCH NORTH COL/NORTHEAST RIDGE EXPEDITION

Leader: Alexander Verrijn Stuart
Jan van Banning, Willem ten Barge, Eelco Dijk, Geert Geuskens, Gerard

Jansen, Ronald Naar, Mathieu van Rijswick, Gerard van Sprang, Johan Taks, Han Timmers, Bart Vos, Robert Weijdert

A high point of 7,850 m. was reached on 7 October (Dijk was badly injured in an avalanche on 29 September).

1982–3

## FRENCH WINTER ATTEMPT

Leader: Michel Metzger
Marc Batard, Alain de Blanchaud, Rene Ghilini, Yves Laulan, Michel Mabilon, Michel Piola, Jean Bourgeois, Pierre-Alain Steiner, Emmanuel Schmutz, Louis Audoubert

Following the Yugoslav route from the Western Cwm via the Lho La, a height of 7,619 m. was reached before strong winds defeated the expedition.

(The Belgian climber Jean Bourgeois, descending alone after becoming unwell, took the easier route down into Tibet from the Lho La. He was detained and interrogated by the Chinese before being returned to the Nepalese border. His companions, meanwhile, had given him up for dead.)

1982–3

## JAPANESE WINTER EXPEDITION

Yasuo Kato was lost on Everest after reaching the summit on 27 December (his third ascent). Toshiaki Kobayashi, who had met him with bivouac supplies just below the South Summit, also failed to return. The climbers had been following the South Col route.

1983

## AMERICAN EVEREST WEST RIDGE EXPEDITION

Leader: Bob Craig
Climbing leader: Galen Rowell
Dr. Gordon Benner, David Carman, Donald Castle, Dallas Clark, Michael Graber, Dr. Robin Houston, Harold Knutson, John Martinek, Steven McKinney, Kim Momb, John Roskelley, Kim Schmitz, Jack Tackle, Christopher Wren

An attempt was made on the West Ridge from Tibet, joining the ridge at the West Shoulder when the highest point reached was 7,925 m.; an attempt via the Hornbein Couloir reached a similar height on 7 May.

1983

## AMERICAN SOUTH COL EXPEDITION

Leader: Gerhard Lenser, W. Germany
Climbing leader: Phil Erschler
On 7 May the summit was reached by Peter Jamieson, Larry Nielson, David Breashears, Sherpa Ang Rita, and Gerald Road; then on 14 May by Gary Neptune, Jim States and Sherpa Lhakpa Dorje.
(Several further attempts were made, notably by Dick Bass and Frank Wells, but were frustrated by high winds. Nielson and Ang Rita climbed without oxygen.)

1983

## CHILEAN NORTH COL EXPEDITION

Claudio Lucero, Ivan Vigoroux, Dagoberto Pena, Gaston Oyarzun, Juan Pardo, Luis Garcia, Gino Casassa, Claudio Galvez, Nelson Rivera, Nelson Nunoz, Eduardo Parvex, Jorge Gassa, Santiago Pavlovic and Danilo Aravena

After three days and nights at Camp VII (8,430 m.) without oxygen, the leader suffered a (non-fatal) cerebral oedema and the expedition was abandoned.

1983

## FRENCH ATTEMPT TO TRAVERSE EVEREST

Leaders: Yannick Seigneur and Patrick Barthe
Jean Afanassieff, Bernard Prud'homme, Louis-Paul Chantelat, Eric Escoffier, Dr. Jean-Louis Etienne, Xavier Fargeas, Bruno Gallen, Serge Koenig, Tom Hargis (USA), Stephane Schaffter (Switzerland)

The objective was to traverse Everest by the West and Northeast Ridges. The first summit attempts were made from Camp II at the foot of the West Ridge of Changtse (5,407 m.) without higher camps or supplementary oxygen. A height of 8,205 m. in the Hornbein Couloir was subsequently reached (where Escoffier and Schaffter bivouacked for 2 nights) before the expedition was abandoned.

1983

## SPANISH POST-MONSOON EXPEDITION

Leader: Conrad Blanch
Joan Massons, Antoni Ricart, Nil Bohigas, Jordi Canals, Jordi Camprubi,

Oscar Cadiach, Josep Maria Duran, Lluis Gomez, Enric Lucas, Miquel Sanchez, Antoni Sors

An attempt via the North Col, North and Northeast Ridges attained a height of 8,300 m.

1983

## ITALO-SWISS POST-MONSOON EXPEDITION

Leader: Romolo Nottaris

An expedition of ten Swiss and two Italian climbers hoped to climb the 1980 Japanese direct North Face route. After three months on the mountain Nottaris broke his ankle near Camp III (7,300 m.) and the expedition was abandoned.

1983

## AMERICAN WEST RIDGE ATTEMPT

Leader: Jim Sano
Climbing leader: Chas Macquarie
Todd Bibler, Sandy Stewart, Claude Fiddler, Alex Moad, Shari Kearney, Lucy Smith, Doug Dalquist, Eric Reynolds, Annie Whitehouse, Rennie Jackson, Sue Giller, Susan Buren (Doctor), Rodney Korich (Base Camp Manager)
Sirdar: Per Temba

The Yugoslav route was followed to the top of the West Shoulder from where the 1963 Hornbein Couloir route was taken. A height of 8,540 m. was reached by R. Jackson and A. Whitehouse before they were turned back by high winds.

1983

## TWO JAPANESE EXPEDITIONS

One team of 5 Japanese with 10 Sherpas, led by Hariuchi Kawamura, originally had permission for the Southwest Face but changed it to the Southeast Ridge. They more or less followed the line of the 1981 American Medical Expedition (to the left of the Lhotse Face) and by the end of September had reached 7,995 m.

By this time another Japanese team had arrived – five climbers and two Sherpas led by Hiroshi Yoshino – and after sitting out a week of bad weather at the beginning of October established camp on the South Col.

On 8 October seven climbers (from the two expeditions) met on the ridge and climbed more or less together until at around 8,500 m. they were met and overtaken by the American Kangshung summiteers (see below). Following in the tracks of the Americans Kawamura, Shomi Suzuki, Yoshino, Hironobu Kamuro and Haruyuki Endo climbed to the summit, while Noburo Sawagami and Sherpa Pasang Temba retreated from just below the South Summit. Pasang Temba slipped and fell to his death and the following day, after a high bivouac, Yoshino and Kamuro must also have fallen, as a body and a boot were later found at the foot of the southwest face. None of the climbers were using artificial oxygen and all appeared to have been climbing independent of the others.

1983

AMERICAN KANGSHUNG FACE EXPEDITION

Leader: James Morrisey
John Boyle, Carlos Buhler, Jay Cassell, David Cheesmond, David Coombs, Andrew Harvard, George Lowe, Christopher Kopczynski, Kim Momb, Louis Reichardt, Daniel Reid, Geoffrey Tabin, Carl Tobin

This expedition made the first ascent of the East/Kangshung Face of Everest. The summit was reached on:

8 October by C. Buhler, K. Momb and L. Reichardt
9 October by J. Cassell, G. Lowe and D. Reid

1983–4

JAPANESE WINTER LHOTSE/EVEREST EXPEDITION

Leader: Kazuyuki Takahashi
A post-monsoon ascent of Lhotse served as acclimatisation for a winter ascent of Everest via the South Col. The summit was reached on 16 December by Takashi Ozaki, Noboru Yamada, Kazunori Murakami and Sherpa Nawang Yonden

(This was the third winter ascent and the first time a Nepalese had climbed the mountain in winter. While the expedition was in progress, the leader's wife was heading another attempt on the mountain, but this time from Tibet – see below.)

1983–4

JAPANESE WINTER ATTEMPT FROM TIBET

Leader: Michiko Imai Takahashi

18 climbers followed the 1980 Japanese route and reached 8,100 m. in the Hornbein Couloir on 30 November. A series of setbacks (frostbite, tent-fire, high winds) prevented further attempts improving on this height.

(The Takahashis had originally hoped their expeditions would meet on the summit of Everest.)

1984

## BULGARIAN WEST RIDGE EXPEDITION

Leader: Avron Avramov

Ognyan Baldjiyski, Dimitar Bardarev, Slavi Dermamdjiev, Trifon Djambazov, Kantcho Dolapchiev, Kiril Doskov, Todor Grigorov, Lyubomir Iliev, Georgi Imov, Stefan Kalayanov, Kostas Kanidis, Zapryan Khorozov, Dr. Stayko Kulaksazov, Milan Milanov, Nikolay Petkov, Christo Prodanov (Deputy Leader), Metodi Savov, Stamen Stanimorov, Dinyo Tomov, Petko Totev, Ivan Valtchev, Doychin Vasilev, Lyudmil Yankov

This 24-man expedition completed the second ascent of the Yugoslav West Ridge Route. The summit was reached on:

20 April by Prodanov alone and without oxygen, but he failed to return after an enforced bivouac during the descent
8 May by Savov and Valtchev
9 May by Doskov and Petkov

All four descended the Southeast Ridge route (assisted by Indian climbers on the South Col – see below) and claimed the first 'complete traverse' of the mountain.

1984

## INDIAN SOUTH COL EXPEDITION

Leader: Major Darshan Kumar Khullar
Dr. Meena Agrawal, Chandra Prabha Aitwal, Jai Bahuguna, Harshwanti Brisht, Magan Bissa, Prem Chand (Deputy Leader), Phu Dorje, Rita Gombu, Kiran I. Kumar, Dorjee Lhatoo, Dr. Minoo Mehta, Bahendri Pal, Sonam Palzor, Sharawati Prabhu, Rekha Sharma, N.D. Sherpa, Rattan Singh, Lopsang Tshering

An expedition with 17 climbing members (including 3 Indian Sherpas and 7 Indian women climbers) succeeded in getting five people to the summit. On 9 May Phu Dorje reached the top alone; on 23 May it was the turn of Dorjee Lhatoo, Sonam Balzor, Bachendri Pal and Ang Dorje Sherpa.

Bachendri Pal thus became the first Indian woman to climb Everest and the fifth overall. For Ang Dorje it was his second ascent of Everest without oxygen. Two sherpas died: one was killed in an avalanche and a member of the cooking staff succumbed to altitude sickness.

1984

DUTCH EVEREST EXPEDITION

Leader: Herman Plugge

Two climbers with a Dutch expedition attempting the South Col route were forced to turn back within 200 mm. of the summit because of deep snow and a shortage of artificial oxygen; Bart Vos continued alone from the South Summit to reach the top (8 October).

1984

AMERICAN 'ULTIMA THULE' EXPEDITION

(Leader: Thomas Fitzsimmons)
Bob Berg, Jim Frush, Donald Goodman, Dave Hambly, Kurt Hanson, Ray Nichols, Greg Thompson, Warren Thompson, John Yaeger

Intent on repeating the classic North Col/Northeast ridge route, this expedition established seven high camps. Fitzsimmons and Greg Thompson reached 8,600 m. on 20 May before the attempt was abandoned.

(It was during the course of this expedition that Goodman, standing at 8,290 m., saw and photographed objects high on the NE Ridge which were non-natural and could only have been relics of the ill-fated 1982 Boardman-Tasker attempt.)

1984

AUSTRALIAN/NEW ZEALAND WEST RIDGE EXPEDITION

Leader: Peter Hillary
Fred From, Kim Logan, John Muir, Craig Nottle

Two Australian climbers of this 6-man expedition, Nottle and From, died in separate falls above Camp 4 (about 8,000 m.) while retreating from an unsuccessful summit bid on 9 October.

1984

CZECH SOUTH PILLAR EXPEDITION

Leader: Frantisek Kele

Z. Brabec, Zoltan Demjan, V. Dudes, Ivan Fiala, J. Just, M. Koncok, V. Launer, M. Matis, R. Mock, M. Neuman, Michal Orolin, J. Orsula, V. Petrik, J. Porvaznik, Josef Psotka, M. Sajnoha, Dr. M. Simonic, Dr. M. Skladany, L. Zahoranhski

A 20-strong expedition which had originally planned to attempt the Southwest Face, opted for the South Pillar route after taking a closer look. The summit was reached on 15 October by Psotka, Demjam and Sherpa Ang Rita without oxygen. Psotka, however, fell into a crevasse and was killed during the descent; at age 50 he was the oldest man to have climbed Everest. (It was the second Everest ascent for Ang Rita.)

1984

NEPALESE POLICE 'CLEAN-UP' EXPEDITION

(Leader: Yogendra Bahadur Thapa)

A 36-member expedition went to the South Col with the stated intent of clearing some of the garbage left by thirty years of expeditions. Once there, it was decided to go higher and try to recover the body of Hannelore Schmatz who died in 1979; during this operation the leader Yogendra Bahadur Thapa and Sherpa Ang Dorje were killed.

1984

AMERICAN NORTH FACE EXPEDITION

Leader: Louis Whittaker
George Dunn, Philip Ershler, Carolyn Gunn (Base Camp Manager), Dr. Edward Hixon, David Mahre, Steve Marts (cameraman), John Roskelley, John Smolich, Peter Whittaker, James Wickwire, Greg Wilson

Erschler reached the summit alone on 20 October, having climbed via the North Col, North Face and Great Couloir. He made it with the use of artificial oxygen; Roskelley, who had set off on the final assault with him but who was not using bottled oxygen was forced back at 8,535 m. (It was Erschler's third attempt on Everest in two years).

1984

AUSTRALIAN NORTH FACE EXPEDITION

Geof Bartram, Lincoln Hall, Andrew Henderson, Tim McCartney-Snape, Greg Mortimer with Dr. Jim Duff and film-makers Mike Dillon, Colin Monteath and Howard Whelan, journalist Simon Balderstone and Nepalese Lobsang Tenzing Sherpa and Narayan Shrestha.

McCartney-Snape and Mortimer became the first Australians to climb Everest when they reached the summit via the Great Couloir on the North Face during October. They followed a line between the Japanese North Face route to the Hornbein Couloir and the North Ridge and they used no artificial oxygen. First complete ascent of the Great Couloir.

(Bartram displayed symptoms of cerebral oedema at 7,385 m. and Henderson sustained severe frostbite injuries to his hands.)

1984

## CUMBRIAN (British) EXPEDITION

Leader: Pat Gunson

This 9-man expedition originally hoped to climb the West Ridge from the North without using supplementary oxygen. Finding the route occupied by a large Bulgarian expedition, the team concentrated their efforts instead on a North Face attempt (Whittaker's 1982 route to the left of the Great Couloir). Camp 4 was established at 7,772 m. on 20 April when bad weather halted progress. Gunson suffered a heart attack at 7,010 m. on 1 May and the expedition had to be abandoned.

1984

## BRITISH SAS EXPEDITION

Leaders: Michael 'Bronco' Lane and 'Brummy' Stokes

14 Britons, mainly from the SAS, called off their spring attempt on the Hornbein Couloir when a massive avalanche hit their Advance Base Camp on 3 April, killing Tony Swierzy and injuring 4 other members of the team. Their high point had been 6,858 m.

1984–5

## SOUTH KOREAN WINTER ATTEMPT

Leader: Oh In-Hwan

The highest point reached by this 13-man expedition attempting the South Col route was 7,850 m. (about an hour below the South Col) by Nam Sun-Woo, Kim Byung-Gil and 5 Sherpas on 20 December and 21 December. They had hoped to pitch their assault camp here, but were driven back by fierce winds which also thwarted a Christmas Day summit bid.

1984–5

## FRENCH WEST RIDGE WINTER EXPEDITION

Leader: Eric Dossin
Bernard Francou, Vincent Fine, Benoit Chamoux, Dr Olivier Callande, Gian-Carlo Grassi (It.) and a Belgian climber

Dossin with Chamoux and Fine established Camp 3 in a crevasse near the West Shoulder early in January, but were subsequently unable to get about 7,500 m. in their attempt on the West Ridge. Strong winds forced a retreat.

1985

## NORWEGIAN SOUTH COL EXPEDITION

Leader: Arne Naess, Jr.

This very successful expedition succeeded in putting a record 17 people on the summit:

21 April Odd Eliasson, Bjorn Mirelund, Chris Bonington (GB), Ang Lakpa, Dawa Nuru and Pertemba
29 April Arne Naess, Stein Aasheim, Havard Nesheim, Ralph Hoibakk, Sun(g) dare (his fourth ascent), Pema Dorje, Ang Rita (his third ascent without oxygen), and Chowang Rinzing
30 April Dick Bass, Dave Breashears (both USA), and Ang Phurba. (At 55 Dick Bass became the oldest man to have reached the summit; he is also the first to have reached the highest points of all seven continents.)

1985

## AMERICAN WEST RIDGE ATTEMPT

Leader: David Saas
Climbing Leader: Jim Bridwell
Robert Anderson, Pete Athens, Heidi Benson, Kim Carpenter, Randall Grandstaff, Rodney Korich, Scott Lankford, Dan Larson, George McLeod (GB), Jim McMillan, John Meyer, Brian O'Malley, John Pelner, Andy Politz, Greg Sapp, Jay Smith, Kevin Swigert, Ed Webster, Fletcher Wilson
Sherpas included: Ang Danu, Fenzo Sherpa and Lhakpa Sherpa

On 10 May Anderson and Smith climbed to 8,595 m., when trouble with oxygen apparatus decided them on a retreat.

1985

## BRITISH NORTHEAST RIDGE EXPEDITION

Leader: Mal Duff
Sandy Allan, Rick Allen, Bob Barton, David Bricknell, Tony Brindle, Terry Dailey, Kurt Diemberger, Liz Duff, Allen Fyffe, Andy Greig, Nick Kekus, Dan Lewis, Andy Nisbet, Sarah Squibb, Jon Tinker, Julie Tullis, Chris Watts, Dr. Urs Wiget

During the spring this second British expedition to attempt the unclimbed Northeast ridge was beaten back from the Pinnacles area (*c.* 8,000 m.) by cold and high winds.

1985

## SPANISH (BASQUE) NORTH COL EXPEDITION

Leader: Mari Abrigo
Jose Manual Casimiro, Juanjo Navarro, Antxon Zamarbide

Navarro was killed and Zamarbide injured in a fall above the North Col during an unsuccessful pre-monsoon attempt by this 4-man expedition attempting the classic northern route.

1985

## SPANISH (CATALAN) EXPEDITION

Leader: Conrad Blanch
Nil Bohigas, Oscar Cadiach, Jordi Camprubi, Jordi Canals, Xavier Perez-Gil, Lluis Gomez, Enric Lucas, Jordi Magrina, Joan Massons, Dr Antoni Ricart, Miquel Sanchez, Antoni Sors, Carles Valles

This expedition, climbing during the monsoon period, succeeded on their fifth attempt in reaching the summit following the classic North Col/NE Ridge line. The top was reached on 28 August by: Cadiach, Valles, and Sors with Tombu Tamang, Narayan and Ang Karma. They did not climb with artificial oxygen.

1985

## FRENCH NORTH FACE ATTEMPT

Pierre and Annie Beghin attempted a new route to the left of the 1984 Australian route. They climbed above 8,100 m. on 11 August, and later the same month made a further attempt, gaining the North Col from the West, but avalanche danger prevented them improving on their earlier height.

1985

## NEW ZEALAND EXPEDITION

Leader: Austin Brookes
Peter Allen, Warwick Anderson, Mike Andrews, Rob Blackbourne, Steve Bruce, Ross Cullen, Graeme Dingle, Bruce Farmer, Shaun Norman, Mike Perry, Dick Price, Mike Rheinberger, Hugh Van Noorden

Snow conditions and avalanches forced withdrawal from an attempt to approach the West Ridge from a spur at the head of the Rongbuk Valley. A new approach to the Great Couloir was then tried, but was similarly avalanched off.

1985

## JAPANESE NORTH FACE/NE RIDGE EXPEDITION

Leader: Tsuneo Hasegawa
Ms M. Hasegawa, K. Hoshino, S. Ishii, Y. Miyaji, M. Nagamachi, K. Ohta, S. Shimada, T. Sasaki, Ms Y. Tanaka

The plan was for Hasegawa to solo the North Face while the others climbed the classic route. Ishii was lost in a snowslide while retreating from the North col. Expedition high point was Camp 5 at 8,200 m., established on 9 September.

1985

## INDIAN EXPEDITION

Leader: Brigadier Jagjit Singh

This 39-man post-monsoon expedition intended to make parallel attempts on the Southwest Face and South Col route. They placed a Camp 3 at 7,770 m. on the face, but thereafter concentrated all energies on the easier Col route. In a prolonged storm during the second week of October, Major Kiran Inder Kumar fell to his death from 8,500 m. and four others – Ranjeet Singh Bakshi, Major Jai Bahuguna, Bhaskar Rao and Vijay Pal Singh Negi – died of exposure in the South Col area. In late October two summit attempts reached 8,400 m.

1985

## JAPANESE 'NAOMI UEMURA FILM EXPEDITION'

Leader: Kuniaki Yagimara

This team moved onto the South Col route after departure of the Indian expedition. On 30 October seven of their members reached the summit: Noboru Yamada (his second ascent and first without oxygen), Hideji Nazuka, Mitsuyoshi Sato, Teruo Saegusa, Etsuo Akutsu, Satoshi Kimoto and Yagimara. Akutsu, who had developed snow-blindness, and Kimoto made an unscheduled bivouac below the S Summit at 8,600 m., as a result of which Kimoto subsequently lost all toes to frostbite.

1985–6

JAPANESE WINTER EXPEDITION

Leader: Michiko Takashi

Attempt on North Face via Hornbein Couloir abandoned at 8,450 m.

1985–6

KOREAN SOUTH COL WINTER ATTEMPT

Leader: Kam Sang-Tae

Deputy Leader Kim Jong-Ho and Park Dong-Seok made two summit attempts; on 21 December, accompanied by Ang Rita, they reached 8,300 m.; the following day the pair pushed to 8,500 m., climbing without oxygen.

1985–6

SOUTH KOREAN SOUTHWEST FACE WINTER ATTEMPT

Leader: Park Young-Bae

High winds and a general lack of resources defeated this attempt on the Bonington-line. A high point of 7,700 m. was reached, first by Sherpas Pasang Dawa and Jimba Jimbu on 13 January, then by Kimi Bo-Youl and Um Hong-Gil two days later. It was the intended site for Camp 5, but the camp was never established.

1985–6

KOREAN WEST RIDGE WINTER ATTEMPT

Leader: Kim Ki-Heyg

The highest point reached was the Camp 3 position at 7,100 m., attained by Lee Jae-Ha, Lim Sam Gyun, Park Gye-Hyun and Sherpas Ang Phurba and Ang Lhakpa Norbu on 8 December. The two Sherpas, whose role was a route-making one, not load-carrying, climbed again to this point two days later before the attempt was abandoned. 12 tents had been destroyed by high wind in the lower camps.

1986

CANADIAN WEST RIDGE EXPEDITION

Leader: Jim Elzinga

Two members of this 18-strong expedition, approaching the West Ridge from the North, Sharon Wood and Dwayne Congden, reached the summit during May. Wood thus became the 6th woman to have climbed Everest.

1986

JAPANESE SOUTH COL EXPEDITION

Leader: Haruyuki Endo

A team of four which included woman climber Takeo Nagao. On 10 May Endo with Tadanori Matsunaga and Sherpa sirdar Pemba Tshering reached 8,600 m. before being turned back by bad snow conditions.

1986

POLISH EXPEDITION

Leader: Tadeusz Karolczak

Karolczak with Aleksander Lwow and an Austrian climber, Helmut Putz, first attempted the West Ridge, approaching from Nepal and the Lho La, but were turned back at around 7,100 m. The two Poles then had a go at the normal (South Col) route, attaining a height of 7,800 m. on the Geneva Spur.

1986

SPANISH (Madrilion) EXPEDITION

Leader: Jeronimo Lopez
Luis-Bernardo Duran, Pedro Nicolas, Angel Sanchez, Carlos Soria

Team attempting North Col route found itself unable to proceed beyond Camp 4 at 7,800 m., just above the Col.

1986

AMERICAN GREAT COULOIR EXPEDITION

Leader: Joseph Murphy

Camp 5 at 7,700 m. was established on 29 April, but five attempts to place a higher camp were repulsed by bad weather.

1986

CHILEAN NORTH COL ATTEMPT (Monsoon)

Leader: Claudio Lucero
Pedro Bralic, Cristian Garcia-Huidobro, Fernando Garcia-Huidobro, Marcelo Grifferos, Rodrigo Jordan, Andres Marambio, Pablo Straub, Victor Hugo Trujillo and four Sherpas

Trujillo was killed on 16 August when he fell into a crevasse on the North Col, triggering an avalanche. The expedition was abandoned.

1986

SOLO ATTEMPT (Monsoon)

Roger Marshall (Br/Canada) with a 3-person support group: his nutritionist Ruth de Cew, photographer Ed Webster and Kristina Kearney

Marshall spent two months camped in the Rongbuk Valley. Attempts on the North Face, approaching from the North Col and later towards the Hornbein Couloir, were unsuccessful in heavy monsoon snow. Webster soloed Northeast flank of Changtse.

1986

FRANCO-SWISS NORTH FACE EXPEDITION

Jean Afanassieff, Annie and Pierre Beghin, Erhard Loretan, Nicole Niquille, Jean Troillet

Troillet and Loretan left base camp in the evening of August 28 and skied to the foot of the North Face. They climbed throughout the night and rested at the foot of the Hornbein Couloir the next day, setting off again in the evening. The summit was reached at 2 pm on August 30 after 31 hours' climbing. Conditions were ideal for glissading, and the descent of the couloir to the foot of the North Face took the pair only three and a half hours!

Pierre Beghin had set off at the same time, hoping to solo the route, but had to turn back because of exhaustion.

1986

BRITISH (EAST-) NORTHEAST RIDGE EXPEDITION

Leader: John 'Brummie' Stokes
Mo Anthoine, Bill Barker, Joe Brown, John English (Doctor), Ronald Faux

(Reporter), Paddy Freaney, Pat Green, Leol Guinness, Philip Horniblow (Doctor), Ali Kellas, Pete Long, Paul Moores (Deputy Leader), Paul Nunn, Trevor Pilling, Sam Roberts, Clive Rowland, Harry Taylor, Will Thompson and Tony Riley with 3-man camera crew

The team made a new approach to the ridge, via 'Bill's Buttress' and avoiding the Rapiu La; after several tries Camp 2 was established in a snow hole at 7,315 m. below the First Buttress on the ridge, from where ropes were fixed to the top of the Second Buttress. Taylor and Pilling attempted to cross the Pinnacles section, but were turned back by hurricane-force winds. No Sherpa support was employed.

1986

## AMERICAN NORTH COL/NE RIDGE EXPEDITION

Leader: Andrew Harvard
Ken Bailey, David Breashears, Mary Kay Brewster, David Cheeseman (Can), Catherine Cullinane, Sue Giller, Tom Holzel, Alistair Macdonald (GB), Al Read, Audrey Salkeld (GB), Steve Shea, David Swanson, Roger Vernon (Can), Mike Weis, Jed Williamson, Mike Yager – and Sherpa team of 15 under Nawang Yonden (Sirdar)

Snow conditions and frequent storms ill-suited a siege-style ascent. High point reached was Camp 5 at 8,010 m. on the NE Ridge. A descending Sherpa, Dawa Nuru, was killed on 17 October when caught in an avalanche on the North Col.

1986

## AMERICAN 'AIR OVER EVEREST' EXPEDITION

Leader: Steve McKinney
Peter Athans, Heidi Benson, Craig Colonica, Kim Carpenter, Bob Carter, Catherine Freer, Peter Hackett (Doctor), Ellen Lapham, Steve Marts, Mark Moeller (Doctor), Andy Politz, Larry Tudor, Andre Ulrych, Jysti Ulrych – and 11 Sherpas

This expedition had the twin objectives of climbing the West Ridge (from the North) and of making a hang-gliding descent from as high on the mountain as possible. Deep snow and avalanche danger bogged down climbers below the shoulder, but Steve McKinney landed his aircraft safely after taking off from the ridge.

1986

## COMMERCIAL SOUTH EAST RIDGE EXPEDITION

Leader: Fredy Graf

Simon Burkhardt (Switzerland) and Sherpa Gayalu died in separate accidents while taking part in an unsuccessful commercial expedition during September and October.

It was an international team of 25; Graf and Serge Koenig and Chuldim Dorje Sherpa reached the South Summit on September 25; Burkhard, Raymond Monnerat and Peter Weber were halted by bad weather at 8600 m. two days later. Burkhard was killed in an avalanche on the Lhotse Face on the way down; Gayalu by falling seracs in the Khumbu Icefall on 4 October.

Eric Escoffier, Savier Murillo, Pierre and Annie Beghin attached themselves to this expedition, arriving in Base Camp on 24 September. Two days later Escoffier started up the mountain and caught up with Graf's party at 8,500 m.; when they turned back at 8,600 m., he continued a further 50 metres. (He was back in Base Camp the next day.)

1986–7

## SOUTH KOREAN WINTER EXPEDITIONS

Although Korean expeditions attempting the South Col route (led by On In-Hwan) and the Southwest Face (led by Park Young-Bae) climbed to 8,000 m. and above, neither met with success. Sherpa Tsuttin Dorje fell to his death from 7,700 m. on 30 January while load-carrying on the Southwest Face climb.

1987

## SPANISH (BASQUE/LATIN) EXPEDITION

Leader: Juanjo San Sebastian
13 Spaniards (Basques and Madrilions, and including Juan-Carlos Tamayo and Ms. Trini Cornellana) with Italians Fausto De Stefani and Almo Giambisi

Expedition failed in its attempt to repeat the South Pillar/Spur route (opened by the Poles in 1980). A high point of *c.* 8,200 m. was reached before the expedition was abandoned because of continuous bad weather. The expedition was reinforced at times with members of the (following) Czech team.

1987

## CZECHOSLOVAK SOUTHWEST FACE EXPEDITION

Leader: Ivan Galfy

Large Czech expedition (23 climbers including Miroslav Smid and Jozef Rakoncaj) was defeated by high winds and bad weather after reaching around 8,300 m. during Spring season.

1987

## AMERICAN NORTH FACE EXPEDITION

Leader Jack Allsup
Bob Allison, Dr John Baumeister, Travis Cannon, George Dunn, Bob East, Craig Van Hoy, Bonnjie Nobori, Eric Simonson (climbing leader), Ann Smith, Ed Viesturs, Greg Wilson, with 5 Sherpas and a cook

Pre-monsoon attempt on Great (Norton) Couloir route, managed to set their highest camp at the top of the couloir (8,400 m.). From there, they deviated towards the West Ridge where highest point reached by summit team was *c.* 8,750 m.

1987

## SOLO ATTEMPT NORTH FACE

Roger Marshall

Roger Marshall was killed on 21 May attempting the Hornbein Couloir; he apparently slipped on blue ice while descending the lower part of the Japanese Direct route.

1987

## SWEDISH NORTH COL/NE RIDGE EXPEDITION

(Leader: Ebbe Wahlund)
Large Swedish team, together with David Breashears (USA) and Mari Abrego and Josimo Casimiro (Spain) – and Sherpas under Nawang Yongden (Sirdar)

After Camp 5 was established at 7,500 m. on the North Ridge, bad weather forced the expedition to traverse across the North Face to the Norton Couloir (where the above American team was active) and where Camp 6 was established at 8,000 m. From here Per Malsten and Sherpa Tenjing climbed to about 8,300–8,400 m. during mid-May and Lasse Cronland to 8,650 m. climbing with the Americans. Bengt Sorvick broke his ankle in the region of

Camp 5, and made an epic descent to the N Col on his own; his hands and feet were badly frostbitten.

[BRITISH NE EXPEDITION, to have been led by Brummie Stokes postponed till 1988 for lack of finance.]

1987

## SPANISH HORNBEIN COULOIR ATTEMPT (MONSOON)

Luis Barcenas, Juan Agustin Casillas, Luis Fraga, Fernando Garrido, Pedro Holst, Bicen Itxaso, Inigo Mauleon, Cristobal Salas, Antonio Ramos Villar.

Eight climbers from different regions of Spain attempted the Hornbein Couloir, but with a variation from the usual line of the lower-section. Pierre Beghin (France), trekking in the area, joined the expedition and climbed the Couloir with Fernando Garrido, emerging onto the West Ridge. Snow conditions prevented them going beyond 8,700 m.

1987

## COMBINED ATTEMPT FROM WESTERN CWM

Active on the classic South Col Route (post-monsoon) were 31 climbers, all but 4 on the permit of Hanns Schell (Austria), but including the American 'Snowbird' Expedition of Peter Athans (leader), Mary Kay Brewster, Karen Fellerhoff, Steve Fossett, Renny Jackson, Elizabeth Haufmann (journalist), Marjorie Lester (film-maker), Robert Link, Sally McCoy, Christopher Noble, Kelly Rhoads, Peter Whittaker and team of Sherpas. Steve Boyer and Murray Rice were a 2-man team from the American Northwest, and there was also a French pair, Bernard Muller and Laurence de la Ferriere.

The highest anyone reached was 8,400 m. on 2 October by Reinhard Patscheider (Italy) and Thomas Schlicher (Austria).

1987

## SOUTH PILLAR ATTEMPT

Leader, Peter Hillary
Kim Logan (NZ) and Australians Jon Muir and Mike Rheinberger

Jet stream winds halted summit attempt at 8,075 m., site of final bivouac.

1987

## KOREAN ASCENT SOUTH COL ROUTE

Leader: Hahm Tak-Young

Heo Young-Ho and Ang Rita Sherpa reached summit on 22 December. Ang Rita used no artificial oxygen. This was his fourth Everest ascent, all without bottled oxygen.

1987

## SOLO ATTEMPT AT NORTH COL ROUTE

Mischa Saleki, Iran, with 2 Sherpas

Saleki failed in September to climb higher than the N Col.

1987

## JAPANESE EXPEDITION TO WEST RIDGE

Leader Takashi Kawakami, Climbing Leader Masao Yokoyama

Post-monsoon expedition. Yokoyama, leader of the very large expedition (about 40 members and 18 Sherpas) was killed crossing a river above Base Camp. Expedition continued but was abandoned at 8,000 m. during last week in October.

1987

## AMERICAN NORTH FACE EXPEDITIONS

N Col team: Steve van Meter (Leader), Paul Briggs, Geoff Creighton (Can), Michael Flynn, Dr. Brack Hattler, Peter Jamieson, Steve Matous, Dr Tom McCullough, Dave Nettle, Greg Sapp, Steven Strain, Rod Willard (BC Manager) and Sherpas Ang Rita and Chuldim Dorje

N Face (Australian Route) team: Scott Fischer (Leader), Stacy Allison, Q. Belk, Dr. David Black, Peter Goldman, Michael Graber, Wes Krause, Evelyn Lees, Bob McConnell, Liz Nichols, Melly Reuling, George Schunk, Mimi Stone, Ben Toland, Rick Wyatt

These two post-monsoon attempts had hoped to link up above the Norton Couloir: Strain of the first team on 13 October climbed alone from Camp 5 as far as the First Step before being turned back by high winds and temperatures of −40 degres; Graber and Stone of the other group made a summit bid on 15 October to be turned back at 8,540 m.

1987

BRITISH NORTHEAST RIDGE EXPEDITION

Leaders: Doug Scott/Rick Allen
Sandy Allan, Nick Kekus, Sharavati Prashu, Robert Schauer, Mike Scott, Steve Susted

Post-monsoon attempt. Snow-cave established at 7,900 m. from where Scott and Allen climbed to 8,100 m. in 100 mph winds. Expedition cook Nima Mangal Sing Tamang died in an avalanche just above Base Camp.

1987–8

JAPANESE WINTER EXPEDITION

Leader: Tsuneo Hasegawa
4-person team, including the leader's wife, attempted Great (Norton) Couloir.

1988

TRI-NATIONAL EXPEDITION

Delegations from China, Japan and Nepal fielded mountaineers to make simultaneous spring ascents of North and South Col routes on what was reputedly a 252-person expedition. Noburu Yamada (Jap), Lhakpa Nuru (Sherpa), Cerni Doji (Chinese) traversed the mountain from North to South, passing the summit on 5 May, the same day as Ang Phurba (Sherpa), Da Cering and Ringen Pungco (both Chinese), who completed the South-North traverse. Additionally, Li Zhixin, Munehiko Yamamoto and Sherpa Lhakpa Sona reached the top from the North (5 May) and Sungdare and Padma Bahadur from the South (10 May). It was Sungdare's fifth Everest ascent and Yamada's third; there was live TV coverage from the summit.

1988

AUSTRALIAN BI-CENTENNIAL EXPEDITION

The South Col Route was climbed without Sherpa support by Paul Bayne and Patrick Cullinan, reaching the summit on 25 May, and John Muir on 28 May.

1988

ANGLO-AMERICAN KANGSHUNG FACE CLIMB

Leader Robert Anderson
Stephen Venables (Br), Ed Webster, Paul Teare (Can), Mimi Zieman (Doctor)

On 12 May Venables reached the summit alone and without oxygen after Webster and Anderson were forced back from the South Summit. They had forged new route up East Face to the South Col.

1988

BRITISH SERVICES WEST RIDGE EXPEDITION

Leader: Dougie Keelan
Ted Atkins, Bill Batson, Martin Bazire, Steve Bell, Henry Day (Deputy Leader), Andy Edington, John Garratt, Simon Gray, Dick Hardie (Chief M.O.), Charlie Hattersley, Dave Howie, Andy Hughes (M.O.), Luke Hughes, Keith Hunter (BC Manager), Steve Last, Simon Lowe, David Maxwell, Al McLeod, Merv Middleton, Alastair Miller (M.O.), Jim Morning, Terry Moore, Dave Nicholls, Dave Orange, Pat Parsons, Richard Pelly, Laurie Skuodas, Kit Spencer, Duncan Strutt, Neville Taylor, Dave Torrington, John Vlasto, Nigel Williams, 'Tug' Wilson, with film crew Mark Anderson, Al Evans, Ian Hills, Nick Plowright, and Sherpa climbers Chowang (Sirdar), Angnema, Gombu, Gopal, Bhadri and Lakpa

A large military team making pre-monsoon attempt on W Ridge (approaching from the Tibetan side) met with failure, but 14 of its 34 climbers went to over 8,000 m., and Nicholls and McLeod to 8,550 m. A 6-part television documentary was made.

1988

BRITISH NORTH EAST RIDGE ATTEMPT

Leader: Brummie Stokes
Mo Anthoine, Bill Barker, Russell Brice (NZ), Joe Brown, Jim Curran (film-maker), Glynn Davis [Glenn Dyson], John English (Doctor), [Gerry Gillespie], Loel Guinness, Philip Horniblow (Doctor), Davey Jones, Ali Kellas, Pete Long, Paul Moores (Deputy Leader), Ian Nicolson, [Dan Noble], Sam Roberts, Graham Stokes (BC Manager), Harry Taylor, David Williams (Film-maker), Trevor Williams, plus eight climbing Sherpas and 2 cooks

Taylor and Brice succeeded in completing the notorious Pinnacles-section to the Northeast Shoulder (*c.* 8,400 m.) before retreating down the North Ridge/North Col route. The complete North East Ridge has now been climbed, but not in a single push. B. Stokes suffered three strokes and was forced to abandon expedition.

1988

## MULTIPLE ACTIVITY

First to arrive at Khumbu Base Camp were American Northwest Expedition (leader: Jim Frush) and large Korean contingent (leader: Sun-Woo Nam); when three separate French groups and a combined Czech/NZ team joined them, they were told to pay for use of fixed ropes through the Icefall. A Spanish team was attempting the W Ridge from the Lho La. They lost a climber in an avalanche at Camp 3 and afterwards abandoned the climb to join other parties on the South Col route.

Czechs Dusan Becik, Peter Bojik, Josef Just, Jaroslav Jasko shared permits for Lhotse and Everest with New Zealanders. Becik and Just climbed Lhotse in an all-night push from Everest Camp III. On 26 September Everest summit was reached by 5 Frenchmen, one Swiss, two Koreans and 4 Sherpas: Koreans had climbed the South Pillar; Michel Metzger had done S Col route without oxygen; Jean-Marc Boivin (who had kept his options open by taking up skis and parapente) jumped from the top and in 11 minutes floated all the way to Camp II; Marc Batard reached summit from base in less than 24 hours. 3 more Koreans reached summit on 29 September as well as Stacy Allison and Sherpa Pasang Gyalzen of the American team. (Allison became first US woman to climb Everest, 7th overall.) On 2 October Peggy Luce, Dawa Tshering, Phu Dorjee and Nima Tashi also reached top (by S Col route); Geoff Tabin summited the same day, as did Sun-Woo Nam (and 4 Koreans climbed Lhotse). 23, in all, to the top of Everest within a week.

On 13 October, in bad weather, Serge Koenig, Pasang Temba and Lakpa Sona reached top, but the two Sherpas perished on the way down. Jeronimo Lopez, Nil Bohigas, Luis Giver, Nima Rita and Ang Rita (his fifth ascent) climbed Everest the next day – as possibly did New Zealander Lydia Bradey (though without a permit – she later denied to Nepalese authorities that the top was reached); in a tricky evacuation involving most of the people on the mountain, Sergei Martinez was dragged and lowered from the South summit to safety.

The 4 Czechs Becik, Bojik, Just and Jasko reached the S summit on 17 October; Just alone got to the top the following day. All four were lost on the descent.

1988

## TIBETAN ACTIVITY

Michel Parmentier (France) was killed attempting a speed ascent of Hornbein Couloir (hoping to outstrip Batard on the S side). French climbers met with no success on the North Face; a large Wyoming team and smaller Canadian one failed on the North Col Route; an American expedition was rebuffed on the East Face.

In all 31 people reached the summit during the 1988 post-monsoon season; and 9 died (7 of whom were climbing without bottled oxygen.) One cannot fail but draw comparisons with the tragic summer of 1986 on K2 when 13 people died. With so many groups attempting the world's highest mountains in a single season, such large-scale tragedies may become a regular feature. Nepal is currently allowing three Everest expeditions to a route per season, and as I write this, 7 expeditions are in progress on the Nepalese side of the mountain, 6 of them going through the Khumbu Icefall.

## ADDENDUM: ASCENTS OF EVEREST, 1988 WINTER-1998 WINTER

Because of the greatly increased activity on the mountain at all seasons in the late 1980s and 1990s, the listings in this addendum give first the year, followed by the season, then the name of the expedition and objective. Only the name of the leader and those making ascents are included. Second or further ascents are indicated by numbers in brackets after an individual's name. For later years, when multiple ascents became commonplace, only the most noteworthy are listed. The spelling of some names continues to be uncertain.

### 1988-9 WINTER

The year tailed off into a poor winter. Hasegawa's party remained behind, trying a new route on the North Face, and actually reached 8,000 m. before abandoning the attempt. The Belgian–Polish teams had no success on Everest, though a Pole, Krzysztof Wielicki, 38, made a daring solo ascent of Lhotse without oxygen. He had made the first winter ascent of Everest 8 years earlier. The final effort of the year was an attempt on the South West Face by a Korean team, which reached the foot of the central couloir before retreating.

### 1989 PRE MONSOON

#### YUGOSLAV—SOUTH EAST RIDGE

Leader: Jovan Poposki
Ascents: Viktor Groselj, Stipe Bozic, Dimitar Ilijevski, Sonam Tshering (2), Ajiwa (2)

All 10 May.
Sonam climbed without oxygen. Ilijevski died from a fall on descent.

AMERICAN–MEXICAN—SOUTH EAST RIDGE
Leader: Walt McConnell
Ascents: Ricardo Torres Nava, Phu Dorje (2), Ang Danu
All 16 May.
Phu Dorje was killed by a fall on the descent.

AMERICAN SNOWBIRD EXPEDITION—SOUTH EAST RIDGE
Leader: Karen Fellerhoff
Ascents: Adrian Burgess (British), Roddy McKenzie (Australian), Ang Lhakpa Nuru (2), Sonam Dendu
All 24 May.

POLISH—WEST RIDGE–HORNBEIN COULOIR
Leader: Eugeniusz Chrobak
Ascents: Eugeniusz Chrobak and Andrzej Marciniak, 24 May
Miroslaw Dasal, Miroslaw Gardzielewski, Waclaw Otreba, Zygmunt Heinrich and Eugeniusz Chrobak were killed by an avalanche whilst attempting to descend via Khumbutse, leading to international rescue attempts.

FRENCH—SOUTH WEST FACE
Leader: Marc Batard (solo)
Reached 7,800 m. before high winds caused him to abandon attempt. He had previously abandoned a solo attempt on Annapurna's South Face—he kept falling in crevasses!

BELGIAN—SOUTH EAST RIDGE
Leader: Karl Huyberechts
Reached 8,500 m.

NEW ZEALAND—SOUTH EAST RIDGE
Leader: Robert Hall
Reached 8,200 m.

AUSTRIAN—SOUTH EAST RIDGE
Leader: Sepp Hassler
Reached 8,500 m.

1989 SUMMER

GREEK—NORTH RIDGE
Leader: Paraskevaidas

ITALIAN—NORTH FACE
Leader: Oreste Forno

SPANISH—NORTH FACE
Leader: Escartin

1989 POST MONSOON

A Polish expedition went to the Lho La from Rongbuk to locate the Polish climbers lost in the spring.

JAPANESE—SOUTH EAST RIDGE
Leader: Ken Kanazawa
Ascents: Toichiro Mitani, Hiroshi Ohnishi, Atsushi Yamamoto, Chumdi (Tchiring Thebe Lama), Chuldin Dorje
All 13 October.

SOUTH KOREAN—SOUTH PILLAR
Leader: Kim In-Tae
Ascent: Cho Kwang-Je, 13 October

MEXICAN—SOUTH EAST RIDGE
Leader: Carlos Carsolio
Ascent: Carsolio, 13 October (without oxygen). (Seven people made the top that day).

SOUTH KOREAN—WEST RIDGE
Leader: Lee Suk-Woo
Ascents: Chung Sang-Yong, Nima Rita (2), Nuru Jangbu
All 23 October.

FRENCH–ITALIAN—SOUTH PILLAR
Leader: Jean-Franck Charlet
Reached 8,450 m.

ARICAN–MEXICAN–AUSTRIAN—NORTH FACE
Leader: Mike Dunn

AMERICAN—NORTH COL–NORTH FACE
Leader: Keith Brown

AMERICAN–BRITISH—NORTH EAST RIDGE
Leader: Gary Speer

CHILE–AMERICAN—WEST RIDGE
Leader: Maramisio

FRENCH–BELGIAN—NORTH COL–NORTH FACE
Leaders: Jaccoux and Vincent

FRENCH–SWISS—NORTH COL–NORTH FACE
Leader: Eric Escoffier

ITALIAN—NORTH FACE
Leader: Mazzoleni

JAPANESE—NORTH COL
Leader: Ogata

SWISS–ITALIAN—NORTH COL
Leader: Joos

YUGOSLAV—NORTH COL–NORTH FACE
Leader: Berljak.
The expedition did not go beyond the col.

SPANISH—NORTH EAST RIDGE
Leader: Arribas

1989-90 WINTER
A Korean expedition led by Kim Ha-Kyung reached the South Col. A Sherpa died from altitude sickness (unusual in Sherpas).

1990 PRE MONSOON

NEPALESE—SOUTH EAST RIDGE
Leader: Chitra Bahadur Gurung
Ascents: Ang Rita (6), Ang Kami (2), Pasang Norbu, Top Bahadur Khatri
All 23 April. Ang Rita did not use oxygen.

INTERNATIONAL—NORTH EAST RIDGE

Leader: Jim Whittaker

Dubbed the Everest International Peace Climb, this large expedition had members from the United States, Russia, Tibet, Kazakhstan and Ukraine. Twenty climbers reached the summit, six without oxygen (indicated below with *).

Ascents: 7 May. Robert Link (US), Steve Gall (US), Sergei Arsentiev* (Russia), Grigori Lunyakov* (Kazakhstan), Da Cheme (Tibet), Gyal Bu (Tibet)
8 May. Ed Viesturs* (US), Mistislav Gorbenko (Ukraine), Andrej Tselishchev* (Kazakhstan)
9 May. Ian Wade (US), Da Qiong (Tibet), Luo Tse (Tibet), Ren Na (Tibet), Gui Sang (Tibet)
10 May: Yekaterina Ivanova (Russia), Anatoli Moshnikov* (Russia), Yervand Ilyinski (Kazakhstan), Aleksandr Tokarev* (Russia), Mark Tucker (US), Wang Ja (Tibet)

AMERICAN—SOUTH EAST RIDGE

Leader: Glenn Porzak

Ascents: Glenn Porzak, Michael Browning, Brent Manning, Peter Athans, Dana Coffield, Nima Tashi (2), Ang Jangbu, Dawa Nuru reached the top on 10 May, followed next day by Andrew Lapkass.

INTERNATIONAL—SOUTH EAST RIDGE

Leader: Rob Hall

Ascents: 10 May. Peter Hillary (New Zealand), Rob Hall (New Zealand), Gary Ball (New Zealand), Rudy Van Snick (Belgium), Apa (Sherpa)
11 May. Mikael Reuterswäld (Sweden), Oskar Kihlbörg (Sweden)
Peter Hillary is the son of Sir Edmund Hillary, the first to ascend.

AUSTRALIAN—SOUTH EAST RIDGE SOLO

The remarkable 'sea to summit' ascent of Tim Macartney-Snape, who started on foot from the Bay of Bengal and reached the top of the world on 11 May, without using oxygen. This was his second ascent—he had climbed Everest by the Norton Couloir 6 years previous (qv).

On 10–11 May the summit of Everest was a pretty crowded place! Not all expeditions were successful, however.

INTERNATIONAL—WEST RIDGE FROM NORTH

Leader: Todd Burleson

BELGIAN—SOUTH EAST RIDGE SOLO
Leader: Karl Huyberechts
Reached 8,500 m.

SWISS—WEST RIDGE
Leader: Beda Fuster
Reached 8,200 m.

NEW ZEALAND–AUSTRALIAN—NORTH EAST RIDGE
Leader: Mike Perry

GERMAN—WEST RIDGE FROM NORTH
Leader: Mischa Saleki
See 1972. 18 years had not dimmed Saleki's enthusiasm.

BRITISH—NORTH COL
Leader: David Breashears
Included the actor Brian Blessed.

1990 POST MONSOON
With several expeditions in the field, there was considerable intermixing of personnel in the various ascents.

AMERICAN (COMMERCIAL)—SOUTH EAST RIDGE
Leader: Hooman Aprin
Ascents: 4 October. Alex Lowe (US), Dan Culver (Canada)
5 October. Hooman Aprin (US), Ang Temba (Sherpa)
7 October. Cathy Gibson (US), Aleksei Krasnokutsky (Russia), Phinzo (Sherpa)
Gibson and Krasnokutsky were married. They were accompanied to the top by a Yugoslav husband and wife team, Andrej and Marija Stremfelj (see later)—the first married couples to reach the summit.

FRENCH (COMMERCIAL)—SOUTH EAST RIDGE
Leader: Laurence de la Ferrière
Ascents: 4 October. Yves Salino (France).
7 October: Jean-Nöel Roche (France), Bertrand 'Zebulon' Roche (France), Alain Desez (France), Denis Pivuot (France), René de Bos (Dutch), Ang Phurba III (Sherpa), Nima Dorje (Sherpa)
At 17, Bertrand Roche was the youngest person to climb Everest and, with

Jean-Nöel, the first father and son team.

FRENCH—SOUTH EAST RIDGE
Leader: Marc Batard
Ascents: 5 October. Erik Decamp, Marc Batard (without oxygen) (2), Christine Janin, Pascal Tournaire, Nawang Thile, Sonam Dendu (2)
6 October. Sherpa Babu Tshering reached the top with the Korean expedition (see below).

SOUTH KOREAN/JAPANESE—SOUTH EAST RIDGE
Leaders: Roh Jong-Baek, Nobuo Kuwahara
Ascents: Bok Jin-Young, Kim Jae-Soo, Park Chang-Woo, Dawa Sange, Pemba Dorje
All 6 October.
Ham Sung-Hun disappeared during a solo attempt from the South Col.

SLOVENIAN—SOUTH EAST RIDGE
Leaders: Tomaz Jamnik, Andrej Stremfelj
Ascents: Andrej Stremfelj (2), Marija Stremfelj, Janez Jeglic, Lhakpa Rita
All 7 October.

FRENCH—SOUTH EAST RIDGE
Leaders: Annie Beghin, Véronique Périllat
Reached 8,500 m.

FRENCH-BRITISH—SOUTH EAST RIDGE
Leader: Pierre Dutrievoz
Reached South Summit.

KOREAN—SOUTH WEST FACE
Leader: Park Young-Bae
Reached 7,700 m.

BASQUE—SOUTH WEST FACE
Leader: José Luis Zuloaga
Reached 8,300 m.

AMERICAN-CANADIAN—NORTH FACE
Leader: Mark Hesse

ITALIAN—NORTH FACE
Leader: Giuseppe Pozzoli

SPANISH—NORTH COL
Leader: Cesar Perez de Tudela
Three members were killed by an avalanche below the North Col.

JAPANESE—EAST FACE RECONNAISSANCE
Leader: Shinichi Hirano (Meiji University)

Bob McConnell led an American team to the north side of Everest as a clean-up expedition, but they did not attempt to climb the mountain.

1991 PRE MONSOON

SHERPA—SOUTH EAST RIDGE
Leader: Lobsang
Ascents: Ang Temba II, Sonam Dendu (3), Apa (2)
All 8 May.

AMERICAN—SOUTH EAST RIDGE
Leader: Rick Wilcox
Ascents: Mark Richey, Rick Wilcox, Barry Rugo, Yves La Forest (Canada)
All 15 May.

AMERICAN—NORTH RIDGE
Leader: Eric Simonson
Ascents: 15 May. Bob Sloezen (US), George Dunn (US), Andy Politz (US), Lhakpa Dorje (2) (Sherpa), Ang Dawa (Sherpa)
17 May. Mike Perry (New Zealand)
21 May. Mark Whetu (New Zealand), Brent Okida (US)
24 May. Greg Wilson (US)

AMERICAN—SOUTH EAST RIDGE
Leaders: Robert Link, Ed Viesturs
Ascent: Viesturs reached the summit on 15 May, his second ascent.

SWEDISH—NORTH FACE
Leader: Jack Berg
Ascents: Two Sherpas, Mingma Norbu and Gyalbu, on 15 May; Lars Cronlund on 20 May
The climb followed the Japanese route and Hornbein Couloir.

ITALIAN—NORTH FACE
Leader: Oreste Forno

Ascents: Battista Bonali (Italy), Leopold Sulovsky (Czechoslovakia) on 17 May
The team, climbing without oxygen, took a partially new route up the Great Couloir that included a difficult wall.

INTERNATIONAL—NORTH EAST RIDGE
Leaders: Harry Taylor (Great Britain), Russell Brice (New Zealand)
Ascents: Two Sherpas, Babu Tshering (2) and Chuldin, 22 May

JAPANESE—NORTH RIDGE AND FACE
Leader: Muneo Nukita
Ascents: Muneo Nukita, Junichi Futagami, Nima Dorje (2), Phinzo Norbu
All 27 May.

NEW ZEALAND SOLO—NORTH RIDGE
Robert Anderson

AUSTRALIAN—WEST RIDGE
Leader: Michael Groom
Reached 7,400 m., then turned to South Col route, reaching 7,900 m.

INTERNATIONAL—NORTH RIDGE
Leader: Marcus Schmuck

FRENCH—SOUTH EAST RIDGE
Leader: Marc Batard
Batard had hoped to stand on the summits of Everest and Lhotse in a single day, but his attempt ended at 8,200 m. on the South East Ridge. Attempts were then abandoned after disputes with the Nepalese authorities.

KOREAN—SOUTH WEST FACE
Leader: Lee Kang-Oh

SWISS-GERMAN—SOUTH EAST RIDGE
Leader: Norbert Joos
Reached South Col.

JAPANESE—EAST RIDGE OF KANGSHUNG FACE
Leader: Shinichi Hirano (Meiji University)

Reconnoitered the previous season, but this 'last great problem' proved altogether too much and the attempt was abandoned.

1991 POST MONSOON

SPANISH—SOUTH EAST RIDGE
Leader: Juan-Carlos Gómez
Ascents: José-Antonio Garcés, Francisco José Perez, Antonio Ubieto, Rafael Vidaurre
All 6 October.

RUSSIAN–AMERICAN—SOUTH EAST RIDGE
Leader: Volodya Balyberdin
Ascents: 7 October. Anatoli Boukreev, Volodya Balyberdin (2)
10 October. Roman Giutashvili, Dan Mazur
Balyberdin and Boukreev climbed without oxygen.

AUSTRALIAN—SOUTH EAST RIDGE
Leader: Michael Groom
Reached 8,200 m.

BELGIAN—NORTH FACE
Leader: Alain Hubert

BRAZILIAN—NORTH COL
Leader: Thomasz Brandolin

BRITISH SOLO—SOUTH EAST RIDGE
Jonathan Pratt

CANADIAN–AMERICAN–FINNISH—NORTH RIDGE
Leader: Peter Austin

FRENCH–BRITISH–BRAZILIAN—SOUTH EAST RIDGE
Leader: Denis Pivot

GERMAN–SWISS—SOUTH EAST RIDGE
Leader: Hans Eitel
Reached 7,900 m.

JAPANESE—SOUTH EAST RIDGE
Leader: Yasuo Iwazoe
Reached South Summit.

NEPALESE–FRENCH–BELGIAN—SOUTH EAST RIDGE
Leader: Pasang Lhamu Sherpa
This was an attempt to get the leader to the top, making her the first Nepalese woman to achieve the feat. The expedition aroused some resentment amongst other groups by trying to charge $300 (£190) for the use of 'their' route through the Icefall!

POLISH INTERNATIONAL—WEST RIDGE FROM SOUTH
Leader: Aleksander Lwow
Reached 7,600 m.

BASQUE—SOUTH EAST RIDGE
Leader: Josu Bereziartua
Reached South Summit.

INDIAN—NORTH FACE
Leader: Chakraborty

1991 WINTER

JAPANESE—SOUTH WEST FACE
Leader: Kuniaki Yagihara
A large team—41 members—spent 12 weeks, but high winds stopped them below the Rock Band.

KOREAN—SOUTH PILLAR
Leader: Kim Kwang-Jin
Reached 8,700 m.

KOREAN—SOUTH EAST RIDGE
Leader: Kim Teuk-Hee
Reached 8,600 m.

1992 PRE MONSOON

Spring saw some extreme ski descents: Reinhard Patschneider from the

South Col, Hans Kammerlander from 7,800 m. and Herbert Jooson from the North Face.

INDIAN—SOUTH EAST RIDGE
Leader: Hukam Singh
Ascents: 10 May. Prem Singh, Sunil Dutt Sharma, Kanhaiya Lal (Pokhriyal)
12 May. Lobsang, Santosh Yadav, Mohan Singh (Gunjyal), Sange Mudok, Wangchuk

NEW ZEALAND (COMMERCIAL)—SOUTH EAST RIDGE
Leader: Rob Hall
Ascents: Ned Gillette (US), Doron Erel (Israel), Cham Yick-Kai (Hong Kong), Gary Ball (2) (New Zealand), Douglas Mantle (US), Rob Hall (2) (New Zealand), Randall Danta (US), Guy Cotter (New Zealand), Ingrid Baeyens (Belgium), and Sherpas Sonam Tshering (3), Ang Dorje II, Tashi Tshering, Apa (3), Ang Dawa (2)
All 12 May.

The ascents were made with the Dutch (see below). Another busy day on Everest—27 climbers on top!

DUTCH—SOUTH EAST RIDGE
Leader: Ronald Naar
Ascents: Ronald Naar, Edmond Oefner, Dawa Tashi, Nima Temba
All 12 May.

RUSSIAN—SOUTH EAST RIDGE
Leader: Vyacheslav Volkov
Ascents: 12 May. Aleksandr Gerasimov, Andrei Volkov, Ilia Sabelnikov, Ivan Dusharin
14 May. Sergei Penzov, Vladimir Zakharov, Yevgeni Vinogradsky, Fedor Konyukhov

AMERICAN—SOUTH EAST RIDGE
Leader: Todd Burleson
Ascents: 12 May. Skip Horner, Louis Bowen, Vernon Tejas, Dawa Temba, Ang Gyalzen
15 May. Peter Athans (3), Keith Kerr (Great Britain), Todd Burleson, Hugh Morton, Lhakpa Rita (2), Man Bahadur Tamang, Dorje
This party placed laser reflectors on the summit for use with an EDM

(electronic distance measuring) laser at Thyangboche.

CHILEAN—EAST FACE
Leader: Rodrigo Jordán
Ascents: Cristián García-Huidobro, Rodrigo Jordán, Juan-Sebastián Montes
All 15 May.
They followed the 1988 route to the South Col (second ascent).

SPANISH—SOUTH PILLAR
Leader: Francisco Soria
Ascents: Francisco Gan, Alfonso Juez, Ramón Portilla, Lhakpa Nuru, Pemba Norbu II
All 15 May.

CHILEAN—SOUTH EAST RIDGE
Leader: Mauricio Purto
Ascents: Mauricio Purto, Ang Rita (7), Ang Phuri
All 15 May.
Ang Rita climbed without oxygen.

INTERNATIONAL—SOUTH EAST RIDGE
Leader: Miroslav Smid
Ascent: Jonathan Pratt with the Chilean team, 15 May

AMERICAN-CANADIAN—NORTH COL-NORTH RIDGE
Leader: Dan Larson

BRITISH—WEST RIDGE-NORTH FACE
Leader: Col Mike Kefford
This British Services expedition reached 8,500 m.

FRENCH—SOUTH EAST RIDGE
Leader: Denis Chatrefou

GERMAN (COMMERCIAL)—NORTH COL-NORTH FACE
Leader: Sigi Hupfauer

INDIAN—SOUTH EAST RIDGE
Leaders: Deepak Kulkarni, Surjit Singh Puri

This two-man expedition failed to return.

JAPANESE-KAZAKHSTAN—NORTH EAST RIDGE
Leader: Motomu Ohmiya
Discovered the remains of Peter Boardman (see 1982).

SPANISH-BRITISH—SOUTH EAST RIDGE
Leaders: Cesar Perez, Juan Luis Salcedo

SPANISH—SOUTH EAST RIDGE
Leader: Albino Quinteiro

1992 POST MONSOON

BASQUE—SOUTH EAST RIDGE
Leader: Pedro Tous
Ascents: 25 September. Juan-Maria Eguillor, Patxi Fernández, Alberto Iñurrategi, Félix Iñurrategi (the latter two without oxygen).
1 October. Josu Bereziartua
3 October. Juan Tomás, Mikel Repáraz, Pedro Tous

FRENCH-ITALIAN—SOUTH EAST RIDGE
Leader: Agostino Da Polenza
Ascents: 28 September. Giuseppe Petigax, Lorenzo Mazzoleni, Mario Panzeri, Pierre Royer, Lhakpa Nuru (2)
29 September. Oswald Santin, Benoît Chamoux
30 September. Abele Blanc, Giampietro Verza
Panzeri did the ascent without oxygen. More measuring equipment was placed on the summit in a French-Italian attempt to remeasure the height. Three stations each in Nepal and Tibet were set up. The results gave 8,848.65 m.—hardly different from the generally accepted figure.

FRENCH—SOUTH EAST RIDGE
Leader: Bernard Muller
Ascent: Eugène Berger, 1 October

GERMAN—SOUTH EAST RIDGE
Leader: Ralf Dujmovits (Germany)

Ascent: Dujmovits and Sonam Tshering (4), 4 October

INTERNATIONAL—SOUTH EAST RIDGE
Leader: Michael Vincent (France)
Ascents: 7 October. Michael Vincent
9 October. Scott Darsney (US)

INTERNATIONAL—SOUTH EAST RIDGE
Leaders: Sergio Watkins, Wally Berg
Ascents: Wally Berg (US), Augusto Ortega (Peru), Alfonso de la Parrá (Mexico), Pasang Kami, Apa (4)
All 9 October.

FRENCH—SOUTH EAST RIDGE
Leader: Michel Pellé
Ascents: Michel Pellé, Philippe Grenier, Thierry Defrance, Alain Roussey, Pierre Aubertin
All 9 October.
Pierre Tardivel made a ski descent from the South Summit, 28 September.

AMERICAN—NORTH FACE
Leaders: Douglas Hansen, Stanton Smith

ITALIAN—NORTH FACE
Leader: Augosto Zanotto

ITALIAN-SWISS—NORTH RIDGE
Leader: Aldo Verzaroli

AMERICAN-LITHUANIAN—NORTH RIDGE
Leader: Alex Bertulis

NEPALESE—SOUTH EAST RIDGE
Leader: Iman Gerung

TAIWANESE NORTH FACE
Leader: Gau Ming-ho

RUSSIAN-UKRAINIAN—SOUTH WEST FACE
Leader: Mikhail Turkevitch

1992 WINTER
Robert McConnell led a clean-up team to the north side of the mountain.

BRITISH—SOUTH EAST RIDGE
Leader: Lt Col Philip Neame
Reached 7,850 m.

SPANISH SOLO—SOUTH EAST RIDGE
Fernando Garrido reached 7,750 m. Ang Tshering Sherpa, helping Garrido, died in a crevasse fall.

1993 PRE MONSOON

SOUTH KOREAN—NORTH RIDGE
Leader: Oh-In-Hwan
Ascents: Heo Young-Ho, Ngati, 13 April
Because of poor weather the pair decided to descend by the South East Ridge, thus completing a north-south traverse of the mountain.

NEPALESE—SOUTH EAST RIDGE
Leader: Pasang Lhamu (Mrs.)
Ascents: Pasang Lhamu (Mrs.), Sonam Tshering, Dawa Tashi, Lhakpa Nuru, Pemba Nuru, Nawang Thile
All 22 April. Lhamu achieved her ambition of being the first Nepalese woman to climb Everest, unfortunately she and Sonam Tshering died on the descent.

CHINESE–TAIWANESE—NORTH RIDGE
Leader: Zeng Shu-Sheng (China)
Ascents: By the Chinese climbers Ji Mi (China), Jia Chuo (China), Kai Zhong (China), Pu Bu (China), Wang Yong Feng (China) and Wu Chin-Hsiung (Taiwan)
All 5 May.

AMERICAN–CANADIAN—SOUTH EAST RIDGE
Leader: Todd Burleson
Ascents: Alex Lowe (US), John Helenek (US), John Dufficy (US), Wally Berg (US), Michael Sutton (Canada), and Sherpas Apa, Dawa Nuru, Chuldin Temba
All 10 May, which was destined to be another busy day on the roof of the

world; 40 climbers made it. See details later.

SOUTH KOREAN WOMEN'S—SOUTH EAST RIDGE
Leader: Ji Hyun-Ok
Ascents: Kim Soon-Joo, Ji Hyun-Ok, Choi Oh-Soon and Sherpas Ang Dawa, Ang Tsering, Sona Dendu, Rinzin
All 10 May.

AUSTRALIAN–INDIAN—SOUTH EAST RIDGE
Leader: Tashi Wangchuk Tenzing
Ascents: Michael Groom (Australia), Lobsang Tshering Bhutia (India), 10 May
Lobsang died on the expedition. Groom climbed without oxygen. Tenzing is a grandson of Tenzing Norgay.

BRITISH—SOUTH EAST RIDGE
Leader: John Barry
Ascents: 10 May. Harry Taylor
17 May. Rebecca Stephens with Sherpas Ang Pasang, Kami Tshering
Taylor was the second British climber to make the summit without oxygen; Rebecca Stephens was the first British woman to climb Everest.

INDIAN–NEPALESE WOMEN'S—SOUTH EAST RIDGE
Leader: Bachendri Pal
Ascents: 10 May. Dicky Dolma, Santosh Yadav, Kunga Bhutia, Baldev Kunwer and Sherpas Ongda Chhiring, Na Temba, Kosang Dorje, Dorje
16 May. Radha Devi Thakur, Rajiv Sharma, Deepu Sharma, Savita Martolia, Nima Norbu Dolma, Suman Kutiyal with Sherpas Nima Dorje, Tenzing, Lobsang Jangbu, Nga Temba
Dicky Dolma was the youngest woman to climb Everest at age 19.

AMERICAN—SOUTH EAST RIDGE
Leaders: Paul Pfau, Michael Sinclair
Ascents: 10 May. Mary (Dolly) Lefever, Mark Selland, Charles Armatys, Pemba Temba, Moti Lal Gurung
16 May. Michael Sinclair, Mark Rabold, Phinzo, Dorje, Durga Tamang

NEW ZEALAND (COMMERCIAL)—SOUTH EAST RIDGE
Leader: Rob Hall
Ascents: Veikka Gustafson (Finland), Ms Jan Arnold (New Zealand), Rob Hall (New Zealand), Jonathan Gluckman (New Zealand), Sherpas Ang

Chumbi, Ang Dorje, Nuru
All 10 May.

LITHUANIAN—SOUTH EAST RIDGE
Leader: Vladas Vitkauskas
Ascent: Vladas Vitkauskas reached the summit on 10 May.

RUSSIAN—SOUTH EAST RIDGE
Leader: Aleksandr Volgin
Ascents: 10 May. Alexei Mouravlev
15 May. Vladimir Janochkine
16 May. Vladimir Bashkirov (without oxygen)
17 May. Vladimir Koroteyev
Originally they tried the West Ridge but failed.

SPANISH—SOUTH EAST RIDGE
Leader: Lluis Belvis
Ascents: 16 May. Josep Pujante, Ang Phurba
17 May. Oscar Cadiach (without oxygen)

BASQUE—SOUTH EAST RIDGE
Leader: Josu Feijoo
Ascents: José Maria Oñate, Alberto Cerain, José Ramon Aguirre, Jangbu, Ang Rita (8)
All 16 May.
Notable for Ang Rita's astonishing eighth ascent of Everest! (He climbed without oxygen.)

AMERICAN—SOUTH EAST RIDGE
Leader: Keith Brown
Ascent: Jan Harris and Keith Brown, 16 May

SOUTH KOREAN—SOUTH EAST RIDGE
Leader: Lee Jong-Ryang
Ascents: Park Young-Seok, An Jin-Seob, Kim Tae-Kon, Kazi
All 16 May. An Jin-Seob died on the expedition.

BRITISH-IRISH—NORTH RIDGE
Leader: Dawson Stelfox
Ascent: Stelfox reached the top on 27 May—the first Irish ascent of Everest and, because of his dual nationality, the first British ascent from the north.

SOUTH KOREAN—SOUTH PILLAR–SOUTH EAST RIDGE
Leader: Jeon Byoung-Mau
Reached 8,600 m.

SWISS–GERMAN—NORTH FACE
Leaders: Gaudenz Bass, Christoph Jezler

1993 SUMMER

AMERICAN—NORTH COL
Leaders: Jim Wickwire, John Roskelley

1993 POST MONSOON

SOUTH KOREAN—NORTH FACE
Leader: Lim Hyung-Chil
Ascents: Park Hyun-Jae, Panuru, 6 October

FRENCH—SOUTH EAST RIDGE
Leader: Alain Estève
Ascents: 6 October. François Bernard, Antoine Cayrol, Eric Gramond, Gyalbu, Dawa Tashi
9 October. Alain Estève, Hubert Giot, Nuru, Nima Gombu
Gramond and Giot climbed without oxygen.

BASQUE—SOUTH PILLAR
Leader: Juanito Oiarzabal
Ascent: Oiarzabal with Sherpa Ongda Chhiring, 7 October
Antonio Miranda died in a fall.

BRITISH–AMERICAN—SOUTH EAST RIDGE
Leader: Stephen Bell
Ascents: 7 October. Ginette Harrison, Gary Pfisterer (US), Ramon Blanco (Spain), Graham Hoyland, Stephen Bell, Scott McIvor, Sherpas Na Temba, Pasang Kami, Dorje
9 October. Martin Barnicott, David Hempleman-Adams,
Lee Nobmann (US), Sherpas Tenzing, Nga Temba, Lhakpa Gelu, Ang Pasang
At 60 years of age, Blanco became the oldest person to make an ascent.

INTERNATIONAL (COMMERCIAL)—NORTH RIDGE
Leader: Jonathan Tinker
Ascents: 9 October. Maciej Berbeka (Poland), Lhakpa Nuru (Sherpa)
10 October. Jonathan Tinker and Sherpa Babu Tshering
They made a variant leading to the Second Step—more or less Norton's attempted route of 1924.

AMERICAN SOLO —NORTH FACE
Ed Viesturs

AMERICAN-CANADIAN SOLO —GREAT COL
Leader: Robert Anderson

GREEK—NORTH COL
Leader: Konstantinos Tsivelekas

INDIAN—NORTH RIDGE
Leader: Amulya Sen

SPANISH—NORTH RIDGE
Leader: Eloy Sanchez

1993 WINTER

JAPANESE—SOUTH WEST FACE
Leader: Kuniaki Yagihara
Ascents: 18 December. Hideji Nazuka, Fumiaki Goto
20 December. Osamu Tanabe, Sinsuke Ezuka
22 December. Yoshio Ogata, Ryushi Hoshino.
The first winter ascent of the face, done remarkably efficiently in just 3 weeks.

1994 PRE MONSOON

JAPANESE—SOUTH PILLAR
Leader: Mitsuyoshi Hongo
Ascents: 8 May. Kiyohiko Suzuki, Wataru Atsuta, Sherpas Nima Dorje, Dawa Tshering, Na Temba, Lhakpa Nuru
13 May. Tomiyasu Ishikawa, Sherpas Nima Temba, Dawa Tashi, Pasang Tshering

Ishikawa was 57 years old.

TAIWANESE—NORTH RIDGE
Leader: Chang Jui-Kong
Ascent: Shih Fang-Fang, 8 May

AMERICAN—SOUTH EAST RIDGE CLEANUP
Leader: Steven Goryl
Ascents: 9 May. Rob Hess, Scott Fischer, Brent Bishop, Sona Dendu, Lobsang Jangbu
13 May. Steven Goryl
Lobsang Jangbu made his second ascent without oxygen—this time in Sherpa costume! Hess and Fischer also climbed without oxygen. Brent Bishop is the son of Barry Bishop (see 1963). The expedition removed 2 tons of rubbish, including 200 discarded oxygen cylinders.

INTERNATIONAL (COMMERCIAL)—SOUTH EAST RIDGE
Leader: Rob Hall
Ascents: Hall Wendel (US), Helmut Seitzl (Germany), David Keaton (US), Ekke Gundelach (Germany), Rob Hall (4) (New Zealand), Ed Viesturs (3) (US), David Taylor (US), Erling Kagge (Norway), Sherpas Nima Gombu, Norbu, Ang Dorje
All 9 May. Kagge claims to be the first person to reach both poles and the top of Everest.

INTERNATIONAL (COMMERCIAL)—SOUTH EAST RIDGE
Leader: Todd Burleson
Ascents: Ryszard Pawlowski (Poland), Robert Cedergreen (US), Paul Morrow (US), Peter Athans (4) (US), Todd Burleson (US), Tamang Man Bahadur, Sherpas Lhakpa Rita, Chuwang Nima, Kami Rita, Dorje
All 13 May.

INTERNATIONAL (COMMERCIAL)—NORTH RIDGE
Leader: Eric Simonson
Ascents: 19 May. David Hahn (US)
25 May. Steve Swenson (US) (without oxygen)
26 May. Mark Whetu (2) (New Zealand), Michael Rheinberger (Australia). Rheinberger died on the expedition.

31 May. Bob Sloezen (2) (US)

AMERICAN—NORTH COL
Leader: Steven Matous

AMERICAN—EAST FACE
Leader: David Breashears

INTERNATIONAL—NORTH COL
Leader: Peter Kowalzik

CANADIAN—GREAT COL
Leaders: Jamie Clarke, Alan Hobson

ITALIAN—NORTH RIDGE
Leader: Giuliano DeMarchi

ITALIAN—NORTH FACE
Leaders: Giuseppe Vigani, Bruno Ongis

BRITISH (COMMERCIAL)—NORTH RIDGE
Leader: Russell Brice

1994 SUMMER

INTERNATIONAL—NORTH FACE
Leaders: Nick Banks, Iain Peter

1994 POST MONSOON

JAPANESE—SOUTH EAST RIDGE
Leaders: Takashi Miyahara
Ascents: Muneo Nukita, Sherpas Apa, Chuang Nima, Dawa Tshering
All 10 October.

BRITISH MEDICAL EXPEDITION—SOUTH EAST RIDGE
Leader: Simon Currin
Ascents: Charlie Hornsby, Roddy Kirkwood, Sherpas Dorje, Dawa Temba

All 11 October.

AMERICAN—NORTH FACE
Leader: Tony Lewis

CZECH–ITALIAN—NORTH FACE
Leader: Josef Rakoncai

FRENCH—NORTH RIDGE
Leader: Daniel Petraud

FRENCH—SOUTH EAST RIDGE
Leader: Bernard Muller

INDONESIAN—SOUTH EAST RIDGE
Leader: Anton Patandung

NEPALESE—SOUTH EAST RIDGE SOLO
Leader: Kaji Sherpa
Attempt to break the speed record for an ascent.

NORWEGIAN—NORTH RIDGE–WEST RIDGE
Leader: Jon Gangdal

RUSSIAN—NORTH RIDGE–NORTH FACE
Leader: Sergai Efimov

SPANISH—NORTH RIDGE
Leader: Rogelio Recio

INTERNATIONAL—NORTH RIDGE
Leader: Peter Kowalzik

1995 PRE MONSOON

Twelve simultaneous expeditions were on the south side of Everest, and there was considerable cooperation. Seventy-four climbers reached the summit in April and May.

NEW ZEALAND (COMMERCIAL)—SOUTH EAST RIDGE
Leader: Rob Hall
Ascent: Sherpa Lobsang Jangbu, 7 May, climbing without oxygen

JAPANESE—NORTH EAST RIDGE
Leader: Tadao Kanzaki
Ascents: Kiyoshi Furuno, Shigeki Imoto, Sherpas Dawa Tshering, Lhakpa Nuru (6), Nima Dorje (5), Pasang Kami
All 11 May.
The first integral ascent of the North East Ridge. 4,000 m. of fixed rope used.

RUSSIAN—NORTH RIDGE
Leader: Kazbek Khamitsayev
Ascents: 11 May. Vladimir Shataev, Iria Projaev, Fedor Shuljev
13 May. Kazbek Khamitsayev, Yevgeni Vinogradski, Sergei Bogomilov, Vladimir Korenkov, Ang Rita (9)
Ang Rita continues his phenomenal career, again without oxygen.

POLISH–ITALIAN—NORTH RIDGE
Leader: Marco Bianchi
Ascents: 12 May. Piotr Pustelnik
13 May. Marco Bianchi, Christian Kuntner
The two Italians did not use oxygen. Pustelnik reached the top with Pawlowski (see next expedition).

INTERNATIONAL (COMMERCIAL)—NORTH RIDGE
Leader: Henry Todd
Ascents: 12 May. Ryszard Pawlowski (see above)
14 May. Mozart Catao (Brazil), Waldemar Niclevicz (Brazil)
17 May. Graham Ratcliffe (UK), Anatoli Boukreev (2) (Russia), Nikolai Sitnikov (Russia)
23 May. Michael Jorgensen (Denmark), Caradoc (Crag) Jones (Wales)
The first Brazilian, Danish, and Welsh ascents. Boukreev again did not use oxygen.

TAIWANESE—NORTH RIDGE
Leader: Liang Ming-Pen
Ascents: Cheng Kuo-Chun, Chiang Hsui-Chen (Miss), Sherpas Mingma Tshering, Lhakpa Dorje, Tenzing
All 12 May. Lhakpa and Tenzing did not use oxygen.

INTERNATIONAL (COMMERCIAL)—NORTH RIDGE
Leader: Russell Brice
Ascents: 13 May. Alison Hargreaves (UK)
17 May. Constantin Lacatusu (Romania)

26 May. Greg Child (Australia), Karsang, Lobsang Temba
Alison Hargreaves climbed solo without oxygen. Lydia Bradey made the first woman's ascent without oxygen but by the South East Ridge (without permission). Lacatusu made the first Romanian ascent.

LATVIAN–ITALIAN—NORTH RIDGE
Leaders: Reinhard Patschneider, Teodors Kirsis
Ascents: Reinhard Patschneider (Italy), Teodors Kirsis (Latvia), Imants Zauls (Latvia)
All 14 May.
Patschneider, climbing without oxygen, set a record for the North Ridge of 21 hours (approximately 2,400 m.). Kirsis and Zauls made the first Latvian ascents.

AMERICAN (COMMERCIAL)—NORTH RIDGE
Leader: Paul Pfau
Ascents: 14 May. George Mallory (Australia), Jeffrey Hall (US), Jim Litch (US), Dan Aguillar (US), Sherpas Kaji, Ongda Chhiring, Wongchu
16 May. Colin Lynch (US), Jay Budnik (US), Steve Reneker (US), Kurt Wedberg (US), Sherpas Phinzo, Jangbu
George Mallory is the grandson of the George Mallory who died on the mountain in 1924.

INTERNATIONAL (COMMERCIAL)—NORTH RIDGE
Leader: Jon Tinker
Ascents: 14 May. Luc Jourjon (France), Babu Tshering
17 May. George Kotov (Russia), Ali Nasuh Mahruki
24 May. Jeff Shea (US), Lhakpa Gelu, Tshering
26 May. Patrick Hache (France), Robert Hempstead (US), Lama Jangbu, Babu Tshering (5)
27 May. Michael Smith (Great Britain), Patrick Falvey (Ireland), James Allen (Australia)
Sherpa Babu Tshering made two ascents in 12 days—his fifth overall and all without oxygen. Mahruki made the first Turkish ascent, and Jourjon's was the first French ascent from the north.

AUSTRIAN—NORTH RIDGE
Leader: Willi Bauer
Ascent: Josef Hinding, 14 May, climbing without oxygen

AMERICAN—SOUTH EAST RIDGE
Leader: Bob Hoffman

Ascents: Brad Bull (US), Tommy Heinrich (Argentina), Sherpas Apa (7), Arita, Nima Rita
The first Argentinian ascent was made by Heinrich.

AMERICAN (COMMERCIAL)—NORTH RIDGE
Leader: Thor Kieser
Ascents: Tony Tonsing (US), Musal Kazi Tamang

AMERICAN (COMMERCIAL)—SOUTH EAST RIDGE
Leader: Todd Burleson

1995 SUMMER

AMERICAN—NORTH RIDGE
Leader: David Breashears

AMERICAN—NORTH FACE
Leader: Robert Anderson

SWISS—NORTH RIDGE
Leader: Aldo Verzarol

1995 POST MONSOON

SOUTH KOREAN—NORTH RIDGE (2 expeditions)
Leader: Kim Jong-Ho
Leader: Lee Dong Ho
These two independent South Korean expeditions decided to join forces.
Ascents: Han Wuang-Yong, Hong Sung-Taek, Jo Yong-Il, Zangbu, Tashi Tshering
All 14 October. Zangbu died on the expedition.

SOUTH KOREAN—SOUTH WEST FACE
Leader: Cho Hyung-Gyu
Ascents: Park Jung-Hun, Kim Young-Tae, Dawa Tamang, Kipa
All 14 October.

INDIAN—NORTH RIDGE
Leader: Atanu Chatterjee

KOREAN—NORTH RIDGE
Leader: Lee Dong-Yeon

SPANISH—NORTH RIDGE
Leader: Albert Castellet

1996 PRE MONSOON

By the spring of 1996, 4,000 climbers had attempted Everest, 660 successfully, and 142 had died (3.5 percent). Fees rose substantially, and a $4,000 (£2,530} bond for garbage clearance was added.

AMERICAN (COMMERCIAL)—SOUTH EAST RIDGE
Leader: Scott Fischer
Ascents (all US except where indicated): Anatoli Boukreev (3) (Russia), Neal Beidleman, Martin Adams, Klev Schoening, Charlotte Fox, Tim Madsen, Sandy Hill Pittman, Scott Fischer, Lena Nielsen-Gammelgaard (Denmark), Sherpas Lobsang Jangbu, Tenzing, Tashi Tshering, Nawang Dorje
All 10 May—a tragic day.
Fischer died. Gammelgaard was the first Danish woman to climb Everest. Boukreev and Lobsang did not use oxygen.

NEW ZEALAND (COMMERCIAL)—SOUTH EAST RIDGE
Leader: Rob Hall
Ascents: Jon Krakauer (US), Andrew Harris (New Zealand), Michael Groom (Australia), Rob Hall (New Zealand), Yasuko Namba (Mrs.) (Japan), Doug Hansen (US), Ang Dorje, Norbu
All 10 May.
The tragedy continues—Harris, Hall, Namba and Hansen died. Namba, at 47, was the oldest woman to reach the summit.

TAIWANESE—SOUTH EAST RIDGE
Leader: Gau Ming-Ho
Ascents: Gau Ming-Ho with Sherpas Nima Gombu, Mingma Tshering, 10 May
A member of this expedition died in the Icefall.

INDIAN–MONGOLIAN—NORTH FACE
Leader: Mohinder Singh
Ascents: 10 May. Tsewang Samanla, Tsewang Paljor, Dorje Morup
17 May. Sange Sherpa, Hira Ram, Tashi Ram, Nadra Ram Sherpa, Kusang Sherpa
It is claimed the 10 May party stopped 150 m. short of the top. Sadly, all died on that fateful day.

JAPANESE—NORTH FACE
Leader: Mitsuo Uematsu
Ascents: 11 May. Hiroshi Hanada, Eisuka Shigekawa, Sherpas Pasang Tshering, Pasang Kami, Ang Gyalzen
13 May. Mamoru Kikuchi, Hirotaka Sugiyama, Sherpas Nima Dorje, Chuwang Nima, Dawa Tshering

JAPANESE—NORTH FACE
Leader: Koji Yamazaki
Ascents: 17 May. Hirotaka Takeyuchi, Sherpas Pemba Tshering, Na Temba
21 May. Koji Yamazaki
Pemba Tshering was 53.

INTERNATIONAL—NORTH FACE
Leader: Jon Gangdal
Ascents: 17 May. Norwegians Sven Gangdal, Olav Ulvund, Sherpas Dawa Tashi, Dawa Tshering
18 May. Morten Rostrup (Norway), Josef Nezerka (Czechoslovakia), Fausto De Stafani (Italy), Gyalbu

BRITISH (COMMERCIAL)—NORTH FACE
Leader: Simon Lowe
Ascents: Alan Hinkes, Matthew Dickinson, Sherpas Lhakpa Gelu, Mingma Dorje, Phur Gyalzen
All 19 May.

RUSSIAN SECONDARY—NORTH FACE
Leader: Sergei Antipin
Ascents: Petr Kouznetsov, Valeri Kohanov, Grigori Semikolenkov
All 20 May. Tough team on difficult new route between North and North East Ridges.

FRENCH—SOUTH EAST RIDGE
Leader: Thierry Renard
Ascents: Renard with Sherpas Dawa, Babu Tshering (6), 23 May
Babu's sixth ascent.

US IMAX FILM—SOUTH EAST RIDGE
Leader: David Breashears
Ascents: Ed Viesturs (US), David Breashears (US), Robert Schauer (Austria), Jamling Tenzing Norgay (India), Araceli Segarra (Miss) (Spain),

Sherpas Lhakpa Dorje, Dorje, Jangbu, Muktu Lhakpa, Thilen
All 23 May. Viesturs and Lhakpa climbed without oxygen.

SWEDISH—SOUTH PILLAR
Leader: Goran Kropp
Ascents: Goran Kropp (with Spanish climber—see below), Ang Rita (10), 23 May
Ang Rita's tenth ascent, done independently of the others. Neither he nor Kropp used oxygen.

SPANISH—SOUTH PILLAR
Leader: Jose Antonio Martinez
Ascent: Jesus Martinez, 23 May (see above), climbed without oxygen.

ITALIAN—NORTH RIDGE
Leader: Hans Kammerlander
Ascent: Hans Kammerlander, 24 May
A fast solo ascent of 17 hours by Kammerlander (without oxygen), who then skied down from the summit (a first).

INTERNATIONAL—NORTH FACE
Leader: Peter Kowalzik
Ascent: Yuri Contreras (Mexico) and Hector Ponce de Leon (Mexico), 24 May

SOUTH AFRICAN—SOUTH EAST RIDGE
Leader: Ian Woodall
Ascents: Ian Woodall, Cathy O'Dowd, Bruce Herrod (United Kingdom), Sherpas Pemba, Ang Dorje, Lama Jangbu
All 25 May.
Herrod later died on the expedition.

GERMAN—NORTH RIDGE
Leader: Goetz Wiegand

GREEK—NORTH RIDGE
Leader: Kostas Tsivelekas

AUSTRO-HUNGARIAN—NORTH RIDGE
Leader: Santor Nagy

Rheinhart Wlasich (Austria) died.

ITALIAN–SWISS—NORTH RIDGE
Leader: Massimo Lugli

NEPALESE CLEAN UP—SOUTH COL
Leader: Sonam Gyaljen Sherpa

NORWEGIAN—SOUTH WEST FACE
Leader: Peter Netby

SLOVENIAN—GREAT COULOIR
Leader: Viktor Groselj

SPANISH—NORTH RIDGE
Leader: Joan Cardona

SWISS-AUSTRIAN—NORTH RIDGE
Leader: Norbert Joos

TAIWANESE—NORTH FACE
Leader: Tsai Fong-Bin

BRITISH (COMMERCIAL)—SOUTH PILLAR
Leader: Mal Duff

AMERICAN (COMMERCIAL)—SOUTH EAST RIDGE
Leaders: Peter Athans, Todd Burleson

MONTENEGRAN—SOUTH EAST RIDGE
Leader: Radosav Nikcevic

INTERNATIONAL—SOUTH EAST RIDGE
Leader: Henry Todd

1996 POST MONSOON

INDONESIAN—NORTH RIDGE–NORTH FACE
Leader: Clara Sumarwati
Ascents: Sumarwati plus Sherpas Kaji, Gyalzen, Ang Gyalzen, Dawa

Tshering, Chuwang Nima, 26 September

SOUTH KOREAN—SOUTH EAST RIDGE
Leader: Lim Hyung-Chil
Ascents: Choi Jong-Tai, Shin Kwang-Chal, Dawa Tamang, Sherpas Paneru, Kipa, 11 October

US–GERMAN–YUGOSLAVIAN—NORTH SIDE
Leader: Craig Calonica
The expedition did not get beyond Advanced Base Camp.

CZECH–UK–SLOVAK—NORTH FACE
Leader: Vaclav Suchel

FRENCH–BELGIAN–SWISS—SOUTH EAST RIDGE
Leader: Bernard Muller
Yves Bouchon died.

AUSTRO-GERMAN—SOUTH EAST RIDGE
Leader: Ralf Dujmogits

JAPANESE—SOUTH EAST RIDGE
Leader: Hirofumi Konishi
Sherpa Lobsang Jangbu, who had climbed Everest four times, died with two expedition members when an avalanche came down Lhotse as they were approaching the South Col.

SOUTH AFRICAN—NORTH RIDGE
Leader: Alex Harris

SWISS (COMMERCIAL)—NORTH RIDGE
Leader: Jean Troillet

BELGIAN—ILLEGAL ATTEMPT FROM SOUTH
Dirk Dansercoer and Daniel Hernadez were apprehended in the Icefall and banished for 10 years.

1997 PRE MONSOON

JAPANESE—SOUTH EAST RIDGE
Leaders: Hiroshi Okura, Kiyohiko Tsujita

High point 7,200 m.

INDONESIAN–RUSSIAN–POLISH—SOUTH EAST RIDGE
Leader: Edhie Wibowo
Ascents: Appa Sherpa (9), Anatoli Boukreev (Russia), Dawa Nuru Sherpa, Vladimir Bashkirov (Russia), Misirin (Indonesia), Asmujiono (Indonesia) All 26 April.
Two weeks later the expedition attempted the North Ridge and reached 8,600 m.

MULTINATIONAL—NORTH RIDGE
Leader: Ervand Ilinski
Nationals involved were Kazakh, Russian, Georgian, Canadian and Australian. Thirteen climbers reached the top.
Ascents: 2 May. Kazakhs Vladimir Frolov, Andrej Molotov, Sergei Ovsharenko, Vladimir Souviga
7 May. Russians Ivan Plotnikov, Nikolai Chevtchenko
20 May. Kazakhs Konstantin Farafonov, Sergei Lavrov, Dimitri Mouravev, Dimitri Grekov, Dimitri Sobolev, Lyudmila Savina
2 May. Andy Evans (Canada–US)
Plotnikov, Chevtchenko and another Russian died on the expedition, one from a fall. Souviga climbed without oxygen.

SOUTH KOREAN—NORTH RIDGE
Leader: Lee Dong-Yeon
Ascents: 7 May. Lee In, Ang Dawa Tamang
A Sherpa died in a fall.

FRENCH–BULGARIAN—NORTH RIDGE
Leader: Antoine de Choudens
Ascents: 8 May. De Choudens (climbing without oxygen) and Stephane Cagnin (France)

20 May. Doytchin Vassilev (Bulgaria)

INTERNATIONAL (COMMERCIAL)—SOUTH EAST RIDGE
Leader: Jon Tinker
Ascents: 21 May. Nikola Kekus (United Kingdom), Bjorn Olafsson (Iceland), Hallgrimur Magnusson (Iceland), Einar Stefansson (Iceland) with Sherpas Babu Tshering and Dawa
23 May. Mark Warham (United Kingdom), Eric Blakeley (United Kingdom),

Hugo Rodriguez (Mexico), and Sherpas Lhakpa Gelu and Da Tenzi
First Icelandic ascents.

NEPALESE— SOUTH EAST RIDGE
Leader: Bhakta Bahadur Thakuri
Ascents: 21 May. Danuri Sherpa
25 May. Kami Rita Sherpa
Technically these two Sherpas were attached to the Burleson expedition (see later)—another example of the increasingly common mix and match!

INTERNATIONAL—NORTH RIDGE
Leader: Darko Berljak
Members from Croatia, Slovenia, Bosnia-Herzegovina, and Germany
Ascents: 22 May. Franc Pepevnik (Slovenia)
23 May. Pavle Kozjek (Slovenia)
Kozjek did not use oxygen.

AMERICAN—SOUTH EAST RIDGE
Leader: David Breashears
Ascents: 23 May. David Breashears, Peter Athans, Sherpas Jangbu, Dorje and Kami
A filming and physiological research expedition during which Liesl Clark and Breashears made *Everest: The Death Zone.*

CANADIAN-AMERICAN—SOUTH EAST RIDGE
Leader: Jason Edwards
Ascents: 23 May. Jamie Clarke (Canada), Alan Hobson (Canada) with Sherpas Lhakpa Tshering, Gyalbu, Tashi Tshering, Kami Tshering

INTERNATIONAL (COMMERCIAL)—SOUTH EAST RIDGE
Leader: Guy Cotter
Ascents: 23 May. Guy Cotter (New Zealand), Ed Viesturs (US), Tashi Tenzing (Australia), David Carter (US), Veikka Gustafsson (Finland), Sherpas Ang Dorje, Mingma Tshering
Cotter took over Rob Hall's company after the latter's death. Gustafsson climbed without oxygen.

MALAYSIAN—SOUTH EAST RIDGE
Leader: Nor Ramlle Sulaiman
Ascents: Mohandas Nagapan, Magendran Munisamy and Sherpas Na Temba, Dawa Temba, Gyalzen, Ang Phuri Gyalzen, Fura Dorje

All 23 May.

INTERNATIONAL (COMMERCIAL)—SOUTH EAST RIDGE
Leader: Mal Duff
Ascents: 23 May. Andres Delgado (Mexico), Tenzing Sherpa
27 May. Brigitte Muir (Australia), Sherpas Kipa and Dorje
The leader died from illness at base camp before the ascents.

RUSSIAN—NORTH RIDGE
Leader: Kazbek Khamitsayev
Ascents: Alexandre Zelinski and Sergei Sokolov, 24 May
They climbed a rib on the North Face to reach the ridge.

AMERICAN–BRITISH—SOUTH EAST RIDGE
Leader: Todd Burleson
Ascents: Wally Berg (US), Sherpas Ang Pasang, Pemba Tenji, Mingma Tshering, Lhakpa Rita, Nima Tashi, Tenzing Nuru, Kami Rita
All 25 May.
The expedition accommodated the scientists engaged in the Everest remeasuring. Tenzing Nuru disappeared, presumed to have fallen.

INTERNATIONAL (COMMERCIAL)—SOUTH EAST RIDGE
Leader: Henry Todd
Ascents: Yuri Contreras (Mexico), Ilgvars Pauls (Latvia), Dawa Sona Sherpa
All 27 May.
No fewer than ten nationalities on this expedition!

INTERNATIONAL (COMMERCIAL)—NORTH RIDGE
Leader: Russell Brice
Ascents: Brice and Richard Price (New Zealand), May 29
CHINESE (TIBETAN)—NORTH RIDGE
Leader: Da Chimyi
Ascents: Da Chimyi, Tenzing Dorje, Kai Zhong, May 29

BELGIAN—NORTH RIDGE
Leader: Pascal Debrouwer
High point 8,200 m.

AUSTRIAN—NORTH RIDGE
Leader: Wilfrid Studer
High point 7,800 m.

BRAZILIAN—NORTH RIDGE
Leader: Paulo Coelho
High point 8,150 m.

GEORGIAN—NORTH RIDGE
Leader: Afi Gigani
High point 8,100 m.

SOLO—NORTH RIDGE
Peter Kowalzik (Germany) disappeared on the climb. Last seen about 8,560 m. on 8 May.

ITALIAN—NORTH RIDGE
Leader: Reinhard Patscheider
High point 7,100 m.

INTERNATIONAL—NORTH RIDGE
A disparate group of Polish, German, Portugese and American climbers without a leader. Joao Garcia reached high point of 8,100 m.

PAKISTANI—NORTH RIDGE
Leader: Nazir Sabir
High point 8,560 m.

SWEDISH—SOUTH EAST RIDGE
Leader: Thomas Sjogren
High point 8,200 m.

1997 POST MONSOON

There were no ascents of Everest during this period.
All the followingattempts were on the North Ridge by the North Col unless stated otherwise.

JAPANESE
Leader: Masufumi Todaka
Attempted North Face–Japanese Couloir and reached 6,400 m. (25 Aug). Later failed on North Ridge at 8,000 m. (27 September).

SOUTH KOREAN
Leader: Kim Teuk-Hee

High point 7,000 m. (8 September)

AMERICAN
Leader: Craig Calonica
High point 7,000 m. (12 September)

BRITISH
Leader:Terry Stubbs
High point 7,000 m. (16 September - 5 October)

SPANISH
Leader: Josef Mario Maixé
High point 7,600 m. (15 September)

COLOMBIAN
Leader: Christobal von Rothkirch
High point 8,200 m. (26 September)

SPANISH
Leader: Jordi Tosas
High point 7,600 m. (27 September)

SWISS
Leader: Jean Troillet
High point 8,700 m. (27 September)

CANADIAN
Leader: George Tumpach
High point 7,800 m. (4 October)

There were only two attempts on the south side, South Col.

FRENCH
Leader:Yvan Estienne
High points: members reached 7,285 m. on 25 September, 6 October, 10 October. Sherpas reached 7,900 m. on 10 October.

SPANISH
Leader: Jose Ramon Madariaga
High points: members reached 7,400 m. on 24, 26 September, 10 October. Sherpas reached 7,900 m. on 8 October.

1998 PRE MONSOON
Some name spellings are unconfirmed at time of compilation.

JAPANESE SOLO—NORTH RIDGE
Hirofumi Konoshi failed at 7,800 m. on 26 April.

NEW ZEALAND SOLO—NORTH RIDGE
Roger Buick died of exposure after reaching 8,350 m. on 7 May.

POLISH—NORTH RIDGE
Leader: Jacek Berbeka
High point 8,350 m. on 7 May.

SPANISH—NORTH FACE
Leader: Joseba Elorrieta
High point 7,500 m. on 14 and 18 May. The attempt was in the vicinity of the Japanese Couloir.

RUSSIAN-BELORUSSIAN—NORTH RIDGE
Leader: Vladimir Shataev
Ascent: Victor Koulbatchenko (Belorussia) on 18 May.

RUSSIAN-INTERNATIONAL—NORTH RIDGE
Leader: Boris Sedusov
Ascents: 18 May. Alexei Bolotov, Valeri Perchine, Sergei Timofeev, Yevgeni Vinogradski (all Russian)
21 May. Anatoli Moshnikov (Russia), Gillies Roman (France)
22 May. Serguei Arsentiev (2) (Rus), Francys Arsentiev (US)
Both Arsentievs died in controversial circumstances.

JAPANESE—NORTH RIDGE
Leader: Hitoshi Onodera
Ascents: 18 May. Shoji Ave, Toshiya Nakajima with Sherpas Pasang Kami, Na Temba, Ang Gyalzen
19 May. Hitoshi Onodera, Hiromichi Kamimura and Sherpas Chuwang Nima, Dawa Tshering

JAPANESE—NORTH RIDGE
Leader: Kazuyoshi Kondo
Ascents: 18 May. Hideoshi Kurashi, Masaru Sato, Koichi Nagata, Hisashi Hashimoto, Shoji Sakamoto and Ang Mingma Sherpa

20 May. Toshiaki Yano, Yoshinori Kawahara, Gyalzen Sherpa
22 May. Kazuyoshi Kondo, Dawa Sherpa

INDIAN—NORTH RIDGE
Leader: Hrishikesh Yadav
Ascents: 18 May. Surendra Chavan with Sherpas Dawa Tashi, Dawa Nuru, Thomting and Tenzing
19 May. Loveraj Dharmshaktu with Sherpas Phinzo Norbu, Nima Gyalzen
Chavan and companions appear to have made the top first on 18 May and were thus the first of the year.

CZECH—NORTH RIDGE
Leader: Zdenek Hruby
Ascents: Radek Jaros and Vladimir Nosek, 19 May
The ascents were made without oxygen. The leader soloed to 8,100 m. before retreating. All six members of this small team reached 8,000 m. Supported by a Sherpa and two others.

SLOVAKIAN–CHINESE—NORTH BUTTRESS
Leaders: Pavol Lazar, Luo Shen
Ascents: 19 May. Peter Hamor, Vladimir Zjoja, Vladimir Plulik (without oxygen).
24 May. Ci Luo (China) possibly with the South African Sherpas (see later)
By all accounts this was not a harmonious expedition.

JAPANESE—NORTH RIDGE
Leader: Noriyuki Muraguchi
Ascents: Muraguchi with Minoru Sawada and Sherpas Migma Tshering, Tshering Dorje, Pasang Kidar, 19 May

POLISH—NORTH RIDGE
Sole Polish climber Anna Czerwinska reached 7,700 m. on 19 May; her Sherpa reached 8,500 m.

SWEDISH—SOUTH EAST RIDGE
Leader: Thomas Sjogren
High point 8,750 m., 19 May.

AMERICAN–BRITISH—SOUTH EAST RIDGE
Leader: Wally Berg
Ascent: Berg reached the summit, possibly with Apa Sherpa (see later) on

20 May
Berg's ascent was part of the attempt to remeasure Everest's height (see Chapter 22).

AMERICAN—SOUTH EAST RIDGE
Leader: Bob Hoffman
Ascents: Bob Hoffman, Donald Beavon, Pasquale Scaturro, Charles Demarest, Mark Cole (all US) and Sherpas Apa (9), Pemba Norbu, Nima Rita, Gyalzen, Chuldim Nuru, Arita
All 20 May.

AMERICAN—SOUTH EAST RIDGE
Leader: Tom Whittaker
Ascents: 20 May. Jeffrey Rhoads, Tashi Tshering Sherpa
27 May. Repeat ascent by Rhoads and Tashi, plus Tom Whittaker, and Sherpas Norbu, Lhakpa Tshering, Dawa Sona
Whittaker became the first disabled climber to reach the summit; he has an artificial right leg. He had tried twice before, in 1989 and 1995.

IRANIAN—SOUTH EAST RIDGE
Leader: Sadegh Aghajani Kalkhoran
Ascents: Jalal Cheshmeh Ghasabani, Mohammed Hassan Majarian, Hamid Reza Olanj, Mohammed Oraz and Sherpas Dawa Tenzi, Chuldim, Pemba Rinzi
All 20 May. The first Iranian ascent of Everest.

UZBEK—NORTH RIDGE
Leader: Anatoli Shabonov
Ascents: 22 May. Rustam Radjapov
23 May. Svetlana Baskakova, Sergei Sokolov, Marat Usaev, Oleg Grigoriev, Angrew Federov
24 May. Aleksai Dokukin, Ilyas Tukhvatullin, Andrew Zaikin
25 May. Khanin Balmagambetov, Roman Mats

SOUTH AFRICAN—NORTH RIDGE
Leader: Ian Woodall
Ascents: Sherpas Lama Jangbu and Lhakpa Gelu, 24 May

NEW ZEALAND-JAPANESE—NORTH RIDGE
Leader: Russell Brice
Ascents: Russell Brice and Sumiyo Tsuzuki with Karsang Sherpa, 25 May

Both had tried Everest several times before.

BRITISH—NORTH RIDGE
Mark Jennings was the only member but said to be on the Brice permit (above). He reached the top on 25 May with Nima Wangchu Sherpa but died of exhaustion on the descent shortly after leaving his top camp.

AMERICAN—NORTH RIDGE
Leader: David Hahn
Ascents: 25 May. Craig John with Sherpas Dawa Nuru, Lhakpa Rita
27 May. Richard Alpert, Robert Sloezen, Panuru Sherpa

BOLIVIAN—SOUTH EAST RIDGE
Leader: Bernardo Guarachi
Ascent: Guarachi reached the summit on 25 May

SINGAPORE–MALAYSIAN—SOUTH EAST RIDGE
Leader: David Lim
Ascents: Khoo Swee-Chiow, Siew Cheok-Wai, Sherpas Kami Rita, Dorje, Fura Dorje, Nawang Phurba
All 25 May.
The first Singaporean ascent of Everest.

BRITISH–INTERNATIONAL (COMMERCIAL)—SOUTH EAST RIDGE
Leader: Dave Walsh
Ascents: Sundeep Dillon (United Kingdom), Dave Walsh (United Kingdom) and Sherpas Nima Gombu, Kusang Dorje, Nima Dorje.
All 25 May.
With this ascent, Dillon became the youngest person to complete the Seven Summits.

BRITISH–INTERNATIONAL (COMMERCIAL)—SOUTH EAST RIDGE
Leader: Henry Todd
Ascents: Alan Silva (Australia), Neil Laughton (United Kingdom), Edward Grylls (United Kingdom) and Sherpas Pasang Dawa, Pasang Tshering
All 26 May.

AUSTRO-GERMAN—NORTH RIDGE
Leader: Heinz Rockenbauer
Ascent: Rockenbauer reached the summit on 26 May

DANISH SOLO—SOUTH EAST RIDGE
Michael Strynoe reached 8,300 m. on 26 May but then withdrew.

AMERICAN—NORTH RIDGE
Leader: Gheorghe Dijmarescu
High point 7,700 m.

INTERNATIONAL—NORTH RIDGE
Leader: Pascal Debrouwer
High point 8,500 m.

1998 POST MONSOON

At the time of compilation the three ascents listed are all disputed, as is the speed-record claim. These were all on the south side:

NEPALESE SPEED ASCENT
October 17. Kaji Sherpa, 35, claimed an ascent by the South East Ridge in 20 hrs 24 mins, thus reducing Marc Batard's 10-year-old record by 2 hours. Japanese climbers on the mountain at the time dispute the ascent.

SPANISH—SOUTH EAST RIDGE
Leader: Juan Corro
Ascent: Carlos Pitarch, October 15
Disputed by both the Nepalese (above) and Matsumoto (below).

JAPANESE—SOUTH EAST RIDGE
Leader: Ken Nogutchi
High point 8,350 m. on October 15.

JAPANESE—SOUTH WEST FACE
Leader: Norichika Matsumoto
High point 8,040 m. on October 12.

There were four attempts from the north:

AMERICAN—NORTH COL
Craig Colonica reached 7,000 m. on September 24. Abandoned an attempt to ski down because of sickness and dangerous snow.

FRENCH—NORTH COL-NORTH FACE
Leader: Jerome Ruby
High point 8,100 m. on September 25 and 4 October. They had hoped to snowboard down.

ITALIAN
Leader: Sergio Martini..
High point 81,00 m. on 25 September.

SPANISH—NORTH COL-NORTH FACE
Leader: Maria Jesus Lago
High point 8,100 m. on 25 September.

JAPANESE—NORTH FACE
Leader: Masafumi Todaka
High points: via Japanese Couloir, 7,100 m. on 29 August; via Great Couloir, 8,500 m. on 16 September

**(Summary compiled by Audrey Salkeld)**

## Routes on Everest

There are so many ways of climbing Everest these days that a summary of the routes might be useful to the reader. Some variants are excluded for clarity.

The list starts at the Lho La and moves clockwise round the mountain.

1. West Ridge Direct (Jugoslav Route), 1979.
2. West Ridge by the Hornbein Couloir (American Route) 1963*
3. North Face by the Hornbein Couloir (Japanese Route), 1980.
4. North Face by the Great Couloir, 1984.
5. North Face from the North Col (Messner Route), 1980.
6. North Ridge from the North Col (Chinese Route), 1960.
7. North East Ridge Integrale, 1988 (incomplete to summit).
8. East Face by the Central Pillar, 1983.
9. East Face and South East Ridge, 1988.
10. South East Ridge from the South Col (Original Route), 1953.
11. South Pillar (Polish Route), 1980.
12. South West Face, 1975.
13. South West Face Central Pillar (Russian Route), 1982.

*The American start to the West Ridge from the Western Cwm (1963) and the Canadian start from the Rongbuk Glacier (1986) are major variants on 1 or 2.

(For a detailed climbing guide to Everest, with all the variants and attempts etc. see J. Kielkowski *Mount Everest – Massiv Nord* [Aree Greul 1986. German text].)

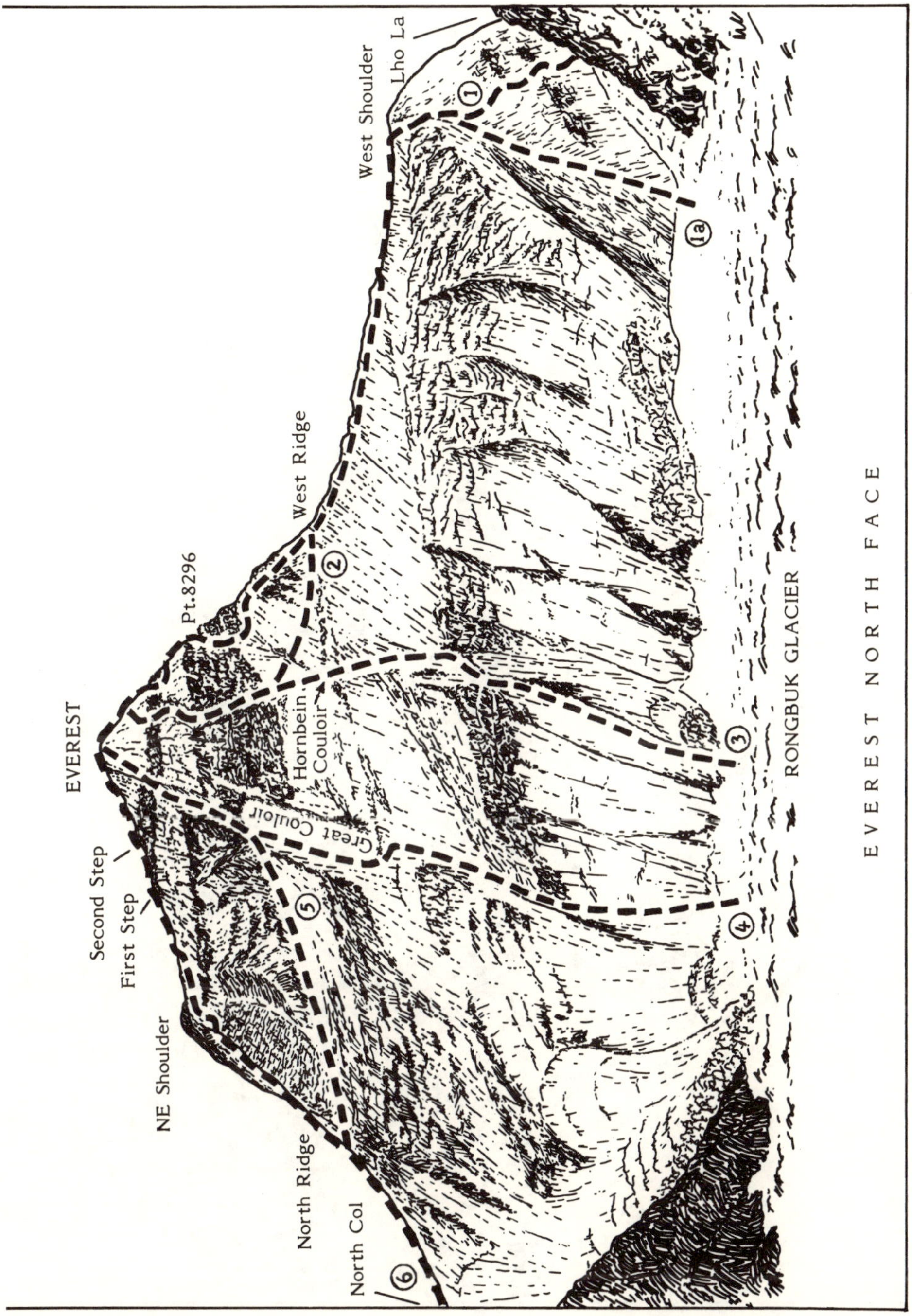
EVEREST
Pt.8296
West Ridge
West Shoulder
Lho La
Hornbein Couloir
Great Couloir
Second Step
First Step
NE Shoulder
North Ridge
North Col
RONGBUK GLACIER
EVEREST NORTH FACE
1
1a
2
3
4
5
6

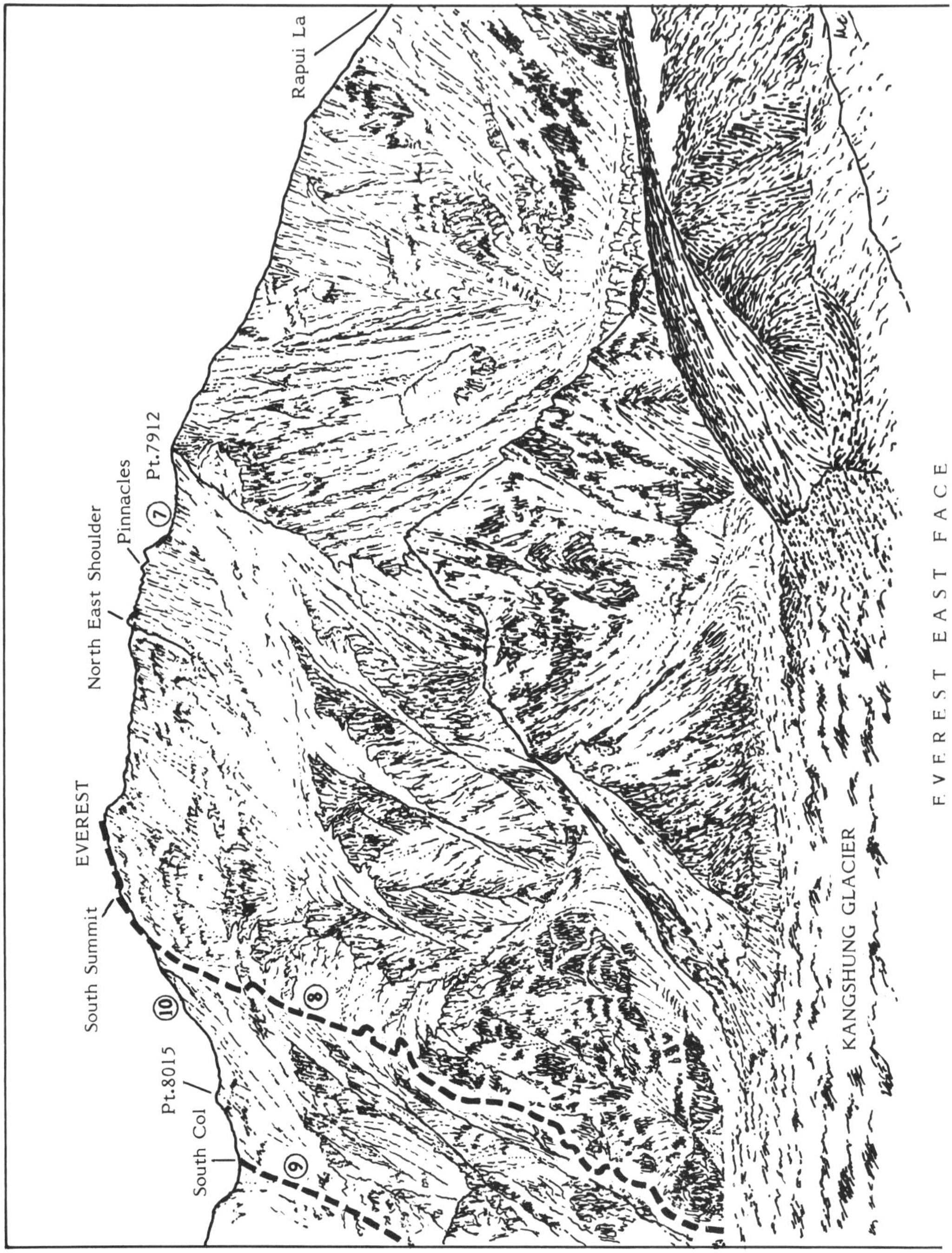
South Col
Pt.8015
South Summit
EVEREST
North East Shoulder
Pinnacles
Pt.7912
Rapui La
7
8
9
10
KANGSHUNG GLACIER
EVEREST EAST FACE

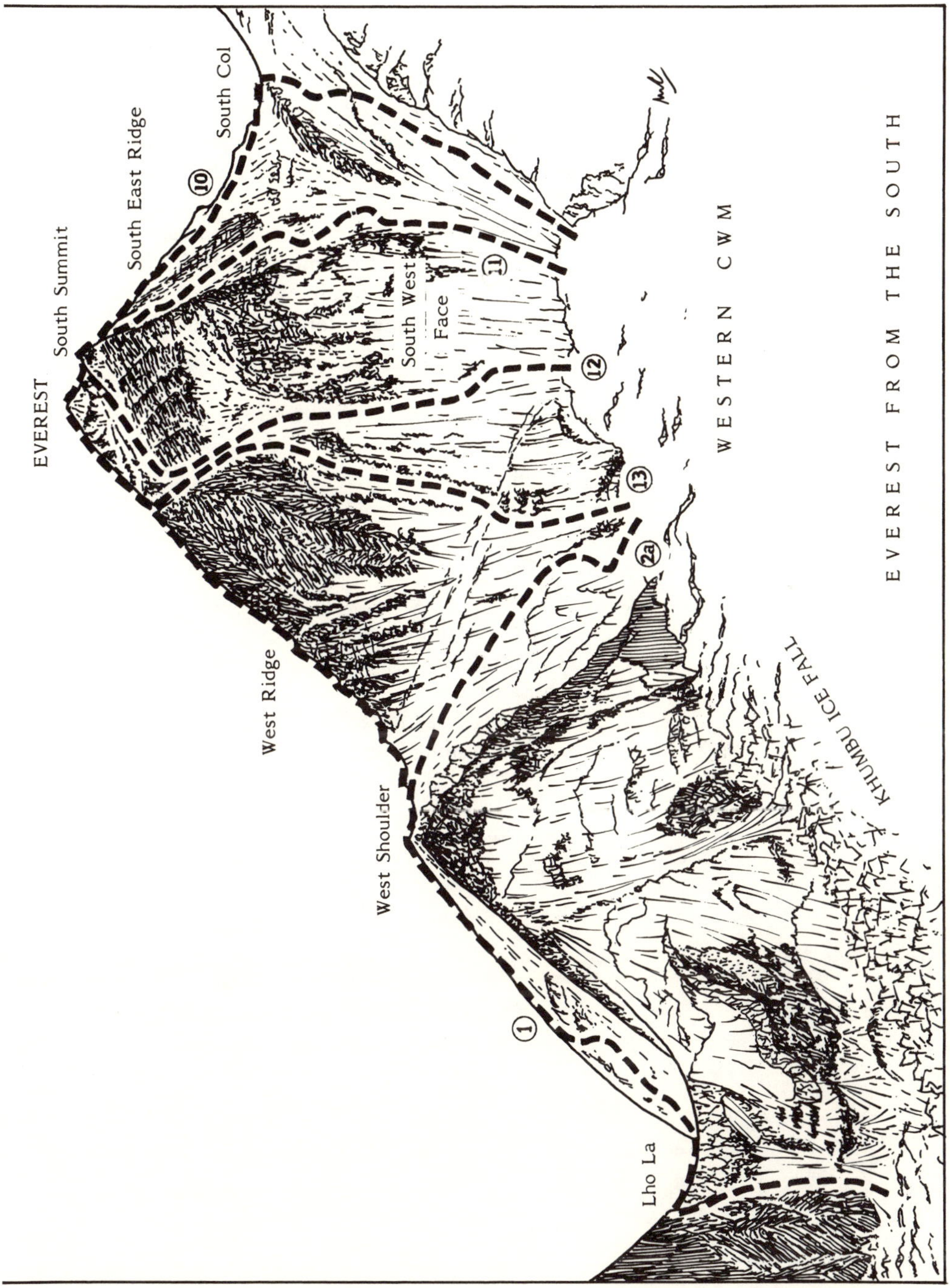


EVEREST FROM THE SOUTH

## On the Naming of The Parts

Now that climbers are starting to examine the mountain in greater detail, some confusion is arising over the names given to the major ridges and faces of Everest. I blame this on the pre-war climbers whose North Ridge is more correctly a north-west ridge and whose North Face is really a north-west face, as the accompanying map shows. In those days such precision didn't matter; now it does.

I think it would be unrealistic to start re-naming things at this late stage but I can see a problem coming up with some parts of the mountain which have not yet attracted climbers but might do so in the future. Therefore I would like to suggest the following names be adopted when referring to the mountain (see map):

1. South East Ridge
2. South Pillar
3. South West Face
4. West Ridge
5. North Face
6. North Ridge
7. Secondary North Face
8. North East Ridge
9. North East Facet
10. East or Kangshung Ridge
11. East or Kangshung Face

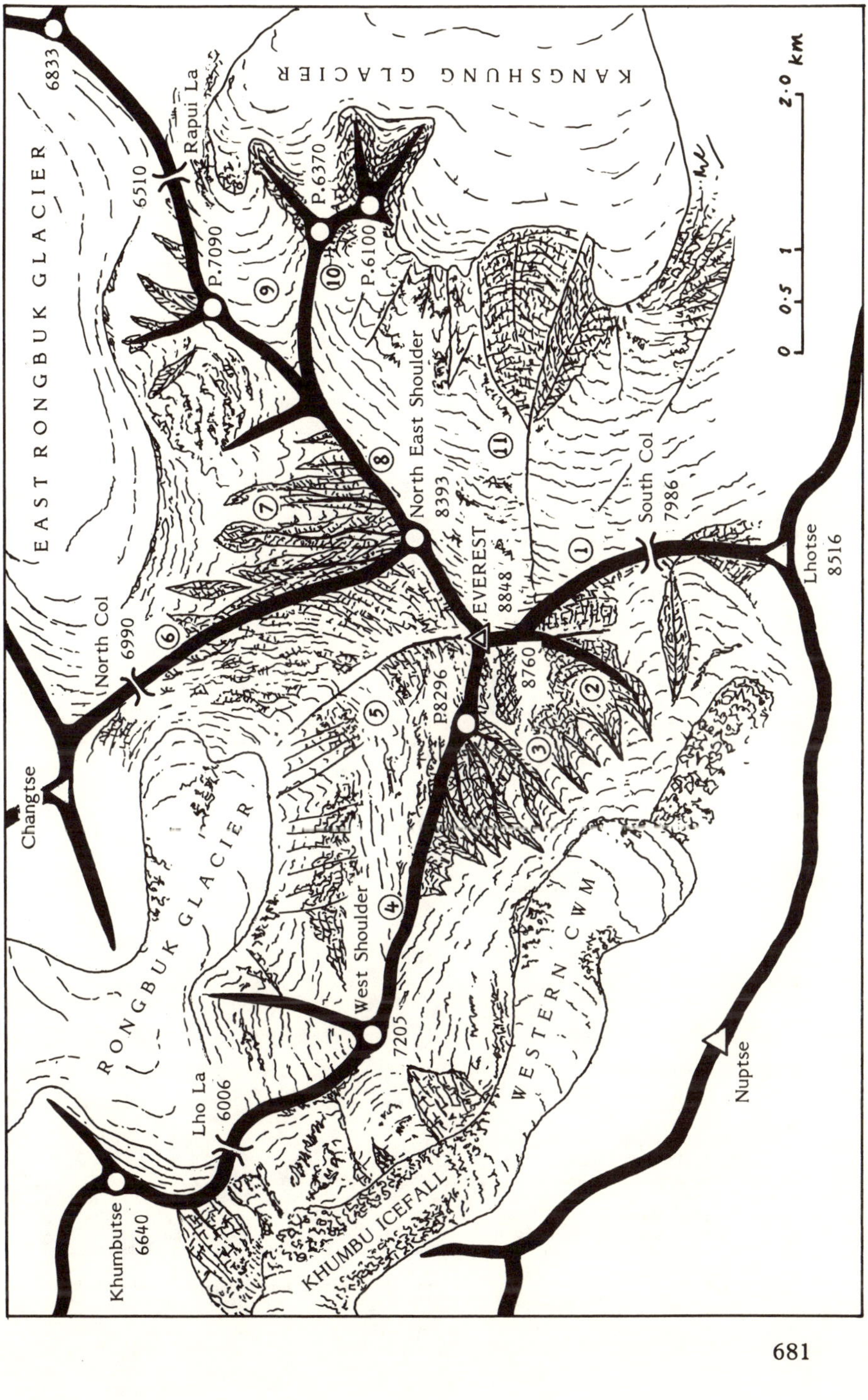
EAST RONGBUK GLACIER
KANGSHUNG GLACIER
RONGBUK GLACIER
WESTERN CWM
KHUMBU ICEFALL
6833
Rapui La
6510
P.7090
P.6370
P.6100
North East Shoulder
8393
EVEREST
8848
South Col
7986
Lhotse
8516
North Col
6990
P.8296
8760
Changtse
West Shoulder
7205
Lho La
6006
Khumbutse
6640
Nuptse
0 0·5 1 2·0 km

# *Appendix 5*
# Ascents of Everest

A = climber's number in the hierarchy. B = number of the ascent. f = woman climber. Multiple ascents in brackets.

| NUMBER A | B | NAME | NATIONALITY | DATE | ROUTE | EXP. | LEADER |
|---|---|---|---|---|---|---|---|
| 1 | 1 | Edmund Hillary | New Zealander | 29-5-1953 | South-East Ridge | BRIT | John Hunt |
| 2 | 2 | Tenzing Norgay | Nepalese Sherpa | " | " | " | " |
| 3 | 3 | Jürg Marmet | Swiss | 23-5-1956 | South-East Ridge | SWISS | Albert Eggler |
| 4 | 4 | Ernst Schmied | " | " | " | " | " |
| 5 | 5 | Hans-Rudolf von Gunten | " | 24-5-1956 | " | " | " |
| 6 | 6 | Adolf Reist | " | " | " | " | " |
| 7 | 7 | Wang Fu-chou | Chinese | 25-5-1960 | North Col to NE Ridge | CHIN | Shih Chan-chun |
| 8 | 8 | Chu Ying-hua | " | " | " | " | " |
| 9 | 9 | Konbu | Tibetan | " | " | " | " |
| 10 | 10 | James Whittaker | American | 1-5-1963 | South-East Ridge | USA | Norman Dyhrenfurth |
| 11 | 11 | Nawang Gombu (1) | Indian Sherpa | " | " | " | " |
| 12 | 12 | Luther Jerstad | American | 22-5-1963 | " | " | " |
| 13 | 13 | Barry Bishop | " | " | " | " | " |
| 14 | 14 | William Unsoeld | " | 22-5-1963 | West Ridge from | " | " |
| 15 | 15 | Thomas Hornbein | " | " | W. Cwm and traverse | " | " |
| 16 | 16 | A. S. Cheema | Indian | 20-5-1965 | South-East Ridge | IND | Mohan S. Kohli |
| * | 17 | Nawang Gombu (2) | Indian Sherpa | " | " | " | " |
| 17 | 18 | Sonam Gyatso | Indian Sikkimese | 22-5-1965 | " | " | " |
| 18 | 19 | Sonam Wangyal | Indian Ladakhi | " | " | " | " |
| 19 | 20 | C. P. Vohra | Indian | 24-5-1965 | " | " | " |
| 20 | 21 | Ang Kami | Indian Sherpa | " | " | " | " |
| 21 | 22 | Hari Pal Singh Ahluwalia | Indian | 29-5-1965 | " | " | " |
| 22 | 23 | Harish Chandra S. Rawat | " | " | " | " | " |
| 23 | 24 | Phu Dorji | Nepalese Sherpa | " | | | |
| 24 | 25 | Teruo Matsuura | Japanese | 11-5-1970 | South-East Ridge | JAP | Saburo Matsukata |
| 25 | 26 | Naomi Uemura | " | " | " | " | " |
| 26 | 27 | Katsutoshi Hirabayashi | " | 12-5-1970 | " | " | " |
| 27 | 28 | Chotare | Nepalese Sherpa | " | " | " | " |
| 28 | 29 | Rinaldo Carrel | Italian | 5-5-1973 | South-East Ridge | ITAL | Guido Monzino |
| 29 | 30 | Mirko Minuzzo | " | " | " | " | " |
| 30 | 31 | Shambu Tamang (1) | Nepalese Tamang | " | " | " | " |
| 31 | 32 | Lahkpa Tenzing | Nepalese Sherpa | " | " | " | " |
| 32 | 33 | Claudio Benedetti | Italian | 7-5-1973 | " | " | " |
| 33 | 34 | Virginio Epis | " | " | " | " | " |
| 34 | 35 | Fabrizio Innamorati | " | " | " | " | " |
| 35 | 36 | Sonam Gyalzen | Nepalese Sherpa | " | " | " | " |
| 36 | 37 | Hisashi Ishiguro | Japanese | 26-10-1973 | South-East Ridge | JAP | Michio Yuasa |
| 37 | 38 | Yasuo Kato (1) | " | " | " | " | " |
| 38 | 39 | Junko Tabei (f) | Japanese | 16-5-1975 | South-East Ridge | JAP | Eiko Hisano (f) |
| 39 | 40 | Ang Tsering | Nepalese Sherpa | " | " | " | " |

| NUMBER A | B | NAME | NATIONALITY | DATE | ROUTE | EXP. | LEADER |
|---|---|---|---|---|---|---|---|
| 40 | 41 | Phantog (f) | Tibetan | 27-5-1975 | North Col to NE Ridge | CHIN | Shih Chan-chun |
| 41 | 42 | Sodnam Norbu | „ | „ | „ | „ | „ |
| 42 | 43 | Lotse | „ | „ | „ | „ | „ |
| 43 | 44 | Samdrub | „ | „ | „ | „ | „ |
| 44 | 45 | Darphuntso | „ | „ | „ | „ | „ |
| 45 | 46 | Kunga Pasang | „ | „ | „ | „ | „ |
| 46 | 47 | Tsering Tobgyal | „ | „ | „ | „ | „ |
| 47 | 48 | Ngapo Khyen | „ | „ | „ | „ | „ |
| 48 | 49 | Hou Sheng-fu | Chinese | „ | „ | „ | „ |
| 49 | 50 | Dougal Haston | Scottish | 24-9-1975 | South-West Face | BRIT | Chris Bonginton |
| 50 | 51 | Doug Scott | English | „ | „ | „ | „ |
| 51 | 52 | Peter Boardman | „ | 29-9-1975 | „ | „ | „ |
| 52 | 53 | Pertemba (1) | Nepalese Sherpa | „ | „ | „ | „ |
|  | ? | Mick Burke | English | „ | „ | „ | „ |
| 53 | 54 | Michael (Bronco) Lane | English | 16-5-1976 | South-East Ridge | BRIT | Tony Streather |
| 54 | 55 | John (Brummy) Stokes | „ | „ | „ | „ | „ |
| 55 | 56 | Chris Chandler | American | 8-10-1976 | South-East Ridge | USA | Phillip Trimble |
| 56 | 57 | Robert Cormack | „ | „ | „ | „ | „ |
| 57 | 58 | Ko Sang-Don | South Korean | 15-9-1977 | South-East Ridge | S.KOR | Kim Young-Do |
| 58 | 59 | Pemba Norbu | Nepalese Sherpa | „ | „ | „ | „ |
| 59 | 60 | Wolfgang Nairz | Austrian | 3-5-1978 | South-East Ridge | AUTR | Wolfgang Nairz |
| 60 | 61 | Robert Schauer | „ | „ | „ | „ | „ |
| 61 | 62 | Horst Bergmann | „ | „ | „ | „ | „ |
| 62 | 63 | Ang Phu (1) | Nepalese Sherpa | „ | „ | „ | „ |
| 63 | 64 | Reinhold Messner (1) | Italian Tyrolean | 8-5-1978 | „ | „ | „ |
| 64 | 65 | Peter Habeler | Austrian | „ | „ | „ | „ |
| 65 | 66 | Reinhard Karl | West German | 11-5-1978 | „ | „ | „ |
| 66 | 67 | Oswald Ölz | Austrian | „ | „ | „ | „ |
| 67 | 68 | Franz Oppurg | „ | 14-5-1978 | „ | „ | „ |
| 68 | 69 | Sepp Mack | West German | 14-10-1978 | South-East Ridge | W.GER | Karl Herrligkoffer |
| 69 | 70 | Hubert Hillmaier | „ | „ | „ | „ | „ |
| 70 | 71 | Hans Engl | „ | „ | „ | „ | „ |
| 71 | 72 | Jean Afanassieff | French | 15-10-1978 | South-East Ridge | FREN | Pierre Mazeaud |
| 72 | 73 | Nicolas Jaeger | „ | „ | „ | „ | „ |
| 73 | 74 | Pierre Mazeaud | „ | „ | „ | „ | „ |
| 74 | 75 | Kurt Diemberger | Austrian | „ | „ | „ | „ |
| 75 | 76 | Wanda Rutkiewicz (f) | Polish | 16-10-1978 | South-East Ridge | W.GER | Karl Herrligkoffer |
| 76 | 77 | Robert Allenbach | Swiss | „ | „ | „ | „ |
| 77 | 78 | Sigi Hupfauer | West German | „ | „ | „ | „ |
| 78 | 79 | Willi Klimek | „ | „ | „ | „ | „ |
| 79 | 80 | Mingma Nuru | Nepalese Sherpa | „ | „ | „ | „ |
| 80 | 81 | Ang Dorje (1) | „ | „ | „ | „ | „ |
| 81 | 82 | Ang Kami | „ | „ | „ | „ | „ |
| 82 | 83 | Georg Ritter | West German | 17-10-1978 | „ | „ | „ |
| 83 | 84 | Bernd Kullman | „ | „ | „ | „ | „ |
| 84 | 85 | Jernej Zaplotnik | Yugoslav | 13-5-1979 | West Ridge Integrale | YUG | Tone Skarja |
| 85 | 86 | Andrej Stremfelj | „ | „ | „ | „ | „ |
| 86 | 87 | Stane Belak | „ | 15-5-1979 | „ | „ | „ |
| 87 | 88 | Stipe Bozik | „ | „ | „ | „ | „ |
| * | 89 | Ang Phu (2) | Nepalese Sherpa | „ | „ | „ | „ |
| 88 | 90 | Gerhard Schmatz | West German | 1-10-1979 | South-East Ridge | W.GER | Gerhard Schmatz |
| 89 | 91 | Hermann Warth | „ | „ | „ | „ | „ |
| 90 | 92 | Hans von Känel | Swiss | „ | „ | „ | „ |
| * | 93 | Pertemba (2) | Nepalese Sherpa | „ | „ | „ | „ |
| 91 | 94 | Lhakpa Gyalzo | „ | „ | „ | „ | „ |
| 92 | 95 | Ray Genet | American | 2-10-1979 | „ | „ | „ |
| 93 | 96 | Hannelore Schmatz (f) | West German | „ | „ | „ | „ |
| 94 | 97 | Sungdare (1) | Nepalese | „ | „ | „ | „ |
| 95 | 98 | Tilman Fischbach | West German | „ | „ | „ | „ |
| 96 | 99 | Günter Kämpfe | „ | „ | „ | „ | „ |
| 97 | 100 | Nick Banks | New Zealander | „ | „ | „ | „ |
| 98 | 101 | Ang Phurba | Nepalese Sherpa | „ | „ | „ | „ |
| 99 | 102 | Ang Jangbo | „ | „ | „ | „ | „ |
| 100 | 103 | Leszek Cichy | Polish | 17-2-1980 | South-East Ridge | POL | Andrzej Zawada |
| 101 | 104 | Kryzysztof Wielicki | „ | „ | „ | „ | „ |
| * | 105 | Yasuo Kato (2) | Japanese | 3-5-1980 | North Col to NE Ridge | JAP | Hyoriko Watanabe |
| 102 | 106 | Tsuneoh Shigehiro | „ | 10-5-1980 | North Face (Hornbein C.) | „ | „ |
| 103 | 107 | Takashi Ozaki (1) | „ | „ | „ | „ | „ |

| NUMBER A | B | NAME | NATIONALITY | DATE | ROUTE | EXP. | LEADER |
|---|---|---|---|---|---|---|---|
| 104 | 108 | Martin Zabaleta | Spanish Basque | 14-5-1980 | South-East Ridge | BASQ | Juan-Ignacio Lorente |
| 105 | 109 | Pasang Temba | Nepalese Sherpa | " | " | " | " |
| 106 | 110 | Andrzej Czok | Polish | 19-5-1980 | South Pillar | POL | Andrzej Zawada |
| 107 | 111 | Jerzy Kukuckzka | " | " | " | " | " |
| * | 112 | Reinhold Messner (2) | Italian Tyrolean | 20-8-1980 | North Col to North Face | SOLO | Reinhold Messner |
| 108 | 113 | Chris Kopczynski | American | 21-10-1981 | South Pillar to SE Ridge | USA | John West |
| * | 114 | Sungdare (2) | Nepalese Sherpa | " | " | " | " |
| 109 | 115 | Chris Pizzo | American | 24-10-1981 | " | " | " |
| 110 | 116 | Yong Tenzing | Nepalese Sherpa | " | " | " | " |
| 111 | 117 | Peter Hackett | American | " | " | " | " |
| 112 | 118 | Vladimir Balyberdin | Soviet Russian | 4-5-1982 | South-West Pillar | USSR | Evgeny Tamm |
| 113 | 119 | Eduard Myslovsky | " | " | " | " | " |
| 114 | 120 | Sergei Bershov | Soviet Ukrainian | 4-5-1982 | " | " | " |
| 115 | 121 | Mikhail Turkevich | " | " | " | " | " |
| 116 | 122 | Valentin Ivanov | Soviet Russian | 5-5-1982 | " | " | " |
| 117 | 123 | Sergei Ephimov | " | " | " | " | " |
| 118 | 124 | Valery Khrishchaty | Soviet Kazakh | 8-5-1982 | " | " | " |
| 119 | 125 | Kazbek Valiev | " | " | " | " | " |
| 120 | 126 | Valery Khomutov | Soviet Russian | 9-5-1982 | " | " | " |
| 121 | 127 | Vladimir Puchkov | " | " . | " | " | " |
| 122 | 128 | Yuri Golodov | Soviet Kazakh | " | " | " | " |
| 123 | 129 | Laurie Skreslet | Canadian | 5-10-1982 | South-East Ridge | CAN | William March |
| * | 130 | Sungdare (3) | Nepalese Sherpa | " | " | " | " |
| 124 | 131 | Khakpa Dorje | " | " | " | " | " |
| 125 | 132 | Pat Morrow | Canadian | 7-10-1982 | " | " | " |
| 126 | 133 | Pema Dorje (1) | Nepalese Sherpa | " | " | " | " |
| 127 | 134 | Lhakpa Tshering | " | " | " | " | " |
| * | 135 | Yasuo Kato (3) | Japanese | 27-12-1982 | South-East Ridge | JAP | Yasuo Kato |
| 128 | 136 | Peter Jamieson | American | 7-5-1983 | South-East Ridge | USA | Gerhard Lenser (W.G.) |
| 129 | 137 | Gerald Roach | " | " | " | " | " |
| 130 | 138 | David Breashears (1) | " | " | " | " | " |
| 131 | 139 | Ang Rita (1) | Nepalese Sherpa | " | " | " | " |
| 132 | 140 | Larry Nielson | American | " | " | " | " |
| 133 | 141 | Gary Neptune | " | 14-5-1983 | " | " | " |
| 134 | 142 | Jim States | " | " | " | " | " |
| 135 | 143 | Lhakpa Dorje | Nepalese Sherpa | " | " | " | " |
| 136 | 144 | Kim Momb | American | 8-10-1983 | East Face to SE Ridge | USA | James Morrissey |
| 137 | 145 | Louis Reichardt | " | " | " | " | " |
| 138 | 146 | Carlos Buhler | " | " | " | " | " |
| 139 | 147 | Haruichi Kawamura | Japanese | 8-10-1983 | South Pillar to SE Ridge | JAP | Haruichi Kawamura |
| 140 | 148 | Shomi Suzuki | " | " | " | " | " |
| 141 | 149 | Haruyuki Endo | Japanese | 8-10-1983 | South-East Ridge | JAP | Hiroshi Yoshino |
| 142 | 150 | Hiroshi Yoshino | " | " | " | " | " |
| 143 | 151 | Hironobu Kamuro | " | " | " | " | " |
| 144 | 152 | George Lowe | American | 9-10-1983 | East Face to SE Ridge | USA | James Morrisey |
| 145 | 153 | Dan Reid | " | " | " | " | " |
| 146 | 154 | Jay Cassell | " | " | " | " | " |
| * | 155 | Takashi Ozaki (2) | Japanese | 16-12-1983 | South-East Ridge | JAP | Yazuyuki Takahashi |
| 147 | 156 | Noboru Yamada (1) | " | " | " | " | " |
| 148 | 157 | Kazunari Murakami | " | " | " | " | " |
| 149 | 158 | Nawang Yonden | Nepalese Sherpa | " | " | " | " |
| 150 | 159 | Hristo Ivanov Prodanov | Bulgarian | 20-4-1984 | West Ridge (Hornbein C.) | BULG | Avram Iliev Avramov |
| 151 | 160 | Ivan G. Valchev | " | 8-5-1984 | W. Ridge, SE Ridge down | " | " " |
| 152 | 161 | Metodi Stefanov Savov | " | " | " | " | " |
| 153 | 162 | Nikolay Petkov | " | 9-5-1984 | " | " | " |
| 154 | 163 | Kiril Doskov | " | " | " | " | " |
| 155 | 164 | Phu Dorjee | Indian Sherpa | 9-5-1984 | South-East Ridge | IND | Darshan Kumar Khullar |
| 156 | 165 | Bachendri Pal (f) | Indian | 23-5-1984 | " | " | |
| 157 | 166 | Dorjee Lhatoo | Indian Sherpa | " | " | " | " |
| * | 167 | Ang Dorje (2) | Nepalese Sherpa | " | " | " | " |
| 158 | 168 | Sonam Palzor | Indian Ladakhi | " | " | " | " |
| 159 | 169 | Tim Macartney-Shape | Australian | 3-10-1984 | North Face (Norton C.) | AUS | Geoffrey Bartram |
| 160 | 170 | Greg Mortimer | " | " | " | " | " |
| 161 | 171 | Bart Vos | Dutch | 8-10-1984 | South-East Ridge | NETH | Herman Plugge |

| NUMBER A | B | NAME | NATIONALITY | DATE | ROUTE | EXP. | LEADER |
|---|---|---|---|---|---|---|---|
| 162 | 172 | Josef Psotka | Czechoslovak | 15-10-1984 | S. Pillar, SE Ridge down | CZECH | Frantisek Kele |
| 163 | 173 | Zoltan Demjan | " | " | " | " | " |
| * | 174 | Ang Rita (2) | Nepalese Sherpa | " | " | " | " |
| 164 | 175 | Philip Ershler | American | 20-10-1984 | North Col to North Face | USA | Louis W. Whittaker |
| 165 | 176 | Bjorn Myrer-Lund | Norwegian | 21-4-1985 | South-East Ridge | NOR | Arne Naess |
| 166 | 177 | Odd Eliassen | " | " | " | " | " |
| * | 178 | Pertemba (3) | Nepalese Sherpa | " | " | " | " |
| 167 | 179 | Ang Lhakpa | " | " | " | " | " |
| 168 | 180 | Chris Bonington | English | " | " | " | " |
| 169 | 181 | Dawa Nuru | Nepalese Sherpa | " | " | " | " |
| 170 | 182 | Arne Naess | Norwegian | 29-4-1985 | " | " | " |
| 171 | 183 | Stein Aasheim | " | " | " | " | " |
| 172 | 184 | Haavard Nesheim | " | " | " | " | " |
| 173 | 185 | Ralph Hölbakk | " | " | " | " | " |
| * | 186 | Sungdare (4) | Nepalese Sherpa | " | " | " | " |
| * | 187 | Ang Rita (3) | " | " | " | " | " |
| * | 188 | Pema Dorje (2) | " | " | " | " | " |
| 174 | 189 | Chowang Rinji | " | " | " | " | " |
| 175 | 190 | Richard Bass | American | 30-4-1985 | " | " | " |
| * | 191 | David Breashears (2) | " | " | " | " | " |
| 176 | 192 | Ang Phurba (1) | Nepalese Sherpa | " | " | " | " |
| 177 | 193 | Oscar Cadiach | Spanish Catalan | 28-8-1985 | North Col to NE Ridge | CATAL | Conrad Blanch |
| 178 | 194 | Toni Sors | " | " | " | " | " |
| 179 | 195 | Carles Valles | " | " | " | " | " |
| 180 | 196 | Ang Karma | Nepalese Gurung | " | " | " | " |
| * | 197 | Shambu Tamang (2) | Nepalese Tamang | " | " | " | " |
| 181 | 198 | Narayan Shrestha | Nepalese Newari | " | " | " | " |
| 182 | 199 | Etsuo Akutsu | Japanese | 30-10-1985 | South-East Ridge | JAP | Kuniaki Yagihara |
| 183 | 200 | Satoshi Kimoto | " | " | " | " | " |
| 184 | 201 | Hideji Nazuka | " | " | " | " | " |
| 185 | 202 | Teruo Saegusa (1) | " | " | " | " | " |
| 186 | 203 | Mitsuyoshi Sato | " | " | " | " | " |
| 187 | 204 | Kuniaki Yagihara | " | " | " | " | " |
| * | 205 | Noboru Yamada (2) | " | " | " | " | " |
| 188 | 206 | Sharon Wood (f) | Canadian | 20-5-1986 | West Ridge (from Tibet) | CAN | Jim Elzinga |
| 189 | 207 | Dwayne Congdon | " | " | " | " | " |
| 190 | 208 | Erhard Loretan | Swiss | 30-8-1986 | North Face (Hornbein C.) | FR-SW | Pierre Béghin |
| 191 | 209 | Jean Troillet | " | " | " | " | " |
| 192 | 210 | Huh Young-Ho | South Korean | 22-12-1987 | South-East Ridge | S.KOR | Hahm Tak-Young |
| * | 211 | Ang Rita (4) | Nepalese Sherpa | " | " | " | " |
| * | 212 | Noboru Yamada (3) | Japanese | 5-5-1988 | N.Col–S.Col Traverse | ASIAN | Tsuneoh Shigehiro |
| 193 | 213 | Lhakpa Nuru (Ang Lhakpa) | Nepalese Sherpa | " | " | " | " |
| 194 | 214 | Cerkin Doji | Tibetan | " | " | " | " |
| * | 215 | Ang Phurba (2) | Nepalese Sherpa | " | S.Col–N.Col Traverse | " | Kunga Sherpa |
| 195 | 216 | Ringen Puncog | Tibetan | " | " | " | " |
| 196 | 217 | Da Cering | " | " | " | " | " |
| 197 | 218 | Susuma Nakamura | Japanese | " | North Col to NE Ridge | " | Tsuneoh Shigehiro |
| 198 | 219 | Shoji Nakamura | " | " | " | " | " |
| * | 220 | Teruo Saegusa (2) | " | " | " | " | " |
| 199 | 221 | Munehiko Yamamoto | " | " | " | " | " |
| 200 | 222 | Li Zhixin | Chinese | " | " | " | " |
| 201 | 223 | Lhakpa Sonam | Nepalese Sherpa | " | " | " | " |
| * | 224 | Sungdare (5) | " | 10-5-1988 | South-East Ridge | " | Kunga Sherpa |
| 202 | 225 | Padma Bahadur | Nepalese Tamang | " | " | " | " |
| 203 | 226 | Stephen Venables | English | 12-5-1988 | East Face to South Col | USA | Robert Anderson |
| 204 | 227 | Paul Bayne | Australian | 25-5-1988 | South-East Ridge | AUS | Austin Brookes |
| 205 | 228 | Patrick Cullinan | " | " | " | " | " |
| 206 | 229 | John Muir | " | 28-5-1988 | " | " | " |
| 207 | 230 | Jean-Marc Boivin | French | 26-9-1988 | South East Ridge | FREN | François Polissonier |
| 208 | 231 | Michel Metzger | " | " | " | " | " |
| 209 | 232 | Jean-Pierre Frachon | " | " | " | " | " |
| 210 | 233 | Gérard Vionnet-Fausset | " | " | " | " | " |
| 211 | 234 | André Georges | Swiss | " | " | " | " |

| NUMBER A | B | NAME | NATIONALITY | DATE | ROUTE | EXP. | LEADER |
|---|---|---|---|---|---|---|---|
| 212 | 235 | Pasang Tshering | Nepalese Sherpa | „ | „ | „ | „ |
| 213 | 236 | Sonam Tshering | „ | „ | „ | „ | „ |
| 214 | 237 | Ajiwa | „ | „ | „ | „ | „ |
| 215 | 238 | Kim Chang-Sun | South Korean | 26-9-1988 | South Pillar to SE Ridge | S.KOR | Choi Chang-Min |
| 216 | 239 | Uh Hong-Gil | „ | „ | „ | „ | „ |
| * | 240 | Pema Dorje (2) | Nepalese Sherpa | „ | „ | „ | „ |
| 217 | 241 | Marc Batard | French | 26-9-1988 | South-East Ridge | SOLO | Marc Batard |
| 218 | 242 | Jang Bong-Wan | South Korean | 29-9-1988 | South Pillar to SE Ridge | S.KOR | Choi Chang-Min |
| 219 | 243 | Chang Byong-Ho | „ | „ | „ | „ | „ |
| 220 | 244 | Chung Seung-Kwon | „ | „ | „ | „ | „ |
| 221 | 245 | Stacy Allison (f) | American | 29-9-1988 | South-East Ridge | USA | James Frush |
| 222 | 246 | Pasang Gyalzen | Nepalese Sherpa | „ | „ | „ | „ |
| 223 | 247 | Peggy Luce (f) | American | 2-10-1988 | „ | „ | „ |
| 224 | 248 | Geoffrey Tabin | „ | „ | „ | „ | „ |
| 225 | 249 | Nima Tashi | Nepalese Sherpa | „ | „ | „ | „ |
| 226 | 250 | Phu Dorje | „ | „ | „ | „ | „ |
| 227 | 251 | Dawa Tshering | „ | „ | „ | „ | „ |
| 228 | 252 | Nam Sun-Woo | South Korean | 2-10-1988 | South Pillar to SE Ridge | S.KOR | Choi Chang-Min |
| 229 | 253 | Serge Koenig | French | 13-10-1988 | South-East Ridge | FREN | Serge Koenig |
| 230 | 254 | Lhakpa Sonam | Nepalese Sherpa | „ | „ | „ | „ |
| 231 | ? | Pasang Temba | „ | „ | „ | „ | „ |
| 232 | 255 | Jerónimo López | Spanish Galician | 14-10-1988 | South-East Ridge | CATAL | Lluis Belvis |
| 233 | 256 | Nil Bohigas | Spanish Catalan | „ | „ | „ | „ |
| * | 257 | Lluis Giner | „ | „ | „ | „ | „ |
| 234 | 258 | Ang Rita (5) | Nepalese Sherpa | „ | „ | „ | „ |
| | 259 | Nima Rita | „ | „ | „ | „ | „ |
| 235 | ? | Lydia Bradey (f) | New Zealander | 14-10-1988 | South-East Ridge | NZ | Rob Hall |
| | 260 | Josef Just | Czechoslovak | 17-10-1988 | South-West Face | CZECH | Ivan Fiala |
| * | 261 | Stipe Bozik (2) | Yugoslav | 10-5-1989 | South-East-Ridge | YUG | Jovan Poposki |
| 236 | 262 | Viktor Groselj | „ | „ | „ | „ | „ |
| 237 | 263 | Dimitar Ilievski | „ | „ | „ | „ | „ |
| * | 264 | Ajiwa (2) | Nep. Sherpa | „ | „ | „ | „ |
| * | 265 | Sonam Tshering (2) | „ | „ | „ | „ | „ |
| 238 | 266 | Ricardo Torres | Mexican | 16-5-1989 | South-East Ridge | USA | Walt McConnel |
| * | 267 | Phu Dorje (2) | Nep Sherpa | „ | „ | „ | „ |
| 239 | 268 | Ang Dannu | „ | „ | „ | „ | „ |
| 240 | 269 | Adrian Burgess | British | 24-5-1989 | South-East Ridge | INT | Karen Fellerhof |
| * | 270 | Lhakpa Nuru (2) | Nep Sherpa | „ | „ | „ | „ |
| 241 | 271 | Sonam Dendu | „ | „ | „ | „ | „ |
| 242 | 272 | Roddy MacKenzie | Australian | „ | „ | „ | „ |
| 243 | 273 | Eugeniusz Chrobak | Polish | 25-5-1989 | West Ridge from Nepal | POL | Eugeniusz Chrobak |
| 244 | 274 | Andrzej Marciniak | „ | „ | „ | „ | „ |

There is no absolute certainty about the ascents of Mick Burke (26-9-75) and Pasang Temba (13-10-88), both of whom died during the descent. Therefore, they do not count for the total figures.

Neither does count Lydia Bradey, who claimed her solo ascent (14-10-88) but later admitted the possibility of having been mistaken about her highest point being the true summit.

Concerning Bart Vos (No. 171), some climbers cast doubt upon his solo ascent, particularly the Czech team that made the following ascent. Nevertheless, he has generally been given the benefit of the doubt.

The number of successful expeditions amounts to 59, of which 9 are from Japan, 8 from USA and the rest from 21 other countries. The total number of expeditions since 1921 amounts to 270, two thirds of which have been unsuccessful. The following seven countries have organized expeditions to Everest, without any success: Denmark, Argentina, New Zealand, Iran, Chile, Sweden and Belgium.

Due to repeated ascents of the summit made by certain climbers, the total number of people who have climbed Everest is smaller than the number of individual ascents (274) that have been listed. Since the number of repetitions is 30, we therefore have total of 244 people who have reached the summit. Of these, 8 are women.

As for the nationalities of the individual climbers and their distribution through the years, they can be resumed in the following table: (to May 1989)

| No. | COUNTRIES | 53 | 56 | 60 | 63 | 65 | 70 | 73 | 75 | 76 | 77 | 78 | 79 | 80 | 81 | 82 | 83 | 84 | 85 | 86 | 87 | 88 | 89 | ASCS | REPS | PEOP |
|---|---|---|---|---|---|---|---|---|---|---|---|---|---|---|---|---|---|---|---|---|---|---|---|---|---|---|
| 1 | NEPAL | — | — | — | — | 1 | 1 | 3 | 2 | — | 1 | 4 | 6 | 1 | 2 | 4 | 3 | 2 | 11 | — | 1 | 16 | 6 | 64 | 20 | 44 |
| 2 | UNITED STATES | — | — | — | 5 | — | — | — | — | 2 | — | — | 1 | — | 3 | — | 12 | 1 | 2 | — | — | 3 | — | 29 | 1 | 28 |
| 3 | JAPAN | — | — | — | — | — | 3 | 2 | 1 | — | — | — | — | 3 | — | 1 | 8 | — | 7 | — | — | 5 | — | 30 | 6 | 24 |
| 4 | CHINA | — | — | 3 | — | — | — | — | 9 | — | — | — | — | — | — | — | — | — | — | — | — | 4 | — | 16 | — | 16 |
| 5 | INDIA | 1 | — | — | 1 | 8 | — | — | — | — | — | — | — | — | — | — | — | 4 | — | — | — | — | — | 14 | 1 | 13 |
| 6 | WEST GERMANY | — | — | — | — | — | — | — | — | — | — | 8 | 5 | — | — | — | — | — | — | — | — | — | — | 13 | — | 13 |
| 7 | U.S.S.R. | — | — | — | — | — | — | — | — | — | — | — | — | — | — | 11 | — | — | — | — | — | — | — | 11 | — | 11 |
| 8 | SWITZERLAND | — | 4 | — | — | — | — | — | — | — | — | 1 | 1 | — | — | — | — | — | — | 2 | — | 1 | — | 9 | — | 9 |
| 9 | FRANCE | — | — | — | — | — | — | — | — | — | — | 3 | — | — | — | — | — | — | — | — | — | 6 | — | 9 | — | 9 |
| 10 | SOUTH KOREA | — | — | — | — | — | — | — | — | — | 1 | — | — | — | — | — | — | — | — | — | 1 | 6 | — | 8 | — | 8 |
| 11 | AUSTRIA | — | — | — | — | — | — | — | — | — | — | 7 | — | — | — | — | — | — | — | — | — | — | — | 7 | — | 7 |
| 12 | UNITED KINGDOM | — | — | — | — | — | — | — | 3 | 2 | — | — | — | — | — | — | — | — | 1 | — | — | 1 | 1 | 8 | — | 8 |
| 13 | SPAIN | — | — | — | — | — | — | — | — | — | — | — | — | 1 | — | — | — | — | 3 | — | — | 3 | — | 7 | — | 7 |
| 14 | ITALY | — | — | — | — | — | — | 5 | — | — | — | 1 | — | 1 | — | — | — | — | — | — | — | — | — | 7 | 1 | 6 |
| 15 | NORWAY | — | — | — | — | — | — | — | — | — | — | — | — | — | — | — | — | — | 6 | — | — | — | — | 6 | — | 6 |
| 16 | POLAND | — | — | — | — | — | — | — | — | — | — | 1 | — | 4 | — | — | — | — | — | — | — | — | 2 | 7 | — | 7 |
| 17 | BULGARIA | — | — | — | — | — | — | — | — | — | — | — | — | — | — | — | — | 5 | — | — | — | — | — | 5 | — | 5 |
| 18 | AUSTRALIA | — | — | — | — | — | — | — | — | — | — | — | — | — | — | — | — | 2 | — | — | — | 3 | 1 | 6 | — | 6 |
| 19 | YUGOSLAVIA | — | — | — | — | — | — | — | — | — | — | — | 4 | — | — | — | — | — | — | — | — | — | 3 | 7 | 1 | 6 |
| 20 | CANADA | — | — | — | — | — | — | — | — | — | — | — | — | — | — | 2 | — | — | — | 2 | — | — | — | 4 | — | 4 |
| 21 | CZECHOSLOVAKIA | — | — | — | — | — | — | — | — | — | — | — | — | — | — | — | — | 2 | — | — | — | 1 | — | 3 | — | 3 |
| 22 | NEW ZEALAND | 1 | — | — | — | — | — | — | — | — | — | — | 1 | — | — | — | — | — | — | — | — | — | — | 2 | — | 2 |
| 23 | NETHERLANDS | — | — | — | — | — | — | — | — | — | — | — | — | — | — | — | — | 1 | — | — | — | — | — | 1 | — | 1 |
| 24 | MEXICO | — | — | — | — | — | — | — | — | — | — | — | — | — | — | — | — | — | — | — | — | — | 1 | 1 | — | 1 |
| | TOTALS | 2 | 4 | 3 | 6 | 9 | 4 | 10 | 15 | 4 | 2 | 25 | 18 | 10 | 5 | 18 | 23 | 17 | 30 | 4 | 2 | 49 | 14 | 274 | 30 | 244 |

Everest Repetitions (up to 31 March 1989)

| No. | CLIMBER | NATIONALITY | DATE | EXP. | ROUTE |
|---|---|---|---|---|---|
| 1 | Sungdare | Nep. Sherpa | 2-10-1979 | W.GERM | South Col and SE Ridge |
| | – Repeated | | 21-10-1981 | USA | South Pillar to SE Ridge |
| | – Repeated | | 5-10-1982 | CAN | South Col and SE Ridge |
| | – Repeated | | 29-4-1985 | NOR | „ |
| | – Repeated | | 10-5-1988 | ASIAN | „ |
| 2 | Ang Rita | Nep. Sherpa | 7-5-1983 | USA | South Col and SE Ridge |
| | – Repeated | | 15-10-1984 | CZECH | South Pillar |
| | – Repeated | | 29-4-1985 | NOR | South Col and SE Ridge |
| | – Repeated | | 22-12-1987 | S.KOR | „ |
| | – Repeated | | 14-10-1988 | CATAL | „ |
| 3 | Pertemba | Nep. Sherpa | 26-9-1975 | BRIT | South-West Face |
| | – Repeated | | 1-10-1979 | W.GER | South Col and SE Ridge |
| | – Repeated | | 21-4-1985 | NOR | „ |
| 4 | Yasuo Kato | Japanese | 26-10-1973 | JAP | South Col and SE Ridge |
| | – Repeated | | 3-5-1980 | „ | North Col to NE Ridge |
| | – Repeated | | 27-12-1982 | „ | South Col and SE Ridge |
| 5 | Pema Dorje | Nep. Sherpa | 7-10-1982 | CAN | South Col and SE Ridge |
| | – Repeated | | 29-4-1985 | NOR | „ |
| | – Repeated | | 26-9-1988 | S.KOR | „ |
| 6 | Noboru Yamada | Japanese | 16-12-1983 | JAP | South Col and SE Ridge |
| | – Repeated | | 30-10-1985 | „ | „ |
| | – Repeated | | 5-5-1988 | ASIAN | N.Col to S.Col Traverse |
| 7 | Nawang Gombu | Ind. Sherpa | 1-5-1963 | USA | South Col and SE Ridge |
| | – Repeated | | 20-5-1965 | IND | „ |
| 8 | Ang Phu | Nep. Sherpa | 3-5-1978 | AUTR | South Col and SE Ridge |
| | – Repeated | | 15-5-1979 | YUG | West Ridge Integrale |
| 9 | Reinhold Messner | It. Tyrolean | 8-5-1978 | AUTR | South Col and SE Ridge |
| | – Repeated | | 20-8-1980 | SOLO | North Col to North Face |
| 10 | Takashi Ozaki | Japanese | 10-5-1980 | JAP | North Face (Hornbein C) |
| | – Repeated | | 16-12-1983 | „ | South Col and SE Ridge |
| 11 | Ang Dorje | Nep. Sherpa | 16-10-1978 | W.GER | South Col and SE Ridge |
| | – Repeated | | 23-5-1984 | IND | „ |
| 12 | David Breashears | American | 7-5-1983 | USA | South Col and SE Ridge |
| | – Repeated | | 30-4-1985 | NOR | „ |
| 13 | Shambu Tamang | Nep. Tamang | 5-5-1973 | ITAL | South Col and SE Ridge |
| | – Repeated | | 28-8-1985 | CATAL | North Col to NE Ridge |
| 14 | Ang Phurba | Nep. Sherpa | 30-4-1985 | NOR | South Col and SE Ridge |
| | | | 5-5-1988 | ASIAN | S. Col to N.Col Traverse |
| 15 | Teruro Saegusa | Japanese | 30-10-1985 | JAP | South Col and SE Ridge |
| | – Repeated | | 5-5-1988 | ASIAN | North Col to NE Ridge |
| 16 | Stipe Bozik | Yugoslav | 15-5-1979 | YUG | West Ridge Integrale |
| | – Repeated | | 10-5-1989 | „ | South Col and SE Ridge |
| 17 | Ajiwa | Nep. Sherpa | 26-9-1988 | FREN | South Col and SE Ridge |
| | – Repeated | | 10-5-1989 | YUG | „ |
| 18 | Sonam Tshering | Nep. Sherpa | 26-9-1988 | FREN | South Col and SE Ridge |
| | – Repeated | | 10-5-1989 | YUG | „ |
| 19 | Phu Dorje | Nep. Sherpa | 2-10-1988 | USA | South Col and SE Ridge |
| | – Repeated | | 16-5-1989 | USA | „ |
| 20 | Lhakpa Nuru | Nep. Sherpa | 5-5-1988 | ASIAN | N.Col to S.Col Traverse |
| | – Repeated | | 24-5-1989 | INT | South Col and SE Ridge |

2.– Ang Rita has made all his ascents without oxygen. Not so Sungdare.
4.– Yasuo Kato disappeared from the South Summit, a few hours after his last climb.
8.– Ang Phu died (16-5-79) while descending from his last climb of Everest.
11.– Ang Dorje was killed (24-10-84) in the SE Ridge, during a cleaning expedition.
13.– Shambu Tamang is the only Nepali climber who has made the ascent from both sides of the mountain (Nepal and Tibet).

**Progressive "Old Men of Everest"**

| N | CLIMBER | NATIONALITY | BIRTH DATE | ASCENT | AGE |
|---|---|---|---|---|---|
| 1 | Tenzing Norgay | Indian Sherpa | Spring 1914 | 29-5-1953 | 39 years |
| 2 | Sonam Gyatso | Ind. Sikkimese | Nov. 1922 | 22-5-1965 | 42 years, 5 months |
| 3 | Pierre Mazeaud | French | 24-8-1929 | 15-10-1978 | 49 years, 52 days |
| 4 | Gerhard Schmatz | West German | 5-6-1929 | 1-10-1979 | 50 years, 118 days |
| 5 | Jósef Psotka | Czechoslovak | 12-2-1934 | 15-10-1984 | 50 years, 246 days |
| 6 | Chris Bonington | English | 6-9-1934 | 21-4-1985 | 50 years, 258 days |
| 7 | Richard Bass | American | 21-12-1929 | 30-4-1985 | 55 years, 130 days |

**The Everest Successful Expeditions to 1988 (55):**

1 Japanese.........9(1970-73-75-**80**-82-83-83-85)
2 American .......8(**1963**-76-81-83-**83**-84-**88**-88)
3 French...........4(1978-88-88-88)
4 British ...........3(**1953-75**-76)
5 South Korean .. 3(1977-87-88)
6 Spanish .......... 3(1980-85-88)
7 Swiss ............ 2(1956-86)
8 Chinese .......... 2(**1960**-75)
9 Indian............ 2(1965-84)
10 Italian............ 2(1973-**80**)
11 West German... 2(1978-79)
12 Polish ............ 2(1980-**80**)
13 Canadian ........ 2(1982-**86**)
14 Australian....... 2(**1984**-88)
15 Czechoslovak... 2(1984-88)
16 Austrian ......... 1(1978)
17 Yugoslav ........ 1(**1979**)
18 Soviet ............ 1(**1982**)
19 Bulgarian........ 1(1984)
20 Dutch............ 1(1984)
21 Norwegian ...... 1(1985)
22 "Asian".......... 1(1988)

The bold dates correspond to expeditions that opened a new route.

**Extreme Dates of Ascent in each Season**

Earliest Pre-Monsoon Ascent ...................... 20 April 1984(Prodanov)
Latest Pre-Monsoon Ascent ......................... 29 May 1953(Hillary, Tenzing)
......................... 29 May 1965(Alhuwalia, Rawat, Phu Dorje)
Earliest Monsoon Ascent ..........................20 August 1980(Messner)
Latest Monsoon Ascent.............................30 August 1986(Loretan, Troillet)
Earliest Post-Monsoon Ascent .............. 15 September 1977(Ko Sang-Don, Pemba Norbu)
Latest Post-Monsoon Ascent ....................30 October 1985(K. Yagihara's 7-man team)
Earliest Winter Official Ascent ..............16 December 1983(Ozaki, Yamada, Murakami, N. Yonden)
Earliest Winter Calendar Ascent.............22 December 1987(Huh Young-Ho, Ang Rita)
Latest Winter Ascent ........................... 17 February 1980(Cichy, Wielicki)

**Statistics by Xavier Eguskitza**

## *Appendix 6*

# Fatalities 1921–89

Verified Deaths on Everest on or above Base Camps (up to 28-2-1989)

| No. | NAME | NATIONALITY | DATE | EXP. | LOCATION | CAUSE |
|---|---|---|---|---|---|---|
| 1 | Norbu | Sherpa | 7-6-1922 | BR | Below North Col | Avalanche |
| 2 | Lhakpa | ,, | ,, | ,, | ,, | ,, |
| 3 | Pasang | ,, | ,, | ,, | ,, | ,, |
| 4 | Pema | ,, | ,, | ,, | ,, | ,, |
| 5 | Sange | ,, | ,, | ,, | ,, | ,, |
| 6 | Dorje | ,, | ,, | ,, | ,, | ,, |
| 7 | Remba | ,, | ,, | ,, | ,, | ,, |
| 8 | Shamsherpun | Gurkha | 15-5-1924 | BR | Above Rongbuk B.C. | Frostbite, brain hem. |
| 9 | Manbahadur | ,, | 25-5-1924 | ,, | At Rongbuk B.C. | Frostbite, pneumonia |
| 10 | George Leigh Mallory | British | 8-6-1924 | ,, | North-east Ridge | Disappeared |
| 11 | Andrew Irvine | ,, | ,, | ,, | ,, | ,, |
| 12 | Maurice Wilson | British | June 1934 | Solo | East Rongbuk glacier | Exhaustion |
| 13 | Mingma Dorje | Sherpa | 31-10-1952 | SW | Lhotse Face | Falling ice |
| 14 | Shao Si-ching | Chinese | May 1960 | CH | North-east Ridge | Not known |
| 15 | Nawang Tsering | Sherpa | 28-4-1962 | IN | Lhotse Face | Falling rocks |
| 16 | John Breitenbach | American | 23-3-1963 | US | Icefall | Falling serac |
| 17 | Phu Dorje | Sherpa | 18-10-1969 | JA | Icefall | Collapsed snow bridge |
| 18 | Mima Norbu | Sherpa | 5-4-1970 | JA | Icefall | Avalanche |
| 19 | Nima Dorje | ,, | ,, | ,, | ,, | ,, |
| 20 | Tshering Tarkey | ,, | ,, | ,, | ,, | ,, |
| 21 | Pasang | ,, | ,, | ,, | ,, | ,, |
| 22 | Kunga Norbu | ,, | ,, | ,, | ,, | ,, |
| 23 | Kami Tshering | ,, | ,, | ,, | ,, | ,, |
| 24 | Kyak Tsering | Sherpa | 8-4-1970 | JA | Icefall | Falling seracs |
| 25 | Kiyoshi Narita | Japanese | 21-4-1970 | ,, | Camp I (icefall) | Heart attack |
| 26 | Harsh Bahuguna | Indian | 18-4-1971 | INT | West Ridge, 6900 m. | Cold, exhaustion |
| 27 | Toni Tighe | Australian | 14-11-1972 | BR | Icefall | Falling serac |
| 28 | Jangbu | Sherpa | 12-10-1973 | JA | South-west Face | Avalanche |
| 29 | Gerard Devouassoux | French | 9-9-1974 | FR | W. Shoulder, 6400 m. | Avalanche |
| 30 | Lapka | Sherpa | ,, | ,, | ,, | ,, |
| 31 | Sanu Wongal | ,, | ,, | ,, | ,, | ,, |
| 32 | Pemba Dorje | ,, | ,, | ,, | ,, | ,, |
| 33 | Nawang Lutuk | ,, | ,, | ,, | ,, | ,, |
| 34 | Nima Wangchu | ,, | ,, | ,, | W. Shoulder, 5800 m. | Avalanche blast |
| 35 | Wu Tsung-yue | Chinese | May 1975 | CH | NE Ridge, 8500 m. | Exhaustion, fall |
| 36 | Liu Lien-man | ,, | 27-5-1975 | ,, | NE Ridge, 8700 m. | Cold, exhaustion |
| 37 | Mick Burke | British | 26-9-1975 | BR | Near summit | Disappeared |
| 38 | Terry Thompson | British | 10-4-1976 | BR | Western Cwm (C II) | Falling in crevasse |
| 39 | Dawa Nuru | Sherpa | 18-4-1978 | A | Icefall | Falling in crevasse |
| 40 | Ang Phu | Sherpa | 16-5-1979 | YU | Hornbein couloir | Fall |
| 41 | Ray Genet | American | 3-10-1979 | WG | SE Ridge, 8400 m. | Cold, exhaustion |
| 42 | Hannelore Schmatz (f) | West German | ,, | ,, | ,, | ,, |
| 43 | Wang Hong-bao | Chinese | 12-10-1979 | CH/JA | Below North Col | Avalanche |
| 44 | Luo Lan | ,, | ,, | ,, | ,, | ,, |
| 45 | Nima Thaxi | Tibetan | ,, | ,, | ,, | ,, |
| 46 | Akira Ube | Japanese | 2-5-1980 | JA | North Face, 7900 m. | Avalanche |

Appendix 6 Fatalities continued.

| No. | NAME | NATIONALITY | DATE | EXP. | LOCATION | CAUSE |
|---|---|---|---|---|---|---|
| 47 | Nawang Kersang | Sherpa | 6-9-1980 | IT/NE | Icefall | Fall |
| 48 | Franco Piana | Italian | 21-9-1980 | „ | Lhotse Face | Falling seracs |
| 49 | Noboru Takenaka | Japanese | 12-1-1981 | JA | Western Cwm, 6900 m. | Fall |
| 50 | Marty Hoey (f) | American | 15-5-1982 | US | North Face, 8000 m. | Fall |
| 51 | Peter Boardman | British | 17-5-1982 | BR | NE Shoulder, 8200 m. | Disappeared |
| 52 | Joe Tasker | „ | „ | „ | „ | „ |
| 53 | Pasang Sonam | Sherpa | 31-8-1982 | CA | Icefall | Avalanche |
| 54 | Ang Tshuling | „ | „ | „ | „ | „ |
| 55 | Dawa Dorje | „ | „ | „ | „ | „ |
| 56 | Blair Griffiths | Canadian | 2-9-1982 | „ | Icefall | Falling seracs |
| 57 | Lhakpa Tshering | Sherpa | 27-9-1982 | SP | West Ridge, 6770 m. | Internal haemorrhage |
| 58 | Nima Dorje | „ | 14-10-1982 | „ | West Ridge, 8300 m. | Fall |
| 59 | Yasuo Kato | Japanese | 27-12-1982 | JA | South summit area | Disappeared |
| 60 | Toshiaki Kobayashi | „ | „ | „ | „ | „ |
| 61 | Pasang Temba | Sherpa | 8-10-1983 | JA | SE Ridge, 8600 m. | Fall |
| 62 | Hironobu Kamuro | Japanese | 8-10-1983 | „ | Hillary Step, 8,800 m. | Fall |
| 63 | Hiroshi Yoshino | „ | 9-10-1984 | „ | „ | Fall |
| 64 | Ang Rinji | Sherpa | 26-3-1984 | IN | Icefall | Avalanche |
| 65 | Tony Swierzy | British | 3-4-1984 | BR | North Face, 6150 m. | Avalanche |
| 66 | Hristo Ivanov Prodanov | Bulgarian | 21-4-1984 | BU | West Ridge, 8500 m. | Exhaustion |
| 67 | Craig Nottle | Australian | 9-10-1984 | AU | Hornbeim Couloir | Fall |
| 68 | Fred From | „ | „ | „ | „ | „ |
| 69 | Jozef Psotka | Czechoslovak | 16-10-1984 | CZ | Lhotse Face | Fall |
| 70 | Ang Dorje | Sherpa | 24-10-1984 | NE | SE Ridge, 8,400 m. | Fall |
| 71 | Yogendra Thapa | Nepalese | „ | „ | „ | „ |
| 72 | Juanjo Navarro | Basque | 12-5-1985 | BA | North Rige, 7,300 m. | Fall |
| 73 | Shinichi Ishii | Japanese | 17-9-1985 | JA | Below North Col | Avalanche |
| 74 | Kiran Kumar | Indian | 7-10-1985 | IN | SE Ridge, 8,500 m. | Slab avalanche |
| 75 | Vijay Pal Singh Negi | „ | 11-10-1985 | „ | South Col | Exposure |
| 76 | Ranjeet Singh Bakshi | „ | „ | „ | „ | „ |
| 77 | Jai Bahuguna | „ | „ | „ | „ | „ |
| 78 | M. U. Bhaskar Rao | „ | „ | „ | „ | „ |
| 79 | Victor Hugo Trujillo | Chilean | 16-8-1986 | CHL | Below North Col | Avalanche |
| 80 | Simon Burkhardt | Swiss | 28-9-1986 | SP | Lhotse Face | Avalanche |
| 81 | Geyalu | Sherpa | 4-10-1986 | „ | Icefall | Falling seracs |
| 82 | Dawa Nuru | Sherpa | 17-10-1986 | US | Below North Col | Avalanche |
| 83 | Tsutten Dorji | Sherpa | 30-1-1987 | SKO | SW Face, 7700 m. | Fall |
| 84 | Roger Marshall | Canadian | 21-5-1987 | Solo | Hornbein Couloir | Fall |
| 85 | Masao Yokoyama | Japanese | 2-9-1987 | JA | Rongbuk B.C. to A.B.C. | Drowned |
| 86 | Mongol Singh Tamal | Nepalese | 20-10-1987 | BR | Above Rongbuk B.C. | Avalanche |
| 87 | Hidetaka Mizusoki | Japanese | 21-4-1988 | JA | Base Camp | Heart attack |
| 88 | Michel Parmentier | French | 20-9-1988 | INT | North Face, 7700 m. | Probably exposure |
| 89 | Narayan Shrestha | Nepalese | 21-9-1988 | SP | West Ridge, 7200 m. | Avalanche |
| 90 | Lhakpa Sonam | Sherpa | 13-10-1988 | FR | SE Ridge, 8200 m. | Fall |
| 91 | Pasang Temba | „ | „ | „ | „ | „ |
| 92 | Dusan Becik | Czechoslovak | 17-10-1988 | CZ | SE Ridge | Disappeared |
| 93 | Peter Bozik | „ | „ | „ | „ | „ |
| 94 | Jaroslav Jasko | „ | „ | „ | „ | „ |
| 95 | Jozef Just | „ | „ | „ | „ | „ |
| 96 | Lhakpa Dorje (Ang L.) | Sherpa | 23-12-1988 | BE | South Col | Cerebral thrombosis |
| 97 | Dimitar Ilievski | Yugoslav | 10-5-1989 | YUG | Descending South Col Route | Fall |
| 98 | Phu Dorje | Sherpa | 16-5-1989 | USA | Descending South Col Route | Fall |
| 99 | Waclaw Otreba | Polish | 27-5-1989 | POL | West Ridge, 7200 m. | Avalanche |
| 100 | Miroslaw Dasal | „ | „ | „ | „ | „ |
| 101 | Miroslaw Gardzielewski | „ | „ | „ | „ | „ |
| 102 | Zygmunt Heinrich | „ | „ | „ | „ | „ |
| 103 | Eugeniusz Chrobak | „ | 28-5-1989 | „ | Lhola camp | Avalanche wound |

**EXPEDITION ABBREVIATIONS**

| | | | |
|---|---|---|---|
| A : Austrian | CH : Chinese | INT : International | SW : Swiss |
| AU : Australian | CHL : Chilean | IT : Italian | US : American |
| BA : Basque | CA : Canadian | JA : Japanese | WG : West Germany |
| BE : Belgian | CZ : Czechoslovak | NE : Nepalese | YU : Yugoslav |
| BR : British | FR : French | SKO : South Korean | |
| BU : Bulgarian | IN : Indian | SP : Spanish | |

**COUNTRIES OF THE VICTIMS**

| | |
|---|---|
| NEPAL[1] | 46 |
| JAPAN | 10 |
| UNITED KINGDOM | 8 |
| INDIA | 6 |
| CHINA[2] | 6 |
| CZECHOSLOVAKIA | 5 |
| POLAND | 5 |
| UNITED STATES | 3 |
| AUSTRALIA | 3 |
| CANADA | 2 |
| FRANCE | 2 |
| WEST GERMANY | 1 |
| ITALY | 1 |
| BULGARIA | 1 |
| SPAIN (Basque) | 1 |
| CHILE | 1 |
| SWITZERLAND | 1 |
| YUGOSLAVIA | 1 |
| Total | 103 |

(1) 41 Sherpas, 2 Ghurkas, 3 others
(2) 5 Chinese, 1 Tibetan

**LOCATIONS**

| | |
|---|---|
| Khumbu Icefall | 19 |
| East Rongbuk glacier to North Col | 17 |
| South-east Ridge (to summit) | 19 |
| West Ridge (and Shoulder) | 16 |
| North Face | 8 |
| North-east ridge | 7 |
| Lhotse Face | 5 |
| South Col | 5 |
| South-west Face | 2 |
| Western Cwm | 2 |
| Base Camps | 2 |
| North Ridge | 1 |
| Total | 103 |

**CAUSES**

| | |
|---|---|
| Avalanches, falling rocks, seracs, etc. | 49 |
| Falls (including into crevasses) | 24 |
| Cold/Exhaustion | 10 |
| Recognised illness | 6 |
| Drowning | 1 |
| Unknown | 13 |
| Total | 103 |

–With the exception of 1977, there have occurred deaths every year since 1969.
–Worst year: 1982, with 11 deaths.

## EVEREST DEATHS BELOW BASE CAMPS

1) Alexander M. Kellas, the Scottish doctor and climber, died of heart failure, in early June 1921, near Kampa Dzong, about 100 miles from Everest, as the crow flies. He was a member of the British expedition led by C.K. Howard-Bury.
2) A coolie also died during the same expedition, June 1921, at Tingri Dzonga, 50 odd miles from Everest.
3) A Sherpa died by drowning when he fell from a rope bridge at Gadong Paga, in June 1936, during the return march of the British expedition that led H. Ruttledge.
4/5) Two Nepalese porters died of exposure in a storm, 23 September 1952, at the Shamung-Namreki-La (4000 m.), during the approach march of the second Swiss expedition, led by G. Chevalley.
6) Harishwar Dayal, Indian Ambassador in Kathmandu, died at Gorak Shep, 19 May 1964, while participating in a publicity trek to promote the Indian 1965 expedition.
7) An old Sherpa porter died of exhaustion near Phakdingma, in the spring of 1970, during the approach march of the Japanese Skiing expedition.
8) Horst Vitt, a West German Consular official, died of pulmonary oedema at Gorak Shep, April 1972, while on his way to take over the post of Base Camp Manager for K. Herrligkoffer's international expedition.
9) Mingma, a deaf-and-dumb Sherpa lad, died on 23 August 1975, by drowning in a glacier stream, two miles short of Base Camp, during the approach march of C. Bonington's SW Face expedition.
10) An Italian reporter, who had been dispatched to cover the Italo-Nepalese expedition led by Francesco Santon, died of pulmonary oedema, near Base Camp, in the autumn of 1980.
11) Jangbir Rai, a Nepalese kitchen boy for the Indian expedition led by D.K. Khullar, died of altitude sickness on 28 March 1984, while descending from Base Camp to Lobuche.

Subsequent Deaths of Everest Summiteers

| No. | NAME | NATIONALITY | ASCENT YEAR | DEATH DATE | LOCATION | CAUSE |
|---|---|---|---|---|---|---|
| 1 | Sonam Gyatso | Ind. Sikkimese | 1965 | 22-4-1968 | New Delhi, India | Liver cancer |
| 2 | Phu Dorji | Nep. Sherpa | 1965 | 18-10-1969 | Everest icefall | Fall in crevasse |
| 3 | Mick Burke | English | 1975 (?) | 26-9-1975 | EVEREST | Disappeared |
| 4 | Dougal Haston | Scottish | 1975 | 17-1-1977 | Riondaz, Leysin Alps | Avalanche, skiing |
| 5 | William Unsoeld | American | 1963 | 4-3-1979 | Mt. Rainier | Avalanche |
| 6 | Ang Phu | Nep. Sherpa | 1978, 79 | 16-5-1979 | EVEREST | Fall to North Face |
| 7 | Ko Sang-Don | South Korean | 1977 | 29-5-1979 | Mt. McKinley | Collective fall |
| 8 | Ray Genet | American | 1979 | 3-10-1979 | EVEREST | Exposure, SE Ridge |
| 9 | Hannelore Schmatz | West German | 1979 | 3-10-1979 | EVEREST | Exposure, SE Ridge |
| 10 | Nicolas Jaeger | French | 1978 | April 1980 | Lhotse, South Face | Disappeared |
| 11 | Franz Oppurg | Austrian | 1978 | 9-3-1981 | Karwendel Mts., Tyrol | Fall |
| 12 | Peter Boardman | English | 1975 | 18-5-1982 | Everest NE Ridge | Disappeared |
| 13 | Reinhard Karl | West German | 1978 | 19-5-1982 | Cho Oyu | Avalanche |
| 14 | Yasuo Kato | Japanese | 1973, 80, 82 | 27-12-1982 | EVEREST | Disappeared |
| 15 | Jernej Zaplotnik | Yugoslav | 1979 | 24-4-1983 | Manaslu | Avalanche |
| 16 | Hironobu Kamuro | Japanese | 1983 | 8-10-1983 | EVEREST | Fall at Hillary Step |
| 17 | Hiroshi Yoshino | Japanese | 1983 | 9-10-1983 | EVEREST | Fall at Hillary Step |
| 18 | Naomi Uemura | Japanese | 1970 | Febr. 1984 | Mt. McKinley | Disappeared |
| 19 | Hristo I. Prodanov | Bulgarian | 1984 | 21-4-1984 | EVEREST | Disappeared |
| 20 | Jozef Psotka | Czechoslovak | 1984 | 16-10-1984 | EVEREST | Fall on Lhotse Face |
| 21 | Ang Dorje | Nep. Sherpa | 1978, 84 | 24-10-1984 | Everest SE Ridge | Fall |
| 22 | Chris Chandler | American | 1976 | 14-1-1985 | Kangchenjunga | Altitude oedema |
| 23 | Andrzej Czok | Polish | 1980 | 11-1-1986 | Kangchenjunga | Altitude oedema |
| 24 | Kim Momb | American | 1983 | 10-2-1986 | B.C. Ranges, Canada | Avalanche, skiing |
| 25 | Tenzing Norgay | Ind. Sherpa | 1953 | 9-5-1986 | Darjeeling, India | Lung infection |
| 26 | Dawa Nuru | Nep. Sherpa | 1985 | 17-10-1986 | Everest, North Col | Avalanche |
| 27 | Phu Dorjee | Ind. Sherpa | 1984 | 25-5-1987 | Kangchenjunga | Disappeared |
| 28 | Toni Sors | Catalan | 1985 | 27-9-1987 | Lhotse Shar | Avalanche |
| 29 | Narayan Shrestha | Nep. Newari | 1985 | 21-9-1988 | Everest, West Ridge | Avalanche |
| 30 | Lhakpa Sonam | Nep. Sherpa | 1988 | 13-10-1988 | EVEREST | Fall from SE Ridge |
| 31 | Pasang Temba | ,, | 1988 (?) | ,, | ,, | ,, |
| 32 | Jozef Just | Czechoslovak | 1988 | 17-10-1988 | EVEREST | Disappeared |
| 33 | Ang Lhakpa | Nep. Sherpa | 1985 | 23-12-1988 | Everest, South Col | Cerebral thrombosis |
| 34 | Noboru Yamada | Japanese | 1983, 85, 88 | Febr. 1989 | Mt. McKinley | Disappeared |
| 35 | Teruo Saegusa | ,, | 1985, 88 | ,, | ,, | ,, |
| 36 | Dimitar Ilievski | Yugoslav | 1989 | 10-5-1989 | EVEREST | Fall |
| 37 | Phu Dorje | Nep. Sherpa | 1988, 89 | 16-5-1989 | EVEREST | Fall |
| 38 | Eugeniusz Chrobak | Polish | 1989 | 28-5-1989 | EVEREST | Avalanche Wound |

## NOTES

Locations given as EVEREST (with capital letters) refer to those cases in which death took place during the descent from the summit.

The ascent of Mick Burke was never totally verified, although he was last seen by Peter Boardman and Pertemba within striking distance of the summit, when the weather conditions were still reasonable. In Boardman's opinion, he probably walked over one of the cornices which overlook the huge Kangshung face, as he came down from the summit, weather conditions having then deteriorated badly.

The two Sherpa brothers, Lhakpa Sonam and Pasang Temba, were found dead on the SE Ridge of Everest, at c.8200 m. by members of a Spanish team on their way to the summit, early on 14 October 1988. They appeared to have suffered a long fall. The previous day, Lhakpa Sonam had reached the summit with French climber, Serge Koenig. A second pair, formed by Pasang Temba and Frenchman Marcus Margaly, stopped at c.8500 m. where Margaly, who had oxygen problems, decided to give up and started the descent. Pasang Temba, alone, kept going and met the summit pair, on their way down, at c.8700 m. While Koenig continued the descent, Lhapka Sonam decided to wait, at c.8500 m., for his brother who had continued towards the summit. From the report of the Spanish climbers who found their bodies, it would appear that Pasang Temba did in all probability reach the summit and, later, rejoined his brother to continue the descent together, with unfortunate results for both of them.

**DEATH LOCATIONS**

a) *On the way down from Everest summit:* 15
Mick Burke (?), Ang Phu, Ray Genet, Hannelore Schmatz, Yasuo Kato, Hironobu Kamuro, Hiroshi Yoshino, Hristo I. Prodanov, Jozef Psotka, Lhakpa Sonam, Pasang Temba (?), Jozef Just, Dimitar Ilievski, Phu Dorje, Eugeniusz Chrobak

b) *On Everest (subsequent attempts)*: 6
Phu Dorji, Peter Boardman, Ang Dorje, Dawa Nuru, Narayan Shrestha, Ang Lhakpa.

c) *On other Eight-Thousanders*: 7
Nicolas Jaeger (Lhotse), Reinhard Karl (Cho Oyu), Jernej Zaplotnik (Manaslu), Chris Chandler (Kangchenjunga), Andrzej Czok (Kangchenjunga), Phu Dorjee (Kangchenjunga), Toni Sors (Lhotse Shar).

d) *In North American mountains:* 6
William Unsoeld (Mt. Rainier), Ko Sang-Don (Mt. McKinley), Naomi Uemura (Mt. McKinley), Kim Momb (B. C. Ranges), Noboru Yamada (Mt. McKinley), Teruo Saegusa (Mt. McKinley)

e) *In the Alps*: 2
Dougal Haston (Riondaz, Leysin), Franz Oppurg (Karwendel, Tyrol)

f) *From terminal disease*: 2
Sonam Gyatso (in New Delhi), Tenzing Norgay (in Darjeeling)

| | | | | | | | |
|---|---|---|---|---|---|---|---|
| NEPALESE | 8 | INDIANS | 3 | FRENCH | 1 | POLISH | 1 |
| JAPANESE | 4 | WEST GERMANS | 2 | AUSTRIANS | 1 | SPANISH | 1 |
| AMERICANS | 4 | CZECHOSLOVAKS | 2 | YUGOSLAVS | 1 | | |
| BRITISH | 3 | SOUTH KOREANS | 1 | BULGARIANS | 1 | | |

**Statistics by Xavier Eguskitza**

# Bibliography

## BOOKS, BOOKLETS ETC

Adamiecki, W., *Zdobyc Everest*, Warsaw, 1984.

Ahluwalia, Major H.P.S., *Higher Than Everest*, New Delhi, 1973.
*Climbing Everest*, New Delhi, 1976.
*Faces of Everest*, New Delhi, 1978.

Alpine Club, The, *Alpine Club Library Catalogue, Volume One 1980*, London, 1982.
*Catalogue of the Exhibition of Photographs and Paintings from The Mount Everest Expedition 1922*.
*Catalogue of paintings and photographs from the Mount Everest Expedition 1924*.
*Catalogue of the Centenary Exhibition (November/December 1957)*.
*Man and Mount Everest* (Inventory of Exhibition of Photographs, Paintings and Memorabilia, held at the Alpine Club December 1978/January 1979 to mark the 25th Anniversary of the First Successful Ascent of Mount Everest. Typescript, prepared by Audrey Salkeld.)
*The Alpine Journal* (Continuous record of mountain adventure from March 1863; now published annually.)

American Alpine Club, *American Alpine Journal* (Continuous record of all mountain activity, published annually.)

Anderson, J.R.L., *High Mountains and Cold Seas*, London, 1980.

Arundale, G.S., *Mount Everest: Its Spiritual Attainment*, Wheaton Il., 1933.

Avramov, A., *Everest – By The West Ridge*, Sofia, 1987.

Barbe Baker, R. St. (and others), *The Lasting Victories*, London, 1948.

Barnes, M., *After Everest: An Autobiography* (of Sherpa Tenzing), London, 1977.

Baroni, Mariani, Nottaris and Quarti, *Finestra Sull'Everest*, Agno, 1984.

Bass, D. and Wells, F. (with Ridgeway, R.), *Seven Summits*, New York, 1986.

Bauer, W., *Mount Everest, Bericht Von Mallory Und Seinen Freunden*, Gutersloh, 1950. (Source-Boyle).

Baume, L., *Sivalaya, The 8000-Metre Peaks of The Himalaya*, Reading, 1978.
*Himalaya Bibliography of The 8000 Metre Peaks*, Reading, 1978.

Benson, C.E., *Mountaineering Ventures*, London, 1928.

Bettembourg, G. and Brame, M., *The White Death*, Seattle, 1981.

Bhanja, K.C., *Darjeeling at a Glance: a handbook, both descriptive and historical of Darjeeling and Sikkim, with thrilling accounts of Everest and Kanchenjunga expeditions by land and air*. Darjeeling, 1941.
*Kinchen-Everest*, Darjeeling, 1942.

Black, C.E.D., *A Memoir of The Indian Surveys 1895–1890*, 1891.

Blanch, C. and Massons, J., *El Everest, Historia de Una Conquista*, Barcelona, 1986.

Boeck, K., *Im Banne des Everest: Erlebnisse in Nepal, Der fur Weisse Verschlossenen Heimat Der Gorkhas im Zentral-Himalaja*, Leipzig, 1923.

Bonington, C.J.S., *The Next Horizon*, London, 1973.
*Everest, South West Face*, London, 1973.
*Everest, The Hard Way*, London, 1976.
*Quest for Adventure*, London, 1981.
*Everest, The Unclimbed Ridge*, London, 1983 (with Clarke, C.).
*The Everest Years*, London, 1986.

Boustead, Col. Sir H., *The Wind of Morning*, London, 1971.

Boyle, J., *Everest 83, An Aerial Tramway*, Privately printed, San Francisco, 1988.

Bridges, T.C. and Tiltman, H.H., *More Heroes of Modern Adventure*, London, 1929.

Briggs, R. and Styles, S., *First up Everest*, London, 1969.

Brook, E. and Donnelly, J., *The Windhorse*, London, 1985.

Broughton, G. (ed.), *Climbing Everest*, Oxford, 1960.

Bruce, Brig.-Gen., The Hon. C.G., *The Assault on Mount Everest, 1922*, London 1923.
*Himalayan Wanderer*, London, 1934.

Bryant, L.V., *New Zealanders and Everest*, Wellington, N.Z., 1953.

Buchan, J., *The Last Secrets, the Final Mysteries of Exploration*, London, 1923.

Burgess, A. and Palmer, J. *Everest, The Ultimate Challenge*, Toronto, 1983.

Burke, B., *Going Back*.

Burrard, Col. (Sir) S.G., *A Sketch of The Geography and Geology of The Himalaya Mountains and Tibet*, Calcutta, 1907–8 (With Hayden, H.J.).
*The Geography and Geology of The Himalayan Mountains and Tibet*, Dehra Dun, 1933–4 (With Heron, A.M.).
*Mount Everest and its Tibetan Names*, Dehra Dun, 1931.

Calvert, H., *Smythe's Mountains, The Climbs of F.S. Smythe*, London, 1985.

Cameron, I. (pseud. for Payne, G.), *To the Farthest Ends of The Earth*, London, 1980.
*Mountains of The Gods*, London, 1984.
*Exploring The Himalayas*, London, 1985.

Carr, H. (ed.), *The Irvine Diaries*, Andrew Irvine and the Enigma of Everest, Reading, 1979.

Chartwell Press, The, *Everest, A Guide to The Climb*, 1953.

China, *The Final Assault on The World's Highest Peak.*
*Mountaineering in China*, Peking, 1965.
*A Photographic Record of The Mount Jolmo Lungma Scientific Expedition 1966–1968*, (Chinese Academy of Science/Science Press) Peking, 1974.
*Another Ascent of The World's Highest Peak – Qomolangma*, Peking, 1975.
*High Mountain Peaks in China – Newly Opened to Foreigners*, Peking/Tokyo, 1981.

Chwascinski, B., *Ku Nie Zdobytym Szczytom*, Warsaw, 1987 (Everest history to 1953. Source-Boyle).

Cichy, W. and Zakoske, *Rozmowy O Everescie*, Warsaw, 1982.
Enlarged edition, 1987.

Clark, R.W., *Six Great Mountaineers*, London, 1956.
*Great Moments in Mountaineering*, London, 1956.
*An Eccentric in The Alps*, London, 1959.
*A Picture History of Mountaineering*, London, 1956.
*Men, Myths and Mountains*, London/New York, 1976.

Clarke, C., *Mountain Medicine and Physiology: Proceedings of an Alpine Club Symposium*. London, 1975 (editor).
*Everest: The Story of Mount Everest and the First Ascent of The South-West Face in 1975* (Epic Adventures Series.) London, 1978.
*Lightweight Expeditions to The Great Ranges*, London, 1984 (edited with Salkeld, A.).

Cleare, J., *Mountains*, London, 1975.

Cobham, Sir A., *Tight Corners*, London, 1940.

Coffey, M., *Fragile Edge*, London, 1989.

Collins, F.A., *Mountain Climbing*, Toronto, 1923.

Corbett, E.V., *Great True Mountain Stories*, London, 1957.

Cremer, R.W., *Mount Everest and other Poems*, Privately printed, 1923.

Cons, G.J., *The Challenge of Everest*, an introductory reader to Climbing Mount Everest, the offical sound film record of the 1933 expedition, London, 1934.

Deck, C. and Mazeaud, P., *La Route de L'Everest avec L'Expedition Française*, Paris, 1979.

Denman, E., *Alone to Everest*, London, 1954.

Dent, C., *Above The Snow Line*, London, 1885.

Desio, Professor A., *Which is the Highest Mountain in the World?* Privately printed, Milan, 1988.

Dias, J., *The Everest Adventure: Story of The Second Indian Expedition*, Delhi, 1965.
*Second Indian Expedition to Mount Everest* (Souvenir brochure.)

Dickinson, L., *Filming the Impossible*, London, 1982.
*Anything is Possible*, London, 1989.

Diemberger, K., *Gipfel und Geheimnisse*, Vienna, 1980.

Dingle, G. and Perry, M. *Chomolungma: Goddess, Mother of the Earth. The North Face of Everest*, Aukland, 1986.

Dittert, R., Chevalley, G. and Lambert, R., *Forerunners to Everest, The Story of The Two Swiss Expeditions of 1952*, London, 1954.

Dolbier, M., *Nowhere Near Everest*, New York, 1955.

Donoughue, C., *Everest* (Jackdaw Pack No. 128).

Douglas & Clydesdale, Sq. Ldr. the Marquess of, and M'Intyre, Flt. Lt. D.F., *The Pilot's Book of Everest*, Edinburgh, 1936.

Douglas-Hamilton, J. *Roof of The World, Man's First Flight over Everest*, Edinburgh, 1983.

Dozois, G. (ed.), *Best New SF2* (for fictional piece *Mother Goddess of the World* by Stanley, R.K.), London, 1988.

Dyhrenfurth, G.O., *To the Third Pole*, London, 1955.

Eggler, A., *The Everest-Lhotse Adventure*, London, 1957.

Ehmer, W., *Um Den Gipfel Der Welt: Die Geschichte Des Bergsteigers Mallory*, Stuttgart, 1936.

Enzinck, W., *Der Grosse Berg: G.L. Mallory und Der Mount Everest* (Roman van een expeditie), The Hague, 1954.

Etherton, P., *The Last Strongholds*, London, 1934.

(Everest), *Everest ein Bildband*

(Explorer Films), *The Epic of Everest* (Programme to accompany the film of the 1924 Expedition).

Evans, C., *Eye of Everest, A Sketch Book from the Great Everest Expedition*, London, 1955.

Fantin, M., *La Lunga Via Che Porta All'Everest*, Bologna, 1971.

Faux, R., *Everest, Goddess of The Wind*, Edinburgh, 1978.
*High Ambition, A Biography of Reinhold Messner*, London, 1982.

Fellowes, Air-Commodore P.F.M. (and others), *First Over Everest, The Houston Mount Everest Expedition*, London, 1933.

Finch, G.I., *The Making of a Mountaineer*, London, 1924; 1989.
*Der Kampf um den Everest*, Leipzig, 1925.
*Climbing Mount Everest*; London, 1930.

Fisher, W.H., *To the Top of The World*, New York, 1926.

Flaig, W., *Im Kampf um Tschomo-Lungma, Den Gipfel Der Erde: Der Himalaya und Sein Hochsten Gipfel*, Stuttgart, 1923.

Fleming, J. and Faux, R., *Soldiers on Everest*, London, 1977.

Fujiki, K., *The Ascent of Everest*, Tokyo, 1954. (In Japanese.)

Gebauer, A.K., *Um den Mount Everest: Fahrten und Abenteur*, Vienna, 1925.

Gillette, N. and Reynolds, J., *Everest Grand Circle: a Climbing and Skiing Adventure through Nepal and Tibet*, Leicester/Seattle, 1985.

Goswami, S.M., *Everest, Is It Conquered?* Calcutta, 1954.

Greene, R. *Moments of Being*, London, 1974.

Gregory, A., *The Picture of Everest*, London, 1954.

Greig, A., *Kingdoms of Experience, Everest the Unclimbed Ridge*, London, 1986.

Grey, B., *The Lost World of Everest*, London, 1950 (children's fiction).

Gruda, K., *Mount Everest – Auf Tod Und Auf Leben*, Gottingen, 1980.

Gulatee, B.L., *Mount Everest, It's Name and Height*, Dehra Dun, 1950.

Gurung, H.B., *Annapurna to Dhaulagiri: A Decade of Mountaineering in The Nepal Himalaya 1950–1960*, Kathmandu, 1968.
*Vignettes of Nepal*, Kathmandu, 1980.

Habeler, P. (transl. by Heald, D.), *Everest, Impossible Victory*, London, 1979.

Hafner, T., *Everest – Ein Schauspiel in Funf Akten*, Lucerne, 1947.

Hagen, T., Dyrhenfurth, G.O., Furer-Haimendorf, C. von, and Schneider, E. (translated by E.N. Bowman), *Mount Everest – Formation, Population and Exploration of The Everest Region*, London, 1963.

Hall, Lincoln, *White Limbo: The first Australian climb of Mount Everest*, McMahons Point, 1985.

Haston, D., *In High Places*, London, 1972.

Hayes, *Trekking to Mount Everest and Solu Khumbu* (Guide).

Hedin, S., *Mount Everest*, Leipzig, 1923.

Helins, T., *Time Markers: The Crowning of Elizabeth II and The Conquest of Mount Everest*. Observations on the historical, spiritual and symbolic significance of these two conjoined events in the starred year of 1953. Los Angeles, 1953.

Hellmich, W. (editor), *Khumbu Himal*, Innsbruck/Munich, 1964–7 (5 vols).

Herrligkoffer, K.M., *Mount Everest, Thron der gotter, Sturm auf den Hochsten Gipfel der Welt*, Stuttgart, 1972; Munich 1982.
*Mount Everest ohne Sauerstoff*, Bamberg, 1979.

Hiebeler, T., *Abenteuer Everest, durchs Sherpaland zur Cholmolongma!* Zurich, 1974.

Hillary, Sir E.P., *High Adventure*, London, 1955.
*East of Everest*, London, 1956 (with Lowe, G.).
*Nothing Venture, Nothing Win*, London, 1975.
*Two Generations*, London, 1984 (with Hillary, P.).

Hindley, G., *The Roof of The World* (Aldus Encyclopaedia of Discovery and Exploration.) London, 1971.

Holzel, T. and Salkeld, A., *The Mystery of Mallory and Irvine*, London, 1986.

Hooker, Sir J.D., *Himalayan Journals, Notes of a Naturalist in Bengal, The Sikkim and Nepal Himalayas, The Khasia Mountains*, etc., London 1854.

Hornbein, T.F., *Everest, The West Ridge*, San Francisco, 1965; London, 1971.

Houston, C., *Going High: The Story of Man and Altitude*, Burlington, Vermont, 1980.
*Going Higher* (revised edition), Burlington, Vermont, 1980.

Howard-Bury, Lt. Col. C.K. (and others) *Mount Everest: The Reconnaissance*, 1921. London, 1922.

Hunt, J. (Brigadier Sir John Hunt, later The Lord Hunt)
*The Ascent of Everest*, London, 1953.
*Our Everest Adventure*, Leicester, 1954.
*My Favourite Mountaineering Stories*, London, 1978 (Ed.).
*Life is Meeting*, London, 1978.

Imai, M., *Macho Quomolungma*, Tokyo, 1986.

Indian Mountaineering Federation, *First Indian Mount Everest Expedition 1960*.
*Second Indian Expedition to Mount Everest 1962*, 1962 (Souvenir Brochure).
*The Indian Mount Everest Expedition 1965*, New Delhi, 1965.

Irving, R.L.G., *The Romance of Mountaineering*, London, 1935.
*Ten Great Mountains*, London, 1940.
*A History of British Mountaineering*, London, 1955.

Izzard, R., *The Innocent on Everest*, London, 1955.

Japanese Alpine Club, *The Japanese Mount Everest Expedition, 1970*, Tokyo, 1970 (with Mainichi Newspaper).
*Official Report of The Japanese Mount Everest 1975*, Tokyo, 1975.
*Everest Expedition, 1969–70*, Tokyo, 1972.
*Chomolangma-Tibet: official account of the Japanese Alpine Club Chomolangma expedition*, Tokyo, 1981.

Japan Everest Skiing Expedition, *Mount Everest: Yuichiro Miura and The Japanese Everest Skiing Expedition*, Tokyo, 1970.

Japan Rock Climbing Club, *Everest 8848: The Japanese Expedition to Mount Everest 1973: The Preliminary Report*, Tokyo, 1974.

Jaros, J. and Kalvoda, J., *Geological Structure of The Himalayas: Mt. Everest-Makalu Section*, Prague, 1978.

(Jefferies, M. and Clarbrough, M.), *Sagarmatha, Mother of The Universe; The Story of Mount Everest National Park*, Auckland, 1985.

Jenkins, P., *Across China*, New York, 1986.

Jones, M., *Canoeing Down Everest*, London, 1979.

Kambara, T., *Nepal Bibliography*, Privately printed, Tokyo, 1959.

Kato, Y., *Everest*, Tokyo, 1984.

Keenlyside, F.H., *Peaks and Pioneers*, London, 1975.

Kele, F., *Everest*, Bratislava, 1986.

Key, C.E., *A Book of Recent Exploration*, London, 1946.

Kielkowski, J., *Mount Everest Massiv Nord: Himalajafuhrer*, Privately printed, Dusseldorf 1985; [Aree Greuil 1986].

Knoop, F.W., *A World Explorer: Sir Edmund Hillary*, Champaign, Il., 1970.

Kogel, *Everest Ansturm*.

Kohli, M.S., *Nine Atop Everest: Story of the Indian Ascent*, Bombay, 1969.

Kononov, I., *Victory Over Everest*, Kiev, 1985.

Kowalewski and Paczkowski, *Mount Everest: Dzieje Zdobycia*; Podboju, Warsaw, 1986.

Kunaver, A. (and others), *Na Vrh Svitjeta, Jugoslavenske Ekspedicije od Trisula do Everesta*, Ljubljana, 1979.

Kurek, Fraciszek, *Mount Everest 1924*, Warsaw, 1933.

Kurz, M., *Chronique Himalayenne, L'Age d'Or 1940–1955*, Zurich, 1959.
*Chronique Himalayenne, Supplement*, Zurich, 1963.

Lambert, R., *A L'Assaut des 'Quatre Mille': Dix Recits de Haute Montagne*, 1946.

Lane, M., *Exercise Pilgrims Return – Everest Expedition 1984*, Aldershot, 1984 (Short report).

Langley, B., *East of Everest*, London, 1984 (Fiction).

Leduc, P. and Stefanie, B., *La Face Cachee de L'Everest*, Paris, 1979.

Link, U., *Mount Everest, Der Kampf um Den Gipfel Der erde*, Munich, 1953.

Lodge, Sir O., *Why I Believe in Personal Immortality*, Privately printed, 1928 (public edition, London 1928, omitted pages referring to the deaths of Mallory and Irvine).

Longstaff, T., *This My Voyage*, London, 1950.

Lowe, G., *Because it is There*, London, 1959.

Lukan, K., *Mountain Adventures*, London/Glasgow/New York, 1972.

Lunn, A., *A Century of Mountaineering 1857–1957*, London, 1957.

McCallum, J.D., *Everest Diary: Based on the Personal Diary of Lute Jerstad*, Chicago, 1966.

MacGregor, J., *Tibet: A Chronicle of Exploration*, London, 1970.

MacIntyre, N., *Attack on Everest*, London, 1936.

Madden, C. (ed.), *Living Dangerously*, London, 1936.

Mainichi Newspaper, *The Ascent of Everest*, Tokyo, 1970 (Photo Album).

Malartic, Y. (transl. by Heller, J.B.), *Tenzing of Everest*, London, 1954.

Markham, C.R., *A Memoir on the Indian Surveys*, 1871.
*A Memoir on The Indian Surveys 1871–1878*, 1878.

Marshall, H.P., *Men Against Everest*, London, 1954.

Mason, K., *Abode of Snow: A History of Himalayan Exploration and Mountaineering*, London, 1955.

Mateu, M., *Everest el Repte D'Un Somni*, Barcelona, 1984.

May, J., *Hillary and Tenzing: Conquerors of Mt. Everest*, 1972.

Mazeaud, P., *Everest '78*, Paris, 1978.

Meiji University, *Everest West Ridge*, Tokyo, 1982.

Messner, R., (transl. by Salkeld, A.), *Everest: Expedition to The Ultimate*, London, 1977.
*All Fourteen Eight-Thousanders*, Marlborough, 1988 (transl. by Neate, J.).
*The Crystal Horizon: Everest – The First Solo Ascent*, Marlborough/Seattle, 1989.

Mila/Tenzing

Mill, H.R., *The Record of The Royal Geographical Society, 1830–1930*, London, 1930.

Milne, M. (ed.), *The Book of Modern Mountaineering*, London, 1968.

Miura, Y., *Skiing on Mount Everest*, Tokyo, 1970.

Miura, Y., *The Man Who Skied Down Everest*, Tokyo, 1974; and San Francisco/New York, 1978 (with Perlman, E.).

Mollier, C., *Everest 74, Le Rendez-Vous du Ciel*, Paris, 1975.

Montgomery, M., *All Out for Everest*, London, 1975 (trekking).

Monzino, G., *La Spedizione Italiana All Everest 1973*, Milan, 1976.

Moon, K., *Man of Everest, Story of Sir Edmund Hillary*, London, 1962.

Mordecai, D., *The Himalayas, an Illustrated Summary of The World's Highest Mountain Ranges*, Calcutta, 1966.

Morin, M., *Everest: From the First Attempt to Final Victory*, London, 1955.

Morris, James, *Coronation Everest*, London, 1958.
*Conundrum*, London, 1974 (written as Jan Morris).

Morris, John, *Hired to Kill*, London, 1960.

Morrow, P., *Beyond Everest: Quest for the Seven Summits*, Camden, Ontario, 1986.

Morshead, I., *The Life and Death of Henry Morshead*, Cambridge, 198x.

(*Mountain* Magazine), *World Climbing* (The 'INFO' pages of *Mountain* 1-64, 1969–78 inclusive, introduced by King, T.), Sheffield, 1980.

(Mount Everest Committee), *Climbing Mount Everest* (Programme to accompany the film of the 1922 expedition).

Mullick, B.N., *The Sky was His Limit*, The Life and Climbs of Sonam Gyatso, Dehra Dun, 1970.

Murray, W.H., *The Story of Everest*, London, 1953.

Naess, Arne, *Drommen om Everest*, Oslo, 1987.

Nairz, W., *Gipfelsieg am Everest: Expedition der Weltrekorde des Alpenvereins 1978*, Vienna/Munich, 1978.

Neate, W.R. (Jill), *Mountaineering and its Literature*, Milnthorpe, 1978.
*Mountaineering Literature*, Milnthorpe/Seattle, 1986.

Neri, I. and Martegani, U., *Terrible Everest*, Bologna, 1953.

Newby, E., *Great Ascents, A Narrative History of Mountaineering*, Newton Abbott, 1977.

Newsome, D. (ed.), *On the Edge of Paradise, A.C. Benson: Diarist*, London, 1980.

Nicolson, N., *The Himalayas* (Time-Life The World's Wild Places Series), Amsterdam, 1975.

Noel, Captain J.B.L., *Through Tibet to Everest*, London, 1927; 1989.

Norton, B.P. (transl. H. Delgrove), *Memoires D'un Sherpa*, 1954.

Norton, Lt. Col. E.F. (and others), *The Fight for Everest: 1924*, London, 1925.

Noyce, C.W.F., *South Col, One Man's Adventure on the Ascent of Everest 1953*, London, 1954.

Noyce, C.W.F., *Everest is Climbed*, Harmonsworth, 1953 (with Taylor, R.)
*World Atlas of Mountaineering*, London, 1969 (with McMorrin, I.).

Oyarzum, G., *Everest de Los Andes al Himalaya*, Santiago, 1984.

Pares, B., *Himalayan Honeymoon*, London, 1940.

Perrin, J. (ed.), *Mirrors in The Cliffs: A Hundred Mountaineering Articles*, London, 1983. (Several Everest references, the most worthwhile being H.W. Tilman's review of *Americans on Everest* by Ullman, J.R.).

Petkov, N., *From Matterhorn to Everest*, Sofia, 1985.

Peyre, J., *Mount Everest*, Paris, 1942.

Phillimore, Col. R.H., *The Historical Records of the Survey of India.*
Vol I (18th Century) Dehra Dun, 1945.
Vol II (1800-1815) Dehra Dun, 1950.
Vol III (1815–1830) Dehra Dun, 1954.
Vol IV (1831–1843) Dehra Dun, 1956.
Vol V (1844–1861) 1964 (suppressed.)

Pye, D., *George Leigh Mallory: A Memoir*, London, 1927.

Rawling, Capt. C.G., *The Great Plateau*, London, 1905.

Rebuffat, G. (transl. Sutton, G.J.), *Mont Blanc to Everest*, London, 1956.

Ridgeway, R., *The Boldest Dream: The Story of the Twelve who Climbed Mount Everest*, New York, 1979.

Roberts, D., *I'll Climb Mount Everest Alone: The Story of Maurice Wilson*, London, 1957.

Robertson, D., *George Mallory*, London, 1969.

Robertson, M. (ed.), *Mountain Panorama*, London, 1955.

Roch, A., *Everest 1952 – Reportage Photographique*, Geneva, 1952.

Rongzu, Zhang, *Mount Qomolangma*, Peking, 1981.

Rost, J., *Everest 82*, Moscow, 1984; Prague, 1984.

Rowell, G., *Mountains of the Middle Kingdom*, San Francisco, 1983.

Royal Geographical Society, *Geographical Journal*, Regular periodical of the Society, of particular interest to the Everest story from the first reconnaissance expedition of 1921 to the successful climb of 1953 (the period of the Mount Everest Committee on which the RGS was strongly represented).

Rudolph, F., *Himalay Tigers*, Berlin, 1955. *Chomolungma und Ihre Kinder*, Moscow, 1983.

Rutkiewicz, Wanda, Na Jednej Linie, Warsaw, 1986.

Ruttledge, H. (and others), *Everest 1933*, London, 1934. *Everest, The Unfinished Adventure*, London, 1937.

Saeki, T., *Diary of Everest Base Camp Headman*, Tokyo, 1971.

Salkeld, A. and Smith, R., *One Step in The Clouds: An Omnibus of Mountain Fiction*, London/Seattle, 1989 (includes number of Everest pieces, including *The Ice Chimney* by Collins, B.).

Salten, F., *Flucht Durch Den Himalaya und Erlebtes Beim Mahardsche U. Bundi*, Salzburg, 1956 (WWII prison escapes).

Sayre, W.W., *Four Against Everest*, New York, 1964.

Schlagintweit, H./Schlagintweit, A./Schlagintweit, R. von, *Results of a Scientific Mission to India and High Asia Undertaken Between the Years 1854 and 1858*, Leipzig/London, 1861–66 (Four volumes and an atlas).

Scott, Col. R.L., *God is My Co-Pilot*, New York, 1943.

Seaver, G., *Francis Younghusband 1863–1942, Explorer and Mystic*, London, 1952.

Serraillier, I., *Everest Climbed*, Oxford, 1955 (Poem).

Shipp, H., *Everest – To all Who Explore New Paths*, London, 1924 (Poem).

Shipton, E.E., *Upon That Mountain*, London, 1943. *The Mount Everest Reconnaissance Expedition 1951*, London, 1952.
*The True Book about Everest*, London, 1955.
*Mountain Conquest*, New York 1966 (in consultation with Bradford Washburn.)
*That Untravelled World*, London, 1969.
*E.E. Shipton: The Six Mountain-Travel Books*, London/Seattle, 1985.

Silva, P., *Le Ascensioni Sull'Everest: Loro Difficolta-Pericoli, Deduzione e Utilia Per le Science*, 1926.

Singh, Brig. Gyan, *Lure of Everest*, Bombay, 1961.

Sircar, S.J., *Himalayan Handbook*, Privately printed, Calcutta, 1979.

Skarja, T., *Everest*, Ljubljana, 1981.

Skuhra, R., *Sturm Auf Die Thron Der Gotter*, Frankfurt, 1950.

Smith, B. Webster, *True Stories of Modern Explorers*, London, undated (c. 1930).

Smythe, R.S., *Camp Six*, London, 1937.

Snaith, S., *At Grips with Everest*, London, 1937.

Somervell, T.H., *After Everest, The Experiences of a Mountaineer and Medical Missionary*, London, 1936.

Spencer, S. (ed.), *Mountaineering*, Lonsdale Library Vol. XVIII, Undated (c. 1934).

Steele, P., *Doctor On Everest*, London, 1972.

Stobart, T. *Adventurer's Eye*, London, 1958.

Styles, S., *The Mountaineer's Weekend Book*, London, 1950.
*Mallory of Everest*, London, 1967.
*On Top of The World; An Illustrated History of Mountaineering and Mountaineers*, London, 1967.
*First on the Summits*, London, 1970.
*The Forbidden Frontiers, The Survey of India from 1765 to 1949*, London, 1970.

Sufrin, M., *To The Top of The World*, New York, 1966.

Swinson, A., *Beyond The Frontiers, The Biography of Colonel F.M. Bailey, Explorer and Special Agent*, London, 1971.

Swiss Foundation for Alpine Research (S.F.R.A.), *Everest, The Swiss Everest Expeditions*, London, 1954.

Tasker, J., *Everest, The Cruel Way*, London 1981.
*The Savage Arena*, London, 1982.

Tchernine, O., *Explorers and Travellers*, 1958.

Temple, P., *The World at Their Feet: The Story of New Zealand Mountaineers in the Great Ranges of the World 1935–1968*, Christchurch, 1969.

Thomas, L., *Lowell Thomas' Book of The High Mountains*, New York, 1964.

Thur, H. and Hanke, *Steig Uber den Everest*, Munich, c. 1953.

Tilman, H.W., *Mount Everest 1938*, Cambridge, 1948. (Also collected in: *H.W. Tilman: The Seven Mountain-Travel Books*, London/Seattle, 1983.)

Tullis, J., *Clouds from Both Sides*, London, 1986.

Turkevich, M., *The Call of The Distant Peaks*, Donetsk, 1984.

Uemura, N., *Beyond Mount Everest*, Tokyo, 1985.

Ullman, J.R., *High Conquest, The Story of Mountaineering*, Philadelphia, 1947.
*Kingdom of Adventure: Everest*, New York, 1947.
*Tiger of The Snows: The Autobiography of Tenzing of Everest*, Philadelphia, 1964.

Unsworth, W., *Because It Is There: Famous Mountainers 1840–1940*, London, 1968.
*Everest: A Mountaineering History*, London/Boston, 1981.

Uriarte, F., *Euskaldunak Everest Mendian/Va Scos en El Everest*, San Sebastian, 1981.

Vanni, M., *Everest (Chomo-Lungma) La Piu Alta Montagna Del Mondo: Suo Conoscnze e Sus Conquista.*, Turin, 1947.

Verghese, B.G. (ed.), *Himalayan Endeavour*, Bombay, 1962.

Ward, M.P., *The Mountaineer's Companion*, London, 1966 (Editor).
*In This Short Span, A Mountaineering Memoir*, London, 1972.
*Mountain Medicine, A Clinical Study of Cold and High Altitude*, London, 1975.
*High Altitude Medicine and Physiology*, London, 1989 (with Milledge, J.S. and West J.B.).

West, J., *Everest, The Testing Place*, New York, 1985.

Wibberley, L., *The Epics of Everest*, London, 1955.

Williams, C., *Women on the Rope: The Feminine Share in Mountain Adventure*, London, 1973.

Wilson, K. (ed.), *The Games Climbers Play*, London, 1978.

Wollaston, M. (ed.), *Letters and Diaries of A.F.R. Wollaston*, Cambridge, 1933.

Yakushi, Y., *Catalogue of The Himalayan Literature*, Privately printed, Kyoto, 1972 (Rev. 1984).

Yamada, K., *The Himalaya from The Air*, Tokyo, 1975.

Yomiuri Newspaper, *Everest: The Glory of Women*, Tokyo, 1975.
*Stood on The Summit of Chomolungma*, Tokyo, 1980.

Yoshizawa, I., *Mountaineering Maps of The World: Himalaya*, Tokyo, 1977.

Young-Do, K., *My Everest*, Seoul, 1980.

Younghusband, Sir F.E., *The Epic of Everest*, London, 1926.
*Everest, The Challenge*, London, 1936.

## JOURNALS

*(A Selected Bibliography of Everest-related Articles)*

*A.J.* *Alpine Journal*
*A.A.J.* *American Alpine Journal*
*G.J.* *Geographical Journal*
*H.J.* *Himalayan Journal*
*N.G.* *National Geographic Magazine*

Anderson, R., 'The Nine Days of Everest', *Mountain*, 124.

(Ang Phu), (?1960–79) Obituary in *Climber and Rambler*, July 1979.

(Bahuguna, Harsh), (1939–71) Obituary in *H.J.*, 1970.

Bell, George (Jr.), 'Video from Heaven', *American Cinematographer*, October 1983 (David Breashears microwaves pictures from summit).

Bere, R., 'Is There an Abominable Snowman?', *A.J.*, 1975.

Bernstein, J., 'The Endless Climb of Reinhold Messner', *Geo*, Vol I, Charter Issue, 1979.

Blacker, L.V.S., 'Flight over Everest'. *The Story of Exploration and Adventure*, Part 3 (Newnes, *c.* 1938).
'The Mount Everest Flights', *H.J.*, 1934.

Blakeney, T.S., 'A.R. Hinks and The First Everest Expedition 1921', *G.J.*, 136, Part 3 (September 1970); also in *H.J.*, 1971.
'The First Steps Towards Mount Everest', *A.J.*, 1971.
'A Tibetan Name for Everest', *A.J.*, 70.
'Maurice Wilson and Everest 1934', *A.J.*, 70.

Blume, R. Duane, and Pace, Nello, 'The Diluter-Demand Oxygen System, Used During the International Himalayan Expedition to Mount Everest', *A.A.J.*, 1971.

Boardman, P., 'Everest Is Not a Private Affair', *Mountain Life*, 23, 1975.
'So You're an Everest Climber', *Mountain*, 76.

Boardman, P., and Richards, R., 'British Everest Expedition, S.W., Face, 1975', *A.J.*, 81.

(Boardman, P.) (1950-82), Obituaries in *The Times*, 7 June 1982; *Climber and Rambler*, August 1982; *High*, 1982; *Mountain*, 1982; *A.J.*, 1983.

Bonington, C., 'Everest South West Face 1972', *H.J.* 1972–3.
'Everest South West Face', *A.A.J.*, 1976.
'Everest South West Face' (with Unsworth, W.), *Climber and Rambler*, January/ February, 1976.
'Hitting The Top at 50', *The Observer*, 28 April 1985 (culminating article in series on Norwegian expedition).

Bourdillon, R. and T., and Harris, E., 'The Closed Circuit Oxygen Apparatus', *A.J.*, 59.

Bourdillon, T., 'The Oxygen Apparatus in Action', A.J., 59.

(Bourdillon, T.) (1924–56), Obituary in *A.J.*, 1961.

Bruce, C.G., 'The Organisation and Start of The Expedition (1924)', *A.J.*, 36.

(Bruce, Brig. Gen. C.G.) (1886–1939), Obituaries *A.J.*, 52; *H.J.*, 1940, 1946.

Bruce, J.G., 'The Journey Through Tibet and the Establishment of the High Camps (1924)', *A.J.*, 36.

(Bruce, J.G.), (1896–1972), Obituaries in *The Times* 2 February 1972; *A.J.*, 1973; *Mountain*, 20.

(Bryant, L.V.) (1905–56), Obituary in *A.J.*, 63.

Bullock, G.H., 'The Everest Expedition, 1921; Diary of G.H. Bullock', *A.J.*, 67.

(Bullock, G.H.) (1887–1956), Obituary in *A.J.*, 61.

(Burke, M.) (1941–75), Obituaries in *Mountain*, 46 and *A.J.*, 1976.

Burrard, S.G., 'Mount Everest: The Story of a Long Controversy', *Nature*, Vo. 71, pp. 42–46.

Chandler, C. and Hornbein, T., 'A. Review of Oxgyen Systems', *A.J.*, 1977.

(Chetin or Chettan, 'Satan') (?–1930), Obituaries in *H.J.* 1931 and A.J., 42.

(China), 'New Information on Chinese Ascents of Mount Everest', *Off Belay*, April 1980.

Clarke, C., 'Contact Lenses at High Altitude: Experiences on Everest South-West Face 1975', *Br. Journal of Ophthalmology*, Vol. 60, No. 6, June 1976.

Clarke, C. and Duff, J., 'Mountain Sickness, Retinal Haemorrhages and Acclimatisation on Mount Everest in 1975', *Br. Medical Journal*, 1976, 2.

Cleare, J., 'Thirteen Nations on Mt Everest', *A.J.*, 77.

Collie, J.N. 'A Short Summary of Mountaineering in The Himalaya, with a Note on The Approaches to Everest', *A.J.*, 33.
'The Ranges North of Mt Everest as seen from Near The Kang La', *A.J.*, 33.
'The Mount Everest Expedition (1921)', *A.J.*, 34.

Crawford, C.G., 'Extracts from Everest Diary of C.G. Crawford', *A.J.*, 46.
(Crawford, C.G.) (1890–1959), Obituary in *A.J.*, 64.

Creighton, G.W., 'The Tibetan Name of Mount Everest', *A.J.*, 69.

Dang, H., 'Mount Everest, 1962', *A.J.*, 68.

(Dias, Maj. J.) (1928–64), Obituary in *H.J.* 1964.

Dickey, P.A. 'Who Discovered Mount Everest', *EOS*, October 1985.

Dubey, S., 'Everest, 1962', *H.J.* 1962–3.

Dyhrenfurth, N.G., 'Six to The Summit', *National Geographic*, October 1963 (with others).
'Americans on Everest, 1963', *A.J.*, LXIX.
'Mount Everest 1963', *H.J.*, 1964 (with Unsoeld, W.).
'Everest Direttissima', *Sierra Club Bulletin*, March 1970.
'Everest Revisited: International Himalayan Expedition 1971', *H.J.*, 1971.
'Everest' (Review of History), *Mountain*, 76.

Eggler, A., 'The Swiss Expedition to Everest and Lhotse 1956', *H.J.* 1957, also *A.J.*, 61.

(Estcourt, N.) (1943–78), Obituaries in *Mountain*, 63 and *A.J.*, 1979.

Evans, R.C., 'Everest, The First Ascent of The South Peak', *H.J.* 1954, also PUA. J., *LIX*.

Farrar, J.P., 'The Everest Expeditions (1921/1922)', *A.J.*, 34.

Faux, R., 'A Breathless Dash to The Top of The World', *The Times*, 27 May 1978.
'Everest Unmasked: The First Ascent Without Oxygen', *Expedition*, Vol. 9, No. 2 (197x).
'Everest NE Ridge – The Seligmann Harris Expedition', *A.J.*, 1987.

Finch, G.I., 'Equipment for High Altitude Mountaineering with Special Reference to Climbing Mount Everest', *G.J.*, LXI.
'The Second Attempt on Mt Everest', *A.J.*, 34.
(Finch, G.I.) (1888–1970), Obituaries in *The Times*, 24 November 1970: *A.J.*, 1972 and 1973.

Freshfield, D.W., 'The Great Peaks of the Himalaya', *A.J.*, XII.
'Notes from Tibet', *A.J.*, 22.
'The Highest Mountain in the World', *A.J.*, 21.
'Mount Everest *v.* Chomolungma', *A.J.*, 34.
'The Last Climb' (verse), *A.J.*, 36.
'The Conquest of Mount Everest', *G.J.* LXIII, also *A.J.*, 36.

George V, His Majesty, 'King's Message of Condolence on Death of Mallory and Irvine', *A.J.*, 36.

Gilbert, L., 'Before Everest', *A.J.*, 81.

Gillman, P., 'These Men Fought Against Everest – And Lost', Captain Noel's story and photographs, *Sunday Times* Magazine, 18 September 1969.
'The Endless Mystery of Mount Everest' (Mallory, Irvine and Holzel), *Sunday Times* 3 October 1971 (and Letters in two subsequent weeks).
'The Show Must Go Up' (profile of Bonington), Sunday Times, 1973.
'Will Mount Everest Yield Up its Ghosts?' *Sunday Times*, 4 January 1981.
'Without a Trace' (Bourgeois mystery), *Sunday Times* Magazine, 18 December 1983.

'The Everest Enigma', *Financial Times*, 15 November 1986.
'Cut Off on Top of The World' (The Venables Story), *Sunday Times* Magazine, 4 December 1988.

Goldie, G.T. and Lord Morley, 'A Himalayan Barrier', *A.J.*, 23.

Goodfellow, B., 'Chinese Everest Expedition 1960: A Further Commentary', *A.J.*, 66.

Graaff-Hunter, J. de 'The Height of Mount Everest and Other Peaks', *Geod. Rep. Surv. India*, I (1924).
'Heights and Names of Mt Everest and other Peaks', *Occ. Notes Royal Astr. Soc.* 3 (1953).
'Various Determinations over a Century of The Height of Mount Everest', *G.J.* CXXI, Part 1 (March 1955).

Greene, R., 'Oxygen and Everest', *Nature*, 28 October 1931. 'Observations on the Composition of Alveolar Air on Everest 1933', *Journal of Physiology*, 1934, Vol 82, No. 4.
'The Everest Oxgyen Apparatus 1933', *The Lancet*, 17 November 1934.
'Mental Performance in Chronic Anoxia', *Brit. Med. Jour.*, 4 May 1957.

(Greene, R.) (1901–82), Obituaries in *The Times*, 8 December 1982; *Climber and Rambler*, February 1983 and *A.J.*, 1983.

Gulatee, B.L., 'Mount Everest, It's Name and Height', *H.J.*, 1952. 'The Height of Mount Everest, A New Determination', *H.J.*, 1955–6.

Habeler, P., 'The Summit Without Oxygen', *Climber and Rambler*, December 1978.

Hall, B., 'Why We Failed on Everest', *Climber and Rambler*, May 1980.
'Everest in Winter', *Climber and Rambler*, October 1981.

Harvard, A. and Morrissey, J.D., 'The Forgotten Face of Everest' and 'Conquest of The Summit' (Kangshung Face), *N.G.*, July 1984.

(Haston, D.) (1940–77), Obituaries in *Mountain*, 53 and *A.J.*, 1978.

(Hazard, J. de Vere) (?–1968), Obituary in *A.J.*, 1969.

Herrligkoffer, Dr. K.M., 'Mount Everest, 1972', *H.J.*, 1973–4.

Hillary, E., 'To The Summit', *H.J.*, 1954.
'The Last Lap', *A.J.*, LIX.

Himalayan Club, Eastern Section, 'The Problem of Mount Everest', *H.J.* 1937.

'Himalayan Traveller, A'
'The Battle with Everest', Morning Post, 14 June 1924; also *A.J.*, 36 (No. 229).

Hingston, R.W.G., 'Physiological Difficulties in The Ascent of Mount Everest', *A.J.*, 37 (No. 230) and *G.J.*, LXV (1925).

(Hingston, Maj. R.W.G.) (1887–1966), Obituary in *A.J.*, 71.

Hinks, A.R., 'The Mount Everest Maps and Photographs', *A.J.*, 34 (No. 224).
'The "Houston Flight"', *A.J.*, XLV.

(Hinks, A.R.) (1873–1945), Obituaries in *G.J.*, March–April 1945 and A.J., 55.

Holzel, T., 'The Mystery of Mallory and Irvine', *Mountain*, 17 (September 1971), and replies, *Mountain*, 21, 26).
'The Search for Mallory and Irvine', *Summit*, Sept–Oct 1981.
'Russians on Everest', *Summit*, March–April 1983.
'The 1960 Chinese Ascent of Everest', *Mountain*, 101.
'Mallory & Irvine: First to The Top of Everest?', *Summit*, Sept–Oct 1987.

Hopkins, T., 'The Menace of Everest' (Canadian Expedition), *Maclean's*, 20 September 1982.

Houston, C.S., 'Operation Everest 1946', *A.A.J.*, 1947.
'Towards Everest 1950', *H.J.*, 1952.

Howard-Bury, Lt Col. C.K., 'The 1921 Mount Everest Expedition', *A.J.*, 34 (No. 224).

(Howard-Bury, Lt Col. C.K.) (1883–1963), Obituaries in *The Times*, 24 September 1963; *A.J.*, 69.

Hunt, J., 'Letters from Everest', *F.R.C.C.*, *Journal*, 1954.
'Everest Ascended', *Mountain World*, 1954.
'Sir John Hunt's Diary (1953)', *A.J.*, 59.

Hunt, J. and Westmacott, M., 'Everest, 1953: Narrative of The Expedition', *A.J.*, 59.

*Illustrated* 'Conquest of Everest: The Full Story in Nine Pages of Vivid Pictures', 4 July 1953.
'How We Made The Everest Film' (Tom Stobart's Story), 24 October 1953.

(Irvine, A.C.O.) (1902–24), Obituary in *A.J.*, 36 (No. 229).

Jayal, N.D., 'Indian Air Force Flights over Everest, 1953', *H.J.*, 1954.

Jeffers, LeRoy, 'Breaking Trail to The Top of The World, The Chances of Conquering Mt Everest', *New York Tribune*, 22 May 1921.

(Kato, Yasuo) (1950–82), Obituary in *Climber and Rambler*, February 1983.

Kellas, A.M., 'Mountains of North Sikkim and Garwhal', *A.J.*, 26.
'The Possibility of Aerial Reconnaissance in the Himalaya', G.J. LI, 6 (June 1918).
'A Consideration of The Possibility of Ascending Mount Everest', Paper presented to the Alpine Congress in Monaco, May 1920, (Copy in AC lib).

(Kellas, Dr. A.M.) (1868–1921), Obituary in *A.J.*, 34.

Khullar D.K., 'Indian Everest Expedition, 1984', *H.J.*, 41.

Krakauer, J., 'Return to The North Face', *Outside*, February 1985 (Climbing Great/Norton Couloir).

Kurz, M., Mount Everest: A Century of History', *Mountain World*, 1953.

Lammer, G., 'The Third Mount Everest Expedition', *A.J.*, 39.

Lester, J.T., 'Personality and Everest', *A.J.*, 74. (1969).

Lloyd, P., 'Oxygen on Mount Everest, 1938' (with note, 'Oxygen and Everest', by G.I. Finch), *A.J.*, 51.

Longland, J.L., 'Between The Wars, 1919–39', *A.J.*, 62.

Longstaff, T.G., 'Lessons from The Mount Everest Expedition of 1933', *A.J.*, 46.
'Some Aspects of The Everest Problem', *A.J.*, 35 (No. 226).

(Longstaff, T.G.) (1875–1964), Obituaries in *A.J.*, 1969 and *H.J.*, 1964.

Lowe, G., 'Everest 1953: The Lhotse Face', *H.J.* 1954.

McNaught Davis, I., 'Why Everest?' *Mountain*, 25, 1973.

Mallory, G.L., 'Mount Everest: The Reconnaissance', *A.J.*, 34 (No. 224).
'The Second Mount Everest Expedition, *A.J.*, 34 (No. 225).

(Mallory, G.L.) (1886–1924), Obituaries in *The Times*, 21 June 1924; The Nation & The Athenaeum, 5 July 1924; A.J., 36.

(Marshall, R.) (1941–87), Obituaries in *Mountain*, 117: *A.A.J.*, 1988.

Marshall, T., 'Everest – The Hell of The Winter Climb', *Observer* Magazine, 15 November 1981.

Martin, S. 'Everest – Pre-Monsoon', *A.J.*, 1985.

Mason, K., Notes as editor of the *Himalayan Journal*, etc.: 'Mount Everest and its "Native" Names'. *H.J.*, 1932.
'Mount Everest Flight, 1933', *H.J.*, 1933.
'The Official Height of Mount Everest', *H.J.*, 1934.
'Tragedy on Mount Everest' (Maurice Wilson), *H.J.*, 1935.
'The Problem of Mount Everest', *H.J.*, 1937 and 1939.
'Map of Mount Everest', *H.J.*, 1958.

Merrick, H., 'Everest: The Chinese Photograph', *A.J.*, 67, 68.

Messner, R., 'I Climbed Everest Alone', *N.G.*, October 1981.

Miller, M.M., 'The Geology and Glaciology Program of The American Mount Everest Expedition 1963', *Harvard Mountaineering*.
'Glacio-Meteorology on Mount Everest in 1963: The Khumbu Glacier of Chomolungma in N.E. Nepal', *Weatherwise*, Vol 17, No. 4, and *H.J.*, 1966.

Monteath, C., 'The Man who Brought "English Air" to Everest', *Geo* (NZ), December 1986.

Moores, P., 'The Boys from The White Stuff', *Mountain*, 124 (N.E. Ridge climb 1988).

Morris, J., 'The Press on Everest', *H.J.*, 1954.

(Morshead, Maj. H.T.) (1882–1931), Obituaries in *A.J.*, 43; *H.J.*, 1932.

*Mountain* magazine, 'Mountain Interview: Sir Edmund Hillary', Nos. 45 and 46.
'Nine Who Climbed Chomolungma Feng' (Official Chinese Report, 1975), No. 46, and photos analysed 'Everest North Ridge Climbed' in No. 47.

Murray, W.H., 'The Reconnaissance of Mount Everest', *H.J.*, 1952; *A.J.*, 58.

Neame, K., 'Flight over Everest', *Lilliput*, No. 185 (1952).

Noel, Maj. J.B., 'A Journey to Tashirak in Southern Tibet, and the Eastern Approaches to Mount Everest', *G.J.*, LIII, No. 5 (May 1919).
'Through Tibet to Everest by Capt. J.B.L. Noel.' Noel's book critically reviewed (anonymously) in *A.J.* 39 (No. 235).

(Noel, Capt. J.B.L.) (1890–1989), Obituaries in *The Times* and *The Daily Telegraph*, 13 March 1989; *Mountain*, 127.

Norton, E.F., The Mount Everest Despatches', *G.J.*, LXIV; also *A.J.* 36 (No. 229).
'Personnel of The Expedition' (1924), *A.J.*, 36 (No. 229).
'The Climb with Mr Somervell to 28,000 ft' (1924), *A.J.*, 36 (No. 229).
'The Problem of Mt Everest'. *A.J.*, 37 (No. 230).
'Mt. Everest: The Last Lap', *A.J.*, 57.

(Norton, Maj. E.F.) (1884–1954), Obituary in *A.J.*, 60.

Noyce, W., Note, as editor of the *H.J.*: The Problem of Mount Everest, 1946.
'Everest 1953: The South Col', *H.J.*, 1954.

(Noyce, C.W.F.) (1917–62), Obituary in *A.J.*, 67.

Nyka J., 'A New Route – South Buttress', *A.A.J.*, 55.

Odell, N.E., 'The Last Climb (1924)', *A.J.*, 36 (No. 229).
(See also *A.J.* 59, 78).
'The Rocks and Glaciers of Mount Everest' *G.J.*, 66, 1925.
'Supposed Fossils from North Face of Mount Everest', *Quar. Jour. Geol. Soc.*, Vol. LXXXII.
'Hypoxia: Some Experiences on Everest and Elsewhere', *Mountain Medicine and Physiology*. (Alpine Club Symposium Proceedings), 1975.
'The Tibetan Name of Mount Everest', a series of notes etc. in *A.J.*, 37, 47, 65, 69.
'Ice Axe Found on Everest', *A.J.*, 46, 68.
'South Summit Versus South Peak', *A.J.*, 59.

(Odell, Prof. N.E.) (1890–1987), Obituaries in *The Times*, 24 February, 1987; *Mountain*, 115; *A.A.J.*, 1988; *A.J.*, 1988–9.

Ohtsuka, Hiromi, The Japanese Mount Everest Expedition, 1969–1970, *H.J.*, 1971.

Pereira, A., 'Personal Reminiscences of The Mount Everest Expedition 1924, *The Year's Photography*, October 1925.

Perrin, J., 'Capt. J.B.L. Noel', *Climber and Rambler*, January 1978.
'H.W. Tilman', *Climber and Rambler*, April 1977.
'Secrets or Intrusions', *High* 1986.

Picture Post, 'Everest, How They Did It' (articles by Wyn Harris, Shipton, Wager and Longland), 4 July 1953.

Pugh, L.G.C.E., 'Scientific Aspects of The Expedition to Mount Everest 1953', *G.J.*, Vol. CXX, Part 2 (June 1954).
'Scientific Problems on Mount Everest 1953, *H.J.*, 1954.
'The Scientific Background of The 1953 Expedition to Mount Everest', *Mountain World*, 1955.
'Himalayan Rations with Special Reference to The 1953 Expedition to Mount Everest', *Proc. Nutr. Soc.*, 13, (pp.60–69).
'Notes on Temperature and Snow Conditions in The Everest Region in Spring 1952 and 1953', *Journal of Glaciology*, Vol. 2, No. 15 (April 1954).
'Technique Employed for Measuring Respiratory Exchanges on Mount Everest 1953', *Journal of Physiology, 123 (pp. 25–26).*
'Some Effects of High Altitude on Man', *(with M. Ward), The Lancet,* 1 December 1956.
'Resting Ventilation and Alveolar Air on Mount Everest: 'with Remarks on The Relation of Barometric Pressure to Altitude in Mountains', *Journal of Physiology*, 135 (1957, pp. 590–610).
'Muscular Exercise on Mount Everest', *Journal of Physiology*, 141 (1958, pp 233–61).
'Physiological and Medical Aspects of The Himalayan Scientific and Mountaineering Expedition, 1960–61', *Brit. Med. Journ.*, 1962, Vol. 2.

Roberts, D., 'The Summit of Hype *Outside Magazine*', October 1988.

Roberts, J.O.M., 'Transport and Sherpas on Mount Everest 1963', *H.J.*, 1962; also *A.J.*, 68.

Roach, G.A., 'Everybody's Everest', *Quest*, 77, March–April 1977.

Roch, A., 'The Swiss Expedition – Spring 1952', *A.J.*, 59.

(Rouse, A.) (1951–1986), Obituaries in *Mountain*, 112; *A.J.*, 1987.

Ruttledge, H., 'The Mount Everest Expedition of 1933', *H.J.*, 1934; also *A.J.*, 45.
'The Mt Everest Expeditions', *United Empire*, Vol. 24 pp. 692–70.
'The Mount Everest Expedition, 1936', *H.J.*, 1937.
'Mount Everest: The 6th Expedition', *A.J.*, 48.

(Ruttledge, H.) (1884–1961), Obituaries in *The Times*, 9 November 1961; *A.J.*, 67; *H.J.*, 1961.

Salkeld, A., 'Important Diaries Come to Light' (A.C. Irvine), *Mountain*, 69.
'(Everest) People', *Mountain*, 76.
'Three Times to Top of Everest' (Sungdare Sherpa), *Mountain*, 88, 89.
'The Unquiet Ghost: Strange Story of Maurice Wilson', *Mountain*, 99.

Sayle, M., 'Up The Face of Everest', *Sunday Times* Weekly Review, 7 February 1971.
'Everest, A Reporter's View', *A.J.*, 77.

Sayre, W.W., 'Commando Raid on Everest', *Life*, 22 March 1963.

Schlagintweit, E., 'Der Name Des Hoechsten Berges der Erde', *Pelermanns Mitteil.*, Vol 47, pp. 40–43.

Schmeid, E., 'Everest 1956', *Mountain World*, 1956–7.

Scott, D., 'To Rest is Not to Conquer', *Mountain*, 23.
'South West Face: Everest The Hard Way', *Expedition*, Vol VI, 5.
'Everest South-West Face Climbed', *Mountain*, 47.
'Man at The Top: The Ultimate View' (with others), Everest photographs in colour, *Sunday Times* Magazine, 26 October 1975.
'The Men, The Women and The Mountain' and 'Five Miles High', accounts of N.E. Ridge Expedition, *Guardian*, 2 and 26 October 1987.
'Everest North-East Ridge', *Climber*, May 1988.

(Shebbeare, E.O.) (1884–1964), Obituaries in *A.J.*, 69; *H.J.*, 1965.

Shi Chan-chun, 'The Conquest of Everest by The Chinese Mountaineering Team' (extensively annotated by T.S. Blakeney and B. Goodfellow), *A.J.*, 66; also *H.J.*, 1961.

Shipton, E.E., 'The Mount Everest Reconnaissance, 1935', *H.J.*, 1936; also *A.J.*, 48.
'The Problem of Mount Everest', H.J., 1937.
'Extracts from The Everest Diary of E.E. Shipton', *A.J.*, 46.

(Shipton, E.E.) (1907–77), Obituaries in *Mountain*, 55; *A.J.*, 1978.

Singh, Brig. G., 'Indians on Mount Everest 1960', *H.J.*, 1959–60; also *A.J.*, 66
'The First Indian Attempt on Mount Everest (1960)', *Mountain World*, 1962–63.

Smythe, F.S., 'Everest: The Final Problem', *A.J.*, 46.

(Smythe, F.S.) (1900–1949), Obituaries in *The Times*, 28 June and 26 July 1949; *A.J.*, 57; *H.J.*, 1949.

(Somervell, Dr. T.H.) (1890–1975), Obituaries in *Mountain*, 42; *A.J.*, 1976.

Spender, M., 'Survey on The Mount Everest Reconnaissance 1935', *H.J.*, 1937.

(Spender, M.) (1907–45), Obituary in *H.J.*, 1946.

Steele, P., 'Acclimatisation', *H.J.*, 1971.

Still, Dr E.W., 'The Defeat of Everest' (based on writings of Dr Still), *Technological News*, (Journal of Normalair-Garrett Ltd), Autumn 1976.

Swiss Expeditions of 1952,
'Mount Everest 1952' (contributions by: M. Kurz, E.S. Cowles, E. Feuz, R. Dittert, R. Aubert, A. Roch, J.-J. Asper L. Flory, R. Lambert, G. Chevalley, E. Hofstetter, E. Wyss-Dunant, A. Lombard, A. Zimmermann), *Mountain World*, 1953. 'Forerunners to Everest', by G. Chevalley and R. Lambert, *Mountain World*, 1954.

(Tasker, J.) (1948–82), Obituaries in *The Times*, 7 June 1982; *A.J.*, 1983.

(Tenzing Norgay) (?1915–1986), Obituaries in *The Times*, 10 May 1986; *A.J.*, 1987.

Thompson, M., 'Out With The Boys Again', *Mountain*, 50.

Tilman, H.W., 'The Mount Everest Expedition of 1938 (plus scientific appendices and discussion notes, *G.J.* XCII, No. 6 (December 1938); other accounts in H.J., 1939, and *A.J.*, 51.
'The Annapurna Himal and The South Side of Everest', *A.J.*, 58.

(Tilman, H.W.) (1898–1978), Obituaries in *Climber and Rambler*, April 1977 and May 1978; *Mountain*, 66; *A.J.*, 1979; *A.A.J.*, 1980.

*The Times*, Special Supplements: 'The Mount Everest Reconnaissance Expedition 1951' (text mainly by Shipton), December 1951; 'Challenge to Mount Everest (The Everest Story told by Eric Shipton), 5 May 1953; 'The First Ascent of Mount Everest', July 1953; 'Everest' (Colour Supplement), 1953.

Town, J., 'Red Rib' *Climber and Rambler*, November 1983.

Trimble, P.R., 'American Bicentennial Everest Expedition' (1976), *A.A.J.*, 1977.

Unna, P.J.H., 'The Oxygen Equipment of The 1922 Everest Expedition, A.J., 34 (No. 224).

Unsoeld, W., 'The West Ridge of Everest', *Mountain World*, 1964–5.

(Unsoeld, W.) (1926–1979), Obituary in *A.A.J.*, 1979.

Venables, S., 'Everest – The Kangshung Face', *High*, September 1988.

Villar, R., 'Everest North Face – A Doctor's View', *A.J.*, 1985.

Wager, L.R., 'Mount Everest: The Chinese Photograph', *A.J.*, 68.
'Mount Everest's Weather in 1933', *H.J.*, 1934.
'The Lachi Series of North Sikkim and The Age of The Rocks Forming Mount Everest', *Rec. Geol. Surv. India*, Vol LXXIV.

(Wager. Prof. L.R.) (1904–65), Obituaries in *The Times*, 22 November 1965; *A.J.*, 71.

Wakefield, A.W., 'The Health of Everest Expeditions', *A.J.*, 46.

Wang Fu-chou and Chu Yin-hua, 'How We Climbed The World's Highest Peak', *Mountain Craft*, July–September 1961.

Ward, Dr. M., 'Everest without Oxygen?' (also a paper on frostbitre) in *Mountain Medicine and Physiology* (Alpine Club Symposium Proceedings), 1975.

Warren, Dr. C.B.M., 'Alveolar Air on Mount Everest', *Journal of Physiology*, 96 (1939 pp.34–5).
'The Medical and Physiological Aspects of The Mount Everest Expeditions', *G.J.*, Vol XC, No 2 (August 1937).

Watanabe, Hyoriki, 'The Chomolangma Project 1980 – North Face and Northeast Ridge', *Sangaku*, 1980.

Webster, Ed, 'Cold Courage', *Sports Illustrated*, 16 January 1989; and 'Up Against It', *Climbing*, April 1989 (both Kangshung Face 1988).

(Wheeler, Maj. E.O.) (1890–1962), Obituary in *A.J.*, 67.

(Whillans, D.) (1933–85), Obituaries and Tributes in *The Times*, 7 August 1985; *Climber and Rambler*, October 1985; *Mountain*, *A.J.*, 1986.

Welford, John Noble, 'Everest, The Old Champion is Crowned', *A New Science Times (NYT)*, October 1987.

Wilson, K., 'Questionable Conclusions in Everest Film', *Mountain*, 17; also *H.J.*, 1971.

(Wollaston, A.F.R.) (1875–1930), Obituary in *A.J.*, 42.

(Wyn-Harris, Sir P.) (1903–79), Obituaries in *The Daily Telegraph*, 28 February 1979; *Mountain*, 69; *A.J.*, 84.

(Younghusband, Sir F.E.) (1863–1942), Obituaries in *A.J.*, 54; *H.J.*, 1946.

Zawada A., 'Mount Everest – The First Winter Ascent' *A.J.* 89.

## MANUSCRIPT MATERIAL

There are numerous private papers, diaries and tapes. These are not listed but some are mentioned in the acknowledgements.

Alpine Club
The A.C. Archives, at present being classified, contain a wealth of documentary material, including the A.C. Minute Books, Maurice Wilson's Diary, and the Longstaff papers.

British Broadcasting Corporation
The B.B.C. Sound Archives have much unique material in the form of interviews etc, dating from 1933 to the present time.

India Office Library and Records
Some early Everest material, including the Morley papers.

Merton College Library
The Irvine Papers and Diary.

Royal Geographical Society
The large collection of box files, named by T.S. Blakeney 'the Everest Archives', contain the best collection of documentary material relating to the British attempts on Everest. There is also a comprehensive photographic archive. Here too are the M.E.C. Minute Book and the H.C. Minute Book.

## MAPS

1811
Manuscript map in the India Office Library of Tibet. (Everest, of course, is not named, but there is reference to the 'highest point').

1856
Survey of India Map of Everest area.

1921
1:253,440 PRELIMINARY MAP OF MOUNT EVEREST made by the 1921 reconnaissance of the area north of Everest, then reduced in scale to 1:750,000 and included in the book *Mount Everest: The Reconnaissance* (C.K. Howard-Bury and others, 1922). Issued by the R.G.S., scale 1:100,000.

1924
1:63,360 MOUNT EVEREST AND THE GROUP OF CHOMO LUNGMA drawn by Charles Jacot-Guillarmod, after E.O. Wheeler, 1921, and Hari Singh, 1924. Published by the Everest Committee and reproduced in the book *The Fight for Everest: 1924* (E.F. Norton and others, 1925).

1935
1:20,000 THE NORTHERN FACE OF MOUNT EVEREST drawn by M. Spender from the 1935 reconnaissance survey, reproduced both in *H.J.*, IX, and in the book *Everest, The Unfinished Adventure* by H. Ruttledge (1937).

1957
1:25,000 CHOMOLONGMA-MOUNT EVEREST drawn by Erwin Schneider and F. Ebster, Vienna, 1957.

1965
1:50,000 NEPAL HIMALAYA-KHUMBU HIMAL drawn by E. Schneider and F. Ebster, Vienna, 1965.

1976
1:100,000 EVEREST REGION drawn by G.S. Holland, R.G.S., 1976.

## FILMS

1922
*Climbing Mount Everest, The Tragedy of Everest*, Captain J.B.L. Noel's record of second Everest Expedition, showing journey from Darjeeling to Tibet, aspects of Tibetan life, and the climb itself. (Unclear whether 2 edited versions of the film exist, or whether it is known under two titles – the copy of *Climbing Mt Everest* in the BFI certainly stops short of tragedy of the loss of 7 porters.)

1924
*Epic of Everest*, Captain J.B.L. Noel's record of third Everest Expedition and the loss of Mallory and Irvine.

1933
*The Fourth Everest Expedition*, 16 mm. film made by Percy Wyn-Harris;

1933
BFI also holds 390 ft unedited 16 mm. footage taken by E.O. Shebbeare of expedition and Tibetan scenery/wildlife.

1933
*Everest Flight, Wings over Everest* (Gaumont British 1934 ed version), film about first flight over Everest, shot by L V Stewart Blacker.

1936
*Everest 1936 – Ruttledge*, 512 ft of 16 mm. footage of this expedition, held by BFI;

1950
Houston (home-movie) footage.

1953
*The Conquest of Everest*, Tom Stobart's film of the successful British expedition of 1953 (Countryman Films, 6910 ft 35 mm.).

*Thin Air* (The World of Life Series No 7), preparations for the 1953 expedition (Countryman films).

*Physiology on Mount Everest*, produced by the Mount Everest Foundation and the Medical Research Council, Division of Human Physiology.

1960
*Conquering The World's Highest Peak*, first ascent of Everest from the North by Chinese mountaineers.

1963
*Americans on Everest*, Norman Dyhrenfurth's film of successful US expedition, narrated by Orson Welles.

1966
*The Challenge of Everest*, 17-minute 35-mm. film of Indian expedition, filmed by G.L. Kaul, directed by Arun Chowdhury for Films Division, Ministry of Information, Government of India.

1968
*Everest*, Indian expedition, filmed by Guru Dayal Singh and H.P.S. Ahluwalia, directed by N.S. Thapa for Films Division, Government of India (90 minutes, 35 mm.).

1970
*Skiing Down Mount Everest*, Japanese television film of Y. Miura's ski descent.

1971
*Surrender on Everest*, Unsuccessful attempt on SW Face, filmed by Ned Kelly and Antony Thomas.

1972
Mick Burke shot about 18,000 ft of film on the SW Face Expedition, this was edited into 20 ITN news items and a half-hour film for Thames TV – *Everest, The Fight for The Face*.

1974
*The Mystery of Mallory and Irvine*, Stephen Peet's BBC documentary (Yesterday's Witness Series) incorporated Noel's films and interviewed Noel, Odell and Somervell.

1974
*Everest*, 1h 40 m film produced by Guido Monzino.

1975
*Another Ascent of The World's Highest Peak*, Chinese film of their multi-ascent from the North.

1975
*Everest The Hard Way*, BBC Film by Ned Kelly and Christopher Ralling of the successful SW Face expedition (incorporates some of Mick Burke's last film).

1977
*Dudh Kosi, Relentless River of Everest*, Leo Dickinson's HTV film of kayaking from Everest Base Camp.

1978
*Everest Unmasked*, Leo Dickinson's film (for HTV) of first ascent of Everest without artificial oxygen by Messner and Habeler.

1978
*Everest '78 – Idee und Erfolg*, Horst Bergmann's film of Austrian expedition which included first oxygen-less ascent by Messner and Habeler.

1978
*The Other Side of The Mountain*, BBC Wales documentary tracing the later fortunes of the successful 1953 Everesters, 25 years on.

1979
*Kore Ga 'Chomolongma' Da!*, Japanese film of Sino-Japanese North Face expedition – 4 men die, Yasuo Kato reaches summit.

1979
*Sagarmatha*, Slavo Vajt's film of Yugoslav W Ridge expedition.

1980–1
*Everest in Winter/Everest The Cruel Way*, British attempt on W Ridge, Chameleon Films.

1981
*Sous L'oeil de Qomolangma*, French TV film by Denis Ducroz/Jean Pierre Chaligne of 1981 military expedition to N Face.

1981
*Mount Everest, The East Face*, ABC Sports (30 minutes) Cameraman: David Breashears with Kurt Diemberger.

1982
*Everest 82 Aresta W – Primer Intent Catala al Sostre del Mon*, Jordi Pons' film of Catalan 1982 attempt on Everest (reaches 8500 m.).

1982
*Everest North Wall*, record of American attempt on N Face, during which Marty Hoey fell to her death, filmed by Steve Marts, directed Laszlo Pal (narrated by Redford).

1982
*Everest, The Last Unclimbed Ridge*, Christopher Ralling's film of attempt on North East Ridge which ended in deaths of Boardman and Tasker, and includes the mountain footage of Tasker.

1982
*Man of Everest*, BBC World About Us film about Sir Edmund Hillary.

1982
*Voshojdenie na Everest*, Soviet film of successful expedition.

1983
*Ascent of Mount Everest*, ABC Sports Film shot by David Breashears. Microwave transmission from summit won him Emmy Award.

1984
*Mount Everest* [Breashears film on Norwegian expedition].

1984
*Winds of Everest*, American China-Everest Expedition filmed by Steve Marts, directed by Laszlo Pal.

1984
*Everest – The Australian Challenge*, Mike Dillon's film of new N Face of Everest climb.

1984
*Die Sudtibet und Mt Everest Expedition 1984 – Geographische Untersuchungen in Hochasien*, film of German-Chinese geographical expedition, directed by Matthias Kuhle.

1985
*Everest: The Final Challenge*, British NE Ridge attempt, filmed by Kurt Diemberger.

1986
*Everest Radost I Maka*, Bulgarian TV film of W Ridge climb and death of Hristo Pradanov (shot by Milan Ognyanov with Metodi Savov).

1986
*Everest le Troisieme Pole*, Jean Afanassieff's film for French TV of successful 1986 Franco Swiss expedition, but only stills of final climb.

1986
*Profession Grimpeur*, Philippe Lallet's TV profile of Eric Escoffier includes footage of Everest expedition.

1986
*No Pay, No Prospects, Not much Pleasure Tilman – An Extraordinary Life* (ITV Title), John Meand's HTV film about H W Tilman.

1987
*The Mystery of Mallory and Irvine*, David Breashears' film for Arcturus and BBC discussing mystery in light of current knowledge, and interviewing Noel, Odell, Longland, Hillary etc (50 minutes). Shortened version shown 1988 by BBC Wideworld.

1987
*Messner: In Nome Della Montagna*, Italian TV film of Messner's 14 × 8,000 metre ascents, including Everest.

1988
*The Everest Years*, profile of Chris Bonington by Chameleon Films.

1988
*First Live Satellite Transmission*, from Everest summit by Friendship Expedition (Chinese/Japanese/Nepalese) for Nippon TV (seen around the world).

1988
*On the Big Hill*, Mark Anderson's 6-part film report of British Services Everest Expedition for Granada TV.

1988
*Everest The Last Ridge*, NE Ridge Expedition and climbing of the Pinnacles, presented and produced by David Williams for HTV (screened in English and Welsh versions).

Also noted—

*Di San Nu Sen*, Chinese feature film about climbing a mythical peak called the Third Goddess, which is patently based on Everest, incorporates actual Everest footage presumably from 1970 expedition.

*Beyond Everest*, Mike Dillon's Australian film of Sir Edmund Hillary's return to Everest for the ?45th time.

*Uemura Naomi Monogatar*, Junya Sato's dramatised documentary of the life of Japanese climber/adventurer Naomi Uemura – includes Everest climbs.

*Rescuing Everest*, Kack Micay's environmental film (Canada).

*Thin Air – White Water*, More Kayaking on Dudh Kosi, film by Nick Downie for Odyssey.

*Return to Everest*, Sir Edmund Hillary's work with the Sherpas of Solu Khumbu.

*Sherpa*, Life and culture of Sherpa family in shadow of Mt Everest. Bob Godfrey and David Breashears, narrated by Robert Redford.

*Japanese Women's Everest Expedition*

**(Bibliography compiled by Audrey Salkeld)**

## OBITUARIES

Ajeeba (1911–?1973), *H.J.*, XXXIII.

Ang Phu (?1960–79), *Climber and Rambler*, July 1979.

Bahuguna, Harsh (?1939–71), *H.J.*, XXX (1970).

Bailey, Col. F.M. (1882–1967), *The Times*, April 1967, *H.J.*, XXXVIII (1967–8).

Bednar, Peter (1943–78), *Mountain*, No. 61.

Beetham, B. (1886–1963), *A.J.*, 68; *H.J.* XXIV.

Bourdillon, T. (1924–56), *A.J.*, 61.

Breitenbach, J., *A.A.J.*

Bruce, Brig. Gen. C.G. (1886–1939), *A.J.*, 52; *H.J.*, XII, XIII.

Bruce, J.G. (1896–1972), *A.J.* 1973; *The Times*, 2 February 1972; *Mountain*, No. 20.

Bryant, L.V. (1905–56), *A.J.*, 63.

Bullock, G.H. (1887–1956), *A.J.*, 61.

Burke, M. (1941–75), *A.J.* 1976; *Mountain*, No. 46.

Chetin or Chettan ('Satan') (?–1930), *H.J.*, III (1931); *A.J.*, 42.

Crawford, C.G. (1890–1959), *A.J.*, 64.

Dias, Maj. J. (1928–64), *H.J.*, XXV (1964).

Estcourt, N. (1943–78), *A.J.*, 1979; *Mountain*, No. 63.

Finch, G. Ingle (1888–1970), *The Times*, 24 November 1970; *A.J.*, 1972 and 1973.

Gaylay (?–1934), *H.J.*, VII.

Haston, D. (1940–77), *A.J.*, 1978.

Hazard, J. de V. (?–1968), *A.J.*, 1969.

Hingston, Maj. R.W.G. (1887–1966), *A.J.*, 71.

Hinks, A.R. (1873–1945), *G.J.*, March-April 1945; *A.J.*, 55.

Houston, O. (1883–1969), *A.A.J.*, 1970; *A.J.*, 1970.

Howard-Bury, Lt Col. C.K. (1883–1963), *The Times*, 24 September 1963; *A.J.*, 69.

Humphreys, G. Noel (?–1966) *The Times*, 12 March 1966; *A.J.*, 71.

Irvine, A.C. (1902–24), *A.J.*, 36.

Kellas, Dr A.M. (1868–1921), *A.J.*, 34.

Kuen, F. (1936–74), *Mountain*, No. 33; *Alpinismus*, 4/74.

Lobsang Bhotia (?–1931), *A.J.*, 44.

Longstaff, Dr T.G. (1875–1964), *A.J.*, 69; *H.J.*, XXV.

Mallory, G. Leigh (1886–1924), *A.J.*, 36.

Morshead, Maj. H.T. (1882–1931), *A.J.*, 43; *H.J.*, IV.

Nima Dorje I (1903–38), *H.J.*, XII.

Nima Dorje II (?–1934), *H.J.*, VII.

Norton, Maj. E.F. (1884–1954), *A.J.*, 60.

Noyce, C.W.F. (1917–62), *A.J.*, 67.

Oliver, P.R. (1909–45), *A.J.*, 55.

Pasang Kikuli (1911–39), *H.J.*, XII.

Phu Dorje (?–1969), *A.J.*, 1970; *The Times*, October 1969.

Raeburn, H. (1865–1926), *A.J.*, 39.

Rawling, Brig. Gen. C. (1870–1917), *The Times*, 7 November 1917; *A.J.*, 32.

Ruttledge, H. (1884–1961), *The Times*, 9 November 1961; *A.J.*, 67; *H.J.*, XXIII.

Shebbeare, E.O. (1884–1964), *A.J.*, 69; *H.J.*, XXVI.

Shipton, E.E. (1907–77), *A.J.*, 1978; *Mountain*, No. 55.

Smythe, F.S. (1900–1949), *The Times*, 28 June 1949, 26 July 1949; *A.J.*, 57; *H.J.*, XV.

Somervell, Dr T.H. (1890–1975), *A.J.*, 1976 (Vol. 81); *Mountain*, No. 42.

Sonam Gyatso (?1923–68), *A.J.*, 1969 (note).

Spender, M. (1907–45), *H.J.*, XIII.

Strutt, Col. E.L. (1874–1948), *A.J.*, 56.

Thompson, T. (?–1976), *Climber and Rambler*, June 1976.

Tilman, H.W. (1898–1978?), *Climber and Rambler*, April 1977 and May 1978; *Mountain*, No. 66; *A.J.*, 84.

Ullman, J.R. (1908–71), *A.A.J.*, 1972.

Unsoeld, W. (?1927–79), *A.A.J.*

Wager, Prof. L.R. (1904–65), *The Times*, 22 November 1965.

Wakefield, Dr A.W. (1876–1949), *A.J.*, 57.

Wheeler, Maj. E.O. (1890–1962), *A.J.*, 67.

Wigram, E.H.L. (1911–45), *A.J.*, 55; *C.U.M.C. Journal*, 1934.

Wollaston, A.F.R. (1875–1930), *A.J.*, 42.

Wood-Johnson, G. (1905–56), *H.J.*, XX.

Wyn Harris, Sir P. (1903–79), *Daily Telegraph*, 28 February 1979; *A.J.*, 84.

Younghusband, Sir F.E. (1863–1942), *A.J.*, 54; *H.J.*, XIII.

# Notes and References

Abbreviations used:

A.C. Alpine Club, London
*A.J. Alpine Journal* (volume numbers of *A.J.* changed from Roman to Arabic numerals in 1969)
E.A. Everest Archives, Royal Geographical Society, London
H.C. Himalayan Committee
M.E.C. Mount Everest Committee, London

INTRODUCTION: GODDESS MOTHER OF THE WORLD (*pages 1–10*)

The chapter heading is a translation of the name Chomolungma.

1. C.K. Howard-Bury, *Mount Everest: The Reconnaissance 1921*, Introduction by Sir Francis Younghusband.
2. Geologists working with the various expeditions over the years have shown that the mountain is built up of three series of rocks. The lowest is a light-coloured massive gneiss, probably metamorphosed from a sedimentary origin. It extends up to about 24,500 ft and is mostly covered with permanent snow and ice. Above this is a dark band of metamorphosed shale, originally clays, with granitic intrusions and bands of more local material such as quartzite, which has been formed from sandstone. Easily eroded, this stratum gives ragged cliffs and fantastic pinnacles – and is very poor climbing material. The third series begins abruptly at 27,500 ft with a 500 ft thick band of yellow schistose limestone almost akin to marble, and known as the Yellow Band. It is most marked on the North Face. Above the Yellow Band the metamorphism tails away, and there is a layer of dark grey massive limestone, which being more durable to erosion is steeper. It shows most distinctively as the First Step and Second Step of the North East Ridge.

   For a more detailed account of the geology of the Everest region see particularly Herron, Odell and Harris in the appendices of the 1921, 1924 and 1933 official volumes, and Miller in *Americans on Everest*.
3. C.K. Howard-Bury, op.cit., Chapter VII (by Mallory).
4. The late Nick Estcourt (conversation with the author).
5. C.K. Howard-Bury, op.cit., Chapter VIII (by Mallory). By 'South Peak', Mallory meant Lhotse.

6. D. Haston, Private document in the author's possession.
7. C. Bonington, *Everest the Hard Way*, Chapter 4.
8 E.E. Shipton, *The Mount Everest Reconnaissance Expedition 1951*, Chapter III.

CHAPTER 1: PEAKS AND LAMAS (*pages 11–29*)

1. C.T. Dent, *Above the Snowline*.
2. The British recognition of Chinese suzerainty over Tibet was to backfire in 1950 when the Communists marched in.
3. Alpine Club Archives, Minute Book 9. The modern spelling of Kingchinjunga is Kangchenjunga. It is now recognized as the third, not the second, highest mountain in the world.
4. ibid.
5. Mumm's firm was Edward Arnold & Co. They published the official volumes of the 1921, 1922 and 1924 Everest expeditions as well as Jack Noel's book and Younghusband's *Epic of Mount Everest*. Mumm died in 1927.
6. T.L. Blakeney, 'The First Steps Towards Mount Everest', *A.J.*, 76, 1971.
7. Goldie/Morley Correspondence, reproduced from *The Times* in *A.J.*, XXIII, 1907.
8. *The Times*, 18 March 1907.
9. *Daily Express*, 6 June 1910.
10. For accounts of this expedition see *Five Months in the Himalaya* by A.L. Mumm (1909) and *This My Voyage* by T.G. Longstaff (1950).
11. Proceedings of the Alpine Club, *A.J.*, XXIV, 1909.
12. ibid.
13. T.G. Longstaff, *This My Voyage*, Chapter 8.
14. J.B. Noel, *Through Tibet to Everest*, Chapter 5.
15. T.G. Longstaff, op. cit., Chapter 8.
16. Noel's substantive rank was actually captain.
17. J.B. Noel, op. cit., Chapter 2.
18. ibid., Chapter 3.
19. ibid., Chapter 3. Taringban was a name Noel gave to one of the intervening peaks.
20. Quoted by Noel. Sir Marcon Tinway is an obvious play on Sir Martin Conway. Some speakers advocated the use of aircraft for reconnaissance (in 1919!), hence the reference to kites and albatrosses.
21. Alpine Club Archives, letter from Farrar to Montagnier, 15 April 1919.
22. ibid., Farrar to Montagnier, 15 May 1919.
23. E.A., Box 1.
24. *The Times*, 1 June 1920.
25. *Observer*, 6 June 1920.
26. *Daily News*, 3 June 1920.
27. *Evening News*, 1 August 1920.
28. D. Robertson, *George Mallory*, Chapter 7.
29. All the letters are from E.A., Box 1. They are reproduced in full in *A.J.*, 76, 1971.

CHAPTER 2: 'WE ARE ABOUT TO WALK OFF THE MAP' (*pages 30–68*)

The chapter heading is taken from a letter home by George Mallory.

1. A.C. Archives, Cuttings File 18.
2. *Daily Mail*, 14 January 1921.

3. Interview with N.E. Odell.
4. ibid.
5. ibid.
6. C.K. Howard-Bury, *Mount Everest: The Reconnaissance, 1921*, Introduction.
7. M.E.C. Minute Book, Item 24.
8. E.A., Box 1.
9. E.A., Box 2.
10. E.A., Box 3.
11. E.A., Box 11.
12. E.A., Box 12.
13. *Daily Telegraph*, 18 October 1921.
14. E.A., Box 4.
15. 'In Memoriam', *A.J.*, XXIII, 1931.
16. D. Robertson, *George Mallory*, Chapter 7.
17. E.A., Box 3.
18. E.A., Box 12.
19. ibid.
20. 'In Memoriam', *A.J.*, XXXIV, 1923.
21. E.A., Box 12.
22. D. Robertson, op. cit., Chapter 7.
23. Incredibly Wollaston, like Morshead, was murdered. He was shot by a student at Cambridge in 1930.
24. E.A., Box 3.
25. ibid.
26. E.A., Box 12.
27. E.A., Box 3.
28. ibid.
29. The Ice Club at Winchester was founded by a young master there, R.L.G. Irving, in 1904. It was a private club with only four members – Mallory, Gibson, Tyndale and Bullock – but interesting as being probably the first-ever school climbing club. It was heavily criticized by the climbing establishment. Mallory was the star member and was known to the others as 'Almer', after the great Grindelwald guide of that name.
30. 'In Memoriam', *A.J.*, LXI, 1956.
31. F. Younghusband, *The Epic of Mount Everest*, Chapter II.
32. D. Robertson, op. cit., Chapter 2.
33. G.W. Young, *Snowdon Biography*, Part II, Chapter 3.
34. E.A., Box 3.
35. D. Robertson, op. cit., Chapter 7.
36. E. A., Box 3.
37. D. Robertson, op. cit., Chapter 7.
38. E.A., Box 12.
39. ibid.
40. ibid. The fault was entirely Mallory's.
41. ibid.
42. J. Morris, *Hired to Kill*, p.144.
43. E.A., Box 18.
44. D. Robertson, op. cit., Chapter 9.
45. E.A., Box 3.
46. C.K. Howard-Bury, op. cit., Chapter I.

47. D. Robertson, op. cit., Chapter 7.
48. ibid.
49. E.A., Box 3.
50. ibid.
51. C.K. Howard-Bury, op. cit., Chapter XII (by Mallory).
52. ibid., Chapter IV.
53. ibid., Chapter XII (by Mallory).
54. ibid.
55. C.K. Howard-Bury, op. cit., Chapter XII (by Mallory).
56. D. Robertson, op. cit.
57. ibid.
58. C.K. Howard-Bury, op. cit., Chapter XII (by Mallory).
59. ibid., Chapter XIII (by Mallory).
60. D. Robertson, op. cit.
61. E.A., Box 3. These two peaks are now called Ri-ring and Pumori respectively.
62. Everest, Chomo Lonzo and Makalu were already known to the climbers. Mallory named Lhotse (literally, South Peak) and Pethangtse (Pethang Peak). He did not see fit to give a separate name to Lhotse Shar, which may be taken as meaning East Summit of the South Peak.
63. D. Robertson, op. cit.
64. C.K. Howard-Bury, op. cit., Chapter XIV (by Mallory).
65. G.H. Bullock, 'The Everest Expedition, 1921. Diary of G.H. Bullock', *A.J.*, LXVII, 1962.
66. C.K. Howard-Bury, op. cit., Chapter XIV (by Mallory).
67. D. Robertson, op.cit.
68. C.K. Howard-Bury, op. cit.
69. D. Robertson, *George Mallory*, Chapter 7.
70. ibid.
71. ibid.
72. C.K. Howard-Bury, *Mount Everest: The Reconnaissance, 1921,* Chapter XV (by Mallory).
73. G.H. Bullock, 'The Everest Expedition, 1921. Diary of G.H. Bullock', *A. J.*, LXVII, 1962.
74. C.K. Howard-Bury, op. cit.
75. E.A., Box 3.
76. C.K. Howard-Bury, op. cit.
77. ibid.
78. G.H. Bullock, op. cit.
79. C.K. Howard-Bury, op. cit.
80. ibid.

CHAPTER 3: ONLY ROTTERS WOULD USE OXYGEN (*pages 69–90*)

The chapter heading is adapted from a letter from Hinks to Farrar in which he says: 'If some of the party do not go to 25,000 ft without oxygen they will be rotters.'

1. E.A., Box 12.
2. E.A., Box 11.
3. D. Robertson, op. cit.
4. ibid.
5. E.A., Box 3.

6. ibid.
7. E.A., Box 12.
8. ibid.
9. Cash in hand was £3,146 and a further £3,463 was owing to the Committee from various sources.
10. E.A., Box 18.
11. ibid.
12. ibid.
13. D. Robertson, op. cit.
14. E.A., Box 18.
15. ibid.
16. Finch was the father of Peter Finch, the well-known actor.
17. ibid.
18. ibid.
19. T.G. Longstaff, *This My Voyage*, Chapter 8.
20. ibid.
21. E.A., Box 18. Bruce was referring to Pope Pius XI, who as a young man had been an enthusiastic mountaineer. After the expedition a piece of rock from Everest, in the form of a paper-weight, was sent to the Pope.
22. ibid.
23. ibid.
24. E.A., Box 11.
25. ibid.
26. It is worth remembering that most of the expeditions to Everest, both before and after the Second World War, picked up additional personnel in India or Nepal, usually as liaison officers. In pre-war years this function was carried out by a cheerful little Tibetan named Karma Paul, who was something of a Darjeeling entrepreneur. A good linguist, he accompanied all the pre-war expeditions except the expedition of 1921 as interpreter and adviser on Tibetan customs and etiquette.

    He organized Sherpas for many expeditions besides Everest, and was still active in 1947 when Earl Denman described him as 'a heavily built man, broad and short, of more than middle age'. He died in Darjeeling in 1984.

    Gurkha soldiers (usually N.C.O.s) also accompanied most pre-war expeditions to Everest. Often they took charge of the lower camps and also guarded the paymaster's treasure chest. Less frequently they have also accompanied some post-war expeditions as signallers etc. All expeditions nowadays have an official Nepalese liaison officer attached to them by the Nepalese Government.
27. With the help of Farrar, Finch developed this into a duvet suit, comprising jacket, trousers and gauntlets, which was made up for him by S.W. Silver & Co. The prototype worked well on the expedition, but the idea was not taken up by the Committee – possibly because Finch was rapidly becoming *persona non grata*.
28. E.A., Box 18.
29. P.J.H. Unna, 'The Oxygen Equipment of the 1922 Everest Expedition', *A.J.*, XXXIV, 1923.
30. E.A., Box 18.
31. ibid.
32. E.A., Box 12.
33. D. Robertson, op. cit.
34. G.I. Finch, *The Making of a Mountaineer*, Chapter 19.
35. ibid.

36. E.A., Box 18. He had delivered a message from Baden-Powell to some Boy Scouts at Kalimpong.
37. ibid.
38. E.A., Box 12. Eaton, representing the Alpine Club, was nominally co-secretary of the Committee with Hinks but seems to have played a subordinate role throughout. The bulk of the work fell on Hinks.

    The funds were £750 overdrawn and the Committee thought the A.C./R.G.S. should guarantee an overdraft of £2,000. The President of the A.C. refused, and the R.G.S. guaranteed the whole sum.
39. C.G. Bruce, *The Assault on Mount Everest, 1922,* Chapter 1.
40. C.G. Bruce, op. cit.
41. J.B.L. Noel, *Through Tibet to Everest,* Chapter 10.
42. Tibetan tea is made of China tea brewed with butter and salt. To western taste it is extremely unpalatable but it is regarded as discourteous to one's host to refuse it.
43. At Khumjung monastery they keep a yeti scalp which has been examined by scientists and pronounced a fake, but the stories about this monster are so numerous and so consistent in detail that nobody can dismiss them out of hand. Tracks have been seen and photographed on several occasions. Quite recently a herd of yaks was killed in Khumjung and the girl tending them struck dumb and bereft of reason with horror. The people are convinced it was the work of a yeti. Whatever one may think of these stories, the fact remains that the Abominable Snowman is one of the great unsolved mysteries of the present day, possibly the last and greatest of them all. Perhaps it should be left a mystery, so that our grandchildren may still have something to wonder at.
44. C.G. Bruce, op. cit., Chapter II.
45. G.I. Finch, op. cit.
46. C.G. Bruce, op. cit. Chapter V (by Mallory).
47. ibid.
48. ibid.
49. In 1922 this was true, but times change – Scott and Haston climbed approximately 2,500 ft to the top of Everest in 1975 from their Camp VI, but were forced to bivouac on the way down. In 1978 Peter Habeler climbed approximately 2,800 ft to the summit in five and a half hours and returned in one hour – without oxygen!
50. ibid., Chapter VI (by Mallory).
51. ibid.
52. ibid.
53. E.A., Box 18.

CHAPTER 4: 'WE WILL STAMP TO THE TOP WITH THE WIND IN OUR TEETH!' (*pages 91–114*)

The chapter heading is taken from a letter by George Mallory to Tom Longstaff.

1. J.B. Noel, *Through Tibet to Everest,* Chapter XIII.
2. The nerve centre controlling involuntary breathing is stimulated by carbon dioxide and as this gas is hardly present in the body at altitude, the smoke replaces it.
3. Geoffrey Bruce's determination was a by-word. In 1924, when discussions about transport were about to take place with the Dzongpen of Shekar, the Tibetan official asked anxiously whether 'that very determined young soldier was to take part'.
4. G.I. Finch, *The Making of a Mountaineer,* Chapter XX.
5. T.G. Longstaff, 'Some Aspects of the Everest Problem', *A.J.*, XXXV, 1923.

6. E.A., Box 18.
7. ibid.
8. ibid.
9. E.A., Box 11.
10. ibid.
11. ibid.
12. ibid.
13. C.G. Bruce, *The Assault on Mount Everest 1922,* Chapter X (by Mallory).
14. T.H. Somervell, *After Everest,* Chapter X.
15. D. Robertson, *George Mallory*, Chapter 7.
16. E.A., Box 11.
17. D. Robertson, op. cit., Chapter 8.
18. ibid.
19. C.G. Bruce, op. cit., Chapter II. Compensation for the men's families was 250R each (about £130). Compare this with the £50 shared by the families of the two men who died with Mummery in 1895, which was reckoned sufficient to make them rich for the rest of their lives.
20. E.A., Box 18.
21. The Mount Everest Suite (Somervell/Dodsworth).
22. D. Robertson, op. cit., Chapter 9.
23. ibid.
24. ibid.
25. ibid.
26. E.A., Box 22. The stolen code was:
    (1) On reaching summit: 'Instructions followed returning [date of month on which summit reached – e.g. 15th] [names of climbers who reached summit] remaining Bruce.'
    (2) Final abandonment: 'Instructions followed continuing send [figure representing difference between 30,000 ft and height reached] rupees Bruce.'
27. E.A., Box 29.
28. E.A., Box 29.
29. The selectors actually stipulated E.F. Norton *or* his brother, J.H. Norton. The latter was forty-three, however, and was turned down by the Committee.
30. D. Robertson, op. cit.
31. K. Mason, interview.
32. D. Robertson, op. cit.
33. E.A., Box 26.
34. E.A., Box 32.
35. ibid. Miss Bernard seems to have been French or Belgian
36. 'In Memoriam', *A.J.*, LXIII, 1958.
37. The initial recommendation for Irvine seems to have come from the Keswick climber George Abraham, who wrote to Meade on the subject. Only a fortnight elapsed between Irvine's name first being mentioned and his selection.
38. 'In Memoriam', *A.J.*, XXXVI, 1924.
39. E.F. Norton, *The Fight for Everest: 1924,* Chapter V.
40. E.A., Box 22.
41. E.A., Box 30.
42. ibid.
43. ibid.
44. ibid.

45. Odell interview (1977).
46. E.A., Box 30.
47. E.A., Box 33.
48. E.F. Norton, op. cit., Part II (Mallory's letters).
49. W.H. Murray, *The Story of Everest,* Chapter X.
50. Letter from Michael Holroyd to author quoting James Strachey (1977).
51. Letter from Duncan Grant (1977).
52. E.A., Box 28. In his autobiography *This My Voyage,* Longstaff altered this to 'stamp to the top with the wind in our teeth'.
53. J.B. Noel, op. cit., Chapter XV.
54. E.F. Norton, op. cit., Chapter II (by J.G. Bruce).
55. J.B. Noel, op. cit., Chapter XVI.

CHAPTER 5: 'THE FINEST CENOTAPH IN THE WORLD' (*pages 115–41*)

'But there are few better deaths than to die in high endeavour, and Everest is the finest cenotaph in the world to a couple of the best of men' – T.H. Somervell, *After Everest.*

1. E.F. Norton, *The Fight for Everest: 1924,* Chapter IV.
2. ibid, Part II (Mallory's letters).
3. Shortly after the formation of the Himalayan Club in 1928 a special Tiger's Badge was created for Sherpas who gave outstanding service. From this the word 'tiger' came into common use amongst British mountaineers at home, meaning anyone who climbed at a high standard. Use of the phrase began to die out in the 1960s and is not much heard today.
4. E.F. Norton, op. cit., Chapter V.
5. ibid.
6. Contrary to earlier reports it was not a 'fossil' that Odell discovered on the North Face but a curious cone-in-cone structure, now in the Natural History Museum, South Kensington.
7. Odell interview (1977).
8. E.A., Box 26.
9. E.F. Norton, op. cit.
10. T.H. Somervell, *After Everest,* Chapter XVII. The obstruction was a body of mucous membrane sloughed off his throat owing to frostbite from continuously inhaling cold air.
11. E.F. Norton, op. cit.
12. ibid.
13. J.B. Noel, *Through Tibet to Everest,* Chapter XVII.
14. F. Younghusband, *The Epic of Mount Everest,* Chapter XXV.
15. E.F. Norton, op. cit., Chapter VI (by Odell).
16. ibid.
17. J.B. Noel, op. cit. (facing p.220). In Odell's note he refers to the oxygen pressure – a full cylinder was 120 atmospheres. Obviously they used oxygen from the North Col to Camp VI. Noel's note refers to photographic arrangements (Noel was using telephoto lenses from Camp III). 8 p.m. is in error for 8 a.m.
18. Lakpa returned to Britain with John Noel and stayed ten months, helping with the promotion of the Everest film (see next chapter).
19. E.F. Norton, op. cit.
20. Norton disagreed over this. He says it was on 'the very backbone of the N arête'. There may be some confusion here – John Noel says Mallory and Irvine moved Camp VI some 500 ft higher than the place where Norton and Somervell pitched

it. On the other hand Noel's account makes it plain that the camp could be seen from Camp IV on the col.

21. E.A., Box 33.
22. J.B. Noel, op. cit. John Noel, in his narrative of the expedition *Through Tibet to Everest*, invariably gives romantic names to the various camps. Snowfield Camp was Camp III.
23. E.A., Box 37.
24. E.A., Box 33.
25. It could be argued that Raeburn's death was also attributable to Everest. The two most seriously ill people of the 1924 expedition, General Bruce and Beetham, both recovered. The 1933 expedition found the memorial badly damaged.
26. E.A., Box 22.
27. E.A., Box 26.
28. E.F. Norton, op. cit.
29. E.A., Box 22.
30. ibid.
31. E.A., Box 28. Originally he wrote 'such absolute fizzers' but crossed it out. The blunt Longstaff would pull Mallory's leg for being an 'intellectual'. 'Mallory, you know the one good thing the Bolsheviks have done in Russia? They've obliterated the Intelligentsia.'
32. E.A., Box 26.
33. E.F. Norton, op. cit.
34. E.A., Box 26.
35. E.A., Box 34.
36. When Odell examined the ice axe in 1934 he found three horizontal nicks 'cut and inked in' upon the shaft. Neither Mallory nor Irvine were known to use such a mark and Wyn Harris thought it likely it was put there by one of the 1924 Sherpas to identify his master's property. Odell was doubtful about this, as it was not the custom of the Sherpas to mark gear in 1924. Wyn Harris's own Sherpa cut another mark in the axe and Wyn Harris recalls:

    'When I picked up the axe there was no mark on it. The cross, over which there has been so much controversy, was not put on either by Mallory or Irvine. It was in fact cut by my personal Sherpa porter, Kusang Pugla, who did it under threats from me that it must not be lost or mixed up with other axes' (P. Wyn Harris, *Sunday Times*, 17 October 1971). Leaving his own axe to mark the place of discovery, Wyn Harris used the 1924 axe during the rest of the 1933 expedition. It is now in the Alpine Club, London.

    When the present author examined the axe in July 1977, there were *four* sets of marks on it. In addition to those already described, there was a single horizontal nick above the three seen by Odell and the 'three nick' emblem was repeated, though fainter, on the side of the axe opposite Pugla's cross. Unfortunately there is no means of knowing whether these marks were there originally or were added later. The axe is light and beautifully balanced.
37. In a letter to the *Alpine Journal* in 1934, Odell suggested that the axe may have been deliberately left behind because the climb was basically a rock climb. He pointed out that there were no marks on it consistent with falling from the ridge.
38. Apart from other evidence, the axe itself could hardly have lain 'free' for nine years subject to the Everest gales if it was on a steep slab.
39. Odell interview (1977).
40. Correspondence, *A.J.*, XLVI, 1934.

41. Shih Chan-chun, 'The Conquest of Mount Everest by the Chinese Mountaineering Team', *A.J.*, LXVI.
42. This happened to Wyn Harris and Wager in 1933.
43. This was not the last time 'the glittering prize', as Peter Boardman has called it, tempted man in such calculated risks – Whittaker and Sherpa Gombu did it successfully in 1966, and Mick Burke, tragically, in 1975.
44. For a detailed account see *Mountain* magazine Nos. 17 and 21. Some of Holzel's arguments and facts are questionable.
45. 'Mitteilung', in *D.O.A.V.*, 15 September 1926.
46. Odell interview (1977).
47. *Morning Post*, 24 June 1924.
48. D. Robertson, *George Mallory*, Chapter 9.

CHAPTER 6: THE AFFAIR OF THE DANCING LAMAS (*pages 142–57*)

1. He infiltrated the Bolshevik ranks and was put in charge of counter-espionage with the specific task of tracking down a British spy called Bailey.
2. It will be noted that he did not object to Morshead returning in 1922.
3. E.A., Box 27.
4. E.A., Box 26.
5. E.A., Box 37.
6. The other directors were Noel, A. Nettlefield, Capt. H. Reeks, Lt Col. H. Fisher and P. Taylor. The company has no connection with any similarly named film companies existing today.
7. E.A., Box 31.
8. *The Statesman* (undated cutting Box 37).
9. A. Pereira, *The Year's Photography*, October 1925.
10. Haddick put some £2,000 into Explorers Films. He was under the impression he would be a regular member of the expedition, according to a note by Hinks.
11. E.A., Box 26.
12. E.A., Box 37.
13. E.A., Box 27.
14. Finch. It was probably only a rumour – the Committee, and Hinks especially, suffered from Finch-mania. Had Hinks but known it there was another scheme afoot, by Captain Angus Buchanan, a desert explorer, who took the line that the claims of the Mount Everest Committee should not exclude indefinitely all other British aspirants. It did, though – throughout the time of British rule in India there was never the slightest chance of any expedition being allowed to attempt Everest except those originated by the Committee.
15. E.A., Box 24.
16. ibid.
17. E.A., Box 17.
18. ibid. David Macdonald, half Scot and half Lepcha, was the former Trade Agent at Yatung and Gyantse. Both he and his son John had been of considerable assistance to the Everest expeditions. Macdonald and Bailey had clashed on several occasions.

    'Laidlaw' was actually Sirdar Bahadur Laden La. As Hinks pointed out it was the Tibetans, not Bailey, who had used the word 'deceitful'. Nevertheless, it was Bailey's translation.
19. E.A., Box 27. Hazard's journey seems to have been overlooked. There is in the Everest files at the R.G.S. a report submitted by Hazard in an almost undecipherable handwriting regretting any trouble he might have caused, accepting all

responsibility personally and putting the whole thing down to a misunderstanding with the local authorities. This was not forwarded to the India Office.

20. The part played by David Macdonald is not clear. Although he disclaimed all knowledge of it, both Noel and the lamas stated that he took part in securing their exit from India.
21. E.A., Box 27.
22. ibid.
23. A. Swinson, *Beyond the Frontiers*, Chapter 13.
24. ibid.
25. E.A., Box 27.
26. A. Swinson, op. cit.

CHAPTER 7: 'ANOTHER BLOODY DAY' (*pages 158–84*)

The chapter heading comes from an entry in Frank Smythe's diary, 6 May 1933.

1. E.A., Box 41.
2. M.E.C. Minute Book, Item 57.
3. E.A., Box 41.
4. E.A., Box 14/15. Somervell got Smythe's age wrong.
5. 'In Memoriam', *A.J.*, LXVII, 1962.
6. ibid.
7. 'In Memoriam', *A.J.*, LXIV. He was called Ferdie because he reputedly resembled Tsar Ferdinand I of Bulgaria! These men were certainly erudite.
8. Brother of Graham Greene, the novelist.
9. When Sit William Goodenough, President of the R.G.S., sent Shipton his invitation telegram it read 'MOUNT EVEREST COMMITTEE INVITE YOU JOIN THE EXPEDITION SUBJECT MEDICAL APPROVAL PLEASE REPLY GOODENOUGH'. A friend intercepted the message and sent a reply cable "GOODENOUGH – SHIPTON'. Shipton was able to cancel the message in time!
10. The tests were done by an R.A.F. medical board and Dr C. Wilson. Crawford only just scraped through.
11. Talented in more ways than one: Longland, Wyn Harris and Brocklebank were Cambridge Blues, while Boustead had taken part in the 1920 Olympics. He, Wyn Harris and Longland ended their careers with knighthoods. They were also extraordinarily literate: Shebbeare wrote a book about elephants, and there are no fewer than six accounts of the 1933 expedition – sometimes as part of longer autobiographies – by Ruttledge, Crawford, Greene, Smythe, Shipton and Boustead.
12. Ruttledge, Shebbeare and Wyn Harris took 16-mm. ciné cameras – with free film from Kodak and Ilford.
13. With one exception (1938), Hodder & Stoughton have published all the official British Everest books since – and many unofficial ones.
14. Named after C.F. Meade (1881–1975), a notable mountaineer of the early part of the century. Meade maintained he had no idea why the tent was named after him.

    The expedition had in fact a wide variety of tentage. Besides those mentioned there were Whympers, a special lightweight tent called the 'Yak', bell tents and the large mess tent.
15. H. Ruttledge, *Everest 1933*, Part I, Chapter II.
16. Possibly the first time oxygen was used in the treatment of frostbite cases.
17. H. Ruttledge, op. cit., Part II, Chapter II (by Greene).
18. E.A., Box 41.

19. The affair did not end happily – Richards got into debt and the Committee paid his passage home at the end of the expedition.
20. Rock climbing to the scratchy tunes of a gramophone was a vogue in England at the time, and this seems like a high-altitude extension of it.
21. H. Boustead, *The Wind of Morning*, p. 101. Boustead's account of the incident differs from others.
22. F.S. Smythe, *Camp Six*, Chapter X.
23. ibid.
24. The party was accompanied by Sirdar Nursang's Tibetan mastiff named Policey (an appropriate name for a guard dog!). Policey reached an altitude of 22,000 ft, which Smythe claimed as a canine height record at the time. Several dogs have since been to the summit of Aconcagua in the Andes, which is some 800 ft higher. Policey disappeared between Camps III and IIIa – she probably fell into a crevasse.
25. F.S. Smythe, op. cit.
26. Smythe says the ledge was forty by twenty feet, but this seems rather small for the number of tents. The estimate given is that of Ruttledge.
27. R. Greene, *Moments of Being*, Chapter 12.
28. F.S. Smythe, op. cit., Chapter XII.
29. According to Jack Longland there was also an 'us and them' attitude between the military and non-military members of the team (conversation with author, 1978).
30. R. Greene, op. cit.
31. E.E. Shipton, *Upon That Mountain*, Chapter VII.
32. R. Greene, op. cit.
33. Smythe's account says one of the tents was a Burns made of Grenfell cloth – superior to the Meade.
34. The camp was moved onto the North Col and was sometimes referred to as IVa to distinguish it from the original camp, which was on the ice shelf 200 ft lower.
35. Greene says Shipton complained of loss of appetite, but that was because he was always eating sweets.
36. H. Ruttledge, op. cit., Chapter VI.
37. Sherpa Kipa Lama, one of the porters who remained at Camp V, lost his senses and held firmly to the belief that he was dead. Some weeks later, finding himself indisputably alive, he attributed his remarkable recovery to Raymond Greene's medical skill.
38. The significance of the axe has been discussed in Chapter 5.
39. F.S. Smythe, op. cit., Chapter XV.
40. ibid.
41. ibid.
42. H. Ruttledge, op. cit., Chapter VIII (by Smythe).
43. *The Listener*, 10 October 1934.
44. H. Ruttledge, op. cit.
45. Verglas is a thin glazing of ice on rock which, naturally, makes the rock slippery and difficult. It does not usually occur on Everest: there is no rain, as such, and snow evaporates directly into the thin, dry, cold air. Similarly there is no rusting, which accounts for the many instances when artefacts from previous expeditions have been found in almost mint condition, the ice axe found by Wyn Harris being a case in point.
46. There seem no real grounds for this in view of subsequent events. Pessimism appears to have been a stock-in-trade for Political Officers in Sikkim.

47. According to Greene there were himself, Crawford, Brocklebank, Smythe, Shipton and Ruttledge.
48. M.E.C. Minute Book, Item 77.

CHAPTER 8: 'WE ARE BEGINNING TO LOOK RIDICULOUS' (*pages 185–209*)

'The present position is that we are beginning to make ourselves look very ridiculous' – G.I. Finch to a newspaper reporter apropos the 1933 expedition.

1. Ruttledge specifically mentioned Marco Pallis's team as well as his own. In 1933 Marco Pallis led a small expedition to the Gangotro Glacier region of Kumaun. The members were F.E. Hicks, C.F. Kirkus, R.C. Nicholson and Dr Charles Warren. At the time Kirkus was regarded by many mountaineers as the finest rock climber in Britain, and he himself fully expected to be chosen for the 1933 Everest team. However, after some winter climbs together in the Alps, Smythe reported unfavourably on him. Of Pallis's team only Charles Warren eventually went to Everest.
2. 'In Memoriam', *A.J.*, LXVII, 1962.
3. ibid.
4. A.C. Archives.
5. A.C. Archives.
6. He later became Head of the B.B.C.'s Third Programme.
7. A.C. Archives.
8. Interview with Raymond Greene.
9. A.C. Archives.
10. A.C. Archives.
11. Meade was a Vice President at the time. Brown would have supported Crawford if only to spite Smythe, whom he disliked intensely. The feeling was mutual.
12. A.C. Archives.
13. K. Mason, *Abode of Snow*, Part V, Chapter 2.
14. E.E. Shipton, *Upon That Mountain*, Chapter XI.
15. K. Mason, op. cit., Part III, Chapter 4.
16. E.E. Shipton, *That Untravelled World*, Chapter 4.
17. E.E. Shipton, *Upon That Mountain*, Chapter XI.
18. Warren interview.
19. *Daily Telegraph*, 2 September 1976.
20. Kempson Diary, 7 July 1935.
21. The heights given in the following paragraphs are from the 1924 Guillarmod map.
22. E.E. Shipton, 'The Mount Everest Reconnaissance, 1935', *A.J.*, XLVIII, 1936.
23. H. Ruttledge, *Everest: The Unfinished Adventure*, Chapter II.
24. Seventeen peaks were climbed by Wigram and Tilman. 'Wigram and I had degenerated into mere peak baggers,' said Tilman.
25. Shipton would have liked to stay behind and test out conditions in the post-monsoon period. Invaluable lessons could have been learned from this. Instead, he was committed to return home to help prepare the 1936 expedition, which was a waste of time.
26. The first ascent was by Longstaff in 1907. Dunagiri was eventually climbed by André Roch in 1939. Another young Army officer, John Hunt, was rejected on medical grounds.
27. This was the porter who almost died of pneumonia during the 1933 expedition.
28. H. Ruttledge, *Everest: The Unfinished Adventure*, Part I, Chapter V.
29. E.E. Shipton, *Upon That Mountain*, Chapter XI.

30. Interviews with Kempson and Warren.
31. *Morning Post*, 17 October 1936. Jean Batten was a famous lady aviator of the period.

CHAPTER 9: SMALL IS BEAUTIFUL (*pages 210–24*)

1. H.W. Tilman, *Mount Everest 1938*, Appendix A.
2. ibid., Chapter I.
3. Longstaff had no intention of losing more money than was necessary. He insisted that there should be a separate banking account for the 1938 expedition with its own treasurer, and not the Committee treasurer. Should a surplus eventually accrue he was to be repaid the £3,000, except for £250 which was a permanent donation to the fund. Any further surplus was to go into the Mount Everest Committee account.

   It seems likely that Longstaff was supported by other guarantors in this, and the £3,000 became £1,700, of which a half was repaid in 1938. In addition *The Times* paid £1,000 and there was rather less than £1,300 in donations. Six months prior to the war there was still about £190 left in the fund.
4. Letter to author, 20 December 1977.
5. H.W. Tilman, op. cit., Appendix A.
6. ibid., Chapter II.
7. ibid.
8. ibid.
9. ibid., Appendix A.
10. ibid.
11. Pemmican is beef, dried, crushed and mixed with melted fat to make a paste which can be pressed into blocks. Currants or raisins are often mixed in and the result is a highly nutritious food which will keep for a very long time. It is said to take 6lb. of beef to make 1 lb. of pemmican.

    From the earliest days pemmican was taken on Arctic exploration. It was first used by certain North American Indian tribes such as the Chepewyans, and the name comes from the Cree word 'pime', meaning fat.
12. H.W. Tilman, op. cit., Chapter V.
13. Long before Tenzing became famous, Tilman described him as 'young, keen and very likeable', and for once we also know what a Sherpa thought of a sahib, because in his autobiography Tenzing describes Tilman as a very fine, quiet man, liked by all the Sherpas. The Sherpas nicknamed Tilman 'Balu' – meaning bear – because of his big eyebrows and shaggy looks.
14. Tenzing was probably the Sherpa avalanched with Oliver. In his biography he gives a vague account of an incident which was probably this.
15. Conservation of energy by the lead climbers became a fetish during early attempts on the South West Face (see Chapter 17). There is no firm evidence that strong climbers burn themselves out by taking part in preparatory work: see Hillary and Tenzing in 1953, Scott and Haston, 1975, and Messner, 1978.
16. H.W. Tilman, op. cit., Chapter VIII.
17. Tenzing, in his autobiography, claims he alone went back for the abandoned loads – and almost slipped to his death on the return. At the end of the expedition he was given a special award of 20 rupees.

    The expedition made the first traverse (west–east) of the North Col. So far as is known it has never been traversed east–west.
18. H.W. Tilman, op. cit., Chapter VIII. In 1938 the Himalayan Club officially

adopted the title of 'Tiger' for Sherpas who performed outstanding service, and issued a Tiger's Badge. According to Tenzing, the idea was Tilman's.

19. ibid., Chapter X.
20. E.E. Shipton, *Upon That Mountain,* Chapter XI.

CHAPTER 10: THE PEGASUS FACTOR (*pages 225–35*)

1. See Howard-Bury's reports to Younghusband in Chapter 1.
2. ibid.
3. J.B. Noel, *Through Tibet to Everest,* Appendix C.
4. Captain C.F. Unwins flying a Vespa (1932). The previous record then stood at 40,000 ft + by Lt Soucek of the U.S.A.A.F., flying a Wright Apache biplane with a Pratt and Whitney engine (1930).
5. P.F.M. Fellowes, L.V.S. Blacker, P.T. Etherton and Lord Clydesdale, *First Over Everest,* Chapter 1.
6. In November 1932 the Irish Government offered two Vickers Vespas free to the Committee. This was the type of aircraft which had recently broken the altitude record. However, the expedition was already committed to the Westlands. One possible reason for the offer is that the Blackers were a prominent Irish family from Co. Armagh.
7. In addition to the survey cameras the equipment was:
   Plane 1: Williamson P14 plate camera 5 ins. by 4 ins.
   Williamson Pistol camera 3½ ins. by 2½ ins.
   Sinclair Newman ciné camera
   Plane 2: 2 Sinclair Newman ciné cameras
   Williamson P14 plate camera 5 ins. by 4 ins.

   Both planes carried spare magazines, plates etc. The first plane concentrated on stills photography, the second on ciné. In addition there was an infra-red camera which could be attached below the fuselage and worked through a trap door in the observer's cockpit, but this was not carried on the actual Everest flights.
8. M.E.C. Minute Book, Item 65.
9. P.F.M. Fellowes, L.V.S. Blacker, P.T. Etherton and Lord Clydesdale, op. cit., Chapter XI.
10. ibid.
11. 'Alpine Notes', *A.J.*, XLV, 1933.
12. Douglas & Clydesdale, the Marquess of, and D.F. McIntyre, *The Pilot's Book of Everest,* Chapter VI.
13. In his first account Clydesdale reckoned he had cleared the summit of Everest by a mere 100 ft, but he later revised his estimate.
14. Fellowes et al., op. cit., Chapter X.
15. Clydesdale and McIntyre, op. cit., Chapter VII.
16. Fellowes et al., op. cit., Chapter X.
17. Clydesdale and McIntyre, op. cit.
18. 'Alpine Notes', *A.J.*, XLVI, 1934.

CHAPTER 11: THE OUTSIDERS (*pages 236–65*)

1. D. Roberts, *I'll Climb Mount Everest Alone,* p.26.
2. Maurice Wilson's Diary, A.C. Archives.
3. ibid.
4. A delightful idiosyncrasy which has not entirely died out. 'I don't trust English guidebooks', an American mountaineer recently wrote. 'If they say something is "just a scramble" I know I'm going to be stretched to the limit.'

5. Wilson's actions are not always explicable to the rational mind. One has only to look at crampons to realize how useful they would be on ice, and a couple of days later in his diary Wilson mentions the fact that crampons would have been useful. Why, then, did he throw them away?
6. Maurice Wilson's Diary.
7. ibid.
8. ibid.
9. In his biography of Wilson, *I'll Climb Mount Everest Alone,* Dennis Roberts gives a detailed account of Wilson's attempt on the col. However, the four camps mentioned by Roberts would not have allowed Wilson to return to Camp III on the 25th, which he did. The diary covering this period is almost impossible to decipher.
10. Maurice Wilson's Diary.
11. ibid.
12. ibid.
13. Charles Warren's Diary.
14. E. Denman, *Alone to Everest,* Chapter I.
15. ibid., Chapter II.
16. J.R. Ullman, *Sherpa Tenzing, Man of Everest,* Chapter 8.
17. ibid.
18. Denman never travelled alone despite the title of his subsequent book, *Alone to Everest,* which Tilman thought was 'ungrateful'. What Denman was planning to do, in fact, was to make an Alpine-style ascent of Everest – a feat yet to be accomplished (1979).
19. J.R. Ullman, op. cit. Denman claimed to have reached 23,500 ft, but in this he was mistaken. The col itself is only 22,990 ft and they got nowhere near it. Tenzing says they made 'a brief try' at the slopes.
20. It is unlikely that Larsen was deliberately misinformed in Namche regarding the Lho La. Glaciers tend to alter over the years, and a century or two ago it is quite likely that the Lho La was a feasible crossing and that a lama did cross it. Time means nothing to these people.
21. K. Becker-Larsen, letter to author, 21 April 1978.
22. Shipton's party crossed the pass in the following year during their attempt on Cho Oyu. Larsen seems to be the only person to have completed the journey between Namche and Kyetrak, however.
23. Using an ice axe as a brake in the event of a slip is a climbing technique fundamental to mountaineering and one of the principal uses of the ice axe. However, it usually requires practice to be effective. Larsen had had no such practice. 'However,' he writes, 'I think I had read of someone in the same situation, and I have a habit of conducting a sort of "mental drill", preparing myself for those eventualities that I can foresee – besides a great deal of luck, of course' (letter to the author).
24. To the author, in 1978, he wrote, 'Today, at the "ripe age" of 50, my judgements are not quite as rash.'
25. K. Becker-Larsen, letter to the author.
26. E. MacAskill, 'Creag Dhu', *Climber and Rambler,* April 1978.
27. W.W. Sayre, *Four Against Everest,* Chapter 2.
28. They had no formal snow and ice training, such as crevasse rescue techniques, which seemed to bother Sayre for much of the Everest trip. Their achievements are all the more remarkable.
29. W.W. Sayre, op. cit.

30. Camp I was above the first step of the Icefall – but bear in mind that 'camps' on this expedition are camp *sites*. The tents are moved on each time.
31. Twenty-five miles on foot, that is. About fifteen miles as the crow flies.
32. Shades of the pre-war Shipton–Tilman expeditions! Like Tilman, Sayre believed in a monotonous but calorie-rich diet.
33. I have retained this name for the camp at the foot of the North Col for the sake of clarity. In actual fact it was Sayre's eleventh camp.
34. W.W. Sayre, op. cit., Chapter 10.
35. ibid.
36. ibid.
37. ibid., Chapter 11.
38. It appeared in *Life*, 22 March 1963.

CHAPTER 12: A FRESH START (*pages 266–94*)

1. Except Gosainthan (Shisha Pangma), which was climbed by the Chinese in 1964. It is inaccessible to Western climbers or it undoubtedly would have been climbed earlier.
2. In 1949 (a year before the Tilman–Houston expedition) a Mr E. St George is rumoured to have made a journey up the Khumbu. Nothing seems known of this highly original adventure.
3. M.P. Ward, letter to the author.
4. E.E. Shipton, *That Untravelled World*, Chapter 8.
5. ibid.
6. E.E. Shipton, *The Mount Everest Reconnaissance Expedition 1951*.
7. E. Hillary, *High Adventure*, Chapter 2.
8. ibid.
9. E.E. Shipton, *Times* Special Supplement, 1951.
10. E. Hillary, op. cit., Chapter 3.
11. N. Estcourt, interview with the author.
12. E.E. Shipton, *Times* Special Supplement, 1951.
13. ibid.
14. ibid.
15. ibid.
16. This journey from the Menlung to the Rongshar was actually in Tibet and they only narrowly escaped capture. In his reports at the time, none of this was mentioned, presumably in case political repercussions might affect the expedition planned for 1952. Shipton considered their discovery of Melungtse the best part of the whole trip.
17. In *That Untravelled World*, published many years after his account in *The Times* quoted here, Shipton said it was Houston who reckoned the odds to be 'forty to one against'.
18. This cut no ice with the War Office, who sent the Himalayan Committee a bill for £479 for lost equipment!
19. E. Hillary, op. cit., Chapter 6.
20. W.H. Murray, *The Story of Everest*, Chapter XIII.
21. The Himalayan Club list makes him three years younger. The Sherpas use the Tibetan calendar, which can cause uncertainties when translated.

    The family title was Gang La, but Sherpas never use their family name. A Sherpa child is named on the third day after birth, but he or she can later change if it turns out to be inappropriate.

22. R. Dittert, G. Chevalley and R. Lambert, *Forerunners to Everest*, Chapter VI.
23. ibid.
24. ibid.
25. ibid., Chapter VII.
26. ibid.
27. ibid., Part Two (Gabriel Chevalley's Journal).

CHAPTER 13: 'RATHER MORE THAN A MOUNTAIN' (*pages 295–313*)

'... we agreed that this was going to be no ordinary climb. For the time being, Everest was rather more than a mountain' – John Hunt, *Life is Meeting*.

1. The north walls of the Matterhorn and Eiger were first climbed by Austro-German climbers. The Eiger in particular saw many deaths before it was climbed in 1938. Climbers who tried such routes were disparagingly called the 'Do or Die School' or the 'Munich School', and the whole movement was associated in the minds of British climbers with the Nazis.
2. H.C. Minute Book, 4 July 1952.
3. Letter to author, 30 July 1978.
4. H.C. Minute Book, 4 July 1952. This was a preliminary report to the Committee. Shipton and Evans were still in Nepal at this date (4 July).
5. The Swiss wanted to discuss the possibility of a joint Anglo-Swiss expedition in 1955, but the Himalayan Committee thought 'it best to have as little to do with them as possible right now'.
6. E.E. Shipton, *That Untravelled World*, Chapter 8.
7. This account is based on the H.C. Minute Book. Shipton's account, in *That Untravelled World*, puts a different emphasis on events. He makes it sound as though the Committee were unanimously in favour of himself as leader and that he proposed the idea of a Deputy Leader. It wasn't and he didn't.
8. Hunt was a pupil at Marlborough where Edwin Kempson was a teacher. In 1933 Kempson and Hunt had a season of guideless climbing at Chamonix – Hunt's first guideless climbs. Kempson was a member of the 1933 Everest reconnaissance and his letters made Hunt think about his own possible participation in 1936.
9. In a letter to the author Hunt describes his position with regard to British climbing circles as 'out of sight, out of mind'.
10. Letter to the author, 23 August 1978.
11. 'This information' presumably means about Hunt's ability. T.G.L. is Tom Longstaff, respected elder statesman of the Alpine Club.
12. E.A., Box 63.
13. ibid.
14. Ingrid Cranfield, 'To Each his Own Everest', *Expedition*, Vol. VIII, No. 4, 1978.
15. E.E. Shipton, op. cit.
16. E.E. Shipton, op. cit.
17. E.E. Shipton, op. cit.
18. I. Cranfield, op. cit.
19. Eric Shipton died in 1977.
20. Letter to the author, 23 August 1978.
21. E. Hillary, *High Adventure*, Chapter 7.
22. J. Morris, *Coronation Everest*, Chapter 4.
23. The British Mountaineering Council was formed in 1944 as the representative body of the sport in England and Wales. There are now over 200 member clubs, and 2,000 individual members, but in 1952 it consisted of a much smaller band of the

older established clubs. Entry to these was fairly restricted, and although it was a widening of horizons on the part of the Himalayan Committee, it was not as wide as it might first appear.

24. Deaken, editor of *The Times*, mischievously suggested that Shipton should be their correspondent.
25. Apropos Bourdillon and this group in general, Hunt stated in *The Ascent of Everest* that 'their standard of performance is comparable with that of the best Continental alpinists'. This was overstating the case. As already mentioned, no British climber at that date had done the Matterhorn Nordwand or the Eigerwand: the two great test pieces of the era. Bourdillon and his contemporaries did however lead a great renaissance of British Alpinism.
26. John Menlove Edwards (1910–58) was a brilliant cragsman, sometimes regarded as the 'father' of modern rock climbing in Britain. Unlike Noyce, he disliked the wider forms of mountaineering. James Morris, the *Times* correspondent and a distinguished author, later underwent a sex change to become Jan Morris.
27. Three climbers earmarked for the autumn were J.H. Emlyn-Jones, J. Jackson and J. Tucker. The fourth was to be chosen from N. Hardie, T.D. McKinnon, A. Rawlinson, D. Bryson and R. Jones.
28. Alf Bridge was one of the best British rock climbers between the wars. His great contribution to the oxygen team, says Lloyd, was 'hard work and enthusiasm'.
29. In feet per hour: Hunt and Da Namgyal (open system), 494: Bourdillon and Evans (closed system) 933. By comparison, twenty-five years later, Messner and Habeler achieved in excess of 550 ft per hour without oxygen.
30. P. Lloyd, letter to the author, 9 October 1978.
31. ibid.
32. ibid. A third type of apparatus was developed by Campbell Secord and the Harwell Atomic Energy Research Station. This supplied oxygen from a chemical source, potassium peroxide. In the event the apparatus was seriously delayed and so could not be tried, even experimentally, by the 1953 expedition. Nothing further seems to have been heard of it.
33. Lloyd's own records were unfortunately destroyed some years ago.
34. J. Hunt, *The Ascent of Everest*, Chapter 7.
35. ibid., Chapter 18.

CHAPTER 14: 'THE LAST INNOCENT ADVENTURE' (*pages 314–42*)

The chapter heading is a description of the 1953 expedition by James Morris in the *Guardian*.

1. According to Jimmy Roberts the Swiss also began the habit of giving Sherpas their equipment – an expensive perk which has several times caused friction between Sherpas and expeditions.
2. J.R. Ullman, *Sherpa Tenzing – Man of Everest*, Chapter 16.
3. J. Hunt, *Life Is Meeting*, Chapter 8.
4. More particularly, rock climbing. Grisly humour is endemic in the sport. From bottom to top of the Icefall the names for particularly difficult or dangerous sections were Mike's Horror (a steep ice pitch), Hillary's Horror (a dangerous crevasse), Hell Fire Alley (unstable seracs), Atom Bomb Area (constantly changing ice), Ghastly Crevasse (dangerous crevasse) and the Nutcracker (a gap between two unstable seracs).
5. E. Hillary, *High Adventure*, Chapter 7.
6. ibid.

7. ibid.
8. J.R. Ullman, op. cit., Chapter 17.
9. E. Hillary, op. cit., Chapter 8.
10. There are discrepancies in the various accounts of this meeting. Hunt and Hillary say it took place on 7 May, but Ward and Noyce put it a day later. Noyce set off up the Icefall on the 8th, but in his book *South Col* he says Hunt told him of his plans privately on the previous evening. In *The Ascent of Everest* Hunt categorically mentions Noyce as being present.
11. This arrangement was modified later.
12. M.P. Ward, *In This Short Span*, Chapter 6.
13. ibid.
14. E. Hillary, op. cit., Chapter 8.
15. J. Hunt, *Ascent of Everest*, Chapter 14.
16. According to Evans, in the *Alpine Journal*, 1.15 p.m., but it is not clear whether he is referring to the actual moment of arrival. They left at 1.30 p.m. and it seems likely that they spent about thirty minutes on the summit.
17. R.C. Evans, letter to the author, 15 January 1979.
18. R.C. Evans, 'The First Ascent of the South Peak', *A.J.*, LIX, 1953/4.
19. E. Hillary, op. cit., Chapter 9.
20. In his autobiography *High Adventure* Hillary admits that sending Lowe down did not fit in with his plans. Had he ideas for a third assault should the second fail? George Lowe writes:

    'There was an element in this that if plans did go wrong we would be near the fulcrum of events – that is natural – and not subversive. We did discuss a third assault – we all had it in mind. John Hunt did – but unvoiced (and he later said he hoped it would be Wilf Noyce and himself). I hoped it might be Wilf Noyce and me. No third assault plan was declared but we all had our unspoken plans for this.

    'I think Ed's words mean we were both keen and rather pushy and wanted to be right up with the action – John Hunt was still not totally accepted by us – that was our fault – we were two New Zealanders and we were brash zealots. Not subversive with secret plans – wild hopes, yes!' The dropping of Shipton still rankled with the two New Zealanders. (Letter to the author, 17 February 1979.)
21. Hunt was in poor shape after three nights on the col but it seems unlikely that this affected his decision. 'John ... was dangerously unaware of how bad his own condition was ...' wrote Ward.
22. In cold weather or high-altitude mountain camping it is usual for the climber to sleep fully dressed. He either keeps his boots on or, more often, removes them from his feet but keeps them warm inside the down sleeping bag. Boots left out of a bag will freeze solid and need to be thawed. The temperature in the tent at 3 a.m. on 28 May 1953 was −27°C.
23. On their return down the ridge Evans and Bourdillon had descended this slope.
24. E. Hillary, op. cit., Chapter 11.
25. Tenzing (whose account of the final climb varies in detail from Hillary's) says the step was only fifteen feet high. What seems certain is that the step varies in difficulty year by year. The Americans in 1963 found it insignificant, yet in 1978 Habeler and Messner thought it worth mentioning in detail.
26. Hillary obviously found the rock step exhausting. In his first written account of it he says that he lay on the top 'gasping like a fish' (*A.J.*, LIX, p.236), but when he came to describe the climb in Hunt's official book *The Ascent of Everest* he unfortunately transferred this description to Tenzing, who took considerable

offence over it. Repeating the story in his autobiography *High Adventure,* Hillary diplomatically dropped all references to fishes. He still maintained that he pulled Tenzing up – something else to which the Sherpa took exception at the time.

27. E. Hillary, op. cit., Chapter 12.
28. Tenzing says he buried some sweets, a little red and blue pencil his daughter Nima had given him, and a small cloth black cat which Hillary gave him and which had come from John Hunt. He did not see any crucifix. Hunt and Hillary do not mention any black cat.
29. Climbers reported the remains of Lambert's Swiss camp still visible many years later, but nobody seems to have seen Hillary's camp again.
30. J. Morris, *Coronation Everest,* Chapter 9.
31. The pepping-up qualities of benzedrine had been exploited during the Second World War with remarkable results. It was tried out on the Sherpas with no apparent effect. The mortar was an idea to dislodge avalanches but was never used on the mountain. The mortar bombs were fired off at Lobuje on the return journey by way of celebration, much to the delight of the porters.
32. Lord Hailsham, Centenary Dinner address to the A.C., 1959.

CHAPTER 15: NEWS FROM THE NORTH (*pages 344–59*)

1. Not all the Communist bloc are so timid. The Poles, for example, have a distinguished post-war Himalayan record.
2. Letter to the author, 24 November 1974.
3. The first ascent was by the Americans T. Moore and K. Burdsall in 1932. The Chinese dispute this.
4. Shih Chan-chun, 'The Conquest of Mount Everest by the Chinese Mountaineering Team', *A.J.*, LXVI, 1961.
5. The Chinese failed to number their camps after Camp 3 on the East Rongbuk Glacier, but this would be Camp 5. It was 340 m. lower than the 1933 Camp V.
6. Shih Chan-chun, op. cit.
7. There are no details regarding the type of set or at what height the Chinese climbers began using them.
8. Shih Chan-chun, op. cit.
9. ibid.
10. Wang Fu-chou and Chu Yin-hua, 'How We Climbed the World's Highest Peak', *Mountain Craft,* July/September 1961.
11. The stiff upper lip school vanished with the war. There are several recorded instances of climbers bursting into tears on post-war Everest expeditions. If this seems strange on the part of fit, tough young men and women, it is worth remembering that nerves are often raw and emotions considerably heightened during an expedition. The strain is considerable.
12. Some years later the ascent was commemorated by a massive jade carving depicting the ascent. Made in Shanghai, it was 4½ ft high and weighed 2½ tons. Eighteen men spent two years four months in making it. 'A monstrosity', commented the *Alpine Journal.*
13. *Mountain,* 8, March 1970.
14. 'Nine Who Climbed Qomolangma Feng', *Mountain,* 46, November/December 1975.
15. Apart from Base Camp (5,000 m.) the lower camps are not mentioned in the Chinese account. However, camps are mentioned at 6,000 m., 6,500 m., 7,000 m. (North Col), 7,600 m., 8,200 m. and 8,600 m.

16. It is not clear whether the Chinese followed their usual practice of establishing these camps in advance, or whether the final assault party moved them. What is always so impossible for Western climbers to understand about the Chinese system is why, having established a top camp, the same people don't go on to the summit next day.
17. *Mountain*, 46, op. cit.
18. The Chinese apparently believe in the restorative effects of oxygen taken at intervals, rather than the Western method of continuous supply. Pre-war Everesters never found this particularly effective, except for momentary relief.
19. When the British found the survey pole in September it was two thirds buried in snow and the fierce Everest winds had stripped it down to bare metal. It was still standing in 1978.
20. *Mountain*, 46, op. cit.

CHAPTER 16: WEST SIDE STORY (*pages 360–92*)

1. Notable landmarks in this trend is Reinhold Messner's incredible solo ascent of Nanga Parbat in 1978, and the ascent of Kangchenjunga – third highest mountain in the world – by Scott, Boardman and Tasker in 1979.
2. The Indian Mountaineering Federation also vets applications from foreign expeditions wishing to climb in India.
3. All the Indian expeditions to Everest marched in from Jaynagar, on the Indian border, rather than the usual route via Kathmandu.
4. H.P.S. Ahluwahlia, *Faces of Everest*, Chapter 5.
5. In *Americans on Everest*, the official expedition book, J.R. Ullman says that permission had been granted in 1961 to a Major O.W. Hackett of the U.S. Army, who asked Dyhrenfurth to join him. The plan fell through because of shortage of time. The version given here is that by Dyhrenfurth himself.
6. J.R. Ullman, *Americans on Everest*, Foreword (by Dyhrenfurth).
7. Readers of this book so far will know that as far as Everest is concerned nationalism has always played a role. In view of Dyhrenfurth's later career there is a certain irony in this. (See Chapter 17.)
8. J.R. Ullman, op. cit, Chapter 3.
9. The *National Geographic* account was written by Barry C. Bishop, an expedition member who already worked for the magazine.
10. Nuptse had been climbed by a British party in 1961, but from the south. It has since been climbed from the Western Cwm (1979) and presents a formidable task from that side. It is extremely unlikely that the Americans would have succeeded in 1963.
11. N.G. Dyhrenfurth, 'Americans on Everest, 1963', *A.J.*, LXIX, 1964.
12. Unsoeld named his daughter 'Nanda Devi' after the mountain of that name. By a cruel irony she was killed on Nanda Devi in 1976. Unsoeld himself was killed by an avalanche on Mount Rainier in 1979.
13. T. Hornbein, *Everest, The West Ridge*, Chapter 8.
14. Gombu (or Gompu) was the 'roly-poly Sherpa' aged seventeen who accompanied the 1953 ascent (see p. 314) – a caterpillar transformed into a butterfly. He eventually became the first man to climb Everest twice.
15. T. Hornbein, op. cit.
16. ibid.
17. The establishing of 3W was a very solid effort on the part of the Sherpas concerned – three continuous hard days. One Sherpa – Tashi – was in his mid-fifties.

18. T. Hornbein, op. cit., Chapter 9.
19. ibid., Chapter 10.
20. ibid.
21. N.G. Dyhrenfurth, op. cit.
22. T. Hornbein, op. cit.
23. In the cause of fitness Corbet and Auten did some load-carrying to Camp III for the South Collers. Emerson was the most seriously affected by altitude and was the last to rejoin the team.
24. Everest's weather seems unpredictably localized. Observers in the Cwm and further afield who saw the summit on 1 May thought it unlikely any attempt would be made that day. Those on the South Col thought the weather too bad for climbing, yet the summit party found conditions acceptable if less than ideal. There are similar examples on other occasions, notably when the Chinese and Indians were on separate sides of the mountain in 1960.
25. T. Hornbein, op. cit., Chapter 11.
26. ibid., Chapter 12.
27. In survival technique the main consideration is to keep out of the wind: wind chill is the prime cause of exposure. A crevasse is frequently used for this purpose, and where no suitable crevasse can be found a climber may have to dig a snow shelter.

    At high altitude oxygen helps to keep up body temperature, and Emerson knew that there was oxygen at the dump before he embarked on his adventure. The equipment dumps on the face had changed from time to time and there were three close together, known as the Old Dump, New Dump and New New Dump. Emerson's bivouac was near the last of these.
28. T. Hornbein, op. cit., Chapter 13.
29. ibid.
30. A descent of this route was accomplished by a Yugoslavian team in 1979.
31. T. Hornbein, op. cit., Chapter 14.
32. Unsoeld's 'promises' were to his wife Jolene that he would never go on another big mountain expedition after Everest. Ironically, he was killed by an avalanche on his own 'backyard' peak, Mt Rainier, in 1979 while with a party of students.

    Frost's poem actually says 'before I sleep' – but Unsoeld was including Hornbein in the sentiment.
33. J.R. Ullman, op. cit., Chapter 14.
34. Bishop lost all his toes and the tips of his little fingers.
35. T. Hornbein, op. cit., Chapter 15.

CHAPTER 17: 'NOT A PRIVATE AFFAIR' (*pages 393–422*)

'. . . as I soon learned, Everest was not a private affair. It belonged to many men' – Tom Hornbein in his Preface to *Everest, The West Ridge*

1. A list of team members for all expeditions will be found in Appendix 4.
2. A scale of fees is charged depending on the height of the mountain. Everest is therefore the most expensive. The fees are revised from time to time and are payable in advance. There are other regulations also – a liaison officer must be taken, there must be insurance for porters, and so on. Some peaks can be attempted only a joint basis with Nepalese climbers and some may not be attempted at all.

    Nepal is not alone in this. Mountaineering in the Himalaya today involves a considerable amount of bureaucratic nonsense.
3. The cost was reported as 100,000 yen.

4. Nanga Parbat (26,658 ft) was by Himalayan tradition a 'German' mountain. The Germans had tried to climb it in 1932, 1934, 1937, 1938 and 1939. Twenty-six climbers and porters were lost in these attempts. Hermann Buhl made the first ascent in 1953 and other German attempts were successful in 1962 and 1970, this last by the Rupal Flank.
5. Dhaulagiri II was climbed by an Austrian expedition in 1971.
6. In view of the events which took place, it is interesting to note that Britain, America and Japan met some 67 per cent of the total bill.
7. C. Bonington, *Everest South West Face,* Chapter 3.
8. Though it might have impressed the sponsors, it seems probable that the *Direttissima* was thought up as a safety net, just in case the 1970 Japanese team climbed the Face by the more probable circuitous route. Expeditions to major peaks are so frequent these days that the second is being planned before the first has actually taken place: contingency planning is therefore necessary.
9. K. Wilson and M. Pearson, 'Post Mortem of an International Expedition', *Mountain,* 17, 1971.
10. The bottles still weighed 16 lb. each: Blume knew the Air Force had special fibreglass bottles at half the weight so he contacted the manufacturers, who wanted 400 dollars apiece for them. When Blume asked for a discount he was told that 400 dollars was half price.
11. C. Bonington, op. cit.
12. ibid.
13. H.P.S. Ahluwalia, *Faces of Everest,* Chapter 9.
14. K. Wilson and M. Pearson, op. cit.
15. ibid.
16. Karrimor is a British firm specializing in mountain equipment. They made the Whillans Box.
17. P. Steele, *Doctor on Everest,* Chapter 14.

CHAPTER 18: 'ALL THE WINDS OF ASIA' (*pages 423–58*)

'All the winds of Asia seemed to be trying to blow us from the ridge' – Peter Boardman

1. J. Cleare, 'Thirteen Nations on Mt Everest', *A.J.*, 77, 1972.
2. ibid.
3. D. Scott, 'To Rest Is Not to Conquer', *Mountain,* 23, 1972.
4. C. Bonington, *Everest South West Face,* Chapter 4.
5. ibid.
6. D. Scott, op. cit.
7. The German press reported this 'flight' by Saleki. Scott points out the difficulty anyone would have in stowing away in a two-seater helicopter, particularly one which was operating near its height limit at Base Camp. He would need to be invisible and almost weightless!
8. Kuen had been to Jirishanca in Peru and to Nanga Parbat.
9. D. Scott, op. cit.
10. ibid.
11. Initially he intended to go to Alaska, because Nepal was temporarily closed to climbers. Fortunately restrictions were lifted before plans were too advanced. Annapurna was chosen on the basis of a photograph he had once seen.
12. I. McNaught Davis, 'Mac the Belly talks to Cassius Bonafide', *Mountain,* 15, 1971.
13. The enormous expense and waste of the International Expedition created the same gut reaction in many climbers as did the huge expeditions of the twenties and

thirties. There was an awakening of interest in the ideas of Shipton and Tilman. At the time of writing, however (1979), no lightweight expedition has succeeded in climbing Everest.

14. I. McNaught Davis, 'Why Everest?', *Mountain*, 25, 1973.
15. Snow anchors are called 'dead men' because they have to be buried in the snow. There is even a smaller variety known as 'dead boys'.
16. C. Bonington, op. cit., Chapter 6.
17. ibid., Chapter 12.
18. ibid., Chapter 16.
19. Bonington interview.
20. As a result of this Barclays Bank make a general annual donation to the Mount Everest Foundation.
21. Bonington interview.
22. Not all the equipment lived up to what was expected of it. Most troublesome was the oxygen gear which was of the Blume/Robertshaw type. The faults were due to defective demand valves. Of the eighteen sets taken all but five broke down – and several of these were not fully efficient.
23. Bonington interview.
24. C. Bonington, *Everest, The Hard Way*, Chapter 2. .
25. Interview with author.
26. C. Bonington, op. cit., Chapter 12.
27. ibid.
28. ibid., Chapter 14.
29. ibid.
30. ibid.
31. ibid.
32. ibid.
33. P. Boardman, 'Everest Is Not a Private Affair', *Mountain Life*, 23, 1976. The 'Blue Peter flag' was a pennant given to the expedition by the children's TV programme of that name.
34. ibid.
35. ibid.

CHAPTER 19: 'NONE BUT OURSELVES' (*pages 459–76*)

'Have we vanquished an enemy? None but ourselves . . . To struggle and to understand – never this last without the other; such is the law . . .' – George Mallory

1. Ang Phu was the second man to have climbed Everest twice (the other was Gombu). He was the only man to have climbed it by two different routes – the South East Ridge in 1978 and West Ridge in 1979.

   At the time of writing full details of the Yugoslavian ascent are not available.
2. The Nepalese protested over the use of helicopters above Base Camp. Helicopters (or other aircraft) are no longer permitted except for medical emergencies.
3. Sambu (or Shambu) Tamang is the youngest person to have reached the summit, being seventeen or eighteen at the time. He is actually not of the Sherpa tribe but a Tamang, as his name suggests.
4. H.P.S. Ahluwalia, *Faces of Everest*, Chapter 12.
5. It is interesting that this straightforward expedition had a budget of 200,000 dollars – almost as much as the successful South West Face team of the previous year. About 90,000 dollars were covered by the climbers themselves.
6. G. Roach, 'Everybody's Everest', *Quest*, 77, March/April 1977.
7. *Climber and Rambler*, July 1977.

8. This statement refers to the country of origin of the expeditions, not of individual climbers. Hillary was a New Zealander, for example, and Mrs Phantog was a Tibetan.
9. Private communication to the author (undated). Cheney also claims in his statement that this expedition proves the Sherpas capable of mounting their own expedition to Everest. One sees no real reason to dispute this.
10. *Mountain*, 60, 1978.
11. After Everest, Messner pressed his philosophy further by climbing Nanga Parbat (8,125 m.) alone and without oxygen.
12. Conversation with the author, 1975.
13. An interesting breakdown of income and expenditure is given in Peter Habeler's *Everest, Impossible Victory*. Perhaps the commonest promotional gimmick used by expeditions these days is the expedition postcard, which is usually a picture card signed by team members and sent to subscribers from Base Camp or Kathmandu.
14. The South Buttress route was Messner's idea and was the route he and Habeler intended to try without oxygen. They considered it too icy to attempt, on inspection.
15. Deposition made to the Hon. Minister of Tourism, Kathmandu, by Mingma Norbu Sherpa of Khumjung Village, 1978.
16. Mingma's accusations can also be considered as part of the 'anti-Messner' campaign waged by some of the Sherpas – see p. 476.
17. There are varying accounts of Messner's return to Base. Messner himself in *Everest, Expedition to the Ultimate* gives the impression he returned alone. Mingma says Messner went down with 'the TV cameraman', and the Sherpas stayed at Camp II. Habeler (already at Base) says Messner arrived with his two Sherpas.
18. Habeler interview, 1978.
19. Eric Jones, conversation with the author, 4 July 1979.
20. Habeler interview.
21. ibid.
22. ibid.
23. Official complaints of this nature by Sherpas are extremely unusual. Nevertheless, none of those people closely associated with Messner at the time – Habeler, Jones and Dickinson – recalled during questioning any incident which might have caused the complaints. It may be that it all stems from the traumatic two nights which Messner spent at the South Col during his first attempt, when he bullied the two Sherpas into saving their own lives.

POSTSCRIPT

1. He actually celebrated his fiftieth birthday in Base Camp after his ascent.

CHAPTER 20: NEW HORIZONS *(pages 477–506)*

1. G. Rowell, *The Mountains of the Middle Kingdom*, Chapter 8. The destruction seems to have taken place in 1974 by a mixture of Red Guards and locals.
2. A. Rouse, 'China News Report', *Mountain*, 76, November/December 1980.
3. Estimated from J. Kielowski, *Mount Everest – Massiv Nord*.
4. Takami reached 6550 m. It was on this expedition that Wang Hongbao was killed (See Appendix 1).
5. Originally sponsored by Mainichi Broadcasting System who pulled out as the costs escalated beyond £800,000. Yomiuri Shimbun Newspapers and Nippon TV Network picked up the tab.

6. Large Japanese expeditions often have extensive command structures involving various 'leaders'. In this case there was a general leader back in Tokyo named Nishibori who was in touch with the expedition by radio, Watanabe in overall command on the spot, Yoshio Hamono in command of the ridge party but with Kato as climbing leader and Miashita and Takami fulfilling the same roles on the North Face.
7. Tsunemichi Ikeda in *The Iwa to Yuki*, quoted by N. Dhyrenfurth in *Mountain*, 76, November/December 1980.
8. R. Messner, *All 14 Eight-Thousanders*, Chapter 1.
9. R. Faux, *High Ambition*, Chapter 16.
10. *ibid.*
11. *ibid.* Dyhrenfurth gives the rucksack weight as 15 kgs in *Mountain*, 76.
12. Nena Holguin, 'A Partner In Myself', *Mountain*, 80, July/August 1981.
13. *ibid.*
14. Due to the build-up of monsoon snow only 30 cm. of the tripod was showing.
15. R. Messner, *op. cit.*
16. O. Ölz (Oelz), 'Reinhold Messner: The Phenomenon', *A.J.* 92, 1987.
17. The tents belonged to the American 'Ultima Thule' expedition of earlier that year (See Appendix 4).
18. L. Hall, *White Limbo*, Chapter 11.
19. J. Wickwire, 'Everest from the North', *A.A.J.*, 1985.
20. Christine Grosjean, 'Suisse, qui est qui?' *AlpiRando*, October 1986. Loretan climbed K2 in 3 days with Eric Escoffier and in the following winter season climbed Dhaulagiri in 4 days with Troillet and Pierre-Alain Steiner.
21. Habeler's descent to the South Col in 1978 (see Chapter 19) was 862 m. in an hour. Troillet and Loretan averaged about 800 m. per hour – but for 3½ times as long and right down to the glacier.
22. Very few climbers had thought of the NE Ridge as an objective. Even Bonington wasn't sure – for some time he referred to it as the ENE Ridge.
23. C. Bonington, *The Everest Years*, Chapter 11.
24. *ibid.*
25. C. Bonington and C. Clarke, *Everest – The Unclimbed Ridge*, Chapter 11.
26. The books were *Everest, The Cruel Way* (1981) and *Savage Arena* (1982), by Joe Tasker, and *The Shining Mountain* (1978) and *Sacred Summits* (1982) by Peter Boardman. *The Shining Mountain* was awarded the John Llewelyn Rhys Memorial Prize in 1979. An annual prize for mountain literature, the Boardman-Tasker Award, was established in their memory.
27. C. Bonington and C. Clarke, *op. cit.*
28. R. Faux, 'Everest NE Ridge – The Seligman Harris Expedition', *A.J.* 92. The expedition gained its name from its sponsor, a city merchant bank.
29. *ibid.* Once the East Face was climbed (1983) one could agree that the NE Ridge was the greatest challenge left on the mountain – but mountain challenges have a habit of appearing from nowhere, and one should not assume Everest is played out. The difficulty of the Pinnacles seems to have been consistently under-rated by observers.
30. D. Scott, 'The Altos North-East Ridge of Everest 1987 Expedition', *A.J.* 93. The name comes from the computer firm sponsoring the expedition.
31. Stokes was able to keep in touch by satellite and even spoke from home in Hereford with Harry Taylor, lodged in Camp 3, 8,000 m. up Everest.
32. A. Alvarez, *Feeding The Rat*, Chapter 11.

33. P. Moores, 'The Boys From The White Stuff', *Mountain* 124, November/December 1988.
34. Polypropylene rope is cheaper and lighter than nylon or perlon climbing rope. Satisfactory for fixed rope, but not really strong enough for climbing.
35. P. Moores, *op. cit.*
36. 'Info', *Mountain* 124, November/December 1988.
37. C.K. Howard-Bury, *Mount Everest, The Reconnaissance 1921*, Chapter XIV.
38. The Americans described present day Kharta as 'lush, green and beautiful, a contrast to the arid Tibetan plains,' but Bonington described it as 'a windswept dusty valley' denuded of trees.
39. A. Harvard, 'The Forgotten Face of Everest', *National Geographic* July 1984.
40. *Ibid.*
41. George Lowe was not the same person as Hillary's New Zealand companion of 1953.
42. G.C. Tabin, 'The Kangshung Face of Everest', *A.A.J.* 1982.
43. The standard was F6 plus A3/A4.
44. *The Seattle Times*, 6 June 1982.
45. *Ibid.*
46. G.C. Tabin, *op. cit.*
47. J. D. Morrissey, 'Conquest of the Summit', *National Geographic*, July 1984.
48. The Americans used a similar device on Everest in 1963 (see Chapter 16).
49. Pasang Temba was with the Japanese party but had retreated just before the South Summit. Two Japanese died in falls next day.
50. Letter from John Pollock to author, dated 8 December 1983.
51. Hunt was expedition patron and the climb was to celebrate the 35th anniversary of the first ascent – a somewhat esoteric anniversary, one would have thought. However, because of this, Hunt suggested a British climber should be in the team and recommended Venables.
52. P. Gillman, 'Cut Off on Top of the World', *Sunday Times Magazine*, 4 December 1988.
53. R. Anderson, 'The Nine Days of Neverest' *Mountain* 124, Nov/Dec 1988.
54. P. Gillman, *op. cit.*
55. R. Anderson, *op. cit.*
56. According to Gillman, Venables bridged up the Step in the way Hillary had done, so presumably the prusik loop was attached to the fixed rope just for safety.
57. R. Anderson, *op. cit.*
58. P. Gillman, *op. cit.*
59. *Ibid.*
60. R. Anderson, *op. cit.*
61. *Ibid.* Venables remembers it as 'Look, you guys, if we don't get down today we're going to die.'
62. P. Gillman, *op. cit.*

CHAPTER 21: 'THE HIGHEST GRADE V IN THE WORLD' *(pages 507-532)*

(The heading is Tone Skarja's description of the West Ridge.)

1. Not including West Ridge attempts.
2. T. Skarja, 'Yugoslav Everest Expedition', *H.J.37*, 1979/80.
3. Early reports (*vide* Chapter 19) called this Camp VI when in fact it was *the sixth camp*, including Base.
4. 'Sponsored by the Bulgarian Tourist Union to commemorate the 40th Anniversary

of Bulgaria's Socialist Revolution and the 80th Anniversary of the Organised Revolutionary Trade Union Movement in Bulgaria,' according to Steve Martin in his valuable article, in *A.J.*90. Martin interviewed Vultchev and Baldjiski in the Khumbu immediately after the expedition.

At that time there was no question of the Bulgarians (or the Russians, to whom they owed political allegiance) attempting Everest from Chinese Tibet.

5. The climb was one of 728 m., which the Yugoslavs, using oxygen, had achieved by 1.15 p.m. – estimated at a little more than 100 m. of ascent per hour. By contrast Prodanov and his companion had only reached 8,500 m. by 11 a.m. – about 75 m. per hour. The summit was reached at 6 p.m. – an average of 60 m. per hour, or almost half that of the Yugoslavs.
6. S. Martin, 'Everest – Pre-monsoon', *A.J.*90, 1985. Ringde was probably badly bruised from his accident as well.
7. *ibid.*
8. This was the first time Everest had been climbed as early as April by a pre-monsoon expedition according to *Indian Mountaineering*, 14, Autumn 1984.
9. Couzy was a famous French mountaineer of the previous generation (1923–58) killed by stonefall in the Alps. He made the first ascent of Makalu in 1955. Why the expedition was named after him is not clear.
10. According to reports in *Mountain* 90, their problems were compounded by poor relations with the Sherpas who did little carrying above Base.
11. Quoted in *Himavanta*, February 1983.
12. But not altogether unique except in that it involved crossing frontiers. At least two other cases of 'missing' Himalayan climbers turning up after all hope was abandoned have been recorded in recent years. There has been some questioning as to just how 'accidental' Bourgeois's escape was; but it does seem a particularly hard way to voluntarily opt out of an expedition!
13. There is a discrepancy of detail regarding the descent of the South East Ridge between the Bulgarian and Indian accounts, but nothing of significance.
14. John Hunt told me he deprecates the use of this term for what is still a considerable achievement.
15. C. Bonington: *The Everest Years*, Chapter 19.
16. The locals had walked past the unconscious Jang Bir with supreme indifference. It cost the Indians 500R to get the body removed.
17. D.K. Khullar, 'Indian Everest Expedition, 1984'. *H.J. 41*, 1983–4.
18. This was an all-Sherpa team, really, for though Phu Dorje and Rita Gombu were technically Indians, his background is Tibet and Nepal and she is the grand-niece of Tenzing.

    There seems no record of the height of the top camp, which consisted of a single tent. Times and distances seem difficult to reconcile but are those from the leader's report.
19. See Note 13.
20. D.K. Khullar, *op. cit.*
21. D.K. Khullar, *op. cit.*
22. In 1983 when Tom Hornbein asked a lecture audience in Seattle how many had climbed on Everest, over thirty stood up. Letter from John Pollock to author, 8/12/83.
23. Quoted in D. Roberts, 'The Summit of Hype', *Outside Magazine*, October 1988.
24. A. Zawada, 'Mount Everest – The First Winter Ascent', *A.J.89*, 1984.
25. During the first ten days of February only four climbers were fit for duty.

26. A. Zawada, *op. cit.*
27. J. Nyka, 'A New Route, South Buttress', *A.A.J.55*, 1981.
28. Once when in the Alps with some Russian climbers the author suggested that the observers were there so that the climbers couldn't defect by descending to another valley. The Russians thought this a huge joke and laughed uproariously.
29. Quoted in *Himavanta*, February 1983. Note: there are minor variations in spelling of the Russian names amongst different sources, due to transliteration from Cyrillic script.
30. Readers will be aware by this that the Icefall is notoriously fickle. It is also likely that the Soviets were taken in by Western understatement.
31. *Himavanta, op. cit.*
32. J. Town, 'Red Rib', *Climber and Rambler*, November 1983.
33. The Russian familiarity with difficult multi-day ridge climbs should make them strong contenders for the great traverse of Nuptse, Lhotse and Everest!
34. New regulations regarding the participation of foreigners in national teams almost denied Bass and Breashears their chance – but not Bonington, for some reason. Nepalese bureaucracy can be quite baffling and regulations seem to change every season.
35. D. Bass, F. Wells, and R. Ridgeway, *Seven Summits*, 1986. The summits are Aconcagua (S. America), Koskiusco (Australia), Everest (Asia), Kilimanjaro (Africa), Elbrus (Europe), Vinson Massif (Antarctica) and Mt McKinley (N. America). Unfortunately there is an error in the list; Koskiusko is not the highest point in Australasia, as distinct from Australia. Bass should have climbed Mt Cook in New Zealand! Unfortunately, Australasia is not properly defined and mountains to challenge Mt Cook can be included in some definitions.
36. C. Bonington, *op. cit.*
37. *Himavanta.*
38. *Mountain*, 124, 1988.
39. The two Swiss climbers rested for 8 hours, so their climbing time was 31 hours.
40. For full details of the South West Face route see Chapter 18.
41. There is probably a reporting error here. Surely Base Camp would have enquired about Bozik if he was missing?
42. Three other top-ranking Czech climbers died in Nepal that month. It was a serious blow to the relatively small Czech climbing community and a matter of grave concern to the Czech government who are said to have ordered all expedition climbing to stop immediately.

CHAPTER 22: 'EVEREST IS ANOTHER BALL GAME' (*pages 533–565*)

'A lot of people are here who shouldn't be here. Even some national teams, not just guided teams, are marginal. They're competent mountaineers, but Everest is another ball game.'

—Ed Viesturs, Everest 1996

1. This is for the South East Ridge. Other routes cost less. In 1993 the Nepalese generally charged $10,000 (£6,400) for up to 20 climbers (not including Sherpas), but after spring of that year, this increased to $70,000 (£45,000) minimum for up to seven climbers plus $10,000 (£6,400) per person extra to a maximum of nine. Later this became $50,000 (£32,000) for seven climbers, plus $10,000 (£6,400) per person to a maximum of 12, plus a surcharge of $20,000 (£13,000) for using the South Col! Initially the idea was to restrict the number of expeditions,

but this was abandoned. The temptation was too great. The Chinese seem to charge $5,000 (£3,200) for up to 20 climbers, but transport and services are controlled and expensive. This is still perhaps marginally cheaper than Nepal. (Based on notes from Steve Bell.)

2. Probably as many as on any other high peak in the world that day.
3. For a satire on these 'firsts,' see Stephen Venables magazine article, 'Everest Climbed by a Dog?', *High,* February 1999.
4. ibid. The ascent has been disputed.
5. A. Boukreev, *The Climb,* Epilogue.
6. ibid. 'Notes and references' section.
7. Joe Simpson quoted in *Dark Shadows Falling,* Chapter 2.
8. Venables. op. cit.
9. Private communication from Ray Huey, a researcher on this subject. These figures are preliminary findings.
10. Adrian Burgess, *American Alpine Journal,* 1990, p. 231.
11. Arthur Hajzer (Poland), Rob Hall (New Zealand), Gary Ball (New Zealand) and Sherpas Zangbu and Shiwa.
12. As of 1999, Ang Rita has climbed Everest ten times, Dhaulagiri four 4 times, Cho Oyu twice and Kangchenjungs once. None used supplementary oxygen.
13. Elizabeth Hawley quoted in *American Alpine Journal,* 1991, p. 223.
14. Jim Whittaker, 'Everest International Peace Climb', *American Alpine Journal,* 1991, p. 47.
15. ibid.
16. Robert Hall, *American Alpine Journal,* 1991, p. 225.
17. *Mountain,* 137, p. 8.
18. ibid.
19. Climbing without a permit in Nepal can carry a 5- to 10-year ban of the offender.
20. Stevan Untch, *American Alpine Journal,* 1992, p. 262.
21. *Mountain,* 140, p. 5.
22. Elizabeth Hawley quoted in *American Alpine Journal,* 1993, p. 213.
23. Three more ascended from the north. This assumes that all the claims are genuine, though there is some doubt.
24. Col M.H. Kefford, *American Alpine Journal,* 1993, p. 216.
25. This grisly sight was apparently photographed by Vladimir Suviga.
26. Ohmiya and Khrishchaty, 'Everest's Northeast Ridge', *American Alpine Journal,* 1993, p. 15.
27. By the selfless sacrifice of a Basque climber who gave up his own oxygen and his chance of success, making it a strange repeat of the same incident in the same place the previous year.
28. The stamp had not appeared by 1995 (*Gibbons,* Part 2 K-Z, 1997). Interestingly, at this time, two other Sherpas have been commemorated: Sungdare and Pasang, with stamps in 1993 and 1994 respectively.
29. Heo claimed to be the first to reach 'all three poles', i.e., North and South Pole and the summit of Everest, the so-called Third Pole. This is disputed by Erling Kagge, who climbed Everest in 1994, because Heo did not start his South Pole attempt from the coast.
30. See Lydia Bradey, 1988.
31. Rumour said the ladder was missing so they brought a portable ladder just in case. This was not used. The account of their climb in *American Alpine Journal* is

rather confusing.

32. Charlotte Fox, 'A Time to Live, A Time to Die,' *American Alpine Journal,* 1997. A fine and lucid account of the tragedy.
33. In 1865, British climber Edward Whymper made the first ascent of the Matterhorn in Switzerland. On the descent the rope broke and four men fell to their deaths. It remains the most famous accident in mountaineering history and there are numerous books on the subject.
34. Jon Krakauer, *Into Thin Air,* Chapter 7.
35. Fox. op. cit.
36. For his rescue attempts on Everest, Boukreev was awarded the American Alpine Club's highest award for valour – the David A. Sowles Award. Sadly, he was killed by an avalanche on Annapurna on Christmas 1997. His friend and companion on Everest, Lopsang Jangbu Sherpa, was killed by an avalanche on Everest in September 1996.
37. Beck and Gau were evacuated from Camp I in a daring helicopter rescue flown by Lt Col Madan Khatri Chhetri. The highest recorded helicopter landing in the Himalaya (20,000 ft) – and perhaps anywhere.
38. Krakauer. op. cit.
39. Nobody can be certain what happened that night at the South Summit, but indications are that Harris had reached Hall at the South Summit then had somehow walked over the edge to oblivion, leaving behind his ice axe. Hansen might have fallen approximately 50 ft above the South Summit where the fixed ropes ended and where *his* axe was found. Shades of 1924!
40. Not since the disappearance of Mallory and Irvine in 1924 (see Chapter 5) has there been such a public interest in an Everest accident as those of 1996. Fuller accounts appear in two books: Jon Krakauer's *Into Thin Air* and Anatoli Boukreev's *The Climb.* Each man has his own perspective.
41. From an interview in the *Financial Times* by Richard Cowper, quoted by Krakauer, op. cit. Chapter 18.
42. Eleven died pre-monsoon, five post-monsoon.
43. A. Boukreev. op. cit.
44. Steven Goodwin quoted in *Out There* Web site.
45. The 'Seven Summits' are the highest points of the seven continents. These are Everest (Asia), Aconcagua (S. America), Denali (N. America), Vinson Massif (Antarctica), Elbrus (Europe) and Kilimanjaro (Africa). There are two schools of thought about Australasia, some claiming Kosciusko (Australia) an easy peak while others Carstenz Pyramid (Irian Jaya) – which is higher but perhaps not in the right continent! The first to climb all seven was Dick Bass, an American, in 1985 (see Chapter 21).
46. Quoted in *Ghosts of Everest: The Search for Mallory and Irvine (The Mountaineers, 1999),* a superb account of the expedition by Jochen Hemmleb, Larry A. Johnson and Eric Simonson.
47. C. Anker, "Mallory and Irvine's Summit Day," *Climbing,* 15 September, 1999.
48. The axe is discussed at length in Chapter 5. I remain unconvinced of the axe's provenance. I examined it at length and very carefully in the Alpine Club more than twenty years ago. See Note 36 for Chapter 5.
49. Two weeks later Andy Politz and climbing cameraman Thom Pollard revisited the body with a metal detector, looking for the missing camera. Politz was able to

examine Mallory's face. There was stubble on his chin and his eyes were closed. There was a wound on his forehead.

50. They had been asked to do this by Mallory's descendants in the event of the body being found.
51. C. Anker. op. cit.
52. ibid.
53. ibid.

APPENDIX 1 *(pages 567–574)*

1. Annie Peck, quoted in *Men, Myths and Mountains*, Chapter 14, by R.W. Clark.
2. G.I. Finch, *The Making of a Mountaineer*. New edition, 1988. Contains Memoir, 'George Finch – the Mountaineer' by Scott Russell.
3. Extracts from Greene's letter appeared in a bookseller's catalogue a few years ago. Several letters were for sale with a copy of *Everest 1933* for £200. Unfortunately the author has only seen a photocopy of the page in question, with no indication of whose catalogue it was, or date. Probably 1982.
4. Greene was with Smythe on the first ascent of Kamet, 1931.
5. The reference to quails in aspic is a dig at the expeditions led by General Bruce, which were noted for gourmet food.
6. In these passages you can feel Smythe's choleric temper rising at the thought of the Crawford-Ruttledge controversy.
7. Letter from Frank Smythe to Raymond Greene dated Tinki Dzong 12 April 1936. Now in AC Archives.
8. Conversation with Sally Nesbitt, Champéry 1985.
9. Ms. history of Chinese mountaineering by Prof. Zhou Zeng.
10. *A Photographic Record of the Mount Jolmo Lungma Scientific Expedition 1966–68*, 1974.
11. Zeng Shusheng, 'Things Left Behind on Mt Qomolangma', from *High Mountain Peaks in China*, 1981.
12. *ibid.*
13. *ibid.*
14. Letters to the author from Nick Clinch, 30 May 1982 and 3 June 1982. Clinch had recently interviewed Shi Zhan Chun in Yosemite.
15. Letter from Hiroyuki Suzuki, Foreign Secretary, Japanese Alpine Club to Tom Holzel, 7 February 1980. Quoted in T. Holzel and A. Salkeld *The Mystery of Mallory and Irvine*, 1986.
16. Article by Shi Zhan Chun, Xu Jing, and Wang Fengtong, in *The Globe* (Peking) 1982.
17. Champak Chatterji: 'End of a Legend – and An Era'. *The Sunday Statesman* (Calcutta), 17 June 1984. A fairly full obituary of Karma Paul.

APPENDIX 2 *(pages 575–579)*

1. W.H. Murray, *The Story of Everest*, Appendix.
2. The stations were Jirol (Jarol) 118 miles; Mirzapur 108 miles, Joafpati (Janjipati) 108 miles; Ladmia 108 miles; Harpur 111 miles; Minai 113 miles.
3. B.L. Gulatee, 'Mount Everest, Its Name and Height', *H.J.*, XVII, 1952.
4. W.W. Graham, letter to the editor, *A.J.*, XI, 1884.
5. S.G. Burrard, 'Mount Everest: the story of a long controversy'. *Nature*, 1904.

6. Parke A. Dickey, 'Who discovered Mount Everest?', *EOS*, 8 October 1985. This article by Professor Dickey is a thorough exposition of the subject, highly recommended.
7. R.H. Phillimore, *Historical Records of the Survey of India*, Vol 5. 1964. Phillimore was himself Surveyor General in 1931.
8. Dickey, *op. cit.*
9. Dickey, *op. cit.*

APPENDIX 3 *(pages 580–584)*

1. D.W. Freshfield, 'The Great Peaks of the Himalaya', *A.J.*, XII, 1886.
2. Where Hodgson found the name Devadhunga is not known, but there has been no further evidence to support it.
3. M. von Dechy, 'Mountain Travel in the Sikkim Himalaya', footnote, *A.J.*, X, 1882.
4. S.G. Burrard, *A Sketch of the Geography and Geology of the Himalaya Mountains and Tibet*, Part 1, p.21.
5. D.W. Freshfield, 'Mount Everest *v.* Chomolungma', *A.J.*, XXXIV, 1923.
6. H. Ruttledge, *Everest: The Unfinished Adventure*, Part II, Chapter 7 (by Kempson).
7. *ibid.* (author's italics).
8. *Morning Post*, 9 November 1920.
9. K. Mason, *Abode of Snow*, Part II, Chapter 3.

# *Glossary*

ABSEIL

A rapid method of descent down a steep rock or ice wall. A doubled rope is hung down the cliff from a rock or ice bollard, or a peg, and the climber makes a controlled slide down it. There are several technical ways he can do this. The rope can then be pulled down after him.

ACCLIMATIZATION

The adaption of the human body to the rarefied air of high altitudes. During acclimatization the breathing becomes deeper and faster and often irregular (Cheyne-Stokes respiration); heartbeat speed and force is increased, while blood thickens because the red cells multiply and plasma becomes less. Individuals differ in their rate and degree of acclimatization, but *generally* the surest method is to gain height slowly and not stay too high, too long, or altitude deterioration sets in.

Almost all Everest expeditions have acclimatization problems: headaches, sleeplessness, sickness. In its most severe form lack of acclimatization can cause pulmonary or cerebral oedema (q.v.).

À CHEVAL

A method of crossing a narrow ridge with one leg on either side, as in riding a horse.

ALP

A high summer pasture above a valley but below the snow line.

ALPINE CLUB

The world's first mountaineering club, founded in 1857 in London. Until fairly recent times it was a somewhat exclusive Establishment club, where the right background counted for as much as, if not more than, ability. Its unique position has always given it an influential voice in mountaineering affairs. Membership is by election.

*Alpine Journal*

The journal of the Alpine Club, now published annually. A unique record of world mountaineering since 1863.

ALPINE STYLE

In high-altitude climbing, a means of tackling a high peak in the same manner as one would tackle an Alpine peak, i.e. without a massive build-up of men and materials and without siege tactics.

ANCHOR

A point of attachment to the mountain for the rope. It may be a rock spike, piton, etc.

ANNAPURNA

Annapurna I (8,078 m.) is important in high-altitude mountaineering history because it was the first peak over 8,000 m. ever climbed – by the French in 1950.
The British expedition of 1970 which climbed the South Face brought a new dimension to high-altitude climbing and was an important forerunner to the attempts on the South West Face of Everest.

ANORAK

An Eskimo word for a windproof smock.

ARÊTE

A sharp rock or ice ridge.

ARTIFICIAL CLIMBING

Sometimes called aid climbing. Where there are no natural holds, or the rock/ice face is too steep, possibly overhanging, the climber hammers in metal pegs or even bolts and uses these in conjunction with footloops known as etriers (q.v.).

AVALANCHE

The sliding-away from a mountain of surface material, commonly snow, but also ice, mud and rocks. The causes of avalanches are various and complex; climbers frequently misjudge conditions and are caught or have narrow escapes. The power of an avalanche is immense, not only because of the speed and volume of the material itself but also because of the air blast associated with it.

BACKING-UP

A method of climbing a chimney (q.v.) by putting one's back against one wall and feet against the other and shuffling up.

BELAYING

Tying on to an anchor in order to safeguard a team of climbers.

BERGSCHRUND

A crevasse between a glacier and the snow slopes of the mountain. Often wide and difficult to cross.

BIVOUAC

A night spent out on the mountain without the benefit of a proper camp. Bivouacs may be deliberately planned or they may be forced on climbers by circumstances. The main aim is to keep out of the wind – under the lee of a rock or in an ice cave. High-altitude climbers often carry lightweight bivouac gear: stove, sleeping bag, bivvy sack etc.

BOLTS

Where no crack exists in which to hammer a piton, a hole is sometimes drilled and an expansion bolt used.

BOOTS

High-altitude mountaineering boots are usually 'double boots', i.e. they have a soft, warm inner boot encased in a tough outer boot. Canvas overboots go over these. The early Everesters had no such luxury and used much the same boots as they used in the Alps.

BRIDGING

A method of climbing a wide chimney by straddling it – having one foot and hand on each wall.

BUTTRESS

A mass of rock bulging out of a mountainside.

CAGOULE

A long, lightweight, windproof outer smock.

CAMP

In high-altitude mountaineering, a staging post: a group of tents where men and materials can spend the night.

CHANG

A white-coloured beer brewed from rice or millet.

CHIMNEY

A wide fissure, usually in rock, but sometimes in ice.

CHOCK

A piece of machined metal to which a nylon or wire loop is attached. It can be jammed in a crack and used as a belay.

CHOCKSTONE

A boulder jammed in a gully or chimney.

CHORTEN

A small wayside shrine.

CLIMBING HELMET

A protective fibre-glass helmet sometimes worn by climbers.

COL

A dip in a ridge, usually between two peaks.

COMBINED TACTICS

One climber assisting another by giving him a 'leg-up' or 'shoulder'.

COMMITTED

Having reached a point in a climb where retreat would be very difficult if not impossible.

CORNICE

A snow lip projecting over the edge of a ridge or top of a gully.

COULOIR

A gully.

CRACK

A fissure in the rock not wide enough to be a chimney.

CRAMPONS

A framework of steel spikes which fits over the sole of a boot and is fastened by straps. Used for climbing ice or snow.

CREVASSE

A crack in the surface of a glacier, which may be very wide and deep. Frequently hidden beneath surface snow, forming a considerable hazard.

CWM

A Welsh word meaning a cirque or corrie.

DEAD MAN

A metal plate which can be buried in the snow to form an anchor.

DESCENDEUR

A metal device to make abseiling quicker and more comfortable.

DUVET

Eiderdown made up into jackets, trousers or overall suit.

DZONG

A fort in Tibet.

ETRIERS

Small portable steps made of webbing or, earlier, little metal steps on ropes, used in artificial climbing.

EXPOSURE

1. A very open position on a mountain where a slip would have serious consequences.
2. A loss of body heat leading to hypothermia: a serious condition which can result in death.

FIRST ASCENT

Climbers take considerable pride in being first to achieve a set goal. The first ascent of a mountain comes top of the list, but each mountain has many other 'firsts' – first solo, first oxygenless, first woman, first traverse, etc.

FIXED ROPES

Ropes fixed for the duration of an expedition to assist climbers and porters over difficult passages or simply to speed up the ferrying between camps.

FREE CLIMBING

Climbing without artificial aids such as etriers, fixed ropes etc.

FROSTBITE

Frostbite is caused by ice crystals forming between cells allied to a constriction of the minor blood vessels. This leads to a reduction in the oxygen supply to the cells and their consequent deterioration and infection. It particularly affects extremities – fingers, toes, ears, nose, lips. Badly frostbitten members may have to be amputated.

GENDARME

A pinnacle on a ridge.

GLACIER

Virtually a river of ice occupying a valley head. The glacier is fed by seasonal snow and flows slowly down the valley. Warmer temperatures in the lower regions cause melting and if the rate of melting is greater than the annual increase of snow the glacier 'retreats' – grows smaller – and vice versa.

GLACIER CREAM

A pigmented face cream used to prevent sunburn.

GLISSADING

A way of sliding down a hard snow slope using the ice axe as a brake.

GROOVE

An open, shallow fissure in rock or ice.

GULLY

A wide fissure in the mountain.

HARNESS

Climbers wear a body harness made of tape, to which the rope can be attached.

HIMALAYAN CLUB

Formed in 1928, the club is based in India and its aim is to encourage Himalayan climbing and exploration.

ICE AXE

An essential climbing tool wherever there is snow and ice. The axe consists of a shaft at one end of which is a spike and ferrule, and at the other the head. The head has one end in the shape of a pick and the opposite end in the shape of an adze. Ice axes have become shorter and lighter over the years, particularly recently.

ICEFALL

The enormous crevasses and pinnacles formed when a glacier falls over a steep declivity and the ice fractures. Because of the downwards movement of the glacier an icefall is unstable and consequently dangerous.

ICE SCREWS

Special pitons for screwing into ice.

JAMMING

Where there are no obvious holds it is sometimes possible for a climber to move by jamming a hand or foot in a crack.

JUMAR CLAMP

A metal device which can be clipped onto a climbing rope, where it can be pushed up but will not slide down. The climber is attached to the Jumar by tapes or cord. Frequently used as a safety device on fixed ropes.

KARABINER

An oval metal ring, one side of which opens as a spring clip. A very useful device for clipping onto ropes, into pitons etc. Often called a 'krab'.

LA

Tibetan word meaning a pass or col.

LEAD CLIMBER

An experienced climber expected to take part in making the actual route.

LEADER

The person ultimately responsible for the conduct of an expedition. In the case of Everest he might be simply a non-climbing executive, as was General Bruce, or he might take an active part in the assault, as did Hunt. Similarly he might be a leader appointed by a committee, like the leaders of all the British expeditions to 1953, or he might be the actual initiator of the enterprise, like Bonington in 1975.

LINE

The route followed up a mountain feature.

MANI STONE

Stones upon which prayers have been carved, common in Tibet and Nepal.

MANTELSHELF

A movement involving pressing up on a ledge until you can get your feet onto it, like trying to climb onto the mantelshelf of a fireplace.

MIXED CLIMBING

Climbing in which the route is partly on snow/ice and partly on rock.

MORAINE

Huge banks of stones and earth pushed out of the way by a glacier. Found at the glacier snout and edges.

MOUNT EVEREST FOUNDATION

A body formed after the first ascent in 1953 to administer the funds accumulated by book and film rights. Grants are made to expeditions.

NAILS

In the years before the Second World War, climbing boots were equipped with special nails round the welts and in the sole.

NEVE

The snow slopes of a mountain above the bergschrund.

OBJECTIVE DANGERS

Dangers which cannot be overcome by climbing skill, e.g. stonefall, serac collapse.

OEDEMA

An acute form of altitude sickness in which water accumulates on the lungs (pulmonary oedema) or brain (cerebral oedema). Retreat to lower altitudes usually results in complete recovery fairly quickly, but failure to take this action is generally fatal.

OVERHANG

Rock or ice which leans out beyond the vertical.

OXYGEN EQUIPMENT

A pack frame usually containing two or three cylinders of gas and equipped with regulators and face mask for counteracting oxygen deficiency at high altitude.

PACK FRAME

A lightweight metal carrying frame, with shoulder straps.

PASS

The way across a mountain ridge from one valley to another. Not always easy and sometimes of considerable altitude.

PILLAR

A narrow column of rock jutting out from the parent mountainside.

PITCH

The distance between two anchors.

PITON

Also called a peg or pin. A metal spike which can be hammered into a crack in the rock and used as an anchor or a runner (q.v.). There are also pitons suitable for driving into ice.

PORTER

A person employed to carry a load. Local porters are used to carry to Base Camp and may be Tamangs, Bhotias, Sherpas or any other tribesmen seeking employment. Above Base Camp the porters are equipped like the climbers. On Everest, Icefall porters ferry goods into the Cwm and high-altitude porters from the Cwm up the mountain. Above Base Camp, porters are usually Sherpas.

PRUSIK KNOT

A knot attaching a sling to the main rope and performing the same function as a Jumar clamp (q.v.), which in the Himalaya has largely superseded it.

RAKSHI

Liquor made from rice.

RIB

A small ridge on a mountain face.

RIDGE

The crest where two opposing faces of a mountain meet.

ROPE

Pre-war climbing ropes were of hemp, or occasionally silk. Modern ropes are of nylon or perlon, which is stronger and more flexible, especially in extreme cold. A group of climbers tied together on a rope is also known as ‘a rope’.

RUNNER (RUNNING BELAY)

As a protection against a long fall, a lead climber will let his rope run through a karabiner clipped to a piton.

RUN-OUT

The length of rope run out by the lead climber from his last anchor.

SACK-HAULING

Hauling rucksacks up separately instead of climbing with them. Sometimes necessary on a difficult pitch.

SCREE

A slope of loose stones.

SERAC

An ice pinnacle.

SHERPA

A race of people, Tibetan in origin, who settled in the Sola Khumbu area near Everest, though many now live in Darjeeling and Kathmandu.

SHERPANI

A Sherpa woman.

SIRDAR

The head Sherpa of an expedition.

SLAB

An area of flat rock tilted up at a fairly steep angle.

SLING

A loop of rope or nylon tape.

SNOWBLINDNESS

The glare from a glacier or snowfield can cause a temporary but painful blindness.

SNOW BRIDGE

A bridge of hard snow often spanning a crevasse and forming a way across. Nice judgement is required to assess its trustworthiness.

SNOW CAVE

A cave dug in the snow as a way of effecting a temporary shelter for a bivouac.

SOLO CLIMBING

Climbing completely alone.

SPINDRIFT

Light powder snow blown about by the wind. It causes discomfort because it penetrates clothing and tents. Sometimes it avalanches, but not usually seriously.

STANCE

A place where a climber can rest and belay.

STEPS

Footholds cut into ice with an ice axe, or kicked into snow with the boot.

**STONEFALL**

The continuous erosion of mountains causes rocks to become loose and fall, particularly down faces and gullies. Stonefall does not seem to be a serious problem on Everest, though it has been reported on the South West Face.

**STUPA**

A Buddhist shrine.

**SUSTAINED CLIMB OR PITCH**

A climb or pitch which never relents in difficulty.

**TAPE**

Nylon tape has numerous uses in climbing, e.g. for slings.

**THIN**

With few holds.

**TIGER**

A name given to the best Sherpas on the 1924 expedition and later extended to any experienced Sherpa. For a time it was also used to describe any good climber, but the term is seldom heard today.

**TRAVERSE**

To go up one side of a peak and down another. In more localized terms, to traverse means to climb more or less horizontally across a feature rather than up it.
climb more or less horizontally across a feature rather than up it.

**TSAMPA**

Barley flour, a staple diet in Tibet and Nepal.

**UNPROTECTED CLIMB**

A climb in which there is no way of preventing a serious accident should a slip occur.

**VERGLAS**

A thin coating of ice on rocks.

**WALL**

A very steep face of rock or ice.

**WHILLANS BOX**

A metal-framed box-like tent, designed for high-altitude camps by Don Whillans.

**WHITE-OUT**

An unpleasant phenomenon of snowscapes in which it is impossible to tell where the earth ends and sky begins. Eerie and dangerous – it is possible to step over an edge unknowingly.

# Index